D1567156

Oracle Tuning
The Definitive Reference
Second Edition

Oracle In-Focus Series

Donald K. Burleson

To Janet, whose love and support helped to make this book a reality.

Oracle Tuning

By Donald K. Burleson

Copyright © 2010 by Rampant TechPress. All rights reserved.

Printed in the United States of America.

Published in Kittrell, North Carolina, USA.

Oracle In-Focus Series: Book #32

Series Editor: Donald K. Burleson

Production Manager: Robin Rademacher

Editors: Valerre Aquitaine, Robin Rademacher, Andrew Burleson

Production Editor: Janet Burleson

Cover Design: Janet Burleson

Printing History: September 2008, December 2009 for First Edition, February 2010 for Second Edition

Oracle, Oracle7, Oracle8, Oracle8i, Oracle9i, Oracle10g and Oracle 11g are trademarks of Oracle Corporation.

Many of the designations used by computer vendors to distinguish their products are claimed as Trademarks. All names known by Rampant TechPress to be trademark names appear in this text as initial caps.

ISBN-13: 978-0-9797951-9-0

Library of Congress Control Number: 2010900994

Table of Contents

Using the Online Code Depot 1
Oracle Script Collection 1
Conventions Used in this Book 2
Are you ready to tune? 2
Acknowledgements 3
Preface 4

Chapter 1: Introduction to Oracle Tuning 7

An Introduction to Oracle Tuning 7
    Throughput vs. Response Time 8
    Top-down Tuning vs. Bottom-up Tuning 9
    Proactive Tuning vs. Reactive Tuning 9
    Reactive Oracle Tuning 10
    Proactive Oracle Tuning 10
Know the Limits: Things that We Can Not Tune 12
Oracle Application-level Tuning 14
    A Historical Review of DBA Job Duties 15
    Oracle Tuning and Server Consolidation 17
    Hardware Technology Drives Database Technology 18
    The Changing Role of an Oracle Tuning Professional 20
The Causes of Poor Oracle Performance 22
The Oracle Tuning Hierarchy 23
    External Hardware Performance Review 25
    Finding Database Bottlenecks 26
    Oracle Instance Tuning 29
    AWR Licensing Options 31
    Tracking your Oracle Option Usage 33
    Oracle SQL Tuning 35
Conclusion 36

Chapter 2: Time Series Tuning for Oracle 38

Managing the Complexity of Oracle 38
The Pros and Cons of Time Series Tuning 39
Data Quality 41
Oracle's Approach to Workload Thresholds 41
Signatures, Workloads and Exceptions 42
    Workloads and Predictive Analysis 43
    What is an Oracle Workload? 43
Using Adaptive Thresholds for Predictive Modeling 44
Using OEM for Predictive Modeling 45
Time Series Tuning Guidelines 47
    Scheduling an SGA Reconfiguration 47
    Trend-based Oracle Reconfiguration 48
    When to Trigger a Dynamic Reconfiguration 49
Approaches to Self-tuning Oracle Databases 51
    Tuning a Constantly Changing Database 51
    Can Oracle Possess Psychic Abilities? 51
    Capturing Time Series Metrics 51
Customized AWR Tuning Reports 52
    Exception Reporting 53
Exception Reporting with the AWR 54
    Exception Reporting with dba_hist_filestatxs 55
Trend Identification with the AWR 58
Conclusion 63
References 64

Chapter 3: The Time Model Tuning Approach 64

Inside the Oracle Time Model Views 64
Displaying Session Details with Time Model Data 66
Real-time Reporting 68
Time Model Tables in AWR 69
Time Model Statistics 74
Conclusion 76

Chapter 4: Predictive Modeling 77

Predicting the Future with Oracle 77
Oracle Data Mining and Predictive Analytics 81
    The Evolution toward Data Mining *82*
    Oracle Data Mining and Predictive Analytics *82*
    Components of the Oracle Data Miner *83*
Predictive Models Made Easy 83
Exception Reporting with the AWR 86
    General Trend Identification with the AWR *88*
Correlation Analysis with AWR and ASH 91
    Predictive Modeling with dba_hist_filestatxs *94*
Conclusion 97

Chapter 5: Oracle Troubleshooting **98**

Introduction to Troubleshooting 98
Emergency Troubleshooting Methods 99
    Why Oracle Shops Lose Their Databases *100*
    The Limitations of the DBA *101*
Case Studies in Oracle Troubleshooting 102
    Accurately Measuring Oracle Performance *110*
Using the BCHR for Performance Tuning 111
    The Danger of Relying on Blanket Ratios *116*
Oracle Bottleneck Analysis 117
    Prerequisites for Bottleneck Analysis *117*
    Combining Bottleneck and Ratio Analysis *123*
    The Number One Oracle Performance Myth *124*
Troubleshooting Oracle Disk Performance 125
    Automatic Growth *126*
Troubleshooting Critical Storage Problems 129
    Detecting Tablespace Fragmentation *129*
    Detecting Object Fragmentation *132*
    Correcting Object Fragmentation *134*
Troubleshooting Table Problems 134
    Index Diagnostics *137*
    Correcting Space-related Object Performance Problems *138*
Troubleshooting Memory Problems 139
    Getting a Handle on Memory Usage *140*
Understanding the SGA 141
    Gaining Insight Into Memory Use *142*
    The Buffer Cache Hit Ratio – Still Worthwhile? *145*
Troubleshooting the Shared Pool 151
    When Does Less Become More? *151*
Troubleshooting the Log Buffer 156
    Log Buffer Related Parameter Issues *158*
    Investigating Sorts *160*
Troubleshooting Oracle Sorting 161
    buffer busy waits *162*
Troubleshooting Latches 163
    Troubleshooting I/O Hotspots *164*
    Global Basic Queries *165*
    Locating Hot I/O Objects *170*
    Examining Background Processes *177*
    Troubleshooting Rollback Activity *179*
Troubleshooting Problem Sessions 180
    Finding Storage Hogs *181*
    Locating Top Resource Sessions *183*
    Pinpointing Sessions with Problem SQL *192*
Troubleshooting Problem SQL 194
    What is Bad SQL? *194*
    Proactive SQL Troubleshooting *196*
    Tricks for SQL Troubleshooting *199*
Troubleshooting Triage 203
Using Active Session History (ASH) for Troubleshooting 207
    Collecting ASH Wait Information *208*
    Using ASH for Troubleshooting *210*
    Inside v$active_session_history *213*

Table of Contents

Display SQL Wait Details in ASH...219
Event Wait Analysis with ASH...220
The Performance Overhead of Collecting ASH Data...222
Inside the v$session_wait_history...226
Signature Analysis of ASH Wait Events...228
Using ASH in OEM..236
Conclusion...240

Chapter 6: Inside STATSPACK and AWR **241**

Introduction to Tuning with STATSPACK..241
Oracle vs. STATSPACK..243
Inside the AWR tables...244
Using STATSPACK for Oracle Tuning..246
The structure of the STATSPACK tables...248
How STATSPACK Works...248
Trend Reports with STATSPACK...252
Inside the AWR Tables..255
The AWR Data Collection Mechanism..256
Customizing AWR snapshots..256
The Mysterious AWR Performance Tables..257
Inside the AWR Tables..258
Inside the dba_hist Tables...258
Database Wait Events in AWR...260
The AWR Metric Tables...267
AWR System Statistics...273
Operating System Statistics in AWR..280
SQL Statistics in AWR..281
Segment Statistics in AWR...284
Datafile I/O Statistics in AWR...286
Conclusion...288

Chapter 7: AWR and STATSPACK Configuration **289**

The Differences between STATSPACK and AWR...289
Installing STATSPACK..290
Install Prerequisites..290
STATSPACK vs. AWR..294
Statistic Management in AWR and STATSPACK...295
The snap_level Parameter..296
The session_id..297
The num_sql...297
What SQL is Captured?..297
STATSPACK SQL Collection Thresholds...298
AWR SQL Collection Thresholds...299
The stats$sql_summary Table..302
Installing AWR...303
The dbms_workload_repository Package...304
Creating an AWR Report...304
Report Naming...305
Conclusion...307

Chapter 8: Reading an AWR or STATSPACK Report... **308**

The Evolution of the Elapsed Time Report..308
What's New in STATSPACK and AWR Reports...310
Generating a STATSPACK Report..310
Generating an AWR Report...312
Reading the STATSPACK / AWR Report..313
STATSPACK / AWR Report Summary...316
Cache Sizes Section...316
Load Profile...317
Instance Efficiency Percentage...320
All about Oracle Ratios...322
Top 5 Timed Events Section of a STATSPACK / AWR Report.............................323
The Wait Events Section of the AWR / STATSPACK Report...............................325
Wait Event Histogram Section...330
Instance Activity Section in the STATSPACK / AWR Report...............................331

Instance Recovery Statistics Section of a STATS/AWR Report...333
PGA Section...333
Process Memory Summary Section...336
Enqueue Statistics..338
Rollback Segments...340
Undo Segments..341
Latch Activity Section of a STATSPACK / AWR report...342
Dictionary and Library Cache Stats 348
The Shared Pool Advisory Section...349
The Time Model Statistics section...355
The Operating System Statistics Section..355
The Top SQL Section..357
The Instance Activity Section..360
The I/O Reports Section..363
The Advisory Sections 365
Buffer Pool Advisory...365
The Buffer Wait Statistics Section...367
Conclusion 375

Chapter 9: Oracle Metrics and *v$* Tuning Views..**376**

Classifying *v$* Views and Metrics...376
Inside the Oracle Metrics...382
Inside the v$metric Tables...382
Database Wait Metrics..386
Oracle File Metrics...388
Oracle Service Metrics..389
The Secret World of the *v$* Views...390
The Active Session History *v$* View...393
Conclusion 397

Chapter 10: Oracle Wait Event Tuning...**399**

The Oracle Wait Event Model 399
The AWR Wait Event Tables 400
Why Wait Event Tuning for Oracle?...402
Addressing Wait Bottlenecks...403
Systemwide Wait Event Tuning..404
Not All Events Are Created Equal..406
Inside the Real-time *V$* Wait Events...408
Inside *v$session_wait* 409
Inside v$session_event...411
Conclusion 420

Chapter 11: Oracle Tuning Tools...**421**

The Evolution of Oracle Tuning Tools 421
The Spirit of Independence..422
A Best Practices Approach to Oracle Tuning...422
The History of Oracle Tuning Techniques...423
An Automated Approach to SQL Tuning..425
How Fully Automated SQL Tuning Works..426
Fully Automated SQL Tuning is not a Panacea...427
Oracle Trace Analyzer (*sqltxplain*) 428
Oracle Lightweight Onboard Monitor (LTOM) 429
LTOM Features...429
Oracle Trace Utility 431
Inside Oracle Event Tracing..431
Setting an Oracle Trace Event...432
Accessing Oracle Trace Records with External Tables...443
Exception Reporting within a Trace File...445
Loading and Analyzing the 10046 Event..449
Inside the Oracle 10046 Trace File Output...449
Conclusions on Tracing...451
Generating Oracle Test Data 452
Gathering a Sample Workload in Oracle 11g..452
Creating Data for Performance Testing...456
Conclusion 460

Chapter 12: Server & Network Tuning **461**

Table of Contents

Oracle Server Tuning..461
Outside the Oracle Instance 462
   Oracle Server Bottlenecks *462*
Oracle Server Monitoring..464
   Capturing Server-side Metrics *464*
   OS Statistics for the Cost-based Optimizer *465*
   OS data inside Oracle views..*465*
The Oracle OS Watcher utility 470
   Starting Oracle OS Watcher...*470*
Oracle CPU Tuning 471
   Viewing CPU Utilization for Oracle *472*
   Identifying High CPU Usage with vmstat *474*
   Storing Information from vmstat *474*
Disk I/O and Oracle 482
   Moore's Law and Disk Speed *483*
   Server RAM and Oracle *486*
   Oracle and the 64-bit Server Technology..*487*
   The New Age of Oracle Server Consolidation *489*
   Oracle Enterprise Manager and Server Metrics *492*
   Server Metrics and SQL Execution..*497*
Oracle Network Tuning 499
Conclusion 502

Chapter 13: Tuning the I/O Subsystem **503**

Inside Oracle Disk Architecture 503
The Plague of Large Oracle Disks 506
   Disk Architectures of the 21st Century...*507*
RAID Technology and Oracle 509
   RAID 5 is Not for Every Database *509*
Oracle and Direct I/O 512
   Enabling Oracle Direct I/O..*512*
Calibrating Disk I/O 514
Monitoring External Disk I/O 515
   Capturing External iostat Information *516*
   Generating iostat Reports *518*
   Solutions to Physical Read Waits *520*
Choosing a default blocksize 521
Using Oracle Multiple Blocksizes 523
   Reducing Data Buffer Waste with multiple blocksizes................................*524*
   Reducing Logical I/O with Multiple Blocksizes...*526*
   Improving Buffer Efficiency with Multiple Blocksizes................................*527*
   Improving SQL Execution with Multiple Blocksizes..................................*527*
   Real World Applications of Multiple Blocksizes...*528*
The *db_file_multiblock_read_count* Parameter..528
   Oracle Blocksize & Index I/O..*534*
   The Latest Consensus on Using Multiple Blocksizes..................................*536*
   Vendor Notes on Oracle Multiple Blocksizes...*538*
Reducing Disk I/O with SSD 540
   2010 Market Survey of SSD Vendors for Oracle *541*
Oracle Disk Monitoring 543
Examining Real-time Disk Statistics 543
   Examining Global I/O *545*
   Tracking I/O for Specific Tables *553*
Analyzing Real Time I/O Waits 555
   Collecting Real-Time Disk Wait Events *556*
Find the Current Disk I/O Session Bandits 564
Measuring Disk I/O Speed..569
Time Series I/O Wait Analysis 571
Time Series Monitoring of the Data Buffers 575
Monitoring Disk I/O with AWR..577
Conclusion 584

Chapter 14: Oracle Instance Tuning **585**

Inside Instance Tuning..585
Instance Tuning Comes First 586
Instance Configuration for High Performance 588
Automatic Memory Management 588

Manual RAM allocation vs. AMM...589
Sizing the Oracle SGA and PGA Regions..590
   Viewing Server RAM Resources..591
   Sizing your SGA..594
   SGA Sizing on a Dedicated Server...594
   RAM and Virtual Memory for Oracle..595
   Finding the High Water Mark of Oracle User Connections..................................597
Determining the Optimal PGA Size..597
   Display PGA Area Sizes...597
   A Script for Estimating Total PGA RAM...599
   Optimizing pga_aggregate_target...601
   Rules for adjusting..601
   Important caveats in PGA management...603
   Sizing your PGA for hash joins..603
   The 11g full hash join...604
   Sizing the PGA for Batch Processing...606
   A case study RAM hash joins...608
   Hidden Parameters for Oracle PGA Regions...609
   Supersizing the PGA...609
   Monitoring Server Resources in MS Windows...611
OS Kernel Parameters..613
   Server Settings for Windows Servers..613
   Kernel Setting for UNIX and Linux Servers..613
Oracle Parameter Tuning...614
   Oracle Hidden Parameters..615
   Oracle Parallel Query Parameters...616
   Hidden Parallel Parameters...618
   SQL Optimizer Parameters...619
   Data Buffer Cache Hidden Parameters...619
Instance Wait Event Tuning...620
Tuning the Oracle Data Buffer Pools...624
   The Problem of Duplicitous RAM Caches...625
   Why is Oracle Logical I/O So Slow?..625
Data Block Caching in the SGA...626
Full Table Caching in Oracle...628
Oracle Data Buffer Metrics..629
   Using AWR for Buffer Pool Statistics..630
   Oracle's Seven Data Buffer Hit Ratios...633
   Viewing Information about SGA Performance...635
   AMM and Oracle Instance Tuning...638
Internals of the Oracle Data Buffers..645
   Finding Hot Blocks inside the Oracle Data Buffers...646
   Viewing the Data Buffer Contents...647
The Downside of Mega Data Buffers..659
   Allocating Oracle Objects into Multiple RAM data buffers...................................660
   Sizing the KEEP Pool..664
Automating KEEP Pool Assignment..666
Tuning the RECYCLE Pool..669
   Large Blocks and Oracle Instance Caching...673
   Finding Baselines..675
   Learning Instance Tuning from Performance Benchmarks.....................................676
   Rules for adjusting shared_pool_size..678
   Sizing the Shared Pool with the Oracle Advisory Utility.......................................680
   Rules for Adjusting the Data Buffer Sizes..681
Monitoring RAM usage..682
   Tracking hash joins...686
   Viewing RAM usage for hash joins in SQL...687
Conclusion...690

Chapter 15: Tablespace & Object Tuning 691

Oracle Tablespace Tuning..691
Inside Oracle Tablespace Tuning...692
   The Issue of pctfree..693
   The Freelist Unlink Process..694
   The Issue of pctused...694
Setting Pctfree and Pctused...695
   Freelists and Performance...696

ASSM and Tablespace Performance 697
    Internal Freelist Management *699*
    Characteristics of Bitmap Segment Management *699*
    New High Watermark Pointers *700*
    Extent Control Header Block *701*
Using ASSM with RAC 702
    Potential Performance Issues with ASSM *704*
    Faster SQL with Database Reorganizations *704*
    Managing Row Chaining in Oracle *706*
    A Summary of Object Tuning Rules *709*
Reorganizing Tables for High Performance 710
    Online Reorganization *711*
    Segment Space Growth Prediction *717*
Tuning SQL Access with *clustering_factor* 718
    Not all Indexes are Used in Range Scans *721*
Rebuilding Indexes 726
    When to Rebuild Indexes *728*
Oracle Parallel DDL 732
    Invoking Parallelism *734*
    Parallel DBA Operations *734*
Conclusion 735

Chapter 16: Inside Oracle SQL Tuning **737**

Introduction to Oracle SQL 737
The Origin of SQL 739
Understanding SQL Tuning 740
Holistic Oracle SQL Tuning 741
    Dealing with Time Constraints *741*
Best Practices for SQL Optimization 741
    Proper Development Environment *741*
    Maintaining A SQL Infrastructure *742*
    A Release-centric Approach to Holistic Optimization *743*
    Oracle 6 – Oracle 7 enhancements *743*
    Oracle 8 – Oracle 8i enhancements *744*
    Oracle 9i enhancements *744*
    Oracle 10g enhancements *744*
    Oracle 10g Release 2 enhancements *745*
    Oracle 11g enhancements *745*
What is the Best Optimizer Philosophy? 746
    The Persistent SQL Philosophy *746*
    The Dynamic SQL Philosophy *747*
Goals of SQL Tuning 748
    Determine Optimal Table Join Order *748*
    Remove Unnecessary Large-table Full-table Scans *748*
Locating full-scan operations 750
    Tuning large-table full-table scans *751*
    Tuning small-table full-table scans *752*
    Optimizing SQL RAM Resources *753*
    Cache Small-table Full-table Scans *753*
    Verify Optimal Index Usage *754*
    Verify Optimal Join Techniques *754*
    Tuning by Simplifying SQL Syntax *754*
Roadblocks to SQL Tuning 756
    SQL Profiles *756*
Tracing SQL Execution History 757
Oracle SQL as a Database Access Method 758
    The rule Hint is still Popular in Oracle 11g *758*
    The Library Cache and Oracle SQL Performance *759*
    Using cursor_sharing=force *761*
Oracle Cursor Sharing Enhancements 762
Oracle ISO 99 Table Syntax 764
    Outer Join Syntax *767*
External Tables and SQL 769
    Defining an External Table *770*

Internals of External Tables *773*
Tuning Distributed SQL Queries 775
Subqueries and SQL *777*
Basic SQL Subqueries *777*
Scalar Subqueries *779*
In-line Views (Subqueries in the from Clause) *782*
Inside Oracle Views 783
Benefits of Oracle Views *784*
The Downside to Using Views *786*
Combining Hints and Views *786*
Parsing SQL Syntax *787*
Create Executable *787*
Interrogating SQL Execution Plans *789*
Oracle SQL Optimizer Statistics 798
The Oracle dbms_stats Package *799*
Managing Schema Statistics with dbms_stats *803*
Column Skew and histograms *808*
Automating Histogram Sampling with dbms_stats *810*
Oracle Workload Statistics and SQL Performance *814*
External Costing with the Optimizer *818*
Tuning SQL with Histograms *818*
Determining the Optimal Table Join Order *818*
How is Join Cardinality Estimated? *819*
Oracle Join Elimination 820
Using Dynamic Sampling *820*
Sampling Table Scans *822*
Oracle Tuning with Hints 823
When hints appear to be ignored *826*
Oracle Indexes – Is Maintenance Required? *828*
Identifying Problem SQL 830
Find the Problem Sessions *830*
AWR and SQL Tuning 838
Viewing Table and Index Access with AWR *847*
Towards Automated SQL Tuning *865*
The Goals of Holistic SQL Tuning *866*
The SQL Tuning Advisor *867*
Using SQL Tuning Advisor Session *868*
Inside the 11g SQL Performance Analyzer *869*
Inside the Oracle 11g SQL Performance Analyzer *871*
Gathering the SQL Tuning Set *872*
Setting the SQL Optimizer Cost Model *884*
Turning on CPU Costing *885*
Tuning SQL with *"rownum"* Filters 887
Using rownum for top-n queries *888*
Using rownum with range bound queries *889*
Alternatives to rownum *890*
Using OPQ in SQL *891*
Optimizing Oracle SQL Insert Performance *894*
Blocksize and Insert Performance *897*
Oracle Delete Tuning 898
Using Bulking for Delete Performance *899*
Oracle Update Tuning 900
CTAS vs. SQL Update statements *900*
Bulking SQL Updates *904*
Bulking SQL Inserts *905*
Oracle tuning with indexes 906
SQL Tuning with Indexes 906
The types of Oracle indexes 907
The Oracle b-tree index *908*
Creating a b-tree index *911*
Does block size matter? *912*
Tuning SQL with bitmapped indexes 913
Distinct key values and bitmap indexes! *914*
SQL Tuning with bitmap join indexes *916*
How bitmap join indexes work *917*
Bitmap join index example *918*
When Oracle SQL chooses the wrong index 920

Table of Contents

Beware of the fast fix *920*
Forcing index usage.. 920
Why doesn't Oracle use my index? *921*
Using nls_date_format with date indexes *924*
Managing complex date comparisons in SQL... 926
Using the months_between date function *926*
Using the add_months date function *926*
Using the last_day date function *927*
Using the next_day date function *927*
Using the round date function.. *928*
Using the trunc date function... *928*
Index usage and built-in functions *929*
Finding BIF's *930*
Tuning SQL with Function-based Indexes (FBI) *930*
Using case statements with a function-based index *934*
Indexing on complex functions *935*
Statistics and function-based indexes *936*
Conclusions on function-based indexes *937*
SQL tuning with regular expression indexes 938
Indexing on regular expressions *938*
Doing case sensitive searches with indexes *940*
*SQL Tuning with Oracle*Text Indexes* *941*
Oracle Text Index re-synchronization *943*
Tuning SQL with Index Organized Tables.. 943
Testing new Oracle indexes 944
Testing SQL workloads with invisible indexes *945*
Monitoring index usage... 946
Monitoring for Index Range Scans *950*
Monitoring SQL workload activity... 964
Verifying optimal index usage *964*
Finding indexing opportunities *966*
Find SQL that uses sub-optimal indexes *969*
Finding SQL with excessive I/O *970*
Finding sub-optimal SQL in the library cache.. *971*
Finding index opportunities in AWR *973*
Locating un-used indexes *975*
Finding un-used indexes in Oracle 8i and earlier... *975*
Finding un-used indexes in Oracle 9i *975*
Finding un-used indexes in Oracle 10g and beyond *976*
Dropping un-used indexes.. 979
Locating infrequently used indexes 979
The problem of too many indexes.. *981*
Determining which index to delete *984*
Large Multi-column Indexes... *985*
Row clustering and SQL Performance 986
Index reorganization and SQL Performance 988
When rebuilding indexes may help SQL performance.. *988*
When rebuilding indexes will hurt performance... *989*
Choosing candidates for index maintenance... *990*
Conclusion.. 992

Chapter 17: Oracle Data Warehouse Tuning... **994**

Oracle Data Warehouse Tuning 994
What Does a Data Warehouse Need?... 995
Oracle *star transformations* and SQL 998
Bad star transformation Plan *999*
Why Oracle for the Data Warehouse?.. 1001
Scaling the Oracle Data Warehouse 1005
Parallel Query for Data Warehouses *1006*
Oracle Data Warehouse Tuning TPC-H Benchmarks.. 1006
Tuning Tricks for Oracle Data Warehouse Configuration.. *1007*
Data Warehouse Design for High Performance 1008
Oracle Data Warehouse Evolution *1009*
End-user Query Approach.. *1009*
Data Warehouse Tuning Skills 1010
Data Warehouse Project Manager *1011*
The Data Warehouse Informaticist *1011*

The Warehouse Statistician *1011*
The Data Warehouse Oracle Tuning Professional *1012*
Conclusion 1013

Chapter 18: OEM Tuning **1014**

Introduction to OEM 1014
The New OEM *1015*
Tuning with Metrics and Exceptions 1017
Active Session History in Enterprise Manager *1020*
Easy Customization of OEM Alerts 1020
Instance Efficiency Metrics 1022
Alerts Notification and Setup *1022*
Overview of *dbms_scheduler* Functions 1026
Throughput Metrics in OEM 1045
OEM Outside the Instance *1046*
Exception Tuning Inside Enterprise Manager 1052
Advisor Central in OEM 1054
ADDM Main Screen 1057
ADDM Recommendations *1059*
Understanding SQL Advisor Recommendations 1067
The SQL Tuning Advisor Links 1069
The Top SQL Screen *1071*
Viewing SQL Details in OEM *1073*
The Execution Plan Tab *1073*
Current Statistics Tab *1074*
Execution History Tab *1075*
Tuning History Tab *1076*
Oracle SQL Tuning Sets 1077
Creating a SQL Tuning Set *1078*
Viewing SQL Tuning Set Details *1078*
Using the SQL Access Advisor 1079
New Features of the SQL Advisors 1080
Inside the SQL Access Advisor 1081
The SQL Access Advisor Workload Definition *1082*
The SQL Access Advisor Recommendation Options *1083*
The SQL Access Advisor Schedule Advisor *1084*
The SQL Access Advisor Review *1085*
SQL Access Advisor Recommendations *1086*
Using the Memory Advisor through OEM 1088
Persistence of Automatically Tuned Values *1094*
Automated Maintenance Tasks *1094*
Resource Management *1094*
Introduction to Online Oracle Tuning Tools 1094
Using Custom Scripts for Oracle Tuning 1095
Shortcomings of OEM 1097
Conclusion 1102

Chapter 19: Oracle RAC and Grid Tuning **1104**

Introduction to Tuning with RAC 1104
Oracle RAC in a Nutshell 1105
Oracle Scalability and Grid Technology 1108
First Scale Up with SMP Servers *1108*
Next Scale Out with Multiple SMP Servers *1109*
Oracle Grid in a Nutshell 1110
Blade Servers and Oracle RAC Tuning 1112
Blade Servers and Oracle App Servers *1112*
The Revolution of Cache Fusion 1113
Overview of RAC and Grid Tuning 1116
RAC Load Balancing *1117*
Managing Inter-instance Data Block Transfers *1119*
Block Spreading 1120
Blocksize Adjustment *1121*
Read-only Tablespaces *1123*
Parallel Processing and RAC Performance *1123*
Conclusion 1124
Index 1125

Table of Contents

Using the Online Code Depot

Purchase of this book provides complete access to the online code depot containing sample code scripts from this book. The code depot scripts in this book are located at the following URL in zip format:

rampant.cc/oracle_tuning2.htm

If technical assistance is needed with downloading or accessing the scripts, please contact Rampant TechPress at rtp@rampant.cc.

Are you ready to tune?

ION for Oracle is the premier Oracle tuning tool. ION provides unparallel capability for time-series Oracle tuning, unavailable anywhere else.

ION can quickly find and plot performance signatures allowing you to see hidden trends, fast. ION interfaces with STATSPACK or AWR to provide unprecedented proactive tuning insights. Get Ion for Oracle now!

www.ion-dba.com

Oracle Script Collection

Packed with over 600 ready-to-use Oracle scripts, this is the definitive collection for every Oracle professional DBA. It would take many years to develop these scripts from scratch, making this download the best value in the Oracle industry.

It's only $79.95.
For purchase and download go to: www.oracle-script.com or call 252-431-0050.

Conventions Used in this Book

It is critical for any technical publication to follow rigorous standards and employ consistent punctuation conventions to make the text easy to read. However, this is not an easy task. Within database terminology, there are many types of notations that can confuse a reader. For example, some Oracle utilities such as STATSPACK and TKPROF are always spelled in CAPITAL letters, while Oracle parameters and procedures have varying naming conventions in the database documentation. It is also important to remember that many database commands are case sensitive, and are always left in their original executable form, and never altered with italics or capitalization.

Hence, all Rampant TechPress books follow these conventions:

Parameters – All database parameters will be *lowercase italics*. Exceptions to this rule are parameter arguments that are commonly capitalized (KEEP pool, TKPROF), these will be left in ALL CAPS.

Variables – All procedural language (e.g. PL/SQL) program variables and arguments will also remain in *lowercase italics* (*dbms_job, dbms_utility*).

Tables & Dictionary Objects – All data dictionary objects are referenced in lowercase italics (*dba_indexes, v$sql*). This includes all *v$* and *x$* views (*x$kcbcbh, v$parameter*) and dictionary views (*dba_tables, user_indexes*).

SQL – All SQL is formatted for easy use in the code depot, and all SQL is displayed in lowercase. The main SQL terms (select, from, where, group by, order by, having) will always appear on a separate line.

Programs & Products – All products and programs that are known to the author are capitalized according to the vendor specifications (CentOS, VMware, Oracle, etc). All names known by Rampant TechPress to be trademark names appear in this text as initial caps. References to UNIX are always made in uppercase.

Acknowledgements

This type of highly technical reference book requires the dedicated efforts of many people. Even though I am the author, my work ends when I deliver the content. After each chapter is delivered, several Oracle DBAs carefully review and correct the technical content. After the technical review, experienced copy editors polish the grammar and syntax.

The finished work is then reviewed as page proofs and turned over to the production manager, who arranges the creation of the online code depot and manages the cover art, printing, distribution, and warehousing.

In short, the author played a small role in the development of this book, and I need to thank and acknowledge everyone who helped bring this book to fruition:

Steve Karam, for reviewing the content for technical correctness.

Robin Rademacher, for the production management, including the coordination of the cover art, page proofing, printing, and distribution.

Valerre Aquitaine, for help editing and in the production of the pages.

Janet Burleson, for exceptional cover design, graphics and editing.

John Lavender, for assistance with the web site, and for creating the code depot and the managing the distribution for this book.

With my sincerest thanks,

Donald K. Burleson

Preface

Oracle tuning has always been a complex task; however, it has become even more complex as Oracle evolves and yields new techniques for achieving optimal performance in the stressed production environment of today's high-tech world. Increasingly robust versions of Oracle continue to drive the business world's expectations to new heights as end-users no longer tolerate slow access to data. Oracle is a main component of the world's information systems, and DBAs are in charge of the mission-critical data.

Today's end-users have no patience for slow databases. They demand databases that support thousands of transactions per second with sub-second response time. It is the job of the Oracle tuning professional to learn these complexities of high-speed Oracle processing.

A key to database tuning success is the ability to leverage the performance history in Oracle in order to locate and fix bottlenecks. The central feature of this book is the Automatic Workload Repository (AWR), an exciting new element introduced in Oracle10g that is a gold-mine of performance insights. The AWR history is crucial for analysis and tuning, providing a knowledge base for other Oracle intelligent tools such as ADDM and the SQL Performance Advisor.

There are several old-time idioms that can be applied to the concepts in this book:

> *"Time takes time"*
>
> *"Those who cannot remember the past are condemned to repeat it."*
>
> *"The further we can look into the past, the further we can see into the future."*
>
> *"You eat an elephant one bite at a time."*

The *"time takes time"* idiom is important in Oracle tuning because if Oracle is waiting on an external event, like a disk read, no amount of internal tuning is going to help.

The saying *"Those who cannot remember the past are condemned to repeat it."* also applies to Oracle tuning. Oracle rarely experience a performance problem without warning and most system have repeating cycles of workload characteristics, changing in predictable ways by hour of the day, and day of the week.

Winston Churchill also said *"The further we can look into the past, the further we can see into the future.",* and this also applies to Oracle tuning. Using Oracle history tables we can analyze historical repeating trends, tease out signatures, and, by applying holistic tuning techniques, adjust the instance just-in-time for the new workload.

I especially like the saying *"You eat an elephant one bite at a time."* While tuning huge Oracle database may seem like an overwhelming task, I will show you where to start and how to be successful in small incremental steps.

This book strives to show you how to leverage upon the wealth of Oracle performance information so that you can create a robust Oracle database engine, one that maximizes computing resources while minimizing overhead.

However, it is not just DBAs who benefit from an understanding of Oracle tuning. Oracle application developers and programmers can also benefit from understanding Oracle internals and Oracle has several easy-to-use tools to quickly find and correct performance bottlenecks.

This book is intended to be an adjunct to the Oracle documentation collection. The information in this reference is leveraged by my decades of experience tuning real-world Oracle systems. Only the tools and techniques that have a proven track record for improving performance have been included. The goal of this book is to show working DBAs how to use these tools to resolve performance problems and predict future database workload.

If you are seeking theory, this is not the book for you. While I cover all of the theoretical foundations for Oracle tuning, I have deliberately made this book pragmatic, a practical tuning book for the professional DBA.

I have given great thought concerning the organization of this book; the chapters are arranged to present Oracle tuning topics in a logical order:

Oracle Tuning: The Definitive Reference

Introduction To Tuning	STATSPACK & AWR	Oracle Internals	Top Down Tuning	Advanced Topics
Chapter 1 Introduction	Chapter 5 Troubleshoot	Chapter 9 Metrics & V$ Views	Chapter 12 Server & net tuning	Chapter 17 Data Warehouse
Chapter 2 Time-series Tuning	Chapter 6 AWR & STATSPACK	Chapter 10 Wait event tuning	Chapter 13 I/O disk tuning	Chapter 18 Tuning with OEM
Chapter 3 Time model tuning	Chapter 7 Configure	Chapter 11 Tuning tools	Chapter 14 Instance tuning	Chapter 19 RAC & Grid tuning
Chapter 4 Predictive modeling	Chapter 8 Reading reports		Chapter 15 Object tuning	
			Chapter 16 SQL tuning	

Architecture of Oracle Tuning: The Definitive Reference

To let you know about my background, I have a Masters Degree in Business Administration with an Information Systems concentration and I been a full-time DBA since 1983. I was a frequent contributor to numerous national database magazines such as Computerworld, Database Design & Programming Magazine, Software Magazine and many others.

After Oracle first became popular in the 1990's, I wrote for Oracle Magazine and I wrote five of the officially authorized Oracle Press books.

My corporate DBA experience has primarily focused on performance tuning, and I am proud to have worked with some of the world's largest and most complex Oracle databases, systems with tens of thousands of end-users that process thousands of transactions per second.

Working with Oracle during the day, I worked at night teaching graduate school courses in Information Systems for the University of New Mexico, Webster University and many others.

I have gone to great effort to ensure this book is error free in all text and script sections. However, we must remember that while the tuning concepts remain static, Oracle technology is constantly changing.

Remember, every system is different and not every technique described in this book will apply to your specific release and version.

We strive to improve this book with each re-printing and welcome your feedback.

If you have any feedback or comments on how I can improve my book, please e-mail me at tune@rampant.cc

Donald K. Burleson

Introduction to Oracle Tuning

A full redesign?

No chance!

I'm tired of throwing money at Oracle problems!

Just move it to a faster server!

Chief
Information
Officer

"The buck stops here"

An Introduction to Oracle Tuning

Oracle tuning is a complex endeavor, and it does not help that Oracle databases are changing constantly. Database transactions come and go at lightning speed. Tuning a busy Oracle database is like trying to tune a car while it is flying down the highway at 80 miles per hour, and things change at breakneck speeds.

This chapter will cover the following topics, explaining the pros and cons of each approach:

- The reactive tuning approach

- The proactive tuning approach

- The oracle tuning hierarchy

- The external review

- The instance review

- Tuning the instance

- Tuning objects

- Tuning SQL

Let's start by removing some of Oracle's marketing hype. Oracle sells itself as an intelligent self-tuning database, and this is quite true for small departmental systems. However, we must understand that the Oracle automated tuning advisors have limitations and the automated tuning tools are not always sufficient to tune large, complex Oracle databases.

While there is no substitute for the human intuition and expertise of a working Oracle DBA, the scripts and techniques in this book will take you a long way in your Oracle tuning endeavors.

There are many approaches to tuning an Oracle database and while every method seeks to remedy a bottleneck, each tuning approach is very different. There are two dimensions to any Oracle tuning approach:

- Throughput vs. response time

- Top-down tuning vs. Bottom-up Tuning

- Proactive tuning vs. Reactive Tuning

Let's look at these different approaches to Oracle database tuning.

Throughput vs. Response Time

At this point we should note that Oracle has two tuning goals, which are very different and sometimes mutually exclusive:

- **Maximize Throughput:** One type of Oracle tuning will maximize Oracle throughput and minimize the use of hardware resources. This tuning approach is associated with the SQL optimizer goal of *all_rows*.

- **Minimize Response Time:** This tuning approach is concerned with delivering data to the end-users quickly, even if it means that the database will consume additional resources. This approach is associated with the SQL optimizer goal of *first_rows_n*.

Top-down Tuning vs. Bottom-up Tuning

Some Oracle DBAs advocate a bottom-up approach; finding the highest impact SQL statements and tuning them and examining system dumps to tease out significant wait events. Other DBAs advocate a top-down approach whereby the system is first tuned as a whole using the existing workloads before tuning individual SQL statements. The top-down approach is taught at Oracle University and is the primary approach covered in this book.

Proactive Tuning vs. Reactive Tuning

Proactive Oracle tuning examines past trends and signatures to forecast changes to the SGA and data structures. Reactive Oracle tuning deals with the present, commonly using $v\$$ views and Active Session History (ASH) tables to diagnose acute performance problems. In proactive Oracle tuning, DBAs strive to address problems as a whole, examining past trends and signatures to forecast changes to the System Global Area (SGA) and data structures. Also, the 11g SQL Performance Advisor (SPA or SQLPA) is a reactive tuning approach where suspicious workloads are identified and tested against real-world workloads. In reactive tuning, changes are made immediately; in proactive tuning, changes are made just in time, usually in anticipation of changes to the workload characteristics.

Please note that all four of these approaches have a valid use, and the trick is to know when they are appropriate!

A good place to start would be reviewing the proactive and reactive tuning approaches and seeking to understand their relative benefits and shortcomings.

Watch the hype!

The Oracle marketing people have touted the 11g SQL Tuning Advisor as the "*Fully automated SQL tuning*". In reality, SQL tuning requires human intuition.

While the SQL Tuning Advisor and SQL Performance Advisor simplify the work by handling the well-structured aspects of SQL tuning, a human tuning expert is still required.

Ever since the rise of the database in the 1980s, experts have tried to automate the highly human-based task of Oracle performance tuning. As of 2009, Oracle tuning remains a skill highly dependent upon human ability and intuition. It is unlikely that a tool will ever be developed that can replace the skill of a competent and experienced DBA. This is testament to the phenomenal complexity of large Oracle-based systems. Remember, while some aspects of Oracle tuning can be automated, the process still requires human intuition.

Reactive Oracle Tuning

As we might surmise, proactive and reactive Oracle tuning methods are very different. While there is a methodology associated with proactive Oracle tuning, reactive tuning usually happens during emergencies. The end-users are complaining, Oracle is slow, and we must rely on tools such as Oracle Enterprise Manager (OEM) to quickly diagnose and solve acute performance problems.

All Oracle DBAs are charged with ensuring that the Oracle database performs at optimal levels using all hardware as efficiently as possible, quite a challenge.

Historically, we would monitor their databases and when a problem occurred, they would be powerless to fix it because many Oracle tuning actions cannot be done in real-time. Hence, we would note the issue and schedule the appropriate action such as SQL Tuning, parameter adjustment and such during a scheduled maintenance window.

The Oracle 11g SQL tuning advisors are a fully automatic SQL tuning approach and that they use a reactive tuning tool approach, waiting watching for problems to occur.

This "wait until the problem occurs" approach is generally limited in benefit, yet it is practiced widely. In reactive tuning, the Oracle DBA fights the symptoms, not the disease. Hence, the DBA is overwhelmed, constantly fighting fires, without any time to fix the root cause of the performance issues. Reactive tuning is also problematic because we wait until the end-users have been inconvenienced.

Proactive Oracle Tuning

Time-based proactive tuning is a proven approach to long term success. This "holistic" tuning methodology has been codified in the Oracle SQL Performance Analyzer (SPA), a framework that examines real-world workloads and makes global tuning recommendations, tuning the entire workload as a whole.

In proactive tuning, the goal is to set a baseline for immutable database settings, finding the "best" tablespace options, table settings and initialization parameters for each SQL workload.

Once the baselines, signatures, and repeating patterns are identified, time-based tuning becomes easy. To be successful, you must recognize that an Oracle database's workload may change dramatically depending on the time of day, day of the week, and week of the month.

With the incorporation of STATSPACK, the Automated Workload Repository (AWR) and the Automated Session History (ASH) tables into Oracle, we have a gold mine of performance information at our fingertips that allows for the leisurely analysis of Oracle performance statistics and trends over time.

The AWR allows us to devise a general tuning strategy that addresses the different kinds of processing that take place within all Oracle applications. When history repeats itself and we can see it coming, corrective actions can be taken before the database is crippled.

"Those who cannot remember the past are condemned to repeat it."

George Santayana

With proactive tuning, our goal is to tune the Oracle database by optimizing the global parameter settings.

By using a proactive approach to Oracle tuning, the Oracle DBA can ensure that the database is optimally tuned for any type of processing that is demanded of it.

Remember, proactive tuning differs from reactive tuning in several fundamental ways:

- **Offline Analysis:** While trying to observe performance problems as they occur, the bulk of the performance data is gleaned from the historical tables in STATSPACK and AWR. It is not necessary to be there when the problems occur.

- **Time Cycle Tuning:** Unlike reactive tuning, proactive tuning takes time into consideration. This dimension of time allows for the observation of performance in a real-world fashion. When the characteristics of a workload change, tests can be performed to determine how to tweak the instance to optimize this new workload. Using this data, we can schedule a just-in-time fix for the next repetition of this change. Obviously, proactive tuning is not meant for decision support systems and data warehouses that lack discernable repeating cycles inside the workloads.

- **Empirically Tested Changes:** Reactive tuning is tuning done in a crisis, often involving shoot-from-the-hip changes meant to remedy acute performance problems. In proactive tuning, signatures and patterns are defined globally, addressing all performance metrics.

In proactive tuning, the historical information is encapsulated into repeating workloads which are fed into statistically valid tests using the 11g SQL Performance Analyzer or 3rd party tools like Quest Benchmark Factory. Tuning changes can be applied to either the instance as a whole, e.g. change an optimizer *init.ora* parameter, or towards specific SQL statements all based on repeatable and statistically valid tests.

Remember, both proactive and reactive tuning rely on the ability of a DBA to dynamically change the System Global Area (SGA) with *alter system* commands, starting in Oracle 9i. But when we combine the dynamic SGA features with the insights that we gather from STATSPACK or AWR, we can examine real-world workloads and reliably perform just-in-time dynamic SGA reconfiguration, fixing performance problems before they impact our end users.

For example, if the AWR shows that the demands on the shared pool increase between 1:00 pm and 2:00 pm, we might trigger a dynamic decrease of *db_cache_size* and a corresponding increase of the *shared_pool_size* parameter during this time period.

In summary, reactive and proactive tuning are both legitimate approaches. The next step is to take a look at the Oracle tuning hierarchy and become more familiar with the top-down nature of large, complex computer systems. Let's start by acknowledging our limitations as a DBA and understand those things that we cannot change.

Know the Limits: Things that We Can Not Tune

Because we rarely have the luxury of altering the design of a system or the application code, Oracle design and application tuning issues are not addressed in this book. Sadly, we must work within the bounds of our existing database and we rarely have the luxury of fixing a poorly designed system. However, this does not mean that the Oracle DBA is helpless.

Application design is the single most important factor in run-time Oracle performance. Sadly, most Oracle DBAs are unable to improve upon a poor application design, either because the application is proprietary software or because the application is already implemented in a production environment.

Many common external causes of poor Oracle performance are often out of our reach. Examples of these external factors are:

- **Poor Schema Design:** Legacy databases from the early 1990s were designed to minimize data redundancy through high normalization, forcing Oracle to perform unnecessary table joins. While materialized views may offer some relief, legacy schemas are often unchangeable for economic reasons.

- **Poor Application Design:** Many serious performance problems may lie at the application level outside the scope of the Oracle database. If poorly designed PL/SQL is encountered, users may be able to tune the database by using array processing such as *bulk collect*, *for all* and *ref cursors*. Unfortunately, the application code is often out of reach, especially when Oracle calls are placed inside procedural code such as C++.

- **Poor External Environment:** In some shops, Oracle professionals do not have root access to the server resources and may not be able to properly tune their server, disk and/or network environment.

While the re-design of an application is almost always economically unfeasible, we do have "tricks" like materialized views or adding faster hardware to increase performance.

Materialized view can be used to pre-join tables from a legacy system to improve performance, and faster hardware is a common technique when tuning a poorly designed application, where fixing the root cause of the performance problem might cost millions of dollars. Let's take a closer look at the problem of tuning poorly designed databases.

Sadly, poorly designed databases are relatively common and there are several causes of a poorly designed table and index architecture:

- **The Offshore Bargain Database:** Some IT managers will be penny-wise and pound foolish and save money by having their Oracle database designed by untrained third world neophytes.

- **Database Neutral Vendor Packages:** Many application packages such as SAP are not optimized for Oracle. Because you cannot change a vendor package, tuning database neutral databases can be very difficult.

- **The Legacy Database:** A database designed in the 20th century is likely to be over normalized, without introducing the data redundancy that is needed to reduce unnecessary table joins. Using Oracle mechanisms such as materialized views, over-normalized designs can introduce redundancy to pre-join read-only tables together for super-fast query performance.

To understand the issues of tuning a legacy Oracle database, we must remember that hardware technology drives Oracle technology, and databases were designed very differently in the 1980's when a single disk drive would cost a quarter of a million dollars.

Back in the 1980s when disk was $200,000 per gigabyte, designing a database in third normal form (3NF) was a perfect approach, since 3NF is non-redundant, and a DBA management goal was to save expensive disk space.

Obviously, the rules of normalization are required to understand the relationships & functional dependencies, but Boyce-Codd Normal Form (BCNF) or Third Normal Form (3NF) is just a starting point, not a completed model.

Nobody can deny that legacy systems tended to be more highly normalized because of the high cost of disk in the 1990s. Today, disk is incredibly cheap, and many Oracle professionals deliberately introduce redundancy (a technique called *denormalization*) to pre-join tables and improve SQL response time by reducing the number of tables involved in a query.

Oracle offers several popular denormalization tools, some that create non first-normal form structures (0NF):

- **Denormalized Object Tables:** Oracle has *nested tables* and *varray tables* whereby repeating groups are stored within a row, violating 1NF. The *varray tables* remove repeating groups are called non-first-normal-form tables (0NF) tables. Oracle also provides *nested tables* that pre-join one-to-many relationships, but they are poorly implemented in Oracle and are not recommended for high performance. For complete details on denormalized tables, see my book *Oracle Physical Design* by CRC Press.

- **Row Co-location:** In direct violation of the relational model, Oracle provides *cluster tables* to co-locate related rows onto the same physical data blocks, dramatically reducing I/O for some SQL. While relational theory says that data location should not matter, it matters a lot! Oracle *sorted cluster tables* are not to be confused with RAC (Oracle cluster databases).

- **Materialized Views:** In materialized views, tables can be pre-joined together into wide flat redundant tables. The Oracle SQL remains unchanged because queries are automatically re-written to access materialization, and a refresh method (Oracle snapshots) keeps the denormalization in-sync with the normalized representation of the data.

While there are some tricks for holistic tuning, a poorly designed application can only be tuned so far, without gutting it and rebuilding it from scratch. Next, let's look at another problematic area, the application layer, which is often off limits to the Oracle DBA.

Oracle Application-level Tuning

It's very difficult to tune a poorly designed Oracle database, and the same applies to a poorly designed application layer. For numerous and sundry reasons, you may not have the ability to tune some of the most important layers of the system:

- **Application Layer Tuning:** There are many reasons why it's not feasible to tune an application. Most commonly, you cannot change source code that comes from a vendor or you do not have the source code to change the application. A third reason is economic feasibility. While the "root cause" of an Oracle performance problem may be a poorly designed application, it's rarely feasible to spend millions of dollars redesigning the application.

- **Database Schema Tuning:** Tuning a vendor schema is very tricky, especially when you do not have direct access to the SQL, which is embedded within the application.

While the greatest opportunity for improving performance is at the application layer, there are many roadblocks to application layer tuning. While all Oracle tuning professionals know that there are many optimization opportunities at the application layer, we don't have the luxury of tuning the SQL statement within an application, nor the ability to tune procedural code that populates the online screens. Other cases where you may not be able to tune the application layer include:

- **Vendor Applications:** If you do not have access to the source code, if can be very challenging to change the SQL execution plans.
- **Ad-Hoc Query Tools:** Tools like Crystal Reports and Oracle Discoverer generate dynamic SQL. Dynamic SQL is created on-the-fly and it is notoriously difficult to intercept and tune because there is no direct access to the SQL source code.
- **Economic Constraints:** If your management will not pay to spend several years tuning 10,000 SQL statements, then you are forced to perform holistic instance tuning, adjust system-wide Oracle parameters to optimize the SQL workload.

In these cases, the best you can hope to do is adjust the global optimizer parameters to optimizer as many SQL statements as possible.

While application level tuning is normally a developer tasks, there are some things that can be done to improve the application layer.

- **Bulk Operations:** If you have access to the PL/SQL at the application layer, you can deploy the *bulk collect* and *forall* operators to improve application performance. See Dr. Hall's book *"PL/SQL Tuning Secrets"* for detailed examples of bulk application fetches and inserts.

- **Reducing Network Round Trips:** A very common application layer issue is a single online screen that makes multiple trips to Oracle to populate the screen values. By encapsulating the SQL into a package and consolidate the screen data into a single request, SQL*Net round trips are reduced and response time is improved.

Remember, while system-wide instance tuning can be extremely helpful in tuning an applications SQL workload, it is not uncommon have shifting workloads. In these cases, we need to adjust the instance parameters need to change, depending on the time-of-day and day-of-week. See Chapter 2, *Time Series Oracle Tuning* for details on how to tune shifting SQL workloads over time.

Before exploring the Oracle tuning hierarchy, we should look into the crystal ball and see how the role of the Oracle professional is going to evolve over the next decade. Consistent advances in hardware, technology and Oracle automation features have affected the job duties of the Oracle professional.

A Historical Review of DBA Job Duties

The Oracle professional of the 21st century will be relieved of the time consuming task of monitoring and tuning and be able to concentrate on less tedious aspects of the DBA role.

When large scale corporate databases first appeared in the late 1970s, all of the applications ran under a single mainframe, and it took only a few DBAs to manage these applications because everything was in a centralized shared environment.

In the 1990s minicomputers appeared and changed the economics of database administration. Shops that used to have a single mainframe now had hundreds of tiny servers to manage and they needed dozens of DBAs to support the systems, which were often placed in a one-server, one-database configuration.

It's true that *"Too many cooks spoil the broth"* and too many DBAs often meant that important tasks were overlooked, often because of miscommunication and job compartmentalization. With hundreds of tiny servers to manage, some DBAs did nothing but apply patches all day, while other DBAs did nothing but install upgrades. This excessive job compartmentalization led to an *"It is not my job"* mentality.

Fortunately, the days of minicomputers are now gone, and we are returning to using large centralized computers, forcing the surviving DBAs to have much broader responsibilities.

As server consolidations caught on in the early 21st century, DBAs were fired by the boatload because corporations no longer needed a large staff. The best DBAs remained in high demand, but marginal DBAs with limited skills had serious employment issues. DBAs who were used for the repetitive tasks like installing upgrades on hundreds of small servers found it hard to stay involved with Oracle.

Job compartmentalization disappeared and the DBA was free to take on more responsibilities in previously disregarded areas such as system design and security.

Hardware advances always drive changes in Oracle technology, and the falling prices of hardware have led to many important changes:

- **Oracle Server Consolidation**: Server consolidation technology has greatly reduced the number of Oracle servers, while providing far better sharing of RAM and CPU resources.

- **Centralized DBA Management:** A single server means a single copy of the Oracle software, so we have less time spent patching and applying upgrades.

- **Transparent High Availability:** If a CPU fails, the monolithic server can re-assign the processing without interruption. This is a more affordable and far simpler solution than Real Applications Clusters (RAC) or Oracle Data Guard, either of which requires duplicate servers.

- **Scalability:** Using a single large server, additional CPU and RAM can be seamlessly added for increased performance.

- **Reduced DBA Workload:** By consolidating server resources, DBAs have fewer servers to manage and need not be concerned with outgrowing the server.

In a centralized server environment, the operating system controls resource allocation for all of the Oracle instances and the server will automatically balance the demands of many Oracle instances for processing cycles and RAM resources. Of course, we still maintain control, and we slice and dice recourses when required. We can dedicate Oracle instances to a single CPU using VMware or processor affinity, and we can control dispatching priority of Oracle tasks with the UNIX *"nice"* command.

What do these changes mean to the DBA's job duties? Clearly, less time is spent installing and maintaining multiple copies of Oracle, and this allows time to pursue more advanced tasks such as SQL tuning and database performance optimization.

The economics of server technology has changed radically over the past 60 years. In the 1960s, IBM dominated the server market with giant mainframe servers costing in the millions of dollars. These behemoth water-cooled mainframes required huge operation centers and a large support staff. Over the decades many things have changed:

- **1960s:** Only the largest of corporations could afford their own data processing center, and all small to mid-sized companies had to rent CPU cycles from a data center in order to automate their business processes.

- **1970s:** By now, all large corporations had a mainframe computer and they were automating simple, repetitive tasks such as payroll processing. Small UNIX-based servers existed, like the PDP-11, but they far too unreliable to be used for a commercial application.

- **1980s:** In 1981, the first commercial personal computer (PC) was unveiled and practically overnight, computing power was in the hands of the masses. Software vendors rushed to develop useful products that would run on a PC, and the introduction of VisiCalc heralded the first business application outside the mainframe domain.

- **1990s:** Oracle is developed, and relational databases dominate the IT market. Large shops have hundreds of small UNIX-based computers for their Oracle databases.

- **2000s:** Monolithic servers reappear, and Oracle shops undertake a massive server consolidation. By 2009, an industrial strength server could support up to 128 processors and run hundreds of Oracle instances.

- **2010s:** In this decade, disks become obsolete and Oracle databases are now solid-state, using disk only for back-end persistence. Hardware costs will fall to the point that less than 30 percent of the IT budget is spent on hardware.

- **2020s:** Largely the results of the advances of hardware technology, Oracle professionals of the year 2020 see a very different landscape:

  - Large mainframe-sized servers will replace minicomputers.

  - Most PC software is accessed over the Internet, and PCs become "dumb terminals". This is Larry Ellison's vision of the "internet appliance", a PC with no local disks, just a Java-enabled web browser. All applications and data are fetched using on-demand cloud computing resources.

  - High-speed network bandwidth will allow instant content delivery and server-to-server communications.

  - Databases become three dimensional, allowing for temporal data presentation, like Oracle Flashback on steroids.

Now that we understand the history, and a glimpse into the future, let's explore how server consolidation will help us tune Oracle databases.

Oracle Tuning and Server Consolidation

At the dawn of the 21st century, server consolidation was well underway when Oracle introduced the idea of Grid computing. In both grid computing and server consolidation, CPU and RAM resources are delivered on-demand. But far and away, the server consolidation movement task surged ahead because there is no better way to share computing resources than to have them instantly available and controlled by the operating system.

This is no *"putting all of your eggs in one basket"* issue either because the new mainframe-like servers are fully redundant, providing high availability for all server components including RAM, CPU, busses and disks. The days of client-server computing are gone and companies are dismantling their ancient server farms and consolidating into large single servers. This means huge savings in both management and hardware costs. During this transition we also see these changing trends:

- **CPU speed outpaces RAM speed:** RAM speed had not improved since the 1970s while CPU speeds gets faster every year. This means that RAM sub-systems must be localized close to the processors to keep the CPUs running at full capacity. This is the special "T1" RAM that the Oracle kernel can address.

- **Flash Disk storage:** Platter disks are being replaced by solid-state RAM disk which can run up to 600 times faster than the spinning platter disks.

- **New bottlenecks:** Oracle databases are shifting from being I/O-bound to CPU-bound as a result of large-scale data caching.

From a historical perspective, it is important to remember that the initial departure from the "glass house" mainframe was not motivated by any compelling technology. Rather, this change was a matter of pure economics. We will soon see that hardware technology drives Oracle technology, so let's take a closer look.

Hardware Technology Drives Database Technology

The new mini-computers of the 1990s were far cheaper than mainframes and provided computing power with a lower hardware cost, but a higher human cost because there were more servers to patch and upgrade. But management found it hard to resist the idea of a $30,000 server, especially when compared to mainframes with costs millions of dollars each.

Hence, the demand increased for more system administrators and DBAs to manage the teeny-tiny mini servers that replaced the giant mainframes. This changing in hardware costs led IT management to begin dismantling their mainframes, replacing them with hundreds of small UNIX-based minicomputers (Figure 1.1).

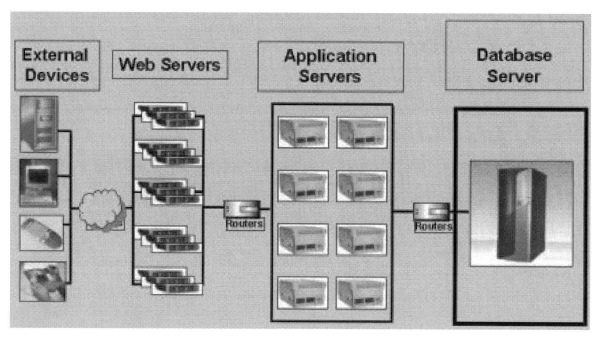

Figure 1.1: *The Multi-server Architecture of the Late 20th Century*

In shops with multiple Oracle instances, consolidating onto a single large server saved thousands of dollars in resource costs and provided better resource allocation. In many cases, the payback period for server consolidation was very short, especially when the existing system had reached the limitations of the 32-bit architecture and a 64-bit solution was needed.

The proliferation of server farms in the 1990s caused a huge surge in demand for Oracle DBA professionals. While multiple database servers gave us job security, they presented an expensive challenge to IT management because they were far less effective than a monolithic mainframe solution:

- **High expense:** In large enterprise data centers, hardware resources were deliberately over-allocated in order to accommodate processing load peaks.

- **High waste:** Because each Oracle instance resided on a single server, there was significant duplication of administration and maintenance and a suboptimal utilization of RAM and CPU resources.

- **Labor intensive:** In many large Oracle shops, a shuffle occurred when a database outgrew its server. A new, larger server would be purchased, and the database would be moved, while another database was migrated onto the old server. This shuffling of databases between servers was a huge headache for Oracle DBAs who were kept busy after hours, moving databases to new server platforms.

When the new 16, 32, and 64-CPU servers were introduced in the early 2000s, it became clear to IT management that the savings in manpower easily outweighed the costs of the monolithic hardware. We soon realized that with a consolidated server we could get more CPU and RAM resources as our processing demands increased. This was a fast, easy, and seamless growth path for the new mainframe computers of the early 21st century (Figure 1.2).

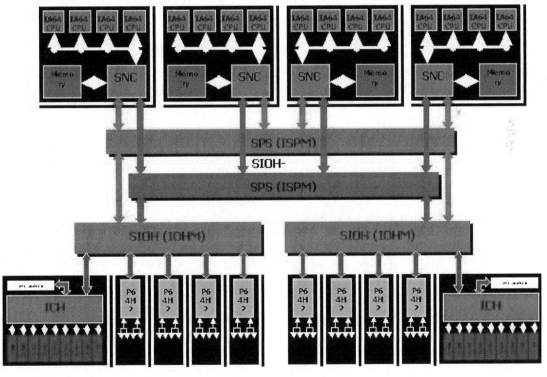

Figure 1.2: *The Intel-CPU Architecture of the Early 21st Century*

A single server meant a single copy of the Oracle software. In addition, the operating system now controlled resource allocation and the server OS automatically balanced the processing demands of all of the Oracle instances. Of course, we still maintain control of the RAM and CPU within the server. As stated in the historical review earlier in this chapter, we can continue to dedicate Oracle instances to a fixed set of CPUs using processor affinity or VMware, and we can adjust the CPU dispatching priority with the UNIX "nice" command.

If any CPU happened to fail, the monolithic server would re-assign the processing without interruption. This offered a solution much more affordable and simple than RAC or Oracle grid computing. By consolidating server resources, we have fewer servers to manage and we are no longer concerned about outgrowing the server. The server consolidation movement also meant that fewer Oracle DBAs were needed.

With the transition to centralized computing, there were fewer job openings for Oracle DBAs, and IT management could now be far more selective, retaining only the best and the brightest Oracle professionals to be the custodians of their mission-critical data. Let's take a closer look at how the job of the Oracle DBA has changed and how it will evolve into a new role in the coming years.

This next section explores the legitimacy of Oracle's automation strategy, the rapid movement towards server consolidation and other important industry trends. As we will learn, the job of Oracle DBA is moving beyond compartmentalized duties into a broader spectrum.

The Changing Role of an Oracle Tuning Professional

In the late 20th century, minicomputers ruled and shops with a hundred instances had to manage a hundred servers, requiring dozens of Oracle DBAs. This decentralization of computer resources led to huge wasted effort. I once spent six months of my life upgrading 370 servers from Oracle 8i to Oracle 9i.

Because of the stress of managing hundreds of servers, important tuning tasks were often overlooked because of "*It is not my job*" or "*I do not have time*" attitudes among Oracle professionals. Fortunately, client-server died in the late 1990s and today we see massive server consolidation, as shops recognize that a large monolithic computer is the best way to share computing resources and minimize redundant DBA work. This changing technology mandated that the 21st century DBA would have more overall responsibility, meaning they were now in charge of the whole operation of the Oracle database.

So, what did this mean to the Oracle DBA of the early 21st century? Clearly, less time was spent installing and maintaining multiple copies of Oracle, and this freed up time to pursue more advanced tasks such as SQL tuning and database performance optimization.

Nevertheless, the sad reality of server consolidation was that thousands of mediocre Oracle DBAs lost their jobs from the return to centralized computing. We also see the technology driving the role of the Oracle tuning professional as hardware prices fall rapidly while the Oracle DBA salary continues to be high, averaging $97,000 per year according to an Oracle 2009 salary survey. This shift in costs has important ramifications for Oracle tuning because hardware becomes cheap relative to the expense of human tuning (Figure 1.3).

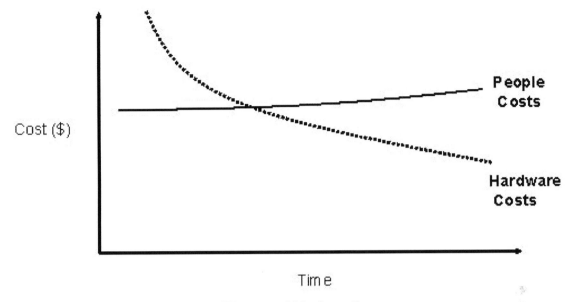

Figure 1.3: *The Changing Dynamics of Human and Hardware Costs*

The surviving Oracle DBAs were relieved of the tedium of managing hundreds of servers, and the Oracle DBA job duties became far more demanding as the DBA became wholly responsible for every aspect of the corporate data, a broad spectrum of duties ranging from security to performance management.

Consequently, the Oracle DBAs of the 21st century are faced with new educational requirements. Today's successful DBAs often have advanced degrees in both computer science and business administration.

As is now evident, the DBA role is becoming broader than ever before. The scope of a DBA's job now encompasses many different areas of data management.

As we see from Figure 1.3, hardware is cheap compared to human effort and it is perfectly reasonable to use faster hardware as a stop-gap solution to Oracle tuning issues. While "*throwing hardware at a tuning problem*" does not address the root-cause, a hardware-based solution is fast, risk free and often cheaper than a root-cause fix.

Using Hardware to Correct a Suboptimal Oracle Database

While an excessive amount of resource consumption may be due to a poorly optimized Oracle database, the perceptive Oracle tuning professional knows that many tuning problems can be solved with the addition of faster hardware. Cost is always an issue in database design. Hardware upgrades offer an inexpensive solution when compared to the expense of database re-design. It is a common choice for managers who need quick, low-risk performance improvements.

For example, tuning 5,000 SQL statements might cost $100,000 in human resources, but moving to faster 64-bit processors might only cost $20,000. Another example is a system that is heavily I/O-bound due to a poorly written application.

Rebuilding the application might cost millions of dollars and take many months, yet a move to super-fast hardware can happen overnight at less cost and risk. The application is still poorly written, but it runs many times faster. It may not be elegant to throw hardware at an Oracle performance problem, but it can often be a safe, cost-effective and timely solution to an acute Oracle performance issue.

So far in this chapter we have introduced proactive and reactive tuning and a historical overview of the evolution of Oracle tuning.

The Causes of Poor Oracle Performance

What are the most common root causes of poor Oracle performance? Below is a list of some common problems:

- **Bad database design:** The number one cause of poor performance is the over-normalization of Oracle tables. This includes excessive and unused indexes and 15-way table joins for what should be simple fetches.

- **Poor server optimization:** Changes to the server kernel parameters and I/O configuration have profound impact on Oracle performance.

- **Bad disk I/O configuration:** Inappropriate use of RAID5, disk channel bottlenecks and poor disk striping all contribute to poor Oracle performance.

- **Poor Optimizer Statistics:** Prior to Oracle 10g and its automatic statistics, a common cause of poor SQL performance was missing/stale CBO statistics and missing histograms. Even in Oracle 11g, the optimizer cannot always be trusted to choose the best statistics in every situation.

- **Object contention:** Failure to set ASSM, freelists or *freelist_groups* for DML-active tables and indexes can cause very slow DML performance.

- **Under-allocated RAM regions:** Not allocating enough RAM for *shared_pool_size, pga_aggregate_target* and *db_cache_size* can cause an I/O-bound database.

- **Non-reentrant SQL:** All SQL should use bind variables, preferably in the code or via *cursor_sharing=force*, to make SQL reusable within the library cache.

- **Un-set initialization parameters:** Many initialization parameters, such as *db_file_multiblock_read_count* before 10gr2 and *optimizer_index_caching,* have been designed to be set by the DBA. Failure to set these parameters properly results in poorly optimized execution plans.

- **Excessive nested loop joins:** In 64-bit Oracle systems, there are gigabytes available for RAM sorts and hash joins. Failure to set *pga_aggregate_target* to allow the CBO to choose hash joins can result in very slow SQL performance.

- **Corporate misfeasance:** A DBA's failure to monitor the database (STATSPACK/AWR), set up exception reporting alerts (OEM) and adjust the instance to match changing workloads can be a major cause of poor performance.

The next section will began exploring Oracle tuning with a look at the natural top-down hierarchy within Oracle tuning.

The Oracle Tuning Hierarchy

It can be tempting to take a shotgun approach to Oracle tuning, applying specific changes to specific problems without regard for the larger environment.

Oracle does not run in a vacuum!

Beware that a large number of Oracle performance problems can be traced to external factors, some of which may be beyond our control.

The many performance areas that are inaccessible to Oracle professionals make it easy to become disheartened with the tuning process. However, it is possible to make a dramatic difference in Oracle performance.

Let's explore the things that can be changed, starting with the Oracle tuning hierarchy; a top-down approach to Oracle tuning is mandatory because of the way global changes impact each tuning layer (Figure 1.4). This method continues the exploration of how the external environment impacts Oracle performance and how CPU, disk, and network effect different areas of Oracle content delivery.

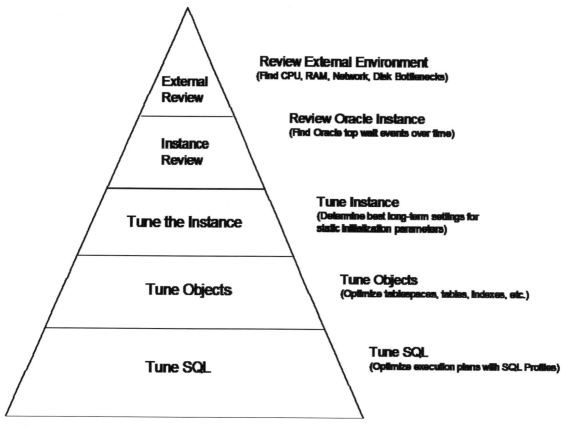

Figure 1.4: *The Oracle Tuning Hierarchy*

Remember, no amount of Oracle tuning is going to remedy poor system design or an improperly configured disk I/O sub-system.

The following is a top-down approach to Oracle tuning that has been very successful for tuning Oracle systems, large and small. This approach starts with a review of server and instance bottlenecks, followed by the application of solutions, moving from global to specific. As we have noted, it is assumed that the design and application performance is untouchable restricting the tuning process to the Oracle database boundary.

The main categories of Oracle tuning include these tasks:

- **Review the external environment:** This is a review of the server, disk and network environment to ascertain if hardware components are over-stressed or under-utilized.

- **Review the instance metrics:** This is a review of the specific events and metrics within AWR over a period of time to understand repeating patterns and the exact nature of a performance problem.

- **Perform the instance tuning:** This is the adjustment of system-wide parameters that affect the behavior of the whole database. Since any Oracle database is in a constant state of flux, it is critical to identify the best overall setting for each of Oracle's 250+ initialization parameters and develop bi-modal instances when necessary.

- **Perform the object tuning:** This is a review of specific wait events that are closely tied to data files, tablespaces, tables and indexes. The source of the stress is examined for each object and then the object characteristics are adjusted in order to remove the bottleneck.

- **Perform the SQL tuning:** This is the most time-intensive of the tuning tasks. The *dba_hist* tables are used to extract suboptimal SQL and search for suboptimal table join order, unnecessary large-table full-table scans, or inefficient execution plans. The SQL is then tuned manually by using hints or with the Oracle SQL Tuning Advisor where SQL profiles can be used to alter execution plans.

The following is a quick overview of these proactive tuning steps, and a subsequent chapter is dedicated to each of these topics later in the book.

External Hardware Performance Review

As stated earlier, Oracle does not run in a vacuum. The performance of an Oracle database depends heavily on external considerations; namely, the Oracle server, disk, and network. The first step when tuning a database is to identify any external bottleneck conditions, which may include:

- **CPU bottleneck:** A shortage of CPU cycles can slow down SQL. Whenever the run queue exceeds the number of CPUs on the Oracle server in the absence of high idle times, the system is said to be CPU-bound. This excessive CPU consumption can be reduced through tuning SQL and reducing library cache contention. However, a CPU shortage may indicate a need to add or upgrade servers.

- **RAM bottleneck:** The amount of available RAM memory can affect the performance of SQL, especially in the regions that control data buffers, in-memory sorts, and hash joins.

- **Network bottleneck:** Large amounts of Oracle*Net traffic can contribute to slow SQL performance.

- **Disk bottleneck:** Disk bottlenecks are common when updates are slow due to channel contention. An example of this is using RAID5 for high update systems.

There are several simple metrics that can be monitored within the external Oracle environment:

- **CPU run queue waits:** When the number of run queue waits exceeds the number of CPUs on the server, the server is experiencing a CPU shortage. This is remedied by increasing the number of CPUs on the server or by disabling high CPU consumers, such as Oracle Parallel Query. Note that a 10% CPU level is not always a concern since modern servers are designed to keep the processors as busy as possible. For more details, see Chapter 12, *Server and Network Tuning with AWR.*

- **RAM page-ins:** When RAM page-in operations are noted along with a prior increase in scan-rate, the non-virtual RAM memory has been exceeded and memory pages are moving into RAM from the swap disk. The remedy for excessive swapping is to add more RAM, reduce the size of the Oracle SGAs, or turn on Oracle Shared Server.

- **Disk enqueues:** Enqueues on a disk device may indicate that the channels are saturated or that the read-write heads cannot move fast enough to keep up with data access requirements

- **Network latency:** Volume-related network latency may indicate either the need to tune the application so that it will make fewer requests or a need for faster network hardware.

Finding Database Bottlenecks

Every Oracle database has at least one physical constraint. Although common, this limitation does not always lie with the disks. The best way to isolate the constraints in the system is to analyze the top five wait events for the database and look for any external waits that might be associated with disk, CPU and network. The best way to see system-level wait summaries is to run the *awrrpt.sql* script from the *$oracle_home/rdbms/admin* directory. This will yield the top five timed events for the specific interval between AWR snapshots.

For a complete treatment of Oracle troubleshooting, see Chapter 5, *Oracle Troubleshooting*. If you don't like managing hundreds of dictionary scripts, the top wait events can also be quickly identified by using the Top Wait Events report in the *Ion for Oracle* tool (Figure 1.5).

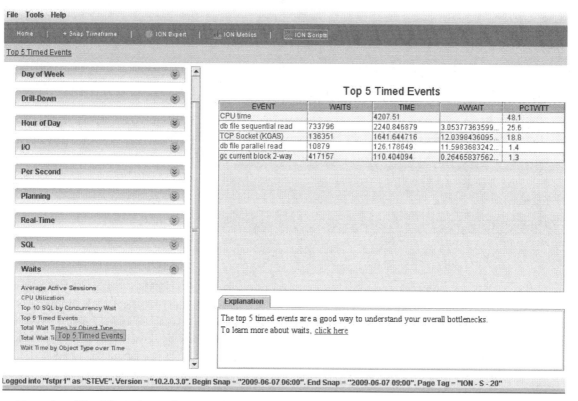

Figure 1.5: *Top Wait Events Report in Ion for Oracle*

Disk Constrained Database

In a disk-bound database, the majority of the wait time is spent accessing data blocks. This can be *db file sequential read* waits, usually index access, and *db file scattered read* waits, usually full-table scans, similar to the following section of a sample AWR report:

```
Top 5 Timed Events

                                                     % Total
Event                         Waits     Time (s)   Ela Time
---------------------------   ---------  ---------  --------
db file sequential read        2,598      7,146      48.54
db file scattered read        25,519      3,246      22.04
library cache load lock          673      1,363       9.26
CPU time                          44      1,154       7.83
log file parallel write       19,157        837       5.68
```

Disk constrained databases were common in the 32-bit world where RAM was constrained to 2**32, or about 2 gigabytes. Today's 64-bit servers have very large RAM caches and disk I/O bottlenecks have been displaced with CPU limitations. (Figure 1.6)

Top 5 Events

control file sequential read - 15.8%	
The control file sequential read Oracle metric indicates the process is waiting for blocks to be read from a control file.	This happens in many cases. For example, you can see a "control file sequential read" when you are making a backup of the controlfiles, sharing information (between instances) from the controlfile, reading other blocks from the controlfiles, and most importantly, when you are reading the header block for a data file.

db file sequential read - 10.1%	
The sequential read event occurs when Oracle reads single blocks of a table or index. Look at the tablespace IO section of the report for tablespaces with less than 2 average blocks per read, high response time, and a large percentage of the total IO.	Moving the data files with the largest amount of time spend waiting on single-block reads to faster storage can significantly reduce the amount of time spent waiting on this event. By reducing the time spent waiting on this event, the database performance could increase 11%.

control file parallel write - 6.0%	
This wait is caused by waiting on writes to the control files.	Moving the control files on to faster storage can help alleviate this wait. It may also be beneficial to investigate the frequency of redo log switching, as new logs and archive generation can cause more control file writes.

db file parallel write - 5.2%	
The DBWR process produces this wait event as it writes dirty blocks to the datafiles. This event can cause poor read performance, and the writes may interfere with reads from the data files.	Moving the tables that are experiencing the highest write activity to faster storage may help to alleviate this wait event. If your datafiles are not striped across multiple spindles, consider better striping or reorganization of files on disks.

Figure 1.6: *Advice for tuning a disk constrained database in Ion for Oracle*

Disk constrained databases are not the only reason for database bottlenecks. Next to be examined is the influence of CPUs on wait time.

CPU Constrained Database

In an Oracle database, the majority of wait time is time spent waiting on I/O or processing computations. As previously indicated, CPU enqueues can be observed when the CPU run queue exceeds the number of CPUs on the database server. This can be seen by looking at the "r" column in the *vmstat* UNIX/Linux utility or within the Windows Performance Manager. If the system is already optimized, having CPU time as a top wait event is a positive because the addition of faster CPUs or more CPUs will relieve the bottleneck.

High CPU usage is also indicative of excessive logical I/O, or *consistent gets*, against the data buffers, which may indicate the need for SQL tuning or shared pool and library cache tuning. High CPU usage may even be reported as a top five timed event in any AWR report, as shown below:

```
Top 5 Timed Events
                                                          % Total
Event                           Waits     Time (s)  Ela Time
------------------------------- ---------- --------- --------
CPU time                          4,851      4,042    55.76
db file sequential read           1,968      1,997    27.55
log file sync                   299,097        369     5.08
db file scattered read           53,031        330     4.55
log file parallel write         302,680        190     2.62
```

Next, let's wrap up the overview of database bottlenecks with a review of network issues within the Oracle database.

Network Constrained Database

Network bottlenecks are common in systems that are disturbed or experience high network traffic. These bottlenecks manifest as SQL*Net wait events as evidenced by this mockup AWR report:

```
Top 5 Wait Events
                                                          % Total
Event                           Waits      Time (cs)  Wt Time
------------------------------- ---------- ---------- -------
SQL*Net more data to client     3,914,935  9,475,372   99.76
db file sequential read         1,367,659      6,129     .06
db file parallel write              7,582      5,001     .05
rdbms ipc reply                        26      4,612     .05
db file scattered read             16,886      2,446     .03
```

Server statistics can be viewed in a variety of ways using standard server-side UNIX and Linux tools. Tools such as *vmstat*, *glance*, *top* and *sar* can be used to ensure that the database server has enough CPU and RAM resources at all times in order to manage the Oracle requests.

Server stress can change depending upon the time. For instance, a system may be CPU-bound in the morning and network-bound in the afternoon. The challenge is to identify server stress over time and learn to interpret any trends in hardware consumption. For example, Oracle Enterprise Manager tracks server run queue waits over time and combines the CPU and paging display into a single OEM screen. This gives DBAs the ability to tell when the system is experiencing server-side waits on hardware resources. Figure 1.7 shows an example of CPU run queue trends over time.

Figure 1.7: *Server CPU Run Queue and RAM Paging Values over Time*

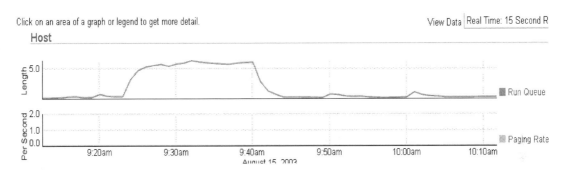

This time-based display is important because it illustrates how Oracle performance issues can be transient with short spikes of excessive hardware consumption. Due to the super fast nature of CPU dispatching, a database might be CPU constrained several times per day, often for minutes at a time. The time series OEM display gives a quick visual clue about those times when the system is experiencing such a bottleneck.

The next step in the process involves drilling down to look at the overall tuning of the Oracle instance.

Oracle Instance Tuning

As a quick review, an Oracle instance is the allocated RAM region on the server, which is called the System Global Area (SGA). Individual Program Global Areas (PGAs) for each session are a set of running programs that do the work for the instance and are referred to as processes.

Instance tuning will be discussed in great detail in Chapter 14, *Oracle Instance Tuning*, but this will provide a quick overview.

Tune the instance first!

Remember that the instance configuration parameters have a profound impact on SQL execution plans and overall performance.

Oracle instance tuning consists of the adjustment of the static global parameters that effect Oracle performance. The process begins with an examination of the instance to locate bottlenecks and sub-optimal settings. The rules for instance tuning vary greatly, depending on the release of the Oracle database software.

Dynamic Instance Parameters

After the release of Oracle9i, it became possible to adjust the values of many important SGA parameters. These include:

- ***shared_pool_size:*** The memory region allocated for the library cache and internal control structures

- ***pga_aggregate_target:*** A shared RAM area, outside the SGA, where Oracle performs sorting and hash joins

- ***db_cache_size:*** The number of data buffers to allocate for the instance

Oracle users can employ the Oracle Automatic Memory Management (AMM) facility for this area of instance tuning. Remember, the more processes that can be automated, the easier it will be to control time-based performance. Many DBAs create their own ad-hoc triggers using *dbms_scheduler* to change these dynamic parameter values, depending on upcoming database stress loads.

The following section is an introduction to the non-changeable parameters.

Static Instance Parameters

The most important parameters for instance tuning are those that are immutable because they cannot be changed without starting and stopping the instance or using *alter session* commands or SQL hints. Because they survive for the entire existence of an instance run, these parameters must be carefully set in order to accommodate the average load on the database during its uptime. The most important of these parameters include:

- ***db_file_multiblock_read_count:*** When set to a high value, the CBO recognizes that scattered (multi-block) reads may be less expensive than sequential reads. This makes the CBO friendlier to full-table scans.

- ***parallel_automatic_tuning*** : When set to ON, full-table scans are parallelized. Since parallel full-table scans are very fast, the CBO will give a higher cost-to-index access and will be friendlier to full-table scans.

- ***optimizer_mode:*** The optimal setting for this important parameter can affect the execution plans for thousands of SQL statements

- ***optimizer_index_cost_adj:*** This parameter controls the relative costs of full-table scans versus index scans

- ***optimizer_index_caching:*** This parameter allows DBAs to tell Oracle how much of an index resides in the RAM data buffer cache on average. This is an important clue when the optimizer makes access decisions.

Inside AWR and STATSPACK

One of the most important Oracle tuning tools is the free STATSPACK utility. In addition the extra-cost AWR tables are available via the purchase of the Oracle Performance Pack and Oracle Diagnostic Pack.

STATSPACK and AWR are almost identical in functionality, they serve to store historical performance information in history tables. Because the SGA internal structures have accumulated statistics, snapshots of these in-memory statistics can be taken. These snapshots are then used to create delta reports showing the changes between a before and after snapshot, creating essentially an elapsed-time performance report.

This is just a brief introduction to the extra-cost AWR and its free cousin, STATSPACK. For complete details, see Chapters 6, 7 and 8.

The AWR utility can trace its ancestry to extensions of the ancient Oracle7 *bstat-estat* utilities and to STATSPACK, which was introduced in Oracle8i. Whenever an AWR snapshot is requested, Oracle interrogates the in-memory *x$* and *v$* structures and stores the information in the appropriate Oracle *dba_hist* views.

Having a historical collection over long periods of time gives the opportunity to accurately simulate and implement an optimal overall performance plan for the database instance. Moreover, Oracle DBAs have the unique ability to visually represent AWR information with either Excel spreadsheet graphics or the Ion for Oracle tool.

Throughout the remainder of this book, details will be provided that will show how the AWR tables can be used to gain insight into the where, what, and how of the optimal tuning plan. The rest of this chapter will include an overview of Oracle tuning starting with general issues such as poor design and suboptimal applications, then move into more Oracle-specific areas.
Now let's take a look at the licensing issues surrounding STATSPACK and the extra-cost AWR. AWR is not inexpensive, but only you can decide whether to use AWR, or the free STATSPACK alternative.

AWR Licensing Options

Oracle Corporation invested millions of dollars to create the Automated Workload Repository (AWR) and the self-tuning features of ADDM and the SQL Tuning Advisor, but they still cannot replicate the skill of a human tuning expert. This is not the fault of Oracle per se; any automated tool is going to be more limited than a human.

It's also important to know that Oracle is does not have any safeguards to prevent you from accidentally using extra-cost features, but they do have an auditing mechanism that will tell them if you have used an extra-cost feature!

Most Oracle licensing agreements give Oracle Corporation the right to audit user databases to ensure that they have paid for all of the Oracle optional tools that are in use.

This includes the Oracle Database Diagnostic Pack and Oracle Tuning Pack (both required fir the AWR), as well as the Automatic Database Diagnostic Monitor (ADDM), including use of the following:

- The *dbms_advisor* package with ADDM as the value to the *advisor_name* parameter

- Access to views starting with *dba_advisor_** of all tasks generated by ADDM, i.e. tasks with ADDM as the *advisor_name* column in *dba_advisor_tasks* view

- Use of the *dbms_workload_repository* package

- Running the *awrrpt.sql* and *awrrpti.sql* reports

- Querying the *dba_hist_** and *v$active_session_history* views

Remember, the extra-cost Database Tuning Pack is required if use any of the SQLTuning Advisor PL/SQL packages (that are located in the *$oracle_home/rdbms/admin* directory). This includes the following packages:

- The *dbms_advisor* package with SQLTuning Advisor as the value to the *advisor_name* parameter

- Using the *addmrpt.sql* or *addmrpti.sql* reports

- Invoking the *dbms_sqltune* package

These features can get expensive. According to oraclestore.oracle.com in 2010, the costs in the U.S. are a total of $7,000.00 per CPU:

- **Oracle Diagnostics pack** - $3,500/processor

- **Oracle Tuning pack** - $3,500/processor

So, if both products are used on a 16-CPU server, the costs for Oracle Performance Pack and Oracle Tuning Pack would be over $100,000, a significant sum of money.

Check your license!

Oracle frequently changes licensing options and it is important to consult your support representative for details about the specific Oracle license options.

Adhering to the Oracle licensing rules is critical to avoid running up a bill for extra licensing fees because of queries to the AWR tables.

Before moving into using AWR, let's quickly review how Oracle tracks usage of these extra-cost features.

Tracking your Oracle Option Usage

Oracle has auditing functions to inform Oracle Corporation if anybody has been querying the AWR or ASH views. The following Oracle views can be used to tell if specific extra-cost Oracle features have been used:

- *dba_feature_usage_statistics*

- *dba_high_water_mark_statistics*

To see details on how Oracle tracks extra-cost feature usage, the *dba_feature_usage_statistics* view can be queried to see usage for the following:

- **Automatic Database Diagnostic Monitor:** An audit record is written when any task for the Automatic Database Diagnostic Monitor has been executed.

- **SQL Access Advisor:** An audit record is written when any task related to the SQL Access Advisor has been executed.

- **SQL Tuning Advisor:** An audit record is written when any task relating to the SQL Tuning Advisor has been used.

- **Automatic Workload Repository:** This auditing event fires when an Automatic Workload Repository (AWR) snapshot was taken in the last sample period.

If the source code to build the *dba_feature_usage_statistics* has been viewed, it becomes apparent that it is composed from three *wri$* tables: *wri$_dbu_usage_sample*, *wri$_dbu_feature_usage*, and *wri$_dbu_feature_metadata*.

```
select
   samp.dbid,
   fu.name,
   samp.version,
   detected_usages,
   total_samples,
   decode(to_char(last_usage_date, 'MM/DD/YYYY, HH:MI:SS'),
        NULL, 'FALSE',
   to_char(last_sample_date, 'MM/DD/YYYY, HH:MI:SS'), 'TRUE',
        'FALSE')
   currently_used,
   first_usage_date,
   last_usage_date,
   aux_count,
   feature_info,
   last_sample_date,
   last_sample_period,
   sample_interval,
   mt.description
 from
   wri$_dbu_usage_sample      samp,
   wri$_dbu_feature_usage     fu,
   wri$_dbu_feature_metadata mt
 where
   samp.dbid    = fu.dbid and
   samp.version = fu.version and
   fu.name      = mt.name and
```

```
fu.name not like '_DBFUS_TEST%' and  /* filter test features */
bitand(mt.usg_det_method, 4) != 4    /* filter disabled feat */;
```

In sum, we must be careful that we have the appropriate licensing before using any of the extra-cost tuning tools.

The next section will provide information on how schema statistics affect SQL execution speed.

Statistics for the Oracle SQL Optimizer

The quality of the execution plans made by the CBO is only as good as the statistics available to it. The old-fashioned *dbms_utility* method for generating CBO statistics is obsolete and somewhat dangerous. The *dbms_stats* package is now the de facto way to get good optimizer statistics.

The better the quality of the statistics, the better the job that the CBO will do when determining SQL execution plans. Unfortunately, doing a complete analysis on a large database could take days, and most shops must sample their database to get CBO statistics. The goal is to take a large enough sample of the database to provide top-quality data for the CBO and to choose the best sampling parameters for the *dbms_stats* utility. Starting in Oracle10g, statistics collections are automated, but users may still need to selectively add histograms and other specialized optimizer statistics.

In Chapter 12, *Server and Network Tuning,* the process for getting the average load values for these important parameters will be presented. By setting the most appropriate baseline values for static initialization parameters, a huge amount of work can be saved when detailed SQL tuning is undertaken. A quick look at object tuning is next.

Oracle Object Tuning

Oracle object tuning is the process of setting characteristics for data files, tablespaces, tables, indexes, hash cluster tables and IOTs (Index Organized Tables) to achieve optimal performance. Each new release of Oracle introduces new object-level features for us to use:

- **Oracle 7:** Bitmap indexes

- **Oracle 8:** Locally Managed Tablespaces (LMTs)

- **Oracle 9i:** Automatic Segment Space Management (ASSM)

- **Oracle 10g:** Automatic Storage Management (ASM)

- **Oracle 11g:** Table compression

Object tuning can be vital to overall system performance because major system wait events such as buffer busy waits are closely tied to the internal structure of the database objects. For example, the following object level adjustments might be called for:

- **Tablespaces:** There are many tablespace options including dictionary managed tablespaces, locally managed tablespaces, and special tablespace options such as Automatic Segment Space Managed (ASSM) tablespaces internally represented by bitmap freelists

- **Indexes:** Users can now choose between b*tree, bitmap and bitmap join indexes

- **Tables/Indexes:** Users can adjust the number of freelists, freelist groups, and the freelist unlink threshold (PCTFREE) for any table or index. Hash cluster tables and IOTs can also be used to reduce I/O for SQL requests.

Adjusting the structure of Oracle objects can help to remove system bottlenecks. For complete information on object-level tuning, see chapter 15, *Tablespace and Object Tuning.*

The value of removing these bottlenecks will be presented in subsequent chapters.

Oracle SQL Tuning

SQL tuning is a complex subject, and entire books have been dedicated to the endeavor. Despite this inherent complexity, there are general guidelines every Oracle DBA follows in order to improve the overall performance of their Oracle system:

- Replace unnecessary large-table full-table scans with index scans

- Cache small-table full table scans

- Verify optimal index usage

- Verify optimal table join order

- Verify optimal JOIN techniques

- Tune complex sub queries to remove redundant access

- Use Oracle's tools

For complete information on object-level tuning, see Chapter 16, *Oracle SQL Tuning.* For a detailed methodology for advanced Oracle SQL tuning, see my new book *Advanced Oracle SQL Tuning: The Definitive Reference.*

In Oracle 11g we have SQL profiles and the SQL Access Advisor to help identify sub-optimal SQL statements. Once identified, the SQL profile utility will allow changes to execution plans without adding hints.

The following section will provide a closer look at the goals listed above as well as how they simplify SQL tuning.

- **Determine optimal table join order:** One of the most common problems with complex SQL is that the tables are not joined in the optimal order. Oracle tries to make the first table join, i.e. the driving table, produce the smallest number of rows to reduce the intermediate row baggage that must be input to later table joins. Extended optimizer statistics, histograms and the ORDERED hint are great ways to verify optimal table join order.

- **Remove unnecessary large-table full table scans:** Unnecessary full table scans (FTS) are an important symptom of suboptimal SQL and cause unnecessary I/O that can drag down an entire database. The tuning expert first evaluates the SQL based on the number of rows returned by the query. The most common tuning tool for addressing unnecessary full table scans is the addition of indexes, especially function-based indexes. The decision about removing a full-table scan should be based on a careful examination of the amount of logical I/O of the index scan versus the costs of the full table scan.

- **Cache small-table full table scans:**   For cases in which a full table scan is the fastest access method, the tuning professional should ensure that a dedicated data buffer is available for the rows. In Oracle 7, an *alter table xxx cache* command can be issued. In Oracle 8 and beyond, the small-table can be cached by forcing it into the KEEP pool.

- **Verify optimal index usage:**   Determining the index usage is especially important for improving the speed of queries with multiple WHERE clause predicates. Oracle sometimes has a choice of indexes, and the tuning professional must examine each index and ensure that Oracle is using the best index, meaning the one that returns the result with the fewest consistent gets.

- **Verify optimal join techniques:** Some queries will perform faster with nested loop joins, some with hash joins, while others favor sort-merge joins. It is difficult to predict what join technique will be fastest, so many Oracle tuning experts will test run the SQL with each different table join method.

- **Tuning by simplifying SQL syntax:** There are several methods for simplifying complex SQL statements:

  - Rewriting the query into a more efficient form

  - Using the WITH clause

  - Using global temporary tables

  - Using materialized views

- **Use Oracle's Tools:** In Oracle 11g, SQL profiles and the SQL Access Advisor can be used to help identify sub-optimal SQL statements. Once identified, the SQL Profile utility will allow changes to execution plans without adding hints.

It is important to know that Oracle 10g will sometimes automatically rewrite SQL to be more efficient.

Another type of Oracle tuning is the Oracle emergency tuning model. Time is of the essence and we must act quickly to relieve an acute performance problem. This will be examined more closely in later chapters.

Conclusion

This chapter focused on a basic overview of reactive, proactive and emergency Oracle tuning. The proactive tuning model will serve as the foundation for later chapters where the value of time-series tuning will be addressed. The main points of this chapter are:

- Reactive tuning is too little, too late. The end-user is already experiencing a loss of service.

- Proactive tuning assumes that DBAs take advantage of the Oracle dynamic tuning features and change the system configuration just in time to meet the change in processing demand.

- All tuning activities start with a global review of the server, e.g. CPU, network, and disk, to isolate the current hardware bottleneck.

- Global tuning is performed through a review of the instance configuration such as initialization parameters and CBO statistics. After the review, the challenge becomes choosing the best overall settings.

- Detailed tuning is performed by tuning the individual SQL statements. Ongoing tuning is the process of adjusting the dynamic Oracle parameters in anticipation of changes in processing profiles.

At this point, it should be clear that the only way to achieve effective Oracle tuning over time is to develop a strategy for monitoring performance trends.

The next chapter provides a closer look at time-series tuning and details on how to develop a sound methodology for tuning any Oracle database.

Time Series Tuning for Oracle

Everyone demands fast response time

Managing the Complexity of Oracle

One of the most common comments from novice Oracle professionals relates to the sheer complexity of Oracle. Many of these professionals learned relational database management in college using a simple relational database such as SQL Server, and they are overwhelmed at the power and complexity of Oracle.

From its humble beginning in the 1980s, Oracle has become the world's most complex, robust and powerful database. Whenever a DBA asks, "*Why does Oracle have to be so hard?*", it is important to remember that along with complexity comes great flexibility and power.

Unlike other relational databases, Oracle gives you complete control over every aspect of the database. You can control how their rows are stored on the data blocks, customize the layout of their data on disk and control every aspect of the Oracle instance.

The ability to leverage the power and sophistication of Oracle is very important to the tuning effort. Because you have complete control over the database, there is no excuse for not maximizing server resources. Server resources depreciate rapidly, regardless of use, and it is important to make sure that Oracle has utilized all of these resources. For example, one of the most common mistakes for a novice DBA is using a 32-bit Windows server with 8 gigabytes of RAM, wasting the RAM because they do not understand how to use /3GB or AWE to utilize "above the line" RAM memory.

Tuning an Oracle database with over 250 initialization parameters and dozens of object configuration options can be overwhelming, even to experienced DBAs. But how do you best manage this type of complexity? Oracle first addressed this problem by developing special advisory utilities in Oracle. These advisory utilities were designed to predict the marginal benefits of changes made to SGA memory region parameters like *db_cache_size*, *pga_aggregate_target* and *shared_pool_size*.

Advisors have limits!

The Oracle advisors are marketed as *"intelligent"*, but no advisor can match the ability of a human expert! Oracle tuning requires in depth knowledge and intuition that cannot be easily automated!

This advisory approach was refined in Oracle10g where the automatic management tools created a simplified umbrella that made Oracle extremely simple, hiding the robust complexities.

This "simple" mode was designed so that Oracle can be used in small departmental applications without an experienced DBA. Oracle can be simplified if the DBA uses only a few tuning parameters and allows Oracle to automate storage and memory management. This automation approach is how Oracle competes against simpler, less robust products such as Microsoft SQL Server.

As a small database grows, these broad-brush automation features can be selectively turned off. This gives you more control over the database. The following section is an overview of time series tuning. Chapters 4 through 8 explore this tuning approach in greater detail.

The Pros and Cons of Time Series Tuning

"Predictions are difficult, especially about the future." — *Yogi Berra*

Predictive modeling is the process of using historical data to predict future values of data items. While forecasting is not new to computer processing, the trend towards using massive data warehouses has created a new vehicle for validating long-term forecasts.

Forecasting has long suffered from a statistical reality called the "trumpet of doom". While it is very easy to generate a forecast for a short-term future value within an alpha of .05 (alpha is a measure of the confidence interval for a forecast), a long-term forecast will see the confidence interval widening as time passes.

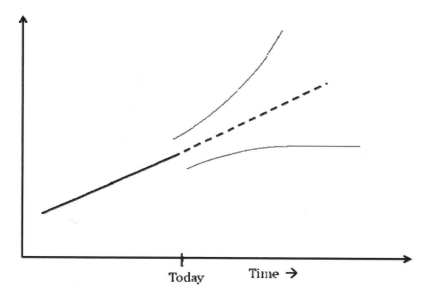

Figure 2.1: *The Trumpet of Doom*

To use a real-world analogy, it is easy for the weatherman to use historical data to predict tomorrow's temperature, but it is quite another story to forecast the temperature for the next month. At some point in the future, the confidence interval widens to the point where the forecast has no predictive validity.

One feature that makes Oracle so powerful is its ability to create predictive models to assist the DBA. These powerful predictive models allow Oracle to forecast the marginal benefit of changes made to the database. Oracle uses rudimentary models in order to create advisors which are great for short-term tuning.

- **SGA Advisors:** Oracle has predictive advisories for the data buffer cache, the shared pool and almost every region within the Oracle RAM heap. In Oracle10g, the Automated Memory Management (AMM) acts upon the predictions and morphs the SGA automatically.

- **Tuning Advisors:** Oracle's Automatic Diagnostic Database Advisor (ADDM) uses artificial intelligence to recommend new materialized views and indexes. Oracle also has a SQL Performance Analyzer and a SQL Access Advisor. These advisors gather real-world empirical execution information from Oracle and recommend actions based upon the execution samples.

There are several important dimensions to time series tuning. Foremost, a DBA must carefully ensure that the data collected is high quality. Also, the length of the snapshots is important. DBAs can take snapshots in more frequent intervals of around five minutes when doing time series tuning while Oracle continues to collect hourly snapshots.

Data Quality

It is important to possess statistically valid performance data, and the frequency of snapshots is critical to data quality. Careful consideration should be taken to ensure that the snapshot is not constrained by the sampling techniques used. For example, when running a post-mortem analysis on yesterday's transient performance hog, snapshots compared over a long period of time may make pin pointing the issue more difficult.

An analysis can only be as good as data used. All else being equal, savvy tuning experts may decide to take a snapshot once every five minutes during busy times while only taking hourly snapshots during lull periods.

While AWR and STATSPACK provide the framework for historical tuning data collection, it is important to remember that how a DBA configures these tools directly affects data quality. For example, many Oracle tuning experts know that some metrics become meaningless when measured over an inappropriate period.

For example, knowing the average yearly temperature for the entire state of Alaska is not particularly helpful to an Eskimo curious about the temperature outside his igloo. The average temperature yesterday, however, provides him with much more useful information. Once there is good data available, the next challenge for the DBA is to use this data to locate repeating patterns inside the workload.

These patterns are collected and analyzed in a time series fashion, organizing by hour-of-the-day and day-of-the-week. When taking snapshots for signature analysis, it is always wise to collect long-term data over many years. The more snapshots a DBA has, the better. More data typically means a more normalized analysis there will be, and one may also be able to identify shifting baselines.

As system load grows, so do the trends that are being measured. Oracle 11g has addressed this tendency with their adaptive threshold. At this point, one needs to know that the object will be to build a reporting infrastructure using the database from STATSPACK/AWR. For beginners, Oracle Enterprise Manager (OEM) is a rudimentary threshold alert mechanism which tests for a range of values on any metrics that one desires.

Oracle's Approach to Workload Thresholds

The Oracle documentation on adaptive thresholds notes that OEM now allows two ways to monitor exception thresholds for any metric alerts:

- **Significance Level:** This uses metric percentages to trigger the alert, e.g. alert when physical reads exceeds 95% of the threshold value.

- **Percentage of Maximum:** Oracle alerts based on a pre-defined threshold number.

Once metric baselines are defined, they can be used to establish alert thresholds that are statistically significant and adapt to expected variations across time. For example, alert thresholds can be defined to be generated based upon significance level.

Alternatively, one can generate thresholds based on a percentage of the maximum value observed within the baseline period. These can be used to generate alerts when performance metric values are observed to exceed normal peaks within that period. The Oracle documents explain that adaptive thresholds will adjust themselves according to historical changes in the database workload:

> *"Adaptive baselines help to significantly improve the accuracy of performance alerting.*
>
> *The adaptive baselines allow for improved manageability since the thresholds adapt to changes in usage and load, and the thresholds do not need to be reconfigured with these changes in load patterns."*

Again, this book is going far beyond the simple approach inside OEM, but the principle is correct. As more about predictive analysis will be learned in the upcoming chapters, we will see how baseline values change over time and how to accommodate these changes in predictions.

Eventually, these patterns will evolve into signatures which are statistically valid repeating events within the application. The next section will cover the relationships between workloads, signatures and exception analysis.

Signatures, Workloads and Exceptions

The old adage "Those who cannot remember the past are condemned to repeat it" is relevant here, and it is only a matter of time before the scientists at Oracle Corporation deploy a predictive model that will analyze historical patterns and proactively change the database before the problem occurs.

Should it ever become a reality, Oracle may become the first "psychic" database, a database that can see into the future and resolve pending performance issues before they become problematic. This is not science fiction. Proactive models are a proven technology. This approach is the same as the Ion for Oracle tool where historical data from STATSPACK and AWR are analyzed to identify any signatures and repeating patterns. These signatures are then interfaced with *dbms_scheduler* to change the database in time to prevent the future outage.

Also, the use of workload-based predictive tuning is taking off and the usage of baselines to capture and adapt thresholds to expected time-dependent workload variations is a core feature of Oracle 11g. According to John Beresniewicz of Oracle Corporation, the metric baselines, first introduced in 10gR2, characterize specific system metrics over time periods, and these time periods can be matched to system usage patterns.

These statistical signatures, dubbed profiles by Oracle, are used to implement adaptive alert thresholds that can signal the DBA when a statistically significant event occurs.

Workloads and Predictive Analysis

Identifying workload characteristics is critical to predictive modeling, and almost all systems will have repeating signatures for each workload. Oracle started to make a commitment to workload-based analysis with the introduction of STATSPACK when Oracle 8i was released. Oracle continued this trend by introducing the SQL Performance Analyzer (SPA) in Oracle 11g. This tool makes it possible to capture a representative Oracle workload from AWR and test it under different configurations.

This is just a brief overview of Oracle predictive modeling power, which will be covered in much greater detail in Chapter 4, *Oracle Predictive Modeling*.

The fundamentals of proactive tuning are predicated on Oracle workload analysis and it is very clear that holistic tuning is the best way to achieve the most efficient allocation of system resources, i.e. disk, RAM, CPU. Another source of data for workloads is the Automatic Workload Repository (AWR), an exciting new extra-cost feature introduced in Oracle10g that is a gold mine of performance insights.

The AWR history is crucial for analysis and tuning, and the AWR forms a knowledge base for linear regression and trend analysis. Of course, one can get much of the same data for free by using STATSPACK as well from other third-party analysis tools such as the Ion for Oracle product.

The AWR workload data can also be used as input to the Oracle Data Mining tool, and Dr. Hamm's book, *Oracle Data Mining*, has some great insights into analyzing workloads with ODM.

What is an Oracle Workload?

To a strategic manager, the Oracle workload is little more than a measure of throughput, often expressed in rows fetched per second and a measure of overall RAM and CPU consumption. Other measures of Oracle workload might include transactions per second, queries per second, or transaction arrival rate, but they all serve a common purpose - to allow management to correlate Oracle performance with hardware utilization.

Oracle Corporation has invested heavily in workload analysis technology for SQL tuning, but they have not yet become sophisticated in identifying full workload signatures for just-in-time predictive modeling. Oracle owns many U.S. patents on their workload capturing technology. The patent is titled "Query optimizer cost model", and it contains some fascinating features of Oracle patented optimizer workload technology.

For example, when the workload on the DBMS is a large number of short, CPU-intensive transactions as is typical for an on-line transaction processing (OLTP) environment, then the demand on the CPU is high relative to the demand on the I/O system. Thus, the optimal execution plan for OLTP is one that favors minimizing CPU usage over minimizing I/O usage.

However, when the workload is a smaller number of long, I/O-intensive transactions as is typical for a night-time batch job processing environment (BATCH), then the demand on the CPU is low relative to the demand on the I/O system. Thus, the optimal execution plan for batch processing is one that favors minimizing I/O usage over minimizing CPU usage.

Conventional cost-based optimizers will not only be inaccurate under these conditions, but they will be inaccurate in different ways at different times as the relative costs change. These variable inaccuracies render the optimization decisions made by conventional optimizers even less useful. Regardless of the metrics used to identify workloads, a full workload analysis is critical to exception-based tuning, predictive modeling, SQL tuning and Oracle trend analysis.

Using Adaptive Thresholds for Predictive Modeling

Once the important metrics have been identified, e.g. physical reads, a baseline can be collected and thresholds can be set up that adapt to the expected workload variations across time. Alternatively, one can generate thresholds based on a percentage of the maximum value observed within the baseline period. These can be used to generate alerts when performance metric values are observed to exceed normal peaks within that period.

It is important to remember that this functionality has been around for more than a decade. DBAs have long been using STATSPACK and other tools to monitor workload baselines and create alerts. The idea is simple.

Because AWR or STATSPACK keeps a historical performance record, Oracle can be configured to detect when a scheduled task is going to cause a resource shortage before it happens! Using the AWR, it is possible to analyze the historical data to find these statistically valid trends and repeating patterns. Many databases have batch job schedules, like implemented via crontabs or *dbms_scheduler*, and workload data has many important uses for batch jobs:

- **Just-in-time Tuning:** A DBA can automatically morph the Oracle instance to anticipate a daily of weekly batch job. The most common example of this is a database that runs in OLTP mode during the day (*first_rows*) and then switches to decision support at night (*all_rows*).

- **Justify Maintenance:** A DBA can predict the reduction in logical I/O and physical I/O from reorganizing a table or index

- **Capacity Planning:** A DBA can use linear regression against resource signatures (CPU usage, RAM usage) to predict a future time when Oracle will exhaust server resources

To understand simple workload identification, look at a simple example. This example is a typical OLTP database that processes orders during the day and runs batch reports in the evening. When SQL full-table scans are plotted versus index scans, the resulting graph would look like this:

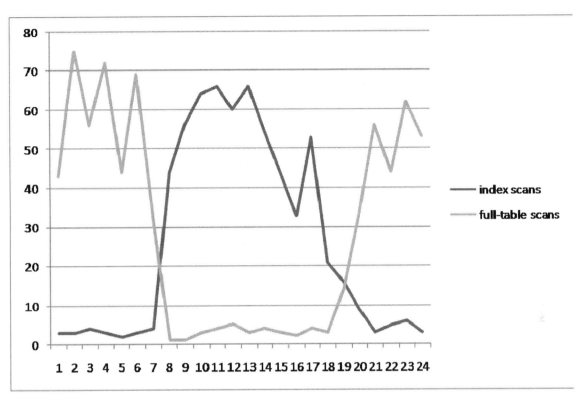

Figure 2.2: *Full scan vs. Index Scan Signature by Hour of the Day*

In the above graph we see two distinct SQL workloads. The first is the day mode, which needs to be optimized for fast OLTP access; for example, *first_rows* optimization. The second is the night mode in which response time is secondary to throughput. The nighttime workload would be optimized to perform queries with a minimum amount of resource consumption, e.g. the *all_rows* optimizer mode. As we will learn in later chapters, we can use this knowledge with *dbms_scheduler* to create just-in-time tuning to change our instance to accommodate these changing workloads.

Using OEM for Predictive Modeling

While the techniques in this book are primarily for senior DBAs with complex databases, Oracle Enterprise Manager (OEM) offers a simple GUI for setting simple alert thresholds for single metrics. While this method is not nearly as powerful as the other techniques described in this book, it is fine for simple databases and for situations where the Oracle professional does not have the necessary experience to build a performance tuning architecture.

This is just a brief overview of using OEM for Oracle tuning, and there is a full discussion in Chapter 18, *Oracle OEM Tuning*.

Build vs. Buy

The Oracle professional must make a choice between buying a tool, which is fast and easy, versus building their own tuning architecture, which is time consuming, but far more powerful than OEM.

One of the best features of OEM is the ability to create thresholds for server metrics such as CPU and RAM consumption. Prior to this functionality, it was necessary for a DBA to write their own tools for performing Oracle threshold alerts and automated corrective actions.

While beginners like OEM because the GUI makes it simple to see data, the OEM tuning Packs are very expensive. The OEM Performance Pack and OEM Diagnostic Pack costs thousands of dollars each, and experienced DBA will use dictionary scripts or tools such as *Ion for Oracle*, a tool which I have spend ten years designing and refining.

As stated earlier, OEM allows one to monitor exception thresholds for alerts in two ways: significance level and percentage of maximum. While OEM is far behind the abilities of a human expert in identifying workloads, there are some new features in OEM for 10gR2. OEM 10gR2 allows for simple time partitioning that can capture common daily or weekly usage/workload cycles. The daily options are:

- **By Hour-of-Day:** Aggregate each hour separately, strong variation across hours

- **By Day and Night:** Aggregate the hours of 7am-7pm as day and 7pm-7am as night

- **By all Hours:** Aggregate all hours together, no strong daily cycle

Oracle OEM also offers weekly time partitioning options. Note that these are quite primitive when compared to the techniques described in later chapters, but it is a good way to start learning predictive modeling. Data can be gathered:

- **By Day-of-Week:** Aggregate days separately, strong variation across days

- **By Weekday and Weekend :** Aggregate Mon-Fri together and Sat-Sun together

- **By all Days:** Aggregate all days together, no strong weekly cycle

The baseline periods can be divided into subintervals of time over which statistical aggregates are computed. These subintervals, or time partitions, allow adaptive baselines that allow baselines that adapt to all workload variations. Time partitioning is fully specified in OEM 10gR2 by selecting both daily and weekly partitioning options.

For example, consider an operational system serving many online users working similar daily schedules and running batch jobs in the evening. For more details on using Enterprise Manager for simple tuning, see Chapter 18, *Oracle OEM Tuning*.

Again, this is just a brief overview of Oracle predictive modeling power, and we go into much greater detail in Chapter 4, *Oracle Predictive Modeling*. Next, let's look at time-series tuning.

Time Series Tuning Guidelines

There are three main areas that affect the decision to resize the Oracle RAM regions. While this book has been devoted to advanced scripts for detecting specific Oracle resource problems, all SGA self-tuning is generally done in one of these three areas:

- *shared_pool_size* : A high value for any of the library cache miss ratios may signal the need to allocate more memory to the shared pool.

- *db_cache_size* : When the data buffer hit ratio falls below a predefined threshold, it might be useful to add RAM to the data buffer cache.

- *pga_aggregate_target* : When there are high values for multi-pass executions, it may be desirable to increase the available PGA memory.

The shops that will benefit most from automated self-tuning are those shops with the following characteristics:

- **Bimodal systems** : Systems that alternate between OLTP and Data Warehouse processing modes will especially benefit from self-tuning RAM regions

- **32-bit shops** : Those shops that are running 32-bit servers are constrained by the size of their RAM regions. This constraint consists of a maximum limit of about 1.7 Gigabytes. For these shops, making the most effective use of RAM resources is especially important.

The following section builds upon the information concerning how to capture performance metrics, providing details about the shared pool. Since everything within the SGA can be modified dynamically, it is critical that the Oracle professional understands how to monitor the Oracle database. It is important to learn how to recognize trends and patterns within the system and proactively reconfigure the database in anticipation of regularly scheduled resource needs.

With respect to ongoing database tuning activities, the Oracle DBA generally looks at these three areas:

- **Normal Scheduled Reconfiguration:** A bimodal instance that performs OLTP and DSS during regular hours will benefit from a scheduled task to reconfigure the SGA and PGA

- **Trend-based Dynamic Reconfiguration:** STATSPACK can be used to predict those times when the processing characteristics change. The *dbms_job* or *dbms_scheduler* packages can be used to fire ad-hoc SGA and PGA changes.

- **Reactive Reconfiguration:** Just as Oracle dynamically redistributes RAM memory for tasks within the *pga_aggregate_target* region, the Oracle DBA can write scripts that steal RAM from an under-utilized area and reallocate these RAM pages to another RAM area.

Scheduling a SGA Reconfiguration

One of the most common techniques for reconfiguring an Oracle instance is to use a shell script. To illustrate a simple example, consider a database that runs in OLTP mode during the day and data warehouse mode at night. For this type of bimodal database, the Oracle DBA can schedule a job to reconfigure the instance to the most appropriate configuration for the type of processing that is being done.

Oracle professionals generally use two tools for scheduling a dynamic reconfiguration. The most common approach is to use a UNIX cron job in order to schedule a periodic reconfiguration while some other Oracle professionals prefer to use the Oracle *dbms_job* (Oracle9i) or *dbms_scheduler* utility. Both of these approaches allow the Oracle professional to schedule a reconfiguration.

In the following example there is a UNIX script that can be used to reconfigure Oracle for decision support processing. One must note the important changes made to the configuration in the *shared_pool*, *db_cache_size*, and *pga_aggregate_target* in order to accommodate data warehouse activity.

The following script changes Oracle into DSS-mode each evening at 6:00 pm:

```
#!/bin/ksh

# First, the environment must be set . . . .
ORACLE_SID=$1
export ORACLE_SID
ORACLE_HOME=`cat /etc/oratab|grep ^$ORACLE_SID:|cut -f2 -d':'`
export ORACLE_HOME
PATH=$ORACLE_HOME/bin:$PATH
export PATH

$ORACLE_HOME/bin/sqlplus -s /nologin<<!
connect system/manager as sysdba;
alter system set db_cache_size=1500m;
alter system set shared_pool_size=500m;
alter system set pga_aggregate_target=4000m;
exit
!
```

This example shows that writing scripts to reconfigure the SGA is easy. The next section presents information on how to use buffer trend reports from Oracle STATSPACK or AWR to predict those times when the data buffers need additional RAM.

Trend-based Oracle Reconfiguration

A common approach to trend-based reconfiguration is to use historical data to proactively reconfigure the database. A good analogy is just-in-time manufacturing where parts appear on the plant floor just as they are needed for assembly. Time series tuning enables the DBA to anticipate processing needs and regularly schedules appropriate intervention, insuring that SGA resources are delivered just in time for processing tasks.

For those who would like to investigate STATSPACK features and abilities at a deeper level, two informative books are available from Oracle Press:

- *Oracle High-Performance Tuning with STATSPACK* - Oracle Press, by Donald K. Burleson.
- *Oracle9i High-Performance Tuning with STATSPACK* - Oracle Press, by Donald K. Burleson.

This section will focus on the examination of STATSPACK reports that indicate trends in the behavior of the data buffer pools. Average values for Oracle performance metrics can be generated along two dimensions:

■ Averages by day-of-the-week

■ Averages by hour-of-the-day

Either of these reports will supply invaluable information for spotting usage trends in the Oracle database. Change occurs in the data buffers rapidly, and sometimes a long-term analysis will provide clues to processing problems within the database.

Almost every Oracle database exhibits patterns that are linked to regular processing schedules called signatures. These signatures allow the DBA to plan long-term solutions based on a database's documented performance over time. Specific details about procedures are presented later in this chapter.

When to Trigger a Dynamic Reconfiguration

The DBA must choose which RAM region to borrow memory from whenever the scripts indicate an overstressed RAM region. Table 2.1 displays the threshold condition for triggering a dynamic memory change.

RAM AREA	OVERSTRESSED CONDITION	OVER-ALLOCATED CONDITION
Shared pool	Library cache misses	No misses
Data buffer cache	Hit ratio < 70%*	Hit ratio > 95%
PGA aggregate	High multi-pass exec	100% optimal executions

Table 2.1: *Threshold Conditions for Dynamic RAM Reallocation*

* The data buffer cache behavior may be meaningless for applications where data is not re-read frequently.

It is easy to schedule tasks that change the RAM memory configuration as the processing needs change on a UNIX platform. For example, it is common for Oracle databases to operate in OLTP mode during normal work hours and to perform the database services memory-intensive batch reports at night. An OLTP database needs a large *db_cache_size* value. Memory-intensive batch tasks require additional RAM in the *pga_aggregate_target* parameter.

The UNIX scripts given next can be used to reconfigure the SGA between the OLTP and DSS without stopping the instance. The example assumes an isolated Oracle server with 8 Gigabytes of RAM, with 10 percent of RAM reserved for UNIX overhead, leaving 7.2 Gigabytes for Oracle and Oracle connections. The scripts are intended either for HP-UX or Solaris and accept the *$oracle_sid* as an argument.

This script will be run at 6:00 p.m. each evening in order to reconfigure Oracle for the memory-intensive batch tasks.

```ksh
#!/bin/ksh

# First, the environment must be set . . . .
ORACLE_SID=$1
export ORACLE_SID
ORACLE_HOME=`cat /etc/oratab|grep ^$ORACLE_SID:|cut -f2 -d':'`
export ORACLE_HOME
PATH=$ORACLE_HOME/bin:$PATH
export PATH

$ORACLE_HOME/bin/sqlplus -s /nologin<<!
connect system/manager as sysdba;
alter system set db_cache_size=1500m;
alter system set shared_pool_size=500m;
alter system set pga_aggregate_target=4000m;
exit
!
```

The script below will be run at 6:00 a.m. each morning to reconfigure Oracle for the OLTP usage during the day.

```ksh
#!/bin/ksh

# First, the environment must be set . . . .
ORACLE_SID=$1
export ORACLE_SID
ORACLE_HOME=`cat /etc/oratab|grep ^$ORACLE_SID:|cut -f2 -d':'`
export ORACLE_HOME
PATH=$ORACLE_HOME/bin:$PATH
export PATH

$ORACLE_HOME/bin/sqlplus -s /nologin<<!
connect system/manager as sysdba;
alter system set db_cache_size=4000m;
alter system set shared_pool_size=500m;
alter system set pga_aggregate_target=1500m;

exit
!
```

Again, the *dbms_job* or *dbms_scheduler* packages can also be used to schedule the SGA reconfigurations.

It should now be clear that the Oracle DBA can develop mechanisms to constantly monitor the processing demands on the database and issue the alter system commands to dynamically respond to these conditions.

Approaches to Self-tuning Oracle Databases

The Oracle administrator must adjust the RAM configuration according to the types of connections the database experiences. Generally, queries against the *v$* structures and STATSPACK will pinpoint those times when Oracle connections change their processing characteristics. The three approaches to automated tuning introduced earlier - normal scheduled reconfiguration, trend-based dynamic reconfiguration and dynamic reconfiguration – are explained further by showing how Oracle may evolve to allow for super-fast dynamic reconfiguration.

Tuning a Constantly Changing Database

Oracle has recognized that it is impossible to create a one-size-fits-all approach to database tuning. Databases are in a constant state of flux, and the ideal tuning approach reacts to changes in processing demands, reallocating resources in real-time.

To the small business user, Oracle automation regulates data file and storage management, changes the sizes of the SGA regions and reactively self-tunes performance issues. However, is a reactive approach enough? It is often too late to make changes after the end user has suffered from poor response time. The real goal of Oracle tuning is to anticipate changes in processing and reallocate resources.

Can Oracle Possess Psychic Abilities?

Just as the name implies, Oracle can indeed predict the future, sometimes with remarkable accuracy. Instead of relying on mystic or spiritual sources, Oracle uses experience to predict the future.

This is the core of time series tuning. Almost all Oracle databases experience repeating patterns of usage, predictable by hour-of-the-day and day-of-the-week. Once Oracle detects a statistically valid pattern of events, the DBA can schedule a reconfiguration just in time to meet the change in requirements and before the end user experiences any degradation in response time. Information in the following section will show how this works.

Capturing Time Series Metrics

The focus of this chapter is the fact that the Oracle DBA now has a wealth of Oracle performance information at their fingertips. More than 100 new dynamic performance tables are stored in the Automatic Workload Repository (AWR) for the DBA to use. These AWR tables feed data to the totally reworked Oracle Enterprise Manager (OEM) to produce stunning time series displays. AWR data is also used by the Automatic Database Diagnostic Monitor (ADDM), the SQL Tuning Advisor, or by the *dbms_sqltune* package to make intelligent performance recommendations.

Instead of running complex scripts to track database performance over time, the Oracle DBA now has detailed time series performance data immediately available for in-depth analysis within OEM. These industrial strength AWR tables are a true blessing for the Oracle tuning DBA. Oracle has introduced new DBMS packages, e.g. *dbms_sqltune*, and *dbms_mview.explain_rewrite* packages, that read the *wrh$* tables and perform sophisticated performance analysis. While not artificial intelligence in the truest sense, these sophisticated tools help simplify the complex task of Oracle tuning.

Customized AWR Tuning Reports

To better explain custom AWR reports, a simple example using the *dba_hist* view and *dba_hist_sysstat* view will be used. The *dba_hist_sysstat* view is one of the most valuable uses of the AWR history tables because it contains instance-wide summaries of many important performance metrics. The following are the most commonly used statistics for Oracle exception reporting:

```
STATISTIC_NAME
----------------------------------------------------
cluster wait time
concurrency wait time
application wait time
user I/O wait time
enqueue waits
enqueue deadlocks
db block gets
consistent gets
physical reads
physical read IO requests
db block changes
physical writes
DBWR buffers scanned
DBWR checkpoints
hot buffers moved to head of LRU
shared hash latch upgrades - wait
redo log space requests
redo log space wait time
table scans (short tables)
table scans (long tables)
table fetch continued row
leaf node splits
leaf node 90-10 splits
index fast full scans (full session cursor cache hits)
buffer is not pinned count
workarea executions - multipass
parse time cpu
parse time elapsed
parse count (total)
SQL*Net roundtrips to/from client
sorts (memory)
sorts (disk)
sorts (rows)
```

The following custom AWR query starts with a simple query to plot the *user I/O wait time* statistic for each AWR snapshot. From this script, it is easy to extract the physical read counts from the AWR.

```
break on begin_interval_time skip 2

column phyrds              format 999,999,999
column begin_interval_time format a25

select
   begin_interval_time,
   filename,
   phyrds
from
   dba_hist_filestatxs
natural join
   dba_hist_snapshot
;
```

Following is a running total of Oracle physical reads from *phys_reads.sql*. The snapshots are collected every half-hour in this example, but many DBAs will increase the default collection frequency of these AWR snapshots. Starting from this script, a WHERE clause criteria can easily be added to create a unique time series exception report.

```
SQL> @phys_reads
```

```
BEGIN_INTERVAL_TIME          FILENAME                                  PHYRDS
--------------------------   ------------------------------------      -----
24-FEB-04 11.00.32.000 PM    E:\ORACLE\ORA92\FSDEV10G\SYSTEM01.DBF     164,700
                             E:\ORACLE\ORA92\FSDEV10G\UNDOTBS01.DBF     26,082
                             E:\ORACLE\ORA92\FSDEV10G\SYSAUX01.DBF     472,008
                             E:\ORACLE\ORA92\FSDEV10G\USERS01.DBF        1,794
                             E:\ORACLE\ORA92\FSDEV10G\T_FS_LSQ.ORA       2,123
```

Now that the basic idea behind custom AWR scripts has been presented, the next step is to look at how the Oracle Enterprise Manager (OEM) can be used to produce powerful exception reports and create even more powerful exception reports with SQL*Plus.

Exception Reporting

Oracle OEM has a fantastic interface, great for easily creating exception alerts and mailing them directly to the Oracle professional; however, the OEM has limitations. Until OEM evolves into a true Decision Support System (DSS) for the Oracle DBA, he or she will still need to use the workload information in the AWR for:

- Complex exception reporting

- Correlation analysis

- Data mining

- Developing metric signatures

- Hypothesis testing

There are more sophisticated exception reports that cannot be provided by OEM. The data inside the AWR *dba_hist* views can be used by the senior DBA to perform sophisticated exception and correlation analysis. For example:

- **Signature Analysis:** The AWR data can be used to plot values of many important performance metrics, averaged by hour-of-the-day and day-of-the-week. For example, plotting physical reads and writes signatures will give the DBA insights into the regular variations in database stress. This information is critical to scheduling just-in-time changes to SGA resources, which is the foundation for creating a self-tuning database.

- **Hypothesis Testing:** The DBA can easily run correlation analysis scripts to detect relationships between important performance metrics. Queries can be developed to show the correlation between buffer busy waits and DML per second for specific tables, all averaged over long periods of time.

- **Comparing a Single Value to a System-wide Value:** Custom scripts can easily be written to compare the relationship between performance values. For example, it can issue an alert when the physical writes for any data file exceeds 25% of total physical writes.

The next section provides information on how the Oracle professional can get valuable exception reports from the AWR.

Exception Reporting with the AWR

Oracle performance exception reporting involves adding a WHERE clause to a query in order to eliminate any values that fall beneath a predefined threshold in the AWR script. For example, this can easily be done with a generic script to read *dba_hist_sysstat*. The following is a simple script that displays a time series exception report for any statistic in *dba_hist_sysstat*. This script accepts the statistics number and the value threshold for the exception report as supplied parameters.

```
prompt
prompt  This will query the dba_hist_sysstat to display all values
prompt  that exceed the value specified in
prompt  the "where" clause of the query.
prompt

set pages 999

break on snap_time skip 2

accept stat_name   char    prompt 'Enter Statistic Name:  ';
accept stat_value  number  prompt 'Enter Statistics Threshold value:  ';

col snap_time    format a19
col value        format 999,999,999

select
   to_char(begin_interval_time,'yyyy-mm-dd hh24:mi') snap_time,
   value
from
   dba_hist_sysstat
  natural join
   dba_hist_snapshot
```

```
where
   stat_name = '&stat_name'
and
   value > &stat_value
order by to_char(begin_interval_time,'yyyy-mm-dd hh24:mi');
```

Note: On 10.2 and beyond, the above script requires SYSDBA connection.

The following script can be run at this point. It will prompt for the statistic name and threshold value:

```
SQL> @rpt_sysatst
```

This will query the *dba_hist_sysstat* view to display all values that exceed the value specified in the *where* clause of the query.

```
Enter Statistic Name:  physical writes

Enter Statistics Threshold value:  200000
```

```
SNAP_TIME                 VALUE
------------------- -----------
2004-02-21 08:00        200,395
2004-02-27 08:00        342,231
2004-02-29 08:00        476,386
2004-03-01 08:00        277,282
2004-03-02 08:00        252,396
2004-03-04 09:00        203,407
```

The listing above indicates a repeating trend where physical writes seem to be high at 8:00 AM on certain days. This powerful script will allow the DBA to quickly extract exception conditions from any instance-wide Oracle metric and see the values changes over time.

The next section examines an even more powerful exception report that compares system-wide values to individual snapshots.

Exception Reporting with *dba_hist_filestatxs*

The *dba_hist_filestatxs* view contains important file-level information about Oracle I/O activities. Because most Oracle databases perform a high amount of reading and writing from disk, the *dba_hist_filestatxs* view can be very useful for identifying high-usage data files.

If the Oracle Automated Storage Management (ASM) is in use, all disks will be striped with the Stripe and Mirror Everywhere (SAME) approach. In ASM, this view is indispensable for locating and isolating hot data files. Many Oracle shops will isolate hot data files onto high-speed solid-state disk (SSD) or relocate the hot files to another physical disk spindle.

If the *dba_hist_filestatxs* table is described as shown in Table 2.2, the important information columns can be viewed. The important information relates to physical reads and writes, the actual time spent performing reads and writes, and the wait count associated with each data file for each snapshot.

COLUMN	DESCRIPTION
snap_id	Unique snapshot ID
filename	Name of the datafile
phyrds	Number of physical reads done
phywrts	Number of times DBWR is required to write
singleblkrds	Number of single block reads
readtim	Time, in hundredths of a second, spent doing reads if the *timed_statistics* parameter is TRUE; 0 if *timed_statistics* is FALSE
writetim	Time, in hundredths of a second, spent doing writes if the *timed_statistics* parameter is TRUE; 0 if *timed_statistics* is FALSE
singleblkrdtim	Cumulative single block read time, in hundredths of a second
phyblkrd	Number of physical blocks read
phyblkwrt	Number of blocks written to disk, which may be the same as PHYWRTS if all writes are single blocks
wait_count	Wait Count

Table 2.2: *Important Metrics on File-level I/O in dba_hist_filestatxs*

The following is another example of a quickly written custom exception report. In this report, the *dba_hist_filestatxs* table is queried to identify hot write datafiles where the file consumed more than 25% of the total physical writes for the instance. A close look at the query reveals that it compares the physical writes, i.e. the *phywrts* column of *dba_hist_filestatxs*, with the instance-wide physical writes (statistic# = 55 from *dba_hist_sysstat*).

This simple, yet powerful, script allows the Oracle professional to track hot write datafiles over time, thereby gaining important insights into the status of the I/O subsystem over time.

```
prompt
prompt   This will identify any single file who's write I/O
prompt   is more than 25% of the total write I/O of the database.
prompt

set pages 999

break on snap_time skip 2

col filename        format a40
```

```
col phywrts        format 999,999,999
col snap_time      format a20

select
   to_char(begin_interval_time,'yyyy-mm-dd hh24:mi') snap_time,
   filename,
   phywrts
from
   dba_hist_filestatxs
natural join
   dba_hist_snapshot
where
   phywrts > 0
and
   phywrts * 4 >
(
select
   avg(value)              all_phys_writes
from
   dba_hist_sysstat
  natural join
   dba_hist_snapshot
where
   stat_name = 'physical writes'
and
  value > 0
)
order by
   to_char(begin_interval_time,'yyyy-mm-dd hh24:mi'),
   phywrts desc;
```

The following is the sample output from this script. This is a useful report because the high-write datafiles are shown as well as those times in which they are hot.

```
SQL> @hot_write_files
```

This will identify any single file whose write I/O is more than 25% of the total write I/O of the database.

```
SNAP_TIME              FILENAME                                        PHYWRTS
----------------       ------------------------------------------      -------
2004-02-20 23:30       E:\ORACLE\ORA92\FSDEV10G\SYSAUX01.DBF            85,543
2004-02-21 01:00       E:\ORACLE\ORA92\FSDEV10G\SYSAUX01.DBF            88,843
2004-02-21 08:31       E:\ORACLE\ORA92\FSDEV10G\SYSAUX01.DBF            89,463
2004-02-22 02:00       E:\ORACLE\ORA92\FSDEV10G\SYSAUX01.DBF            90,168
2004-02-22 16:30       E:\ORACLE\ORA92\FSDEV10G\SYSAUX01.DBF           143,974
                       E:\ORACLE\ORA92\FSDEV10G\UNDOTBS01.DBF           88,973
```

This type of time series exception reporting is extremely useful for detecting those times when an Oracle database is experiencing I/O related stress. Many Oracle professionals will schedule these types of exception reports using *dbms_scheduler* and send them via automatic e-mail every day.

Now move on to the identification and examination of repeating trends.

Trend Identification with the AWR

Once the creation of simple *dba_hist* queries has been mastered, the DBA should be prepared to move on to trend identification with the AWR views. The Oracle professional knows that aggregating important Oracle performance metrics over time, i.e. day-of-the-week and hour-of-the-day, allows them to see hidden signatures.

These signatures are extremely important for proactive tuning because they show regularly occurring changes in processing demands. This knowledge allows the DBA to anticipate upcoming changes and reconfigure Oracle just in time to meet the changes.

The following report shows the signature for any Oracle system statistic, averaged by hour-of–the-day.

```
prompt  This will query the dba_hist_sysstat view to
prompt  display average values by hour of the day

set pages 999

break on snap_time skip 2

accept stat_name char prompt 'Enter Statistics Name:  ';

col snap_time    format a19
col avg_value    format 999,999,999

select
   to_char(begin_interval_time,'hh24') snap_time,
   avg(value)                          avg_value
from
   dba_hist_sysstat
  natural join
   dba_hist_snapshot
where
   stat_name = '&stat_name'
group by
   to_char(begin_interval_time,'hh24')
order by
   to_char(begin_interval_time,'hh24');
```

In the output, there is an average for every hour of the day. This information can be easily pasted into an MS Excel spreadsheet and plotted with the chart wizard or the Ion tool, which is included free with this book:

```
SQL> @rpt_sysstat_hr
```

This will query the *dba_hist_sysstat* view to display average values by hour- of-the-day:

```
Enter Statistics Name:   physical reads

SNAP_TIME                AVG_VALUE
```

```
------------------------    -----------
00                          120,861
01                          132,492
02                          134,136
03                          137,460
04                          138,944
05                          140,496
06                          141,937
07                          143,191
08                          145,313
09                          135,881
10                          137,031
11                          138,331
12                          139,388
13                          140,753
14                          128,621
15                          101,683
16                          116,985
17                          118,386
18                          119,463
19                          120,868
20                          121,976
21                          112,906
22                          114,708
23                          116,340
```

Figure 2.3 shows the data after it has been pasted into an MS Excel spreadsheet and plotted with the Excel chart wizard:

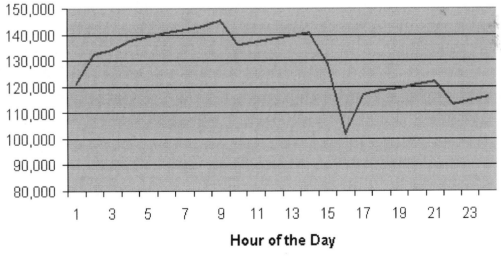

Figure 2.3: *An Hourly Signature Can Show Hidden Trends*

Open source products such as RRDtool and Ion for Oracle can also be used to automate the plotting of data from the AWR and ASH.

The Ion for Oracle tool is a great way to quickly plot Oracle time series data and gather signatures for Oracle metrics. Figure 2.4 shows how the Ion tool displays this data. Ion is also able to plot performance data on a daily or hourly basis.

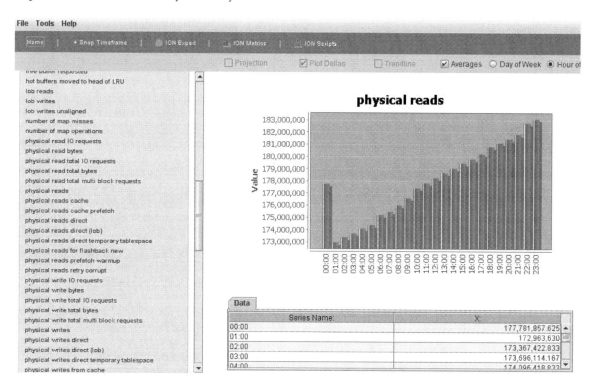

Figure 2.4: *Disk reads by hour of the day from Ion for Oracle*

The same types of reports aggregated by day-of-the week can also be used to see ongoing daily trends. Over long periods of time, almost all Oracle databases will develop distinct signatures that reflect the regular daily processing patterns of the end user community.

The following script will accept any of the values from *dba_hist_sysstat* and plot the average values by hour-of-the-day:

```
prompt
prompt   This will query the dba_hist_sysstat view to display
prompt   average values by day-of-the-week
prompt

set pages 999

accept stat_name char prompt 'Enter Statistic Name:  ';
```

```
col snap_time    format a19
col avg_value    format 999,999,999

select
   to_char(begin_interval_time,'day')    snap_time,
   avg(value)                            avg_value
from
   dba_hist_sysstat
natural join
   dba_hist_snapshot
where
   stat_name = '&stat_name'
group by
   to_char(begin_interval_time,'day')
order by
   decode(
   to_char(begin_interval_time,'day'),
    'sunday',1,
    'monday',2,
    'tuesday',3,
    'wednesday',4,
    'thursday',5,
    'friday',6,
    'saturday',7
   )
;
```

The following is the output from this script:

```
SQL> @rpt_sysstat_dy
```

This will query the *dba_hist_sysstat* view to display average values by day-of-the-week

```
Enter Statistics Name:  physical reads


SNAP_TIME                AVG_VALUE
------------------       ------------
sunday                     190,185
monday                     135,749
tuesday                     83,313
wednesday                  139,627
thursday                   105,815
friday                     107,250
saturday                   154,279
```

These results provide an average for every day of the week as shown graphically in Figure 2.5. These types of signatures will stabilize for most Oracle databases and can be used to develop a predictive model for proactive tuning activities.

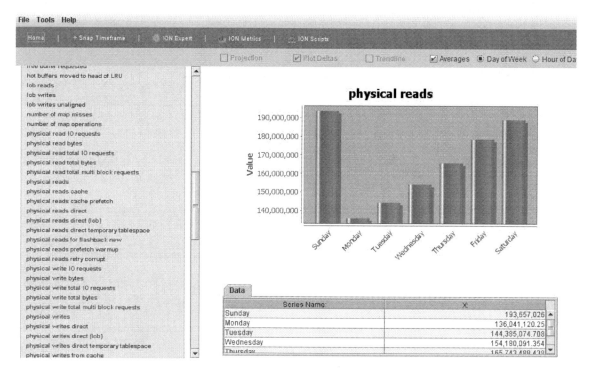

Figure 2.5: *An Ion Signature for Average Physical Reads by Day of the Week*

Oracle allows a DBA to use the STATSPACK and AWR data tables to perform fast and easy exception reporting.

Conclusion

Now that Oracle 11g has embraced time series tuning techniques, this proactive approach is a legitimate supplement to the reactive tuning approach. Furthermore, having the ability to identify trends and cyclic signatures allows a DBA to create just-in-time tuning mechanisms that adjust the instance immediately before a change to the workload.

As DBAs get more sophisticated in their self-tuning endeavors, many more Oracle metrics may become self-tuning. In Oracle, the self-tuning capability increases greatly, and it becomes even easier to write detection scripts and schedule tasks to adjust Oracle based on the processing needs.

The main points of this chapter include:

- Time series tuning has been wholeheartedly endorsed by Oracle Corporation

- Proactive tuning involves analyzing historical performance data seeking repeating trends and patterns of usage

- Statistical analysis tools can be used to predict future behavior based on historical activity

- Oracle 11g SQL Performance Analyzer performs holistic tuning using real-world workloads

- Once signatures are identified, just-in-time tuning can be scheduled to morph Oracle to accommodate the upcoming workload changes

The next chapter will introduce the Oracle time model tables and show how time model analysis can help with diagnosing acute performance problems.

The Time Model
Tuning Approach

Time model tuning involves advanced statistics!

Inside the Oracle Time Model Views

When performing reactive Oracle tuning it's always been hard to get good instrumentation on Oracle metrics. This is not a fault of Oracle; it was done deliberately because the overhead of collecting data can actually hurt performance!

Oracle 10g first introduced important time-series *v$* views and *dba_hist* tables, information that give us a uniform picture of actual time spent performing work within the database.

Oracle provides these *v$* time model views:

- **v$sys_time_model:** This view shows cumulative database processing times for the whole instance. The *v$sys_time_model* view displays cumulative times, all expressed in microseconds, which are collected from every non-idle database session.

```
desc v$sys_time_model

Name                     Null?     Type
----------------         --------  ------------
STAT_ID                            NUMBER
STAT_NAME                          VARCHAR2(64)
VALUE                              NUMBER
```

- **_v$sess_time_model:_** This view report on cumulative database processing times on a per session basis.

```
desc v$sess_time_model

Name                     Null?     Type
----------------         --------  ------------
SID                                NUMBER
STAT_ID                            NUMBER
STAT_NAME                          VARCHAR2(64)
VALUE                              NUMBER
```

Look Out!

Know your stats!

The cumulative approach in *v$sys_time_model* is not used in the *v$sess_time_model* view! Also, the background process timings are not included in *v$sess_time_model* unless the statistic is specific for background processes.

As we see, these are "flattened" tables with one row for each statistic and the table rows measure cumulative processing times for the following database operations (the *stat_name* column):

- DB CPU
- DB time
- Java execution elapsed time
- PL/SQL compilation elapsed time
- PL/SQL execution elapsed time
- Background CPU time
- Background elapsed time
- Connection management call elapsed time
- Failed parse (out of shared memory) elapsed time
- Failed parse elapsed time
- Hard parse (bind mismatch) elapsed time
- Hard parse (sharing criteria) elapsed time
- Hard parse elapsed time
- Inbound PL/SQL rpc elapsed time

- Parse time elapsed
- Sequence load elapsed time
- SQL execute elapsed time

The greatest benefit of this time model approach is that every statistic is measured in terms of time so that we can evaluate metrics on an "apples-to-apples" basis. This approach is best suited for situations in which there is a CPU-bound system and we need to know what steps to take to remove or at least decrease this time dependence.

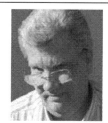

Time series tables are extra-cost licenses!

While you can freely query the ASH tables, this is audited in the *dba_usage_features_statistics* table. To query these tables you must purchase the Oracle Tuning pack and Oracle diagnostic packs, thousands of dollars each!

Please note that there are other ways to get this time model data, and 3rd party tools like *Confio Ignite* and *Ion for Oracle* can replace much of this functionality, and with a lower total cost of ownership (TCO).

Next, let's explore how we can look into session details using the time series tables.

Displaying session details with time model data

One great benefit of using the *v$sess_time_model* view is that it allows the quick identification of what part of the session's processing work spends the most time. If a user is complaining about poor response times, once the SID for the user session has been grabbed, a query like *sess_waits_ash.sql* can be used to find out exactly what areas of work are causing the degradation:

🖫 **sess_waits_ash.sql**

```
select
   b.username,
   a.stat_name,
   round((a.value / 1000000),3) time_secs
from
   v$sess_time_model a,
   v$session          b
where
   a.sid = b.sid
and
   b.sid = 123
order by
   3 desc;
```

The sample output looks like this, showing each statistic and the number of seconds spent performing each operation!

```
USERNAME    STAT_NAME                                          TIME_SECS
----------  -------------------------------------------------  --------
SPV         DB time                                              23,133
SPV         sql execute elapsed time                              6,035
SPV         DB CPU                                                3,399
SPV         parse time elapsed                                    3,205
SPV         hard parse elapsed time                               2,976
SPV         connection management call elapsed time                ,168
SPV         background elapsed time                                    0
SPV         PL/SQL execution elapsed time                             0
SPV         PL/SQL compilation elapsed time                          0
SPV         Java execution elapsed time                               0
SPV         inbound PL/SQL rpc elapsed time                          0
SPV         hard parse (bind mismatch) elapsed time                  0
SPV         background cpu time                                       0
SPV         failed parse elapsed time                                0
SPV         hard parse (sharing criteria) elapsed time               0
SPV         failed parse (out of shared memory) elapsed time         0
SPV         sequence load elapsed time
```

The time model statistics give insight about where the processing time is actually spent during the snapshot interval.

```
Time Model Statistics
DB/Inst: LSQ/lsq  Snaps: 1355-1356
-> ordered by Time (seconds) desc
                                                   Time      % Total
                                                (seconds)      DB
Statistic Name                                                Time
-------------------------------------------  -------------  -----------
DB time                                         7,274.60      100.00
sql execute elapsed time                        7,249.77       99.66
background elapsed time                           778.48       10.70
DB CPU                                            150.62        2.07
parse time elapsed                                 45.52         .63
hard parse elapsed time                            44.65         .61
PL/SQL execution elapsed time                      13.73         .19
background cpu time                                 8.90         .12
PL/SQL compilation elapsed time                     3.80         .05
connection management call elapsed time              .15         .00
Java execution elapsed time                          .05         .00
hard parse (bind mismatch) elapsed time              .00         .00
hard parse (sharing criteria) elapsed time           .00         .00
sequence load elapsed time                           .00         .00
failed parse (out of shared memory) elapsed          .00         .00
inbound PL/SQL rpc elapsed time                      .00         .00
failed parse elapsed time                            .00         .00
```

Take a closer look at this report output.

- The system spends the most processing time executing SQL and very little on parsing SQL statements.
- If a high PL/SQL execution elapsed time is discovered, the system may benefit from optimizing the PL/SQL programs
- The most important statistics within the time model views is the *DB time* and *DB CPU*. The *DB time* statistic in the *v$sess_time_model* view determines the total elapsed processing time spent by database

for a particular session, while the same statistic in the *v$sys_time_model* view represents the total cumulative time spent by Oracle for all sessions' CPU times and wait times spent for non-idle wait events.

Watch for excessive hard parses!

This report is great for locating non-reentrant SQL statements (excessive hard parsing). If found, you might implement *cursor_sharing=force* or *cursor_sharing=similar*, as appropriate.

Most of the extra-cost Oracle advisor utilities use some of this time model data to produce their output, and *DB time* is just one of the statistics used for producing their recommendations.

Real-time reporting

It is also useful to monitor *DB time* and *DB CPU* statistics in real time so that you can see short-term fluctuations that are hidden in a busy database. Visualization of performance is critical to understand any Oracle database and a real-time monitoring approach allows the DBA to immediately identify possible system overload problems or stress when an exceptional event occurs. For example, The Ion tool allows the DBA to monitor database time in real time as shown in Figure 3.1:

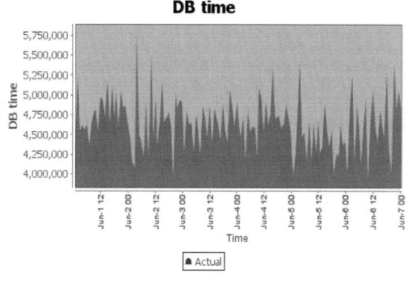

Figure 3.1: *Monitoring Real-time Database Processing with the Ion Tool*

While real-time reporting is great for spotting trends and signatures, we also need to implement an exception reporting mechanism and make exception scripts to give a warning if any database workload metric exceeds the pre-defined threshold. For example, the script below lists sessions that experience high workload and consume significant processing resources:

```
select
   s.sid,
   s.username,
   s.module,
   round(t.value/1000000,2) "elapsed processing time (sec)"
from
   v$sess_time_model t,
   v$session        s
where
   t.sid = s.sid
and
   t.stat_name = 'db time'
and
   s.username IS NOT NULL
and
   t.value/1000000 >= 1;
```

Here is a sample output for the actual elapsed time for current tasks.

```
       SID USER  MODULE       Elapsed Processing Time (Sec)
---------- ----- ------------ -----------------------------
       137 DONB  SQL*Plus                              5,93
       135 SYS   SQL*Plus                              6,36
       141 DONB  SpMon.exe                            23,42
       150 DONB  spvent.exe                            8,3
       152 SYS   SQL*Plus                              8,13
       156 SYS   SQL*Plus                              1,43
```

In the script above, note how the output has been restricted (*where t.value/1000000>1*) to only show user sessions that consume processing time of more than one second.

Next, let's move out of the time model tables and look into the long term retained data inside the Automatic Workload Repository.

Time Model Tables in AWR

In AWR there are equivalent tables for the *v$sys_time_model* view, namely the *dba_hist_sys_time_model* table. As with other AWR and STATSPACK metrics, the *dba_hist_sys_time_model* stores cumulative values since instance startup time. Hence, we must compare two snapshots to get meaningful information on the elapsed-time changes to our time model statistics.

It's easy to build time series trend charts of database workload and particular processing parts based on history stored in the AWR. These charts allow the DBA to get signatures of the database workload and identify hot periods when the database is most stressed. For example, the query below displays the database workload for a particular snapshot interval using the *dba_hist_sys_time_model* view:

⊟   **pct_of_tot_elapsed_time.sql**

```
select
```

```
    e.stat_name "E.STAT_NAME"
      , Round((e.value - b.value)/1000000,2)"Time (s)"
      , Round(decode( e.stat_name,'DB time'
              , to_number(null)
              , 100*(e.value - b.value)
              )/
   (SELECT NVL((e1.value - b1.value),-1)
      FROM dba_hist_sys_time_model  e1
         , dba_hist_sys_time_model  b1
       WHERE b1.snap_id                 = b.snap_id
       AND e1.snap_id                   = e.snap_id
       AND b1.dbid                      = b.dbid
       AND e1.dbid                      = e.dbid
       AND b1.instance_number           = b.instance_number
       AND e1.instance_number           = e.instance_number
       AND e1.stat_name                 = 'DB time'
       AND b1.stat_id                   = e1.stat_id ),2) "Percent of Total DB Time"
from
   dba_hist_sys_time_model e,
   dba_hist_sys_time_model b
 WHERE
   b.snap_id                 = &pBgnSnap
   AND e.snap_id             = &pEndSnap
   AND b.dbid                = &pDbId
   AND e.dbid                = &pDbId
   AND b.instance_number     = &pInstNum
   AND e.instance_number     = &pInstNum
   AND b.stat_id             = e.stat_id
   AND e.value - b.value > 0
 ORDER BY 2 DESC
```

The output of this script is very useful since it shows each metric as a percentage of total elapsed time.

E.STAT_NAME	Time (s)	Pct Tot DB Time
DB time	21,204.90	
sql execute elapsed time	20,934.21	98.72
background elapsed time	16,202.46	76.41
DB CPU	8,761.48	41.32
parse time elapsed	5,007.8	23.62
hard parse elapsed time	4,788	22.58
background cpu time	2,785.09	13.13
PL/SQL execution elapsed time	2,495.51	11.77
failed parse elapsed time	933.21	4.4
PL/SQL compilation elapsed time	280.73	1.32
Java execution elapsed time	123.52	.58
hard parse (sharing criteria) elapsed ti	84.84	.4
connection management call elapsed time	23.05	.11
hard parse (bind mismatch) elapsed time	10.75	.05
sequence load elapsed time	2.21	.01

The above output reports the overall database workload activity and shows the particular part of database processing that consumes significant CPU resources.

This time series database workload trend report is also available in Ion for immediate visualization so that the main bottlenecks in a database can be easily identified:

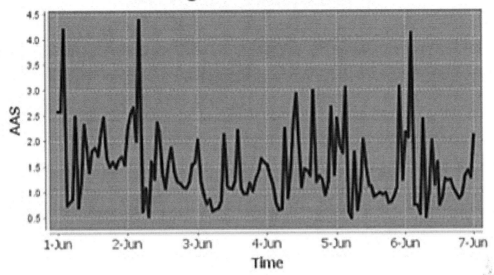

Figure 3.2: *Time Model Overview Report (Graph Section) in the Ion Tool*

Using the *dba_hist_sys_time_model* view, you can also write trend reports that describe the workload, aggregated by hour-of-the-day and day-of-the-week. For example, the query below returns the average database workload by hour-of-the-day:

🖫 **avg_workload_hour_of_the_day.sql**

```
select
   to_char(end_interval_time,'HH24') "Hour of Day",
   Round(avg(newtime.value-oldtime.value)/1000000,2) "Avg DB Time (Sec)"
from
   dba_hist_sys_time_model oldtime,
   dba_hist_sys_time_model newtime,
   dba_hist_snapshot       sn
where
   newtime.snap_id = sn.snap_id
and
   oldtime.snap_id = sn.snap_id-1
and
   newtime.stat_name = 'DB time'
and
   oldtime.stat_name = 'DB time'
having
   avg(newtime.value-oldtime.value) > 0
group by
   to_char(end_interval_time,'HH24');
```

The sample output, showing a signature of *DB time* by hour-of-the-day, looks like the following:

```
Ho Avg DB Time (Sec)
-- ----------------
00           55.21
```

01	54.68
02	53.38
03	52.79
04	53.8
05	52.98
06	53.62
07	52.51
08	53.26
09	61.27
10	515.71
11	484.96
12	103.26
13	88.07
14	121.25
15	134.94
16	90.56
17	70.51
18	73.53
19	53.32
20	53.89
21	53.61
22	53.47
23	53.91

It is important to visualize this output in order to see the trends, and the Ion for Oracle tool can be used or simply paste the output into an MS-Excel chart Wizard to visualize the trends (Figure 3.3).

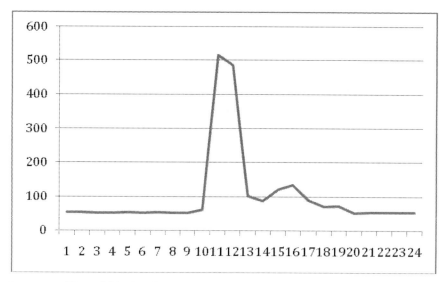

Figure 3.3: *Using MS Excel to Chart Trends*

Now that the data is plotted, a DBA can clearly see that this workload experiences high *DB time* every day between 10:00 AM to 3:00 PM.

Trend charts of averages can easily be generated by hours-of-the-day, days-of-the-week, or months using the Ion tool. Figure 3.4 shows such a report from the Ion tool:

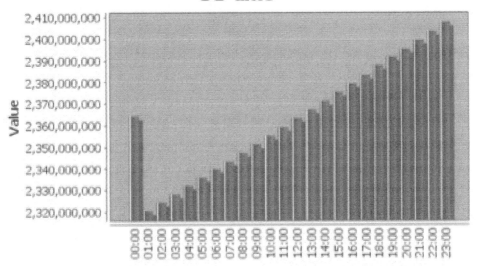

Figure 3.4: *Hourly Averages for Database Time in the Ion Tool*

In this case, the DBA would review the jobs in *dba_jobs* and try to re-schedule large batch jobs away from the peak workload times.

The Ion for Oracle tool can also be used to produce trend charts of time model statistics (Figure 3.5):

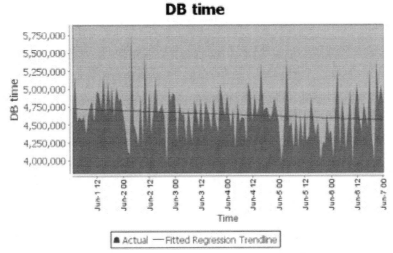

Figure 3.5: *Sample Time Model Trend Report in the Ion Tool*

Now examine the time model sections of an AWR/STATSPACK report.

Time Model Statistics

The standard AWR/STATSPACK reports now contain a Time Model Statistics report, and it breaks down exactly how the system spent the timeframe for the report. The following listing shows an example from the test runs:

```
Time Model Statistics  DB/Inst: SSD/ssd2  Snaps: 3-4
-> ordered by Time (seconds) desc
```

Statistic Name	Time (seconds)	%Total DB Time
DB time	592.04	100.00
sql execute elapsed time	586.23	99.02
DB CPU	203.60	34.39
background elapsed time	45.51	7.69
background cpu time	22.46	3.79
PL/SQL execution elapsed time	1.63	.28
connection management call elapsed time	1.30	.22
parse time elapsed	.58	.10
sequence load elapsed time	.02	.00
hard parse (sharing criteria) elapsed time	.00	.00
hard parse (bind mismatch) elapsed time	.00	.00
hard parse elapsed time	.00	.00
Java execution elapsed time	.00	.00
failed parse elapsed time	.00	.00
PL/SQL compilation elapsed time	.00	.00
inbound PL/SQL rpc elapsed time	.00	.00
failed parse (out of shared memory) elapsed t	.00	.00

```
Operating System Statistics  DB/Inst: SSD/ssd2  Snaps: 3-4
```

Statistic Name	Value
AVG_BUSY_TICKS	11,641
AVG_IDLE_TICKS	349,688
AVG_IN_BYTES	851,628,032
AVG_NICE_TICKS	0
AVG_OUT_BYTES	1,107,304,448
AVG_SYS_TICKS	2,335
AVG_USER_TICKS	9,306
BUSY_TICKS	23,282
IDLE_TICKS	699,377
IN_BYTES	1,703,256,064
NICE_TICKS	0
OUT_BYTES	2,214,608,896
RSRC_MGR_CPU_WAIT_TIME	0

```
SYS_TICKS                                   4,670
USER_TICKS                                 18,612
```

Between the supplied Oracle internal statistics and the system time ticks values, one can quickly determine how the system spent it's time for the report interval. In the example report, the time was spent running SQL. This example was for a 2-CPU system, so the total time calculates out to 200% rather than 100%.

The next section of the AWR report was also new in 10g. It reports on the various services and shows their activity levels. The following listing is an example from the report:

```
Service Statistics  DB/Inst: SSD/ssd2  Snaps: 3-4
-> ordered by DB Time


                                      Physical    Logical
Service Name     DB Time (s)  DB CPU (s)   Reads     Reads
---------------- -----------  ----------- ---------- ----------ssd      591.9      203.5     5,468
6,041,482
SYS$USERS            0.1         0.1          0         36
SYS$BACKGROUND       0.0         0.0         52     96,198
ssdXDB               0.0         0.0          0          0

-------------------------------------------------------
```

```
Service Wait Class Stats  DB/Inst: SSD/ssd2  Snaps: 3-4


-> Wait Class info for services in the Service Statistics section.
-> Total Waits and Time Waited displayed for the following wait
   classes: User I/O, Concurrency, Administrative, Network
-> Time Waited (Wt Time) in centisecond (100th of a second)
```

```
Service Name
  User I/O  User I/O  Concurcy Concurcy   Admin    Admin   Network Network

Total Wts  Wt Time Total Wts  Wt Time Total Wts Wt Time Total Wts Wt Time
--------- --------- --------- -------- --------- ------- --------- -------
ssd
    7806       242      1411     4114         0        0     31702    2628
SYS$USERS
       0         0         0        0         0        0        72       0
SYS$BACKGROUND
   49003         1       147       16         0        0         1       0
```

This report shows exactly which services spent the most time waiting, and in general, what they waited for. Some times are reported in units of centiseconds while others are in seconds. In this report, the SSD service dominates the time utilized. This was the service used to run the test cases. Note that the high percentages of reads that are logical reads indicate an almost fully cached system.

Time Model Statistics   **75**

Conclusion

When tuning Oracle, DBAs have a wealth of available statistics; it is important to understand the benefits and limitations of each. Oracle 10g introduced the time model statistics to open a window into the time spent by sessions and background processes, an invaluable tool for the Oracle tuning expert. The main points of this chapter include:

- Oracle has two time model views with cumulative numbers in *v$sys_time_model* and point-in-time metrics in the *v$sess_time_model* view
- Oracle AWR has the *dba_hist_sys_time_model* table with historical time model information.
- The standard AWR report has several sections dedicated to time model statistics.
- The time model statistics can be used to identify repeating periods of high workload activity (aggregated by day-of-the-week and hour-of-the-day). Workload overload problems can be remedied by load-balancing jobs, i.e. moving large scheduled tasks to other times.

The next chapter will put together concepts already covered and explore how to study past performance and how to use predictive modeling techniques to spot repeating Oracle performance issues.

Predictive Modeling

The trend is clear!

Tomorrow we will see lightly-scattered I/O bottlenecks clearing into afternoon latch contention.

Predicting the Future with Oracle

Predictive modeling is the study of the past to predict the future, a well-established statistical technique that is used in many industries. While everyone knows that predictive modeling saves lives in medical research and saves us from credit card fraud, is it possible for Oracle to predict a future problem and prevent it?

Predictive models are widely used in the credit card industry, and it's scary how using statistics can reveal all sorts of personal information:

- Predictive models exist that will accurately determine your age, gender and race only from examining your credit card purchase history.

- Using predictive modeling we can even "guess" your income range, number of dependant and even your weight.

- Credit card companies can calculate the odds you will eat at McDonald's today, considering your history of eating at McDonald's.

- The credit card companies use "cohorts", statistical groupings of related purchasers. They give these cohorts cute names like "dinks (double income, no kids).

- Credit card fraud prevention software is so sophisticated that if you order products a person in your group never ordered, your card will get automatically locked.

- Credit card use is never private. It can be used by law enforcement to prove a DUI indirectly if the suspect spent a large amount on a credit card at a bar shortly before.

Predictive modeling is one of the best ways to perform long term Oracle instance tuning, and the AWR (Automated Workload Repository) tables are very helpful in this pursuit. In the predictive model of Oracle tuning, the DBA is charged with taking the existing AWR statistics and predicting the future needs for all instance and I/O areas within the Oracle database.

With Oracle performance data in STATSPACK or AWR it's possible to develop a predictive model that will analyze historical patterns and "proactively" change the database before the problem occurs.

"Those who cannot remember the past are condemned to repeat it."

George Santayana

While most DBAs will run scripts to find important trends and signatures, it can also be automated. The Oracle data buffer cache advisor is a primitive predictive modeling tool that forecasts the marginal reduction in disk I/O when you add more RAM, and the predictive modeling approach is codified in the *Ion for Oracle* tool, where historical data from STATSPACK and AWR is analyzed to identify important trends and signatures within any SQL workload.

While it's not easy to implement, predictive modeling with Oracle is very easy to describe. Once you identify your SQL workloads (called "cohorts" in statistical analysis), you create jobs with *dbms_scheduler* to change the database just-in-time to prevent an impending performance problem.

Most databases have repeating workloads that change over time in predictable ways:

- **OLTP system workloads:** These databases tend to have a daytime workload and another distinct workload for evening batch processing. Some shops also have distinct end-of-week and end-of-month workloads.

- **VLDB system workloads:** Decision Support and Data Warehouse applications tend to have many distinct workloads depending on the current stage of processing. You might have a workload for loading data, another for aggregating summaries and building indexes and another workload for warehouse queries.

Of course, every database is different and some systems have only a single workload, but the vast majority of databases will have repeating "signatures", identifiable trends in SQL processing.

Oracle can be psychic!

Just like medical researchers can use predictive modeling to predict disease before they kill you, you can use predictive modeling with Oracle performance data to predict changes and fix the database before it kills your response time!

In a nutshell, these are the steps for Oracle predictive modeling:

- **Step 1, Identify workloads:** Use STATSPACK or AWR scripts to identify your distinct workloads.

- **Step 2, Optimize workloads:** Once you have isolated workloads, you run empirical tests to find the optimal parameters and statistics for each workload. While expert DBAs will do this with customized scripts, Oracle 11g and beyond offers tools to capture workloads into SQL Tuning Sets (STS), you can replay them using the SQL Performance Analyzer (SPA) with Real Application Testing (RAT) to determine the optimal settings for the workload variables:

  o **Find optimal instance pool parameters:** Each workload needs an optimal setting for *db_cache_size, shared_pool_size, pga_aggregate_target* and other RAM region parameters.

  o **Find optimal optimizer parameters:** It's not uncommon for different SQL workload to have different values for *optimizer_mode, optimizer_index_caching* and *optimizer_index_cost_adj.*

  o **Find optimal optimizer statistics:** It's a good idea to save your optimizer statistics (via *dbms_stats*), and import and export them immediately before the workload changes.

- **Step 3, Change the instance:** Once you have identified the workloads and when they change, you use *dbms_scheduler* to implement just-in-time changes, morphing the instance to accommodate the new workload, fixing problems before they occur!

Oracle has started to build primitive predictive models to assist the DBA, predicting the marginal changes to various pool sizing parameters, "silver bullet" settings where making changes will have a profound impact on your SQL workload.

Oracle has predictive advisors for the data buffer cache, the shared pool, PGA, large pool, almost every region within the Oracle SGA RAM heap.

However, not all advisors are predictive. It's important to note that many of Oracle "automated" tool are not predictive, they are reactive. With a reactive tool, the software waits until a problem occurs before attempting a remedy. These are some of Oracle non-predictive advisors:

- **Tuning advisors**: Oracle's automatic diagnostic database advisor (ADDM) uses applied artificial intelligence to recommend new materialized views and indexes. Oracle also has a primitive extra-cost SQLTuning advisor and a SQLAccess advisor that gather real-time execution information your SQL workload and recommends actions like index and materialized view opportunities. Using the scripts from this book you will be able to develop your own custom advisors that work better than these one-size-fits-all solutions from Oracle.

- **Memory Advisor**: Starting in Oracle 10g, we saw the Automated Memory Management (AMM) software that detects problems and re-size the SGA regions. This one-size-fits-all approach is OK for tiny departmental databases that have no DBA, but the constant re-sizing of the RAM pools can actually cause performance problems!

For example, the AWR physical reads could be analyzed and compared to the memory usage within the Oracle *db_cache_size*. The information from the comparison could be extrapolated and used to predict the times at which the Oracle data buffers would need to be increased in order to maintain the current levels of performance.

There are also third-party vendors offering predictive modeling tools for Oracle:

- **Ion for Oracle:** Designed by Donald K. Burleson, and Steve Karam, Ion is a tool to model and predict future changes in Oracle workloads.

- **SPSS:** The Statistical Package for the Social Sciences (SPSS, a.k.a. Clementine) supports Oracle Data Mining.

- **SAS:** The SAS (Statistical Analysis System) "SAS/Access" software and SAS Enterprise Miner for Oracle is very popular because it has been used for data mining for more than thirty (30) years.

- **Quest Central:** Quest says that their tool has *"A non-intrusive database object and source code scanner that identifies possible performance problems offline or online from the System Global Area, enabling users to be proactive in troubleshooting bottlenecks before they arise"*.

- **ProfitLogic:** A predictive modeling tool recently purchased by Oracle.

- **Confio Ignite:** Confio Ignite claims to have *"performance intelligence"* and predictive profiling capabilities.

Let's start our in-depth discussion of Oracle predictive modeling by examining Oracle's premier predictive modeling tool, Oracle Data Miner (ODM).

Oracle Data Mining and Predictive Analytics

Data mining is the capstone of Oracle data queries, a method for defining cohorts of related data items and tracking them over time. The basic goal of data mining is to identify hidden correlations, and the data mining expert must identify populations, and then track this population across various external factors, e.g. treatments and drugs.

In a nutshell, ODM serves as a Decision Support System (DSS) interface, allowing the DBA to create and refine decision rules as well as test changes the salient parameters of the problem domain.

"Predictions are difficult, especially about the future."

Yogi Berra

Data mining is a great method for finding patterns in huge amounts of data. The Gartner Group is an information technology research firm that defines data mining as:

"...the process of discovering meaningful new correlations, patterns and trends by sifting through large amounts of data stored in repositories, using pattern recognition technologies as well as statistical and mathematical techniques."

This is a wonderful yet somewhat obtuse definition of data mining! When faced with a data mining issue, it can often be difficult to know where to start. First let's look at some information about the Oracle data warehousing tools.

ODM is one of the most challenging areas of Oracle. As disk prices fall by orders of magnitude every few years, many shops find themselves with multi-terabyte online archives of historical information. This is a virtual gold mine of information. Data mining can be used to sift through massive amounts of data and find hidden information — valuable information that can help you better understand your customers and anticipate behavior.

Historical Oracle information is so valuable that a typical data warehouse can often pay for itself in just a few months by providing nuggets of information that saves the company money.

Data mining has evolved much over the past decades. The next section takes a look at the evolution of Oracle data mining, as well as reviewing Dr. Hamm's new book, *Oracle Data Mining.*

The Evolution toward Data Mining

Once a new data warehouse and ETL (extract, transform, and load) has been created, Oracle data experts implement data queries, starting with simple queries and culminating in data mining:

- **Ad-hoc query:** The Discoverer end-user layer will be configured to allow for the ad-hoc display of summary and detailed data.

- **Aggregation and multidimensional display:** Develop Oracle Warehouse Builder structures to summarize, aggregate and rollup salient information for display using the Oracle 10g Discoverer interface.

- **Basic correlations:** The front end should allow the end-user to specify dimensions and request a correlation matrix between the variables with each dimension. The system will start with one-to-one correlations and evolve to support multivariate chi-square methods.

- **Hypothesis testing:** The data warehouse is used to validate theories about the behavior of the customer universe, and curve formulation techniques allow data mining experts to derive valid formulae to describe the data. Hypothesis testing in data mining often involves simulation modeling using the Oracle data as input.

- **Oracle Data Mining:** This is the capstone of Oracle data queries, a method for defining cohorts of related data items and tracking them over time. The basic goal of data mining is to identify hidden correlations. The data mining expert must identify a population; for example, all Eskimos with alcoholism, and then track this population across various external factors, like whether or not the Eskimos went to rehab. These DSS interfaces require the ability for the end-user to refine the decision rules and change the salient parameters of the domain, i.e. the confidence interval for the predictions.

Performing Oracle data mining requires advanced statistics skills including multivariate (chi-square) techniques for identifying hidden correlations. Many shops employ professionals with advanced degrees in areas that are statistics-centered, drawing from people with doctorates in Economics, Experimental Psychology and Sociology. To perform complex and valid studies, the warehouse team must have a statistician with the following skills:

- **Multivariate statistics:** Even a simple longitudinal study requires knowledge of the application of applied multivariate statistics.

- **Artificial Intelligence:** ODM is heavily centered around the application of AI for mining algorithms. The statistician should have a firm grounding in fuzzy logic, pattern matching and the use of advanced Boolean logic.

The ODM tools are complex by nature and ODM professionals must understand how to apply Oracle's powerful tools to the data mining process.

Oracle Data Mining and Predictive Analytics

Oracle started with predictive modeling by developing ODM tools, and is currently developing the Automatic Maintenance Tasks (AMT) feature, starting in Oracle 10g, that will *"automatically detect and re-build suboptimal indexes."*

There has been great discussion about using the scientific method with Oracle databases and how mathematical models are developed for Oracle. Predicting the future without historical justifications is the realm of psychics, not scientists. Virtually every predictive model used in Oracle relies on data from the database to create the predictive framework.

Oracle provides a powerful data mining infrastructure embedded directly into the database. The data mining infrastructure, accessed through Java API, automates the performance of all the phases of data. Even though data mining is based on statistics, machine learning and artificial intelligence, you don't have to have to be a statistical genius to run a data mining analysis with Oracle.

The approach to Oracle data mining follows these straightforward steps:

1. Sample from a larger database or data warehouse
2. Explore, clean, preprocess and reduce the data, including treatment of outliers and missing data
3. Develop an understanding of variables and selection of variables for building a model
4. Data is partitioned into training, validation and test data sets
5. Run several modeling techniques, choosing one on the basis of its performance on the validation data. Results with the test data are an indicator of how well it will do with new data.

Fortunately, one of the strengths of data mining is the algorithms available to help capture the important fields that are needed to build successful models of good customers. So do not worry about deciding which fields will be needed. Include as many as can reasonably be loaded into the table and let ODM help mine the gold from the data.

Components of the Oracle Data Miner

To help with steps one and two above, ODM has an impressive array of tools for sampling, exploring, and cleaning the data. These tools can import files, recode existing fields, derive new fields, and filter all this data using *where* queries. In addition to these tools, there are utilities for creating views, creating tables from views, copying tables, joining tables together, and importing text files. Displaying summary statistics and histograms assists in step three, thereby developing an understanding of the data.

For a full treatment of this exciting area, see Dr. Carolyn Hamm's book, *Oracle Data Mining*. Now, let's drill deeper into Oracle predictive modeling toolkit.

Predictive Models Made Easy

As we covered in Chapter 1, almost all of the Oracle SGA components can be changed at will with *alter system* statements. DBAs can dynamically change the Oracle database RAM regions and other instance parameters depending upon the performance needs of the applications. By making many initialization parameters alterable, Oracle is moving towards a dynamic database configuration, whereby the configuration of the system can be adjusted according to the needs of the Oracle application. The AWR can identify these changing needs.

There are four main predictive utilities included with the standard STATSPACK and AWR reports, one for each major SGA and PGA memory region:

- **PGA advisor:** Oracle 9i introduced an advisory utility dubbed *v$pga_target_advice*. This utility shows the marginal changes in optimal, one-pass, and multi-pass PGA execution for different sizes of *pga_aggregate_target*, ranging from 10% to 200% of the current value.

- **Shared pool advisor:** This advisory functionality does predictive modeling, showing various sizes of the *shared_pool_size* parameter. This utility can also be invoked manually and results viewed in *v$shared_pool_advice*.

- **Data cache advisor:** The *v$db_cache_advice* utility shows the marginal changes in physical data block reads for different sizes of *db_cache_size*. The data from STATSPACK can provide similar data as *v$db_cache_advice*, and most Oracle tuning professionals use STATSPACK and *v$db_cache_advice* to monitor the effectiveness of their data buffers.

- **Java pool advisor:** Oracle now has an advisor for the Java pool usage.

These advisory utilities are extremely helpful for the Oracle DBA who must adjust the sizes of the RAM areas to meet processing demands. The following query can be used to perform the cache advice function once the *v$db_cache_advice* has been enabled and the database has run long enough to give representative results.

🖫 **cache_advice.sql**

```
column c1    heading 'Cache Size (meg)'      format 999,999,999,999
column c2    heading 'Buffers'               format 999,999,999
column c3    heading 'Estd Phys|Read Factor' format 999.90
column c4    heading 'Estd Phys| Reads'      format 999,999,999

select
   size_for_estimate          c1,
   buffers_for_estimate       c2,
   estd_physical_read_factor  c3,
   estd_physical_reads        c4
from
   v$db_cache_advice
where
   name = 'DEFAULT'
and
   block_size  = (select value from v$parameter
                  where name = 'db_block_size')
and
   advice_status = 'ON';
```

The output from the script is shown below. The values range from ten percent of the current size to double the current size of the *db_cache_size*.

Cache Size (meg)	Buffers	Estd Phys Read Factor	Estd Phys Reads

```
------------------ ------------- ----------- ------------
      30              3,802         18.70    192,317,943  <== 10% size
      60              7,604         12.83    131,949,536
      91             11,406          7.38     75,865,861
     121             15,208          4.97     51,111,658
     152             19,010          3.64     37,460,786
     182             22,812          2.50     25,668,196
     212             26,614          1.74     17,850,847
     243             30,416          1.33     13,720,149
     273             34,218          1.13     11,583,180
     304             38,020          1.00     10,282,475  Current Size
     334             41,822           .93      9,515,878
     364             45,624           .87      8,909,026
     395             49,426           .83      8,495,039
     424             53,228           .79      8,116,496
     456             57,030           .76      7,824,764
     486             60,832           .74      7,563,180
     517             64,634           .71      7,311,729
     547             68,436           .69      7,104,280
     577             72,238           .67      6,895,122
     608             76,040           .66      6,739,731  <== 2x size
```

From the previous listing, it is clear that increasing the *db_cache_size* from 304 megabytes to 334 megabytes would result in approximately 700,000 less physical reads. This can be plotted as a 1/x function and the exact optimal point computed as the second derivative of the function 1/x as shown in Figure 4.1:

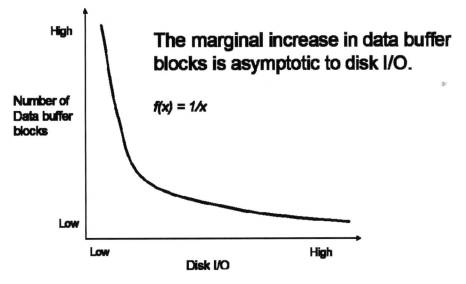

Figure 4.1: *The Relationship between Buffer Size and Disk I/O*

Once it is possible to recognize cyclic performance patterns in the Oracle database, the DBA is in a position to reconfigure the database in order to meet the specific processing needs of that Oracle database.

While the predictive models are new, the technique dates back to Oracle 6. Old-timer Oracle professionals would often keep several versions of their initialization parameter file and bounce in a new version when processing patterns were expected to change. For example, it was not uncommon to see a special Oracle instance configuration that was dedicated exclusively to the batch processing tasks that might occur every Friday, while another version of the *init.ora* file would be customized for OLTP transactions.

Additional *init.ora* files could be created that were suited to data warehouse processing that might occur on the weekend. In each of these cases, the Oracle database had to be stopped and restarted with the appropriate *init.ora* configuration file.

Starting with Oracle 10g, the AWR tables can be used to identify all specific times when an instance-related component of Oracle is stressed, and the new *dbms_scheduler* package can be used to trigger a script to dynamically change Oracle during these periods. In sum, AWR data is ideally suited to work with the dynamic SGA features of Oracle.

Next, let's examine another type of time-series reporting, the tracking of exceptional conditions within our database.

Exception Reporting with the AWR

The DBA can also make a detailed analysis of Oracle's data buffer caches, including the KEEP pool, DEFAULT pool, the RECYCLE pool, and the pools for multiple block sizes like *db_32k_cache_size*. With that information, the DBA can accurately measure the performance of each one of the buffer pools, summarized by day-of-the-week and hour-of-the-day over long periods of time. Based upon existing usage, the DBA can accurately predict at what time additional RAM memory is needed for each of these data buffers.

The AWR tables also offer the DBA an opportunity to slice off the information in brand new ways. In the real world, all Oracle applications follow measurable, cyclical patterns called signatures. For example, an Oracle Financials application may be very active on the first Monday of every month when all of the books are being closed and the financial reports are being prepared. Using AWR data, information can be extracted from every first Monday of the month for the past year, which will yield a valid signature of the specific performance needs of the end- of-the-month Oracle financials applications.

At the highest level, exception reporting involves adding a *where* clause to a data dictionary query to eliminate values that fall beneath a pre-defined threshold. For a simple example, this can be done quite easily with a generic script to read *dba_hist_sysstat*.

The following simple script displays a time series exception report for any statistic in *dba_hist_sysstat*. The script accepts the statistics number and the value threshold for the exception report.

🖫 **display_stat.sql**

```
prompt
prompt   This will query the dba_hist_sysstat view to display all values
prompt   that exceed the value specified in
prompt   the "where" clause of the query.
prompt

set pages 999

break on snap_time skip 2

accept stat_name    char    prompt 'Enter Statistic Name:   ';
accept stat_value   number  prompt 'Enter Statistics Threshold value:   ';


col snap_time       format a19
col value           format 999,999,999

select
   to_char(begin_interval_time,'yyyy-mm-dd hh24:mi') snap_time,
   value
from
   dba_hist_sysstat
  natural join
   dba_hist_snapshot
where
   stat_name = '&stat_name'
and
  value > &stat_value
order by
   to_char(begin_interval_time,'yyyy-mm-dd hh24:mi')
;
```

This simple script will prompt for the statistic name and threshold value which allow for ad-hoc AWR queries:

```
SQL> @rpt_sysatst
```

This will query the *dba_hist_sysstat* view to display all values that exceed the value specified in the *where* clause of the query.

```
Enter Statistic Name:  physical writes
Enter Statistics Threshold value:  200000


SNAP_TIME                   VALUE
-------------------   -----------
2004-02-21 08:00          200,395
2004-02-27 08:00          342,231
2004-02-29 08:00          476,386
2004-03-01 08:00          277,282
2004-03-02 08:00          252,396
2004-03-04 09:00          203,407
```

To see the signature, it is useful to plot this data, and here is a visualization of this data using Ion Oracle (Figure 4.2):

Exception Reporting with the AWR

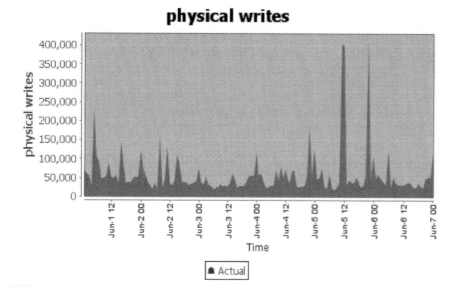

Figure 4.2: *Physical Writes over Time*

The listing above indicates a repeating trend where physical writes seem to be high at 8:00 AM on certain days. This powerful script will allow the DBA to quickly extract exception conditions from any instance-wide Oracle metric and see its behavior over time.

The next section provides a more powerful exception report that compares system-wide values to individual snapshots.

General Trend Identification with the AWR

Once the *dba_hist* scripts have been mastered, the next step is to look at the more complex task of trend identification with the AWR tables. By now, it should be clear that aggregating important Oracle performance metrics over time, day-of-the-week and hour-of-the-day, allows the DBA to see the hidden signatures. These signatures are extremely important because they show regularly occurring changes in processing demands. This knowledge allows the DBA to anticipate upcoming changes and reconfigure Oracle just in time to meet the changes.

The following is a simple example. A script can be used to show the signature for any Oracle system statistic, averaged by hour-of-the-day. Figure 4.3 shows how the output of such a script might appear.

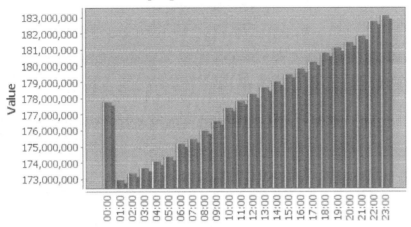

Figure 4.3: *An Hourly Signature for Physical Disk Reads*

Plotting the data makes it easy to find trends. Of course, open source products such as RRDTool can also be used to automate the plotting of data from the AWR and ASH tables and make nice web screens to see the data. Finally, the Ion for Oracle tool can be used and, with just a few clicks, comprehensive charts can be produced for any snapshot period as well as trend charts for month, day, or hourly periods. Figure 4.4 below shows a sample Ion view:

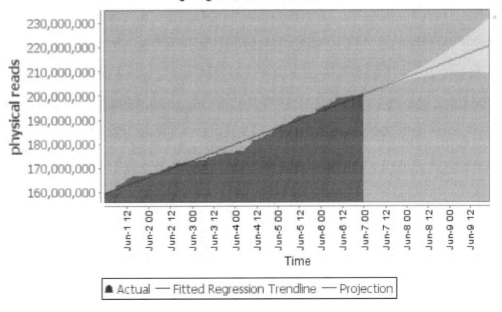

Figure 4.4: *Time Series Charts in the Ion Tool*

As we see in this linear regression, we must be cautious in time-series modeling since the farther we go into the future, the wider the confidence interval. Statisticians call this widening confidence interval the "trumpet of Doom" because it spells doom for long-range forecasting (Figure 4.5):

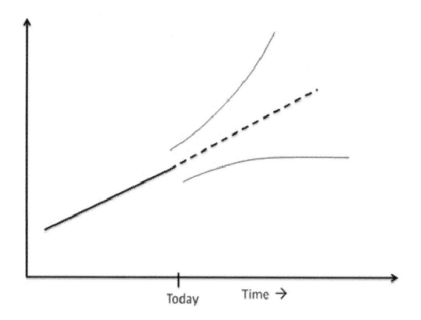

Today   Time →

Figure 4.5: *The trumpet of doom*

The script that we introduced in the Chapter 2 section titled *Exception Reporting with the AWR* will accept any of the values from *dba_hist_sysstat*. This data can now be plotted for trend analysis as shown in Figure 4.6. These types of signatures will become very stable for most Oracle databases and can be used to develop a predictive model for proactive tuning activities.

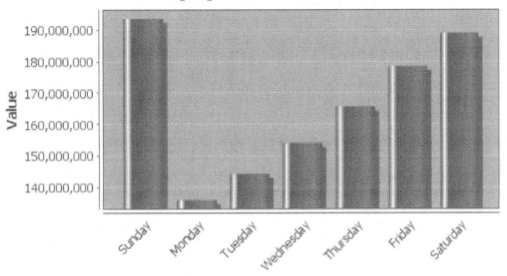

Figure 4.6: *The Signature for Average Physical Reads by Day-of-the-Week*

The same types of reports, aggregated by day-of-the week, can be created to show daily trends. Over long periods of time, almost all Oracle databases will develop distinct signatures that reflect the regular daily processing patterns of the end-user community.

Next, examine how a DBA can perform rudimentary correlation analysis using data from AWR and ASH.

Correlation Analysis with AWR and ASH

For those who like Oracle tuning with the Oracle Wait Interface (OWI), there are interesting statistics that relate to system-wide wait events from the *dba_hist_waitstat* table as shown in Table 4.1 that provide detailed wait event information from the *dba_hist_active_sess_history*.

COLUMN	DESCRIPTION
snap_id	Unique snapshot ID
dbid	Database ID for the snapshot
instance_number	Instance number for the snapshot
class	Class of the block

COLUMN	DESCRIPTION
wait_count	Number of waits by the OPERATION for this CLASS of block
time	Sum of all wait times for all the waits by the OPERATION for this CLASS of block

Table 4.1: *The dba_hist_waitstat Statistics Used to Wait Event Analysis*

To understand correlation analysis for an Oracle database, a simple example may be helpful. For advanced correlation analysis, the DBA can seek to identify correlations between instance-wide wait events and block-level waits. This is a critical way of combining human insight with the AWR and ASH (Active Session History) information to isolate the exact file and object where the wait contention is occurring.

The ASH stores the history of a recent session's activity in *v$active_session_history* with the AWR history view *dba_hist_active_sess_history*. This data is designed as a rolling buffer in memory, and earlier information is overwritten when needed. To do this, the AWR *dba_hist_active_sess_history* view is needed. This view contains historical block-level contention statistics as shown in Table 4.2 below.

COLUMN	DESCRIPTION
snap_id	Unique snapshot ID
sample_time	Time of the sample
session_id	Session identifier
session_serial#	Session serial number. This is used to uniquely identify a session's objects.
user_id	Oracle user identifier
current_obj#	Object ID of the object that the session is currently referencing
current_file#	File number of the file containing the block that the session is currently referencing
current_block#	ID of the block that the session is currently referencing
wait_time	Total wait time for the event for which the session last waited (0 if currently waiting)
time_waited	Time that the current session actually spent waiting for the event. This column is set for waits that were in progress at the time the sample was taken.

Table 4.2: *Selected Columns from the Dba_hist_active_sess_history View*

The *wait_time_detail.sql* script below compares the wait event values from *dba_hist_waitstat* and *dba_hist_active_sess_history*. This script quickly allows the identification of the exact objects that are experiencing wait events.

🖫 wait_time_detail_10g.sql

```
prompt
prompt   This will compare values from dba_hist_waitstat with
prompt   detail information from dba_hist_active_sess_history.
prompt

set pages 999
set lines 80

break on snap_time skip 2

col snap_time      heading 'Snap|Time'    format a20
col file_name      heading 'File|Name'    format a40
col object_type    heading 'Object|Type'  format a10
col object_name    heading 'Object|Name'  format a20
col wait_count     heading 'Wait|Count'   format 999,999
col time           heading 'Time'         format 999,999

select
   to_char(begin_interval_time,'yyyy-mm-dd hh24:mi') snap_time,
   object_type,
   object_name,
   wait_count,
   time
from
   dba_hist_waitstat              wait,
   dba_hist_snapshot              snap,
   dba_hist_active_sess_history   ash,
   dba_data_files                 df,
   dba_objects                    obj
where
   wait.snap_id = snap.snap_id
and
   wait.snap_id = ash.snap_id
and
   df.file_id = ash.current_file#
and
   obj.object_id = ash.current_obj#
and
   wait_count > 50
order by
   to_char(begin_interval_time,'yyyy-mm-dd hh24:mi'),
   file_name;
```

This script is also enabled to join into the *dba_data_files* view to get the file names associated with the wait event. This is a very powerful script that can be used to quickly drill in to find the cause of specific waits. Below is a sample output showing time-slices and the corresponding wait counts and times:

```
SQL> @wait_time_detail_10g
```

This will compare values from *dba_hist_waitstat* with detailed information from *dba_hist_active_sess_hist.*

```
Snap                   Object      Object         Wait
Time                   Type        Name           Count     Time
-----------------      ---------   ------------   -------   -------
2004-02-28 01:00       TABLE       ORDOR           4,273       67
                       INDEX       PK_CUST_ID     12,373      324
                       INDEX       FK_CUST_NAME    3,883       17
                       INDEX       PK_ITEM_ID      1,256      967

2004-02-29 03:00       TABLE       ITEM_DETAIL        83       69

2004-03-01 04:00       TABLE       ITEM_DETAIL     1,246       45

2004-03-01 21:00       TABLE       CUSTOMER_DET    4,381      354
                       TABLE       IND_PART          117       15

2004-03-04 01:00       TABLE       MARVIN         41,273       16
                       TABLE       FACTOTUM        2,827       43
                       TABLE       DOW_KNOB          853        6
                       TABLE       ITEM_DETAIL        57      331
                       TABLE       HIST_ORD        4,337      176
                       TABLE       TAB_HIST          127       66
```

This example demonstrates how the AWR and ASH data can be used to create an almost infinite number of sophisticated custom performance reports.

The AWR can also be used with the ODM product to analyze trends. Using ODM, the AWR tables can be scanned for statistically significant correlations between metrics. Sophisticated multivariate Chi-Square techniques can also be applied to reveal hidden patterns within the AWR treasury of Oracle performance information. The Oracle ODM uses sophisticated Support Vector Machines (SVM) algorithms for binary, multi-class classification models and has built-in linear regression functionality.
As we learned in Chapter 1, disk I/O is the single most expensive operation within Oracle. Let's take a look at how we can use AWR to predict changes in disk I/O activity.

Predictive Modeling with *dba_hist_filestatxs*

The *dba_hist_filestatxs* table contains important file level information about Oracle I/O activities. Because most Oracle databases perform a high amount of reading and writing from disk, the *dba_hist_filestatxs* view can be very useful for identifying high use data files. For Oracle customers who are not using the Stripe and Mirror Everywhere (SAME) approach, this view is indispensable for locating and isolating hot data files. Many Oracle shops will isolate hot data files onto high-speed solid-state disk (SSD), or relocate the hot files to another physical disk spindle.

If the *dba_hist_filestatxs* is described as shown in Table 4.3, the important information columns can be seen next. The important information relates to physical reads and writes, the actual time spent performing reads and writes, and the wait count associated with each data file for each snapshot.

COLUMN	DESCRIPTION
snap_id	Unique snapshot ID
filename	Name of the datafile
phyrds	Number of physical reads done
phywrts	Number of times DBWR is required to write
singleblkrds	Number of single block reads
readtim	Time, in hundredths of a second, spent doing reads if the *timed_statistics* parameter is TRUE; 0 if *timed_statistics* is FALSE
writetim	Time, in hundredths of a second, spent doing writes if the *timed_statistics* parameter is TRUE; 0 if *timed_statistics* is FALSE
singleblkrdtim	Cumulative single block read time, in hundredths of a second
phyblkrd	Number of physical blocks read
phyblkwrt	Number of blocks written to disk, which may be the same as *phywrts* if all writes are single blocks
wait_count	Wait Count

Table 4.3: *The Metrics Relating to File I/O in Dba_hist_filestatxs*

It is easy to write a customized exception report with AWR data. In this simple report called *hot_write_files_10g.sql*, the *dba_hist_filestatxs* table is queried to identify hot write datafiles, which is any condition where any individual file consumed more than 25% of the total physical writes for the whole instance. Especially when RAID is not being used, identification of hot datafiles is important because the objects inside the file cache can be cached with the KEEP pool or by moving the hot data file onto high-speed solid-state RAM disks.

The query below compares the physical writes in the *phywrts* column of *dba_hist_filestatxs* with the instance-wide physical writes *statistic# = 55* from the *dba_hist_sysstat* table. This simple, yet powerful, script allows the Oracle professional to track hot-write datafiles over time, thereby gaining important insight into the status of the I/O subsystem over time.

file_io_hogs.sql

```
prompt  This will identify any single file who's write I/O
prompt  is more than 25% of the total write I/O of the database.
prompt

set pages 999

break on snap_time skip 2
```

```
col filename        format a40
col phywrts         format 999,999,999
col snap_time       format a20

select
    to_char(begin_interval_time,'yyyy-mm-dd hh24:mi') snap_time,
    filename,
    phywrts
from
    dba_hist_filestatxs
natural join
    dba_hist_snapshot
where
    phywrts > 0
and
    phywrts * 4 >
(
select
    avg(value)                  all_phys_writes
from
    dba_hist_sysstat
  natural join
    dba_hist_snapshot
where
    stat_name = 'physical writes'
and
  value > 0
)
order by
    to_char(begin_interval_time,'yyyy-mm-dd hh24:mi'),
    phywrts desc;
```

The following is the sample output from this powerful script. This is a useful report because the high-write datafiles are identified as well as those specific times in which they are hot.

```
SQL> @hot_write_files
```

This will identify any single file whose write I/O is more than 25% of the total write I/O of the database.

```
SNAP_TIME          FILENAME                                        PHYWRTS
-------------      ---------------------------------------------   --------
2004-02-20 23:30   E:\ORACLE\ORA92\FSDEV10G\SYSAUX01.DBF            85,540
2004-02-21 01:00   E:\ORACLE\ORA92\FSDEV10G\SYSAUX01.DBF            88,843
2004-02-21 08:31   E:\ORACLE\ORA92\FSDEV10G\SYSAUX01.DBF            89,463
2004-02-22 02:00   E:\ORACLE\ORA92\FSDEV10G\SYSAUX01.DBF            90,168
2004-02-22 16:30   E:\ORACLE\ORA92\FSDEV10G\SYSAUX01.DBF           143,974
                   E:\ORACLE\ORA92\FSDEV10G\UNDOTBS01.DBF           88,973
```

This type of time series exception reporting is extremely useful for detecting those times when an Oracle database is experiencing I/O stress. Many Oracle professionals will schedule these types of exception reports for automatic e-mailing every day. AWR can also be used to aggregate this information to spot trends.

Conclusion

If we take the time to become familiar with the wealth of metrics within the AWR and ASH tables, it becomes easy to get detailed correlation information between any of the 500+ performance metrics captured by the AWR.

As the Oracle database evolves, Oracle will continue to enhance the mechanisms for analyzing the valuable performance information in AWR. At the present rate, future releases of Oracle may have true artificial intelligence built in to detect and correct even the most challenging Oracle optimization issues.

The AWR provides the foundation for sophisticated performance analysis, including exception reporting, trend analysis, correlation analysis, hypothesis testing, data mining, and best of all, the ability to anticipate future stress on the database. The main points of this chapter include:

- The AWR *dba_hist* views are similar to well-known STATSPACK tables, making it easy to migrate existing performance reports to Oracle 10g and beyond.

- The *dba_hist* views are fully documented and easy to use for writing custom scripts.

- The creation of AWR and ASH provides a complete repository for diagnosing and fixing any Oracle performance issue.

- The AWR and ASH are the most exciting performance optimization tools in Oracle's history and provide the foundation for the use of artificial intelligence techniques to be applied to Oracle performance monitoring and optimization.

- As Oracle evolves, the AWR and ASH will likely automate the tedious and time-consuming task of Oracle tuning.

Now that the basic idea behind proactive time series and correlation analysis has been revealed, the next step is to take a look at how the ASH data can be used as a real-time monitor for diagnosing acute performance bottlenecks.

Oracle Troubleshooting

A good DBA is also a good detective

Introduction to Troubleshooting

One of the most stressful aspects of the Oracle DBA job role is troubleshooting acute performance problems. In a serious emergency, there could be thousands of end-users waiting for the DBA to provide access to the database. While the proactive techniques described in this book serve to prevent future performance problems, there is always the possibility of a rare exception, a rogue process, or an unplanned increase in system usage.

This chapter will focus on the "now" issues of Oracle emergency support and examine techniques to quickly locate and relieve transient Oracle bottlenecks.

It is also important to understand the scope of unplanned outages. The DBA may be troubleshooting a locked session for a single end-user or could be troubleshooting a system-wide outage that affects thousands of end-users. This chapter will describe proven techniques and provide scripts to allow ease in ascertaining the cause of an acute performance problem, but problem identification is only a small part of the solution.

Even with all of Oracle's flexibility, some performance problems cannot be quickly corrected. These global lockups are often related to resource shortages that impact the entire database, and the solutions to these problems are often mandated by management.

While the DBA has a vested interest in finding the root cause of a performance problem, it is impractical to inconvenience an entire end-user community while performing diagnostics. Some mission-critical Oracle databases such as Amazon or eBay have downtime costs exceeding $100,000 per minute and time is of the essence when disaster strikes.

Don't be scared to bounce production!

If a production database has crashed, quickly abort and warm start. Bouncing a locked up instance will frequently fix the issue.

Oracle troubleshooting is significant part of Oracle tuning, an approach whereby the Oracle professional quickly diagnoses the root cause of an acute performance problem. Huge stress levels and late night hours are an inevitable part of life for an emergency support DBA. Most of the databases will be unfamiliar and there will only be a few minutes to view the problem and create a plan to quickly relieve the bottleneck.

Only when the easy remedies have failed is the emergency support DBA called in because when a production database is in crisis, minimizing downtime is critical. At this point, clients demand quick fixes, and this often requires unconventional methods.

There are many global remedies for Oracle performance troubleshooting including "silver bullets", which are defined as any single action or small set of commands that has a profound impact on system wide performance.

It is important to make a distinction between a proactive just-in-time tuning techniques and a too-late tuning technique like those in the Automatic Shared Memory Management (ASMM) facility, where Oracle detects an problem and morphs the SGA regions to meet changing demands of processing. A true proactive solution will fix the problem before it interferes with the end-user community.

The following section will illustrate some common emergency troubleshooting methods.

Emergency Troubleshooting Methods

When the telephone rings at the Oracle support desk, it is usually an irate end-user complaining that their database is down. From this point forward, time is of the essence, and the emergency support DBA must be ready to perform fast detective work to get the database online again quickly.

Functioning as an emergency Oracle support DBA can be great fun for an adrenaline junky or maddening for those who cannot tolerate stress. The case studies that follow will show that emergency Oracle support often requires a very different set of goals and techniques from time-series Oracle tuning:

- **Fix the symptom first:** The goal is to get the database available as soon as possible, and it may be necessary to deliberately ignore the root cause and fix the symptom. The root cause can be addressed later, after the database is available to the end-user community.

- **Time is critical:** When a quick fix is required, instance-wide changes are often the best hope for a fast resolution.

- **Be creative:** Traditional time consuming tuning methods do not always apply in an emergency.

My company, Burleson Consulting, has an Oracle emergency support center (www.remote-dba.net) where we get calls from clients all over the world. They never call just to say "hello"; it is always a crisis, with a serious loss of availability to their mission-critical Oracle databases. I have personally worked on systems where an Oracle failure has shut down entire factories, leaving thousands of workers sitting on their hands waiting for me to restart their assembly line.

The stress is high, and fast troubleshooting can help save lives. I have worked with hospital image delivery systems when patients and doctors were waiting for the information that they needed to save lives.

Oracle troubleshooting is not for the faint hearted. I have supported financial systems for which downtime is measured in tens of thousands of dollars per minute.

Working late nights as an emergency support DBA comes with huge stress levels. It is common to get calls from brand new clients and have only a few minutes to assess their crisis and devise a plan to quickly relieve the problem. This is the core of Oracle troubleshooting, hours of boredom punctuated by sheer terror.

Why Oracle Shops Lose Their Databases

For many shops, Oracle troubleshooting support is a last resort, and the DBAs call us only after the obvious remedies have already been tried.

While it is true that Oracle is unbreakable, it takes an experienced Oracle DBA to make sure that a mission-critical database never crashes.

It is not uncommon to get calls from shops that have no DBA or an inexperienced or inept DBA who cannot figure out the predicament! Here are some common reasons reported for having little or no on-site support:

- **Outsourced DBA:** Penny wise and pound foolish, shops fire their in-house DBA and buy cheap offshore support, and then call us after their database is hopelessly corrupted.

- **No DBA:** Having a good DBA can create the illusion that the company does not need a DBA because they never experience a database crash. This often slows the efforts to hire a replacement. For instance, it is frequently reported that the previous DBA quit six months ago, and there has not been time to find a replacement. Of course, this call follows the inevitable crash of their production instance.

- **Oracle Certified Beginners:** In many cases, the company has hired an Oracle ACE or an Oracle OCP, but despite their certificates, they do not know what they are doing. This is usually caused by their lack of any significant experience with real database systems.

When Time Is of the Essence

When a production database is in crisis, minimizing downtime is of the essence. A fast fix is demanded, which often requires unconventional methods.

The main theme of this chapter is *"there are no rules in Oracle troubleshooting"*, so if the search is on to find a well-structured checklist, it will not be found here because it does not exist! Oracle tuning is not well-structured, and any DBA who relies on a checklist is probably unable to assist effectively in a downtime emergency.

Emergency support is the most exciting and challenging area of Oracle performance tuning, and one that relies largely on intuition and experience. All methodologies are thrown by the wayside and it is critical to do whatever it takes to get the database online as soon as possible.

Emergency support is also no place for Oracle Scientists, rigid thinkers who insist on applying some inflexible methodology to an acute performance problem.

Most real-world production systems have hundreds of segments and thousands of concurrent users, and trying to test a hypothesis on a busy database is a ludicrous waste of time and effort.

The Limitations of the DBA

There are many database problem areas that are beyond the scope of the Oracle DBA's control, and this can be very frustrating. The following is a short list of Oracle problems that the DBA may be prohibited from fixing:

- Poorly designed application or schema
- Inefficient PL/SQL within the application
- Excessive Transparent Network Substrate (TNS) calls within the application
- Dynamic SQL
- SQL without host variables
- Poorly-formed SQL statements
- Sub-optimal server kernel parameters
- Stupid management

One of the most maddening issues in Oracle troubleshooting is IT managers who do not understand the issues surrounding Oracle databases, especially when money is involved.

Management will commonly be unwilling to pay to solve the root cause of an Oracle performance problem. Managers are driven by cost savings, and they are extremely averse to taking risks.

For example, instead of paying $100,000 to tune 1,000 SQL statements, the manager may instead spend $50,000 to move poor SQL to a faster server.

I have also seen embarrassed managers, who are not going to admit that their offshore bargain was not such a bargain after all. When these poorly designed Oracle systems circle the bowl, these managers will never acknowledge their poor choices. Even if the DBA proves that the root cause of a chronic performance problem required rebuilding the schema from the ground-up, the embarrassed manager will never admit culpability for poor judgment.

Another frequent occurrence involves issues from embarrassed vendors who do not want to admit that their product was not optimized for Oracle. Most vendor packages are designed with "vanilla SQL" so that the product can be easily ported to a variety of database platforms such as Sybase, MySQL and DB2; however, vendors rarely make customization for Oracle-centric performance. Worst of all, most vendors do not like being told that their database layer needs to be tuned.

Vendors control the schema structures and the application layers. Even if a user finds sub-optimal SQL statements, they often cannot access the SQL source code in order to tune it.

These quirky vendor packages are the primary reason that Oracle offers specialized features such as *optimizer plan stability* in the form of stored outlines and the new Oracle10g SQL Profiles feature. In fact, Oracle has a wealth of tools for tuning vendor applications when the source code cannot be altered.

So, do these limitations render DBAs powerless to tune these databases? Oracle provides a variety of tuning tools. Many of the global tools are very powerful and have a positive effect on an entire database.

Oracle has many silver bullet parameters and settings, where changing a single item has a profound impact on the whole system. Some of these silver bullets allow tuning of vendor applications when the code cannot be changed directly. For example, a poorly designed application that does not use bind variables in their SQL can be fixed by adjusting the *cursor_sharing* parameter, a single act that can change the behavior of thousands of SQL statements.

To see how Oracle troubleshooting works in the real world, it will be helpful to examine some case studies in Oracle emergency techniques.

Case Studies in Oracle Troubleshooting

Unlike traditional tuning where the performance changes are justified with benchmark testing and quality assurance, an unplanned downtime offers no such luxury. The emergency DBA must use every weapon at their disposal to get the client's database running as quickly as possible, and unconventional methods are driven by a panicked client who does not appreciate the time and money it might take to fix the root cause of the problem. They need their performance back right away, as fast and as inexpensively as possible!

Clients are impatient, and they often insist on treating the symptom, using stop-gap remedies that are neither elegant nor comprehensive. In many cases, the client does not want to even hear about the time and effort that is required to address the root cause of an acute Oracle performance problem.

Take a close look at some case studies in emergency Oracle support. The following stories are representative of many real-world cases where a fast fix was used to relieve an acute performance problem:

- sub-optimal optimizer mode
- Replace an obsolete statistics gathering method
- Add missing indexes
- Implement *cursor_sharing=force*
- Implement the KEEP pool
- Add additional SGA RAM
- Employ materialized views
- Create bitmap indexes
- Add freelists
- Windows Oracle issues

It is impossible to reproduce the conditions of a complex performance breakdown, and the emergency support DBA is forced to rely on experience and anecdotal evidence as a guide. Examine each of these silver bullets and see how a well placed silver bullet can save the day.

Case Study: Sub-optimal Optimizer Mode

The call came in from an Oracle client who had just migrated their system into production and was experiencing a serious performance problem. Upon inspection, I found that they were using the default *optimizer_mode=all_rows* even though this was an OLTP database where the end-user wanted rows back as quickly as possible.

Their DBA did not understand the difference between the optimizer goal of *all_rows*, which minimizes computing resources and favors full-tale scans and the *first_rows_n* optimizer which sacrifices fast throughput in favor of fast access via indexes.

After inspecting the SQL, the *optimizer_mode* parameter was set to *optimizer_mode=first_rows_100*. The instance was then restarted with dramatically improved system performance!

Case Study: Obsolete Optimizer Statistics

In this emergency, an Oracle9i shop called complaining about a serious degradation in SQL performance right after implementing a partitioned tablespace.

They said that they thoroughly tested the change in their development and QA instances, and they could not understand why their system was grinding to a halt in production.

Upon inspection, it turned out that they were using *analyze table* and *analyze index* commands to gather their CBO statistics instead of invoking the *dbms_stats* package. Only the *dbms_stats* utility gathers partition-wise statistics.

There was not time to pull a deep-sample collection, so a *dbms_stats* was issued with a 10 percent sample size. Note that it was parallelized with 15 parallel processes to speed up the statistics collection:

```
exec dbms_stats.gather_schema_stats( -
   ownname          => 'SAPR3', -
   options          => 'GATHER AUTO', -
   estimate_percent => 10, -
   method_opt       => 'for all columns size repeat', -
   degree           => 15 -
)
```

This took less than 30 minutes and the improved CBO statistics tripled the performance of the entire database.

Case Study: Troubleshoot Missing Indexes

An Oracle financial application shop in New York called and reported that their performance degraded as more data was entered into the tables. A quick check of *v$sql_plan* using the *plan9i.sql* script looked like this, with load of unnecessary large-table full-table scans:

```
                    Full table scans and counts

OWNER      NAME                     NUM_ROWS  C  K    BLOCKS   NBR_FTS
---------- ----------------------   --------  -  -  --------   -------
APPLSYS    FND_CONC_RELEASE_DISJS     14,293  N      4,293   498,864
APPLSYS    FND_CONC_RELEASE_PERIODS  384,173  N     67,915   134,864
DONALD     PERSON_LOGON_ID        18,263,390  N    634,272    96,212
DONALD     SITE_AMDMNT             2,371,232  N     51,020    50,719
DONALD     CLIN_PTCL_VIS_MAP      23,123,384  N    986,395    11,273
```

This shows a huge number of large-table, full-table scans. A quick look into *v$sql* revealed that the rows returned by each query was small, and a common WHERE clause for many queries looked like this:

```
where customer_status = ':v1' and customer_age > :v2;
```

A quick creation of a concatenated index on *customer_status* and *customer_age* resulted in a 50x performance improvement and reduced disk I/O by over 600 percent.

In another memorable case on an 8.1.6 database, the *access.sql* script revealed suspect large-table, full-table scans:

```
                Full table scans and counts

OWNER        NAME                    NUM_ROWS   C K   BLOCKS   NBR_FTS
----------   --------------------   ---------- - - --------  --------
APPLSYS      FND_CONC_RELEASE_DISJS  1,293,292 N K  65,282   498,864
APPLSYS      FND_CONC_RELEASE_PERIODS 4,373,362 N K 62,282   122,764
APPLSYS      FND_CONC_RELEASE_STATES  974.193 N K   9,204    98,122
APPLSYS      FND_CONC_PP_ACTIONS      715,021 N     6,309    52,036
APPLSYS      FND_CONC_REL_CONJ_MEMBER  95,292 N K   4,409    23,122
```

The DBA had created an index on the *order_date* column and was surprised that their *order_date* index was not being used, primarily because their boss was not willing to pay for him to attend an Oracle new features class. Creating the function-based index on *to_char(order_date,'MON-DD')* resulted in an immediate 5x performance improvement.

Case Study: Troubleshoot *cursor_sharing=force*

I worked on an Oracle database in Toronto where the end users complained about poor performance right after a new manufacturing plant was added to the existing database. A quick look at the STATSPACK top five timed events looked something like this:

```
Top 5 Wait Events

~~~~~~~~~~~~~~~~~~~                            Wait       % Total
Event                               Waits    Time (cs)   Wt Time
-----------------------------------  ----------- -----------  -------
enqueue                               25,901    479,654     46.71
db file scattered read            10,579,442    197,205     29.20
db file sequential read              724,325    196,583      9.14
latch free                         1,150,979     51,084      4.97
log file parallel write              148,932     39,822      3.88
```

My first look was into the SQL section of the STATSPACK report, where I noted that almost all of the SQL used literals in the WHERE clause of all queries.

```
where customer_state = 'Alabama' and customer_type = 'REDNECK';
```

This was a vendor package with dynamically generated SQL, so *cursor_sharing* was the only fast solution. Setting *cursor_sharing=force* greatly reduced the contention on the library cache and reduced CPU consumption. In this emergency, the end users reported a 75 percent improvement in overall performance. Note that in Oracle 11g, *cursor_sharing=similar* has been debugged, and it is now possible to use cursor sharing with bind variable peeking.

Case Study: Use the KEEP Pool

I worked on a database complaint was that performance had been degrading since the last production change. A STATSPACK top five timed events report showed that over 80 percent of system waits related to *db file scattered* reads.

A quick review of *v$sql_plan* using *plan9i.sql* showed quite a few small-table, full-table scans with many of the tables not assigned to the *KEEP* pool, as denoted by the "K" column in the following listing:

```
              Full table scans and counts


OWNER        NAME                    NUM_ROWS C K   BLOCKS   NBR_FTS
----------   --------------------    -------- - -  --------  --------
APPLSYS      FND_CONC_RELEASE_DISJS       39  N        44    98,864
APPLSYS      FND_CONC_RELEASE_PERIODS     39  N K      21    78,232
APPLSYS      FND_CONC_RELEASE_STATES       1  N K       2    66,864
APPLSYS      FND_CONC_PP_ACTIONS       7,021  N     1,262    52,036
APPLSYS      FND_CONC_REL_CONJ_MEMBER      0  N K     322    50,174
APPLSYS      FND_FILE_TEMP                 0  N       544    48,611
APPLSYS      FND_RUN_REQUESTS             99  N        98    48,606
INV          MTL_PARAMETERS                6  N K      16    21,478
APPLSYS      FND_PRODUCT_GROUPS            1  N        23    12,555
APPLSYS      FND_CONCURRENT_QUEUES_TL     13  N K      10    12,257
AP           AP_SYSTEM_PARAMETERS_ALL      1  N K       6     4,521
```

Rows fetched into the *db_cache_size* from full-table scans are not pinged to the Most Recently Used (MRU) end of the data buffer. Running my *buf_blocks.sql* script confirmed that the FTS blocks were falling off the least recently used end of the buffer and had to be frequently reloaded into the buffer.

```
                   Contents of Data Buffers

           Number of Percentage
                                      Blocks in of object
              Object        Object    Buffer   Buffer Buffer  Block
Owner         Name          Type      Cache    Blocks Pool    Size
-----------   -------------- --------- -------- ------ ------- -------
DW01          WORKORDER      TAB PART  94,856        6 DEFAULT  8,192
DW01          HOUSE          TAB PART  50,674        7 DEFAULT 16,384
ODSA          WORKORDER      TABLE     28,481        2 DEFAULT 16,384
DW01          SUBSCRIBER     TAB PART  23,237        3 DEFAULT  4,096
ODS           WORKORDER      TABLE     19,926        1 DEFAULT  8,192
DW01          WRKR_ACCT_IDX  INDEX      8,525        5 DEFAULT 16,384
DW01          SUSC_SVCC_IDX  INDEX      8,453       38 KEEP    32,768
```

In this case, I ran my *buf_keep_pool.sql* script to reassign all tables that experienced small-table, full-table scans into the KEEP pool. The output looks like this and can be fed directly into SQL*Plus:

```
alter TABLE BOM.BOM_OPERATIONAL_ROUTINGS storage (buffer_pool keep);
alter INDEX BOM.CST_ITEM_COSTS_U1 storage (buffer_pool keep);
alter TABLE INV.MTL_ITEM_CATEGORIES storage (buffer_pool keep);
alter TABLE INV.MTL_ONHAND_QUANTITIES storage (buffer_pool keep);
alter TABLE INV.MTL_SUPPLY_DEMAND_TEMP storage (buffer_pool keep);
alter TABLE PO.PO_REQUISITION_LINES_ALL storage (buffer_pool keep);
```

```
alter TABLE AR.RA_CUSTOMER_TRX_ALL storage (buffer_pool keep);
alter TABLE AR.RA_CUSTOMER_TRX_LINES_ALL storage (buffer_pool keep);
```

With more efficient buffer caching, I fixed the problem in less than one hour and overall database performance more than doubled.

Case Study: Troubleshoot Wasted RAM on a 32-bit Server

One of the most common candidates for a silver bullet solution is a database that has a working set of frequently referenced data that cannot fit into the data buffer cache. While this is rarely an issue on large 64-bit Oracle servers, there are still older departmental Intel-based Oracle servers that run Linux and Windows on 32-bit PCs.

I hate waste, especially expensive RAM. One of the most common wastes I see are 32-bit servers with a small SGA, thereby wasting most of the server RAM resources.

This used to be a huge problem for the 32-bit Oracle server in which the total SGA size was difficult to grow beyond 1.7 gigabytes without special tools like PAE, AWE and 4GT. These are tools designed especially to address the memory limitations of Intel-based 32-but servers.

I still routinely see databases on dedicated servers with eight gigabytes RAM with an SGA size less than three gigabytes.

A quick increase in *db_block_buffers* or *db_cache_size* and performance improves dramatically, but the issue that a 32-bit server can only address 2**32 ~= 4 gigabytes still remains. In these databases, Oracle buffers can be moved "above the line" using PAE in Linux or 4GT or AWE in a Windows server.

Case Study: Tune with Materialized Views

Once there was a call from a point-of-sale data warehouse in Germany that was largely read-only with a short batch window every night for batch updates. Once I connected to the database, I immediately noticed that virtually every query in the system was performing a *sum()* or *avg()* function against several important tables.

The *v$sql_plan* view as shown in Figure 5.1 below, via *plan9i.sql*, showed loads of very-large-table, full-table scans, and the system was crippled with db file scattered read waits.

```
Top 5 Timed Events
~~~~~~~~~~~~~~~~~~~~~~~               % Total
Event                       Waits    Time (s)  Ela Time
------------------------- ------------- ------------- --------
db file scattered read      325,519     3,246    82.04
library cache load lock       4,673     1,363     9.26
db file sequential read     534,598     7,146     4.54
CPU time                      1,154       645     3.83
log file parallel write      19,157       837     1.68
```

Figure 5.1: *Example of db File Scattered Read Waits*

Subsequent chapters in this book will show that materialized views are wonderful for pre-joining tables together and pre-summarizing aggregations in read-only data warehouse and decision support system applications.

In this case, it was easy to create three materialized views, and by using Oracle query re-write feature, I was able to reduce physical disk I/O by over 2,000 percent; this improved performance by more than 30x — a real silver bullet! More importantly, all of this was done in only a few hours without altering any SQL and with no changes to the application layer

Case Study: Implement Bitmap Indexes

I was called upon to troubleshoot and fix a State police automobile lookup system that was experiencing slow SQL performance. The system was read-only except for a 30-minute window at night when new vehicle data was loaded. Upon inspection of the SQL, I noted complex combinational WHERE clauses:

```
where color='BLU' and make='CHEVY' and year=1997 and doors=2;
```

The distinct values for each of these columns were less than 200, and concatenated indexes were employed.

Because of this low cardinality and the use of combinations of many low cardinality columns in the SQL, I replaced the b-tree indexes with bitmap indexes which were rebuilt each night after the data loads. This new bitmap index resulted in a stunning performance improvement for the entire system, taking queries from three seconds down to under one-tenth of a second.

Case Study: Adding Freelists

A client called with a complaint that their company order processing center was unable keep up with adding new orders into Oracle. The client had just expanded its telephone order processing department and had doubled the order processing staff to meet a surge in market interest.

The VP was frantic, saying that 400 order-entry clerks were getting 30-second response time and they were forced to manually write down order information. They needed relief, and they need it right away!

Upon checking *v$session,* I found 450 connected users, and a quick review of *v$sql* revealed that at virtually all the DML were inserts into a *customer_order* table. The top timed event was *buffer busy wait* and it was clear that there were enqueues on the segment header blocks for the table and its indexes.

The supposedly proper fix for this issue is to create a new tablespace for the table and index using Automatic Segment Space Management (ASSM), also known as bitmap freelists and then reorganize the table online with the *dbms_redefinition* utility and *alter index cust_pk rebuild* the index into the new tablespace.

However, it could take several hours to build and execute the jobs and the VP said that they were losing over $500 per minute. A faster solution was needed!

I was able to immediately relieve the segment header contention with these commands:

```
alter table customer_order freelists 5;

alter index cust_pk freelists 5;
```

> **Note:** I did not know the length of the enqueues on the segment header, so I added the additional freelists, one at a time, until the buffer busy waits disappeared.

Adding the additional freelists did the trick and the segment header contention disappeared. However, I knew that this was only a stop-gap fix and as soon as they ran their weekly purge (a single process), that only one of the five freelists would get the released blocks, causing the table to extend unnecessarily.

Case Study: Troubleshoot Windows Issues

Windows Oracle databases are always the most fun to tune because they are often implemented by someone with a very limited knowledge of Oracle. The following are my favorite Windows Oracle silver bullets.

- **Norton Anti-Virus:** I got a call from a new client in England who said that their database had slowed to the point where sub-second queries were taking 15 minutes. A review of a STATSPACK report showed giant waits of up to 10 seconds on read I/O. A review of the external Windows environment revealed that a well-intentioned support person was told to install Norton Antivirus on all Windows servers. Upon every block read, Norton was conducting a virus check!

- **A really cool screen saver:** Another case involved a Windows Oracle system that was experiencing sporadic CPU shortages, periods when over half of the CPU was being consumed by some external process. Because I was dialed in, I could not see the obvious. An on-site person informed me that the screen saver was called *3D Flowerbox*. This was a CPU intensive screen saver that performed thousands of calculations per second to generate the cool display.

Case Study Conclusion

For adrenaline junkies, being an emergency Oracle support DBA is great fun. As illustrated in this section, this kind of support often requires a unique set of techniques:

- **Fix the symptom first:** The root cause can be addressed later.

- **Time is of the essence:** When a quick fix must be provided, instance-wide adjustments are often the best hope.

- **Be creative:** Traditional, i.e. time consuming, tuning methods do not apply in an emergency.

There are about a dozen silver bullet parameters which have a profound impact on performance, both good and bad. Adjusting these powerful throttles such as *optimizer_index_cost_adj* and *_optimizer_cost_model* should only be done by experts and ONLY after the CBO statistics have been optimized, especially intelligent histogram placement.

The following section will provide a closer look at Oracle troubleshooting.

Accurately Measuring Oracle Performance

Every Oracle professional would like to be thought of as a performance tuning expert but it is truly all about real-world experience. There are no shortcuts and no training that will make it happen instantly.

Slow systems are the bane of existence for any critical business, and DBAs and developers alike constantly strive to improve their diagnostic skills. The highest paid Oracle consultants are the ones who can take a lethargic system and quickly turn it into one that runs as fast as greased lightning.

With the Internet, there is a wealth of information about Oracle troubleshooting and some of it is good, while most of it is absolute garbage. Every self-anointed Oracle expert is touting their own methodology for Oracle troubleshooting, and some are absolute zealots in proclaiming their approach as the "best" method. In the real world, an Oracle troubleshooting expert uses a variety of tools and techniques and there is no single best way to diagnose an acute performance problem.

Oracle analysts use one of two methods for examining the performance levels of a database in crisis. Note that this is not about the holistic, proactive tuning approaches which are used for long-term tuning. This is about the reactive methods to see what the problem may be in real-time.

- **Wait event analysis:** Advocates of the Oracle wait interface (OWI and ASH) sample the instance to see where Oracle is spending the most time.

- **Trace dump analysis:** Some Oracle experts say that the only way to see what is going on is to collect a detailed trace dump (event 10046) and analyze where Oracle is spending its time.

- **Ratio-based analysis:** Some experts use short-term ratios to pinpoint areas of poor performance.

- **Bottleneck analysis:** This seems to be more in vogue today, with many experts on database performance deriding those who still dare to practice any ratio-based analysis. Instead of using ratios, this methodology focuses on finding the things that cause the database to wait, and removing them where possible.

It is best to start by separating the fact from the fiction. Whether it is about the buffer cache hit ratio or the data buffer cache advisory (see *v$db_cache_advice*), it is good to remember that they are just different formulas for twiddling the same metrics, namely the elapsed-time deltas for logical I/O (consistent gets) and physical I/O (disk reads). Hence, any computations are fundamentally flawed:

- **One point:** A single delta value does not provide enough information for any meaningful estimates.

- **Too long:** Using the standard one-hour snapshots loses much detail, making most extrapolations meaningless. Of course, it is a different story when multiple snapshots are being taken, especially at high-granularity, e.g. 10 minutes or less.

If the problem is decomposed, elapsed logical I/O vs. physical reads is the main concern. The formulas are incidental.

Most experts agree that the *buffer cache hit ratio* (BCHR) is of limited value, and it is only one of hundreds of metrics that indicate database performance. In general, all ratios are limited because they only measure a probability; in the instance case, the overall probability that a data block will be found in the data buffer cache upon re-read, i.e. the BCHR has no bearing on blocks that are brand new to the data cache.

Another issue with the BCHR is its high variability. For example, while an overall hourly BCHR may be 96%, the value swings wildly. When examined at a finer level of granularity, the BCHR could be 20% one minute and 95% the next as shown in Figure 5.2. It is all dependent on the current workload.

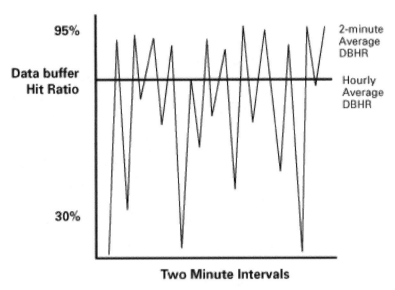

Figure 5.2: *High Variability of BCHR*

So, can it be concluded that the ratios are totally useless? This will be examined next.

Using the BCHR for Performance Tuning

The *buffer cache hit ratio* is no longer touted as a standalone measure of system performance, but it is not completely useless either. From the Oracle documentation on memory usage, it can be seen that Oracle continues to recommend using the BCHR in conjunction with other metrics, namely the predictive ratios displayed in the 10g buffer cache advisory:

> *"The buffer cache hit ratio can be used to verify the physical I/O as predicted by v$db_cache_advice."*

In a well-tuned production database, adding RAM to the data buffers can make a difference in overall throughput via a reduction in physical disk reads, one of the most time-consuming operations in any Oracle database.

The Oracle AWR report contains a buffer advisory utility that shows predictions of the marginal changes to physical disk reads with changes to the buffer size:

```
Buffer Pool Advisory

-> Only rows with estimated physical reads >0 are displayed
```

P	Size for Estimate (M)	Size Factr	Buffers for Estimate	Est Physical Read Factor	Estimated Physical Reads
D	4	.1	501	2.10	1,110,930
D	8	.2	1,002	1.84	970,631
D	12	.2	1,503	1.75	924,221
D	16	.3	2,004	1.62	857,294
D	20	.4	2,505	1.61	850,849
D	24	.5	3,006	1.59	837,223
D	28	.5	3,507	1.58	831,558
D	32	.6	4,008	1.57	829,083
D	36	.7	4,509	1.56	825,336
D	40	.8	5,010	1.56	823,195
D	44	.8	5,511	1.06	557,204
D	48	.9	6,012	1.01	534,992
D	52	1.0	6,513	1.00	527,967
D	56	1.1	7,014	0.78	411,218
D	60	1.2	7,515	0.35	186,842
D	64	1.2	8,016	0.28	148,305
D	68	1.3	8,517	0.26	134,969
D	72	1.4	9,018	0.23	123,283
D	76	1.5	9,519	0.23	121,878
D	80	1.5	10,020	0.23	120,317

For a well-tuned database, the goal of setting the data buffer size is to cache the working set of frequently referenced data blocks, the point at which there is a marginal decline in the amount of RAM needed to reduce disk reads as shown in Figure 5.3.

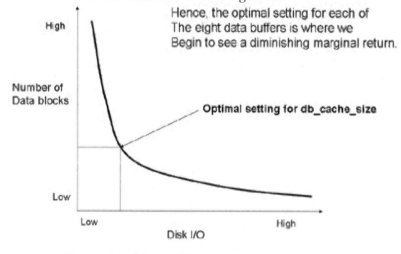

Figure 5.3: *Diminishing Marginal Returns and Buffer Utilization*

Oracle Enterprise Manager also displays the data buffer advisor, and it has an interactive feature whereby the cache size can be changed in real-time as shown in Figure 5.4.

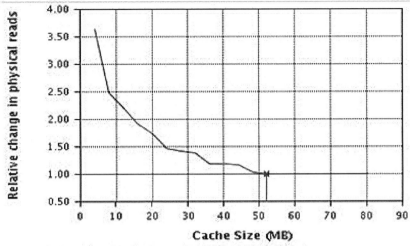

Cache Size (MB) |52

☑ **TIP** You can click on the curve in the graph to set new value.

Figure 5.4: *Data Buffer Advisor in OEM*

However, there are some serious limitations to the Oracle data buffer cache advisor:

- **Only one delta:** Using only two observations for logical reads and physical I/O are not enough data for a meaningful prediction. The current workload assumption has a wide variance, and the numbers for a one-minute report will be quite different from a one hour report.

- **Only two metrics:** All of the advice from the data buffer cache advisory is limited to logical I/O and physical I/O at the system-wide level.

- **Assumption of optimization:** The AWR data buffer cache advisor, and possibly the related *v$db_cache_advice* utility, only has two data points to consider and it assumes that the existing data buffer size is optimal, the point at which the working set of frequently-used data blocks are cached and additions to the data buffer result in marginally declining reductions in physical reads.

Hence, on the margin, the data buffer cache advisory is inaccurate for databases with an undersized *db_cache_size* and *db_keep_cache_size* and such. With the data buffer set to a very small size, a small increase to the size of the RAM data buffers results in a large reduction in Disk I/O as illustrated in Figure 5.5.

.

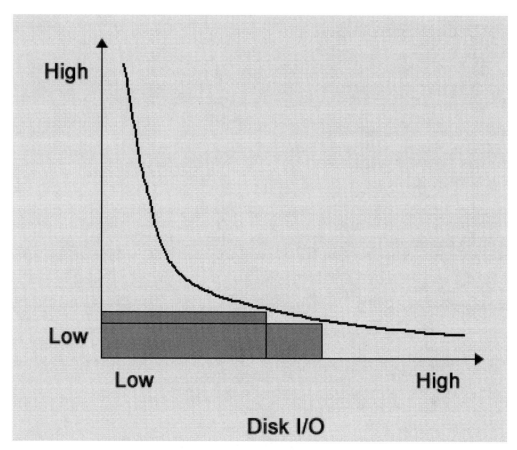

Figure 5.5: *The Buffer Advisory in Regards to Small Cache*

However, the high reduction in Disk I/O does not continue ad infinitum. As the RAM size approaches the database size, the marginal reduction in Disk I/O is smaller because all databases have infrequently accessed data, as shown in Figure 5.6.

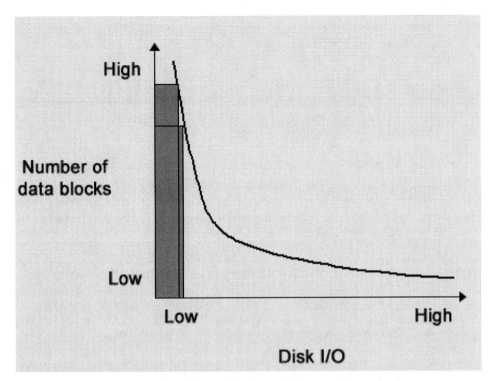

Figure 5.6: *Data Buffer Cache Advisory Not Knowing Cache is Oversized*

In sum, the usefulness of a data buffer cache advisory is undisputed, but the true way to a successful predictive model is to use the proactive tuning scripts. These provide valid time-series analyses since the single delta values in the advisory are not sufficient. Using STATSPACK data for consistent gets and physical reads, statistically significant trends can be established.

When done properly, ratio-based analysis definitely has a place in the performance tuning arsenal. Performance ratios are very good roll-up mechanisms for busy DBAs, making analysis possible at a glance. Many DBAs have large database farms to contend with and cannot spend time checking detailed wait-based analysis outputs for each and every database they oversee.

For example, take a look at one of the common queries used to report the database's buffer cache hit ratio:

```
select
   100 -
   100 *
   (round((sum (decode (name, 'physical reads', value, 0)) -
   sum (decode (name, 'physical reads direct', value, 0))) /
   (sum (decode (name, 'db block gets', value, 1)) +
   sum (decode (name, 'consistent gets', value, 0))),3))
from
   sys.v_$sysstat
where
```

```
name in ('db block gets',  'consistent gets',
         'physical reads', 'physical reads direct')
```

If a database has been up for many weeks, the numbers representing the I/O statistics above will likely be enormous. The counts of block gets and consistent gets will be very large and, in most systems, exceed the count of physical reads by a wide margin. Such a situation can skew the buffer cache hit ratio if it is computed solely with cumulative value counts in *v$sysstat*.

If an inefficient SQL query is issued that causes many physical reads, adding them to the *v$sysstat* counters will probably not cause a meaningful dip in the overall buffer cache hit ratio as long as cumulative statistics are used. However, if delta statistics are used, taking, for a specified sampling period, the before and after counts of each statistic that make up the ratio, then the portrayal of the buffer cache hit ratio will be more current and accurate.

There are some ratios that do not rely on *v$sysstat*, and therefore, can be derived from current/cumulative values. One example of this is the blocking lock ratio, which computes the percentage of user sessions that are currently blocked on a system. Because locks in a database are repeatedly obtained and released, the ratio can be computed with cumulative numbers from several performance views without the need for taking a before-and-after statistical snapshot.

In addition to using delta statistics to compute many of the key metrics in ratio-based performance analysis, the DBA must also be committed to examining all the database categories that contribute to its overall health and well-being. This can mean employing ratios and analytic percentages that have historically been neglected by DBAs.

For instance, many DBAs do not use ratios when examining their object structures in a database because they have not seen how such a technique can be applied to objects. However, ratio-based analysis can definitely be utilized to determine if objects like tables and indexes are disorganized. For example, finding the global percentage of tables that contain chained rows may help the DBA realize that he is not properly defining the table storage parameters in a dynamic database.

A final thing to remember about using ratio-based analysis is that while there are several rules of thumb that can be used as starting points in the evaluation of database performance, each database has an individual personality. Some hard and fast rules simply will not apply to every database.

The Danger of Relying on Blanket Ratios

The danger in using blanket ratio standards is that they can lead a DBA to take action haphazardly, often contributing nothing to the situation and sometimes even degrading performance! For example, one rule of thumb says that the library cache hit ratio should never fall below 95%, and if it does, the standard remedy is to increase the amount of memory assigned to the shared pool.

However, it is never that simple, and this kind of lazy approach to performance tuning can actually lead to more problems. Oftentimes, a database that is very ad-hoc in nature will experience many queries that are almost always unique with respect to their WHERE clause predicates and the literals used as qualifying filters.

So, does ratio-based analysis still sound like old hat or can it be thought of as adding value to the performance analysis arsenal? Now that the benefits and shortcomings of ratio-based analysis are understood, continue into the next section and discover the ins-and-outs of Oracle bottleneck analysis.

Oracle Bottleneck Analysis

When an Oracle database is up and running, every connected process is either busy doing work or waiting to perform work. A process that is waiting may be idle, or it can be an indicator that a database bottleneck exists. How can you tell? This is where bottleneck analysis comes into play. This form of performance analysis is used to determine if perceived bottlenecks in a database are contributing to a performance problem.

Bottleneck analysis is a valid method of measuring performance because it helps track where the database has been spending its time. If latch contention or heavy table-scan activity has been dragging a database's performance down, bottleneck analysis should be used to confirm the actual root cause.

Once one or more wait events or other bottlenecks have been pinpointed as possible performance vampires, it is then possible to drill down and often discover a fair amount of detail about the sessions and objects that are causing the problem.

Prerequisites for Bottleneck Analysis

What is the proper way to practice bottleneck or wait-based analysis? First, it is imperative that the *timed_statistics* initialization parameter be set to *true*, if the Oracle wait events are to be examined. By default, this parameter is set to *false*, which disallows the collection of wait times for each wait event defined in the Oracle engine.

To really understand the impact of wait events on database performance, the DBA needs to not only discover what the database is or has been waiting on but the durations of the waits. Having both allows a complete picture to be formed regarding the magnitude of wait-initiated performance degradations.

Almost all Oracle experts now agree that collecting time statistics adds little, if anything, to database overhead, so setting *timed_statistics* to *true* should not be a worry. The parameter can be dynamically altered at both the system and session levels, so the database does not have to be shut down and then restarted for the change to take effect. A simple *alter system set timed_statistics= true* should do the trick.

The next prerequisite to using bottleneck analysis is that certain wait events should be filtered out of any metrics used to diagnose performance bottlenecks. For example, Oracle will record a wait statistic that represents how long a particular user sits at their SQL*Plus prompt between each issued database request.

Such a statistic provides no real value to a DBA who is trying to figure out where a database bottleneck exists. Any SQL scripts that are used to collect database wait statistics should exclude such events. A listing of these Oracle events, normally dubbed idle events, to eliminate includes:

- lock element cleanup

- pmon timer

- rdbms ipc message

- smon timer

- SQL*Net message from client

- SQL*Net break/reset to client

- SQL*Net message to client

- SQL*Net more data to client

- dispatcher timer

- Null event

- parallel query dequeue wait

- parallel query idle wait - slaves

- pipe get

- PL/SQL lock timer

- slave wait

- virtual circuit status

When collecting wait statistics, there are several levels of detail that can be penetrated. The first level is the system view, which provides a global, cumulative snapshot of all the waits that have occurred on a system.

Viewing these numbers can help determine which wait events have caused the most commotion in a database thus far. A query that can be used to collect these metrics is the *syswaits.sql* script:

💾 **syswaits.sql**

```
select
       event,
       total_waits,
       round(100 * (total_waits / sum_waits),2) pct_tot_waits,
       time_wait_sec,
       round(100 * (time_wait_sec / sum_secs),2) pct_secs_waits,
       total_timeouts,
       avg_wait_sec
from
(select
       event,
       total_waits,
       round((time_waited / 100),2) time_wait_sec,
       total_timeouts,
       round((average_wait / 100),2) avg_wait_sec
from
       sys.v_$system_event
where
       event not in
       ('lock element cleanup',
        'pmon timer',
        'rdbms ipc message',
```

```
            'smon timer',
            'SQL*Net message from client',
            'SQL*Net break/reset to client',
            'SQL*Net message to client',
            'SQL*Net more data to client',
            'dispatcher timer',
            'Null event',
            'parallel query dequeue wait',
            'parallel query idle wait - Slaves',
            'pipe get',
            'PL/SQL lock timer',
            'slave wait',
            'virtual circuit status',
            'WMON goes to sleep') and
            event not like 'DFS%' and
            event not like 'KXFX%'),
(select
            sum(total_waits) sum_waits,
            sum(round((time_waited / 100),2)) sum_secs
 from
            sys.v_$system_event
 where
            event not in
            ('lock element cleanup',
            'pmon timer',
            'rdbms ipc message',
            'smon timer',
            'SQL*Net message from client',
            'SQL*Net break/reset to client',
            'SQL*Net message to client',
            'SQL*Net more data to client',
            'dispatcher timer',
            'Null event',
            'parallel query dequeue wait',
            'parallel query idle wait - Slaves',
            'pipe get',
            'PL/SQL lock timer',
            'slave wait',
            'virtual circuit status',
            'WMON goes to sleep') and
            event not like 'DFS%' and
            event not like 'KXFX%')
order by
    2 desc;
```

	EVENT	TOTAL_WAITS	PCT_TOT_WAITS	TIME_WAIT_SEC	PCT_TIME_WAITS	TOTAL_TIMEOUTS	AVG_WAIT_SEC
1	control file parallel write	77154	64.69	67.18	37.74	0	0
2	direct path write	18271	15.32	28.54	16.03	0	0
3	control file sequential read	10531	8.83	24.74	13.9	0	0
4	direct path read	7758	6.5	34.86	19.58	0	0
5	db file sequential read	2627	2.2	5.33	2.99	0	0
6	refresh controlfile command	1401	1.17	10.94	6.15	0	.01
7	log file parallel write	477	.4	.45	.25	1	0
8	log file sync	276	.23	1.4	.79	0	.01
9	db file parallel write	266	.22	1.94	1.09	0	.01
10	file open	156	.13	.99	.56	0	.01
11	db file scattered read	125	.1	.11	.06	0	0
12	latch free	97	.08	1.11	.62	89	.01
13	file identify	47	.04	.18	.1	0	0
14	buffer busy waits	22	.02	.02	.01	0	0
15	library cache pin	21	.02	0	0	0	0
16	LGWR wait for redo copy	9	.01	.03	.02	3	0
17	rdbms ipc reply	7	.01	0	0	0	0
18	log file sequential read	5	0	0	0	0	0
19	log file single write	5	0	0	0	0	0
20	single-task message	5	0	.18	.1	0	.04
21	SQL*Net more data from client	4	0	0	0	0	0
22	reliable message	1	0	0	0	0	0
23	library cache load lock	1	0	0	0	0	0
24	instance state change	1	0	0	0	0	0

Figure 5.7: *Sample Output Showing System Waits*

What is a db file sequential read anyway? Database file sequential reads normally indicate index lookup operations or ROWID fetches from a table. If the requested Oracle blocks are not already in memory, the initiating process must wait for them to be read in. Such activity seems to be the main source of contention in the above listing.

After looking at system level wait activity, drill down further to discover which current connections may be responsible for any reported waits that are being observed at the system level. One query that can be used to collect such data is the *sesswaits.sql* script:

sesswaits.sql

```
select
      b.sid,
      decode(b.username,NULL,c.name,b.username) process_name,
      event,
      a.a.total_waits,
      round((a.time_waited / 100),2)
      time_wait_sec,a.total_timeouts,
      round((average_wait / 100),2)
      average_wait_sec,
      round((a.max_wait / 100),2) max_wait_sec
  from
      sys.v_$session_event a,
      sys.v_$session b,
      sys.v_$bgprocess c
where
      a.event not in
        ('lock element cleanup',
        'pmon timer',
        'rdbms ipc message',
        'smon timer',
        'SQL*Net message from client',
        'SQL*Net break/reset to client',
        'SQL*Net message to client',
        'SQL*Net more data to client',
```

```
          'dispatcher timer',
          'Null event',
          'parallel query dequeue wait',
          'parallel query idle wait - Slaves',
          'pipe get',
          'PL/SQL lock timer',
          'slave wait',
          'virtual circuit status',
          'WMON goes to sleep'
          )
   and a.event not like 'DFS%'
   and a.event not like 'KXFX%'
   and a.sid = b.sid
   and b.paddr = c.paddr (+)
order by
   4 desc;
```

	SID	PROCESS_NAME	EVENT	TOTAL_WAITS	TIME_WAIT_SEC	TOTAL_TIMEOUTS	AVERAGE_WAIT_SEC	MAX_WAIT_SEC
1	4	CKPT	control file parallel write	729	8.77	0	.01	.86
2	11	SYS	control file sequential read	262	2.54	0	.01	.14
3	4	CKPT	control file sequential read	228	10.31	0	.05	.23
4	5	SMON	db file scattered read	124	13.08	0	.11	.22
5	9	SCHED	db file sequential read	111	8.84	0	.08	.19
6	11	SYS	db file sequential read	73	3.69	0	.05	.15
7	3	LGWR	log file parallel write	69	1.92	64	.03	.13
8	5	SMON	db file sequential read	68	6.13	0	.09	.19
9	2	DBW0	control file sequential read	35	1.74	0	.05	.25
10	3	LGWR	control file sequential read	30	1.91	0	.06	.16
11	2	DBW0	direct path read	18	.22	0	.01	.15
12	2	DBW0	db file parallel write	16	.22	16	.01	.08
13	3	LGWR	control file parallel write	14	1.43	0	.1	.26
14	3	LGWR	direct path read	9	0	0	0	0
15	8	SYS	db file sequential read	8	.25	0	.03	.08
16	3	LGWR	direct path write	8	.17	0	.02	.17
17	3	LGWR	log file single write	7	.33	0	.05	.07
18	3	LGWR	log file sequential read	6	.22	0	.04	.07
19	9	SCHED	log file sync	3	.08	0	.03	.03
20	11	SYS	library cache pin	3	.12	0	.04	.12
21	2	DBW0	async disk IO	2	.22	0	.11	.15
22	3	LGWR	async disk IO	2	.17	0	.09	.17
23	11	SYS	buffer busy waits	1	.01	0	.01	.01
24	6	RECO	db file sequential read	1	.12	0	.12	.12

Figure 5.8: *Sample Historical Wait Output at the Session Level*

Such a query, for example, could indicate the Oracle processes responsible for most of the *db file sequential waits* that were reported in the global system overview query. Like the system level query, the above query shows cumulative wait statistics for each session since it has been connected. Note that all data for that session is lost once it disconnects from the database.

A final level of detail can be obtained by checking for any active Oracle processes that are currently waiting. One query that can be used to uncover such data is the *csesswaits.sql* script:

csesswaits.sql

```
select
        a.sid,
        decode(b.username,null,c.name,b.username) process_name,
        a.event,
        a.seconds_in_wait,
        a.wait_time,
        a.state,
        a.p1text,
```

```
        a.p1,
        a.p1raw,
        a.p2text,
        a.p2,
        a.p2raw,
        a.p3text,
        a.p3,
        a.p3raw
  from
        sys.v_$session_wait a,
        sys.v_$session b,
        sys.v_$bgprocess c
  where
        a.event not in
            ('lock element cleanup',
             'pmon timer',
             'rdbms ipc message',
             'smon timer',
             'SQL*Net message from client',
             'SQL*Net break/reset to client',
             'SQL*Net message to client',
             'SQL*Net more data to client',
             'dispatcher timer',
             'Null event',
             'parallel query dequeue wait',
             'parallel query idle wait - Slaves',
             'pipe get',
             'PL/SQL lock timer',
             'slave wait',
             'virtual circuit status',
             'WMON goes to sleep'
             )
    and a.event not like 'DFS%'
    and a.event not like 'KXFX%'
    and a.sid = b.sid
    and b.paddr = c.paddr (+)
  order by
        4 desc;
```

SID	PROCESS_NAME	EVENT	SECONDS_IN_WAIT	WAIT_TIME	STATE	P1TEXT	P1	P1RAW	P2TEXT	P2	P2RAW	P3TEXT	P3	P3RAW
1	10 ERADMIN	enqueue	3	0	WAITING	name|mode	1415053316	54580006	id1	524312	00080018	id2	31373	00007A8D

Figure 5.9: *Output Showing a Session Currently Waiting on a Resource*

If a current process is noticed with a *db file sequential read wait*, data contained in the parameter columns of the above query, i.e. *p1text, p1* and such, can be used to locate the exact file and block of the object being used by Oracle to satisfy the end user's request.

If enqueue waits are found present when the output of current session waits is examined, the *objwait.sql* script can be used to find which object and datafile are causing the holdup:

💾 **objwaits.sql**

```
select
        sid,
        username,
        machine,
        program,
        b.owner,
```

```
        b.object_type,
        b.object_name,
        c.file_name
from    sys.v_$session a,
        sys.dba_objects b,
        sys.dba_data_files c
where   a.row_wait_obj# > 0 and
        a.row_wait_obj# = b.object_id and
        a.row_wait_file# = c.file_id
order by sid;
```

	SID	USERNAME	MACHINE	PROGRAM	OWNER	OBJECT_TYPE	OBJECT_NAME	FILE_NAME
1	10	ERADMIN	MSHOME\ROBINS	sqlplusw.exe	ERADMIN	TABLE	ADMISSION_TEST	C:\ORACLE\ORA90\RMSD\USERS01.DBF

Figure 5.10: *Uncovering the Objects and Datafiles / Enqueue Wait*

When using bottleneck analysis, the DBA cannot rely only on the information contained in the wait event views that Oracle provides. For example, an object may attempt to extend into another extent of space in a tablespace, and yet be denied if no such free space exists.

Such a failure will not be reflected in any wait event but still represents a very real bottleneck to the database. In the same way that it is impossible to depend on only a few ratios to properly carry out ratio-based performance analysis, several statistical metrics must be included in the overall bottleneck analysis framework to obtain an accurate performance risk assessment.

For example, in the aforementioned object extension failure, it would be advisable to include a query in the bottleneck analysis framework that returns a count of any object that has reached, or better yet, approaches its maximum extent limit or is housed in a tablespace with insufficient free space to accommodate its next extent. Now that method for bottleneck and ration analysis have been reviewed, the next step is to examine an effective approach that combines both techniques.

Combining Bottleneck and Ratio Analysis

To provide the best possible coverage for a database, it is best to utilize both ratio-based and bottleneck analysis in an effective performance-monitoring toolkit. While there are many ways to accomplish this, one approach is to categorize each area of performance interest, and then list out the metrics that should be used for both ratio-based and bottleneck analysis.

Realize that some ratio-based metrics can be represented as bottleneck metrics and vice versa; for example, while a ratio could be used to indicate how full an Oracle archive log destination has become, such a measure could also be used as a bottleneck metric that represents an approaching space-related blockage, and some metrics can overlap categories.

To summarize the strength and weakness of each approach:

Performance Area: Memory

Ratio-Based Metrics	Bottleneck-Based Metrics
Buffer Cache Hit Ratio	Buffer Busy

Data Dictionary Cache Hit Ratio	Enqueue Waits
Free Shared Pool Percent	Free Buffer Waits
Library Cache Hit Ratio	Latch Free Waits
Memory/Disk Sort Ratio	Library Cache Pin Waits
Parse/Execute Ratio	Library Cache Load Lock Waits
Leading Memory Session Percentage	Log Buffer Space Waits
	Library Object Reloads Count
	Redo Log Space Waits
	Redo Log Space Wait Time

Table 5.1: *Ratio-Based Metrics to Bottleneck-Based Metrics*

Needless to say, there is a need to be able to quickly pinpoint resource-intensive SQL code that is causing undo strain on the database. Understanding current and historical SQL execution patterns will enable the DBA to have the second set of data necessary to properly perform workload analysis.

Chapter 17 of this book covers techniques and provides scripts to help interrogate Oracle and find SQL calls that might require optimization. It will become evident that optimizing the SQL code will produce some of the best performance enhancements, but always remember that global tuning must happen first.

Keep in mind that while locating SQL calls that are racking up expensive statistics is not hard since this is an integral part of all STATSPACK and AWR reports, the actual process of optimizing SQL can be quite complicated. While there are third-party software products that can help in rewriting SQL queries, it is difficult to find one that will tell that a particular SQL statement should not be executed.

Only by understanding a particular application's needs can this be accomplished. Removing SQL "waste" in a database can produce dramatic results as, believe it or not, sometimes the best SQL query is the one that is not executed.

Using a singular diagnostic approach to database performance analysis may, under the right conditions, result in pinpointing a database slowdown, but a more holistic approach is to utilize metrics and collection methods from both ratio-based and bottleneck analysis as well as techniques found in workload analysis. As with investing in the stock market, a person might not be right every time, but they can limit most losses by staying true to a combined and proven methodology.

The Number One Oracle Performance Myth

Whether it is in the realm of database technology or any other discipline, some maxims are whispered around the campfire so much that they are taken for gospel on face value and never questioned, especially when supposed experts mouth the words. Such is the case with a database performance myth that has been around for as long as most can remember. It goes something like this:

> *"Eighty percent of a database's overall performance is derived from the code that is written against it."*

This is a complete untruth, or at the very least, an overestimation of the impact that properly written SQL code has against a running physical database. Good coding practices definitely count, often heavily, toward the success of any database application, but to state affirmatively that they make a contribution of over two-thirds is a stretch.

The reason this proverb cannot pass the reality test is that it is stated independently of what good or bad code can do in the face of poor physical design. The real-world case that opened this chapter is a shining example of how wrong this adage is.

The physical design constrains all code, good or bad, and has the capability to turn even the best written SQL into molasses. After all, how can a SQL developer obtain unique key index access unless the physical index has been created and is in place?

How can a database coder scan only the parts of a table that they need unless that table has been partitioned to accommodate such a request? Only when a solid physical design is put in place - a design that fits the application like a glove - can SQL code really take off and make for some impressive response times. However, good design comes first.

What about the link between availability and design? According to Oracle Corporation's own studies of client downtime, the largest percentage, up to 36%, are design-related issues. If no one has been very serious about the database design until now, consider this a wake-up call.

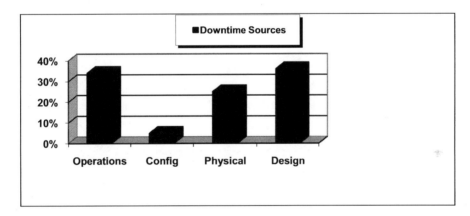

Figure 5.11: *Downtime Statistics Provide by Oracle Corporation*

Disk I/O is the single most expensive operation on any Oracle database, so at the following section will delve more into how to troubleshoot Oracle disk I/O problems.

Troubleshooting Oracle Disk Performance

If the reason that most DBAs' pagers go off at night could be tracked, it would be a fair bet to say that a leading cause would be storage-related problems. However, the good news is that this does not have to be the case if proactive techniques are used.

Automatic Growth

Way back in version 7, Oracle introduced the concept of auto-extendable datafiles. This simple addition to Oracle has silenced many emergency pagers. It basically allows Oracle to automatically grow a datafile to meet the need of incoming or changed data if not enough free space currently exists in the tablespace. To enable this feature, either create a tablespace with *autoextend* enabled or alter a tablespace after creation to turn the feature on. An example of creating a tablespace with *autoextend* initially enabled would be:

```
create tablespace
   users
datafile
   'd:\oracle\ora92\o92\users01.dbf' size 25600k
autoextend on next 1280k maxsize unlimited
extent management local autoallocate
logging
online;
```

Some DBAs have an aversion to using *autoextend* and instead prefer to preallocate space to a tablespace. If proper capacity planning measures are used, this approach can work just fine. However, if the database is very dynamic and unpredictable, then *autoextend* should be enabled for most tablespaces, especially temporary tablespaces that can be the object of large sort operations.

Some DBAs may not know whether *autoextend* is enabled for their tablespaces and datafiles. Furthermore, they may not know how much total space their storage structures are currently taking up. Depending on the Oracle version being used, one of the two following scripts can give these exact facts.

🖫 spacesum.sql

```
select
      tablespace_name,
      autoextend,
      round ((total_space / 1024 / 1024), 2) as
      total_space,
      round ((total_free_space /
      1024 / 1024), 2) as total_free,
      round (((total_space - total_free_space) /
      1024 / 1024), 2) as used_space,
      to_char (
        nvl (
          round (
            (100 *
                sum_free_blocks /
                sum_alloc_blocks),2),0)) || '%'
          as pct_free
 from (select
            tablespace_name,
            max (autoextensible) autoextend,
            sum (blocks) sum_alloc_blocks,
            sum (bytes) as total_space
      from
            dba_data_files
      group by tablespace_name),
```

```
       (select
               b.tablespace_name fs_ts_name,
               nvl (sum (bytes), 0) as total_free_space,
               sum (blocks) as sum_free_blocks
           from
               dba_free_space a, dba_tablespaces b
         where
               a.tablespace_name (+) = b.tablespace_name
         group by b.tablespace_name,  status)
 where
       tablespace_name = fs_ts_name
union all
select
       d.tablespace_name, autoextend,
       round ((a.bytes / 1024 / 1024), 2),
       round ((a.bytes / 1024 / 1024) -
       (nvl (t.bytes, 0) / 1024 / 1024), 2),
       round (nvl (t.bytes, 0) / 1024 / 1024, 2),
       to_char (100 - (nvl (t.bytes /
       a.bytes * 100, 0)), '990.00')
  from
       sys.dba_tablespaces d,
       (select
               tablespace_name,
               max (autoextensible) autoextend,
               sum (bytes) bytes
           from
               dba_temp_files
         group by tablespace_name) a,
       (select
               tablespace_name, sum (bytes_cached) bytes
           from
               sys.v_$temp_extent_pool
         group by tablespace_name) t
 where
       d.tablespace_name = a.tablespace_name (+)
   and d.tablespace_name = t.tablespace_name (+)
   and d.extent_management like 'LOCAL'
   and d.contents like 'TEMPORARY'
order by 1;
```

	TABLESPACE_NAME	AUTOEXTEND	TOTAL_SPACE	TOTAL_FREE	USED_SPACE	PCT_FREE
1	AUTOSEG	NO	5	4.94	.06	98.75%
2	DRSYS	YES	20	15.19	4.81	75.94%
3	INDX	YES	25	24.88	.13	99.5%
4	OEM_REPOSITORY	YES	35.01	3	32.01	8.57%
5	SYSTEM	YES	300	3.63	296.38	1.21%
6	TEMP	YES	556	1	555	0.18
7	TOOLS	YES	10	7.75	2.25	77.5%
8	UNDOTBS1	YES	210	208.69	1.31	99.38%
9	USERS	YES	25	15.13	9.88	60.5%
10	XDB	YES	38.13	.19	37.94	.49%

Figure 5.12: *Output Displaying Summary Space Information and Autoextend Properties for Tablespaces*

While the queries above will let the DBA know if a tablespace has *autoextend* enabled, it will not tell which datafile if the tablespace has multiple datafiles. For that you will need the *datafileae.sql* script, which will work for all Oracle versions:

💾 **datafileae.sql**

```
select
       b.file_name,
       b.tablespace_name,
       decode(c.inc,null,'no','yes') autoextend
  from
       sys.dba_data_files b,
       sys.filext$ c
 where
       c.file# (+)= b.file_id
 order by
       2, 1;
```

	FILE_NAME	TABLESPACE_NAME	AUTOEXTEND
1	D:\ORACLE\ORA92\O92\AUTOSEG.ORA	AUTOSEG	NO
2	D:\ORACLE\ORA92\O92\DRSYS01.DBF	DRSYS	YES
3	D:\ORACLE\ORA92\O92\INDX01.DBF	INDX	YES
4	D:\ORACLE\ORA92\O92\OEM_REPOSITORY.DBF	OEM_REPOSITORY	YES
5	D:\ORACLE\ORA92\O92\SYSTEM01.DBF	SYSTEM	YES
6	D:\ORACLE\ORA92\O92\TOOLS01.DBF	TOOLS	YES
7	D:\ORACLE\ORA92\O92\UNDOTBS01.DBF	UNDOTBS1	YES
8	D:\ORACLE\ORA92\O92\USERS01.DBF	USERS	YES
9	D:\ORACLE\ORA92\O92\XDB01.DBF	XDB	YES

Figure 5.13: *Information Regarding What Datafiles Have Autoextend Enabled*

The last thing to remember about using unlimited extents is that it is still possible for an object not to be able to extend. There are three primary reasons an object will fail to extend:

- **No file** *autoextend***:** The tablespace that the object resides in does not have *autoextend* enabled, and there is not enough room in the tablespace to add the object's new extent.

- **No filesystem space:** The tablespace that the object resides in has *autoextend* enabled, but the drive/file system that the tablespace is on is out of free space and will not allow the tablespace to automatically grow.

- **Fragmentation problem:** The dictionary managed tablespace that the object resides in has enough total free space to add the object's new extent, but the free space is not contiguous in nature because of bubble fragmentation, and therefore, the object cannot extend.

Troubleshooting Critical Storage Problems

I always recommend trying to adopt a proactive approach to Oracle storage management, and the first step is to ensure that the design includes intelligent planning for the current and future space needs of the database. It is necessary to manage storage both inside and outside on the Oracle server, making certain to use all the space-related features that Oracle provides.

While this is all well and good for new databases, an existing database may have sub-optimal storage structures. So, what sort of investigating should be done on existing systems to determine their storage health, and how should any new databases be kept free from space-related headaches? The following section will provide some insight.

Detecting Tablespace Fragmentation

How is it possible to tell if the tablespaces are suffering from fragmentation problems and then identify the type of fragmentation? The detection and diagnosis is not hard to make, if the right scripts are used. To determine if the tablespaces are having a problem with fragmentation, use the *tsfrag.sql* script:

🖫 tsfrag.sql

```
select
      tablespace_name,
      count(*) free_chunks,
      decode(round((max(bytes) / 1024000),2),null,0,
      round((max(bytes) / 1024000),2)) largest_chunk,
      nvl(round(sqrt(max(blocks)/sum(blocks))*
   (100/sqrt(sqrt(count(blocks)) )),2),0)
      fragmentation_index
from
      sys.dba_free_space
group by
      tablespace_name
order by
      2 desc, 1;
```

	TABLESPACE_NAME	FREE_CHUNKS	LARGEST_CHUNK	FRAGMENTATION_INDEX
1	TEMP	2208	.44	.81
2	USER_DATA	73	63.23	31.33
3	RBS	36	18.94	15.77
4	USER_DATA2	8	4.66	57.06
5	ER_DATA	5	2.47	47.33
6	BROKER_DATA	3	8.26	72.94
7	BROKER_INDEXES	1	10.18	100
8	OEM_REPOSITORY	1	2.82	100
9	USER_DATA3	1	12.28	100
10	SYSTEM	1	.24	100
11	TEST	1	1.02	100
12	TEST_TS	1	14.27	100
13	TOOLS	1	5.08	100
14	USER_INDEXES	1	.38	100

When the script output is examined, a couple of columns in particular attract attention. First, notice the fragmentation index column. This will give the tablespace an overall ranking with respect to how badly it is actually fragmented. A 100% score indicates no fragmentation at all. Lesser scores verify the presence of fragmentation.

The free chunks count column will tell how many segments of free space are scattered throughout the tablespace. One thing to keep in mind is that tablespaces with multiple datafiles will always show a free chunk count greater than one because each datafile will likely have at least one pocket of free space.

The dffrag.sql script can be used to drill down a little further and find out how badly fragmented each datafile in the database is.

🖫 dffrag.sql

```
select
      b.file_name, b.tablespace_name,
      nvl(round(sqrt(max(a.blocks)/
      sum(a.blocks))*(100/sqrt(sqrt(count(a.blocks)) )),2),0)
      fragmentation_index,
      decode(c.inc,null,'no','yes') autoextend,
      count (*) free_chunks,
      decode (
          round ((max (a.bytes) / 1024000), 2),
          null, 0,
          round ((max (a.bytes) / 1024000), 2)) largest_chunk
 from
      sys.dba_free_space a,
      sys.dba_data_files b,
      sys.filext$ c
where
      b.tablespace_name = a.tablespace_name (+) and
      c.file# (+)= a.file_id and
      b.file_id = a.file_id (+)
group
      by b.file_name,
      decode(c.inc,null,'no','yes'),
      b.tablespace_name
order
      by 5 desc, 1;
```

	FILE_NAME	TABLESPACE_NAME	FRAGMENTATION_INDEX	AUTOEXTEND	FREE_CHUNKS	LARGEST_CHUNK
1	D:\ORACLE\ORADATA\O817\TEMP01.DBF	TEMP	.81	YES	2208	.44
2	D:\ORACLE\ORADATA\O817\USERS01.DBF	USER_DATA	32.08	YES	68	63.23
3	D:\ORACLE\ORADATA\O817\RBS01.DBF	RBS	15.77	YES	36	18.94
4	D:\ORACLE\ORADATA\O817\USER_DATA2.DBF	USER_DATA2	57.06	NO	8	4.66
5	D:\ORACLE\ORADATA\O817\ER_DATA.DBF	ER_DATA	47.33	NO	5	2.47
6	D:\ORACLE\ORADATA\O817\USERS02.DBF	USER_DATA	43.98	YES	5	.38
7	D:\ORACLE\ORADATA\O817\BROKER_DATA.DBF	BROKER_DATA	72.94	YES	3	8.26
8	D:\ORACLE\ORADATA\O817\BIGADMIN.DBF	BIG_ADMISSION	0	NO	1	0
9	D:\ORACLE\ORADATA\O817\BROKER_INDEXES.DBF	BROKER_INDEXES	100	YES	1	10.18
10	D:\ORACLE\ORADATA\O817\INDX01.DBF	USER_INDEXES	100	YES	1	.38
11	D:\ORACLE\ORADATA\O817\OEM_REPOSITORY.ORA	OEM_REPOSITORY	100	YES	1	2.82
12	D:\ORACLE\ORADATA\O817\USER_DATA3.DBF	USER_DATA3	100	NO	1	12.28
13	D:\ORACLE\ORADATA\O817\SYSTEM01.DBF	SYSTEM	100	YES	1	.24
14	D:\ORACLE\ORADATA\O817\TEST01.DBF	TEST	100	YES	1	1.02
15	D:\ORACLE\ORADATA\O817\TEST_TS.ORA	TEST_TS	100	YES	1	14.27
16	D:\ORACLE\ORADATA\O817\TOOLS01.DBF	TOOLS	100	YES	1	5.08

Figure 5.15: *Checking for Datafile Fragmentation*

One last thing to remember in detecting tablespace fragmentation is that even if numerous free chunk counts are found in locally managed tablespaces, it really is not an issue.

Since every object placed in the tablespace will have the same extent size, sooner or later the pockets of free space will be reused, whether new objects are placed into the tablespace or existing objects extend. If fragmentation is indeed found in the tablespaces, it will be necessary to identify whether it is of the honeycomb or bubble variety.

To answer this question, produce a tablespace map that plots the entire tablespace in datafile/block id order. Doing so will show a number of interesting things, including where the actual objects in the tablespace reside along with where the pockets of free space are located.

A clean tablespace will normally show one large segment of free space at the end. A badly fragmented tablespace will show bubbles of free space interspersed throughout. Two free space segments that reside next to one another can identify honeycombs.

🖫 tsmap.sql

```
select
        'free space' object_owner,
        '    ' object_type,
        '    ' object_name,
        file_id,
        block_id,
        bytes / 1024 size_kb,
        blocks
from
        sys.dba_free_space
where
        tablespace_name = '&tablespacename'
union all
select
        owner,
        segment_type,
        decode (partition_name,null,segment_name,segment_name ||
        '.' || partition_name),
        file_id,
        block_id,
        bytes / 1024,
        blocks
from
        sys.dba_extents
where
        tablespace_name = '&tablespacename'
order by
        4,5;
```

	OBJECT_OWNER	OBJECT_TYPE	OBJECT_NAME	FILE_ID	BLOCK_ID	SIZE_KB	BLOCKS
1	USER21	TABLE	TAB1	3	2	128	16
2	ERADMIN	INDEX	PK22	3	18	128	16
3	free space			3	34	128	16
4	USER21	TABLE	INDEX1	3	50	128	16
5	EMBT_CP	INDEX	REF61	3	66	128	16
6	EMBT_CP	INDEX	REF63	3	82	128	16
7	EMBT_CP	INDEX	REF62	3	98	128	16
8	free space			3	114	128	16
9	ERADMIN	LOBSEGMENT	SYS_LOB0000034196C00001$$	3	130	128	16
10	free space			3	146	128	16
11	EMBT_CP	TABLE	CP_TABLE	3	162	128	16
12	EMBT_CP	INDEX	REF67	3	178	128	16
13	ERADMIN	TABLE	TEST_RAW	3	194	128	16
14	BILLY	TABLE	PLAN_TABLE	3	210	128	16
15	ERADMIN	TABLE	EMP_BKP	3	226	128	16
16	ERADMIN	TABLE	CREATE$JAVA$LOB$TABLE	3	242	128	16
17	BAD_GUY	TABLE	ROB	3	258	128	16
18	ERADMIN	TABLE	DOCTOR_PROCEDURE	3	274	128	16
19	ERADMIN	INDEX	PK10	3	290	128	16
20	ERADMIN	TABLE	EMPLOYEE	3	306	128	16
21	ERADMIN	TABLE	MEDICATION	3	322	128	16
22	ERADMIN	INDEX	PK11	3	338	128	16
23	ERADMIN	TABLE	MEDICATION_DISP	3	354	128	16
24	ERADMIN	INDEX	PK12	3	370	128	16
25	ERADMIN	TABLE	MEDICATION_DISPM	3	386	128	16
26	ERADMIN	INDEX	PK13	3	402	128	16
27	ERADMIN	TABLE	NURSE	3	418	128	16
28	ERADMIN	LOBINDEX	SYS_IL0000034196C00002$$	3	434	128	16

Figure 5.16: *Mapping the Contents of a Tablespace*

The next section will provide a look into object fragmentation.

Detecting Object Fragmentation

Object fragmentation can damage the performance in one of two ways. First, if there are objects in dictionary-managed tablespaces that have a maximum extent limit set to something other than unlimited, the objects could run out of space.

As a result of repeated insert and delete activity, tables can become internally fragmented and contain a lot of wasted space. In the same way, indexes can become fragmented so that their depth reaches unacceptable levels. This predicament will be covered in the next section.

Is it possible to tell if the objects are getting close to hitting their maximum extent limit? Yes, this is quite easy to do. If version 7 of Oracle is being used, then execute the *maxext7.sql* script, which will find all objects that are within five extents of their limit:

🖫 **maxext.sql**

```
select
      owner,
      decode(partition_name,NULL,segment_name,segment_name ||
      '.' || partition_name) segment_name,
      segment_type,
      extents,
      max_extents,
      initial_extent,
      next_extent,
```

```
        tablespace_name
from
        sys.dba_segments
where
        max_extents - extents <= 5 and
        segment_type <> 'CACHE'
order by
     1,2,3;
```

	OWNER	SEGMENT_NAME	SEGMENT_TYPE	EXTENTS	MAX_EXTENTS	INITIAL_EXTENT	NEXT_EXTENT	TABLESPACE_NAME
1	ERADMIN	CANT_EXTEND	TABLE	3	4	131072	131072	USER_DATA
2	USER21	TABLE1	TABLE	1	1	16384	6144000	USER_DATA
3	USER21	TABLE2	TABLE	1	1	106496	8192	USER_DATA
4	USER21	TABLE3	TABLE	1	1	106496	8192	USER_DATA

Figure 5.17: *Output Showing Objects Nearing Their Maximum Extent Limit*

Another extent problem arises when an object in a dictionary-managed tablespace cannot extend because of a lack of contiguous free space. To uncover these types of problems, use the *objdef.sql* script:

🖫 objdef.sql

```
select
    a.owner,
    a.segment_name,
    a.segment_type,
    a.tablespace_name,
    a.next_extent,
    max(c.bytes) max_contig_space
from
    sys.dba_segments a,
    sys.dba_free_space c
where
    a.tablespace_name = c.tablespace_name and
    a.next_extent >
    (select
            max(bytes)
        from
            sys.dba_free_space b
        where
            a.tablespace_name = b.tablespace_name and
            b.tablespace_name = c.tablespace_name)
group by
        a.owner,
        a.segment_name,
        a.tablespace_name,
        a.segment_type,
        a.next_extent;
```

	OWNER	SEGMENT_NAME	SEGMENT_TYPE	TABLESPACE_NAME	NEXT_EXTENT	MAX_CONTIG_SPACE
1	BAD_GUY	ADMISSION	TABLE PARTITION	USER_DATA	104857600	64749568
2	ERADMIN	ADMISSION	TABLE PARTITION	USER_DATA	104857600	64749568
3	ERADMIN	REF440	INDEX	USER_DATA	102400000	64749568
4	USER21	TABLE1	TABLE	USER_DATA	6144000	4767744
5	SYS	C_FILE#_BLOCK#	CLUSTER	SYSTEM	335872	245760
6	SYS	EMBARCADERO_EXPLAIN_PLAN	TABLE	SYSTEM	507904	245760
7	SYS	I_IDL_SB41	INDEX	SYSTEM	335872	245760
8	SYS	I_IDL_UB11	INDEX	SYSTEM	1146880	245760
9	SYS	I_IDL_UB21	INDEX	SYSTEM	335872	245760
10	SYS	JAVANM	TABLE	SYSTEM	507904	245760

Correcting Object Fragmentation

The prescription for correcting object fragmentation is reorganization with the *dbms_redefinition* package or CTAS. Such a procedure used to be fraught with errors and fear, even when third party software products were used. Fortunately, this is not really the case any longer as Oracle has provided more built-in reorganization capabilities with each new release. Oracle has even gone so far as to grant online reorganization abilities for certain object types.

The next section will cover in detail the reorganization techniques and methods that can be used to fix the objects that need to be reorganized.

Troubleshooting Table Problems

The problem of wasted space in a table and a corresponding misleading high water mark has already been covered in this chapter. Needless to say, tables that suffer from high levels of wasted space could definitely be causing the database to spin in undesirable ways. The other problem that might exist in the tables is one of chained/migrated rows.

Under normal circumstances, a row of data should fit completely inside one Oracle block. Sometimes, however, this is not the case, and the table suddenly finds itself containing chained or migrated rows, which are rows that span more than one data block.

Chaining occurs when a row is initially too large to fit inside one block. Two or more blocks are used by Oracle to hold the row. Migration deals with rows that have grown so much that they can no longer be contained within their original block. When this occurs, Oracle relocates the row out of its original block into another block, but leaves a pointer behind to indicate the relocation.

Both chaining and migration force Oracle to perform more than one I/O to retrieve data that could normally be obtained with a single I/O operation. The end result is degraded performance. How can the levels of wasted space in the tables be determined in addition to finding out if they suffer from a chained/migrated row problem? The following scripts will provide all the necessary answers. They locate tables that contain 25% or more wasted space.

As a bonus, the scripts also calculate the chained row ratio for a table, the percentage of used extents to maximum extents, and determine if the object can extend into its next block of free space.

In other words, these are nice reorganization diagnostic scripts.

🖫 **tabreorg.sql**

```
select
        /*+ RULE */
        owner,
```

```
        segment_name table_name,
        segment_type,
        round(bytes/1024,2) table_kb,
        num_rows,
        blocks,
        empty_blocks,
        hwm highwater_mark,
        avg_used_blocks,
        greatest(round(100 * (nvl(hwm - avg_used_blocks,0) /
        greatest(nvl(hwm,1),1) ),2),0) block_inefficiency,
        chain_pct,
        max_extent_pct,
        extents,
        max_extents,
        decode(greatest(max_free_space -
        next_extent,0),0,'n','y') can_extend_space,
        next_extent,
        max_free_space,
        o_tablespace_name tablespace_name
from
(select
        a.owner owner,
        segment_name,
        segment_type,
        bytes,
        num_rows,
        a.blocks blocks,
        b.empty_blocks empty_blocks,
        a.blocks - b.empty_blocks - 1 hwm,
        decode(round((b.avg_row_len * num_rows *
        (1 + (pct_free/100))) /
        c.blocksize,0),0,1,round((b.avg_row_len * num_rows *
        (1 + (pct_free/100))) / c.blocksize,0)) + 2
        avg_used_blocks,
        round(100 * (nvl(b.chain_cnt,0) /
        greatest(nvl(b.num_rows,1),1)),2)
        chain_pct,
        a.extents extents,
        round(100 * (a.extents / a.max_extents),2) max_extent_pct,
        a.max_extents max_extents,
        b.next_extent next_extent,
        b.tablespace_name o_tablespace_name
   from
        sys.dba_segments a,
        sys.dba_all_tables b,
        sys.ts$ c
  where
        ( a.owner = b.owner ) and
        ( segment_name = table_name ) and
        ( ( segment_type = 'TABLE' ) ) and
        b.tablespace_name = c.name
 union all
 select
        a.owner owner,
        segment_name || '.' || b.partition_name,
        segment_type,
        bytes,
        b.num_rows,
        a.blocks blocks,
        b.empty_blocks empty_blocks,
        a.blocks - b.empty_blocks - 1 hwm,
        decode(round((b.avg_row_len * b.num_rows * (1 +
        (b.pct_free/100))) /
        c.blocksize,0),0,1,round((b.avg_row_len * b.num_rows *
        (1 + (b.pct_free/100))) / c.blocksize,0)) + 2
```

```
            avg_used_blocks,
            round(100 * (nvl(b.chain_cnt,0) /
            greatest(nvl(b.num_rows,1),1)),2)
            chain_pct,
            a.extents extents,
            round(100 * (a.extents / a.max_extents),2) max_extent_pct,
            a.max_extents max_extents,
            b.next_extent,
            b.tablespace_name o_tablespace_name
        from
            sys.dba_segments a,
            sys.dba_tab_partitions b,
            sys.ts$ c,
            sys.dba_tables d
    where
            ( a.owner = b.table_owner ) and
            ( segment_name = b.table_name ) and
            ( ( segment_type = 'TABLE PARTITION' ) ) and
            b.tablespace_name = c.name and
            d.owner = b.table_owner and
            d.table_name = b.table_name and
            a.partition_name = b.partition_name),
(  select
            tablespace_name f_tablespace_name,
            max(bytes) max_free_space
    from
            sys.dba_free_space
    group by tablespace_name)
    where
            f_tablespace_name = o_tablespace_name and
            greatest(round(100 * (nvl(hwm - avg_used_blocks,0) /
            greatest(nvl(hwm,1),1) ),2),0) > 25
order by 10 desc, 1 asc,2 asc;
```

	OWNER	TABLE_NAME	SEGMENT_TYPE	TABLE_KB	NUM_ROWS	BLOCKS	EMPTY_BLOCKS	HIGHWATER_MARK	AVG_USED_BLOCKS	BLOCK_INEFFICIENCY	CHAIN_PCT
1	ERADMIN	EMP	TABLE	19072	0	2384	120	2263	3	99.87	0
2	SYS	OBJ$	TABLE	2440	4387	305	1	303	43	85.81	0
3	SYS	ADMISSION_NO	TABLE	256	1520	32	0	31	5	83.87	0
4	USER21	TABLE1	TABLE	256	0	32	15	16	3	81.25	0
5	USER21	TABLE2	TABLE	256	130	32	12	19	4	78.95	0
6	USER21	TABLE3	TABLE	176	40	22	0	21	11	47.62	82.5
7	ERADMIN	EMBARCADERO	TABLE	384	2217	48	6	41	27	34.15	0
8	SYS	PROCEDURE$	TABLE	80	418	10	3	6	4	33.33	0
9	BRKADMIN	INVESTMENT	TABLE	64	412	8	0	7	5	28.57	0

Figure 5.19: *Partial Output Showing the Wasted Space Amounts and Chained Row Percentage of Database Tables*

To see the shape that all his database tables are in, remove the WHERE clause that restricts the output to only those tables having a block efficiency ranking of 25% or higher.

There are a couple of columns in Figure 5.19 that should be honed in on. The block inefficiency ranking will highlight any table that suffers from a lot of wasted space. For example, the *eradmin.emp* table has no rows in it but sports a very high watermark.

Therefore, it tops the list in terms of tables with high amounts of wasted space. Also, notice the chain percent column. This column indicates how badly the table suffers from chained or migrated rows. In Figure 5.19, the *user21.table3* table appears to be in bad shape with respect to chained/migrated rows.

Generally, if a table appears to have a chain percent of 25% or more, it would be worth it to reorganize it.

Index Diagnostics

Like tables, indexes can become disorganized due to heavy DML activity. There has been much debate in the DBA world as to what a DBA should look for when determining if an index is in poor shape, but the *idxreorg.sql* script below should help.

The script displays the level and clustering factor of the index, calculates the percentage of used extents to maximum extents and also determines if the index can extend into its next block of free space.

💾 **idxreorg.sql**

```
select
        /*+ RULE */
        owner,
        segment_name index_name,
        segment_type,
        round(bytes/1024,2) index_kb,
        num_rows,
        clustering_factor,
        blevel,
        blocks,
        max_extent_pct,
        extents,
        max_extents,
        decode(greatest(max_free_space -
        next_extent,0),0,'n','y') can_extend_space,
        next_extent,
        max_free_space,
        o_tablespace_name
from
(select
        a.owner owner,
        segment_name,
        segment_type,
        bytes,
        num_rows,
        b.clustering_factor,
        b.blevel,
        a.blocks blocks,
        a.extents extents,
        round(100 * (a.extents / a.max_extents),2)
        max_extent_pct,
        a.max_extents max_extents,
        b.next_extent next_extent,
        b.tablespace_name o_tablespace_name
    from
        sys.dba_segments a,
        sys.dba_indexes b,
        sys.ts$ c
    where
        ( a.owner = b.owner ) and
        ( segment_name = index_name ) and
        ( ( segment_type = 'INDEX' ) ) and
        b.tablespace_name = c.name
union all
select
```

```
        a.owner owner,
        segment_name || '.' || b.partition_name,
        segment_type,
        bytes,
        b.num_rows,
        b.clustering_factor,
        b.blevel,
        a.blocks blocks,
        a.extents extents,
        round(100 * (a.extents / a.max_extents),2)
        max_extent_pct,
        a.max_extents max_extents,
        b.next_extent,
        b.tablespace_name o_tablespace_name
    from
        sys.dba_segments a,
        sys.dba_ind_partitions b,
        sys.ts$ c,
        sys.dba_indexes d
    where
        ( a.owner = b.index_owner ) and
        ( segment_name = b.index_name ) and
        ( ( segment_type = 'INDEX PARTITION' ) ) and
        b.tablespace_name = c.name and
        d.owner = b.index_owner and
        d.index_name = b.index_name and
        a.partition_name = b.partition_name),
(  select
        tablespace_name f_tablespace_name,
        max(bytes) max_free_space
    from
        sys.dba_free_space
    group by tablespace_name)
where
    f_tablespace_name = o_tablespace_name
order
    by 1,2;
```

	OWNER	INDEX_NAME	SEGMENT_TYPE	INDEX_KB	NUM_ROWS	CLUSTERING_FACTOR	BLEVEL	BLOCKS	MAX_EXTENT_PCT	EXT
7	AURORAJISUTILITY$	SNS$NODE_INDEX	INDEX	64	84	10	0	8	0	
8	AURORAJISUTILITY$	SNS$PERM_INDEX	INDEX	64	312	1	0	8	0	
9	AURORAJISUTILITY$	SNS$REFADDR_INDEX	INDEX	64	291	5	0	8	0	
10	AURORAJISUTILITY$	SNS$SHARED$OBJ_INDEX	INDEX	64	0	0	0	8	0	
11	AURORAJISUTILITY$	SYS_C0011031	INDEX	64	117	1	0	8	0	
12	AURORAJISUTILITY$	SYS_C0011032	INDEX	64	0	0	0	8	0	
13	BILLY	SYS_C0011859	INDEX	128	0	0	0	16	.02	
14	BILLY	SYS_C0011860	INDEX	128	1	1	0	16	.02	
15	BRKADMIN	BROKER_COMMISSION_N1	INDEX	32	0	0	0	4	0	
16	BRKADMIN	BROKER_N1	INDEX	32	20	1	0	4	0	
17	BRKADMIN	CLIENT_N1	INDEX	32	500	8	0	4	0	

Figure 5.20: *Partial Output Showing Index Reorganization Diagnostics*

Seeing index levels beyond four, or bad clustering factors for indexes with supposed high cardinality, should lead to an investigation whether the index should be reorganized or even maintained in the system.

Correcting Space-related Object Performance Problems

While use of locally managed tablespaces can just about make full tablespace reorganizations a thing of the past, object reorganizations are still necessary to remove headaches like wasted table space, chained/migrated table rows, deep index levels and more.

Oracle used to leave reorganization capabilities to third party software vendors, but newer versions of the RDBMS engine provide a number of built-in features that allow performing object reorganizations with simple DDL commands or packages.

The following section covers the other side of the I/O spectrum: RAM.

Troubleshooting Memory Problems

When the subject of Oracle performance tuning comes up, almost every database professional thinks of tweaking the RAM memory settings. After all, is it not true that servers with more RAM run faster than comparable servers with less memory? Should not databases work the same?

Not surprisingly, the general answer is yes. Databases operating with more memory will usually run hundreds of times faster than those whose RAM allocations are rationed out in smaller portions. There are, of course, exceptions to every rule, and those will be covered in this chapter.

Those who think that throwing memory at a database is always going to solve serious performance problems are setting themselves up for a rude awakening. It takes a careful blend of balance and investigation to determine exactly how much memory a database needs and where those allocations should be made. It is also critically important not to over allocate a database's memory allotment. Doing so can cause a server to page swap and thrash to a point where all operations come to a complete standstill.

Without a doubt, a small book could be written on the subject of memory concepts and tuning within Oracle. Instead of trying to cover every nook and cranny with respect to memory optimization, this chapter will focus on getting the most bang for the buck when the DBA begins to turn Oracle's memory knobs. There is nothing more irritating than spending an hour and a half reading an in-depth white paper on something like Oracle latch analysis, and then discovering that following the author's advice yields no noticeable benefit on the database.

This chapter will hopefully give the reader the knowledge to maximize memory inside and outside the database by focusing on the following topics:

- How to determine if Oracle is being given the right amount of memory.

- What new memory options in Oracle offer the most potential for improving performance.

- How to keep data, code, and object definitions in memory so response times are the fastest possible.

- How to quickly pinpoint user sessions that degrade response times by using excessive memory resources.

Once these things are understood, the reader will be in a better position to ensure that the Oracle database is properly configured from a memory standpoint. To begin, analyze the current memory configuration and usage of the database.

Getting a Handle on Memory Usage

Not surprisingly, each release of Oracle has featured additional memory parameters that can be tweaked to create an optimal memory configuration for the database. And in trained hands, these parameters can make a dramatic difference in how well the database runs.

Happily, Oracle has now made these key memory settings dynamic in version 9i and above, meaning that it is now possible to size the SGA without having to start and stop the database.

With an existing database, the place to start is by gaining an understanding of how much RAM the database server offers and then determine the current settings of the Oracle SGA. This provides a basis for judging whether Oracle can benefit from adding or manipulating memory and how much headroom exists. Obtaining the memory configuration of the server will depend on the hardware/operating system platform. Most operating systems have decent GUI interfaces that allow for such configuration information to be obtained through pointing and clicking.

Once the memory amounts for the server are known, diagnostics should be performed to investigate the metrics of the paging/swapping situation on the server. Again, getting such information will depend on the hardware platform. However, regardless of the platform, it is best to avoid excessive paging and swapping. They tend to degrade the overall performance of anything that runs on the server since data is constantly transferred from RAM to physical swap files and then back again.

After there is a comfort level for the memory behavior on the database server, now attention will need to be turned to Oracle. The first step is to find the size of the current SGA that controls the database. To get such information, use the *sgasize.sql* script. Note that this script can be used on all Oracle versions. However, some of the columns may be null or zero because certain memory regions are not available in all versions.

🖫 sgasize.sql

```
select
        db_size_in_mb - db_caches db_buffers_in_mb,
        db_caches db_caches_mb,
        fixed_size_in_mb,
        lb_size_in_mb,
        sp_size_in_mb,
        lp_size_in_mb,
        jp_size_in_mb
from
(select
        round (max(a.bytes) / 1024 / 1024, 2)  db_size_in_mb
  from
        sys.v_$sgastat a
 where
        (a.name = 'db_block_buffers' or a.name = 'buffer_cache')),
(select
        nvl(round (sum (b.value) / 1024 / 1024, 2),0) db_caches
  from
        sys.v_$parameter b
 where
        b.name like '%k_cache_size'),
(select
        round (sum (b.bytes) / 1024 / 1024, 2) fixed_size_in_mb
  from
```

```
          sys.v_$sgastat b
 where
          b.name = 'fixed_sga'),
(select
          round (sum (c.bytes) / 1024 / 1024, 2) lb_size_in_mb
   from
          sys.v_$sgastat c
 where
          c.name= 'log_buffer' ),
(select
          round (sum (d.value) / 1024 / 1024, 2) sp_size_in_mb
   from
          sys.v_$parameter d
 where
          d.name = 'shared_pool_size'),
(select
          round (sum (e.value) / 1024 / 1024, 2) lp_size_in_mb
   from
          sys.v_$parameter e
 where
          e.name = 'large_pool_size' ),
(select
          round (sum (f.value) / 1024 / 1024, 2) jp_size_in_mb
   from
          sys.v_$parameter f
 where
          f.name = 'java_pool_size');
```

	DB_BUFFERS_IN_MB	DB_CACHES	FIXED_SIZE_IN_MB	LB_SIZE_IN_MB	SP_SIZE_IN_MB	LP_SIZE_IN_MB	JP_SIZE_IN_MB
1	56	16	.43	.63	48	8	32

Figure 5.21: *Getting a Summary of Oracle SGA Settings*

This script delivers more detailed information than the standard *show sga* command in the server manager or SQL*Plus because it breaks down the standard buffer cache, showing the total amount of memory given to the special 9i and above data caches and displaying information for the large and java pools.

Exactly what each of these areas is and how Oracle uses them is the topic of the next section.

Understanding the SGA

Most DBAs know all about the Oracle System Global Area (SGA). The SGA is Oracle's structural memory area that facilitates the transfer of data and information between clients and the Oracle database. Long gone are the days when only four main tunable components existed. When using Oracle9i or above, expect to deal with the following memory regions:

- **Default buffer cache:** This is the default memory cache that stores data blocks when they are read from the database. If objects are not specifically placed in another data cache, then any data requested by clients from the database will be placed into this cache. This memory area is controlled by the *db_block_buffers* parameter in Oracle8i and below and *db_cache_size* in Oracle9i and above.

- **Keep buffer cache:** Beginning with Oracle 8, objects can be assigned to a special cache that will retain those objects' requested blocks in RAM for as long as the database is up. The *keep* cache's main function is to hold frequently referenced lookup tables that should always be kept in memory for quick access. The *buffer_pool_keep* parameter controls the size of this cache in Oracle 8, while the *db_keep_cache_size* parameter handles the cache in Oracle9i and above. The KEEP pool is a sub-pool of the default buffer cache.

- **Recycle buffer cache:** Imagine the opposite of the *keep* cache, and this is the *recycle* cache. When large table scans occur, the data filling a memory cache is unlikely to be needed again and should be quickly discarded from RAM. By placing this data into the *recycle* cache, it will neither occupy valuable memory space nor prevent blocks that are needed from being placed in a buffer. However, should it be requested again, the discarded data is quickly available. The *buffer_pool_recycle* parameter controls the size of this cache in Oracle 8 and below, while the *db_recycle_cache_size* parameter handles the cache in Oracle9i and above.

- **Specific block size caches:** Beginning in Oracle9i, tablespaces can be created whose blocksize differs from the overall database blocksize. When data is read into the SGA from these tablespaces, their data has to be placed into memory regions that can accommodate their special blocksize. Oracle9i and above has memory settings for 2K, 4K, 8K, 16K and 32K caches. The configuration parameter names are in the pattern of *db_nk_cache_size*.

- **Shared pool:** this familiar area holds object structures and code definitions as well as other metadata. Setting the proper amount of memory in the shared pool assists a great deal in improving overall performance with respect to code execution and object references. The *shared_pool_size* parameter controls this memory region.

- **Large pool:** Starting in Oracle 8, the DBA can configure an optional, specialized memory region called the large pool that holds items for shared server operations, backup and restore tasks and other miscellaneous things. The *large_pool_size* parameter controls this memory region. The large pool is also used for sorting when the multi-threaded server (MTS) is implemented.

- **Java pool:** This area handles the memory for Java methods, class definitions and such. The *java_pool_size* parameter controls the amount of memory for this area.

- **Redo log buffer:** This area buffers modifications that are made to the database before they are physically written to the redo log files. The *log_buffer* configuration parameter controls this memory area.

Note that Oracle also maintains a fixed area in the SGA that contains a number of atomic variables, pointers, and other miscellaneous structures that reference areas of the SGA.

Gaining Insight Into Memory Use

Once the current settings of the SGA are understood, the next task is to see how well it is being utilized. Use a number of key ratios and wait metrics to assemble a global picture of SGA performance.

Before using the scripts below to obtain key memory metrics, be aware that some database professionals passionately believe that ratio-based analysis is a worthless endeavor and only favor a wait-based or bottleneck approach instead. There are certainly valid reasons for not relying solely on ratios to determine if the database is functioning properly. However, when practiced correctly, ratio-based analysis is indeed worthwhile and can contribute to the understanding of system performance. Chapter 10, which covers ratio-based and bottleneck analysis, provides more information on this topic.

That said, what are some of the key indicators of memory efficiency and usage? Rather than list each metric in a single script, the *memsnap.sql* script below obtains many key memory metrics in a single query and presents them all at once.

🖫 **memsnap.sql**

```
select
       buffer_hit_ratio,
       percent_shared_pool_free,
       lib_cache_hit_ratio,
       object_reloads,
       dd_cache_hit_ratio,
       redo_log_space_waits,
       redo_log_space_wait_time,
       mem_sort_ratio,
       parse_execute_ratio,
       buffer_busy_waits,
       latch_miss_ratio
from
(select
       100 -
       100 *
       (round ((sum (decode (name, 'physical reads', value, 0)) -
        sum (decode (name, 'physical reads direct', value, 0)) -
        sum (decode (name,
        'physical reads direct (lob)', value, 0))) /
        (sum (decode (name,
        'session logical reads', value, 1))),3)) buffer_hit_ratio
 from
       sys.v_$sysstat
 where
       name in ('session logical reads',
                'physical reads direct (lob)',
                'physical reads', 'physical reads direct')),
(select
       round (100 * (free_bytes / shared_pool_size), 2)
       percent_shared_pool_free
  from
       (select
               sum (bytes) free_bytes
          from
               sys.v_$sgastat
         where
               name = 'free memory'
           and
               pool = 'shared pool'),
       (select
               value shared_pool_size
          from
               sys.v_$parameter
         where
               name = 'shared_pool_size')),
(select
       100 - round ((sum (reloads) /
       sum (pins)) * 100, 2) lib_cache_hit_ratio
  from
       sys.v_$librarycache),
(select
       100 - round ((sum (getmisses) /
       (sum (gets) + sum (getmisses)) * 100), 2) dd_cache_hit_ratio
from    sys.v_$rowcache),
(select round (
```

```
            (100 * b.value) /
            decode ((a.value + b.value), 0, 1, (a.value + b.value)),
            2)mem_sort_ratio
  from
        v$sysstat a,
        v$sysstat b
  where
        a.name = 'sorts (disk)'
    and b.name = 'sorts (memory)'),
(select
        round(100 * (sum (sys.v_$latch.misses) /
        sum (sys.v_$latch.gets)),2) latch_miss_ratio
  from
        sys.v_$latch),
(select
        round (100 * (a.value - b.value) /
        decode (a.value, 0, 1, a.value), 2) parse_execute_ratio
  from
        sys.v_$sysstat a,
        sys.v_$sysstat b
  where
        a.name = 'execute count'
    and b.name = 'parse count (hard)'),
(select
        nvl(sum(total_waits),0) buffer_busy_waits
from
        sys.v_$system_event a,
        sys.v_$event_name b
where
        a.event = 'buffer busy waits' and
        a.event (+) = b.name),
(select
        sum(reloads) object_reloads
  from
        sys.v_$librarycache),
(select
        value redo_log_space_waits
  from
        sys.v_$sysstat
where
        name = 'redo log space requests'),
(select
        value redo_log_space_wait_time
  from
        sys.v_$sysstat
where
        name = 'redo log space wait time');
```

BUFFER_HIT_RATIO	LIB_CACHE_HIT_RATIO	OBJECT_RELOADS	DB_CACHE_HIT_RATIO	MEM_SORT_RATIO	PARSE_EXECUTE_RATIO	PERCENT_SHARED_POOL_FREE
99.9	99.99	9	94.93	99.89	98.12	69.33

Figure 5.22: *Partial Output Showing Key Memory Usage Metrics*

The buffer cache hit ratio is the first statistic shown in the above script. As mentioned, many maintain that this measure is not a good indicator of performance, but is this actually true?

The Buffer Cache Hit Ratio – Still Worthwhile?

The buffer cache hit ratio indicates how often data is found in memory versus disk. Critics of this ratio complain that it is not a good indicator of performance because (a) many analysts use cumulative numbers for the computations, which can artificially inflate the value to a meaningless measure, and (b) it does not negatively reflect excessive logical I/O activity, which, although faster than disk I/O, can certainly suppress performance on any database.

These complaints have merit. Delta statistics must be used over time to come up with a meaningful value for the ratio, and high logical I/O values can definitely be a leading cause of bad execution times. However, when properly computed, the buffer cache hit ratio is an excellent indicator of how often the data requested by users is found in RAM instead of disk, a fact of no small importance.

The global statistic shown above is a good place to start, but it does not have to stop there. Penetrate deeper to find cache hit ratios at the buffer pool, session and SQL statement level. If a *keep* and *recycle* buffer pool is used in addition to the default buffer cache, utilize the *poolhit.sql* script to find the hit rates in each pool:

🖫 poolhit.sql

```
select
        name,
        100 * (1 - (physical_reads / (db_block_gets +
        consistent_gets))) hit_ratio
from
        sys.v$buffer_pool_statistics
where
        db_block_gets + consistent_gets > 0;
```

Output from the above query might look like the following:

```
NAME        HIT_RATIO
---------- ---------
DEFAULT        92.82
KEEP           93.98
RECYCLE        85.05
```

From the overall buffer caches, turn to the cache hit ratios for user processes. The *sesshitrate.sql* script below will provide a buffer cache hit ratio for all currently connected sessions:

🖫 sesshitrate.sql

```
select
        b.sid sid,
        decode (b.username,null,e.name,b.username)
        user_name,
        d.spid os_id,
        b.machine machine_name,
        to_char(logon_time,'mm/dd/yy hh:mi:ss pm')
        logon_time,
        100 - 100 *
        (round ((sum (decode (c.name,
        'physical reads', value, 0)) -
        sum (decode (c.name,
        'physical reads direct', value, 0)) -
```

```
        sum(decode (c.name,
        'physical reads direct (lob)', value, 0))) /
        (sum (decode (c.name,
        'db block gets', value, 1)) +
        sum (decode (c.name,
        'consistent gets', value, 0))),3)) hit_ratio
from
        sys.v_$sesstat a,
        sys.v_$session b,
        sys.v_$statname c,
        sys.v_$process d,
        sys.v_$bgprocess e
where
        a.statistic#=c.statistic# and
        b.sid=a.sid  and
        d.addr = b.paddr and
        e.paddr (+) = b.paddr  and
        c.name in ('physical reads',
                   'physical reads direct',
                   'physical writes direct (lob)',
                   'physical reads direct (lob)',
                   'db block gets',
                   'consistent gets')
group by
        b.sid,
        d.spid,
        decode (b.username,null,e.name,b.username),
        b.machine,
        to_char(logon_time,'mm/dd/yy hh:mi:ss pm')
order by
        6 desc;
```

	SID	USER_NAME	OS_ID	MACHINE_NAME	LOGON_TIME	HIT_RATIO
1	1	PMON	292	EBT2K11	01/03/03 01:01:16 pm	100
2	2	DBW0	1148	EBT2K11	01/03/03 01:01:16 pm	100
3	3	LGWR	304	EBT2K11	01/03/03 01:01:16 pm	100
4	6	RECO	1136	EBT2K11	01/03/03 01:01:17 pm	100
5	8	SYS	2552	EBT2K\BILLYWS	01/17/03 02:59:01 pm	100
6	9	QVIN	2420	EBT2K\BILLYWS	01/17/03 02:39:55 pm	100
7	12	SYSMAN	2948	EBT2K\EBT2K11	01/07/03 10:29:04 am	100
8	14	SYSMAN	2800	EBT2K\EBT2K11	01/07/03 10:29:05 am	100
9	15	SYSMAN	1424	EBT2K\EBT2K11	01/07/03 10:29:05 am	100
10	24	ERADMIN	452	EBT2K\ROBINWS	01/16/03 10:27:14 am	100
11	23	USER21	3176	EBT2K\EBT2K12	01/17/03 03:59:10 pm	100
12	22	SYS	2312	EBT2K\BILLYWS	01/17/03 03:32:51 pm	100
13	21	USER21	2136	EBT2K\EBT2K12	01/14/03 11:12:56 am	100
14	19	SYSMAN	1560	EBT2K\EBT2K11	01/07/03 10:29:05 am	100
15	18	SYS	3972	EBT2K\BILLYWS	01/17/03 03:02:23 pm	100
16	17	SYSMAN	2000	EBT2K\EBT2K11	01/07/03 10:29:05 am	100
17	13	SYSMAN	236	EBT2K\EBT2K11	01/07/03 10:29:05 am	100
18	30	SYS	3752	EBT2K\ROBINWS	01/16/03 09:27:38 am	100
19	29	SYS	3620	EBT2K\BILLYWS	01/17/03 02:57:11 pm	100
20	27	SYS	1884	EBT2K\ROBINWS	01/17/03 03:55:18 pm	100
21	26	SYS	3128	EBT2K\ROBINWS	01/17/03 03:59:45 pm	100
22	11	SYSMAN	2952	EBT2K\EBT2K11	01/07/03 10:29:04 am	100
23	4	CKPT	1176	EBT2K11	01/03/03 01:01:17 pm	100
24	5	SMON	1236	EBT2K11	01/03/03 01:01:17 pm	99.8
25	25	SYSTEM	612	EBT2K\EBT2K11	01/07/03 10:29:44 am	99.5

Figure 5.23: *Sample Output Showing Session Hit Ratio Information*

After examining the session hit ratio information, move into SQL statement analysis with the *sqlhitrate.sql* script:

💾 sqlhitrate.sql

```
select
        sql_text ,
        b.username ,
        100 - round(100 *
        a.disk_reads/greatest(a.buffer_gets,1),2) hit_ratio
from
        sys.v_$sqlarea a,
        sys.all_users b
where
        a.parsing_user_id=b.user_id and
        b.username not in ('SYS','SYSTEM')
order by
        3 desc;
```

	SQL_TEXT	USERNAME	HIT_RATIO
1	SELECT 1035, COUNT(*) FROM SYS.SEG$ S,SYS.TS$ TS WHERE S.TS# = TS.TS# AND DECODE(BITAND(TS.FLAGS, 3), 1, TO_NUMBER(NULL),S.EXTSIZE	USER1	100
2	COMMIT	QVIN	100
3	SELECT 980, CHAINEDFETCHES,TOTALFETCHES FROM (SELECT VALUE AS CHAINEDFETCHES FROM SYS.V_$SYSSTAT A WHERE NAME='table fetch	USER1	100
4	SELECT 1036, COUNT(*) FROM (SELECT ROUND((100*Sum_Free_Blocks / Sum_Alloc_Blocks),2) PCT_FREE FROM (SELECT Tablespace_Name,SUM(Blocks) Sum_Alloc_Blocks,SUM(bytes) AS Total_space FROM SYS.DBA_DATA_FILES GROUP BY Tablespace_Name), (SELECT	USER1	100
5	SELECT /*+ ALL_ROWS IGNORE_WHERE_CLAUSE */ NVL(SUM(C1),0), NVL(SUM(C2),0), COUNT(DISTINCT C3) FROM (SELECT /*+	QVIN	100
6	COMMIT WORK	QVIN	100
7	/* OracleOEM */ UPDATE smp_vdp_node_info SET status = 'N', DOWN_TIME = :1, DOWN_TIMEZONE = :2 WHERE (status = 'Y') AND (node = :3) AND	SYSMAN	100
8	begin PERFCNTR_DRILLDOWN_QUERIES.fetchcursor_10(QUERY_LIST_IN=>'914',MAX _ROWS_IN=>500,VAR1_OUT=>:R001C001,VAR2_OUT=>:R001C002,VAR3_OU	USER1	100
9	SELECT 976, ROUND(A.VALUE/1048576,2) DB,ROUND(B.VALUE/1048576,2) FS,ROUND(C.VALUE/1048576,2) RB,ROUND(D.VALUE/1048576,2) VS FROM	USER1	100
10	LOCK TABLE smp_vdp_node_oms_map IN EXCLUSIVE MODE	SYSMAN	100
11	LOCK TABLE smp_vdg_gateway_map in EXCLUSIVE MODE	SYSMAN	100
12	SELECT 1033, b.USERNAME,b.SID,b.SERIAL#,B.STATUS,DECODE((SUBSTR(B.MACHINE,LENG TH(B.MACHINE),1)),CHR(0),(SUBSTR(B.MACHINE,1,LENGTH(B.MACHINE)-1)),RT RIM(B.MACHINE)) MACHINE,ROUND(SUM(DECODE(c.NAME,'session pga memory',VALUE,0))/1024,2) pga_memory,ROUND(SUM(DECODE(c.NAME,'session uga memory',VALUE,0))/1024,2) uga_memory,ROUND(SUM(DECODE(c.NAME, 'sorts	USER1	100

Figure 5.24: *Sample Output Showing SQL Statement Hit Ratio Analysis*

One nuance in the SQL hit ratio script, as well as the buffer pool script which calculates hit rates for the different buffer pools, that the DBA should be aware of is that the Oracle *v$sqlarea* view does not provide a way to filter direct reads, i.e. physical reads that do not pass through the buffer cache, and consequently do not increment any logical I/O counters. This means it is possible to have a SQL statement that prompts a lot of direct reads, while the hit ratio shows *negative*.

Exploiting Non-standard Data Caches

In Oracle9i and above, tablespaces can be created with blocksizes that differ from the overall database blocksize. To use this feature the DBA must also enable one or more of the new *db_nk_cache_size* parameters so that blocks read in from tablespaces that have a different blocksize than the regular database blocksize have a cache to reside. For example, if a tablespace is created with a 16K blocksize, then the DBA must also set aside RAM for those blocks using the *db_16k_cache_size* parameter. Note that such allocations are in addition to the memory allotments specified by the *db_cache_size* parameter.

This feature allows database to be tuned in ways that were impossible in earlier versions of Oracle. For example, use the large (16-32K) blocksize data caches to store data from indexes or tables that are the object of repeated large scans. Does such a thing really help performance? A small but revealing test can answer that question.

For the test, the following query will be used against a 9i database that has a database block size of 8K, but also has the 16K cache enabled along with a 16K tablespace:

```
select
      count(*)
from
      eradmin.admission
where
      patient_id between 1 and 40000;
```

The *eradmin.admission* table has 150,000 rows in it and has an index build on the *patient_id* column. An *explain* of the query reveals that it uses an index range scan to produce the desired end result:

```
Execution Plan
------------------------------------------------------------
SELECT STATEMENT Optimizer=CHOOSE
(Cost=41 Card=1 Bytes=4)
   1    0   SORT (AGGREGATE)
   2    1     INDEX (FAST FULL SCAN) OF 'ADMISSION_PATIENT_ID'
              (NON-UNIQUE) (Cost=41 Card=120002 Bytes=480008)
```

Executing the query twice to eliminate parse activity and to cache any data with the index residing in a standard 8K tablespace produces these runtime statistics:

```
Statistics
------------------------------------------------------------
         0  recursive calls
         0  db block gets
       421  consistent gets
         0  physical reads
         0  redo size
       371  bytes sent via SQL*Net to client
       430  bytes received via SQL*Net from client
         2  SQL*Net roundtrips to/from client
         0  sorts (memory)
         0  sorts (disk)
         1  rows processed
```

To test the effectiveness of the new 16K cache and 16K tablespace, the index used by the query will be rebuilt into the larger tablespace, while everything else remains the same:

```
alter index
     eradmin.admission_patient_id
     rebuild nologging noreverse tablespace indx_16k;
```

Once the index is nestled firmly into the 16K tablespace, the query is re-executed (again, twice) with the following runtime statistics being produced:

```
Statistics
----------------------------------------------------
         0   recursive calls
         0   db block gets
       211   consistent gets
         0   physical reads
         0   redo size
       371   bytes sent via SQL*Net to client
       430   bytes received via SQL*Net from client
         2   SQL*Net roundtrips to/from client
         0   sorts (memory)
         0   sorts (disk)
         1   rows processed
```

The amount of logical reads has been cut in half simply by using the new 16K tablespace and accompanying 16K data cache. Clearly, the benefits of the proper use of the data caches and multi-block tablespace features of Oracle9i are worth investigating and testing.

Other Interesting Buffer Cache Metrics

There are a few additional queries that can be used to gain deeper insight into buffer cache utilization. If the *keep* and *recycle* buffer caches are being used, the *cacheobjcnt.sql* query can be run to get an idea on how many objects have been assigned to each cache:

🖫 cacheobjcnt.sql

```
select
      decode(cachehint, 0, 'default', 1,
      'keep', 2, 'recycle', null) cache,
      count(*) objects
from
      sys.seg$ s
where
      s.user#  in
      (select
          user#
       from
          sys.user$
       where
          name not in ('sys','system'))
group by
      decode(cachehint, 0, 'default', 1,
      'keep', 2, 'recycle', null)
order by
   1;
```

Output may resemble something like the following:

```
CACHE       OBJECTS
----------------
default        2023
keep              5
```

Finally, it will be helpful to analyze the buffer cache activity from time to time to see how it is being utilized. The *buffutl.sql* script will show how full the cache currently is along with the state of the buffers in the cache:

💾 buffutl.sql

```
select
        'free' buffer_state,
        nvl(sum(blocksize) / 1024 ,0) amt_kb
from
        sys.x$bh a,
        sys.ts$ b
where
        state = 0  and
        a.ts#  =  b.ts#
union all
select
        'read/mod' buffer_state,
        nvl(sum(blocksize) / 1024 ,0) amt_kb
from
        sys.x$bh a,
        sys.ts$ b
where
        state = 1  and
        a.ts#  =  b.ts#
union all
select
        'read/notmod',
        nvl(sum(blocksize) / 1024 ,0) amt_kb
from
        sys.x$bh a,
        sys.ts$ b
where
        state = 2  and
        a.ts#  =  b.ts#
union all
select
        'being read' buffer_state,
        nvl(sum(blocksize) / 1024 ,0) amt_kb
from
        sys.x$bh a,
        sys.ts$ b
where
        state = 3  and
        a.ts#  =  b.ts#
order by
        1;
```

Output from the above query might look something like this:

```
BUFFER_STATE       AMT_KB
----------------------
being read           5920
```

```
free              23568
read/mod          47952
read/notmod           0
```

Hopefully this has provided a good overview of how to interrogate the buffer cache, so now the next area to be examined is the shared pool.

Troubleshooting the Shared Pool

The four metrics below are revealed by the *memsnap.sql* query, after the buffer cache hit ratio and concern the shared pool. Execution response times can be adversely affected if Oracle has to handle parse activity, perform object definition lookups or manage other code-related or reference tasks. The shared pool helps Oracle keep these reference-related activities to a minimum by holding SQL statements, along with code and object definitions, in memory.

As with the data cache, properly sizing the shared pool can be tricky and often involves trial and error. The *memsnap.sql* query reveals that a shared pool that is sized too small has the following characteristics:

- Zero or near-zero percent free in the pool after the database has only been up a short while.

- A library cache hit ratio that is below average (95% or below).

- Many object reloads due to definitions being forced from the pool prematurely.

- A below average data dictionary cache hit ratio (95% or below).

The last three metrics mentioned above should be viewed in the same light as the buffer cache hit ratio, in that delta measurements often produce more meaningful results than cumulative measurements, and some databases will perform quite well with measures that appear non-optimal.

With respect to the percent free in the shared pool, a near zero reading after the database has been up for some time is probably fine. But if the pool drops to zero free shortly after Oracle is started, there is a strong indication that it may be sized too small.

When Does Less Become More?

So, why not just size the shared pool to some huge number and be done? First, as with sizing the data cache, it is important keep an eye on available memory at the server level, so that paging or swapping is not induced when RAM is added to the shared pool.

However, the main reason to not oversize the shared pool is that sometimes a large pool actually causes reduced response times. How can this happen? The simple explanation is that it takes Oracle longer to search for object definitions or SQL statements in a shared pool that is gargantuan.

Oracle will always try and reuse SQL statements to keep from re-parsing a query, and while this can certainly reduce execution times when a shared pool is sized correctly, it can actually hinder progress when the pool is so large that Oracle wastes time interrogating it.

Viewing Shared Pool Usage Internals

While the global ratios and metrics can provide a rough idea of how efficient the shared pool is, looking deeper will provide more details on how the pool is being utilized and whether it is sized correctly.

The two main areas of the shared pool are the library and data dictionary caches. The library cache holds commonly used SQL statements, basically database code objects. One excellent method of improving performance in Oracle is to encourage the reuse of SQL statements so that expensive parse operations are avoided. The library cache assists this tuning effort.

The data dictionary cache enables the sharing of object definition information. The dictionary cache stores the description of database structures so that needed structure references can be resolved as quickly as possible.

There are three queries that can be used to extract the details of library cache usage. The *libdet.sql* script will show which object types are taking longer to find than others:

🖫 **libdet.sql**

```
select
        namespace,
        gets,
        round(gethitratio*100,2) gethitratio,
        pins,
        round(pinhitratio*100,2) pinhitratio,
        reloads,
        invalidations
from
        sys.v_$librarycache
order by
        1;
```

	NAMESPACE	GETS	GETHITRATIO	PINS	PINHITRATIO	RELOADS	INVALIDATIONS
1	BODY	7755	99.47	7761	99.34	0	0
2	CLUSTER	9962	99.84	6838	99.62	0	0
3	INDEX	682	54.99	408	20.34	0	0
4	JAVA DATA	16	62.5	61	73.77	2	0
5	JAVA RESOURCE	0	100	0	100	0	0
6	JAVA SOURCE	16	81.25	22	50	2	0
7	OBJECT	0	100	0	100	0	0
8	PIPE	0	100	0	100	0	0
9	SQL AREA	2491828	99.56	11586427	99.8	1039	5494
10	TABLE/PROCEDURE	499978	99	3052161	99.64	1338	0
11	TRIGGER	44032	99.92	44039	99.91	0	0

Figure 5.25: *Extracting the Library Cache Details*

Bottleneck or wait-based analysis can be used in addition to ratios and drill down queries to get an idea of overall library cache health.

The *libwait.sql* query provides clues about whether Oracle has been waiting for library cache activities:

libwait.sql

```
select
        b.name,
        nvl(max(a.total_waits),0)
from
        sys.v_$system_event a,
        sys.v_$event_name b
where
        a.event (+)  = b.name and
        b.name in ('latch free','library cache load lock',
                   'library cache lock','library cache pin')
group by
        b.name
```

Output from the above script might resemble the following:

```
NAME                         WAITS
---------------------------------
latch free                      16
library cache load lock          2
library cache lock               0
library cache pin                0
```

Seeing increasing numbers of waits for the above events could indicate an undersized shared pool. Dig even deeper into the library cache and uncover exactly which objects currently reside in the cache.

The *libobj.sql* script will show everything a DBA needs to know on this front, but be forewarned as this script can return large amounts of data in databases with large shared pools and many references to code and data objects:

libobj.sql

```
select
        owner,
        name,
        type,
        sharable_mem,
        loads,
        executions,
        locks,
        pins,
        kept
from
        sys.v_$db_object_cache
order by
        type asc;
```

	OWNER	NAME	TYPE	SHARABLE_MEM	LOADS
8	[NULL]	select i.obj#, i.flags, u.name, o.name from sys.obj$ o, sys.user$ u, ind$ idx, sys.indpart$ i	CURSOR	11416	1
9	[NULL]	select /*+ rule */ bucket_cnt, row_cnt, cache_cnt, null_cnt, timestamp#, sample_size, minimum,	CURSOR	10468	1
10	[NULL]	select i.obj#, i.flags, u.name, o.name from sys.obj$ o, sys.user$ u, ind$ idx, sys.indpart$ i	CURSOR	1064	1
11	[NULL]	select /*+ rule */ bucket_cnt, row_cnt, cache_cnt, null_cnt, timestamp#, sample_size, minimum,	CURSOR	1068	1
12	[NULL]	select grantee#,privilege#,nvl(col#,0),max(nvl(opti	CURSOR	1003	1
13	[NULL]	SELECT 1 FROM SYS.OBJ$ WHERE OWNER# =1	CURSOR	920	1
14	[NULL]	select privilege#,nvl(col#,0),max(nvl(option$,0))fro	CURSOR	982	1
15	[NULL]	select signature from triggerjavas$ where obj#=:1	CURSOR	4224	1
16	[NULL]	select class_name, class_factory, class_factory_	CURSOR	966	1
17	[NULL]	select class_name, class_factory, class_factory_	CURSOR	5516	1
18	[NULL]	select flags from triggerjavaf$ where obj#=:1	CURSOR	903	1
19	[NULL]	select flags from triggerjavaf$ where obj#=:1	CURSOR	4524	1
20	[NULL]	select text from view$ where rowid=:1	CURSOR	895	1
21	[NULL]	select text from view$ where rowid=:1	CURSOR	4252	1
22	[NULL]	select privilege#,nvl(col#,0),max(nvl(option$,0))fro	CURSOR	6848	1
23	[NULL]	SELECT 1 FROM SYS.OBJ$ WHERE OWNER# =1	CURSOR	6960	1
24	[NULL]	insert into uet$ (segfile#,segblock#,ext#,ts#,file#,b	CURSOR	5756	1
25	[NULL]	select count (*), state from SYSTEM.DEF$_AQER	CURSOR	940	1

Figure 5.26: *Drilling Down into the Library Cache*

Using the above script, it is possible to see how often an object has been loaded into the cache. The presence of many loads could indicate that the object is continuously being forced from the cache, which would potentially degrade performance.

If the object is a code object, such as a procedure or package, the code should be pinned in the cache to stop it from being removed. In the above query, reference the *kept* column to see which code objects, if any, have already been pinned.

The *dbms_shared_pool* package is used to pin or unpin code objects to and from the library cache. For example, if there is a frequently referenced procedure called *eradmin.add_admission* and the goal is to make sure that it would always be found in the library cache for quick reference, the following code would be used:

```
exec sys.dbms_shared_pool.keep('ERADMIN.ADD_ADMISSION','P');
```

Performing a pin keeps the code handy at all times. Pinned objects are also impervious to an *alter system flush shared_pool* command.

While this technique works well for code objects, what about regular SQL statements? How can they be kept in the shared pool so that parse operations are minimized? The easiest method is to ensure that user sessions are launching identical SQL statements, which allows reuse to occur in the cache.

If Oracle detects that a user process has launched an identical SQL statement that is already present in the cache, it will reuse the statement rather than parse and load it into memory. Using literals in SQL statements instead of bind variables can greatly hinder this process from occurring. Again, the key to statement reuse is that the SQL has to be identical, and the use of literals in SQL statements can entirely negate this.

If a DBA is not able to encase the user's SQL in applications or stored code objects to ensure bind variables are being used instead of literals, what should be done? In version 8.1.6, Oracle quietly introduced the *cursor_sharing* parameter, which can deal with the problem of literals in otherwise identical SQL statements in a hurry.

If this parameter is set to *force*, Oracle will substitute bind variables in the place of literals in any SQL statement and place it into the library cache. This permits any statement submitted subsequently to be reused, as long as the only difference is its bind variable(s).

Is there anything else that should be looked into with respect to the shared pool? One other area of interest is the data dictionary cache.

More Shared Pool Metrics

To see how often Oracle is finding the system references it needs in the data dictionary, the *dictdet.sql* script below can be used. The results will be sorted from best-hit ratio to worst:

🖫 dictdet.sql

```
select
        parameter,
        usage,
        gets,
        getmisses,
        100 - round((getmisses/
        (gets + getmisses) * 100),2) hit_ratio
from
        sys.v_$rowcache
where
        gets + getmisses <> 0
order by
        5 desc;
```

	PARAMETER	USAGE	GETS	GETMISSES	HIT_RATIO
1	dc_profiles	1	37318	1	100
2	dc_tablespaces	20	287977	20	99.99
3	dc_users	39	393939	42	99.99
4	dc_rollback_segments	12	106272	11	99.99
5	dc_user_grants	36	172771	48	99.97
6	dc_files	14	35355	14	99.96
7	dc_usernames	18	94137	35	99.96
8	dc_sequences	5	3426	18	99.48
9	dc_global_oids	19	1477	19	98.73
10	dc_tablespace_quotas	14	974	16	98.38
11	dc_object_ids	1037	82692	1521	98.19
12	dc_segments	629	41262	916	97.83
13	dc_objects	1638	77893	4367	94.69
14	dc_histogram_defs	1262	19592	2241	89.74
15	dc_constraints	1	1482	748	66.46
16	dc_table_scns	0	6	6	50

Figure 5.27: *Drilling Down into the Dictionary Cache*

Just as with the library cache, a high data dictionary cache hit ratio is desirable. Strive for a hit ratio between 90 - 100% with 95% being a good rule-of-thumb benchmark.

Note that when a database is first started, the overall data dictionary cache hit ratio, as well as the individual hit ratios in the above query, will not be at an optimal level. This is because all references to object definitions will be relatively new and as such, must be placed into the shared pool. Look for hit ratios between eighty and ninety percent for new database startups.

If, however, after a solid hour or two of steady database time, the data dictionary cache hit ratio has not increased to desirable levels, it is time to look into the possibility of increasing the *shared_pool_size* parameter.

While there is certainly more that can be investigated regarding shared pools, the areas covered in the above sections are the normal hot spots. Another related SGA issue that should be checked periodically is the redo log buffer.

Troubleshooting the Log Buffer

Sometimes a user process must wait for space in the redo log buffer. Oracle uses the log buffer to cache redo entries prior to writing them to disk, and if the buffer area is not large enough for the redo entry load, waits can occur. The log buffer is normally small in comparison with other regions of the SGA, and a small increase in size can significantly enhance throughput.

In high-update databases, no amount of disk tuning may relieve redo log bottlenecks because Oracle must push all updates, for all disks, into a single redo location as illustrated in Figure 5.28:

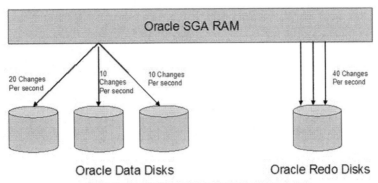

Redo is a natural bottleneck for high-update databases because Oracle redo disk must accept the sum of all disk update rates.

After redo and disk are optimized, the only way to relieve redo bottlenecks is faster redo storage

Figure 5.28: *Oracle Redo Bottleneck*

The *memsnap.sql* script contains two main numbers to watch for the log buffer, which are:

- *redo log space requests*; and
- *redo log wait time*

If either statistic strays too far from 0, then it may be desirable to increase the *log_buffer* parameter and add more memory to the redo log buffer.

The *log_buffer* is one of the most complex Oracle RAM region parameters to optimize, but it is a low resource parameter, only using a few megabytes of RAM. As a result, the goal in sizing the *log_buffer* is to set a value that results in the least overall amount of log-related wait events. The big issue with the log buffer is determining the optimal sizing for the *log_buffer* in a busy, high-DML database. Common wait events related to a too small *log_buffer* size include high *redo log space requests* and a too large *log_buffer* may result in high *log file sync* waits.

The following is an excerpt from an AWR report showing a database with an undersized *log_buffer*, in this case, where the DBA did not set the *log_buffer* parameter in their *init.ora* file:

Event	Waits	Timeouts	Avg Total Wait Time (s)	wait (ms)	Waits /txn
log file sequential read	4,275	0	229	54	0.0

log buffer space	12	0	3	235	0.0

```
Top 5 Timed Events
~~~~~~~~~~~~~~~~~~~                                      % Total
Event                             Waits     Time (s) Ela Time
-------------------------------- ----------- ----------- --------
CPU time                                      163,182    88.23
db file sequential read          1,541,854      8,551     4.62
log file sync                    1,824,469      8,402     4.54
log file parallel write          1,810,628      2,413     1.30
SQL*Net more data to client     15,421,202        687      .37
```

It is important to note that log buffer shortages do not always manifest in the Top 5 timed events, especially if there are other SGA pool shortages. The next example includes an Oracle10g database with an undersized log buffer of 512k, where there was a serious data buffer shortage causing excessive disk I/O:

```
Top 5 Timed Events
~~~~~~~~~~~~~~~~~~~                               % Total
Event                     Waits   Time (s)  DB Time     Wait Class
------------------------- --------- --------- --------- -----------
log file parallel write    9,670      291     55.67 System I/O
log file sync              9,293      278     53.12 Commit
CPU time                              225     43.12
db file parallel write     4,922      201     38.53 System I/O
control file parallel write 1,282      65     12.42 System I/O
```

Log Buffer Related Parameter Issues

In addition to resizing *log_buffer*, the hidden Oracle10g parameter *_log_io_size* can also be adjusted, but only at the direction of Oracle technical support, and then the *transactions_per_rollback_segment* parameters are adjusted. In 10g, the *_log_io_size* parameter governs the offload threshold and it defaults to *log_buffer/3*.

The *transactions_per_rollback_segment* parameter specifies the number of concurrent transactions each rollback segment is expected to handle. Today, most large databases use a log buffer between five and 10 megabytes. It is important to note that log buffer shortages do not always manifest in the Top 5 timed events, especially if there are other SGA pool shortages. It is important to remember that the optimal *log_buffer* size is a function of the commit rate and redo log volume.

After determining how the SGA is performing globally, the next step might be to look into memory usage at the session level to see which processes are consuming the most resources and making life miserable for everyone.

Investigating Session Memory Usage

Even though Oracle has built-in governors, it is not uncommon for one or two users to cause runtime problems that plague an entire database. The problem could be a runaway process, an untuned batch procedure or other user-initiated operation. Sometimes user connection memory consumption can get out of hand, and extreme cases can cause headaches at both the database and operating system level, causing ORA-4030 errors.

If the database server does not have an overabundance of memory, it is good practice to periodically check to see who the heavy memory users are, along with the total percentage of memory each user consumes. If there are one or two users who have more than 15-50% of the total memory usage, then the sessions should be investigated further to see the kind of activities they are performing.

The *memhog.sql* script can be used to find the sessions that use the most memory in a database:

🖫 memhog.sql

```
select
        sid,
        username,
        round(total_user_mem/1024,2) mem_used_in_kb,
        round(100 * total_user_mem/total_mem,2) mem_percent
from
(select
    b.sid sid,
    nvl(b.username,p.name) username,
    sum(value) total_user_mem
from
    sys.v_$statname c,
    sys.v_$sesstat a,
    sys.v_$session b,
    sys.v_$bgprocess p
where
        a.statistic#=c.statistic# and
        p.paddr (+) = b.paddr and
        b.sid=a.sid and
        c.name in ('session pga memory','session uga memory')
group by
        b.sid, nvl(b.username,p.name)),
(select
        sum(value) total_mem
from
        sys.v_$statname c,
        sys.v_$sesstat a
where
        a.statistic#=c.statistic# and
        c.name in ('session pga memory','session uga memory'))
order by
        3 desc;
```

	SID	USERNAME	MEM_USED_IN_KB	MEM_PERCENT
1	2	DBW0	740.92	18.28
2	14	SYS	685.63	16.91
3	7	SNP0	417.76	10.31
4	3	LGWR	295.21	7.28
5	5	SMON	275.42	6.79
6	13	SYS	232.14	5.73
7	8	SNP1	217.38	5.36
8	11	SNP4	216.77	5.35
9	9	SNP2	200.73	4.95
10	10	SNP3	200.73	4.95
11	12	DBSNMP	188.45	4.65
12	4	CKPT	172.29	4.25
13	6	RECO	150.95	3.72
14	22	SYS	86.88	2.14
15	1	PMON	76.39	1.88

Figure 5.29: *Sample Output Showing the Top Memory Users in a Database*

Another metric shown in the *memsnap.sql* script is the parse to execute ratio. It shows the percentage of SQL executed that did not incur a hard parse. Low values might indicate that users are executing SQL with many hard coded literals instead of bind variables within the application. High values (90% +) generally indicate Oracle is saving precious CPU resources by avoiding heavy parse tasks.

While the above figures illustrate the session memory usage within Oracle's program global areas (PGA) and user global areas (UGA), another area that should be checked into is sort activity.

Investigating Sorts

The SGA is not the only memory structure used by Oracle for database work. One of the other memory regions used by Oracle8i and below for normal activity is an area set aside for sort actions. When a sort operation occurs, Oracle attempts to perform the sort in a memory space that exists at the operating system level. If the sort is too large to be contained within this space, it will continue the sort on disk; specifically, in the user's assigned temporary tablespace.

Techniques to include in the overall performance strategy are those that relate to minimizing the amount of overall sort activity, and especially sort activity that takes place on disk. A good place to start is to understand what things cause sorts in the first place. A list of sort-related commands and SQL-related options include:

- CREATE, ALTER INDEX … REBUILD
- DISTINCT
- ORDER BY

- GROUP BY

- UNION

- INTERSECT

- MINUS

- IN, NOT IN

- Certain unindexed joins

- Certain correlated subqueries

All of these SQL commands have the potential to create a sort. The probability of knowing which queries will sort entirely in memory and which ones will be forced to go to disk is low; however, it is possible to get a feel for the overall sort performance by looking at the memory sort ratio that is contained in the output from the *memsnap.sql* query.

As has already been mentioned, when a sort exhausts its memory allotment, it will then be forced to go to disk, the actual place being the user's temporary tablespace assignment. Oracle records the overall number of sorts that are satisfied in memory as well as those that end up being finalized on disk. These numbers can be used to calculate the percentage of memory sorts versus disk sorts and get a feel for how fast the sort activity is being resolved.

If the memory sort ratio falls below 90%, increasing the parameters devoted to memory sorts, *sort_area_size* and *sort_area_retained_size*, may help. In some cases, individual users may possess the ability to alter their own sessions and increase their *sort_area_size* assignments. As a DBA, it may be desirable to restrict users that have the *alter session* privilege so that this does not occur.

Troubleshooting Oracle Sorting

As has been noted, a serious problem in Oracle8i was the requirement that all dedicated connections use a one-size-fits-all *sort_area_size*. Oracle9i introduced the option of running automatic PGA memory management using the *pga_aggregate_target* parameter.

When the *pga_aggregate_target* parameter is set and dedicated Oracle connections are being used, Oracle will ignore all of the PGA parameters in the Oracle file including *sort_area_size*, *hash_area_size* and *sort_area_retained_size*. Oracle recommends that the value of *pga_aggregate_target* be set to the amount of remaining memory (less a 10 % overhead for other UNIX tasks) on the UNIX server after the instance has been started.

Once the *pga_aggregate_target* has been set, Oracle will automatically manage PGA memory allocation based upon the individual needs of each Oracle connection. Oracle allows the *pga_aggregate_target* parameter to be modified at the instance level with the *alter system* command, thereby allowing the total RAM region available to Oracle to be adjusted dynamically.

Oracle9i also introduced a new parameter called *workarea_size_policy*. When this parameter is set to *automatic*, all Oracle connections will benefit from the shared PGA memory. When *workarea_size_policy* is set to *manual*, connections will allocate memory according to the values for the *sort_area_size* parameter. Under the automatic mode, Oracle tries to maximize the number of work areas that are using optimal memory and uses one-pass memory for the others.

In addition to increasing the amount of memory devoted to sorting, it is also good to hunt down inefficient SQL that cause needless sorts. For example, *union all* does not cause a sort, whereas *union* does in a SQL query to eliminate duplicate rows. The *distinct* keyword is often coded inappropriately, especially by folks transferring from Microsoft Access, which has historically used *distinct* for nearly every query.

The two final metrics shown in the *memsnap.sql* script deal with *buffer busy waits* and the *latch miss ratio*.

buffer busy waits

buffer busy waits occur when a process needs to access a data block in the buffer cache but cannot because it is being used by another process. So, it must wait. *buffer busy waits* normally center around contention for rollback segments, too small an *initrans* setting for tables or insufficient *freelists* for tables.

The remedy for each situation would be to increase the number of rollback segments or to alter tables for larger *initrans* settings to allow for more transactions per data block and more *freelists*. With the automatic segment management feature in Oracle9i, locally managed tablespaces can make the *freelist* problem a thing of the past, while the UNDO tablespace feature of 9i can help remedy any rollback contention problem.

However, segment header contention will still occur when concurrent tasks attempt to insert into the same table, and multiple *freelists* are required to remove these sources of *buffer busy waits*.

When using Oracle9i and above, the *bufobjwaits.sql* script below can be used to reveal what objects have been the sources of buffer busy waits.

🖫 bufobjwaits.sql

```
select
        owner,
        object_name,
        object_type,
        value waits
from
        sys.v_$segment_statistics
where
        (statistic_name = 'buffer busy waits' and value > 0)
order by
        1,2;
```

OWNER	OBJECT_NAME	OBJECT_TYPE	WAITS
USR1	TAB1	TABLE	3
USR1	TAB2	TABLE	2
USR1	TAB3	TABLE	2

Troubleshooting Latches

Latches protect the many memory structures in Oracle's SGA. They ensure that one and only one process at a time can run or modify any memory structure at the same instant. Much more restrictive than locks, which at least allow for some collective user interaction, latches have no queuing mechanism. Therefore, if the first attempt is not successful, it will be necessary to continually retry until successful.

Common indicators of latch contention are a *latch miss ratio*, which records willing-to-wait mode latch requests, and the *latch immediate miss ratio*, which records no-wait mode latch requests. These statistics reflect how often latch requests were made and satisfied without waiting. If either of these exceeds 1%, the next step is to drill down further into latching details to identify what latches are responsible for the contention. To drill down into latch miss details, use the *latchdet.sql* script:

💾 latchdet.sql

```
select
      name,
      gets,
      round(misses*100/decode(gets,0,1,gets),2) misses,
      round(spin_gets*100/decode(misses,0,1,misses),2) spins,
      immediate_gets igets,
      round(immediate_misses*100/
      decode(immediate_gets,0,1,immediate_gets),2) imisses,
      sleeps
from
      sys.v_$latch
order by
      2 desc;
```

	HAME	GETS	MISSES	SPINS	IGETS	IMISSES	SLEEPS
1	cache buffers chains	44409592	0	0	4724	0	30
2	cache buffers lru chain	2374631	0	0	0	0	0
3	library cache	572680	.01	0	306	0	155
4	row cache objects	399355	0	0	155	0	52
5	session idle bit	198677	0	0	0	0	0
6	shared pool	164652	0	0	0	0	1
7	enqueues	149031	0	0	0	0	0
8	messages	134876	0	0	0	0	0
9	checkpoint queue latch	82846	0	0	0	0	0
10	redo writing	82507	0	0	0	0	7
11	session allocation	66204	0	0	0	0	0
12	enqueue hash chains	63572	0	0	0	0	0
13	undo global data	29407	0	0	0	0	0
14	redo allocation	23957	.01	0	0	0	8
15	active checkpoint queue latch	20344	0	0	0	0	0
16	session timer	20297	0	0	0	0	0
17	sort extent pool	8813	0	0	0	0	0
18	JOX SGA heap latch	3720	0	0	3120	0	0
19	virtual circuit queues	3046	0	0	0	0	0
20	library cache load lock	2526	0	0	0	0	0
21	cache buffer handles	2453	.08	0	0	0	2
22	shared java pool	2289	0	0	0	0	0
23	transaction allocation	1991	.1	0	0	0	2
24	dml lock allocation	1252	0	0	0	0	0
25	longop free list	998	0	0	0	0	0
26	session switching	983	0	0	0	0	0
27	transaction branch allocation	976	0	0	0	0	0

To see whether any sessions are currently waiting for latches, use the *currlwaits.sql* script:

currlwaits.sql

```
select
     a.sid,
     username,
     a.event,
     a.p1text,
     a.p1,
     a.p2text,
     a.p2,
     a.seq#,
     a.wait_time,
     a.state
from
     sys.v_$session_wait a,
     sys.v_$session b,
     sys.v_$latchname c
where
     a.sid = b.sid and
     a.p2 = c.latch# and
     a.event in
     (select
            name
       from
         sys.v_$event_name
 where
         name like '%latch%')
order by
        1;
```

It can be difficult to catch an actual session latch wait since they rarely consume much time.

Troubleshooting I/O Hotspots

When complaints begin to surface about the database's performance, the root cause can often be traced to one or more issues with I/O. The one thing to keep in mind when the I/O of the database is beginning to be monitored is that the success of the physical design model is what is really being reviewed.

All the physical storage characteristics and placements, the table and index designs and the speed with which it all works are on display when I/O is monitored. Because a database's main index of performance is measured by how fast I/O needs are satisfied, it is the DBA's responsibility to quickly interrogate Oracle to determine if a reported database slowdown is I/O related.

How can such a task be accomplished quickly? While it is true that every situation is different in some regard, one roadmap that can be regularly used is the following:

- Obtain global measures regarding the I/O of the database and note any standout values.

- Examine global statistics regarding how database objects are being accessed.

- Move deeper by examining the I/O of the storage structures and noting where the hotspots appear to be on the disk.

- From storage, uncover what objects appear to be the most in demand.

- If the reported slowdown is currently active, obtain metrics regarding the leading sessions with respect to I/O.

Once the objects and users that are responsible for the most I/O issues are identified, drill further into the situation by locating the SQL being issued. Next, walk through each of these steps in detail and see how they can quickly pinpoint the I/O hotspots and bottlenecks in the database.

Global Basic Queries

The first step in unraveling any I/O puzzles in the database is to make a quick check of some of the global database I/O metrics. A query such as the *globiostats.sql* script can be used to get a bird's eye view of a database's I/O:

🖫 globiostats.sql

```
select
   name,
   value
from
   sys.v_$sysstat
where
   name in
     ('consistent changes',
      'consistent gets',
      'db block changes',
      'db block gets',
      'physical reads',
      'physical writes',
      'sorts (disk)',
      'user commits',
      'user rollbacks'
     )
 order by
 1;
```

Output from the above query might look like the following:

```
NAME                         VALUE
----------------------------
consistent changes           1
consistent gets     70983
db block changes      243
db block gets         612
physical reads      11591
physical writes        52
sorts (disk)            0
user commits           26
user rollbacks          1
```

It is also a good idea to do a cursory, global check of the system-level wait events to get an idea of the I/O bottlenecks that may be occurring. A script like the *syswaits.sql* script can be used to perform such a check:

🖫 **syswaits.sql**

```
select
   event,
   total_waits,
   round(100 * (total_waits / sum_waits),2) pct_waits,
   time_wait_sec,
   round(100 * (time_wait_sec / greatest(sum_time_waited,1)),2)
   pct_time_waited,
   total_timeouts,
   round(100 * (total_timeouts / greatest(sum_timeouts,1)),2)
   pct_timeouts,
   average_wait_sec
from
(select
      event,
      total_waits,
      round((time_waited / 100),2) time_wait_sec,
      total_timeouts,
      round((average_wait / 100),2) average_wait_sec
from
      sys.v_$system_event
where
      event not in
('lock element cleanup',
 'pmon timer',
 'rdbms ipc message',
 'rdbms ipc reply',
 'smon timer',
 'SQL*Net message from client',
 'SQL*Net break/reset to client',
 'SQL*Net message to client',
 'SQL*Net more data from client',
 'dispatcher timer',
 'Null event',
 'parallel query dequeue wait',
 'parallel query idle wait - Slaves',
 'pipe get',
 'PL/SQL lock timer',
 'slave wait',
 'virtual circuit status',
 'WMON goes to sleep') and
event not like 'DFS%' and
event not like 'KXFX%'),
(select
      sum(total_waits) sum_waits,
      sum(total_timeouts) sum_timeouts,
      sum(round((time_waited / 100),2)) sum_time_waited
from
      sys.v_$system_event
where
      event not in
('lock element cleanup',
 'pmon timer',
 'rdbms ipc message',
 'rdbms ipc reply',
 'smon timer',
 'SQL*Net message from client',
 'SQL*Net break/reset to client',
 'SQL*Net message to client',
```

```
 'SQL*Net more data from client',
 'dispatcher timer',
 'Null event',
 'parallel query dequeue wait',
 'parallel query idle wait - Slaves',
 'pipe get',
 'PL/SQL lock timer',
 'slave wait',
 'virtual circuit status',
 'WMON goes to sleep') and
 event not like 'DFS%' and
 event not like 'KXFX%')
order by
   2 desc, 1 asc;
```

Output from this query could resemble something like the following:

	EVENT	TOTAL_WAITS	PCT_WAITS	TIME_WAIT_SEC	PCT_TIME_WAITED	TOTAL_TIMEOUTS	PCT_TIMEOUTS	AVERAGE_WAIT_SEC
1	control file parallel write	13763	66.1	11.8	43.77	0	0	0
2	direct path write	2216	10.64	4.18	15.5	0	0	0
3	db file sequential read	1874	9	1.76	6.53	0	0	0
4	control file sequential read	1805	8.67	3.86	14.32	0	0	0
5	direct path read	319	1.53	1.11	4.12	0	0	0
6	refresh controlfile command	231	1.11	1.7	6.31	0	0	.01
7	log file parallel write	165	.79	.1	.37	0	0	0
8	db file scattered read	130	.62	.11	.41	0	0	0
9	file open	130	.62	.75	2.78	0	0	.01
10	log file sync	51	.24	.5	1.85	0	0	.01
11	db file parallel write	46	.22	.39	1.45	0	0	.01
12	file identify	35	.17	.06	.22	0	0	0
13	latch free	22	.11	.52	1.93	21	100	.02
14	library cache pin	12	.06	0	0	0	0	0
15	buffer busy waits	10	.05	.12	.45	0	0	.01
16	log file sequential read	5	.02	0	0	0	0	0
17	log file single write	5	.02	0	0	0	0	0
18	instance state change	1	0	0	0	0	0	0
19	library cache load lock	1	0	0	0	0	0	0
20	reliable message	1	0	0	0	0	0	0

Figure 5.31: *System Event Waits Output*

A few quick things to note about the output from the waits SQL script:

- Numerous waits for the *db file scattered read* event may indicate a problem with table scans.

- Many waits for the *latch free* event could indicate excessive amounts of logical I/O activity.

- High wait times for the *enqueue* event pinpoint a problem with lock contention.

After getting a feel for the I/O numbers at a global level, it is possible to begin to work further down into what is really going on under the covers.

Determine Global Object Access Patterns

Oracle has come a long way in helping the database professional determine how objects in the database are being accessed. Oracle9i, in particular, introduced some wonderful new statistical views that can be queried to get a handle on object access patterns. For databases older and version 9i, there are still methods that can be used to investigate the I/O occurring against the database.

A global sweep of access pattern activity is a good starting place. A query such as the *globaccpatt.sql* script can be used to get that information:

⊟ globaccpatt.sql

```
select
   name,
   value
from
   sys.v_$sysstat
where
   name in
   ('table scans (cache partitions)',
    'table scans (direct read)',
    'table scans (long tables)',
    'table scans (rowid ranges)',
    'table scans (short tables)',
    'table fetch by rowid',
    'table fetch continued row')
order by
   1;
```

Results from such a query might look like this:

```
NAME                                    VALUE
-------------------------------------
table fetch by rowid             146540
table fetch continued row           698
table scans (cache partitions)        0
table scans (direct read)                    0
table scans (long tables)             0
table scans (rowid ranges)                   0
table scans (short tables)          262
```

When reviewing the output from the above query, the following items should be the focus:

- Large-table full-table scans can indicate sub-optimal SQL and/or missing indexes, cases where the SQL needlessly reads all blocks in the table.

- The Ion for Oracle tool can also help identify the database signature over time.

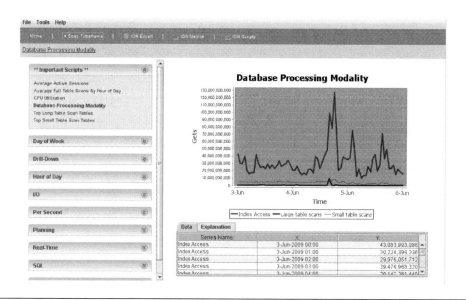

Examine Storage-level Statistics

Understanding where the storage-level hot spots of a database are is beneficial for a couple of reasons. First, it offers a good way to get a feel for overworked physical disks by viewing I/O statistics at the tablespace and datafile levels. If a particular disk or set of disks is under too much strain, the tablespaces can be relocated to less-used devices or new tablespaces can be created on different disks and hot objects can be moved onto them, assuming, of course, that there are extra disks available. Also, if standard DBA practices have been followed and indexes are placed in their own tablespace, the I/O statistics for that tablespace can be examined to determine if the indexes are actually being used. The *fileio.sql* below can be used to gather this information:

🖫 **fileio.sql**

```
select
    d.name file_name,
    c.name tablespace_name,
    b.phyrds,
    b.phywrts,
    b.phyblkrd,
    b.phyblkwrt,
    b.readtim,
    b.writetim
from
    sys.v_$datafile a,
    sys.v_$filestat b,
    sys.ts$ c,
    sys.v_$dbfile d,
    sys.file$ e
 where
    a.file# = b.file#
 and
    a.file# = d.file#
 and
    e.ts# = c.ts#
 and
    e.file# = d.file#
union all
select
    v.fnnam file_name,
    c.name tablespace_name,
    b.phyrds,
    b.phywrts,
    b.phyblkrd,
    b.phyblkwrt,
    b.readtim,
    b.writetim
from
    sys.v_$tempfile a,
    sys.v_$tempstat b,
    sys.ts$ c,
    sys.x$kccfn v,
    sys.x$ktfthc hc
where
    a.file# = b.file#
and
    a.file# = hc.ktfthctfno
and
    hc.ktfthctsn = c.ts#
```

```
and
   v.fntyp = 7
and
   v.fnnam is not null
and
   v.fnfno = hc.ktfthctfno
and
   hc.ktfthctsn = c.ts#
order by
   3 desc;
```

Output from one of the previous queries would look like this:

	FILE_NAME	TABLESPACE_NAME	PHYRDS	PHYWRTS	PHYBLKRD	PHYBLKWRT	READTIM	WRITETIM
1	D:\ORACLE\ORA92\O92\SYSTEM01.DBF	SYSTEM	22735	1318	29987	1318	6581	331
2	D:\ORACLE\ORA92\O92\XDB01.DBF	XDB	2979	2	2990	2	850	5
3	D:\ORACLE\ORA92\O92\OEM_REPOSITORY.DBF	OEM_REPOSITORY	1582	2	1582	2	487	5
4	D:\ORACLE\ORA92\O92\USERS01.DBF	USERS	554	55	619	55	213	20
5	D:\ORACLE\ORA92\O92\DRSYS01.DBF	DRSYS	282	2	282	2	129	3
6	D:\ORACLE\ORA92\O92\TOOLS01.DBF	TOOLS	84	0	84	0	48	0
7	D:\ORACLE\ORA92\O92\UNDOTBS01.DBF	UNDOTBS1	46	8567	46	8567	709	484
8	D:\ORACLE\ORA92\O92\INDX01.DBF	INDX	11	2	11	2	49	5
9	D:\ORACLE\ORA92\O92\AUTOSEG.ORA	AUTOSEG	6	2	6	2	24	2

Figure 5.33: *Datafile and Tablespace I/O Details*

Some issues to consider when viewing the output of these queries include:

- A lot of activity in the SYSTEM tablespace and datafiles may indicate a lot of recursive calls (space management, etc.). Temporary tablespaces devoted to sort activity, thereby showing higher volumes of physical I/O, could indicate a problem with excessive disk activity.

- A quick review of all the physical I/O for each drive/file system will help the DBA get a feel for the overworked disks on the server. If there are underutilized disk drives with their own controllers, it would be prudent to consider relocating some tablespaces that exhibit high I/O characteristics to those drives.

Now that tablespace and datafile hotspots can be identified, the next step is to determine the actual objects under constant pressure.

Locating Hot I/O Objects

Once the locations of the hotspots in the database are known with respect to storage structures, it is time to drill further down and locate the objects that are most in demand. There is no doubt that hub tables in a system can cause a major I/O bottleneck if they are not correctly designed and implemented.

To get an idea of which objects have been the favorite of a database's SQL calls, run the following *toptables.sql* query, which gets the top 100 objects as determined by SQL statement execution:

🖫 **toptables.sql**

```
select
   table_owner "table owner",
   table_name "table name",
```

```
   command "command issued",
   0 - executions   "executions",
   disk_reads "disk reads",
   gets "buffer gets",
   rows_processed "rows processed"
from
(select
        distinct executions,
                command,
                table_owner,
                table_name,
                gets,
                rows_processed,
                disk_reads
 from
(select
        decode (a.command_type ,
                2, 'insert ' ,
                3,'select ',
                6, 'update  ' ,
                7, 'delete ' ,
                26,'table lock  ') command ,
                c.owner table_owner,
                c.name table_name ,
                sum(a.disk_reads) disk_reads ,
                sum(0 - a.executions) executions ,
                sum(a.buffer_gets) gets  ,
                sum(a.rows_processed) rows_processed
 from
        sys.v_$sql  a ,
        sys.v_$object_dependency b ,
        sys.v_$db_object_cache   c
where
        a.command_type in (2,3,6,7,26)and
        b.from_address = a.address and
        b.to_owner = c.owner and
        b.to_name= c.name and
        c.type = 'table' and
        c.owner not in ('SYS','SYSTEM')
group by
        a.command_type , c.owner  , c.name )  )
where
        rownum <= 100;
```

Output from the above query might look like the results depicted in Figure 5.34:

	TABLE OWNER	TABLE NAME	COMMAND ISSUED	EXECUTIONS	DISK READS	BUFFER GETS	ROWS PROCESSED
1	ERADMIN	TESTXML_927	SELECT	13	2	131	0
2	ERADMIN	ADMISSION	SELECT	7	13	184	2508
3	ERADMIN	TESTXML_927NEW2	SELECT	4	0	94	0
4	ERADMIN	TESTLOB_NEW	SELECT	2	5	127	2
5	ERADMIN	ADMISSION_TEST	SELECT	1	1	111	0
6	ERADMIN	MEDICATION_DISP	SELECT	1	1	32	0
7	ERADMIN	PATIENT_PROCEDURE	SELECT	1	5	23	0
8	ERADMIN	TESTXML_927NEW	SELECT	1	0	53	3
9	WMSYS	WM$ENV_VARS	SELECT	1	8	403	1
10	WMSYS	WM$VERSIONED_TABLES	SELECT	1	8	403	1
11	WMSYS	WM$VERSION_HIERARCHY_TABLE	SELECT	1	8	403	1

Figure 5.34: *Top Tables Query Output*

Observing a single table with a lot of DML activity provides a clue that it may be a potential bottleneck for the system. Other things to consider when reviewing output from this query include:

- Small, frequently accessed tables should be considered candidates for the Oracle KEEP buffer pool.

- Large tables that are often accessed and scanned should be reviewed to determine if they could be partitioned. Partitioning can reduce scan times if only one or a handful of partitions can be scanned instead of the entire table.

- High amounts of disk reads for tables in the above query are red flags that can help identify partitioning possibilities.

If a DBA using Oracle9i or greater thinks that large tables are being scanned, the *v_$sql_plan* view can be used to validate those suspicions. The *largescan9i.sql* query uses this view to show which large tables, defined in the query as tables over 1MB, are being scanned in the database:

🖫 **largescan.sql**

```
select
   table_owner,
   table_name,
   table_type,
   size_kb,
   statement_count,
   reference_count,
   executions,
   executions * reference_count total_scans
from
   (select
       a.object_owner table_owner,
       a.object_name table_name,
       b.segment_type table_type,
       b.bytes / 1024 size_kb,
       sum(c.executions ) executions,
       count( distinct a.hash_value ) statement_count,
       count( * ) reference_count
   from
       sys.v_$sql_plan a,
       sys.dba_segments b,
       sys.v_$sql c
   where
       a.object_owner (+) = b.owner
   and
          a.object_name (+) = b.segment_name
and
          b.segment_type IN ('TABLE', 'TABLE PARTITION')
and
          a.operation LIKE '%TABLE%'
and
          a.options = 'FULL'
and
          a.hash_value = c.hash_value
and
          b.bytes / 1024 > 1024
group by
   a.object_owner,
   a.object_name,
   a.operation,
   b.bytes / 1024,
   b.segment_type
order by
   4 desc, 1, 2 );
```

Figure 5.35: *Output From the Large Table Scan Query*

After finding out what table is being accessed the most, the next move is to find out who is causing all the activity.

Find the Current I/O Session Bandits

If the complaint of poor performance is ongoing, connected sessions can be checked to see which users are impacting the system in undesirable ways.

First, get an idea of the percentage that each session is/has taken up with respect to I/O. One rule of thumb is that if any session is currently consuming 50% or more of the total I/O, that session and its SQL need to be investigated further to determine what activity it is engaged in.

If the concerns is just with physical I/O, the *physpctio.sql* query will provide the information needed:

💾 **physpctio.sql**

```
select
   sid,
   username,
   round(100 * total_user_io/total_io,2) tot_io_pct
from
(select
    b.sid sid,
    nvl(b.username,p.name) username,
    sum(value) total_user_io
 from
    sys.v_$statname c,
    sys.v_$sesstat a,
    sys.v_$session b,
    sys.v_$bgprocess p
 where
    a.statistic#=c.statistic# and
    p.paddr (+) = b.paddr and
    b.sid=a.sid and
    c.name in ('physical reads',
               'physical writes',
               'physical writes direct',
               'physical reads direct',
               'physical writes direct (lob)',
               'physical reads direct (lob)')
group by
    b.sid, nvl(b.username,p.name)),
(select
    sum(value) total_io
 from
    sys.v_$statname c,
    sys.v_$sesstat a
 where
    a.statistic#=c.statistic# and
```

```
        c.name in ('physical reads',
                   'physical writes',
                   'physical writes direct',
                   'physical reads direct',
                   'physical writes direct (lob)',
                   'physical reads direct (lob)'))
order by
     3 desc;
```

To see the total I/O picture, meaning both logical and physical I/O, the *totpctio.sql* query would be used instead:

💾 totpctio.sql

```
SELECT
     SID,
     USERNAME,
     ROUND(100 * TOTAL_USER_IO/TOTAL_IO,2) TOT_IO_PCT
FROM
(SELECT
        b.SID SID,
        nvl(b.USERNAME,p.NAME) USERNAME,
        SUM(VALUE) TOTAL_USER_IO
FROM
     sys.V_$STATNAME c,
     sys.V_$SESSTAT a,
     sys.V_$SESSION b,
     sys.v_$bgprocess p
WHERE
     a.STATISTIC#=c.STATISTIC# and
     p.paddr (+) = b.paddr and
     b.SID=a.SID and
     c.NAME in ('physical reads','physical writes',
                'consistent changes','consistent gets',
                'db block gets','db block changes',
                'physical writes direct',
                'physical reads direct',
                'physical writes direct (lob)',
                'physical reads direct (lob)')
GROUP BY
     b.SID, nvl(b.USERNAME,p.name)),
(select
        sum(value) TOTAL_IO
from
        sys.V_$STATNAME c,
        sys.V_$SESSTAT a
WHERE
        a.STATISTIC#=c.STATISTIC# and
        c.NAME in ('physical reads','physical writes',
                'consistent changes',
                'consistent gets','db block gets',
                'db block changes',
                'physical writes direct',
                'physical reads direct',
                'physical writes direct (lob)',
                'physical reads direct (lob)'))
ORDER BY
        3 DESC;
```

Regardless of which query is being used, the output might resemble something like the following:

```
SID USERNAME       TOT_IO_PCT
--------------------------------
 9  USR1               71.26
20  SYS                15.76
 5  SMON                7.11
 2  DBWR                4.28
12  SYS                 1.42
 6  RECO                 .12
 7  SNP0                 .01
10  SNP3                 .01
11  SNP4                 .01
 8  SNP1                 .01
 1  PMON                   0
 3  ARCH                   0
 4  LGWR                   0
```

In the above example, it would be prudent to examine the USR1 session to see what SQL calls are being made. In a subsequent chapter, how to do this will be shown in detail. The above queries are excellent weapons that can be used to quickly pinpoint problem I/O sessions.

If more detail with respect to the top I/O session in a database is required, use the rather large *topiousers.sql* query instead to see all the actual I/O numbers:

🖫 **topiousers.sql**

```
select
    b.sid sid,
    decode (b.username,null,e.name,b.username)
    user_name,
    d.spid os_id,
    b.machine machine_name,
    to_char(logon_time,'mm/dd/yy hh:mi:ss pm')
    logon_time,
    (sum(decode(c.name,'physical reads',value,0))
    +
    sum(decode(c.name,'physical writes',value,0))
    +
    sum(decode(c.name,
    'physical writes direct',value,0)) +
    sum(decode(c.name,
    'physical writes direct (lob)',value,0)) +
    sum(decode(c.name,
    'physical reads direct (lob)',value,0)) +
    sum(decode(c.name,
    'physical reads direct',value,0)))
    total_physical_io,
    (sum(decode(c.name,'db block gets',value,0))
    +
    sum(decode(c.name,
    'db block changes',value,0))  +
    sum(decode(c.name,'consistent changes',value,0)) +
    sum(decode(c.name,'consistent gets',value,0)) )
    total_logical_io,
    100 - 100 *(round ((sum (decode
    (c.name, 'physical reads', value, 0)) -
    sum (decode (c.name,
    'physical reads direct', value, 0))) /
    (sum (decode (c.name, 'db block gets',
```

```
    value, 1)) +
    sum (decode (c.name, 'consistent gets',
     value, 0))),3)) hit_ratio,
    sum(decode(c.name,'sorts (disk)',value,0))
    disk_sorts,
    sum(decode(c.name,'sorts (memory)',value,0))
    memory_sorts,
    sum(decode(c.name,'sorts (rows)',value,0))
    rows_sorted,
    sum(decode(c.name,'user commits',value,0))
    commits,
    sum(decode(c.name,'user rollbacks',value,0))
    rollbacks,
    sum(decode(c.name,'execute count',value,0))
    executions,
    sum(decode(c.name,'physical reads',value,0))
    physical_reads,
    sum(decode(c.name,'db block gets',value,0))
    db_block_gets,
    sum(decode(c.name,'consistent gets',value,0))
    consistent_gets,
    sum(decode(c.name,'consistent changes',value,0))
    consistent_changes
from
    sys.v_$sesstat a,
    sys.v_$session b,
    sys.v_$statname c,
    sys.v_$process d,
    sys.v_$bgprocess e
where
    a.statistic#=c.statistic#
and
    b.sid=a.sid
and
    d.addr = b.paddr
and
    e.paddr (+) = b.paddr
and
    c.name in
    ('physical reads',
     'physical writes',
     'physical writes direct',
     'physical reads direct',
     'physical writes direct (lob)',
     'physical reads direct (lob)',
     'db block gets',
     'db block changes',
     'consistent changes',
     'consistent gets',
     'sorts (disk)',
     'sorts (memory)',
     'sorts (rows)',
     'user commits',
     'user rollbacks',
     'execute count'
)
group by
    b.sid,
    d.spid,
    decode (b.username,null,e.name,b.username),
        b.machine,
        to_char(logon_time,'mm/dd/yy hh:mi:ss pm')
order by
    6 desc;
```

Output from the query above could look like the following:

	SID	USER_NAME	OS_ID	MACHINE_NAME	LOGON_TIME	TOTAL_PHYSICAL_IO	TOTAL_LOGICAL_IO	HIT_RATIO	DISK_SORTS	MEMORY_SORTS	ROWS_SORTED	COMMIT
1	2	DEMO	1064	EBT2K11	12/05/02 03:12:10 PM	9982	0	100	0	0	0	
2	12	ORA_MONITOR	2488	EBT2K\EBT2K08	12/12/02 05:28:18 PM	8527	59015775	100	0	289379	126302548	
3	5	SMON	296	EBT2K11	12/05/02 03:12:11 PM	2657	465527	99.4	0	78	175	
4	3	LGWR	980	EBT2K11	12/05/02 03:12:10 PM	34	0	100	0	0	0	
5	6	RECO	1220	EBT2K11	12/05/02 03:12:11 PM	1	1753	99.9	0	8	48	
6	1	PMON	1032	EBT2K11	12/05/02 03:12:09 PM	0	0	100	0	0	0	
7	4	CKPT	1144	EBT2K11	12/05/02 03:12:10 PM	0	0	100	0	0	0	
8	16	SYS	3956	EBT2K\ROBINAS	12/17/02 04:55:29 PM	0	4	100	0	0	0	
9	11	SYS	3096	EBT2K\ROBINAS	12/17/02 05:26:31 PM	0	235	100	0	66	27449	

Figure 5.36: *Sample Top I/O Users Detail Output*

Such a query can provide details about the actual, raw I/O numbers for each connected session. Armed with this information, it is then possible to drill down into each heavy-hitting I/O session to determine what SQL calls they are making and which sets of SQL are the I/O hogs.

While how to troubleshoot I/O from a user standpoint has been covered, it is best not to forget about all the system activity that is caused by Oracle itself. The next section will help with peering into those areas and uncovering any I/O issues that reside there.

Before leaving the topic of I/O hotspots, there are a couple of remaining items to mention in passing - examining background processes and monitoring rollback activity.

Examining Background Processes

How can a DBA tell if Oracle's DBWR, LGWR, ARCH or other background processes are experiencing I/O bottlenecks? The first step is to issue the *bgact.sql* query to get a general handle on DBWR and LGWR activity:

bgact.sql

```
select
   name,
   value
from
   sys.v_$sysstat
where
   (name like '%DBWR%'
or
    name in
       ('dirty buffers inspected',
        'summed dirty queue length',
        'write requests'))
or
       (name like '%redo%')
order by
    1;
```

The output from the above query might look like this:

```
NAME                                     VALUE
-----------------------------------------------
DBWR buffers scanned                         0
DBWR checkpoint buffers written            438
```

```
DBWR checkpoints                          0
DBWR cross instance writes                0
DBWR free buffers found                   0
DBWR lru scans                            0
DBWR make free requests                   0
DBWR revisited being-written buffer       0
DBWR summed scan depth               0
DBWR transaction table writes           151
DBWR undo block writes              154
dirty buffers inspected                   0
redo blocks written                     804
redo buffer allocation retries            0
redo entries                           1297
redo log space requests                   0
redo log space wait time                  0
redo log switch interrupts                0
redo ordering marks                       0
redo size                            329192
redo synch time                          54
redo synch writes                       116
redo wastage                          69528
redo write time                          79
redo writer latching time                 0
redo writes                             237
summed dirty queue length                 0
```

Seeing non-zero values for the DBWR summed dirty queue length typically indicates that buffers are being left in the write queue after a write request. This could signal that the DBWR process is falling behind and that more DBWR processes should be added to the system. Non-zero values for the *redo log space wait requests* and *redo log space wait time* statistics could indicate the log buffer setting is too low.

Archive log I/O problems can usually be viewed in the form of entries in the Oracle alert log, as in messages indicating waits for the archive log files to complete. Issuing a query like the *archhist.sql* script, which shows the number of logs written per day for the last 30 days, can yield an idea of how many logs the archive process writes per day:

💾 **archhist.sql**

```
select
   to_char(completion_time,'mm/dd/yy') completion_time,
   count(*)                            log_count
from
   sys.v_$archived_log
where
   sysdate - completion_time < 31
group by
   to_char(completion_time,'mm/dd/yy')
order by
   1 desc;
```

Once the overall I/O picture of Oracle's background processes has been reviewed, it is time to delve into specific areas like rollback segments.

Troubleshooting Rollback Activity

Undo segments can become hotspots for I/O activity, especially if a lot of DML activity is occurring in the database. Oracle writes data to individual undo segments to undo changes made to the Oracle database from within a transaction. Undo segments are also used to maintain read consistency for multiple users of modified data.

The *rolldet.sql* below can be used to check the amount of rollback I/O the database is experiencing:

🖫 rolldet.sql

```
select
   name,
   round ((rssize / 1024), 2) size_kb,
   shrinks,
   extends,
   gets,
   waits,
   writes,
   xacts,
   status,
   round ((hwmsize / 1024), 2) hw_kb
from
   sys.v_$rollstat a,
   sys.v_$rollname b
where
   (a.usn = b.usn)
order by
   name;
```

Figure 5.37 below shows a sample of the query output:

	NAME	SIZE_KB	SHRINKS	EXTENDS	GETS	WAITS	WRITES	XACTS	STATUS	HW_KB
1	RBS0	4088	0	0	3572	0	3624	0	ONLINE	4088
2	RBS1	4088	0	0	3573	0	6194	0	ONLINE	4088
3	RBS10	4088	0	0	3569	0	8252	0	ONLINE	4088
4	RBS11	4088	0	0	3568	0	1650	0	ONLINE	4088
5	RBS12	4088	0	0	3566	0	1266	0	ONLINE	4088
6	RBS13	4088	0	0	3566	0	1150	0	ONLINE	4088
7	RBS14	4088	0	0	3566	0	1420	0	ONLINE	4088
8	RBS15	4088	0	0	3566	0	1152	0	ONLINE	4088
9	RBS16	4088	0	0	3566	0	1480	0	ONLINE	4088
10	RBS17	4088	0	0	3566	0	4448	0	ONLINE	4088
11	RBS18	4088	0	0	3566	0	1436	0	ONLINE	4088
12	RBS19	4088	0	0	3567	0	4266	0	ONLINE	4088
13	RBS2	4088	0	0	3575	0	3874	0	ONLINE	4088
14	RBS20	4088	0	0	3566	0	994	0	ONLINE	4088
15	RBS21	4088	0	0	3566	0	1054	0	ONLINE	4088
16	RBS22	4088	0	0	3566	0	1044	0	ONLINE	4088
17	RBS23	4088	0	0	3566	0	1214	0	ONLINE	4088
18	RBS24	4088	0	0	3568	0	1556	0	ONLINE	4088
19	RBS25	4088	0	0	3568	0	1528	0	ONLINE	4088

Figure 5.37: *Rollback Activity Details*

To properly tune rollback I/O, first make sure that there are enough segments to accommodate the workload of the database. Constantly seeing a count of active undo segments equal to or near the number of rollbacks defined for the database is an indicator that more should be created.

An overall rollback contention ratio of 1% or higher is an indicator of too few rollbacks as well. Seeing wait counts greater than zero for each rollback segment is further evidence that more rollback segments should be created. When using Oracle9i or above, the UNDO tablespace feature can be used. It allows Oracle to automatically manage all rollback activity, including dynamically allocating more rollback segments when it becomes necessary.

After ensuring that enough rollback segments exist in the database, it is time to turn attention to the question of sizing. Dynamic rollback extension can take a toll on performance if segments are being consistently enlarged to accommodate heavy transaction loads.

Seeing undo segments undergoing numerous extends and shrinks as Oracle returns a segment back to its optimal setting, as well as rollback segments with current or high watermark sizes greater than their optimal setting, usually is a good indicator that they should be permanently enlarged.

It is certainly not easy keeping track of all the I/O activity in a heavy-duty database, but by following the roadmap provided in this chapter and using the included scripts, a good DBA should be able to quickly uncover all the hotspots in any Oracle database. By starting with global I/O statistics and moving through I/O at the storage structure, object, and user levels, the I/O hotspots can be identified and then work can begin on making things better. The next section in this chapter will cover how the major bottlenecks in the system can be eliminated by using both wait-based and extended analytical techniques.

Troubleshooting Problem Sessions

It is an old joke among database administrators that databases would run just fine if no users were allowed to connect to them. Of course this is not really the case, and with internet-enabled database applications, it is possible to have databases with virtually no limit to the number of users that can connect to the system. Also, as user load increases, there is an increased need to manage the performance of the database with respect to user and code activity.

Today, the bar has been raised for high-usage databases. It is not uncommon to see large eCommerce systems that support thousands of transactions per second, and many of these databases have strict service level agreements (SLAs) mandating sub-second response time. The DBA's performance strategy should include solid techniques for quickly identifying database sessions that are using excessive resources or causing system bottlenecks. It was shown earlier that it is best to use ratio-based and bottleneck analysis techniques when troubleshooting Oracle databases.

When session and SQL activity is being examined, a third analytic technique referred to as *workload analysis* is also very helpful. The following sections will cover how to perform workload analysis by looking at session activity using a variety of analysis techniques and scripts. The main topics to be covered are:

- Finding storage hogs
- Locating top resource sessions

- Pinpointing sessions with problem SQL

Looking at security holes is a logical place to start because the user accounts that belong on a system should be the only accounts allowed on the system.

Finding Storage Hogs

One thing that should be tracked in the database is the amount of storage space that each user account is consuming. It is not uncommon for developers to create object backups of their object backups when working on a critical project. If those objects are left in the database indefinitely, they might create a considerable amount of unusable space that may be needed at a later time.

A good query to run to see how much space each user account has consumed is the *totuserspace.sql* script:

🖫 totuserspace.sql

```
select
        owner,
        round((byte_count / 1024 / 1024),2) space_used_mb,
        round(100 * (byte_count / tot_bytes),2) pct_of_database
from
(select
        owner ,
        sum(bytes) as byte_count
from
        sys.dba_segments
where
        segment_type not in ('TEMPORARY','CACHE')
group by
        owner
order by
        2 desc),
(select
        sum(bytes) as tot_bytes
from
        sys.dba_segments);
```

Partial output from the above query might look something like this:

```
OWNER           SPACE_USED_MB       PCT_OF_DATABASE
----------------------------------------------------
ERADMIN             807.10              58.48
SYS                 322.36              23.36
USER1                45.47               3.29
REPO                 27.19               1.97
SYSTEM               22.88               1.66
```

This script should be run periodically to see if any user accounts are hogging the majority of space in a database. Of course, some databases only have one schema account that contains application objects; so in that case, there should not be anything to worry about. If, however, a number of accounts with large amounts of data have been identified, each user should be checked to ensure that bogus objects have not been left behind in the database that both clutter up the user database files and add to the size of the Oracle data dictionary.

Another storage issue to examine from time to time is the amount of temporary space connected sessions are using. Many DBAs have experienced the sad fact that large disk sorts can cause out of space conditions to manifest quickly at both the database and operating system level. The *sortusage.sql* below and be used to get an idea of historical temporary tablespace (sort) usage:

🖫 sortusage.sql

```
select
        tablespace_name,
        current_users,
        total_extents,
        used_extents,
        free_extents,
        max_used_size,
        max_sort_size
from
        sys.v_$sort_segment
order by 1;
```

	TABLESPACE_NAME	CURRENT_USERS	TOTAL_EXTENTS	USED_EXTENTS	FREE_EXTENTS	MAX_USED_SIZE	MAX_SORT_SIZE
1	TEMP	0	3	0	3	3	2

Figure 5.38: *Output from the Sortusage.sql Query*

The output will tell how many users are currently using space in each temporary tablespace along with the currently used extent and free extent numbers. The last two columns will tell the largest number of total extents ever used for all sorts and the size of the single largest sort in extents since the database has been up.

Such knowledge can help in planning the size of the temporary tablespace(s). Many DBAs will size the temporary tablespaces very large in anticipation of heavy sort activity only to find that such sorts do not occur. If heavy temporary tablespace usage is not seen, it may be possible to resize the temporary tablespace datafiles and reclaim space on the server.

If the *sortusage* query shows that users are currently using space in a temporary tablespace, it may be necessary to dig deeper and see exactly what they are doing. The *sortdet.sql* query can give this exact detail:

🖫 sortdet.sql

```
select
        sql_text,
        sid,
        c.username,
        machine,
        tablespace,
        extents,
        blocks
from
        sys.v_$sort_usage a,
        sys.v_$sqlarea b,
        sys.v_$session c
where
        a.sqladdr = b.address and
        a.sqlhash = b.hash_value and
        a.session_addr = c.saddr
```

```
order by
      sid;
```

Output from the previous query might look like this:

```
SQL_TEXT     SID    USERNAME  MACHINE  TABLESPACE EXTENTS    BLOCKS
---------------------------------------------------------------------
SELECT * FROM  10    ERADMIN   ROBS     TEMP          10        80
```

This query returns the SQL call, current session information, and details on how much temporary space the SQL call is using. Red flags should begin to run up the flagpole if continuous large disk sorts are occurring on the system.

Sort activity that occurs on disk is much slower than sorts that occur in memory, so begin to examine the memory settings, as well as the SQL statements that are uncovered from this query, to see if unnecessary sorts are occurring or if the *init.ora/spfile* parameters relating to sorting are set too low.

Locating Top Resource Sessions

When the phone starts ringing with complaints of performance slowdowns, one of the first things that should happen is a cursory examination of the workload that exists on the database. This is done by checking:

- What sessions are connected to the database

- What and how much resources each session is using

- What the resource-heavy sessions are/have been executing

There are a number of database monitors on the market that give a 'Top Sessions' view of system activity. Even if there is not a third-party monitor available, all the various metrics that will be needed can quickly be pinpointed with just a few queries. The rather large *topsess.sql* query can be used to get a bird's eye view of the top resource users with respect to physical I/O, logical I/O, memory, and CPU:

🖫 topsess.sql

```
select
       'top physical i/o process' category,
       sid,
       username,
       total_user_io amt_used,
       round(100 * total_user_io/total_io,2) pct_used
from
(select
       b.sid sid,
       nvl(b.username,p.name) username,
       sum(value) total_user_io
from
     sys.v_$statname c,
     sys.v_$sesstat a,
     sys.v_$session b,
     sys.v_$bgprocess p
where
       a.statistic#=c.statistic# and
       p.paddr (+) = b.paddr and
       b.sid=a.sid and
```

```
        c.name in ('physical reads','physical writes',
                   'physical reads direct',
                   'physical reads direct (lob)',
                   'physical writes direct',
                   'physical writes direct (lob)')
group by
      b.sid, nvl(b.username,p.name)
order by
      3 desc),
(select
      sum(value) total_io
from
      sys.v_$statname c,
      sys.v_$sesstat a
where
      a.statistic#=c.statistic# and
      c.name in ('physical reads','physical writes',
                 'physical reads direct',
                 'physical reads direct (lob)',
                 'physical writes direct',
                 'physical writes direct (lob)'))
where
      rownum < 2
union all
select
      'top logical i/o process',
      sid,
      username,
      total_user_io amt_used,
      round(100 * total_user_io/total_io,2) pct_used
from
(select
       b.sid sid,
       nvl(b.username,p.name) username,
       sum(value) total_user_io
from
    sys.v_$statname c,
    sys.v_$sesstat a,
    sys.v_$session b,
    sys.v_$bgprocess p
where
      a.statistic#=c.statistic# and
      p.paddr (+) = b.paddr and
      b.sid=a.sid and
      c.name in ('consistent gets','db block gets')
group by
      b.sid, nvl(b.username,p.name)
order by
      3 desc),
(select
      sum(value) total_io
from
       sys.v_$statname c,
       sys.v_$sesstat a
where
      a.statistic#=c.statistic# and
      c.name in ('consistent gets','db block gets'))
where
      rownum < 2
union all
select
      'top memory process',
      sid,
      username,
      total_user_mem,
```

```
          round(100 * total_user_mem/total_mem,2)
from
(select
        b.sid sid,
        nvl(b.username,p.name) username,
        sum(value) total_user_mem
from
        sys.v_$statname c,
        sys.v_$sesstat a,
        sys.v_$session b,
        sys.v_$bgprocess p
where
      a.statistic#=c.statistic# and
      p.paddr (+) = b.paddr and
      b.sid=a.sid and
      c.name in ('session pga memory','session uga memory')
group by
      b.sid, nvl(b.username,p.name)
order by
      3 desc),
(select
      sum(value) total_mem
from
    sys.v_$statname c,
    sys.v_$sesstat a
where
    a.statistic#=c.statistic# and
    c.name in ('session pga memory','session uga memory') )
where
    rownum < 2
union all
select
        'top cpu process',
        sid,
        username,
        total_user_cpu,
        round(100 * total_user_cpu/greatest(total_cpu,1),2)
from
(select
        b.sid sid,
        nvl(b.username,p.name) username,
        sum(value) total_user_cpu
from
        sys.v_$statname c,
        sys.v_$sesstat a,
        sys.v_$session b,
        sys.v_$bgprocess p
where
      a.statistic#=c.statistic# and
      p.paddr (+) = b.paddr and
      b.sid=a.sid and
      c.name = 'CPU used by this session'
group by
      b.sid, nvl(b.username,p.name)
order by
      3 desc),
(select
        sum(value) total_cpu
from
        sys.v_$statname c,
        sys.v_$sesstat a
where
        a.statistic#=c.statistic# and
        c.name = 'CPU used by this session'  )
where
```

```
   rownum < 2;
```

Output from this query might look like this:

```
CATEGORY                SID    USERNAME     AMT_USED    PCT_USED
--------------------------------------------------------------------
Top Physical I/O Process 19   ORA_USR1    120,423,120 99.68
Top Logical I/O Process   5   SMON          2,774,880 25.50
Top Memory Process       19   ORA_USR1      6,198,492 27.83
Top CPU Process          19   ORA_USR1     15,435,557 99.75
```

From the above example, SID 19 would be the focus as it seems to have a stranglehold on the system in terms of overall resource consumption. A rule of thumb is that no session should consume more than 25-50% of the overall resources in a particular category. If there is no one session clearly hogging the resources, it will be necessary to examine each session in more detail to gain insight into what each might be doing.

To drill down and get more detail on across-the-board resource consumption, run a query such as the *topsessdet.sql* script:

🖫 topsessdet.sql

```
select *
       from
(select
       b.sid sid,
       decode (b.username,null,e.name,b.username) user_name,
       d.spid os_id,
       b.machine machine_name,
       to_char(logon_time,'mm/dd/yy hh:mi:ss pm') logon_time,
       (sum(decode(c.name,'physical reads',value,0)) +
       sum(decode(c.name,'physical writes',value,0)) +
       sum(decode(c.name,'physical writes direct',value,0)) +
       sum(decode(c.name,'physical writes direct (lob)',value,0))
       +
       sum(decode(c.name,'physical reads direct (lob)',value,0))
       +
       sum(decode(c.name,'physical reads direct',value,0)))
       total_physical_io,
       (sum(decode(c.name,'db block gets',value,0))  +
       sum(decode(c.name,'db block changes',value,0))  +
       sum(decode(c.name,'consistent changes',value,0)) +
       sum(decode(c.name,'consistent gets',value,0)) )
       total_logical_io,
       100 -
       100 *
       (round ((sum (decode (c.name, 'physical reads', value,
       0)) -
       sum (decode (c.name, 'physical reads direct', value,
       0))) /
       (sum (decode (c.name, 'db block gets', value, 1)) +
       sum (decode (c.name, 'consistent gets', value, 0))
       ),3)) hit_ratio,
       (sum(decode(c.name,'session pga memory',value,0))+
       sum(decode(c.name,'session uga memory',value,0)) )
       total_memory_usage,
       sum(decode(c.name,'parse count (total)',value,0)) parses,
       sum(decode(c.name,'CPU used by this session',value,0))
```

```
        total_cpu,
        sum(decode(c.name,'parse time cpu',value,0)) parse_cpu,
        sum(decode(c.name,'recursive cpu usage',value,0))
        recursive_cpu,
        sum(decode(c.name,'CPU used by this session',value,0)) -
        sum(decode(c.name,'parse time cpu',value,0)) -
        sum(decode(c.name,'recursive cpu usage',value,0))
        other_cpu,
        sum(decode(c.name,'sorts (disk)',value,0)) disk_sorts,
        sum(decode(c.name,'sorts (memory)',value,0)) memory_sorts,
        sum(decode(c.name,'sorts (rows)',value,0)) rows_sorted,
        sum(decode(c.name,'user commits',value,0)) commits,
        sum(decode(c.name,'user rollbacks',value,0)) rollbacks,
        sum(decode(c.name,'execute count',value,0)) executions,
        sum(decode(c.name,'physical reads',value,0))
        physical_reads,
        sum(decode(c.name,'db block gets',value,0)) db_block_gets,
        sum(decode(c.name,'consistent gets',value,0))
        consistent_gets,
        sum(decode(c.name,'consistent changes',value,0))
        consistent_changes
from
        sys.v_$sesstat a,
        sys.v_$session b,
        sys.v_$statname c,
        sys.v_$process d,
        sys.v_$bgprocess e
where
        a.statistic#=c.statistic# and
        b.sid=a.sid  and
        d.addr = b.paddr and
        e.paddr (+) = b.paddr  and
        c.name in ('physical reads',
                'physical writes',
                'physical writes direct',
                'physical reads direct',
                'physical writes direct (lob)',
                'physical reads direct (lob)',
                'db block gets',
                'db block changes',
                'consistent changes',
                'consistent gets',
                'session pga memory',
                'session uga memory',
                'parse count (total)',
                'CPU used by this session',
                'parse time cpu',
                'recursive cpu usage',
                'sorts (disk)',
                'sorts (memory)',
                'sorts (rows)',
                'user commits',
                'user rollbacks',
                'execute count'
)
group by
        b.sid,
        d.spid,
        decode (b.username,null,e.name,b.username),
        b.machine,
        to_char(logon_time,'mm/dd/yy hh:mi:ss pm')
order by
        6 desc);
```

	SID	USER_NAME	OS_ID	MACHINE_NAME	LOGON_TIME	TOTAL_PHYSICAL_IO	TOTAL_LOGICAL_IO	HIT_RATIO	TOTAL_MEMORY_USAGE	PARSES	TOTAL_CPU	PARSE
1	13	USR1	344	EBT2K\EBT2K08	12/17/02 11:12:45 PM	7209	26147999	100	1646676	39406	52671	
2	2	DBW0	1484	EBT2K04	12/17/02 11:10:30 PM	762	0	100	758700	0	0	
3	5	SMON	2316	EBT2K04	12/17/02 11:10:31 PM	731	38035	98.1	282028	437	0	
4	18	SYS	2512	EBT2K\ROBINWS	12/18/02 01:44:59 PM	343	32345	100	541740	48	112	
5	3	LGWR	2492	EBT2K04	12/17/02 11:10:30 PM	66	0	100	302300	0	0	
6	4	CKPT	2580	EBT2K04	12/17/02 11:10:30 PM	64	0	100	358424	0	0	
7	15	DBSNMP	2304	EBT2K\EBT2K04	12/17/02 11:10:57 PM	37	349	89.9	192968	53	0	
8	12	SYS	2240	EBT2K\ROBINWS	12/18/02 04:26:29 PM	19	101	99.2	434232	20	5	
9	6	RECO	2404	EBT2K04	12/17/02 11:10:31 PM	1	162	99.5	154576	41	0	
10	1	PMON	2628	EBT2K04	12/17/02 11:10:29 PM	0	0	100	78220	0	0	
11	7	SNP0	2416	[NULL]	12/18/02 04:26:17 PM	0	0	100	367832	0	20	
12	8	SNP1	2040	[NULL]	12/18/02 04:26:18 PM	0	0	100	361780	0	14	
13	9	SNP2	2368	[NULL]	12/18/02 04:26:16 PM	0	0	100	214108	0	19	
14	10	SNP3	1668	[NULL]	12/18/02 04:26:17 PM	0	0	100	138300	0	6	
15	11	SNP4	2500	[NULL]	12/18/02 04:26:18 PM	0	0	100	138300	0	6	

Figure 5.39: *Partial Top Sessions Detail Output*

The output from this query is pretty large, but it can be seen from the selected columns that a lot more detail can be obtained from this query than the top session's summary query. For example, the CPU usage is broken down by parse, recursive and other CPU usage.

Such details will help determine the exact nature of the work each session has been doing. Once the top sessions have been located, the next step is to locate the SQL calls they have made and determine what 'killer' queries each session has submitted. It may be a case of untuned SQL or inappropriately submitted SQL such as SQL used for a report that should be run during off hours.

The above queries and scripts are the traditional way of locating problem sessions in the database. However, there are some newer techniques that can be used to uncover user sessions that might be contributing to an overall decrease in database performance. For example, it is often preferable to avoid the continuous scanning of large tables because of the heavy logical and physical I/O cost.

There are a couple of different ways to locate the currently connected sessions causing such scans. The *userscans.sql* query can be used on Oracle to pick out the worst large table scan offenders:

userscans.sql

```
select
       sid,
       username,
       total_user_scans,
       round(100 * total_user_scans/total_scans,2) pct_scans
from
(select
        b.sid sid,
        nvl(b.username,p.name) username,
        sum(value) total_user_scans
from
     sys.v_$statname c,
     sys.v_$sesstat a,
     sys.v_$session b,
     sys.v_$bgprocess p
where
      a.statistic#=c.statistic# and
      p.paddr (+) = b.paddr and
      b.sid=a.sid and
      c.name = 'table scans (long tables)'
group by
      b.sid,
      nvl(b.username,p.name)
```

```
order by
     3 desc),
(select
     sum(value) total_scans
from
     sys.v_$statname c,
     sys.v_$sesstat a
where
     a.statistic#=c.statistic# and
     c.name = 'table scans (long tables)');
```

Sample output from this query might look like this:

```
SID       USERNAME    TOTAL_USER_SCANS   PCT_SCANS
--------------------------------------------------
19   ORA_USER1    2286724                   99.94
5    SMON            1397                     .06
21   ERADMIN           47                       0
1    PMON               0                       0
```

Needless to say, if output has been received like that shown above, there should not be too much trouble in identifying which SID had some explaining to do. Keep in mind that a DBA would normally focus on large table scans vs. small table scans. Often, Oracle can actually digest a small table much easier if it scans it rather than if it uses an index.

Another way of getting a handle on sessions that are causing table scans is to look at wait events. The *db file scattered read* wait event is generally thought to be an indicator of table scan activity.

The *scatwait.sql* query will yield historical information regarding sessions that have caused *db file scattered read* wait events since the database has been up:

🖫 scatwait.sql

```
select
     b.sid,
     nvl(b.username,c.name) username,
     b.machine,
     a.total_waits,
     round((a.time_waited / 100),2)
     time_wait_sec,a.total_timeouts,
     round((average_wait / 100),2)
     average_wait_sec,
     round((a.max_wait / 100),2) max_wait_sec
  from
     sys.v_$session_event a,
     sys.v_$session b,
     sys.v_$bgprocess c
 where
     a.event = 'db file scattered read'
     and a.sid = b.sid
     and c.paddr (+) = b.paddr
order by
     3 desc,
     1 asc;
```

Again, it is not hard to find the table scan glutton on this system:

	SID	USERNAME	MACHINE	TOTAL_WAITS	TIME_WAIT_SEC	TOTAL_TIMEOUTS	AVERAGE_WAIT_SEC	MAX_WAIT_SEC
1	13	USR1	EBT2K\EBT2K08	16	.04	0	0	.01
2	5	SMON	EBT2K04	93	0	0	0	0

Figure 5.40: *Detailed Wait Output for Sessions with Possible Table Scans*

Note that the drawback of using the above query is that it does not accurately determine if the waits have been caused by small or large table scans.

While the above queries will work well on Oracle8i and above, utilize some new *v$* views if Oracle9i or later is being used. They give more flexibility identifying problem table scan situations.

The *large_scanusers.sql* query can help ferret out the parsing users submitting SQL calls that have scanned tables over 1MB:

large_scanusers.sql

```
select
       c.username username,
       count(a.hash_value) scan_count
from
     sys.v_$sql_plan a,
     sys.dba_segments b,
     sys.dba_users c,
     sys.v_$sql d
where
     a.object_owner (+) = b.owner
     and   a.object_name (+) = b.segment_name
     and   b.segment_type in ('TABLE', 'TABLE PARTITION')
     and   a.operation like '%TABLE%'
     and   a.options = 'FULL'
     and   c.user_id = d.parsing_user_id
     and   d.hash_value = a.hash_value
     and   b.bytes / 1024 > 1024
group by
      c.username
order by
       2 desc;
```

Output from such a query might look like this:

```
USERNAME    SCAN_COUNT
---------- ------------
SYSTEM              15
SYS                 13
ORA_USR1             2
```

To use the above query to locate scans on larger tables can be tweaked by changing the *b.bytes / 1024 > 1024* clause. Large-table scans identified in the *v$sessstat* view are generally thought to be scans that were performed on a table of five blocks or greater.

The *large_scanusers.sql* query allows the flexibility to define 'large' in the user's own terms. However, regardless of what query is used, if indication are that certain sessions appear to be causing a lot of table scans, the next step is to capture the SQL calls those sessions are issuing and begin the SQL examination/tuning process.

One final area to examine with respect to problem sessions that are using/holding resources is blocking locks. If the phone calls received about performance concern complaints about complete gridlock, it is a sure bet that a blocking lock situation exists. When that is the case, there are a few queries that can be issued that should get right to the heart of the matter.

To get an idea if any blocking locks exist on the database, submit the *lockcnt.sql* query:

🖫 lockcnt.sql

```
select
      count(*)
from
      sys.v_$session
where
      lockwait is not null;
```

The return of any non-zero number indicates a current blocking lock situation and can be investigated further by running this query:

```
select
      a.username blocked_user,
      b.username blocking_user,
      w.sid waiting_session,
      h.sid holding_session,
      w.type,
      decode(h.lmode, 1,'no lock',
                      2,'row share',
                      3,'row exclusive',
                4,'share',
                5,'share row exclusive',
                6,'exclusive','none') lmode,
      decode(w.request, 1,'no lock',
                      2,'row share',
                      3,'row exclusive',
                      4,'share',
                      5,'share row exclusive',
                      6,'exclusive','none') request,
      a.row_wait_row# row_waited_on,
      w.id1,
      w.id2,
      w.ctime blocked_user_wait_secs,
      u1.name || '.' || t1.name locked_object
from
      sys.v_$lock w,
      sys.v_$lock h,
      sys.v_$session a,
      sys.v_$session b,
      sys.v_$locked_object o,
      sys.user$ u1,
      sys.obj$ t1
where
      h.lmode != 0 and
      w.request != 0 and
      w.type = h.type and
      w.id1 = h.id1 and
      w.id2 = h.id2 and
      b.sid = h.sid and
```

```
      a.sid = w.sid and
      h.sid = o.session_id and
      o.object_id = t1.obj# and
      u1.user# = t1.owner#
order by
      4,3;
```

Pinpointing Sessions with Problem SQL

Although this section mentions finding problem SQL and the sessions that are making the problem SQL calls, the bulk of the topic about finding the most resource intensive SQL code that has run on a database will be saved for the next chapter. The focus here is to pinpoint the problem sessions that are currently issuing bad SQL calls rather than create a historical analysis of the worst SQL issued on a system.

For example, to see the SQL currently running in a database session that has caused the most physical I/O, a query like the *curriosql.sql* script would do the trick for Oracle8i and above.

💾 **curriosql.sql**

```
select
      sid,
      username,
      sql_text
from
      sys.v_$sqltext a,
      sys.v_$session b
where
      b.sql_address = a.address
      and b.sid =
(select
      sid
from
(select
      b.sid sid,
      nvl(b.username,p.name) username,
      sum(value) total_user_io
from
      sys.v_$statname c,
      sys.v_$sesstat a,
      sys.v_$session b,
      sys.v_$bgprocess p
where
      a.statistic#=c.statistic# and
      p.paddr (+) = b.paddr and
      b.sid=a.sid and
      c.name in ('physical reads','physical writes',
                 'physical reads direct',
                 'physical reads direct (lob)',
                 'physical writes direct',
                 'physical writes direct (lob)')
group by
      b.sid,
      nvl(b.username,p.name)
order by
      3 desc)
where
      rownum < 2)
order by
      a.piece;
```

Output from such a query might look like this:

```
SID USERNAME      SQL_TEXT
----------------------------------------------------------
19  ORA_MONITOR   SELECT COUNT(*) FROM ADMISSION
19  ORA_MONITOR    WHERE PATIENT_ID BETWEEN 1 AND 100;
```

Similar queries could be issued to uncover the SQL that the current memory or CPU is running as well. Of course, the previous query will give only the currently running SQL for a session, which may or may not be the code that has contributed to the session's resource consumption.

Some higher-level analysis can be done to answer questions like "What sessions have parsed Cartesian join statements?" by issuing the *cartsession.sql* script.

⊟ cartsession.sql

```
select
      username,
      count(distinct c.hash_value) nbr_stmts
from
    sys.v_$sql a,
    sys.dba_users b,
    sys.v_$sql_plan c
where
      a.parsing_user_id = b.user_id
      and    options = 'cartesian'
      and    operation like '%join%'
      and    a.hash_value = c.hash_value
group by
      username
order by
      2 desc;
```

Running this query on an Oracle9i server may yield results similar to this:

```
USERNAME    NBR_STMTS
---------   ---------
ORA_USR1            2
SYSMAN             2
ERADMIN            1
```

Once it has been determined that Cartesian joins have occurred on a system, look further and find the actual SQL statements themselves by using a query like the *cartsql.sql* script; again, only on Oracle9i or above:

⊟ cartsql.sql

```
select
    *
from
    sys.v_$sql
where
    hash_value in
(select
    hash_value
```

```
from
      sys.v_$sql_plan
where
      options = 'CARTESIAN'
      and operation LIKE '%JOIN%' )
order by
      hash_value;
```

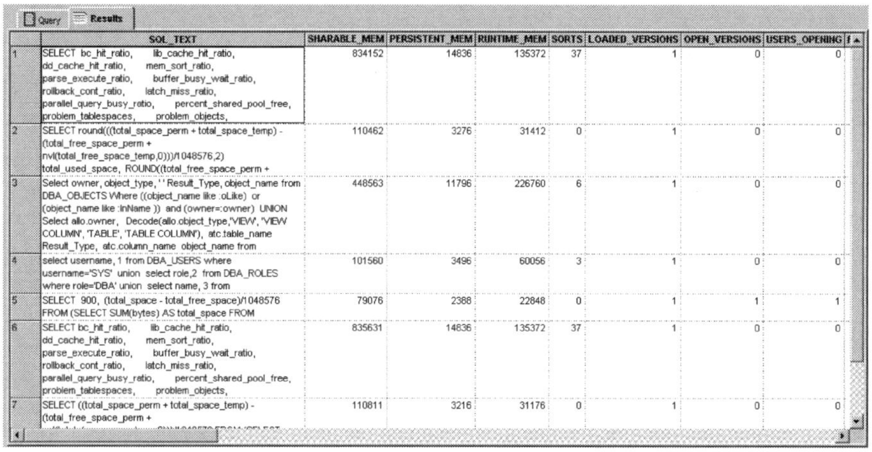

	SQL_TEXT	SHARABLE_MEM	PERSISTENT_MEM	RUNTIME_MEM	SORTS	LOADED_VERSIONS	OPEN_VERSIONS	USERS_OPENING
1	SELECT bc_hit_ratio, lib_cache_hit_ratio, dd_cache_hit_ratio, mem_sort_ratio, parse_execute_ratio, buffer_busy_wait_ratio, rollback_cont_ratio, latch_miss_ratio, parallel_query_busy_ratio, percent_shared_pool_free, problem_tablespaces, problem_objects,	834152	14836	135372	37	1	0	0
2	SELECT round(((total_space_perm + total_space_temp) - (total_free_space_perm + nvl(total_free_space_temp,0)))/1048576,2) total_used_space, ROUND((total_free_space_perm +	110462	3276	31412	0	1	0	0
3	Select owner, object_type, ' ' Result_Type, object_name from DBA_OBJECTS Where ((object_name like :oLike) or (object_name like :lnName)) and (owner=:owner) UNION Select allo.owner, Decode(allo.object_type,'VIEW', 'VIEW COLUMN', 'TABLE', 'TABLE COLUMN'), atc.table_name Result_Type, atc.column_name object_name from	448563	11796	226760	6	1	0	0
4	select username, 1 from DBA_USERS where username='SYS' union select role,2 from DBA_ROLES where role='DBA' union select name, 3 from	101560	3496	60056	3	1	0	0
5	SELECT 900, (total_space - total_free_space)/1048576 FROM (SELECT SUM(bytes) AS total_space FROM	79076	2388	22848	0	1	1	1
6	SELECT bc_hit_ratio, lib_cache_hit_ratio, dd_cache_hit_ratio, mem_sort_ratio, parse_execute_ratio, buffer_busy_wait_ratio, rollback_cont_ratio, latch_miss_ratio, parallel_query_busy_ratio, percent_shared_pool_free, problem_tablespaces, problem_objects,	835631	14836	135372	37	1	0	0
7	SELECT ((total_space_perm + total_space_temp) - (total_free_space_perm +	110811	3216	31176	0	1	0	0

Figure 5.41: *SQL Statements That Contain at Least One Cartesian Join*

The above script is quite valuable as Cartesian joins can cause unnecessary system workload and be difficult to spot in SQL queries with many join predicates.

While there is no way to totally prevent users from accessing the database in ways that are not desired, it is possible to limit the users' resource privileges, uncover problem access patterns, and find excessive usage by applying the techniques and scripts highlighted in these sections. When doing so, the starting techniques of another valuable form of performance analysis, termed workload analysis, will be applied.

Once the problem sessions are identified, attention should be turned to finding and either removing or tuning the problem SQL calls that are causing any system slowdowns. This second set of workload analysis techniques will be covered in the next chapter.

Troubleshooting Problem SQL

As a DBA, the right game plan needs to be in place for finding and fixing problem SQL code in the database. Fortunately, Oracle is better than most DBMSs at providing information in the data dictionary to help locate and analyze potentially bad SQL. By using the roadmap and scripts provided in this section, short work can be made of pinpointing any bad SQL that is run though the system.

What is Bad SQL?

Before problem SQL can be identified in the database, the question to ask is "What is bad SQL?" What criteria should be used when beginning the hunt for problem SQL in the critical systems?

Even the seasoned experts disagree on what constitutes efficient and inefficient SQL, so there is no way to sufficiently answer this question to every Oracle professional's satisfaction. What follows are some general criteria that can be used when evaluating the output from various database monitors or personal diagnostic scripts:

- **Overall Response (Elapsed) Time:** This is how much time the query took to parse, execute and fetch the data needed to satisfy the query. It should not include the network time needed to make the round trip from the requesting client workstation to the database server.

- **CPU Time:** This is how much CPU time the query took to parse, execute, and fetch the data needed to satisfy the query

- **Physical I/O:** Often used as the major statistic in terms of identifying good vs. bad SQL, this is a measure of how many disk reads the query caused to satisfy the user's request. While the goal certainly is to control disk I/O where possible, it is important that focus is not put solely on physical I/O as the single benchmark of inefficient SQL. Make no mistake, disk access is slower than memory access and also consumes processing time making the physical to logical transition, but it is important to look at the entire I/O picture of a SQL statement, which includes looking at a statements' logical I/O as well.

- **Logical I/O:** This is a measure of how many memory reads the query took to satisfy the user's request. The goal of tuning I/O for a query should be to examine both logical and physical I/O and use appropriate mechanisms to keep both to a minimum.

- **Repetition:** This is a measure of how often the query has been executed. A problem in this area is not as easy to spot as the others unless the DBA knows the application well. A query that takes a fraction of a second to execute may still be causing a headache on the system if it is executed erroneously. One example might be a query that executes in a runaway PL/SQL loop over and over again.

There are other criteria that can be examined, like sort activity or access plan statistics, that show items such as Cartesian joins and the like, but more often than not, these measures are reflected in the criteria listed above.

Fortunately, Oracle records all of the above measures which makes tracking the SQL that has been submitted against an Oracle database a lot easier.

Pinpointing Bad SQL

When looking for inefficient SQL in the library cache, the DBA must start by defining what constitutes inefficient SQL. Remember, Oracle has two separate optimizer goals, each with different definitions of what it means to be best:

- *first rows:* Fetch the desired rows with a minimum amount of block touches (favors indexes).

- *all rows:* Fetch the desired rows using the least amount of computing resources (favors full scans).

Far and away, most Oracle systems will want to optimize the SQL using *first_rows* optimization, configuring the optimizer to use indexes to fetch results as quickly as possible, even if the index access means more computing resources.

Proactive SQL Troubleshooting

The best way to tune the database is by tuning the workload as a whole, examining historical SQL execution patterns. The easiest way to perform historical SQL analysis is to use STATSPACK or AWR and set the SQL collection thresholds to capture exceptional SQL, based on the system's characteristics.

To find inefficient SQL in real-time, a good top SQL script to use for Oracle is the *topsql.sql* query. It will pull the top 20 SQL statements as determined initially by disk reads per execution, but the sort order can be changed to sort on logical I/O, elapsed time and such:

🖫 **topsql.sql**

```
select
        sql_text ,
        username ,
        disk_reads_per_exec,
        buffer_gets_per_exec,
        buffer_gets ,
        disk_reads,
        parse_calls ,
        sorts ,
        executions ,
        loads,
        rows_processed ,
        hit_ratio,
        first_load_time ,
        sharable_mem ,
        persistent_mem ,
        runtime_mem,
        cpu_time_secs,
        cpu_time_secs_per_execute,
        elapsed_time_secs,
        elapsed_time_secs_per_execute,
        address,
        hash_value
from
(select
        sql_text ,
        b.username ,
        round((a.disk_reads/
        decode(a.executions,0,1,a.executions)),2)
        disk_reads_per_exec,
        a.disk_reads ,
        a.buffer_gets ,
        round((a.buffer_gets/
        decode(a.executions,0,1,a.executions)),2)
        buffer_gets_per_exec,
        a.parse_calls ,
        a.sorts ,
        a.executions ,
        a.loads,
        a.rows_processed ,
        100 - round(100 *
        a.disk_reads/
        greatest(a.buffer_gets,1),2) hit_ratio,
        a.first_load_time ,
        sharable_mem ,
        persistent_mem ,
        runtime_mem,
        round(cpu_time / 1000000,3) cpu_time_secs,
        round((cpu_time / 1000000)/
```

```
        decode(a.executions,0,1,a.executions),3)
        cpu_time_secs_per_execute,
        round(elapsed_time / 1000000,3) elapsed_time_secs,
        round((elapsed_time /
        1000000)/decode(a.executions,0,1,a.executions),3)
        elapsed_time_secs_per_execute,
        address,
        hash_value
from
        sys.v_$sqlarea a,
        sys.all_users b
where
        a.parsing_user_id=b.user_id and
        b.username not in ('SYS','SYSTEM')
        order by 3 desc)
where
     rownum < 21;
```

Output from this query might resemble Figure 5.42:

	SQL_TEXT	USERNAME	DISK_READS_PER_EXEC	BUFFER_GETS_PER_EXEC	BUFFER_GETS	DISK_READS	PARSE_CALLS	SORTS	EX
1	begin PERFCNTR_24x7_QUERIES.fetchcursor20_2(VAR1_	USR1	122.5	78886.5	157773	245	2	0	
2	SELECT 956, (INVALID_OBJECTS + UNUSABLE_INDEXES) AS TOTAL FROM (SELECT	USR1	94	45723.5	91447	188	1	0	
3	SELECT 'PERFCNTR_24x7_QUERIES', PERFCNTR_24x7_QUERIES.GetVersion from DUAL UNION	USR1	67	975	975	67	1	1	
4	SELECT 900, (total_space - total_free_space)/1048576 FROM (SELECT SUM(bytes) AS total_space FROM	USR1	18.5	238	476	37	1	0	
5	select 99 /100, 1 - to_number(to_char(to_date('1997-11-0	USR1	11	86	86	11	1	0	
6	SELECT 955, COUNT(*) FROM SYS.DBA_TABLES WHER	USR1	5.5	30784	61568	11	1	0	
7	SELECT 998, COUNT(*) FROM (SELECT USERNAME FROM SYS.DBA_USERS WHERE	USR1	3.5	239.5	479	7	1	16	
8	select a.machine, b.count from (SELECT DISTINCT MACHINE FROM V$SESSION WHERE TYPE =	USR1	3	63	63	3	1	1	
9	SELECT 977, a.active active_jobs,b.due-a.active jobs_waiting,c.snp_processes - a.active idle_jobs,c.snp_processes total_jobs FROM (SELECT	USR1	2.5	70.5	141	5	1	2	
10	begin PERFCNTR_24x7_QUERIES.fetchcursor22_5(VAR1_	USR1	2.5	70.5	141	5	2	0	
11	begin PERFCNTR_24x7_QUERIES.fetchcursor16_3(VAR1_	USR1	1.67	114.5	687	10	6	0	
12	SELECT 948, ACTIVE_COUNT,ROUND(100 * (ACTIVE_COUNT / TOTAL_COUNT),2) AS ACTIVE_PCT	USR1	1.67	76.17	457	10	1	0	
13	begin PERFCNTR_24x7_QUERIES.fetchcursor1_2(VAR1_	USR1	1.33	156.17	937	8	6	0	
14	begin PERFCNTR_24x7_QUERIES.fetchcursor3_3(VAR1_	USR1	.83	107.83	647	5	6	0	

Figure 5.42: *Output from the Top 20 SQL Query*

It is important to examine the output of this query and see how it uses the criteria set forth at the beginning of this chapter to pinpoint problematic SQL.

First, start by looking at Figure 5.43 and focus on the circled columns.

	PERSISTENT_MEM	RUNTIME_MEM	CPU_TIME_SECS	CPU_TIME_SECS_PER_EXECUTE	ELAPSED_TIME_SECS	ELAPSED_TIME_SECS_PER_EXECUTE	ADDRESS	HASH_VALUE
1	540	276	1.642	.821	4.814	2.407	672621C0	3077230681
2	696	30300	.521	.26	1.204	.602	6746A26C	2965734772
3	1400	3684	.11	.11	.399	.399	674D57CC	2741343822
4	2388	22848	.06	.03	1.368	.684	6746A848	3829441909
5	700	876	.02	.02	.079	.079	674FA26C	1276527007
6	660	12748	.26	.13	.293	.147	6746A460	2911359602
7	892	100596	.05	.025	.07	.035	67469D84	3547812303
8	664	4036	.02	.02	.034	.034	674F4504	2966647892
9	852	4388	.02	.01	.054	.027	674688A0	482951707

Figure 5.43: *Output From the Top 20 SQL Query That Shows Timing Statistics*

The output displays both CPU and elapsed times for each SQL query. The times are shown both cumulatively in seconds and per execution indicating, for example, that the first query in the result set has accumulated almost five seconds of total execution time and runs for about two and half seconds each time it is executed. The query to sort by any of these timed statistics can be changed depending on the criteria needed to bubble the worst running SQL to the top of the result set. Again, sadly, these metrics are lost when any database version prior to Oracle9i is used.

Looking back at Figure 5.43, the columns that will help with examining the I/O characteristics of each SQL statement are visible. The number of disk reads (physical I/O) and buffer gets (logical I/O) are shown along with numbers that display the average I/O consumption of each SQL statement.

Watch out for single execution SQL!

Queries that have only been executed once may have misleading statistics with respect to disk reads as the data needed for the first run of the query was likely read in from disk to memory.

Therefore, the number of disk reads per execution should drop for subsequent executions and the hit ratio should rise.

The executions column of the top SQL's result set will provide clues to the repetition metric for the query. When troubleshooting a slow system, be on the lookout for any query that shows an execution count that is significantly larger than any other query on the system. It may be that the query is in an inefficient PL/SQL loop or other problematic programming construct. Bring the query to the attention of the application developers to help determine if the query is being mishandled from a programming standpoint.

Once the problematic SQL statements are found through Oracle's diagnostic views, the next step is to get the entire SQL text for the statements that appear inefficient. This can be accomplished by noting the *hash_value* values for each SQL statement and then issuing the *fullsql.sql* script to obtain the full SQL statement:

🖫 **fullsql.sql**

```
select
      sql_fulltext
from
      sys.v_$sqlarea
where
      sql_id = '&sqlid';
```

One of the first activities in Oracle troubleshooting is to quickly check to see what SQL is currently executing to understand if any resource intensive SQL is dragging down the database's overall performance levels. This is very easy to do and only involves making one change to the already explained *topsql.sql* query. Add the following filter to the main query's WHERE clause:

```
where
      a.parsing_user_id=b.user_id and
```

```
      b.username not in ('SYS','SYSTEM') and
      a.users_executing > 0
      order by 3 desc;
```

This query change will display the worst SQL that is currently running in the database to quickly tell if any queries are to blame for a dip in database performance.

Tricks for SQL Troubleshooting

The troubleshooting techniques that have been shown so far are traditional ways of pinpointing problem SQL in Oracle. However, there are some newer methods that can be used to get a handle on how well the SQL in the database is executing.

For example, the DBA may want to know how many total SQL statements are causing Cartesian joins on the system. The following *cartcount.sql* query can find all Cartesian joins:

🖫 cartcount.sql
```
select
      count(distinct hash_value) carteisan_statements,
      count(*) total_cartesian_joins
from
      sys.v_$sql_plan
where
      options = 'CARTESIAN' and
      operation like '%JOIN%';
```

Output from this query might resemble the following. Note that it is possible for a single SQL statement to contain more than one Cartesian join:

```
CARTEISAN_STATEMENTS      TOTAL_CARTESIAN_JOINS
----------------------    ----------------------
                     4                          6
```

It is the possible to view the actual SQL statements containing the Cartesian joins along with their performance metrics by using the *cartsql.sql* query:

🖫 cartsql.sql
```
select
      *
from
      sys.v_$sql
where
      hash_value in
(select
      hash_value
 from
      sys.v_$sql_plan
 where
      options = 'CARTESIAN'
 and  operation like '%JOIN%' )
order by hash_value;
```

Another big area of interest is monitoring table scan activity. Small-table scans are generally not a worry since Oracle can often access small tables more efficiently through a full scan than through index access; the small table is just cached and accessed. Large table scans, however, are another matter. While large-table full-table scans are sometimes justified, i.e. reading the majority of blocks in the table, they also indicate missing indexes or sub-optimal SQL optimization. In OLTP environments all large-table full-scans are commonly removed with smart index placement or intelligent partitioning. The *v$sql_plan* view can be used to quickly identify any SQL statement that contains one or more large-table scans and even define large in the DBA's own terms.

The following *tabscan.sql* query shows any SQL statement that contains a large-table scan, defined in this query as a table over 1MB, along with a count of how many large scans it causes for each execution, the total number of times the statement has been executed, and then the sum total of all scans it has caused on the system:

💾 **tabscan.sql**

```
select
        sql_text,
        total_large_scans,
        executions,
        executions * total_large_scans sum_large_scans
from
(select
        sql_text,
        count(*) total_large_scans,
        executions
from
     sys.v_$sql_plan a,
     sys.dba_segments b,
     sys.v_$sql c
where
        a.object_owner (+) = b.owner
and    a.object_name (+) = b.segment_name
and    b.segment_type in ('TABLE', 'TABLE PARTITION')
and    a.operation like '%TABLE%'
and    a.options = 'FULL'
and    c.hash_value = a.hash_value
and    b.bytes / 1024 > 1024
group by
        sql_text, executions)
order by
        4 desc;
```

	SQL_TEXT	TOTAL_LARGE_SCANS	EXECUTIONS	SUM_LARGE_SCANS
1	select o.owner#,o.obj#,decode(o.linkname,null, decode(u.name,null,'SYS',u.name),o.remoteowner),	1	19	19
2	SELECT 1 FROM SYS.DBA_OBJECTS WHERE ROWNUM = 1 MINUS SELECT 1 FROM SYS.DBA_EXTENTS WHERE ROWNUM = 1 MINUS	2	2	4
3	SELECT 1 FROM SYS.DBA_OBJECTS WHERE ROWNUM = 1 MINUS SELECT 1 FROM SYS.DBA_EXTENTS WHERE ROWNUM = 1 MINUS	2	1	2
4	SELECT OWNER,TABLE_NAME,NUM_ROWS,PCT_FREE,PCT_USED,TA	1	2	2
5	EXPLAIN PLAN SET STATEMENT_ID='10118429' INTO EMBARCADERO	1	1	1
6	SELECT OWNER,TABLE_NAME,NUM_ROWS,PCT_FREE,PCT_USED,TABLESPA	1	1	1
7	select count(*) from eradmin.emp	1	1	1
8	select distinct i.obj# from sys.idl_ub1$ i where i.obj#>=:1 and i.obj# not	1	1	1

Figure 5.44: *Output Showing Large Table Scan Activity*

This query provides important output and yields a number of interesting questions. Should there be more worry about a SQL statement that causes only one large-table scan, but has been executed 1,000 times, or a SQL statement that has ten large scans in it, but has only been executed a handful of times? Every Oracle tuning professional will likely have an opinion on this, but regardless, it is vital to have such a query that can assist with identifying SQL statements that have the potential to cause system slowdowns.

Oracle 9.2 introduced another new performance view, *v$sql_plan_statistics,* that can be used to get even more statistical data regarding the execution of inefficient SQL statements. This view can tell how many buffer gets, disk reads and such that each step in a SQL execution plan caused, and even goes so far as to list the cumulative and last executed counts of all held metrics.

This view can be referenced to get a great perspective of which step in a SQL execution plan is really responsible for most of the resource consumption. To enable the collection of data for this view, the Oracle configuration parameter *statistics_level* must be set to ALL.

An example that utilizes this view is the following *planstats.sql* script that shows the statistics for one problem SQL statement:

🖫 planstats.sql

```
select
        operation,
        options,
        object_owner,
        object_name,
        executions,
        last_output_rows,
        last_cr_buffer_gets,
        last_cu_buffer_gets,
        last_disk_reads,
        last_disk_writes,
        last_elapsed_time
from
        sys.v_$sql_plan a,
        sys.v_$sql_plan_statistics b
where
        a.sql_id = b.sql_id and
        a.id = b.operation_id and
        a.sql_id = '&sql_id'
order by a.id;
```

	OPERATION	OPTIONS	OBJECT_OWNER	OBJECT_NAME	EXECUTIONS	LAST_OUTPUT_ROWS	LAST_CR_BUFFER_GETS	LAST_CU_BUFFER_GETS	LAST_DISK_READS	LAST
1	MERGE JOIN	CARTESIAN	[NULL]	[NULL]	1	31849	48	0	18	
2	TABLE ACCESS	FULL	ERADMIN	PATIENT	1	22	24	0	5	
3	BUFFER	SORT	[NULL]	[NULL]	1	31849	22	0	13	
4	PARTITION RANGE	ALL	[NULL]	[NULL]	1	1507	22	0	13	
5	TABLE ACCESS	FULL	ERADMIN	ADMISSION	1	1507	22	0	13	

Figure 5.45: *Example Output Showing Statistical Metrics for Each Step in a Query Execution Plan*

Understanding the current state and shape of the objects being used in the queries being tuned can unlock clues about how the SQL code might need to be restructured. For example, a DBA may realize that critical foreign keys that are used over and over again in various sets of join operations have not been indexed. Another scenario might be that there is a million row table that is a perfect candidate for a bitmap index given the current WHERE predicate.

Object-based solutions are another option for SQL tuning analysts. This route involves things like intelligent index creation, partitioning and more. In order to do this, it is necessary to first find the objects that will benefit from such modification, which in turn will enhance the overall runtime performance.

For example, to investigate better use of partitioning, the first step would be to locate large tables that are the consistent targets of full-table scans. The *tabscan.sql* query below will identify the actual objects that are the target of such scans. It displays the table owner, table name, the table type (standard, partitioned), the table size in KB, the number of SQL statements that cause a scan to be performed, the number of total scans for the table each time the statement is executed, the number of SQL executions to date and the total number of scans that the table has experienced (total single scans * executions):

💾 tabscan.sql

```
select
    table_owner,
    table_name,
    table_type,
    size_kb,
    statement_count,
    reference_count,
    executions,
    executions * reference_count total_scans
from
    (select
    a.object_owner table_owner,
    a.object_name table_name,
    b.segment_type table_type,
    b.bytes / 1024 size_kb,
    sum(c.executions ) executions,
    count( distinct a.hash_value ) statement_count,
    count( * ) reference_count
from
    sys.v_$sql_plan a,
    sys.dba_segments b,
    sys.v_$sql c
where
    a.object_owner (+) = b.owner
    and a.object_name (+) = b.segment_name
    and b.segment_type in ('TABLE', 'TABLE PARTITION')
    and a.operation like '%TABLE%'
    and a.options = 'FULL'
    and a.hash_value = c.hash_value
    and b.bytes / 1024 > 1024
group by
    a.object_owner, a.object_name, a.operation,
    b.bytes / 1024, b.segment_type
order by
    4 desc, 1, 2 );
```

	TABLE_OWNER	TABLE_NAME	TABLE_TYPE	SIZE_KB	STATEMENT_COUNT	REFERENCE_COUNT	EXECUTIONS	TOTAL_SCANS
1	ERADMIN	EMP	TABLE	19456	2	2	2	4
2	ERADMIN	PATIENT	TABLE	3496	1	1	1	1
3	ERADMIN	ADMISSION	TABLE	3136	4	7	31	217

Figure 5.46: *Identifying Tables or Table Partitions That Have Been Scanned in Oracle*

The above query will help determine what tables might benefit from better indexing or partitioning. When reviewing such output, to the question might come to mind as to whether the tables being scanned have indexes, and if so, why are the queries that are scanning the tables not making use of them?

While only examination of the actual SQL statements can answer the second part of that question, the first part can be answered through the following *unused_indx.sql* query:

unused_indx.sql

```
select distinct
    a.object_owner table_owner,
    a.object_name table_name,
    b.segment_type table_type,
    b.bytes / 1024 size_kb,
    d.index_name
from
     sys.v_$sql_plan a,
     sys.dba_segments b,
     sys.dba_indexes d
where
    a.object_owner (+) = b.owner
    and a.object_name (+) = b.segment_name
    and b.segment_type in ('TABLE', 'TABLE PARTITION')
    and a.operation like '%TABLE%'
    and a.options = 'FULL'
    and b.bytes / 1024 > 1024
    and b.segment_name = d.table_name
    and b.owner = d.table_owner
order by
    1, 2;
```

Query | Results

	TABLE_OWNER	TABLE_NAME	TABLE_TYPE	SIZE_KB	INDEX_NAME
1	ERADMIN	ADMISSION	TABLE	2048	I_ADMISSION1
2	ERADMIN	ADMISSION	TABLE	2048	I_ADMISSION2
3	ERADMIN	PATIENT	TABLE	3072	I_PATIENT1
4	ERADMIN	PATIENT	TABLE	3072	I_PATIENT2
5	ERADMIN	PATIENT	TABLE	3072	I_PATIENT3

Figure 5.47: *Output Showing Unused Indexes for Tables Being Scanned*

Such a query can create a mini *unused indexes* report that can be used to ensure that any large tables being scanned on the system have the proper indexing scheme.

Troubleshooting Triage

To optimally cache the working set of frequently accessed data, the data buffers can be monitored for short periods of time. An experienced DBA can measure the buffer efficiency with either the

Automated Workload Repository (AWR) or STATSPACK with the script below. An overall system-wide data buffer hit ratio is not much help.

The scripts that follow in this section can be used to get an idea what is happening currently in the database. The DBA will be prompted for a wait period, two STATSPACK snapshots will be taken and then a quick time period summary of database changes will be performed. This is just a quick overview of SGA tuning. Chapter 14, *Oracle Instance Tuning*, provides significantly more detail on the subject.

Before revealing the script, the following is a sample of the output:

```
*************************************************************
This will identify any single file whose read I/O
is more than 10% of the total read I/O of the database.

*************************************************************
MYDATE               FILE_NAME                                READS
----------------     ------------------------------------     ---------
2000-12-20 11        /u03/oradata/PROD/pod01.dbf              1,766

*************************************************************
When the data buffer hit ratio falls below 90%, you
should consider adding to the db_block_buffer init.ora parameter

*************************************************************

MYDATE               phys_writes BUFFER HIT RATIO
----------------     ----------- ----------------
20 Dec 11:23:47          101,888               91


*************************************************************
When there are high disk sorts, you should investigate
increasing sort_area_size, or adding indexes to force index_full scans
*************************************************************


MYDATE               SORTS_MEMORY  SORTS_DISK        RATIO
----------------     ------------  ------------  ---------------
20 Dec 11:23:47               109           1    .0091743119266


*************************************************************
Buffer busy wait most frequently signal incorrectly configured database writer (DBWR) or
freelist cointention. This event means simply that another session has the buffer pinned and
that the session recording this event must wait.

*************************************************************

MYDATE               BUFFER_BUSY_WAIT
----------------     ----------------
20 Dec 11:23:47                    20

*************************************************************
Table fetch continued row indicates chained rows, or fetches of
long datatypes (long raw, blob)

Investigate increasing db_block_size or reorganizing tables
with chained rows.
*************************************************************
```

```
MYDATE              TABLE_FETCH_CONTINUED_ROW
---------------     -------------------------
20 Dec 11:23:47                         1,551


****************************************************************
Long-table full table scans might indicate a need to:

- Make the offending tables parallel query
(alter table xxx parallel degree yyy;)
- Place the table in the RECYCLE pool
- Build an index on the table to remove the FTS

****************************************************************

MYDATE              FTS
---------------     -----------
20 Dec 11:23:47          148
```

The listing above shows the significant value of this report. It shows a time-series report of Oracle behavior and the DBA even gets to choose the time interval. An experienced DBA would likely run the *quick.ksh* script below using a five-minute time interval.

🖫 awr_quick.ksh (partial)

```
spool rpt_last.lst

set pages 9999;
set feedback on;
set verify off;

column reads  format 999,999,999
column writes format 999,999,999

select
   to_char(sn.end_interval_time,'yyyy-mm-dd HH24'),
   (newreads.value-oldreads.value) reads,
   (newwrites.value-oldwrites.value) writes
from
   dba_hist_sysstat oldreads,
   dba_hist_sysstat newreads,
   dba_hist_sysstat oldwrites,
   dba_hist_sysstat newwrites,
   dba_hist_snapshot    sn
where
   newreads.snap_id = (select max(sn.snap_id)
from dba_hist_snapshot)
   and newwrites.snap_id = (select max(sn.snap_id)
from dba_hist_snapshot)
   and oldreads.snap_id = sn.snap_id-1
   and oldwrites.snap_id = sn.snap_id-1
   and oldreads.stat_name = 'physical reads'
   and newreads.stat_name = 'physical reads'
   and oldwrites.stat_name = 'physical writes'
   and newwrites.stat_name = 'physical writes'
;

prompt ****************************************************************
prompt  This will identify any single file who's read I/O
prompt  is more than 10% of the total read I/O of the database.
prompt
prompt  The "hot" file should be examined, and the hot table/index
prompt  should be identified using STATSPACK.
```

```
prompt
prompt   - The busy file should be placed on a disk device with
prompt     "less busy" files to minimize read delay and channel
prompt     contention.
prompt
prompt   - If small file has a hot small table, place the table
prompt     in the KEEP pool
prompt
prompt   - If the file has a large-table full-table scan, place
prompt     the table in the RECYCLE pool and turn on parallel query
prompt     for the table.
prompt   ************************************************************

column mydate     format a16
column file_name  format a40
column reads      format 999,999,999

select
   to_char(sn.end_interval_time,'yyyy-mm-dd HH24')  mydate,
   new.filename                          file_name,
   new.phyrds-old.phyrds                 reads
from
   dba_hist_filestatxs old,   dba_hist_filestatxs new,   dba_hist_snapshot   snwhere
sn.snap_id = (select max(snap_id) from dba_hist_snapshot) and   new.snap_id = sn.snap_id
and
   old.snap_id = sn.snap_id-1
and
   new.filename = old.filename
--and
--   new.phyrds-old.phyrds > 10000
and
   (new.phyrds-old.phyrds)*10 >
(
select
   (newreads.value-oldreads.value) reads
from
   dba_hist_sysstat oldreads,
   dba_hist_sysstat newreads,
   dba_hist_snapshot    sn1
where
   sn.snap_id = sn1.snap_id
and newreads.snap_id = sn.snap_id
and oldreads.snap_id = sn.snap_id-1
and oldreads.stat_name = 'physical reads'
and newreads.stat_name = 'physical reads'
and (newreads.value-oldreads.value) > 0)
;

prompt   ************************************************************
prompt   This will identify any single file who's write I/O
prompt   is more than 10% of the total write I/O of the database.
prompt
prompt   The "hot" file should be examined, and the hot table/index
prompt   should be identified using STATSPACK.
prompt
prompt   - The busy file should be placed on a disk device with
prompt     "less busy" files to minimize write delay and channel
prompt     channel contention.
prompt
prompt   - If small file has a hot small table, place the table
prompt     in the KEEP pool
prompt
prompt   ************************************************************
```

Now that the basic methods for troubleshooting have been covered, the following section will provide a look into the extra cost Active Session History (ASH) tables.

Using Active Session History (ASH) for Troubleshooting

Prior to Oracle10g, capturing wait event information was a cumbersome process involving the setting of special events (e.g. 10046) and the reading of complex trace dumps. Fortunately, Oracle10g simplified the way that wait event information is captured and there are a wealth of *v$* and *wrh$* views relating to Oracle wait events.

While this chapter concentrates on the ASH tables, Chapter 10, *Oracle Wait Event Tuning*, is dedicated to examining complete wait analysis techniques.

Check your license!

To view the ASH tables it is necessary to purchase the extra-cost Oracle Diagnostic Pack. There is nothing to prevent a user from querying these tables, but the access is audited and reported.

Oracle has already developed a great data collection infrastructure within the Automated Workload Repository (AWR) which is built into the Oracle kernel. AWR snapshots will rarely impose any measurable system load and by default, Oracle collects AWR data in hourly snapshots for long periods of time that are determined by the DBA.

To complement AWR, Oracle has created the Automated Session History (ASH) data collection mechanism which keeps highly detailed session information for a short period of time, usually specified as an hour or 30 minutes.

Within the core software, Oracle Corporation balances the issue of statistics detail and overall system performance with AWR (long-term proactive) versus ASH (short-term reactive). Oracle's own monitoring and statistics collection mechanisms, STATSPACK and AWR, are built to be very unobtrusive because they quickly extract snapshots of accumulators from the *x$* fixed tables. Oracle now offers wait event statistics on more than 800 specific wait events. These wait events are the result of Oracle breaking out their latch waits into their individual components and breaking-out enqueue waits (locks) into a finer level of granularity.

The foundation concept of the ASH architecture is called the time model, and Oracle10g introduced several important wait event v$ views.

v$ view	dba_hist view
v$active_sess_hist	dba_hist_active_sess_history
v$sys_time_model	dba_hist_sys_time_model
v$active_session_history	dba_hist_active_sess_history

v$event_histogram	No equivalent DBA view

Table 5.2: *v$ views and dba_hist Views*

Unlike the old-fashioned *v$session* and *v$session_wait* views where waits can only be seen at the exact instant when they occurred, the new *v$session_wait_history* and *v$sys_time_model* views allow Oracle to capture system waits details in a time-series mode.

The ASH is one of the most important areas of Oracle10g wait event tuning. ASH data is visualized through the *v$active_sess_hist* view and the *wrh$active_session_history* tables.

Collecting ASH Wait Information

The ASH tables can be used for both real time and historical trend analysis, but the real value is in time-series trend analysis. However, ASH views such as *v$active_session_history* and *v$session_wait_history* only report sessions' histories for a short, sliding period of time in a SGA buffer. The *v$* views are good for real-time monitoring using OEM, but they are not very good for showing wait-related performance trends over a long time interval.

The AWR that holds ASH history is sampled every second and stored inside *x$* structures that are materialized by the *v$active_session_history* and *v$session_wait_history* views and stored inside a circular SGA buffer. When an AWR snapshot is taken, only the current session wait information that exists at that precise moment is transferred from the *v$active_session_history* in-memory view into the persistent *dba_hist_active_sess_history* table.

The default collection retention for AWR data is only seven days, but the retention period can be increased by using the new dbms package called *dbms_workload_repository.modify_snapshot_settings*. Many Oracle DBAs will increase the storage of detail information over longer time periods. Once transferred to AWR tables, the data can be used for longer periods of time and the length of these time periods can be adjusted as needed. In order to track historical data longer than a few minutes or seconds in earlier Oracle versions, it would be necessary to increase the retention period for the ASH tables. This will change the retention period and collection frequency, thereby providing users with longer time periods of data:

```
begin
  dbms_workload_repository. modify_snapshot_settings (
    retention => 43200,        -- Minutes (= 30 Days).
    interval  => 30);          -- Minutes.
end;
/
```

In the above script, the retention period is indicated as 30 days (43200 minutes) while the interval between each snapshot is 30 minutes. Changes to these settings will be apparent if the *dba_hist_wr_control* view is queried after this procedure is executed. Typically, the retention period should capture at least one complete workload cycle for the database. Some databases have hourly cycles, daily cycles and monthly processing cycles.

The retention argument of the *dbms_workload_repository. modify_snapshot_settings* procedure specifies how long all of the AWR data is retained, and many shops will keep at least two calendar years in order to capture repeating monthly workload cycles.

For wait event troubleshooting, the *interval* parameter is the most important. If the interval is longer than the amount of real-time session wait information stored in the circular buffer for the *v$active_session_history* and *v$session_wait_history* views, some wait session data will be lost.

Another innovation is the ability to use the Oracle10g hash key for tracking session identification. This hash key allows tracking of common session processes and allows inter-cal session tracking in cases like OCI session bouncing, where each call to Oracle has a different session ID. The ASH samples for wait events every second and tracks the waits in the new *v$active_sess_hist* view. New data values are written to the *wrh$* tables every hour or when a new AWR snapshot is taken. The following are the Oracle *wrh$* wait event tables:

- *wrh$_active_session_history*
- *wrh$_active_session_history_bl*
- *wrh$_bg_event_summary*
- *wrh$_event_name*
- *wrh$_metric_name*
- *wrh$_sessmetric_history*
- *wrh$_sys_time_model*
- *wrh$_sys_time_model_bl*
- *wrh$_sysmetric_history*
- *wrh$_sysmetric_summary*
- *wrh$_sysstat*
- *wrh$_sysstat_bl*
- *wrh$_system_event*
- *wrh$_system_event_bl*
- *wrh$_waitclassmetric_history*
- *wrh$_waitstat*
- *wrh$_waitstat_bl*

The next section will detail the new Oracle *dba_hist* views that are used to create time-series performance reports, both manually and within Oracle Enterprise Manager (EM). The information will start with an overview of the *dba_hist* views and move on to examples of custom Oracle performance exception reports that can be easily generated from these views with SQL*Plus.

Using ASH for Troubleshooting

At a basic level, the ASH stores the history of a recent session's activity and facilitates the analysis of the system performance at the current time. The ASH is designed as a rolling buffer in memory, and earlier information is overwritten when needed. The ASH uses the memory of the SGA. Oracle keeps session history in the circular memory buffer in the SGA. This means that the greater the database activity is, the smaller the amount of time session history is that is available in the ASH view.

For long-term retention there is the *dba_hist_active_sess_history* view which stores the ASH history. However, *dba_hist_active_sess_history* is highly transient with sessions coming and going constantly. Remember, AWR only stores ASH data snapshots when an AWR snapshot is taken.

Once the AWR table data and inter-table relationships between AWR and performance metrics have been explained thoroughly, it will be important to understand how the *wrh$* tables are used as input to the Automatic Memory Manager (AMM), the Automatic Database Diagnostic Monitor (ADDM) and the SQL Tuning Advisor.

The creation of the AWR and the ASH provides a complete repository for diagnosing and fixing any Oracle performance issue. The AWR provides the foundation for sophisticated performance analysis including exception reporting, trend analysis, correlation analysis, hypothesis testing and data mining. A good place to start is with time-series wait event analysis using the Oracle ASH tables.

Oracle's Graham Wood, inventor of ASH, notes in his presentation titled *Sifting through the ASHes: Performance Analysis with the Oracle10g Active Session History*:

> *"Internally, Oracle stores ASH data in ASH RAM buffers within the shared pool before writing the data to the ASH data files."*

```
select * from v$sgastat where name like 'ASH buffers';

POOL          NAME                        BYTES
-----------   -------------------------   ----------
shared pool   ASH buffers                 65011712
```

The ASH samples every 10 seconds and then writes every one of ten samples to the *dba_hist_active_sess_history* table as illustrated in Figure 5.48 below:

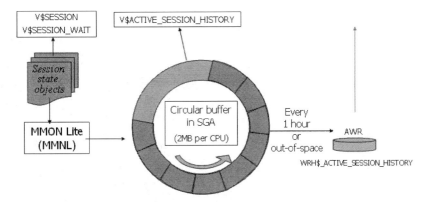

Figure 5.48: *Oracle's ASH Process*

This collection process answers many important tuning questions:

- Where is time being spent?

- What events were taking the most time?

- What was a session doing?

- What does a SQL statement wait for?

ASH reports on active, non-idle sessions such as sessions waiting on a non-idle event, and this might be a small portion of the Oracle sessions. The design goal of ASH is to hold one hour of activity information in memory. The ASH component keeps this data:

- Wait event detail

- Session details

- SQL details such as the execution plan and step costs

- Tables and indexes like *Object#, File#,* and *Block#*

- Application information such as *program, module, action* and *client_id*

Dumping ASH Data to a Flat File:

The ability to dump ASH data to a flat file provides a useful tool for analyzing transaction waits at a super-detailed level.

The following commands are designed to dump the ASH data to a flat file:

```
SQL>oradebug setmypid

SQL>oradebug dump ashdump 10

SQL>alter session set events 'immediate trace name ashdump level 10';
```

Figure 5.49 shows the relationships between the ASH structures:

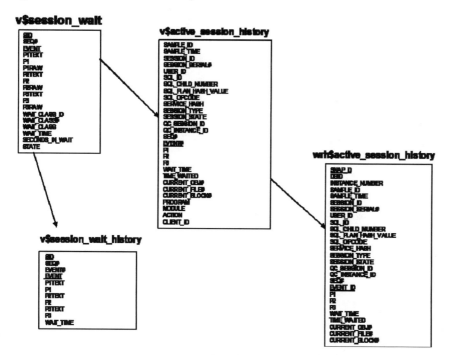

Figure 5.49: *The Relationship Between v$ views and wrh$ Event Tables*

It will be helpful to look at examples of how the *v$session_event* view might be used in real life. In this example, end users have begun complaining that they recently started to experience large delays when running a production application.

In some ERP applications like Oracle Applications and SAP, a single user account is used to connect to the database. In these cases, the following *session_waits.sql* statement can be issued to determine the particular event application for which the sessions are waiting:

🖫 **session_waits.sql**

```
select
   se.event,
   sum(se.total_waits),
   sum(se.total_timeouts),
   sum(se.time_waited/100) time_waited
from
   v$session_event se,
   v$session        sess
where
   sess.username = 'SAPR3'
and
   sess.sid = se.sid
group by
   se.event
order by 2 DESC;
```

The output of this script might look like the following:

```
                      Waits for user SAPR3

                           SUM   SUM            TIME
    EVENT                  WAITS TIMEOUTS       WAITED
    --------------------   ----- --------       ------
    SQL*Net message to client    7,824  0             .06
    SQL*Net message from client  7,812  0      312,969.73
    db file sequential read      3,199  0           16.23
    SQL*Net more data to client    590  0             .08
    SQL*Net break/reset to client  418  0              .2
    direct path read               328  0             .01
    SQL*Net more data from client   78  0            3.29
    latch free                      62  10            .08
    db file scattered read          56  0             .75
    log file sync                   47  0             .96
    direct path write               32  0              .4
    file open                       32  0               0
    library cache pin               13  0               0
    log file switch completion       3  0             .53
```

From the listing above, it can be concluded that end users of this particular system spend most of their wait time waiting on the event SQL*Net message from client. This could be an indication that there is some network-related issue causing clients too much wait time to send data to the database server.

Inside *v$active_session_history*

Oracle10g first introduced the *v$active_session_history* view that keeps a history for recent active sessions' activity. Oracle takes snapshots of active database sessions every second without placing serious overhead on the system. A database session is considered active by Oracle when it is consuming CPU time or waiting for an event that does not belong to the idle wait class.

This view contains a considerable amount of information that is available in the *v$session* view, but it also has the *sample_time* column that points to a time in the past when a session was doing some work or waiting for a resource. The *v$active_session_history* view contains a single row for each session when sampling was performed.

The next query against the *dba_hist_active_sess_history* view reports a list of resources that were in high demand in the last hour. This query does not reflect idle wait events.

```
select
   e.name                       "Wait Event",
   sum(h.wait_time + h.time_waited  ) "Total Wait Time"
from
   v$active_session_history     h,
   v$event_name                 e
where
   h.event_id = e.event_id
and
   e.wait_class <> 'Idle'
group by
   e.name
```

```
order by 2 DESC;
```

This query produces a listing like the following, showing aggregate wait time for each event:

```
Wait Event                              Total Wait Time
-----------------------------           ---------------
log buffer space                             9,638,484
db file sequential read                      8,442,918
log file switch completion                   5,231,711
write complete waits                         5,200,368
db file scattered read                       4452,153
process startup                              3623,464
rdbms ipc reply                                917,765
log file sync                                  662,224
latch free                                     550,241
latch: library cache                           370,696
db file parallel write                         364,641
free buffer waits                              319,151
latch: redo allocation                          64,984
LGWR wait for redo copy                         63,647
read by other session                           52,757
log file sequential read                        46,126
null event                                      33,011
log file parallel write                         26,280
SQL*Net E "SQL*Net" more data to client          8,894
latch: cache buffers chains                      7,005
control file sequential read                     3,966
direct path read temp                              395
direct path write temp                             229
SQL*Net E "SQL*Net" message to client               74
```

The results listing shows an issue with the *log buffer space* wait event that may indicate the need to increase the *log_buffer* parameter to increase the cache in order to minimize this possible bottleneck.

Using the AWR ASH view, a list of database users who have experienced high wait times during the time period between any two snapshots can be retrieved. The *ash_user_wait_time.sql* query can be used to identify these target users:

🖫 ash_user_wait_time.sql

```
select
   s.sid,
   s.username,
   sum(h.wait_time + h.time_waited ) "total wait time"
from
   v$active_session_history        h,
   v$session                       s,
   v$event_name                    e
where
   h.session_id = s.sid
and
   e.event_id = h.event_id
and
   e.wait_class <> 'Idle'
and
   s.username IS NOT NULL
```

```
group by
   s.sid, s.username
order by 3;
```

This sample output shows the total wait time, both by process ID (SID) and by individual users.

```
       SID   USERNAME            total wait time
----------   ----------------    ---------------
       261   SYS                       1,537,288
       259   SYS                      12,247,007
       254   SYS                      18,640,736
```

The *ash_event_rollup.sql* query that follows is commonly used for exception reporting of wait events:

ash_event_rollup.sql

```
title 'High waits on events|Rollup by hour'


column mydate heading 'Yr. Mo Dy Hr' format a13;
column event format a30;
column total_waits heading 'tot waits' format 999,999;
column time_waited heading 'time wait' format 999,999;
column total_timeouts heading 'timeouts' format 9,999;
break on to_char(snap_time,'yyyy-mm-dd') skip 1;

select
to_char(e.sample_time,'yyyy-mm-dd HH24') mydate,
e.event,
count(e.event) total_waits,
sum(e.time_waited) time_waited
from
v$active_session_history e
where
e.event not like '%timer'
and
e.event not like '%message%'
and
e.event not like '%slave wait%'
having
count(e.event) > 100
group by
to_char(e.sample_time,'yyyy-mm-dd HH24'),
e.event
order by 1
;
```

The output from this script is shown next. A time-series report is the result, showing those days and hours when the thresholds are exceeded. Notice where every evening between 10:00 PM and 11:00 PM high I/O waits on the Oracle redo logs are being experienced.

```
Wed Aug 21 page 1
High waits on events
Rollup by hour

Yr.  Mo Dy Hr EVENT                        tot waits   time wait
------------ ----------------------------- ---------   ---------
2002-08-18 22 LGWR wait for redo copy 9,326            1,109
2002-08-18 23 LGWR wait for redo copy 8,506              316
2002-08-18 23 buffer busy waits               214        21,388
```

```
2002-08-19 00 LGWR wait for redo copy 498           5
2002-08-19 01 LGWR wait for redo copy 497          15
2002-08-19 22 LGWR wait for redo copy 9,207     1,433
2002-08-19 22 buffer busy waits          529        53,412
2002-08-19 23 LGWR wait for redo copy 9,066       367
2002-08-19 23 buffer busy waits          250        24,479
2002-08-20 00 LGWR wait for redo copy 771          16
2002-08-20 22 LGWR wait for redo copy 8,030     2,013
2002-08-20 22 buffer busy waits          356        35,583
2002-08-20 23 LGWR wait for redo copy 8,021       579
2002-08-20 23 buffer busy waits          441        44,677
2002-08-21 00 LGWR wait for redo copy 1,013        26
2002-08-21 00 rdbms ipc reply           160     30,986
2002-08-21 01 LGWR wait for redo copy 541          17
```

The following *ash_object_wait_time.sql* sample query against the AWR ASH table shows a list of database objects that caused the most wait times during time interval stored in AWR. Idle wait times are not included in the output.

ash_object_wait_time.sql

```
select
   o.owner,
   o.object_name,
   o.object_type,
   sum(h.wait_time + h.time_waited ) "total wait time"
from
   v$active_session_history      h,
   dba_objects                   o,
   v$event_name                  e
where
   h.current_obj# = o.object_id
and
   e.event_id = h.event_id
and
   e.wait_class <> 'Idle'
group by
   o.owner,
   o.object_name,
   o.object_type
order by 4 DESC;
```

This report produces a list of hot objects which might be candidates for further tuning investigations:

OWNER	Object Name	Object Type	total wait time
SYSMAN	MGMT_OMS_PARAMETERS	TABLE	1,1232E+10
SYS	SCHEDULER$_WINDOW_DE TAILS	TABLE	2989867
SYSMAN	MPVV_PK	INDEX	1333198
SYSMAN	MGMT_DELTA_ENTRY_SHO ULD_BE_UK	INDEX	835641
SYSMAN	MGMT_DB_LATEST_HDM_F INDINGS	TABLE	397504

SYS	CDEF$	TABLE	116853
SYS	I_LINK1	INDEX	46922
SYS	SYS_IOT_TOP_8542	INDEX	25469
SYS	I_COM1	INDEX	24908
SYS	I_CDEF3	INDEX	23125
SYSMAN	MGMT_DB_LATEST_HDM_F INDINGS	INDEX	11325
SYS	I_OBJ2	INDEX	5953
SYS	WRH$_ACTIVE_SESSION_ HISTORY_BL	TABLE	304
SYSTEM	SQLPLUS_PRODUCT_PROF ILE	TABLE	3

With *v$active_session_history*, the DBA is now able to trace sessions without the need to use the 10046 event to extended trace.

How can the information available through the *v$active_session_history* view be used? If a session that is experiencing delays or hangs have been identified and the goal is to identify the SQL statement(s) the session is issuing, along with the wait events being experienced for a particular time period, a query similar to this one can be issued:

```
select  c.sql_text,
        b.name,
        count(*),
        sum(time_waited)
from    v$active_session_history a,
        v$event_name b,
        v$sqlarea c
where   a.sample_time between '10-JUL-04 09:57:00 PM' and
                             '10-JUL-04 09:59:00 PM' and
        a.event# = b.event# and
        a.session_id= 123 and
        a.sql_id = c.sql_id
group by c.sql_text, b.name
```

The *current_obj#* column can be joined with the *dba_objects* view to get name of the object, or it can be joined with the *current_file#* column using *dba_data_files* to see the name of the datafile that was accessed. Even a particular block that caused a wait event can be identified using the *current_block#* column.

It is also possible to identify hot datafiles, objects or even data blocks that are being accessed by sessions more frequently than others and thus could be candidates for additional investigations. The *hot_files_ash.sql* query shows hot datafiles that caused the most wait times during session access:

🖫 hot_files_ash.sql

```
select
  f.file_name       "Data File",
  count(*)          "Wait Number",
  sum(h.time_waited) "Total Time Waited"
from
  v$active_session_history h,
  dba_data_files            f
```

```
where
  h.current_file# = f.file_id
group by f.file_name
order by 3 desc
```

The sample output looks like:

```
Data File                                  Wait Number Total Time Waited
---------------------------------------- ----------- -----------------
D:\ORACLE\ORADATA\DBDABR\SYSAUX01.DBF           5514         994398837
D:\ORACLE\ORADATA\DBDABR\SYSTEM01.DBF           2579         930483678
D:\ORACLE\ORADATA\DBDABR\UNDOTBS01.DBF           245           7727218
D:\ORACLE\ORADATA\DBDABR\USERS01.DBF            141           1548274
```

The *v$active_session_history* view does not catch session activity that is extremely fast, but it should catch activity that causes the most waits and resource consumption.

Below are several helpful queries that run against the *v$active_session_history* view. The first query, *events_waits_hr_ask.sql*, shows resources that were in high demand in the last hour.

🖫 events_waits_hr_ash.sql

```
select
  h.event "Wait Event",
  sum(h.wait_time + h.time_waited) "Total Wait Time"
from
  v$active_session_history h,
  v$event_name e
where
      h.sample_time between sysdate - 1/24 and sysdate
  and h.event_id = e.event_id
  and e.wait_class <> 'Idle'
group by h.event
order by 2 desc
```

The output will look like the following:

```
Wait Event                  Total Wait Time
-------------------------- ---------------
Queue Monitor Task Wait         10,256,950
class slave wait                10,242,904
log file switch completion       5,142,555
control file parallel write      4,813,121
db file sequential read            334,871
process startup                    232,137
log file sync                      203,087
latch free                          36,934
log buffer space                    25,090
latch: redo allocation              22,444
db file parallel write                 714
db file scattered read                 470
log file parallel write                182
direct path read temp                  169
control file sequential read           160
direct path write temp                 112
```

Display SQL Wait Details in ASH

This section will cover how ASH data can be transformed to give a complete picture of system wait details. The following ASH script can be used to find details about the most active SQL in the past 10 minutes:

🖫 ash_sql_counts.sql

```
col c1 heading "invocation|count"   format 9,999
col c2 heading "percentage|of|load" format 99

select
   sql_id, count(*)                        c1,
   round(count(*)/sum(count(*)) over (), 2) c2
from
   v$active_session_history
where
   sample_time > sysdate - 1/24/60
and
   session_type <> 'BACKGROUND'
group by
   sql_id
order by
   count(*) desc;
```

SQL_ID	COUNTS	PCTLOAD
25wtt4ycbtkyz	456	32.95
7umwqvcy7tusf	123	8.89
01vunx6d35khz	119	8.6
bdyq2uph07cmp	102	7.37

In this example, the script's output shows that the *sql_id* of 25wtt4ycbtkyz was the most active SQL during the past 10 minutes, executed 456 times. This *sql_id* can be used to join into other ASH views to see more details about that specific SQL statement.

The *ash_sql_waiting_io.sql* can be used to join *v$active_session_history* into *v$event_name* to display SQL with the most I/O. The results will show the SQL ID for all SQL statements that are waiting on user I/O.

🖫 ash_sql_waiting_io.sql

```
select
   ash.sql_id,
   count(*)
from
   v$active_session_history ash,
   v$event_name             evt
where
   ash.sample_time > sysdate - 1/24/60
and
   ash.session_state = 'WAITING'
and
   ash.event_id = evt.event_id
and
   evt.wait_class = 'User I/O'
group by
   sql_id
```

```
order by
   count(*) desc;
```

```
SQL_ID          COUNT(*)
------------ ----------
5a8s3s46u2ra7        1
```

This ASH report is useful for finding the root causes of sudden spikes or transient performance problems, but the query must be run quickly, within five minutes of the slowdown. Note that this ASH report has information that includes current transaction IDs (the key) plus blocking session details, top sessions, SQL details and wait event details.

Even though these ASH queries look quite simple, their complexity and value as a reactive tuning aid should not be underestimated. There are many complexities buried in ASH. Although ASH provides innovative ways to collect and use real-time performance information, it is not perfect, and there are special cases where ASH might not yield the expected information. For example, the times in the *dba_hist_active_sess_history* are the sampled times, and as such, they are not statistically valid for the SQL *avg, min,* or *max* operators.

 ***Do not be fooled by similar sounding ASH metrics!***

Some ASH metrics sound very similar, such as *wait_time* and *time_waited*. It is important understand and use the correct metric.

For example, the difference between *wait_time* and *time_waited* in the *v$active_session_history* are:

- ***wait_time***: The *wait_time* metric is the same as the *wait_time* found in *v$session_wait*. A value of zero (0) indicates "waiting", while any other non-zero value means "on CPU".

- ***time_waited***: The *time_ waited* metric is the actual time waited for any in-flight event, and it is updated when the event is completed.

The next section will delve even deeper into how to conduct a wait event analysis using the ASH.

Event Wait Analysis with ASH

With ASH tables, a snapshot of Oracle wait events can be collected every hour and all of the changes in wait behavior can be plotted over time, yielding visual trends. It is also possible to set thresholds and report only on wait events that exceed a predefined threshold. For example, the following script can be used for exception reporting of wait events:

💾 **ash_high_wait_events.sql**
```
ttitle 'High waits on events|Rollup by hour'

column mydate heading 'Yr.  Mo Dy Hr'     format a13;
column event                              format a30;
column total_waits     heading 'tot waits' format 999,999;
```

```
column time_waited      heading 'time wait' format 999,999;
column total_timeouts heading 'timeouts'   format 9,999;

break on to_char(snap_time,'yyyy-mm-dd') skip 1;
 select
   to_char(e.sample_time,'yyyy-mm-dd HH24')   mydate,
   e.event,
   count(e.event)                             total_waits,
   sum(e.time_waited)                         time_waited
from
   v$active_session_history e
where
   e.event not like '%timer'
and
   e.event not like '%message%'
and
   e.event not like '%slave wait%'
having
   count(e.event) > 100
group by
   to_char(e.sample_time,'yyyy-mm-dd HH24'),
   e.event
order by 1
;
```

The output below is from this script. The result is a time series, showing those days and hours when set thresholds are exceeded. From this listing, it is easy to see that every evening between 10:00 PM and 11:00 PM, the system experiences high waits on the redo logs.

```
Wed Aug 21                                        page      1
                     High waits on events
                       Rollup by hour


Yr.  Mo Dy Hr EVENT                      tot waits time wait
------------ ------------------------- --------- ---------
2002-08-18 22 LGWR wait for redo copy       9,326     1,109
2002-08-18 23 LGWR wait for redo copy       8,506       316
2002-08-18 23 buffer busy waits              214    21,388
2002-08-19 00 LGWR wait for redo copy        498         5
2002-08-19 01 LGWR wait for redo copy        497        15
2002-08-19 22 LGWR wait for redo copy       9,207     1,433
2002-08-19 22 buffer busy waits              529    53,412
2002-08-19 23 LGWR wait for redo copy       9,066       367
2002-08-19 23 buffer busy waits              250    24,479
2002-08-20 00 LGWR wait for redo copy        771        16
2002-08-20 22 LGWR wait for redo copy       8,030     2,013
2002-08-20 22 buffer busy waits              356    35,583
2002-08-20 23 LGWR wait for redo copy       8,021       579
2002-08-20 23 buffer busy waits              441    44,677
2002-08-21 00 LGWR wait for redo copy       1,013        26
2002-08-21 00 rdbms ipc reply                160    30,986
2002-08-21 01 LGWR wait for redo copy        541        17
```

The Oracle Wait Event Interface within Ion gives the ability to monitor database bottlenecks in real time and Ion becomes even more powerful when used together with the AWR tables as shown in Figure 5.50.

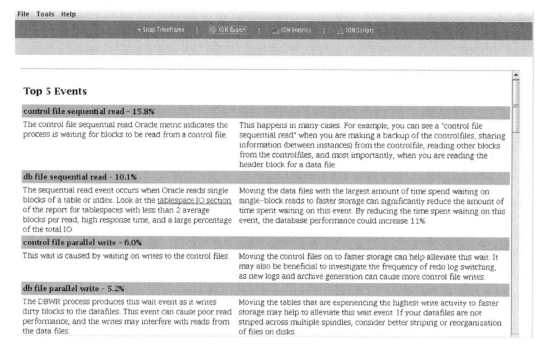

+ Snap Timeframe | ION Expert | ION Metrics | ION Scripts

Top 5 Events

control file sequential read – 15.8%

The control file sequential read Oracle metric indicates the process is waiting for blocks to be read from a control file.	This happens in many cases. For example, you can see a "control file sequential read" when you are making a backup of the controlfiles, sharing information (between instances) from the controlfile, reading other blocks from the controlfiles, and most importantly, when you are reading the header block for a data file.

db file sequential read – 10.1%

The sequential read event occurs when Oracle reads single blocks of a table or index. Look at the tablespace IO section of the report for tablespaces with less than 2 average blocks per read, high response time, and a large percentage of the total IO.	Moving the data files with the largest amount of time spend waiting on single-block reads to faster storage can significantly reduce the amount of time spent waiting on this event. By reducing the time spent waiting on this event, the database performance could increase 11%.

control file parallel write – 6.0%

This wait is caused by waiting on writes to the control files.	Moving the control files on to faster storage can help alleviate this wait. It may also be beneficial to investigate the frequency of redo log switching, as new logs and archive generation can cause more control file writes.

db file parallel write – 5.2%

The DBWR process produces this wait event as it writes dirty blocks to the datafiles. This event can cause poor read performance, and the writes may interfere with reads from the data files.	Moving the tables that are experiencing the highest write activity to faster storage may help to alleviate this wait event. If your datafiles are not striped across multiple spindles, consider better striping or reorganization of files on disks.

Figure 5.50: *Ion Display of Wait Event Details*

Now it is time to explore the subtleties of the ASH tables. Prior to Oracle10g there was no standard way to keep and analyze the history for a session's wait events into the Oracle database kernel. Instead, custom code had to be written to vacuum wait information from the *v$* views and store it inside STATSPACK extension tables.

This inability to capture information was a critical flaw in evaluating database performance because most wait events that occurred in real time were not caught using manual queries. This lack of a quick interface caused Oracle DBAs to develop custom tools to monitor their wait events in an automated manner.

The Performance Overhead of Collecting ASH Data

The ASH data collection mechanism keeps highly detailed session information for a short period of time. ASH data is filtered out by writing it to permanent AWR tables using the MMON background process every 30 minutes. However, also recognize that ASH is part of the extra-cost performance pack and diagnostic packs, costing $6,000 per CPU, as of 2009. While Oracle ASH relieves the DBA from the problem of collecting the dynamic performance information, there are alternatives, and many shops choose to collect the data directly from the SGA, the *x$* structures and from the *v$* views.

Within the world of molecular physics, the scientists say that the act of observing a subatomic behavior will alter the behavior, and that is the same problem with Oracle system monitoring. In the nanosecond world of the Oracle SGA, the act of running SQL to collect statistics from the *v$* views can easily exceed the cost of the instruction itself.

Before investing in real-time monitors to replace or supplement ASH, be aware of several potential problems:

- On stressed systems, greedy real-time monitors can create more performance problems than they reveal.

- There are few options to remedy an acute performance problem. It can be difficult, if not impossible, to correct some acute performance problems.

Using ASH to Trace a Session

The *v$active_session_history* view can fully replace the 10046 trace event. To accomplish this, the *v$active_session_history* columns *wait_time*, *session_state* and *time_waited* should be reviewed.

If *wait_time* is zero, the session currently has a *session_state* of waiting, and the event listed is the event that is the last event waited for before this sample. The *time_waited* is the amount of time that the session waited for the event listed in the *event* field.

If *wait_time* is greater than zero, the session currently has a *session_state* of 'on CPU', and the event listed is the event that was last waited for before this sample. The *time_waited* will be zero. *Time_waited* will only contain a value when waits are occurring at the instant the sample is taken.

For clarity, this means that if *wait_time* in one row is two, the *session_state* will be on CPU and the *time_waited* will be zero. The value of two in *wait_time* represents the time spent waiting the last time it waited before the current time on the CPU.

In order to use ASH, it is critical to understand the layout of the views. Figure 5.51 shows the connection between the *v$session* data, the key ASH view named *v$active_session_history*, and the Automated Workload Repository (AWR) structure named *wrh$_active_session_history*. The underlined fields can be used to join the other views to gather the specific information needed to diagnose performance problems.

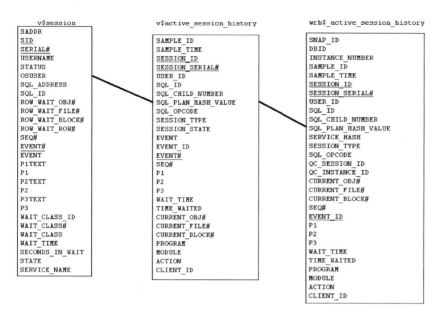

Figure 5.51: *Relationships Among V$session and Other Structures*

Due to the volume of data that can be found in *v$active_session_history* during times of heavy activity, not all of the data is stored in the AWR tables. This is because of the dirty read mechanism which reads data even though it may belong to an in-process transaction. This allows the impact on the database to be negligible. In spite of this limitation, enough data is kept to allow the ASH information to be statistically accurate and useful for historical review.

For example, the query below identifies SQL statements that accessed the *orders* table for session number 74 on the current day:

```
select
   h.sql_id,
   s.sql_text
from
   dba_hist_active_sess_history h,
   v$sql                        s
where
   h.session_id = 74
and
   h.sql_id = s.sql_id
and
   trunc(h.sample_time) = trunc(SYSDATE)
and
   s.sql_fulltext like '%orders%';
```

The output of this query shows the actual SQL statements executed against the *orders* table. Due to the large amount of data available for this query, the output has been truncated to include only one sample record that was retrieved:

```
SQL_ID        SQL_TEXT
------------- ------------------------------------------------------------
4g5qdabvfumhc select c.c_day wrk_date, c.day_type, nvl(c.rl_day, 'N') rl_day, nvl(c.short_day,
              'N') short_day, c.week_day,           p.id ewp_id, p.emp_id, p.dep_id, p.flag_main,
              p.eca_id, p.emp_sal, p.sal_prc,          nvl(d.start_date, p.start_date) start_date,
              nvl(nvl(d.finish_date, p.finish_date), to_date('9999', 'yyyy')) finish_date,
              d.id wpd_id, d.wsc_id, d.team_num, d.ept_id,          (select decode(c.day_type, 'W',
```

The output above shows the SQL that was issued against the *orders* table. Since this application produces the same set of SQL statements against the database, the DBA can go further and determine what SQL statements issued against the *orders* table were issued most frequently in the recent past.

These SQL statements are the most likely candidates for further investigations in order to find an effective way to reduce *buffer busy waits* events. The following is the query that retrieves the most frequent SQL statements identifiers against the *orders* table:

Do not cause a performance problem!

Repeated querying of the *v$sql* view causes memory access against the library latch once for each retrieved row. Be careful!

🖫 ash_count_table_usage.sql

```
select
   h.sql_id,
   count(*)
from
   dba_hist_active_sess_history h,
   v$sql                        s
where
   h.sql_id = s.sql_id
and
   s.sql_fulltext like '%orders%'
having
   count(*) > 1
group by
   h.sql_id
order by
   2 desc;
```

The output of the above query yields the following results:

```
SQL_ID        COUNT(*)
------------- ----------
3ta4tz9xbn4gf    2,678
fxr47mpnpc2yx      740
```

Now, actual SQL statements can be retrieved from the *v$sql* view using the SQL identifiers retrieved above and then a deeper investigation of those suspect SQL statements can be conducted. The example above gives an idea of one possible usage of the ASH feature in a real tuning session.

The next section will offer a look into the *v$* views that accumulate task-level data and outline how ASH is built up from this data.

Inside the *v$session_wait_history*

Now that *v$active_session_history* has been covered, it can be compared to the *v$session_wait_history* view. As the name would suggest, *v$session_wait_history* is a history table and it contains the last ten wait events for every current database session. The columns are:

```
SQL> desc v$session_wait_history

Name                     Null?    Type
------------------------  --------  ------------
SID                                 NUMBER
SEQ#                                NUMBER
EVENT#                              NUMBER
EVENT                               VARCHAR2(64)
P1TEXT                              VARCHAR2(64)
P1                                  NUMBER
P2TEXT                              VARCHAR2(64)
P2                                  NUMBER
P3TEXT                              VARCHAR2(64)
P3                                  NUMBER
WAIT_TIME                           NUMBER
WAIT_COUNT                          NUMBER
```

Focusing on any session in *v$session_wait_history*, using the SID, it will show the wait event details for that session.

In this example, assume that session 74 had high *buffer busy waits*. Drill into the session by running *v$session_wait_history* where *v$session_wait_history.sid=74*. Also, note the join into *v$session* to get the username, and the extraction of some special columns, namely *p1* and *p2*:

🖫 **session_wait_history_events.sql**

```
select
   swh.seq#       seq_nbr,
   sess.sid       sid,
   sess.username  username,
   swh.event      event,
   swh.p1,
   swh.p2
from
   v$session               sess,
   v$session_wait_history  swh
where
   sess.sid = 74
and
   sess.sid = swh.sid
order by
   swh.seq#;
```

The results show some additional latch events:

```
SEQ# SID USERNAME EVENT                              P1          P2
---- --- -------- -------------------------- ---------- ----------
   1  74 PCS      buffer busy waits                   3      21277
   2  74 PCS      latch: cache buffers chains 1556332118       172
   3  74 PCS      latch: cache buffers chains 1556332118       172
   4  74 PCS      buffer busy waits                   4        155
```

By querying the *v$session_wait_history* view, it becomes clear that session 74 experienced some additional waits.

But where? Is it possible to determine what table or index block is experiencing this contention?

In this example, *P1* and *P2* were resolved for the *object_name* and *object_type* for the block, and it is apparent that these were *buffer busy waits* for an UNDO segment. Also, it appears that the session had many waits for *cache buffer chain latch*. This type of contention has two likely causes: very long buffer chains; or very heavy access to the same data blocks. Usually, this flavor of buffer contention is caused by identical SQL queries being issued by numerous sessions, all of which retrieve rows from the same set of data blocks.

The tuning options available in this situation are to either tune the SQL statement or application so that it will access the data blocks less often, i.e. cache the data inside the application. Another approach is to spread the data across many data blocks by setting *pctused* to a high value such as 90, thereby allowing only a few rows in each data block before the block is taken off the freelist. This spreads the hot rows across more data blocks.

The next step in reactive troubleshooting is to determine what SQL statements the session executed the fetches from in the *orders* table. Finally, the exact block number is found within the table. This is where *v$active_session_history* comes to the rescue. Unlike the *v$session_wait_history*, the extra-cost *v$active_session_history* table has much finer sampling, and snapshots of a session's activities can be seen every second. Nevertheless, ASH does not have to be used. This is where the free view, *v$event_name*, comes into play.

It will be necessary to distinguish between active and idle states to understand the state changes during task execution. A database session is active when it waits for any non-idle event or when it is waiting on CPU. Idle events are indicated by the *wait_class* column for the corresponding wait event in the *v$event_name* view. This view reports one row per active session for every snapshot taken. Table 5.3 shows the contents of *v$event_name*:

CONTENTS	DESCRIPTION
snap_id	Unique snapshot ID
dbid	Database ID for the snapshot
instance_number	Instance number for the snapshot
sample_id	ID of the sample
sample_time	Time of the sample
session_id	Session identifier
session_serial#	Session serial number

user_id	Oracle user identifier
sql_id	identifier of the SQL statement
sql_child_number	Child number of the SQL statement
sql_opcode	Indicates what phase of operation the SQL statement is in
current_obj#	Object ID of the object that the session is currently referencing
current_file#	File number of the file containing the block that the session is currently referencing
current_block#	ID of the block that the session is currently referencing
event_id	Identifier of the resource or event for which the session is waiting or for which the session last waited
wait_time	Total wait time for the event for which the session last waited
time_waited	Time that the current session actually spent waiting for the event
program	Name of the operating system program
module	Name of the currently executing module
client_id	Client identifier of the session

Table 5.3: *Contents of the v$event_name View*

The information available in this view allows the determination of which SQL statement was executed at a given time, what wait event the sessions waited for, and what database file, object, or data block was accessed.

Now that how to extract wait events has been shown, the next step will be to learn how they can be used for signature analysis.

Signature Analysis of ASH Wait Events

There are many more benefits that can be achieved using information provided by the ASH as it is a useful tool for database activity analysis and performance tuning. The two sample analytical reports below make use of the ASH *v$active_session_history* view.

Signature analysis is an important area of Oracle tuning and one that especially applies to time-series wait event analysis. Just as Socrates said "Know Thy Self", the Oracle DBA must "Know Thy Database". Signature analysis is ideal for wait event tuning, particularly in the areas of:

- Spotting hidden trends

- Allowing holistic tuning

- Allowing just-in-time anticipation and self-tuning using the *dbms_scheduler* package

- Allowing adjustment of object characteristics such as freelists, file placement, caching, and block population

The following script compares the wait event values from *dba_hist_waitstat* and *dba_hist_active_sess_history*. This allows the identification of the exact objects that are experiencing wait events.

🖫 **ash_display_table_index_wait_counts.sql**

```
set pages 999
set lines 80

break on snap_time skip 2

col snap_time      heading 'Snap|Time'    format a20
col file_name      heading 'File|Name'    format a40
col object_type    heading 'Object|Type'  format a10
col object_name    heading 'Object|Name'  format a20
col wait_count     heading 'Wait|Count'   format 999,999
col time           heading 'Time'         format 999,999

select
   to_char(begin_interval_time,'yyyy-mm-dd hh24:mi') snap_time,
--    file_name,
   object_type,
   object_name,
   wait_count,
   time
from
   dba_hist_waitstat            wait,
   dba_hist_snapshot            snap,
   dba_hist_active_sess_history ash,
   dba_data_files               df,
   dba_objects                  obj
where
   wait.snap_id = snap.snap_id
and
   wait.snap_id = ash.snap_id
and
   df.file_id = ash.current_file#
and
   obj.object_id = ash.current_obj#
and
   wait_count > 50
order by
   to_char(begin_interval_time,'yyyy-mm-dd hh24:mi'),
   file_name
;
```

This script is enabled to join into the *dba_data_files* view to get the file names associated with the wait event. This is a very powerful script that can be used to quickly drill in to find the cause of specific waits. Below is a sample output:

```
SQL> @ash_display_table_index_wait_counts.sql
```

This will compare values from *dba_hist_waitstat* with detailed information from *dba_hist_active_sess_history*.

Using Active Session History (ASH) for Troubleshooting   **229**

```
Snap                    Object      Object          Wait
Time                    Type        Name            Count       Time
--------------------    ----------  ------------    --------    --------
2004-02-28 01:00        TABLE       ORDOR           4,273       67
                        INDEX       PK_CUST_ID      12,373      324
                        INDEX       FK_CUST_NAME    3,883       17
                        INDEX       PK_ITEM_ID      1,256       967

2004-02-29 03:00        TABLE       ITEM_DETAIL     83          69

2004-03-01 04:00        TABLE       ITEM_DETAIL     1,246       45

2004-03-01 21:00        TABLE       CUSTOMER_DET    4,381       354
                        TABLE       IND_PART        117         15

2004-03-04 01:00        TABLE       MARVIN          41,273      16
                        TABLE       FACTOTUM        2,827       43
                        TABLE       DOW_KNOB        853         6
                        TABLE       ITEM_DETAIL     57          331
                        TABLE       HIST_ORD        4,337       176
                        TABLE       TAB_HIST        127         66
```

The first analytic trend report yields total wait times by the hour of the day. The *ash_cpu_foreground_events.sql* script shows when database sessions have to wait for resources that decrease response time:

🖫 ash_cpu_foregound_events.sql

```
select
   TO_CHAR(h.sample_time,'HH24')  "Hour",
   Sum(h.wait_time/100)           "Total Wait Time (Sec)"
from
   v$active_session_history       h,
   v$event_name                   n
where
   h.session_state = 'ON CPU'
and
   h.session_type = 'FOREGROUND'
and
   h.event_id = n.EVENT_ID
and
   n.wait_class <> 'Idle'
group by
   TO_CHAR(h.sample_time,'HH24');
```

The output of this query might look like the results listed below, and it shows a distinct signature or repeating wait event pattern within the database. This signature will be valid for the entire range of ASH snapshots that the DBA chooses to retain. Many DBAs will retain several months' worth of ASH data so they can perform system-wide wait event tuning.

```
SQL> @ash_cpu_foregound_events.sql

Hr Total Wait Time (Sec)
-- --------------------
1                   219
2               302,998
```

```
3                60,982
4               169,716
5                39,593
6               299,953
7               122,933
8                 5,147
```

From the above listing, it appears that the database had the most wait times at 12AM and 4PM.

Most Oracle databases also have daily signatures with regularly repeating trends in wait events. In the same manner, the following query that reports total wait times by the day of the week could be run:

🖫 ash_cpu_foregound_events_dow.sql

```
select
   TO_CHAR(h.sample_time,'Day') "Hour",
   sum(h.wait_time/100)         "Total Wait Time (Sec)"
from
   v$active_session_history      h,
   v$event_name                  n
where
   h.session_state = 'ON CPU'
and
   h.session_type = 'FOREGROUND'
and
   h.event_id = n.EVENT_ID
and
   n.wait_class <> 'Idle'
group by
   TO_CHAR(h.sample_time,'Day');
```

This query produces a listing that looks like the one shown below:

```
Hour         Total Wait Time (Sec)
---------    ---------------------
Monday                     679,089
Tuesday                    141,142
Wednesday                  181,226
Thursday                   241,711
Friday                     319,023
Saturday                    93,362
Sunday                      81,086
```

From this output, it is clear that the database is most stressed on Monday, and the numbers can be visualized by pasting them into a spreadsheet and plotting them with the chart wizard. The results from the two trend reports just given allow further investigation into ASH data in order to get more detailed information. The query below retrieves a list of wait events that had high wait time from 12AM to 1PM.

A previous report on the same system showed that sessions experienced high wait times during this time period.

```
select
   h.event           "Wait Event",
   SUM(h.wait_time/100) "Wait Time (Sec)"
from
   v$active_session_history      h,
   v$event_name                  n
```

```
where
   h.session_state = 'ON CPU'
and
   h.session_type = 'FOREGROUND'
and
   h.event_id = n.EVENT_ID
and
   to_char(h.sample_time,'HH24') = '12'
and
   n.wait_class <> 'Idle'
group by
   h.event
order by
  2 DESC;
```

This query returns results that look like the following, showing aggregate totals for important wait events.

```
Wait Event                     Wait Time (Sec)
------------------------------ ---------------
buffer busy waits                      522,152
db file sequential read                299,572
SQL*Net more data to client                317
SQL*Net more data from client              201
SQL*Net message to client                   55
```

From the listing above, the DBA can conclude that between 12AM and 1PM the database sessions waited most for *buffer busy waits* and *db file sequential read* events indicating table access by index.

After these results are acquired, it is possible to determine what SQL statements were issued during this time period and probably find ones that may cause buffer cache contention or heavy disk read access. The ASH provides the Oracle DBA with the ability to build different trend reports in order to observe database activity from various points of view.

The AWR repository stores snapshots for the ASH view called *v$active_session_history* in its internal table *wrh$_active_session_history*. This table is available through the *dba_hist_active_sess_history* view. The AWR does not store snapshots of ASH activity on a continuous basis. This means that the *wrh$_active_session_history* table stores sessions' activity records that were in the SGA circular buffer at the time the AWR snapshot was taken.

This data archiving approach does not allow the monitoring of activity for particular sessions because the AWR misses all the activity that occurred in the session during the period of time between two AWR snapshots. However, trend reports based on data exposed by *dba_hist_active_sess_history* view can be built. The following sections will present information on valuable trend analysis that can be performed against the AWR concerning ASH activity.

It is possible to identify hot datafiles or database objects that were accessed by sessions more frequently than others. These hot datafiles or database objects could be candidates for additional tuning investigations. The following query shows hot datafiles that caused the most wait times during access:

```
select
   f.file_name          "Data File",
   COUNT(*)             "Wait Number",
   SUM(h.time_waited)   "Total Time Waited"
from
   v$active_session_history    h,
   dba_data_files              f
where
   h.current_file# = f.file_id
group by
   f.file_name
order by 3 DESC;
```

This query produces output like the following:

```
Data File                                   Wait Number  Total Time Waited
----------------------------------------    -----------  -----------------
D:\ORACLE\ORADATA\DBDABR\SYSAUX01.DBF               153         11,169,771
D:\ORACLE\ORADATA\DBDABR\SYSTEM01.DBF               222          6,997,212
D:\ORACLE\ORADATA\DBDABR\UNDOTBS01.DBF               45          1,758,065
```

The datafile named *d:\oracle\oradata\dbdabr\sysaux01.dbf* had the highest wait time during access to its data. This might indicate the need to further investigate SQL statements that are accessing data within this datafile or the need to spread its content between several datafiles, thus eliminating a possible hot spot.

The Oracle multiple data buffers or the KEEP pool could also be used to reduce waits on these objects by caching them in the data buffers. If there are high waits on in-buffer reads, the SQL that accesses the hot object needs to be tuned to reduce the amount of logical I/O.

The next query against the *dba_hist_active_sess_history* view reports a list of resources that were in high demand in the last hour. This query does not reflect idle wait events.

```
select
   e.name                           "Wait Event",
   sum(h.wait_time + h.time_waited) "Total Wait Time"
from
   v$active_session_history    h,
   v$event_name                e
where
   h.event_id = e.event_id
and
   e.wait_class <> 'Idle'
group by
   e.name
order by 2 DESC;
```

This query produces a listing like the one below, showing aggregate wait time for each event:

```
Wait Event                     Total Wait Time
-----------------------------  ---------------
log buffer space                     9,638,484
db file sequential read              8,442,918
log file switch completion           5,231,711
write complete waits                 5,200,368
```

Using Active Session History (ASH) for Troubleshooting   **233**

```
db file scattered read                  4452,153
process startup                          3623,464
rdbms ipc reply                           917,765
log file sync                             662,224
latch free                                550,241
latch: library cache                      370,696
db file parallel write                    364,641
free buffer waits                         319,151
latch: redo allocation                     64,984
LGWR wait for redo copy                    63,647
read by other session                      52,757
log file sequential read                   46,126
null event                                 33,011
log file parallel write                    26,280
SQL*Net more data to client                 8,894
latch: cache buffers chains                 7,005
control file sequential read                3,966
direct path read temp                         395
direct path write temp                        229
SQL*Net message to client                      74
```

The results listing above indicates an issue with the *log buffer space wait* event that may indicate the need to increase the *log_buffer* parameter to increase the cache in order to minimize this possible bottleneck.

Using the AWR ASH view, the DBA can also retrieve a list of database users who have experienced high wait times during the time period between any two snapshots. The following query can be used to identify these target users:

```
select
   s.sid,
   s.username,
   sum(h.wait_time + h.time_waited) "total wait time"
from
   v$active_session_history      h,
   v$session                     s,
   v$event_name                  e
where
   h.session_id = s.sid
and
   e.event_id = h.event_id
and
   e.wait_class <> 'Idle'
and
   s.username IS NOT NULL
group by
   s.sid, s.username
order by 3;
```

This sample output shows the total wait time, both by process ID (SID) and by individual users.

```
       SID   USERNAME          total wait time
---------- --------------    ---------------
       261   SYS                  1,537,288
       259   SYS                 12,247,007
       254   SYS                 18,640,736
```

The next sample query against the AWR ASH table shows a list of database objects that caused the most wait times during time interval stored in AWR. Idle wait times are not included in the output.

```
select
   o.owner,
   o.object_name,
   o.object_type,
   SUM(h.wait_time + h.time_waited) "total wait time"
from
   v$active_session_history     h,
   dba_objects                  o,
   v$event_name                 e
where
   h.current_obj# = o.object_id
and
   e.event_id = h.event_id
and
   e.wait_class <> 'Idle'
group by
   o.owner,
   o.object_name,
   o.object_type
order by 4 DESC;
```

This report produces a list of hot objects which might be candidates for further tuning investigations:

OWNER	Object Name	Object Type	total wait time
SYSMAN	MGMT_OMS_PARAMETERS	TABLE	1,1232E+10
SYS	SCHEDULER$_WINDOW_DE TAILS	TABLE	2989867
SYSMAN	MPVV_PK	INDEX	1333198
SYSMAN	MGMT_DELTA_ENTRY_SHO ULD_BE_UK	INDEX	835641
SYSMAN	MGMT_DB_LATEST_HDM_F INDINGS	TABLE	397504
SYS	CDEF$	TABLE	116853
SYS	I_LINK1	INDEX	46922
SYS	SYS_IOT_TOP_8542	INDEX	25469
SYS	I_COM1	INDEX	24908
SYS	I_CDEF3	INDEX	23125
SYSMAN	MGMT_DB_LATEST_HDM_F INDINGS	INDEX	11325
SYS	I_OBJ2	INDEX	5953
SYS	WRH$_ACTIVE_SESSION_ HISTORY_BL	TABLE	304
SYSTEM	SQLPLUS_PRODUCT_PROF ILE	TABLE	3

As part of Oracle's commitment to time-series tuning, 10g contains major changes in the *x$* structures as well as many new and modified *v$* performance views. Figure 5.52 shows the 10g *v$* views relating to database events.

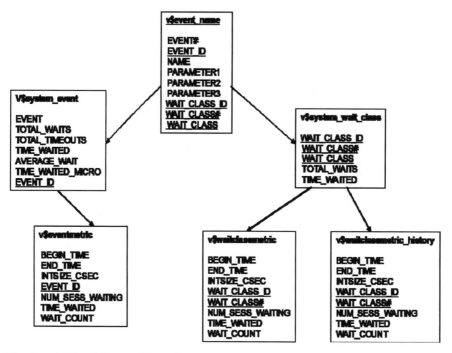

Figure 5.52: *The Oracle10g v$ System Event Structure*

The following section will explore how the ASH information can be viewed from inside Oracle Enterprise Manager (OEM).

Using ASH in OEM

Together, the AWR and ASH metrics form the foundation for a complete Oracle tuning framework, and the Enterprise Manager provides a great tool for visualizing the bottlenecks. Now that the underlying wait event collection mechanism has been explained, it is time to explore how OEM gives an intelligent window into this critical Oracle tuning information.

Before the use of OEM to identify a performance issue is examined, it must be noted that the AWR and ASH information can be used inside OEM to create customized exception alerts. Even when no one is watching, OEM can send an e-mail warning about any impending performance issue. Figure 5.53 shows the ASH alert threshold screen:

▼ Wait Bottlenecks	None
Active Sessions	Not Set
Active Sessions Using CPU	Not Set
Active Sessions Using CPU (%)	Not Set
Active Sessions Waiting: I/O	Not Set
Active Sessions Waiting: I/O (%)	Not Set
Active Sessions Waiting: Other	Not Set
Active Sessions Waiting: Other (%)	Not Set
Average Instance CPU (%)	Not Set
CPU Time (sec)	Not Set
Wait Time (%)	Not Set
Wait Time (sec)	Not Set

Figure 5.53: *OEM ASH Wait Bottleneck Metrics*

This is an especially important screen for customizing OEM alerts because thresholds can be set based on changes with either absolute or delta-based metrics. For example, it may be desirable to have OEM alert when the following session metrics are exceeded:

- **Active Sessions Waiting I/O:** Alert when there are more than 500 active sessions waiting on I/O.

- **Active Sessions Waiting I/O (%):** Alert when active sessions waiting on I/O increase by more than 10%.

- **Wait Time (sec):** Alert when wait time exceeds two seconds.

- **Wait Time (%):** Alert when wait time increases by more than 25%.

The OEM also allows the viewing of session wait information at the metric level. For example, if OEM informs the DBA that the major wait event in the database is related to concurrency such as locks, latches and pins, the DBA can drill down on the concurrency link to go to the OEM Active sessions waiting screen as shown in Figure 5.54.

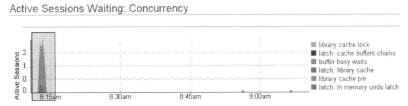

Figure 5.54: *The OEM Display for Active Sessions Waiting on Concurrency*

This display is also a learning aid because OEM lists all of the sources of concurrency waits including library cache lock, latch and buffer busy waits, and it also displays the values associated with each concurrency component. After a double click on the chosen snapshot, OEM delivers a summary histogram of the response time components for the top ten SQL statements and top ten sessions that were identified during the AWR snapshot as shown in Figure 5.55.

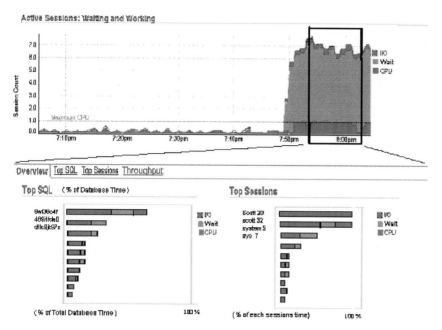

Figure 5.55: *The OEM Top Ten SQL and Top Ten Session Response Time Component Display*

This visual display of summary information allows the quick identification of the most resource-intensive tasks. In addition, it is instantly possible to see if the main response time component is I/O, CPU or Oracle internal wait events. Oracle performance investigations that used to take hours are now completed in a matter of seconds.

While this functionality of OEM is amazing in its own right, Oracle10g took the AWR model beyond the intelligent display of performance metrics. Using true Artificial Intelligence (AI), OEM also has a built-in interface to the Automatic Database Diagnostic Monitor (ADDM), and the intelligent SQL Tuning Advisor, both of which are explored in other chapters.

The main OEM performance screen displays a summary of session wait time server-side components as shown in Figure 5.56. Understanding the components involved in total response time can give huge insight into the root cause of a performance bottleneck.

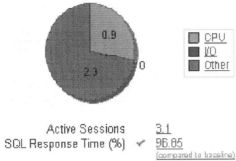

Active Sessions   3.1
SQL Response Time (%) ✓ 96.85
(compared to baseline)

Figure 5.56: *Active Session Response Time OEM Summary Display*

In this figure, there are currently 3.1 active sessions with approximately one-third of the response time being consumed in CPU activities. This is a very common profile for 10g databases with large data caches. The figure also includes the important SQL Response Time (%) delta metric that displays marginal changes on overall SQL performance.

The OEM interface to ASH also facilitates drilling down to view details on any of the active Oracle session. Figure 5.57 shows the hyperlinks to detailed session statistics, wait events, open cursors and locks associated with the task.

Session Details: SID 42

Collected From Target

General | Statistics Wait Events Open Cursors Locks

Serial Number **52801**	Logged On Since **2003-08-13 08:22:58.0**
Current Status **INACTIVE**	Last Activity On **2003-08-13 09:09:57.0**
Wait Event **IDLE**	Connection Type **DEDICATED**
OS Server Process ID **2445**	SQL ID **No currently executing SQL**
DB User Name **OLAF**	
Resource Consumer Group **0**	

Application Information

Program **JDBC Thin Client**
Module **Oracle Enterprise Manager**
Command **UNKNOWN**

Client Information

OS Client Process ID **1234**
OS User Name **0**
Terminal **0**

Figure 5.57: *Session Level Detail Display in OEM*

Conclusion

This chapter has shown that real-time wait event information is captured in *v$* views and 10046 trace files. For an extra cost, Oracle provides the Active Session History views which can relieve the DBA from the tedium of detailed trace setup. The main points of this chapter include:

- **ASH is not required:** All ASH functionality can be captured with free, traditional techniques.

- **ASH captures wait event details:** The *v$active_session_history* view collects wait state details every 60 seconds and stores them in a rolling buffer.

- **Long-term retention:** The data from *v$active_session_history* is transferred to *dba_hist_active_sess_history* whenever an AWR snapshot is taken.

- **OEM performance pack and diagnostic pack:** The Oracle tools have a visual interface into the ASH views, but specialized trending tools such as Ion for Oracle can also be used to identify trends and signatures in wait events.

Now it is time to begin taking a wider view and exploring all of the wait event details and metrics in the following chapters.

Inside STATSPACK and AWR

AWR and STATSPACK give you insight into your database

Introduction to Tuning with STATSPACK

As we have previously discussed, STATSPACK and AWR provide us with invaluable time-series information for Oracle tuning, and we are now ready to take a closer look at the specific tables within this goldmine of historical performance data. For those who do not wish to purchase the extra-cost AWR (via licensing the Oracle diagnostic pack and Oracle performance pack), a STATSPACK remains a great no extra-cost alternative.

Before diving into the details of these utilities, let's see how Oracle has evolved these historical data collection mechanisms.

- **Oracle 7:** In the early 1990s, the first effective proactive time-series method for Oracle performance appeared in Oracle 7 and involved begin and end snapshots using the *utlbstat* and *utlestat* utilities which related a time-series report that still resembles the 11g STATSPACK and AWR reports.

- **Oracle 8:** Back in Oracle 8, this author published scripts to alter the *estat* utility to store the report data inside DBA defined extension tables.

- **Oracle 8i:** Starting in 1998 with Oracle 8i, Oracle Corporation codified this approach with the STATSPACK utility.

- **Oracle 10g:** Starting in Oracle 10g, AWR was built into the Oracle kernel and offered as an extra-cost supplement to STATSPACK.

- **Oracle 11g:** Oracle continues to build intelligent advisor tools that use the AWR data. As of 2010, none of these tools are as good as a human expert.

STATSPACK remains popular in 11g and there is talk at Oracle Corporation of discontinuing the free STATSPACK in the next major release of Oracle. However, this will not succeed since the scripts to take snapshots are easily lifted and moved between releases. When STATSPACK first came out in Oracle8i, a smart DBA could backport it to Oracle 8, and if STATSPACK were to be removed from a future release, scripts could be created to replicate the STATSPACK functionality.

Oracle Corporation works with remarkable predictability, and historically we see a new major release of Oracle about every 3.16 years (Figure 6.1):

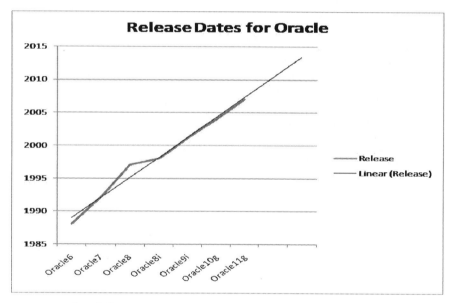

Figure 6.1: *Oracle Does a New Release Every Three Years*

Remember, while primitive time-series reports are available within Oracle Enterprise Manager (OEM), the expert Oracle DBA will go beyond the limited functionality of ADDM and the SQLTuning Advisor. Advanced time series analysis, hypothesis testing and correlation analysis still require special techniques and custom queries against the STATSPACK or AWR tables.

Oracle vs. STATSPACK

Because AWR branched off from STATSPACK in Oracle 10g, they remain remarkably similar and undergo many of the same enhancements. Table 6.1 below shows the comparison of Oracle STATSPACK tables to their AWR equivalents. Note that the *wrh$* fixed views are the building blocks for AWR, built into the Oracle software. Fortunately, many of the names of the *wrh$* tables are identical to their *stats$* equivalents making it easy to migrate STATSPACK scripts to AWR.

DBA HIST TABLE	WRH$ VIEW	STATSPACK TABLE
dba_hist_event_summary	wrh$_bg_event_summary	stats$bg_event_summary
dba_hist_buffer_pool_statistics	wrh$_buffer_pool_statistics	stats$buffer_pool_statistics
dba_hist_filestatxs	wrh$_filestatxs	stats$filestatxs
dba_hist_latch	wrh$_latch	stats$latch
dba_hist_latch_children	wrh$_latch_children	stats$latch_children
dba_hist_librarycache	wrh$_librarycache	stats$librarycache
dba_hist_rowcache_summary	wrh$_rowcache_summary	stats$rowcache_summary
dba_hist_sgastat	wrh$_sgastat	stats$sgastat
dba_hist_sql_summary	wrh$_sql_summary	stats$sql_summary
dba_hist_sysstat	wrh$_sysstat	stats$sysstat
dba_hist_system_event	wrh$_system_event	stats$system_event
dba_hist_waitstat	wrh$_waitstat	stats$waitstat

Table 6.1: *STATSPACK, DBA HIST and wrh$ Equivalencies*

Fortunately, Oracle has kept the column definitions almost identical between STATSPACK and AWR, making it easy to downgrade to STATSPACK if you don't want to pay the thousands of dollars to license AWR. Conversely, if you have just purchased an AWR license, it's easy to port your STATSPACK scripts to AWR.

To begin, let's revisit this simple example of an AWR query. The script below gathers physical disk read counts, the phyrds column of *dba_hist_filestatxs*. It then joins this data into the *dba_hist_snapshot* view to get the *begin_interval_time* column.

🖫 awr_disk_reads.sql

```
break on begin_interval_time skip 2

column phyrds  format 999,999,999
column begin_interval_time format a25

select
```

```
   begin_interval_time,
   filename,
   phyrds
from
   dba_hist_filestatxs
 natural join
   dba_hist_snapshot;
```

Executing this script shows a running total of physical reads, organized by datafile. In this case, the AWR snapshots are collected every half-hour, but it is possible to adjust the snapshot collection interval depending on data needs.

```
SQL> @reads
```

```
BEGIN_INTERVAL_TIME        FILENAME                                     PHYRDS
------------------------    -----------------------------------------   ----------
24-FEB-04 11.00.32.000 PM  E:\ORACLE\ORA92\FSDEV10G\SYSTEM01.DBF         164,700
                           E:\ORACLE\ORA92\FSDEV10G\UNDOTBS01.DBF         26,082
                           E:\ORACLE\ORA92\FSDEV10G\SYSAUX01.DBF         472,008
                           E:\ORACLE\ORA92\FSDEV10G\USERS01.DBF            1,794
                           E:\ORACLE\ORA92\FSDEV10G\T_FS_LSQ.ORA           2,123


24-FEB-04 11.30.18.296 PM  E:\ORACLE\ORA92\FSDEV10G\SYSTEM01.DBF         167,809
                           E:\ORACLE\ORA92\FSDEV10G\UNDOTBS01.DBF         26,248
                           E:\ORACLE\ORA92\FSDEV10G\SYSAUX01.DBF         476,616
                           E:\ORACLE\ORA92\FSDEV10G\USERS01.DBF            1,795
                           E:\ORACLE\ORA92\FSDEV10G\T_FS_LSQ.ORA           2,244


25-FEB-04 12.01.06.562 AM  E:\ORACLE\ORA92\FSDEV10G\SYSTEM01.DBF         169,940
                           E:\ORACLE\ORA92\FSDEV10G\UNDOTBS01.DBF         26,946
                           E:\ORACLE\ORA92\FSDEV10G\SYSAUX01.DBF         483,550
                           E:\ORACLE\ORA92\FSDEV10G\USERS01.DBF            1,799
                           E:\ORACLE\ORA92\FSDEV10G\T_FS_LSQ.ORA           2,248
```

This small, simple script is quite powerful. This script can be enhanced by adding to the *where* clause to create a unique time-series exception report on any specific data file or any specific time periods.

Of course, with a few minor adjustments to this script, physical writes, read time, write time, single block reads, and a host of other metrics from *dba_hist_filestatxs* view can also be displayed.
Now, let's drill deeper into the AWR tables and see how they store time series tuning information.

Inside the AWR tables

Oracle has over 60 *dba_hist* views, each one mapping to underlying *x$* and *wrh$* component fixed tables. For example, the listing below shows the internal creation syntax for the *dba_hist_sysstat* view.

Let's look at how these tables are assembled. Figure 6.2 shows how the *dba_hist_sysstat* view is built from *wrm$_snapshot*, *wrh$_sysstat* and *dba_hist_stat_name* tables:.

```
create table
   dba_hist_sysstat
```

```
as
select
    s.snap_id,
    s.dbid,
    s.instance_number,
    s.statistic#,
    s.statistic_hash,
    nm.statistic_name, value
from
    wrm$_snapshot        sn,
    wrh$_sysstat          s,
    dba_hist_stat_name nm
where
    s.statistic_hash = nm.statistic_hash
and s.statistic# = nm.statistic#
and s.dbid = nm.dbid
and s.snap_id = sn.snap_id
and s.dbid = sn.dbid
and s.instance_number = sn.instance_number
and sn.status = 0
and sn.bl_moved = 0
union all
select
    s.snap_id,
    s.dbid,
    s.instance_number,
    s.statistic#,
    s.statistic_hash,
    nm.statistic_name, value
from
    WRM$_SNAPSHOT sn,
    WRH$_SYSSTAT_BL s,
    DBA_HIST_STAT_NAME nm
where
    s.statistic_hash = nm.statistic_hash
and s.statistic# = nm.statistic#
and s.dbid = nm.dbid
and s.snap_id = sn.snap_id
and s.dbid = sn.dbid
and s.instance_number = sn.instance_number
and sn.status = 0
and sn.bl_moved = 1;
```

Figure 6.2: *The Creation Script for dba_hist_sysstat*

Remember, AWR and STATSPACK are close cousins, and they capture a lot of the same information. Due to the common types of performance data captured by AWR and STATSPACK, the *dba_hist* views have columns that are also in STATSPACK and table 6.2 lists a few of the more familiar views.

The column names in the AWR tables are different from the STATSPACK tables, but the types of performance data collected by these STATSPACK tables is essentially the same as that found inside the *dba_hist* views.

DBA_HIST VIEW	STATSPACK TABLE
dba_hist_bg_event_summary	stats$bg_event_summary
dba_hist_buffer_pool_statistics	stats$buffer_pool_statistics

DBA_HIST VIEW	STATSPACK TABLE
dba_hist_filestatxs	stats$filestatxs
dba_hist_latch	stats$latch
dba_hist_latch_children	stats$latch_children
dba_hist_librarycache	stats$librarycache
dba_hist_rowcache_summary	stats$rowcache_summary
dba_hist_sgastat	stats$sgastat
dba_hist_sql_summary	stats$sql_summary
dba_hist_sysstat	stats$sysstat
dba_hist_system_event	stats$system_event
dba_hist_waitstat	stats$waitstat

Table 6.2: *STATSPACK vs. AWR Tables*

Now move on and examine some of the most important *dba_hist* views for time-series and exception reporting. Since the data is common to both tools, let's start with STATSPACK, the free tool.

Using STATSPACK for Oracle Tuning

Just like AWR, STATSPACK stores performance and workload data inside specialized tables, and STATSPACK has a set of 25 tables that can be used to analyze historical performance trends. By querying these tables with standard SQL, we can gain tremendous insight into the performance of our databases.

As seen in Figure 6.3, the 25 STATSPACK tables provide a complete picture of everything that is going on within the Oracle database.

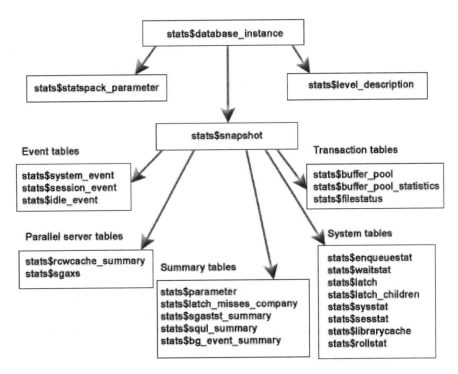

Figure 6.3: *The Structure of the STATSPACK Tables*

The STATSPACK schema contains several control tables. The *stats$parameter* tables control the thresholds for snapshot collection, and a table called *stats$level_description* provides information regarding the level of detail within a snapshot.

Watch the SQL history tables!

The *stats$sql_summary* table will grow very rapidly because STATSPACK will extract SQL from the library cache every time a snapshot is executed, based on one's collection thresholds settings.

Look Out!

Because of rapid growth, we need to be careful to set the appropriate threshold values for *stats$sql_summary* data collection and also run a periodic script to delete older rows from STATSPACK when the SQL details are no longer needed. A good recommendation is to keep the current month's worth of SQL and then delete the older rows from the STATSPACK tables.

The structure of the STATSPACK tables

The main anchor for STATSPACK is the table called *stats$snapshot*. This table contains the snapshot ID for all of the subordinate tables and the *snap_time* indicating when the snapshot was taken.

Oracle also implements all of the subordinate tables with referential integrity using the *on cascade delete* option. This means that the *stats$snapshot* table can be deleted in order to delete rows from all of the subordinate tables after they have passed their useful lives within the database.

Underneath the *stats$snapshot* table, there are several categories of system tables. These categories include *event* tables, *parallel server* tables, *SGA summary* tables, *system* tables, and *transaction* tables:

- **Event tables:** These tables contain information about system, session, and idle events within the Oracle region.

- **Parallel server tables:** These tables are used in an OPS environment to store information about row caching in the Integrated Distributed Lock Manager (IDLM) as well as SGA information.

- **SGA summary tables:** These tables store information about latches, SGA statistics, SQL statements, and the background events within Oracle.

- **System tables:**   The system table section of the STATSPACK utility contains information on enqueue stats, waits stats, and latch stats as well as system and session statistics, including information on the library cache and rollback statistics.

- **Transaction tables:** The STATSPACK transaction tables contain information about the buffer pool, the buffer pool statistics, and most importantly, the I/O activity against every file within the system.

Taken together, these 25 STATSPACK tables provide a huge amount of information regarding the performance of the Oracle database. It is the challenge of the Oracle DBA to understand these tables and the value of the information they contain and then to apply this information to satisfy the performance tuning needs.

How STATSPACK Works

As we have noted, the Oracle STATSPACK utility was the natural outgrowth of Oracle's earlier utilities that compared beginning snapshots with ending snapshots.

Starting with STATSPACK in Oracle 8.1.6, the STATSPACK utility can take the output of elapsed-time reports and store the results in Oracle tables where they can be used for time-series analysis. The STATSPACK tables are easy to create and define, and it is also easy to set up collection mechanisms for any Oracle system.

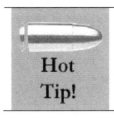

Remember to turn off AWR!

If you choose to use the free STATSPACK utility, you should disable the automatic AWR snapshot collection.

Hot Tip!

Once the STATSPACK software and snapshots collector is installed, you can use the STATSPACK data to create many types of reports including elapsed time reports, alert reports for out-of-bounds conditions, and trend reports.

Installing the STATSPACK utility is simple and straightforward and will be covered in detail in Chapter 7, *AWR and STATSPACK Configuration*.

To create the STATSPACK tables, simply go to the *$oracle_home/rdbms/admin* directory and run the scripts beginning with *stats*. The scripts create a set of 25 STATSPACK tables and also install several PL/SQL packages and procedures that are used by the STATSPACK utility to run elapsed-time reports and store the resulting information into the STATSPACK tables.

Understand the STATSPACK Levels

There are three snapshot collection levels used in STATSPACK, each level capturing increasingly detailed information. Level 5 is the default:

- **Level 0: General performance statistics**: This level collects general performance statistics such as wait statistics, system events, system statistics, rollback segment data, row cache, SGA, background events, session events, lock statistics, buffer pool statistics, and parent latch statistics.

- **Level 5: Add SQL statements**: This level includes all level 0 statistics plus SQL statements in the *stats$sql_summary* table.

- **Level 10: Add child latch statistics:** This level includes everything in the level 5 statistics plus child latches in the *stats$latch_children* table. We rarely, if ever, need this level of detail and should do a level 10 snapshot only when directed by Oracle technical support.

Once STATSPACK is installed, there are several ways to activate it. The most common way is to go into SQL*Plus as the *perfstat* user and execute *statsauto.sql*. This will schedule a STATSPACK data collection snapshot every hour. Most Oracle professionals can install and configure STATSPACK in a few hours. The real challenge is deciding how to use the information that has been collected. The information gathered in the STATSPACK tables can be used in several general areas of Oracle reporting.

Specifying snapshot ranges

To get reports from the snapshots, you need to manually specify the range of snapshots for any STATSPACK and AWR reports. The Ion for Oracle tool has a GUI that allows you to choose your snapshot ranges (Figure 6.4).

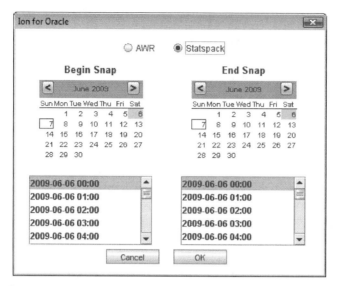

Figure 6.4: *Ion Display Screen for STATSPACK Collections*

Once the data is collected into STATSPACK or AWR, we can use standard SQL to get all sorts of reports about the historical performance.

Generating reports with SQL and Scripts

There are many techniques for running STATSPACK and AWR queries and you can even use Oracle analytic functions to display changes over time. Oracle guru Dan Fink has these examples of using Oracle analytic SQL for STATSPACK trend reports. This script compares the changes between snapshot periods, in this case the time period between snapshots 313 and 320:

```
select
   s1.ucomment,
   w1.event,
   s1.snap_id,
   w1.total_waits,
   lag(w1.total_waits)
   over (order by s1.snap_id) prev_val,
   w1.total_waits -
   lag(w1.total_waits)
   over (order by s1.snap_id) delta_val
from
   stats$snapshot      s1,
   stats$system_event w1
where
   s1.snap_id between 313 and 320
and
   s1.snap_id = w1.snap_id
and
   w1.event = 'db file sequential read'
```

```
order by
   w1.event, s1.snap_id;
```

You can also use Oracle analytic functions for comparing two periods in STATSPACK. In this example, out SQL specifies a list of valid snapshots.

```
select
   sy.snap_id,
   sy.statistic# statistic#,
   sy.name statname,
   sy.value - (LAG(sy.value)
   over (partition by sy.name
   order by sy.snap_id)) statdelta
from
   stats$sysstat sy
where
   sy.snap_id in (12208,12599,13480,13843)
and
   sy.name IN
   ('consistent gets','consistent changes',
   'db block gets', 'db block changes')
order by
   sy.name, sy.snap_id;
```

It's also easy to put a STATSPACK or AWR alert into a UNIX/Linux shell script that will e-mail the DBA whenever an exceptional condition is detected. Below is a script that will look for significant wait events in STATSPACK and e-mail the alert to the DBA.

💾 wait_alert_email.ksh

```
#!/bin/ksh

# First, we must set the environment . . . .
ORACLE_SID=proderp
export ORACLE_SID
ORACLE_HOME=`cat /var/opt/oracle/oratab|grep \^$ORACLE_SID:|cut -f2 -d':'`
export ORACLE_HOME
PATH=$ORACLE_HOME/bin:$PATH
export PATH

SERVER_NAME=`uname -a|awk '{print $2}'`
typeset -u SERVER_NAME
export SERVER_NAME

# sample every 10 seconds
SAMPLE_TIME=10

while true
do

   #***************************************************************
   # Test to see if Oracle is accepting connections
   #***************************************************************
   $ORACLE_HOME/bin/sqlplus -s /<<! > /tmp/check_$ORACLE_SID.ora
   select * from v\$database;
   exit
```

```
!

#*****************************************************************
# If not, exit immediately . . .
#*****************************************************************
check_stat=`cat /tmp/check_$ORACLE_SID.ora|grep -i error|wc -l`;
oracle_num=`expr $check_stat`
if [ $oracle_num -gt 0 ]
 then
 exit 0
fi

rm -f /export/home/oracle/statspack/busy.lst

$ORACLE_HOME/bin/sqlplus -s perfstat/perfstat<<!> /tmp/busy.lst

set feedback off;
select
   sysdate,
   event,
   substr(tablespace_name,1,14),
   p2
from
   v\$session_wait a,
   dba_data_files  b
where
   a.p1 = b.file_id
;
!

var=`cat /tmp/busy.lst|wc -l`

echo $var
if [[ $var -gt 1 ]];
 then
  echo
*****************************************************************"
  echo "There are waits"
  cat /tmp/busy.lst|mailx -s "Prod block wait found"\
  info@remote-dba.net \
  Larry_Ellison@oracle.com
  echo
*****************************************************************"
 exit
fi

sleep $SAMPLE_TIME
done
```

Next, look at the other area of STATSPACK reporting that makes use of STATSPACK for long-term trend analysis.

Trend Reports with STATSPACK

While STATSPACK is great for comparing short-time ranges, STATSPACK reports are even more interesting for doing long-term trend analysis. Because STATSPACK can be configured to take hourly reports of the entire Oracle database, it is extremely useful for doing long-term planning in trend analysis and developing predictive models for future resource consumption.

Unlike any other Oracle tool, the STATSPACK and AWR utilities can be used to provide insight into both hourly and daily trends, unobtrusive events that are hard to see without a specialized tool. Predictive trends can be visualized by running STATSPACK reports to see trends by the day of the week or the hour of the day and plotting these in a graph.

Almost all Oracle databases have repeating SQL workload characteristics, and it is the job of the Oracle DBA to identify those patterns and plan for the changes in database activity. By knowing those repeating periods when our database changed workload characteristics we can take appropriate action in order to alleviate the problem.

The most common uses of STATSPACK reports for trend analysis have to do with creating predictive models to determine when their Oracle databases are going to run short of CPU, memory, or disk hardware resources. These types of resources can usually be predicted for several different kinds of STATSPACK reports, such as the one shown in Figure 6.5.

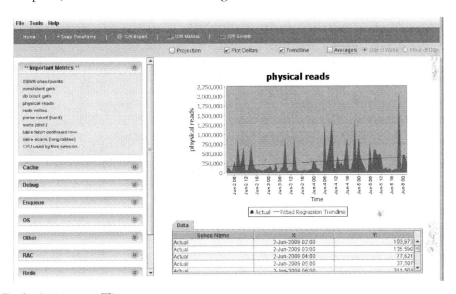

Figure 6.5: *Disk Activity over Time*

This report was created by querying the *stats$filestatxs* table, and it shows a long-term trend report for physical disk reads, the single most time-consuming operation ion any database.

However, you don't need to buy a tool to plot STATSPACK and AWR data. Your script output can be easily extracted, pasted into a Microsoft Excel spreadsheet, and then you can use the chart wizard can to create a linear regression to see future needs of the Oracle database. These types of reports are indispensable for Oracle managers charged with capacity planning, ordering hardware resources before the Oracle database suffers any significant performance degradation.

This query from the *Oracle Sponge* web site shows a technique that computes wait times for sequential and scattered reads:

💾 event_read_waits.sql

```
select to_char(snap_time,'mm/dd/yyyy hh24:mi:ss') snaptime
, max(decode(event,'db file scattered read', nvl(wait_ms,0), null)) wait_ms_dbfscatrd
, max(decode(event,'db file sequential read',nvl(wait_ms,0), null)) wait_ms_dbfseqrd
, max(decode(event,'db file scattered read', nvl(waits,0), null)) waits_dbfscatrd
, max(decode(event,'db file sequential read',nvl(waits,0), null)) waits_dbfseqrd
from
(
select ps.snap_time
, event
, case
when (total_waits - lag_total_waits > 0)
then round(( (time_waited_micro - lag_time_waited_micro) / (total_waits - lag_total_waits))
/ 1000)
else -1
end wait_ms
, (total_waits - lag_total_waits) waits
, (time_waited_micro - lag_time_waited_micro) time_waited
from (
select se.snap_id
, event
, se.total_waits
, se.total_timeouts
, se.time_waited_micro
, lag(se.event) over (order by snap_id, event) lag_event
, lag(se.snap_id) over (order by snap_id, event) lag_snap_id
, lag(se.total_waits) over (order by snap_id, event) lag_total_waits
, lag(se.total_timeouts) over (order by snap_id, event) lag_total_timeouts
, lag(se.time_waited_micro) over (order by snap_id, event) lag_time_waited_micro
from perfstat.stats$system_event se
where event = 'db file sequential read'
and snap_id in (select snap_id from stats$snapshot
where snap_time > trunc(sysdate) - 1
)
union all
select se.snap_id
, event
, se.total_waits
, se.total_timeouts
, se.time_waited_micro
, lag(se.event) over (order by snap_id, event) lag_event
, lag(se.snap_id) over (order by snap_id, event) lag_snap_id
, lag(se.total_waits) over (order by snap_id, event) lag_total_waits
, lag(se.total_timeouts) over (order by snap_id, event) lag_total_timeouts
, lag(se.time_waited_micro) over (order by snap_id, event) lag_time_waited_micro
from perfstat.stats$system_event se
where event = 'db file scattered read'
and snap_id in (select snap_id from stats$snapshot
where snap_time > trunc(sysdate) -1
)
order by event, snap_id
) a
, perfstat.stats$snapshot ss
, perfstat.stats$snapshot ps
where a.lag_snap_id = ps.snap_id
and a.snap_id = ss.snap_id
and a.lag_total_waits != a.total_waits
and a.event = a.lag_event
order by a.snap_id, event
)
group by snap_time
;
```

SNAPTIME	RD	WAIT_MS	WAITS_DBFSCATRD	WAITS_DBFSEQRD
06/06/2009 03:00:00		5		52911
06/06/2009 05:00:02		5		39646
06/06/2009 06:00:04	1	2	3966	1191959
06/06/2009 07:00:00		2		130977
06/06/2009 09:00:03		3		367850
06/06/2009 20:00:03	4	3	1	562774

This type of STATSPACK data can also be summarized by day of the week to show overall trends on a daily basis. Now, that we get the general idea about using STATSPACK, let's move on and look at the AWR tables.

Inside the AWR Tables

Originally, the AWR was added in Oracle 10g to provide data for Oracle's extra-cost diagnostic and performance packs, but it has much of the same information as the free STATSPACK utility. We also discussed that the *dba_hist* views that comprise AWR are built from their underlying *wrh$* equivalents. These views serve to provide the data source for a wealth of customizable reports for identification of trends and time-series performance optimization.

All custom queries that are written against the *dba_hist* views require a join into the *dba_hist_snapshot* view, which is the main anchor for the AWR history views. Figure 6.6 shows the anchor *dba_hist_snapshot* view and samples of summary and detail *dba_hist* views.

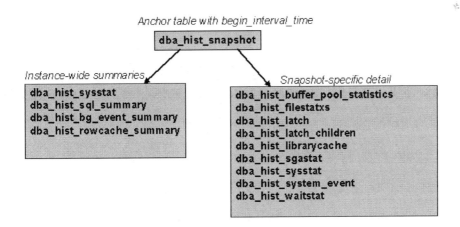

Figure 6.6: *A Sample of the dba_hist Views for the AWR*

Within these *dba_hist* views, there are thousands of possible statistics to examine, a virtual gold mine of performance data. The trick to success with AWR reports is to start simple and add successive detail.

From the simple reports, more sophisticated reports can be created for exception reporting, trend identification, correlation analysis, and hypothesis testing.

The AWR Data Collection Mechanism

While the Oracle STATSPACK utility remains idle until activated, the AWR automated polling mechanism is automatic, and collects a huge amount of performance data from Oracle and automatically stores it for time-based analysis. The AWR data collection process is fast and simple. It is essentially the transfer of in-memory statistics from the *x$* fixed tables into the corresponding *wrh$* tables.

Starting in 10g, Oracle introduced the new Manageability Monitor (MMON) background process to handle data collection for AWR and ASH. In addition to the accumulated metrics from the *x$* fixed tables, MMON also collects average event metrics such as consistent gets per second or user calls per transaction.

There are approximately 180 metrics that are gathered by AWR automatically, and these metrics are instantly available by querying *v$* dynamic views such as *v$sysmetric_history* or *v$sysmetric_summary*. The AWR keeps the history for metrics in its special *wrh$* internal tables and provides *dba_hist* views to access them. These wait event metrics are presented in more detail later in this book.

Now that we are armed with information on AWR data collection, the following section will show us all about custom AWR scripts.

Customizing AWR snapshots

The default retention period for AWR data is only seven days and adjustments must be made in the AWR to perform time-based tuning.

The adjustment to increase the retention periods and interval can be made by invoking the *dbms_workload_.modify_snapshot_settings* procedure.

Also, the *recodify_snapshot_settings* procedure will change the AWR retention period and collection frequency to make the date available for longer periods of time. For example:

```
execute dbms_workload_repository.modify_snapshot_settings (
   interval => 60,
   retention => 43200);
```

In this example, the retention period is specified as 30 days (43,200 minutes) and the interval between each snapshot is 60 minutes.

The architecture of the AWR is quite simple, as shown in Figure 6.7. The MMON background process polls the *x$* fixed tables from the SGA region and stores them in the AWR tables.

From there, the performance data is instantly available for analysis and the Oracle Enterprise Manager GUI can be used for graphical data display. Alternatively, the Automatic Database Diagnostic Monitor (ADDM) can be used for automated tuning analysis, or SQL*Plus can be used if customized Oracle tuning size reports are desired.

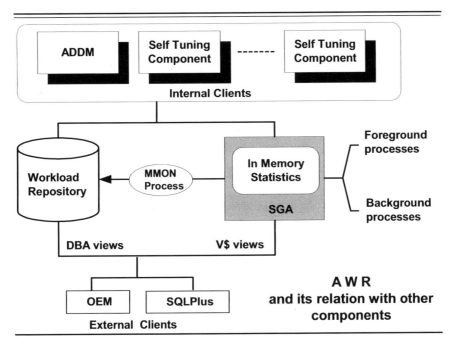

Figure 6.7: *The AWR Architecture*

The AWR is very comprehensive and there are thousands of distinct metrics that we can examine, some important, some trivial. For example, the *dba_hist_systat* table contains over 300 individual performance metrics and it's our job to figure out which of these metrics will help us tune our database. Next, let's move on and get a brief overview of the AWR tables and then introduces ways that customized reports can be extracted from the AWR tables.

The Mysterious AWR Performance Tables

Oracle has fixed RAM structures inside the SGA that provide the raw data for STATSPACK and AWR. These Oracle dynamic performance tables (the x$ fixed tables) constitute the foundation of sophisticated automations such as Automatic Memory Management (AMM) as well as intelligent advisory tools such as ADDM and the SQLTuning Advisor. The AWR is a core feature of the 10g database kernel and automatically collects and stores important run-time performance information for historical analysis.

The tables that store this information are prefixed with *wrh$* and are very similar in function to the STATSPACK tables. At first glance, it might seem like STATSPACK is obsolete, but it is still available in the *$oracle_home/rdbms/admin* directory and almost as powerful as AWR.

For beginners, the OEM display of AWR data allows them to misunderstand their system performance far more efficiently than with STATSPACK. Unlike the more cumbersome STATSPACK utility, which requires knowledge of the table structure and creation of complex query scripts, the Oracle Enterprise Manager (OEM) Performance Pack and Diagnostic Pack instantly displays time-series performance data.

Whether it's for STATSPACK or AWR, each snapshot is a capture of the in–memory *x$* fixed tables (and other control structures) at a certain point in time. Each of the internal AWR table names is prefixed with *wrm$* (Metadata tables), *wrh$* (History tables), or *wri$* (Advisory tables).

- The *wrm$* tables store metadata information for the Workload Repository.

- The *wrh$* tables store historical data or snapshots.

- The *wri$* tables: these 49 tables store data related to advisory functions.

Next, let's take a closer look at the underlying data structures and see how the AWR tables store important time-series performance information.

Inside the AWR Tables

Due to the transient nature of the data in the *x$* fixed tables, the goal of AWR and STATSPACK is to make this information persistent. As we have already seen, much of the information collected by the AWR comes from the *x$* fixed table structures in the Oracle heap.

Prior to Oracle 10g, there was no automatic collection of time-series performance data. To get proactive tuning data, we had to take snapshots with the BSTAT-ESTAT utility (in Oracle 6 and Oracle 7). In Oracle8i we got the STATSPACK utility to see our performance over time.

In Oracle 10g and beyond, there are new *v$* metric tables including *v$eventmetric*, *v$waitclassmetric* and *v$waitclassmetric*_history, which offer persistent storage of elapsed time Oracle performance data. These metrics tables are easy to identify because they contain *begin_time* and *end_time* data columns. As a standard, any *v$* views that contain *begin_time* and *end_time* columns are used to store proactive time-series performance information. Next is a quick tour of the basic *dba_hist* tables.

Inside the *dba_hist* Tables

Oracle provides the following *dba_hist* data dictionary tables (Figure 6.8), something for almost every possible statistic:

DBA_HIST_ACTIVE_SESS_HISTORY	DBA_HIST_SEG_STAT
DBA_HIST_BASELINE	DBA_HIST_SEG_STAT_OBJ
DBA_HIST_BG_EVENT_SUMMARY	DBA_HIST_SERVICE_NAME
DBA_HIST_BUFFER_POOL_STAT	DBA_HIST_SERVICE_STAT
DBA_HIST_CLASS_CACHE_TRANSFER	DBA_HIST_SERVICE_WAIT_CLASS
DBA_HIST_CR_BLOCK_SERVER	DBA_HIST_SESSMETRIC_HISTORY
DBA_HIST_CURRENT_BLOCK_SERVER	DBA_HIST_SGA
DBA_HIST_DATABASE_INSTANCE	DBA_HIST_SGASTAT
DBA_HIST_DATAFILE	DBA_HIST_SHARED_POOL_ADVICE
DBA_HIST_DB_CACHE_ADVICE	DBA_HIST_SNAPSHOT
DBA_HIST_DLM_MISC	DBA_HIST_SNAP_ERROR
DBA_HIST_ENQUEUE_STAT	DBA_HIST_SQLBIND
DBA_HIST_EVENT_NAME	DBA_HIST_SQLSTAT
DBA_HIST_FILEMETRIC_HISTORY	DBA_HIST_SQLTEXT
DBA_HIST_FILESTATXS	DBA_HIST_SQL_PLAN
DBA_HIST_INSTANCE_RECOVERY	DBA_HIST_SQL_SUMMARY
DBA_HIST_JAVA_POOL_ADVICE	DBA_HIST_SQL_WORKAREA_HSTGRM
DBA_HIST_LATCH	DBA_HIST_STAT_NAME
DBA_HIST_LATCH_CHILDREN	DBA_HIST_SYSMETRIC_HISTORY
DBA_HIST_LATCH_MISSES_SUMMARY	DBA_HIST_SYSMETRIC_SUMMARY
DBA_HIST_LATCH_NAME	DBA_HIST_SYSSTAT
DBA_HIST_LATCH_PARENT	DBA_HIST_SYSTEM_EVENT
DBA_HIST_LIBRARYCACHE	DBA_HIST_SYS_TIME_MODEL
DBA_HIST_LOG	DBA_HIST_TABLESPACE_STAT
DBA_HIST_METRIC_NAME	DBA_HIST_TBSPC_SPACE_USAGE
DBA_HIST_MTTR_TARGET_ADVICE	DBA_HIST_TEMPFILE
DBA_HIST_OPTIMIZER_ENV	DBA_HIST_TEMPSTATXS
DBA_HIST_OSSTAT	DBA_HIST_THREAD
DBA_HIST_OSSTAT_NAME	DBA_HIST_UNDOSTAT
DBA_HIST_PARAMETER	DBA_HIST_WAITCLASSMET_HISTORY
DBA_HIST_PARAMETER_NAME	DBA_HIST_WAITSTAT
DBA_HIST_PGASTAT	DBA_HIST_WR_CONTROL
DBA_HIST_PGA_TARGET_ADVICE	
DBA_HIST_RESOURCE_LIMIT	
DBA_HIST_ROWCACHE_SUMMARY	

Figure 6.8: *The AWR Data Dictionary List*

The *dba_hist* tables are grouped by the types of performance data available inside the tables, and the Oracle AWR repository collects the history for the following types of database statistics:

- Database wait events

- Metric statistics

- Time model statistics

- System statistics

- Operating system statistics

- SQL statistics

- Segment statistics

- Datafile I/O statistics

The following section presents more details about the statistics provided in the most popular *dba_hist* tables.

Inside the AWR Tables

Database Wait Events in AWR

Database wait event statistics are critical to tuning because they show us how much time a process had to wait for a particular resource. These wait events are grouped by Oracle into several categories including Administrative, Application, Cluster, Commit, Concurrency, Configuration, Idle, Network, Other, Scheduler, System I/O, and User I/O events.

Wait event data is most effective when they are ordered by wait time. This way, the most significant wait events are displayed first as the lead candidates for further investigation. Even though there is a standard AWR report which contains a wait events section that displays top wait events, I like to use the following query to retrieve the top wait events for a particular AWR snapshot interval:

🖫 wt_events_int.sql

```
select event
    , waits "Waits"
    , time "Wait Time (s)"
    , pct*100 "Percent of Tot"
    , waitclass "Wait Class"
from (select e.event_name event
                , e.total_waits - nvl(b.total_waits,0)  waits
                , (e.time_waited_micro - nvl(b.time_waited_micro,0))/1000000  time
                , (e.time_waited_micro - nvl(b.time_waited_micro,0))/
                  (select sum(e1.time_waited_micro - nvl(b1.time_waited_micro,0)) from
dba_hist_system_event b1 , dba_hist_system_event e1
                  where b1.snap_id(+)            = b.snap_id
                    and e1.snap_id               = e.snap_id
                    and b1.dbid(+)               = b.dbid
                    and e1.dbid                  = e.dbid
                    and b1.instance_number(+)    = b.instance_number
                    and e1.instance_number       = e.instance_number
                    and b1.event_id(+)           = e1.event_id
                    and e1.total_waits           > nvl(b1.total_waits,0)
                    and e1.wait_class            <> 'Idle'
    )  pct
                , e.wait_class waitclass
            from
              dba_hist_system_event b ,
              dba_hist_system_event e
        where b.snap_id(+)            = &pBgnSnap
          and e.snap_id               = &pEndSnap
          and b.dbid(+)               = &pDbId
          and e.dbid                  = &pDbId
          and b.instance_number(+)    = &pInstNum
          and e.instance_number       = &pInstNum
          and b.event_id(+)           = e.event_id
          and e.total_waits           > nvl(b.total_waits,0)
          and e.wait_class            <> 'Idle'
      order by time desc, waits desc
    );
```

The sample output of this query looks like:

```
SQL> @ wt_events_int.sql
```

EVENT	Waits	Wait Time(s)	Percent of Tot	Wait Class
control file parallel write	11719	119.13	34,1611762	System I/O
class slave wait	20	102.46	29,3801623	Other
Queue Monitor Task Wait	74	66.74	19,1371008	Other
log file sync	733	20.60	5,90795938	Commit
db file sequential read	1403	16.27	4,09060416	User I/O
log buffer space	178	10.17	2,91745801	Configuration
process startup	114	7.65	2,19243344	Other
db file scattered read	311	2.14	,612767501	User I/O
control file sequential read	7906	1.33	,380047642	System I/O
latch free	254	1.13	,324271668	Other
log file switch completion	20	1.11	,319292495	Configuration

The output of the script displays the wait events ordered by wait times in seconds.

The Ion tool has a report named Top Wait Events that yields output and advice for top wait events that occurred for the particular snapshot interval.

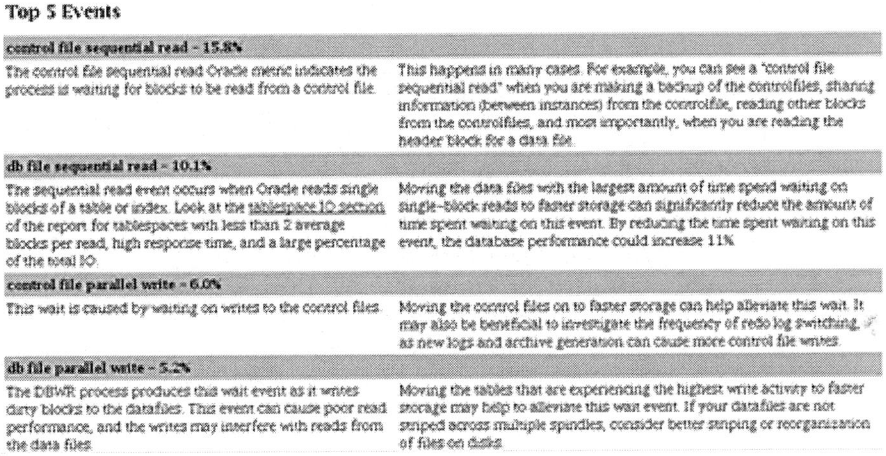

Figure 6.9: *AWR Top Wait Events in Ion*

The following *dba_hist* tables are available for accessing wait events statistics in the AWR. Let's take a closer look.

The dba_hist_system_event table

The *dba_hist_system_event* table displays information about the count of total waits and time waited in microseconds, gathering the data from the *v$system_event* view. The following query can be used to retrieve wait events data for a particular snapshot interval:

```
select
     event "Event Name",
     waits "Waits",
     timeouts "Timeouts",
     time "Wait Time (s)",
     avgwait "Avg Wait (ms)",
     waitclass "Wait Class"
from
     (select e.event_name event
          , e.total_waits - nvl(b.total_waits,0)  waits
          , e.total_timeouts - nvl(b.total_timeouts,0) timeouts
          , (e.time_waited_micro - nvl(b.time_waited_micro,0))/1000000  time
          ,  decode ((e.total_waits - nvl(b.total_waits, 0)), 0, to_number(NULL),
               ((e.time_waited_micro - nvl(b.time_waited_micro,0))/1000) / (e.total_waits -
nvl(b.total_waits,0)) ) avgwait
          , e.wait_class waitclass
     from
          dba_hist_system_event b ,
          dba_hist_system_event e
     where
                    b.snap_id(+)             = &pBgnSnap
            and e.snap_id                    = &pEndSnap
            and b.dbid(+)                    = &pDbId
            and e.dbid                       = &pDbId
            and b.instance_number(+)         = &pInstNum
            and e.instance_number            = &pInstNum
            and b.event_id(+)                = e.event_id
            and e.total_waits                > nvl(b.total_waits,0)
            and e.wait_class                 <> 'Idle' )
order by time desc, waits desc;
```

In the above and some subsequent queries, the following parameters need to have appropriate values substituted for them:

- *BgnSnap*: the start snapshot number for the AWR snapshot interval of interest

- *EndSnap*: the finish snapshot number for the AWR snapshot interval of interest

- *DbId*: the database identified of the target database

- *InstNum*: the instance number of the target database

The sample output for this query looks like the following:

```
SQL> @ Sys_event_int.sql
```

Event Name	Waits	Timeouts	Wait Time (s)	Avg Wait (ms)	Wait Class
control file parallel write	11719	0	119.13	10.17	System I/O
class slave wait	20	20	102.46	5,122.91	Other
Queue Monitor Task Wait	74	0	66.74	901.86	Other
log file sync	733	6	20.60	28.11	Commit
db file sequential read	1403	0	16.27	10.17	User I/O
log buffer space	178	0	10.17	57.16	Configurat
process startup	114	0	7.65	67.07	Other
db file scattered read	311	0	2.14	6.87	User I/O
control file sequential read	7906	0	1.33	.17	System I/O
latch free	254	0	1.13	6.45	Other
log file switch completion	20	0	1.11	55.67	Configurat

The Ion tool has a report named System Wait Events which shows these results as well.

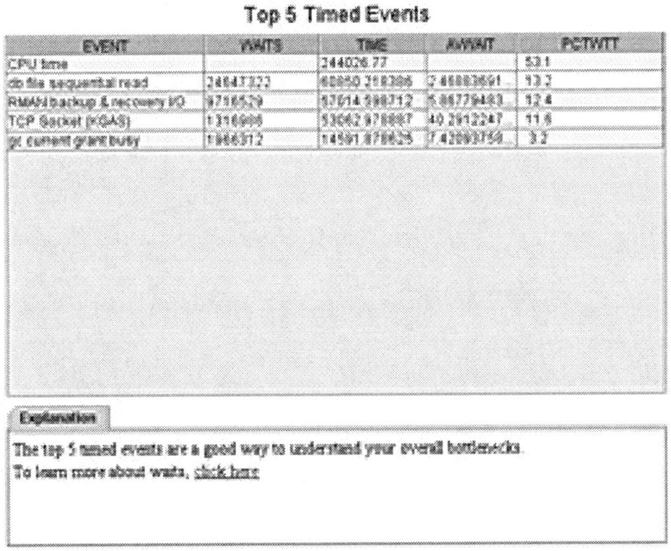

Top 5 Timed Events

EVENT	WAITS	TIME	AWAIT	PCTWTT
CPU time		244026.77		53.1
db file sequential read	24647322	60850.218306	2.46883691	13.2
RMAN backup & recovery I/O	9716529	57014.398712	5.86779483	12.4
TCP Socket (KGAS)	1316986	53062.978687	40.2912247	11.6
gc current grant busy	1966312	14591.878625	7.42093759	3.2

Explanation

The top 5 timed events are a good way to understand your overall bottlenecks.
To learn more about waits, click here.

Figure 6.10: *AWR System Wait Events Output in Ion*

The dba_hist_event_name table

The *dba_hist_event_name* table shows information about all wait events available in the database. This table contains the history of snapshots for the *v$event_name* view. This table allows users to find out the wait class to which every wait event belongs.

The dba_hist_bg_event_summary table

The *dba_hist_bg_event_summary* data dictionary table is very similar to the *dba_hist_system_event* table. The difference is that the *dba_hist_bg_event_summary* table displays historical information about wait events caused by Oracle background process activities.

These OS background processes form the "kernel software" of an Oracle instance, and they interface with the SGA memory region and perform many types of important jobs.

In a concurrent access environment, these Oracle background processes can see contention for shared system resources in much the same way as the foreground user processes might experience contention. Hence, we may need to know what part of database waits are caused by background Oracle processes.

The following query can be used to retrieve background wait event data for a particular snapshot interval:

show_background_waits.sql

```
select
    event       "Event Name",
    waits       "Waits",
    timeouts    "Timeouts",
    time        "Wait Time (s)",
    avgwait     "Avg Wait (ms)",
    waitclass   "Wait Class"
from
    (select e.event_name event
        , e.total_waits - nvl(b.total_waits,0)  waits
        , e.total_timeouts - nvl(b.total_timeouts,0) timeouts
        , (e.time_waited_micro - nvl(b.time_waited_micro,0))/1000000  time
        ,  decode ((e.total_waits - nvl(b.total_waits, 0)), 0, to_number(NULL),
          ((e.time_waited_micro - nvl(b.time_waited_micro,0))/1000) / (e.total_waits -
nvl(b.total_waits,0)) ) avgwait
        , e.wait_class waitclass
    from
        dba_hist_bg_event_summary b ,
        dba_hist_bg_event_summary e
    where
                        b.snap_id(+)         = &pBgnSnap
            and e.snap_id                    = &pEndSnap
            and b.dbid(+)                    = &pDbId
            and e.dbid                       = &pDbId
            and b.instance_number(+)         = &pInstNum
            and e.instance_number            = &pInstNum
            and b.event_id(+)                = e.event_id
            and e.total_waits                > nvl(b.total_waits,0)
            and e.wait_class                 <> 'Idle' )
order by time desc, waits desc;
```

The output of this script looks similar to the output of the script shown in the previous *dba_hist_system_event* section with the exception that wait events are displayed for background processes.

The dba_hist_waitstat table

The *dba_hist_waitstat* table displays historical statistical information about block contention, and the AWR gets this information from the *v$waitstat* view. This table is useful if we see buffer busy waits with a large wait time because we can query *dba_hist_waitstat* to see what block has DML contention.

As seen in Chapter 5 in the section *Collecting ASH Wait Information*, the *dba_hist_active_sess_history* table can be queried to identify particular sessions and objects that caused the high contention. In AWR, the datafile and object's IDs can be found in the *v$session_wait* dynamic view. The following query can be used to retrieve historical block contention statistics:

wait_stat_int.sql

```
select e.class                               "E.CLASS"
    , e.wait_count  - nvl(b.wait_count,0)    "Waits"
    , e.time        - nvl(b.time,0)          "Total Wait Time (cs)"
```

```
      , (e.time        - nvl(b.time,0)) /
        (e.wait_count  - nvl(b.wait_count,0))     "Avg Time (cs)"
  from dba_hist_waitstat b
     , dba_hist_waitstat e
 where b.snap_id            = &pBgnSnap
   and e.snap_id            = &pEndSnap
   and b.dbid               = &pDbId
   and e.dbid               = &pDbId
   and b.dbid               = e.dbid
   and b.instance_number    = &pInstNum
   and e.instance_number    = &pInstNum
   and b.instance_number    = e.instance_number
   and b.class              = e.class
   and b.wait_count         < e.wait_count
 order by 3 desc, 2 desc;
```

The sample query output looks like this and total waits over time are seen:

```
SQL> @wait_stat_int.sql
```

E.CLASS	Waits	Total Wait Time (cs)	Avg Time (cs)
undo header	97	121	1,24742268
file header block	2	114	57

The output of the script shows which particular buffer wait events play a significant role.

The dba_hist_enqueue_stat table

The *dba_hist_enqueue_stat* table displays statistical information about requests for various types of enqueues or locks. At snapshot time, *dba_hist_enqueue_stat* gets its data from the *v$enqueue_statistics* view.

Oracle enqueues provide a lock mechanism for the coordination of concurrent access to numerous database resources. The name of the enqueue is included as part of the wait event name and takes the form *enq: enqueue_type-related_details*. There are several types of enqueues available:

- **ST enqueues:** The ST enqueues control dynamic space allocation.

- **HW enqueues:** HW enqueues are used to serialize the allocation of space beyond the high water mark (HWM).

- **Waits for TM locks:** These are usually caused by missing indexes on foreign key constraints.

- **TX locks:** The TX locks are placed in various modes on data blocks when a transaction modifies data within this block. There are several types of TX locks: *enq: TX - allocate ITL entry; enq: TX – contention; enq: TX - index contention; enq: TX - row lock contention.*

If you see any wait events appear with "enqueue" in their name, the *dba_hist_enqueue_stat* table can be used to drill down to details about what particular enqueue has a long wait time. Here is a script to see these important enqueue statistics:

💾 enq_stat_int.sql

```
select
  ety "Enqueue",
  reqs "Requests",
  sreq "Successful Gets",
  freq "Failed Gets",
  waits "Waits",
  wttm "Wait Time (s)",
  awttm "Avg Wait Time(ms)"
from (
select /*+ ordered */
        e.eq_type || '-' || to_char(nvl(l.name,' '))
     || decode( upper(e.req_reason)
              , 'CONTENTION', null
              , '-',          null
              , ' ('||e.req_reason||')')              ety
   , e.total_req#   - nvl(b.total_req#,0)            reqs
   , e.succ_req#    - nvl(b.succ_req#,0)             sreq
   , e.failed_req#  - nvl(b.failed_req#,0)           freq
   , e.total_wait#  - nvl(b.total_wait#,0)           waits
   , (e.cum_wait_time - nvl(b.cum_wait_time,0))/1000 wttm
   , decode(  (e.total_wait#   - nvl(b.total_wait#,0))
           , 0, to_number(NULL)
           , (  (e.cum_wait_time - nvl(b.cum_wait_time,0))
              / (e.total_wait#   - nvl(b.total_wait#,0))
             )
           )                                         awttm
  from dba_hist_enqueue_stat e
     , dba_hist_enqueue_stat b
     , v$lock_type            l
where b.snap_id(+)           = &pBgnSnap
  and e.snap_id              = &pEndSnap
  and b.dbid(+)              = &pDbId
  and e.dbid                 = &pDbId
  and b.dbid(+)              = e.dbid
  and b.instance_number(+)   = &pInstNum
  and e.instance_number      = &pInstNum
  and b.instance_number(+)   = e.instance_number
  and b.eq_type(+)           = e.eq_type
  and b.req_reason(+)        = e.req_reason
  and e.total_wait# - nvl(b.total_wait#,0) > 0
  and l.type(+)              = e.eq_type
 order by wttm desc, waits desc);
```

The output will look like the following:

```
SQL> @Enq_stat_int.sql
```

Enqueue	Requests	Successful Gets	Failed Gets	Waits	Wait Time (s)	Avg Wait Time(ms)
RO-Multiple Object	1806	1806	0	153	4,554	29,7647059
TC-Tablespace Checkpoint	81	81	0	27	4,016	148,740741

TQ-Queue table 224,75 enqueue	19878	19878	0	16	3,596
CF-Controlfile 346 Transaction	308733	308732	1	2	,692

This script output shows activity statistics for particular types of enqueues which allows users to find the enqueues that cause most waits and wait times. Now, let's take a look at the AWR metric tables.

The AWR Metric Tables

The metric *dba_hist* data dictionary tables are organized into several groups: system, session, service, file, tablespace, and event metrics. All available metric groups can be found in the *v$metricgroup* dynamic view:

```
SQL> select * from V$METRICGROUP;

GROUP_ID NAME                            INTERVAL_SIZE MAX_INTERVAL
-------- ------------------------------- ------------- ------------
       0 Event Metrics                            6000            1
       1 Event Class Metrics                      6000           60
       2 System Metrics Long Duration             6000           60
       3 System Metrics Short Duration            1500           12
       4 Session Metrics Long Duration            6000           60
       5 Session Metrics Short Duration           1500            1
       6 Service Metrics                          6000           60
       7 File Metrics Long Duration              60000            6
       9 Tablespace Metrics Long Duration         6000            0
```

All of the metrics in AWR and kept in the *dba_hist_metric_name* table that stores snapshots for the *v$metric_name* view. There are over 180 different metrics in Oracle 11g, a whole lot of information!

These metrics are actively used by Oracle's automation features, providing the data that drives AMM as well as advisory engines such as ADDM and the SQLTuning and SQLAccess Advisors. For example, the ADDM uses a goal-based algorithm designed to minimize db time. This metric is computed as a cumulative time spent.

```
select
   metric_name
from
   dba_hist_metric_name;
```

The following is a list of several metrics that are computed by the AWR snapshot engine; however, the list is not exhaustive.

```
METRIC_NAME
-------------------------------------
Average File Read Time (Files-Long)
Average File Write Time (Files-Long)
Average Users Waiting Counts
Background Checkpoints Per Sec
Blocked User Session Count
Branch Node Splits Per Sec
Branch Node Splits Per Txn
Buffer Cache Hit Ratio
CPU Time (Session)
CPU Time Per User Call
CPU Usage Per Sec
```

The usage of metric statistics in time-series tuning approach will be presented later in this book. This next section provides a general overview of metric *dba_hist* tables that are available and a short description of information they provide.

The dba_hist_filemetric_history table

The *dba_hist_filemetric_history* table collects metrics history for datafile I/O related activity such as average file read/write times, number of physical read/write operations, and blocks. Along with this *dba_hist_filemetric_history* table, there is a corresponding AWR data dictionary table called *dba_hist_sysmetric_summary* that contains several useful datafile I/O related metrics.

```
select
   metric_name
from
   dba_hist_metric_name
where
   group_name like 'File Metrics%';
```

```
METRIC_NAME
-------------------------------------
Physical Block Writes (Files-Long)
Physical Block Reads (Files-Long)
Physical Writes (Files-Long)
Physical Reads (Files-Long)
Average File Write Time (Files-Long)
Average File Read Time (Files-Long)
```

The above query output shows all of the metrics available for datafile I/O activity.

The *dba_hist_sessmetric_history* table

The *dba_hist_sessmetric_history* table collects history information for important session related metrics such as:

```
select
   metric_name
from
   dba_hist_metric_name
where
   group_name like 'Session Metrics%';
```

```
METRIC_NAME
-------------------------------------
Blocked User Session Count
Logical Reads Ratio (Sess/Sys) %
Physical Reads Ratio (Sess/Sys) %
Total Parse Count (Session)
Hard Parse Count (Session)
PGA Memory (Session)
Physical Reads (Session)
CPU Time (Session)
User Transaction Count (Session)
```

The *dba_hist_sessmetric_history* table can be queried to find additional metric details about particular sessions of interest. This table contains a *metric_unit* column that helps identify the units of measure for every metric.

The dba_hist_sysmetric_history table

The *dba_hist_sysmetric_history* table collects history for all system-wide metrics which belong to such metric groups as System Metrics Long Duration and System Metrics Short Duration, gathering its data from the *v$sysmetric_history* view.

This *dba_hist_sysmetric_history* table contains important metrics for database time-series tuning approach such as:

- Buffer cache hit ratio

- Database CPU time ratio

- Database time per sec

- Database wait time ratio

- Physical reads per sec

- Response time per TXN

- SQL service response time

This table also contains a *metric_unit* column that helps identify measure units for every metric.

The dba_hist_sysmetric_summary table

The *dba_hist_sysmetric_summary* table shows a history for system-wide metrics that belong to the System Metrics Long Duration metric group. This table stores snapshots for the *v$sysmetric_summary* dynamic view.

The following simple query can be used to retrieve metrics for a particular snapshot.

🖫 **metric_summary.sql**

```
select
  metric_name "Metric Name",
  metric_unit "Metric Unit",
  minval "Minimum Value",
  maxval "Maximum Value",
  average "Average Value"
from
  dba_hist_sysmetric_summary
where
  snap_id          = &pEndSnap
and
  dbid             = &pDbId
and
  instance_number  = &pInstNum;
```

This table contains pre-computed metric values as they appeared in *v$sysmetric_summary* dynamic view. The sample output of this script shows the minimum and maximum values for the chosen metric:

```
SQL> @ metric_summary.sql
```

Metric Name Average Value	Metric Unit	Minimum Value	Maximum Value
Host CPU Utilization (%) 16	% Busy/(Idle+Busy)	1	55
Database Time Per Sec 0	CentiSeconds Per Second	0	9
Txns Per Logon 4	Txns Per Logon	1	17
Executions Per Sec 1	Executes Per Second	0	17
Executions Per Txn 28	Executes Per Txn	10	357
Session Limit % 10	% Sessions/Limit	10	12
Process Limit % 10	% Processes/Limit	9	12
PGA Cache Hit % 97	% Bytes/TotalBytes	97	97
Shared Pool Free % 10	% Free/Total	10	11
Library Cache Miss Ratio 0	% Misses/Gets	0	6

```
Library Cache Hit Ratio    % Hits/Pins                      93          100
99
Row Cache Miss Ratio       % Misses/Gets                     0           24
1
```

The output from *dba_hist_sysmetric_summary* can be easily retrieved directly from the AWR for any time interval, without any additional computing overhead.

The dba_hist_waitclassmet_history table

The *dba_hist_waitclassmet_history* table displays the metric history for wait event classes such as application, commit, concurrency, configuration, and others. The metrics stored in this table include average waiter count, database time spent in the wait, time waited, and number of wait times.

Time Model Statistics *dba_hist* Tables

Time model statistics show the amount of CPU time that it takes to complete each type of database processing work. Examples include SQL execute elapsed time, parse time elapsed and PL/SQL execution elapsed time statistics. The time model statistics shows where Oracle spends the most CPU time.

The most important time model statistic is db time, which represents the total time spent by Oracle in processing all database calls; thus, it describes the total database workload. Db time is calculated by aggregating the CPU and all non-idle wait times for all sessions in the database after last startup. Since it is an aggregate value, it is possible that the db time statistic could be larger than the total instance runtime.

One common objective in Oracle performance tuning is the reduction of database workload or db time by minimizing specific components such as the session's SQL parse and processing times, sessions wait times, and so on.

The *dba_hist_sys_time_model* table

The *dba_hist_sys_time_model* table displays snapshots for the *v$sys_time_model* dynamic view and stores history for system time model statistics.

The statistic names are also available in the *dba_hist_stat_name* table that displays all the statistic names gathered by the AWR and stores snapshots for the *v$statname* view. The *dba_hist_stat_name* table is also used with the *dba_hist_sysstat* table as shown below where information from *dba_hist_sys_time_model* table for a particular AWR snapshot interval is retrieved.

🖫   **sys_time_model_int.sql**

```
column "Statistic Name" format A40
```

```
column "Time (s)" format 999,999
column "Percent of Total DB Time" format 999,999

select e.stat_name "Statistic Name"
     , (e.value - b.value)/1000000        "Time (s)"
     , decode( e.stat_name,'DB time'
             , to_number(null)
             , 100*(e.value - b.value)
             )/
     ( select nvl((e1.value - b1.value),-1)
       from dba_hist_sys_time_model   e1
          , dba_hist_sys_time_model   b1
       where b1.snap_id               = b.snap_id
       and e1.snap_id                 = e.snap_id
       and b1.dbid                    = b.dbid
       and e1.dbid                    = e.dbid
       and b1.instance_number         = b.instance_number
       and e1.instance_number         = e.instance_number
       and b1.stat_name               = 'DB time'
       and b1.stat_id                 = e1.stat_id
)
     "Percent of Total DB Time"
  from dba_hist_sys_time_model e
     , dba_hist_sys_time_model b
 where b.snap_id                = &pBgnSnap
   and e.snap_id                = &pEndSnap
   and b.dbid                   = &pDbId
   and e.dbid                   = &pDbId
   and b.instance_number        = &pInst_Num
   and e.instance_number        = &pInst_Num
   and b.stat_id                = e.stat_id
   and e.value - b.value > 0
 order by 2 desc;
```

The output of this query looks like:

```
SQL> @sys_time_model_int.sql

Statistic Name                          Time (s) Percent of Total DB Time
-------------------------------------   --------  ------------------------
DB time                                      169
sql execute elapsed time                     156                        93
DB CPU                                       153                        90
PL/SQL execution elapsed time                 77                        46
background cpu time                           53                        31
parse time elapsed                             6                         4
hard parse elapsed time                        4                         3
connection management call elapsed time        0                         0
Java execution elapsed time                    0                         0
PL/SQL compilation elapsed time                0                         0
sequence load elapsed time                     0                         0
hard parse (sharing criteria) elapsed ti       0                         0
hard parse (bind mismatch) elapsed time        0                         0
```

This simple script provides valuable information about the percentage of total database processing time and actual the time (in seconds) for each metric. With this query, we can quickly identify the areas in which Oracle consumes processing time (not wait time) and, thereby, isolate the most resource intensive tasks.

The next section will provide an overview of performance information that the AWR stores about instance-wide system activity.

AWR System Statistics

The AWR stores history for a large number of instance cumulative statistics. These statistics are generally available through the *v$sysstat* dynamic view. The AWR stores snapshots for this table in the *dba_hist_sysstat* table. The following sections provide more details on these system statistics AWR tables.

The *dba_hist_sysstat* table

The *dba_hist_sysstat* table contains a history for system statistics from the *v$sysstat view*. Statistic names can be retrieved from the *dba_hist_statname* table where more than 300 statistics are available.

System statistics for a particular snapshot interval can be viewed using the following query.

🖫   **sys_stat_int.sql**

```
select e.stat_name         "Statistic Name"
     , e.value - b.value  "Total"
     , round((e.value - b.value)/
     ( select
       avg( extract( day from (e1.end_interval_time-b1.end_interval_time) )*24*60*60+
            extract( hour from (e1.end_interval_time-b1.end_interval_time) )*60*60+
            extract( minute from (e1.end_interval_time-b1.end_interval_time) )*60+
            extract( second from (e1.end_interval_time-b1.end_interval_time)) )
     from dba_hist_snapshot  b1
         ,dba_hist_snapshot  e1
     where b1.snap_id          = b.snap_id
       and e1.snap_id          = e.snap_id
       and b1.dbid             = b.dbid
       and e1.dbid             = e.dbid
       and b1.instance_number  = b.instance_number
       and e1.instance_number  = e.instance_number
       and b1.startup_time     = e1.startup_time
       and b1.end_interval_time < e1.end_interval_time ),2) "Per Second"
from  dba_hist_sysstat  b
    , dba_hist_sysstat  e
where b.snap_id            = &pBgnSnap
  and e.snap_id            = &pEndSnap
  and b.dbid               = &pDbId
  and e.dbid               = &pDbId
  and b.instance_number    = &pInstNum
  and e.instance_number    = &pInstNum
  and b.stat_id            = e.stat_id
  and e.stat_name not in (  'logons current'
                    , 'opened cursors current'
                    , 'workarea memory allocated'
                  )
  and e.value              >= b.value
  and e.value              > 0
order by 1 asc;
```

The query output will look like this:

```
SQL> @sys_stat_int.sql

Statistic Name                                  Total Per Second
----------------------------------------- ---------- ----------
CPU used by this session                        4,307          1
CPU used when call started                      4,307          1
CR blocks created                                 200          0
DB time                                       959,909        115
DBWR checkpoint buffers written                 3,228          0
DBWR checkpoints                                    9          0
DBWR object drop buffers written                   75          0
DBWR tablespace checkpoint buffers written         71          0
DBWR transaction table writes                      92          0
DBWR undo block writes                            822          0
IMU CR rollbacks                                   20          0
IMU Flushes                                       103          0
IMU Redo allocation size                      761,060         92
IMU commits                                       383          0
IMU contention                                      0          0
IMU ktichg flush                                    4          0
IMU pool not allocated                          1,702          0
IMU undo allocation size                    1,772,624        213
```

This script allows users to easily identify all instance activity statistics for a particular snapshot interval in two representations: cumulative and per second.

The *dba_hist_latch* table

The *dba_hist_latch* table contains historical latch statistics, gathered at snapshot time from *v$latch*. The statistics in the *dba_hist_latch* table are grouped by latch names and allows us to tune applications whenever wait events show a significant amount of latch contention. For example, latch resource usage can be greatly reduced if the application is properly tuned and shared pool is configured optimally. Methods for reducing latch contention will be covered in Chapter 14, *Oracle Instance Tuning*.

The following query can be used to retrieve historical data about latches from AWR.

🖫 latch_int.sql

```
select e.latch_name "Latch Name"
    , e.gets    - b.gets  "Get Requests"
    , to_number(decode(e.gets, b.gets, null,
      (e.misses - b.misses) * 100/(e.gets - b.gets)))    "Percent Get Misses"
    , to_number(decode(e.misses, b.misses, null,
      (e.sleeps - b.sleeps)/(e.misses - b.misses)))     "Avg Sleeps / Miss"
    , (e.wait_time - b.wait_time)/1000000 "Wait Time (s)"
    , e.immediate_gets - b.immediate_gets "No Wait Requests"
    , to_number(decode(e.immediate_gets,
                  b.immediate_gets, null,
                    (e.immediate_misses - b.immediate_misses) * 100 /
                    (e.immediate_gets   - b.immediate_gets)))    "Percent No Wait Miss"
 from  dba_hist_latch  b
     , dba_hist_latch  e
 where b.snap_id        = &pBgnSnap
```

```
   and e.snap_id          = &pEndSnap
   and b.dbid             = &pDbId
   and e.dbid             = &pDbId
   and b.dbid             = e.dbid
   and b.instance_number  = &pInstNum
   and e.instance_number  = &pInstNum
   and b.instance_number  = e.instance_number
   and b.latch_hash       = e.latch_hash
   and e.gets - b.gets    > 0
 order by 1, 4;
```

The results of the query show latch activity statistics and identify the particular type of latch that produces miss events that cause processes to wait.

```
SQL> @latch_int.sql

Latch Name                     Get Requests
------------------------- ------------
Percent Get Misses Avg Sleeps / Miss Wait Time (s) No Wait Requests
------------------ ------------------ ------------- ----------------
Percent No Wait Miss
--------------------
Consistent RBA            5,670           0           0                0

FOB s.o list latch          203           0           0                0

In memory undo latch     22,929           0           0            5,163

JOX SGA heap latch        1,173           0           0                0
```

The *dba_hist_latch_misses_summary* table

The *dba_hist_latch_misses_summary* table displays historical summary statistics about missed attempts to get latches.

The following query can be used to get statistics on latch misses for a particular snapshot interval.

💾 latch_miss_int.sql

```
select    latchname "Latch Name",
          nwmisses "No Wait Misses",
          sleeps "Sleeps",
              waiter_sleeps "Waiter Sleeps"
From (
select e.parent_name||' '||e.where_in_code  latchname
    , e.nwfail_count - nvl(b.nwfail_count,0) nwmisses
    , e.sleep_count  - nvl(b.sleep_count,0)  sleeps
    , e.wtr_slp_count - nvl(b.wtr_slp_count,0)   waiter_sleeps
  from dba_hist_latch_misses_summary  b
    , dba_hist_latch_misses_summary  e
  where b.snap_id(+)        = &pBgnSnap
    and e.snap_id           = &pEndSnap
    and b.dbid(+)           = &pDbId
    and e.dbid              = &pDbId
    and b.dbid(+)           = e.dbid
```

```
   and b.instance_number(+) = &pInstNum
   and e.instance_number    = &pInstNum
   and b.instance_number(+) = e.instance_number
   and b.parent_name(+)     = e.parent_name
   and b.where_in_code(+)   = e.where_in_code
   and e.sleep_count        > nvl(b.sleep_count,0)
)
order by 1, 3 desc;
```

The output of the query provides additional details about sleeps that occur while the database attempts to acquire a particular latch.

```
SQL> @latch_miss_int.sql
```

Latch Name	No Wait Misses	Sleeps	Waiter Sleeps
KWQMN job cache list latch kwqmnuji: update job it	0	8	0
cache buffers chains kcbgcur: kslbegin	0	2	0
cache buffers chains kcbgtcr: fast path	0	2	0
cache buffers lru chain kcbzgws_1	0	1	1
latch wait list No latch	0	1,163	1,163
library cache kgldti: 2child	0	3	0
library cache kglhdgc: child:	0	1	0
library cache kglic	0	3	0
library cache kglobld	0	1	2
library cache kglobpn: child:	0	11	15
library cache kglpin	0	4	0
library cache kglpnc: child	0	51	1,606
library cache kglpndl: child: after processing	0	7	0
library cache kglpndl: child: before processing	0	1,016	40

There is other data inside the library cache, and AWR has a view for this information.

The *dba_hist_librarycache* table

The *dba_hist_librarycache* table contains the statistical history of library cache activity, and it gets its data from the *v$librarycache* view. As we know from DBA 101 class, the library cache stores SQL, Java classes, and PL/SQL programs in an executable form. If our library cache contention is significant, *dba_hist_librarycache* can be queried to get more details about particular library objects that may cause such a contention. These details will give us clues on how to reduce library cache contention.

In order to understand the importance of library cache tuning, we must remember that a library and dictionary cache miss is more expensive, in terms of resources, than a data buffer miss. This is because it involves a significant amount of CPU.

The following query can be used to get a report for library cache statistics.

🖫 **lib_cache_int.sql**

```
select b.namespace "Name Space"
    , e.gets - b.gets  "Get Requests"
    , to_number(decode(e.gets,b.gets,null,
        100 - (e.gethits - b.gethits) * 100/(e.gets - b.gets))) "Get Pct Miss"
```

```
         , e.pins - b.pins "Pin Requests"
         , to_number(decode(e.pins,b.pins,null,
           100 - (e.pinhits - b.pinhits) * 100/(e.pins - b.pins)))  "Pin Pct Miss"
         , e.reloads - b.reloads                                    "Reloads"
         , e.invalidations - b.invalidations                        "Invalidations"
  from dba_hist_librarycache  b
         , dba_hist_librarycache  e
  where b.snap_id             = &pBgnSnap
    and e.snap_id             = &pEndSnap
    and b.dbid                = &pDbId
    and e.dbid                = &pDbId
    and b.dbid                = e.dbid
    and b.instance_number     = &pInstNum
    and e.instance_number     = &pInstNum
    and b.instance_number     = e.instance_number
    and b.namespace           = e.namespace;
```

The following is a result of this query.

```
SQL> @lib_cache_int.sql
```

Name Space	Get Req	Get Pct Miss	Pin Requests	Pin Pct Miss	Reloads	Invalidat
BODY	1840	5,76086957	3117	4,39525184	24	0
CLUSTER	216	2,31481481	532	1,12781955	1	0
INDEX	37	97,2972973	41	87,804878	0	0
JAVA DATA	3	33,3333333	5	40	0	0
JAVA RESOURCE	0		0		0	0
JAVA SOURCE	0		0		0	0
OBJECT	0		0		0	0
PIPE	0		0		0	0
SQL AREA	31706	7,459156	120148	2,84482472	495	60
TABLE/PROCEDURE	13926	17,6576188	83460	5,5415768	425	0
TRIGGER	119	14,2857143	488	3,89344262	2	0

The report shows what particular types of library cache contents have the highest miss percentage.

The *dba_hist_rowcache_summary* table

The *dba_hist_rowcache_summary* table stores history summary statistics for data dictionary cache activity, gathered at snapshot time from *v$rowcache*. This data dictionary cache stores information about schema objects that participate in SQL parsing or compilation of PL/SQL programs.

The following query can be used to retrieve historical statistical data for the data dictionary cache:

💾 rowcache_int.sql

```
select
  param    "Parameter",
  gets     "Get Requests",
  getm     "Pct Miss"
From
(select lower(b.parameter)                                      param
     , e.gets - b.gets                                          gets
     , to_number(decode(e.gets,b.gets,null,
       (e.getmisses - b.getmisses) * 100/(e.gets - b.gets)))    getm
     , e.scans - b.scans                                        scans
     , to_number(decode(e.scans,b.scans,null,
```

```
        (e.scanmisses - b.scanmisses) * 100/(e.scans - b.scans)))  scanm
    , e.modifications - b.modifications                             mods
    , e.usage                                                       usage
  from dba_hist_rowcache_summary  b
    , dba_hist_rowcache_summary  e
 where b.snap_id           = &pBgnSnap
   and e.snap_id           = &pEndSnap
   and b.dbid              = &pDbId
   and e.dbid              = &pDbId
   and b.dbid              = e.dbid
   and b.instance_number   = &pInstNum
   and e.instance_number   = &pInstNum
   and b.instance_number   = e.instance_number
   and b.parameter         = e.parameter
   and e.gets - b.gets     > 0   )
 order by param;
```

The following is a sample output from this script that displays details about dictionary cache activity for a particular snapshot interval.

```
SQL> @rowcache_int.sql
```

Parameter	Get Requests	Pct Miss
dc_awr_control	23,167	.00
dc_constraints	558	33.51
dc_files	2,748	.00
dc_global_oids	3,018,842	.00
dc_histogram_data	55,080	15.47
dc_histogram_defs	225,507	16.29
dc_object_ids	3,269,890	.05
dc_objects	265,208	1.34
dc_profiles	29,205	.00
dc_rollback_segments	155,231	.00
dc_segments	348,808	.31
dc_sequences	763	1.31
dc_table_scns	38	100.00
dc_tablespace_quotas	6	.00
dc_tablespaces	582,952	.00
dc_usernames	65,451	.02
dc_users	3,753,587	.00
outstanding_alerts	13,822	3.43

The *dba_hist_buffer_pool_stat* table

The *dba_hist_buffer_pool_stat* table contains statistical history for all buffer pools configured for the instance. Additional non-default buffer caches can be used as keep and recycle caches in order to address atypical access patterns to data segments. This query can be used to review the statistical history of buffer pools for a particular snapshot interval:

🖫 buf_pool_int.sql

```sql
select
      name
    , numbufs      "Number of Buffers"
    , buffs        "Buffer Gets"
    , conget       "Consistent Gets"
    , phread       "Physical Reads"
    , phwrite      "Physical Writes"
    , fbwait       "Free Buffer Waits"
    , bbwait       "Buffer Busy Waits"
    , wcwait  "Write Complete Waits"
    , poolhr  "Pool Hit %"
From
(select e.name
     , e.set_msize                                          numbufs
     , decode(    e.db_block_gets      - nvl(b.db_block_gets,0)
             +  e.consistent_gets   - nvl(b.consistent_gets,0)
           , 0, to_number(null)
           , (100* (1 - (  (e.physical_reads - nvl(b.physical_reads,0))
                        / (  e.db_block_gets      - nvl(b.db_block_gets,0)
                          + e.consistent_gets    - nvl(b.consistent_gets,0)))
                   )
              )
          )
        )                                                   poolhr
     ,     e.db_block_gets       - nvl(b.db_block_gets,0)
       +  e.consistent_gets     - nvl(b.consistent_gets,0)   buffs
     , e.consistent_gets        - nvl(b.consistent_gets,0)   conget
     , e.physical_reads         - nvl(b.physical_reads,0)     phread
     , e.physical_writes        - nvl(b.physical_writes,0)   phwrite
     , e.free_buffer_wait       - nvl(b.free_buffer_wait,0)  fbwait
     , e.write_complete_wait  - nvl(b.write_complete_wait,0)  wcwait
     , e.buffer_busy_wait       - nvl(b.buffer_busy_wait,0)  bbwait
  from dba_hist_buffer_pool_stat  b
     , dba_hist_buffer_pool_stat  e
 where b.snap_id(+)            = &pBgnSnap
   and e.snap_id              = &pEndSnap
   and b.dbid(+)              = &pDbId
   and e.dbid                 = &pDbId
   and b.dbid(+)              = e.dbid
   and b.instance_number(+)   = &pInst_Num
   and e.instance_number      = &pInst_Num
   and b.instance_number(+)   = e.instance_number
   and b.id(+)                = e.id)
 order by 1;
```

The output of the query looks like:

```
SQL> @buf_pool_int.sql


NAME                Number of Buffers Buffer Gets Consistent Gets
------------------- ----------------- ----------- ---------------
Physical Reads Physical Writes Free Buffer Waits Buffer Busy Waits
-------------- --------------- ----------------- -----------------
Write Complete Waits Pool Hit %
-------------------- ----------

DEFAULT                          8016   5,354,123       4,347,376
       100,070          41,865                 0                24
```

The script output provides users with valuable history information about activity in their data buffers. Analysis of buffer cache usage can determine if the pools are configured correctly and whether or not tables need to be reassigned to a particular cache.

The next section provides more details about a *dba_hist* table that exposes operating system performance statistics gathered by database server.

Operating System Statistics in AWR

Oracle does not run in a vacuum, and it's critical to search outside the box and see what is happening with your CPU, RAM, network and disk I/O subsystems. Operating system (OS) statistics such as CPU, disk input/output (I/O), virtual memory, and network statistics help identify possible bottlenecks where system hardware is stressed.

The AWR has a table called *dba_hist_osstat* that stores snapshots of the *v$osstat* dynamic view. OS statistics indicate how the hardware and OS are working, and thus, they reflect the workload placed on the database. To view history statistics for a particular snapshot interval, the following query can be used:

os_stat_int.sql

```
select e.stat_name "Statistic Name"
     , decode(e.stat_name, 'NUM_CPUS', e.value, e.value - b.value) "Total"
     , decode( instrb(e.stat_name, 'BYTES'), 0, to_number(null)
             , round((e.value - b.value)/( select
         avg( extract( day from (e1.end_interval_time-b1.end_interval_time) )*24*60*60+
             extract( hour from (e1.end_interval_time-b1.end_interval_time) )*60*60+
             extract( minute from (e1.end_interval_time-b1.end_interval_time) )*60+
             extract( second from (e1.end_interval_time-b1.end_interval_time)) ) )
       from dba_hist_snapshot  b1
          ,dba_hist_snapshot  e1
      where b1.snap_id          = b.snap_id
        and e1.snap_id          = e.snap_id
        and b1.dbid             = b.dbid
        and e1.dbid             = e.dbid
        and b1.instance_number = b.instance_number
        and e1.instance_number = e.instance_number
        and b1.startup_time    = e1.startup_time
        and b1.end_interval_time < e1.end_interval_time ),2)) "Per Second"
 from  dba_hist_osstat  b
    , dba_hist_osstat  e
 where b.snap_id          = &pBgnSnap
   and e.snap_id          = &pEndSnap
   and b.dbid             = &pDbId
   and e.dbid             = &pDbId
   and b.instance_number = &pInstNum
   and e.instance_number = &pInstNum
   and b.stat_id          = e.stat_id
   and e.value           >= b.value
   and e.value           >  0
 order by 1 asc;
```

The query output looks like the following, a valuable peek outward into the operating system:

```
SQL> @os_stat_int.sql

Statistic Name                      Total    Per Second
------------------------------ ----------   ----------
AVG_BUSY_TICKS                  1,974,925
AVG_IDLE_TICKS                  7,382,241
AVG_IN_BYTES                2,236,256,256    23,881.91
AVG_OUT_BYTES                 566,304,768      6047.8
AVG_SYS_TICKS                     727,533
AVG_USER_TICKS                  1,247,392
BUSY_TICKS                      1,974,925
IDLE_TICKS                      7,382,241
IN_BYTES                    2,236,256,256    23,881.91
NUM_CPUS                                1
OUT_BYTES                     566,304,768     6,047.8
SYS_TICKS                         727,533
USER_TICKS                       1247,392
```

This script allows a OS statistics in two forms, both cumulative and per second. With the per-second rates, we can identify hot areas in the OS and hardware, possible external bottlenecks.

The next section describes the very important *dba_hist* tables that contain performance history information for SQL statements executed in the Oracle database.

SQL Statistics in AWR

At the highest level, Oracle is just a SQL statement processor, so SQL optimization is a critical area of Oracle tuning. Almost all performance problems are related to sub-optimal SQL statements and it is important to learn how the AWR helps identify SQL statements that are candidates for tuning. The SQL tuning process usually consists of three steps:

6. Find "bad" SQL statements that place a high workload on an Oracle database

7. Determine that the cost-based optimizer (CBO) created a sub-optimal execution plan for those statements

8. Implement actions which lead to alternative execution plans that provide better response times and lower workload for poor SQL statements

The goals of SQL tuning can be identified as the minimization of SQL response time or reduction of the workload on an Oracle database while performing the same amount of work. In previous Oracle releases, SQL tuning work was mostly a manual process, tuning the workload as a whole by adjusting init.ora parameters and CBO statistics, followed by individual SQL tuning where we found a sub-optimal execution plan, fixed it, and moved on to the next SQL statement.

Oracle 10g first offered primitive automated SQL tuning tools in the form of the SQLTuning advisor and the SQLAccess advisor, tools which aid beginners by providing simplistic recommendations and advice. These recommendations may suggest simple things like replacing poor CBO statistics, adding missing indexes or materialized views and rewriting SQL statements into a more efficient form, but they are nowhere near replacing the ability of a human expert.

As q review, there are several tools to gather information about poorly performing SQL statements:

- Use of the AWR / STATSPACK
- Use of SQL related *v$* dynamic performance tables as *v$sql*
- Use of the TKPROF SQL trace facility

The AWR can be used to find resource-intensive SQL statements and plot them over time. The AWR repository contains several SQL related tables:

- The *dba_hist_sqlstat* table contains a history for SQL execution statistics and stores snapshots of *v$sql* table
- The *dba_hist_sqltext* table stores actual text for SQL statements captured from *v$sql* view
- The *dba_hist_sql_plan* table stores execution plans for SQL statements available in dba_hist_sqlstat table

The *dba_hist_sqlstat* is the table that helps us identify candidates for tuning. Let's take a closer look at the *dba_hist_sqlstat* table and see how it helps us identify of poorly optimized SQL statements.

The *dba_hist_sqlstat* Table

This table contains more than 20 statistics related to SQL statement execution. The statistics for every SQL statement are stored in two separate columns:

- *<Statistic Name>_total* column stores the total values of statistics since the last instance startup
- *<Statistic Name>_delta* column reflects the change in a statistic's value between *end_interval_time* and *begin_interval_time* that is stored in the *dba_hist_snapshot* table.

Using this core *dba_hist_sqlstat* table, poor SQL statements can be identified using such criteria as:

- High buffer gets
- High physical reads
- Large execution count
- High shared memory usage
- High version count
- High parse count
- High elapsed time
- High execution CPU time
- High number of rows processed
- High number of sorts

This table does not contain the actual text of SQL statements; however, it does contain a *sql_id* column. The SQL text can be retrieved by joining *dba_hist_sqlstat* with the *dba_hist_sqltext* table. For example, the *high_sql_buf_gets.sql* script below retrieves high buffer gets SQL statements for a particular snapshot interval.

🖫 high_sql_buf_gets.sql

```
select
           sql_id
         , buffer_gets_total                    "Buffer Gets"
         , executions_total                     "Executions"
         , buffer_gets_total/executions_total   "Gets / Exec"
         , pct*100                              "% Total"
         , cpu_time_total/1000000              "CPU Time (s)"
         , elapsed_time_total/1000000         "Elapsed Time (s)"
         , module                               "SQL Module"
         , stmt                                 "SQL Statement"
from
(select
            e.sql_id sql_id
          , e.buffer_gets_total - nvl(b.buffer_gets_total,0) buffer_gets_total
          , e.executions_total - nvl(b.executions_total,0) executions_total
          , (e.buffer_gets_total - nvl(b.buffer_gets_total,0))/
            ( select e1.value - nvl(b1.value,0)
              from dba_hist_sysstat b1 , dba_hist_sysstat e1
                  where b1.snap_id(+)           = b.snap_id
                    and e1.snap_id              = e.snap_id
                    and b1.dbid(+)              = b.dbid
                    and e1.dbid                 = e.dbid
                    and b1.instance_number(+)   = b.instance_number
                    and e1.instance_number      = e.instance_number
                    and b1.stat_id              = e1.stat_id
                    and e1.stat_name            = 'session logical reads'

) pct
          , e.elapsed_time_total - nvl(b.elapsed_time_total,0) elapsed_time_total
          , e.cpu_time_total - nvl(b.cpu_time_total,0) cpu_time_total
          , e.module
          , t.sql_text   stmt
     from dba_hist_sqlstat   e
        , dba_hist_sqlstat   b
        , dba_hist_sqltext   t
    where b.snap_id(+)            = @pBgnSnap
      and b.dbid(+)              = e.dbid
      and b.instance_number(+)   = e.instance_number
      and b.sql_id(+)            = e.sql_id
      and e.snap_id             = &pEndSnap
      and e.dbid               = &pDBId
      and e.instance_number     = &pInstNum
      and (e.executions_total - nvl(b.executions_total,0)) > 0
      and t.sql_id             = b.sql_id
)
     order by 2 desc;
```

Aas we see, the *dba_hist_sqlstat* view provides valuable information about SQL statements that are querying the database. By regularly checking this table, the primary causes of most performance problems can easily be identified. The next section of this chapter introduces the segment-related AWR tables.

Segment Statistics in AWR

The AWR repository stores table-level statistics such as logical reads, physical reads and writes, buffer busy waits and row lock waits in *dba_hist_seg_stat*, gathering this data at snapshot time from data inside *v$segstat*.

Oracle also has a more view called *v$segment_statistics* which shows the basic table and index statistics along with additional owner and segment names and tablespace name. These segment-level statistics can be selected from the *v$segstat_name* view:

```
SQL> select name from V$SEGSTAT_NAME;

NAME
-------------------------------------
logical reads
buffer busy waits
gc buffer busy
db block changes
physical reads
physical writes
physical reads direct
physical writes direct
gc cr blocks received
gc current blocks received
ITL waits
row lock waits
space used
space allocated
segment scans
```

Reviewing the segment-level statistics history helps us to identify hot segments, revealing those tables and indexes that are experiencing performance problems. For example, if the database has a high value of TX enqueue waits, the *dba_hist_seg_stat* table can be queried to find actual segments that are experiencing high row lock activity.

We can query the *dba_hist_seg_stat* table using various criteria to identify hot segments. For example, the *seg_top_logreads.sql* script retrieves top segments that have high logical reads activity:

🖫 seg_top_logreads.sql

```
select
    object_name "Object Name"
  , tablespace_name "Tablespace Name"
  , object_type "Object Type"
  , logical_reads_total "Logical Reads"
  , ratio "%Total"
from(
select n.owner||'.'||n.object_name||decode(n.subobject_name,null,null,'.'||n.subobject_name)
object_name
```

```
    , n.tablespace_name
    , case when length(n.subobject_name) < 11 then
            n.subobject_name
        else
            substr(n.subobject_name,length(n.subobject_name)-9)
      end subobject_name
    , n.object_type
    , r.logical_reads_total
    , round(r.ratio * 100, 2) ratio
  from dba_hist_seg_stat_obj  n
    , (select *
        from (select e.dataobj#
                   , e.obj#
                   , e.dbid
                   , e.logical_reads_total - nvl(b.logical_reads_total, 0)
logical_reads_total
                   , ratio_to_report(e.logical_reads_total - nvl(b.logical_reads_total,
0)) over () ratio
                from dba_hist_seg_stat   e
                   , dba_hist_seg_stat   b
              where b.snap_id   = 2694
                and e.snap_id   = 2707
                and b.dbid      = 37933856
                and e.dbid      = 37933856
                and b.instance_number   = 1
                and e.instance_number   = 1
                and e.obj#            = b.obj#
                and e.dataobj#        = b.dataobj#
            and e.logical_reads_total - nvl(b.logical_reads_total, 0)  > 0
              order by logical_reads_total desc) d
        where rownum <= 100) r
  where n.dataobj# = r.dataobj#
    and n.obj#     = r.obj#
    and n.dbid     = r.dbid
)
order by logical_reads_total desc;
```

This script allows the identification of hot segments which experience high logical reads activity. This information may help with the selection of tuning actions such as the optimization of corresponding queries that access these segments, redistribute segments across different disks, and more.

```
SQL> @seg_top_logreads.sql

Object Name                        Tablespace Object Type Logical Reads %Total
--------------------------------   ---------- ----------- ------------- ------
SYSMAN.MGMT_METRICS_RAW_PK         SYSAUX     INDEX              46,272   8.68
SYS.SMON_SCN_TIME                  SYSTEM     TABLE              43,840   8.23
SYS.JOB$                           SYSTEM     TABLE              30,640   5.75
SYS.I_SYSAUTH1                     SYSTEM     INDEX              27,120   5.09
PERFSTAT.STATS$EVENT_HISTOGRAM     SYSAUX     INDEX              26,912   5.05
```

The Ion tool also has several reports for the retrieval of hot segments using the following criteria:

- Top logical reads

- Top physical reads

- Top physical writes

- Top buffer busy waits

- Top row lock waits

AWR System Statistics

- Top block changes

The *dba_hist_seg_stat* table has two columns for each statistic: the accumulated total and the delta values. The *total* column shows the cumulative value of the statistic and the *delta* column shows change in the statistic value between *begin_interval_time* and *end_interval_time.*

The next chapter section introduces the *dba_hist* tables that are related to the I/O activity of the database.

Datafile I/O Statistics in AWR

The AWR has several tables that can be used to isolate datafile I/O statistics as well as tablespace space usage statistics. The *dba_hist_filestatxs* and *dba_hist_tempstatxs* tables display information about I/O activity over time.

The *dba_hist_tempstatxs* table has the identical structure to *dba_hist_filestatxs.* Both tables can be queried to monitor overall database I/O activity for a particular snapshot interval grouped by tablespaces using the *db_tbsp_io.sql* query.

💾 db_tbsp_io.sql

```
select tbsp "Tablespace"
     , ios "I/O Activity"
From (
select e.tsname tbsp
     , sum (e.phyrds  - nvl(b.phyrds,0))  +
       sum (e.phywrts - nvl(b.phywrts,0)) ios
  from dba_hist_filestatxs  e
     , dba_hist_filestatxs  b
 where b.snap_id(+)            = &pBgnSnap
   and e.snap_id              = &pEndSnap
   and b.dbid(+)              = &pDbId
   and e.dbid                 = &pDbId
   and b.dbid(+)              = e.dbid
   and b.instance_number(+)  = &pInstNum
   and e.instance_number     = &pInstNum
   and b.instance_number(+)  = e.instance_number
   and b.file#               = e.file#
   and ( (e.phyrds  - nvl(b.phyrds,0) ) +
         (e.phywrts - nvl(b.phywrts,0)) ) > 0
 group by e.tsname
union
select e.tsname tbsp
     , sum (e.phyrds  - nvl(b.phyrds,0))  +
       sum (e.phywrts - nvl(b.phywrts,0)) ios
  from dba_hist_tempstatxs  e
     , dba_hist_tempstatxs  b
 where b.snap_id(+)            = &pBgnSnap
   and e.snap_id              = &pEndSnap
   and b.dbid(+)              = &pDbId
   and e.dbid                 = &pDbId
   and b.dbid(+)              = e.dbid
   and b.instance_number(+)  = &pInstNum
   and e.instance_number     = &pInstNum
   and b.instance_number(+)  = e.instance_number
```

```
    and b.file#             = e.file#
    and ( (e.phyrds  - nvl(b.phyrds,0) ) +
          (e.phywrts - nvl(b.phywrts,0) ) ) ) > 0
  group by e.tsname
);
```

This script allows users to look at the I/O activity on a per tablespace basis. It assists in finding hot tablespaces that experienced a large workload and may be candidates for further tuning consideration.

```
SQL> @db_tbsp_io.sql

Tablespace                      I/O Activity
------------------------------  ------------
SYSAUX                                 9,630
SYSTEM                                 3,658
UNDOTBS1                               1,104
USERS                                     14
```

The Ion tool offers the following I/O related reports that build time-series charts for I/O database activity:

- I/O by datafiles

- I/O by tablespaces

- Total database I/O activity

- Total tablespace I/O activity

For instance, the following Ion screenshot demonstrates a sample report available in Ion. The screenshot shows a database's physical reads by particular tablespace.

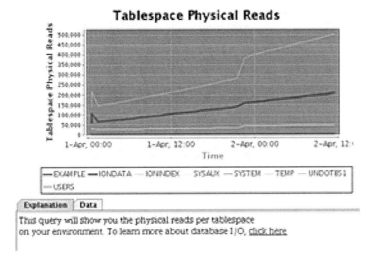

Figure 6.11: *AWR Physical Reads by Tablespace Chart in Ion*

Conclusion

This chapter is a quick overview of the evolution of time-series tuning from STATSPACK to AWR. We should now understand how the AWR table data creates the foundation from the *wrh$* tables for input to the intelligent ADDM and the SQLTuning Advisor.

The main points of this chapter include:

- Before STATSPACK and AWR were invented, we were able to create time-series tables using the BSTAT and ESTAT utilities.

- STATSPACK was introduced in Oracle 8i as a free tool for collecting rime-series data and it remains in Oracle 11g.

- AWR was built into Oracle 10g and beyond as an extra-cost feature requiring the purchase of the Oracle Performance Pack and Oracle Diagnostic Pack

- The AWR *dba_hist* views are similar to well-known STATSPACK tables, making it easy to migrate existing performance reports between these utilities.

- STATSPACK and AWR provides the foundation for sophisticated performance analysis including exception reporting, trend analysis, correlation analysis, hypothesis testing and data mining

- The AWR data is used as input to "intelligent advisor" tools such as ADDM, the SQLTuning Advisor, the SQLAccess Advisor and the SQL Performance Analyzer. As of 2010, none of these tools can replicate the ability of a human tuning expert, but these tools are an excellent way for a beginner to get started.

- STATSPACK remains an excellent low-cost alternative to the expensive AWR

- AWR and STATSPACK provide a set of history tables, and the AWR tables are actually views built upon the *wrh$* tables, all prefixed with *dba_hist*

- The AWR and STATSPACK repository stores time-series history for all major performance database statistics

- The AWR information can be easily accessed using simple SQL queries

- Third party tools can be used to visualize important trends within AWR and/or STATSPACK query results

Now that we have some basic knowledge on STATSPACK and AWR, it's time to dive deeper and explore how to install and configure STATSPACK and AWR.

AWR and STATSPACK Configuration

The Differences between STATSPACK and AWR

This chapter will show how to install and configure AWR and STATSPACK to meet specific monitoring and tuning requirements. The AWR is similar to STATSPACK in that it takes time-based snapshots of the all-important performance tuning $v\$$ dynamic views and stores these snapshots in its repository.

Unlike STATSPACK, AWR is installed by default in Oracle 10g and beyond in the hopes that DBAs will use it and pay the $3,000 per CPU licensing fee for the required performance and diagnostic packs. By design, the AWR is created at the same time as the database and is included in the data dictionary. AWR is part of the Oracle kernel while STATSPACK is a stand-alone utility that can be installed or removed from the database at any time. By default, the STATSPACK utility is not installed in the Oracle database. STATSPACK must be manually loaded into the database in order to start monitoring performance and gathering statistic history.

Fortunately, the STATSPACK utility is very functional and with a little tweaking, Oracle professionals can get almost as much information using STATSPACK as they can from AWR without incurring additional license fees.

The first section will show how to install and configure STATSPACK.

Installing STATSPACK

Install Prerequisites

The following steps must be taken before attempting to install STATSPACK:

1. Run *catdbsyn.sql* when connected as SYS
2. Run *dbmspool.sql* when connected as SYS
3. Allocate a tablespace called *perfstat* with at least 180 megabytes of storage

Step 1: Create the *perfstat* Tablespace

The STATSPACK utility requires an isolated tablespace to contain all of the objects and data. For uniformity, it is suggested that the tablespace be called *perfstat*, the same name as the schema owner for the STATSPACK tables. Note that the *autoextend* option has not been used. It is important for the Oracle DBA to closely watch the STATSPACK data to ensure that the *stats$sql_summary* table is not taking an inordinate amount of space. Adjusting the STATSPACK thresholds will be covered later in this chapter.

The next step is to create a tablespace called *perfstat* with at least 180 megabytes of space in the datafile:

```
[oracle@dbserver ~]$ sqlplus / as sysdba

SQL*Plus: Release 10.2.0.3.0 - Production on Sun Jun 7 21:31:30 2009

Copyright (c) 1982, 2006, Oracle.  All Rights Reserved.


Connected to:
Oracle Database 10g Release 10.2.0.3.0 - 64bit Production
With the Real Application Clusters option

SQL> create tablespace perfstat datafile '+/u01/app/oracle/oradata/prod/perfstat01.dbf' size
500M;
```

Tablespace created.

Step 2: Run the Create Scripts

Now that the tablespace exists, the STATSPACK software installation process can begin.

The *statscre.sql* script creates a user called *perfstat*, executes the script to create all of the STATSPACK tables, and installs the STATSPACK PL/SQL package. After running this script, Oracle will ask for the following information:

*   Specify *perfstat* user's default tablespace: *perfstat*

- Specify *perfstat* user's temporary tablespace: *temp*

- Enter tablespace where STATSPACK objects will be created: *perfstat*

NOTE: The STATSPACK scripts are designed to stop whenever an error is encountered. The *statsctab.sql* script contains the SQL*Plus directive *whenever sqlerror exit*. This means that the script will cease execution if an error is encountered. If an error is encountered and the script needs to be restarted, it is necessary to comment out the *whenever sqlerror exit* line and run the script again. Also, be aware that the STATSPACK install script contains SQL*Plus commands. Because of this, DBAs should run the script from SQL*Plus rather than in SVRMGRL or SQL*Worksheet.

Once the *spcreate.sql* script has completed, it is necessary to ensure that no errors have occurred. The STATSPACK utility creates a series of files with the *.lis* extension as shown here:

```
prodb2-/u01/app/oracle/product/8.1.6_64/rdbms/admin

>ls -al *.lis
-rw-r--r--   1 oracle    oinstall    4170 Dec 12 14:28 spctab.lis
-rw-r--r--   1 oracle    oinstall    3417 Dec 12 14:27 spcusr.lis
-rw-r--r--   1 oracle    oinstall     201 Dec 12 14:28 spcpkg.lis
```

To check for errors, look for any lines that contain "ORA-" or the word "error", since the presence of these strings indicates an error. If using Windows NT, it is possible check for errors by searching the output file in MS Word. However, most Oracle administrators on NT get a freeware grep for DOS, which is readily available on the Internet.

The code here shows the UNIX *grep* commands that are used to check for creation errors.

```
mysid-/u01/app/oracle/product/9.0.2/rdbms/admin> grep ORA- *.lis

mysid-/u01/app/oracle/product/9.0.2/rdbms/admin> grep -i error *.lis

spctab.lis:SPCTAB complete. Please check spctab.lis for any errors.
spcusr.lis:STATSCUSR complete. Please check spcusr.lis for any errors.
spcpkg.lis:No errors.
```

Now that the user, tables, indexes and the package have been installed, STATSPACK data can now be collected. The next step is to test STATSPACK functionality.

Step 3: Test the STATSPACK Install

To help ensure that everything is installed correctly, a DBA can demand two snapshots and then request an elapsed-time report. To execute a STATSPACK snapshot, enter the *statspack.snap* procedure. If done twice, this procedure will result in two snapshots. The *statsrep.sql* report can then be run to ensure that everything is working properly. If *statsrep* returns a meaningful report, then the install was successful. Also, note that the *statsrep.sql* script has an EXIT statement, so it will return to the UNIX prompt when it has completed:

```
SQL> execute statspack.snap

PL/SQL procedure successfully completed.
```

```
SQL> execute statspack.snap

PL/SQL procedure successfully completed.

SQL> @spreport
. . .
```

Step 4: Schedule Automatic STATSPACK Data Collections

Now that STATSPACK is installed and working, the next step is to schedule automatic data collection. By using the *spauto.sql* script, the user can automatically schedule an hourly data collection for STATSPACK. The *spauto.sql* script contains the following directive:

```
SQL> execute dbms_job.submit(:jobno, 'statspack.snap;',
trunc(sysdate+1/24,'HH'), 'trunc(SYSDATE+1/24,''HH'')', TRUE, :instno);
```

The important thing to know in this call to *dbms_job.submit* is the execution interval. The SYSDATE+1/24 is the interval that is stored in the *dba_jobs* view to produce hourly snapshots. This interval can be changed to allow for different sample times. There are 1,440 minutes in a day, and the divisors from Table 7.1 can be used to adjust the execution times.

Minutes per Day	Minutes between Snapshots	Required Divisor
1,440	60	24
1,440	30	48
1,440	10	144
1,440	5	288

Table 7.1: *Determining the Snapshot Interval*

For example, the following command can be issued to get a snapshot every ten minutes:

```
SQL> execute dbms_job.submit(:jobno, 'statspack.snap;',
trunc(sysdate+1/144,'MI'), 'trunc(SYSDATE+1/144,''MI'')', TRUE, :instno);
```

In the real world, there may be times when it is necessary to sample the database over short time intervals. For example, if a DBA notices that a performance problem happens every day between 4:00 p.m. and 5:00 p.m., they can request a more frequent snapshot schedule during this period.

For normal use, it is usually appropriate to accept the hourly default and execute a snapshot every hour. Below is the standard output from running the *spauto.sql* script:

```
SQL> connect perfstat/perfstat;

Connected.

SQL> @spauto

PL/SQL procedure successfully completed.
```

```
Job number for automated statistics collection for this instance
~~~~~~~~~~~~~~~~~~~~~~~~~~~~~~~~~~~~~~~~~~~~~~~~~~~~~~~~~~~~~~~~~~~~~

Note that this job number is needed when modifying or removing the job:

      JOBNO  1

Job queue process
~~~~~~~~~~~~~~~~~~
```

Below is the current setting of the *job_queue_processes* *init.ora* parameter. The value for this parameter must be greater than 0 to use automatic statistics gathering:

```
NAME                                  TYPE     VALUE
------------------------------------- -------  ---------------------------
job_queue_processes                   integer  1
```

```
Next scheduled run
~~~~~~~~~~~~~~~~~~~
```
The next scheduled run for this job is:

```
      JOB NEXT_DATE NEXT_SEC
---------- --------- --------
        1 12-MAY-02 16:00:00
```

Here, the STATSPACK snapshot will automatically be executed every hour. The snapshot is scheduled as job number 1. You can use this job number to cancel this collection at any time using the *dbms_job.remove* procedure:

```
SQL> execute dbms_job.remove(1);
```

```
PL/SQL procedure successfully completed.
```

The STATSPACK utility consists of 20 SQL scripts located in the *$oracle_home/rdbms/admin* directory. The following files form STATSPACK, as distributed in Oracle:

- The *spcreate.sql* script is a primary script for STATSPACK utility installation and should be run by user *sys*. This script calls some of the other creation scripts described below.

- The *spcusr.sql* script creates the *perfstat* schema. *Perfstat* is the owner of all STATSPACK database objects that form the STATSPACK repository. This script also grants all the necessary authorities to user PERFSTAT.

- The *spctab.sql* script creates all the STATSPACK objects under schema *perfstat*.

- The *spcpkg.sql* script creates a special statistics package that is necessary for snapshot and report generation.

- The *spdrop.sql* script uninstalls the STATSPACK utility from the database. This script calls the scripts *spdtab.sql* and *spdusr.sql*.

- The *spauto.sql* script is used to schedule the STATSPACK procedure called *statspack.snap* that gathers STATSPACK snapshots. In the AWR, this job performs a new background process called the Manageability Monitor (MMON).

- The *sppurge.sql* script purges old STATSPACK data from the repository. The snapshot range for the data to be cleared must be specified by the user.

- The *sprepcon.sql* is a new script in STATSPACK that is used to specify selected parameters that are related to report generation invoked by *spreport.sql* script.

- The *spreport.sql* and *sprepins.sql* are the scripts used for report generation. The *spreport.sql* script must be called to produce the STATSPACK report for a specified snapshot range.

- The *sprepsql.sql* and *sprsqins.sql* scripts are used to generate the STATSPACK report for SQL statements, statistics and plan usage.

- The *sptrunc.sql* script can be used to clear all the STATSPACK tables, thereby reclaiming space for the database.

- The *spuexp.par* is the name of the export parameter file which is used to export the whole STATSPACK user.

- The *sp*.sql* scripts are the upgrade scripts used to convert existing STATSPACK repository information to the latest Oracle version.

STATSPACK vs. AWR

In Chapter 6, many of the internal AWR tables that have a structure similar to the corresponding STATSPACK tables that store snapshots from the same *v$* dynamic views were viewed. This similarity enables the easy conversion of existing performance reports originally designed for STATSPACK to new AWR views.

The AWR repository holds all of the statistics available in STATSPACK as well as some additional statistics. The following information on statistics is specific to those stored in the AWR that are not part of the STATSPACK utility. STATSPACK does not store the Active Session History (ASH) statistics available in the AWR *dba_hist_active_sess_history* view. The ASH allows DBAs to perform time-series analyses of wait events for a particular session history.

An important difference between STATSPACK and the AWR is that STATSPACK does not store history for new metric statistics introduced in Oracle10g. The key AWR views, *dba_hist_sysmetric_history* and *dba_hist_sysmetric_summary*, help the DBA build time-series reports for important database performance metrics such as *Total Time Waited* or *Response Time Per Txn*. The AWR also contains views such as *dba_hist_service_stat*, *dba_hist_service_wait_class* and *dba_hist_service_name*, which store history for performance cumulative statistics tracked for specific services.

Starting with STATSPACK in Oracle 10g, tables are provided for monitoring Oracle Streams. These tables are *stats$streams_capture*, *stats$streams_apply_sum*, *stats$buffered_subscribers*, *stats$rule_set*, *stats$propagation_sender*, *stats$propagation_receiver* and *stats$buffered_queues*. The AWR does not contain the specific tables that reflect Oracle Streams activity; therefore, if a DBA relies heavily on the Oracle Streams feature, it would be useful to monitor the database performance using the STATSPACK utility.

Now that the basic functionality of the AWR and the STATSPACK utility have been introduced, it will be helpful to see how database statistics are managed using each.

Statistic Management in AWR and STATSPACK

Both STATSPACK and AWR take a snapshot of the *v$* dynamic view and store it in repositories.

The AWR has a special background process, MMON, which is responsible for gathering regular snapshots. The DBA is able to specify the frequency at which MMON gathers snapshots via the *dbms_workload_repository.modify_snapshot_settings* procedure:

```
SQL> desc dbms_workload_repository

PROCEDURE MODIFY_SNAPSHOT_SETTINGS

 Argument Name        Type             In/Out Default?
 ---------------      ---------------  ------ --------
 RETENTION            NUMBER           IN     DEFAULT
 INTERVAL             NUMBER           IN     DEFAULT
 DBID                 NUMBER           IN     DEFAULT
```

The first *dbms_workload_repository.modify_snapshot_settings* procedure parameter is *retention*. This parameter allows the DBA to specify the time period in minutes. The AWR will preserve that particular snapshot in the repository. The valid range of values for this parameter ranges from 10 minutes to 52,560,000 minutes, or 100 years. The *dbms_workload_repository* package has the global variables *min_retention* and *max_retention*, which set the lower and upper limits for the *retention* parameter. If a zero value is specified for retention, snapshots will be stored for an unlimited time.

The *interval* parameter sets the time interval, in minutes, between the snapshots. The default interval between snapshots is 60 minutes. The valid range of values for this parameter ranges from 10 minutes to 52,560,000 minutes, or 100 years. The *dbms_workload_repository* package has the global variables *min_interval* and *max_interval*, which set the lower and upper limits for this parameter. If the value specified for the interval is zero, automatic and manual snapshots will be prohibited.

The current settings for AWR *retention* and *interval* parameters can be viewed using *dba_hist_wr_control* data dictionary view with this script:

```
select
     extract( day from snap_interval) *24*60+
     extract( hour from snap_interval) *60+
     extract( minute from snap_interval ) "Snapshot Interval",
     extract( day from retention) *24*60+
     extract( hour from retention) *60+
     extract( minute from retention ) "Retention Interval"
from dba_hist_wr_control;
```

This script returns the current AWR interval values in minutes:

```
Snapshot Interval Retention Interval
---------------- -----------------
             60             10080
```

STATSPACK has many more settings that can be configured. These are kept in the *stats$statspack_parameter* table. This table stores a single row for the database parameters with the corresponding STATSPACK settings. These settings influence the amount of information STATSPACK gathers from the *v$* views.

```
SQL> desc stats$statspack_parameter

Name                                      Null?     Type
----------------------------------------- --------  -------------
DBID                                      NOT NULL  NUMBER
INSTANCE_NUMBER                           NOT NULL  NUMBER
SESSION_ID                                NOT NULL  NUMBER
SNAP_LEVEL                                NOT NULL  NUMBER
NUM_SQL                                   NOT NULL  NUMBER
EXECUTIONS_TH                             NOT NULL  NUMBER
PARSE_CALLS_TH                            NOT NULL  NUMBER
DISK_READS_TH                             NOT NULL  NUMBER
BUFFER_GETS_TH                            NOT NULL  NUMBER
SHARABLE_MEM_TH                           NOT NULL  NUMBER
VERSION_COUNT_TH                          NOT NULL  NUMBER
PIN_STATSPACK                             NOT NULL  VARCHAR2(10)
ALL_INIT                                  NOT NULL  VARCHAR2(5)
LAST_MODIFIED                                       DATE
UCOMMENT                                            VARCHAR2(160)
JOB                                                 NUMBER
```

The *stats$statspack_parameter* configuration table stores the following settings for STATSPACK.

The *snap_level* Parameter

Snapshot level zero captures general statistics including rollback segment, row cache, SGA, system events, background events, session events, system statistics, wait statistics, lock statistics and latch information.

- Level 5 includes the capture of high resource usage SQL statements along with all data captured by lower levels.

- Level 6, only available in version 9.0.1 or later, includes the capture of SQL plan and SQL plan usage information for high resource usage SQL statements in addition to all data captured by lower levels.

- Level 7, also only available in version 9.2 or later, captures segment level statistics, including logical and physical reads, row lock, itl and buffer busy waits, as well as all data captured by lower levels.

- Level 10 includes the capture of child latch statistics along with all data captured by lower levels.

The session_id

This is the Session ID of the Oracle session for which session granular data is captured. The valid value is from the *sid* column in *v$* session. The default value is zero, which means no session.

The num_sql

This is the number of SQL statements to be gathered for Top Resource SQL reports. The default value is 50.

What SQL is Captured?

People who use AWR and STATSPACK to track historical SQL patterns often wonder why some SQL does not appear in the STATSPACK and AWR tables. The snap process collects information from *v$sqlarea* for SQL statements. Because this part is wrapped code, it is invisible to the DBA. If the library cache no longer has the SQL statement in it, then it will not get snapped. If the SQL statement is not snapped on both the begin snap and end snaps, Oracle will not be able to report on it.

This can be seen in the *sprepins.sql* script, which is the real body of *spreport.sql*. An example of one of the SQL reports is seen here:

```
display_sql_captured.sql

select aa, hv
  from ( select /*+ ordered use_nl (b st) */
           decode( st.piece
                 , 0
                 , lpad(to_char((e.buffer_gets - nvl(b.buffer_gets,0))
                             ,'99,999,999,999')
                     ,15)||' '||
                   lpad(to_char((e.executions - nvl(b.executions,0))
                             ,'999,999,999')
                     ,12)||' '||
                   lpad((to_char(decode(e.executions - nvl(b.executions,0)
                               ,0, to_number(null)
                               ,(e.buffer_gets - nvl(b.buffer_gets,0)) /
                                 (e.executions - nvl(b.executions,0)))
                             ,'999,999,990.0'))
                     ,14) ||' '||
                   lpad((to_char(100*(e.buffer_gets - nvl(b.buffer_gets,0))/:gets
                             ,'990.0'))
                     , 6) ||' '||
                   lpad(  nvl(to_char(  (e.cpu_time - nvl(b.cpu_time,0))/1000000
                             , '9990.00')
                     , ' '),8) ||' ' ||
                   lpad(  nvl(to_char(  (e.elapsed_time - nvl(b.elapsed_time,0))/1000000
                             , '99990.00')
                     , ' '),9) ||' ' ||
                   lpad(e.old_hash_value,10)||''||
                   decode(e.module,null,st.sql_text
                               ,rpad('Module: '||e.module,80)||st.sql_text)
                 , st.sql_text) aa
             , e.old_hash_value hv
         from stats$sql_summary e
            , stats$sql_summary b
```

```
        , stats$sqltext        st
   where b.snap_id(+)          = :bid
     and b.dbid(+)             = e.dbid
     and b.instance_number(+)  = e.instance_number
     and b.old_hash_value(+)   = e.old_hash_value
     and b.address(+)          = e.address
     and b.text_subset(+)      = e.text_subset
     and e.snap_id             = :eid
     and e.dbid                = :dbid
     and e.instance_number     = :inst_num
     and e.old_hash_value      = st.old_hash_value
     and e.text_subset         = st.text_subset
     and st.piece              <= &&num_rows_per_hash
     and e.executions          > nvl(b.executions,0)
     and 100*(e.buffer_gets - nvl(b.buffer_gets,0))/:gets > &&top_pct_sql
   order by (e.buffer_gets - nvl(b.buffer_gets,0)) desc, e.old_hash_value, st.piece
   )
where rownum < &&top_n_sql;
```

STATSPACK SQL Collection Thresholds

The *executions_th*, *parse_calls_th*, *disk_read_th*, *buffer_gets_th*, *sharable_mem_th*, and *version_count_th* settings allow the DBA to set thresholds for SQL statements. If any of the thresholds are exceeded, the information will be stored by STATSPACK in the repository.

These STATSPACK parameters can be set manually using the *statspack.modify_statspack_parameter* procedure:

```
SQL> desc statspack

PROCEDURE MODIFY_STATSPACK_PARAMETER

Argument Name            Type            In/Out Default?
--------------------     -------------   ------ --------
I_DBID                   NUMBER          IN     DEFAULT
I_INSTANCE_NUMBER        NUMBER          IN     DEFAULT
I_SNAP_LEVEL             NUMBER          IN     DEFAULT
I_SESSION_ID             NUMBER          IN     DEFAULT
I_UCOMMENT               VARCHAR2        IN     DEFAULT
I_NUM_SQL                NUMBER          IN     DEFAULT
I_EXECUTIONS_TH          NUMBER          IN     DEFAULT
I_PARSE_CALLS_TH         NUMBER          IN     DEFAULT
I_DISK_READS_TH          NUMBER          IN     DEFAULT
I_BUFFER_GETS_TH         NUMBER          IN     DEFAULT
I_SHARABLE_MEM_TH        NUMBER          IN     DEFAULT
I_VERSION_COUNT_TH       NUMBER          IN     DEFAULT
I_ALL_INIT               VARCHAR2        IN     DEFAULT
I_PIN_STATSPACK          VARCHAR2        IN     DEFAULT
I_MODIFY_PARAMETER       VARCHAR2        IN     DEFAULT
```

With the release of Oracle10g, the use of STATSPACK now requires more configuration settings than those required with the AWR.

In the STATSPACK utility, the *statspack.snap* procedure must be executed manually as an Oracle job in order to gather history for *v$* statistics on a regular basis. The *statspack.snap* procedure must be called to take a new STATSPACK snapshot:

```
SQL> desc statspack

PROCEDURE SNAP

Argument Name          Type          In/Out Default?
-------------------    ------------  ------ --------
I_SNAP_LEVEL           NUMBER        IN     DEFAULT
I_SESSION_ID           NUMBER        IN     DEFAULT
I_UCOMMENT             VARCHAR2      IN     DEFAULT
I_NUM_SQL              NUMBER        IN     DEFAULT
I_EXECUTIONS_TH        NUMBER        IN     DEFAULT
I_PARSE_CALLS_TH       NUMBER        IN     DEFAULT
I_DISK_READS_TH        NUMBER        IN     DEFAULT
I_BUFFER_GETS_TH       NUMBER        IN     DEFAULT
I_SHARABLE_MEM_TH      NUMBER        IN     DEFAULT
I_VERSION_COUNT_TH     NUMBER        IN     DEFAULT
I_ALL_INIT             VARCHAR2      IN     DEFAULT
I_PIN_STATSPACK        VARCHAR2      IN     DEFAULT
I_MODIFY_PARAMETER     VARCHAR2      IN     DEFAULT
```

The parameters for the *statspack.snap* procedure allow the DBA to specify the level of statistics gathered as well as the specific thresholds for the new snapshot. The settings specified in the call of the *statspack.snap* procedure will be valid only for this single new snapshot.

AWR SQL Collection Thresholds

By default, the AWR requires no DBA intervention because the Top-n SQL collection threshold is controlled by the *statistics_level* parameter where TYPICAL means top-30 SQL statements.

Unlike STATSPACK, AWR uses a "Top N" method which defaults to collect the Top-30 SQL statements for each SQL category.
If you set *statistics_level* = "all", AWR will collect the top 100 SQL statements.

While the AWR is fully automated with regard to statistic history storage, it also allows for a DBA to take new snapshots manually using the *dbms_workload_repository.create_snapshot* procedure.

```
SQL> desc dbms_workload_repository
...
PROCEDURE CREATE_SNAPSHOT

Argument Name                     Type          In/Out Default?
-------------------------------   ------------  ------ --------
FLUSH_LEVEL                       VARCHAR2      IN     DEFAULT
FUNCTION CREATE_SNAPSHOT RETURNS NUMBER
```

```
Argument Name                         Type          In/Out   Default?
-------------------------------       ------------  ------   --------
    FLUSH_LEVEL                       VARCHAR2      IN        DEFAULT
```

The only parameter listed in the procedures is the *flush_level,* which configures the amount of information the AWR gathers. This parameter can have either the default value of TYPICAL or a value of ALL. When the statistics level is set to ALL, the AWR gathers the maximum amount of performance data possible. Usually, the TYPICAL level is enough for performance analysis and tuning purposes. The AWR uses the *spfile* initialization parameter *statistics_level* to specify the snapshots level for snapshots gathered by MMON process. The possible values for this parameter are the same, TYPICAL (Top-30 SQL) and ALL (Top-100 SQL).

The *dbms_workload_repository* package has an overloaded function, called *create_snapshot,* which has the same parameter level and utility as the *create_snapshot* procedure. The difference is that *dbms_workload_repository* only returns the number of the newly created snapshots.

Another essential difference between AWR and STATSPACK is the way that old statistical history is removed from the database. The AWR removes old snapshots from its repository based on the *retention* parameter, which specifies the length of time that any snapshot is stored in the database. Thanks to this feature, DBAs using AWR do not need to manually clear the database of old information.

Because of this scheduled cleanup, the total space consumed by the AWR remains relatively constant depending on the *statistics_level* parameter. However, the AWR also has a procedure for the manual removal of historical data called *dbms_workload_repository.drop_snapshot_range.*

```
SQL> desc dbms_workload_repository
```

```
PROCEDURE DROP_SNAPSHOT_RANGE

Argument Name        Type          In/Out   Default?
-----------------    ------------  ------   --------
LOW_SNAP_ID          NUMBER        IN
HIGH_SNAP_ID         NUMBER        IN
DBID                 NUMBER        IN        DEFAULT
```

STATSPACK, on the other hand, does not automatically remove old data from the database. DBAs must manually remove old STATSPACK data using either the *sppurge.sql* script.

The summary reports for the AWR and STATSPACK can be built using SQL scripts such as *awrrpt.sql* for the AWR and *spreport.sql* for STATSPACK. In addition, the AWR is able to produce summary reports in HTML format. If using STATSPACK, a DBA can use the Ion tool to convert the summary text report files to HTML format. This feature is one of many helpful tools Ion provides to analyze processed STATSPACK reports.

Another interesting point in the comparison of AWR and STATSPACK is that both utilities support the ability to store historical performance information from several databases in a single repository. This repository can be checked using *dba_hist* views or the underlying *wrh$* data dictionary tables. Each table contains *dbid* and *instance_number* columns, which are included as primary keys on *wrh$* data dictionary tables.

In the case of STATSPACK, most *stats$* repository tables contain the *dbid* and *instance_number* columns. This combination of columns allows for the storage of different subsets of performance history data from several databases into a single repository. It is important to remember, however, that the current release of Oracle 11g does not support any documented methods for exporting/importing AWR data between databases. Perhaps this functionality will be provided in a future release of the Oracle software.

Unlike AWR, the STATSPACK utility has a documented method for moving data between different repositories. This is done using Oracle Export/Import utilities. A special parameter file called *spuexp.par* is delivered with STATSPACK as a sample export parameter file. Although possible, the process of moving STATSPACK data between databases using the Export/Import approach is complex.

The Ion tool provides a simple method for moving STATSPACK data across databases. The process can be automated and scheduled to run on a regular basis. Once scheduled, the Ion tool will move data from the STATSPACK repositories to a single place without manual intervention. STATSPACK's ability to store performance data from multiple databases allows DBAs to establish a single STATSPACK storage database that will store data from all relevant Oracle databases.

The last important difference between AWR and STATSPACK concerns the use of baselines. The AWR supports the creation and ability to work with Oracle-defined baselines, while STATSPACK does not. A baseline is a set of statistics that is defined by a beginning and ending pair of snapshots. A baseline can be created using the *dbms_workload_repository.create_baseline* procedure, as demonstrated here:

```
SQL> desc dbms_workload_repository

PROCEDURE CREATE_BASELINE

Argument Name          Type                    In/Out Default?
--------------------   --------------------    ------ --------
START_SNAP_ID          NUMBER                  IN
END_SNAP_ID            NUMBER                  IN
BASELINE_NAME          VARCHAR2                IN
DBID                   NUMBER                  IN     DEFAULT

FUNCTION CREATE_BASELINE RETURNS NUMBER

Argument Name          Type                    In/Out Default?
--------------------   --------------------    ------ --------
START_SNAP_ID          NUMBER                  IN
END_SNAP_ID            NUMBER                  IN
BASELINE_NAME          VARCHAR2                IN
DBID                   NUMBER                  IN     DEFAULT
```

All of the created baselines are visible in the *dba_hist_baselines* view:

```
SQL> desc dba_hist_baseline
```

```
Name              Null?     Type
---------------   --------  ----
DBID              NOT NULL  NUMBER
BASELINE_ID       NOT NULL  NUMBER
BASELINE_NAME               VARCHAR2(64)
START_SNAP_ID               NUMBER
START_SNAP_TIME             TIMESTAMP(3)
END_SNAP_ID                 NUMBER
END_SNAP_TIME               TIMESTAMP(3)
```

Once two baselines have been created, statistics related to the two baselines can be compared. The AWR automatically preserves the snapshots, which are part of any existing baseline.

The *dbms_workload_repository.drop_baseline* procedure can be used to remove existing baselines from the data dictionary, and the *baseline_name* parameter identifies the baseline to be dropped. The default setting for the *cascade* parameter is FALSE, and in order to remove the snapshots associated with the baseline to be removed, the *cascade* parameter will have to be set to TRUE:

```
desc dbms_workload_repository
```

```
PROCEDURE DROP_BASELINE

Argument Name                     Type                    In/Out Default?
------------------------------    --------------------    ------ --------
BASELINE_NAME                     VARCHAR2                IN
CASCADE                           BOOLEAN                 IN     DEFAULT
DBID                              NUMBER                  IN     DEFAULT
```

STATSPACK, on the other hand, does not support the functionality of baselines. The Ion tool provides Oracle DBAs with the ability to create and work with baselines employing an easy-to-use GUI interface. With the Ion tool, a DBA can compare a current statistic's behavior with a recorded baseline. The next section will cover the *SQL statistics summary* table, which is a vital STATSPACK feature.

The *stats$sql_summary* Table

The *SQL statistics summary* is one of the most important tables within the STATSPACK utility. The process of tuning SQL can often have a profound impact on the performance of an Oracle system. The *stats$sql_summary* table provides the text of each SQL statement. In addition, this table gives the DBA a detailed description of the resources used by each and every SQL statement that meets the necessary threshold conditions.

The table tracks the number of executions, parse calls, and data blocks that are read and written for each SQL statement. This information can be an invaluable tool when tuning the SQL within an Oracle database.

It is also important to note that the *stats$sql_summary* table is the most highly populated of all of the STATSPACK tables. If the threshold values are set relatively low in a busy database, it is not uncommon to get 300 to 500 rows added to the *stats$sql_summary* table every time STATSPACK requests a snapshot. Hence, it is very important that a DBA remove unwanted rows from the *stats$sql_summary* table after the rows are no longer used for SQL tuning.

```
SQL> desc STATS$SQL_SUMMARY
 Name                                     Null?    Type
 ---------------------------------------- -------- --------------
 SNAP_ID                                  NOT NULL NUMBER(6)
 DBID                                     NOT NULL NUMBER
 INSTANCE_NUMBER                          NOT NULL NUMBER
 TEXT_SUBSET                              NOT NULL VARCHAR2(31)
 SQL_TEXT                                          VARCHAR2(1000)
 SHARABLE_MEM                                      NUMBER
 SORTS                                             NUMBER
 MODULE                                            VARCHAR2(64)
 LOADED_VERSIONS                                   NUMBER
 EXECUTIONS                                        NUMBER
 LOADS                                             NUMBER
 INVALIDATIONS                                     NUMBER
 PARSE_CALLS                                       NUMBER
 DISK_READS                                        NUMBER
 BUFFER_GETS                                       NUMBER
 ROWS_PROCESSED                                    NUMBER
 COMMAND_TYPE                                      NUMBER
 ADDRESS                                           RAW(8)
 HASH_VALUE                               NOT NULL NUMBER
 VERSION_COUNT                                     NUMBER
 CPU_TIME                                          NUMBER
 ELAPSED_TIME                                      NUMBER
 OUTLINE_SID                                       NUMBER
 OUTLINE_CATEGORY                                  VARCHAR2(64)
```

Within a STATSPACK installation, the *stats$sql_summary* table will grow very rapidly. This is because STATSPACK will extract SQL from the library cache every time a snapshot is executed. Hence, the Oracle administrator must be careful to set the appropriate threshold values for *stats$sql_summary* data collection to ensure that the database does not run wild. Refer to the listing and description of the STATSPACK SQL threshold parameters provided earlier in this chapter.

Now it is time to cover the steps to install and configure the AWR.

Installing AWR

There are only two AWR installation scripts, which are also located in the *$oracle_home/rdbms/admin* directory:

- The *catawr.sql* script creates data dictionary catalog objects for the AWR.

- The *dbmsawr.sql* script creates the *dbms_workload_repository* package for database administrators.

In later versions of Oracle, STATSPACK is shipped without the *spdoc.txt* file, which was a guide for working with STATSPACK that was included in previous versions. This is another mechanism by which Oracle Corporation urges the use of the AWR for performance tuning purposes rather than STATSPACK.

Many utilities of AWR have been covered earlier in this chapter, such as, *dbms_workload_repository.drop_snapshot_range*, the *dbms_workload_repository.create_baseline* procedure, the *dba_hist_baselines* view and the *dbms_workload_repository.drop_baseline* procedure. Additional information about working with AWR follows.

The *dbms_workload_repository* Package

The *dbms_workload_repository* package allows the DBA to manage the AWR using a handy PL/SQL API. This functionality can be used to configure AWR settings such as snapshot interval and data retention to create or remove baselines for trend performance analysis purposes, to gather AWR snapshots manually or programmatically, and to generate reports.

The *dbms_workload_repository.modify_snapshot_settings* procedure was also covered earlier in this chapter, as were its variables *min_interval* and *max_interval*. As stated before, these two variables set the lower and upper limits for the *interval*. If a zero value is specified for *interval*, automatic and manual snapshots will be prohibited.

An interesting fact about the AWR is that the base *wrh$_* history and *wrm$_* AWR data dictionary metadata tables support *dbid* and *instance_number* columns that store the current database identifier and the *instance* number. Furthermore, some procedures and functions in the *dbms_workload_repository* package contain the *dbid* parameter that defaults to the current database identifier and can be omitted. The popular theory is that these parameters are reserved for future use when a single AWR will be able to store data from multiple databases.

The new MMON Oracle background process, as shown earlier, is responsible for the creation of new snapshots at the specified snapshot interval; however, the DBA is able to programmatically take new snapshots using the *dbms_workload_repository.create_snapshot* procedure.

The MMON background process is also responsible for removing old historical data from the AWR. As was stated previously, the amount of retention time after which data will be removed from the database is determined by the *retention* setting. However, data can be cleared from the AWR tables by using the *dbms_workload_repository.drop_snapshot_range* procedure.

This concludes the explanation of how to invoke the workload repository packages directly. The following section will take a look at how to generate a standard AWR report using the *dbms_workload_repository* package.

Creating an AWR Report

The remaining procedures in the *dbms_workload_repository* package are *awr_report_text* and *awr_report_html*, which generate the AWR report for the specified snapshot range in text or HTML formats, respectively. The following script segment shows how to retrieve the AWR text report for any snapshot range or duration:

```
SELECT
   output
FROM    TABLE(dbms_workload_repository.awr_report_text (37933856,1,2900,2911 ));
```

The sample output below shows the typical report generated for AWR data. The output display shows the four arguments to the *awr_report_text* stored procedure:

- The database ID is 37933856

- The instance number for RAC is 1

- The starting snapshot number is 2900

- The ending snapshot number is 2911

Report Naming

The standard Oracle elapsed time report has evolved over the past 12 years and has had several names:

- **report.txt:** In Oracle 7 and Oracle 8, this *bstat-estat* was taken by running the *utlbstat.sql* followed by *utlestat.sql* in the *$oracle_home/rdbms/admin* directory.

- **spreport:** From Oracle 8i to Oracle 10g, this is an enhanced *bstat-estat* report where the user chooses the beginning and ending snapshot numbers.

- **AWR Report:** In Oracle 10g, this is the latest time-series report, and it is produced by running a SQL*Plus script in the *$oracle_home/rdbms/admin directory*. *Awrrpt.sql* is a text-based report. *Awrrpti.sql* is a HTML-based report for online publishing of time-series reports.

```
OUTPUT
-------------------------------------------------------------
WORKLOAD REPOSITORY report for

DB Name        DB Id      Instance      Inst Num Release      Cluster Host
------------ ----------- ------------ -------- ---------- ------ 
DBDABR         37933856 dbdabr              1 10.1.0.2.0  NO     Host1

               Snap Id       Snap Time        Sessions Curs/Sess
             --------- ------------------- -------- ---------
Begin Snap:      2900 19-Aug-04 11:00:29       18      7.2
  End Snap:      2911 19-Aug-04 22:00:16       18      4.6
   Elapsed:            659.78 (mins)
   DB Time:             10.08 (mins)

Cache Sizes (end)
~~~~~~~~~~~~~~~~~
Buffer Cache:      48M     Std Block Size:        8K
Shared Pool Size:  56M        Log Buffer:      256K

Load Profile
~~~~~~~~~~~~          Per Second        Per Transaction
                   --------------       -----------
      Redo size: 1,766.20             18,526.31
  Logical reads:    39.21                411.30
  Block changes:    11.11                116.54
 Physical reads:     0.38                  3.95
```

```
Physical writes:    0.38           3.96
   User calls:      0.06           0.64
      Parses:       2.04          21.37
 Hard parses:       0.14           1.45
       Sorts:       1.02          10.72
      Logons:       0.02           0.21
    Executes:       4.19          43.91
```

This is very similar to the old STATSPACK reports from Oracle 9i, and it contains vital elapsed-time change information for what happened during the particular snapshot range.

A more detailed look at reading the standard AWR report is included in the next chapter.

Conclusion

A comparison of the AWR to the STATSPACK utility shows that the AWR presents a much more comprehensive and advanced tool than STATSPACK. The AWR gathers and stores history for an extended set of performance data that is available in Oracle. The main points of this chapter include:

- The primary benefit of the AWR is that it requires minimal administration efforts from the Oracle DBA.

- The AWR utility gives Oracle DBAs a powerful tool for performance tuning and trend analysis. It is simple enough to be used as a monitoring tool by junior DBAs, yet powerful enough to be used as an advanced data-mining source for detailed time-series analysis, trend identification and capacity planning.

- The AWR forms an analysis base for Oracle intelligent self-tuning features such as ADDM, the SQL Tuning Advisor, Automatic Segment Management and ASM.

Now that the similarities and differences between the AWR and the STATSPACK utility have been introduced, the next chapter will provide a detailed look into Oracle $v\$$ views.

Reading an AWR or STATSPACK Report

I'm here to divine the secret meaning within your AWR report

The Evolution of the Elapsed Time Report

This chapter focuses on creating, reading and interpreting the Oracle time-series report from STATSPACK and AWR. Originally created exclusively for use by Oracle Technical Support Services, this time-series report was originally named "*report.txt*", and the basic format has remained the same since Oracle 7. Since then, Oracle continues to add new report sections such as the SGA sizing advisors, and this has become the de-facto standard report from STATSPACK and AWR.

Ever since our DBA ancestors began monitoring Oracle databases (circa 1988), we have struggled to wade through the plethora of statistics in the Oracle time-series performance report. These reports have taken several forms over the years, but the core content has remained identical, an elapsed-time view of database activity between two snapshot periods:

- ***bstat-estat* reports:** The original elapsed time report was introduced in Oracle 6 and used through Oracle 8. For storing the time-series snapshots, I created a special routine that would store the intermediate values and published it in Oracle Magazine in the 1990's, serving as a forerunner of STATSPACK.

- **STATSPACK reports:** Oracle 8i to present. The STATSPACK report is an offshoot of the original *bstat-estat* report, which was created for Oracle internal-use only and it is not documented by Oracle. Many of the performance metrics are undocumented also and requires detailed knowledge of Oracle internals, and reading a STATSPACK report requires considerable knowledge.

- **Automated Workload Repository (AWR) reports:** Oracle 10g to present.

Now, this might look like AWR supersedes STATSPACK, but this is not the case, and STATSPACK is alive and well in the 2010 current releases.

STATSPACK is current in 11g

If you don't want to purchase AWR, STATSPACK has been updated for the new 11g view, and serves as a great, free alternative to the expensive AWR option.

Originally, Oracle's elapsed-time reports were intended solely for Oracle technical support and they remain full of undocumented performance metrics, with page after page of undocumented gobbledygook, like this example:

```
Statistic                          Total      per Second    per Trans
-------------------------------- ---------  -------------- ----------
DFO trees parallelized                   1           0.0        0.0
calls to get snapshot scn: kcmgss   55,918          15.5      860.3
calls to kcmgas                      9,929           2.8      152.8
calls to kcmgcs                         59           0.0        0.9
cleanout - number of ktugct calls   11,057           3.1      170.1
```

Every Oracle tuning expert has their own method for reading and interpreting STATSPACK reports, but it's all about separating the wheat from the chaff, sifting through reams of data to glean out important details to create valid tuning recommendations.

It's not easy, and the challenge is to focus on those metrics that are the most important for understanding the nature of your performance problem.

Interpreting an Oracle STATSPACK/AWR report will always be complex and it is only a few tools have invested the thousands of hours of work required to replicate the analysis of a human expert.

I have been refining my STATSPACK/AWR report interpreter component in *Ion for Oracle* for almost a decade, and I can say firsthand that automating the interpretation of an elapsed time report is a significant software engineering challenge! If you are a raw beginner, one good way to learn how to read a STATSPACK/AWR report is to use the Ion Expert system analysis tool.

Again, this elapsed-time report was originally designed for use by Oracle Corporation and it has many undocumented metrics. Hence, understanding all of the sections of a STATSPACK report is quite complicated, but if you know where to look, the STATSPACK/AWR report has valuable information. While the learning curve is steep, it is worth the time investment to understand how to read this important report.

There are many applications of expert systems and applied artificial intelligence with Oracle, but the Oracle community has always desired a software tool that could apply the well-structured decision rules to the generic STATSPACK and AWR reports.

What's New in STATSPACK and AWR Reports

As each new release brings new features to the database, these enhancements are translated into the AWR and STATSPACK reports. As of Oracle 10g, these are the following new report sections:

- **Operating system statistics:** Beginning in Oracle 10g, Oracle realized that the database does not run in a vacuum and started to include OS statistics on RAM and CPU consumption in addition to filing I/O timings.

- **Time model statistics:** The time model statistics were covered at length in Chapter 3, and the time model details are now presented for elapsed time reports.

- **Wait event histograms:** By presenting wait events in a histogram format, we can quickly see the distribution of wait event wait times.

- **File read histograms:** Oracle has taken the histogram format to show the distribution of disk reads along a millisecond time dimension. This histogram format makes it easy to spot transient disk enqueues and cases where high activity is causing disk I/O latency.

Remember, analyzing a thousand-line report is not trivial, and many dozens of observation points may be required to formulate a decision rule. Further, the generalization of these complex rules may make them prone to false positives such as the reporting of a non-existent bottleneck.

Obviously, no tool will ever be able to model the intuition of an expert because it is impossible to quantify those "*I have a feeling*" hunches that distinguish the real experts, but this tool shows great promise as a research tool.

While there is only enough room in this chapter to cover the highlights of reading a STATSPACK and AWR report, this important chapter should give users a good idea what to look for in an AWR report and how to use this data to identify performance problems.

Generating a STATSPACK Report

Back in the days before STATSPACK, the original time-series report was generated when we ran the *end statistics* utility (*estat*) and it was stored on the server as a flat file named *report.txt*.

Today, the method for creating a STATSPACK report has changed little, so follow these basic steps:

1. **Take the snapshots:** If a STATSPACK report is being taken for an acute performance problem, the recommendation is to take short duration snapshots at 5, 10 or 15-minute intervals

2. **Generate the report:** It is easy to invoke the STATSPACK/AWR report, with the begin snapshot and end snapshot being passed as parameters

Also use Ion for Oracle to generate an intelligent elapsed time report by specifying the starting and end snapshots (Figure 8.1):

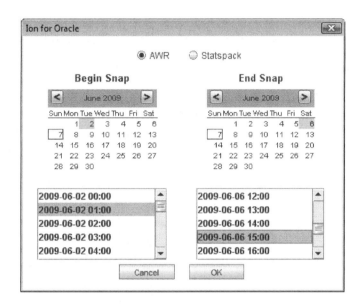

Figure 8.1: *Choosing a Snapshot Range in Ion*

Comparing the Ion intelligent analysis to the Oracle provided elapsed time report is a great way to learn how to read the standard STATSPACK/AWR report because the Ion report is in plain English and points to the core sections of the STATSPACK/AWR report where the data was collected.

To get a STATSPACK report, simply execute *spreport.sql* in SQL*Plus. Start by connecting as the *perfstat* user (the owner of the STATSPACK schema), run *spreport.sql* and specify the start and end snapshot numbers:

```
SQL>  connect perfstat/my_password

Connected.

SQL>  @?/rdbms/admin/spreport

DB Id       DB Name      Inst Num Instance
----------- ------------ -------- ------------
2659362428  DIOGENES            1 DIO1

Completed Snapshots
```

```
                    Snap              Snap
Instance      DB Name      Id   Snap Started     Level Comment
-----------   -----------  ----- ----------------- ----- ----------------
dio1          DIOGENES       1 11 May 2000 12:07     5
                             2 11 May 2000 12:08     5

Specify the Begin and End Snapshot Ids
~~~~~~~~~~~~~~~~~~~~~~~~~~~~~~~~~~~~~~~

Enter value for begin_snap: 1

Begin Snapshot Id specified: 1

Enter value for end_snap: 2

End   Snapshot Id specified: 2
```

The final report is written to the flat file that was named when executing *spreport.sql*, and we can then exit SQL*Plus and view the report.

Generating an AWR Report

The procedure for getting an AWR report is quite different than STATSPACK. The final AWR report can be built by using the PL/SQL API provided in the *dbms_workload_repository* package. The procedures that generate AWR reports are *awr_report_text* and *awr_report_html*. These procedures generate the AWR report for the specified snapshot range in TEXT or HTML formats, respectively. The following script shows one way of retrieving the AWR text report for the particular snapshot range:

```
select
   output
from
   table
   (dbms_workload_repository.awr_report_text
      (37933856,1,2900,2911 )
   );
```

```
OUTPUT
-----------------------------------------------------------------------
WORKLOAD REPOSITORY report for

DB Name      DB Id      Instance   Inst Num Release       Cluster Host
----------   ----------- ---------- -------- ----------    ------- -----
DBDABR       37933856 dbdabr             1 10.1.0.2.0    NO      Host1

             Snap Id        Snap Time       Sessions Curs/Sess
             ---------  ------------------  -------- ---------
Begin Snap:    2900 19-Aug-04 11:00:29        18       5.2
  End Snap:    2911 19-Aug-04 22:00:16        18       4.6
  Elapsed:           659.78 (mins)
  DB Time:            10.08 (mins)
```

The old-fashioned AWR report generation procedure has also been preserved from STATSPACK. The *awrrpt.sql* script in SQL*Plus can simply be run, and the parameters necessary to build the AWR report can be provided. In fact, the *awrrpt.sql* script calls the corresponding procedure from the *dbms_workload_repository* package and stores its output in the target report file.

Now that we know how to create the report, it is time to look at the major sections of the STATSPACK and AWR report.

Reading the STATSPACK / AWR Report

This section contains detailed guidance for evaluating each section of a STATSPACK/AWR report. As has been noted, both the AWR and STATSPACK reports are very similar and both contain vital elapsed-time information.

Remember, the raw data in an AWR or STATSPACK are accumulated values and the process of creating the report calculates the changes between the snapshots. The main sections in an AWR report include:

- **Report summary:** This gives an overall summary of the instance during the snapshot period, and it contains important aggregate summary information.

- **Cache sizes (end):** This shows the size of each SGA region after AMM has changed them. This information can be compared to the original *init.ora* parameters at the end of the AWR report.

- **Load profile:** This section shows important rates expressed in units of per second and per transaction.

- **Instance efficiency percentages:** With a target of 100%, these are high-level ratios for activity in the SGA.

- **Shared pool statistics:** This is a good summary of changes to the shared pool during the snapshot period.

- **Top 5 timed events:** This is the most important section in the AWR report. It shows the top wait events and can quickly show the overall database bottleneck.

- **Wait events statistics section:** This section shows a breakdown of the main wait events in the database including foreground and background database wait events as well as time model, operating system, service, and wait classes statistics.

- **Wait events:** This AWR report section provides more detailed wait event information for foreground user processes which includes Top 5 wait events and many other wait events that occurred during the snapshot interval.

- **Background wait events:** This section is relevant to the background process wait events.

- **Time model statistics:** Time model statistics report how database-processing time is spent. This section contains detailed timing information on particular components participating in database processing.

- **Operating system statistics:** The stress on the Oracle server is important, and this section shows the main external resources including I/O, CPU, memory, and network usage.

- **Service statistics:** The service statistics section gives information about how particular services configured in the database are operating.

- **SQL section:** This section displays top SQL, ordered by important SQL execution metrics.

  - **SQL ordered by elapsed time:** This includes SQL statements that took significant execution time during processing.

  - **SQL ordered by CPU time:** This section includes SQL statements that consumed significant CPU time during its processing.

  - **SQL ordered by gets:** These SQL statements performed a high number of logical reads while retrieving data.

  - **SQL ordered by reads:** These SQL statements performed a high number of physical disk reads while retrieving data.

  - **SQL ordered by parse calls:** These SQL statements experienced a high number of reparsing operations.

  - **SQL ordered by sharable memory:** This includes SQL statement cursors which consumed a large amount of SGA shared pool memory.

  - **SQL ordered by version count**: These SQL statements have a large number of versions in shared pool.

- **Instance activity stats:** This section contains statistical information describing how the database operated during the snapshot period.

  - **Instance activity stats (absolute values):** This section contains statistics that have absolute values not derived from end and start snapshots

  - **Instance activity stats (thread activity):** This report section reports a log switch activity statistic

- **I/O section:** This section shows the all important I/O activity for the instance and shows I/O activity by tablespace, data file, and includes buffer pool statistics.

  - Tablespace I/O stats

  - File I/O stats

  - Buffer pool statistics

- **Advisory section:** This section shows details of the advisories for the buffer, shared pool, PGA and Java pool.

  - Buffer pool advisory

  - **PGA aggregate summary:** This is the PGA aggregate target stats, PGA aggregate target histogram, and PGA memory advisory

  - Shared pool advisory

  - Java pool advisory

- **Buffer wait statistics:** This important section shows buffer cache waits statistics.

- ***Enqueue* activity:** This important section shows how *enqueue* operates in the database. *Enqueues* are special internal structures which provide concurrent access to various database resources.

- ***Undo segment* summary:** This section gives a summary about how *undo segments* are used by the database.

- ***Undo segment* stats:** This section shows detailed history information about *undo segment* activity.

- ***Latch* activity:** this section shows details about *latch* statistics. *Latches* are a lightweight serialization mechanism that is used to single-thread access to internal Oracle structures.

    - Latch sleep breakdown

    - Latch miss sources

    - Parent latch statistics

    - Child latch statistics

- **Segment section:** this report section provides details about hot segments using the following criteria:

    - **Segments by logical reads:** This includes top segments which experienced high number of logical reads.

    - **Segments by physical reads:** This includes top segments which experienced high number of disk physical reads.

    - **Segments by buffer busy waits:** These segments have the largest number of buffer waits caused by their data blocks.

    - **Segments by row lock waits:** This includes segments that had a large number of row locks on their data.

    - **Segments by ITL waits:** This includes segments that had a large contention for Interested Transaction List (ITL). The contention for ITL can be reduced by increasing *initrans* storage parameter of the table.

- **Dictionary cache stats:** This section exposes details about how the data dictionary cache is operating.

- **Library cache activity:** Includes library cache statistics describing how shared library objects are managed by Oracle.

- **SGA memory summary:** This section provides summary information about various SGA regions.

- **Initialization parameters:** This section shows the original *init.ora* parameters for the instance during the snapshot period.

Now let's explore these main sections and see what we should look for when troubleshooting and tuning our Oracle database. Let's start by reviewing the first report section, the elapsed-time summary.

STATSPACK / AWR Report Summary

The first part of the STATSPACK/AWR report includes general information about the database as a whole. The report summary section contains the identification of the database on which the report was run along with the time interval of the STATSPACK/AWR report.

```
WORKLOAD REPOSITORY report for

DB Name        DB Id      Instance      Inst Num Release     Cluster Host
-----------  -----------  ------------  -------- ----------- ------- -
ABC          2787970997 abc                   1 10.1.0.2.0  NO      BASK

               Snap Id      Snap Time        Sessions Curs/Sess
             ---------  -------------------  -------- ---------
Begin Snap:     1355 24-Jun-04 18:00:10          29     14.8
  End Snap:     1356 24-Jun-04 19:00:39          28     15.0
  Elapsed:             60.49 (mins)
  DB Time:            121.24 (mins)
```

The most important part of the introduction section is the elapsed time interval. If this elapsed time period is too great, there may not be enough granularity in the delta values and important details may be lost. In general, we take hourly snapshots for time-series tuning and close-together (every minute) snapshots for diagnosing acute performance problems.

Cache Sizes Section

This report section contains the cache sizes at the end of the snapshot period. Remember, if Automatic Shared Memory Management (ASMM or AMM) is being used, AMM may adjust the cache sizes between the snapshots and you will see this at the end of the report, under initialization parameters, where you will see the starting and ending values.

This information about the cache size always shows only the endpoint values since Oracle has no way of knowing what changes may have been done between the snapshot periods.

```
Cache Sizes (end)
~~~~~~~~~~~~~~~~~
            Buffer Cache:    11,504M    Std Block Size:       8K
        Shared Pool Size:       592M       Log Buffer:   1,280K
```

Be careful if you enable automatic memory management

Remember, we do not recommend using Automatic Shared Memory Management for large mission-critical databases because a good DBA can do a better job than an automated utility.

Watch out for ASMM resizing problems!

When you see the automatic shared memory management in a STATSPACK/AWR report, consider manually monitoring your SGA regions.

By enabling AMM, you allow Oracle to dynamically change the sizes of the major SGA pools such as the *shared_pool_size, db_32k_cache_size, db_16k_cache_size, large_pool_size* and so on. While this may sound like a good idea on the surface, look deeper and understand the nature of AMM detection.

Unlike the proactive technique where we anticipate an upcoming problem and change the SGA before the problem begins, AMM is a reactive tool that only changes the SGA after detecting that the database has experienced degradation. There are also verified complaints in Oracle 10g and 11g where AMM can cause a performance problem!

AMM has been enhanced in 11g, but it is still primarily designed for small databases where it is not feasible to proactively optimize the major RAM pools.

Load Profile

The load profile section gives us a glimpse of the database workload activity that occurred within the snapshot interval. For example, below we see a typical OLTP database doing 89,000 logical I/Os per second and 3,000 disk I/Os per second:

```
Load Profile
~~~~~~~~~~~~                            Per Second           Per Transaction
                                     ---------------          ---------
              Redo size:              1,816,614.40             6,098.30
          Logical reads:                 89,851.90               301.63
          Block changes:                  7,266.68                24.39
         Physical reads:                  3,227.66                10.84
        Physical writes:                  1,233.78                 4.14
             User calls:                  4,044.55                13.58
                Parses:                     154.38                 0.52
            Hard parses:                      3.64                 0.01
                 Sorts:                     330.61                 1.11
                Logons:                       0.22                 0.00
              Executes:                   2,885.80                 9.69
          Transactions:                     297.89
```

The Ion for Oracle tool also shows per-second statistics, in a graphical format to make it easier to spot trends:

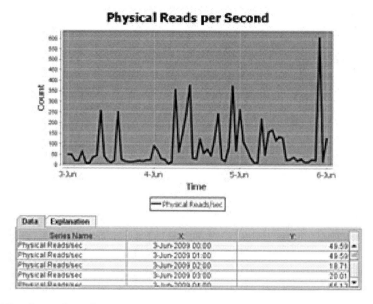

Figure 8.2: *Physical Reads per Second in Ion for Oracle*

These statistics give an idea about the characteristics of the workload during the snapshot period. However, it does not indicate the reason for the problem. For example, if there are a high number of physical reads per second, this does not necessarily mean that the SQL statements are poorly tuned.

The STATSPACK/AWR report can quickly tell us if our database is experiencing a typical OLTP or data warehouse workload.

- **OLTP Workload:** To test for an OLTP workload, look to see if there is more than one transaction per second and if the *db file sequential reads* wait in the three top-5 timed events is greater than ten reads per second.

- **OLAP Workload:** To test for a data warehouse workload, which typically have lots of small-table full-table scans, check the instance efficiency section of the STATSPACK/AWR report where we see more than one *table scans – (short tables)* or *table scans – (short tables)* per second.

Also, a decision support system/data warehouse will often have batch-oriented SQL statements that return more than 500 rows, and this is shown in the "*SQL ordered by Executions*" STATSPACK/AWR report section by looking at the *rows per execution* metric.

Remember, this workload information is intended to be used along with information from other sections of the STATSPACK/AWR report in order to learn the details about the nature of the applications running on the system.

Our goal is to get a correct picture of database performance, and the following list includes detailed descriptions for particular statistics:

- **Redo size:** The amount of redo generated during this report

- **Logical reads:** calculated as (consistent gets + DB block gets = Logical Reads).

- **Block changes:** The number of blocks modified during the sample interval.

- **Physical reads:** The number of requests for a block that caused a physical I/O operation.

- **Physical writes:** The number of physical writes performed.

- **User calls:** The number of user queries generated.

- **Parses:** The total of all parses, both hard and soft parses.

- **Hard parses:** The parses requiring a completely new parse of the SQL statement. These consume both latches and shared pool area.

- **Soft parses:** Soft parses are not listed but derived by subtracting the hard parses from parses. A soft parse reuses a previous hard parse; hence, it consumes far fewer resources.

- **Sorts, logons, executes and transactions:** All self-explanatory.

The parse activity statistics should be checked carefully because they can indicate a performance problem within the application layer. For example, a database has been running several days with a fixed set of applications should have parsed most SQL statements and these hard parsing statistics should be low, assuming that your *shared_pool_size* is large enough to cache all frequently executed SQL statements.

If there are high values for hard parses, this might be an indication that the applications make little use of bind variables and produce large numbers of unique SQL statements. In these cases we might consider implementing *cursor_sharing* to make these SQL statements reentrant and reusable.

The following information is also available in the workload section:

```
% Blocks changed per Read:    4.85    Recursive Call %:    89.89
Rollback per transaction %:   8.56      Rows per Sort:    13.39
```

In this listing, the *% blocks changed per read* statistic indicates that only 4.85 percent of all blocks are retrieved for update. We also see that the *recursive call %* statistic is extremely high, at almost 90 percent.

The concept of "recursive" SQL can be confusing, and Oracle considers all SQL statements executed within PL/SQL programs to be recursive. Hence, if there are applications making use of a large number of stored PL/SQL programs, high recursive calls may be good for performance. However, we do not expect to see high recursive calls in applications that do not use PL/SQL.

It is also useful to check the value of the *rollback per transaction %* statistic. This statistic reports the percent of transactions that are rolled back, usually by the application issuing a "*rollback*" command after an end-user error. In a properly designed production application, rollbacks should be very low.

Load Profile

If the output indicates a high percentage of transactions rolled back, the database expends a considerable amount of effort and this should be investigated in order to see why the application issues rollback statements.

Instance Efficiency Percentage

The *instance efficiency percentage* report section contains ratios or calculations that may provide us with information regarding different structures and operations in our Oracle instance. Back in the early days of Oracle, Oracle Education (later Oracle University) taught tuning students to carefully watch and tune from these instance-wide ratios. Today we know that Oracle tuning must never be driven by hit ratios, but ratios are nonetheless important for telling us when the characteristics of our workload changes, knowledge which is critical to proactive Oracle tuning.

For example, in a Decision Support System (DSS), a low cache hit ratio may be acceptable because a DSS does not have "popular" data blocks and there is a large amount of random data being accessed.

Increasing the *db_cache_size* for a VLDB DSS will not help performance, and expensive RAM memory resources may be wasted. The following is a sample instance efficiency percentage section of an STATSPACK/AWR report:

```
Instance Efficiency Percentages (Target 100%)
~~~~~~~~~~~~~~~~~~~~~~~~~~~~~~~~~~~~~~~~~~~~~~~
            Buffer Nowait %:   99.99      Redo NoWait %:  100.00
            Buffer  Hit  %:   97.39   In-memory Sort %:   99.97
            Library Hit  %:   99.83      Soft Parse %:    97.65
         Execute to Parse %:   94.65       Latch Hit %:    99.68
Parse CPU to Parse Elapsd %:   54.02    % Non-Parse CPU:   99.32
```

Parse rations are important to Oracle tuning. In this example above, about 95 percent of the parses are soft as indicated by the *soft parse %*. This indicates that the SQL statements are actively being reused by Oracle.

Also note the *parse CPU to parse elapsd %* statistic. In this case, it is about three percent, which is very low. This fact reveals that Oracle waits for some resources during parsing of SQL statements.

This should be investigated further to find the cause. In this case, the *% non-parse CPU* statistic is about 97 percent, which is quite high. This indicates Oracle utilizes the CPU mostly for statement execution but not for parsing. As a rule of thumb, we should always minimize the number of hard parses in a production database. This reduction yields the benefit of minimizing CPU overhead spent performing costly parse work.

Take a closer look at these ration metrics:

- **Buffer hit ratio:** This measures how many times a required block was found in memory rather than having to execute an expensive read operation on disk to get the block.

- **Buffer nowait %:** This shows the percentage of times when data buffers were accessed directly without any wait time.

- **Library hit %:** This shows the percentage of times when SQL statements and PL/SQL packages were found in the shared pool.

- **Execute to parse %:** This shows how often parsed SQL statements are reused without reparsing.

- **Parse CPU to parse elapsd %:** This gives the ratio of CPU time spent to parse SQL statements.

- **Redo noWait %:** This shows whether the redo log buffer has sufficient size.

- **In-memory sort %:** This shows the percentage of times when sorts are performed in memory instead of using temporary tablespaces.

- **Soft parse %:** This shows how often sessions issued a SQL statement that is already in the shared pool and how it can use an existing version of that statement.

- **Latch hit %:** This shows how often latches were acquired without having to wait.

- **% Non-parse CPU:** This shows the percentage of how much CPU resources were spent on the actual SQL execution.

Again, while ratios have limited value for tuning, they can be symptomatic of deeper problems within the instance. Here are some ratios to look for:

- **When *library hit* < 90:** A low library cache hit percentage could mean SQL is prematurely aging out of the shared pool as the shared pool may be small, or that unsharable SQL is being used. Also compare with the soft parse ratio; if they are both low, investigate whether there is a parsing issue. Since we never know in advance how many SQL statements need to be cached, the Oracle DBA must set *shared_pool_size* large enough to prevent excessive re-parsing of SQL.

- **When *Buffer Hit* < 90:** The buffer hit ratio measures the probability that a data block will be in the buffer cache upon a re-read of the data block. If a database has a large number of frequently referenced table rows, i.e. a large working set, then investigate increasing the *db_cache_size*. See the output from the data buffer cache advisory utility for specific recommendations using the *v$db_cache_advice* utility. Also, a low buffer hit ratio is normal for applications that do not frequently re-read the same data blocks. Moving to SSD will alleviate the need for a large data buffer cache.

- **When *Latch Hit %* < 95:** The latch hit percentage is below the recommended value of 99%. Investigate the specific latches in the latch activity section and tune to reduce library cache contention.

This following sample report section shows shared pool related statistics:

```
Shared Pool Statistics        Begin    End
                              ------   ------
         Memory Usage %:      92.70    92.49
```

```
% SQL with executions>1:    86.73    84.20
% Memory for SQL w/exec>1:   84.12    71.86
```

In this example, the *memory usage* % statistic shows that almost all (92 percent) of the shared pool memory is consumed. This could indicate that the system experiences some overhead while aging-out old shared memory structures like cursors, PL/SQL programs, and so on.

A too small *shared_pool_size* imposes additional overhead on the CPU to perform reparsing aging-out. The size of the shared pool should be increased appropriately to eliminate such overhead. In general, this statistic should be near 70 percent after the database has been running a long time. If it is quite low, memory is being wasted.

The *% SQL with executions>1* statistic indicates how many SQL statements are executed more than one time. This measures how well production applications are tuned and how well they make use of bind variables.

Before we move on, let's go over ratios again, so that you clearly understand the benefits and limitations of ratio information.

All about Oracle Ratios

Ever since the Oracle 7 performance tuning classes recommended keeping the buffer hit ratio above 95%, the myth has been perpetuated, and this over-generic advice was later adopted by SAP and other ERP vendors. Over the years there has been a huge amount of misunderstanding about the Buffer Cache Hit Ratio (BCHR), and the value of ratios in general as a tool for Oracle monitoring and tuning.

Most experts agree that the Oracle ratios, by themselves, are of limited value, and they are only one of hundreds of metrics that indicate database performance. In general, all ratios have limited predictive value because they only measure a probability that a data block will be found in the data buffer cache upon re-read. Hence, the BCHR has no bearing on blocks that are brand new to the data cache.

Another issue with ratios is their high variability. For example, while an overall hourly BCHR may be 96%, the value swings wildly minute-by-minute. When we look at the BCHR at a finer level of granularity, the BCHR could be 20% one minute and 95% the next (Figure 8.3).

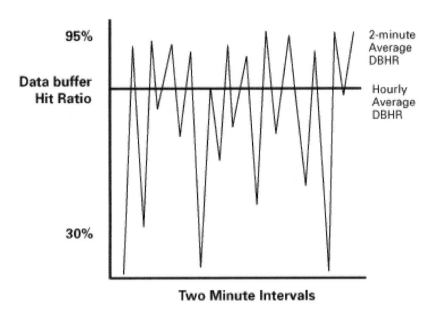

Figure 8.3: *Ratio values become more volatile in short durations*

Remember, ratios can be very valuable, provided that their natural limitations are understood. Now let's move on and look at one of the most important sections of any AWR/STATSPACK report, the top 5 timed events section.

Top 5 Timed Events Section of a STATSPACK / AWR Report

The AWR/STATSPACK report provides a super-detailed view of all elapsed-time metrics, and one of the most important sections is the top 5 timed events as shown in the output below. This report is critical because it shows those database events that might constitute the bottleneck for the system.

```
Top 5 Timed Events
~~~~~~~~~~~~~~~~~~
                                                    % Total
Event                      Waits     Time (s)     Ela Time
-------------------------  -------  -----------   --------
CPU time                    4,851        4,042       55.76
db file sequential read     1,968        1,997       27.55
log file sync             299,097          369        5.08
db file scattered read     53,031          330        4.55
log file parallel write   302,680          190        2.62
```

In the above example, it is clear that this system spends over half its time in processing activity (CPU time). We can also infer from the wait time that this server may be experiencing CPU enqueues, which happens when we have more concurrent work than we have CPU to handle the work. In these cases, multiple processes must queue up to be dispatched by the CPUs as we can see this in the *vmstat* runqueue (r) column when the runqueue exceed the *cpu_count* for the server.

The STATSPACK/AWR reports top 5 timed events is one of the most important sections and reveals many important details about the database.

- **When latch free > 25%:** This indicates high latch free waits. Check the later section for the specific latch waits. Latch free waits are usually due to SQL without bind variables, but they can also be caused by buffer chains and redo generation.

- **When CPU time > 50%:** This indicates high CPU activity. This is common for 64-bit servers with large data buffer caches, and we can tune-down CPU consumption by optimizing our SQL. In an optimized database, the only remedy for CPU time > 50% may be to move to more of faster processors.

- **Disk reads > 50%:** Whenever *db file scattered read* or *db file sequential read* values are over 50%, an investigation is needed.

- **SQL*Net message > 50%:** Whenever there are SQL*Net waits, especially *SQL*Net message from client*, there may be a network bottleneck.

- **Control file sequential read > 25%:** The *control file sequential read* Oracle metric indicates the process is waiting for blocks to be read from a control file. This happens in many cases. For example, we can see a control file sequential read when a backup of the control files is being made, sharing information between instances from the control file, reading other blocks from the control files, and most importantly, when the header block for a data file is being read.

- **Enqueue waits > 25%:** High enqueue waits are related to Oracle internal locks. Investigate by querying the *v$lock, v$transaction* and *v$session* views to drill in and see the exact queries that are causing the locks.

Look at another example of top 5 timed events. Below a large OLTP database which is disk I/O bound can be seen. In the AWR sample report section below, the system is clearly constrained by disk I/O.

```
Top 5 Timed Events
~~~~~~~~~~~~~~~~~~                                             % Total
Event                                   Waits    Time (s) Ela Time
------------------------------------- ------------ ----------- -------
db file sequential read                 568,948       4,375   66.15
CPU time                                              1,983   29.99
db file scattered read                  106,287          65     .99
log file sync                             7,053          50     .75
log buffer space                          1,717          47     .71
```

Here it can be seen that disk reads and writes constitute the majority of the total database wait time. In this case, we might consider increasing the RAM size of the *db_cache_size* to reduce disk I/O, tune the SQL to reduce disk I/O, or invest in a faster solid-state disk.

Tips for 100% CPU

Please note that it is not uncommon to see the CPU utilization on an Oracle server peg at 100 percent even when the server is not overwhelmed with processing activities.

The reason that CPU drives to 10% utilization is because the UNIX internal dispatchers will always attempt to keep the CPUs as busy as possible. This maximizes task throughput, but it can be misleading for a neophyte. Remember, it is not a cause for concern when the user + system CPU values approach 100 percent. This just means that the CPUs are working to their full potential.

As a general rule, a server is CPU-bound when the number of processes in the execution queue exceeds the number of CPUs on the server, the *r* value in the UNIX/Linux *vmstat* utility. The only metric that identifies a CPU bottleneck is when the run queue (*r* value) exceeds the number of CPUs on the server. In the output below, the 16-CPU server is not experiencing a CPU shortage because the (r) *runqueue* value is 12, meaning that all Oracle asks are getting prompt service.

```
vmstat 5 1
```

```
kthr      memory              page                   faults        cpu
-----  -----------  ------------------------  ------------  -----------
 r  b    avm    fre  re  pi  po  fr   sr  cy  in   sy   cs us sy id wa
12  0  217485   386   0   0   0   4   14   0 202  300  210 20 75  3  2
```

In general, the causes of these top wait events should be investigated in order to minimize database wait time as much as possible.

The Wait Events Section of the AWR / STATSPACK Report

The wait events section of a STATSPACK/AWR report shows where the database spends most of its wait time, and this report has a breakdown of the main wait events including the wait event details for all foreground user processes.

The wait events STATSPACK/AWR report section displays all wait events that occurred during the snapshot interval and displays wait events statistics for only foreground end-user processes. All the idle events are placed at the end of this report. The following is a sample of the wait events section:

```
Wait Events for DB: 123456 Instance: 123456 Snaps: 7150 -7151

-> s  - second

-> cs - centisecond -     100th of a second
```

```
-> ms - millisecond -    1000th of a second

-> us - microsecond - 1000000th of a second

-> ordered by wait time desc, waits desc (idle events last)
```

| | | | | Avg | |
Event	Waits	Timeouts	Total Wait Time (s)	wait (ms)	Waits /txn
db file sequential read	568,948	0	4,375	8	3.2
db file scattered read	106,287	0	65	1	0.6
log file sync	7,053	0	50	7	0.0
log buffer space	1,717	0	47	27	0.0
SQL*Net message from dblink	37	0	22	591	0.0
direct path read	12,871	0	18	1	0.1
db file parallel write	618	0	13	21	0.0
log file sequential read	984	0	11	11	0.0
library cache pin	7	3	9	1,286	0.0
buffer busy waits	4,490	0	7	2	0.0
db file parallel read	309	0	5	16	0.0
latch free	1,673	325	2	1	0.0
async disk IO	2,840	0	2	1	0.0
control file parallel write	431	0	1	3	0.0
enqueue	19	0	1	54	0.0
SQL*Net more data to client	151,977	0	1	0	0.8
LGWR wait for redo copy	563	4	1	1	0.0
log file switch completion	39	0	0	12	0.0
direct path write	1,020	0	0	0	0.0
SQL*Net break/reset to clien	416	0	0	0	0.0
control file sequential read	1,232	0	0	0	0.0
log file parallel write	8,263	8,091	0	0	0.0
log file single write	16	0	0	2	0.0
process startup	1	0	0	21	0.0
direct path read (lob)	36	0	0	0	0.0
SQL*Net message to dblink	37	0	0	0	0.0
buffer deadlock	7	7	0	0	0.0
SQL*Net message from client	2,450,615	0	214,735	88	13.7
PX Idle Wait	1,175	1,175	2,350	2,000	0.0
pipe get	179	175	700	3,908	0.0
virtual circuit status	20	20	586	29,297	0.0
wakeup time manager	19	19	570	30,000	0.0
SQL*Net more data from clien	654	0	15	24	0.0
SQL*Net message to client	2,450,615	0	1	0	13.7

When examining the wait events section of the STATSPACK report, remember the old saying "*time takes time*" and recognize that every database will inevitably wait for some resources when running. Remember, no section of an AWR/STATSPACK report stands alone, and other sections of the AWR report must be reviewed to find the real bottleneck in the system. The following are the most common causes of wait events:

- **DB file scattered read:** The *scattered reads* are read for full-scan multi-block I/O operations, and they can be tuned by seeking missing indexes and speeding up the full-scans with parallel query

- **DB file sequential read:** The *sequential reads* are single block reads, usually an index block fetch. A high number of db file sequential read waits could be from non-selective indexes, poorly optimized SQL or a suboptimal *hash_area_size*.

- **Buffer busy:** The *buffer busy* wait is caused by concurrent access to the same buffer by competing processes, and the remedy is to increase *freelists* if not using ASSM or *freelist groups* if using RAC. This statistic should be correlated with the buffer waits section of the AWR report.

- **Free buffer:** The *free buffer* waits indicates that a server process was unable to find a free buffer and has posted the database writer to make free buffers by writing out dirty buffers. A dirty buffer is a buffer whose contents have been modified. Dirty buffers are freed for reuse when DBWR has written the blocks to disk and free buffer waits should be regarded as a database writer (DBWR) tuning issue.

- **Log buffer space:** The *log buffer space* waits shows that the log writer (LGWR) process is not fast enough to free log cache for new blocks. This could be caused by slow log switches, slow disks serving the online redo logs, or a suboptimal size for the online redo logs or the *log_buffer* RAM area in the SGA.

- **Latch free:** The *latch free* wait occurs when a process is waiting for a latch held by another process. Note that the latch free wait is a true wait; it does not apply to processes that are spinning while waiting for a latch. Latch free waits are often caused by not using bind variables in SQL statements and manifests as library cache latch waits in the latches section of the AWR/STATSPACK report. There are other latches that can cause this wait event to be high such as redo allocation latch, cache buffers LRU chain, and cache buffers chain.

The wait events for background processes are separated in the background wait events section:

```
Background Wait Events for DB: 123456 Instance: 123456

Snaps: 7150 -7151

-> ordered by wait time desc, waits desc (idle events last)
```

Event	Waits	Timeouts	Total Wait Time (s)	Avg wait (ms)	Waits /txn
db file parallel write	616	0	13	21	0.0
log file sequential read	984	0	11	11	0.0
direct path read	3,068	0	4	1	0.0
async disk IO	2,840	0	2	1	0.0
control file parallel write	430	0	1	3	0.0
enqueue	1	0	1	963	0.0
LGWR wait for redo copy	563	4	1	1	0.0
db file scattered read	90	0	0	4	0.0

Instance Efficiency Percentage

log file parallel write	8,256	8,084	0
0 0.0			
db file sequential read	71	0	0
1 0.0			
log file single write	16	0	0
2 0.0			
direct path write	720	0	0
0 0.0			
control file sequential read	590	0	0
0 0.0			
process startup	1	0	0
21 0.0			
log buffer space	8	0	0
2 0.0			
latch free	2	0	0
0 0.0			
rdbms ipc message	25,892	17,240	5,966
230 0.1			
smon timer	2	2	600
300,000 0.0			
pmon timer	202	202	586
2,901 0.0			

Tips for interpreting wait event times:

The times for wait events can be indicators of database bottlenecks and following are some generalized rules for the wait time section.

- **When *free buffer wait time (ms)* > 50:** There is high free buffer wait time. *Free buffer* waits commonly happen when the application is insert-intensive, among many other factors, and Oracle requests a new block from the freelist. With a *free buffer* wait, Oracle requests RAM heap space for the new block but no space is available within the data buffer cache region. The remedy is tuning the data buffer cache which might include: using faster disks, rebuilding with larger blocksizes, tuning the DBWR process, segregating hot tables into separate data buffers using the multiple blocksize feature, optimizing the SQL to reduce data block requests using highly-selective function-based indexes or materialized views or by increasing the speed of our back-end disks. We can also optimize the *db_cache_size* by moving the hot objects to high-speed solid-state disks.

- **When *latch free waits/txn* > 5:** There are high latch free waits. The *latch free* wait occurs when the process is waiting for a latch held by another process. Check later in this chapter for the specific latch waits. *Latch free* waits are usually due to SQL without bind variables, but they can also be caused by buffer chains and redo generation.

- **When *log buffer space waits/txn* > 5:** There is a high value for log buffer space waits. If the *log_buffer* is too small, then high *log buffer space* waits will be seen during high DML periods (redo generation). Consider moving the redo log data files to solid-state disk, or increase the size of the redo log buffer (*log_buffer*).

- **When *log file switch completion* wait time (ms) > 50:** There is a high value for log file switch waits. If there is a large SGA full of dirty buffers and small redo log files, a log switch must wait for DBWR to write dirty buffers to disk before continuing. Consider allocating larger online redo log files or move the redo logs to faster disk with SSD.

- **When *log file sync waits/txn* > 5:** There is a high value for *log file sync* waits. Check to ensure that the application does frequent commits and consider moving the redo log files to faster SSD disk. Also consider increasing the *log_buffer* size.

- **When *SQL*Net message from* wait time (ms) > 50:** The average wait time for SQL*Net from client events is too high. Check the application to see if it might benefit from bulk collection using PL/SQL *forall* or *bulk collect* operators. Also optimize the TNS settings in our *tnsnames.ora* file and investigate if our Oracle requests can be consolidated into larger TNS packets.

- **When *db file sequential read* avg. wait time *(ms)* > 50:** The average wait time for *db file sequential read* is very slow. The sequential read event occurs when Oracle reads single blocks of a table or index. Index reads are a typical cause of this event. Also, check to ensure that non-buffered direct I/O is being used. If these steps fail to reduce the disk wait times, moving some of the datafiles to solid-state disk will reduce the amount of time spent waiting for this event.

- **When *db file scattered read* avg. wait time (ms) > 50:** The average wait time for *db file scattered read* is very slow. The *scattered read events* occur when Oracle reads multiple blocks of a table or index, i.e. a full-table scan of fast full index scan. Full-table scans may indicate missing indexes. Check for missing indexes and verify that the *db_file_multiblock_read_count* has been optimized. If these steps fail to reduce the disk wait times, moving some of the datafiles to solid-state disk will reduce the amount of time spent waiting for scattered disk reads.

- **When *buffer busy wait* avg. wait time (ms) > 50 or *buffer busy wait* > 1 wait per transaction:** There may be excessive *buffer busy* waits. *Buffer busy* waits are most commonly caused by segment header contention and can be remedied by increasing the value of the tables and index freelists or *freelist groups* parameters, tuning the database writer (DBWR process) or using ASSM in the tablespace definition. Using super-fast SSD will also reduce *buffer busy* waits because transactions are completed many times faster.

- **When *SQL*Net message from client* > 50 ms:** The SQL*Net message from client waits indicates high network latency. Tune the network by optimizing the TNS settings and optimize the TCP/IP settings. A faster network bandwidth can also remedy this wait condition.

- **When *enqueue* avg. wait time (ms) > 50 or *waits/txn* > 1:** There are excessive enqueue wait times. Oracle locks protect shared resources and allow access to those resources via a queuing mechanism. A large amount of time spent waiting for enqueue events can be caused by various problems, such as waiting for individual row locks or waiting for exclusive locks on a table. We should also ensure that we are using locally-managed tables if *enqueue ST* waits can be seen, and review our settings for *initrans* and *maxtrans* if there are *enqueue TX* waits. If *enqueue TX* waits can be seen, check for DML locks and ensure that all foreign keys are indexed.

In most cases, Oracle background processes place very little overhead on the system, but any time that background events experience more than 100 time-outs per hour, there may be a locking problem. However, it makes sense to monitor the database's wait events activity in order to see how they operate.

Wait Event Histogram Section

The wait event histogram section of a STATSPACK/AWR report displays the percentage of waits, distributed by the time waited for each event.

```
Wait Event Histogram  DB/Inst: LIMBO01/limbo01  Snaps: 651-652

-> Total Waits - units: K is 1000, M is 1000000, G is 1000000000

-> % of Waits - column heading: <=1s is truly <1024ms,
   >1s is truly >=1024ms

-> % of Waits - value: .0 indicates value was <.05%, null is truly 0

-> Ordered by Event (idle events last)
```

Event	Total Waits	<1ms	<2ms	<4ms	<8ms	<16ms	<32ms	<=1s	>1s
Data file init write	3	66.7			33.3				
LGWR wait for redo copy	3	100.0							
Log archive I/O	74	35.1		64.9					
SQL*Net break/reset to cli	302	100.0							
SQL*Net more data to clien	71	100.0							
buffer busy waits	3	100.0							
control file parallel writ	1244	99.6	.2	.2	.1				
control file sequential re	4472	95.0	2.4	.4	1.2	1.0	.0		
db file parallel write	249	100.0							
db file scattered read	15	53.3			33.3	13.3			
db file sequential read	1736	39.9	5.4	15.1	33.9	5.4	.2		
db file single write	1	100.0							
direct path read	51	78.4	2.0	5.9	11.8		2.0		
direct path write	78	100.0							
enq: RO - fast object reus	12	58.3	8.3	16.7	16.7				
latch free	1				100.0				
latch: In memory undo latc	1	100.0							
latch: library cache	6	100.0							
latch: shared pool	10	100.0							
log buffer space	12	100.0							
log file parallel write	6097	100.0							
log file sequential read	53	7.5		5.7	1.9	9.4	30.2	45.3	
log file single write	2	100.0							
log file switch completion	2				50.0	50.0			
log file sync	3637	99.0	.5	.4	.2				
os thread startup	45				100.0				
rdbms ipc reply	58	100.0							
reliable message	12	100.0							
undo segment extension	1	100.0							
SQL*Net message from clien	52K	85.9	1.3	.5	.4	.2	3.6	1.7	6.3
SQL*Net message to client	52K	100.0							
SQL*Net more data from cli	538	100.0							
Streams AQ: qmn coordinato	264	48.9							51.1
Streams AQ: qmn slave idle	129								100.0
Streams AQ: waiting for me	720								100.0
Streams AQ: waiting for ti	5							60.0	40.0
class slave wait	1	100.0							
dispatcher timer	60								100.0
jobq slave wait	1202							.2	99.8
pmon timer	1211	.9							99.1
rdbms ipc message	17K	9.4	14.1	3.4	1.5	1.1	.8	24.0	45.8
smon timer	28				3.6	14.3	17.9	7.1	57.1
virtual circuit status	120								100.0
wait for unread message on	3600				.0			100.0	

In this report, start by examining the total number of waits during the elapsed time, since tuning for uncommon waits is not very useful. Especially important is the far right-hand column which shows the percentage of the waits that exceeded one second.

Instance Activity Section in the STATSPACK / AWR Report

The instance activity section gives rates for many important statistics, showing the totals and the rate expressed in a per-second value. This is one of the report sections that contain lots of undocumented metrics and our primary job is to separate-out the meaningful statistics. The most important statistics in this report section are highlighted below:

```
Instance Activity Stats for DB: 123456 Instance: 123456

Snaps: 7150 -7151
```

Statistic	Total	per Second	per Trans
CPU used by this session	198,333	330.0	1.1
CPU used when call started	198,374	330.1	1.1
CR blocks created	2,957	4.9	0.0
DBWR buffers scanned	266,470	443.4	1.5
DBWR checkpoint buffers written	204,356	340.0	1.1
DBWR checkpoints	4	0.0	0.0
DBWR free buffers found	266,432	443.3	1.5
DBWR lru scans	93	0.2	0.0
DBWR make free requests	93	0.2	0.0
DBWR revisited being-written buff	0	0.0	0.0
DBWR summed scan depth	266,470	443.4	1.5
DBWR transaction table writes	100	0.2	0.0
DBWR undo block writes	69,080	114.9	0.4
Parallel operations downgraded to	0	0.0	0.0
SQL*Net roundtrips to/from client	2,427,484	4,039.1	13.6
SQL*Net roundtrips to/from dblink	47	0.1	0.0
active txn count during cleanout	68,741	114.4	0.4
background checkpoints completed	4	0.0	0.0
background checkpoints started	4	0.0	0.0
background timeouts	1,265	2.1	0.0
branch node splits	14	0.0	0.0
buffer is not pinned count	25,816,192	42,955.4	144.2
buffer is pinned count	87,025,454	144,801.1	486.1
bytes received via SQL*Net from c	315,280,030	524,592.4	1,761.0
bytes received via SQL*Net from d	11,821	19.7	0.1
bytes sent via SQL*Net to client	710,726,648	1,182,573.5	3,969.9
bytes sent via SQL*Net to dblink	12,036	20.0	0.1
calls to get snapshot scn: kcmgss	2,100,631	3,495.2	11.7
calls to kcmgas	42,867	71.3	0.2
calls to kcmgcs	72,357	120.4	0.4
change write time	6,668	11.1	0.0
cleanout - number of ktugct calls	69,837	116.2	0.4
cluster key scan block gets	16,341	27.2	0.1
cluster key scans	8,128	13.5	0.1
commit cleanout failures: block l	0	0.0	0.0
commit cleanout failures: buffer	4,955	8.2	0.0
commit cleanout failures: callbac	2,675	4.5	0.0
commit cleanout failures: cannot	8	0.0	0.0
commit cleanout failures: hot bac	0	0.0	0.0
commit cleanouts	203,358	338.4	1.1
commit cleanouts successfully com	195,720	325.7	1.1
commit txn count during cleanout	21,874	36.4	0.1
consistent changes	25,984	43.2	0.2
consistent gets	49,593,708	82,518.7	277.0
consistent gets - examination	19,464,027	32,386.1	108.7
current blocks converted for CR	0	0.0	0.0
cursor authentications	308	0.5	0.0
data blocks consistent reads - un	25,900	43.1	0.1
db block changes	4,367,273	7,266.7	24.4
db block gets	4,405,293	7,329.9	24.6
deferred (CURRENT) block cleanout	89,733	149.3	0.5
dirty buffers inspected	72	0.1	0.0
enqueue conversions	745	1.2	0.0

Instance Efficiency Percentage

enqueue releases	1,962,502	3,265.4	11.0
enqueue requests	1,962,495	3,265.4	11.0
enqueue timeouts	0	0.0	0.0
enqueue waits	16	0.0	0.0
exchange deadlocks	7	0.0	0.0
execute count	1,734,365	2,885.8	9.7
free buffer inspected	2,350	3.9	0.0
free buffer requested	1,518,574	2,526.8	8.5
hot buffers moved to head of LRU	338,881	563.9	1.9
immediate (CR) block cleanout app	5,557	9.3	0.0
immediate (CURRENT) block cleanou	32,067	53.4	0.2
index fast full scans (full)	798	1.3	0.0
index fetch by key	2,817,840	4,688.6	15.7
index scans kdiixs1	6,262,938	10,420.9	35.0
leaf node 90-10 splits	61	0.1	0.0
leaf node splits	2,970	4.9	0.0
logons cumulative	131	0.2	0.0
messages received	8,905	14.8	0.1
messages sent	8,905	14.8	0.1
no buffer to keep pinned count	0	0.0	0.0
no work - consistent read gets	23,695,478	39,426.8	132.4
opened cursors cumulative	76,615	127.5	0.4
parse count (failures)	97	0.2	0.0
parse count (hard)	2,185	3.6	0.0
parse count (total)	92,782	154.4	0.5
parse time cpu	1,351	2.3	0.0
parse time elapsed	2,501	4.2	0.0
physical reads	1,939,822	3,227.7	10.8
physical reads direct	531,883	885.0	3.0
physical reads direct (lob)	36	0.1	0.0
physical writes	741,500	1,233.8	4.1
physical writes direct	537,034	893.6	3.0
physical writes non checkpoint	736,637	1,225.7	4.1
pinned buffers inspected	2,175	3.6	0.0
prefetched blocks	735,317	1,223.5	4.1
prefetched blocks aged out before	39	0.1	0.0
process last non-idle time	149,599,768,883	248,918,084.7	835,608.2
recursive calls	882,456	1,468.3	4.9
recursive cpu usage	111,279	185.2	0.6
redo blocks written	2,202,134	3,664.1	12.3
redo buffer allocation retries	1,740	2.9	0.0
redo entries	2,343,003	3,898.5	13.1
redo log space requests	39	0.1	0.0
redo log space wait time	47	0.1	0.0
redo ordering marks	3	0.0	0.0
redo size	1,091,785,252	1,816,614.4	6,098.3
redo synch time	5,114	8.5	0.0
redo synch writes	7,062	11.8	0.0
redo wastage	1,983,996	3,301.2	11.1
redo write time	6,075	10.1	0.0
redo writer latching time	52	0.1	0.0
redo writes	8,159	13.6	0.1
rollback changes - undo records a	1,178	2.0	0.0
rows fetched via callback	2,257,493	3,756.2	12.6
session connect time	149,599,768,883	248,918,084.7	835,608.2
session logical reads	54,000,990	89,851.9	301.6
session pga memory	47,913,536	79,723.0	267.6
session uga memory	41,663,280	69,323.3	232.7
session uga memory max	9,094,517,624	15,132,308.9	50,798.6
shared hash latch upgrades - no w	6,202,999	10,321.1	34.7
shared hash latch upgrades - wait	1,790	3.0	0.0
sorts (disk)	66	0.1	0.0
sorts (memory)	198,630	330.5	1.1
sorts (rows)	206,783,146	344,065.1	1,155.0
summed dirty queue length	111	0.2	0.0
switch current to new buffer	25,886	43.1	0.1
table fetch by rowid	49,085,557	81,673.1	274.2
table fetch continued row	447,404	744.4	2.5
table scan blocks gotten	6,289,478	10,465.0	35.1
table scan rows gotten	343,127,765	570,928.1	1,916.6
table scans (cache partitions)	2	0.0	0.0
table scans (long tables)	11	0.0	0.0
table scans (short tables)	87,400	145.4	0.5
transaction rollbacks	33	0.1	0.0
transaction tables consistent rea	0	0.0	0.0
transaction tables consistent rea	0	0.0	0.0
user calls	2,430,777	4,044.6	13.6
user commits	7,237	12.0	0.0
user rollbacks	171,794	285.9	1.0
workarea executions - onepass	130	0.2	0.0

```
workarea executions - optimal          278,674          463.7          1.6
write clones created in backgroun             0            0.0          0.0
write clones created in foregroun           323            0.5          0.0
```

The main information in this section is related to disk activity, physical disk reads and writes, but there are also other important details such as the number of cumulative logons, the number of sorts to disk and table access details, i.e. number of full scans and index scans.

Instance Recovery Statistics Section of a STATSPACK / AWR Report

The instance recovery section is small and shows the begin and end values for the estimated I/O required to do a database recovery.

```
Instance Recovery Stats for DB: 123456 Instance: 123456

Snaps: 7150 -7151

-> B: Begin snapshot,  E: End snapshot
```

	Targt MTTR (s)	Estd MTTR (s)	Recovery Estd IOs	Actual Redo Blks	Target Redo Blks	Log File Size Redo Blks	Log Ckpt Timeout Redo Blks	Log Ckpt Interval Redo Blks
B	300	27	41222	454012	442368	442368	1131577	
E	300	31	52876	442083	442368	442368	1366902	

This information is useful for disaster recovery planning.

PGA Section

The PGA section of a STATSPACK/AWR report is very critical because the PGA sizes directly control the amount of disk sorts and hash joins used by any Oracle session.

```
PGA Aggr Target Stats for DB: 123456 Instance: 123456

Snaps: 7150 -7151

-> B: Begin snap   E: End snap (rows dentified with B or E contain data which is absolute
i.e. not diffed over the interval)

-> PGA cache hit % - percentage of W/A (WorkArea) data processed only in-memory

-> Auto PGA Target - actual workarea memory target

-> W/A PGA Used    - amount of memory used for all Workareas (manual + auto)

-> %PGA W/A Mem    - percentage of PGA memory allocated to workareas

-> %Auto W/A Mem   - percentage of workarea memory controlled by Auto Mem Mgmt

-> %Man W/A Mem    - percentage of workarea memory under manual control
```

```
PGA Cache Hit %  W/A MB Processed  Extra W/A MB Read/Written
--------------   ----------------  ------------------------
       79.1              19,461                       5,143
```

```
                                             %PGA  %Auto  %Man
      PGA Aggr   Auto PGA   PGA Mem   W/A PGA  W/A   W/A   W/A   Global Mem
      Target(M)  Target(M)  Alloc(M)  Used(M)  Mem   Mem   Mem   Bound(K)
-     ---------  ---------  --------  -------  ----- ----- ----- ----------
B       2,500      1,701    1,288.9    117.7    9.1 100.0    .0   102,400
E       2,500      1,687    1,314.9    155.2   11.8 100.0    .0   102,400
      --------------------------------------------------------------
```

PGA Aggr Target Histogram for DB: 123456 Instance: 123456

Snaps: 7150 -7151

-> Optimal Executions are purely in-memory operations

```
    Low    High
Optimal Optimal   Total Execs Optimal Execs 1-Pass Execs M-Pass Execs
------- -------   ----------- ------------- ------------ ------------
     8K     16K       230,854       230,854            0            0
    16K     32K        45,231        45,231            0            0
    32K     64K         1,365         1,365            0            0
    64K    128K           180           180            0            0
   128K    256K           452           452            0            0
   256K    512K            35            35            0            0
   512K   1024K             1             1            0            0
     2M      4M             8             8            0            0
     4M      8M             4             4            0            0
     8M     16M            12            12            0            0
    32M     64M           129             0          129            0
    64M    128M           155           155            0            0
   512M   1024M             1             0            1            0
      --------------------------------------------------------------
```

PGA Memory Advisory for DB: 123456 Instance: 123456

End Snap: 7151

-> When using Auto Memory Mgmt, minimally choose a pga_aggregate_target value where Estd PGA
Overalloc Count is 0

```
                                         Estd Extra    Estd PGA   Estd PGA
PGA Target    Size          W/A MB    W/A MB Read/     Cache     Overalloc
  Est (MB)    Factr      Processed  Written to Disk    Hit %       Count
----------   ------   -------------  --------------  --------   ---------
       313      0.1   20,773,882.2     28,614,489.1     42.0        91,104
       625      0.3   20,773,882.2     19,223,130.1     52.0        30,864
     1,250      0.5   20,773,882.2      9,384,356.6     69.0             0
     1,875      0.8   20,773,882.2      3,192,034.6     87.0             0
     2,500      1.0   20,773,882.2      3,183,089.0     87.0             0
     3,000      1.2   20,773,882.2        391,786.0     98.0             0
     3,500      1.4   20,773,882.2        391,786.0     98.0             0
     4,000      1.6   20,773,882.2        391,786.0     98.0             0
     4,500      1.8   20,773,882.2        391,786.0     98.0             0
     5,000      2.0   20,773,882.2        391,786.0     98.0             0
     7,500      3.0   20,773,882.2        391,786.0     98.0             0
    10,000      4.0   20,773,882.2        391,786.0     98.0             0
    15,000      6.0   20,773,882.2        391,786.0     98.0             0
```

| 20,000 | 8.0 | 20,773,882.2 | 391,786.0 | 98.0 | 0 |

As we will see in later chapters, the PGA statistics for one-pass and multi-pass give an indication of the PGA efficiency and memory allocation details. Remember, the PGA sizing is complex and controlled by many *init.ora* parameters including *pga_aggregate_target, sga_max_size, sort_area_size, hash_area_size* and others.

Oracle also has a PGA advisor in Oracle Enterprise Manager, using data from AWR. The PGA advisor is run by clicking on the PGA property page in OEM, and it produces a similar report as the one above. Note that the cache hit percentage is plotted against memory size. Higher hit ratios in the range of 75% to 100% indicate better cache performance.

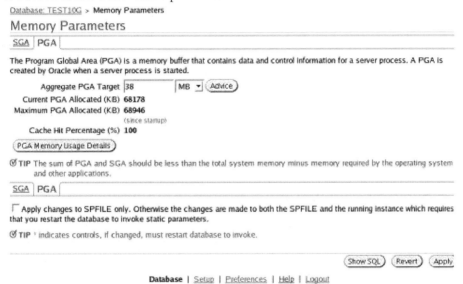

Figure 8.4: *PGA Memory*

Once PGA Memory Usage Details is clicked on, the statistics for one-pass and multi-pass executions are shown:

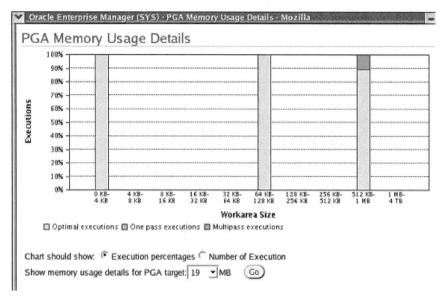

Figure 8.5: *PGA Memory Display in OEM*

Next, examine the process memory section of a STATSPACK report and see how it relates to PGA usage.

Process Memory Summary Section

The process memory summary section of a STATSPACK/AWR report shows the beginning and ending values for several major categories of memory usage, including SQL memory, PL/SQL memory and all freeable memory:

```
Process Memory Summary Stats  DB/Inst: MMLIMS01/mmlims01

Snaps: 651-652

-> B: Begin snap   E: End snap

-> All rows below contain absolute values (i.e. not diffed over the interval)

-> Max Alloc is Maximum PGA Allocation size at snapshot time
   Hist Max Alloc is the Historical Max Allocation for still-
   connected processes

-> Num Procs or Allocs:  For Begin/End snapshot lines, it is the
   number of processes. For Category lines, it is the number of
   allocations

-> ordered by Begin/End snapshot, Alloc (MB) desc
```

                                                         Hist   Num

Category	Alloc (MB)	Used (MB)	Freeable (MB)	Avg Alloc (MB)	Std Dev Alloc (MB)	Max Alloc (MB)	Max Alloc (MB)	Procs or Allocs
B	296.9	195.1	57.9	2.3	3.1	28	28	130
Other	226.4			1.7	2.8	25	25	130
Freeable	57.9	.0		.9	.4	2		67
SQL	9.6	4.8		.1	.1	0	11	95
PL/SQL	2.9	1.3		.0	.0	0	0	128
E	283.2	189.2	57.8	2.2	3.0	28	28	128
Other	213.1			1.7	2.7	25	25	128
Freeable	57.8	.0		.9	.4	2		65
SQL	9.4	4.6		.1	.1	0	11	94
PL/SQL	2.9	1.3		.0	.0	0	0	126

Top Process Memory (by component)   DB/Inst: MMLIMS01/mmlims01
Snaps: 651-652

-> ordered by Begin/End snapshot, Alloc (MB) desc

	PId	Category	Alloc (MB)	Used (MB)	Freeabl (MB)	Max Alloc (MB)	Hist Max Alloc (MB)
B	72	SHAD --------	27.7	25.3	2.2	27.7	27.7
		Other	25.0			25.0	25.0
		Freeable	2.2	.0		2.2	
		SQL	.4	.2		.4	2.3
		PL/SQL	.2	.0		.2	.2
	22	J000 --------	13.7	6.7	.6	13.7	13.7
		Other	12.9			12.9	12.9
		Freeable	.6	.0		.6	
		SQL	.2	.1		.2	1.4
		PL/SQL	.1	.0		.1	.1
	16	ARC0 --------	9.2	4.4	.0	9.2	9.2
		Other	9.2			9.2	9.2
		PL/SQL	.0	.0		.0	.0
	17	ARC1 --------	9.2	4.4	.0	9.2	9.2
		Other	9.2			9.2	9.2
		PL/SQL	.0	.0		.0	.0
	18	ARC2 --------	9.2	4.4	.0	9.2	9.2
		Other	9.2			9.2	9.2
		PL/SQL	.0	.0		.0	.0
	19	ARC3 --------	9.2	4.4	.0	9.2	9.2
		Other	9.2			9.2	9.2
		PL/SQL	.0	.0		.0	.0
	6	LGWR --------	9.2	4.4	.0	9.2	12.1
		Other	9.2			9.2	12.1
		PL/SQL	.0	.0		.0	.0
	49	SHAD --------	4.6	3.5	1.1	4.6	8.8
		Other	2.9			2.9	2.9
		Freeable	1.1	.0		1.1	
		SQL	.5	.3		.5	5.3
		PL/SQL	.1	.0		.1	.1
	15	SHAD --------	3.7	2.6	1.0	3.7	9.6
		Other	2.5			2.5	2.5
		Freeable	1.0	.0		1.0	
		SQL	.2	.1		.2	6.9
		PL/SQL	.1	.0		.1	.1
	25	SHAD --------	3.6	2.6	.9	3.6	7.7
		Other	2.4			2.4	2.4
		Freeable	.9	.0		.9	
		SQL	.3	.2		.3	5.0
		PL/SQL	.0	.0		.0	.0
	123	SHAD --------	3.5	2.5	1.1	3.5	10.1
		Other	2.2			2.2	2.2
		Freeable	1.1	.0		1.1	

Instance Efficiency Percentage

```
      SQL                      .2        .1                     .2         7.0
      PL/SQL                   .0        .0                     .0          .1
  11  MMON --------           3.5       1.8        1.0         3.5         3.6
      Other                   2.3                              2.3         2.3
      Freeable               1.0        .0                    1.0
      SQL                     .1        .1                     .1          .8
      PL/SQL                  .0        .0                     .0          .1
 107  SHAD --------          3.4       2.3        1.1         3.4         8.2
      Other                  2.1                              2.1         3.8
      Freeable              1.1        .0                    1.1
```

This report also shows the in-flight memory usage for all processes that were active at begin snapshot time.

Enqueue Statistics

Enqueue statistics show waits for specific enqueues within Oracle:

```
Enqueue activity for DB: 123456 Instance: 123456 Snaps: 7150 -7151

-> Enqueue stats gathered prior to 9i should not be compared with 9i data

-> ordered by Wait Time desc, Waits desc
```

```
                                                    Avg Wt         Wait
Eq      Requests    Succ Gets Failed Gets    Waits  Time (ms)      Time (s)
--   ------------ ------------ ----------- ----------- ------------- -----------
CF        363          363           0           1       987.00           1
TX     13,878       13,880           0          14         4.79           0
SQ        205          205           0           1          .00           0
```

There are many types of Oracle enqueues, so below is a sample of the most common types:

- **CF enqueue:** The CF enqueue is a Control File enqueue (a.k.a. *enq: CF – contention*) and happens during parallel access to the control files. The CF enqueue can be seen during any action that requires reading the control file such as redo log archiving, redo log switches and *begin backup* commands.

- **CI enqueue:** The CI enqueue is the Cross Instance enqueue (a.k.a. *enq: US - contention*) and happens when a session executes a cross instance call such as a query over a database link.

- **FB enqueue:** This is the Format Block enqueue, used only when data blocks are using ASSM (Automatic Segment Space Management or bitmapped freelists). As might be expected, common FB enqueue relates to buffer busy conditions, especially since ASSM tends to cause performance problems under heavily DML loads.

- **HV enqueue:** The HV enqueue (a.k.a. *enq: HV - contention*) is similar to the HW enqueue but for parallel direct path inserts.

- **HW enqueue:** The High Water enqueue (a.k.a. *enq: HW – contention*) occurs when competing processes are inserted into the same table and are trying to increase the high watermark of a table simultaneously. The HW enqueue can sometimes be removed by adding freelists or moving the segment to ASSM.

- **KO enqueue:** The KO enqueue (a.k.a. enq: *KO - fast object checkpoint*) is seen in Oracle STAR transformations and high enqueue waits can indicate a suboptimal DBWR background process.

- **PE enqueue:** The PE enqueue (a.k.a. *enq: PE – contention*) is the Parameter Enqueue, which happens after *alter system* or *alter session* statements.

- **PS enqueue:** The PS enqueue is the Parallel Slave synchronization enqueue (a.k.a *enq: PS – contention*), which is only seen with Oracle parallel query. The PS enqueue happens when pre-processing problems occur while allocating the factotum (slave) processes for oracle parallel query.

- **RO Enqueue:** this is the Reuse Object enqueue and is a cross-instance enqueue related to *truncate table* and *drop table* DDL operations.

- **SQ enqueue:** this is the Sequence Cache enqueue (a.k.a. *enq: SQ – contention*) used to serialize access to Oracle sequences.

- **SS enqueue:** The SS enqueue is the Sort Segment enqueue (a.k.a. *enq: SS – contention*), and these are related to the sorting of large result sets, i.e. when a process is performing a large sort operation.

- **ST enqueue:** The ST enqueue can be seen in a partitioned environment when a large number of partitions are created simultaneously.

- **TC enqueue:** The TC enqueue is related to the DBWR background process and occur when *alter tablespace* commands are issued. We will also see the TC enqueue when doing parallel full-table scans where rows are accessed directly without being loaded into the data buffer cache.

- **TM enqueue:** The TM enqueue related to Transaction Management (a.k.a. *enq: TM - contention*) and can be seen when tables are explicitly locked with reorganization activities that require locking of a table.

- **TQ enqueue:** The TQ enqueue is the Table Queue enqueue (a.k.a. *enq: TQ - DDL contention*) and happens during Data Pump (export import) operations.

- **TS enqueue:** The TS enqueue is the temporary segment enqueue (a.k.a. *enq: TS – contention*) and these enqueues happen during disk sort operations.

- **TT enqueue:** The TT enqueue (a.k.a. *enq: TT – contention*) is used to avoid deadlocks in parallel tablespace operations. The TT enqueue can be seen with parallel create tablespace and parallel point in time recovery (PITR).

- **TX runqueue:** The TX enqueue is the transaction enqueue (a.k.a. *enq: TX – contention*) and is commonly related to buffer busy waits in conditions where multiple transaction attempt to update the same data blocks.

  - enq: TX - row lock contention

  - enq: TX - allocate ITL entry

  - enq: TX - row lock contention

- **UL enqueue:** The UL enqueue is a User Lock enqueue (a.k.a. *enq: UL – contention*) and happens when a lock is requested in *dbms_lock.request*. The UL enqueue can be seen in Oracle Data Pump.

- **US Enqueue:** The US enqueue happens with Oracle automatic undo management when undo segments are moved online and offline.

Next, examine the rollback segment statistics.

Instance Efficiency Percentage

Rollback Segments

The rollback segments section of the STATSPACK/AWR report shows activity details for each rollback segment for the instance.

Rollback Segment Storage for DB: 123456 Instance: 123456

Snaps: 7150 -7151

->Optimal Size should be larger than Avg Active

RBS No	Segment Size	Avg Active	Optimal Size	Maximum Size
0	385,024	30,222		385,024
1	61,005,824	999,518		1,610,735,616
2	75,620,352	1,078,156		4,227,981,312
3	43,114,496	945,706		1,979,834,368
4	58,843,136	1,051,742		700,571,648
5	59,891,712	34,609,720		4,227,981,312
6	66,183,168	3,700,772		788,652,032
7	35,774,464	1,241,147		861,003,776
8	77,717,504	252,393,963		805,429,248
9	92,397,568	2,444,808		1,543,626,752
10	193,060,864	59,828,097		4,227,981,312
11	59,891,712	1,152,799		59,891,712
12	184,672,256	53,017,799		184,672,256
13	100,786,176	6,823,932		218,226,688
14	16,900,096	990,490		31,580,160
15	203,546,624	73,950,674		268,558,336
16	92,397,568	162,591,770		873,586,688
17	46,260,224	918,311		46,260,224
18	30,531,584	999,105		30,531,584
19	59,891,712	1,049,916		59,891,712
20	209,838,080	53,503,116		209,838,080
21	31,580,160	2,013,934		31,580,160
22	35,774,464	1,012,863		35,774,464
23	49,405,952	1,039,950		49,405,952
24	8,511,488	0		8,511,488
25	55,697,408	1,044,243		55,697,408
26	59,891,712	3,338,330		159,506,432
27	29,483,008	987,066		29,483,008
28	29,483,008	988,279		29,483,008
29	27,385,856	1,005,955		27,385,856
30	20,111,360	884,335		20,111,360
31	7,462,912	460,498		7,462,912
32	49,405,952	1,040,263		49,405,952
33	33,546,240	1,111,236		33,546,240
34	12,574,720	701,514		12,574,720
35	167,763,968	147,535,220		167,763,968
36	6,283,264	395,521		6,283,264
37	59,760,640	1,045,554		59,760,640
38	59,760,640	1,045,543		59,760,640
39	26,206,208	960,354		26,206,208
40	27,254,784	1,783,204		27,254,784
41	52,420,608	1,042,239		52,420,608
42	36,691,968	1,017,812		36,691,968
43	9,428,992	581,242		9,428,992
44	19,914,752	883,753		19,914,752

The Oracle documentation on rollback segment sizing is wrong in many spots, especially regarding the *optimal* parameter. The *optimal* parameter assumes growth, followed by a shrink. If the rollback segment is sized properly, they should never grow. Hence, using the *optimal* parameter is not recommended.

The optimal size of the rollback segment occurs when we do not get "*snapshot too old*" errors, and the rollback segment does not grow; it must then shrink later to optimal size.

Undo Segments

Oracle uses undo records, (called rollback segments prior to Oracle 9i), to maintain the "before" images for updated rows. Whenever a task terminates with an abort or a rollback, Oracle goes to the undo records and reapplies the previous images for the rows.

Oracle 9i and beyond supports both rollback segments or undo records, but rollback segments for managing undo space is being deprecated in Oracle 9i. We recommend using automatic undo management and manage undo space using an undo tablespace.

Undo segment statistics show space utilization for system undo segments, including the counts of all ORA-01555 "*snapshot too old*" errors, and the six different status flags for undo segments, unexpired stolen, unexpired released, unexpired reused, expired stolen, expired released and expired reused:

```
Undo Segment Summary for DB: 123456 Instance: 123456

Snaps: 7150 -7151

-> Undo segment block stats:

-> uS - unexpired Stolen,   uR - unexpired Released,   uU - unexpired reused

-> eS - expired   Stolen,   eR - expired   Released,   eU -
   expired   reused
```

Undo TS#	Undo Blocks	Num Trans	Max Qry Len (s)	Max Tx Concurcy	Snapshot Too Old	Out of Space	uS/uR/uU/ eS/eR/eU
1	43,298	20,132,631	2,263	29	0	0	0/0/0/0/0/0

```
Undo Segment Stats for DB: 123456 Instance: 123456

Snaps: 7150 -7151

-> ordered by Time desc
```

Undo End Time	Num Blocks	Max Qry Trans Len (s)	Max Tx	Snap Concy	Out of Too Old	uS/uR/uU/ Space	eS/eR/eU
04-Dec 11:54	43,298	########	2,263	29	0	0	0/0/0/0/0/0

Back before there was Oracle automatic undo, the undo segments were managed manually, and tuning would be done to reduce undo extends and the subsequent shrinks which resulted after a transaction is completed.

Inside the database instance there needs to be enough undo record space to accommodate all concurrent update tasks. In addition, the undo record tablespace must be large enough to hold all of the before images between the start and the end (commit or rollback) checkpoints.

There is a direct relationship between the undo segments and system latches. A transaction writing rollback data has to first access the transaction table stored in the undo segment header and acquire a slot in that table. This requires momentary latching of the table to serialize concurrent updates to it. If the database is update-intensive and has a small number of rollback segments, user transactions will wait on the latch to access the transaction table.

Now take a look at latch statistics and understand how serialization locking can affect system wide performance.

Latch Activity Section of a STATSPACK / AWR report

Latches are serialization mechanisms, like semaphores, locking structures that ensure that sequential operations happen one-at-a-time within Oracle.

There have been volumes written about Oracle latches because these latches protect the many memory structures in Oracle's SGA. Latches ensure that one and only one process at a time can run or modify any memory structure at the same instant. Latches are much more restrictive than locks, (which at least allow for some collective user interaction) because latches have no queuing mechanism.

Mutex latches are here!!

Starting in 10gR2 Oracle has replaced latches and library cache pins with a new construct called a "mutex". Mutexes are used in shared cursor operations as cursor pins.

A latch is all or nothing. You either acquire a latch or you wait and retry.

There are more than a dozen types of latches, but there are only a few that impact Oracle performance. Here is a brief listing of some important latches and the remedy to shortages. There are more than a dozen types of latches, but there are only a few that impact Oracle performance. Here is a brief listing of some important latches and the remedy to shortages.

Latch Name	Willing-to-wait?	Action
Redo copy	Yes	Increase redo log size
Redo allocation	No	Increase log_small_entry_max_size
Library cache	Yes	Increase shared_pool_size
Shared pool	Yes	Increase shared_pool_size

Table 8.1: *Latches and Remedies to Shortage*

Common indicators of latch contention are a latch miss ratio, which records willing-to-wait mode latch requests, and latch immediate miss ratio, which records no-wait mode latch requests.

The latch statistics reflect how often latch requests were made and satisfied without waiting. Remember, any latch wait is a bad for performance, and any latch wait exceeds 1%, you need to drill down into the latching details to identify what latches are responsible for the contention.

For a complete treatment of locks, latches and mutexes, see Chapter 14, *Oracle Instance Tuning*.

Here is a sample latch activity report section from a STATSPACK/AWR report. There are three sections for latch activity, latch sleeps and latch misses.

Below, in the first report there are many undocumented latches such as *"mostly latch-free SCN"* and other cryptic latch items. From a tuning perspective, the most important latches relate to cache buffer chains, library cache, redo and process latches.

```
Latch Activity for DB: 123456 Instance: 123456 Snaps: 7150 -7151

->"Get Requests", "Pct Get Miss" and "Avg Slps/Miss" are statistics
   for willing-to-wait latch get requests

->"NoWait Requests", "Pct NoWait Miss" are for no-wait latch get
   requests

->"Pct Misses" for both should be very close to 0.0
```

Latch	Get Requests	Pct Get Miss	Avg Slps /Miss	Wait Time (s)	NoWait Requests	Pct NoWait Miss
Consistent RBA	8,165	0.0		0	0	
FAL request queue	8	0.0		0	0	
FIB s.o chain latch	70	0.0		0	0	
FOB s.o list latch	6,672	0.0		0	0	
SQL memory manager latch	1	0.0		0	193	0.0
SQL memory manager worka	54,976	0.0	0.0	0	0	
active checkpoint queue	1,495	0.2	0.0	0	0	
alert log latch	20	0.0		0	0	
archive control	261	0.0		0	0	
archive process latch	36	5.6	0.5	0	0	
cache buffer handles	340,828	0.0	0.0	0	0	
cache buffers chains	100,446,295	0.1	0.0	0	2,393,142	0.0
cache buffers lru chain	231,007	0.1	0.0	0	2,017,747	0.5
channel handle pool latc	270	0.0		0	0	
channel operations paren	793	0.0		0	0	
checkpoint queue latch	519,585	0.0	0.0	0	220,487	0.1
child cursor hash table	17,182	0.0		0	0	
dml lock allocation	116,216	0.0	0.0	0	0	
dummy allocation	272	0.0		0	0	
enqueue hash chains	3,924,464	2.9	0.0	0	0	
enqueues	3,965,960	4.5	0.0	0	0	
event group latch	130	0.0		0	0	
global tx hash mapping	89	0.0		0	0	
hash table column usage	127	0.0		0	9,148	0.0
internal temp table obje	8	0.0		0	0	
job workq parent latch	1	0.0		0	0	
job_queue_processes para	9	0.0		0	0	
ktm global data	2	0.0		0	0	
kwqit: protect wakeup ti	19	0.0		0	0	
lgwr LWN SCN	8,179	0.0	0.0	0	0	

Instance Efficiency Percentage

Latch Name	Gets	Get/Miss	Get/Sleep	Sleeps	NoWait	NoWait/Miss
library cache	7,149,229	0.4	0.0	1	7,694	3.4
library cache load lock	1,338	0.0		0	0	
library cache pin	5,503,478	0.1	0.0	0	0	
library cache pin alloca	802,800	0.0	0.0	0	0	
list of block allocation	10,430	0.0	0.0	0	0	
loader state object free	972	0.0		0	0	
longop free list parent	6	0.0		0	6	0.0
messages	61,532	0.2	0.0	0	0	
mostly latch-free SCN	8,321	0.7	0.0	0	0	
multiblock read objects	311,007	0.2	0.0	0	0	
ncodef allocation latch	10	0.0		0	0	
post/wait queue	11,277	0.0		0	8,706	0.1
process allocation	130	0.0		0	130	0.0
process group creation	268	0.0		0	0	
redoallocation	359,370	2.3		0	0	0.0
redo copy	0			0	2,341,557	0.0
redo writing	26,422	0.0	0.0	0	0	
resmgr group change latc	1,885,097	0.3	0.0	0	0	
resmgr:actses active lis	270	0.0		0	0	
resmgr:actses change gro	126	0.0		0	0	
resmgr:actses change sta	7	0.0		0	0	
resmgr:plan CPU method	239	0.0		0	0	
resmgr:resource group CP	525	0.4	0.0	0	0	
resmgr:schema config	1,883,994	0.0		0	1,263	0.0
row cache enqueue latch	279,462	0.0	0.0	0	0	
row cache objects	287,274	0.0	0.0	0	648	0.0
sequence cache	18,406	0.1	0.0	0	0	
session allocation	374,347	0.0	0.2	0	0	
session idle bit	5,050,157	0.0	0.0	0	0	
session switching	40	0.0		0	0	
session timer	202	0.0		0	0	
shared pool	3,107,447	0.2	0.0	0	0	
sim partition latch	0			0	691	0.0
simulator hash latch	3,216,603	0.0	0.0	0	0	
simulator lru latch	135,442	0.0	0.0	0	12,632	0.8
sort extent pool	544	0.0		0	0	
spilled msgs queues list	19	0.0		0	0	
temp lob duration state	2	0.0		0	0	
transaction allocation	3,350	0.0		0	0	
transaction branch alloc	65	0.0		0	0	
undo global data	141,171	0.0	0.0	0	0	
user lock	552	0.0		0	0	

Next is the latch sleep section. When a process requests a latch and one is not available, the process spins, waiting for a latch to become available. This spinning is known as a latch sleep, and high numbers of sleeps for a particular latch indicate that some tuning effort may be required in the area of the Oracle system in which the latch is located.

In a STATSPACK/AWR report, it is not uncommon to see the highest sleeps are in the area of the buffer cache and library caches. These latch sleeps could be due to transaction serialization issues.

```
Latch Sleep breakdown for DB: 123456 Instance: 123456

Snaps: 7150 -7151

-> ordered by misses desc
```

Latch Name	Get Requests	Misses	Sleeps	Spin & Sleeps 1->4
enqueues	3,965,960	179,594	33	179561/33/0/0/0
enqueue hash chains	3,924,464	114,517	20	114497/20/0/0/0
redo allocation	2,359,370	55,300	23	55277/23/0/0/0
cache buffers chains	100,446,295	55,023	318	0/0/0/0/0

library cache	7,149,229	31,981	1,185 30796/1185/0/0/0
shared pool	3,107,447	5,816	29 5787/29/0/0/0
resmgr group change latch	1,885,097	5,534	24 5510/24/0/0/0
library cache pin	5,503,478	3,086	1 3085/1/0/0/0
session idle bit	5,050,157	693	13 0/0/0/0/0
session allocation	374,347	61	12 49/12/0/0/0
archive process latch		36	2 1 1/1/0/0/0

The *dba_hist_latch_misses_summary* view displays historical summary statistics about missed attempts to get latches. Remember, in the latch miss section of a STATSPACK or AWR report, we should look for the redo allocation line where *pct get miss* > 0.1 or *pct nowait miss* > 1.0.

The redo allocation latch controls the allocation of space for redo entries in the redo log buffer as defined by the *log_buffer* parameter. The redo allocation latch is a serialization latch that enforces the sequence of entries in the log buffer. A process can only write a redo entry after the redo allocation latch, which is why it is a will-to-wait latch.

Undocumented latches!
Remember, the STATSPACK/AWR report was originally created for internal use only, and it is packed with undocumented latch names. These are known as G.O.K. latches (God only knows).

- FAL request queue

- FIB s.o chain latch

- FOB s.o list latch

- resmgr:schema config

- sim partition latch

Redo allocation latches are a willing-to-wait latch, and the traditional remedy was to increase the size of the *log_small_entry_max_size* parameter, but this parameter was removed in Oracle 8i. Redo allocation latch misses can be measured with this query:

🖫 **Redo_allocation_latches.sql**

```
select
round(
   greatest(
     (sum(decode(ln.name,'redo allocation',misses,0))
/greatest(sum(decode(ln.name,'redo allocation',gets,0)),1)),
(sum(decode(ln.name,'redo allocation',immediate_misses,0))
/greatest(sum(decode(ln.name,'redo allocation',immediate_gets,0))
+sum(decode(ln.name,'redo allocation',immediate_misses,0)),1))
)*100,2)
from
   v$latch l,
   v$latchname ln
where
   l.latch#=ln.latch#;
```

When latch misses are observed, remember that there are two types of latches:

- **Willing-to-wait latch:** A willing-to-wait latch will repeatedly try to reacquire the latch. The redo allocation latch is a good example.

- **Immediate latch:** The immediate latches must acquire a latch immediately or the task will abort. The redo copy latch is a good example of an immediate latch.

Latch sleeps are very important because they indicate the number of times they had to sleep because they could not get a latch. The latches with the highest sleep values are the latches that are the most important. Latch misses are recorded in the *nwfail_count* column of this table, and misses are important because they indicate system resource shortages:

```
Latch Miss Sources for DB: 123456  Instance: 123456

Snaps: 7150 -7151

-> only latches with sleeps are shown

-> ordered by name, sleeps desc
```

Latch Name	Where	NoWait Misses	Sleeps	Waiter Sleeps
archive process latch	kcrrpa	0	1	0
cache buffers chains	kcbgtcr: kslbegin excl	0	187	157
cache buffers chains	kcbrls: kslbegin	0	67	104
cache buffers chains	kcbgcur: kslbegin	0	13	10
cache buffers chains	kcbgtcr: fast path	0	12	28
cache buffers chains	kcbget: pin buffer	0	9	6
cache buffers chains	kcbzgb: scan from tail. nowait	0	7	0
cache buffers chains	kcbget: exchange	0	6	2
cache buffers chains	kcbzib: multi-block read: nowait	0	6	0
cache buffers chains	kcbzwb	0	3	2
cache buffers chains	kcbchg: kslbegin: bufs not pinne	0	2	3
cache buffers chains	kcbchg: kslbegin: call CR func	0	2	1
cache buffers chains	kcbzib: finish free bufs	0	2	4

cache buffers chains	kcbnew	0		
	2	0		
cache buffers chains	kcbget: exchange rls	0		
	1	2		
enqueue hash chains	ksqrcl	0		
	19	2		
enqueue hash chains	ksqgtl3	0		
	1	18		
enqueues	ksqdel	0		
	21	6		
enqueues	ksqgel: create enqueue	0		
	12	26		
library cache	kglpnc: child	0		
	522	593		
library cache	kglpin: child: heap processing	0		
	141	1		
library cache	kglupc: child	0		
	122	211		
library cache	kglpndl: child: before processin	0		
	110	114		
library cache	kglhdgc: child:	0		
	106	3		
library cache	kgllkdl: child: cleanup	0		
	45	2		
library cache	kglpnp: child	0		
	43	155		
library cache	kglpndl: child: after processing	0		
	32	0		
library cache	kglobpn: child:	0		
	22	0		
library cache	kglhdgn: child:	0		
	21	65		
library cache	kglic	0		
	9	16		
library cache	kgldte: child 0	0		4
	17			
library cache	kgldti: 2child	0		
	1	0		
library cache	kglpin	0		
	1	3		
library cache pin	kglupc	0		
	1	0		
redo allocation	kcrfwr	0		
	21	22		
redo allocation	kcrfwi: more space	0		
	1	1		
redo allocation	kcrfwr: redo allocation 0	0		
	1	0		
resmgr group change latc	kskincrstat1	0		
	24	24		
session allocation	ksufap: active sessions	0		
	12	0		
session idle bit	ksupuc: clear busy	0		
	10	6		
session idle bit	ksupuc: set busy	0		
	3	7		
shared pool	kghalo	0		
	16	2		

```
shared pool              kghupr1                          0
7       25
shared pool              kghfrunp: alloc: wait            0
6        0
shared pool              kghfrunp: clatch: nowait         0
4        0
shared pool              kghfrunp: clatch: wait           0
2        3
```

Here are some general tuning guidelines for latch activity waits:

- When *cache buffers chains pct get miss* > 0.1 or *pct nowait miss* > 1.0, then hawse have high cache buffer chain latches. See MetaLink about increasing the hidden parameter *_db_block_hash_buckets*.

- When *cache buffers lru chains pct get miss* > 0.1 or *pct nowait miss* > 1.0, then we have a high value for cache buffer LRU chain waits, and one needs to reduce the length of the hash chains for popular data blocks in the RAM buffer. Investigate the specific data blocks that are experiencing the latches and reduce the popularity of the data block by spreading the rows across more data blocks through reorganizing with a higher value for *pctfree*.

- When *library cache pct get miss* > 0.1 or *pct nowait miss* > 1.0, then we may have high library cache waits. Consider pinning the frequently used packages in the library cache with *dbms_shared_pool.keep*.

- When *redo allocation pct get miss* > 0.1 or *pct nowait miss* > 1.0, then we may have high redo allocation misses. The redo allocation latch controls the allocation of space for redo entries in the redo log buffer as defined by the *log_buffer* parameter. The redo allocation latch is a serialization latch that enforces the sequence of entries in the log buffer. A process can only write a redo entry after the redo allocation latch, which is why it is a will-to-wait latch. Investigate increasing the *log_buffer* parameter.

- When *redo copy pct get miss* > 0.1 or *pct nowait miss* > 1.0, then we may have high redo copy latch wait times. Check MetaLink for increasing the hidden parameter *_log_simultaneous_copies*.

Dictionary and Library Cache Stats

Just like tables are cached in RAM, Oracle caches rows from the data dictionary using a RAM buffer to relieve the need to re-read dictionary rows from disk whenever they are needed. All of the data dictionary caching is managed on one's behalf by the database kernel, so there are no tuning remedies for high dictionary cache misses other than increasing the size of the shared pool via *shared_pool_size*.

The query below shows the data dictionary cache stats and library cache activity for a typical STATSPACK/AWR report:

```
Dictionary Cache Stats for DB: 123456 Instance: 123456

Snaps: 7150 -7151

->"Pct Misses"  should be very low (< 2% in most cases)

->"Cache Usage" is the number of cache entries being used

->"Pct SGA"     is the ratio of usage to allocated size for that
    cache
```

Cache	Get Requests	Pct Miss	Scan Reqs	Pct Miss	Mod Reqs	Final Usage
dc_database_links	9	0.0	0		0	6
dc_global_oids	54	0.0	0		0	20
dc_histogram_defs	48,739	0.0	0		0	4,562
dc_object_ids	20,470	0.0	0		0	1,063
dc_objects	12,261	4.6	0		0	13,801
dc_profiles	135	0.0	0		0	4
dc_rollback_segments	2,909	0.0	0		0	314
dc_segments	13,429	0.1	0		0	1,006
dc_sequences	206	0.0	0		206	25
dc_tablespace_quotas	4	0.0	0		1	3
dc_tablespaces	2,061	0.0	0		0	68
dc_user_grants	5,662	0.0	0		0	220
dc_usernames	7,928	0.1	0		0	246
dc_users	33,287	0.0	0		7	466

```
Library Cache Activity for DB: 123456 Instance: 123456

Snaps: 7150 -7151

->"Pct Misses" should be very low
```

Namespace	Get Requests	Pct Miss	Pin Requests	Pct Miss	Reloads	Invali- dations
BODY	7,120	0.0	7,120	0.0	1	0
CLUSTER	6	0.0	8	0.0	0	0
INDEX	76	0.0	76	0.0	0	0
PIPE	66	1.5	70	1.4	0	0
SQL AREA	81,986	2.5	1,980,968	0.2	185	0
TABLE/PROCEDURE	290,943	0.3	845,688	0.1	169	0
TRIGGER	1,970	0.0	1,970	0.1	2	0

The Shared Pool Advisory Section

The Oracle shared pool contains Oracle's library cache, which is responsible for collecting, parsing, interpreting, and executing all of the SQL statements that go against the Oracle database. Hence, the shared pool is a key component, so it is necessary for the Oracle database administrator to check for shared pool contention.

The shared pool is like a buffer for SQL statements. Oracle's parsing algorithm ensures that identical SQL statements do not have to be parsed each time they are executed. The shared pool is used to store SQL statements, and it includes the following components:

- the library cache

- the dictionary cache

- control structures

The following lists the different areas stored in the shared pool and their purpose:

- **Shared SQL area:** The shared SQL area stores each SQL statement executed in the database. This area allows SQL execution plans to be reused by many users.

- **Private SQL area:** Private SQL areas are non-shared memory areas assigned to unique user sessions

- **PL/SQL area:** This is used to hold parsed and compiled PL/SQL program units, allowing the execution plans to be shared by many users.

- **Control structures:** This has common control structure information, like lock information.

The dictionary cache stores metadata and the dictionary cache is also known as the row cache. In a nutshell, the dictionary cache is used to cache data dictionary related information in RAM for quick access. The dictionary cache is like the data buffer cache, except it is exclusively for Oracle data dictionary information instead of user information.

Staring in Oracle 9i release 2 we saw the shared pool advisor (implemented via *v$shared_pool_advice*), and this utility is now included in all STATSPACK and AWR reports. The *v$shared_pool_advice* view shows the marginal difference in SQL parses as the shared pool changes in size from 10% of the current value to 200% of the current value.

The Oracle documentation contains a complete description for the setup and use of shared pool advice, and it is very simple to configure. Once it is installed, a simple script can be run to query the *v$shared_pool_advice* view and locate the marginal changes in SQL parses for different *shared_pool_size* values.

The Oracle shared pool advisory utility indicates "A" cached memory objects during the sample interval. Oracle estimates that doubling the shared pool size by increasing *shared_pool_size* will allow for ("A"-"C") extra cached objects and have mated library cache time saved of ("B"-"D").

```
Shared Pool Advisory for DB: 123456 Instance: 123456 End Snap: 7151

-> Note there is often a 1:Many correlation between a single logical object in the Library
Cache, and the physical number of memory objects associated with it.

Therefore comparing the number of Lib Cache objects (e.g. in v$librarycache), with the
number of Lib Cache Memory Objects is invalid
```

Shared Pool Size for Estim (M)	SP Size Factr	Estd Lib Cache Size (M)	Estd Lib Cache Mem Obj	Estd Cache Time Saved (s)	Estd Lib LC Time Saved Factr	Estd Lib Cache Mem Obj Hits
352	.6	337	39,058	2,460,632	1.0	3,836,117

```
    416      .7        400      46,632   2,460,637      1.0      3,836,826
    480      .8        462      54,529   2,460,637      1.0      3,837,105
    544      .9        525      63,837   2,460,647      1.0      3,837,192
    608     1.0        590      74,834   2,460,650      1.0      3,837,223
    672     1.1        653      85,805   2,460,650      1.0      3,837,238
    736     1.2        716      95,196   2,460,650      1.0      3,837,239
    800     1.3        779     105,732   2,460,650      1.0      3,837,239
    864     1.4        843     114,716   2,460,650      1.0      3,837,249
    928     1.5        906     123,815   2,460,650      1.0      3,837,261
    992     1.6        969     132,807   2,460,650      1.0      3,837,270
  1,056     1.7      1,032     140,841   2,460,650      1.0      3,837,276
  1,120     1.8      1,096     149,069   2,460,650      1.0      3,837,276
  1,184     1.9      1,138     153,402   2,460,650      1.0      3,837,276
  1,248     2.1      1,186     156,730   2,460,650      1.0      3,837,276
          ------------------------------------------------------------------
```

Here is the SGA size summary:

```
SGA Memory Summary for DB: 123456 Instance: 123456 Snaps: 7150 -7151


SGA regions                          Size in Bytes
-----------------------------        ----------------
Database Buffers                     12,062,818,304
Fixed Size                                  764,208
Redo Buffers                              1,585,152
Variable Size                         3,154,116,608
                                     ----------------
sum                                  15,219,284,272
-------------------------------------------------------
```

In this report example below we see all of the individual RAM areas, most of which are not documented by Oracle. It's also interesting to see how Oracle managers the sub-pools within the SGA. Even without Automatic Shared Memory Management enabled, Oracle will grow and shrink areas within *shared_pool_size*, and this report will show us some details of the changes to the SGA sub-pools.

In this example we see the *KGLS shared heap* and *shared PL/SQL DIANA* shrinking between the snapshot times.

```
SGA breakdown difference for DB: 123456 Instance: 123456

Snaps: 7150 -7151


Pool   Name                        Begin value        End value    % Diff
------ --------------------------  ----------------  ----------------  ----------
java   free memory                 79,433,728        79,433,728        0.00
java   memory in use                4,452,352         4,452,352         0.00
large  PX msg pool                    983,040           983,040         0.00
large  free memory                 49,348,608        49,348,608         0.00
shared Checkpoint queue            10,246,400        10,246,400         0.00
shared DML lock                     7,260,072         7,260,072         0.00
shared FileIdentificatonBlock         899,080           899,080         0.00
shared FileOpenBlock               16,270,720        16,270,720         0.00
shared KGK heap                        26,200            26,200         0.00
shared KGLS heap                    4,935,968         4,402,344       -10.81
shared KGSK scheduler                 623,000           623,000         0.00
shared KGSKI schedule                  43,512            43,512         0.00
shared KQR L PO                    15,680,976        15,717,840         0.24
shared KQR M PO                     3,538,696         3,543,856         0.15
shared KQR M SO                        95,440            96,464         1.07
shared KQR S SO                        56,816            57,072         0.45
```

Dictionary and Library Cache Stats

```
shared KQR X PO                        569,424        569,424     0.00
shared KSXR receive buffers          1,034,000      1,034,000     0.00
shared MTTR advisory                 4,517,632      4,517,632     0.00
shared PL/SQL DIANA                  4,183,200      3,859,392    -7.74
shared PL/SQL MPCODE                 6,322,376      6,447,072     1.97
shared PLS non-lib hp                    2,944          2,944     0.00
shared PX subheap                       73,496         73,496     0.00
shared Temporary Tables State Ob     1,992,664      1,992,664     0.00
shared UNDO INFO SEGMENTED ARRAY     1,667,000      1,667,000     0.00
shared VIRTUAL CIRCUITS             17,275,680     17,275,680     0.00
shared XDB Schema Cac                7,318,136      7,318,136     0.00
shared branch                        3,031,632      3,031,632     0.00
shared constraints                   2,116,280      2,116,280     0.00
shared db_block_hash_buckets        50,520,304     50,520,304     0.00
shared db_handles                      928,000        928,000     0.00
shared dictionary cache              3,229,952      3,229,952     0.00
shared dummy                           690,024        690,024     0.00
shared enqueue                      12,075,416     12,075,416     0.00
shared enqueue resources             4,972,088      4,972,088     0.00
shared enqueue_hash                    817,680        817,680     0.00
shared errors                          206,856        166,896   -19.32
shared event statistics per sess    95,472,000     95,472,000     0.00
shared fixed allocation callback           960            960     0.00
shared free memory                  30,221,176     29,829,608    -1.30
shared joxlod: in ehe                  272,384        272,384     0.00
shared joxs heap init                      480            480     0.00
shared ktlbk state objects           5,011,600      5,011,600     0.00
shared library cache               207,085,696    207,344,336     0.12
shared miscellaneous                70,470,832     71,023,848     0.78
shared parameters                      128,352        141,216    10.02
shared qmps connections              3,604,000      3,604,000     0.00
shared replication session stats     2,584,000      2,584,000     0.00
shared sessions                     22,984,000     22,984,000     0.00
shared sim memory hea               11,957,424     11,957,424     0.00
shared sql area                    290,896,456    291,209,768     0.11
shared subheap                         102,312        102,312     0.00
shared table definiti                   28,832         25,176   -12.68
shared transaction                  15,358,928     15,358,928     0.00
shared trigger defini                  102,736         92,568    -9.90
shared trigger inform                   10,128          7,080   -30.09
shared trigger source                      872            872     0.00
shared type object de                    9,264          9,264     0.00

       buffer_cache             12,062,818,304 12,062,818,304     0.00
       fixed_sga                       764,208        764,208     0.00
       log_buffer                    1,573,888      1,573,888     0.00
```

As we see, this report shows us the major SGA RAM regions as well as a breakdown of the sub-components in the SGA RAM heap.

The OEM memory advisor

Oracle Enterprise Manager also has a Memory Advisor can be used only when the Automatic Memory Management (AMM) feature is disabled. The Memory Advisor has three advisors that give recommendations on: the shared pool in the System Global Area (SGA), the buffer cache in the SGA, and the PGA. The following steps can be used to access the Memory Advisor and tune its underlying structures.

The first step is to click on the Memory Advisor in the Advisor Central Page.

Figure 8.6: *Memory Advisor*

The SGA page will appear as shown in Figure 8.7. This page has all the details on memory usage for the SGA. The shared pool and the buffer cache are part of the SGA. Help can be clicked for more information on the structure shown here.

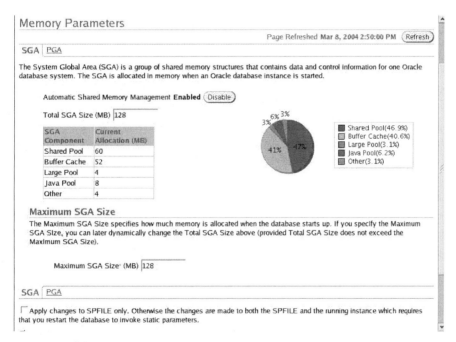

Figure 8.7: *Memory Parameters*

Remember, if you are using AMM, it must has to be disabled to run the PGA advisor. To accomplish this, the shared pool or the buffer cache should be chosen and the Advice link next to it should be clicked.

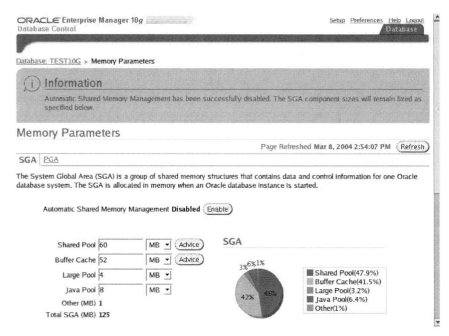

Figure 8.8: *Memory Parameters Screen*

For the Shared Pool size, the graph reveals that a shared pool size larger than 60 MB will not improve the performance much. So the recommended optimal shared pool size is 60 MB.

Figure 8.9: *Shared Pool Size Advice*

Now we can look at the time model report section. The Oracle time model was reviewed in Chapter 3, so now take a closer look at some of the time model data in a STATSPACK/AWR report.

The Time Model Statistics section

The next report section is new starting in Oracle 10g. The time model statistics give insight about where the processing time is actually spent during the snapshot interval.

```
Time Model Statistics DB/Inst: ABC/abc Snaps: 1355-1356

-> ordered by Time (seconds) desc
```

	Time	% (seconds)	Total DB Time
Statistic Name			
DB time		7,274.60	100.00
sql execute elapsed time		7,249.77	99.66
background elapsed time		778.48	10.70
DB CPU		150.62	2.07
parse time elapsed		45.52	.63
hard parse elapsed time		44.65	.61
PL/SQL execution elapsed time		13.73	.19
background cpu time		8.90	.12
PL/SQL compilation elapsed time		3.80	.05
connection management call elapsed time		.15	.00
Java execution elapsed time		.05	.00
hard parse (bind mismatch) elapsed time		.00	.00
hard parse (sharing criteria) elapsed time		.00	.00
sequence load elapsed time		.00	.00
failed parse (out of shared memory) elapsed		.00	.00
inbound PL/SQL rpc elapsed time		.00	.00
failed parse elapsed time		.00	.00

In the sample output of the AWR Time Model Statistics Report shown above, it can be seen that the system spends the most processing time on actual SQL execution but not on parsing. This is very good for production systems.

The Operating System Statistics Section

The stress on the Oracle server is important, and no amount of internal tuning can relieve an external bottleneck. The OS section explores the main external resources including I/O, CPU, memory, and network usage. This information helps us to see performance in a more complex way, giving us the whole picture of internal and external system bottlenecks.

```
Operating System Statistics   DB/Inst: SSD/ssd2  Snaps: 3-4


Statistic Name                             Value
----------------------------------- ------------------
```

```
AVG_BUSY_TICKS                          11,641
AVG_IDLE_TICKS                         349,688
AVG_IN_BYTES                       851,628,032
AVG_NICE_TICKS                               0
AVG_OUT_BYTES                    1,107,304,448
AVG_SYS_TICKS                            2,335
AVG_USER_TICKS                           9,306
BUSY_TICKS                              23,282
IDLE_TICKS                             699,377
IN_BYTES                         1,703,256,064
NICE_TICKS                                   0
OUT_BYTES                        2,214,608,896
RSRC_MGR_CPU_WAIT_TIME                       0
SYS_TICKS                                4,670
USER_TICKS                              18,612
```

In order to isolate a performance bottleneck at the database level, the information from the next section may be used.

The Service Statistics Section

The service statistics section gives information about how particular services configured in the database are operating. A sample of the AWR Service Report may look like the following:

```
Service Statistics   DB/Inst: ABC/abc   Snaps: 1355-1356

-> ordered by DB Time

-> us - microsecond - 1000000th of a second
```

| | | | Physical | Logical |
Service Name	DB Time (s)	DB CPU (s)	Reads	Reads
SYS$USERS	3,715.8	67.7	191,654	525,164
ABC	3,572.4	83.1	187,653	544,836
ABCXDB	0.0	0.0	0	0
SYS$BACKGROUND	0.0	0.0	1,927	70,537

```
Service Wait Class Stats   DB/Inst: ABC/abc   Snaps: 1355-1356

-> Wait Class info for services in the Service Statistics section.

-> Total Waits and Time Waited displayed for the following wait
   classes:  User I/O, Concurrency, Administrative, Network

-> Time Waited (Wt Time) in centisecond (100th of a second)
```

Service Name							
User I/O	User I/O	Concurcy	Concurcy	Admin	Admin	Network	Network
Total Wts	Wt Time	Total Wts	Wt Time	Total Wts	Wt Time	Total Wts	Wt Time

```
SYS$USERS
   36370    360380 73 66        0          0       1313         4
ABC
   35514    346409 85 95        0          0       8057         7
SYS$BACKGROUND
    1226     29322  4  4        0          0          0         0
          --------------------------------------------------
```

If particular production databases are configured for different database services, the above report section allows the DBA to quickly isolate which application places the most overhead on the system. Furthermore, the report indicates where the application waits most of the time. The report shows that applications that use the SYS$USERS service are spending most of the time performing I/O operations.

It is necessary to notice that this SYS$USERS service is a default service for all applications. To take advantage of isolating applications performance, some DBAs will configure separate services for each kind of production application. The DBA is now ready to find which particular SQL statements may cause that stress.

The Top SQL Section

This section displays top SQL ordered by important SQL execution metrics, and it is critical for finding low-hanging fruit, namely frequently executed high-impact SQL statements.

The top SQL section in the AWR report contains lists of SQL statements ordered by the following criteria:

- **Elapsed time:** SQL statements are ordered according to elapsed execution times.

- **CPU time:** SQL statements are ordered according to CPU time.

- **Buffer gets:** SQL statements are ordered according to logical reads number.

- **Physical reads:** SQL statements are ordered according to physical reads number.

- **Execution number:** SQL statements are ordered according to execution number.

- **Parse calls:** SQL statements are ordered according to parse number.

- **Version count:** SQL statements are ordered according to version number.

- **Sharable memory:** SQL statements are ordered according to sharable memory consumption.

Here is a sample of a top SQL in a STATSPACK/AWR report section, showing the actual SQL source code:

```
   Elapsed      CPU                    Elap per  % Total
   Time (s)   Time (s)   Executions   Exec (s)   DB Time   SQL Id
   ---------- ---------- ------------ ---------- --------  ------------
      4,504         78            2     2251.9     61.9  6zmdns6h6xm5p

Module: SQL*Plus
```

Dictionary and Library Cache Stats   **357**

```
DECLARE
feeval NUMBER;
BEGIN
  FS_ABC.sp_funds_val(Feeval,'1003');
  dbms_output
.put_line('Feeval = '||TO_CHAR(Feeval));
END;

     3,434          62          74        46.4      47.2 dahmxun9ngx14
Module: SQL*Plus
SELECT NVL(SUM(PAYMENTS.AMT) * :B4 ,0) FROM PAYMENTS, TRANSACTIONS WHERE ( (TRAN
SACTIONS.TRANSKEY = PAYMENTS.TRANSKEY) AND (TRANSACTIONS.CLIENTKEY = :B3 ) AND (
PAYMENTS.TYPE_ <> 7) AND PAYMENTS.AMT>0 AND (PAYMENTS.COLSTATUS = 2) AND (PAYMEN
TS.POSTDATE=:B2 +:B1 ) )

     3,408          54          74        46.1      46.8 0fzfwb0szmgss
Module: SQL*Plus
SELECT PAYMENTS.POSTDATE FROM TRANSACTIONS, PAYMENTS WHERE ( (TRANSACTIONS.CLIEN
TKEY = :B3 ) AND (TRANSACTIONS.TRANSKEY = PAYMENTS.TRANSKEY) AND (PAYMENTS.TYPE_
 <> 7) AND (PAYMENTS.COLSTATUS = 2) AND (PAYMENTS.POSTDATE=:B2 +:B1 )) GROUP BY
PAYMENTS.POSTDATE

        87           2          56         1.6       1.2 6gvch1xu9ca3g
DECLARE job BINARY_INTEGER := :job; next_date DATE := :mydate;  broken BOOLEAN :
= FALSE; BEGIN EMD_MAINTENANCE.EXECUTE_EM_DBMS_JOB_PROCS(); :mydate := next_date
; IF broken THEN :b := 1; ELSE :b := 0; END IF; END;

        74           2           1        74.1       1.0 d92h3rjp0y217
begin prvt_hdm.auto_execute( :db_id, :inst_id, :end_snap ); end;

        52           1           2        25.8       0.7 gfwfn87avpfq8
Module: SQL*Plus
DECLARE
checkval NUMBER;
BEGIN
  FS_ABC.Sp_get_res_checkval(checkval,'844');
  d
bms_output.put_line('checkval = '||TO_CHAR(checkval));
END;

        52           1           2        25.8       0.7 cv2n8rfpnzdza
Module: SQL*Plus
SELECT NVL(SUM(CHECKDTL.AMT),0) FROM CHECKHDR , CHECKDTL,ACCOUNTS WHERE (CHECKDT
L.CHECKHDRKEY = CHECKHDR.CHECKHDRKEY) AND (CHECKDTL.ACCTNO = ACCOUNTS.ACCTNO) AN
D (ACCOUNTS.ACCOUNTS = 5) AND CHECKTYPE<>1 AND CHECKTYPE<>2 AND CHECKTYPE<>12 AN
D CHECKTYPE<>5 AND CLIENTKEY=:B1 ORDER BY CHECKHDR.CHECKDATE ASC
```

The top SQL by elapsed time report is most useful when it is ordered according to the our top-5 timed events, so that we can correlate SQL activity with the total time spent for different activities.

This information should be used in conjunction with other sections of the STATSPACK/AWR report. For example, if the system experiences a high number of parses, the Top SQL should be checked by parse number section to find the particular statements with a large number of parses (Figure 8.10):

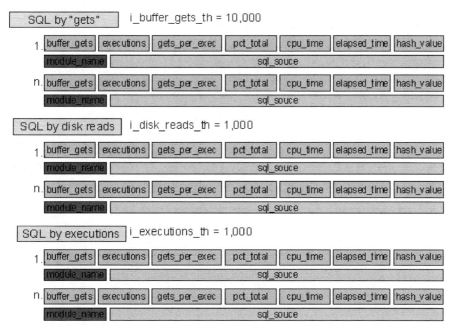

Figure 8.10: *Top SQL Section Summary*

The Top SQL section alone cannot reveal which particular statements have suboptimal execution. This decision is completely dependent on other factors and the DBAs knowledge about the system and applications.

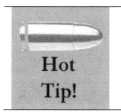

You control the number of SQL statements!

The number of SQL statements that you see is dependent upon your SQL collection threshold value for each metric (*executions, disk reads*, &c).

Below, we can see the SQL collection thresholds for STATSPACK, to allow you to govern the criteria for SQL to appear in the elapsed time report.

```
SQL> desc statspack

PROCEDURE MODIFY_STATSPACK_PARAMETER

Argument Name            Type            In/Out Default?
--------------------     -------------   ------ --------
I_DBID                   NUMBER          IN     DEFAULT
I_INSTANCE_NUMBER        NUMBER          IN     DEFAULT
I_SNAP_LEVEL             NUMBER          IN     DEFAULT
I_SESSION_ID             NUMBER          IN     DEFAULT
I_UCOMMENT               VARCHAR2        IN     DEFAULT
I_NUM_SQL                NUMBER          IN     DEFAULT
```

Dictionary and Library Cache Stats

I_EXECUTIONS_TH	NUMBER	IN	DEFAULT
I_PARSE_CALLS_TH	NUMBER	IN	DEFAULT
I_DISK_READS_TH	NUMBER	IN	DEFAULT
I_BUFFER_GETS_TH	NUMBER	IN	DEFAULT
I_SHARABLE_MEM_TH	NUMBER	IN	DEFAULT
I_VERSION_COUNT_TH	NUMBER	IN	DEFAULT
I_ALL_INIT	VARCHAR2	IN	DEFAULT
I_PIN_STATSPACK	VARCHAR2	IN	DEFAULT
I_MODIFY_PARAMETER	VARCHAR2	IN	DEFAULT

The next STATSPACK/AWR report section allows the DBA to acquire an overview of the system in a more complex way.

The Instance Activity Section

This section of the STATSPACK/AWR report contains useful instance-wide statistical information about the database. I have highlighted some of the most important statistics.

Instance Activity Stats for DB: ENAZZ   Instance: enactexm

Snaps: 775 -778

Statistic	Total	per Second	per Trans
CPU used by this session	189,919	17.6	9.6
CPU used when call started	189,880	17.6	9.6
CR blocks created	2,377	0.2	0.1
DBWR checkpoint buffers written	19,753	1.8	1.0
DBWR checkpoints	12	0.0	0.0
DBWR transaction table writes	85	0.0	0.0
DBWR undo block writes	15,097	1.4	0.8
SQL*Net roundtrips to/from client	2,069,324	191.6	105.1
buffer is not pinned count	102,951,598	9,531.7	5,227.6
buffer is pinned count	86,169,269	7,977.9	4,375.4
bytes received via SQL*Net from c	547,898,802	50,726.7	27,820.6
bytes sent via SQL*Net to client	665,185,598	61,585.6	33,776.1
cleanouts and rollbacks - consist	380	0.0	0.0
cleanouts only - consistent read	162	0.0	0.0
cluster key scan block gets	3,389	0.3	0.2
cluster key scans	1,531	0.1	0.1
consistent changes	2,803	0.3	0.1
consistent gets	122,696,942	11,359.8	6,230.2
consistent gets - examination	57,548,324	5,328.1	2,922.1
cursor authentications	2,878	0.3	0.2
data blocks consistent reads - un	2,732	0.3	0.1
db block changes	310,932	28.8	15.8
db block gets	324,644	30.1	16.5
deferred (CURRENT) block cleanout	51,582	4.8	2.6
enqueue conversions	1,489	0.1	0.1
enqueue deadlocks	0	0.0	0.0
enqueue releases	99,016	9.2	5.0
enqueue requests	99,040	9.2	5.0
enqueue timeouts	25	0.0	0.0
enqueue waits	1,000	0.1	0.1
execute count	694,029	64.3	35.2
free buffer inspected	1	0.0	0.0
free buffer requested	256,282	23.7	13.0
hot buffers moved to head of LRU	1,163	0.1	0.1
immediate (CR) block cleanout app	542	0.1	0.0
immediate (CURRENT) block cleanou	12,057	1.1	0.6
index fast full scans (full)	107	0.0	0.0
index fetch by key	20,039,881	1,855.4	1,017.6
index scans kdiixs1	17,551,582	1,625.0	891.2
logons cumulative	298	0.0	0.0
messages received	25,515	2.4	1.3

messages sent	25,515	2.4	1.3
no buffer to keep pinned count	0	0.0	0.0
no work - consistent read gets	47,066,576	4,357.6	2,389.9
opened cursors cumulative	682,972	63.2	34.7
parse count (failures)	0	0.0	0.0
parse count (hard)	12,618	1.2	0.6
parse count (total)	690,401	63.9	35.1
parse time cpu	9,250	0.9	0.5
parse time elapsed	11,033	1.0	0.6
physical reads	251,776	23.3	12.8
physical reads direct	522	0.1	0.0
physical writes	25,464	2.4	1.3
physical writes direct	5,711	0.5	0.3
physical writes non checkpoint	9,742	0.9	0.5
redo blocks written	346,104	32.0	17.6
redo buffer allocation retries	8	0.0	0.0
redo entries	169,075	15.7	8.6
redo log space requests	5	0.0	0.0
redo log space wait time	13	0.0	0.0
redo size	165,165,732	15,291.7	8,386.6
redo synch time	2,404	0.2	0.1
redo synch writes	19,738	1.8	1.0
redo wastage	6,558,844	607.2	333.0
redo write time	2,156	0.2	0.1
redo writer latching time	0	0.0	0.0
redo writes	23,955	2.2	1.2
rollback changes - undo records a	573	0.1	0.0
rollbacks only - consistent read	2,309	0.2	0.1
rows fetched via callback	19,384,082	1,794.7	984.3
session connect time	292,579,879,221	27,088,221.4	############
session logical reads	123,021,586	11,389.8	6,246.7
session pga memory	15,101,664	1,398.2	766.8
session pga memory max	59,106,600	5,472.3	3,001.3
session uga memory	5,146,640	476.5	261.3
session uga memory max	495,289,832	45,855.9	25,149.3
sorts (disk)	1	0.0	0.0
sorts (memory)	79,989	7.4	4.1
sorts (rows)	15,024,130	1,391.0	762.9
switch current to new buffer	1,867	0.2	0.1
table fetch by rowid	65,112,693	6,028.4	3,306.2
table fetch continued row	7,745	0.7	0.4
table scan blocks gotten	21,882,135	2,025.9	1,111.1
table scan rows gotten	2,005,167,162	185,646.4	101,816.2
table scans (long tables)	3,041	0.3	0.2
table scans (short tables)	235,223	21.8	11.9
transaction rollbacks	5	0.0	0.0
user calls	2,519,861	233.3	128.0
user commits	19,691	1.8	1.0
user rollbacks	3	0.0	0.0
workarea executions - onepass	1	0.0	0.0
workarea executions - optimal	88,125	8.2	4.5
write clones created in foregroun	7	0.0	0.0

The information in the instance activity STATSPACK/AWR report section is used to compute numerous ratios and percentages contained in other report sections. For example, the statistics in this section are used to calculate hit ratios for the instance efficiency load profile report sections, and so on.

Additional attention should be paid to the *parse count (hard)* statistic. Too high a value of this statistic could indicate that the DBA should consider tuning SQL statements to make the SQL reentrant by using bind variables. If the *Redo log space wait time* statistic is high enough, the DBA should consider tuning the redo log files.

Here are some things to look for in the instance activity section:

- **Table scans:** High numbers of the statistics *table scans (long tables)* and *physical reads* may indicate that SQL statements perform a large number of unnecessary full table scans.

- **SQL*Net roundtrips:** When *SQL*Net roundtrips to/from client* > 50 per trans or > 50 per sec, then there may be high network activity with high SQL*Net roundtrips to/from client per transaction. Review the application to reduce the number of calls to Oracle by encapsulating data requests into larger pieces, i.e. make a single SQL request to populate all online screen items. Also check the application to see if it might benefit from bulk collection by using PL/SQL *forall* or *bulk collect* operators.

- **Block changes:** When *db block changes* > 50 per trans or > 50 per sec, then there may be high update activity and high db block changes. The DB block changes are a rough indication of total database work. This statistic indicates, on a per-transaction level, the rate at which buffers are being dirtied and one may want to optimize the database writer (DBWR) process. Which sessions and SQL have the highest db block changes can be found by querying the *v$session* and *v$sessstat* views.

- **Disk reads:** When *physical reads* or *physical reads direct* > 50 per trans or > 50 per sec, then there may be high disk reads. Disk reads can be reduced by increasing the data buffer size or speeding up the disk read speed by moving to SSD storage. The physical disk reads can be monitored by hour of the day using AWR to see when the database has the highest disk activity.

- **Disk writes:** When *physical writes* or *physical writes direct* > 50 per trans or > 50 per sec, then there may be high disk write activity. So drill down and identify the sessions that are performing the disk writes as they can cause locking contention within Oracle. Also investigate moving the high-write datafiles to a smaller data buffer to improve the speed of the database writer process. Also, the disk write speed can be dramatically improved by up to 300x by moving the high-write datafiles to solid-state disk.

- **Small-table full-table scans:** When *table scans – (short tables)* > .5 per second, then there may be high small-table full-table scans. Verify that the KEEP pool is sized properly to cache frequently referenced tables and indexes. Moving frequently referenced tables and indexes to SSD will significantly increase the speed of small-table full-table scans.

- **Large-table full-table scans:** When *table scans – (long tables)* > .5 per second, then there may be high long-table full-table scans per second. This might indicate missing indexes, and we can run *plan9i.sql* to identify the specific tables and investigate the SQL to see if an index scan might result in faster execution. If the large-table full-table scans are legitimate, look at optimizing our *db_file_multiblock_read_count* parameter.

- **PGA workareas:** When *workarea executions – onepass* > 20, then there may be excessive onepass PGA workarea executions with xxx non-optimal executions during this elapsed period. It is better to have workarea executions – optimal, and one might consider optimizing the *pga_aggregate_target* parameter.

- **Disk sorts:** When *sorts (disk)* > 0, then there may be excessive disk sorts during this period. Disk sorts are very expensive and increasing the PGA, *sort_area_size* or *pga_aggregate_target*, may allow us to perform these sorts in RAM.

- **Chained rows:** When *table fetch continued row* > 1,000 total, then there may be high migrated/chained rows which always cause double the I/O for a row fetch and *table fetch continued row* (chained row fetch) happens when BLOB/CLOB columns are fetched (if the *avg_row_len* > *db_block_size*), when there are tables with > 255 columns, and when *pctfree* is too small. We may need to reorganize the affected tables with the *dbms_redefintion* utility and re-set the *pctfree* parameters to prevent future row chaining.

- **Logical I/O:** When *consistent gets – examination* > 1,000 per second, then there may be high *consistent gets examination* per second. *Consistent gets – examination* are a different kind of consistent get that is used to read undo blocks for consistent read purposes, but they also do it for the first part of an index read and hash cluster I/O.

The following section allows the DBA to estimate how the I/O subsystem works, and gives the DBA a way to find possible hot spots in I/O operation.

The I/O Reports Section

The following sections of the STATSPACK/AWR report show the distribution of I/O activity between the tablespaces and data files.

```
Tablespace IO Stats  DB/Inst: ABC/abc  Snaps: 1355-1356

-> ordered by IOs (Reads + Writes) desc
```

Tablespace

	Av	Av	Av			Av	Buffer	Av Buf
Reads	Reads/s	Rd(ms)	Blks/Rd	Writes	Writes/s	Waits	Wt(ms)	

T_FS_ABC

| 26,052 | 7 | 132.5 | 14.5 | 1 | 0 | 43,931 | 78.3 |

SYSAUX

| 1,730 | 0 | 123.5 | 1.1 | 1,139 | 0 | 0 | 0.0 |

SYSTEM

| 814 | 0 | 305.1 | 2.0 | 95 | 0 | 0 | 0.0 |

USERS

| 262 | 0 | 15.2 | 1.0 | 1 | 0 | 290 | 12.1 |

UNDOTBS1

| 14 | 0 | 86.4 | 1.0 | 129 | 0 | 3 | 0.0 |

TEMP

| 1 | 0 | 80.0 | 1.0 | 0 | 0 | 0 | 0.0 |

```
File IO Stats DB/Inst: ABC/abc Snaps: 1355-1356
-> ordered by Tablespace, File
```

Tablespace	Filename
------------------------	--

	Av	Av	Av			Av	Buffer	Av Buf
Reads	Reads/s	Rd(ms)	Blks/Rd	Writes	Writes/s	Waits	Wt(ms)	

SYSAUX   G:\ORACLE\ABC\ABC\SYSAUX01.DBF

| 1,730 | 0 | 123.5 | 1.1 | 1,139 | 0 | 0 | 0.0 |

SYSTEM   G:\ORACLE\ABC\ABC\SYSTEM01.DBF

| 814 | 0 | 305.1 | 2.0 | 95 | 0 | 0 | 0.0 |

TEMP   G:\ORACLE\ABC\ABC\TEMP01.DBF

| 1 | 0 | 80.0 | 1.0 | 0 | 0 | 0 | |

T_FS_ABC   G:\ORACLE\ABC\ABC\T_FS_ABC01.DBF

| 26,052 | 7 | 132.5 | 14.5 | 1 | 0 | 43,931 | 78.3 |

UNDOTBS1   G:\ORACLE\ABC\ABC\UNDOTBS01.DBF

```
          14 0    86.4     1.0            129      0    3    0.0
USERS                 G:\ORACLE\ABC\ABC\USERS01.DBF
         262 0    15.2     1.0              1      0  290   12.1
         --------------------------------------------------
```

In general, the information presented in the I/O section shown above is intended to help us identify "hot spots" of the database I/O subsystem. Remember, if we are using RAID (or SAME, Stripe and mirror everywhere), our disk I/O is randomized and we do not have to worry about disk level I/O load balancing.

When any tablespace *av rd(ms)* > 25 then we have a disk performance issue, as 25 milliseconds is way too slow. This tablespace might have disk enqueues, or the tablespace delay might be caused by excessive read-write head movement or disk channel contention. In cases where we see slow I/O (any I/O slower than 20 milliseconds), consider distributing the frequently referenced objects to a less busy disk or moving the tablespace to a faster storage device such as SSD.

Oracle considers average disk read times of greater than 20 milliseconds to be unacceptable. If data files, as in the example above, consistently have average read times of 20 ms or greater, a number of possible approaches can be followed:

- **Better SQL management**: A database with no user SQL being run generates little or no I/O. Ultimately, all I/O generated by a database is directly or indirectly due to the nature and amount of user SQL being submitted for execution. This means that it is possible to limit the I/O requirements of a database by controlling the amount of I/O generated by individual SQL statements. This is accomplished by tuning SQL statements so that their execution plans result in a minimum number of I/O operations. Typically in a problematic situation, there will only be a few SQL statements with suboptimal execution plans generating a lot more physical I/O than necessary and degrading the overall performance for the database.

- **Using memory caching to limit I/O:** The amount of I/O required by the database is limited by the use of a number of memory caches; e.g., the buffer cache, the log buffer, various sort areas and more. Increasing the buffer cache, up to a point, results in more buffer accesses by database processes, i.e. logical I/Os, being satisfied from memory instead of having to go to disk (physical I/Os). With larger sort areas in memory, the likelihood of them being exhausted during a sorting operation and having to use a temporary tablespace on disk is reduced.

- **Tuning the size of multi-block I/O:** The size of individual multi-block I/O operations can be controlled by instance parameters. Up to a limit, multi-block I/Os are executed faster when there are fewer larger I/Os than when there are many smaller I/Os.

- **Index management:** If the tablespace contains indexes, another option is to compress the indexes so that they require less space and hence, less I/O.

- **Optimizing I/O at the operating system level:** This involves making use of I/O capabilities such as asynchronous I/O or using file systems with advanced capabilities such as direct

I/O, bypassing the operating system's file caches. Another possible action is to raise the limit of maximum I/O size per transfer.

- **Load balancing:** Balancing the database I/O by use of striping, RAID, Storage Area Networks (SAN) or Network Attached Storage (NAS). This approach relies on storage technologies such as striping, RAID, SAN and NAS to automatically load balance database I/O across multiple available physical disks in order to avoid disk contention and I/O bottlenecks when there is still available unused disk throughput in the storage hardware.

- **I/O management:** Database I/O by manual placement of database files across different file systems, controllers and physical devices. This is an approach used in the absence of advanced modern storage technologies. Again, the aim is to distribute the database I/O so that no single set of disks or controller becomes saturated from I/O requests when there is still unused disk throughput. It is harder to get right than the previous approach and most often less successful.

- **Hardware:** Investing in faster hardware will remedy many problems, especially the new 11g flash_cache for solid-state disk, which perform I/O hundreds of times faster than disks.

The Advisory Sections

This section shows details of the advisories for the buffer, shared pool, PGA and Java pool. Let's start with the buffer pool advisory.

Buffer Pool Advisory

This portion of the AWR report shows the estimates from the buffer pool advisory, which are computed based on I/O activity that occurred during the snapshot interval.

```
Buffer Pool Statistics for DB: 123456 Instance: 123456

Snaps: 7150 -7151

-> Standard block size Pools  D: default,  K: keep,  R: recycle

-> Default Pools for other block sizes: 2k, 4k, 8k, 16k, 32k
```

P	Number of Buffers	Cache Hit %	Buffer Gets	Physical Reads	Physical Writes	Free Buffer Waits	Write Complete Waits	Buffer Busy Waits
D	1,427,215	97.4	54,746,567	1,396,413	206,245	0	0	4,881

```
Buffer Pool Advisory for DB: 123456 Instance: 123456 End Snap: 7151

-> Only rows with estimated physical reads >0 are displayed

-> ordered by Block Size, Buffers For Estimate
```

| | Size for | Size | Buffers for | Est Physical | Estimated |
P	Estimate (M)	Factr	Estimate	Read Factor	Physical Reads
D	1,152	.1	142,920	2.98	396,571,233
D	2,304	.2	285,840	2.33	310,016,650
D	3,456	.3	428,760	1.86	247,924,478
D	4,608	.4	571,680	1.57	209,136,872
D	5,760	.5	714,600	1.37	182,801,899
D	6,912	.6	857,520	1.24	164,654,121
D	8,064	.7	1,000,440	1.14	152,061,901
D	9,216	.8	1,143,360	1.08	143,454,688
D	10,368	.9	1,286,280	1.03	137,575,270
D	11,504	1.0	1,427,215	1.00	133,139,478
D	11,520	1.0	1,429,200	1.00	133,076,790
D	12,672	1.1	1,572,120	0.97	128,691,089
D	13,824	1.2	1,715,040	0.94	125,196,307
D	14,976	1.3	1,857,960	0.92	121,922,155
D	16,128	1.4	2,000,880	0.90	119,663,650
D	17,280	1.5	2,143,800	0.89	117,887,942
D	18,432	1.6	2,286,720	0.87	116,379,898
D	19,584	1.7	2,429,640	0.86	115,024,183
D	20,736	1.8	2,572,560	0.86	113,833,108
D	21,888	1.9	2,715,480	0.85	112,858,656
D	23,040	2.0	2,858,400	0.84	111,966,259

In general, this report shows estimates of how physical read operations can be reduced if the buffer cache is increased by a fixed amount of memory. For example, the sample Buffer Advisory Report above shows that at the existing buffer cache size, there will likely be about 133,000,000 physical reads and that doubling the buffer size results in 111,000,000 physical reads, a drop of 22 million disk reads.

Also, note that most databases have popular, frequently referenced data and unpopular, rarely access data, resulting in a 1/x distribution (Figure 8.11).

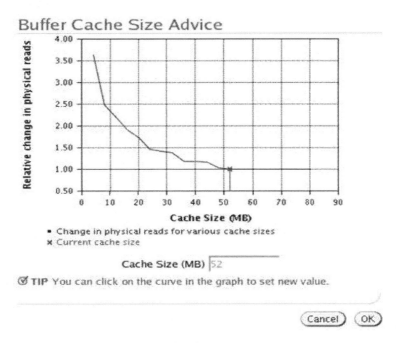

Figure 8.11: *OEM Screenshot of Data Buffer Pool Advisory*

The AWR report contains sections related to other advisories like PGA, shared pool, and java pool advisories. Enabling the AMM feature of Oracle allows the DBA freedom from fine-grained tuning of components within SGA. This data is used with the automatic memory management if you specify the total SGA size target that is used by Oracle as the upper limit of SGA size. This target is specified by the *init.ora* parameter *sga_target*, but again, we do not always recommend this approach.

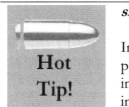

Hot Tip!

_shared_pool_size_ is used with AMM!

In cases where *sga_target* is set, the *shared_pool_size* parameter serves as the minimum value and increasing *sga_target* causes the shared pool to be increased without resetting the *shared_pool_size*.

The following AWR report section gives details about data buffer cache waits.

The Buffer Wait Statistics Section

This section of the AWR report exposes the wait activity that occurred within the data cache.

```
Buffer Wait Statistics  DB/Inst: ABC/abc  Snaps: 1355-1356

-> ordered by wait time desc, waits desc


Class                Waits Total Wait Time (s)  Avg Time (ms)
------------------   -----------  -------------------  --------------
data block           44,213                 3,445             78
segment header           1                      0             20
undo header              2                      0              0
                     -------------------------------------------------
```

In the above sample buffer wait Report listing, we can see that the database experiences a large wait time waiting for data blocks. This may indicate that there are some hot blocks applications are concurrently using. The following actions can be considered in order to reduce such contention:

■ Eliminate hot blocks from the application by redistributing the data

■ Check for repeatedly scanned / unselective indexes

  ■ Change *pctfree* / *pctused*

■ Check for right-hand-indexes. These are indexes that get inserted at the same point by many processes.

■ Increase *initrans*. Reduce the number of rows per block.

If there is a high number of waits for segment header blocks and you are not using bitmap freelists (with automatic segment space management, not recommended), the number of *freelists* can be increased or use made of *freelist groups*. In the case of high undo header waits, we may want to increase the number of undo/rollback segments.

The Enqueue Activity Section

This important section shows how *enqueues* operate in the database. *Enqueues* are special internal structures which provide concurrent access to various database resources. In general, this view can be used to determine how optimally applications are tuned for concurrent access of data. If there are a large number of waits for TX or TS, the applications may need to be revised to identify a reason for the frequent locks.

The Undo Segment Summary Section

This section provides summary information about *undo* segments usage by Oracle. In this section, we can see how evenly Oracle distributes work between *undo* segments along with statistics about the *undo* errors that occurred.

The Undo Segment Stats Section

This section helps identify possible time periods when extra rollback activity occurred in the database. This could be very useful when the DBA has identified that the database sometimes experiences a large number of rollbacks. This section can help find exact times when such an activity took a place.

Latch Statistics Section

The latch statistics STATSPACK/AWR report section shows the activity statistics of latches, which are lightweight serialization devices to provide concurrent access to the internal Oracle structures.

```
Latch Activity  DB/Inst: ABC/ABC  Snaps: 1355-1356

-> "Get Requests", "Pct Get Miss" and "Avg Slps/Miss" are statistics
   for willing-to-wait latch get requests

-> "NoWait Requests", "Pct NoWait Miss" are for no-wait latch get
   requests

-> "Pct Misses" for both should be very close to 0.0
```

Latch Name	Get Requests	Pct Get Miss	Avg Slps /Miss	Wait Time (s)	NoWait Requests	Pct NoWait Miss
Consistent RBA	728	0.0		0	0	
FOB s.o list latch	86	0.0		0	0	
In memory undo latch	8,641	0.0		0	1,563	
JOX SGA heap latch	23	0.0		0	0	
JS queue state obj latch	24,588	0.0		0	0	
JS slv state obj latch	2	0.0		0	0	
KTF sga enqueue	10	0.0		0	977	

In this report, the NoWait Get Miss column should be checked carefully. This column indicates the percentage of requests to get a latch that were finished successfully. It also indicates which latch was acquired. For example, if the application does not widely use bind variables, there will be a low ratio in Pct Get Miss column for library cache latch.

The next report section allows the identification of hot segments by using the criteria described below.

Segment Statistics Section

The segment statistics section exposes the hot segments ordered by the following criteria:

- Top segments by logical reads
- Top segments by physical reads
- Top segments by buffer busy waits

- Top segments row lock waits

| | Tablespace | | Obj. | Logical | |
Owner	Name	Object Name	Type	Reads	%Total
FS_ABC	T_FS_ABC	PAYMENTS	TABLE	751,616	67.93
FS_ABC	T_FS_ABC	TRANSACTIONS	TABLE	113,696	10.28
FS_ABC	T_FS_ABC	CHECKHDR	TABLE	54,048	4.88
FS_ABC	USERS	CHECKHDRKEY_1	INDEX	29,136	2.63
SYS	SYSAUX	SYS_IOT_TOP_8547	INDEX	22,560	2.04

Segments by Physical Reads DB/Inst: ABC/ABC Snaps: 1355-1356

| | Tablespace | | Obj. | Physical | |
Owner	Name	Object Name	Type	Reads	%Total
FS_ABC	T_FS_ABC	PAYMENTS	TABLE	374,984	98.59
FS_ABC	T_FS_ABC	CHECKDTL	TABLE	1,210	.32
SYS	SYSTEM	TAB$	TABLE	801	.21
FS_ABC	T_FS_ABC	CHECKHDR	TABLE	763	.20
SYSMAN	SYSAUX	MGMT_METRICS_INDEX	498	.13

The top segments section allows the quick identification of segments which may pose a potential bottleneck or create a hot spot in the application.

In the example Top Segments Report above, the payments table experiences the most physical reads and the DBA might want to investigate why this table has such a high number of physical reads.

Perhaps the SQL statements that retrieve data are not optimized, or this table has stale statistics that causes the optimizer to use a wrong execution plan. On the other hand, perhaps this table has a large number of analytic reports running against it. In this case, it's also possible that the large number of physical reads might be normal.

This report section, in conjunction with other AWR report sections, should be used to identify the primary cause of really hot segments. The next report section contains information about the data dictionary cache.

The Dictionary Cache Stats Section

This section contains statistics describing the dictionary cache activity. In real life, a lot of useful information cannot be gained here since the dictionary cache is completely managed by Oracle and there is no direct mechanism available for tuning. The only way it can be managed is via the *init.ora* parameter, *shared_pool_size*.

The next section gives more useful information about the library cache.

The Library Cache Activity Section

The library cache AWR report section provides details about the library cache activity. Oracle stores in the library cache, which is part of the shared pool SGA component, many parsed objects such as cursors, packages, procedures, and such.

Below is a sample of the library cache report section:

```
Library Cache Activity  DB/Inst: ABC/abc  Snaps: 1355-1356

-> "Pct Misses"  should be very low
```

Namespace	Get Requests	Pct Miss	Pin Requests	Pct Miss	Reloads	Invalidations
BODY	700	0.4	6,038	0.0	0	0
CLUSTER	17	5.9	33	9.1	2	0
INDEX	34	17.6	78	7.7	0	0
JAVA DATA	1	0.0	0		0	0
SQL AREA	3,777	3.4	37,955	1.2	107	9
TABLE/PROCEDURE	639	1.7	11,907	3.9	252	0
TRIGGER	33	6.1	2,943	0.1	0	0

The most important information listed in this section is that the Pct Miss columns indicate how often Oracle finds cached objects in the cache. If there are enough high values in these columns, you may want to increase *shared_pool_size*. If the ASMM feature is being used, you should consider increasing the values of the *sga_target* parameter and also note the warnings about ASMM thrashing earlier in this chapter.

The next report section gives more details about the SGA regions and their size.

The SGA Memory Summary Section

This section is mostly informational, providing detailed size information of memory caches as shown below:

SGA regions	Size in Bytes
Database Buffers	54,525,952
Fixed Size	787,828
Redo Buffers	262,144
Variable Size	82,836,108

```
SGA breakdown difference  DB/Inst: ABC/abc  Snaps: 1355-1356
```

Pool	Name	Begin value	End value	% Diff

The Advisory Sections

```
------ -------------------------------   ----------------  -------
java    free memory            2,675,264          2,675,264     0.00
java    joxlod exec hp         5,471,424          5,471,424     0.00
java    joxs heap                241,920            241,920     0.00
large   PX msg pool              206,208            206,208     0.00
large   free memory            3,988,096          3,988,096     0.00
shared  ASH buffers            2,097,152          2,097,152     0.00
shared  KGLS heap              1,669,884          2,272,852    36.11
shared  KQR L SO                 144,384            146,432     1.42
shared  KQR M PO               2,279,792          2,323,860     1.93
shared  KQR M SO                 610,864            610,864     0.00
shared  KQR S PO                 229,728            192,856   -16.05
shared  KQR S SO                   6,400              6,400     0.00
shared  KSPD key heap              4,220              4,220     0.00
shared  KSXR pending message     841,036            841,036     0.00
shared  KSXR receive buffer    1,033,000          1,033,000     0.00
shared  PL/SQL DIANA             861,124            932,120     8.24
shared  PL/SQL MPCODE          3,382,696          3,352,036    -0.91
shared  PLS non-lib hp            29,160             29,160     0.00
shared  PX subheap                68,668             68,668     0.00
shared  alert threshol               728                728     0.00
shared  event statistics pe    2,966,080          2,966,080     0.00
shared  fixed allocation ca          260                260     0.00
```

The Initialization Parameters Section

Table 8.2 shows the original *init.ora* parameters for the instance during the snapshot period. One interesting feature in AWR is the use of *begin* values and *end* values for those parameters that are changed dynamically or via the Automatic Shared Memory Manager (ASMM) facility.

Also, note that this report does not list all of the 200+ *init.ora* parameters, only those that have been changed from their default values.

PARAMETER NAME	BEGIN VALUE	END VALUE (IF DIFFERENT)
background_dump_dest	D:\ORACLE\ADMIN\DB\ DUMP	
compatible	10.1.0.2.0	
db_block_size	8192	
db_cache_size	364904448	455210668
db_domain		
db_file_multiblock_read_count	8	
db_name	dbdabr	
db_recovery_file_dest	D:\oracle\flash_recovery_area	
db_recovery_file_dest_size	2147483648	
dispatchers	(protocol=TCP)(mul=ON)	
java_pool_size	8388608	2000000

PARAMETER NAME	BEGIN VALUE	END VALUE (IF DIFFERENT)
pga_aggregate_target	104857600	2038570
shared_pool_size	138412032	
sga_max_size	578813952	
sga_target	524288000	
shared_servers	1	
sort_area_size	1500000	
undo_management	AUTO	

Table 8.2: *The Init.ora Parameters for the Instance During the Snapshot Period*

Here are some general tuning guidelines from the parameters sections:

- **PGA:** When no setting for *pga_aggregate_target* and *sort_area_size* = 65536, then one is using the default *sort_area_size*, usually too small. Examine the statistics for high disk sorts and low hash joins and reset *sort_area_size* or enable *pga_aggregate_target*. When *pga_aggregate_*target > 2,000,000,000, then the PGA region may have been over-allocated. No RAM sort may use more than 5% of *pga_aggregate_target* or *_pga_max_size*, whichever is smaller. This means that no task may use more than 200 megabytes for sorting or hash joins. See *pga_aggregate_target* for more details, and consider increasing *_pga_max_size* high disk sorts or low hash joins are being experienced.

- **Sort area size:** When *sort_area_size* < 500,000 and not set *pga_aggregate_target* and not set (*mts_servers* or *shared_servers*), then there may be an unusually small *sort_area_size*. Examine the statistics for high disk sorts and low hash joins and reset *sort_area_size* or enable *pga_aggregate_target*.

- **Hash joins:** Hash joins are a powerful alternative to nested loop joins. When *hash_area_size* < 1,000,000 and not set *pga_aggregate_target* and not set (*mts_servers* or *shared_servers*), then there may be an unusually small *hash_area_size* = xx. Setting a larger *hash_area_size* (or enabling *pga_aggregate_target*) may improve SQL performance. When *hash_join_enabled* = *false,* then hash joins are not enabled.

- **Optimizer mode:** When *(optimizer_mode=all_rows* and release > 10), then there may be a suboptimal default optimizer mode and we might consider setting it to *first_rows* or *first_rows_n* if we have an online transaction processing system

- **Multiblock reads:** When *db_file_multiblock_read_count* = 16 and *release* < 10g and *DB File Scattered Reads* is in the top 5 waits, then there may be the default value for *db_file_multiblock_read_count* = 16. This parameter is used by the CBO to determine the cost of a full-table scan. The default value is sometimes too large, and scripts can be run to determine the optimal setting.

- **Materialized views:** When *query_rewrite_enabled* = FALSE, then hawse have not enabled materialized views and function-based indexes, very powerful features that require us to set *query_rewrite_integrity* and *query_rewrite_enabled*.

- **Parallelism:** When *parallel_automatic_tuning* = TRUE and *release* < 10, then we have enabled system-level parallel query. This can influence the CBO to favor full-table scans over index access. Consider using parallel hints instead, or invoking parallelism at the session level.

The Advisory Sections

- **Workarea policy**: When *sort_area_size* >0 and *pga_aggregate_target* >0 and *workarea_size_policy* =auto and *not found* (mts_servers or shared_servers), then the *sort_area_size* is ignored when *pga_aggregate_target* is set and when *workarea_size_policy* =auto, unless a specialized feature is being used such as the MTS. If dedicated server connections are used, the *sort_area_size* parameter is ignored. See *pga_aggregate_target* for more details.

- **Shared pool**: When *shared_pool_size* < 100,000, then the shared pool may not be large enough to hold our working set of frequently reused SQL. See the shared pool advisory for further details. When *shared_pool_size* > 10,000,000, then the shared pool is set at an unusually large value. Allocating excessive shared pool resources can adversely impact Oracle performance. See the sh*ared pool adviso*ry for further details.

Conclusion

The AWR/STATSPACK time series report is a great tool for monitoring day-to-day database activity and for planning a proactive tuning strategy. Careful use of this report allows us to quickly overview the health of our system and to identify possible hot spots, as well as the characteristics of the current database workload. The main points of this chapter include:

- The STATSPACK/AWR report has become the de-facto standard within Oracle for elapsed-time reports

- The AWR and STATSPACK reports were originally designed for Oracle Technical Support Staff, and all of the metrics are not fully described in the Oracle documentation

- The AWR and STATSPACK reports are invoked from the scripts in the *$oracle_home/rdbms/admin* directory

- The AWR and STATSPACK reports provide detailed elapsed-time reports to expose the root cause of Oracle performance slowdowns and bottlenecks

- The shorter the elapsed time between AWR or STATSPACK snapshots, the finer the granularity. Hence, frequent snapshot collection is advised during those times when a performance problem manifests itself.

Of course, reading the time series report is just the beginning and the DBA must clearly understand what steps to undertake according to the information contained in the report to proactively react to the problems identified by an AWR or STATSPACK report.

In the next chapter, we will look at the *v$* views and see how they are used for reactive tuning activities.

Oracle Metrics and *v$* Tuning Views

Dictionary Internals can be very mysterious

Classifying *v$* Views and Metrics

Before we begin exploring the *v$* views it is important to understand the metrics inside the *v$* views. Oracle metrics can be classified along two dimensions, long duration and short duration metrics. Oracle computes the long duration metrics at 60-second intervals while the short duration metrics are computed every 15 seconds. For more complete details on using the *v$* dynamic performance views, see Chapter 5, *Oracle Troubleshooting*.

Oracle metrics are further broken down by functionality. For an example, the *v$metricgroup* view can be used to see available metric groups using the following query:

```
select
   name,
   interval_size
from
   v$metricgroup
order by
   interval_size;
```

Table 9.1 below shows the Oracle metrics and their associated interval sizes, listed in hundredths of seconds. Fortunately, Oracle has designed the metric group names to be self-explanatory. To help identify the metrics, Oracle has included the duration for the metric in the *interval_size* column, which is very handy.

NAME	Interval size (1/100th of a second)
System Metrics Short Duration	1,500 centiseconds
Session Metrics Short Duration	1,500 centiseconds
Event Metrics	6,000 centiseconds
Event Class Metrics	6,000 centiseconds
Service Metrics	6,000 centiseconds
Tablespace Metrics Long Duration	6,000 centiseconds
Session Metrics Long Duration	6,000 centiseconds
System Metrics Long Duration	6,000 centiseconds
File Metrics Long Duration	60,000 centiseconds

Table 9.1: *Metric groups and interval sizes*

The *v$metricname* view can be used to show all of the hundreds of metrics. This *v$metricname* view also displays the corresponding metric group and the metric unit that exposes the meaning of the particular metric.

```
select
   group_name,
   metric_name,
   metric_unit
from
   v$metricname
order by
   group_name,
   metric_name;
```

This view returns information about the metrics including the group, descriptive name and the units in which the metric is reported by Oracle. A partial output of the results of the above view statement lists some of the metrics available:

```
GROUP_NAME                       METRIC_NAME                                       METRIC_UNIT
------------------------------   ------------------------------------------------  ------------
-----
Event Class Metrics              Average Users Waiting Counts                      Users
                                 Database Time Spent Waiting(%)                    % TimeWaited /
DBTime)
                                 Total Time Waited                                 CentiSeconds
                                 Total Wait Counts                                 Waits
Event Metrics                    Number of Sessions Waiting (Event)                Sessions
```

	Total Time Waited	CentiSeconds
	Total Wait Counts	Waits
File Metrics Long Duration Per Read	Average File Read Time (Files-Long)	CentiSeconds
Per Write	Average File Write Time (Files-Long	CentiSeconds
	Physical Block Reads (Files-Long)	Blocks
	Physical Block Writes (Files-Long)	Blocks
	Physical Reads (Files-Long)	Reads
	Physical Writes (Files-Long)	Writes
Service Metrics Per Call	CPU Time Per User Call	Microseconds
Per Call	Elapsed Time Per User Call	Microseconds
Session Metrics Long Duration	Blocked User Session Count	Sessions
Session Metrics Short Duration	CPU Time (Session)	CentiSeconds
	Hard Parse Count (Session)	Parses
	Logical Reads Ratio (Sess/Sys) %	%
SessLogRead/SystemLogRead		
	PGA Memory (Session)	Bytes
	Physical Reads (Session)	Reads
	Physical Reads Ratio (Sess/Sys) %	%
SessPhyRead/SystemPhyRead		
	Total Parse Count (Session)	Parses
	User Transaction Count (Session)	Transactions
System Metrics Long Duration Per Second	Background Checkpoints Per Sec	Check Points
Second	Branch Node Splits Per Sec	Splits Per
Txn	Branch Node Splits Per Txn	Splits Per
PhyRead)/LogRead	Buffer Cache Hit Ratio	% (LogRead -
Per Second	CPU Usage Per Sec	CentiSeconds
Per Txn	CPU Usage Per Txn	CentiSeconds
Second	CR Blocks Created Per Sec	Blocks Per
Txn	CR Blocks Created Per Txn	Blocks Per
Per Second	CR Undo Records Applied Per Sec	Undo Records
Txn	CR Undo Records Applied Per Txn	Records Per
Second	Consistent Read Changes Per Sec	Blocks Per

It is important to understand that Oracle uses a circular memory buffer to maintain the history of database metrics.

Several *v$* views can be used to access historical information, which Oracle retains by default for a one-hour duration. Internally, the Oracle Manageability Monitor (MMON) background process gathers these metrics, periodically saving metric history into the Automated Workload Repository (AWR) tables.

The *v$* views *v$sysmetric_history*, *v$waitclassmetric_history*, and *v$filemetric_history* offer a history of database metrics. For starters, the *v$sysmetric_history* view displays the history for all of the system database metrics, punching them from memory to disk for the last hour. To identify the time interval that was computed for a metric, we use the *begin_time* and *end_time* columns.

For example, the following query reveals the data buffer hit ratio history for last hour:

💾 **display_metric_values.sql**

```
select
    'buffer cache hit ratio'        "metric name",
    to_char(begin_time,'hh24:mi:ss') "begin",
    to_char(end_time,'hh24:mi:ss')   "end",
    round(value,2) "value"
from
  v$sysmetric_history
where
 metric_name = 'buffer cache hit ratio'
order by
  begin_time desc;
```

Here is a sample of the output:

```
Metric Name          Begin    End         Value
-------------------- -------- --------  ----------
Buffer Cache Hit Ratio 13:56:15 13:56:32      99
                     13:56:00 13:56:15     100
                     13:55:45 13:56:00     100
                     13:55:32 13:56:32      99
                     13:55:32 13:55:45     100
                     13:55:17 13:55:32     100
                     13:55:02 13:55:17     100
                     13:54:46 13:55:02     100
                     13:54:31 13:55:32     100
                     13:54:31 13:54:46     100
                     13:54:15 13:54:31     100
                     13:54:03 13:54:15     100
                     13:53:45 13:54:03     100
                     13:53:32 13:54:31     100
                     13:53:32 13:53:45     100
                     13:53:17 13:53:32     100
                     13:52:31 13:53:32     100
                     13:51:33 13:52:31      99
                     13:50:31 13:51:33     100
                     13:49:33 13:50:31     100
                     13:48:31 13:49:33     100
                     13:47:32 13:48:31     100
                     13:46:32 13:47:32      99
                     13:45:33 13:46:32     100
                     13:44:31 13:45:33     100
                     13:43:30 13:44:31     100
                     13:42:31 13:43:30     100
                     13:41:32 13:42:31     100
                     13:40:31 13:41:32      99
                     13:39:33 13:40:31     100
                     13:38:31 13:39:33     100
```

```
13:37:33 13:38:31          100
13:36:31 13:37:33           99
13:35:33 13:36:31          100
```

The *v$waitclassmetric_history* table is another source of performance metrics that gives an outline of the totals of wait database metrics for all wait classes. Here are some metrics that are presented in the *v$waitclassmetric_history* view:

- **average_waiter_count:** Displays the average number of waits for the sample time interval for wait class events.

- **db_time_in_wait:** States the total database wait time spent for the specific wait class.

- **time_waited:** Shows time waited during the sample interval.

- **wait_count:** Presents the number of waits that occurred during the sample interval.

The history for recent database wait activity can be recreated by querying *v$waitclassmetric_history*, and the following query is useful for viewing the recent history for an individual wait class:

🖫 **display_file_avg_io_wait_time.sql**

```
select
   c.wait_class                 "Wait Class",
   to_char(h.begin_time,'hh24:mi:ss') "Begin",
   to_char(h.end_time,'hh24:mi:ss')   "End",
   h.average_waiter_count       "Average|Waiter",
   h.time_waited                "Time|Waited",
   h.wait_count                 "Wait|Count"
from
   v$waitclassmetric_history h,
   v$system_wait_class        c
where
   c.wait_class_id = h.wait_class_id
and
   c.wait_class = 'User I/O'
order by
   h.begin_time desc;
```

The output will look something like this:

Wait Class	Begin	End	Average Waiter	Time Waited	Wait Count
ser I/O	15:39:31	15:40:30	0	24	15
	15:38:30	15:39:31	0	0	0
	15:37:32	15:38:30	0	0	1
	15:36:30	15:37:32	0	3	7
	15:35:32	15:36:30	0	8	125
	15:34:30	15:35:32	0	66	63
	15:33:32	15:34:30	0	0	0
	15:32:30	15:33:32	0	0	1
	15:31:32	15:32:30	0	2	5
	15:30:31	15:31:32	0	1	8
	15:29:32	15:30:31	0	0	0
	15:28:31	15:29:32	0	3	2

```
15:27:32 15:28:31        0            0            0
15:26:32 15:27:32        0            0            1
15:25:32 15:26:32        0            0            0
15:24:31 15:25:32        0            0            0
15:23:32 15:24:31        0            0            8
15:22:31 15:23:32        0            0            1
15:21:33 15:22:31        0            1            9
15:20:31 15:21:33        0            2           77
15:19:33 15:20:31        0            0            5
15:18:32 15:19:33        0         2117          944
15:17:30 15:18:32        1         3210         2310
```

The *v$filemetric_history* view also allows estimation of the datafile I/O activity that has occurred during the last hour. I/O metrics such as the number of physical reads and writes for operations and blocks are reported in this view as well as averages for file reads and write times. For a particular datafile, the following query retrieves the I/O metrics:

🖫 display_file_io_avg_read_time.sql

```
select
    f.file_name,
    to_char(h.begin_time,'hh24:mi:ss') "Begin",
    to_char(h.end_time,'hh24:mi:ss') "End",
    h.average_read_time,
    h.physical_reads
from
    v$filemetric_history h,
    dba_data_files f
where
    h.file_id = f.file_id
and
    f.file_id = 3
order by
    h.begin_time desc;
```

The following is a sample of the output. This is handy, showing the average read time for each data file and the number of reads by data file:

```
FILE_NAME                 Begin     End       AVERAGE_READ_TIME PHYSICAL_READS
------------------------- --------- --------- ----------------- --------------
D:\ORACLE\SYSAUX01.DBF    15:46:30 15:56:33                  0              6
D:\ORACLE\SYSAUX01.DBF    15:36:30 15:46:30                  0              2
D:\ORACLE\SYSAUX01.DBF    15:26:32 15:36:30                  0             16
D:\ORACLE\SYSAUX01.DBF    15:16:31 15:26:32                  1           2156
D:\ORACLE\SYSAUX01.DBF    15:06:32 15:16:31                  0            314
D:\ORACLE\SYSAUX01.DBF    14:56:32 15:06:32                  1            821
D:\ORACLE\SYSAUX01.DBF    14:46:30 14:56:32                  0              0
```

Now that the basics of the *v$* performance metrics have been covered, we can take a deeper look into the *v$* views to see the advanced queries that are helpful when tuning.

Inside the Oracle Metrics

If you like to use a GUI, the Oracle Enterprise Manager (OEM) console explains and activates custom thresholds for the database metrics. Using OEM, it's possible to create custom metrics that, like predefined metrics, can be monitored by MMON. Figure 9.1 shows a sample OEM screen that offers access to database metrics.

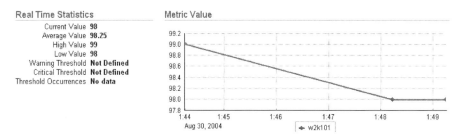

Figure 9.1: *Access database metrics in the OEM console*

If the initialization parameter *statistics_level* is set to *basic*, Oracle will not compute the database metrics, and Oracle will not collect AWR or metric statistics. To enable database metrics, set the *statistics_level* parameter to *typical*, or it can be set to a value of *all*.

Inside the *v$metric* Tables

Staring in Oracle 10g, the MMON background procedure that is used for gathering database metrics. As mentioned earlier in this chapter, MMON calculates short duration metrics every 15 seconds and long duration metrics every 60 seconds.

Database metrics are grouped by their meaning and duration. Groups of metric values based on their importance; the most important of these metrics are shown in Table 9.2:

METRIC_NAME	METRIC_UNIT
Average Users Waiting Counts	Users
Blocked User Session Count	Sessions
PGA Memory (Session)	Bytes

Table 9.2: *PGA Usage Metrics*

Below are the Oracle wait event metrics (Table 9.3):

METRIC_NAME	METRIC_UNIT
Database Time Spent Waiting (%)	% (TimeWaited /
Total Time Waited	CentiSeconds

Total Wait Counts	Waits
Number of Sessions Waiting (Event)	Sessions
Total Time Waited	CentiSeconds
Total Wait Counts	Waits

Table 9.3: *Wait Metrics*

We also have sundry I/O metrics, showing us the I/O landscape for our I/O sub-system (Table 9.4)

METRIC_NAME	METRIC_UNIT
Average File Read Time (Files-Long)	CentiSeconds Per Read
Average File Write Time (Files-Long)	CentiSeconds Per Write
Physical Block Reads (Files-Long)	Blocks
Physical Block Writes (Files-Long)	Blocks
Physical Reads (Files-Long)	Reads
Physical Writes (Files-Long)	Writes
Physical Reads (Session)	Reads
Physical Reads Ratio (Sess/Sys) %	%
Logical Reads Ratio (Sess/Sys) %	%

Table 9.4: *I/O Metrics*

We also see CPU metrics, including averages for CPU per second and CPU time per session (Table 9.5):

METRIC_NAME	METRIC_UNIT
CPU Time Per User Call	Microseconds Per Call
Elapsed Time Per User Call	Microseconds Per Call
CPU Time (Session)	CentiSeconds
CPU Usage Per Sec	CentiSeconds Per
CPU Usage Per Txn	CentiSeconds Per Txn

Table 9.5: *CPU Metrics*

While these numbers are self-explanatory, we will see how these are used in Oracle diagnostic scripts in later chapters. Now, let's move on and look at the database workload metrics.

Database Workload Metrics

Information about database workload metrics can be found in the *v$sysmetric_history*, *v$sysmetric*, and *v$sysmetric_summary* dynamic performance views. The extra-cost AWR tables (those with *dba_hist* in the names) captures snapshots of *v$sysmetric_history,* but this can also be obtained for free using the STATSPACK tables. This information can be obtained via the *dba_hist_sysmetric_history* view.

The *v$sysmetric_history* view is especially helpful because it monitors the Oracle workload in real time, and we can use this data to create real time charts based on this view. For example, the Ion for Oracle tool can be used to plot real time charts for metrics with both short and long durations. The example in Figure 9.2 shows how Ion for Oracle monitors metrics over time:

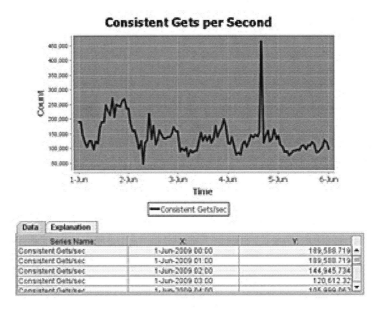

Figure 9.2: *Monitoring Workload Database Metrics using Ion*

The following code listing will retrieve database metrics with more than 10% growth in their current value compared to their average value:

💾 **metrics_growing.sql**

```
select
  to_char(m.begin_time,'hh24:mi')  "start time",
  to_char(m.end_time,'hh24:mi')    "end time",
  m.value                          "current value",
  s.average                        "average value",
  m.metric_name,
  m.metric_unit
from
  v$sysmetric          m,
  v$sysmetric_summary s
where
  m.metric_id = s.metric_id
and
  s.average > 0
and
  ((m.value - s.average)/s.average)*100 >= 10
and
  lower(m.metric_name) not like '%ratio%';
```

The current and average values for metrics meeting the criteria of interest are then displayed:

```
Start End T Curr Val Avg Val METRIC_NAME              METRIC_UNIT
----- ----- -------- ------- ----------------------- ----------------------
15:42 15:43       29      18 User Calls Per Txn       Calls Per Txn
15:42 15:43       63      31 Rows Per Sort            Rows Per Sort
15:42 15:43        5       3 CPU Usage Per Sec        CentiSeconds Per Second
15:42 15:43      294     180 CPU Usage Per Txn        CentiSeconds Per Txn
15:42 15:43       29      26 Current Logons Count     Logons
15:42 15:43      301     225 Response Time Per Txn    CentiSeconds Per Txn
15:42 15:43       17      15 Process Limit %          % Processes/Limit
15:42 15:43       18      16 Session Limit %          % Sessions/Limit
15:42 15:43        5       3 Database Time Per Sec    CentiSeconds Per Second
15:43 15:43       21      18 User Calls Per Txn       Calls Per Txn
15:43 15:43        7       3 Database Time Per Sec    CentiSeconds Per Second
```

By using the above script output, we can identify the database metrics that have changed from their average values and use this script to create exception reports.

This is done using exception thresholds in the queries. The AWR also takes snapshots for the *v$sysmetric_summary* view which can be found through the *dba_hist_sysmetric_summary* view. It is possible to view usual activity occurring in the database by using this report, which provides a window into the database.

Oracle metrics can also be monitored on a session-level basis. The *v$sessmetric* view has a single row per current session, which gives an account of the following metrics:

- CPU usage by session

- Number of physical reads

- PGA memory consumption

- Numbers of hard and soft parses

- Physical and logical read ratios

Oracle sessions can be monitored to alert for unusual resource utilization using the *v$sessmetric* view. Using the following query, DBAs can view a list of all sessions where CPU time greater than one percent of total database CPU time is consumed.

🖫 high_cpu_session.sql

```
select
   s.sid,
   s.username
from
  v$sessmetric sm,
  v$session   s
where
```

```
        s.sid = sm.session_id
and
    (sm.cpu/(select decode(value,0,-1)
     from
        v$sysmetric
     where
        metric_name = 'cpu usage per sec')
     *100) > 1;
```

A sample output of the query is displayed below:

```
SID     USERNAME
------  ---------------------------
33      SCOTT
19      SYSTEM
```

This query is important as it allows DBAs to quickly identify sessions that consume excess CPU resources.

Database Wait Metrics

Database wait metrics deal with database wait activity that has occurred in the recent past. The *v$sysmetric* view can be used as shown below to access the list of wait metrics that are available:

```
select
    group_name,
    metric_name,metric_unit
from
    v$metricname
where
    group_name IN ('Event Metrics', 'Event Class Metrics');
```

The following is a sample output:

```
GROUP_NAME           METRIC_NAME                         METRIC_UNIT
-------------------  ----------------------------------  -------------
Event Metrics        Total Wait Counts                   Waits
Event Metrics        Total Time Waited                   CentiSeconds
Event Metrics        Number of Sessions Waiting(Event)   Sessions
Event Class Metrics  Total Wait Counts                   Waits
Event Class Metrics  Total Time Waited                   CentiSeconds
Event Class Metrics  Database Time Spent Waiting (%)     % (TimeWaited / DBTime)
Event Class Metrics  Average Users Waiting Counts        Users
```

We can also use the *v$waitclassmetric_history* view to follow the total wait activity by grouping wait events into specific wait classes. To query the recent history for the wait class called *application*, the following code can be used:

🖫 **display_wait_class_details.sql**

```
select
   c.wait_class                        "wait class",
   to_char(h.begin_time,'hh24:mi:ss') "begin",
   to_char(h.end_time,'hh24:mi:ss')   "end",
   h.average_waiter_count,
   h.time_waited,
   h.wait_count
from
   v$waitclassmetric_history h,
   v$system_wait_class         c
where
   c.wait_class_id = h.wait_class_id
and
   c.wait_class = 'application' -- plug-in your metric name here
order by
   h.begin_time desc;
```

Below we see a running count of total user I/O for each snapshot interval:

Wait Class	Begin	End	AVERAGE_WAITER_COUNT	TIME_WAITED	WAIT_COUNT
Application	16:47:58	16:48:56	0	0	4
	16:46:56	16:47:58	0	0	26
	16:45:58	16:46:56	0	0	4
	16:44:57	16:45:58	0	0	4
	16:43:58	16:44:57	0	0	4
	16:42:57	16:43:58	0	0	4
	16:41:58	16:42:57	0	0	10
	16:40:57	16:41:58	0	0	4
	16:39:55	16:40:57	0	0	2
	16:38:57	16:39:55	0	0	4
	16:37:56	16:38:57	0	1	30
	16:36:57	16:37:56	0	0	4
	16:35:56	16:36:57	0	0	4
	16:34:58	16:35:56	0	0	4
	16:33:56	16:34:58	0	0	4
	16:32:58	16:33:56	0	0	4
	16:31:57	16:32:58	0	0	8
	16:30:59	16:31:57	0	0	4
	16:29:57	16:30:59	0	0	4
	16:28:58	16:29:57	0	0	4
	16:27:58	16:28:58	0	0	4
	16:26:56	16:27:58	0	1	38
	16:25:58	16:26:56	0	0	4
	16:24:58	16:25:58	0	0	4
	16:23:59	16:24:58	0	0	4
	16:22:58	16:23:59	0	0	4
	16:21:59	16:22:58	0	2	30

The *v$waitclassmetric* view and the *v$waitclassmetric_history* view have many of the same characteristics, except that *v$waitclassmetric* only shows wait class metrics for the most current data sample.

The *v$eventmetric* view contains a single row for every wait event, and its purpose is to deliver detailed wait metrics such as the number of waits, the number of sessions waiting during the sample interval and the wait time. The next example yields a list of non-idle wait events that have experienced the most wait time:

display_wait_event_details.sql

```
select
   to_char(m.begin_time,'hh24:mi') "start time",
   to_char(m.end_time,'hh24:mi')   "end time",
```

```
    n.name,
    m.time_waited,
    m.num_sess_waiting,
    m.wait_count
from
    v$eventmetric m,
    v$event_name  n
where
      m.event_id = n.event_id
  and n.wait_class <> 'idle'  -- add your event metric name here
  and m.time_waited > 0
order by 4 desc;
```

The resulting output shows a breakdown of all of the wait events by time. It also includes a count of the number of times each event waited during the AWR snapshot period:

```
start end t NAME                       TIME_WAITED NUM_SESS_WAITING WAIT_COUNT
----- ----- ------------------------- ----------- ---------------- --------
17:29 17:30 control file parallel write         29                0         19
17:29 17:30 latch free                           4                0          8
17:29 17:30 db file parallel write               1                0          7
```

Oracle File Metrics

The *v$filemetric_history* and the *v$filemetric* views are views that can be used for short-term datafile access alerts. For example, the *v$filemetric_history* view shows file metrics snapping data at ten-minute intervals for the preceding hour, whereas the *v$filemetric* view supplies the datafile metrics for only the most recent sample. Here is a list of the metrics in the *v$filemetric_history* view:

- Current numbers of physical read and write operations

- Current numbers of physical block reads and writes

- Average file read and write times

To see data files that experience a high current read/write I/O time exceeding the average I/O time computed, the following query can be used:

🖫 display_file_avg_io_wait_time.sql

```
select
  to_char(m.begin_time,'hh24:mi') "start time",
  to_char(m.end_time,'hh24:mi')   "end time",
  f.file_name,
  s.lstiotim                      "last i/o time",
  m.average_read_time + m.average_write_time "average i/o time"
from
  v$filemetric    m,
  dba_data_files  f,
  v$filestat      s
where
      m.file_id = f.file_id
  and s.file# = f.file_id
```

```
and s.lstiotim > (m.average_read_time + m.average_write_time);
```

The average I/O time and the last I/O time are shown in the output:

```
start end t FILE_NAME                                   Last I/O Time Avg I/O
----- ----- --------------------------------------------- ---- ---------------
12:36 12:46 D:\ORACLE\ORADATA\JANETB\SYSTEM01.DBF            6               3
12:36 12:46 D:\ORACLE\ORADATA\JANETB\UNDOTBS01.DBF           3               2
12:36 12:46 D:\ORACLE\ORADATA\JANETB\SYSAUX01.DBF           12               5
12:36 12:46 D:\ORACLE\ORADATA\JANETB\USERS01.DBF             4               7
```

Snapshots of *v$filemetric_history* views are captured within the corresponding AWR table, *wrh$_filemetric_history*.

It's important to note that the MMON process does not write a history to the AWR repository for all datafile metrics and MMON only writes snapshots of the current history that is there at the moment of the snapshot.

Therefore, you cannot use *v$filemetric_history* to recreate a sequential, all-inclusive file I/O access history. For this, you want to use *stats$filestatxs* or *dba_hist_filemetric_history*.

Oracle Service Metrics

Oracle metrics for database services are also tracked by Oracle. For example, several services for different applications accessing Oracle can be seen with the *v$services* dynamic view:

```
select * from v$services;
```

The following is a sample output:

```
SERVICE_ID NAME                     NAME_HASH NETWORK_NAME
---------- -------------------- ---------- ------------
         5 janetb               3608862068 janetb
         1 SYS$BACKGROUND        165959219
         2 SYS$USERS            3427055676
```

Two other *v$* views, *v$servicemetric_history* and *v$servicemetric*, can be employed for reporting metrics for database services. The *v$servicemetric* view shows the most recent samples for the services while the *v$servicemetric_history* view exhibits metrics for all samples during the last hour. The metrics collected for services are:

- Elapsed time per call issued through a given service
- CPU time per call issued through a given service

It is often advantageous to use the *v$servicemetric_history* view to check on database workload on a per-instance basis. The query below is an example of how recent history can be retrieved for a certain network service that was configured:

Classifying v$ Views and Metrics

389

```
select
  to_char(m.begin_time,'hh24:mi')  "start time",
  to_char(m.end_time,'hh24:mi')    "end time",
  m.service_name,
  m.elapsedpercall                 "elapsed time",
  m.cpupercall                     "cpu time"
from
  v$servicemetric_history m
where
  m.service_name = 'janetb' - add your service name here
order by
  m.end_time desc;
```

The output of this particular script might look like the following:

```
start end t service_na Elapsed Time    CPU Time
----- ----- ---------- ------------    ----------
13:16 13:17 janetb              0              0
13:15 13:16 janetb           4532           3926
13:14 13:15 janetb           5478           4897
13:13 13:14 janetb              0              0
13:12 13:13 janetb         604549         408964
13:11 13:12 janetb          13901           3111
13:10 13:11 janetb           9687           5356
13:09 13:10 janetb           7296           6533
13:08 13:09 janetb              0              0
13:07 13:08 janetb              0              0
13:06 13:07 janetb              0              0
13:05 13:06 janetb              0              0
13:04 13:05 janetb              0              0
13:03 13:04 janetb              0              0
13:02 13:03 janetb              0              0
13:01 13:02 janetb              0              0
13:00 13:01 janetb           2160           2160
12:59 13:00 janetb          11080           5270
```

Using this method, it is possible to pinpoint which application is placing a burden on the database. With this information, DBAs can correlate specific database services with their workloads.

Now that we see the metric tables, let's move into the world of the *v$* views and see what useful information they have to help us tune our Oracle database.

The Secret World of the *v$* Views

Oracle offers several wait classes that allow DBAs to evaluate wait activities. For example, a DBA can use the following statement to group all events by class in order to have a basic idea of the performance issues:

🖫 **wait_class_times.sql**

```
select
   e.wait_class,
   sum(s.total_waits),
   sum(s.time_waited)
from
   v$event_name   e,
   v$system_event s
where
   e.name = s.event
group by
   e.wait_class;
```

The output will look like this, showing each wait class, the total waits and the sum of the time waited for each class.:

WAIT_CLASS	SUM(S.TOTAL_WAITS)	SUM(S.TIME_WAITED)
Application	354	925
Commit	10,715	18,594
Concurrency	584,360	16,525
Configuration	94,415	28,140
Idle	2691,962	911,122,390
Network	99,645	2,278
Other	225,773	445,863
System I/O	467,075	275,631
User I/O	298,723	335,344

Oracle introduced several new views which also help us by providing more thoroughly analyzing wait-related statistics:

- *v$system_wait_class:* This provides the instance-wide time totals for each class of wait events.

- *v$session_wait_class:* This provides the total time spent in each class of the wait event on a per session basis. DBAs could use this view as one of the primary methods for identifying where an individual session waits the longest amount of time.

- *v$event_histogram:* This shows a histogram of the number of waits, the total wait time and the maximum wait on a wait event basis. The DBA can also create a histogram that displays the frequency of wait events for a wide range of durations, as well as giving information that helps determine whether a wait event is a repeating problem or a unique event. The following query can be used in viewing this type of information. Note that idle events are filtered out.

```
select
   event,
   wait_time_milli,
   wait_count
from
   v$event_histogram
where
   event in
        (select name
         from   v$event_name
         where  wait_class not in ('idle'))
order by 1,2
```

The Secret World of the v$ Views

- **_v$session_wait_history_:** Displays the last ten wait events for each active session. The last ten wait events for all sessions, as they occurred for every session, can be retrieved using a code listing like the following:

```
select
    a.sid,
    b.username,
    a.seq#,
    a.event,
    a.wait_time
from
    v$session_wait_history a,
    v$session b
where
    a.sid = b.sid
and
    b.username is not null
order by 1,3
```

- **_v$file_histogram_:** This shows a histogram of all single block reads on a per file basis. This histogram can be used to determine whether a unique issue or a regular occurrence causes a specific bottleneck. The _v$file_histogram_ view displays the number of I/O wait events over a range of values which provides more in-depth data.

- **_v$temp_histogram_:** This displays, on a per tempfile basis, a histogram of all single block reads

When examining where a database is spending most of its time, the best place to start is with the _v$system_wait_class_ view. To take a quick glimpse at system-wide wait activity, the following query can be used to quickly identify potential problem areas:

🖫 display_wait_class_pct.sql

```
column total_waits  format 999,999,999
column pct_waits     format 99.99
column time_waited  format 999,999,999
column pct_time      format 99.99
column wait_class    format a20

select   wait_class,
         total_waits,
         round(100 * (total_waits / sum_waits),2) pct_waits,
         time_waited,
         round(100 * (time_waited / sum_time),2) pct_time
from
(select wait_class,
        total_waits,
        time_waited
from     v$system_wait_class
where    wait_class != 'idle'),
(select  sum(total_waits) sum_waits,
         sum(time_waited) sum_time
from     v$system_wait_class
where    wait_class != 'idle')
order by 5 desc;
```

The output of the query might look like this:

```
WAIT_CLASS           TOTAL_WAITS  PCT_WAITS  TIME_WAITED  PCT_TIME
-------------------- ------------ ---------- ------------ --------
Other                     747,485       4.50      957,039    50.37
System I/O              4,182,722      25.18      771,654    40.62
User I/O                  188,448       1.13       81,534     4.29
Commit                    341,861       2.06       53,797     2.83
Application             1,216,251       7.32       15,341      .81
Configuration             262,214       1.58        7,640      .40
Network                 9,664,173      58.17        7,623      .40
Concurrency                10,618        .06        5,279      .28
```

This listing sums up information about the wait events by wait classes. It also provides an overview of the involvement of every wait class in relation to the total database response time. For example, in the query above, it can be seen that the wait events that belong to the wait class "Other" were causing the most database wait time.

The Active Session History *v$* View

The *v$active_session_history* view was introduced by Oracle in 10g to maintain a history for recent active sessions' activity. A database session is deemed to be active when it is utilizing CPU time or waiting for an event that does not belong to the idle wait class. Snapshots of active database sessions are taken every second without placing any serious overhead on the system.

This view also contains quite a bit of information from the *v$session* view, and it also includes the *sample_time* column. This *sample_time* column indicates a time in the past when a session was waiting for a resource or doing some work. When sampling is performed, the *v$active_session_history* view contains a single row for each session.

With the *v$active_session_history* tool, the DBA can now trace sessions without using the 10046 extended tracing events. By employing only SQL queries, all tracing can be performed without reviewing raw trace files or using the cumbersome TKPROF utility.

Session history is maintained by Oracle in the SGA via a circular memory buffer. Because of this, the higher the workload, the smaller the amount of time session history that is available in the *v$active_session_history* ASH view.

It is important to remember that the *dba_hist_active_sess_history* view stores ASH history for a longer time period, and the *dba_hist_active_sess_history* view only stores ASH data snapshots for the times that AWR snapshots were also taken.

For example, if a session is experiencing delays, a DBA would need to identify the SQL statement that the session is executing along with the wait events associated with that session for the desired time period. To gather that information for a particular time period, the following query can be used:

💾 display_sql_time_range.sql

```
select
   c.sql_text,
   b.name,
   count(*),
   sum(time_waited)
from
   v$active_session_history a,
   v$event_name b,
   v$sqlarea c
where
   a.sample_time between '10-JUL-09 09:57:00 PM' and
                         '10-JUL-09 09:59:00 PM'
and
   a.event# = b.event#
and
   a.session_id= 123
and
   a.sql_id = c.sql_id
group by
   c.sql_text, b.name;
```

In order to get the name of the object, simply join the *current_obj#* column with the *dba_objects* view. To see the name of the datafile accessed, join the *current_obj#* column with the *current_file#* column using *dba_data_files*. To identify a particular block that caused a wait event, the *current_block#* column can be used.

Busy data blocks, hot datafiles and objects that are being accessed by sessions more frequently than others can also be identified. The listing below will reveal hot datafiles that triggered the most wait times while the session was being accessed:

💾 display_ash_file_waits.sql

```
select
  f.file_name         "data file",
  count(*)            "wait number",
  sum(h.time_waited) "total time waited"
from
  v$active_session_history h,
  dba_data_files          f
where
  h.current_file# = f.file_id
group by f.file_name
order by 3 desc;
```

The sample output looks like:

Data File	Wait Number	Total Time Waited
D:\ORACLE\ORADATA\JANETB\SYSAUX01.DBF	5514	994398837
D:\ORACLE\ORADATA\JANETB\SYSTEM01.DBF	2579	930483678
D:\ORACLE\ORADATA\JANETB\UNDOTBS01.DBF	245	7727218

Statistically, the *v$active_session_history* view is the most useful because it reliably catches the activity that is causing the most waits and resource consumption in a database. However, the *v$active_session_history* view is not as reliable as the 10046 trace for catching fast, transient activity.

The following queries are examples of how to use the *v$active_session_history* view to find acute performance problems. This view shows those resources that were in high demand during the previous hour. Note that none of the following four queries in this section include idle wait events.

🖫 **display_wait_event_tot_time.sql**

```
select
  h.event "wait event",
  sum(h.wait_time + h.time_waited) "total wait time"
from
  v$active_session_history h,
  v$event_name e
where
      h.sample_time between sysdate - 1/24 and sysdate
  and h.event_id = e.event_id
  and e.wait_class <> 'idle'
group by h.event
order by 2 desc;
```

The output looks like the following:

```
Wait Event                        Total Wait Time
------------------------------    ---------------
Queue Monitor Task Wait                10,256,950
class slave wait                       10,242,904
log file switch completion              5,142,555
control file parallel write             4,813,121
db file sequential read                   334,871
process startup                           232,137
log file sync                             203,087
latch free                                 36,934
log buffer space                           25,090
latch: redo allocation                     22,444
db file parallel write                        714
db file scattered read                        470
log file parallel write                       182
direct path read temp                         169
control file sequential read                  160
direct path write temp                        112
```

This query reveals database users who experienced, in the last hour, the most wait times.

🖫 **display_ash_high_wait_time.sql**

```
select
  s.sid,
  s.username,
  sum(h.wait_time + h.time_waited) "total wait time"
```

```
from
  v$active_session_history h,
  v$session              s,
  v$event_name           e
where
      h.sample_time between sysdate - 1/24 and sysdate
  and h.session_id = s.sid
  and e.event_id = h.event_id
  and e.wait_class <> 'idle'
  and s.username is not null
group by
  s.sid, s.username
order by 3;
```

Here is the output, showing total wait time by user ID:

```
       SID USERNAME                            Total Wait Time
---------- ------------------------------- ---------------
       137 DABR                                      17,955
       144 SPV                                       12,334
       152 SCOTT                                      3,449
```

This third query retrieves the SQL statements that experienced high wait time during the last hour:

🖫 display_ash_sql_last_hour_time.sql

```
select
   h.user_id,
   u.username,
   sql.sql_text,
   sum(h.wait_time + h.time_waited) "total wait time"
from
  v$active_session_history h,
  v$sqlarea sql,
  dba_users u,
  v$event_name e
where
      h.sample_time between sysdate - 1/24 and sysdate
  and h.sql_id = sql.sql_id
  and h.user_id = u.user_id
  and h.sql_id is not null
  and e.event_id = h.event_id
  and e.wait_class <> 'idle'
group by
  h.user_id,sql.sql_text, u.username
order by 4 desc;
```

The output below shows the SQL with the highest wait time, a super useful report when seeking SQL tuning opportunities:

```
  USER_ID USERNAME   SQL_TEXT                                                  total wait time
--------- ---------- -------------------------------------------------------- ---------------
        0 SYS        begin prvt_hdm.auto_execute( :db_id, :inst_id, :end              37107
                      _snap ); end;

        0 SYS                begin          dbms_rcvman.setDatabase(upper             35378
                      (:dbname:dbname_i),:rlgscn,:rlgtime,:fhdbi:fhdbi_i);
                      end;

       69 DABR       select   h.history.user_id,   u.username,     sql           8004
                      .sql_text,    sum(h.wait_time + h.time_waited) "To
                      tal Wait Time" from   v$active_session_history h,
```

		v$sqlarea sql, dba_users u where h.sample_time between sysdate - 1/24 and sysdate and h.sql_id = sql.sql_id and h.user_id = u.user_id and h.SQL_ID is not null group by h.user_id,sql.sql_text, u.username order by 4	
0	SYS	select pos#,intcol#,col#,spare1,bo#,spare2 from icol$ where obj#=:1	594
0	SYS	select /*+ rule */ bucket_cnt, row_cnt, cache_cnt, null_cnt, timestamp#, sample_size, minimum, maximum, distcnt, lowval, hival, density, col#, spare1, spare2, avgcln from hist_head$ where obj#=:1 and intcol#=:2	142
69	DABR	select h.user_id, u.username, sql.sql_text, sum(h.wait_time + h.time_waited) "Total Wait Time" from v$active_session_history h, v$sqlarea sql, dba_users u where h.sample_time between sysdate - 1/24 and sysdate and h.sql_id = sql.sql_id and h.user_id = u.user_id and h.SQL_ID is not null group by h.user_id,sql.sql_text, u.username order by 4	121
69	DABR	select s.sid, s.username, sum(h.wait_time + h.time_waited) "Total Wait Time" from v$active_session_history h, v$session s, v$event_name e where h.sample_time between sysdate - 1/24 and sysdate and h.session_id = s.sid and e.EVENT_ID = h.EVENT_ID and e.WAIT_CLASS <> 'Idle' and s.username is not null group by s.sid, s.username order by 3	11

Lastly, this query shows a list of the database objects that have caused the most wait times during the last hour.

🖫 display_ash_object_waits_last_hour.sql

```
select
  o.owner,
  o.object_name,
  o.object_type,
  sum(h.wait_time + h.time_waited) "total wait time"
from
  v$active_session_history h,
  dba_objects o,
  v$event_name e
where
     h.sample_time between sysdate - 1/24 and sysdate
  and h.current_obj# = o.object_id
  and e.event_id = h.event_id
  and e.wait_class <> 'idle'
group by
  o.owner, o.object_name, o.object_type
order by 4 desc
```

Conclusion

Oracle has many powerful tools within the data dictionary dynamic performance views, perfect for short-term Oracle monitoring. The *v$* dynamic views serve as sources for real-time troubleshooting of the current database workload and health.   For more complete details on using the dynamic performance views, see Chapter 5, *Oracle Troubleshooting*.

This chapter contained examples of how the *v$* views and ASH views provide valuable performance reports. It should now be clear that Oracle's innovative time model approach and corresponding *v$* views provide detailed information about where Oracle spends its processing time. These are extremely powerful tools in the hands of an astute Oracle DBA since the key to performance tuning is the ability to successfully identify, isolate, and correct performance issues.

The next chapter will examine the wait event approach to Oracle tuning.

Oracle Wait Event Tuning

Fighting excessive waits requires dexterity and skill!

The Oracle Wait Event Model

There are many different approaches to Oracle tuning. Although some people may favor one approach over another, the true Oracle tuning professional uses every Oracle tuning tools in the arsenal.

We were first introduced to wait events in Oracle 7 via the cumbersome 10046 trace dumps. Wait events have become increasingly popular with the introduction of the Oracle Wait Interface (OWI), a somewhat complex and cumbersome wait exposure interface that began with *v$* tables. This wait event interface got a major boost in Oracle with the advent of the metrics tables and the ASH tables, where the Oracle MMON process directly gathers Oracle wait details for current and recent sessions.

Chapter 5 showed us how to work with Automated Session History (ASH) tables and we know that these tables show how Oracle collects statistics for real-time wait events. This chapter will examine how to tune Oracle by examining these wait events.

The Oracle wait event interface has changed and evolved with each new release of Oracle, and the OWI provides us with valuable insights into where time is being consumed by SQL statements and sessions.

As a quick review, we know that wait event information is gathered by the Oracle MMON background process, stored in intermediate *x$* structures in a circular SGA buffer and later transferred to the Oracle metric tables and if you have purchased AWR, the *dba_hist* tables. Prior to Oracle 10g, capturing wait event information was a cumbersome process involving the setting of special events like 10046 and the reading of complex trace dumps as shown below:

```
PARSING IN CURSOR #1 len=42 dep=0 uid=47 oct=3 lid=47
                     tim=2941832446 hv=1811837456 ad='69b05900'
select *
from sapr3.vbap
where vlelm < sysdate
END OF STMT
PARSE #1:c=0,e=870,p=0,cr=0,cu=0,mis=1,r=0,
        dep=0,og=0,tim=2941832432
BINDS #1:
 bind 0: dty=2 mxl=22(22) mal=00 scl=00 pre=00
         oacflg=03 oacfl2=0 size=24 offset=0
   bfp=04af96b8 bln=22 avl=01 flg=05
   value=0
EXEC #1:c=0,e=950,p=0,cr=0,cu=0,mis=0,r=0,dep=0,
        og=4,tim=2941835605
WAIT #1: nam='SQL*Net message to client' ela= 6
        p1=1111838976 p2=1 p3=0
FETCH #1:c=0,e=148,p=0,cr=3,cu=0,mis=0,r=1,dep=0,
        og=4,tim=2941836146
WAIT #1: nam='SQL*Net message from client' ela= 543
        p1=1111838976 p2=1 p3=0
WAIT #1: nam='SQL*Net message to client' ela= 4
        p1=1111838976 p2=1 p3=0
```

The Automated Session History (ASH) tables revolutionized Oracle wait event tuning. For more details on wait event tuning with ASH, see Chapter 5, *Oracle Troubleshooting*.

The AWR Wait Event Tables

Before the release of Oracle 10g, we had to rely on the *v$session_wait* and *v$system_event* views in order to examine detailed information about the wait state for ongoing Oracle transactions. Additionally, capturing wait event information was an awkward process. This process involved the setting of special events such as the 10046 trace dump as well as the reading of other complex trace dumps. Fortunately, Oracle has simplified the way that wait event information is captured by creating a wealth of new *v$* and *wrh$* views relating to Oracle wait events.

Oracle's Automatic Session History (ASH) captures statistics on more than 800 specific wait events. New wait events are the result of Oracle breaking down the latch waits into their individual components and dividing enqueue waits (locks) into a finer level of granularity.

The foundation concept of the ASH architecture is called the time model, and Oracle has introduced several important wait event *v$* views as shown in Table 10.1:

v$ VIEW	dba_hist VIEW
v$active_sess_hist	dba_hist_active_sess_history
v$sys_time_model	dba_hist_sys_time_model
v$active_session_history	dba_hist_active_sess_history
v$event_histogram	No equivalent DBA view

Table 10.1: *The Oracle wait event v$ views*

Unlike the old-fashioned *v$session* and *v$session_wait* views where waits could only be seen at the exact instant in which they occurred, the *v$session_wait_history* and *v$sys_time_model* views allow Oracle to capture details on system waits in a time-series mode. Fortunately, Oracle has simplified the way that wait event information is captured and there is a wealth of *v$* and *wrh$* views relating to Oracle wait events as shown in Figure 10.1.

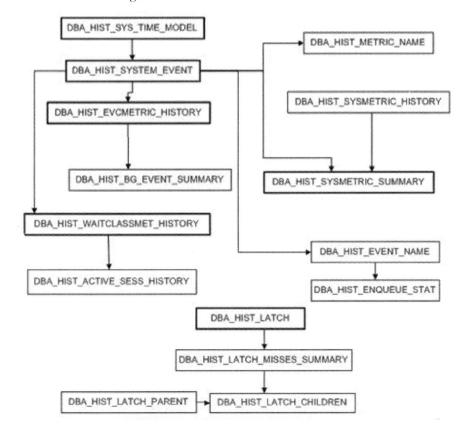

Figure 10.1: *Some common dba_hist views of Oracle event data*

Each new release has introduced some new wait events, and the 11g database kernel now captures statistics on more than 800 specific wait events. These new wait events are the result of Oracle breaking out their latch waits into their individual components and breaking out enqueue waits, or locks, into a finer level of granularity.

Get the proper license!

Remember, the AWR and ASH tables are separate, extra cost components, requiring the Oracle Tuning Pack and Oracle Diagnostic Pack. See your CSR for pricing details.

After the *x$* structures are materialized in the *v$active_session_history* and *v$session_wait_history* views, a new AWR snapshot transfers and aggregates the events into corresponding *dba_hist_active_sess_history* and other *dba_hist* tables. Table 10.2 below shows some of the most important Oracle ASH wait event tables:

dba_hist_active_session_history	dba_hist_active_session_history_bl
dba_hist_bg_event_summary	dba_hist_event_name
dba_hist_metric_name	dba_hist_sessmetric_history
dba_hist_sys_time_model	dba_hist_sys_time_model_bl
dba_hist_sysmetric_history	dba_hist_sysmetric_summary
dba_hist_sysstat	dba_hist_sysstat_bl
dba_hist_system_event	dba_hist_system_event_bl
dba_hist_waitclassmetric_history	dba_hist_waitstat
dba_hist_waitstat_	

Table 10.2: *Oracle wait event dba_hist tables*

The following section begins with a quick review of Oracle wait events in order to assist users' understanding of how they can help identify and tune bottlenecks in the database. This involves stepping back and exploring why wait event tuning is a useful tool for Oracle tuning. As a reminder, there is no single Oracle tuning technique, SQL tuning, parameter tuning, ratio tuning and such that does it all, and wait event tuning is just another weapon in the Oracle tuning arsenal.

Why Wait Event Tuning for Oracle?

Wait event tuning has always been mysterious, mainly because wait events happen so fast that it is often difficult to see what is happening without taking a detailed task dump. When using ASH, not only can specific details about individual sessions, SQL statements, and users be seen, but wait information can be tracked over periods of time revealing the all important signatures that help schedule just-in-time resources to relieve instance related wait bottlenecks.

Time-based wait tuning is especially useful for tracking changes to SQL execution over time as well as database-wide stress. The Oracle ASH tables can be used to show trends in wait events over long time periods, and fluctuations in waits can often provide useful information.

A top-down approach starts at a high level and shows scripts that can be used to track system wide events and show events for background processes. Time-based wait event analysis for Oracle can be broken down into several areas:

- **External wait event analysis:** The advent of the new mainframe-like SMP servers means that servers may share hardware resources with dozens of other applications and databases. These external resources demand server resources such as RAM, CPU, and disk channels, which can have an effect on Oracle waits. The ASH tables provide insights into the external network waits; for example, the SQL*Net waits, in addition to disk waits like the db file sequential and scattered read waits.

- **Internal wait event analysis:** Oracle internal mechanisms like buffer busy waits and latch waits can change over time, depending on the overall database load. Time-series analysis with the ASH tables allows the DBA to find the cause of internal bottlenecks, even after the transaction has completed.

- **Session-level wait event analysis:** Oracle resources associated with a session can be traced to the exact external or internal wait event.

- **SQL event analysis:** In most OLTP systems, the same SQL statements may execute thousands of times per hour. Because SQL is the interface between applications and Oracle, tracing waits on an SQL statement over time can be especially useful.

When running the system-wide time-based wait event scripts, the DBA will be able to identify areas where the database is spending most of its time waiting.

Addressing Wait Bottlenecks

High waits on events do not always indicate a bottleneck or a problem. As database users say: "*time takes time.*" Every Oracle database, no matter how well tuned, spends time performing activities, and every database has a bottleneck. High waits may indicate a bottleneck, but some waits are a normal part of database operations.

Do not lose the wait data!

Oracle wait information is collected in a circular SGA buffer and wait event information may be lost if this buffer rolls over between the AWR snapshot interval.

In general, the system wide wait events show where the database spends most of its time. For example, high waits on *db file sequential reads* events may indicate a disk bottleneck, but the average disk queue length for each disk spindle must be checked to be sure that these waits are abnormal.

In one case, an Oracle shop ran the script for system-wide wait events and discovered that their RAID-5 configuration was causing a huge amount of disk enqueues. This shop reorganized their disk to RAID 0+1 and experienced a 300% performance improvement for the whole database. The following is just a small sample of some common wait bottlenecks:

- **SQL*Net waits:** High SQL*Net waits could be due to poor encapsulation of SQL statements within the application. For example, a screen may need data from six different tables, and there is much less network traffic and database overhead if all of the information for an online screen is captured in a single trip to the database. High SQL*Net waits can also signify an error in the application programming logic or a serious network problem.

- *parallel query dequeue* **waits:** The default degree of parallelism for database objects needs to be checked, and parallelism at the system level should be turned off using specific parallel hints. The value of *parallel_threads_per_cpu* should be checked and adjusted to reduce *automatic parallel query* and its influence on the CBO.

- *db file scattered reads* **waits:** These are caused by competing demands for large-table full-table scans and are the most common waits found in data warehouse and decision support systems.

- *db file sequential reads* **waits:** These waits are sometimes due to segment header contention on hot rows or indexes, but can also be due to disk-level contention. The first step when addressing this bottleneck is to increase the number of freelists on the indexes. If the waits persist, the offending index should be striped across multiple disk spindles. The DBA should check for segment header contention/waits on index headers or create multiple segment header blocks for stressed indexes using *alter index xxx storage (freelists 4)*. The DBA could also distribute heavy impact tables and indexes onto a faster disk or stripe the rows across more data blocks by setting a high *pctfree* for a table and reorganizing the table.

These are very general wait conditions, and they can sometimes be fixed by changing parameters or object characteristics.

Systemwide Wait Event Tuning

Sometimes, a major external problem such as bad disk RAID can cause an entire database to run slowly. Because of this, it is always a good idea to start with a listing of the AWR top five wait event listing. Detailed wait event tuning will not do much good until all database-wide issues have been fixed.

Common database-wide wait bottleneck issues often include network, CPU, disk and instance bottlenecks. The following sections will provide a closer look at using the top five timed event list from the AWR report to search for global wait issues.

Network Wait Bottlenecks

A slow network can be a nightmare. Network overload can be caused by Oracle TNS issues or by an inefficient application that makes too many trips to the Oracle database to fetch screen data. Network bottlenecks are very common in distributed systems and those with high network traffic. They are manifested as SQL*Net wait events, similar to this example where 99% of the time is being spent in SQL*net activities:

```
Top 5 Timed Events
~~~~~~~~~~~~~~~~~~~                                     % Total
Event                         Waits    Time (cs)   Wt Time
-----------------------      --------   ---------   --------
SQL*Net more data to client  3,914,935  9,475,372    99.76
db file sequential read      1,367,659      6,129      .06
db file parallel write           7,582      5,001      .05
rdbms ipc reply                     26      4,612      .05
db file scattered read          16,886      2,446      .03
```

CPU Wait Bottlenecks

A database may be CPU-bound due to a real overload of the CPU banks. In this case, the problem can be remedied by upgrading to faster processors or adding more processors to the system. High CPU consumption can also be due to un-tuned SQL causing excessive logical I/O in the form of consistent gets or by contention within the shared pool, such as the total lack of SQL bind variables. The following top five events list shows a CPU-constrained database.

```
Top 5 Timed Events
~~~~~~~~~~~~~~~~~~~                                    % Total
Event                         Waits    Time (s)   Ela Time
-----------------------      --------   ---------   --------
CPU time                        4,851      4,042     55.76
db file sequential read         1,968      1,997     27.55
log file sync                 299,097        369      5.08
db file scattered read         53,031        330      4.55
log file parallel write       302,680        190      2.62
```

In this example, it is easy to see that this system is clearly CPU-bound with 55% of the processing time being spent in the CPU.

As a general rule, a server is CPU-bound when the number of processes in the execution queue exceeds the number of CPUs on the server. Also note that recursive SQL is a factor. CPU consumption is measured even though the single invocation of a stored procedure may have a dozen CPU-intensive SQL statements within the body of the procedure. For a complete treatment of finding CPU enqueues, see the *vmstat* scripts in Chapter 12, *Server and Network Tuning*.

To verify that a top-five wait event of the CPU is not caused by bad recursive SQL, you will need to explore the details for *"parse time CPU"*, *"CPU used by this session"* and *"recursive CPU usage"*. In other words, a top-five wait event may not show *"CPU other"* as a major event. This can be very misleading.

Disk Wait Bottlenecks

A suboptimal RAID configuration can make even a well-tuned Oracle database slow to a crawl. The following example shows an I/O bound database:

```
Top 5 Timed Events
```

```
                                                   % Total
Event                       Waits      Time (s)    Ela Time
-------------------------   --------   ----------  --------
db file sequential read     2,598 7,146     48.54
db file scattered read      25,519 3,246    22.04
library cache load lock     673    1,363           9.26
CPU time                           1,154           7.83
log file parallel write     19,157 837            5.68
```

Excessive *db file sequential read* waits on an OLTP database might indicate a suboptimal disk subsystem or configuration issues with the disk array. High I/O waits on *db file scatter read* waits associated with large-table full-table scans may not always indicate a problem, but they are most commonly found on these kinds of databases:

- Data warehouse and Decision Support applications

- 32-bit Oracle systems with SGAs of less than 1.5 gigabytes

- Databases that do not have enough buffer cache space to cache their working set of frequently referenced objects

For more details on tuning disk I/O bottlenecks, see Chapter 13, *Tuning the I/O Subsystem*, or the book *Oracle Disk I/O Tuning*, from Rampant TechPress.

Instance Wait Bottlenecks

Suboptimal settings for *init.ora* parameters, like *optimizer_mode*, *optimizer_index_cost_adj*, and *cursor_sharing*, can precipitate database-wide wait problems. It is also possible to see object-level waits caused by suboptimal settings for *freelists*, *freelist_groups*, and other *object* parameters.

Now that holistic wait exploration has been covered, it is time to explore the Oracle *dba_hist* views that are used to create time-series performance reports, both manually and within Oracle Enterprise Manager. The next section will look at the wait events classification hierarchy.

Not All Events Are Created Equal

The information contained in the AWR is substantial, tracking over 800 distinct wait events. These events are organized into groups called Wait Classes in order to help organize the large number of wait events. These classes are listed in Table 10.3.

ADMINISTRATIVE WAIT CLASS EVENTS	APPLICATION WAIT CLASS EVENTS
Cluster	Commit
Concurrency	Configuration
Idle	Network
Other	Scheduler
System I/O	User I/O

Table 10.3: *Oracle wait event classes*

Detailed information on the waits that are occurring in a specific wait class is available in other areas of the repository. The following script lists the specific wait events that are part of each wait class.

💾 wait_class_events.sql

```
break on wait_class skip 1

column event_name format a40
column wait_class format a20

select
  wait_class,
  event_name
from
  dba_hist_event_name
order by
  wait_class,

  event_name;
```

Because of the large number of events, it is often advisable to use a *where* clause to restrict the output of the wait class to what is most relevant to the DBA. Some of the events for the System I/O and User I/O are shown below as an example:

```
WAIT_CLASS     EVENT_NAME
----------     -----------------------------
System I/O     db file parallel write
               io done
               kfk: async disk IO
               ksfd: async disk IO
               log file parallel write
               log file sequential read
               log file single write
               recovery read

User I/O       BFILE read
               buffer read retry
               db file parallel read
               db file scattered read
               db file sequential read
               db file single write
```

The listing above is useful if the AWR top five timed events report indicates a significant amount of time spent on I/O related waits.

Wait events that are superfluous to the DBA's tuning effort can also be filtered out. For example, idle events can be filtered out by adding *where wait_class <> 'Idle'* into the ASH queries. Table 10.4 below shows the system idle wait events that usually have no meaningful information to DBAs performing Oracle bottleneck analysis.

Why Wait Event Tuning for Oracle?   **407**

dispatcher timer	lock element cleanup
Null event	parallel query dequeue wait
parallel query idle wait - Slaves	pipe get
PL/SQL lock timer	pmon timer
rdbms ipc message	slave wait
smon timer	SQL*Net break/reset to client
SQL*Net message from client	SQL*Net message to client
SQL*Net more data to client	virtual circuit status

Table 10.4: *Oracle idle events*

The next section will provide a look inside the most useful ASH tables for time-series wait event tuning.

Inside the Real-time *V$* Wait Events

As covered in Chapter 3, the foundation of the ASH architecture is the time model, and Oracle has introduced several important wait event *v$* views relating to ASH. Table 10.5 shows some *v$* equivalents to *dba_hist* views.

v$ VIEW	dba_hist VIEW
v$active_sess_hist	dba_hist_active_sess_history
v$sys_time_model	dba_hist_sys_time_model
v$active_session_history	dba_hist_active_sess_history
v$event_histogram	No equivalent DBA view

Table 10.5: *Oracle v$ equivalents to ASH wait event tables*

The main components of the OWI interface are the dynamic performance views: *v$session_wait* and *v$session_event* as shown in Figure 10.2.

Figure 10.2: *The v$ event structures in Oracle*

These *v$* views are in-memory structures that feed data to the ASH tables which provide time-series wait event information.

The ASH samples data for wait events every second and tracks the waits in the new *v$active_sess_hist* view. Before looking into the *wrh$* and ASH tables, it will be useful to take a quick tour of the important *v$* wait event views. For more details on wait event tuning with ASH, see Chapter 5, *Oracle Troubleshooting*.

Inside *v$session_wait*

The *v$session_wait* view displays information about wait events for which active sessions are currently waiting. The following is the description of this view, and it contains some very useful columns, especially the *P1* and *P2* columns, which can be de-referenced with other views to find the specific objects associated with the wait events.

```
SQL> desc v$session_wait
```

```
Name                           Null?    Type
------------------------------ -------- -----------
SID                                     NUMBER
SEQ#                                    NUMBER
EVENT                                   VARCHAR2(64)
P1TEXT                                  VARCHAR2(64)
P1                                      NUMBER
P1RAW                                   RAW(4)
P2TEXT                                  VARCHAR2(64)
P2                                      NUMBER
P2RAW                                   RAW(4)
P3TEXT                                  VARCHAR2(64)
P3                                      NUMBER
P3RAW                                   RAW(4)
WAIT_CLASS_ID                           NUMBER
WAIT_CLASS#                             NUMBER
WAIT_CLASS                              VARCHAR2(64)
WAIT_TIME                               NUMBER
SECONDS_IN_WAIT                         NUMBER
STATE                                   VARCHAR2(19)
```

With *v$session_wait*, wait class columns show how various wait events can be grouped into the related areas of processing, including network waits, application waits, idle waits and concurrency waits.

The *v$session_wait* view also provides a dynamic snapshot of the wait events for specific sessions, and each wait event contains other parameters that provide additional information about the event. For example, if a particular session waits for a *buffer busy waits* event, the database object causing this wait event can easily be determined using the following query:

```
select
   username,
   event,
   p1,
   p2
from
   v$session_wait
where
   sid = 74;
```

The output of this query for a particular session with SID 74 would look something like this:

```
USERNAME   EVENT               SID   P1   P2
---------- ----------------    ---   --   ---
PCS        buffer busy waits    74    4   155
```

Columns *P1* and *P2* allow the DBA to determine the file and block numbers that caused this wait event. The query below retrieves the object name that owns data block 155, the value of *P2* above:

```
select
  segment_name,
  segment_type
from
  dba_extents
where
  file_id = 4
and
  155 between
  (block_id and block_id + blocks - 1);
```

```
SEGMENT_NAME                         SEGMENT_TYPE
------------------------------------ ---------------
orders                               TABLE
```

The above output shows that the table named *orders* caused this wait event, a very useful clue when tuning the SQL within this session.

Inside *v$session_event*

The *v$session_event* view shows the cumulative time that each session has spent waiting for a particular event to complete. Unlike the *v$session_wait* view, the *v$session_event* view collects aggregate wait information and organizes this information by System ID (SID) and a named event.

```
SQL> desc v$session_event
```

```
Name              Null?     Type
----------------- --------- -----------
SID                         NUMBER
EVENT                       VARCHAR2(64)
TOTAL_WAITS                 NUMBER
TOTAL_TIMEOUTS              NUMBER
TIME_WAITED                 NUMBER
AVERAGE_WAIT                NUMBER
MAX_WAIT                    NUMBER
```

The *v$session_event* view is very helpful when used in real life tuning. In this example, the end users are plagued by slow response time when running a production application.

In some ERP applications, like Oracle Applications and SAP, a single user account is used to pre-spawn multiple connections to Oracle. Because of this, individual users connect via the application server and not directly to Oracle. In these cases, a DBA can issue the following statement to determine the particular event application for which the sessions are waiting:

🖫   **session_time_waited.sql**

```
select
   se.event,
   sum(se.total_waits),
   sum(se.total_timeouts),
   sum(se.time_waited/100) time_waited
from
   v$session_event se,
   v$session       sess
where
   sess.username = 'SAPR3'
and
   sess.sid = se.sid
group by
   se.event
order by 2 desc;
```

The output of this script might look like the following:

```
                    Waits for user SAPR3

                         SUM    SUM          TIME
EVENT                    WAITS  TIMEOUTS     WAITED
----------------------   -----  ---------    ------
SQL*Net message to client    7,824  0              .06
SQL*Net message from client  7,812  0       312,969.73
db file sequential read      3,199  0            10.23
SQL*Net more data to client    590  0              .08
SQL*Net break/reset to client  418  0               .2
direct path read               328  0              .01
SQL*Net more data from client   78  0             3.29
latch free                      62  10             .08
db file scattered read          56  0              .75
log file sync                   47  0              .96
direct path write               32  0               .4
file open                       32  0                0
library cache pin               13  0                0
log file switch completion       3  0              .53
```

From the listing above, it can be figured that end users spend most of their wait time waiting on the event "SQL*Net message from client". This may indicate that there is some network-related issue causing clients excessive wait time when sending data to the database server.

The old-fashioned *v$session* and *v$session_wait* accumulation views were designed where waits could only be seen at the exact instant when they occurred. The new *v$session_wait_history* and *v$sys_time_model* views, on the other hand, allow Oracle to capture system waits details in a time-series mode. The following scripts will utilize ASH and AWR tables and show how time series wait event tuning can give DBAs unprecedented insights.

The *dba_hist_waitclassmet_history* table contains summary information for these categories. There are often instances when summary information can provide clues as to the nature of a performance problem. The following script provides one way to look at this summary level data, grouped by the AWR snapshot and wait class.

🖫 wait_class_db_time_in_wait.sql

```
break on begin_time skip 1

column wait_class format a15

select
  begin_time,
  wait_class,
  average_waiter_count,
  dbtime_in_wait
from
  dba_hist_waitclassmet_history
where
  dbtime_in_wait >10
order by
  begin_time,
  wait_class,
  average_waiter_count desc;
```

The following is a sample output:

BEGIN_TIM	WAIT_CLASS	AVERAGE WAITER COUNT	DBTIME IN WAIT
12-NOV-04	Commit	0	18
	Other	0	100
	Commit	0	17
	Other	0	100
	Other	0	100
	Commit	0	17
	Commit	0	14
	Commit	0	18
	Other	0	100

The AWR can provide valuable information about cumulative statistics like file I/O. The following script demonstrates the physical read statistics gathered for each datafile.

🖫 physical_reads.sql

```
break on begin_interval_time skip 1

column phyrds              format 999,999,999
column begin_interval_time format a25
column file_name           format a45

select
  begin_interval_time,
  filename,
  phyrds
from
  dba_hist_filestatxs
  natural join
  dba_hist_snapshot
order by
  begin_interval_time;
```

The sample output below shows a running total of physical reads for each datafile. Starting from this script, it would be easy to add a *where* clause criteria and create a unique time-series exception report of disk reads, an important component of overall response time.

```
BEGIN_INTERVAL_TIME        FILENAME                          PHYRDS
-------------------------  -------------------------------   -----
10-NOV-04 09.00.01.000 PM  /oradata/test10g/system01.dbf      3,982
                           /oradata/test10g/undotbs01.dbf        51
                           /oradata/test10g/users01.dbf           7
                           /oradata/test10g/example01.dbf        14
                           /oradata/test10g/sysaux01.dbf        551
                           /oradata/test10g/tbsalert.dbf          7

10-NOV-04 09.11.06.131 PM  /oradata/test10g/system01.dbf      6,120
                           /oradata/test10g/users01.dbf          21
                           /oradata/test10g/tbsalert.dbf         21
                           /oradata/test10g/example01.dbf        28
                           /oradata/test10g/sysaux01.dbf      4,786
                           /oradata/test10g/undotbs01.dbf       231

10-NOV-04 10.00.10.672 PM  /oradata/test10g/system01.dbf     10,950
                           /oradata/test10g/undotbs01.dbf       262
                           /oradata/test10g/users01.dbf          22
                           /oradata/test10g/tbsalert.dbf         22
                           /oradata/test10g/example01.dbf        40
                           /oradata/test10g/sysaux01.dbf      6,320
```

Latch contention can also be a source of performance problems. When faced with latch issues, the following script can help to identify the biggest latch issues from this repository. Rather than providing transient data, this script allows the DBA to examine recent data and determine trend information, as well as data from a specific point in the recent past. How far in the past depends on the settings that have been used for the database.

latch_stats.sql

```
break on begin_interval_time skip 1

column begin_interval_time format a25
column latch_name          format a40

select
   begin_interval_time,
   latch_name,
   gets,
   misses,
   sleeps
from
   dba_hist_latch
natural join
   dba_hist_snapshot
where
   (misses + sleeps ) > 0
```

```
order by
   begin_interval_time,
   misses desc,
   sleeps desc;
```

This listing is important because sporadic latch misses can be tracked over time. Since Oracle is very dynamic and latch related performance problems happen quickly, they often disappear before a DBA is even aware of them.

BEGIN TIME	LATCH NAME	GETS	MISSES	SLEEPS
6 AM	library cache	4,451,177	856	943
	shared pool	3,510,651	482	611
	redo allocation	146,500	139	139
	cache buffers chains	13,050,732	52	104
	session allocation	8,176,366	43	43
	slave class create	2,534	41	41
	cache buffers lru chain	347,142	33	33
	row cache objects	2,556,877	24	26
	library cache pin	2,611,493	8	8
	messages	1,056,963	7	5
	library cache lock	1,483,983	4	4
	object queue header operation	1,386,809	3	3
	enqueue hash chains	2,915,290	3	3
	enqueues	2,693,816	2	2
	client/application info	11,578	1	3
	JOX SGA heap latch	43,033	1	2
	simulator lru latch	17,806	1	1
	JS slv state obj latch	85	1	1
7 AM	library cache	4,540,521	862	950
	shared pool	3,582,239	485	614
	redo allocation	149,434	140	140
	cache buffers chains	13,214,066	53	105
	session allocation	8,342,651	43	43
	slave class create	2,590	42	42
	cache buffers lru chain	352,002	33	33
	row cache objects	2,606,652	24	26
	library cache pin	2,663,535	8	8
	messages	1,079,305	7	5
	library cache lock	1,514,016	4	4
	object queue header operation		1,412,733	3

These trends can be expanded by examining the changes, or delta values, between the ASH statistics. This is done using the *dba_hist_sys_time_model* view:

🖫 **sys_time_model_stat.sql**

```
break on begin_interval_time skip 0

column stat_name format a25

select
  begin_interval_time,
  new.stat_name,
  (new.value - old.value) "Difference"
from
  dba_hist_sys_time_model old,
  dba_hist_sys_time_model new,
  dba_hist_snapshot       ss
where
  new.stat_name = old.stat_name
and
  new.snap_id = ss.snap_id
and
  old.snap_id = ss.snap_id - 1
and
  new.stat_name like '%&stat_name%'
order by
  begin_interval_time;
```

This report was run for the event *hard parse elapsed time,* and the output can be analyzed to detect repeating patterns of specific wait events.

Below, a huge increase can be seen at 11 PM when the wait time delta nearly doubled from the previous hour. This is an important clue for further investigation.

```
BEGIN_INTERVAL_TIME         STAT_NAME                      Difference
-------------------------    -------------------------      ----------
12-NOV-04 08.00.20.745 PM   hard parse elapsed time        10,605,028
12-NOV-04 09.00.48.205 PM   hard parse elapsed time        15,628,615
12-NOV-04 10.00.13.470 PM   hard parse elapsed time        54,707,455
12-NOV-04 11.00.41.412 PM   hard parse elapsed time        96,643,842
13-NOV-04 12.00.06.899 AM   hard parse elapsed time        16,890,047
```

Similarly, ASH keeps information on enqueues. This allows a query to produce a report on enqueue waits, as shown below:

💾 enqueue_stat.sql

```
column begin_interval_time format a10
column req_reason          format a25
column cum_wait_time       head CUM|WAIT|TIME
column total_req#          head TOTAL|REQ#
column total_wait#         head TOTAL|WAIT#
column failed_req#         head FAILED|REQ#

select
  begin_interval_time,
  eq_type,
  req_reason,
  total_req#,
  total_wait#,
  succ_req#,
  failed_req#,
  cum_wait_time
```

```
from
   dba_hist_enqueue_stat
 natural join
   dba_hist_snapshot
where
   cum_wait_time > 0
order by
   begin_interval_time,
   cum_wait_time;
```

The following sample results display waits by time period:

```
                                         TOT SUCCESS     FAILED    CUM
               REQ               TOT      WT  REQ         REQ      WAIT
 TIME EQ       REASON            REQUEST  NUM NUM         NUM      TIME
 ---- --       ----------------  -------  --- ----------  --       ----
 1 PM JS       slave enq get lock1    11    2         11   0      2,990
 1 PM RO       fast object reuse   1,960   31      1,960   0      1,940
 1 PM SQ       contention            244    4        244   0        550
 1 PM TM       contention        121,391    1    121,370  21        100
 1 PM TX       contention         66,793    1     66,793   0         60
 1 PM TX       index contention        1    1          1   0         50

 2 PM JS       slave enq get lock1    22    4        233   0      4,332
 2 PM RO       fast object reuse   1,960   31      1,960   0      5,730
 2 PM SQ       contention            244    4        244   0        950
 2 PM TX       row lock contention     1    1          1   0        870
 2 PM JS       queue lock       1151,724    1   1151,724   0        790
 2 PM SQ       contention            247    4        247   0        550
 2 PM TM       contention        122,513    1    122,492  21        450
 2 PM TX       contention         67,459    1     67,459   0        360
 2 PM TX       index contention        1    1          1   0        250
 2 PM TX       row lock contention     1    1          1   0        170
```

In the above samples, it is clear that a savvy DBA can use AWR and ASH together to get precise time-series trend pictures of database performance.

Correlation Analysis Reports with the AWR and ASH Views

The Oracle Wait Interface automatically collects interesting statistics that relate to system-wide wait events from *dba_hist_waitstat* using detailed wait event information from *dba_hist_active_sess_history*, as seen below in Table 10.6.

COLUMN	DESCRIPTION
snap_id	Unique snapshot ID
Dbid	Database ID for the snapshot
instance_number	Instance number for the snapshot
Class	Class of the block

COLUMN	DESCRIPTION
wait_count	Number of waits by the operation for this class of block
Time	Sum of all wait times for all the waits by the operation for this class of block

Table 10.6: *The dba_hist_waitstat statistics used for wait event analysis*

When doing advanced correlation analysis, a DBA will often try to identify correlations between instance-wide wait events and the associated block-level waits. This process uses AWR and ASH information to isolate the exact file and object where the wait contention is occurring.

The ASH *wrh$* tables store the history of a recent session's activity in *dba_hist_active_sess_history* and this data is designed as a rolling buffer in memory. Because of this buffer, earlier information is overwritten when necessary.

The *dba_hist_active_sess_history* view contains historical block-level contention statistics. The contents are shown in Table 10.7.

COLUMN	DESCRIPTION
snap_id	Unique snapshot ID
sample_time	Time of the sample
session_id	Session identifier
session_serial#	Session serial number which is used to uniquely identify a session's objects
user_id	Oracle user identifier
current_obj#	Object ID of the object that the session is currently referencing
current_file#	File number of the file containing the block that the session is currently referencing
current_block#	ID of the block that the session is currently referencing
wait_time	Total wait time for the event for which the session last waited. 0 if currently waiting.
time_waited	Time that the current session actually spent waiting for the event. This column is set for waits that were in progress at the time the sample was taken.

Table 10.7: *Selected columns from the dba_hist_active_sess_history view*

In the following script, the wait event values from *dba_hist_waitstat* and *dba_hist_active_sess_history* are compared. This comparison allows the identification of the exact objects that are experiencing wait events.

🖫 **waitstat_ash_objects.sql**

```
prompt
prompt   This will compare values from dba_hist_waitstat with
prompt   detail information from dba_hist_active_sess_history.
prompt

set pages 999
set lines 80

break on snap_time skip 2

col snap_time       heading 'Snap|Time'     format a20
col file_name       heading 'File|Name'     format a40
col object_type     heading 'Object|Type'   format a10
col object_name     heading 'Object|Name'   format a20
col wait_count      heading 'Wait|Count'    format 999,999
col time            heading 'Time'          format 999,999

select
   to_char(begin_interval_time,'yyyy-mm-dd hh24:mi') snap_time,
--    file_name,
   object_type,
   object_name,
   wait_count,
   time
from
   dba_hist_waitstat             wait,
   dba_hist_snapshot             snap,
   dba_hist_active_sess_history  ash,
   dba_data_files                df,
   dba_objects                   obj
where
   wait.snap_id = snap.snap_id
and wait.snap_id = ash.snap_id
and df.file_id = ash.current_file#
and obj.object_id = ash.current_obj#
and wait_count > 50
order by
   to_char(begin_interval_time,'yyyy-mm-dd hh24:mi'),
   file_name;
```

Note that this script joins into the *dba_data_files* in order to get the file names that are associated with the wait event. This is a very powerful script that can be used to find the root cause of specific waits. Below is a sample output from *wait_time_detail*:

```
SQL> @wait_time_detail
```

This will compare values from *dba_hist_waitstat* with detail information from *dba_hist_active_sess_hist*.

| Snap | Object | Object | Wait |

```
Time                   Type         Name                Count     Time
-------------------    ----------   ---------------    --------  --------
2004-02-28 01:00       TABLE        ORDOR               4,273       67
                       INDEX        PK_CUST_ID         12,373      324
                       INDEX        FK_CUST_NAME        3,883       17
                       INDEX        PK_ITEM_ID          1,256      967
2004-02-29 03:00       TABLE        ITEM_DETAIL            83       69
2004-03-01 04:00       TABLE        ITEM_DETAIL         1,246       45
2004-03-01 21:00       TABLE        CUSTOMER_DET        4,381      354
                       TABLE        IND_PART              117       15
2004-03-04 01:00       TABLE        MARVIN             41,273       16
                       TABLE        FACTOTUM            2,827       43
                       TABLE        DOW_KNOB              853        6
                       TABLE        ITEM_DETAIL            57      331
                       TABLE        HIST_ORD            4,337      176
```

This simple example demonstrates how AWR and ASH data can be used to create a seemingly infinite number of sophisticated custom performance reports.

The wealth of metrics within the STATSPACK, AWR and ASH can be very useful for getting detailed correlation information between any of the wait event performance metrics captured by the AWR.

Conclusion

The Active Session History (ASH) and Oracle Wait Event Interface tools provide details into the wait events experienced by the database. The main points of this chapter are:

- The wait time model approach is only one of several approaches for tuning Oracle, and the savvy DBA will use all of the available techniques and not rely on any single approach.

- The wait event interface was completely overhauled in Oracle 10g, and it is now easier than ever to identify and track wait-related database bottlenecks.

- Wait events are extremely transient, making it difficult to see bottlenecks. The wait-related *v$* views and Active Session History (ASH) tables can provide trend analysis of wait-related performance data.

- The ASH tables are useful for identifying wait event information at many levels including individual sessions, specific SQL statements, specific users, or the database as a whole.

The next chapter will explore more Oracle tools that can be used to tune the Oracle database.

Oracle Tuning Tools

Don't get burned by using the wrong tuning tool

The Evolution of Oracle Tuning Tools

Each new release of Oracle brings new tools and techniques for performance optimization, but it is a formidable challenge to create tools that can identify and correct database bottlenecks for every possible situation. I run a large remote DBA operation and I monitor and tune mission-critical databases around the globe. Because I have a large base of experience, I am in a unique position to see hundreds of systems in-action and understand the best approaches to achieve optimal performance.

This chapter will begin with a review of a "best practices" approach to Oracle tuning; a practical approach and then see a historical perspective by looking at the evolution of Oracle tuning tools and techniques, and wrap up with a pragmatic tuning approach which has worked well in my company.

The Spirit of Independence

This chapter will attempt to present the unvarnished truth about those Oracle tuning tools and techniques are the most effective and expose those tools that are not so helpful.

Oracle Corporation is always like a cheerleader, saying that all of their features are wonderful, and they are not always forthcoming about the risks and rewards of using new tools and techniques. This is especially true for the Oracle "evangelists", the Oracle ACE shills who will never say anything bad about Oracle tools.

For example, back in the last days of Oracle 7, word came forth from Oracle Corporation that the rule-based optimizer was being removed from Oracle 8, and all shops must move quickly to adopt the cost-based optimizer (CBO). The CBO was not quite ready for primetime, much to the consternation of those shops who had attempted to migrate to the CBO. This is when I learned that Oracle's goals were not necessarily the same as mine, and I remember that our boss nearly switched to Informix because they were so angry at Oracle.

Even in 11g, rule-based optimization is alive and well, and despite Oracle's dire warnings that the RBO will disappear, *rule* hints appear in hundreds of Oracle's own internal SQL statements.

In any case, let's move on and see some of the approaches to Oracle tuning and evaluate the benefits and drawbacks of each approach.

A Best Practices Approach to Oracle Tuning

Over the years, Oracle tuning experts have introduced many different tuning methodologies and tools, each with their own benefits and shortcomings. Each proponent zealously advocated that their approach is the "best" approach, and until Oracle 11g, Oracle Corporation remained silent about an approved approach to Oracle tuning.

All of that changed in Oracle 11g when Oracle's toolset made definite recommendations of a holistic tuning approach with their fully automated SQL Tuning feature. Implemented via the SQL Performance Advisor, Oracle attempts to automate a proven approach that has been used for more than a decade by Oracle tuning experts:

- **Top-down tuning:** The Oracle University performance tuning classes have always recommended tuning to the global parameters before diving in to tune specific SQL statements, but this has now become codified in the 11g SQL Performance Analyzer (SPA), a tool which allows the DBA to capture real-world workloads and test them in a controlled environment.

- **Empirical tuning:** Rather than rely on artificially contrived test cases for tuning, Oracle 11g now endorses a workload-based approach, where the guesswork is eliminated by testing your changes with real-world data.

- **Separation of proactive vs. reactive tuning activities:** With the introduction of the Automated Session History (ASH) tables and the AWR tables, Oracle Corporation made a clear distinction between proactive and reactive tuning. Reactive tuning involves reacting to an acute tuning crisis, while Oracle gives the AWR tables to use for long-term tuning using predictive analytics to forecast repeating performance bottlenecks.

Before exploring the top-down approach to Oracle tuning in detail, start with a quick review of the evolution of Oracle tuning tools and techniques.

The History of Oracle Tuning Techniques

To fully appreciate the enhancements within Oracle 11g, it is important to take a historical perspective and understand the context of the enhancements. Performance tuning has not changed much since Oracle 7, but there is a wealth of new tools and techniques with each new release.

The Oracle 7 Tuning Approach

In Oracle 7, Oracle Education (later Oracle University) advocated instance tuning, an approach whereby the database is tuned as a whole by optimizing the critical *init.ora* parameters, CBO statistics and object parameters. These specific tuning features included:

- Bitmap indexes

- Partitioned views

- Sequential prefetch for full table scans (asynchronous read ahead)

- *alter index xx rebuild* syntax

- Advanced replication

The Oracle 8 Tuning Approach

Oracle 8 was originally dubbed "Oracle Universal Server" (OUS), a relational database with object-oriented features. Incidentally, despite the great quality of Oracle implementation of OODFBMS, the object-oriented features never caught-on expect within Oracle Corporation itself. Oracle 8 improved upon many of the Oracle 7 tuning features, some of which were too buggy for production, and gave these meager new tuning features:

- Table and index partitioning enhancements

- Reverse key indexes

- Updatable views

- Oracle parallel query for DML (insert, update, delete)

The Oracle 8i Tuning Approach

Dubbed "The Internet enabled database", Oracle 8i concentrated on enhancements to existing tuning features:

- Function-based indexes (FBI)

- KEEP pool replaces *alter table xxx cache* syntax

- Hash and composite partitioning

- SQL*Loader direct load API (direct=y)

- Online index rebuilds

- Cache Fusion added to Oracle Parallel Server (OPS)

- The Oracle HTTP server allows faster Apache extensions

- Oracle JVM Accelerator

The Oracle 9i Tuning Approach

Oracle 9i saw major improvements in performance tuning tools, most notably STATSPACK, an improvement on the old *bstat-estat* utility which allowed for elapsed-time reports to be stored within the database. Oracle also introduced advisory utilities, tools which showed the marginal benefits for different SGA pool sizes. The following important new tuning features were also introduced:

- Multiple blocksize support

- Separate data buffers allow for segregation of critical tables & indexes

- Oracle *upsert* statement improves warehouse loads

- SQL case statement replaces decode syntax

- Oracle external tables allow SQL access to flat files

- Real Application Clusters (RAC) replaces OPS

- List partitioning and multi-level list-hash partitioning

The Oracle 10g Tuning Approach

Oracle 10g was a major improvement in all areas of Oracle performance. The optimizer undertook a major overhaul, the entire kernel was improved and PL/SQL performance was improved by over 20%. As the Grid database, Oracle redefined the traditional definition of grid computing, allowing for blade servers to be brought in as needed to accommodate changes in the workload. 10g also had several important tuning features including the Automated Workload Repository (AWR) and the Automatic Session History (ASH) tables:

- Oracle 10g Grid and RAC is enhanced for dynamic scalability with server blades

- Completely reworked 10g Enterprise Manager (OEM)

- AWR and ASH tables incorporated into OEM Performance Pack and Diagnostic Pack options

- Automated Session History (ASH) materializes the Oracle Wait Interface over time

- Automatic Database Diagnostic Monitor (ADDM)

- Automatic Workload Repository (AWR) enhances STATSPACK

- SQL Tuning Advisor

- SQL Access Advisor

Oracle 10g Release 2 showed another major tuning improvement, *mutexes*. To improve cursor execution and also hard parsing, a new memory serialization mechanism has been created in 10gR2. For certain shared-cursor related operations, *mutexes* are used as a replacement for library cache latches and library cache pins. Using *mutexes* is faster, uses less CPU and also allows significantly improved concurrency over the existing latch mechanism. The use of *mutexes* for cursor pins can be enabled by setting the init.ora parameter *_use_kks_mutex* to true.

The Oracle 11g Tuning Approach

Oracle 11g was not a revolutionary release for Oracle tuning, it concentrated mostly upon improvements to existing features and the introduction of semi-automated tools to replicate the steps taken by a human tuning expert. Here is a list of the major performance tuning new features of Oracle 11g:

- **SQL Performance Analyzer:** This is the codification of Oracle's holistic approach, an empirical technique whereby SQL is tuned in a real-world environment. Designed for testing silver bullet impact of global changes such as *init.ora* parameters, new indexes and materialized views, SPA provides real-world evidence of the performance impact of major changes.

- **11g compression:** With a late start out of the gate (other DBMS tools have had compression for decades), Oracle's compression promises to improve the speed of full-scans operations, which is important to batch jobs and data warehouses.

- **SQL optimization improvements:** The CBO is continuously evolving, and there is now extended optimizer statistics and the problem of bind peeking has been fixed.

- **Automatic memory tuning:** Automatic PGA tuning was introduced in Oracle 9i. Automatic SGA tuning was introduced in Oracle 10g. In 11g, all memory can be tuned automatically by setting one parameter. The DBA literally tells Oracle how much memory it has and Oracle determines how much to use for PGA, SGA and OS processes.

- **AWR baselines:** The AWR baselines of 10g have been extended to allow automatic creation of baselines for use in other features.

- **Adaptive metric baselines:** Notification thresholds in 10g were based on a fixed point. In 11g, notification thresholds can be associated with a baseline, so the notification thresholds vary throughout the day in line with the baseline.

Now that we see the major tuning features within each successive release, let's take a close look at Oracle's data collection sources so that we can understand how Oracle gathers their performance statistics.

An Automated Approach to SQL Tuning

Starting with Oracle 11g, Oracle has touted their new 11g holistic approach to SQL tuning as "fully automated SQL tuning", but the marketing hype must be separated from the reality. The main benefit is that the DBA can now test changes to global parameters against a real-world workload, using a SQL Tuning Set (STS).

Holistic tuning in Oracle 11g is offered through several functional areas, most importantly the SQL Performance Advisor and the automated SQL Plan Management (SPM) facility. SPA is the natural evolution of the SQL Access advisor:

- **10g SQL Access Advisor:** The 10g SQL Access advisor tests real-world SQL workloads, recommending missing indexes and materialized views.

- **11g SQL Performance Analyzer:** The SPA takes the SQL Access advisor one step further and implements tuning recommendations for any SQL statements that run 3x faster when tested with a new workload.

It is important to note that while these tools are new, the techniques have been used for decades to tune large databases. There are several third-party vendors who sell tools for capturing workloads, and the expert DBA can lift high-use SQL statements directly from the *v$* views using standard SQL.

In sum, Oracle is attempting to make it easier on the tuning professional and enforce a standard methodology for performance tuning. Tuning has always been one of the most complex and challenging areas of database administration, and Oracle is no exception.

Oracle has often been criticized by neophytes as being too hard when compared to less robust and flexible databases such as SQL Server, but these newbies fail to appreciate that with great power comes great complexity. As the world's most robust and flexible database, Oracle has been seeking automated techniques.

Oracle's first attempt at an intelligent advisor was in Oracle8, the "Oracle Expert", a silly tool that often made ludicrous recommendations, and was mocked by DBA's calling it "Oracle Idiot". In Oracle 10g there was the extra-cost performance pack and diagnostic pack, which contained primitive tools for performance forecasting, none of which could completely replicate a human expert. But Oracle continues in their quest to automate the tedious, well-structured components of the tuning process.

How Fully Automated SQL Tuning Works

In a nutshell, the 11g fully automated SQL tuning is a series of processes and tools, loosely coupled for maximum flexibility.

A – The setup for fully automatic SQL tuning: Here representative SQL workloads (SQL tuning sets) are captured and set up in a testing environment:

1. **Define the SQL workload:** The DBA defines a set of problematic SQL statements or chooses a representative workload. This is called the SQL Tuning Set, or STS. This uses the *dbms_sqltune.create_sqlset* package.

2. **Set up a changed environment:** The DBA can choose to change the initialization parameters, test the performance against a previous release of the CBO, a very useful feature when testing upgrades, or conduct custom experiments on the effect of environmental changes on the SQL tuning set.

B – Initial SQL tuning: Using the SQL Performance Analyzer, the environment is optimized using the SQL tuning set.

1. **Schedule & run workload tests:** The workload is scheduled for execution during low usage periods so that an empirical sample of real-world execution times can be collected and compared using different execution plans from the two SQL tuning sets. To do this, run the *dbms_sqlpa* package. The OEM SPA Guided Workflow wizard can also be used.

2. **Implement the changes:** Oracle has the Real Application Testing (RAT) framework for empirical testing of SQL workloads. For any statements that execute more than 3x faster, after out global changes, Oracle 11g will automatically implement the changes via "SQL Profiles", a replacement for stored outlines that bypasses the generation of an execution plan for incoming SQL, replacing it with the pre-tuned access plan.

C – Gather Baseline: Create the SQL Plan Baseline; to enable automatic SQL plan capture, set the *optimizer_capture_sql_plan_baselines* initialization parameter to *true*.

D – Regression testing and implementation: This stage allows us to test global changes with the SQL Plan Manager (SPM). As the system characteristics change, use the SQL Plan Manager to test against real workloads and ensure that all changed execution plans result in at least 3x faster performance.

This is a huge improvement over the hit-and-miss SQL tuning techniques of the past, but it is not truly a fully-automated approach either. Remember that there will always be "outlier" SQL statements that must be tuned manually.

Fully Automated SQL Tuning is not a Panacea

There are many internal and external factors that influence the response time for a given SQL statement and with 11g the SQL Performance Analyzer (SPA) and the SQL Plan Management (SPM), can help us establish an optimal baseline before tuning individual SQL statements. Remember, system-wide workload tuning always comes first:

- **Optimize the server kernel:** Always tune the disk and network I/O subsystem, i.e. RAID, DASD/Fibre bandwidth, network, to optimize the I/O time, network packet size and dispatching frequency. Kernel settings have an indirect effect on SQL performance. For example, a kernel setting may speed up I/O, a change which is noted by the CBO workload statistics using *dbms_stats.gather_workload_stats*. This, in turn, directly influences the optimizer's access decisions.

- **Adjust the optimizer statistics:** Always collect and store optimizer statistics to allow the optimizer to learn more about the distribution of the data in order to produce more intelligent SQL access plans. Also, histograms can hypercharge SQL when determining optimal table join order, and when making access decisions on skewed *where* clause predicates. Also new in 11g, multi-column statistics can be gathered for use by the optimizer to determine optimal ways to run queries based upon multiple column criteria.

- **Adjust optimizer parameters:** One of the most common SQL problems is using the default optimizer_mode for a OLTP database. Before tuning individual SQL statements, the DBA can empirically determine their optimal settings for *optimizer_mode, optimizer_index_caching,* and *optimizer_index_cost_adj.*

- **Optimize the instance:** The choice of *db_block_size, db_cache_size,* and OS parameters, such as *db_file_multiblock_read_count,* and *cpu_count,* can greatly influence SQL performance.

- **Tune with indexes and materialized views:** Just as the 10g SQLAccess advisor recommends missing indexes and missing materialized views, it is always best to optimize the SQL workload with indexes, especially function-based indexes, a godsend for SQL tuning.

Now that we have reviewed the evolution of Oracle tuning, it's time to move on and explore those tools and techniques which have survived the test of time.

Oracle provides a wealth of tools for collecting data to tune the Oracle database:

- Oracle Trace Analyzer – For Metalink users only

- Oracle LTOM

- SQL*Trace (TKPROF)

- Oracle STATSPACK and AWR

Let's start by examining the Oracle Trace Analyzer.

Oracle Trace Analyzer (*sqltxplain*)

The *sqltxplain* utility was written by Carlos Sierra, a brilliant developer at Oracle Corporation. This script is an enhancement to the Center of Excellence (COE) script to produce a super-detailed trace of SQL execution. Carlos' *sqltxplain* utility script enhances standard execution plan analysis by providing:

- **Enhanced Explain Plan:** Including execution order, indexed columns, rows count and blocks for tables.

- **Schema Object Attributes for all tables and indexes accessed by the SQL statement being diagnosed including:** Object dependencies, tables, indexes, columns, partitions, sub-partitions, synonyms, policies, triggers and constraints.

- **CBO Statistics for levels:** Table, index, partition, sub-partition and column.

- **Histograms:** Including table, partition and sub-partition levels.

- **Space utilization and administration:** For tables, indexes, partitions and sub-partitions.

- **Objects, segments, extents, tablespaces and datafiles:** Including current performance of datafiles.

- **Oracle initialization parameters:** *init.ora*, required, recommended and default for an APPS 11i database, and all other parameters set on the *init.ora* file.

- **Source code:** In which the SQL statement and accessed tables depend on, i.e. triggers description and body, views columns and text, packages specs and bodies, procedures and functions.

Remember, the Oracle Trace Analyzer is exclusively for metal-level (bronze, silver or gold) customers and complete usage details are available in MetaLink note 224270.1.

Oracle also offers LTOM (Lightweight Onboard Monitor), a specialized tuning monitor. How LTOM can aid in tuning Oracle is covered next.

Oracle Lightweight Onboard Monitor (LTOM)

Oracle LTOM is an embedded real-time data collection and diagnostics platform which was designed exclusively for highly experienced Oracle database administrators. Oracle LTOM is described as an OS independent (Java front-end) tool that works to trigger detailed trace collection whenever a LTOM user-defined threshold event like a non-idle wait event and/or CPU usage occurs. The LTOM documentation notes:

> "The Lightweight Onboard Monitor (LTOM) is a java program designed as a real-time diagnostic platform for deployment to a customer site. . ."

> *"LTOM runs on the customer's UNIX server, is tightly integrated with the host operating system and provides an integrated solution for detecting and collecting trace files for system performance issues."*

The ability of LTOM to detect problems and collect data in real-time will reduce the amount of time it takes to solve problems and reduce customer downtime. For more details on using LTOM, see Metalink Note 352363.1.

LTOM Features

The new Oracle LTOM tool has the following features centered around the concept of threshold-based data recording (trace files):

- Automatic hang detection
- Manual data recording
- Automatic data recording
- Automatic session tracing

LTOM creates no footprint on the database. All data is written to ASCII text files, either Oracle session trace files located in the *udump* or to a specific log file associated with the respective service that is being used, i.e. manual recorder, auto recorder, hang detection or session recorder. The manual recorder writes *vmstat*, *mpstat* and *top* command info to an ASCII log file.

The session recorder uses an in-memory trace buffer for the 10046 trace. Sessions are traced in-memory until they violate either a CPU or wait event rule and, at that time, the contents of the memory buffer is dumped to disk.

LTOM Wait Event Rules

LTOM implements a rule-based approach to allow the DBA to specify collection-triggering threshold rules based on the scalar values for Oracle non-idle wait events.

LTOM External Data Recording

LTOM notes the major shortcoming of STATSPACK and its inability to gather data about the external server environment including disk enqueues, CPU enqueues, RAM paging and such.

One of the problems with relying solely on STATSPACK is the inability to look at performance from a holistic point of view. Information about non-Oracle processes and the health of the operating system in terms of memory, CPU and I/O for example, is not collected. LTOM also notes the issue with deriving high-detail from hourly STATSPACK snapshots when more frequent elapsed-time metrics are needed.

Further, all static data collectors are problematic in that single sample snapshots or multiple snapshots taken at 15- or 30-minute intervals can miss problems which can occur briefly during a snapshot interval and will be averaged out over the duration of the snapshot.

The data for the LTOM in-RAM data repository includes data from both the UNIX/Linux *top* and *vmstat* commands. Note that many Oracle professionals have implemented external scripts to capture UNIX/Linux *vmstat* information.

LTOM Automatic Data Recording

LTOM has rule definition components called automatic data recording that allows the DBA to set thresholds by providing specific values for non-idle wait events. When the LTOM thresholds are triggered, data collection is enabled. LTOM allows the DBA to define rules for external CPU thresholds. This is important because many 64-bit databases become CPU-bound with large RAM regions. This CPU tracing, by recording amount of CPU used, is also important if the SQL optimizer (CBO) has been changed to consider CPU by setting the *_optimizer_cost_model=cpu* parameter.

LTOM Automatic Session Tracing

LTOM has a method to collect the *session_id* for offending SQL statements and a method to fire a 10046 SQL trace dump. LTOM uses the Oracle extended SQL*Trace utility, turning on a 10046 super-detailed trace on a target SQL statement. Automatic session tracing uses a set of rules to determine when to turn on SQL trace for individual Oracle sessions, using event 10046 level 12 trace.

In sum, LTOM is an exciting new proactive Oracle utility that overcomes many of the problems with existing reactive database monitors. Next, let's have a look at the Oracle Trace utility.

Oracle Trace Utility

Setting special Oracle events is a technique designed to signal Oracle to create detailed trace information, a very expensive and time-consuming process, it is sometimes necessary to troubleshoot a problem. These tracing events are used for debugging and examining SQL execution details, but they are only used in very rare cases when less resource intensive methods have failed.

This section will review the Oracle 10046 trace event and show how it can be useful in performance tuning efforts. We begin with an overview on Oracle database events in general and then cover the 10046 event in more detail.

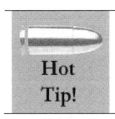

Watch your release level!

Trace dumps are release specific! Beware, that 10046 trace file contents differ greatly between different versions of Oracle.

Inside Oracle Event Tracing

Oracle trace dumps were originally designed only for Oracle internal staff, and they were once considered dangerous because of their high resource consumption. Over time, a number of Oracle experts have experimented with these events and discovered that not all events are dangerous, and some can be useful as a diagnostic tool. There are four main types of Oracle events:

- **Process trace events:** The 10053 and 10046 events are called process trace events. These dumps will trace certain system operations continuously until the tracing is canceled, or the trace file directory becomes full.

- **Events to change default Oracle behavior:** These events are designed to modify the default behavior of Oracle. For example, trace event 10262 causes Oracle to stop reporting memory smaller than a predefined size threshold.

- **On-demand events:** Immediate events that will dump diagnostic information such as system state dumps and dumps of file headers.

- **On-error events:** These trace dumps are triggered by an error event. These events dump information immediately, producing a dump file that can be used to discover the cause of the error.

Inside the 10046 Trace Event

The 10046 event allows DBAs to trace the execution of any set of SQL statements. The 10046 event can be set at both the session level for tracing a specific session or at a database level. The 10046 event can

---

be set via a parameter file setting or dynamically for the database, the current session or even another session.

The 10046 event can also be set to cause the trace output to be generated with differing levels of detail. For example, level 1 tracing is equivalent to the output generated when enabling the *sql_trace* facility within Oracle (*alter session set sql_trace=true*).

The real bang from the 10046 trace results comes with enabling the higher levels of detail. With these higher levels of detail wait related information and bind variable related information is visible. The following table lists the typically used event levels present in the 10046 trace event in Oracle Database 11g:

10046 Trace Level	Description
1	Basic trace level. Like the standard *sql_trace* trace file. Provides statistics for parse, execute, fetch, commit and rollback database calls.
4	Displays bind variables
8	Displays wait statistics
12	Displays wait statistics and bind variables

Table 11.1: *10046 Trace Event Levels*

The higher levels of trace detail are only used in rare cases and they are seldom applicable for overall Oracle tuning efforts. For detailed SQL tuning, you might want to capture a detailed trace to see how long a SQL statement waits for disk reads or how long it waits on the redo allocation latch. It would also be nice to know exactly what it is that makes month-end processing take so long!

These trace files are full of information, making their interpretation a daunting task. Some ideas on using the Oracle database to get at the information stored in these trace files will be presented here. Since the trace files must be created first, let's look at how to create a 10046 trace event in Oracle.

Setting an Oracle Trace Event

Setting an event means telling Oracle to generate information in the form of a trace file in the context of the event. The trace file is usually located in a directory specified by the initialization parameter *user_dump_dest*. By examining the resulting trace file, detailed information about the event traced can be deduced. The general format for an event is as follows:

```
EVENT = "
   <trace class>
   <event name>
   <action>
   <name>
   <trace name>
   <qualifier>"
```

There are two types of events: session events and process events. Process events are initialized in the parameter file; session-events are initialized with the *alter session...* or *alter system* command. When checking for posted events, the Oracle Server first checks for session events, then for process events.

Oracle Trace Event Classes

There are four traceable event classes:

- **Class 1: "Dump something":** Traces are generated upon so-called unconditioned immediate events. This is the case when Oracle data has to be dumped; for example, the headers of all *redolog* files or the contents of the *controlfile*. These events cannot be set in the *init<sid>.ora,* but must be set using the *alter session* or the *dbms_session.set_ev()* procedure.

- **Class 2: "Trap on Error":** Setting this class of (error-) events causes Oracle to generate an error stack every time the event occurs.

- **Class 3: "Change execution path":** Setting such an event will cause Oracle to change the execution path for some specific Oracle internal code segment. For example, setting event 10269 prevents SMON from doing free-space coalescing.

- **Class 4: "Trace something":** Events from this class are set to obtain traces that are used, for example, for SQL tuning. A common event is 10046, which will cause Oracle to trace the SQL access path on each SQL statement.

The *set events* Trace Command Settings

The *set events* command in an *init<sid>.ora* file is normally enabled only with the direction of Oracle Technical Support when the DBA needs to gather internals, usually to diagnose a bug for Oracle. These alerts turn on more advanced levels of tracing and error detection than are commonly available. Source 2.6 lists some of the more common events.

The syntax to specify multiple events in the *init.ora* is:

```
EVENT="
   <event 1>:
   <event 2>:
   <event 3>:
   <event n>"
```

We can also split the events on multiple lines by using the continuation backslash character (\) at the end of each event and continue the next event on the next line.

```
EVENT="<event 1>:\
      <event 2>:\
      <event 3>:\
      <event n>"
```

For Example, here we use the backslash characters:

```
EVENT="\
10210 trace name context forever, level 10:\
10211 trace name context forever, level 10:\
10231 trace name context forever, level 10:\
10232 trace name context forever, level 10"
```

After setting the events in the initialization file, the instance must be restarted. Be sure to check the *alert.log* and verify that the events are in effect. Almost all event settings can be specified at the session level using the *alter session* command or a call to the *dbms_sysytem.set_ev* set event procedure; doing so does not require an instance bounce for the event to take effect.

The *alert.log* should show the events that are in effect; for example:

```
event = 10210 trace name context forever, level 10:10211 trace name context for ever, level
10:10231 trace name context forever, level 10:10232 trace name context forever, level 10
```

Here are example uses of the *event* parameter:

1. To enable block header and trailer checking to detect corrupt blocks:

```
event="10210 trace name context forever, level 10"  -- for tables
event="10211 trace name context forever, level 10"  -- for indexes
event="10210 trace name context forever, level 2" -- data block checking
event="10211 trace name context forever, level 2" -- index block checking
event="10235 trace name context forever, level 1" -- memory heap checking
event="10049 trace name context forever, level 2" -- memory protect cursors
```

And to go with these settings, this undocumented parameter setting is included:

```
_db_block_cache_protect=TRUE
```

This will prevent corruption from getting to the disks at the cost of a database crash.

2. For tracing of a *max_cursors* exceeded error:

```
event="1000 trace name ERRORSTACK level 3"
```

3. To get an error stack related to a SQLNet ORA-03120 error:

```
event="3120 trace name error stack"
```

4. To work around a memory space leak problem:

```
event="10262 trace name context forever, level x"

where x is the size of space leak to ignore.
```

5. To trace memory shortages:

```
event="10235 trace name context forever, level 4"

event="600 trace name heapdump, level 4"
```

6. To take a shared pool heap dump:

This will track ORA-04031 as the error occurs; set the following event in the *init.ora* file:

```
event = "4031 trace name heapdump forever, level 2"
```

7. Tracing ORA-04030 errors:

Take a dump by setting this event in the *init* file and analyze the trace file. This will clearly pinpoint the problem.

```
event="4030 trace name errorstack level 3"
```

In addition, these undocumented SQL statements can be used to obtain information about internal database structures. Remember; only use these with the express permission of Oracle Technical Support.

* To dump the control file:

```
alter session set events 'immediate trace name CONTROLF level 10'
```

* To dump the file headers:

```
alter session set events 'immediate trace name FILE_HDRS level 10'
```

* To dump redo log headers:

```
alter session set events 'immediate trace name REDOHDR level 10'
```

* To dump the system state:

```
alter session set events 'immediate trace name SYSTEMSTATE level 10'
```

* To dump the optimizer statistics whenever a SQL statement is parsed:

```
alter session set events '10053 trace name context forever'
```

* To prevent db block corruptions:

```
event = "10210 trace name context forever, level 10"

event = "10211 trace name context forever, level 10"

event = "10231 trace name context forever, level 10"
```

* To enable the maximum level of SQL performance monitoring:

```
event = "10046 trace name context forever, level 12"
```

* To enable a memory-protect cursor:

```
event = "10049 trace name context forever, level  2"
```

* To perform data-block checks:

```
event = "10210 trace name context forever, level  2"
```

* To perform index-block checks:

```
event = "10211 trace name context forever, level  2"
```

* To perform memory-heap checks:

```
event = "10235 trace name context forever, level  1"
```

* To allow 300 bytes memory leak for each connection:

```
event = "10262 trace name context forever, level 300"
```

Note the sequence of event arguments!

The sequence of events is important! The first argument in the event is the error code followed by the suggested action to take upon receiving the error code, and the last argument is the trace level number.

Look Out!

Setting Events at the Session Level

Events are also implemented as the *session* level using the *alter session* command or calls to the *dbms_system.set_ev* set event procedure. The general format for the *alter session* command is:

```
alter session SET EVENTS 'ev_number ev_text level x';

where:

  Ev_number = the event number.
```

```
Ev_text = is any required text (usually "trace name context
          forever").

     x = is the required level setting corresponding to the
         desired action, file, or other  required data.
```

For example, to provide more detailed SQL trace information:

```
alter session SET EVENTS '10046 trace name context forever level NN'

where NN:

1 is same as a regular trace.

4 means also dump bind variables

8 means also dump wait information

12 means dump both bind and wait information
```

Here are some example uses for the *alter session set event* command.

1. To coalesce free space in a tablespace defined as temporary:

```
alter session
   SET EVENTS 'immediate trace name drop_segments level &x';

where:

  x is the value for file# from ts$ plus 1.
```

2. To get the information out of the db block buffers regarding order of LRU chains:

```
alter session
   SET EVENTS 'immediate trace name buffers level x';

where:

  x  is 1-3 for buffer header order or 4-6 for LRU chain order.
```

3. To cause "QKA Disable GBY sort elimination"

This impacts how Oracle will process sorts:

```
alter session SET EVENTS'10119 trace name context forever';
```

The SQL optimizer can also be altered with events:

- Disable index fast full scans using the event 10156. In this case, CBO will eliminate the index FFS and use full-scans of index scans instead.

- Hash joins can also be eliminated by setting event 10092 which disables the hash joins completely.

The internals of the CBO are not a mystery when the time is taken to trace the internals. Use event 10053 to give the detail of the various plans considered, depending on the statistics available. The data density, sparse characteristics, index availability, and index depth all lead the optimizer to make its decisions. The running commentary can be seen in trace files generated by the 10053 event.

In addition, event 10015 shows how SMON cleans up rollback entries. Event 10235 can be used to check how the memory manager works internally.

Enabling the 10046 Event - Setup

As is now known, the 10046 trace creates a huge output dump file. Therefore, before enabling the 10046 trace event, it is necessary to set some database parameters that control the output of the dump file. These parameters include:

- **timed_statistics:** This must be set to true to get timing information in the trace files.

- **max_dump_file_size:** This controls the maximum size of the trace file. For 10046 trace files, the default setting is generally too small.

- **user_dump_dest:** This is the location where the 10046 trace file(s) are written.

- **statistics_level:** This should be set, at a minimum, to *typical*. When set to *all*, more information will be collected in the resulting trace files. All examples in this white paper are with *statistics_level* set to *typical*.

Watch your directory size!

The default value of *max_dump_file_size* is unlimited, and it is important to be very careful not to fill up the *user_dump_dest* directory.

Remember to ensure that the *user_dump_dest* is set to a location that has gigabytes of free space. Other filesystem locations, such as *$oracle_home* and the root directory, are not recommended for *user_dump_dest*.

Here are some examples of setting *trace* parameters with *alter session* commands:

```
alter system set timed_statistics=true
```

By default, only those who have access to the Oracle user account or are members of the operating system level Oracle DBA group will be able to read the output of the 10046 trace event. To access these files, set the hidden Oracle parameter _trace_files_public to true.

Consider the security implications of this setting however, as this makes a great deal of information available to the entire user community.

Setting the 10046 Event in the Parameter File

Oracle offers a regular plethora of ways of setting the 10046 event. The 10046 can be set for the entire database via:

- Changing the parameter file manually

- Changing the *spfile* via the *alter system* command

It has already been shown that the 10046 event can be set for the session with the *alter session* command, but the 10046 event can also be set for sessions other than the DBA's current session using a number of different methods. Take a closer look at each of these methods.

If a manual *init.ora* parameter file is being used, the *event* parameter can be used to set the 10046 event as seen in this example:

```
Event='10046 trace name context forever, level 12';
```

If there are multiple events in the *init.ora* pfile, they should all be in the same sequences; so if there is another parameter set between the events, only one set of event specifications will be taken. Using this method of setting the 10046 database event requires a shutdown and restart of the database for it to take effect.

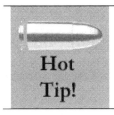

Be selective in tracing!

Setting the 10046 event for the entire database is never recommended! Always try to confine the trace as specifically as possible.

When using a *spfile*, the *alter system* command can be used to add the event record:

```
alter system
   set event='10046 trace name context forever, level 4'
scope=spfile;
```

Note that Oracle does not support the *scope=both* or *scope=memory* parameters when setting the 10046 event in this manner. To remove this setting from the *spfile*, issue this command and then cycle the database:

```
alter system set event='' scope=spfile;
```

Setting the 10046 Event Using the Alter Session Command

A common way to set the 10046 event is to enable tracing for a specific session. To trace a specific session, use the *alter session* command:

```
alter session
   set event='10046 trace name context forever, level 12';
```

To stop the trace, exit the session or use the *alter session* command to stop the trace:

```
alter session
   set event='10046 trace name context off';
```

Setting the 10046 Event for User Sessions

Most of the time, it is not going to be the DBA's session that needs to be traced. It will be the session of a user who has called with complaints that things are taking too long. There are a couple of ways to enable tracing for another user's session. The preferred method is to use the Oradebug utility to enable 10046 tracing on other sessions. There are other methods, such as *dbms_system.set_ev*, but Oradebug is easiest to use, so it is the one covered in this section. For more details on using Oradebug, see Bert Scalzo's book, *Advanced Oracle Utilities*, published by Rampant TechPress.

To enable tracing of another user's system with Oradebug the DBA needs to know some information about that user. Finding the required user session information will be covered first, and then we will take a look at using Oradebug to set the 10046 events in different sessions.

Locating Oracle Sessions

To trace a user session, the SID and serial number of that session is required. The SID is the Serial Identifier of a session, and it is unique for each concurrently running session. A session is assigned to a SID when it connects to the database. That SID is released when the session disconnects from the database.

Since SIDs can be reused by subsequent sessions, Oracle includes a serial# column to make each session associated with a SID unique. Thus, if the DBA queries *v$session* and sees SID 100 and serial# 101, and queries it again and sees SID 100 and serial# 103, then we know that the original SID 100 disconnected, and a new SID 100 connected to the database. The username may be the same, but the session is different.

To discover the SID and serial# of a session, use the following SQL query:

display_session_process_details.sql

```
select
   a.sid,
   a.serial#,
   b.spid,
   b.pid,
   a.username,
   a.osuser,
   a.machine
from
   v$session a,
   v$process b
where
   a.username IS NOT NULL
and
   a.paddr=b.addr;
```

Note that several columns are included in this query. Sometimes, common user logins might be used in a database, and it is suggested to include the *osuser* and *machine* columns to make identifying the correct session easier. Here is an example of some output for this command:

```
sid serial# SPID PID USERNAME OSUSERMACHINE
--- ------- ---- --- -------- -------------
162   7 3072 13 SYS    Robert      ROBERTS1
144 36 1864 21 SCOTT Robert      ROBERTS2
146 29 1868 22 SCOTT Robert      ROBERTS3
```

Other *v$session* columns might also help identify the correct session such as *command, server, terminal, program, logon_time,* and *last_call_et.* Also, when familiar with the system, joining *v$session* to *v$sqlarea* might help identify the correct session.

Next, examine a technique for using Oracle external tables for reading an Oracle trace file.

The Wait Event External Table

The first external table is designed to load all of the wait events that are listed in the 10046 trace file. Notice each of the external tables uses the *trace_row_num* pseudo column to track the actual row number of the event in the trace file. This will allow visibility of the records in the sequence that they appeared in the trace file.

Also note that the *create directory* command needs to be used to create the *load_directory* directory that is referenced in these external tables. Here is the SQL for that command:

create_10046_wait_table.sql

```
create directory
   load_directory
as
   'c:\oracle\product\admin\BOOKTST\udump';
```

And here is the first external table DDL code. Note that the variables related to the particular events to external table columns have all been loaded:

```
drop table ext_10046_table_wait_events;

create table ext_10046_table_wait_events
(event_type              varchar2(10),
 cursor_number           number,
 wait_event_name         varchar2(60),
 total_elapsed_time       number,
 p1                      varchar2(100),
 p2                      varchar2(100),
 p3                      varchar2(100),
 trace_row_num           number
)
ORGANIZATION EXTERNAL
(TYPE oracle_loader
 DEFAULT DIRECTORY load_directory
 access parameters
         ( RECORDS DELIMITED BY NEWLINE
           badfile load_directory:'bad_10046.log'
           logfile load_directory:'load_10046.log'
           skip 24
           LOAD WHEN event_type="WAIT"
           FIELDS RTRIM
               (
                   event_type CHAR terminated by '#',
                   cursor_number CHAR terminated by ': nam=',
                   wait_event_name CHAR terminated by 'ela=',
                   total_elapsed_time CHAR terminated by 'p1=',
                   p1  CHAR terminated by 'p2=',
                   p2  CHAR terminated by 'p3=',
                   p3  CHAR terminated by WHITESPACE,
                   trace_row_num recnum
               )
         )
     location ('booktst_ora_3640.trc')
)
reject limit unlimited;
```

The *parse, execute and fetch* Events External Table

Because the *parse, execute and fetch* record formats are almost identical, they are loaded into a single external table:

⊟ create_10046_wait_format.sql

```
drop table ext_10046_table_pef_events;

create table ext_10046_table_pef_events
(event_type              varchar2(10),
 cursor_number           number,
 pef_cpu_time            number,
 pef_elap                number,
 pef_blocks              number,
```

```
   pef_blocks_cm          number,
   pef_blocks_curmode     number,
   pef_lib_cache_misses   number,
   pef_rows_returned      number,
   pef_depth              number,
   pef_goal               number,
   pef_tim                number,
   trace_row_num          number
   )
ORGANIZATION EXTERNAL
(TYPE oracle_loader
  DEFAULT DIRECTORY load_directory
  access parameters
           ( RECORDS DELIMITED BY NEWLINE
             badfile load_directory:'bad_10046.log'
             logfile load_directory:'load_10046.log'
             skip 24
             LOAD WHEN (    event_type="EXEC"
                         or event_type="FETCH"
                         or event_type="PARSE" )
             FIELDS RTRIM
                (
                     event_type            CHAR terminated by '#',
                     cursor_number         CHAR terminated by ':c=',
                     pef_cpu_time          CHAR terminated by ',e=',
                     pef_elap              CHAR terminated by ',p=',
                     pef_blocks            CHAR terminated by ',cr=',
                     pef_blocks_cm         CHAR terminated by ',cu=',
                     pef_blocks_curmode    CHAR terminated by ',mis=',
                     pef_lib_cache_misses  CHAR terminated by ',r=',
                     pef_rows_returned     CHAR terminated by ',dep=',
                     pef_depth             CHAR terminated by ',og=',
                     pef_goal              CHAR terminated by ',tim=',
                     pef_tim               CHAR terminated by WHITESPACE,
                     trace_row_num recnum
                )
            )
        location ('booktst_ora_3640.trc')
 )
reject limit unlimited;
```

Accessing Oracle Trace Records with External Tables

Collecting the trace data is just the first step; now the DBA needs to be able to read and analyze the trace file contents.   Here is a view to make accessing the trace records easier:

💾   **view_10046_trace.sql**

```
create or replace view

   vw_10046_view as
select
   trace_row_num,
   event_type,
   cursor_number,
   wait_event_name,
   to_char(total_elapsed_time) wait_time,
   -1 command
```

```
from
   ext_10046_table_wait_events
union
select
   trace_row_num,
   event_type,
   cursor_number,
   null,
   to_char(pef_tim),
   -1
from
   ext_10046_table_pef_events
union
select
   distinct
b.trace_row_num,
   null,
   null,
   null,
   sql_text,
   to_number(cur_oct) command
from
   v$sql
a,
   ext_10046_table_cursor_events b
where
   upper(b.cur_ad)=a.address (+)
order by 1;
```

While this view makes it easier to read the trace file, there is still a performance problem. External table access to large 10046 trace files is very slow. Creating a table to dump the 10046 trace data into helps improve the access speed.

```
create table tab_10046 as
select * from vw_10046_view;

Create index ix_tab_10046_01 on tab_10046(trace_row_num);
Create index ix_tab_10046_02 on tab_10046(command);
Create index ix_tab_10046_03 on tab_10046(event_type);
Create index ix_tab_10046_04 on tab_10046
(event_type, trace_row_num, cursor_number, wait_time);
```

These indexes help tremendously with overall access times for queries. Next arc some more queries that will help with real world 10046 trace problem solving. The first query uses the analytical functions of Oracle to provide some insight into the run times of various operations:

🖫 trace_exec_parse_fetch_sql.sql

```
column time_between_events heading "Time|Between|Events"
column wait_time format 9999999999

select
   event_type,
   cursor_number,
   to_number(wait_time) wait_time,
   (wait_time/1000000)-lag(wait_time/1000000, 1)
over
   (order by trace_row_num) "time_between_events"
```

```
from
   tab_10046
where
   event_type in ('EXEC','FETCH','PARSE')
order by
   trace_row_num;
```

Next is a trace file listing that shows each *exec, fetch* and *parse* operation for a SQL statement, showing the elapsed time between the operations. It is a lot of detail! For example, this 10046 trace file produced over five million output records:

```
   Time
   Cursor  Between
EVENT_TYPE  Number  WAIT_TIME  Events
----------  ----------  -----------  ----------
PARSE   3   3889179528
EXEC    3   3889180002   .000474
PARSE   3   3889182412   .00241
EXEC    3   3889182891   .000479
PARSE   3   3889185178   .002287
EXEC    3   3889185634   .000456
PARSE   3   3889188020   .002386
EXEC    3   3889188437   .000417
PARSE   3   3923555525   34.367088
EXEC    3   3923556292   .000767
PARSE   3   3923559154   .002862
EXEC    3   3923559754   .0006
PARSE   3   3923562154   .0024
EXEC    3   3923562690   .000536
PARSE   3   3923565068   .002378
EXEC    3   3923565564   .000496
```

Exception Reporting within a Trace File

Five million records of trace detail is clearly overkill, but how can the size of the trace results be reduced while still seeing the details that are needed? One option is to do exception reporting.

Below, modify the trace query to add some additional run time criteria to only show significant wait events (over a quarter second):

💾 **filter_trace_file.sql**

```
select
   trace_row_num,
   event_type,
   cursor_number,
   to_number(wait_time) wait_time,
   event_time
from
  (select trace_row_num, event_type, cursor_number, wait_time,
  (wait_time/1000000)-lag(wait_time/1000000, 1)
   over (order by trace_row_num) "EVENT_TIME" from tab_10046
```

```
   where
      event_type in ('EXEC','FETCH','PARSE')
   order by
      trace_row_num  )
where
   trace_row_num in
   ( select trace_row_num
     from
       (select trace_row_num,
         (wait_time/1000000)-
         lag(wait_time/1000000, 1)
     over (order by trace_row_num)
     "EVENT_TIME"
     from
     tab_10046
     where
       event_type in ('EXEC','FETCH','PARSE') )
where
   event_time > .25 );
```

This complex SQL query will limit the trace result to those events that experienced a lag time of greater than .25 seconds. This will significantly reduce the row set and produce a manageable trace file. Here is a partial result of this trace file exception report:

```
TRACE_ROW_NUM EVENT_TYPE   Number  WAIT_TIME EVENT_TIME
------------- ----------  ---------- ----------- ----------
   2298019 PARSE   3  2881178580   32.95
   2425666 PARSE   3  2939522206   34.07
   2553299 PARSE   3  2994920152   31.08
   2680751 PARSE   3  3054787045   33.54
   2808832 PARSE   3  3110536030   32.24
   2936778 PARSE   3  3167765847   31.58
   3064266 PARSE   3  3227249876   33.48
   3191935 PARSE   3  3284241535   32.12
   3319636 PARSE   3  3341259394   31.84
   3447092 PARSE   3  3400515679   33.46
   3574826 PARSE   3  3457276827   33.02
   3702529 PARSE   3  3515651502   33.09
   3829993 PARSE   3  3575157371   34.83
   3957662 PARSE   3  3630381367   31.68
   4085349 PARSE   3  3689283680   33.62
   4106254 EXEC    3  3695989891     .45
   4213359 PARSE   3  3750297980   35.12
   4341185 PARSE   3  3805701373   31.61
   4468887 PARSE   3  3865174711   33.78
   4596361 PARSE   3  3923555525   34.37
```

This ability to do exception reporting on trace file output makes it easier to pinpoint problem areas, but there is still a piece missing. It would be even easier if it would be possible to see the operation prior to this operation, the one on which the lag time is actually predicated. This query will enable us to determine a range of records that are of interest. Here the query is modified to provide this information:

💾 **filter_trace_file_range.sql**

```
select
   'E' operation,
   trace_row_num,
   event_type,
   cursor_number,
   wait_time,
   event_time
from
   select
      trace_row_num,
      event_type,
      cursor_number,
      to_number(wait_time) wait_time,
      (wait_time/1000000)-lag(wait_time/1000000, 1)
       over (order by trace_row_num) "EVENT_TIME" from tab_10046
   where
      event_type in ('EXEC','FETCH','PARSE')
       order by trace_row_num  )
where
   trace_row_num in
   ( select trace_row_num
     from
      (select trace_row_num,
       (wait_time/1000000)-
        lag(wait_time/1000000, 1)
     over (order by trace_row_num) "EVENT_TIME"
    from tab_10046
     where event_type in ('EXEC','FETCH','PARSE') )
  where event_time > .25 )
UNION
select
   'B' Operation,
   trace_row_num,
   event_type,
   cursor_number,
   to_number(wait_time) wait_time,
   event_time
from
  (select
      trace_row_num,
      event_type,
      cursor_number,
      wait_time,
      (wait_time/1000000)-lag(wait_time/1000000, 1)
   over (order by trace_row_num) "EVENT_TIME"  from tab_10046
   where
      event_type in ('EXEC','FETCH','PARSE')
   order by trace_row_num  )
where
   rowid in
      (select q_rowid
        from (select trace_row_num,
        (wait_time/1000000)-
         lag(wait_time/1000000, 1)
         over (order by trace_row_num) "EVENT_TIME",
         lag(rowid) over
        (order by trace_row_num) q_rowid
  from tab_10046
  where
   event_type in ('EXEC','FETCH','PARSE') )
where event_time > .25  )
order by trace_row_num;
```

This complex query gives this useful trace report showing the begin and end activity for each step:

```
        Cursor
O   TRACE_ROW_NUM  EVENT_TYPE   Number   WAIT_TIME EVENT_TIME
-   -------------  ----------   ------   ----------- ----------
B   4661621        PARSE        3        3936743204  .01
E   4661624        EXEC         3        3937120555  .38

B   4724009        EXEC         3        3948848444  .00
E   4724035        PARSE        3        3981191796  32.34

B   4851699        EXEC         3        4006419477  .00
E   4851727        PARSE        3        4040119254  33.70

B   4979646        EXEC         3        4063701927  .00
E   4979674        PARSE        3        4096337840  32.64

B   5033307        PARSE        3        4107294796  .01
E   5033311        EXEC         3        4107692394  .40
```

Note that this report reveals the *beginning* operation, denoted with the B, and the *ending* operation number, denoted with the E. The *ending* operation is the one reporting the lag, the *beginning* operation is the one where the lag timing started. So, the bottom line is that somewhere between these operations, trouble has occurred.

Now that the range of interest has been isolated, it is time to run another query to drill-down and see all of the waits that occurred in between those events:

🖫 **trace_detail.sql**

```
select
   trace_row_num,
   event_type,
   wait_event_name,
   cursor_number,
   wait_time/1000000 wait_time
from
   tab_10046
where
   trace_row_num between 4851699 and 4851727
order by
   trace_row_num;
```

```
Cursor
TRACE_ROW_NUM EVENT_TYPE WAIT_EVENT_NAME          Number  WAIT_TIME
------------- ---------- ---------------          ------  ---------
    4851699 EXEC   3   4006
    4851700 WAIT   'SQL*Net message to client'     3    0
    4851701 WAIT   'SQL*Net message from client'   3    0
    4851703 WAIT   'log file sync'                  0    0
    4851704 WAIT   'SQL*Net message to client'     0    0
    4851705 WAIT   'SQL*Net message from client'   0    0
    4851708 WAIT   'SQL*Net message to client'     3    0
```

```
4851709 WAIT    'SQL*Net message from client'  3   0
4851710 WAIT    'SQL*Net message to client'    0   0
4851712 WAIT    'SQL*Net message from client'  0   34

4851713 WAIT    'SQL*Net message to client'    0   0
4851714 WAIT    'SQL*Net message from client'  0   0
4851715 WAIT    'SQL*Net message to client'    3   0
4851716 WAIT    'SQL*Net message from client'  3   0
4851718
4851727 PARSE  3  4040
```

In this case, there was a wait event, a SQL*Net message from the client that lasted for 34 seconds. This may be a normal situation, waiting for user feedback perhaps, or it might demonstrate some sort of problem with the application or network.

Loading and Analyzing the 10046 Event

Oracle provides the TKPROF utility for reviewing trace dumps, a tool that will analyze a trace file generated via a 10046 event, and TKPROF collects summary wait information for each event.

But TKPROF has limitations. Sometimes it is necessary to be able to load critical 10046 trace information into the database so that SQL extraction and analysis methods can be used. In these examples, three external tables are created that load specific event information from within the trace file. These external tables have been tested on Oracle Database 10g on a Windows XP platform. They should work on 11g databases.

Inside the Oracle 10046 Trace File Output

As has been seen, a 10046 trace file contains a great deal of information. Each cursor that is opened after tracing has been enabled and will be recorded in the trace file. Here is a sample excerpt from a trace file:

```
====================
PARSING IN CURSOR #2 len=79 dep=0 uid=73 oct=3 lid=73 tim=259898785365
hv=4060294543 ad='1cd62f00'
SELECT a.emp_first_name, b.job_name
FROM emp a, job b
WHERE a.job_key=b.job_key
END OF STMT
PARSE #2:c=0,e=154,p=0,cr=0,cu=0,mis=0,r=0,dep=0,og=1,tim=259898785352
BINDS #2:
EXEC #2:c=0,e=12571,p=0,cr=0,cu=0,mis=0,r=0,dep=0,og=1,tim=259898883135
WAIT #2: nam='SQL*Net message to client' ela= 10 p1=1111838976 p2=1 p3=0
FETCH #2:c=0,e=854,p=0,cr=14,cu=0,mis=0,r=1,dep=0,og=1,tim=259898908178
WAIT #2: nam='SQL*Net message from client' ela= 2120 p1=1111838976 p2=1 p3=0
WAIT #2: nam='SQL*Net message to client' ela= 6 p1=1111838976 p2=1 p3=0
FETCH #2:c=0,e=12470,p=0,cr=1,cu=0,mis=0,r=9,dep=0,og=1,tim=259898947719
WAIT #2: nam='SQL*Net message from client' ela= 1353028 p1=1111838976 p2=1 p3=0
XCTEND rlbk=0, rd_only=1
STAT #2 id=1 cnt=10 pid=0 pos=1 obj=0 op='HASH JOIN (cr=15 pr=0 pw=0 time=850 us)'
STAT #2 id=2 cnt=4 pid=1 pos=1 obj=55218 op='TABLE ACCESS FULL OBJ#(55218) (cr=7
pr=0 pw=0 time=168 us)'
```

```
STAT #2 id=3 cnt=10 pid=1 pos=2 obj=55217 op='TABLE ACCESS FULL OBJ#(55217) (cr=8
pr=0 pw=0 time=60 us)'
```

Break down this trace file into its constituent pieces:

Parse Phase of a 10046 Oracle Trace

In this section of the trace file, the SQL statement and the parse record are found to be associated with the parse statement. This line provides information on the cursor itself. It shows the length of the cursor (len=79), the user id of the person parsing the cursor (uid=73), the time the parse began (tim=) and the SQL address of the cursor (ad=). As will be shown shortly, referencing the ad= line to *v$sqlarea* provides the text of this cursor.

```
=====================
PARSING IN CURSOR #2 len=79 dep=0 uid=73 oct=3 lid=73 tim=259898785365
hv=4060294543 ad='1cd62f00'
```

This is the SQL statement itself. Note that terminator, END OF STMT.

```
SELECT a.emp_first_name, b.job_name
FROM emp a, job b
WHERE a.job_key=b.job_key
END OF STMT
```

This is the actual parse record. Note that many of the variables documented in this comment are reused in the *execute* and *fetch* records. The variables are: c= cpu time, e=elapsed time, p=number of database blocks read, cr=number of consistent mode blocks read, cu=number of current mode blocks read, mis=number of library cache misses, r=number of rows, og=optimizer goal (1=all_rows, 2=first_rows, 3=rule and 4=choose.

Also note that the cursor number is 2. Each cursor will be assigned its own number. Cursor numbers can be reused, so be careful about that!

```
PARSE #2:c=0,e=154,p=0,cr=0,cu=0,mis=0,r=0,dep=0,og=1,tim=259898785352
```

Notice that the parse record is accompanied by the cursor number; #2 in this case.

Execute Phase of a 10046 Oracle Trace

Just in case a SQL statement has bind variables, tracing has been enabled with a level 12, so Oracle will capture the bind variable information. The bind variables will show up in the trace file at this point. Since bind variables are not being used, it is time to move onto the execution (*exec*) phase which is represented by this line:

```
EXEC #2:c=0,e=12571,p=0,cr=0,cu=0,mis=0,r=0,dep=0,og=1,tim=259898883135
```

Fetch Phase of a 10046 Oracle Trace

Next is the fetch phase. Notice that the variables listed in the fetch record are the same as the parse and execute records though, of course, some values may be different.

```
FETCH #2:c=0,e=854,p=0,cr=14,cu=0,mis=0,r=1,dep=0,og=1,tim=259898908178
```

Those Evil Wait Events in the 10046 Trace File

The trace file contains lots of details and it is important to seek out the wait event notes as the wait events are interspersed throughout the 10046 trace file.

```
WAIT #2: nam='SQL*Net message to client' ela= 10 p1=1111838976 p2=1 p3=0
```

This wait record shows that the wait event (*nam*) is a SQL*Net message to client. These wait events are the same wait events that can be found in the database in the *v$* views like *v$session_wait* or *v$event_name*.

The elapsed time (*ela*) is in microseconds since this database is Oracle 10g, so this wait was a whole 10 microseconds. This is nothing to worry about because 1 second = 1,000,000 microseconds. Please note the *P1, P2* and *P3* variables are specific to each event.

Here are some other examples of possible wait events:

```
WAIT #7:  nam='db file scattered read' ela= 1046 p1=10 p2=166987 p3=2
WAIT #7:  nam='db file sequential read' ela= 509 p1=10 p2=166994 p3=1
WAIT #7:  nam='buffer busy waits' ela= 26 p1=2 p2=1341 p3=231
WAIT #13: nam='latch free' ela= 0 p1=-2147427600 p2=103 p3=0
WAIT #15: nam='log buffer space' ela= 4 p1=0 p2=0 p3=0
WAIT #38: nam='file open' ela= 0 p1=0 p2=0 p3=0
```

Conclusions on Tracing

As has been shown, Oracle tracing provides an extremely fine granularity where each and every minute detail of execution can be seen. In the real world, the DBA seldom requires this level of detail, but it is good to know how to look under the covers when needed.

As we know, carefully benchmark testing is the only recognized method for testing changes to our database and it's critical to understand how to create test data, so that we can make our changes confidentially.

Generating Oracle Test Data

Getting valid data for testing Oracle systems is critical to proactive tuning. To eliminate the guesswork from global changes like optimizer parameters or optimizer stats, the DBA must be able to test against representative workloads that closely approximate the real-world transactions.

Gathering a Sample Workload in Oracle 11g

While workloads are identified for instance-wide tuning, Oracle also offers a workload-based approach for SQL tuning. Starting with Oracle 10g, Oracle introduced database replay where using artificial test data can be avoided by grabbing real-world workloads. This allows the DBA more flexibility than ever before, and increases the validity of pre-production testing.

Workload-based optimization is an important part of global SQL optimization, and Oracle codified the holistic approach to Oracle tuning, most directly in the 11g SQL Performance Analyzer, called SPA. See these related notes on workload-based testing:

- Important notes for global SQL optimization
- Inside Oracle 11g database replay
- Oracle 10g SQL Access advisor
- Oracle regression testing tips

Workload management is a major new approach for Oracle, away from contrived test cases, and into testing with empirical, real-world workloads. First, see 11g SQL Performance Analyzer tips for detailed coverage on capturing a STS. Ahmed Baraka notes these steps in capturing a SQL workload in 11g.

Preparing to Capture a SQL Workload

Before capturing the workload, perform the following steps:

1. Backup database data before testing. Use either RMAN, user-managed online backup, Data Pump utilities or a snapshot standby. Output files of this backup will be used for the replay process.

2. Any transaction that is underway when capture of the workload is being started may not be captured. To capture all transactions, restart the database in restricted mode, start the capture process, and open the database for users.

3. Create directory object for storing captured workload.

```
create directory
   workload_dir
as
   'C:\Oracle\admin\ora11g\workload';
```

4. Decide whether some of the user sessions should not be captured. It may not be necessary to capture DBA sessions, Oracle Enterprise Manager sessions or any sessions created by third party sessions. To achieve this task, use the *dbms_workload_capture* package as in the following guidelines:

a. Use *add_filter* procedure to add any eliminating sessions based on *user, module, action, program, service* or *instance_number.*

```
begin
dbms_workload_capture.add_filter(
fname => 'FILTER_DBA1',
fattribute => 'USER',
fvalue => 'SYSTEM,DBSNMP' );
end;
```

b. Use *delete_filter* procedure to delete any existing filter:

```
exec dbms_workload_capture.delete_filter( fname => 'filter_dba1');
```

Capturing the Workload

Use the *start_capture* procedure in the *dbms_workload_capture* package to start capturing the workload:

```
begin
dbms_workload_capture.start_capture(
name => '1JAN_WORKLOAD',
dir => 'WORKLOAD_DIR',
duration => 40); -- duration in minutes
end;
```

To stop the capture process before the ending of duration period, issue the following command:

```
begin
dbms_workload_capture.finish_capture;
end;
```

After the capture process finishes, issue a query about workload captures using the following command:

```
select
    id,
    name,
    status,
    error_message
from
    dba_workload_captures;
```

A report can be generated about the workload capture that has been made:

```
DECLARE
v_capture_id number;
v_capture_rpt clob;
BEGIN

v_capture_id := DBMS_WORKLOAD_CAPTURE.GET_CAPTURE_INFO(DIR => 'WORKLOAD_DIR');

v_capture_rpt := DBMS_WORKLOAD_CAPTURE.REPORT( CAPTURE_ID => v_capture_id , FORMAT =>
DBMS_WORKLOAD_CAPTURE.TYPE_TEXT); -- format could also be TYPE_HTML

-- display contents of v_capture

END;
```

Alternatively, the following statements can be used:

```
select id, name, status from dba_workload_captures:

select dbms_workload_capture.report(1, 'HTML') from dual;
```

To delete from its data dictionary views, use the procedure *delete_capture_info*. However, this procedure does not delete the workload capture files in its directory. To take a new workload capture with the same name, manually get rid of the files; otherwise, an error will be returned when the *start_capture* procedure is executed.

External Workload Metrics in Oracle

Oracle knows that the external environment has a profound impact on SQL performance, and the Oracle CBO now has the ability to consider real-world timings for multi-block reads (*mreadtim*) and sequential read I/O times (*sreadtim*) within the *dbms_stats.gather_system_stats* procedure.

Oracle has two types of CBO statistics for estimating disk read times workload and *noworkload* statistics. The *noworkload* statistics gather data by submitting random reads against all data files while the *workload* statistics increments internal counters to measure database I/O activity:

- **Noworkload statistics:** These include *cpuspeednw, ioseektim* and *iotfrspeed*.

- **Workload statistics:** These are gathered by *dbms_stats.gather_system_stats* and include *sreadtim, mreadtim, cpuspeed, mbrc, maxthr,* and *slavethr* that represent workload statistics.

If both *workload* and *noworkload* statistics are available, the optimizer uses the *workload* statistics in hopes of getting the best execution plan for the SQL. Run this query to see the current values for the database:

```
select
   sname,
   pname,
   pval1
from
   sys.aux_stats$;
```

```
SNAME          PNAME                      PVAL1
-------------- ---------- ----------
SYSSTATS_INFO  STATUS
SYSSTATS_INFO  DSTART
SYSSTATS_INFO  DSTOP
SYSSTATS_INFO  FLAGS                          1
SYSSTATS_MAIN  CPUSPEEDNW               502.005
SYSSTATS_MAIN  IOSEEKTIM                     10
SYSSTATS_MAIN  IOTFRSPEED                  4096
SYSSTATS_MAIN  SREADTIM                   7.618
SYSSTATS_MAIN  MREADTIM                  14.348
SYSSTATS_MAIN  CPUSPEED                     507
SYSSTATS_MAIN  MBRC                           6
SYSSTATS_MAIN  MAXTHR                     32768
SYSSTATS_MAIN  SLAVETHR
```

Oracle *workload* statistics that are gathered with *dbms_stats.gather_system_stats* now gather real-workload I/O performance metrics in Oracle 10g and beyond:

- **Sreadtim:** Single block read time in milliseconds

- **mreadtim:** Multiblock read time in ms

- **cpuspeed:** CPU speed

- **mbrc:** Average blocks read per *multiblock* read (see *db_file_multiblock_read_count*)

- **maxthr:** Maximum I/O throughput (for OPQ only)

- **slavethr:** This is for Oracle Parallel Query (OPQ) factotum (slave) throughput and indicates when the multiblock read time is less than single block disk read time (*mreadtim* <= *sreadtim*), then the query plan costing will not use the workload statistics.

The Oracle Performance Tuning Guide notes that the timing of the workload sample is important and that it is best to run samples during a time when legitimate multiblock reads are being performed or stage a workload that performs full-table scans:

> *"During the gathering process of workload statistics, it is possible that mbrc and mreadtim will not be gathered if no table scans are performed during serial workloads, as is often the case with OLTP systems. On the other hand, FTS occur frequently on DSS systems but may run parallel and bypass the buffer cache. In such cases, sreadtim will still be gathered since index lookup are performed using the buffer cache."*

The docs also note that bad timing of a system statistics sample can cause less than optimal estimates for the timings of full-table scan I/O:

"If Oracle cannot gather or validate gathered mbrc or mreadtim, but has gathered sreadtim and cpuspeed, then only sreadtim and cpuspeed will be used for costing.

FTS cost will be computed using analytical algorithms implemented in previous releases. Another alternative to computing mbrc and mreadtim is to force FTS in serial mode to allow the optimizer to gather the data."

While everyone agrees that real-world workloads are best, brand-new systems require the generation of artificial testing data. Take a closer look at how to generate volume data for testing performance.

Creating Data for Performance Testing

It's always prudent to test any changes in a QA environment before migrating them into production and there are many tools to assist us in generating test data. There are two general approaches, gathering real-world SQL workloads (preferred), and generative "junk" data for testing purposes.

For complete details on running Oracle benchmark test, see the book: *Database Benchmarking: Practical methods for Oracle & SQL Server.* There are several tools and methods for generating test data for Oracle:

- **STATSPACK:** You can easily write your own SQL capture, directly from the STATSPACK *stats$sqlstat* table.
- **AWR:** AWR captures historical SQL in the *dba_hist_sqlstat* table.
- **SQL Tuning Sets:** This 10g tool grabs SQL from the library cache or Oracle.
- **Real Application Testing (RAT) and SQL Performance Analyzer (SPA):** This new 11g tool captures representative SQL workloads.
- **Mercury LoadRunner:** This is a popular tools for simulating the real-world effect of an Oracle system change.
- **Quest Benchmark Factory:** This tool has s complete environment for showing the effects of an Oracle change.
- **DBGEN:** This is a TPC-H tools, dbgen and qgen allow for the development of anywhere from a gig to a terabyte databases.
- **Hammerora:** The Hammerora product provides a means to create a pseudo-TPC-C database and generate loads against it.

For simple testing, there are many techniques to generate junk tables. Using junk data is useful when doing capacity planning for a new environment. It is not uncommon to get capacity planning specifications long before the Oracle schema is designed, and using junk data is a good way to loads-down your server with transactions.

Junk data is great for testing hardware. Because no single client's workloads will ever be the same, using junk data is good for generating a fairly consistent load on different clients' hardware as opposed to benchmarking application performance.

Determining the future size of Oracle tables, the size of Oracle indexes, and the overall tablespace size is a formidable challenge which depends on many factors. Most notable is the blocksize for each object, the average row length, the pctfree threshold and the freelist mechanism (traditional vs. ASSM).

Oracle capacity planning generally involves determining tablespace sizes, sizing for individual tables, but more important, capacity planning is used to size the server resources, all of which must be measured at the high-watermark of concurrent transactions:

- How much SGA and PGA are required for optimal performance?

- What is the optimal blocksize for high-impact tables and indexes?

- What are the optimal TNS settings for maximum network throughput?

Using artificial test data can help determine a first stab at these sizings until there are real-world workloads to use for testing. Here is a simple test data generation script:

```
create table test (
  pkey number(15) not null,
  pdate date not null,
  pchar varchar2(4000) not null
);

create sequence test_seq;

create procedure pop_test(p_pass in number)
as begin
  for i in 1 .. p_pass loop
    insert into test
      select test_seq.nextval, sysdate, object_name||'.'||object_type||'.'||owner
      from sys.dba_objects;
    commit;
  end loop;
end;
/

exec pop_test(500);
```

Example:

```
SQL> create table test (
  pkey number(15) not null,
  pdate date not null,
  pchar varchar2(4000) not null
); 2   3   4   5
```

```
Table created.
```

```
SQL> create sequence test_seq;
```

```
Sequence created.
```

```
SQL> create procedure pop_test(p_pass in number)
as begin
  for i in 1 .. p_pass loop
    insert into test
      select test_seq.nextval, sysdate, object_name||'.'||object_type||'.'||owner
      from sys.dba_objects;
    commit;
  end loop;
end;
/  2    3    4    5    6    7    8    9    10
```

```
SQL> exec pop_test(10);
```

PL/SQL procedure successfully completed.

```
SQL> select count(*) from test;
```

```
  COUNT(*)
----------
    127150
```

This will insert 100k test records into a table.

```
-- Insert into varchar and number columns:

create table junk table (
   char_col varchar(200),
   num_col number);

begin
for i in 1..100000
loop
   insert into junk_table values(
     dbms_random.string('U',20),
     dbma_random.value(1,1000)
   );
end loop;
end;
```

Here is one (sample loads 1,000,000 rows):

```
create table
  test_a as
select
  a.*
from
  dba_objects a,
  ( select 1 from dba_objects where rownum <= (select
    ceil(1000000/count(*)) from dba_objects ) )
where
  rownum <1000000+1
```

Here is another way to generate testing data, this one Oracle Corporation:

```
create table number_test
(
c_number_32 number(32,0) not null,
c_number_6 number(6,0) not null,
c_number number not null)
pctfree 10
/
insert into number_test
select c_number,c_number,c_number from source_test;
create index fon.test_32 on number_test(c_number_32);
create index fon.test_6 on number_test(c_number_6);
create index fon.test_ on number_test(c_number);
select segment_name,sum(bytes)/1024/1024
from dba_segments
where segment_name like 'test%'
group by segment_name;
```

And there is this script which will create six gigabytes of test data:

```
create table t1 as
select a.*
from
    dba_objects a
  cross join
    dba_objects b;
```

If that is not enough data, then add another cross join:

```
create table t1 as
select a.*
from
    dba_objects a
  cross join
    dba_objects b
  cross join
    dba_objects c;
```

Conclusion

Oracle provides a host of performance tuning tools, some are spectacular while some are ridiculous, and some are free while others are extra-cost. With each new release, Oracle makes the tuning tools more sophisticated and easier to use, but no tools will ever completely replace the ability of a human tuning expert. The main points of this chapter include:

- Oracle 11g introduced a new holistic approach to Oracle tuning, whereby real-world workloads and text performance are captured using a scientific approach. This removes the guesswork and makes test cases obsolete.

- Oracle has the SQL Performance Advisor, an enhancement of the SQL Access and SQL Tuning advisors, to make simple tuning recommendations about a given SQL workload.

- For super-detailed analysis, Oracle offers specialized trace dumps that reveals all internal processing. Oracle tracing is very expensive and should be run selectively, and only when needed, usually at the bequest of Oracle technical support.

- Oracle offers internal tools such as the Oracle Trace Analyzer and LTOM to aid in specific tuning tasks.

Now it is time to move on and take a look at environmental tuning with Oracle. Oracle does not run in a vacuum, and the DBA must understand how the Oracle instance interacts with the server, disk and network.

Server & Network Tuning

"Mom! It's the server again!"

Oracle Server Tuning

Oracle became one of the world's leading databases because it is optimized to work on any database server from a mainframe to a Macintosh. However, Oracle does not run in a vacuum and the DBA must be careful to avoid server overload conditions.

Fortunately, the Oracle Automated Workload Repository (AWR) tracks server performance over time and allows the production of detailed management reports that show exactly when the server was overloaded. AWR trend reports on RAM, disk I/O, and CPU can be generated to help isolate hardware stress and predict when new hardware is needed. Careful attention to server utilization is required to maintain good performance.

The first step in evaluation of server utilization is the examination of the influence of the external environment on server performance. The DBA is then free to deploy specific monitoring techniques for evaluating the external environment.

Outside the Oracle Instance

While server overload conditions may indicate a sub-optimal Oracle component, overload of a pre-tuned database indicates that more hardware resources are needed.

But what about a crappy vendor application? Is it legitimate to throw hardware at an atrocious Oracle application that is loaded with sub-optimal SQL and inferior code? The answer has to do more with economics than with theory.

For example, consider a database with thousands of suboptimal SQL statements and 100,000 lines of poorly written PL/SQL. Assume that the database is heavily I/O bound with a large amount of unnecessary logical and physical I/O. Sadly, systems like this are not that unusual, and IT management might be presented with the following options:

5. The code could be repaired for $50,000 and it will take 8 weeks; or

6. The tablespaces could be moved to a high-speed solid-state disk for $20,000 and the problem could be remedied tomorrow. Of course, adding solid-state disks will only serve to eliminate disk I/O, but it will fix their immediate issue quickly and without risk.

Whenever a hardware fix is used to address a software issue, the lousy code will still be inefficient, but it might run 20 times faster! It does not address the root cause of the I/O problem (crappy SQL), but the faster hardware is cheaper and less risky, very appealing to IT managers.

This approach of "throwing hardware at the problem" is more common than you might think. Now that we see how economic often drive they type of tuning solution that we implement, let's move on and take a closer look at common server tuning issues.

Oracle Server Bottlenecks

Oracle does not run in a vacuum, and a poorly designed Oracle system will clobber any server. You can only tune Oracle so far, and it's not uncommon for systems to outgrow their servers as they take on heavier workloads with more end-users and higher volumes of transactions per second.

While the amount of server stress ranges widely, if our SQL workload has not been completely optimized, the following server overload conditions may appear:

- **I/O overload:** An I/O overload is sometimes evidenced by high *db file sequential read* and *db file scattered read* waits and can be detected in the Oracle *dba_hist_filestatxs* view. SQL that issues unnecessary table block access, possibly due to missing indexes or poor statistics, should be investigated. Assuming that the SQL is optimized, the only remaining solutions are the addition of RAM for the data buffers or a switch to solid-state disks.

- **CPU overhead:** With the advent of 64-bit Oracle and large data block buffers such as *db_cache_size* and *db_keep_cache_size*, the main bottleneck for many databases has shifted from I/O to CPU

If CPU is listed in the top wait events, suboptimal SQL that may be causing unnecessary logical I/O against the data buffers should be investigated. The library cache can also be investigated to see if excessive parsing might be causing the CPU consumption.

Assuming that Oracle has been optimized, the options to relieve a CPU bottleneck are to add more CPUs or faster CPU processors. This is an extremely rare event. On most installations which have paid only minimal attention to sizing, a CPU bottleneck is suffered only as a consequence of bad SQL.

- **Network overload:** In many Oracle-based applications, the largest component of end-user response time is network latency. Oracle captures important metrics that will show if the Oracle database is network bound, specifically using the SQL*Net statistics from the *dba_hist_sysstat* view. Due to the Oracle Transparent Network Substrate (TNS) isolation, there are only a few network tuning options and most network issues, such as packet sizes, are usually external to the Oracle database.

- **RAM overload:** The Oracle Automatic Memory Management (AMM) utility has facilities for resizing the *db_cache_size, shared_pool_size*, and *pga_aggregate_target* regions and Oracle Enterprise Manager for detecting memory regions that are too small. RAM can be reallocated within these regions, which will reduce *pga_aggregate_target* if there are no disk sorts or hash joins, reduce *shared_pool_size* if there is no library cache contention, and reduce *db_cache_size* if there is low disk I/O activity.

Historically, tiny data buffers meant that disk I/O was the most common wait event, but this has changed with the introduction of Solid State RAM disk and 64-bit Oracle where large RAM data buffer caches can be implemented to reduce disk reads.

This has shifted many databases from I/O to CPU constraints, and it is one of the reasons that Oracle introduced CPU based costing into the SQL optimizer.

External bottleneck can cause system wide outages!

Let's take a look at some of Oracle's tools for monitoring our server environment.

Oracle Server Monitoring

We are going to take a look at two types of server-side statistics, the "real" external server metrics from OS-level tools, and Oracle's internal measurements of the amount of OS resources that are being used.

It is important to frequently monitor the resource consumption on our Oracle server and most server-side monitoring is done with scripts. Since very dew production database run on personal computers, we will focus on the UNIX/Linux implementation that comprises the vast majority of Oracle shops.

For UNIX systems, most shops capture OS data from the *vmstat* utility every few minutes and place them into an Oracle table. From this server data, you can correlate the server utilization with Oracle internal usage and create exception reports:

- **Exception reports:** These reports show the time period where predefined thresholds are exceeded

- **Daily trend reports:** These reports are often run and used with Excel spreadsheets to produce trending graphs

- **Hourly trend reports:** These reports show the median utilization, averaged by the hour of the day. These reports are very useful for showing peak usage periods in a production environment

- **Long-term predictive reports:** These reports generate a long-term trend line for performance. The data from these reports is often used with a linear regression to predict when additional RAM memory or CPU power is required for the server.

Following is a closer look at how a DBA can capture server-side performance metrics in UNIX and Linux.

Capturing Server-side Metrics

When capturing server-side RAM and CPU consumption, it makes sense to capture the information outside of the Oracle instance using a generic utility such as *vmstat*. If the extra-cost AWR has been purchased, some primitive external tuning metrics are captured in OEM.

Oracle knows that the database does not run in a vacuum and that external environmental events have a huge impact on Oracle performance.

The speed of disk access, the backlog of CPU enqueues, network latency and RAM swapping can all be the root cause of an Oracle performance problem, and no amount of tuning can fix a problem that is at the OS layer, external to Oracle. Oracle has two main ways to collect OS information:

- **The *dbms_stats* procedure:** The *gather_system_stats* procedure samples important OS metrics.

- **The *v$* Views:** The Oracle background processes also collect OS information and store them in *v$osstat*.

- **STATSPACK:** In STATSPACK we have OS information in *stats$osstat* and *stats$osstatname*
- **AWR:** In the extra-cost AWR we have OS statistics inside the *dba_hist_osstat* table.

Let's take a closer look at the operating system statistics captured by Oracle.

OS Statistics for the Cost-based Optimizer

The *dbms_stats.gather_system_stats* procedure measures important timings within the database and adjusts the optimizer's propensity to choose indexes vs. full-scans. Oracle captures these OS statistics:

Here are the data items collected by *dbms_stats.gather_system_stats*:

Non Workload (NW) OS statistics:

- o   CPUSPEEDNW - CPU speed
- o   IOSEEKTIM - The I/O seek time in milliseconds
- o   IOTFRSPEED - I/O transfer speed in milliseconds

Workload-related OS statistics:

- o   SREADTIM - Single block read time in milliseconds
- o   MREADTIM - Multiblock read time in ms
- o   CPUSPEED - CPU speed
- o   MBRC - Average blocks read per multiblock read
- o   MAXTHR - Maximum I/O throughput (for OPQ only)
- o   SLAVETHR - OPQ Factotum (slave) throughput (OPQ only)

While it's one thing to get statistics to help the SQL optimizer, it's quite different than collecting OS statistics to help us tune our environment.

OS data inside Oracle views

Oracle has several views that collect OS information, namely *v$osstat*, *stats$osstat*, *stats$osstatname* and *dba_hist_osstat*. Let's start with the free STATSPACK OS data tables and then look at scripts that use the extra-cost AWR equivalents.

However, these are rarely used in the real-world because it is easier to capture external OS statistics from *vmstat*.

STATSPACK OS table Scripts

For those who do not want to spend thousands of dollars to purchase a license to access the *dba_hist* tables, the free STATSPACK utility has very much the same OS information as AWR. The *stats$osstat* table is quite simple, showing the values for all statistics in the *stats$osstatname* table:

```
select
   snap_id,
   stat_name,
   value
from
   stats$osstat       st1,
   stats$osstatname st2
where
   st1.osstat_id = st2.osstat_id
and
   and snap_id between 10046 and 10047;
```

This query also uses stats$osstat to roll-up OS statistics between snapshot periods:

📄 statspack_osstats_rollup.sql

```
select *
from
(select
   snap_id,
   osstat_id,
value
from
   stats$osstat
where
   snap_id in (10046, 10047))
pivot
   sum(value) for osstat;
```

AWR OS statistics Scripts

The extra-cost AWR has two tables with OS information, *dba_hist_system_event* and *dba_hist_osstat*. Here is a script to display these Oracle OS statistics from *dba_hist_system_event*:

📄 display_os_stats.sql

```
select
   sum(a.time_waited_micro)/sum(a.total_waits)/1000000 c1,
   sum(b.time_waited_micro)/sum(b.total_waits)/1000000 c2,
   (
```

```
      sum(a.total_waits) /
      sum(a.total_waits + b.total_waits)
   ) * 100 c3,
   (
      sum(b.total_waits) /
      sum(a.total_waits + b.total_waits)
   ) * 100 c4,
   (
      sum(b.time_waited_micro) /
      sum(b.total_waits)) /
      (sum(a.time_waited_micro)/sum(a.total_waits)
   ) * 100 c5
from
   dba_hist_system_event a,
   dba_hist_system_event b
where
   a.snap_id = b.snap_id
and
   a.event_name = 'db file scattered read'
and
   b.event_name = 'db file sequential read';
```

Here is a script that queries the AWR for OS statistics using *dba_hist_osstat*:

🖫 awr_osstats.sql

```
select e.stat_name "Statistic Name"
     , decode(e.stat_name, 'NUM_CPUS', e.value, e.value - b.value) "Total"
     , decode( instrb(e.stat_name, 'BYTES'), 0, to_number(null)
             , round((e.value - b.value)/( select

      avg( extract( day from (e1.end_interval_time-b1.end_interval_time) )*24*60*60+

          extract( hour from (e1.end_interval_time-b1.end_interval_time) )*60*60+
          extract( minute from (e1.end_interval_time-b1.end_interval_time) )*60+
          extract( second from (e1.end_interval_time-b1.end_interval_time)) )
    from dba_hist_snapshot  b1
        ,dba_hist_snapshot  e1
   where b1.snap_id          = b.snap_id
     and e1.snap_id          = e.snap_id
     and b1.dbid             = b.dbid
     and e1.dbid             = e.dbid
     and b1.instance_number  = b.instance_number
     and e1.instance_number  = e.instance_number
     and b1.startup_time     = e1.startup_time
     and b1.end_interval_time < e1.end_interval_time ),2)) "Per Second"
 from
   dba_hist_osstat  b,
   dba_hist_osstat  e
where b.snap_id       = &pBgnSnap
  and e.snap_id       = &pEndSnap
  and b.dbid          = &pDbId
order by 1 asc;
```

The query output looks like the following:

```
Statistic Name                   Total      Per Second
------------------------------   ----------  ----------
```

```
AVG_BUSY_TICKS                   1,974,925
AVG_IDLE_TICKS                   7,382,241
AVG_IN_BYTES                 2,236,256,256   23,881.91
AVG_OUT_BYTES                 566,304,768      6047.8
AVG_SYS_TICKS                      727,533
AVG_USER_TICKS                   1,247,392
BUSY_TICKS                       1,974,925
IDLE_TICKS                       7,382,241
IN_BYTES                     2,236,256,256   23,881.91
NUM_CPUS                                 1
OUT_BYTES                     566,304,768     6,047.8
SYS_TICKS                          727,533
USER_TICKS                        1247,392
```

We can also join *dba_hist_osstat* against itself to produce a time line showing the OS load averages and RAM. However, on dedicated server where only one instance is running, OS statistics are better captured outside of Oracle using standard OS utilities.

🖫 awr_os_stats_load_cpu_ram.sql

```
select
    s1t0.snap_id,
    to_char(s0.BEGIN_INTERVAL_TIME,'YYYY-Mon-DD HH24:MI:SS') time,
    s1t1.value - s1t0.value as busy_time,
    s2t1.value as load,
    s3t1.value as num_cpus,
    s4t1.value as physical_memory_bytes
        from dba_hist_snapshot s0,
             dba_hist_snapshot s1,
             dba_hist_osstat s1t0,
             dba_hist_osstat s1t1,
             dba_hist_osstat s2t1,
             dba_hist_osstat s3t1,
             dba_hist_osstat s4t1
        where
          s0.dbid = (select dbid from v$database)
          and s1t0.dbid = s0.dbid
          and s1t1.dbid = s0.dbid
          and s2t1.dbid = s0.dbid
          and s3t1.dbid = s0.dbid
          and s4t1.dbid = s0.dbid
          and s0.instance_number = 1
          and s1t0.instance_number = s0.instance_number
          and s1t1.instance_number = s0.instance_number
          and s2t1.instance_number = s0.instance_number
          and s3t1.instance_number = s0.instance_number
          and s4t1.instance_number = s0.instance_number
          and s1.snap_id = s0.snap_id + 1
          and s1t0.snap_id = s0.snap_id
          and s1t1.snap_id = s0.snap_id + 1
          and s2t1.snap_id = s0.snap_id
          and s3t1.snap_id = s0.snap_id
          and s4t1.snap_id = s0.snap_id
          and s1t0.stat_name = 'BUSY_TIME'
          and s1t1.stat_name = s1t0.stat_name
          and s2t1.stat_name = 'LOAD'
          and s3t1.stat_name = 'NUM_CPUS'
          and s4t1.stat_name = 'PHYSICAL_MEMORY_BYTES'
        order by snap_id asc;
```

Here is the output:

```
    SNAP_ID TIME                   BUSY_TIME        LOAD   NUM_CPUS PHYSICAL_MEMORY_BYTES
---------- --------------------  ----------  ----------  ---------- ---------------------
      49303 2010-Jan-24 22:00:54      35460           0           8            1.6692E+10
      49304 2010-Jan-24 23:00:55      32737   .26953125           8            1.6692E+10
      49305 2010-Jan-25 00:00:57      36409  .079101563           8            1.6692E+10
      49306 2010-Jan-25 01:00:58      34126  .159179688           8            1.6692E+10
      49307 2010-Jan-25 02:00:59      40046  .159179688           8            1.6692E+10
      49308 2010-Jan-25 03:01:01      39088    .0390625           8            1.6692E+10
      49309 2010-Jan-25 04:00:02      43388  .309570313           8            1.6692E+10
      49310 2010-Jan-25 05:00:03      87001  .759765625           8            1.6692E+10
```

We cal also produce OS delta reports showing changes between sampling periods.

💾 awr_stats_deltas.sql

```sql
select
   to_char(s.end_interval_time,'DD-MON-YYYY HH24:MI') SNAP_TIME,
   os.stat_name,
   os.value,
   lag(os.value,1) over
   (PARTITION BY os.STAT_NAME order by os.snap_id) prev,
case
when os.stat_name = 'LOAD'
   then os.value
when os.stat_name = 'PHYSICAL_MEMORY_BYTES'
   then os.value
else
   os.value - lag(os.value,1) over
   (PARTITION BY os.STAT_NAME order by
 os.snap_id)
end value
from
   dba_hist_snapshot s,
   dba_hist_osstat   os
where
   s.snap_id = os.snap_id
order by
   os.snap_id,os.stat_name;
```

Here is the output, showing the delta values between the snapshot periods:

```
SNAP_TIME             STAT_NAME                           VALUE        PREV        VALUE
-------------------   ----------------------------   ----------  ----------  ----------
24-JAN-2010 23:00     BUSY_TIME                        76302487
24-JAN-2010 23:00     IDLE_TIME                      2422533267
24-JAN-2010 23:00     IOWAIT_TIME                      22618114
24-JAN-2010 23:00     LOAD                                    0                        0
24-JAN-2010 23:00     NICE_TIME                             652
24-JAN-2010 23:00     NUM_CPUS                                8
24-JAN-2010 23:00     NUM_CPU_SOCKETS                        2
24-JAN-2010 23:00     PHYSICAL_MEMORY_BYTES          1.6692E+10               1.6692E+10
24-JAN-2010 23:00     RSRC_MGR_CPU_WAIT_TIME                 0
24-JAN-2010 23:00     SYS_TIME                          7954878
24-JAN-2010 23:00     USER_TIME                        67653069
25-JAN-2010 00:00     BUSY_TIME                        76337947    76302487       35460
```

Oracle Server Monitoring

```
25-JAN-2010 00:00    IDLE_TIME              2425377745 2422533267    2844478
25-JAN-2010 00:00    IOWAIT_TIME              22629280   22618114      11166
25-JAN-2010 00:00    LOAD                    .26953125          0  .26953125
25-JAN-2010 00:00    NICE_TIME                     652        652          0
25-JAN-2010 00:00    NUM_CPUS                        8          8          0
25-JAN-2010 00:00    NUM_CPU_SOCKETS                 2          2          0
25-JAN-2010 00:00    PHYSICAL_MEMORY_BYTES   1.6692E+10 1.6692E+10 1.6692E+10
25-JAN-2010 00:00    RSRC_MGR_CPU_WAIT_TIME          0          0          0
25-JAN-2010 00:00    SYS_TIME                  7963310    7954878       8432
25-JAN-2010 00:00    USER_TIME                67678911   67653069      25842
25-JAN-2010 01:00    BUSY_TIME                76370684   76337947      32737
25-JAN-2010 01:00    IDLE_TIME              2428224903 2425377745    2847158
25-JAN-2010 01:00    IOWAIT_TIME              22637834   22629280       8554
25-JAN-2010 01:00    LOAD                   .079101563  .26953125 .079101563
```

Again, these utilities have limited value because the best place to sample OS resource consumption is directly on the OS, and not inside Oracle. For this purpose, many shops use OS scripts. Let; start with Oracle's script collection, the OS watcher and then move on to move sophisticated scripts to monitor Oracle.

The Oracle OS Watcher utility

The Oracle OS watcher is a collection of UNIX shell scripts that reports on CPU, RAM and Network stress, and is a new alternative for monitoring Oracle servers.

MetaLink note 301137.1 has the users guide for Oracle OS Watcher (OSW), a collection of UNIX C shell scripts that help diagnose server and network bottlenecks. The Oracle OS watcher is user-configurable, collecting one hour worth of OS data at one minute intervals, and then writing the hour's data to an archive flat file...

Oracle OS watcher is useful for Linux/UNIX-based RAC systems where monitoring the OS is important for identifying CPU, RAM or network stress. Oracle OS Watcher may invoke these popular UNIX/Linux utilities, depending on the platform (Solaris, HP/UX, Linux and Tru64):

- *vmstat*

- *iostat*

- *top*

- *netstat*

- *traceroute*

Starting Oracle OS Watcher

You can start Oracle OS Watcher with a *nohup* command to submit the OS collection job, specifying the data collection interval (in seconds) and the max number of hours to keep archive files. In this example we submit the collector as a background job to collect every 5 minutes and keep 24 hours of archive files, writing all messages to oswatcher.log:

```
nohup /u01/app/oracle/scripts/startOSW.sh 300 24 & > /u01/app/oracle/scripts//oswatcher.log
```

You can download Oracle OSWatcher here:

Using Oracle OS Watcher requires knowledge of UNIX and Linux C shell commends syntax, but it removes much of the tedium from OS monitoring for those who are not licensed to use AWR automatic OS statistics collection.

Now, let's move on and take a look at he issues surrounding the tuning of Oracle CPU consumption.

Oracle CPU Tuning

You can always tell somebody who did not take college courses in computer science because they will misinterpret the CPU statistics on the server. When they see CPU activity at 100% they wrongly assume that there is a CPU bottleneck.

In reality, SMP servers are designed to drive CPU and all virtual memory servers are designed to have their dispatchers drive processing to 100% as quickly as possible. A state of 100% CPU utilization is optimal, and means that the processors are working at peak efficiency.

We only have CPU problems when there are more tasks waiting for CPU, than CPUs available (the *cpu_count*), and the only way to tell if the server has a CPU bottleneck is when the CPU *runqueue* values (per *vmstat*) exceeds the number of processors on the server (*cpu_count*). The *vmstat* utility is a great way to see if the server has CPU enqueues.

The following are some of the cryptic commands the Oracle UNIX professional would have to know in order to display the number of CPUs on the Oracle server:

- Linux command:
  ```
  cat /proc/cpuinfo|grep processor|wc -l
  ```
- Solaris command:
  ```
  psrinfo -v|grep "Status of processor"|wc -l
  ```
- AIX command:
  ```
  lsdev -C|grep Process|wc -l
  ```
- HP/UX command:
  ```
  ioscan -C processor | grep processor | wc -l
  ```

To learn how to monitor CPU at the operating system level using *glance*, *top*, *watch* and *vmstat*, see Monitoring CPU with UNIX.

There is a "Chicken Little" myth among neophytes who panic when they see that CPU is 100%, and they do not understand that 100% CPU utilization is the desired, and optimal, behavior. Take a closer look at CPU and Oracle databases.

The Myth of 100% CPU Being a Bottleneck

Please note that it is not uncommon to see the CPU approach 100 percent even when the server is not overwhelmed with work. This is because the UNIX internal dispatchers will always attempt to keep the CPUs as busy as possible. This maximizes task throughput, but it can be misleading for a neophyte.

Here is justification from IBM that 100% CPU utilization is optimal (from the IBM documentation):

> "Optimum use would have the CPU working 100 percent of the time. This holds true in the case of a single-user system with no need to share the CPU.
>
> Generally, if us + sy time is below 90 percent, a single-user system is not considered CPU constrained. However, if us + sy time on a multiuser system exceeds 80 percent, the processes may spend time waiting in the run queue. Response time and throughput might suffer.
>
> To check if the CPU is the bottleneck, consider the four cpu columns and the two kthr (kernel threads) columns in the *vmstat* report. It may also be worthwhile looking at the faults column."

Viewing CPU Utilization for Oracle

Server statistics can be viewed in a variety of ways using standard server-side UNIX and Linux tools such as *vmstat, glance, top* and *sar* . The goal is to ensure that the database server has enough CPU and RAM resources at all times in order to manage the Oracle requests.

Oracle has many operations that are CPU intensive, and tuning can reduce CPU:

- **Buffer touches:** Logical I/O (consistent gets) has high CPU overhead, and buffer touches can be reduced via SQL tuning, adding more selective indexes, materialized views and such

- **Shared pool contention:** Library cache contention (high parses) drives-up CPU

Remember, having 100% CPU is not always a problem; it is normal for virtual memory servers to drive CPU consumption to 100%. Also note that starting in Oracle 10g, there is the *_optimizer_cost_model* parameter which is set to CPU from the default in 9i and earlier of I/O. This parameter is for Oracle databases which are CPU-bound, and it tells Oracle to create the CBO decision tree weights with estimated CPU consumption, not estimated I/O costs.

When analyzing *vmstat* output, there are several metrics to which you should pay attention. For example, keep an eye on the CPU run queue column. The run queue should never exceed the number of CPUs on the server. If it is noticed that the run queue is exceeding the amount of CPUs, it is a good indication that the server has a CPU bottleneck.

Monitoring CPU on Linux & UNIX

The *vmstat* utility provides a wealth of information about CPU usage in an Oracle instance. Tasks that are waiting for CPU resources can be shown in UNIX *vmstat* command output as the second column under the *kthr* (kernel thread state change) heading. Other task states include the wait queue (b) if they are waiting on a resource, while other in-flight tasks appear in the run queue (r) column.

But it is easy to know when there is a CPU bottleneck. Any Oracle server is experiencing a CPU bottleneck when "r" is greater than the number of CPUs on the server.

Always remember that the vmstat *runqueue* value must never exceed the number of CPUs. For example, a *runqueue* value of 32 is perfectly acceptable for a 36-CPU server, while a value of 32 would be a serious problem for a 16-CPU server.

In the example below, run the *vmstat* utility, gathering five samples at five second intervals. Interest is shown in the first two columns: the run queue "r", and the *kthr* wait "b" column. In the listing below, we see that there are about eight new tasks entering the run queue every five seconds (see the "r" column), while there are five other tasks that are waiting on resources (the "b" column). Also, a nonzero value in the ("b") column may indicate a bottleneck.

```
root> vmstat 5 5

kthr      memory            page                  faults          cpu
----- ----------- ------------------------ ------------- -----------
 r  b   avm   fre  re  pi  po  fr   sr  cy   in     sy   cs  us sy id wa
 7  5 220214  141   0   0   0  42   53   0  1724  12381 2206  19 46 28  7
 9  5 220933  195   0   0   1 216  290   0  1952  46118 2712  27 55 13  5
13  5 220646  452   0   0   1  33   54   0  2130  86185 3014  30 59  8  3
 6  5 220228  672   0   0   0   0    0   0  1929  25068 2485  25 49 16 10
```

There are several solutions to managing CPU overload, and these alternatives are presented in their order of desirability:

- Tune SQL to consume less CPU cycles

- Add more processors (CPUs) to the server

- Load balance the system tasks by rescheduling large batch tasks to execute during off-peak hours

- Adjust the dispatching priorities (*nice* values) of existing tasks

To understand how CPU dispatching priorities work, remember that not all incoming tasks are equal, and that tasks are placed in the CPU execution queue according to their dispatching priority (*nice* value).

To make it more confusing, tasks with a low *nice* value are scheduled for execution above those tasks with a higher *nice* value. Now that how to tell when the CPUs are overloaded is known, check into *vmstat* further and see how to tell when the CPUs are running at full capacity.

Identifying High CPU Usage with *vmstat*

How does a DBA distinguish between a busy database and a database that has excessive CPU usage? Whenever the "us" (user) column plus the "sy" (system) column times approach 100%, the CPUs are operating at full capacity. This often leads to a false panic. Remember, processors are designed to throttle to 100% as quickly as possible and 100% CPU utilization maximizes throughout and it DOES NOT always indicate a CPU shortage!

Note below that the CPU is at 100%, yet the run queue ("r" value) is zero.

```
root> vmstat 5 1

kthr      memory              page                faults        cpu
-----  -----------  -----------------------  -------------  -----------
 r  b    avm    fre  re  pi  po  fr   sr  cy   in   sy  cs  us sy id wa
 0  0 217485    386   0   0   0   4   14   0  202  300 210  25 75  3
```

When the *user + system* CPU values approach 100 percent, the CPUs are working to their full potential. In this output below, the 16-CPU server is not experiencing a CPU shortage because the (r) *runqueue* value is 12, meaning that all Oracle asks are getting prompt service.

```
vmstat 5 1

kthr      memory              page                faults        cpu
-----  -----------  -----------------------  -------------  -----------
 r  b    avm    fre  re  pi  po  fr   sr  cy   in   sy  cs  us sy id wa
12  0 217485    386   0   0   0   4   14   0  202  300 210  20 80  3  2
```

Storing Information from *vmstat*

To keep server side information, create an Oracle table to store *vmstat* data and create a simple script to populate the table. Creating the automated *vmstat* monitor begins by creating an Oracle table to contain the *vmstat* output.

🖫 cr_vmstat_tab.sql

```
connect perfstat/perfstat;

drop table stats$vmstat;
create table stats$vmstat
(
     start_date          date,
     duration            number,
     server_name         varchar2(20),
     runque_waits        number,
     page_in             number,
     page_out            number,
     user_cpu            number,
     system_cpu          number,
     idle_cpu            number,
```

```
      wait_cpu            number
)
tablespace perfstat;
```

Now that an Oracle table to capture the *vmstat* information has been defined, write a shell script that will execute *vmstat*, capture the *vmstat* output, and place it into the Oracle table. To learn more about writing shell scripts for Oracle, see the book, *Oracle Shell Scripting,* by Jon Emmons.

The main script to collect the *vmstat* information is a Korn shell script called *get_vmstat.ksh*. Each dialect of UNIX displays *vmstat* information in different columns, so the DBA needs slightly different scripts for each dialect of UNIX and Linux. The idea is to write a script that continually runs the *vmstat* utility and then directs the results into the Oracle table.

The script shows the *vmstat capture* utility script for the Linux operating system. Note that the DBA must change this script in several places to make it work:

- set the *oracle_home* to the directory:

    ```
    ORACLE_HOME=/u01/app/oracle/product/11.2.0/db_1
    ```

- set the destination database in the *sqlplus* command:

    ```
    $ORACLE_HOME/bin/sqlplus -s perfstat/perfstat@testsys1<<EOF
    ```

- The DBA can change the duration of samples by resetting *sample_time* UNIX variable:

    ```
    SAMPLE_TIME=300
    ```

🖫 get_vmstat.ksh (Linux version)

```
#!/bin/ksh

# This is the Linux version

#!/bin/ksh

# This is the Linux version

ORACLE_HOME=/usr/app/oracle/admin/product/8/1/6
export ORACLE_HOME

PATH=$ORACLE_HOME/bin:$PATH
export PATH
SERVER_NAME=`uname -a|awk '{print $2}'`
typeset -u SERVER_NAME
export SERVER_NAME

# sample every five minutes (300 seconds) . . . .
SAMPLE_TIME=300

while true
do
   vmstat ${SAMPLE_TIME} 2 > /tmp/msg$$


# run vmstat and direct the output into the Oracle table . . .
cat /tmp/msg$$|sed 1,3d | awk  '{ printf("%s %s %s %s %s %s\n", $1, $8, $9,
14, $15, $16) }' | while read RUNQUE PAGE_IN PAGE_OUT USER_CPU SYSTEM_CPU
```

```
DLE_CPU
   do

      $ORACLE_HOME/bin/sqlplus -s perfstat/perfstat@testsys1<<EOF
      insert into perfstat.stats\$vmstat
                          values (
                            sysdate,
                            $SAMPLE_TIME,
                            '$SERVER_NAME',
                            $RUNQUE,
                            $PAGE_IN,
                            $PAGE_OUT,
                            $USER_CPU,
                            $SYSTEM_CPU,
                            $IDLE_CPU,
                            0
                                  );
      EXIT
EOF
   done
done

rm /tmp/msg$$
```

Because of the differences in implementations of *vmstat* in different dialects, the first task is to identify the columns of the *vmstat* output that contain the information that the DBA wants to capture. Once the columns are known, add these columns to the *vmstat* script to put the output into the table (Table 12.1).

Dialect	Run Queue Column	Page-In Column	Page-Out Column	User Column
HP/UX	1	8	9	16
AIX	1	6	7	14
Solaris	1	8	9	20
Linux	1	8	9	14
	System Column	Idle Column	Wait Column	
HP/UX	17	18	NA	
AIX	15	16	17	
Solaris	21	22	NA	
Linux	15	16	NA	

Table **12.1:**
Differences in vmstat Data by Operating System

Using the new *vmstat* table, adjust the capture script according to the operating system. Customize the script by changing the line in the script that reads the vmstat output and places it into the *stats$vmstat* table. Here is a summary of the UNIX dialect changes to this line.

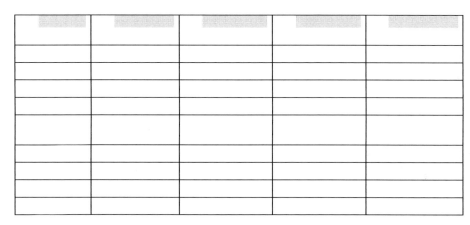

HP/UX vmstat columns:

```
cat /tmp/msg$$|sed
1,3d |\
 awk  '{ printf("%s %s
%s %s %s %s\n", $1,
$8, $9, $16, $17, $18)
}' |\
 while read RUNQUE
PAGE_IN PAGE_OUT
USER_CPU SYSTEM_CPU
IDLE_CPU
```

IBM AIX vmstat columns:

```
cat /tmp/msg$$|sed 1,3d |\
 awk  '{ printf("%s %s %s %s %s %s\n", $1, $6, $7, $14, $15, $16, $17) }' |\
 while read RUNQUE PAGE_IN PAGE_OUT USER_CPU SYSTEM_CPU IDLE_CPU WAIT_CPU
```

Sun Solaris vmstat columns:

```
cat /tmp/msg$$|sed 1,3d |\
 awk  '{ printf("%s %s %s %s %s %s\n", $1, $8, $9, $20, $21, $22) }' |\
 while read RUNQUE PAGE_IN PAGE_OUT USER_CPU SYSTEM_CPU IDLE_CPU
```

Linux vmstat columns:

```
cat /tmp/msg$$|sed 1,3d |\
 awk  '{ printf("%s %s %s %s %s %s\n", $1, $8, $9, $14, $15, $16) }' |\
 while read RUNQUE PAGE_IN PAGE_OUT USER_CPU SYSTEM_CPU IDLE_CPU
```

Internals of the *vmstat* Capture Script

It is important to understand how the *get_vmstat.ksh* script works. Here are the main steps:

1.   Execute the *vmstat* utility for the specified elapsed-time interval (in this case, where *sample_time=300*).

2.   The output of the *vmstat* is directed into the */tmp* directory

3.   The output is then parsed using the *awk* utility, and the values are inserted into the *stats$vmstat* table

---

Once this *daemon* is started (a constant-running process), the *get_vmstat.ksh* script will run continually and capture the *vmstat* information into the table. This script will run continually to sample the server status at whatever interval is desired without making any impact on server performance.

This script will stop when the server is rebooted, so it is a good idea to place a *crontab* entry to make sure that the *get_vmstat* script is always running. Below is a script called *run_vmstat.ksh* that will ensure that the *vmstat]|[po-0* utility is always running on the server.

Note that it is important to make the following changes to this script:

- Set the file location variable vmstat to the directory that contains the *get_vmstat.ksh* script:

```
vmstat=`echo ~oracle/vmstat`
```

- Create a small file in the UNIX file directory (*$vmstat*) called *mysid*. This file will contain one line and specify the name of the *oracle_sid*.

```
ORACLE_SID=`cat ${vmstat}/mysid`
```

💾 run_vmstat.ksh

```
#!/bin/ksh

# First, we must set the environment . . . .
vmstat=`echo ~oracle/vmstat`
export vmstat
ORACLE_SID=`cat ${vmstat}/mysid`
export ORACLE_SID

ORACLE_HOME=`cat /etc/oratab|grep $ORACLE_SID:|cut -f2 -d':'`
export ORACLE_HOME
PATH=$ORACLE_HOME/bin:$PATH
export PATH

#-------------------------------------
# If it is not running, then start it . . .
#-------------------------------------
check_stat=`ps -ef|grep get_vmstat|grep -v grep|wc -l`;
oracle_num=`expr $check_stat`
if [ $oracle_num -le 0 ]
 then nohup $vmstat/get_vmstat_linux.ksh > /dev/null 2>&1 &
fi
```

On my systems, *run_vmstat.ksh* is scheduled to run hourly via cron. Each hour, the script checks to see if the *get_vmstat.ksh* script is executing. If it is not executing, the script resubmits it for execution. In practice, the *get_vmstat.ksh* script will never abort, but if the server is shut down and restarted, the script will need to be restarted.

Here is an example of the UNIX crontab file for this hourly check. Note that it schedules the *run_vmstat.ksh* script every hour, and runs a *vmstat* exception report every day at 7:00 a.m.

```
00 * * * * /home/vmstat/run_vmstat.ksh > /home/vmstat/r.lst

00 7 * * * /home/vmstat/run_vmstat_alert.ksh prodb1 > /home/vmstat/v.lst
```

Now that how to monitor the Oracle database server has been given, examine how to use the new vmstat table to report on server-side RAM and CPU issues.

Server-side *vmstat* Reports

The alert script below, *vmstat_alert.sql*, will produce a complete exception report on all of the important server conditions, according to the user-defined thresholds, and this report will display those times when the CPU and RAM memory exceed the predefined thresholds:

🖫 **vmstat_exception_rpt.sql**

```
set lines 80;
set pages 999;
set feedback off;
set verify off;

column my_date heading 'date          hour' format a20
column c2         heading runq    format 999
column c3         heading pg_in    format 999
column c4         heading pg_ot    format 999
column c5         heading usr      format 999
column c6         heading sys      format 999
column c7         heading idl      format 999
column c8         heading wt       format 999


ttitle 'run queue > 2|May indicate an overloaded CPU|When runqueue exceeds
the number of CPUs| on the server, tasks are waiting for service.';

select
 server_name,
 to_char(start_date,'YY/MM/DD     HH24') my_date,
 avg(runque_waits)       c2,
 avg(page_in)            c3,
 avg(page_out)           c4,
 avg(user_cpu)           c5,
 avg(system_cpu)         c6,
 avg(idle_cpu)           c7
from
perfstat.stats$vmstat
WHERE
runque_waits > 2
and start_date > sysdate-&&1
group by
 server_name,
 to_char(start_date,'YY/MM/DD     HH24')
ORDER BY
 server_name,
 to_char(start_date,'YY/MM/DD     HH24')
;

ttitle 'page_in > 1|May indicate overloaded memory|Whenever Unix performs
a page-in, the RAM memory | on the server has been exhausted and swap pages are being
used.';

select
 server_name,
 to_char(start_date,'YY/MM/DD     HH24') my_date,
 avg(runque_waits)       c2,
 avg(page_in)            c3,
 avg(page_out)           c4,
```

```
 avg(user_cpu)              c5,
 avg(system_cpu)            c6,
 avg(idle_cpu)              c7
from
perfstat.stats$vmstat
WHERE
page_in > 1
and start_date > sysdate-&&1
group by
 server_name,
 to_char(start_date,'YY/MM/DD     HH24')
ORDER BY
 server_name,
 to_char(start_date,'YY/MM/DD     HH24')
;

ttitle 'user+system CPU > 70%|Indicates periods with a fully-loaded CPU subssystem.|Periods
of 100% utilization are only a | concern when runqueue values exceeds the number of CPs on
the server.';

select
 server_name,
 to_char(start_date,'YY/MM/DD     HH24') my_date,
 avg(runque_waits)          c2,
 avg(page_in)               c3,
 avg(page_out)              c4,
 avg(user_cpu)              c5,
 avg(system_cpu)            c6,
 avg(idle_cpu)              c7
from
perfstat.stats$vmstat
WHERE
(user_cpu + system_cpu) > 70
and start_date > sysdate-&&1
group by
 server_name,
 to_char(start_date,'YY/MM/DD     HH24')
ORDER BY
 server_name,
 to_char(start_date,'YY/MM/DD     HH24')
;
```

This *vmstat* alert report is used to alert the on-call staff whenever any out-of-bounds condition occurs on each Oracle server. These conditions include:

- **CPU waits > 40% (AIX version only):**   This may indicate I/O-based contention. The solution is to spread files across more disks or add buffer memory.

- **Run queue > xxx – (where xxx is the number of CPUs on the server, 2 in this example):** This indicates an overloaded CPU. The solution is to add additional processors to the server.

- **Page_in > 2 with correlated scan rates:**   Page-in operations can indicate overloaded memory. The solution is to reduce the size of the Oracle SGA, PGA, or add additional RAM memory to the server.

- **User CPU + System CPU > 90%:**   This indicates periods where the CPU is highly utilized

While the SQL here is self-explanatory, look at a sample report and see how it will help the systems administrator monitor the server's behavior:

```
SQL> @vmstat_alert 7
```

                                run queue > 2
                        May indicate an overloaded CPU.
                    When runqueue exceeds the number of CPUs
                  on the server, tasks are waiting for service.

SERVER_NAME	date	hour	runq	pg_in	pg_ot	usr	sys	idl
AD-01	01/13/04	17	3	0	0	87	5	8

                                page_in > 1
                        May indicate overloaded memory.
              Whenever Unix performs a page-in, the RAM memory
          on the server has been exhausted and swap pages are being used.

SERVER_NAME	date	hour	runq	pg_in	pg_ot	usr	sys	idl
AD-01	01/12/13	16	0	5	0	1	1	98
AD-01	01/12/14	09	0	5	0	10	2	88
AD-01	01/12/15	16	0	6	0	0	0	100
AD-01	01/12/19	20	0	29	2	1	2	98
PROD1DB	01/12/13	14	0	3	43	4	4	93
PROD1DB	01/12/19	07	0	2	0	1	3	96
PROD1DB	01/12/19	11	0	3	0	1	3	96
PROD1DB	01/12/19	12	0	6	0	1	3	96
PROD1DB	01/12/19	16	0	3	0	1	3	96
PROD1DB	01/12/19	17	0	47	68	5	5	91

                                user+system > 70%
                  Indicates periods with a fully-loaded CPU sub-system.
                      Periods of 100% utilization are only a
          concern when runqueue values exceeds the number of CPUs on the server.

SERVER_NAME	date	hour	runq	pg_in	pg_ot	usr	sys	idl
AD-01	01/12/13	14	0	0	2	75	2	22
AD-01	01/12/13	17	3	0	0	87	5	8
AD-01	01/12/15	15	0	0	0	50	29	22
AD-01	01/12/15	16	0	0	0	48	33	20
AD-01	01/12/19	07	0	0	0	77	4	19
AD-01	01/12/19	10	0	0	0	70	5	24
AD-01	01/12/19	11	1	0	0	60	17	24
PROD1	01/12/19	12	0	0	1	52	30	18
PROD1	01/12/19	13	0	0	0	39	59	2
PROD1	01/12/19	14	0	0	0	39	55	6
PROD1	01/12/19	15	1	0	0	57	23	20

You may notice that this exception report gives the hourly average for the *vmstat* information with the data being captured every 300 elapsed seconds, or five-minute intervals.

It is important to note that while the above report shows hourly figures, the data is being captured in five-minute increments, so drill in whenever a past problem is seen. This report can also be run in conjunction with other STATSPACK or AWR reports to identify what tasks may have precipitated the server problem. The *stats$sql_summary* table is especially useful for this purpose.

Monitoring CPU on Windows Servers

Windows was originally designed for personal computers and it falls far behind the more robust platforms for server-side monitoring utilities. Those utilities that do exist for Windows are poorly implemented and far less useful than their Linux equivalents.

For Windows, there is the Windows Task Manager, and the DBA should look at the Processor Queue Length to detect CPU enqueue conditions. The processor queue length is displayed in the system monitor and task manager. Microsoft notes:

"Processor Queue Length (System): this is the instantaneous length of the processor queue in units of threads. All processors use a single queue in which threads wait for processor cycles. After a processor is available for a thread waiting in the processor queue, the thread can be switched onto a processor for execution. A processor can execute only a single thread at a time. Note that faster CPUs can handle longer queue lengths than slower CPUs.

The number of threads in the processor queue: shows ready threads only, not threads that are running. Even multiprocessor computers have a single queue for processor time; thus, for multiprocessors, you need to divide this value by the number of processors servicing the workload.

A sustained processor queue of less than two threads per processor is normally acceptable, depending upon the workload."

Now move on to the subject of disk I/O. Remember the next chapter is entirely devoted to disk I/O tuning within Oracle.

Disk I/O and Oracle

While the entire next chapter is being devoted to Oracle disk I/O, this brief introduction will explain the basics of disk I/O for Oracle. The first point is that storage, both disk and solid-state disk, fall rapidly in price every year. In 1985, a 1.2 gigabyte disk sold for more than $250,000. Today, users can buy 100 gigabytes disks for $200 and 100 gigabytes of RAM-disk for $100,000. The following statements show how storage trends change over time:

- Disk storage improves tenfold every year

- Storage media becomes obsolete every 25 years

- RAM-SAN will replace disks by 2006

In Oracle, physical disk I/O can be measured by querying STATSPACK and the AWR for the physical disk reads information that is captured inside the *stats$filestatxs* and *dba_hist_filestatxs* tables. For example, the following Oracle script detects all files with physical reads over 10,000 during the snapshot period:

```
break on begin_interval_time skip 2
```

```
column phyrds format 999,999,999
column begin_interval_time format a25

select
   begin_interval_time,
   filename,
   phyrds
from
   dba_hist_filestatxs
natural join
   dba_hist_snapshot
where
   phyrds > 10000;
```

The results yield a running total of Oracle physical reads. The snapshots are collected every hour in this example, and many DBAs will increase the default collection frequency of AWR snapshots. Starting from this script, users could easily add a *where* clause criteria and create a unique time-series exception report.

```
SQL> @phys_reads

BEGIN_INTERVAL_TIME FILENAME PHYRDS
----------------------- ------------------------------------------- ----
24-FEB-04 11.00.32.000 PM E:\ORACLE\ORA92\FSDEV10G\SYSTEM01.DBF    164,700
                          E:\ORACLE\ORA92\FSDEV10G\UNDOTBS01.DBF     26,082
                          E:\ORACLE\ORA92\FSDEV10G\SYSAUX01.DBF     472,008
                          E:\ORACLE\ORA92\FSDEV10G\USERS01.DBF       21,794
                          E:\ORACLE\ORA92\FSDEV10G\T_FS_LSQ.ORA      12,123

24-FEB-04 12.00.32.000 PM E:\ORACLE\ORA92\FSDEV10G\SYSTEM01.DBF    164,700
                          E:\ORACLE\ORA92\FSDEV10G\UNDOTBS01.DBF     26,082
```

This concept is particularly true when considering Moore's Law, which essentially states that processor capacity increases steadily while hardware costs fall. While Moore's Law does not apply to RAM chip characteristics, RAM is steadily falling in cost, but the speed has remained the same for more than 30 years, hovering at about 50 nanoseconds.

Moore's Law and Disk Speed

Back in the mid-1960's, Gordon Moore, the director of the research and development labs at Fairchild Semiconductor, published a research paper titled, *Cramming More Components into Integrated Circuits.* In his paper, Moore performed a linear regression on the rate of change in server processing speed and costs and noted an exponential growth in processing power and an exponential reduction of processing costs. This landmark paper gave birth to Moore's Law, which postulated that CPU power will get four times faster every three years as illustrated in Figure 12.1.

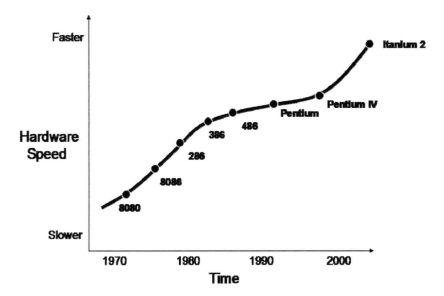

Figure 12.1: *Moore's Law for CPU Speed*

In the 1970s, a 4-way Symmetric Multiprocessing (SMP) processor cost over three million dollars. Yet today, the same CPU can be purchased for less than three thousand dollars. CPUs will increase in speed four times every three years and only increase in cost by 50%.

While Moore's Law is generally correct, the curve is not linear. The formerly marginal rate of advances in CPU speed has increased dramatically in the past decade, most notably with the introduction of the Itanium 2 processors.

The large RAM data buffers enabled by 64-bit operating systems have shifted the bottleneck for many Oracle databases from I/O to CPU. Oracle accommodates this shift to CPU consumption by providing a new *cpu_cost* feature that allows Oracle's cost-based SQL optimizer to evaluate SQL execution plan costs based on predicted CPU costs as well as I/O costs. This is an adjustable feature in Oracle, and it is controlled by the *_optimizer_cost_model* hidden parameter.

While Moore's Law is quite correct for processor speed and cost, many have over-generalized this principle as it applies to disks and RAM. It is true that costs are continually falling for RAM and disk, but the speed assumptions do not apply.

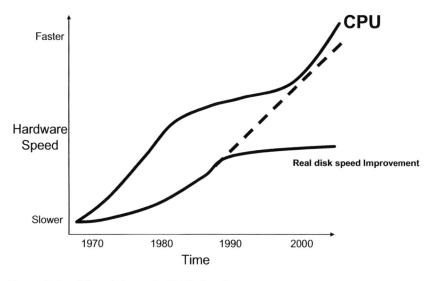

Figure 12.2: *Moore's Law for Disk Speed*

The old-fashioned spinning platters of magnetic-coated metal disks have an upper limit of spin speed, and the read/write head movement speed is limited. In the early 1990s, it became apparent that the 1950s disk technology had reached the limits of its physical capabilities. It became necessary for disk manufacturers to add on-board RAM caches to disk arrays and include asynchronous writing mechanisms to continue to improve disk speed.

One glaring exception to Moore's Law is RAM speed as shown in Figure 12.3.

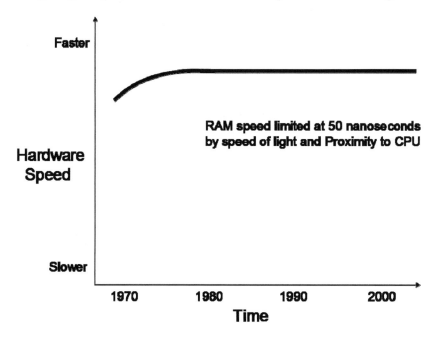

RAM has not made many significant gains in speed since the mid 1970s. This is due to the limitations of silicon and the fact that access speed in nanoseconds approaches the speed of light. The only way to further improve the speed of RAM would be to employ a radical new medium such as Gallium Arsenide.

This flat speed curve for RAM has important ramifications for Oracle processing. Since CPU speed continues to outpace RAM speed, RAM subsystems must be localized to keep the CPUs running at full capacity. This type of approach is evident in the new Itanium 2 servers where the RAM is placed as close to the CPU as possible as shown in Figure 12.4.

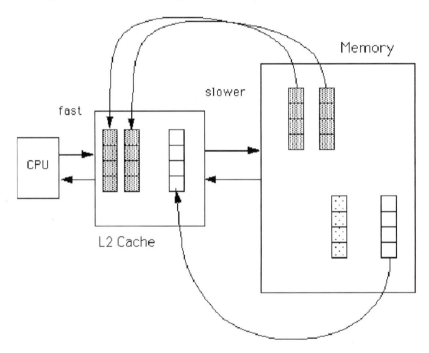

Figure 12.4: *Localizing RAM in Itanium2 Servers*

This represents the Oracle servers of the 21st century, e.g. the UNISYS ES7000 series, which have a special L2 RAM that is placed near the processors for fast RAM access. Low-cost RAM technology has dramatically changed the way that Oracle databases are tuned.

Server RAM and Oracle

Today, 100 gigabytes of RAM disk can be purchased for as little as $100,000 and can deliver access times 6,000 times faster than traditional disk devices. By 2013, a gigabyte of RAM is projected to cost the same as a gigabyte of disk today, which is definitely under $200. RAM I/O bandwidth is projected to grow one bit every 18 months, making 128 bit architecture due in about 2010 according to the data in Table 12.2.

8 bit	1970's
16 bit	1980's
32 bit	1990's
64 bit	2000's
128 bit	2010's

Table 12.2: *RAM Bandwidth Evolution*

The fact that RAM does not get faster means that CPU speed continues to outpace memory speed. This means that RAM subsystems must be localized close to the processors to keep the CPUs running at full capacity, and this architecture impacts Oracle performance.

Oracle and the 64-bit Server Technology

The advent of 64-bit CPUs has lead to a dramatic change in the way that Oracle databases are managed and tuned. To understand the issues, it is important to understand the advantages of a 64-bit server, especially the ability to have large data buffer caches. The following are the architectural benefits of the 64-bit processors listed in order of importance to Oracle shops:

- **Improved RAM addressing:** A 32-bit word size can only address approximately four gigabytes of RAM (2 to the 32nd power). All 64-bit servers have a larger word size that allows for up to 18 billion gigabytes (2 to the 64th power or 16 exabytes). These servers allow for huge scalability as the processing demand grows.

- **Faster processors:** Intel's 64-bit architecture is more powerful than the older 32-bit chipsets. While faster chips are not a direct result of the 64-bit architecture, they are an important consideration for shops with computationally-intensive databases.

- **High parallelism:** Multiple CPU and SMP support allows large scale parallel processing. For example, the Unisys 64-bit ES7000 servers support up to 32 processors which yields large parallel benefits.

- **Cluster architecture:** The 64-bit servers, such as the Unisys 64-bit ES7000 servers, are generally cluster-ready.

While having a 64-bit processor might be an attractive option, a large number of Oracle shops continued to run 32-bit versions of the Oracle database on their servers.

The new Intel and AMD processor architecture now rivals the proprietary UNIX systems with the ability to house CPUs and over 20 gigabytes of RAM capacity as shown in Figure 12.6. This architecture can support thousands of users while providing sub-second response time.

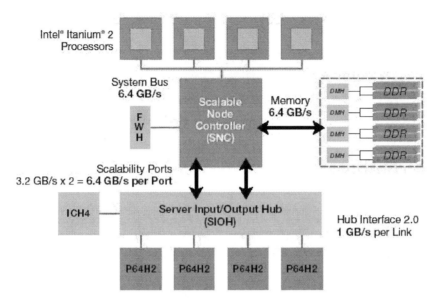

Figure 12.6: *The Intel E8870 Chipset Supporting the Itanium 2 Processor*

Intel also allows architecture to be scaled to a 16-way SMP configuration as shown in Figure 12.7, and it is apparent that Intel will continue to pursue the hardware-level expansion of this architecture.

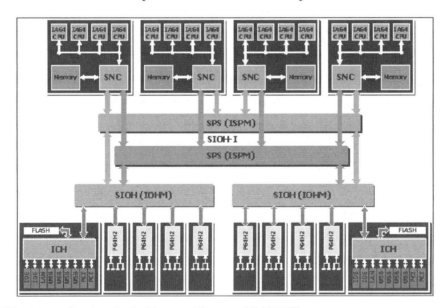

Figure 12.7: *The 16-way Itanium 2 Architecture (Courtesy UNISYS)*

With the 16-way processors using Itanium 2, there exists server architecture reminiscent of the larger servers offered by Sun, HP, and IBM. As all the vendors are offering 64-bit servers, the greatest benefit to Oracle shops occurs in these areas:

- **High transactions processing rates:** For systems with more than 200 disk I/Os per second, disk I/O is reduced by caching large amounts of data and system performance skyrockets.

- **Declining performance:** **T**32-bit limitations prevent continued growth beyond a certain point. The 64-bit architecture raises the ceiling on that growth.

- **Anticipating rapid growth:** For systems that require uninterrupted growth and scalability, the 64-bit architecture allows almost infinite scalability. Many large enterprise resource planning (ERP) systems have been able to scale successfully on Windows 64 platforms.

- **Computationally intensive system:** If an Oracle database is CPU-bound or if it performs multiple parallel full-table scans, the faster processors in a 64-bit architecture are very appealing.

What does this mean to the Oracle professional? Larry Ellison, CEO of Oracle, noted at OracleWorld in 2003 that:

"If you want the world's faster processors, then you will be forced to pay less."

He was referring to the Intel Itanium 2 chips which appear to be making strong advances in the displacement of the proprietary UNIX environments, especially HP/UX and Solaris. The major operating environments for Itanium 2 servers are Linux and Microsoft Windows:

- **Linux:** Offers large-scale uptake but is hindered by non-open source costs and lackluster support.

- **Windows:** Increasing in popularity but suffering from unreliable past performance.

These large inexpensive servers provide the ultimate in resource sharing. With many Oracle instances on a single server, processes that need more CPU will automatically be allocated cycles from the server run queue. Likewise, an instance that requires additional RAM for the SA or PGA can easily get the resources without cumbersome manual intervention.

In summary, 16-way and 32-way SMP servers are leading the way into a new age of Oracle database consolidation.

The New Age of Oracle Server Consolidation

It is ironic that the old mainframe architectures of the 1970s and 1980s are now brand new again. Back in the days of data processing, it was not uncommon for a single server to host a dozen databases. The advent of the inexpensive 64-bit servers is leading the way back to server consolidation. There was nothing inherently wrong with a centralized server environment, and in many ways it was superior to the distributed client-server architectures of the 1990s.

When companies first started to leave the mainframe environment, it was not because there were particular benefits to having a number of tiny servers. Instead, it was a pure economic decision based on the low cost of the UNIX-based minicomputers of the day.

These minicomputers of the 1980s could be purchased for as little as $30k, which was a bargain when compared to the three million dollar cost of a mainframe. As minicomputers evolved into the UNIX-centric Oracle servers of the 1990s, some shops found themselves with hundreds of servers, one for each Oracle database. In fact, the breakdown of the mainframe was a nightmare for the Oracle DBA.

Instead of a single server to manage, the DBA had dozens or even hundreds of servers, each with its own copy of the Oracle software.

The 1990s was the age of client/server computing, where multi-tiered applications were constructed with dozens of small servers. Systems might have been comprised of a Web server layer, an application server layer, and a database layer, each with dozens of individual servers as shown in Figure 12.8.

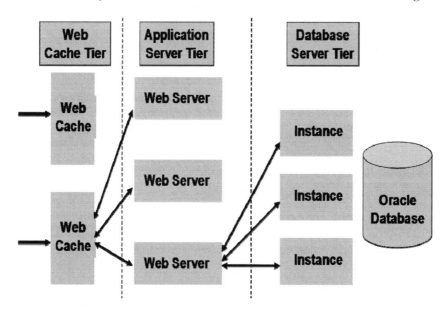

Figure 12.8: *The Multi-server Oracle Architectures of the 1990s*

The example in Figure 12.8 shows a multi-server architecture that employs Oracle Real Application Clusters (RAC), which is a processing architecture that allows multiple Oracle instances on separate servers that access a common Oracle database.

One of the issues associated with single server Oracle systems was the deliberate over-allocation of computing resources. Each system would experience periodic processing spikes, and each server had to be equipped with additional resources to accommodate the irregular frequency of the demands of various applications. This led to a condition in which Oracle servers had unused CPU and RAM resources that could not be easily shared.

The client/server Oracle paradigm had many serious problems:

- **High Expense:** in large enterprise data centers with many servers and many instances, hardware resources must be deliberately over-allocated in order to accommodate the sporadic peaks in CPU and RAM resources

- **High Waste:** since each Oracle instance resides on a separate single server, there is a significant duplication of work which results in suboptimal utilization of RAM and CPU resources

- **Very Time Consuming for the Oracle DBA:** in many large Oracle shops, a shuffle occurs when a database outgrows its server. When a new server is purchased, the Oracle database is moved to the new server, leaving the older server to accept yet another smaller Oracle database. This shuffling consumes considerable time and attention from the DBA.

This waste and high DBA overhead have lead IT managers to recognize the benefits of a centralized server environment, and there is now resurgence in popularity of large monolithic servers for bigger Oracle shops. There is also a rapid depreciation rate for servers, which has also contributed to the movement towards server consolidation. For example, three year-old Oracle servers that cost over $100k brand new are now worth less than five thousand dollars.

These new mainframes may contain 16, 32, or even 64 CPUs and have processing capabilities that dwarf the traditional mainframe ancestors of the 1980s. The new Oracle benchmarks of server performance make use of many of the new features of Oracle including:

- Multiple blocksizes

- Large buffer caches

- KEEP and other non-default pools

- Multi-core 64-bit CPUs

There are those who argue that it is not a good idea to throw everything onto a single server because it introduces a single point of failure. Even Oracle Corporation says that it is not a good idea to place all of the proverbial eggs in one basket; therefore, they advocate the grid approach in Oracle. Many of these concerns are unfounded. In reality, these large systems have redundant everything, and with the use of Oracle Streams for replication at different geographical locations, they are virtually unstoppable.

In the new server architectures, everything from disk, CPU, RAM, and internal busses are fully fault tolerant and redundant, which makes the monolithic approach appealing to large corporations for the following reasons:

- **Lower costs:** Monolithic servers are extremely good at sharing computing resources between applications, making grid computing unnecessary.

- **Lower Oracle DBA maintenance:** Instead of maintaining 30 copies or more of Oracle and the OS, DBAs only need to manage a single copy.

Cost savings aside, there are other compelling reasons to consolidate Oracle instances onto a single server:

1. Oracle server consolidation: server consolidation technology can greatly reduce the number of Oracle database servers.

2. Centralized management: a single server means a single copy of the Oracle software. Plus, the operating system controls resource allocation and the server will automatically balance the demands of many Oracle instances for processing cycles and RAM resources. Of course, the Oracle DBA still maintains control and can dedicate Oracle instances to a single CPU, thereby utilizing processor affinity or adjust the CPU dispatching priority using the UNIX nice command.

3. Transparent high availability: if any server component fails, the monolithic server can reassign the processing without interruption. This is a more affordable and far simpler

solution than Real Applications Clusters or Oracle Data Guard, either of which requires duplicate servers.

4. Scalability: using a single large server, additional CPU and RAM can be added seamlessly for increased performance

5. Reduced DBA workload: by consolidating server resources, the DBA has fewer servers to manage and need not be concerned with outgrowing server capacity.

So, what does this mean to the Oracle DBA? Clearly, less time will be spent installing and maintaining multiple copies of Oracle. This will free time for the DBA to pursue more advanced tasks such as SQL tuning and database performance optimization.

Following this information on the impact of the new server environments for Oracle, it is logical to look at the overhauled Oracle Enterprise Manager and see how it now displays AWR server-side metrics.

Oracle Enterprise Manager and Server Metrics

Using the new Oracle 10g Enterprise Manager (OEM) interface, the Oracle professional can now get access to external information that has never before been available in a single interface. This is important because it removes the need for the DBA to have any experience with the cumbersome OS command syntax that is required to display server-side information.

In UNIX for example, the DBA would need to know the command-line syntax of various UNIX utilities such as *sar*, *glance*, *top*, *lsattr*, and *prtconf* to display server metrics. The Oracle OEM screens allow seamless access server-side performance metrics including:

■ Oracle server-side file contents such as *alert log* and *trace dumps*

■ Oracle archives redo log file performance

■ Server OS kernel performance parameter values

■ Server OS characteristics such as the number of CPUs, the amount of RAM, and the network

■ Historical capture of CPU and RAM activity

A quick look at the Oracle 10g OEM display screens for external information reveals how the DBA is relieved of the burden of having to know and recall hundreds of server-side commands. Oracle 10g OEM allows DBAs to quickly see the status of Oracle server-side file performance and error messages, including the alert log file, archived redo log status and file system status as shown in Figure 12.9.

All Metrics

Expand All | Collapse All

Metrics	Thresholds	Collection Stat
▼FSDEV10G		
▼Alert Log	Some	Not Collected
Alert Log Error Trace File	Not Set	Not Collected
Alert Log Name	Not Set	Not Collected
Archiver Hung Alert Log Error	Set	Not Collected
Data Block Corruption Alert Log Error	Set	Not Collected
Generic Alert Log Error	Set	Not Collected
Session Terminated Alert Log Error	Set	Not Collected
▼Alert Log Content	None	Not Collected
Content	Not Set	Not Collected
▼Alert Log Error Status	All	Last Collected
Archiver Hung Alert Log Error Status	Set	Last Collected
Data Block Corruption Alert Log Error Status	Set	Last Collected
Generic Alert Log Error Status	Set	Last Collected
Session Terminated Alert Log Error Status	Set	Last Collected
▼Archive Area	Some	Last Collected
Archive Area Used (%)	Set	Last Collected
Archive Area Used (KB)	Not Set	Last Collected
Free Archive Area (KB)	Not Set	Last Collected

Figure 12.9: *Partial Listing of the AWR Metrics from Inside Oracle 10g Enterprise Manager*

The ability of OEM to monitor server-side metrics makes it a one-stop tool for monitoring both Oracle and the server. In addition, a systems administrator may no longer be required to buy separate, expensive tools to monitor the server and the data files. Best of all, the Oracle professional does not have to worry about a server-side problem, i.e. file-system full, causing an Oracle interruption.

From these OEM interfaces, server-side Oracle components can be displayed and managed without having to sign on to the server. This is an advantage for those Oracle professionals running UNIX servers who may not be fluent in UNIX commands and the complex *vi* editor. Figure 12.10 shows the display of server OS details including all of the OS kernel parameters.

Figure 12.10: *The Oracle 10g OEM Display of Server-side Performance Parameters*

Users can also throw away existing checklists of cumbersome OS commands required to display server hardware characteristics. The OEM issues server commands and displays all hardware characteristics in an easy-to-read display as shown in Figure 12.11.

OEM does much more than simply display the server parameters and configuration information. A shortage of server resources may cause slow performance, and the OEM now quickly displays the relevant CPU and RAM metrics. The main performance display screen in the OEM now displays a current summary of the CPU run queue and RAM paging as shown in Figure 12.12.

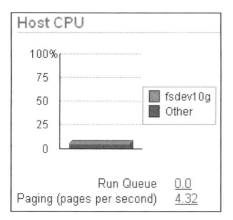

Figure 12.12: *The HOST CPU Section of the Main OEM Performance Screen*

If a shortage of Oracle server resources is causing a performance bottleneck, it quickly becomes evident. If the instance and SQL have already been optimized, this server-side information can give immediate insight into server resource shortages such as:

- **CPU dispatcher run queue:** whenever the server processors are overstressed, the run queue will exceed the number of CPUs. For example, a *runqueue* value of nine on an 8-CPU server indicates the need to add more, or faster, CPUs.

- **Server RAM Paging:** whenever the RAM demands of a server exceed the real RAM capacity, the server's Virtual Memory (VM) utility will page, thereby transferring RAM frames to a special swap-disk on the server. Assuming the SGA and PGA regions are optimized, paging indicates the need to add RAM resources to the server.

The Oracle OEM also tracks server usage over time, allowing quick access to information regarding those times when a hardware-related constraint occurs as shown in Figure 12.13. This figure displays the historical CPU usage as well as user defined threshold alert status which is defined by setting a threshold alert for the *average CPU (%)* OEM metric.

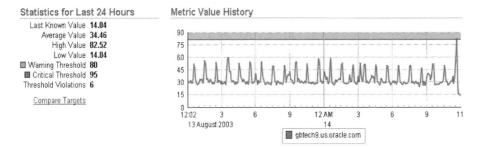

Figure 12.13: *The Oracle 10g OEM Historical Tracking of CPU Consumption*

The OEM also tracks server run queue waits over time and combines the CPU and paging display into a single screen. This allows users to determine when there are server-side waits on hardware resources as shown in Figure 12.14. This is important because Oracle performance issues are often transient in nature as evidenced by short spikes indicating excessive CPU demands.

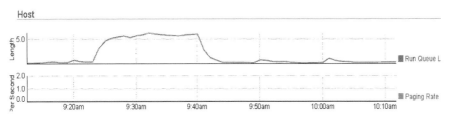

Figure 12.14: *Server CPU Run Queue and RAM Paging Values Over Time*

Due to the fast nature of CPU dispatching, a database might be CPU constrained for a few minutes at a time at different times of the day. The time series OEM display can give a quick visual clue about those times when the system is experiencing a CPU or RAM bottleneck. Further detailed information can be obtained by using the OEM drill-down function and clicking on any area of the graph.

Due to Oracle's commitment to extending the OEM beyond the boundaries of the Oracle instance, virtually all areas of server utilization can be tracked over time as shown in Figure 12.15. The chart shows specific times when the server exceeded the maximum CPU capacity along with the total time spent by active Oracle sessions for both waiting and working.

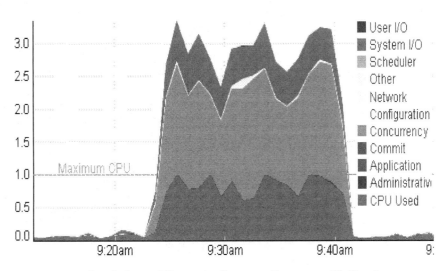

Figure 12.15: *Oracle Server Time-series Resource Component Utilization*

The legend indicates the components of Oracle wait times including CPU time, concurrency management overhead in the form of locks and latches, and I/O. This display also shows the times when CPU usage exceeds the server capacity.

The same AWR data that is rendered within OEM can also be used as input to more sophisticated scripts for covariate analysis and trending of server-side AWR and ASH data. New server-side abilities of AWR clearly influence the execution of SQL within Oracle.

Server Metrics and SQL Execution

When determining the best execution plan for an SQL query, the newly enhanced cost-based optimizer (CBO) considers external influences. Since the Oracle database does not run in a vacuum, the CBO must have the ability to factor in the costs of external disk I/O as well as the cost of CPU cycles for each SQL operation. This is a significant step forward in making the CBO one of the most sophisticated software packages in the world. Choosing the best execution plan for any SQL statement is always the job of the CBO and is no small challenge.

According to Oracle documentation, the I/O and CPU costs are estimated as shown below:

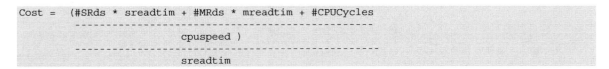

```
Cost =  (#SRds * sreadtim + #MRds * mreadtim + #CPUCycles
        -------------------------------------------------
                        cpuspeed )
        -------------------------------------------------
                        sreadtim
```

where:

- **#SRDs:** number of single block reads

- **#MRDs:** number of multi-block reads

- **#CPUCycles:** number of CPU cycles

- **sreadtim:** single block read time

- **mreadtim:** multi-block read time

- **cpuspeed:** CPU cycles per second

The external costing is markedly influenced by the calculated cost of disk reads as measured by the *v$* tables and the estimated CPU costs associated with each internal operation. By storing the details regarding the costs of many components of SQL execution, Oracle can use these average costs to influence the choices made by the CBO. Here are some examples:

- **Hash join costs:** Oracle records the average amount of RAM memory consumed by a hash join

- **Sort costs:** Oracle tracks the RAM necessary for sorting and aggregation operations

- **Table scan costs:** Oracle keeps information about the amount of time that is essential to performing a multi-block read such as *db file scatter reads*

- **Index block access costs:** Oracle stores the average time required to fetch a single block such as *db file sequential reads*

Depending on the *optimizer_mode* choice, Oracle costs are weighed differently. If the *all_rows* optimizer mode is utilized for a data warehouse, the CBO will be heavily influenced by external factors due to the fact that the *all_rows* mode is designed to minimize resource consumption. On the other hand, if there is an OLTP system with the *first_rows* optimizer mode, the CBO deems it more imperative to return rows quickly than to minimize resource costs.

CPU Based Optimizer Costing

The recently added CPU costing feature, controlled by the *_optimizer_cost_model* = hidden parameter, enhances the CBO's capabilities by allowing it to estimate the number of machine cycles necessary for an operation. This cost subsequently counts in the execution plan calculation. The CPU costs affiliated with servicing an Oracle query hinge on the current server load, which Oracle cannot see. Generally, CPU costs are not considered significant unless the entire Oracle instance is using excessive CPU resources.

I/O Costing

While the CBO is now enhanced to figure the number of physical block reads required for an operation, it has not yet been quite perfected. For example, the CBO is not yet aware of the percentage of a table's blocks that reside in the data buffer.

The I/O cost is proportional to the number of physical data blocks read by the operation. However, the CBO has no prior information on the data buffer contents and cannot distinguish between a logical read (in-buffer) and a physical read. Due to this shortcoming, the CBO cannot know if the data blocks are already in the RAM data buffers. The best environment for using CPU costing is for *all_rows* execution plans, where cost is more noteworthy than with *first_rows* optimization.

External costing does not take into account the number of data blocks residing in the RAM data buffers; however, a future release of the CBO is likely to incorporate this element. Additionally, costs are a function of the number of reads and the relative read times plus the CPU cost estimate for the query. In evaluating the execution plan, Oracle uses both the CPU and I/O cost estimations. This equation becomes even more complex when parallel querying is factored in when several concurrent processes are servicing the query. Oracle Network affects Oracle performance and the AWR data can help users detect and fix data transmission issues.

Oracle Network Tuning

Oracle databases are often shared across dispersed geographical locations, so it is imperative that the Oracle professional comprehend how database performance is affected by network communications. In response to this, Oracle provides the Transparent Network Substrate (TNS), which allows distributed communications between databases.

As a distributed protocol, the TNS allows for transparent database communications between remote systems. The TNS serves the physical communications between the remote servers and acts as an insulator between Oracle's logical data requests. This allows the network administrator to control much of the network performance tuning; however, it also subsequently leaves the Oracle administrator little control over the network settings that can affect overall database performance, as shown in Figure 12.16.

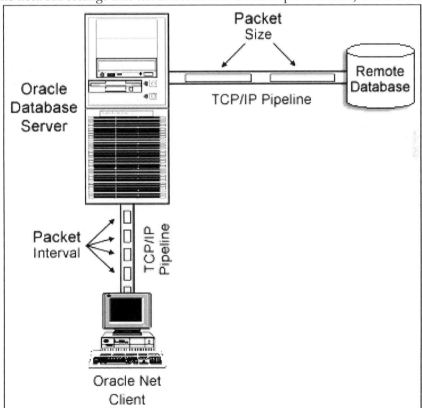

Figure 12.16: *The SQL*Net architecture*

By using some network parameter settings, several of which are presented in this chapter, the performance of distributed transactions can be improved. This review of the network tuning parameters should indicate that the *init.ora* parameters relate to distributed communications, while the TCP parameters, such as *tcp.nodelay*, can be used to change the packet shipping mechanisms such as size and frequency of packet transmission.

The parameters within the *sqlnet.ora*, *tnsnames.ora*, and *protocol.ora* files can also be used to change the configuration and size of TCP packets. The setting for these parameters can have a profound impact on the underlying network transport layer's ability to improve the throughput of all Oracle transactions. SQL*Net is a layer in the OSI model that resides above the network specific protocol stack. SQL*Net prohibits the Oracle administrator from tuning Oracle network parameters to improve network performance. SQL*Net takes the data and gives it to the protocol stack for transmission in response to a data request. The protocol stack then creates a packet from this data and transmits it over the network. Passing data to the protocol stack is SQL*Net's sole task, so there is little allowance for the DBA to improve network performance.

The DBA does have the ability to control the frequency and size of network packets. Oracle offers a number of tools that are used to change packet frequency and size. Changing the refresh interval for a snapshot to ship larger amounts of data at less frequent intervals is a simple example.

Using several parameters, SQL*Net connections between servers can be tuned; however, network tuning is outside the scope of Oracle and a qualified network administrator should be consulted for tuning the network. By using settings contained in the following parameter files, the frequency and size of packets shipping across the network can be impacted:

FILE	PARAMETER
sqlnet.ora	tcp.nodelay
sqlnet.ora	automatic_ipc
sqlnet.ora	break_poll_skip
tnsnames.ora	SDU and TDU
listener.ora	SDU, TDU, and queuesize

Table 12.2: *Oracle Network Parameter Locations*

While limited in power, the settings for these parameters can still make a huge difference in the performance of distributed Oracle databases. A closer look at these parameters is warranted.

The *Tcp.nodelay* Parameter

By default, SQL*Net waits until the buffer is full before transmitting data; therefore, requests are not always sent immediately to their destinations. This is most commonly found when large amounts of data are streamed from one location to another, and SQL*Net does not transmit the packet until the buffer is full. Adding a *sqlnet.ora* file and specifying a *tcp.nodelay* to stop buffer flushing delays can sometimes remedy this problem. The parameter can be used both on the client and server. The *sqlnet.ora* statement is:

```
tcp.nodelay = YES
```

As of Oracle 10g, this parameter defaults to a value of YES. TCP buffering is skipped so that every request is sent immediately. Slowdowns in the network may be caused by an increase in network traffic due to smaller and more frequent packet transmission.

The *Automatic_ipc* Parameter

Speeding local connections to the database occurs when the *automatic_ipc* parameter bypasses the network layer. When *automatic_ipc* is set to ON, SQL*Net checks to see if a local database is defined by the same alias:

```
automatic_ipc=ON
```

Only when an SQL*Net connection must be made to the local database should the *automatic_ipc* parameter be used on the database server. Set this parameter to OFF if local connections are not needed or required. This will improve the performance of all SQL*Net clients.

The SDU and TDU Parameters

The session data unit (SDU) specifies the size of the packets to send over the network. The maximum transmission unit (MTU) is a fixed value that depends on the actual network implementation used. Ideally, SDU should not surpass the size of the MTU. Oracle recommends that SDU be set equal to the MTU. The *tnsnames.ora* and *listener.ora* files house the SDU and TDU parameters.

To group data together, the TDU value is the default packet size used within SQL*Net. The default value for both SDU and TDU is 2,048 bytes and the maximum value is 32,767 bytes. The TDU parameter should ideally be a multiple of the SDU parameter. For SDU and TDU, the following guidelines apply:

- On fast network connections such as T1 or T3 lines, SDU and TDU should be set equal to the MTU for the network. On standard Ethernet networks, the default MTU size should be set to 1,514 bytes. On standard token ring networks, the default MTU size is 4,202 bytes.

- If the users are connecting via dial-up modem lines, it may be desirable to set SDU and TDU to smaller values in consideration of the frequent resends that occur over modem connections

- The dispatchers must also be set with the proper MTU-TDU configuration if Oracle Shared Server is used

- As a rule, SDU should not be set greater than the TDU because network resources will be wasted by shipping wasted space in each packet.

This brief review of network-related parameters was intended to provide an introduction to the scope and complexity of network tuning. It is important to understand that SQL*Net is simply a layer in the OSI model that is above the network-specific protocol stack and therefore, virtually all network tuning is external to Oracle.

Conclusion

The future of Oracle database administration is constantly changing. These changes will forever alter the way that Oracle DBAs perform their work. The following are examples of some expected changes:

- **Fully cached databases:** just as the UNISYS benchmark used 115 gigabyte data buffers, many Oracle systems will become fully cached. This is largely a result of decreasing RAM costs and the advent of 64-bit Oracle servers. As of 2009, all Sun Microsystems servers contain solid-state disk, and by 2012 the majority of Oracle databases will be fully cached.

- **Solid-state Oracle:** the advent of Solid-State Disk (SSD) will produce a faster replacement for the archaic spinning platters of magnetic coated media and will someday relieve the need for data buffers

- **Back to the mainframe:** the Oracle system of the future will run an entire corporate enterprise on a two-server system consisting of a main server and a geographically distant failover server, which provides both failover and disaster recovery

- **Changing role of the DBA:** a single DBA will be able to manage dozens of Oracle instances in a consolidated environment. This is reminiscent of the 1980s when the DBA for a large corporation was required to have credentials including advanced degrees and skills far exceeding those of the typical Oracle DBA of the late 1990s.

Having experienced the huge wave of demand for Oracle DBAs in the early 1990s as the direct result of server deconsolidation, many DBAs would welcome the return to the old days where they could manage dozens of Oracle instances within a single server environment.

The next step is to take a look at disk I/O tuning issues with Oracle and see how the new AWR and ASH views can help.

Tuning the I/O Subsystem

"Yeah, it's a hot disk problem"

Inside Oracle Disk Architecture

Disk I/O is the single slowest operation in any computer system, and databases applications are especially vulnerable to I/O performance issues. Back in the 1990s when RAM was very expensive and data buffer caches were tiny, nearly all Oracle databases were I/O-bound. A primary responsibility of the 1990's DBA was to load balance the I/O subsystem to maximize disk throughput, a critical task in any data intensive Oracle applications.

But times have changed. Today, the mapping of the tablespace to the disk spindles is obfuscated by RAID 10 striping, plaiding, and other esoteric disk access technologies, making it nearly impossible to track a single hot disk without resorting to vendor supplied tools.

It's odd that the old-fashioned magnetic-coated spinning platters of yesteryear are still here today, even though they are slowly being replaced by solid-state disk. Who would have guessed that computers in the 21st century would still contain moving parts? Disk technology is aging-out, being replaced by solid-state storage, but disks remain a critical tertiary components, replacing magnetic tape for long-term offline data storage.

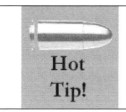

Disk I/O is a critical management component within Oracle, and this chapter only provides a basic overview of Oracle disk I/O tuning. For an in-depth overview, see the book *Oracle Disk I/O Tuning* by Rampant TechPress.

In this chapter, we will learn why disk I/O is so important to Oracle tuning and explore the use of the STATSPACK and AWR tables for locating disk I/O-related problems. We will start with an overview of the basic disk I/O mechanisms followed by a look at the use of the *dba_hist* tables for tracking disk I/O.

On the ancient IBM mainframes of the 1980s, we had far more control over file placement on disk than we do today. On IBM mainframe disks, the placement of all of our data files can be controlled with a very high degree of granularity, placing data files directly on the track that we desire using the absolute track (ABSTR) JCL argument.

Prior to the advent of RAID and the Oracle SAME standard (Stripe and Mirror Everywhere), we were constantly on the lookout for hot disks and data file placement was a very important part of Oracle tuning.

If RAID striping is not in use, the manual disk placement rules remain important. The rules for manual data file placement include:

File Placement: On large disks where the data cannot be fully cached in the data buffers, we might consider placing high I/O data files in the middle absolute track number to minimize read-write head movement. This is a situation in which the low access data files reside on the inner and outer cylinders of the disk. As shown next, high impact data files should be placed to minimize read-write head movement.

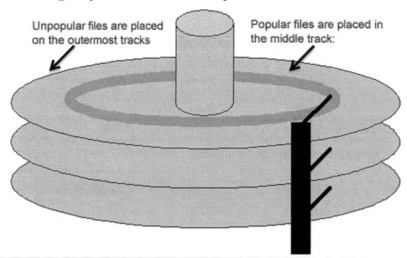

File Striping: High impact data files could extend across many disk drives to spread the load and relieve disk and channel contention. Today RAID does this, depending upon the stripe size.

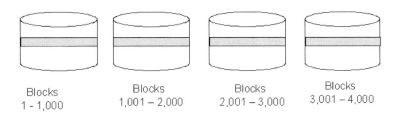

Figure 13.2: *High Impact Data Files Extended Across Disk Drives*

File Segregation: To relieve disk contention, the redo files and data files should be placed on separate disk spindles. This is also true for the archived redo log file directory and the undo log files.

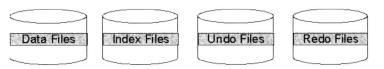

Figure 13.3: *File Segregation*

All of these disk I/O rules still apply even if hardware or software RAID, Solid-state Disk (SSD), or 100 percent data caching are not in use. Now look at how advances of the past decade have simplified this important task of disk I/O management.

Today's disks still have extremely slow access speed and there can be wide variations in disk access speed even though the average disk latency is 8-15 milliseconds. Internally, disks have changed little in the past 40 years. They are the last remaining electro-mechanical device in a computer, with spinning platters and mechanical read-write heads.

Platter disks suffer from three sources of delay:

- **Read-write head delay (seek delay):** The time required to position the read-write head under the disk cylinder can consume 90 percent of the total disk access time. With today's super-large 1 terabyte disks, it is unwise to place competing files in outermost cylinders because of the read-write head motion. This read-write head movement will actually make the disk drive vibrate as the read-write heads swing back and forth!

- **Data transmission delay:** Data transmission time remains a huge source of delay for distributed databases and databases on the Internet. For instance, many worldwide Oracle shops use replication techniques and place systems staggered across the world to reduce data transmission time.

- **Rotational delay:** The rotational delay is the RPM speed of the platter divided by two, and assumes that a platter will have to spin a half-revolution to access any given track header. Once on the proper cylinder, the read-write heads must wait until the track header passes beneath them.

Before large data buffer caches and RAID, we had to manually place data files on the disk and monitor I/O patterns to ensure there was no disk contention. But technology marches on, and the rules for Oracle data files are far different than they were 20 years ago. Explore how the evolving technology has changed Oracle disk I/O tuning.

The Plague of Large Oracle Disks

Oracle is a data delivery engine, and accessing data from disks often imposes a system bottleneck, especially when the entire database resides on a single disk drive.

In my book *Oracle Disk I/O Tuning* I note that placing too much data on a single disk spindle will impose enqueues because the mechanical device can only locate to a single cylinder at a time. On busy Oracle databases on a single disk spindle, the disk can shake like an out-of-balance washing machine as competing tasks enqueue for data service.

Originally, RAID was an acronym for Redundant Arrays of INEXPENSIVE DISKS, and Oracle professionals enjoyed the ability of spreading their Oracle data across multiple disks and spreading the load. Today's large disk arrays commonly utilize asynchronous write and multi-gigabyte RAM buffers to minimize this latency, but it still is a major concern for thousands of Oracle shops.

According to the book *Oracle Solid State Disk Tuning*, smaller solid-state RAM disks have far less bandwidth issues because the RAM architecture of SSD allow high concurrent access that is impossible on a mechanical platter. This issue of single channel access also imposes a bottleneck on Oracle disk devices, and the large disks (over 144 gigabytes) often perform more slowly for high concurrent access than their smaller predecessors.

Oracle's standard SAME (Stripe and Mirror Everywhere, RAID 10) is largely useless for load balancing if the whole database resides on just a few physical disks. Remember, the seek delay (movement of the read-write heads) composes well over 80% of disk access latency, and high concurrent requests against large devices make them very slow.

Remember, disk enqueues will kill Oracle performance because the read-write heads cannot move fast enough to service concurrent requests, and disk load balancing may be required, where popular Oracle data files can be placed on the middle absolute track of the device to minimize read-write head movement.

Obviously, the Oracle professional must take action to relieve disk I/O bottlenecks. As manufacturing costs continue to fall, disk vendors are offering larger and larger disks and this is imposing some serious large disk performance issues with seek delay is 1.5 times slower.

As a result of this trend towards super-large disk devices, many Oracle professionals experience external I/O waits and they see that the top-5 waits events (from a STATSPACK or AWR Report) show "*db file sequential reads*" and "*db file scattered reads*" as a main system bottleneck.

But it's rarely as simple as a few disks. Today's storage arrays may have dozens of disk platters, and a complex architecture that make it hard for us to manage our I/O latency. Let's take a closer look.

Disk Architectures of the 21st Century

During the 1980s, all databases were I/O bound and countless DBAs spent their days managing the disk I/O subsystem with cumbersome and complex file placement rules. However, there are several advancements in disk technologies that have changed the approach to data file placement:

- **Solid-State Disk:** With a cost of only $1k per gigabyte in 2010, the new solid-state disks retrieve data hundreds of time faster than traditional platter-based disks. In shops too large to go 100% SSD, they use SSD technology for their high impact files such as their TEMP tablespace, undo files, and redo log files.

- **Large RAM Caching:** In 64-bit Oracle, the *db_cache_size* is only limited by the server, allowing many shops to run fully cached databases. Prices of RAM should fall in the next five years such that most systems can be fully cached, thereby making disk management obsolete.

Oracle has an insatiable appetite for RAM, but we must remember that almost all databases have "popular" files and "unpopular" files. If we have limited RAM we will only want to increase our data buffer caches up to the point of diminishing marginal returns, the "*sweet spot*" where all of the frequently-referenced data blocks are in the data buffer cache.

Oracle has a utility called *v$db_cache_advice* that allows us to predict the benefit of adding RAM buffers. This same concept has been incorporated into the Oracle Automatic Memory Management (AMM) as shown in Figure 13.4.

Cache Size (meg)	Buffers	Estd Phys Read Factor	Estd Phys Reads
30	3,802	18.70	192,317,943 <== 10% size
60	7,604	12.83	131,949,536
91	11,406	7.38	75,865,861
121	15,208	4.97	51,111,658
152	19,010	3.64	37,460,786
182	22,812	2.50	25,668,196
212	26,614	1.74	17,850,847
243	30,416	1.33	13,720,149
273	34,218	1.13	11,583,180
304	38,020	1.00	10,282,475 <== Current Size
334	41,822	.93	9,515,878
364	45,624	.87	8,909,026
395	49,426	.83	8,495,039
424	53,228	.79	8,116,496
456	57,030	.76	7,824,764
486	60,832	.74	7,563,180
517	64,634	.71	7,311,729

```
547        68,436        .69    7,104,280
577        72,238        .67    6,895,122
608        76,040        .66    6,739,731 <== 2x size
```

Figure 13.4: *Output from the v$db_cache_advice Utility*

Oracle estimates the physical reads for different sizes of the *db_cache_size*. In Figure 13.4, it is clear that doubling the *db_cache_size* from 856 to 1,672 will cut disk I/O by more than 80 million disk reads. However, as full caching is approached, less frequently referenced data becomes cached, and the marginal benefit of caching decreases, as shown in Figure 13.5.

The marginal increase in data buffer blocks is asymptotic to disk I/O.

This is a y = 1/x function where:

$$RAM\ buffers = \frac{1}{physical\ reads}$$

Plotted, it looks like this:

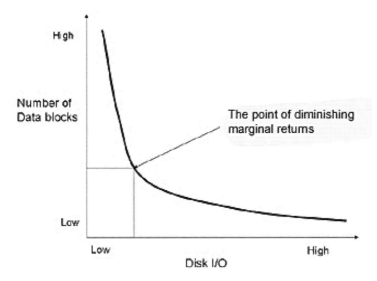

Figure 13.5: *The Marginal Gains from Large RAM Caches*

Take a close look at Figure 13.5. At first, with a tiny *db_cache_size* a marginal increase to the buffer results in a greater decline in disk I/O because popular blocks become cached. As full data caching is approached and unpopular data is accessed, the marginal benefit of adding blocks to *db_cache_size* decreases.

Oracle 10g introduced the Automatic Shared Memory Management (ASMM) feature, which reactively tracks the usage of RAM within the *shared_pool_size, pga_aggregate_target* and *db_cache_size* and automatically adjusts the sizes of these SGA regions based on current usage.

Beware of ASMM resize operations!

ASMM is a one-sized-fits-all approach, and some databases will experience performance problems with ASMM resizing operations.

Look Out!

In large mission-critical databases, the DBA almost always manages the RAM manually because they have far more control than an automated method.

Full details on tuning the RAM data buffers are covered in chapter 14, *Oracle Instance Tuning.* Now take a look at the influence of RAID on Oracle databases.

RAID Technology and Oracle

The need to manually stripe the data files across multiple disk spindles has been lessened with the advent of hardware and software RAID. The two most common levels of RAID for Oracle are RAID 10 (mirroring and striping) and RAID 5.

For all low-update systems, Oracle recommends using SAME (Stripe and Mirror Everywhere, a.k.a., RAID 1+0), and this SAME approach is the foundation of the Oracle Automatic Storage Management (ASM) approach.

RAID 5 is Not for Every Database

Many disk vendors persist in pushing RAID 5 as a viable solution for highly updated systems even though using RAID 5 for an Oracle system with a high update rate can be disastrous to performance because of the inherent update "penalty", a core part of the RAID 5 architecture.

As of 2010, many disk vendors have made advances that overcome the "write penalty" associated with high update activity and there are now RAID 5 storage devices that can accommodate high update databases without the high write penalty latency.

One such product is the Hitachi TagmaStore RAID 5 Universal Storage Platform, which uses a huge 256-gigabyte cache to overcome the RAID 5 write penalty. Because this cache is so huge, the database can write to disk and move on; the parity is calculated from the data in cache asynchronously. Therefore, unless the cache is over-extended, the database will not suffer the RAID 5 write penalty.

But even with RAID, disk I/O remains a critical component, and we must still understand disk I/O at a very detailed level. The main points of this section include:

- **Not everyone uses RAID:** In some systems, the DBA may choose to manually stripe and mirror their data without RAID. In these systems, the Oracle data files must be manually placed across the disk spindles to relieve I/O contention.

- **Watch out for RAID 5:** RAID 5 is not always recommended for high-update Oracle systems. The performance penalty from the parity checking will greatly diminish Oracle performance.

- **Use SAME:** Using a RAID 10 approach (striping and mirroring) distributes data blocks across all of the disk spindles, making hot disks a random and transient event.

- **Consider large buffers:** Oracle continues to expand support for very large RAM data buffers and buffer monitoring with the *v$db_cache_advice* utility and ASMM.

- **Watch our bottlenecks:** Improving disk access speed will not help if disk is not the source of the bottleneck. The top 5 STATSPACK wait events should be checked to ensure that disk I/O is the bottleneck prior to undergoing expensive changes to the disk I/O subsystem.

- **Consider solid-state disk:** Many Oracle customers are using solid-state disk for high I/O data files such as TEMP, UNDO, and REDO files. Solid-state disk is becoming less expensive and may soon replace traditional disk devices.

In sum, Oracle DBAs must be steadfast in attempting to understand their disk I/O subsystem and making sure that disk I/O does not impede the high performance of their systems.

RAID 5 can be deadly for high-update databases!

Even with lots of caching, the goal of almost all Oracle tuning activities is to reduce I/O. Tuning the instance parameters, sizing the library cache, and tuning SQL statements all have the common focus of reducing disk I/O overhead.

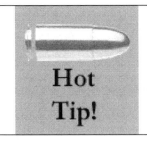

Hot Tip!

Logical I/O is also important

After our physical disk I/O is minimized, logical I/O is still a major contributor to response time. Also, even fully cached databases are slow if sub-optimal SQL statements force high LIOs against the buffer .

Time and time again, we spend our time and energy tuning a component of our database that is not a top 5 wait event, and we would be surprised to find that a change did not make a huge difference in performance! For example, getting a faster CPU does not help an I/O-bound system, and moving to faster disk does not help a CPU-bound system.

Remember, time takes time. All Oracle databases have some physical constraint, and it is not always disk I/O. The best way to find the constraints for our own system is to examine the top five wait events on the STATSPACK/AWR report.

The system is disk I/O-bound if the majority of the wait time is spent accessing data blocks. This can be *db file sequential read waits*, usually index access, and *db file scattered read waits*, usually full-table scans:

```
Top 5 Timed Events

                                                   % Total
Event                            Waits           Ela Time
--------------------------    ------------    ----------  --------
db file sequential read           2,598           48.54
db file scattered read           25,519           22.04
library cache load lock             673            9.26
CPU time                             44            7.83
log file parallel write          19,157            5.68
```

An I/O bottleneck may also manifest itself with high CPU run queue values combined with high idle times.

```
SERVER_NAME     date      hour   runq  pg_in pg_ot  usr  sys    idl
------------    -------  ------   ----  ----- ----   ----- ----- ----
CSS-HP1         04/06/15   22     10      4     0     11    2     87
CSS-HP1         04/06/15   09      9      4     0     11    2     87
CSS-HP1         04/06/14   22     10      2     0     46    6     50
CSS-HP1         04/06/14   07      9      4     0     10    2     88
```

Normally, a high *vmstat* run queue, where the run queue values exceed the number of CPUs on the server, indicates CPU overload. However, when combined with high CPU idle times, the run queue values indicate that the CPU is backed up waiting for I/O to complete.

Once it has been determined that the Oracle database is I/O-bound, we need to understand the internals of our disk devices, layers of caching, and the configuration of the disk controllers and physical disk spindles. The mapping all the way from the logical tablespace to the physical disk spindle also needs to be known.

Oracle and Direct I/O

Many Oracle shops are plagued with I/O intensive databases, and direct I/O can help anyone whose top 5 timed events shows disk I/O as a major wait event:

```
Top 5 Timed Events
                                           % Total
Event                       Waits         Ela Time
-------------------------   -----------   ----------- ---
db file sequential read       2,598           48.54
db file scattered read       25,519           22.04
library cache load lock         673            9.26
CPU time                      2,154            7.83
log file parallel write      19,157            5.68
```

It is important to note that deploying direct I/O is an OS-level solution, but the root cause of high disk I/O is often un-tuned SQL, and Oracle starts by tuning the SQL to reduce unnecessary large-table full-table scans before employing direct I/O.

File I/O is easy to see. Disk activity can be monitored using the AWR *dba_hist_filestatxs* table or the STATSPACK *stats$filestatxs* table and there are other supplemental tables that will be covered later in this chapter. For optimal disk performance, Oracle should always use direct I/O for data files, bypassing any journal files system (JFS) caching at the OS layer. Remember, direct I/O must be enabled both in Oracle and in the operating system.

Oracle controls direct I/O with a parameter named *filesystemio_options*. According to the Oracle documentation, the *filesystemio_options* parameter must be set to *setall* or *directio* in order for Oracle to read data blocks directly from disk. Using *directio* allows the enhancement of I/O through the bypassing of the redundant OS block buffers, reading the data block directly into the Oracle SGA. Using direct I/O also allows the creation of multiple blocksize tablespaces.

Enabling Oracle Direct I/O

Methods for configuring the OS will vary depending on the operating system and file system in use. The following sections contain some examples of quick checks that anyone can perform to ensure that direct I/O is being used by your Oracle database.

Oracle recommends that all database files use direct I/O, which is a disk access method that bypasses the additional overhead on the OS buffer. One important exception to this rule is the archived redo log filesystem, which should use OS buffer caching. The following information details the method for ensuring that the OS uses Direct I/O.

Direct I/O for Windows

The Windows uses direct I/O by default, and there is no special configuration to ensure that the database files use Direct I/O.

Direct I/O for IBM AIX

The *filesystemio_options* initialization parameter should be set to configure a database to use either direct I/O or concurrent I/O when accessing datafiles, depending on the file system.

Specification of the value setall for this parameter ensures that:

- Datafiles on a JFS file system are accessed using direct I/O

- Datafiles on a JFS2 file system are accessed using concurrent I/O

In Oracle 9i Server Release 2, *filesystemio_options* was a hidden parameter, but in 10g and beyond, this parameter is externally available. The *filesystemio_options* can be set to any of the following values:

- **asynch:** Set by default. This allows asynchronous I/O to be used where supported by the OS.

- *directio:* This allows direct I/O to be used where supported by the OS. Direct I/O bypasses any UNIX buffer cache.

- *setall:* Enables both ASYNC and direct I/O

- **None:** This disables asynch I/O and direct I/O so that Oracle uses normal synchronous writes without any direct I/O options.

Direct I/O for Linux

Direct I/O support is not available and is not supported on Red Hat Enterprise Linux 2.1. However, dissect I/O is available and is supported on Red Hat Enterprise Linux 3 also over NFS, if the driver being used on the system supports *varyio*. To enable direct I/O support:

- Set the *filesystemio_options* parameter in the parameter file to *directio (filesystemio_options = directio)*.

- If the asynchronous I/O option is in use, the *filesystemio_options* parameter in the parameter file should be set to *setall*.

Also with 10g, this feature is already working, which means that is does not require any patch. For Oracle 9i, we will need to download <patch:2448994> - Abstract: direct I/O support over NFS.

Direct I/O for Sun Solaris

For Sun Solaris servers, you need to set the *forcedirectio* option. Oracle DBAs claim this option makes a tremendous difference in I/O speed for Sun servers.

Direct I/O for Veritas

For Veritas VxFS, including HP-UX, Solaris and AIX Veritas, the following setting should be used: *convosync* = direct. It is also possible to enable direct I/O on a per file basis using Veritas QIO. Please refer to the *qiostat* command and corresponding manual page for hints.

Now that we have addressed direct I/O, let's look at a nice package that shows us the average response time and throughput for our disk platters.

Calibrating your disk I/O

We must remember that Oracle does not run in a vacuum, and that disk I/O is the single most expensive operation in any Oracle database. For software than executes procedures in microseconds, waiting a millisecond for a disk read is an eternity, and while the *dbms_stats.gather_system_stats* procedure measure I/O averages as a whole for the SQL optimizer, it does not drill-down to the device level.

If you are responsible for your Oracle performance you will want to know the maximum throughput of your disk spindles and the average response time from each disk. Remember, disk platters have moving parts, and response time is not uniform!

The *dbms_resource_manager* package has a nice procedure called *calibrate_io* which is perfect for calibrating disk latency and throughout.

You can pass several arguments to *dbms_resource_manager.calibrate_io*:

- **Maximum latency tolerance:** This is the I/O per second target for the disks (milliseconds).
- **The number of disk spindles:** This is the number of physical disk devices.

Here is a working example of the *calibrate_io* procedure. Note the use of *dbms_output.put_line* to display the disk calibration results:

```
set serveroutput on

declare
  lat  integer;
  iops integer;
  mbps integer;
begin
  dbms_resource_manager.calibrate_io (2, 10, iops, mbps, lat);
  dbms_output.put_line ('max_iops = ' || iops);
  dbms_output.put_line ('latency  = ' || lat);
  dbms_output.put_line('max_mbps = ' || mbps);
end;
/
```

After running this procedure you can view the results using the *v$io_calibration_status* and for RAC, the *gv$io_calibration_status* views.

You can view the output from this procedure in the *dba_rsrc_io_calibrate* view and see important disk speed metrics:

- Maximum I/O per second for the disk (or group of disks)
- Maximum throughout (in megabytes per second)
- Average Disk response time (in milliseconds)

```
select
   *
from
   dba_rsrc_io_calibrate;
```

In the output below we see the maximum I/O per second and throughput in megabytes per second:

```
START_TIME   END_TIME    MAX_IOPS   MAX_MBPS   MAX_PMBPS   LATENCY   DISKS
------------ ----------- ---------- ---------- ----------- --------- --------
28-JUL-2008  28-JUL-2008 556        48         48          17        1
```

Calibrate_io is not used by the SQL optimizer

While *dbms_stats.gather_system_stats* samples disk I/O speed for use by the SQL optimizer, the information gathered by *dbms_resource_manager.calibrate_io* is not used by the SQL optimizer.

Look Out!

Now that we see how to calibrate disk I/O, let's move on and explore how to monitor disk I/O at the external level.

Monitoring External Disk I/O

Oracle runs on over 60 different platforms, but the majority of Oracle databases run on some variant of Linux and UNIX. For these platforms, measuring external disk I/O is best done using the industry standard *iostat* utility.

Because the *iostat* utility is slightly different on every server, create separate versions of a shell script to capture the disk information. Regardless of the differences in display format, a single Oracle table can be defined to hold the *iostat* information. Here is the syntax for this table:

```
drop table perfstat.stats$iostat;

create table
perfstat.stats$iostat
(
   snap_time          date,
   elapsed_seconds    number(4),
   hdisk              varchar2(8),
   kb_read            number(9,0),
   kb_write           number(9,0)
```

```
)
tablespace perfstat
storage (initial 20m next 1m );

create index
   perfstat.stats$iostat_date_idx
on
   perfstat.stats$iostat
  (snap_time)
tablespace perfstat
storage (initial 5m next 1m);

create index
   perfstat.stats$iostat_hdisk_idx
on
   perfstat.stats$iostat
   (hdisk)
tablespace perfstat
storage (initial 5m next 1m);
```

Capturing external *iostat* Information

The *get_iostat.ksh* script below is a Korn shell script that runs *iostat* to collect disk-level I/O information at five-minute intervals. Note that this script runs the *iostat* utility and captures the output into the user-defined *stats$iostat* table using the data from the *vol_grp* table to create the *sum_iostat* table. Once this script has been run, the data required to identify the system's hot disks and mount points appears, externally from Oracle.

💾 **get_iostat_solaris.ksh**

```
#!/bin/ksh
while true
do
   iostat -x  300 1|\
      sed 1,2d|\
      awk '{ printf("%s %s %s\n", $1, $4, $5) }' |\
   while read HDISK VMSTAT_IO_R VMSTAT_IO_W
   do
      if [ $VMSTAT_IO_R -gt 0 ] and [ $VMSTAT_IO_W -gt 0 ]
      then
          sqlplus -s perfstat/perfstat <<!
          insert into
             perfstat.stats\$iostat
          values
             (SYSDATE, 5, '$HDISK', $VMSTAT_IO_R,$VMSTAT_IO_W);
          exit
!
      fi
   done
   sleep 300
done
```

Note that this script does not store *iostat* null rows where the values for reads and writes are zero. This is because the *stats$iostat* table will grow very rapidly, and it is only useful to keep non-zero information. To keep the *iostat* utility running at all times like a daemon process, add a script to the crontab file:

```
#!/bin/ksh
# First, we must set the environment . . . .
ORACLE_SID=prodz1
ORACLE_HOME=`cat /var/opt/oracle/oratab|grep $ORACLE_SID|cut -f2 -d':'`
PATH=$ORACLE_HOME/bin:$PATH
MON=`echo ~oracle/iostat`
#-----------------------------------
# If it is not running, then start it . . .
#-----------------------------------
check_stat=`ps -ef|grep get_iostat|wc -l`;
oracle_num=`expr $check_stat`
if [ $oracle_num -ne 2 ]
 then nohup $MON/get_iostat_solaris.ksh > /dev/null 2>&1 &
fi
```

Once the *iostat* scripts are created, an entry can be placed into the crontab file to ensure that the *iostat* monitor is always running. Following is a sample of this crontab file:

```
#*********************************************************************
# This is the daily iostat collector & report for the DBAs and SAs
#*********************************************************************
00 * * * * /home/oracle/iostat/run_iostat_solaris.ksh > \ /home/oracle/iostat/r.lst
```

I like to synchronize my AWR/STATSPACK snapshots with *get_iostat.ksh* so that my file-level and disk-level data are collected during the same time periods. One drawback of this approach is that the data collection tables will eventually become very large. However, table size can be managed by deleting low-I/O datafile entries. For example, inactive-file entries can be deleted with the following SQL:

```
delete from
   perfstat.stats$iostat
where
   phys_read < 10 and phys_write < 10;
```

Although the information collected in *stats$iostat* and *stats$filestatxs* is somewhat redundant, the two sets of disk data complement each other. When the *iostat* results identify a "hot" disk, turn to the *stats$filestatxs* results to look at the activity for each datafile residing on the mount point.

At that point, we can reference the *stats$filestatxs* data to see more-in-depth information, including the overall time required to perform the reads and writes. From elapsed-time information, we can quickly identify the files that are waiting on disk I/O and see the actual number of physical reads and writes.

Now that extending *iostat* for disk information has been explained, let's examine some other useful AWR and STATSPACK reports that can provide details about contention within the I/O subsystem.

Generating *iostat* Reports

In very large shops with hundreds of gigabytes of Oracle files, having *iostat* data is critical to disk load balancing, but *iostat* data is also useful for spotting transient bottlenecks, especially when RAID is not being used.

Remember, an application's disk I/O workload patterns can vary greatly according to daily or weekly processing needs, so the optimal file placement on disk may not always be obvious.

For example, it is possible that relocating a datafile may relieve I/O contention for one process only to cause contention for an unrelated process. I like to note that disk load balancing is like pressing our fist into an overstuffed pillow: when one area goes down, another area bulges. With the scripts and tables detailed in this section, a procedure can be quickly set up to alter the disk enqueues and the resulting slow response time.

Using the I/O information from the stats$iostat table, we can generate trend and alert reports. Both types of reports are easy to generate using SQL, and the combination of the reports will help identify current bottlenecks as well as spot potential future issues:

- **High disk I/O:** For each five-minute interval, we can display the name of any Oracle database file with an I/O value - defined in this case by number of reads - that is more than 50 percent of the total I/O during that interval.

- **High file I/O:** The alert reports, on the other hand, are intended to identify current bottleneck possibilities; that is, specific datafiles experiencing a disproportionate amount of I/O. For example, those experiencing 20% more activity than the average for the mount point.

Often, companies use these types of automated procedures to generate alerts which send e-mail. For example, the following script will generate a figure of all of the I/O summed by day, hour, or every five minutes.

🖫 rpt_disk.sql

```
column hdisk            format a10;
column mydate           format a15;
column sum_kb_read      format 999,999;
column sum_kb_write     format 999,999;
set pages 999;
break on hdisk skip 1;
select
   hdisk,
--   to_char(snap_time,'yyyy-mm-dd HH24:mi:ss') mydate,
--   to_char(snap_time,'yyyy-mm-dd HH24') mydate,
   to_char(snap_time,'day') mydate,
   sum(kb_read)  sum_kb_read,
   sum(kb_write) sum_kb_write
from
   stats$iostat
group by
```

Oracle Tuning

```
   hdisk
  ,to_char(snap_time,'day')
-- ,to_char(snap_time,'yyyy-mm-dd HH24:mi:ss')
-- ,to_char(snap_time,'yyyy-mm-dd HH24');
```

This report produces a daily summary of disk activity from this script. Note that there is a clear picture of disk I/O activity by physical disk, and the changes are seen by the day of the week:

```
HDISK        MYDATE           SUM_KB_READ SUM_KB_WRITE
----------   ----------------  ----------- ------------
atf0         tuesday                    33        1,749
             wednesday                 150        7,950
atf2         tuesday                     0            4
atf289       tuesday                    33          330
             wednesday                 150        1,500
atf291       tuesday                     0            0
atf293       tuesday                    32        1,696
             wednesday                 150        7,950
atf4         tuesday                     0            0
atf6         tuesday                     1           10
atf8         tuesday                     0            0
sd0          tuesday                    96          160
             wednesday                 450          750
```

Note that this script allows the display of iostat information using several different data formats:

```
to_char(snap_time,'day')
to_char(snap_time,'yyyy-mm-dd HH24:mi:ss')
to_char(snap_time,'yyyy-mm-dd HH24')
```

To change the aggregation of the display information, simply substitute the date format. For example, to see the I/O aggregated by the hour of the day, substitute the 'day' format string with the 'HH24' format string. Here is the same report aggregating by hour of the day:

```
HDISK        MYDATE           SUM_KB_READ SUM_KB_WRITE
----------   ----------------  ----------- ------------
atf0         2000-12-26 21               9          477
             2000-12-26 22              12          636
             2000-12-26 23             112        14636
             2000-12-27 07             382         3636
             2000-12-27 08             433          641
atf2         2000-12-26 21               0            4
atf289       2000-12-26 21               9           90
             2000-12-26 22              12          120
             2000-12-26 23             132         5655
atf291       2000-12-26 21               0            0
atf293       2000-12-26 21               8          424
             2000-12-26 22              12          636
             2000-12-26 23             412         1646
             2000-12-27 00             574         4745
             2000-12-27 01             363         3736
             2000-12-27 02             332          432
atf4         2000-12-26 21              23           23
atf6         2000-12-26 21               1           10
```

```
atf8        2000-12-26 21           0           9
sd0         2000-12-26 21          24          40
            2000-12-26 22          36          60
```

Solutions to Physical Read Waits

Once the objects that experience the physical read waits have been identified, STATSPACK can be used to extract the SQL associated with the waits. The following actions can then be taken to correct the problem. These corrective actions are presented in the order in which they are most likely to be effective. Some may not apply to a particular environment:

- **Tune the SQL statement:** Tuning the SQL is the single most important factor in reducing disk I/O contention. If an SQL statement can be tuned to reduce disk I/O by using an index to remove an unnecessary large-table full-table scan, the amount of disk I/O and associated waits are dramatically reduced. Other SQL tuning might include:

    - **Change table join order:** For sequential read waits, the SQL may be tuned to change the order that the tables are joined, often using the *ordered* hint.

    - **Change indexes:** The SQL can be tuned by adding function-based indexes or using an *index* hint to make the SQL less I/O-intensive by using a more selective index.

    - **Change table join methods:** Often, nested loop joins have fewer I/O waits than hash joins, especially for sequential reads. Table join methods can be changed with SQL hints; *use_nl*, for example. Prior to Oracle 9i with *pga_aggregate_target*, the propensity for hash join must be changed by adjusting the *hash_area_size* parameter.

The database can also be tuned at the instance level with these techniques:

- **Get better CBO statistics:** Stale or non-representative statistics can cause suboptimal SQL execution plans, resulting in unnecessary disk waits. The solution is to use the *dbms_stats* package to analyze the schema. Also, it should be noted if column data values are skewed, the addition of histograms may also be necessary.

- **Distribute disk I/O across more spindles:** Disk channel contention is often responsible for physical read waits, and they will show up in the ASH data. If the system experiences disk waits as a result of hardware contention and RAID is not in use, the DBA may consider segregating the table of indexes into a separate tablespace with many data files and striping the offending data file across multiple disk spindles by reorganizing the object and using the *minextents* and *next* parameters.

- **Use the KEEP pool:** Many experts recommend implementing the KEEP pool for reducing scattered reads. In the Oracle Magazine article, *Advanced Tuning with STATSPACK* (Jan/Feb. 2003), the author notes that small-table full-table scans should be placed in the KEEP pool to reduce scattered read waits.

- **Increase the *db_cache_size*:** The more data blocks in the RAM buffer, the smaller the probability of physical read wait events.

The *dba_hist_sqltext* table keeps a record of historical SQL source statements, and it is easy to extract the SQL that was executing at the time of the read waits. From there, the execution plans for the SQL statements can be gathered. The DBA can then verify they are using an optimal execution plan.

Choosing a default blocksize

When you first create your Oracle database you are prompted for a very important decision, the blocksize for the physical data files. While the default of 8K is fine for many small departmental databases, the blocksize determines the unit of data storage and this can have a profound impact on performance, especially with databases that use block size boundaries for their components:

- **Indexes:** The boundary for an Oracle b-tree index node is the blocksize.

- **11g data compression:** Oracle uses the blocksize as the boundary for data compression

- **Real Application Clusters:** Pinging can be minimized over an Oracle cluster by using a small 2K blocksize.

If we look at the various tuning activities within Oracle database, we will see that the common goal of Oracle tuning has the directed and immediate goal of reducing disk I/O. For example, tuning an SQL statement to remove full-table scans makes the query run faster because of the direct reduction in the amount of data blocks that are read from the disk. Adjusting instance tuning parameters such as *db_cache_size* also has the goal of reducing the amount of disk overhead. To understand how using different blocksizes can improve performance of the Oracle database, first start by taking a look at the basic nature of disk I/O.

Anytime an Oracle data block is accessed from disk, there are commonly three sources of delay. The first and most important source of delay is the read-write head movement time. This is the time required for the read-write head to position itself under the appropriate cylinder. There is also rotational delay as the read-write head waits for the desired block to pass beneath it, and the third source of delay is the data transmission time from the disk back to the Oracle SGA.

If the premise is accepted that 99 percent of the latency is incurred prior to actually accessing the desired data block, then it makes sense that the marginal cost for reading a 32K block is not significantly greater than the cost of reading a 2K block. In other words, the amount of disk delay is approximately the same regardless of the size of the block. Therefore, it should follow that the larger the block that can be read in on a single I/O, the less overall I/O will be performed on the Oracle database.

Prior to Oracle, Oracle professionals noticed that by moving the entire database to a larger blocksize, they reduce disk I/O and improve the performance of the entire system. This is somewhat counterintuitive, and people ask, "If I only need an 80-byte row, where do I get the benefit of reading 16K block?"

The answer has to do with indexes. Most well-tuned Oracle databases have indexes based roughly equal to the space of the table data. There is no question that a large blocksize for indexes is going to reduce I/O, and therefore improve the overall performance of the entire database.

Oracle has codified the benefits of different blocksizes, and the *Oracle 11g Performance Tuning Guide* notes that multiple blocksizes are indeed beneficial in large databases to eliminate superfluous I/O and isolate critical objects into a separate data buffer cache:

> "With segments that have atypical access patterns, store blocks from those segments in two different buffer pools: the KEEP pool and the RECYCLE pool.
>
> A segment's access pattern may be atypical if it is constantly accessed (that is, hot) or infrequently accessed (for example, a large segment accessed by a batch job only once a day).
>
> Multiple buffer pools let you address these differences. You can use a KEEP buffer pool to maintain frequently accessed segments in the buffer cache, and a RECYCLE buffer pool to prevent objects from consuming unnecessary space in the cache. By allocating objects to appropriate buffer pools, you can:
>
> - Reduce or eliminate I/Os
> - Isolate or limit an object to a separate cache"

When all of the advanced features are stripped away, Oracle's job is to deliver data, and the management of disk I/O is a very critical component and tuning of any Oracle database. Anything that can be done to reduce the amount of disk I/O is going to have a positive impact on the throughput of the Oracle database system.

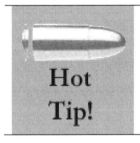

Multiple blocksizes mean multiple buffers!

Multiple blocksizes are sometimes used to segregate I/O, such as placing a high DML tablespace into a separate blocksize so that it can have an isolated data buffer..

For most databases, creating multiple blocksizes is not going to make a measurable difference, and the deployment of multiple blocksizes must be carefully evaluated on a case-by-case basis. The DBA must carefully evaluate the database for I/O patterns and buffer efficiency to see if multiple blocksizes are right for your system.

While it is generally accepted that multiple blocksizes are not for every shop, they may be appropriate for large multi-terabyte databases where the DBA wants to incur the additional monitoring complexity to be able to control their I/O buffers at a lower level of granularity.

For example, insert-intensive databases will perform less write I/O (via the DBWR process) with larger blocksizes. This is because more logical inserts can take place within the data buffer before the block becomes full and requires writing it back to disk. Some shops define their high-insert tablespaces in a larger blocksize to minimize I/O, and some use SSD to achieve insert speeds of over 10,000 rows per second.

For these very large, high activity databases, some DBAs will choose to create a 32K tablespace, a corresponding 32K data buffer, and then migrate all of the indexes, but only those that experience multiblock reads, from their existing blocks into the 32K tablespace. Upon having done this, the Oracle database can read a significant amount of index note branches in a single disk I/O, thereby reducing stress on the system and improving overall performance.

Using Oracle Multiple Blocksizes

Databases with multiple blocksizes have been around for more than 20 years and were first introduced in the 1980s as a method to segregate and partition data buffers. Once Oracle adopted multiple blocksizes in Oracle 9i in 2001, the database foundation for using multiple blocksizes was already a well-tested and proven approach. Non-relational databases such as the CA IDMS/R network database have been using multiple blocksizes for nearly two decades.

The introduction of Oracle 9i brought an amazing amount of complexity to the Oracle database engine. Oracle introduced many new internal features including bitmap freelists, redo log based replication, dynamic SGA, and perhaps the most important feature of all, the ability to support multiple blocksizes.

Watch out for multi-block reads!

One danger with Oracle multiple blocksizes is the setting for *db_file_multiblock_read_count* because this value influences the SQL optimizer about the costs of a full-table scan.

Look Out!

Originally implemented to support transportable tablespaces, Oracle DBAs quickly realized the huge benefit of multiple blocksizes for improving the utilization and performance of Oracle systems. These benefits fall into several general areas, which are detailed in the following sections.

The Oracle® Database Administrator's Reference 10g Release 2 (10.2) for UNIX-Based Operating Systems notes these guidelines for choosing the best Oracle blocksizes:

> Oracle recommends smaller Oracle Database block sizes (2 KB or 4 KB) for online transaction processing (OLTP) or mixed workload environments and larger block sizes (8 KB, 16 KB, or 32 KB) for decision support system (DSS) workload environments.

The use of multiple blocksizes in very large databases (VLDB) is more than 20 years old, and corporations have been using multiple blocksizes in the IDMS database with proven success since the 1980's. There are well-documented reports of different response times using identical data and workloads with multiple block sizes.

Multiple blocksizes are only for large systems!

For small databases, creating multiple blocksizes is not going to make a measurable difference, and the deployment of multiple blocksizes must be carefully evaluated on a case-by-case basis.

Look Out!

In general, different blocksizes can improve performance in a variety of ways:

- **Contention reduction:** Small rows in a large block perform worse under heavy DML than large rows in a small blocksize.

- **Faster updates:** Heavy insert/update tables can see faster performance when segregated into another blocksize which is mapped to a small data buffer cache. Smaller data buffer caches often see faster throughput performance.

- **Reduced pinging:** RAC can perform far faster with smaller blocksizes, reducing cache fusion overhead.

- **Less RAM waste:** Moving random access small row tables to a smaller blocksize, with a corresponding small blocksize buffer, will reduce buffer waste and improve the chance that other data blocks will remain in the cache.

- **Faster scans:** Tables and indexes that require full scans can see faster performance when placed in a large blocksize.

Let's take a closer look at each of these benefits.

Reducing Data Buffer Waste with multiple blocksizes

By performing block reads of an appropriate size, the DBA can significantly increase the efficiency of the data buffers. For example, consider an OLTP database that randomly reads 80-byte customer rows. If there is a 16k *db_block_size*, Oracle must read all of the 16k into the data buffer to get the 80 bytes, which is a waste of data buffer resources.

If this customer table is migrated into a 2k blocksize, only 2k needs to be read in to get the row data. This results in eight times more available space for random block fetches as shown in Figure 13.6.

One 16k block per row fetch

Eight 2k blocks – Same storage area, better utilization

Figure 13.6: *Improvements in Data Buffer Utilization*

Also note that the overall percentage of RAM cache is an influence in the choice to deploy multiple blocksizes. Concerning a large database with a tiny percentage of RAM, the DBA may want to maximize the efficiency of the buffers (Figure 13.7):

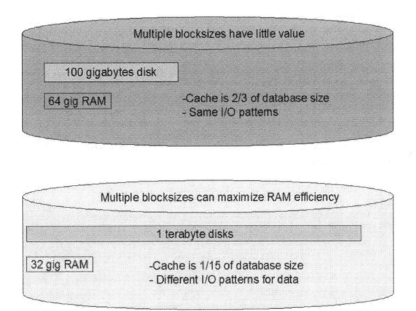

Figure 13.7: *Using Multiple Blocksizes to Improve RAM Buffer Efficiency*

One of the greatest problems of very large data buffers is the overhead of Oracle in cleaning out direct blocks that result from truncate operations and high activity DML. This overhead can drive up CPU consumption of databases that have large data buffers.

By segregating high activity tables into a separate, smaller data buffer, Oracle has far less RAM frames to scan for dirty block, improving the throughout and also reducing CPU consumption. This is especially important for super-high update tables with more than 100 row changes per second.

Reducing Logical I/O with Multiple Blocksizes

As more and more Oracle databases become CPU-bound as a result of solid-state disks and 64-bit systems with large data buffer caches, minimizing logical I/O consistent gets from the data buffer has become an important way to reduce CPU consumption. This can be illustrated with indexes. Oracle performs index range scans during many types of operations such as nested loop joins and enforcing row order for result sets with an *order by* clause. In these cases, moving Oracle indexes into large blocksizes can reduce both the physical I/O (disk reads) and the logical I/O (buffer gets).

Robin Schumacher has proven in his book, *Oracle Performance Troubleshooting* (2003, Rampant TechPress), that Oracle *b-tree* indexes are built in flatter structures in 32k blocksizes. There is also evidence that bitmap indexes will perform faster in a 32k blocksize. There is also a huge reduction in logical I/O during index range scans and sorting within the temp tablespace because adjacent rows are located inside the same data block as shown in Figure 13.8.

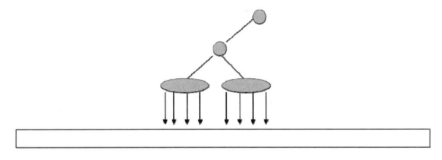

Index Range scan on 32k block – One consistent get

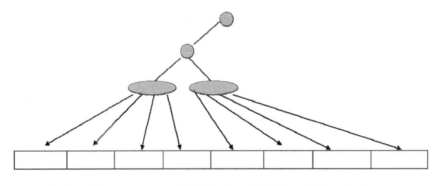

Index Range scan on 2k blocks – Eight consistent gets

Figure 13.8: *Improvements Logical I/O*

Improving Buffer Efficiency with Multiple Blocksizes

One of the greatest problems with very large data buffers is the overhead of Oracle in cleaning out direct blocks that result from truncate operations and high activity DML. This overhead can drive up CPU consumption of databases that have large data buffers as shown in Figure 13.9.

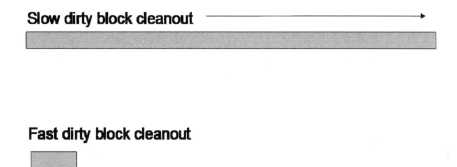

Figure 13.9: *Dirty Block Cleanup in a Large vs. Small Data Buffer*

By segregating high activity tables into a separate, smaller data buffer, Oracle has far less RAM frames to scan for dirty block, improving the throughput and also reducing CPU consumption. This is especially important for high update tables with more than 100 row changes per second.

Improving SQL Execution with Multiple Blocksizes

Intelligent buffer segregation improves overall execution speed by reducing buffer gets, but there are also some other important reasons to use multiple blocksizes.

In general, the Oracle CBO is unaware of buffer details, except when the *optimizer_index_caching* parameter is set where using multiple data buffers will not impact SQL execution plans. When data using the new *cpu_cost* reported metric, the Oracle SQL optimizer builds the SQL plan decision tree based on the execution plan that will have the lowest estimated CPU cost. For example, if a 32k data buffer is implemented for the index tablespaces, the DBA can ensure that the indexes are cached for optimal performance and minimal logical I/O in range scans.

For example, if a database has 50 gigabytes of index space, a 60-gigabyte *db_32k_cache_size* can be defined and then the *optimizer_index_caching* parameter can be set to 100, telling the SQL optimizer that all of the Oracle indexes reside in RAM. When Oracle makes the index versus table scan decision, knowing that the index nodes are in RAM will greatly influence the optimizer because the CBO knows that a logical I/O is often 100 times faster than a physical disk read.

In sum, moving Oracle indexes into a fully cached 32k buffer will ensure that Oracle favors index access, reducing unnecessary full table scans and greatly reducing logical I/O because adjacent index nodes will reside within the larger 32k block.

Real World Applications of Multiple Blocksizes

The use of multiple blocksizes is most important for very large databases with thousands of updates per second and thousands of concurrent users accessing terabytes of data. In these super large databases, multiple blocksizes have proven to make a huge difference in response time.

The largest benefit of multiple blocksizes can be seen in the following types of databases:

- **Large OLTP databases:** Databases with a large amount of index access (*first_rows optimizer_mode*) and databases with random fetches of small rows are ideal for buffer pool segregation.

- **64-bit Oracle databases:** Oracle databases with 64-bit software can support very large data buffer caches and these are ideal for caching frequently referenced tables and indexes.

- **High-update databases:** In databases where a small subset of the database receives large update activity, i.e. a single partition within a table, there will be a large reduction in CPU consumption when the high update objects are moved into a smaller buffer cache.

On the other hand, there are specific types of databases that may not benefit from the use of multiple blocksizes:

- **Small node Oracle grid systems:** Since each data blade in an Oracle grid node has only two to four gigabytes of RAM, data blade grid applications do not show a noticeable benefit from multiple blocksizes.

- **Solid-state databases:** Oracle databases using solid-state disks (RAM-SAN) perform fastest with super small data buffers that are just large enough to hold the Oracle serialization locks and latches.

- **Decision Support Systems (DSS):** Large Oracle data warehouses with parallel large-table full-table scans do not benefit from multiple blocksizes. Parallel full-table scans bypass the data buffers and store the intermediate rows sets in the PGA region. As a general rule, databases with the *all_rows optimizer_mode* may not benefit from multiple blocksizes.

Even though Oracle introduced multiple blocksizes for an innocuous reason, their power has become obvious in very large database systems. The same divide and conquer approach that Oracle has used to support very large databases can also be used to divide and conquer Oracle data buffers.

The db_file_multiblock_read_count parameter

The *db_file_multiblock_read_count* parameter controls the number of blocks that are pre-fetched into the buffer cache if a cache miss is encountered for a particular block.

Oracle Database 10g Release 2 and beyond automatically selects the appropriate value for the *db_file_multiblock_read_count* parameter depending on the operating system optimal I/O size and the size of your buffer cache.

Important 11g Tip!

In Oracle 10gr2 and beyond, it's critical to un-set the *db_file_multiblock_read_count* parameter and remove it from your pfile or spfile. If not, the CBO may choose unnecessary large table full-table scans.

As a review, "multi-block" reads are commonly db file scattered read operations, where the disk read-write head locates itself under the proper cylinder, and sits there, as the disks rotation feeds the data blocks into the Oracle SGA (or PGA if using parallel full-scans).

The value of *db_file_multiblock_read_count* can have a significant impact on the overall performance and prior to automating this setting it was not easy to determine the optimal value.

The value of *db_file_multiblock_read_count* can have a significant impact on the overall database performance and it is not easy for the administrator to determine its most appropriate value. The maximum effective setting for *db_file_multiblock_read_count* is OS and disk dependent. Steve Adams, an independent Oracle performance consultant has published a helpful script to assist in setting an appropriate level:

multiblock_read_test.sql

```
------------------------------------------------------------------
-- Script:  multiblock_read_test.sql
-- Purpose: find largest actual multiblock read size
--
-- Copyright:      (c) Ixora Pty Ltd
-- Author:  Steve Adams
--
-- Description: This script prompts the user to enter the name of a
-- table to scan, and then does so with a large multiblock read
-- count, and with event 10046 enabled at level 8.  The trace file
-- is then examined to find the largest multiblock
-- read actually performed.
--
------------------------------------------------------------------

@save_sqlplus_settings

alter session set db_file_multiblock_read_count = 32768;
/
column value heading "Maximum possible multiblock read count"
select
  value
from
  sys.v_$parameter
where
  name = 'db_file_multiblock_read_count'
/
```

```
prompt
@accept Table "Table to scan" SYS.SOURCE$
prompt Scanning ...
set termout off
alter session set events '10046 trace name context forever, level 8'
/
select /*+ full(t) noparallel(t) nocache(t) */ count(*) from &Table t
/
alter session set events '10046 trace name context off'
/

set termout on


@trace_file_name


prompt
prompt Maximum effective multiblock read count
prompt -------------------------------------

host sed -n '/scattered/s/.*p3=//p' &Trace_Name | sort -n | tail -1

@restore_sqlplus_settings
```

Remember, the *db_file_multiblock_read_count* parameter is used to tell Oracle how many blocks to retrieve in the single I/O operation and the setting is platform-dependent. The most common settings ranged from 4 to 64 blocks per single multi-block I/O execution.

The "automatically tuned" *db_file_multiblock_read_count* in 10gr2 and beyond uses external disk workload statistics that are gathered via the *dbms_stats.gather_system_stats* package to determine the optimal setting.

A sub-optimal setting for *db_file_multiblock_read_count* can running SQL performance because it can cause the optimizer to favor full-scan access. This would cause some beginners to adjust for this by turning the wrong knob, lowering the setting for *optimizer_index_cost_adj* instead of using *dbms_stats.gather_system_stats*.

10gr2 and beyond, the *db_file_multiblock_read_count* is not used to estimate the average number of blocks read and a separate metric for the estimated number of actual block reads. Instead, the optimizer computes two new values, one for optimizer costing and another for the number of I/O requests.

- **_db_file_optimizer_read_count:** The average block reads for optimizer costing

- **_db_file_exec_read_count:** The actual number of block to read in real I/O operations

For sophisticated shops that want to control multi-block I/O at a very granular level, we see special hidden parameters relating to multiblock file I/O. Of course, hidden parameters should only to be changed after careful testing in a development environment:

- *_db_file_exec_read_count*

- *_db_file_noncontig_mblock_read_count*

- *_db_file_optimizer_read_count*

- *_sort_multiblock_read_count*

In sum, it's important to "unset" *db_file_multiblock_read_count* (by removing it from the spfile), so that the optimizer can independently compute these two estimates for multiblock I/O.

Setting the *db_block_size* with Multiple Blocksizes

By now, the importance of multiple blocksizes and multiple RAM caches should be clear. Understanding the salient issues associated with blocksizes enables us to intelligently assign blocksizes to tables and indexes.

When multiple blocksizes are implemented, the *db_block_size* should be set based on the size of the tablespace where the large object full scans will be occurring. The *db_file_multiblock_read_count* parameter is only applicable for tables/indexes that are full scanned.

With the implementation of multiple blocksizes, Oracle MetaLink notes that the *db_file_multiblock_read_count* should always be set to a value that sums to the largest supported blocksize of 32k:

db_block_size	db_file_multiblock_read_count
2k	16
4k	8
8k	4
16k	2

Table 13.1: *Oracle Blocksize and Corresponding Read Count*

One issue with Oracle multiple blocksizes is the setting for *db_file_multiblock_read_count*. This value influences the SQL optimizer about the costs of a full table scan. According to Oracle, the following formula can be used for setting *db_file_multiblock_read_count*:

$$db\_file\_multiblock\_read\_count = \frac{max\ I/O\ chunk\ size}{db\_block\_size}$$

But what is the maximum I/O chunk size?

Here is a handy script to display the data blocks associated with the data buffers, using the *x$* fixed tables:

🖫 blocks_to_buffers.sql

```
select
   decode(
   pd.bp_id,
     1,'KEEP',
     2,'RECYCLE',
     3,'DEFAULT',
     4,'2K SUBCACHE',
     5,'4K SUBCACHE',
     6,'8K SUBCACHE',
     7,'16K SUBCACHE',
     8,'32K SUBCACHE',
     'UNKNOWN') subcache,
   bh.object_name,
   bh.blocks
from
   x$kcbwds ds,
   x$kcbwbpd pd,
   (select /*+ use_hash(x) */
      set_ds,
      o.name object_name,
      count(*) BLOCKS
   from
      obj$ o,
      x$bh x
   where
      o.dataobj# = x.obj
   and
      x.state !=0
   and
      o.owner# !=0
   group by
      set_ds,o.name) bh
where
   ds.set_id >= pd.bp_lo_sid
and
   ds.set_id <= pd.bp_hi_sid
and
   pd.bp_size != 0 and ds.addr=bh.set_ds;
```

Next, take a look at how the physical file blocksize can impact disk performance.

Allocating Objects into Multiple Block Buffers

So given that we have the ability to create multiple data buffers within the Oracle database, how do we decide what data is wanted in each of these data buffers? Start with some of the more common techniques.

- **Segregate large-table full-table scans:** Tables that experience large-table full-table scans will benefit from the largest supported blocksize and should be placed in a tablespace with the largest blocksize, setting *db_file_multiblock_read_count* according to this blocksize.

- **Set *db_recycle_cache_size* carefully:** If we are not setting *db_cache_size* to the largest supported blocksize for the server, we should not use the *db_recycle_cache_size* parameter. Instead, create a *db_32k_cache_size* or whatever the max is, and assign all tables that experience frequent large-table full-table scans to the largest buffer cache in the database.

- **The data dictionary uses the default cache:** Ensure that the data dictionary, e.g. our SYSTEM tablespace, is always fully cached in a data buffer pool. Remember, the blocksize of the data dictionary is not as important as ensuring that the data buffer associated with the SYSTEM tablespace has enough RAM to fully cache all data dictionary blocks.

- **Segregate indexes:** In many cases, Oracle SQL statements will retrieve index information via an index range scan, scanning the *b-tree* or *bitmap* index for ranges of values that match the SQL search criteria. Hence, it is beneficial to have as much of an index residing in RAM as possible.

- **Segregate random access reads:** For those databases that fetch small rows randomly from the disk, the Oracle DBA can segregate these types of tables into 2K tablespaces. Keep in mind that while disk is becoming cheaper every day, do not waste any available RAM by reading in more information to RAM number than is actually going be used by the query. Hence, many Oracle DBAs will use small blocksize in cases of tiny, random access record retrieval.

- **Segregate LOB column tables:** For those Oracle tables that contain raw, long raw, or in-line LOBs, moving the table rows to large blocksize will have an extremely beneficial effect on disk I/O. Experienced DBAs will check *dba_tables.avg_row_len* to make sure that the blocksize is larger than the average size. Row chaining will be reduced while at the same time the entire LOB can be read within a single disk I/O, thereby avoiding the additional overhead of having Oracle to go out of read multiple blocks.

- **Check the average row length:** The blocksize for a tables' tablespace should always be greater than the average row length for the table (*dba_tables.avg_row_len*). If the blocksize is smaller than the average row length, row chaining occurs and excessive disk I/O is incurred because we double the I/O to fetch the block.

Because the benefits from a tuning activity can be hard to measure, except with the SQL Performance Analyzer, many DBAs adopt a successive empirical approach to disk I/O tuning. For example, if the I/O increases after a table is moved into a 2K tablespace, it can simply be moved into a larger tablespace. In the real world, minimizing I/O by adjusting blocksizes is an iterative process.

The list below is a summary of rules for sizing objects into tablespaces of multiple blocksizes:

- **Some index access likes large blocksizes:** *B-tree* indexes with frequent index range scans perform best in the largest supported blocksize. This facilitates retrieval of as many index nodes as possible with a single I/O, especially for SQL during index range scans. Some indexes do not perform range scans, so the DBA should make sure to identify the right indexes.

- **Consider the average row length:** A tablespace should always have a larger blocksize than the average row length of the tables that reside in the tablespace as noted by the avg_row_len column in the *dba_tables* view. Excessive I/O is incurred when the blocksize is smaller than the average row length due to row chaining.

The blocksize is especially important for Oracle indexes because the blocksize affects the b-tree structure and the amount of physical I/O required to fetch a ROWID.

Oracle Blocksize & Index I/O

Within the Oracle index, each data block hold nodes to the index tree with the bottom-level nodes, called leaf blocks, containing pairs of symbolic keys and ROWID values. Oracle controls the allocation of pointers within each data block to properly manage the blocks. As an Oracle tree grows by inserting rows into the table, Oracle fills the block. When the block is full, it splits, creating new index nodes or data blocks to manage the symbolic keys within the index. Therefore, an Oracle index block may contain two types of pointers:

- ROWID pointers to specific table rows

- Pointers to other index nodes

As may be recalled from DBA 101 class, the freelist *pctused* (the re-link threshold) for indexes cannot be specified because Oracle manages the allocation of pointers within index blocks.

By studying an index block structure, it is possible to see that the number of entries within each index node is a function of two values:

- The blocksize for the index tablespace

- The length of the symbolic key

The blocksize affects the number of keys within each index block, hence the blocksize will have an effect on the structure of the index tree. All else being equal, large 32K blocksizes will have more index keys, resulting in a flatter index structure. In any event, there appears to be evidence that blocksize affects the tree structure, which supports the argument that the size of the data blocks affects the structure of the Oracle index tree.

Do larger index blocks actually help performance of range scans? A small but enlightening test can reveal the answer. The following query for the test will be used against a database that has a database blocksize of 8K, but also has the 16K cache enabled along with a 16K tablespace:

```
select
      count(*)
from
      scott.hospital
where
      patient_id between 1 and 40000;
```

The *scott.hospital* table has 150,000 rows and has an index built on the *patient_id* column. An *explain plan* of the query shows it uses an index fast full scan to manifest the desired end result:

```
Execution Plan
--------------------------------------------------------
0    SELECT STATEMENT Optimizer=CHOOSE
1    (Cost=41 Card=1 Bytes=4)
   1    0    SORT (AGGREGATE)
   2    1        INDEX (FAST FULL SCAN) OF 'HOSPITAL_PATIENT_ID'
                 (NON-UNIQUE) (Cost=41 Card=120002 Bytes=480008)
```

Executing the query twice to eliminate parse activity and to cache any data with the index residing in a standard 8K tablespace produces these runtime statistics:

```
Statistics
--------------------------------------------------
          0  recursive calls
          0  db block gets
        421  consistent gets
          0  physical reads
          0  redo size
        371  bytes sent via SQL*Net to client
        430  bytes received via SQL*Net from client
          2  SQL*Net roundtrips to/from client
          0  sorts (memory)
          0  sorts (disk)
          1  rows processed
```

To see if a 16K tablespace and 16k blocksize will help this query, the index that is used by the query will be rebuilt into the 16K tablespace, which has the exact same aspects as the original 8K tablespace, except for the larger blocksize:

```
alter index
    scott.hospital_patient_id
rebuild
    nologging noreverse
tablespace
    indx_16k;
```

When the index is lodged firmly into the 16K tablespace, the query is re-executed, again twice, with the following runtime statistics being produced:

```
Statistics
--------------------------------------------------
          0  recursive calls
          0  db block gets
        211  consistent gets
          0  physical reads
          0  redo size
        371  bytes sent via SQL*Net to client
        430  bytes received via SQL*Net from client
          2  SQL*Net roundtrips to/from client
          0  sorts (memory)
          0  sorts (disk)
          1  rows processed
```

Simply by using the new 16K tablespace and accompanying 16K data cache, the amount of logical reads has been reduced by half (Figure 13.10).

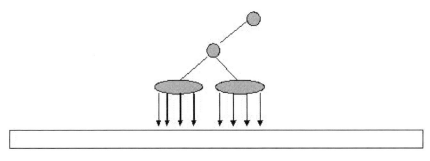

Index Range scan on 32k block — One consistent get

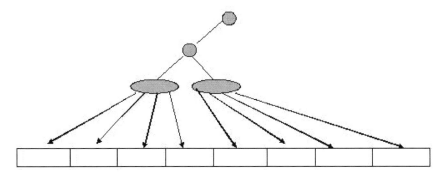

Index Range scan on 2k blocks — Eight consistent gets

Figure 13.10: *The Impact of Blocksize on Index I/O*

Most assuredly, the benefits of properly using the new data caches and multi-block tablespace feature of Oracle 9i and later are worth examination and trials in a database.

The Latest Consensus on Using Multiple Blocksizes

The use of multiple blocksizes in very large databases (VLDB) is more than 20 years old, and corporations have been using multiple blocksizes in the IDMS database with proven success since the 1980s. There are well-documented reports of different response times using identical data and workloads with multiple blocksizes.

Multiple blocksize is not for everyone!

For most databases, creating multiple blocksizes is not going to make a measurable difference, and the deployment of multiple blocksizes must be carefully evaluated on a case-by-case basis.

The DBA must carefully evaluate the database for I/O patterns and buffer efficiency to see if multiple blocksizes are right for the unique system. While it is generally accepted that multiple blocksizes are not for every shop, they may be appropriate for large multi-terabyte databases where the DBA wants to incur the additional monitoring complexity to be able to control the I/O buffers at a lower level of granularity.

For example, insert-intensive databases will perform less write I/O, via the DBWR process, with larger blocksizes. This is because more logical inserts can take place within the data buffer before the block becomes full and requires writing it back to disk. Some shops define their high-insert tablespaces in a larger blocksize to minimize I/O, and some shops use SSD to achieve insert speeds of over 10,000 rows per second.

I have seen dozens of cases where changing the blocksize can have a profound impact on overall performance, both in response time and throughput performance, and the choice of blocksize is one of the most important tuning considerations. I recently saw a server running Oracle 9.2.0.8 with two instances on the machine, each with the exact same parameters except for *db_block_size*, with all files located on the exact same mounts.

When the 16k instance runs an 850,000 row update (no *where* clause), it finishes in 45 minutes. When the 4k instance runs an 850,000 row update (no *where* clause), it finishes in 2.2 minutes. The change in blocksize caused the job to run twenty times faster.

A client has an update that they must run, unfortunately, which updates ~830,000 rows, setting one column equal to the other, i.e. two-column table. On their development environment, this was taking roughly twenty seconds to perform. However, on their soon-to-be production environment, it was taking roughly 45 minutes.

Explain plans were checked, trace files examined, and not much popped up except that the production machine was attempting larger I/Os during the update and was consequently taking much longer. Comparing the initialization parameters between production and development showed the exact same parameters, except that the upcoming production box was using a 16k blocksize and development was using a 4k blocksize.

The final result: When the update was run against the 16k blocksize DB, it took 45 minutes. Against the 4k blocksize DB on the same box with the same parameters and the same FS mounts, it took 2 minutes 20 seconds. I even took it a step further to see if any more performance could be squeezed out of it. Setting *filesystemio_options*='setall' (instead of none), I was able to get the update down to 1.5 minutes. By turning off *db_block_checking* (not recommended), I was able to get it down to 10 seconds.

By going from a 16k blocksize to a 4k blocksize with all other things being equal, roughly a twenty times improvement was experienced. Even more time was shaved off setting *filesystemio_options* = setall. Then *db_block_checking* was changed, a parameter Oracle documentation says only adds a 1 to 10% overhead depending on concurrency of DML, which made the update six times faster alone.

The final result was a 270 times improvement over the original, changing only the *db_block_size*. To be fair, I also tried setting the *filesystemio_options* and *db_block_checking* the same on the 16k blocksize instance, which resulted in the update taking 30 minutes as opposed to 45. The results were better, but

The db_file_multiblock_read_count parameter

the 4k blocksize database still won by 180 times. In addition, all queries both large and small performed the same or better than in production, and a test insert of 100,000 rows went from 20 seconds on the 16k blocksize to 3 seconds on the 4k.

While this experiment definitely shows that changing only blocksize can have a profound effect, more thorough analysis will help get to the core of why changing blocksizes had such a positive tuning effect.

Over the years, there have been heated discussions about the benefits of using multiple blocksizes, especially in these areas:

- Faster performance: Some claim up to 3x faster elapsed times with a larger index blocksize and numerous TPC benchmarks can be found which employed multiple blocksizes. Vendors spend huge sums of money optimizing their systems for TPC benchmarks, so this indicates that they employed multiple blocksizes for a performance reason.

- Faster updates: In 64-bit database with large data buffers, over 50 gig, some shops claim a benefit from segregating high-impact DML tables into a separate blocksize, assigned to a separate, small buffer. They claim that this improved DML throughput because there are fewer RAM buffer chains to inspect for dirty blocks.

- Data segregation: Some DBAs use separate 2k data buffers for tablespaces that randomly fetch small rows, thereby maximizing RAM by not reading in more data than required by the query.

-

Vendor Notes on Oracle Multiple Blocksizes

There are many Oracle TPC benchmarks that thoroughly tested multiple blocksizes vs. one-size fits all. Because a benchmark is all about maximizing performance, it appears that these world-record Oracle benchmarks chose multiple blocksizes because it provided the fastest performance for their hardware. These benchmarks are fully reproducible, so the performance gains can be proven independently.

A 2003 UNISYS Oracle benchmark used multiple blocksizes to achieve optimal performance, with these initialization parameters:

```
db_cache_size = 4000M

db_recycle_cache_size = 500M

db_8k_cache_size = 200M

db_16k_cache_size = 4056M

db_2k_cache_size = 35430M
```

The IBM Oracle Technical Brief titled *Oracle Architecture and Tuning on AIX* (November 2006) notes that careful evaluation is required before implementing multiple blocksizes:

"While most customers only use the default database blocksize, it is possible to use up to five different database blocksizes for different objects within the same database. Having multiple database blocksizes adds administrative complexity and, if poorly designed and implemented, can have adverse performance consequences. Therefore, using multiple blocksizes should only be done after careful planning and performance evaluation."

The paper continues with specific examples of differing I/O patterns that are related to the database blocksize. Some possible blocksize considerations are as follows:

- Tables with a relatively small row size that are predominantly accessed one row at a time may benefit from a smaller *db_block_size*, which requires a smaller I/O transfer size to move a block between disk and memory, takes up less memory per block and can potentially reduce block contention.

- Similarly, indexes with small index entries that are predominantly accessed via a matching key may benefit from a smaller *db_block_size*.

- Tables with a large row size may benefit from a large *db_block_size*. A larger *db_block_size* may allow the entire row to fit within a block and/or reduce the amount of wasted space within the block. Tables or indexes that are accessed sequentially may benefit from a larger *db_block_size*, because a larger blocksize results in a larger I/O transfer size and allows data to be read more efficiently.

- Tables or indexes with a high locality of reference, i.e. the probability that once a particular row/entry has been accessed, a nearby row/entry will subsequently be accessed, may benefit from a larger *db_block_size* since the larger the size of the block, the more likely the nearby row/entry will be on the same block that was already read into database cache.

But what is Oracle's official position on multiple blocksizes? For Oracle metal-level customers, there is the Oracle Metalink system which provides the official position of Oracle's own experts.

Metalink Note: 46757.1, titled *Notes on Choosing an Optimal Db Blocksize,* says that there are some benefits from having larger blocksizes, but only under specific criteria (paraphrased from Metalink):

- Large blocks give more data transfer per I/O call.

- Larger blocksizes provides less fragmentation, i.e. row chaining and row migration, of large objects (LOB, BLOB, CLOB).

- Indexes like big blocks because index height can be lower and more space exists within the index branch nodes.

Moving indexes to a larger blocksize saves disk space. Oracle says "you will conserve about 4% of data storage (4 GB on every 100GB) for every large index in your database by moving from a 2 KB database blocksize to an 8 KB database blocksize."

Metalink goes on to say that multiple blocksizes may benefit shops that have "mixed" blocksize requirements:

"What can be done if there are mixed requirements of the above blocksizes? Oracle 9i Multiple Blocksizes new feature comes into the rescue here, it allows the same database to have multiple blocksizes at the same time . . . "

In the IOUG 2005 conference proceeding titled *OMBDB: An Innovative Paradigm for Data Warehousing Architectures*, Anthony D. Noriega notes evidence that his databases benefited greatly from employing multiple blocksizes and notes that multiple blocksizes are commonly used in large databases with limited RAM resources in applications such as marketing, advertisement, finance, pharmaceutical, document management, manufacturing, inventory control, and entertainment industry:

> "The paper and presentation will discuss how to best utilize multiple blocksize databases in conjunction with table partitioning and related techniques, . . .
>
> Utilizing Oracle multiblock databases in data warehousing based systems will prove in the long-term to be a reliable methodology to approach the diversity of information and related business intelligence applications processes when integrating existing systems, consolidating older systems with existing or newly created ones, to avoid redundancy and lower costs of operations, among other factors.
>
> The input received from those already using multiblock databases is highly satisfactory in areas such as marketing, advertisement, finance, pharmaceutical, document management, manufacturing, inventory control, and entertainment industry."

Are Multiple Blocksizes Right for my Database?

As we have repeatedly noted, multiple blocksizes are exclusive for very large mission-critical databases, usually systems that have high processing loads, and they may not be right for your system.

Remember, every database is unique, and all prudent DBAs will test any changes to standard blocksizes with a representative test using a real-world workload. When considering deploying multiple blocksizes we must be aware that they require more management and we need to carefully check to see if our database will benefit by performing workload test in our QA instance.

Most shops will use tools such as the Quest *Oracle Benchmark Factory* or the Oracle SQL Tuning Set (STS) to capture and replay a representative SQL workload. For more details, see the book *Database Benchmarking* for complete details on best practices for SGA changes. Also, note the 11g Real Application Testing (RAT) and SQL Performance Analyzer (SPA) tools which can be used to validate any blocksize changes.

Now we understand how disk latency remains a major contributor to slow performance, let's explore how the faster solid-state disks are being used in Oracle databases.

Reducing Disk I/O with SSD

As RAM storage becomes cheaper than ever, many companies are exploring the issue of fully cached Oracle databases. As noted in an earlier Oracle tip, solid-state disk is changing the way that Oracle professionals manage and tune their databases.

I have been deploying SSD for several years, and some I/O-intensive Oracle systems can see up to 600x faster performance. SSD is also very popular with Oracle RAC databases because it reduces cache fusion overhead that can be defined by very small data buffer caches on each node.

One of the issues is the relatively high cost of fetching an Oracle data block from disk. In theory, RAM is 10,000 times faster than disk with speeds in the milliseconds versus nanoseconds; however, when the overhead of lock serialization and latches is added in, a logical I/O might be less than a thousand times faster than a physical disk I/O.

SSD is especially useful for Oracle undo logs, redo logs and the TEMP tablespace, but it can be used with any Oracle data file for high-speed access. In a real world setting, SSD has been used to set a new record for table load rates using SQL*Loader to get over 500,000 rows per second into a table! Yes, that is 30 million rows per minute!

Oracle speeds are very high with SSD, and SSD is also cheap at only $1k/gig USD. The existing TPC-C benchmark is always under challenge in hopes of setting the new world record by exceeding one million transactions per minute using Oracle with SSD. Companies are now offering solid-state disk replacement for the Oracle data buffer cache to speed up I/O at the physical level. Companies such as UNISYS are getting blistering performance from Oracle using 100-gigabyte *db_cache_size* and *db_keep_cache_size*.

Physical disk I/O is measured in milliseconds, an eternity when compared to the faster operations within other server components such as network RAM and CPU speeds. For many years, Oracle shops have been embracing solid-state disks, RAM disks that operate hundreds of time faster than the old-fashioned platter technology from the 1960s. SSD also has no channel contention, and as prices fall, SSD will eventually displace the ancient magnetic spinning platters of the past century.

Now Sun Solaris is offering 32 gigabytes in internal SSD technology in almost all of the new Sun servers and SSD is especially useful for database application where I/O can be a major bottleneck. Sun notes that their internal SSD consumes one-fifth the power and is a hundred times faster than the magnetic-coated spinning platter disk.

Sun also notes that all the major hardware vendors are predicting big things for SSD, and predicts that flash SSD disks will be adopted quickly for anyone developing systems using database products like Oracle:

- "The majority of enterprises building I/O-intensive applications will use some amount of flash within a year, Fowler predicted.
- Databases like Oracle, MySQL and IBM DB2 are ideal candidates."

2010 Market Survey of SSD Vendors for Oracle

There are many vendors who offer rack-mount solid-state disk that work with Oracle databases, and the competitive market ensures that product offerings will continuously improve while prices fall. The SearchStorage web site notes that SSD will soon replace platter disks and that hundreds of SSD vendors may enter the market:

"The number of vendors in this category could rise to several hundred in the next three years as enterprise users become more familiar with the benefits of this type of storage."

As of June 2008, many of the major hardware vendors, including Sun and EMC, are replacing slow disks with RAM-based disks, and Sun announced that all of their large servers will offer SSD.

Here are some of the major rack-mount SSD vendors for Oracle databases (vendors are listed alphabetically):

- Advanced Media Inc.
- EMC software
- MTron
- Pliant Technology
- SeaChange
- Solid Access Technologies
- Sun Microsystems
- Texas Memory Systems

2008 Rack Mount SSD Performance Statistics

SearchStorage.com has done a comprehensive survey of rack mount SSD vendors, and lists these SSD rack mount vendors with this showing the fastest rack-mount SSD devices (as of May 15, 2008):

Manufacturer				
Texas Memory Systems				
Violin Memory				
Solid Access Technologies	USSD 200FC	RAM SSD	Fibre Channel SAS SCSI	59 MB/s random sustained read or write per port (full duplex is 719MB/s), with 8 x 4Gbps FC ports aggregated throughput is approx 2,000MB/s, 320,000 IOPS
Curtis	HyperXCLR R1000	RAM SSD	Fibre Channel	197MB/s sustained R/W transfer rate, 35,000 IOPS

Table 13.2: *Rack Mount Vendors and SSD Devices*

Choosing the Right SSD for Oracle

When evaluating SSD for Oracle databases, consider performance (throughput and response time), reliability (Mean Time Between failures) and TCO (total cost of ownership). Most SSD vendors will provide a test RAM disk array for benchmark testing so that the vendor can be chosen who offers the best price/performance ratio.

Now let's move on and look at scripts for real-time Oracle disk monitoring and view information on the STATSPACK, AWR and ASH tables as they relate to Oracle disk I/O monitoring.

Oracle Disk Monitoring

Everyone has better things to do than sit around and run disk performance scripts, and many shops automate the disk monitoring using scripts and the *crontab* in UNIX and Linux. By doing a simple web search we can find any number of OS scripts to monitor using *iostat, vmstat* and *sar*.

Rather than recreating the wheel, the web can be used to find examples of scripts. The book, *Oracle Shell Scripting*, provides a wealth of scripts and examples of disk I/O monitoring techniques.

It's clear that disk I/O remains a major bottleneck for the vast majority of Oracle systems, but is it really important to monitor for transient hot disk conditions?

Unless the system is running in single disk sets (*jbod* technology), monitoring for disk hot spots is not quite as important, but we must still monitor I/O, either through Oracle, through the OS, or via performance monitoring tools provided by the disk array or storage system software vendors such as Veritas.

We must keep in mind that disk I/O remains an important issue and understand the internals of disk management to maximize the performance of their I/O-bound systems. Let's take a look at how to examine our real-time disk performance.

Examining Real-time Disk Statistics

The following scripts can be run anytime against the dynamic *v$* performance views to get a summary of instance wide activity for the database. Knowing the locations of the database's storage level hot spots is beneficial for a several reasons:

- By viewing I/O statistics at the tablespace and datafile levels, the DBA can get a feel for overworked physical disks. Should a particular disk or set of disks be under too much strain, the tablespaces can be relocated to less used devices or create new tablespaces on different disks and move hot objects into them if extra disks are available.

- The I/O statistics can be viewed for that tablespace to see if the indexes are actually being used if the users have followed standard DBA practice and placed indexes in their own tablespace.

To get a feel for physical I/O at the tablespace and datafile level, the following query can be used with Oracle 7.3.4 through 8.0:

🖫 ora7_8_phys_io.sql

```
select
    d.name file_name,
    c.name tablespace_name,
    b.phyrds,
    b.phywrts,
    b.phyblkrd,
    b.phyblkwrt,
    b.readtim,
    b.writetim
from
    sys.v_$datafile  a,
    sys.v_$filestat  b,
    sys.ts$          c,
    sys.v_$dbfile    d,
    sys.file$        e
where
    a.file# = b.file#
and
    a.file# = d.file#
and
    e.ts# = c.ts#
 and
    e.file# = d.file#
 order by
    b.phyrds desc;
```

When using Oracle 8i or higher, this query can be used since these versions of Oracle have temp files in addition to regular datafiles:

🖫 ora_phys_io.sql

```
select
    d.name file_name,
    c.name tablespace_name,
    b.phyrds,
    b.phywrts,
    b.phyblkrd,
    b.phyblkwrt,
    b.readtim,
    b.writetim
from
    sys.v_$datafile  a,
    sys.v_$filestat  b,
    sys.ts$ c,
    sys.v_$dbfile d,
    sys.file$ e
 where
    a.file# = b.file#
 and
    a.file# = d.file#
 and
    e.ts# = c.ts#
 and
    e.file# = d.file#
```

```
union all
select
   v.fnnam file_name,
   c.name tablespace_name,
   b.phyrds,
   b.phywrts,
   b.phyblkrd,
   b.phyblkwrt,
   b.readtim,
   b.writetim
from
   sys.v_$tempfile a,
   sys.v_$tempstat b,
   sys.ts$ c,
   sys.x$kccfn v,
   sys.x$ktfthc hc
where
   a.file# = b.file#
and
   a.file# = hc.ktfthctfno
and
   hc.ktfthctsn = c.ts#
and
   v.fntyp = 7
and
   v.fnnam is not null
and
   v.fnfno = hc.ktfthctfno
and
   hc.ktfthctsn = c.ts#
order by
   3 desc;
```

The following are a few areas to consider when examining the output of these queries:

- When temporary tablespaces devoted to sort activity show higher volumes of physical I/O, it could indicate a problem with excessive disk activity.

- If there are underutilized disk drives with their own controllers, consideration should be given to relocating some tablespaces that exhibit high I/O characteristics to those drives. The physical I/O for each drive/file system should be quickly reviewed in order to get a feel for the overworked disks on the server.

- Too much activity in the SYSTEM tablespace and datafiles may indicate a lot of recursive calls such as space management. Space management problems incurred from data dictionary references can be alleviated by implementing locally managed tablespaces in Oracle 8i and higher.

Now that locating tablespaces and datafiles hotspots has been added to the DBA's list of tools, the next step is to determine the actual objects under constant pressure.

Examining Global I/O

The first step in unraveling any I/O puzzles in Oracle is to make a quick check of some of the global database I/O metrics. A query such as this script uses the *v$* views to get a bird's eye view of a database's I/O:

💾 io_overview.sql

```
select
   name,
   value
from
   sys.v_$sysstat
where
   name in
     ('consistent changes',
      'consistent gets',
      'db block changes',
      'db block gets',
      'physical reads',
      'physical writes',
      'sorts (disk)',
      'user commits',
      'user rollbacks'
     )
 order by
1;
```

The script queries the *sys.v_$sysstat* view and output from the query might look like the following:

```
NAME                        VALUE
----------------------------------
consistent changes              1
consistent gets             70983
db block changes              243
db block gets                 612
physical reads              11591
physical writes                52
sorts (disk)                    0
user commits                   26
user rollbacks                  1
```

Although there are some database experts who do not believe the buffer cache hit ratio is of much value anymore, a cursory check can still be performed to get an idea of overall disk I/O activity by using this script:

💾 v_dollar_phys_reads_ratio.sql

```
select
   100 -
   100 *
      (round ((sum (decode (name, 'physical reads',
      value, 0))
        -
      sum (decode (name, 'physical reads direct',
      value, 0)) -
         sum (decode (name,
      'physical reads direct (lob)',
          value, 0))) /
         (sum (decode (name, 'session logical reads',
         value, 1))
           ),3)) hit_ratio
   from
      sys.v_$sysstat
   where
      name in
```

```
     ('session logical reads',
      'physical reads direct (lob)',
      'physical reads',
      'physical reads direct');
```

This script also queries the *sys.v_$sysstat* view and some quick items to look for in the statistics include:

- Increasing numbers of physical reads and a low hit ratio may indicate insufficient settings for *db_cache_size*. The hit ratio reading, in particular, should be observed over a time period sufficient to see if the ratio is representative of the database's personality. Readings below the normal rule of thumb of 90% can be OK.

- High volumes of disk sorts could be indicative of a too low setting for *pga_aggregate_target*. Large numbers of user rollbacks can be undesirable since it indicates that user transactions are not completing for one reason or another.

The *fileio.sql* script listed below shows an example select statement to generate both regular and temporary file IO.

💾 fileio.sql

```
rem
rem NAME: fileio.sql
rem
rem FUNCTION: Reports on the file io status of all of the
rem FUNCTION: datafiles in the database.

rem
column sum_io1 new_value st1 noprint
column sum_io2 new_value st2 noprint
column sum_io new_value divide_by noprint
column Percent format 999.999 heading 'Percent|Of IO'
column brratio format 999.99 heading 'Block|Read|Ratio'
column bwratio format 999.99 heading 'Block|Write|Ratio'
column phyrds heading 'Physical | Reads'
column phywrts heading 'Physical | Writes'
column phyblkrd heading 'Physical|Block|Reads'
column phyblkwrt heading 'Physical|Block|Writes'
column name format a45 heading 'File|Name'
column file# format 9999 heading 'File'
column dt new_value today noprint
select to_char(sysdate,'ddmonyyyyhh24miss') dt from dual;
set feedback off verify off lines 132 pages 60 sqlbl on trims on
rem
select
    nvl(sum(a.phyrds+a.phywrts),0) sum_io1
from
    sys.v_$filestat a;
select nvl(sum(b.phyrds+b.phywrts),0) sum_io2
from
        sys.v_$tempstat b;
select &st1+&st2 sum_io from dual;
rem
@title132 'File I/O Statistics Report'
spool rep_out\&db\fileio&&today
select
    a.file#,b.name, a.phyrds, a.phywrts,
    (100*(a.phyrds+a.phywrts)/&divide_by) Percent,
    a.phyblkrd, a.phyblkwrt, (a.phyblkrd/greatest(a.phyrds,1)) brratio,
```

```
        (a.phyblkwrt/greatest(a.phywrts,1)) bwratio
from
    sys.v_$filestat a, sys.v_$dbfile b
where
    a.file#=b.file#
union
select
    c.file#,d.name, c.phyrds, c.phywrts,
    (100*(c.phyrds+c.phywrts)/&divide_by) Percent,
    c.phyblkrd, c.phyblkwrt,(c.phyblkrd/greatest(c.phyrds,1)) brratio,
    (c.phyblkwrt/greatest(c.phywrts,1)) bwratio
from
    sys.v_$tempstat c, sys.v_$tempfile d
where
    c.file#=d.file#
order by
    1
/
spool off
pause Press enter to continue
set feedback on verify on lines 80 pages 22
clear columns
ttitle off
```

The output from the above script is shown below. This report is important because it shows the percent of total I/O for each datafile.

```
Date: 11/09/03                                                              Page:    1
Time: 01:24 PM                        File I/O Statistics Report            PERFSTAT
                                          testdb database

                                                        Physical  Physical  Block    Block
          File                  Physical  Physical Percent Block    Block     Read     Write
File Name                        Reads     Writes  Of I/O   Reads    Writes    Ratio    Ratio
----- ---------------------------- -------- -------- ------- -------- -------- ------- -------
    1 /data001/oradata/testdb/system01.dbf  27396    2992  53.526  55735    2992     2.03     1.00
    1 /data001/oradata/testdb/temp01.dbf     1703    1357   5.390   7184    7177     4.22     5.29
    2 /data001/oradata/testdb/undotbs01.dbf   151   18034  32.032    151   18034     1.00     1.00
    3 /data001/oradata/testdb/drsys01.dbf     116     107    .393    116     107     1.00     1.00
    4 /data001/oradata/testdb/indx01.dbf      117     107    .395    117     107     1.00     1.00
    5 /data001/oradata/testdb/tools01.dbf     890    1403   4.039   1137    1403     1.28     1.00
    6 /data001/oradata/testdb/users01.dbf     115     107    .391    115     107     1.00     1.00
    7 /data001/oradata/testdb/xdb01.dbf       183     107    .511    194     107     1.06     1.00
    8 /data001/oradata/testdb/olof_data01.dbf 1045     620   2.933   1242     620     1.19     1.00
    9 /data001/oradata/testdb/olof_idx01.dbf   116     107    .393    116     107     1.00     1.00
```

Another important measurement is the actual timing. On some systems and some disk subsystems, the I/O timing data can be bad, so it should always be compared against actual *iostat* numbers. An example of an I/O timing report is shown next.

```
Date: 11/21/03                                                              Page:    1
Time: 09:56 AM                        I/O Timing Analysis                   PERFSTAT
                                          testdb database

    FILE# NAME                                PHYRDS   PHYWRTS READTIM/PHYRDS WRITETIM/PHYWRTS
    ----- ------------------------------------ -------- ------- -------------- ----------------
        5 /oracle/oradata/testdb/tools01_01.dbf      318     153  .377358491     .150326797
        1 /oracle/oradata/testdb/system01.dbf       3749     806  .332622033    2.3101737
        9 /oracle/oradata/testdb/tcmd_data01_03.dbf 442389    1575  .058064283    6.90095238
        8 /oracle/oradata/testdb/tcmd_data01_02.dbf 540596    2508  .057647485    5.11961722
        7 /oracle/oradata/testdb/tcmd_data01_01.dbf 14446868   1177  .036516842    2.62531861
       10 /oracle/oradata/testdb/tcmd_idx01_02.dbf  15694    5342  .035746145    6.50074878
        3 /oracle/oradata/testdb/rbs01_01.dbf         757   25451  .034346103   10.7960002
       11 /oracle/oradata/testdb/tcmd_data01_04.dbf   1391     606  .023005032    6.66336634
        6 /oracle/oradata/testdb/tcmd_idx01_01.dbf 1148402   10220  .015289942    6.35831703
        2 /oracle/oradata/testdb/temp01_01.dbf      34961    8835   0              0
        4 /oracle/oradata/testdb/users01_01.dbf        78      76   0              0
```

The output in the listing above shows that all of the I/O timing is at or below 10 milliseconds, within normal tolerances for platter disks without an onboard RAM buffer. Normally, this would be considered as good performance for disks; however, most modern arrays can give sub-millisecond response times by use of caching and by spreading I/O across multiple platters.

While many experts say anything less than 10-20 milliseconds is good, that was based on old disk technology. If the disk system is not giving response times that are at five milliseconds or less, we should consider tuning the I/O subsystems.

Another interesting statistic is the overall I/O rate for the system as it relates to Oracle. This is easily calculated using PL/SQL as shown in the *get_io.sql* script below.

🖫 get_io.sql

```
set serveroutput on
declare
cursor get_io is select
        nvl(sum(a.phyrds+a.phywrts),0) sum_io1,to_number(null) sum_io2
from sys.gv_$filestat a
union
select
        to_number(null) sum_io1, nvl(sum(b.phyrds+b.phywrts),0) sum_io2
from
        sys.gv_$tempstat b;
now date;
elapsed_seconds number;
sum_io1 number;
sum_io2 number;
sum_io12 number;
sum_io22 number;
tot_io number;
tot_io_per_sec number;
fixed_io_per_sec number;
temp_io_per_sec number;
begin
open get_io;
for i in 1..2 loop
fetch get_io into sum_io1, sum_io2;
if i = 1 then sum_io12:=sum_io1;
else
sum_io22:=sum_io2;
end if;
end loop;

select sum_io12+sum_io22 into tot_io from dual;
select sysdate into now from dual;
select ceil((now-max(startup_time))*(60*60*24)) into elapsed_seconds from gv$instance;
fixed_io_per_sec:=sum_io12/elapsed_seconds;
temp_io_per_sec:=sum_io22/elapsed_seconds;
tot_io_per_sec:=tot_io/elapsed_seconds;
dbms_output.put_line('Elapsed Sec :'||to_char(elapsed_seconds, '9,999,999.99'));
dbms_output.put_line('Fixed IO/SEC:'||to_char(fixed_io_per_sec,'9,999,999.99'));
dbms_output.put_line('Temp IO/SEC :'||to_char(temp_io_per_sec, '9,999,999.99'));
dbms_output.put_line('Total IO/SEC:'||to_char(tot_io_Per_Sec, '9,999,999.99'));
end;
/
```

An example of the output from this report is shown below.

```
SQL> @io_sec

Elapsed Sec :     43,492.00
Fixed IO/SEC:        588.33
Temp IO/SEC :         95.01
```

```
Total IO/SEC:       683.34
```

By examining the total average IO/SEC for the database, we can determine if the I/O subsystem is capable of handling the load. For example, if the above listing was for a RAID 10 system with 10 disks in a five-way stripe in a two-way mirror array, then the DBA will know that they do not have any problems with I/O rate:

```
(10 DISKS * 110 IO/SEC/DISK = ~1100 IO/SEC max rate)
```

However, if there are only six disks in a RAID 5, then there are probably periods when I/O is saturated (5 DISKS * 90 IO/SEC/DISK = ~ 450 IO/SEC max rate). The above I/O rate is an average, which means that if there is an equal distribution about the mean, then 50% of the time the I/O rate was higher than this reported value of 683 IO/SEC.

The other indication of possible I/O related problems with Oracle is examination of I/O related wait events from the wait interface of the Oracle kernel. If the STATSPACK reports or homegrown reports show that any of the following waits are the majority wait on the system, look at tuning the I/O system in relationship to Oracle:

- ***db file sequential read***: An event generated during index and other short term read events

- ***db file scattered read***: An event generated during full-table and index scans

- ***db file parallel write***: An event generated during writes to multiple extents across multiple datafiles

- **Log file or control file writes:** Events generated during waits to write to a log or control file

- **Direct path read or write:** Events generated during hash, sort, global temporary table I/O or other direct operations

- **LGWR waits:** Events generated during writes to the redo logs

These events must be reviewed in relationship to their overall contribution to the total service time. The following is a sample Wait Report in Comparison to CPU Time.

```
Date: 02/03/04
Page:  1
Time: 08:31 AM                System Events Percent
MAULT
                                testdb database
```

Event Name	Total Waits	Average Waits	Time Waited	Percent Of Non-Idle Waits	Percent of Total Uptime
CPU used when call started	0	0	3,580,091	52.659	3.8499
db file sequential read	9,434,983	0	1,278,929	18.811	1.3753
enqueue	302	2,899	875,552	12.878	.9415
wait for stopper event to be increased	1,526	194	295,860	4.352	.3182
db file scattered read	430,041	1	261,103	3.841	.2808
log file parallel write	339	590	199,881	2.940	.2149
db file parallel write	32,240	5	170,070	2.502	.1829
...			------------		
sum			6,798,684		

So even if all I/O related wait times in the above report are eliminated, the service time would only be reduced by about 27%. Remember, it cannot always be assumed that fixing I/O will give large performance returns. If there are CPU usage issues, adding the fastest disks in the world may not help performance that much.

This directs the focus to the major turning point for any Oracle or other database system: Tune the code first! Make the SQL as optimized as possible for both Logical and Physical IO, then tackle other issues.

The wait report shown above was generated using the following script.

💾 **wait_report.sql**

```
col event         format a30        heading 'Event Name'
col waits         format 999,999,999 heading 'Total|Waits'
col average_wait  format 999,999,999 heading 'Average|Waits'
col time_waited   format 999,999,999 heading 'Time Waited'
col total_time new_value divide_by noprint
col value new_value val noprint
col percent format 999.990 heading 'Percent|Of|Non-Idle Waits'
col duration new_value millisec noprint
col p_of_total heading 'Percent|of Total|Uptime' format 999.9999

set lines 132 feedback off verify off pages 50

select to_number(sysdate-startup_time)*86400*1000 duration from v$instance;

select
sum(time_waited) total_time
from v$system_event
where total_waits-total_timeouts>0
```

```
       and event not like 'SQL*Net%'
    and event not like 'smon%'
    and event not like 'pmon%'
    and event not like 'rdbms%'
        and event not like 'PX%'
        and event not like 'sbt%'
        and event not in ('gcs remote message','ges remote message','virtual circuit
status','dispatcher timer') ;

select value from v$sysstat where name ='CPU used when call started';

@title132 'System Events Percent'

break on report
compute sum of time_waited on report
spool rep_out/&db/sys_events

select name event,
          0 waits,
   0 average_wait,
   value time_waited,
   value/(&&divide_by+&&val)*100 Percent,
   value/&&millisec*100 p_of_total
from v$sysstat
where name ='CPU used when call started'
union
select event,
       total_waits-total_timeouts waits,
       time_waited/(total_waits-total_timeouts) average_wait,
       time_waited,
       time_waited/(&&divide_by+&&val)*100 Percent,
       time_waited/&&millisec*100 P_of_total
from v$system_event
where total_waits-total_timeouts>0
    and event not like 'SQL*Net%'
    and event not like 'smon%'
    and event not like 'pmon%'
    and event not like 'rdbms%'
        and event not like 'PX%'
        and event not like 'sbt%'
        and event not in ('gcs remote message','ges remote message','virtual circuit
status','dispatcher timer')
        and time_waited>0
order by percent desc
/
spool off
clear columns
ttitle off
clear computes
clear breaks
```

The following section shows how we can track down disk I/O against specific tables and indexes. This can give great insight into the internal operations of the Oracle database application.

After the disk hot spots in the database have been found, it is time to drill further down and find the objects that are most in demand. The hub tables in a system will undoubtedly cause a major I/O bottleneck if they are not correctly designed and implemented.

Tracking I/O for Specific Tables

If STATSPACK on Oracle 9i release 2 or beyond is used, I/O can be tracked for specific Oracle tables and indexes. This allows us to see the specific sources of physical disk I/O.   Starting in Oracle 9i release 2, the most notable enhancements to Oracle STATSPACK are:

- Track reads or writes for specific segments

- Track buffer busy waits by table or index

- Collect historical SQL execution plans using the level 8 snapshot

Using the level 7 STATSPACK collection, it is now possible to track I/O at the individual segment level, showing disk I/O for any Oracle table or index.

```
execute statspack.snap (i_snap_level=>7, i_modify_parameter=>'true');
```

A level 7 STATSPACK snapshot collects all segment level statistics, including logical and physical reads, row locks, and buffer busy waits. The ability to track buffer busy waits at the table and index level is especially important for removing segment header contention.

To get an idea of which objects have been the favorite of a database's SQL calls, look at the following *toptables.sql* query which retrieves the top 100 objects as determined by SQL statement execution that can be run:

💾 toptables.sql

```
select
   table_owner "table owner",
   table_name "table name",
   command "command issued",
   0 - executions    "executions",
   disk_reads "disk reads",
   gets "buffer gets",
   rows_processed "rows processed"
from
(select
      distinct executions,
               command,
               table_owner,
               table_name,
               gets,
               rows_processed,
               disk_reads
 from
(select
      decode (a.command_type ,
               2, 'insert ' ,
               3,'select ',
               6, 'update  ' ,
               7, 'delete ' ,
               26,'table lock  ') command ,
               c.owner table_owner,
               c.name table_name ,
               sum(a.disk_reads) disk_reads  ,
```

```
                       sum(0 - a.executions) executions ,
                       sum(a.buffer_gets) gets ,
                       sum(a.rows_processed) rows_processed
   from
               sys.v_$sql                  a ,
               sys.v_$object_dependency b ,
               sys.v_$db_object_cache    c
   where
               a.command_type in (2,3,6,7,26)and
               b.from_address = a.address and
               b.to_owner = c.owner and
               b.to_name= c.name and
               c.type = 'table' and
               c.owner not in ('SYS','SYSTEM')
   group by
               a.command_type , c.owner  , c.name )  )
   where
               rownum <= 100;
```

One way to uncover a potential bottleneck for any system is to observe a single table with a lot of DML activity. Other things to consider when reviewing output from this query include:

- Small, regularly accessed tables should be reviewed as candidates for the Oracle KEEP buffer pool.

- To determine if they can be partitioned, large tables that are often accessed and scanned should be reviewed. Partitioning can reduce scan times, but only one or a handful of partitions can be scanned instead of the entire table.

If it is suspected that there are unnecessary large-table full-table scans, use the *v$sql_plan* view to get details. The following query uses this *v$sql_plan* to reveal which large tables, defined in the query as tables over 1MB, are being scanned since instance startup time:

💾 sql_to_tables.sql

```
select
   table_owner,
   table_name,
   table_type,
   size_kb,
   statement_count,
   reference_count,
   executions,
   executions * reference_count total_scans
from
   (select
      a.object_owner table_owner,
      a.object_name table_name,
      b.segment_type table_type,
      b.bytes / 1024 size_kb,
      sum(c.executions ) executions,
      count( distinct a.hash_value ) statement_count,
      count( * ) reference_count
   from
      sys.v_$sql_plan  a,
      sys.dba_segments b,
      sys.v_$sql        c
   where
      a.object_owner (+) = b.owner
   and
         a.object_name (+) = b.segment_name
```

```
and
        b.segment_type IN ('TABLE', 'TABLE PARTITION')
and
        a.operation LIKE '%TABLE%'
and
        a.options = 'FULL'
and
        a.hash_value = c.hash_value
and
        b.bytes / 1024 > 1024
group by
   a.object_owner,
   a.object_name,
   a.operation,
   b.bytes / 1024,
   b.segment_type
order by
   4 desc, 1, 2 );
```

The following is the sample output:

	TABLE_OWNER	TABLE_NAME	TABLE_TYPE	SIZE_KB	STATEMENT_COUNT	REFERENCE_COUNT	EXECUTIONS	TOTAL_SCANS
1	ERADMIN	EMP	TABLE	19456	2	2	2	4
2	SYS	DEPENDENCY$	TABLE	3496	1	1	1	1
3	SYS	OBJ$	TABLE	3136	4	7	25	175

Figure 13.12: *Sample Output of Sql_to_tables.sql*

Once we uncover what is being accessed the most, we can then attempt to reveal the source of the activity.

Analyzing Real Time I/O Waits

The majority of activity in a database involves reading data. Therefore, the ability to analyze and correct Oracle database physical read wait events is critical in any tuning project. This type of tuning can have a huge, positive impact on performance.

Since it can show those wait events that are the primary bottleneck for the system, system wait tuning has become very popular. Certain expert techniques like the 10046 wait event (level 8 and higher) analysis and Oracle MetaLink now have an analysis tool called *trcanlzr.sql* written by Carlos Sierra to interpret bottlenecks via 10046 trace dumps. Details are available in MetaLink note 224270.1.

In theory, any Oracle database will run faster if access to hardware resources associated with waits is increased. It is critical to remember all Oracle databases experience wait events, and the presence of waits does not always indicate a problem. In reality, every well-tuned database experiences some bottleneck. For example, a computationally intensive database may be CPU-bound and a data warehouse may be bound by disk read waits.

While this section explores a small subset of wait analysis, it also illustrates the critical concept of Oracle tuning that every task waits on specific events. It is the DBA's job to find out whether the Oracle database is I/O-bound, CPU-bound, memory-bound, or bound waiting on latches or locks. Once the source of the bottleneck has been identified, ASH data can be used to determine the causes of these events and attempt to remove them.

The Oracle database provides numerous views such as *v$system_event* and *v$session_wait* to give insight into the wait events and to aid in their identification. The *v$system_event* dictionary views provide information regarding the total number of I/O-related waits within the Oracle database, but it does not identify the specific object involved. In Oracle 9i Release 2, the *v$segment_statistics* view gives this information. The *v$session_wait* view offers detailed file and block data, from which the object can be extracted from the block number.

Oracle event waits occur quite swiftly, and it is difficult to get data unless the query is run at the exact moment the database is experiencing the wait. For this reason, a method for using the *v$session_wait* view must be created so a sample of the transient physical I/O waits can be captured.

If the *v$system_event* view is used, there are over 300 specific wait events. There are two critical I/O read waits within any Oracle database:

- ***db file scattered read waits***: Scattered read waits happen whenever multiblock (full scan) I/O is invoked by an SQL statement. When the Oracle database performs a full-table scan or sort operation, multiblock block read is automatically invoked.

- ***db file sequential read waits***: A db file sequential read wait occurs within an Oracle database when a single block is requested, usually via index access. A single read is most commonly an index probe by ROWID into an individual table or the access of an index block. Sequential reads are single block reads, as opposed to multiblock (scattered) reads.

First, those objects that experience physical read waits and when they do so must be identified in order to tune these wait events. The issue would then be addressed with tuning techniques. The following section starts by studying the solutions and then looks at ways to identify wait conditions.

Collecting Real-Time Disk Wait Events

While tuning disk I/O waits is an important task, it should not be considered as a comprehensive approach to Oracle tuning. Start by learning about the specific tables and indexes that are associated with the waits. Since the *v$* views are accumulators, we can only see the sum of the total number of waits since the instance started.

The *v$session_wait* view is a great place to start. As disk read waits occur within the Oracle database, they appear in the *v$session_wait* view for a very short period of time.

Prior to the Automated Session History (ASH) table starting in Oracle 10g, it was impossible to catch all of the run time waits because of the transient appearance of read waits. Regardless, it is possible to take a frequent sample of the *v$session_wait* view and catch a representative sample of the system-waits details at the exact moment that the events occur.

Determining the exact table or index where the wait occurred, when the file and block number are available, is also credible. Therefore, the enticing thing about the *v$session_wait* view is that the exact time the wait occurred can be captured as well as the file and block number that was being waited upon.

This view, shown below, provides the name of the wait event, the total number of waits and timeouts, the total time waited, and the average wait time per event.

```
select *
from
    v$system_event
where
    event like '%wait%';
```

EVENT	TOTAL_WAITS	TOTAL_TIMEOUTS	TIME_WAITED	AVERAGE_WAIT
buffer busy waits	636528	1557	549700	.863591232
write complete waits	1193	0	14799	12.4048617
free buffer waits	1601	0	622	.388507183

The type of buffer that causes the wait can be queried using the *v$waitstat* view. This view lists the waits per buffer type for buffer busy waits, where *count* is the sum of all waits for the class of block, and *time* is the sum of all wait times for that class:

```
select * from v$waitstat;
```

CLASS	COUNT	TIME
data block	1961113	1870278
segment header	34535	159082
undo header	233632	86239
undo block	1886	1706

Buffer busy waits occur when an Oracle session needs to access a block in the buffer cache, but cannot because the buffer copy of the data block is locked. This buffer busy wait condition can happen for either of the following reasons:

- The block is being read into the buffer by another session, so the waiting session must wait for the block read to complete.

- Another session has the buffer block locked in a mode that is incompatible with the waiting session's request.

Since buffer busy waits are due to contention between particular blocks, there is nothing that can be done until it is known which blocks are in conflict and why the conflicts are happening. Disk I/O tuning involves identifying and eliminating the cause of the block contention.

```
SQL> desc v$session_wait
```

Name	Null?	Type
---	--------	----------------

```
SID                                    NUMBER
SEQ#                                   NUMBER
EVENT                                  VARCHAR2(64)
P1TEXT                                 VARCHAR2(64)
P1                                     NUMBER
P1RAW                                  RAW(4)
P2TEXT                                 VARCHAR2(64)
P2                                     NUMBER
P2RAW                                  RAW(4)
P3TEXT                                 VARCHAR2(64)
P3                                     NUMBER
P3RAW                                  RAW(4)
WAIT_TIME                              NUMBER
SECONDS_IN_WAIT                        NUMBER
STATE                                  VARCHAR2(19)
```

The columns of the *v$session_wait* view that are of particular interest for a buffer busy wait event are:

- *P1:* The absolute file number for the data file involved in the wait

- *P2:* The block number within the data file referenced in P1 that is being waited upon

- *P3:* The reason code describing why the wait is occurring

The following is an Oracle data dictionary query for these values:

```
select
   p1 "File #".
   p2 "Block #",
   p3 "Reason Code"
from
   v$session_wait
where
   event = 'buffer busy waits';
```

If the output from repeatedly running the above query shows that a block or range of blocks is experiencing waits, the following query should be used to show the name and type of the segment:

```
select
   owner,
   segment_name,
   segment_type
from
   dba_extents
where
   file_id = &P1
and
   &P2 between block_id and block_id + blocks -1;
```

Once the segment is identified, the *v$segment_statistics* performance view facilitates real time monitoring of segment level statistics. This enables a DBA to identify performance problems associated with individual tables or indexes, as shown below.

```
select
   object_name,
   statistic_name,
   value
from
   V$SEGMENT_STATISTICS
where
   object_name = 'SOURCE$';
```

The output looks like the following:

```
OBJECT_NAME    STATISTIC_NAME              VALUE
-----------    ------------------------    ----------
SOURCE$        logical reads                    11216
SOURCE$        buffer busy waits                  210
SOURCE$        db block changes                    32
SOURCE$        physical reads                   10365
SOURCE$        physical writes                      0
SOURCE$        physical reads direct                0
SOURCE$        physical writes direct               0
SOURCE$        ITL waits                            0
SOURCE$        row lock waits
```

Now dive deeper and examine system waits.

🖫 total_waits.sql

```
select event,
       total_waits,
       round(100 * (total_waits / sum_waits),2) pct_waits,
       time_wait_sec,
       round(100 * (time_wait_sec / greatest(sum_time_waited,1)),2)
       pct_time_waited,
       total_timeouts,
       round(100 * (total_timeouts / greatest(sum_timeouts,1)),2)
       pct_timeouts,
       average_wait_sec
from
(select event,
       total_waits,
       round((time_waited / 100),2) time_wait_sec,
       total_timeouts,
       round((average_wait / 100),2) average_wait_sec
from sys.v_$system_event
where event not in
('lock element cleanup',
 'pmon timer',
 'rdbms ipc message',
 'rdbms ipc reply',
 'smon timer',
 'SQL*Net message from client',
 'SQL*Net break/reset to client',
 'SQL*Net message to client',
 'SQL*Net more data from client',
 'dispatcher timer',
 'Null event',
 'parallel query dequeue wait',
 'parallel query idle wait - Slaves',
 'pipe get',
 'PL/SQL lock timer',
```

```
 'slave wait',
 'virtual circuit status',
 'WMON goes to sleep',
 'jobq slave wait',
 'Queue Monitor Wait',
 'wakeup time manager',
 'PX Idle Wait') AND
 event not like 'DFS%' AND
 event not like 'KXFX%'),
(select sum(total_waits) sum_waits,
       sum(total_timeouts) sum_timeouts,
       sum(round((time_waited / 100),2)) sum_time_waited
from sys.v_$system_event
where event not in
('lock element cleanup',
 'pmon timer',
 'rdbms ipc message',
 'rdbms ipc reply',
 'smon timer',
 'SQL*Net message from client',
 'SQL*Net break/reset to client',
 'SQL*Net message to client',
 'SQL*Net more data from client',
 'dispatcher timer',
 'Null event',
 'parallel query dequeue wait',
 'parallel query idle wait - Slaves',
 'pipe get',
 'PL/SQL lock timer',
 'slave wait',
 'virtual circuit status',
 'WMON goes to sleep',
 'jobq slave wait',
 'Queue Monitor Wait',
 'wakeup time manager',
 'PX Idle Wait') AND
 event not like 'DFS%' AND
 event not like 'KXFX%')
order by 4 desc, 1 asc;
```

The output of this script, in the Ion tool, looks like the following:

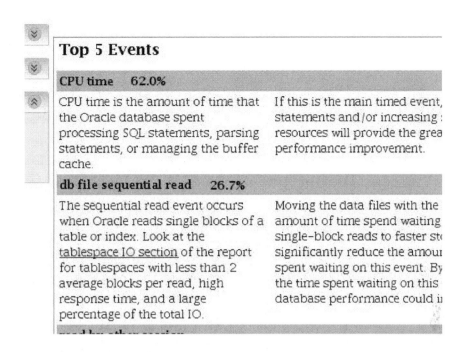

Top 5 Events

CPU time   62.0%

CPU time is the amount of time that the Oracle database spent processing SQL statements, parsing statements, or managing the buffer cache.

If this is the main timed event, statements and/or increasing resources will provide the grea performance improvement.

db file sequential read   26.7%

The sequential read event occurs when Oracle reads single blocks of a table or index. Look at the tablespace IO section of the report for tablespaces with less than 2 average blocks per read, high response time, and a large percentage of the total IO.

Moving the data files with the amount of time spend waiting single-block reads to faster st significantly reduce the amour spent waiting on this event. By the time spent waiting on this database performance could i

Figure 13.13: *System Waits from Ion Tool*

The main wait class within ASH that relates to user I/O can be determined with the following script.

💾 **ash_waits.sql**

```
select  A.SID,
        B.USERNAME,
        A.WAIT_CLASS,
        A.TOTAL_WAITS,
        A.TIME_WAITED
from    V$SESSION_WAIT_CLASS A,
        V$SESSION B
where   B.SID = A.SID
and
        B.USERNAME IS NOT NULL
and
            A.WAIT_CLASS like '%I/O%'
order by 1,2,3;
```

The output shows total waits by user and wait class:

SID	USERNAME	WAIT_CLASS	TOTAL_WAITS	TIME_WAITED
131	SYSMAN	User I/O	11	5
132	SYSMAN	User I/O	3	2
133	SYSMAN	User I/O	13	7
134	SYSMAN	User I/O	173	97
138	SPV	User I/O	10	3

```
140 SYSMAN              User I/O              387          413
141 DBSNMP              User I/O              201          433
142 SYSMAN              User I/O               36           71
144 SYSMAN              User I/O                6            7
146 SYSMAN              User I/O               35           28
149 SYSMAN              User I/O               46           42
154 DBSNMP              System I/O             84           68
160 SYS                 System I/O              5            3
162 SYSMAN              User I/O               16           10
```

The ASH tables can also be queried to find all of the wait conditions for a specific session. Once the Session ID (SID) is acquired for the session, the value can be plugged into the query below to identify all of the wait conditions for that SID.

```
select
   a.sid,
   b.username,
   a.stat_name,
   round((a.value / 1000000),3) time_secs
from
   v$sess_time_model a,
   v$session b
where
   a.sid = b.sid
and
   b.sid = < input sid here >
order by 4 desc;
```

The result is shown below.

```
SID USERNAME    STAT_NAME                                            TIME_SECS
---- ---------- --------------------------------------------------- ----------
 160 SYS        DB time                                                 18,592
 160 SYS        sql execute elapsed time                                18,168
 160 SYS        DB CPU                                                  17,139
 160 SYS        parse time elapsed                                          456
 160 SYS        PL/SQL compilation elapsed time                            447
 160 SYS        hard parse elapsed time                                    317
 160 SYS        PL/SQL execution elapsed time                               93
 160 SYS        connection management call elapsed time                     66
 160 SYS        background elapsed time                                       0
 160 SYS        Java execution elapsed time                                  0
 160 SYS        inbound PL/SQL rpc elapsed time                              0
 160 SYS        hard parse (bind mismatch) elapsed time                     0
 160 SYS        background cpu time                                          0
 160 SYS        failed parse elapsed time                                   0
 160 SYS        hard parse (sharing criteria) elapsed time                  0
 160 SYS        failed parse (out of shared memory) elapsed time            0
 160 SYS        sequence load elapsed time                                  0
```

The following section shows how to track I/O wait events for specific database objects.

Tracking I/O Waits on Specific Tables and Indexes

It should be clear that the DBA still must be able to translate the file number and block number into a specific table or index name. This can be accomplished by using the *dba_extents* view to determine the start block and end block for every extent in every table.

Using *dba_extents* to identify the object and its data block boundaries, it becomes a trivial matter to read through the new table and identify those specific objects experiencing read waits or buffer busy waits. The next step is to add the segment name by joining into the *dba_extents* view.

The following is the output from this script. Here we can see all of the segments that have experienced more than 10 disk read wait events:

Wait Event	Segment Name	Segment Type	Wait Count
SEQ_READ	SYSPRD.S_EVT_ACT_F51	INDEX	72
SEQ_READ	SYSPRD.S_ACCNT_POSTN_M1	INDEX	41
SEQ_READ	SYSPRD.S_ASSET_M3	INDEX	24
SEQ_READ	SYSPRD.S_ASSET_M51	INDEX	19
SEQ_READ	SYSPRD.S_COMM_REQ_U1	INDEX	11

This shows the exact indexes that are experiencing sequential read waits, and now there is an important clue for SQL tuning or object redistribution strategy.

The next step is to identify all hot blocks to complete the analysis. This can be accomplished by examining the *dba_hist_waitstat* table for any data blocks that have experienced multiple waits. In this sample output, each segment, the exact block where the wait occurred, and the number of wait events can be seen:

Wait Event	Segment Name	Segment Type	Block Number	Multiple Block Wait Count
SEQ_READ	SYSPRD.S_EVT_ACT_F51	INDEX	205,680	7
SEQ_READ	SYSPRD.S_EVT_ACT	TABLE	401,481	5
SEQ_READ	SYSPRD.S_EVT_ACT_F51	INDEX	471,767	5
SEQ_READ	SYSPRD.S_EVT_ACT	TABLE	3,056	4
SEQ_READ	SYSPRD.S_EVT_ACT_F51	INDEX	496,315	4
SEQ_READ	SYSPRD.S_DOC_ORDER_U1	INDEX	35,337	3

Since it identifies those data blocks that have experienced multiple block waits, this report is critical. It is then possible to go to each data block and see the contention on a segment header.

Find the Current Disk I/O Session Bandits

To see which users are impacting the system in undesirable ways, the first thing to check is the connected sessions, especially if there are current complaints of poor performance. In this case, there are a few different avenues that can be taken. Getting an idea of the percentage that each session has taken up with respect to I/O is one of the first steps.

If any session consumes 50% or more of the total I/O, that session and its SQL should be investigated further to determine the activities in which it is engaged. If the DBA is just concerned with physical I/O, the *physpctio.sql* query will provide the information needed:

🖫   **physpctio.sql**

```
select
   sid,
   username,
   round(100 * total_user_io/total_io,2) tot_io_pct
from
(select
    b.sid sid,
    nvl(b.username,p.name) username,
    sum(value) total_user_io
 from
    sys.v_$statname c,
    sys.v_$sesstat a,
    sys.v_$session b,
    sys.v_$bgprocess p
 where
     a.statistic#=c.statistic# and
     p.paddr (+) = b.paddr and
     b.sid=a.sid and
     c.name in ('physical reads',
                'physical writes',
                'physical writes direct',
                'physical reads direct',
                'physical writes direct (lob)',
                'physical reads direct (lob)')
group by
     b.sid, nvl(b.username,p.name)),
(select
     sum(value) total_io
 from
     sys.v_$statname c,
     sys.v_$sesstat a
 where
     a.statistic#=c.statistic# and
     c.name in ('physical reads',
                'physical writes',
                'physical writes direct',
                'physical reads direct',
                'physical writes direct (lob)',
                'physical reads direct (lob)'))
order by
     3 desc;
```

If the DBA wants to see the total I/O picture, the *totpctio.sql* query should be used instead:

```
SELECT
      SID,
      USERNAME,
      ROUND(100 * TOTAL_USER_IO/TOTAL_IO,2) TOT_IO_PCT
FROM
(SELECT
      b.SID SID,
      nvl(b.USERNAME,p.NAME) USERNAME,
      SUM(VALUE) TOTAL_USER_IO
FROM
    sys.V_$STATNAME c,
    sys.V_$SESSTAT a,
    sys.V_$SESSION b,
    sys.v_$bgprocess p
WHERE
    a.STATISTIC#=c.STATISTIC# and
    p.paddr (+) = b.paddr and
    b.SID=a.SID and
    c.NAME in ('physical reads','physical writes',
               'consistent changes','consistent gets',
               'db block gets','db block changes',
               'physical writes direct',
               'physical reads direct',
               'physical writes direct (lob)',
               'physical reads direct (lob)')
GROUP BY
    b.SID, nvl(b.USERNAME,p.name)),
(select
    sum(value) TOTAL_IO
from
    sys.V_$STATNAME c,
    sys.V_$SESSTAT a
WHERE
    a.STATISTIC#=c.STATISTIC# and
    c.NAME in ('physical reads','physical writes',
               'consistent changes',
               'consistent gets','db block gets',
               'db block changes',
               'physical writes direct',
               'physical reads direct',
               'physical writes direct (lob)',
               'physical reads direct (lob)'))
ORDER BY
    3 DESC;
```

The output might resemble the following, regardless of which query is used:

```
SID USERNAME       TOT_IO_PCT
--------------------------------
9   USR1                71.26
20  SYS                 15.76
5   SMON                 7.11
2   DBWR                 4.28
12  SYS                  1.42
6   RECO                  .12
7   SNP0                  .01
```

Find the Current Disk I/O Session Bandits   **565**

```
10  SNP3                 .01
11  SNP4                 .01
 8  SNP1                 .01
 1  PMON                   0
 3  ARCH                   0
 4  LGWR                   0
```

Following the above example, a DBA would indeed be wise to study the USR1 session to see what SQL calls were made. The above queries are excellent resources that can be used to quickly pinpoint problem I/O sessions.

To see all the actual I/O numbers, the rather large *topiousers.sql* query can be used if the goal is to gather more detail with respect to the top I/O session in a database:

🖫 **topiousers.sql**

```
select
    b.sid sid,
    decode (b.username,null,e.name,b.username)
    user_name,
    d.spid os_id,
    b.machine machine_name,
    to_char(logon_time,'mm/dd/yy hh:mi:ss pm')
    logon_time,
    (sum(decode(c.name,'physical reads',value,0))
    +
    sum(decode(c.name,'physical writes',value,0))
    +
    sum(decode(c.name,
    'physical writes direct',value,0)) +
    sum(decode(c.name,
    'physical writes direct (lob)',value,0)) +
    sum(decode(c.name,
    'physical reads direct (lob)',value,0)) +
    sum(decode(c.name,
    'physical reads direct',value,0)))
    total_physical_io,
    (sum(decode(c.name,'db block gets',value,0))
    +
    sum(decode(c.name,
    'db block changes',value,0))   +
    sum(decode(c.name,'consistent changes',value,0)) +
    sum(decode(c.name,'consistent gets',value,0)) )
    total_logical_io,
    100 - 100 *(round ((sum (decode
    (c.name, 'physical reads', value, 0)) -
    sum (decode (c.name,
    'physical reads direct', value, 0))) /
    (sum (decode (c.name, 'db block gets',
    value, 1)) +
    sum (decode (c.name, 'consistent gets',
    value, 0))),3)) hit_ratio,
    sum(decode(c.name,'sorts (disk)',value,0))
    disk_sorts,
    sum(decode(c.name,'sorts (memory)',value,0))
    memory_sorts,
    sum(decode(c.name,'sorts (rows)',value,0))
    rows_sorted,
    sum(decode(c.name,'user commits',value,0))
    commits,
```

```
      sum(decode(c.name,'user rollbacks',value,0))
      rollbacks,
      sum(decode(c.name,'execute count',value,0))
      executions,
      sum(decode(c.name,'physical reads',value,0))
      physical_reads,
      sum(decode(c.name,'db block gets',value,0))
      db_block_gets,
      sum(decode(c.name,'consistent gets',value,0))
      consistent_gets,
      sum(decode(c.name,'consistent changes',value,0))
      consistent_changes
from
   sys.v_$sesstat a,
   sys.v_$session b,
   sys.v_$statname c,
   sys.v_$process d,
   sys.v_$bgprocess e
where
   a.statistic#=c.statistic#
and
   b.sid=a.sid
and
   d.addr = b.paddr
and
   e.paddr (+) = b.paddr
and
   c.name in
   ('physical reads',
    'physical writes',
    'physical writes direct',
    'physical reads direct',
    'physical writes direct (lob)',
    'physical reads direct (lob)',
    'db block gets',
    'db block changes',
    'consistent changes',
    'consistent gets',
    'sorts (disk)',
    'sorts (memory)',
    'sorts (rows)',
    'user commits',
    'user rollbacks',
    'execute count'
)
group by
   b.sid,
   d.spid,
   decode (b.username,null,e.name,b.username),
        b.machine,
        to_char(logon_time,'mm/dd/yy hh:mi:ss pm')
order by
   6 desc;
```

Output from the query above could look like the following:

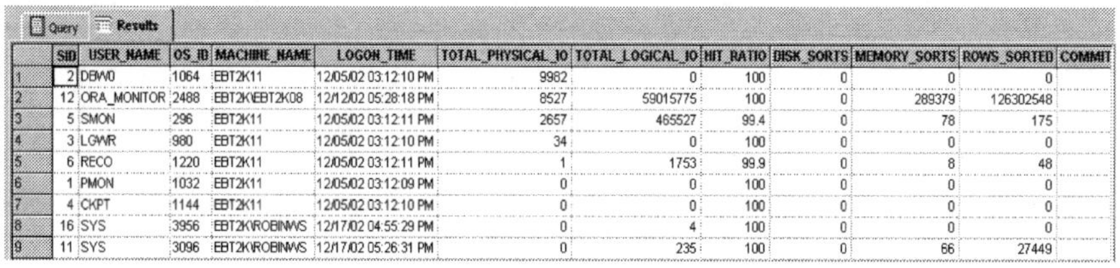

Query | Results

	SID	USER_NAME	OS_ID	MACHINE_NAME	LOGON_TIME	TOTAL_PHYSICAL_IO	TOTAL_LOGICAL_IO	HIT_RATIO	DISK_SORTS	MEMORY_SORTS	ROWS_SORTED	COMMIT
1	2	DBW0	1064	EBT2K11	12/05/02 03:12:10 PM	9982	0	100	0	0	0	
2	12	ORA_MONITOR	2488	EBT2K\EBT2K08	12/12/02 05:28:18 PM	8527	59015775	100	0	289379	126302548	
3	5	SMON	296	EBT2K11	12/05/02 03:12:11 PM	2657	465527	99.4	0	78	175	
4	3	LGWR	980	EBT2K11	12/05/02 03:12:10 PM	34	0	100	0	0	0	
5	6	RECO	1220	EBT2K11	12/05/02 03:12:11 PM	1	1753	99.9	0	8	48	
6	1	PMON	1032	EBT2K11	12/05/02 03:12:09 PM	0	0	100	0	0	0	
7	4	CKPT	1144	EBT2K11	12/05/02 03:12:10 PM	0	0	100	0	0	0	
8	16	SYS	3956	EBT2K\ROBINWS	12/17/02 04:55:29 PM	0	4	100	0	0	0	
9	11	SYS	3096	EBT2K\ROBINWS	12/17/02 05:26:31 PM	0	235	100	0	66	27449	

Figure 13.14: *Output of Topiousers.sql Query*

A query such as this reveals details about the actual raw I/O numbers for each connected session. Armed with this information, it is then possible to drill down into each heavy-hitting I/O session to evaluate what SQL calls are made and which sets of SQL are the I/O hogs.

Even though troubleshooting I/O from a user standpoint has been explained, we should not forget about all the system activity caused by Oracle itself. A cursory, global check of the system level wait events should be performed to get an idea of the I/O bottlenecks that may be occurring. A script like the *syswaits.sql* script can be used to perform such a check:

syswaits.sql

```
select
       event,
       total_waits,
       round(100 * (total_waits / sum_waits),2) pct_tot_waits,
       time_wait_sec,
       round(100 * (time_wait_sec / sum_secs),2) pct_secs_waits,
       total_timeouts,
       avg_wait_sec
from
(select
       event,
       total_waits,
       round((time_waited / 100),2) time_wait_sec,
       total_timeouts,
       round((average_wait / 100),2) avg_wait_sec
from
      sys.v_$system_event
where
      event not in
      ('lock element cleanup ',
       'pmon timer ',
       'rdbms ipc message ',
       'smon timer ',
       'SQL*Net message from client ',
       'SQL*Net break/reset to client ',
       'SQL*Net message to client ',
       'SQL*Net more data to client ',
       'dispatcher timer ',
       'Null event ',
       'parallel query dequeue wait ',
       'parallel query idle wait - Slaves ',
       'pipe get ',
       'PL/SQL lock timer ',
       'slave wait ',
       'virtual circuit status ',
       'WMON goes to sleep') and
       event not like 'DFS%' and
```

```
        event not like 'KXFX%'),
(select
        sum(total_waits) sum_waits,
        sum(round((time_waited / 100),2)) sum_secs
 from
        sys.v_$system_event
 where
        event not in
        ('lock element cleanup ',
         'pmon timer ',
         'rdbms ipc message ',
         'smon timer ',
         'SQL*Net message from client ',
         'SQL*Net break/reset to client ',
         'SQL*Net message to client ',
         'SQL*Net more data to client ',
         'dispatcher timer ',
         'Null event ',
         'parallel query dequeue wait ',
         'parallel query idle wait - Slaves ',
         'pipe get ',
         'PL/SQL lock timer ',
         'slave wait ',
         'virtual circuit status ',
         'WMON goes to sleep') and
         event not like 'DFS%' and
         event not like 'KXFX%')
order by
   2 desc;
```

The script queries the *sys.v_$system_event* view and here are a few quick things to note about the output from the waits SQL script:

- Numerous waits for the *db file scattered read* event may indicate a problem with table scans.

- Many waits for the latch free event could indicate excessive amounts of logical I/O activity.

- High wait times for the enqueue event pinpoints a problem with lock contention.

Once the DBA has a feel for the I/O numbers at a global level, it is possible to begin working further down into what is really going on below the surface.

Measuring Disk I/O Speed

The relative cost of physical disk access is an important topic since all Oracle databases retrieve and store data. A significant factor in weighing these costs is physical disk speed. Quicker disk access speeds can diminish the costs of a full table scan versus single block reads to a negligible level.

In a solid-state disk environment, disk I/O is far more rapid and multiblock reads become far cheaper compared to traditional disks. The new solid-state disks provide up to 100,000 I/Os per second, six times faster than traditional disk devices.

The standard STATSPACK report can be generated when the database is processing a peak load, and it is also possible to get a detailed report of all elapsed time metrics. The STATSPACK top-five timed event report is the most important of these metrics. The report is critical for it displays the database events that constitute the bottleneck for the system. The listing below from a STATSPACK report shows that the system is clearly constrained by disk I/O.

```
Top 5 Timed Events
                                                    % Total
Event                      Waits        Time (s)   Ela Time
-------------------------  -----------  ----------- ---------
db file sequential read     2,598         7,146       48.54
db file scattered read     25,519         3,246       22.04
library cache load lock       673         1,363        9.26
CPU time                                  1,154        7.83
log file parallel write    19,157           837        5.68
```

Reads and writes constitute the majority of the total database time as shown above. In such a case, the RAM size of the *db_cache_size* should be increased in order to reduce disk I/O, the SQL tuned to reduce disk I/O, or a faster disk I/O subsystem should be invested in.

Not only do the ideal optimizer settings rely on the environment, they are heavily swayed by the system's costs for *scattered disk reads* versus *sequential disk reads*. A great script to measure these I/O costs on the database is shown below.

```
col c1 heading 'Average Waits|forFull| Scan Read I/O'   format 9999.999
col c2 heading 'Average Waits|for Index|Read I/O'       format 9999.999
col c3 heading 'Percent of| I/O Waits|for Full Scans'   format 9.99
col c4 heading 'Percent of| I/O Waits|for Index Scans'  format 9.99
col c5 heading 'Starting|Value|for|optimizer|index|cost|adj' format 999

select
   a.average_wait                                c1,
   b.average_wait                                c2,
   a.total_waits /(a.total_waits + b.total_waits) c3,
   b.total_waits /(a.total_waits + b.total_waits) c4,
   (b.average_wait / a.average_wait)*100          c5
from
  v$system_event  a,
  v$system_event  b
where
   a.event = 'db file scattered read'
and
   b.event = 'db file sequential read';
```

While there are varied opinions regarding full-table scans, they are not necessarily a detriment to performance. Indeed, they are often the quickest way to access the table rows. The CBO option of performing a full-table scan depends on many factors, some being the settings for Oracle Parallel Query, the *db_block_size,* the *clustering_factor,* and the estimated percentage of rows returned by the query according to the CBO statistics.

Once Oracle selects a full-table scan, the speed of performing a full-table scan (SOFTS) rests with internal and external factors:

- Table partitioning
- The number of CPUs on the system

- The setting for Oracle Parallel Query (parallel hints, alter table)

- The speed of the disk I/O subsystem, e.g. hardware-cached I/O, solid-state disk RAM 3

When factoring in all these elements, it may be impossible to decide the exact best setting for the weight in *optimizer_index_cost_adj*. In reality, the decision to petition a full-table scan is heavily influenced by run-time factors such as:

- The present demands on the CPUs

- The attainability of free blocks in the data buffers

- The amount of TEMP tablespace if the FTS has an order by clause

No two database systems are the same and good DBAs must adjust *optimizer_index_cost_adj* according to database configuration and data access patterns. The encompassing amount of time performing full-table scans is equal to the percentage of *db file sequential read* waits as a percentage of total I/O waits from *v$system_event*.

The following section will introduce how to measure system I/O wait events in real-time.

The next section will explore how the data needed to fix the causes of the physical read waits can be acquired now that the solutions have been identified.

Time Series I/O Wait Analysis

Every database will have signatures, which are typically caused by regularly scheduled processing. When these signatures are identified, STATSPACK must be used to extract the SQL and ensure that it is properly optimized. When the detailed event waits data has been acquired, it is a trivial task to roll up the data and create trend reports.

If the read waits persist, the next step is to manipulate the schedule to execute the colliding SQL at different times. Some of the workload can be moved to a different time window if there is not sufficient I/O bandwidth to run the full workload all at once. To display a trend by day, a similar query may be run that will average the number of sequential read waits by day of the week.

More importantly, there is the detailed wait information in the *dba_hist_waitstat* table, so the exact table or index that is experiencing the real time wait can be investigated. By doing that in conjunction with AWR, the SQL may also be collected in the AWR table such that it is clear what SQL is precipitating the disk wait events.

DB time

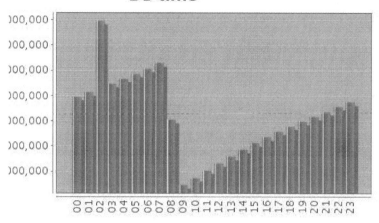

Figure 13.15: *Plotting Real-time Waits Averages by Hour of the Day*

Figure 13.15 shows a high number of real time *db file sequential read* waits between 2:00 AM and 3:00 AM with another spike between 9:00 PM and midnight. This information can go to STATSPACK for use in extracting the SQL that was running during this period.

The DBA can also average the read waits by day of the week as shown in Figure 13.16. The figure shows that there is an obvious increase in scattered read waits every Tuesday and Thursday and the SQL can be extracted during these periods.

physical reads

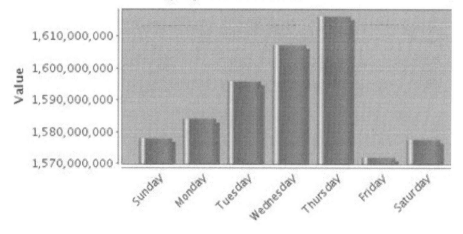

Ordinarily, this insight would be ineffective because the source of the waits would not be obvious. Of course, with Oracle 9i release 2 and beyond, the *v$segment_statistics* view can be used to see some of this information if the *statistics_level* parameter is set to a value of seven or higher.

Now, the DBA can drill in and see those specific tables and indexes that were experiencing the sequential read waits.

```
                                                            Block
                        Segment                  Segment    Wait
Date         Hr.        Name                     Type       Count
------------ ---------- ------------------------ ---------- ----
23-jan-2003  21         SYSPRD.S_COMM_REQ_SRC_U1 INDEX      23
23-jan-2003  21         SYSPRD.S_EVT_ACT         TABLE      44
23-jan-2003  21         SYSPRD.S_EVT_ACT_F51     INDEX      16
23-jan-2003  22         SYSPRD.S_EVT_ACT         TABLE      32
```

The specific object that experiences the physical read wait must be identified since the goal may be to distribute the object over additional disk spindles.

The details about the objects that experience physical read waits can be easily captured using a real time wait sampling method. Once they are recognized, STATSPACK can be used to find the problematic SQL and begin the tuning. The tuning of physical read waits involves SQL tuning, object striping across multiple disks, employing the KEEP pool for small objects, rescheduling the SQL to relieve the contention, or increasing the data buffer cache size.

A simple query can be used to plot the user I/O wait time statistic for each AWR snapshot. Using the following script, the physical read counts can be extracted from the AWR.

```
break on begin_interval_time skip 2

column phyrds               format 999,999,999
column begin_interval_time format a25

select
   begin_interval_time,
   filename,
   phyrds
from
   dba_hist_filestatxs
natural join
   dba_hist_snapshot
;
```

The output below shows a running total of Oracle physical reads. The snapshots are collected every half-hour. Starting from this script, a *where* clause criteria could easily be added to create a unique time series exception report.

```
SQL> @phys_reads
```

Time Series I/O Wait Analysis

```
BEGIN_INTERVAL_TIME          FILENAME                                         PHYRDS
------------------------     ----------------------------------------    ------------
24-FEB-04 11.00.32.000 PM    E:\ORACLE\ORA92\FSDEV10G\SYSTEM01.DBF            164,700
                             E:\ORACLE\ORA92\FSDEV10G\UNDOTBS01.DBF            26,082
                             E:\ORACLE\ORA92\FSDEV10G\SYSAUX01.DBF            472,008
                             E:\ORACLE\ORA92\FSDEV10G\USERS01.DBF               1,794
                             E:\ORACLE\ORA92\FSDEV10G\T_FS_LSQ.ORA              2,123
```

The next step is to take a look at how these simple scripts can be enhanced to produce powerful exception reports.

In the simple report generated with the following script, the *dba_hist_filestatxs* is queried to identify hot write datafiles where the file consumed more than 25% of the total physical writes for the instance. The query compares the physical writes in the *phywrts* column of *dba_hist_filestatxs* with the instance-wide physical writes on *statistic#* = 55 from *dba_hist_sysstat*.

This simple yet powerful script allows the Oracle professional to track hot-write datafiles over time, thereby gaining important insights into the status of the I/O subsystem over time.

🖫 high_disk_writes.sql

```
prompt
prompt   This will identify any single file who's write I/O
prompt   is more than 25% of the total write I/O of the database.
prompt

set pages 999

break on snap_time skip 2

col filename        format a40
col phywrts         format 999,999,999
col snap_time       format a20

select
   to_char(begin_interval_time,'yyyy-mm-dd hh24:mi') snap_time,
   filename,
   phywrts
from
   dba_hist_filestatxs
natural join
   dba_hist_snapshot
where
   phywrts > 0
and
   phywrts * 4 >
(
select
   avg(value)               all_phys_writes
from
   dba_hist_sysstat
  natural join
   dba_hist_snapshot
where
   stat_name = 'physical writes'
```

```
and
  value > 0
)
order by
  to_char(begin_interval_time,'yyyy-mm-dd hh24:mi'),
  phywrts desc
;
```

The following is a sample output. This is a very useful report because the high write datafiles as well as the times when they are hot are revealed.

```
SQL> @hot_write_files
```

This will identify any single file whose write I/O is more than 25% of the total write I/O of the database.

```
SNAP_TIME              FILENAME                                        PHYWRTS
-------------------    --------------------------------------------    ----------
2004-02-20 23:30       E:\ORACLE\ORA92\FSDEV10G\SYSAUX01.DBF            85,540

2004-02-21 01:00       E:\ORACLE\ORA92\FSDEV10G\SYSAUX01.DBF            88,843

2004-02-21 08:31       E:\ORACLE\ORA92\FSDEV10G\SYSAUX01.DBF            89,463

2004-02-22 02:00       E:\ORACLE\ORA92\FSDEV10G\SYSAUX01.DBF            90,168

2004-02-22 16:30       E:\ORACLE\ORA92\FSDEV10G\SYSAUX01.DBF           143,974
                       E:\ORACLE\ORA92\FSDEV10G\UNDOTBS01.DBF           88,973
```

Time series exception reporting is extremely useful for detecting those times when an Oracle database is experiencing stress. Many Oracle professionals will schedule these types of exception reports for automatic e-mailing every day.

Time Series Monitoring of the Data Buffers

Before we can self-tune the data buffers, there needs to be a mechanism for monitoring the data buffer hit ratio (DBHR) for all pools that have been defined. All seven data buffers can be monitored with this script; but remember, unless objects are segregated into separate buffers, aggregate DBHR values are largely meaningless.

```
select
  name,
  block_size,
  (1-(physical_reads/ decode(db_block_gets+consistent_gets, 0, .001,
db_block_gets+consistent_gets)))*100   cache_hit_ratio
from
  v$buffer_pool_statistics;
```

The following is a sample output from this script. The names of the sized block buffers remain DEFAULT, and the *block_size* column must be selected to differentiate between the buffers. The sample output shows all seven data buffers.

```
NAME            BLOCK_SIZE  CACHE_HIT_RATIO
----------      ----------  ---------------
DEFAULT          32,767              .97
RECYCLE          16,384              .61
KEEP             16,384             1.00
DEFAULT          16,384              .92
DEFAULT           4,096              .99
DEFAULT           8,192              .98
DEFAULT           2,048              .86
```

Of course, this report is not extremely useful because the *v$sysstat* view only shows averages since the instance was started. To perform self-tuning of the data buffers, Oracle's AWR views can be used to measure the data buffer hit ratios every hour.

To do this, an AWR data buffer exception report table can be used. Figure 13.17 shows the output from a time-based data buffer hit ratio report.

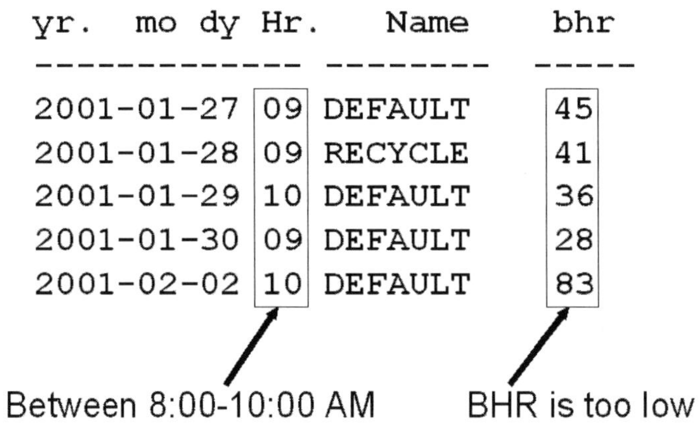

```
yr.   mo dy Hr.    Name      bhr
-------------      --------   -----
2001-01-27  09   DEFAULT     45
2001-01-28  09   RECYCLE     41
2001-01-29  10   DEFAULT     36
2001-01-30  09   DEFAULT     28
2001-02-02  10   DEFAULT     83
```

Between 8:00-10:00 AM   BHR is too low

Figure 13.17: *Time-based Proactive Problem Detection*

In Figure 13.17, it appears that the database regularly experiences a decline in the data buffer hit ratio between 9:00 and 11:00 AM. Once it has been confirmed that this is a signature and repeats on a regular basis, action can be taken to correct the deficiency as follows:

- Review and tune all SQL between 9:00 - 11:00 AM using the SQL source captured in the *stats$sql_summary* table.

- Schedule a job (*dbms_job* or *dbms_scheduler*) to increase the *db_cache_size* during this period.

The following section provides a look at time series disk monitoring and analysis using the powerful AWR tables.

Monitoring Disk I/O with AWR

One of the great features of AWR is that it can directly monitor disk input and output (I/O). The following is a great technique that can be used for extending the capabilities of Oracle's STATSPACK performance utility to report statistics on I/O activity at the disk and file level in a UNIX environment.

Statistics ordinarily captured by an AWR snapshot are related only to the read and write activity at the Oracle data file level. Normally, AWR cannot show I/O at the disk or mount point level, which can be valuable information in determining hyperactivity on particular files or disks.

Instead of using standard utilities to generate a report for a single time period, utilities can be modified to collect I/O data over consistent intervals, storing the results in Oracle tables for easy access and reporting. The following is an outline of requirements.

The *dba_hist_filestatxs* table contains I/O data collected by snapshots taken at consistent intervals. I/O data captured includes the actual number of physical reads, physical writes, block reads, block writes, and the time required for each operation. Disk activity over time is represented in Figure 13.18.

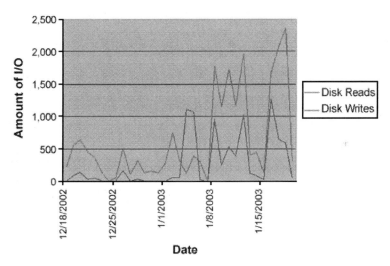

Figure 13.18: *Disk Activity Over Time*

Holistic data, which yields the status internal to Oracle and external with the various UNIX and Linux commands, can be gathered and analyzed using just STATSPACK and system utilities.

The data collected by STATSPACK can be accessed with normal scripts such as the *snapfileio_10g.sql* listed here:

💾 **Snapfileio_awr.sql**

```
rem
```

```
rem NAME: snapfileio.sql

rem FUNCTION: Reports on the file io status of all of the
rem FUNCTION: datafiles in the database for a single snapshot.


column sum_io1 new_value st1 noprint
column sum_io2 new_value st2 noprint
column sum_io new_value divide_by noprint
column Percent format 999.999 heading 'Percent|Of IO'
column brratio format 999.99 heading 'Block|Read|Ratio'
column bwratio format 999.99 heading 'Block|Write|Ratio'
column phyrds heading 'Physical | Reads'
column phywrts heading 'Physical | Writes'
column phyblkrd heading 'Physical|Block|Reads'
column phyblkwrt heading 'Physical|Block|Writes'
column filename format a45 heading 'File|Name'
column file# format 9999 heading 'File'

set feedback off verify off lines 132 pages 60 sqlbl on trims on

select
    nvl(sum(a.phyrds+a.phywrts),0) sum_io1
from
    dba_hist_filestatxs a where snap_id=&&snap;

select nvl(sum(b.phyrds+b.phywrts),0) sum_io2
from
        dba_hist_tempstatxs b where snap_id=&&snap;

select &st1+&st2 sum_io from dual;

rem
@title132 'Snap&&snap File I/O Statistics Report'

spool rep_out\&db\fileio&&snap

select
    a.filename, a.phyrds, a.phywrts,
    (100*(a.phyrds+a.phywrts)/&divide_by) Percent,
    a.phyblkrd, a.phyblkwrt, (a.phyblkrd/greatest(a.phyrds,1)) brratio,
     (a.phyblkwrt/greatest(a.phywrts,1)) bwratio
from
    dba_hist_filestatxs a
where
    a.snap_id=&&snap
union
select
    c.filename, c.phyrds, c.phywrts,
    (100*(c.phyrds+c.phywrts)/&divide_by) Percent,
    c.phyblkrd, c.phyblkwrt,(c.phyblkrd/greatest(c.phyrds,1)) brratio,
     (c.phyblkwrt/greatest(c.phywrts,1)) bwratio
from
    dba_hist_tempstatxs c
where
    c.snap_id=&&snap
order by
    1
/

spool off
pause Press enter to continue
set feedback on verify on lines 80 pages 22
clear columns
ttitle off
```

```
undef snap
```

Of course, a single AWR reading suffers from the same limitations that a single read of the *v$* or *gv$* dynamic performance views. It only gives the cumulative data from when the database was started to the time that the snapshot was taken. A better methodology is shown in *snapdeltafileio_awr.sql*.

🖫 snapdeltafileio_awr.sql

```
rem FUNCTION: Reports on the file io status of all of
rem FUNCTION: the datafiles in the database across
rem FUNCTION: two snapshots.

column sum_io1 new_value st1 noprint
column sum_io2 new_value st2 noprint
column sum_io new_value divide_by noprint

column Percent format 999.999 heading 'Percent|Of IO'
column brratio format 999.99  heading 'Block|Read|Ratio'
column bwratio format 999.99  heading 'Block|Write|Ratio'
column phyrds                 heading 'Physical | Reads'
column phywrts                heading 'Physical | Writes'
column phyblkrd               heading 'Physical|Block|Reads'
column phyblkwrt              heading 'Physical|Block|Writes'
column filename format a45    heading 'File|Name'
column file# format 9999      heading 'File'

set feedback off verify off lines 132 pages 60 sqlbl on trims on

select
    nvl(sum((b.phyrds-a.phyrds)+(b.phywrts-a.phywrts)),0) sum_io1
from
    dba_hist_filestatxs a, dba_hist_filestatxs b
where
        a.snap_id=&&first_snap_id and b.snap_id=&&sec_snap_id
        and a.filename=b.filename;

select
    nvl(sum((b.phyrds-a.phyrds)+(b.phywrts-a.phywrts)),0) sum_io2
from
    dba_hist_tempstatxs a, dba_hist_tempstatxs b
where
        a.snap_id=&&first_snap_id and b.snap_id=&&sec_snap_id
        and a.filename=b.filename;

select &st1+&st2 sum_io from dual;

rem
@title132 'Snap &&first_snap_id to &&sec_snap_id File I/O Statistics Report'
spool rep_out\&db\fileio'&&first_snap_id'_to_'&&sec_snap_id'

select
    a.filename, b.phyrds -a.phyrds phyrds, b.phywrts-a.phywrts phywrts,
    (100*((b.phyrds-a.phyrds)+(b.phywrts-a.phywrts))/&divide_by) Percent,
    b.phyblkrd- a.phyblkrd phyblkrd, b.phyblkwrt-a.phyblkwrt phyblgwrt,
        ((b.phyblkrd-a.phyblkrd)/greatest((b.phyrds-a.phyrds),1)) brratio,
        ((b.phyblkwrt-a.phyblkwrt)/greatest((b.phywrts-a.phywrts),1)) bwratio
from
    dba_hist_filestatxs a, dba_hist_filestatxs b
where
        a.snap_id=&&first_snap_id and b.snap_id=&&sec_snap_id
```

```
          and a.filename=b.filename
union
select
    c.filename, d.phyrds-c.phyrds phyrds, d.phywrts-c.phywrts phywrts,
    (100*((d.phyrds-c.phyrds)+(d.phywrts-c.phywrts))/&divide_by) Percent,
    d.phyblkrd-c.phyblkrd phyblkrd, d.phyblkwrt-c.phyblkwrt phyblgwrt,
        ((d.phyblkrd-c.phyblkrd)/greatest((d.phyrds-c.phyrds),1)) brratio,
        ((d.phyblkwrt-c.phyblkwrt)/greatest((d.phywrts-c.phywrts),1)) bwratio
from
    dba_hist_tempstatxs c, dba_hist_tempstatxs d
where
        c.snap_id=&&first_snap_id and d.snap_id=&&sec_snap_id
        and c.filename=d.filename
order by
    1
/
spool off
pause Press enter to continue
set feedback on verify on lines 80 pages 22
clear columns
ttitle off
undef first_snap_id
undef sec_snap_id;
```

Figure 13.19 shows a representation of a daily disk delta report.

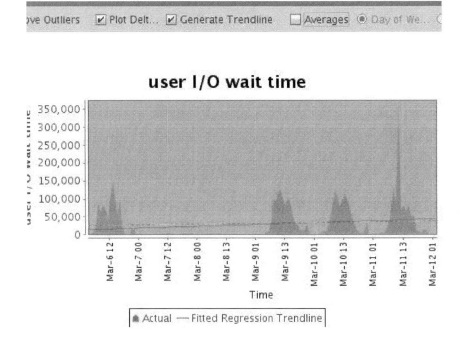

Figure 13.19: *A Daily Disk Delta Report in Ion*

The report accepts two snapshot IDs and uses them to calculate the delta between the I/O readings. This I/O delta information is vital to help pinpoint real I/O problems for a given time period.

Combined with *iostat* and *vmstat* readings from the same time period, we can get a complete picture of the I/O profile of the database. A similar technique can be used for I/O timing and other useful delta statistics. These scripts and many others are available from oracle-script.com.

Scripts can be written to show the signature for any Oracle system statistic, averaged by hour of the day. This information is great for plotting disk activity. The following shows an average for every hour of the day. This information can then be easily pasted into an MS Excel spreadsheet and plotted with the chart wizard as shown in Figure 13.20.

```
SQL> @rpt_10g_sysstat_hr
```

This will query the *dba_hist_sysstat* view to display average values by hour of the day:

```
Enter Statistics Name:   physical reads

SNAP_TIME                 AVG_VALUE
-------------------       -----------
00                          120,861
01                          132,492
02                          134,136
03                          137,460
04                          138,944
05                          140,496
06                          141,937
07                          143,191
08                          145,313
09                          135,881
10                          137,031
11                          138,331
12                          139,388
13                          140,753
14                          128,621
15                          101,683
16                          116,985
17                          118,386
18                          119,463
19                          120,868
20                          121,976
21                          112,906
22                          114,708
23                          116,340
```

physical reads

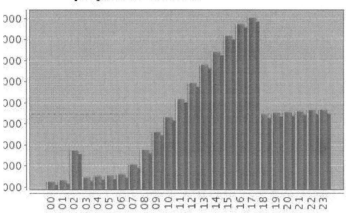

Figure 13.20: *An Hourly Disk Read I/O Trend Signature*

The following script will generate results aggregated by day of the week instead of hour of the day.

💾 **avg_stats_doy.sql**

```
prompt  This will query the dba_hist_sysstat view to
prompt  display average values by hour of the day
prompt

set pages 999

break on snap_time skip 2

accept stat_name char prompt 'Enter Statistics Name:  ';


col snap_time    format a19
col avg_value    format 999,999,999

select

decode(snap_time1,1,'Monday',2,'Tuesday',3,'Wednesday',4,'Thursday',5,'Friday',6,'Saturday',
7,'Sunday') snap_time,
   avg_value
from (
select
   to_char(begin_interval_time,'d') snap_time1,
   avg(value)                       avg_value
from
   dba_hist_sysstat
   natural join
   dba_hist_snapshot
```

```
where
    stat_name = 'physical reads'
group by
    to_char(begin_interval_time,'d')
order by
    to_char(begin_interval_time,'d')
)
;
```

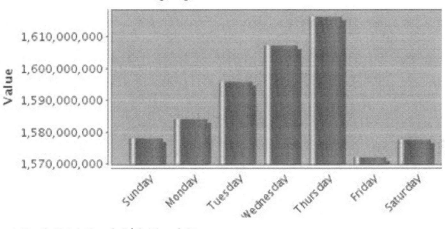

Figure 13.21: *A Daily Disk Reads I/O Trend Signature*

In Figure 13.21, the daily aggregation of disk read I/O shows that the database experiences the most physical read I/O activity on Saturday. This allows the isolation of routines and applications which are performed mainly on Saturday in order to check them for possible I/O tuning.

This chapter will conclude with a review and summary of the major points regarding disk I/O tuning.

Conclusion

Disks have evolved over the past 40 years but remain an archaic component of Oracle. Disk array manufacturers are now homogenizing disk arrays to the point where they can get I/O rates to match the disk capacity. This results in the spread of the I/O across many more platters than ever before, but it makes tracking Oracle I/O problems more difficult.

The main points of this chapter include:

- Databases used to be largely I/O-bound but this is changing as a result of falling RAM process, larger data buffer caches and solid-state disks. Many databases in Oracle have shifted to being CPU-bound.

- Solid-state disk is making inroads with Oracle and many systems are now using SSD instead of disk.

- Verify that the database is I/O-bound before undertaking the tuning of the I/O subsystem. Check the top 5 wait events for the database.

- Oracle *v$* views and the AWR tables provide time series I/O tracking information so that read and write I/O signatures can be plotted, aggregated by hour of the day and day of the week.

Our next step is to dive into the Oracle instance and look at how the AWR and ASH tables can give insight into tuning the SGA processes and RAM regions.

Oracle Instance Tuning

Inside Instance Tuning

This is one of the most important chapters in this book because the configuration of the System Global Area (SGA) and instance is critical to performance. At the lowest level, an Oracle instance is nothing more than a chunk of reserved RAM, i.e. the SGA and PGA areas, plus a set of constantly running programs such as background processes and user processes.

An improperly configured instance can cripple Oracle performance. Some of the most common problems in Oracle instance management include:

- **Wasted RAM:** Wasting RAM is one of the most common causes of poor performance. Oracle has an insatiable appetite for RAM, especially when the SGA pools are undersized. The main goal is to use the entire available RAM without exceeding the swap threshold and causing page-in operations.

- **Improper parameter settings:** The *init.ora* parameters have a profound impact on database performance, especially the parameters that govern how Oracle uses server resources like RAM and CPU.

- **Improper SQL optimization environment:** Oracle can be thought of as a SQL processing engine, and the settings for the optimizer parameters, i.e. *optimizer_mode* and such, and optimizer statistics via *dbms_stats* have a profound impact on system-wide performance.

When diving into instance tuning, remember that there is no single optimal configuration! Workloads change from minute-to-minute, and it is the DBA's job to identify these workloads and ensure that the instance is properly optimized for that workload. For example, Oracle databases frequently have b-modal workloads, a daytime OLTP mode and a nighttime batch mode. In these cases, it is important to create two optimizations and change the instance configuration when the workload changes.

The increasing sophistication and flexibility of Oracle offers complex new challenges when the DBA attempts to optimize the sizes of the SGA pools like buffer and library cache, and utilize the super-fast and super-expensive RAM to the best advantage.

Tuning saves money!

Making the proper decisions required to efficiently utilize RAM resources for the SGA and PGA can save millions of dollars in computing resources.

This chapter will address the following areas of Oracle instance tuning:

- **Operating system configuration:** There are many settings on the server that affect the performance of the Oracle database.

- **Oracle instance parameters:** Oracle has over 250 documented and over one hundred undocumented instance configuration parameters.

- **Oracle data caching:** Properly defining data buffer caches, i.e. KEEP pool and multiple data buffers, has a tremendous impact on reducing disk I/O.

Start by understanding why instance tuning must precede other areas of Oracle tuning.

Instance Tuning Comes First

Some beginners advocate tuning individual SQL statements before optimizing the instance parameters. This can be a huge waste of effort. Changing instance parameters after SQL tuning can undo a lot of hard work.

Instance tuning is the process of determining the optimal settings for over 250 instance initialization parameters. Some instance parameters, such as *optimizer_mode* and *optimizer_index_caching*, control how Oracle configures itself to process and optimize SQL statements. These parameters must be preset to optimize the bulk of the SQL statements before any individual SQL tuning takes place.

Tune the root cause first!

Sub-optimal SQL plans are most commonly caused by incorrect system statistics (*dbms_stats*), or by an incorrect *optimizer_mode*. Only alter the optimizer

If individual SQL statements were tuned prior to determining the instance parameter settings, much of that hard work would have to be redone.

For example, *v$bh* can be sampled with AWR and STATSPACK tables used to determine the average amount of index segments in the data buffers. The parameter *optimizer_index_caching* can be reset from its default value of 0. From Oracle's *10g Performance Tuning Guide*, we see the following advice on setting *optimizer_index_caching*:

> *"optimizer_index_caching: This parameter controls the costing of an index probe in conjunction with a nested loop.*
>
> *The range of values 0 to 100 for optimizer_index_caching indicates percentage of index blocks in the buffer cache, which modifies the optimizer's assumptions about index caching for nested loops and IN-list iterators.*
>
> *A value of 100 infers that 100% of the index blocks are likely to be found in the buffer cache and the optimizer adjusts the cost of an index probe or nested loop accordingly.*
>
> *Use caution when using this parameter because execution plans can change in favor of index caching."*

Here, the Oracle 10g Reference suggests that this instance parameter should be set according to average system workload:

> *"The cost of executing an index using an IN-list iterator or of executing a nested loops join when an index is used to access the inner table depends on the caching of that index in the buffer cache.*
>
> *The amount of caching depends on factors that the optimizer cannot predict, such as the load on the system and the block access patterns of different users.*
>
> *You can modify the optimizer's assumptions about index caching for nested loops joins and IN-list iterators by setting this parameter to a value between 0 and 100 to indicate the percentage of the index blocks the optimizer should assume are in the cache."*

To see how *optimizer_index_caching* works, consider the following scenario. The default value for *optimizer_index_caching* was left unchanged and 10 weeks were spent tuning 5,000 SQL statements using hints, adding histograms, and more. Later on, it comes to light that *optimizer_index_caching* is set at the default value of zero. This means that the CBO assumes that there are no index data blocks in the cache.

Inspections of *x$bh* confirm that an average of 80% of all indexes are in the data buffer. This factor will greatly influence the CBO's decision about the speed of index vs. table scan access. So, *optimizer_index_caching* is reset to a more real-world value. Suddenly, thousands of SQL execution plans change, undoing all of that hard tuning work.

The moral: Always set good baseline values for instance parameters BEFORE tuning any individual SQL statements.

Instance Configuration for High Performance

With the introduction of Oracle 11g, we see benchmarks using multi-million dollar servers with up to 64 processors and over a terabyte of RAM. The vendors want their benchmarks to dazzle, so they hire the best experts to hypercharge benchmarks using Oracle high performance techniques. There are many Oracle parameters that can have a profound impact on database performance, and reading full-disclosure benchmarks from www.tpc.org is a great place to learn Oracle tuning secrets.

One of the most common mistakes made by the Oracle tuning professional is diving into specific tuning issues before tuning the instance. The instance is always changing, but the proper configuration of initialization parameters can make a tremendous difference in overall database performance. These all-important parameters include OS kernel parameters and Oracle initialization parameters.

Oracle 10g first introduced Automatic Memory Management (AMM), but this feature is reactive, only reallocating the memory regions after problems are detected. The single most important region for purposes of Oracle tuning is the data buffer cache, and a proactive approach is often better than AMM, where we detect repeating SQL workloads and automate just-in-time instance tuning by the *dbms_scheduler* utility to change the size of the SGA regions immediately before the workload changes. This way, we anticipate the problem and fix it before our end-user community sees any slow response time.

Automatic Memory Management

When Oracle9i first allowed "*alter system*" commands to morph the SGA, Oracle 10g introduced Automatic Memory Management, a reactive tool to re-size the RAM regions.

Oracle Database 10g now has Automatic Memory Management (ASMM) in the form of the one-size-fits-all parameter called sga_target, which replaces many individual parameters and automates the allocation of RAM between the data buffers, shared pool, and log buffers.

The tuning of these SGA memory regions used to be complex and time consuming, until ASMM automated the tuning. Using predictive models derived from *v$db_cache_advice* and *v$shared_pool_advice*, Oracle automatically monitors changing demands on the SGA regions and re-allocates RAM memory based on the existing workload.

It's a common misunderstanding that when using AMM by setting *sga_target* and *sga_memory_max*, the values for the "traditional" pool parameters (*db_cache_size, shared_pool_size*, &c) are not ignored. Rather, they will specify the minimum size that Oracle will always maintain for each sub-area in the SGA.

Beware!

Beware of Automatic memory management!

Oracle's automatic memory management (AMM) is not appropriate for large mission-critical databases, were a human expert can always do a better job in optimizing RAM resources. AMM is designed for small databases.

In sum, most shops continue to use self-created memory management tools because of the performance hits and the reactive nature of AMM, which does not anticipate upcoming changes in possessing, predictions which can now be made by analyzing STATSPACK and AWR data.

In 11g and beyond, Oracle automatic memory management is configured using the *memory_target* and *memory_max_target* initialization parameters. The memory_target parameter specifies the amount of shared memory available for Oracle to use when dynamically controlling the SGA and PGA. The *memory_max_target* AMM parameter specifies the max size that *memory_target* may take.

Manual RAM allocation vs. AMM

In an effort to complete with simple databases such as SQL Server, Oracle has undertaken to remove much of the inherent complexity by building automated tools to manage storage, RAM and tuning.

This "umbrella of simplicity" is amazing and has allows the world's most flexible ad robust database to be as simple to use as the lesser databases, using this one-sized-fits-all technique of automation.

However, it's critical to understand that the Oracle automation tools were developed for hands-off, small departmental applications, and automation is not always the best approach for a large mission-critical database with thousands of concurrent users. Remember, with today's technology, any automated tool will never be able to optimize your database as well as a human expert.

A competent Oracle professional will always be able to do a better job than an automated tool at forecasting and optimizing RAM resources for SQL statements. This is true for all automated tools, not just Oracle AMM, and there is no automated substitute for human intuition and experience.

Oracle designed AMM to simplify operations on small to midsize databases where it does an adequate job in managing the Ram pool in the absence of a DBA. However, in case after case on large systems, I have seen frequent AMM re-size operations cause performance problems on Oracle databases, as per Oracle 11g, I do not recommend using automatic memory management for large or for mission-critical databases.

The biggest issue with AMM is that it is a "reactive" tool. Unlike a proactive approach, AMM waits until it detects a problem before changing the SGA pool sizes. But on the other hand, developing a proactive approach is not easy either.

To be effective in proactive RAM tuning for an instance, you must understand basic statistical techniques such as linear and non-linear regression modeling, and be able to analyze STATSPACK or AWR reports to identify RAM usage trends (called "signatures"). Once the repeating patterns of workload usage are identified (repeating in cycles of hour-of-the-day, day-of-the-week, and day-of the-month), you can automate scripts to re-optimize your SGA pools immediately before the workload changes.

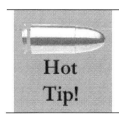

Never use MTS with AMM!

Using shared servers (MTS) with AMM and PL/SQL can hog all of the RAM on the Oracle instance!.

This is especially true in cases when AMM is used with obsolete tools like shared servers (the multi-threaded server, or MTS). Quest Software's Guy Harrison has this excellent warning about using the AMM with MTS:

"When you use MTS and AMM (or ASMM) together, PL/SQL programs that try to create large collections can effectively consume all available server memory with disastrous consequences.

AMM allocates virtually all memory on the system to the large pool in order to accommodate the PL/SQL memory request. First it consumes the buffer cache, then it reduces the *pga_aggregate_target* - all the way to zero!"

As we see, there are many pitfalls and perils to using automated tools, and we must always understand the limits of automation.

To briefly review, the Oracle data buffers use RAM to cache incoming data blocks from disk. The data can then be retrieved from RAM hundreds of times faster than a disk access. Disk access is the slowest activity in any database, and managing these RAM buffers intelligently will have a huge positive impact on Oracle performance.

Sizing the Oracle SGA and PGA Regions

In a shared environment, it is important to observe the optimal sizes for each *shared_pool_size* (*v$shared_pool_advice*) and the optimal data buffer size using *v$db_cache_advice*. Estimating SGA size is critical for all capacity planning activities and estimating the SGA size ensures that precious and expensive RAM is not wasted. The goal of server optimization for any Oracle database is to manage the RAM and CPU resources of the machine and make sure that expensive RAM is not under allocated.

In simple databases, consider using AMM and set the *sga_max_size* parameter to give the total SGA allocation, but there are well-documented issues where ASMM resize operations can hurt performance! Wasting expensive RAM resources is a bad thing and the goal of the Oracle DBA is to maximize the SGA region with intelligent SGA sizing techniques.

If there is only Oracle on the server, start by reserving 10% of RAM for Linux or 20% or RAM for Windows. With whatever RAM is left over:

- **SGA sizing:** Optimize the instance by determining the optimal size for *db_cache_size*, *shared_pool_size*, and such.

- **PGA sizing:** Determine the optimal total RAM for PGA regions (*pga_aggregate_target*) to minimize disk sorts and maximize hash joins.

Viewing Server RAM Resources

On each UNIX dialect, there are specific commands that are required to display the RAM usage (Table 14.1).

Dialect	RAM display command
DEC-UNIX	`uerf -r 300	grep -i mem`
Solaris	`prtconf|grep -i mem`
AIX	`lsdev -C|grep mem`
Linux	`free`
HP/UX	`swapinfo -tm`

Table 14.1: *Commands Used to Display RAM Usage*

On most Oracle servers, a DBA can issue a few commands to see the amount of RAM. Look at a few examples.

In the IBM AIX dialect of UNIX, there is a two-step command to display the amount of available RAM memory. Start with the *lsdev* command to show all devices that are attached to the UNIX server. The *lsdev* command produces a large listing of all devices, but the output can be piped from *lsdev* to the *grep* command to refine the display to only show the name of the device that has the RAM memory.

```
root> lsdev -C|grep mem

mem0        Available 00-00          Memory
```

Here it can be seen that *mem0* is the name of the memory device on this AIX server. Now issue the *lsattr -El* command, passing *mem0* as an argument, to see the amount of memory on the server. Below is shown that this server has 2 gigabytes of RAM memory attached to the mem0 device.

```
root> lsattr -El mem0

size      2048 Total amount of physical memory in Mbytes  False
goodsize  2048 Amount of usable physical memory in Mbytes False
```

Oracle RAM in Linux

In Linux, seeing available RAM is easy. The *free* command can be used to quickly display the amount of RAM mcmory on the server.

```
root> free

              total       used       free     shared    buffers     cached
Mem:        3728668     504688    3223980      41316     430072      29440
-/+ buffers/cache:        45176    3683492
Swap:        265032        608     264424
```

Oracle RAM on MS Windows

To see how much RAM is on the MS-Windows server, go to Start --> Settings > Control Panel --> System, and click on the General tab (Figure 14.1). Here it can be seen that this server has 1,250 megabytes of RAM.

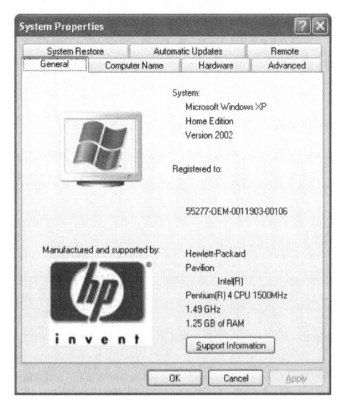

Figure 14.1: *The MS Windows System Display Screen*

Now that you know how to tell the size of the MS Windows RAM and the size of the SGA, consider the RAM usage for Oracle connections.

Reserving RAM for Database Connections

The Oracle DBA can use math to determine the optimal RAM allocation for a MS Windows server. For the purposes of this example, assume that the database is on a dedicated MS Windows Oracle server, and Oracle will be the only program running on the server. The total RAM demands for Oracle on MS Windows are as follows:

- **OS RAM:** I like to allow 20 percent of total RAM for MS Windows, 10% of RAM for UNIX.

- **Oracle SGA RAM:** Is determined with the *show sga* command.

- **Oracle database connections RAM:** Each Oracle connection, when not using the Oracle multi-threaded server, will use two megabytes of RAM plus *sort_area_size* plus *hash_area_size* or *pga_aggregate_target* allocation.

Important Windows Note!

If the server is 32-bit Windows, it cannot address more than 2**32 bits (about 1.7 gig), and you will need to use AWE to use all of the RAM on the Windows server.

Once the total available RAM memory is known, subtract 20 percent from this value for MS Windows overhead. Even in an idle state, Windows services use RAM resources, and you must subtract 20% to get the real free RAM on an idle server.

Sizing your SGA

The SGA sizing tasks include optimizing settings for *sga_max_size* and the various configuration parameters for *db_cache_size, db_xk_cache_size, shared_pool_size, large_pool_size,* and other memory objects give better control of SGA component sizing. Some parameters to consider in SGA sizing include:

- **sga_max_size:** This parameter sets the hard limit up to which *sga_target* can dynamically adjust sizes. Usually, *sga_max_size* and *sga_target* will be the same value, but there may be times when the DBA wants to have the capability to adjust for peak loads. By setting this parameter higher than *sga_target*, dynamic adjustment of the *sga_target* parameter is allowed.

- **sga_target:** This parameter was new with Oracle 10g and reflects the total size of memory footprint a SGA can consume. It includes in its boundaries the fixed SGA and other internal allocations, the (redo) log buffers, the shared pool, Java pool, streams pool, buffer cache, keep/recycle caches, and if they are specified, the non-standard blocksize caches.

SGA Sizing on a Dedicated Server

For dedicated Oracle servers, the maximum total RAM SGA size can be computed as follows:

- **OS reserved RAM:** This is the RAM required to run the OS kernel and system functions, 20% of total RAM for MS Windows, and 10% of total RAM for UNIX/Linux.

- **Oracle database connections RAM:** Each Oracle connection requires OS RAM regions for sorting and hash joins. Note that this does not apply when using the Oracle multi-threaded server or *pga_aggregate_target*. The maximum amount of RAM required for a session is as follows:

  - 2 megabytes RAM session overhead

  - + *sort_area_size*

  - + *hash_area_size*

- **Oracle SGA sizing for RAM:** This is determined by the Oracle parameter settings. The total is easily found by either the *show sga* command or the value of the *sga_max_size* parameter.

Subtract 20 percent from the total available RAM to allow for MS Windows overhead. Windows uses RAM resources even when idle, and the 20 percent deduction is necessary to get the real free RAM on an idle server. Once the amount of RAM on the server is determined, the DBA will be in a position to size the Oracle SGA for optimal RAM usage.

For PGA sizing, it's important to know the high water mark (HWM) of Oracle connections and the average RAM needs to minimize disk sorts and maximize hash joins.

The HWM of connected Oracle sessions can be determined in several ways. One popular method uses Oracle login and logoff system-level triggers to record sessions in a statistics table. Another method uses Oracle STATSPACK to display the values from the *stats$sysstat* table, or the *v$resource_limit* view, but only after release 8.1.7 because of a bug.

In sum, SGA sizing is a relatively straightforward push-pull of the competing RAM needs of the internal SGA pools (buffer, library cache), the external RAM for PGA, and the OS overhead.

The goal of server optimization for any Oracle database is to manage the RAM and CPU resources of the machine and make sure that expensive RAM is not under allocated. When optimizing Oracle database performance in a MS Windows environment is talked about, the techniques that are used are very similar to those used on larger UNIX/Linux platforms.

In my experience as an Oracle consultant, I see millions of dollars worth of RAM being wasted by Oracle shops. Because the Oracle DBA does not know how to accurately compute the RAM demands of the database, they under allocate the RAM. On larger servers, RAM is still very expensive and depreciates regardless of use. The savvy Oracle professional knows how to accurately predict the high water mark of RAM demands for their database, and fully allocates the RAM, reserving only enough to accommodate spikes in user connections.

RAM and Virtual Memory for Oracle

On all platforms, it is best to ensure that the RAM processing demands of the Oracle database do not exceed the real RAM memory of the server. As may be known, all large servers use a Virtual Memory (VM) scheme to allow sharing of RAM resources. Oracle servers, i.e. Windows, UNIX, and OS390, have special swap disks to manage excessive RAM demands.

Virtual memory is an internal trick that relies on the fact that not every executing task is always referencing its RAM memory region. Since all RAM regions are not constantly in use, vendors have developed a paging algorithm that move RAM memory pages to the swap disk when it appears that they will not be needed in the immediate future.

A special area of disk called a swap disk is required to provide for the sharing of RAM. The primary purpose of the swap disk is to hold page frames from inactive programs on disk and to offload the least-frequently-used (LRU) RAM page frames so that many applications can concurrently share the same memory.

Once RAM pages from inactive programs are written to disk, i.e. a *page-out*, the operating system can make the freed RAM memory available for another active task. Later, when the inactive program resumes execution, the RAM pages are reloaded from the swap disk into RAM, i.e. a *page-in*. This reloading of RAM pages is called swapping, and we must always remember that swapping is evil to performance and it degrades the performance of the target program.

While having the swap disk ensures concurrent RAM usage above the real amount of RAM, optimal performance requires that the swap disk is never used for active programs. This is because reading RAM pages off of the swap disk is about 14,000 times slower than reading the memory pages directly from RAM. As is likely known, disk access is measured in milliseconds, or thousandths of a second, while RAM access is measured in nanoseconds, or billionths of a second.

In virtual memory (VM) architecture, the OS will write RAM to the swap disk even though the real RAM has not been exceeded. This is done in anticipation of a RAM shortage, and if a real RAM shortage occurs, the LRU RAM frames are already on the swap disk.

For an Oracle server, the goal is to keep all of the RAM memory demands of the database and database connections beneath the amount of physical RAM memory. In an Oracle environment, the DBA can accurately control the amount of RAM memory that is used by the database instance SGA. This is because the Oracle database administrator can issue the *alter system* command to change the RAM memory areas allowing the RAM memory areas to grow and shrink on an as needed basis.

The allocated size of the SGA in the Oracle alert log can now be seen, and it is also displayed on the console when Oracle is started as shown here:

```
SQL> startup

ORACLE instance started.

Total System Global Area   143421172 bytes
Fixed Size                    282356 bytes
Variable Size              117440512 bytes
Database Buffers            25165824 bytes
Redo Buffers                  532480 bytes
Database mounted.
Database opened.
```

The DBA can also see the SGA RAM region by issuing the *show sga* command. In the example below, the total SGA size is 143 megabytes:

```
SQL> connect system/manager as sysdba

Connected.

SQL> show sga

Total System Global Area   143421172 bytes
Fixed Size                    282356 bytes
```

```
Variable Size              117440512 bytes
Database Buffers            25165824 bytes
Redo Buffers                 532480 bytes
```

Next, see how the DBA can quickly find out how many users are connected to the instance. This is critical for finding the proper size for *pga_aggregate_target*.

Finding the High Water Mark of Oracle User Connections

Once the amount of available RAM for Oracle is known, the HWM for the number of Oracle connections must be known. For systems that are not using Oracle's multi-threaded server architecture, each connected session to the Windows server is going require an area of memory for the Program Global Area, or PGA.

There is no easy way to determine the high water mark of connected Oracle sessions. If Oracle STATSPACK is used, this information can be obtained from the stats$sysstat table, but most Oracle DBAs make a generous guess for this value.

Determining the Optimal PGA Size

In this example, there is 1,250 megabytes of RAM memory on the MS Windows server so subtracting 20 percent leaves the total available allocation for Oracle of one gig.

The size for each PGA RAM region is computed as follows:

- **OS overhead:** Reserve 2 meg for Windows and 1 meg for UNIX.
- *sort_area_size* **parameter value:** This RAM is used for data row sorting inside the PGA.
- *hash_area_size* **parameter value:** This RAM defaults to 1.5 time *sort_area_size* and is used for performing hash joins of Oracle tables.

Use the Oracle show parameters command to quickly see the values for *sort_area_size* and *hash_area_size* if not using *pga_aggregate_target*:

```
SQL> show parameters area_size

NAME                                     TYPE         VALUE
---------------------------------------- -----------  ---------
bitmap_merge_area_size                   integer      1048576
create_bitmap_area_size                  integer      8388608
hash_area_size                           integer      1048576
sort_area_size                           integer      524288
workarea_size_policy                     string       MANUAL
```

Display PGA Area Sizes

Here the values for *sort_area_size* and *hash_area_size* for the Oracle database can be seen. To compute the value for the size of each PGA RAM region, write a quick data dictionary query against the *v$parameter* view:

🖫 display_pga_size.sql

```
set pages 999;

column pga_size format 999,999,999

select
    1048576+a.value+b.value    pga_size
from
    v$parameter a,
    v$parameter b
where
    a.name = 'sort_area_size'
and
    b.name = 'hash_area_size';
```

The output from this data dictionary query shows that every connected Oracle session will be about 2.5 megabytes of RAM memory for the Oracle PGA.

```
PGA_SIZE
------------
   2,621,440
```

Now, by multiplying the number of connected users by the total PGA demands for each connected user, the DBA will know exactly how much RAM memory to reserve for connected sessions.

Getting back to the example, assume that there is a high water mark of 100 connected sessions to the Oracle database server. Multiply 100 by the total area for each PGA memory region, and the maximum size of the SGA can be determined:

Total RAM on Windows Server	1250 MB
Less:	
Total PGA regions for 10 users:	250 MB
RAM for Windows (20 %)	250 MB

RAM for SGA & buffers	750 MB

Hence, the desire is to adjust the RAM to the data buffers in order to make the SGA size less than 750 MB. Any SGA size greater than 750 MB, and the server might start RAM paging, adversely affecting the performance of the entire server. The final task is to size the Oracle SGA such that the total memory involved does not exceed 750 MB.

Remember, RAM is an expensive server resource, and it is the DBA's job to fully allocate RAM resources on the database server. Unallocated RAM wastes expensive hardware resources, and RAM depreciates regardless of usage.

As a review, the size of an Oracle SGA is based upon the following parameter settings:

- *shared_pool_size*: This sizes the administrative RAM for Oracle and the library cache.

- *db_cache_size*: This parameter determines the size of the RAM for the data buffers.

- *large_pool_size*: The size used for shared servers (MTS, not recommended) and parallel queries. Parallel execution allocates buffers out of the large pool only when *parallel_automatic_tuning* = true.

- *log_buffer*: The size of the RAM buffer for redo logs

In general, the most variable of these parameters is *db_cache_size*. Because Oracle has an almost insatiable appetite for RAM data buffers, most DBAs add additional RAM to the *db_cache_size*.

A Script for Estimating Total PGA RAM

In SQL*Plus, a parameter can be accepted and then it can be referenced inside the query by placing an ampersand (&) in front of the variable name. In the simple example below, declare a variable called *myparm* and direct SQL*Plus to accept this value when the script is executed:

```
set heading off
set echo on

accept myparm number prompt 'Choose a number between 1 and 10: '

select 'You chose the number '||&myparm from dual;
```

The goal is to create a script called *pga_size.sql*. This script will prompt for the high water mark of connected users, and then compute the sum of all PGA RAM to be reserved for dedicated Oracle connections. In this example, there is a two meg overhead for MS Windows PGA sessions.

Here is the finished script:

```
set pages 999;
column pga_size format 999,999,999

accept hwm number prompt 'Enter high-water mark of connected users:'

select
    &hwm*(2048576+a.value+b.value) pga_size
from
    v$parameter a,
    v$parameter b
where
    a.name = 'sort_area_size'
and
    b.name = 'hash_area_size';
```

When the script is run, there is a prompt for the HWM, and Oracle takes care of the math needed to compute the total RAM to reserve for Oracle connections.

```
SQL> @pga_size
```

```
Enter the high-water mark of connected users: 100

old   2:        &hwm*(2048576+a.value+b.value) pga_size
new   2:           100*(2048576+a.value+b.value) pga_size


    PGA_SIZE
 ------------
  362,144,000
```

When sizing the PGA, it is easy to minimize the disk sorts metric using a STATSPACK or AWR report, but there is a need to account for *hash joins*. The more PGA, the higher the propensity for Oracle to choose hash joins. Use a script like this to track *nested loops* vs. *hash joins*, tracking rows processed, disk reads and CPU consumption:

💾 **track_hash_joins.sql**

```
col c1 heading 'Date'               format a20
col c2 heading 'Nested|Loops|Count' format 99,999,999
col c3 heading 'Rows|Processed'     format 99,999,999
col c4 heading 'Disk|Reads'         format 99,999,999
col c5 heading 'CPU|Time'           format 99,999,999



accept nested_thr char prompt 'Enter Nested Join Threshold: '

ttitle 'Nested Join Threshold|&nested_thr'

select
   to_char(sn.begin_interval_time,'yy-mm-dd hh24')  c1,
   count(*)                                          c2,
   sum(st.rows_processed_delta)                      c3,
   sum(st.disk_reads_delta)                          c4,
   sum(st.cpu_time_delta)                            c5
from
   dba_hist_snapshot sn,
   dba_hist_sql_plan  p,
   dba_hist_sqlstat   st
where
   st.sql_id = p.sql_id
and
   sn.snap_id = st.snap_id
and
   sn.dbid = st.dbid
and
   p.operation = 'NESTED LOOPS'
having
   count(*) > &hash_thr
group by
   begin_interval_time;
```

The output below shows the number of total nested loop joins during the snapshot period along with a count of the rows processed and the associated disk I/O. This report can be used to learn if increasing *pga_aggregate_target* will improve performance.

```
             Nested Loop Join Thresholds
```

Date	Nested Loops Count	Rows Processed	Disk Reads	CPU Time
04-10-10 16	22	750	796	4,017,301
04-10-10 17	25	846	6	3,903,560
04-10-10 19	26	751	1,430	4,165,270
04-10-10 20	24	920	3	3,940,002

Optimizing *pga_aggregate_target*

Almost every Oracle professional agrees that the old-fashioned *sort_area_size* and *hash_area_size* parameters imposed a cumbersome one-size-fits-all approach to sorting and hash joins. Different tasks require different RAM areas, and the trick has been to allow enough PGA RAM for sorting and hash joins without having any high-resource task hog all of the PGA, to the exclusion of other users.

Oracle 9i first introduced the *pga_aggregate_target* parameters to fix this resource issue, and by-and-large *pga_aggregate_target* works very well for most systems. Check the overall PGA usage with the *v$pga_target_advice* advisory utility or a STATSPACK or AWR report. High values for multi-pass executions, high disk sorts, or low hash join invocation might indicate a low resource usage for PGA regions.

Prior to Oracle 11g, the *sga_target* and *sga_max_size* parameters were manually set, allowing Oracle to reallocate RAM within the SGA. The PGA was independent, as governed by the *pga_aggregate_target* parameter. Now in Oracle 11g, the *memory_max_target* parameter governs the total maximum RAM for both the PGA and SGA regions and the *memory_target* parameter governs the existing sizes. This allows RAM to be de-allocated from the SGA and transferred to the PGA.

Take a look at the issues surrounding the hidden limits of *pga_aggregate_target*.

Rules for adjusting *pga_aggregate_target*

It is appropriate to consider dynamically changing the *pga_aggregate_target* parameter when any one of the following conditions is true:

1. Whenever the value of the *v$sysstat* statistic "estimated PGA memory for one-pass" exceeds *pga_aggregate_target*, the *pga_aggregate_target* should be increased.

2. Whenever the value of the *v$sysstat* statistic "workarea executions – multipass" is greater than 1 percent, the database may benefit from additional RAM memory.

It is possible to over-allocate PGA memory, and so consider reducing the value of *pga_aggregate_target* whenever the value of the *v$sysstat* row "*workarea executions—optimal*" consistently measures 100 percent.

Hidden Parameters for Oracle PGA Regions

With proper understanding and knowing that these undocumented parameters are not supported by Oracle, the PGA regions can be adjusted to allow for system-specific sorting and hash joins.

- **_pga_max_size**: This hidden parameter defaults to 200 megabytes, regardless of the setting for *pga_aggregate_target*.

- **_smm_px_max_size**: This parameter is used for Oracle parallel query, and defaults to 30% of the *pga_aggregate_target* setting, divided by degree of parallelism as set by a *parallel* hint, *alter table xxx parallel* command, or the *parallel_automatic_tuning* initialization parameter. For example, by default a *degree*= 4 parallel query would have a maximum sort area value of 15 megabytes per session with a 200 megabyte *pga_aggregate_target* setting. Remember, parallel full-table scans bypass the data buffers and store the incoming data rows in the PGA region and not inside the data buffers, as defined by the *db_cache_size* parameter.

The Limits of Sorting and Hashing

There are important limitations of *pga_aggregate_target*:

- The total work area cannot exceed 200 megabytes of RAM because of the default setting for *_pga_max_size*.

- No RAM sort may use more than 5% of *pga_aggregate_target* or *_pga_max_size*, whichever is smaller. This means that no task may use more than 200 megabytes for sorting or hash joins. The algorithm further reduces this to (200/2) for sorts, so the actual limit for pure sorts will be 100 megabytes.

These restrictions were made to ensure that no large sorts or hash joins hog the PGA RAM area, but there are some secrets to optimize the PGA. For example, the following set of parameters may be mutually exclusive:

- **sort_area_size = 1048576 <--:** *sort_area_size* is ignored when *pga_aggregate_target* is set and when *workarea_size_policy* = auto, unless the DBA is using a specialized feature such as the MTS. If dedicated server connections are used, the *sort_area_size* parameter is ignored.

- **pga_aggregate_target = 500m <--:** The maximum default allowed value is 200 megabytes. This limits sorts to 25 megabytes (5% of 500m).

- **mts_servers<>0 <--:** If a multi-threaded server is being used, the *pga_aggregate_target* setting would be ignored in all versions prior to Oracle 10g.

Note: there may be some cases where *sort_area_size* is used in Oracle utilities, but these have not been documented, even with *pga_aggregate_target*.

Important caveats in PGA management

Do not adjust any hidden parameters without opening a Service Request (SR) and getting the consent and advice of Oracle Technical Support. These are undocumented, hidden parameters you must be willing to accept full responsibility for any issues. Some hidden parameters have no effect when set at session level and you must issue "*alter system*" commands for them to take effect.

These PGA rules do not apply to shared server environments using Oracle Shared Server (formerly known as MTS). However, the vast majority of Oracle shops do not use shared server sessions.

Each process (with one PGA area) may have multiple work areas. For example, a query might perform a parallel full-table scan followed by an ORDER BY sort, having one PGA and two workareas. The *_pga_max_size* controls the PGA size and *_smm_max_size* controls the size for each workarea.

Now that the basics of instance tuning have been presented, it is a good time to take a look at Oracle's new SQL tuning advisor functions.

Before Oracle10g, it was extremely difficult to track index usage and see how SQL statements behaved except when they were in the library cache. With Oracle10g and beyond, it is now possible to track SQL behavior over time and ensure that all SQL is using an optimal execution plan, and Oracle provides the ability to track SQL execution metrics with new *dba_hist* tables, most notably *dba_hist_sqlstat* and *dba_hist_sql_plan*.

It is important to track the relationship between database objects, such as tables, indexes, and the SQL that accesses the objects.

Oracle SQL execution plans for any given statement may change if the system statistics change, dynamic sampling is used, materialized views are created, or indexes are created or dropped.

Sizing your PGA for hash joins

The rules are quite different depending on your release, and you need to focus on the *hash_area_size* OR the *pga_aggregate_target* parameters.

Unfortunately, the Oracle hash join is more memory intensive than a nested loop join. To be faster than a nested loop join, we must set the *hash_area_size* large enough to hold the entire hash table in memory (about 1.6 times the sum of the rows in the table).

If the Oracle hash join overflows the *hash_area_size* memory, the hash join will page into the TEMP tablespace, severely degrading the performance of the hash join. You can use the following script, to dynamically allocate the proper *hash_area_size* for your SQL query in terms of the size of your hash join driving table.

```
select
```

```
    'alter session set hash_area_size='||trunc(sum(bytes)*1.6)||';'
from
   dba_segments
where
   segment_name = upper('&1');

spool off;

@run_hash
```

Here is the output from this script with the suggested hash area size calculation for the driving table. As you see, we pass the driving table name, and the script generates the appropriate alter session command to ensure that we have enough space in *hash_area_size* RAM to hold the driving table.

```
SQL> @hash_area customer

alter session set hash_area_size=3774873;
```

In addition to seeing the *hash_area_size*, we must also be able to adjust the degree of parallelism in cases where we use a full-table scan to access the tables in a hash join.

The 11g full hash join

The new Oracle 11g "*hash join full*" execution plan that uses RAM to create results that use less than 50% of the logical I/O (consistent gets) than a traditional full join.

For more on the 11g *hash join full outer* execution plan, we note that the full outer join was introduced with the SQL99 standard, but due to bugs it was not ready for production usage until Oracle 11g.

The Oracle 11g documentation has these notes on the hash join full outer execution plan, and explains the internal machinations of the full hash join:

> "The optimizer uses hash joins for processing an outer join if the data volume is high enough to make the hash join method efficient or if it is not possible to drive from the outer table to inner table.
>
> The order of tables is determined by the cost. The outer table, including preserved rows, may be used to build the hash table, or it may be used to probe one. . . "

A full outer join retrieves rows from both tables, whether or not they have a matching row, and is used in cases where you want non-matching rows from both tables. There are many ways to formulate a full join, and here is an example using the *with* clause.

In the example below, because we have lots of RAM defined in PGA (more than 5% of *pga_aggregate_target*), the standard full join is replaced by a *hash full join outer* operation:

```
with
  emp
as
(
  select
    'joel' ename,
    40 deptno
  from
    dual
  union all
  select
    'mary' ename,
    50 deptno
  from
    dual
)
select
  e.ename,
  d.dname
from
  emp e
full join
  dept d
using
(
  deptno
);
```

```
ENAM DNAME
---- --------------
JOEL OPERATIONS
MARY
     SALES
     RESEARCH
     ACCOUNTING
```

```
------------------------------------------------------------------------------------
---
| Id  | Operation               | Name     | Rows  | Bytes | Cost (%CPU)| Time
|
------------------------------------------------------------------------------------
---
|   0 | SELECT STATEMENT        |          |    8  |  120  |   8  (13)|
00:00:01 |
|   1 |  VIEW                   | VW_FOJ_0 |    8  |  120  |   8  (13)|
00:00:01 |
|*  2 |   HASH JOIN FULL OUTER  |          |    8  |  176  |   8  (13)|
00:00:01 |
|   3 |    VIEW                 |          |    2  |   18  |   4   (0)|
00:00:01 |
|   4 |     UNION-ALL           |          |       |       |          |
|
|   5 |      FAST DUAL          |          |    1  |       |   2   (0)|
00:00:01 |
|   6 |      FAST DUAL          |          |    1  |       |   2   (0)|
00:00:01 |
|   7 |     TABLE ACCESS FULL   | DEPT     |    4  |   52  |   3   (0)|
00:00:01 |
```

```
-------------------------------------------------------------------------------
---
```

As we have noted, the *hash full outer join* is much faster (and safer!) than in release 10.2 because the optimizer uses a new operation called *hash join full outer* that scans each table only once instead of doing a union of two joins. Here are the results from 10gr2 showing the older *hash join outer* operator.

```
------------------------------------------------------------------------------------
| Id | Operation                  | Name                    | Rows | Bytes | Cost (%CPU)| Time     |
------------------------------------------------------------------------------------
|   0 | SELECT STATEMENT           |                         |    5 |    75 |   13   (24)| 00:00:01 |
|   1 |  TEMP TABLE TRANSFORMATION |                         |      |       |            |          |
|   2 |   LOAD AS SELECT           |                         |      |       |            |          |
|   3 |    UNION-ALL               |                         |      |       |            |          |
|   4 |     FAST DUAL              |                         |    1 |       |    2    (0)| 00:00:01 |
|   5 |     FAST DUAL              |                         |    1 |       |    2    (0)| 00:00:01 |
|   6 |   VIEW                     |                         |    5 |    75 |    9   (12)| 00:00:01 |
|   7 |    UNION-ALL               |                         |      |       |            |          |
|*  8 |     HASH JOIN OUTER        |                         |    2 |    44 |    5   (20)| 00:00:01 |
|   9 |      VIEW                  |                         |    2 |    18 |    2    (0)| 00:00:01 |
|  10 |       TABLE ACCESS FULL    | SYS_TEMP_0FD9D6601_2C2CE3 |    2 |    38 |    2    (0)| 00:00:01 |
|  11 |      TABLE ACCESS FULL     | DEPT                    |    4 |    52 |    2    (0)| 00:00:01 |
|* 12 |     HASH JOIN ANTI         |                         |    3 |    48 |    5   (20)| 00:00:01 |
|  13 |      TABLE ACCESS FULL     | DEPT                    |    4 |    52 |    2    (0)| 00:00:01 |
|  14 |      VIEW                  |                         |    2 |     6 |    2    (0)| 00:00:01 |
|  15 |       TABLE ACCESS FULL    | SYS_TEMP_0FD9D6601_2C2CE3 |    2 |    38 |    2    (0)| 00:00:01 |
------------------------------------------------------------------------------------

   8 - access("E"."DEPTNO"="D"."DEPTNO"(+))
  12 - access("E"."DEPTNO"="D"."DEPTNO")
```

As we noted, Oracle must detect that there is enough PGA RAM to allow the optimizer to invoke the hash join, and it's up to the DBA to monitor PGA to ensure that SQL queries always have enough RAM for these faster internal operations.

For active queries you can use this script to watch the RAM memory consumption of a hash join full operation

📟 **monitor_hash_join_ful_ram.sql**

```
select
   tempseg_size
from
   v$sql_workarea_active;
```

Sizing the PGA for Batch Processing

For certain Oracle applications, the Oracle professional will want to allow individual tasks to exceed the default limits imposed by Oracle. For example, PC-based 64 bit Oracle servers, i.e. one or two CPUs with eight gigabytes of RAM, will often have unused RAM available. For example, a fully cached five-gigabyte database on an eight-gigabyte dedicated Oracle server will have approximately one gigabyte available for the PGA, thereby allowing 20% for the OS and other SGA regions:

- O/S: 1.6 gig
- SGA: 5 gig
- PGA Space: 1 gig
- Total: 8 gig

Assume that the database has a *pga_aggregate_target* setting of one gigabyte and the undocumented parameters are at their default settings. While it is unusual for an online system to require super-sized regions for sorting because the result sets for online screens are normally small, there can be a benefit to having large RAM regions available for the Oracle optimizer.

The Oracle cost-based optimizer will determine whether a hash join would be beneficial over a nested loop join, so making more PGA available for hash joins will not have any detrimental effect since the optimizer will only invoke a super-sized hash join if it is better than a nested loop join. In a system like the example above, the following settings would increase the default sizes for large sorts and hash joins while limiting those for parallel sorts.

- *pga_aggregate_target* = 4g
- *_pga_max_size* = 400m
- *_smm_px_max_size* = 333m

With these hidden parameters set, a significant size increase can be seen for serial sorts and a throttling effect for parallel queries and sorts. To see a reproducible, artificial test case demonstrating sort throttling, Mike Ault has prepared a 230-page artificial test case: *Validation of Sort Sizes in a Linux Oracle10g Database*. However, bear in mind that it is only valid for a specific release of Oracle 10g, on a specific hardware and OS environment when not using any optional features such as the MTS.

A RAM sort or hash join may now have up to the full 200 megabytes, which is 5% of *pga_aggregate_target*, a 400% increase over a one-gigabyte *pga_aggregate_target* setting. With the default settings, only a 200%, or 100-megabyte size increase would be possible.

Parallel queries are now limited to 333 megabytes of RAM, 30% of *pga_aggregate_target* or *_smm_px_max_size*, such that a *degree* = 4 parallel query would have a maximum of 83 megabytes (333 meg/4) per slave, which may actually be less due to internal sizing algorithms that set the memory increments used in setting sort areas. This throttling is to prevent one parallel query from using all the available memory since *_smm_px_max_size* would default to 1.2 gigabytes with the setting for *pga_aggregate_target* at four gigabytes.

Be careful in setting the *pga_aggregate_target* to greater than the available memory, calculate the maximum number of users who would be sorting/hashing and multiply that times the predicted size to get the actual limitations; otherwise, ORA-4030 errors or swapping may occur.

In conclusion, overriding the built-in safeguards of *pga_aggregate_target* can make more efficient use of RAM resources in cases where large RAM regions are available on the database server. When used with care and the blessing of Oracle Technical Support, it can often make sense to override these default values to make better use of expensive RAM resources.

There is also lots of evidence that changing these parameters will have a positive effect on large, batch-oriented Oracle jobs, but the DBA must be careful to fully understand the limitations of the PGA parameters.

A case study RAM hash joins

Oracle author Laurent Schneider notes that overriding the PGA defaults made a large batch processes run more than 8x faster with a *use_hash* hint:

"I set appropriate values for *pga_aggregate_target* and *_pga_max_size*...

```
alter system set pga_aggregate_target=6G;
alter system set "_pga_max_size"=2000000000;
```

...and I gave the query some hints *"norewrite full use_hash ordered"*.

As a result, it boosted my query performance from 12 hours to 1.5 hour."

Ah, if only it were that easy, just change a setting and batch jobs run six times faster. Laurent Schneider goes on to note some perils and reliability issues relating to this parameter and says

"This parameter often leads to an ORA-4030, even when plenty of memory available, for some obscure reasons".

There are other tricks for overcoming the built-in governor for PGA usage. Oracle has a 5% limit for any individual process, and by using parallel DML any single batch job can consume 30% of the PGA without touching any of the undocumented parameters. Oracle author Laurent Schneider noted a more stable solution for his hash join:

"I finally opted for a more maintainable solution.

No more hints, no more undocumented parameter, but parallel processing up to 16 threads on a 4 CPU server.

As discussed in metalink thread 460157.996, a supported way to increase the maximum PGA memory per single SQL query is to increase the degree of parallelism."

While Laurent abandoned the undocumented approach, the promise of eight times faster execution speeds are very tempting. Once you get permission from Oracle Technical Support to set an undocumented parameter, they can work with to resolve errors. While they may not address bugs, they may be able to provide alternatives and workarounds.

Hidden Parameters for Oracle PGA Regions

With proper understanding and clear knowledge that these undocumented parameters are not supported by Oracle, it is possible for the experienced DBA to adjust their PGA regions to allow for system-specific sorting and hash joins.

- **_pga_max_size**: This hidden parameter defaults to 200 megabytes, regardless of the setting for *pga_aggregate_target*.

- **_smm_px_max_size:** This parameter is used for Oracle parallel query and defaults to 30% of the *pga_aggregate_target* setting, divided by degree of parallelism as set by a parallel hint, *alter table xxx parallel* command, or the *parallel_automatic_tuning* initialization parameter. For example, by default a degree=4 *parallel* query would have a maximum sort area value of 15 megabytes per session with a 200 megabyte *pga_aggregate_target* setting. Remember, parallel full-table scans bypass the data buffers and store the incoming data rows in the PGA region and not inside the data buffers as defined by the *db_cache_size* parameter.

Note these additional undocumented parameters:

- *_smm_advice_enabled*: If TRUE, enable *v$pga_advice*.

- *_smm_advice_log_size:* This overwrites default size of the PGA advice workarea history log .

- *_smm_auto_cost_enabled:* If TRUE, use the auto size policy cost functions.

- *_smm_auto_max_io_size:* The maximum IO size (in KB) used by sort/hash-join in auto mode

- *_smm_auto_min_io_size:* The minimum IO size (in KB) used by sort/hash-join in auto mode

- *_smm_bound:* This overwrites memory manager automatically computed bound

- *_smm_control:* This provides controls on the memory manager.

- *_smm_max_size:* This is the maximum work area size in auto mode (serial).

- *_smm_min_size:* The minimum work area size in auto mode

- *_smm_px_max_size:* The maximum work area size in auto mode (global)

- *_smm_trace:* The on/off tracing for SQL memory manager

WARNING!

These are unsupported parameters and should not be used unless someone in the know has opened an SR and tested the behavior on the database first. Plus, there must be someone willing to accept full responsibility for any issues.

Supersizing the PGA

In certain situations, the informed Oracle professional will want to allow individual tasks to exceed the default limits imposed by Oracle. For example, PC based, 64-bit Oracle servers, i.e. one or two CPUs

---

with eight gigabytes of RAM, will often have unused RAM available. A fully-cached five-gigabyte database on an eight-gigabyte dedicated Oracle server will have approximately one gigabyte available for the PGA, therefore allowing 20% for the OS and other SGA regions:

- O/S   1.6 gig
- SGA   5 gig
- PGA Space   1 gig
- Total   8 gig

The system has a *pga_aggregate_target* setting of one gigabyte, and the undocumented parameters are at their default settings.

While it is unusual for an online system to require supersized regions for sorting because the result sets for online screens are normally small, there can be a benefit to having large RAM regions available for the Oracle optimizer.

The Oracle CBO will determine whether a *hash* join would be beneficial over a *nested loop* join, so making more PGA available for *hash* joins will not have any detrimental effect since the optimizer will only invoke a supersized *hash* join if it is better than a *nested loop* join. In a system like the example above, the following settings would increase the default sizes for large sorts and Are these the same or different examples? joins while limiting those for parallel sorts:

- *pga_aggregate_target = 4g*
- *_pga_max_size = 400m*
- *_smm_px_max_size = 333m*

With these hidden parameters set, there is a significant size increase for serial sorts and a throttling effect for parallel queries and sorts. However, bear in mind that it is only valid for a specific release of Oracle 10g, on a specific hardware and OS environment, and not using any optional features such as the MTS.

A RAM sort or *hash* join may now have up to the full 200 megabytes (5% of *pga_aggegate_target*) a 400% increase over a one gigabyte *pga_aggregate_target* setting. With the default settings, only a 200% (100 megabyte size) increase would be possible.

Parallel queries are now limited to 333 megabytes of RAM (30% of *pga_aggegate_target* or *_smm_px_max_size*), such that a degree=4 *parallel* query would have a maximum of 83 megabytes (333 meg/4) per slave which may actually be less due to internal sizing algorithms that set the memory increments used in setting sort areas. This throttling is to prevent one *parallel* query using all available memory since *_smm_px_max_size* would default to 1.2 gigabytes with the setting for *pga_aggregate_target* at four gigabytes.

It is important to be careful when setting the *pga_aggregate_target* to greater than the available memory. Calculate the maximum number of users who would be sorting/hashing and multiply that times the predicted size to get the actual limitations; otherwise, ORA-4030 errors or swapping may occur.

In conclusion, overriding the built-in safeguards of *pga_aggregate_target* can make more efficient use of RAM resources in cases where large RAM regions are available on the database server. When used with care, and with the blessing of Oracle Technical Support, it can often make sense to override these default values to make better use of expensive RAM resources. There is also much evidence that changing these parameters will have a positive effect on large, batch-oriented Oracle jobs. It is important to understand the limitations of the PGA parameters.

Important Caveats in PGA Management

This cannot be stressed enough: do not adjust any hidden parameters without opening a Service Request (SR) and getting the consent and advice of Oracle Technical Support. These are undocumented parameters and anyone willing to work with them must be willing to accept full responsibility for any issues. Some hidden parameters have no effect when set at session level, and *alter system* commands must be issued for them to take effect. These PGA rules do not apply to shared server environments using Oracle Shared Server, formerly known as MTS. However, the vast majority of Oracle shops do not use shared server sessions.

Each process with one PGA area may have multiple work areas. For example, a query might perform a parallel full-table scan followed by an *order by* sort, having one PGA and two workareas. The *_pga_max_size* controls the PGA size and *_smm_max_size* controls the size for each workarea.

Now that the basics of instance tuning have been presented, it is a good time to take a look at Oracle's updated SQL Tuning Advisor functions. Before Oracle 10g, it was extremely difficult to track index usage and see how SQL statements behaved except when they were in the library cache. With Oracle 10g and beyond, it is now possible to track SQL behavior over time and ensure that all SQL is using an optimal execution plan, and Oracle provides the ability to track SQL execution metrics with new *dba_hist* tables, most notably *dba_hist_sqlstat* and *dba_hist_sql_plan*.

It is important to track the relationship between database objects, such as tables, indexes, and the SQL that accesses the objects. Oracle SQL execution plans for any given statement may change if the system statistics change, dynamic sampling is used, materialized views are created, or indexes are created or dropped.

Now that sizing RAM regions for Oracle on Windows is understood, look at how the RAM used by Windows during Oracle activities can be examined.

Monitoring Server Resources in MS Windows

In MS Windows, the performance manager screen can be used to observe the resource consumption of the Oracle Windows server. The performance manager is hidden deep inside the Windows menus, but can be found by following Start > Settings > Control Panel > Administrative Tools > Performance (Figure 14.2):

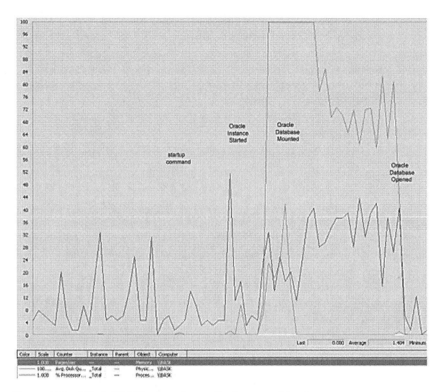

Figure 14.2: *The MS Windows Server Performance Monitor*

The MS Windows performance monitor plots three metrics:

- **CPU:** The percentage of CPU resources consumed.

- **RAM:** The number of RAM pages per seconds used.

- **DISK:** The disk I/O queue length percentage.

Take a closer look at the MS Windows performance monitor. Figure 14.2 is a time-based snapshot of the Oracle database's resource consumption at startup time. These lines form signatures, i.e. known usage patterns that reveal some interesting patterns inside Oracle:

- **RAM usage:** The first spike in the RAM is visible when the SGA is allocated and there ia another short spike in RAM as the database is mounted.

- **DISK usage:** The disk I/O activity peg is seen at the point where the database is mounted. This is because Oracle must touch every data file header to read the system change number (SCN).

- **CPU usage:** The CPU shows that the CPU never goes above 50% during Oracle database startup.

In sum, the allocation of RAM memory for an Oracle server can be done solely with mathematics and no expensive performance monitors are required. The most difficult part of Oracle RAM optimization in any environment is accurately predicting the high water mark of connected user sessions. If there is an unexpected spike of connected sessions, it is possible that a session would exceed the amount of RAM on the server, causing an active program's RAM regions to go out to the swap disk. The goal is to fully allocate RAM without ever experiencing RAM paging.

Now explore the kernel parameters and see how they affect overall performance.

OS Kernel Parameters

Environmental issues have already been addressed in Chapter 12, *Server & Network Tuning*, but the most important OS parameters for Oracle instance tuning will be reiterated. Oracle's OS specific installation instructions provide guidelines for the OS configuration, but the settings for the OS parameters can make an enormous difference in Oracle performance.

Because Oracle runs on over 60 different operating systems from a mainframe to a Macintosh, it is impossible to cover every single platform. However, the common configuration issues for UNIX and Microsoft Windows platforms will be presented.

Server Settings for Windows Servers

Windows servers for Oracle are relatively simple when compared to UNIX-based servers. There are only a few major points to cover to ensure that the Windows server is optimized for an Oracle database. The larger Windows servers, e.g. the UNISYS ES7000 servers, can have up to 32 CPUs and hundreds of gigabytes of RAM. They can support dozens of Oracle instances, but many third party applications can hog server resources, causing Oracle performance issues.

Kernel Setting for UNIX and Linux Servers

In UNIX and Linux, there is much more flexibility in configuration and hundreds of kernel settings that can benefit database performance. Table 14.2 lists some of the most common kernel parameters that influence Oracle:

PARAMETER NAME	DESCRIPTION	DEFAULT VALUE	SET BY THE DBA
shmmax	The maximum size, in bytes, of a single shared memory segment. For best performance, it should be large enough to hold the entire SGA.	1048576	YES
shmmin	The minimum size, in bytes, of a single shared memory segment.	1	YES
shmseg	The maximum number of shared memory segments that can be attached (i.e. used) by a single process.	6	YES
shmmni	This determines how many shared memory segments can be on the system.	100	YES

PARAMETER NAME	DESCRIPTION	DEFAULT VALUE	SET BY THE DBA
shmmns	The amount of shared memory that can be allocated system-wide.	N/A	NO

Table 14.2: *OS Parameters*

For details, the OS-specific Oracle installation guide should be consulted for details. One of the most common problems with Oracle server configuration is suboptimal I/O. For example, the most important thing with Linux is enabling direct I/O on the underlying file system. Without that being enabled, Linux will cache files both in the system buffer cache and in SGA. That double caching is unnecessary and will deprive the server of RAM resources. The following section provides a closer look by outlining some of the important Oracle parameters for performance.

Oracle Parameter Tuning

Oracle has more than 250 initialization parameters, and these parameters govern the overall behavior of the Oracle instance. When set to suboptimal values, Oracle parameters can cause serious performance problems. This is especially true for the parameters that govern the SQL optimizer.

The following is a list of some of the most important parameters for Oracle SQL tuning:

- *optimizer_mode*
- *optimizer_index_cost_adj*
- *optimizer_index_caching*
- *optimizer_percent_parallel*

There are parameters that control the sizes of the SGA regions and the proper configuration and settings for these parameters can have a profound impact on database performance. These parameters include:

- *db_cache_size*
- *db_keep_cache_size*
- *shared_pool_size*
- *pga_aggregate_target*
- *log_buffer*
- *query_rewrite_enabled*
- *cursor_sharing*
- *db_file_multiblock_read_count*
- *hash_multiblock_io_count*

If the Oracle Automatic Shared Memory Management (ASMM) is utilized, Oracle will automatically change the relative sizes of the SGA regions, such as *db_cache_size*, *pga_aggregate_target* and *shared_pool_size*, based on current demands; however, the overall parameters for the instance must be set.

Oracle Hidden Parameters

There are also a number of hidden parameters that greatly impact Oracle performance. For example, a recent Linux world record benchmark used the following hidden Oracle parameters:

- *_in_memory_undo* = false
- *_cursor_cache_frame_bind_memory* = true
- *_db_cache_pre_warm* = false
- *_in_memory_undo* = false
- *_check_block_after_checksum* = false
- *_lm_file_affinity*

Warning!

These are unsupported parameters and they should not be used in production unless a service request has been opened and the parameter's behavior has been tested on a test database.

Oracle will not provide support if any of these values are modified, so DBAs must do careful research in a test database before making any production database changes.

Hidden Latch Parameters

- **_db_block_hash_buckets:** Defaults to two times *db_block_buffers* but should be the nearest prime number to the value of two times *db_block_buffers*.

- **_db_block_hash_latches:** Defaults to 1024, but 32768 is sometimes a better value.

- **_kgl_latch_count:** This defaults to zero and lock contention can often be reduced by resetting this value to 2*CPUs +1.

- **_latch_spin_count:** This parameter shows how often a latch request will be taken.

- **_db_block_write_batch:** Formerly documented, this parameter is now undocumented. It is the number of blocks that the database writers will write in each batch. It defaults to 512 or *db_files*db_file_simultaneous_writes/2 up* to a limit of one-fourth the value of *db_cache_size*.

Oracle Parallel Query Parameters

There are several initialization parameters that pertain to parallel query.
The following are some of the parameters that Oracle sets at install time, based upon the *cpu_count*:

- *fast_start_parallel_rollback*
- *parallel_max_servers*
- *log_buffer*
- *db_block_lru_latches*
- *parallel_automatic_tuning (PAT)*

There are also these parameters that control parallel query function:

- *parallel_adaptive_multi_user*
- *optimizer_percent_parallel*
- *fast_start_parallel_rollback*

Now examine these parameters more closely.

The *parallel_automatic_tuning* Parameter

Oracle Parallel Query (OPQ) is a great way to speed full full-scan operations, but Oracle parallelism can be problematic if it is not implemented properly.

Oracle provides a general method for implementing parallelism with the *parallel_automatic_tuning* = true parameter setting, but there are cases when using PAT can actually degrade Oracle's performance. The Oracle documentation says that *parallel_automatic_tuning* = true will result in optimal parallelism for full-scan operations.

The *parallel_automatic_tuning* parameter feature was created for DSS and Data Warehouse environments using the *all_rows* optimizer mode on servers with many CPU processors to ensure that the common full-table scans are parallelized to an optimal degree. However, *parallel_automatic_tuning* is not always appropriate for OLTP and online systems where setting *parallel_automatic_tuning* may change the SQL optimizer's perception of the costs of full scan operations, causing indexes not to be used.

For non-warehouse environments, I do not recommend setting *parallel_automatic_tuning* or turning on parallel queries at the system or table level. I get the best performance by manually adding the *parallel* hint to query where I want the full scan to be done in parallel.

The *parallel_adaptive_multi_user* Parameter

This defaults to FALSE, and when set to TRUE enables an adaptive algorithm designed to improve performance in multi-user environments that use Parallel Query (PQ). It does this by automatically

---

reducing the requested degree of parallelism based on the current number of active PQ users on the system.

The effective degree of parallelism will be based on the degree of parallelism from the table or hint divided by the total number of PQ users. The algorithm assumes that the degree of parallelism provided has been tuned for optimal performance in a single user environment.

At Oracle OpenWorld 2007, Oracle recommended never to turn on the *parallel_adaptive_multi_user* parameter.

The *optimizer_percent_parallel* Parameter

This specifies the amount of parallelism that the optimizer uses in its cost functions. With the default value of 0 the optimizer chooses the best serial plan. With a value of 100 the optimizer uses each object's degree of parallelism in computing the cost of a full-table scan operation. Low values favor indexes, and high values favor table scans.

Cost-based optimization will always be used for any query that references an object with a nonzero degree of parallelism. For such queries, a *rule* hint or optimizer mode or goal will be ignored. Use of a *first_rows* hint or optimizer mode will override a nonzero setting of *optimizer_percent_parallel*.

The *parallel_min_percent* Parameter

This specifies the minimum percent of threads required for parallel query. Setting this parameter ensures that a parallel query will not be executed sequentially if adequate resources are not available. The default value of 0 means that this parameter is not used.

If too few query slaves are available, an error message is displayed and the query is not executed. Consider the following settings:

- *parellel_min_percent* = 50
- *parallel_min_servers* = 5
- *parallel_max_servers* = 10

In a system with 20 instances up and running, the system would have a maximum of 200 query slaves available. If 190 slaves are already in use and a new user wants to run a query with 40 slaves; for example, degree two instances 20, an error message would be returned because 20 instances, or 50% of 40, are not available.

The *fast_start_parallel_rollback* Parameter

One exciting new area of Oracle parallelism is the ability to invoke parallel rollbacks in cases of system crashes. In those rare cases when an Oracle database crashes, Oracle automatically detects in-flight transactions and rolls them back at startup time. This is called a parallel warmstart, and Oracle uses the *fast_start_parallel_rollback* parameter to govern the degree of parallelism for in-flight transactions based on the *cpu_count*.

Parallel data-manipulation-language (DML) recovery will dramatically speed up the time required to restart the Oracle database after an instance crash. The default value is two times the number of CPUs in the system, but some DBAs recommend setting this value to four times the *cpu_count*.

The *parallel_max_servers* Parameter

One significant enhancement within Oracle is the ability to automate the degree of parallelism for OPQ. Because Oracle is aware of the number of CPUs on the server, Oracle will automatically allocate the appropriate number of slave processes to maximize the response time of the parallel queries. Of course, there are other external factors, such as the use of table partitioning and the layout of the disk I/O subsystem, but setting the *parallel_max_servers* parameter will give Oracle a reasonable idea of the best degree of parallelism for the system based on *cpu_count*.

Because Oracle parallel is heavily dependent on the number of CPUs on the server, the default value for *parallel_max_servers* is set to the number of CPUs on the server. If multiple instances are being run on the same server, this default may be too high, in which case there will be excessive server paging and high CPU utilization. The degree of parallelism is also dependent upon the number of partitions in the target table, so *parallel_max_servers* should be set high enough to allow Oracle to choose the best number of parallel query slaves for each query.

SQL queries and subqueries can be paralleled in *select* statements. The query portions of DDL statements and DML statements, such as *insert, update* and *delete*, can also be paralleled. However, the query portion of a DDL or DML statement cannot be paralleled if it references a remote object. A *select* statement can be paralleled only if the following conditions are satisfied.

If a table has both a parallel hint specification in the query and a parallel declaration in its table specification, the hint specification takes precedence over the parallel declaration specification. Also, note that the parallel hint is used only for operations on a table and the *parallel_index* hint parallels an index range scan of a partitioned index.

Remember, the degree of parallelism (DOP) can be specified within a table or index definition by using one of the following statements: *create table, alter table, create index* or *alter index*.

Hidden Parallel Parameters

The most important of the hidden parallel parameters is the *_parallelism_cost_fudge_factor*. This parameter governs the invocation of OPQ by the cost-based SQL optimizer when *parallel_automatic_tuning* = true. By adjusting this parameter, the threshold for invoking parallel queries can be controlled.

```
NAME                                VALUE
----------------------------------- --------
_parallel_adaptive_max_users        1
_parallel_default_max_instances     1
_parallel_execution_message_align   FALSE
_parallel_fake_class_pct            0
_parallel_load_bal_unit             0
```

```
_parallel_load_balancing          TRUE
_parallel_min_message_pool        64560
_parallel_recovery_stopat         32767
_parallel_server_idle_time        5
_parallel_server_sleep_time       10
_parallel_txn_global              FALSE
_parallelism_cost_fudge_factor    350
```

While the Oracle hidden parameters are wonderful for the high level DBA, all others need to make sure they thoroughly test any changes to hidden parameters before using them in the production environment. The Oracle benchmarks are a great way to see Oracle hidden parameters in action, as hardware vendors often know secrets for optimizing their servers. The following section will examine some Oracle SQL parameters.

SQL Optimizer Parameters

Despite the name Oracle, the Cost Based Optimizer (CBO) is not psychic, and it can never know the exact load on the system in advance. Hence, the Oracle professional must adjust the CBO behavior, and most Oracle professionals adjust the CBO with two parameters: *optimizer_index_cost_adj* and *optimizer_index_caching*.

The parameter named *optimizer_index_cost_adj* controls the CBO's propensity to favor index scans over full-table scans. In a dynamic system, the ideal value for *optimizer_index_cost_adj* may change radically in just a few minutes as the type of SQL and load on the database changes.

SQL Optimizer Undocumented Parameters

These parameters control the internal behavior of the cost-based SQL optimizer.

- *_fast_full_scan_enabled*: This enables or disables fast full index scans if only indexes are required to resolve the queries.

- *_always_star_transformation*: This parameter helps tune data warehouse queries, provided that the warehouse is designed properly.

- *_small_table_threshold*: This sets the size definition of a small table. A small table is automatically pinned into the buffers when queried. In Oracle 9i and beyond, this parameter defaults to two percent.

Data Buffer Cache Hidden Parameters

For the brave DBA, the caching and aging rules within the Oracle *db_cache_size* can be changed. This will modify the way that Oracle keeps data blocks in RAM memory. While modifying these parameters is somewhat dangerous, some savvy DBAs have been able to get more efficient data caching by adjusting these values:

- **_db_aging_cool_count:** Touch count set when buffer cooled.

- **_db_aging_freeze_cr:** Make consistent read buffers always be FALSE; too cold to keep in cache.

- **_db_aging_hot_criteria:** Adjust aging for the touch count which sends a buffer to the head of the replacement list.

- **_db_aging_stay_count:** Adjust aging stay count for touch count.

- **_db_aging_touch_time:** Touch time that sends a buffer to the head of LRU.

- **_db_block_cache_clone:** Always clone data blocks on get, for debugging.

- **_db_block_cache_map:** Map/unmap and track reference counts on blocks, for debugging.

- **_db_block_cache_protect:** Protect database blocks. This is true only when debugging.

- **_db_block_hash_buckets:** Number of database block hash buckets.

- **_db_block_hi_priority_batch_size:** Fraction of writes for high priority reasons.

- **_db_block_max_cr_dba:** Maximum allowed number of CR buffers per DBA.

- **_db_block_max_scan_cnt:** Maximum number of buffers to inspect when looking for free space.

- **_db_block_med_priority_batch_size:** Fraction of writes for medium priority reasons,

Oracle does not support changing the hidden parameters, and any change should be carefully tested prior to being employed in any production database. After this introduction to the importance of setting instance wide parameters, it is time to look at a general approach to Oracle instance tuning.

Instance Wait Event Tuning

The use of the Active Session History (ASH) data collection within Oracle provides a wealth of excellent instance tuning opportunities. The dba_hist_sys_time_model table can be queried to locate aggregate information on where Oracle sessions are spending most of their time.

The v$active_session_history table can be used to view specific events with the highest resource waits.

🖫 **ash__view_events.sql**

```
select
   ash.event,
   sum(ash.wait_time +
   ash.time_waited) ttl_wait_time
from
   v$active_session_history ash
where
   ash.sample_time between sysdate - 60/2880 and sysdate
group by
   ash.event
order by 2;
```

The following is sample output from this script:

```
EVENT                                TTL_WAIT_TIME
------------------------------------ -------------
SQL*Net message from client                    218
db file sequential read                      37080
control file parallel write                 156462
jobq slave wait                            3078166
Queue Monitor Task Wait                    5107697
rdbms ipc message                         44100787
class slave wait                         271136729
```

The v$active_session_history table can be used to view users, and see which users are waiting the most time for database resources:

🖫 ash_session_details.sql

```
col wait_time format 999,999,999
select
   sess.sid,
   sess.username,
   sum(ash.wait_time + ash.time_waited) wait_time
from
   v$active_session_history ash,
   v$session                   sess
where
   ash.sample_time > sysdate-1
and
   ash.session_id = sess.sid
group by
   sess.sid,
   sess.username
order by 3;
```

The following is sample output from this script:

```
SID USERNAME                                  WAIT_TIME
---------- -------------------------------------- ----------
       140 OPUS                                     30,055
       165                                          30,504
       169                                       9,234,463
       167                                      27,089,994
       160                                      34,145,401
       168                                      40,033,486
       152                                      45,162,031
```

```
        159                                      81,921,987
        144 OPUS                                129,249,875
        150 SYS                                 134,263,687
        142                                     163,752,689
        166                                     170,700,889
        149 OPUS                                195,664,013
        163                                     199,860,105
        170                                     383,992,930
```

For a given session, an Oracle user may issue multiple SQL statements and it is the interaction between the SQL and the database that determines the wait conditions. The v$active_session_history table can be joined into the *v$sqlarea* and *dba_users* to quickly see the top SQL waits as well as the impacted user and session with which they are associated:

🖫 **ash_display_sql_wait_time.sql**

```
select
   ash.user_id,
   u.username,
   sqla.sql_text,
   sum(ash.wait_time + ash.time_waited) wait_time
from
   v$active_session_history ash,
   v$sqlarea                sqla,
   dba_users                u
where
   ash.sample_time > sysdate-1
and
   ash.sql_id = sqla.sql_id
and
   ash.user_id = u.user_id
group by
   ash.user_id,
   sqla.sql_text,
   u.username
order by 4;
```

The following is sample output from this script:

```
    USER_ID USERNAME
---------- ------------------------------
SQL_TEXT
--------------------------------------------------------------------------------
 WAIT_TIME
----------
        54 SYSMAN
DECLARE job BINARY_INTEGER := :job; next_date DATE := :mydate;  broken BOOLEAN :
= FALSE; BEGIN EMD_MAINTENANCE.EXECUTE_EM_DBMS_JOB_PROCS(); :mydate := next_date
; IF broken THEN :b := 1; ELSE :b := 0; END IF; END;
         0

        58 DABR
select tbsp       , reads "Reads"        , rps  "Reads / Second"      , atpr    "Avg
 Reads (ms)"      , bpr   "Avg Blks / Read"       , writes  "Writes"       , wps
"Avg Writes / Second"      , waits  "Buffer Waits"        ,  atpwt"Avg Buf Wait (m
```

```
s)" From ( select e.tsname tbsp        , sum (e.phyrds - nvl(b.phyrds,0))
        reads        , Round(sum (e.phyrds - nvl(b.phyrds,0))/awr101.getEla( :
pDbId,:pInstNum,:pBgnSnap,:pEndSnap,'NO' ),3)    rps       , Round(decode( sum(e.p
hyrds - nvl(b.phyrds,0))          , 0, 0       , (sum(e.readtim - nvl
(b.readtim,0)) /          sum(e.phyrds   - nvl(b.phyrds,0)))*10),3)
atpr     , Round(decode( sum(e.phyrds - nvl(b.phyrds,0))          , 0, to_n
umber(NULL)          , sum(e.phyblkrd - nvl(b.phyblkrd,0)) /
sum(e.phyrds   - nvl(b.phyrds,0)) ),3)          bpr     , sum (e.phywrts   - n
vl(b.phywrts,0))          writes     , Round(sum (e.phywrts   - nvl(b.ph
ywrts,0))/awr101.getEla( :pDbId,:pInstNu
        174


        58 DABR
select e.stat_name                "E.STAT_NAME"    , (e.value - b.value
)/1000000      "Time (s)"      , decode( e.stat_name,'DB time'          ,
to_number(null)          , 100*(e.value - b.value)          )/awr101.get
DBTime(:pDbId,:pInstNum,:pBgnSnap,:pEndSnap) "Percent of Total DB Time"   from d
ba_hist_sys_time_model e      , dba_hist_sys_time_model b  where b.snap_id
        = :pBgnSnap     and e.snap_id          = :pEndSnap     and b.dbid
        = :pDbId     and e.dbid          = :pDbId     and b.ins
tance_number      = :pInstNum    and e.instance_number      = :pInstNum    a
nd b.stat_id          = e.stat_id    and e.value - b.value > 0   order by 2
 desc
```

Once the SQL details have been identified, drill down deeper by joining *v$active_session_history* with *dba_objects* and find important information about the interaction between the SQL and specific tables and indexes. What follows is an ASH script that can be used to show the specific events that are causing the highest resource waits. Some contention is not caused by SQL but by faulty network, slow disk, or some other external causes. Also, frequent deadlocks may be caused by improperly indexed foreign keys.

```
select
   obj.object_name,
   obj.object_type,
   ash.event,
   sum(ash.wait_time + ash.time_waited) wait_time
from
   v$active_session_history ash,
   dba_objects            obj
where
   ash.sample_time > sysdate -1
and
   ash.current_obj# = obj.object_id
group by
   obj.object_name,
   obj.object_type,
   ash.event
order by 4 desc;
```

The following is sample output from this script:

OBJECT_NAME	OBJECT_TYPE	EVENT	WAIT_TIME
SCHEDULER$_CLASS	TABLE	rdbms ipc message	199,853,456
USER$	TABLE	rdbms ipc message	33,857,135
USER$	TABLE	control file sequential read	288,266

```
WRI$_ALERT_HISTORY      TABLE       db file sequential read       26,002
OL_SCP_PK               INDEX       db file sequential read       19,638
C_OBJ#                  CLUSTER     db file sequential read       17,966
STATS$SYS_TIME_MODEL    TABLE       db file scattered read        16,085
WRI$_ADV_DEFINITIONS    INDEX       db file sequential read       15,995
```

It is apparent that table *wri$_alert_history* experiences a high wait time on a *db file sequential read* wait event. Based on this fact, the DBA can further investigate causes of such behavior in order to find the primary problem. It could be, for example, a non-optimal SQL query that performs large full-table scans on this table.

Now that it has been shown how ASH information can enlighten DBAs about specific wait events for active sessions, it is time to return to the detailed information on instance-wide tuning and see how to optimize the Oracle data buffer pools.

Tuning the Oracle Data Buffer Pools

Oracle's ability to support multiple blocksizes is a small and misunderstood feature. As a result, the important role that multiple blocksizes play in the reduction of disk I/O was less appreciated than it might have been. For the Oracle administrator, multiple blocksizes are extremely significant and exciting. For the first time, data buffer sizes can be customized to fit the specific needs of the database.

Prior to the introduction of multiple blocksizes, the entire Oracle database had a single blocksize, and this size was determined at the time the database was created. Historically, Oracle 8i allowed tables and index blocks to be segregated into three separate data buffers, but the buffer caches had to be the same size. The KEEP pool stored table blocks that were referenced frequently, the RECYCLE pool held blocks from large-table full-table scans, and the DEFAULT pool contained miscellaneous object blocks.

Oracle opened up a whole new world of disk I/O management with its ability to configure multiple blocksizes. Tablespaces can be defined with blocksizes of 2K, 4K, 8K, 16K, and 32K. These tablespaces can be matched with similar sized tables and indexes, thus minimizing disk I/O and efficiently minimizing wasted space in the data buffers. In Oracle, there are a total of seven separate and distinct data buffers that are used to segregate incoming table and index rows.

Many Oracle professionals still fail to appreciate the benefits of multiple blocksizes and do not understand that the marginal cost of I/O for large blocks is negligible. A 32K block fetch costs only one percent more than a 2K block fetch because 99 percent of the disk I/O is involved with the read-write head and rotational delay in getting to the cylinder and track. It also depends on the file system, since some file systems cannot handle multi-block I/O well.

This is an important concept for Oracle indexes because indexes perform better when stored in large blocksize tablespaces. The indexes perform better because the b-trees may have a lower height and mode entries per index node, resulting in less overall disk overhead with sequential index node access. The exploration of this important new feature begins with a review of data caching in Oracle.

The Problem of Duplicitous RAM Caches

As hardware evolved though the 1990s, independent components of database systems started to employ their own RAM caching tools as shown in Figure 14.3.

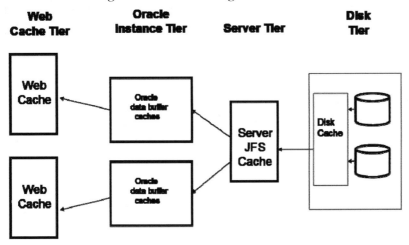

Figure 14.3: *Multiple RAM Caches in an Oracle Enterprise*

In this figure, the Oracle database is not the only component to utilize RAM caching. The disk array employs a RAM cache, the servers have a Journal File System (JFS) RAM cache, and the front-end web server also serves to cache Oracle data. This concept is important because many enterprises may inadvertently double cache Oracle data. Even more problematic are the fake statistics reported by Oracle when multiple level caches are employed:

- **Fake physical I/O times:** If a disk array with a built-in RAM cache is in use, the disk I/O subsystem may acknowledge (ack) a physical write to Oracle, when in reality the data has not yet been written to the physical disk spindle. This false ack can skew timing of disk read/write speeds.

- **Wasted Oracle data buffer RAM:** In a system that employs web servers, the Apache front end may cache frequently used data. Thus, significant Oracle resources may be wasted by caching data blocks that are already cached on the web server tier.

The next step is to take a look at the best way to use SSD in an Oracle environment. First is the examination of the relationship between physical disk I/O (PIO) and Oracle logical I/O (LIO).

Why is Oracle Logical I/O So Slow?

Disk latency is generally measured in milliseconds while RAM access is expressed in nanoseconds. In theory, RAM is four orders of magnitude, 10,000 times, faster than disk; however, this is not true when using Oracle. In practice, logical I/O is seldom more than 1,000 times faster than disk I/O. Most Oracle experts say that logical disk I/O is only 15 times to 100 times faster than a physical disk I/O.

Oracle has internal data protection mechanisms that cause a RAM data block access, a consistent get, to be far slower due to internal locks and latch serialization mechanisms. This overhead is required in order to maintain read consistency and data concurrency.

If Oracle logical I/O is expensive, can this expense be avoided by reading directly from disk? The answer to this question is important to the discussion about the most appropriate placement for SSD in an Oracle environment. There are also issues associated with super large disks. With 144 gigabyte disks becoming commonplace, I/O intensive databases will often see disk latency because many tasks are competing to read blocks on different parts of the super large disk.

An Oracle physical read must read the disk data block and then transfer it into the Oracle RAM buffer before the data is passed to the requesting program as shown in Figure 14.4.

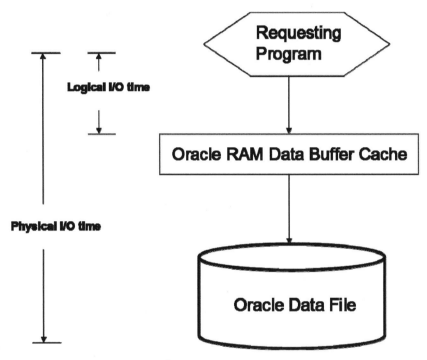

Figure 14.4: Physical *Reads Include Logical* I/O *Latency*

So if it is accepted that LIO expense is going to happen regardless of whether or not a PIO is performed, valuable insight can be gained into the proper placement for SSD in an Oracle environment. In the next section, information will be presented on the KEEP and RECYCLE data buffers and how objects are selected for inclusion.

Data Block Caching in the SGA

When a SQL statement makes a fetch request for a row, Oracle first checks the internal memory to see if the data block that contains the row is already in a data buffer, thereby avoiding unnecessary disk I/O.

Now that very large SGAs are available with 64-bit versions of Oracle, small databases can be entirely cached, and one data RAM buffer can be defined for each database block.

For databases that are too large to be stored in data buffers, Oracle has developed a touch count algorithm to retain the most popular RAM blocks. The touch count algorithm is an approximation of the LRU algorithm. Certain types of uses, like the full-table scan, do not add to the touch count so that blocks keep losing the touch count and the probability of them being replaced increases significantly. Blocks maintain so-called touch count and only blocks with touch counts lower than prescribed by an undocumented parameter are eligible for replacement. While it is not exactly a queue structure, as was the case with the proper LRU method, latch contention is significantly reduced since no LRU queue latches are needed.

When the data buffer does not have enough room to cache the whole database, Oracle utilizes a least recently used algorithm that selects pages to flush from memory. Oracle assigns each block in the data buffer an in-memory control structure, and each incoming data block is placed in the middle of the data buffer. Every time the block is requested, it moves to the front of the buffer list, shifting all other RAM blocks toward the age out area. Data blocks referenced infrequently will eventually reach the end of the data buffer where they will be erased, thereby making room for new data blocks as shown in Figure 14.5.

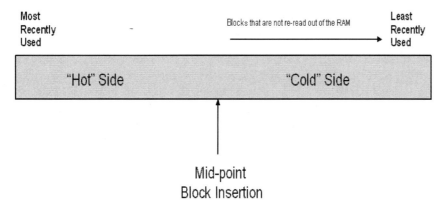

Figure 14.5: Aging Data Blocks From the RAM Block Buffer

Oracle 7 always placed incoming blocks at the most recently used end of the buffer. Beginning with Oracle 8, Oracle provided three separate pools of RAM, the KEEP, RECYCLE, and DEFAULT pools, in the *db_cache_size* region to hold incoming data blocks. With Oracle 8i, Oracle dramatically changed the way data blocks were handled within the buffers by inserting them into the midpoint of the block and dividing the block into HOT and COLD areas.

With Oracle, the highly efficient technique of prioritizing data blocks within the buffers has been combined with the additional flexibility of multiple blocksizes. To view the current database buffer parameters, SQL*Plus can be used to issue the *show parameters buffer* command. A list of parameters from an Oracle 8i database is shown below.

```
SQL> show parameters buffer
```

```
NAME                                TYPE     VALUE
----------------------------------- -------  ----------------------
buffer_pool_keep                    string   500
buffer_pool_recycle                 string
db_block_buffers                    integer  6000
log_archive_buffer_size             integer  64
log_archive_buffers                 integer  4
log_buffer                          integer  2048000
sort_write_buffer_size              integer  32768
sort_write_buffers                  integer  2
use_indirect_data_buffers           boolean  FALSE
```

This output shows the KEEP pool (*buffer_pool_keep*), the RECYCLE pool (*buffer_pool_recycle*) and the DEFAULT pool (*db_cache_size*). The same listing for Oracle 11g is shown below. Note the renaming of *db_block_buffers* to *db_cache_size*.

```
SQL> show parameters buffer
```

```
NAME                                TYPE     VALUE
----------------------------------- -------  ------
buffer_pool_keep                    string
buffer_pool_recycle                 string
db_block_buffers                    integer  0
log_buffer                          integer  524288
use_indirect_data_buffers           boolean  FALSE
```

Full Table Caching in Oracle

The large RAM region within Oracle 8i made it possible to fully cache an entire database. Before Oracle introduced 64-bit versions, the maximum size of the SGA was 1.7 gigabytes on many UNIX platforms. With the introduction of 64-bit addressing, there is no practical limitation on the size of an Oracle SGA, and there are enough data buffers to cache the whole database.

The benefits of full data caching become clear when the savvy DBA recalls that retrieving data from RAM is an order of magnitude faster than reading it from disk. Access time from disks is expressed in milliseconds, while RAM speed is expressed in nanoseconds. In Oracle, RAM cache access is at least 100 times faster than disk access and sometimes as much as 600 times faster.

Also, remember that solid-state disk is a viable alternative to a large data buffer. As of 2009, Sun Microsystems is offering 32 gigabytes in internal SSD technology in almost all of the new Sun servers, and that SSD is especially useful for database application where I/O can be a major bottleneck. Sun notes that their internal SSD consumes one-fifth the power and is a hundred times faster than the magnetic-coated spinning platter disk. They note that SSD is perfect for I/O intensive systems like Oracle applications

If the intention is to fully cache the Oracle database, there must be careful planning. The multiple data buffer pools are not needed, and most DBAs cache all the data blocks in the DEFAULT pool. In general, any database that is less than 20 gigabytes is fully cached, while larger databases still require partial data buffer caches. The following simple command can be issued to calculate the number of allocated data blocks:

```
SQL> select
  2      sum(blocks)
  3  from
  4      dba_data_files;


SUM(BLOCKS)
-----------
     217360

SQL> select
  2      sum(blocks)
  3  from
  4*     dba_extents

SUM(BLOCKS)
-----------
     127723
```

As the database grows, the buffers must be carefully monitored in order to increase the *db_cache_size* to match the database size. Another common approach is to use solid-state disks (RAM-SAN) and use a small data buffer. This technique ensures that all data blocks are cached for reads, but write activity still requires disk I/O. With RAM becoming cheaper each year, the trend of fully caching smaller databases will continue.

Oracle Data Buffer Metrics

The data buffer hit ratio (DBHR) measures the propensity for a data block to be cached in the buffer pool. The goal is to keep as many of the frequently used Oracle blocks in buffer memory as possible. However, this goal is clouded by the use of SSD and the on-board RAM caches of the newer disk arrays. Oracle may appear to be performing a disk I/O, when in reality the data block is already in RAM on the disk subsystem cache. Hence, the DBHR has become a largely meaningless number except in cases of predicting changes in system processing patterns and the initial sizing of the *db_cache_size*.

As the hit ratio approaches 100 percent, more data blocks are found in memory which normally results in fewer I/Os and faster overall database performance. On the other hand, if the DBHR falls below 50 percent, fewer data blocks are resident in memory which requires Oracle to perform additional, often expensive disk I/O to move the data blocks into the data buffer. The formula for calculating the DBHR in Oracle 8 is:

```
1 - (Physical Reads - Physical Reads Direct)
--------------------------------------------
           (session logical reads)
```

The formula for calculating the hit ratio in Oracle 7 and Oracle 8 does not include direct block reads. Direct block reads became a separate statistic in Oracle 8i.

The hit ratio for Oracle 8i can be gathered from the *v$* views, as shown below. However, this particular value is not very useful because it shows the total buffer hit ratio since the beginning of the instance.

```
select
    1 - ((a.value - (b.value))/d.value) "Cache Hit Ratio"
from
    v$sysstat a,
    v$sysstat b,
    v$sysstat d
where
    a.name='physical reads'
and
    b.name='physical reads direct'
and
    d.name='session logical reads';
```

Many novice DBAs make the mistake of using the DBHR from the *v$* views. The *v$buffer_pool_statistics* view does contain the accumulated values for data buffer pool usage, but computing the DBHR from the *v$* tables only provides the average since the database was started.

The next section explains how the AWR can provide a wealth of information for tracking buffer pool utilization and computing the data buffer hit ratio.

Using AWR for Buffer Pool Statistics

AWR uses the *dba_hist$buffer_pool_statistics* table for monitoring buffer pool statistics. This table contains the following useful columns:

- **name:** Shows the name of the data buffer; KEEP, RECYCLE, or DEFAULT

- **free_buffer_wait:** A count of the number of waits on free buffers.

- **buffer_busy_wait:** The number of times a requested block was in the data buffer but was unavailable because of a conflict.

- **db_block_gets:** The number of database block gets which are either logical or physical.

- **consistent_gets:** The number of logical reads.

- **physical_reads:** The number of disk block fetch requests issued by Oracle - not always a real read because of disk array caching.

- **physical_writes:** The number of physical disk write requests from Oracle. If there is a disk array, the actual writes are performed asynchronously.

These AWR columns provide information that can be used to measure several important metrics including the most important, the DBHR.

Data Buffer Monitoring with STATSPACK and AWR

There are two ways to use the AWR to compute the DBHR. In Oracle, there is the *dba_hist_buffer_pool_stat* table. In Oracle 9i and Oracle 8i, the *stats$buffer_pool_statistics* table can be used, and for Oracle 8.0, the *stats$sesstat* table should be used.

The *rpt_bhr_all.sql* script listed below is used for Oracle 8.1 and beyond:

💾 rpt_bhr_all.sql

```
column bhr format 9.99
column mydate heading 'yr.  mo dy Hr.'

select
   to_char(snap_time,'yyyy-mm-dd HH24')        mydate,
   new.name                                    buffer_pool_name,
   (((new.consistent_gets-old.consistent_gets)+
   (new.db_block_gets-old.db_block_gets))-
   (new.physical_reads-old.physical_reads))
   /
   ((new.consistent_gets-old.consistent_gets)+
   (new.db_block_gets-old.db_block_gets))     bhr
from
   dba_hist_buffer_pool_stat old,
   dba_hist_buffer_pool_statnew,
   dba_hist_sgasn
where
   (((new.consistent_gets-old.consistent_gets)+
   (new.db_block_gets-old.db_block_gets))-
   (new.physical_reads-old.physical_reads))
   /
   ((new.consistent_gets-old.consistent_gets)+
   (new.db_block_gets-old.db_block_gets)) < .90
and
   new.name = old.name
and
   new.snap_id = sn.snap_id
and
   old.snap_id = sn.snap_id-1
;
```

The following is a similar method using the AWR tables:

💾 rpt_bhr_all_awr.sql

```
column bhr format 9.99
column mydate heading 'yr.  mo dy Hr.'

select
   to_char(end_interval_time,'yyyy-mm-dd HH24')        mydate,
   new.name                                            buffer_pool_name,
   (((new.consistent_gets-old.consistent_gets)+
   (new.db_block_gets-old.db_block_gets))-
   (new.physical_reads-old.physical_reads))
   /
   ((new.consistent_gets-old.consistent_gets)+
   (new.db_block_gets-old.db_block_gets))     bhr
from
   dba_hist_buffer_pool_stat old,
   dba_hist_buffer_pool_stat new,
   dba_hist_snapshot sn
where
   (((new.consistent_gets-old.consistent_gets)+
   (new.db_block_gets-old.db_block_gets))-
   (new.physical_reads-old.physical_reads))
   /
```

```
   ((new.consistent_gets-old.consistent_gets)+
   (new.db_block_gets-old.db_block_gets)) < .90
and
   new.name = old.name
and
   new.snap_id = sn.snap_id
and
   old.snap_id = sn.snap_id-1
;
```

Sample output from this script is shown below:

```
yr.  mo dy Hr     BUFFER_POOL_NAME       BHR
-------------     --------------------   -
2001-12-12 15     DEFAULT                .92
2001-12-12 15     KEEP                   .99
2001-12-12 15     RECYCLE                .75

2001-12-12 16     DEFAULT                .94
2001-12-12 16     KEEP                   .99
2001-12-12 16     RECYCLE                .65
```

This script provides the DBHR for each of the buffer pools at one-hour intervals. It is important that the KEEP pool always has a 99-100 percent DBHR. If this is not the case, data blocks should be added to the KEEP pool to make it the same size as the sum of all object data blocks that are assigned to the KEEP pool. It is easy to size the KEEP pool, and the DBA should add up all of the data blocks that are assigned, such as BUFFER-POOL=KEEP, adding a 20% overhead in case of growth.

 The Data Buffer Hit ratio may be meaningless for Data Warehouse and Decision Support systems that perform frequent large-table full-table scans or any database with all_rows optimization.

This DBHR is also of little value in databases that perform parallel large-table full-table scans which bypass the data buffer, storing the retrieved rows in their PGA region.

In practice, it is obvious that the variation in the DBHR will increase with the frequency of measured intervals, such as the snapshot collection interval. For example, the AWR may report a DBHR of 92% at hourly intervals, but there may be a wide variation in DBHR values when the ratio is sampled in two-minute intervals, as shown in Figure 14.6.

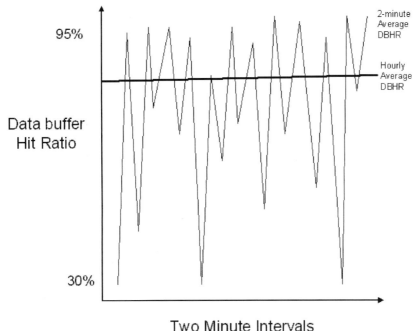

Figure 14.6: *Sampling the DBHR Over Two-minute Intervals*

This variation can be illustrated with a simple example. In this case, a database instance is started, and the first ten tasks read ten separate blocks. At this point, the DBHR is zero because all the requested blocks had to be retrieved via a physical disk I/O. Also, the Oracle 10g Automatic Memory Manager (AMM) will continuously change the sizes of the data buffer pools to accommodate existing processing needs.

In general, data warehouses will have lower buffer hit ratios because they are exposed to large-table full-table scans, while Online Transaction Processing (OLTP) databases will have higher buffer hit ratios because the indexes used most frequently are cached in the data buffer.

A good guiding principle for the Oracle DBA is that as much RAM as possible should be allocated to the data buffers without causing the server to page-in RAM.

Oracle's Seven Data Buffer Hit Ratios

The DBHR is a common metric used by Oracle tuning experts to measure the propensity of a row to be in the data buffer. For example, a hit ratio of 95 percent means that 95 percent of row requests were already present in the data buffer, thereby avoiding an expensive disk I/O. In general, as the size of the data buffers increases, the DBHR will also increase and approach 100 percent.

Oracle has a separate DBHR for all seven data buffer caches. For optimum performance, the Oracle DBA might consider a manual approach, such as turning off AMM, and monitor all seven data buffers

---

and adjust their sizes based on each DBHR. Oracle provides the exciting feature of allowing the number of RAM buffers within any of the data buffer caches to be changed dynamically.

This is done through *alter system* commands that allow the size of the buffers to be changed while Oracle remains available. This means that performance can be maximized in response to current statistics by manually de-allocating RAM from one data buffer and shifting it to another buffer cache.

The general rule is that the more data that can be retrieved from a single I/O, the better the overall hit ratio. However, it is important to delve a little deeper to get a more complete understanding of how multiple data buffers operate.

Allocating Oracle Data Buffer Caches

It is imperative to know how multiple data buffers actually work. As an example, the following buffer cache allocations might be defined in the initialization parameters.

- **db_block_size** = 32768: The system-wide default block size

- **db_cache_size** = 3G: Allocates a total of 3 gigabytes for all of the 32K data buffers

- **db_keep_cache_size** = 1G: Use 1 gigabyte for the KEEP pool

- **db_recycle_cache_size** = 500M: 500 meg for the RECYCLE pool

Hence, the DEFAULT pool is 1,500 meg. The caches below are all additional RAM memory (total=3.1 gig) that are above and beyond the allocation from db_cache_size:

- **db_2k_cache_size** = 200M: This cache is reserved for random block retrieval on tables that have small rows.

- **db_4k_cache_size** = 500M: This 4K buffer will be reserved exclusively for tables with a small average row length and random access.

- **db_8k_cache_size** = 800M: This is a separate cache for segregating I/O for specific tables.

- **db_16k_cache_size** = 1600M: This is a separate cache for segregating I/O for specific tables.

What is the total RAM allocated to the data buffer caches in the example above? The total RAM is the sum of all the named buffer caches plus *db_cache_size*. Hence, the total RAM in the example is 6,100 megabytes, or 6.1 gigabytes.

Before Oracle 9i, these were subsets of the DEFAULT pool, and the *db_keep_cache_size* and *db_recycle_cache_size* are subtracted from the *db_cache_size*. After subtracting the allocation for the KEEP and RECYCLE pools, the DEFAULT pool in the example is 1.5 gigabytes. Of course, the total size must be less than the value of *sga_max_size*. In Oracle 9i and beyond, the KEEP and RECYCLE became separate RAM areas.

At this point, the basic concepts behind the data buffers should be a little clearer, so it is an appropriate time to go deeper into the internals and see how AWR data can allow the monitoring and self-tuning of the data buffers. Remember, AMM is reactive and only changes the pool sizes after performance has degraded.   By identifying trends in buffer utilization, the *dbms_scheduler* package can be used to anticipate and self-tune the data buffers, thereby supplementing and improving AMM.

Viewing Information about SGA Performance

The following views provide information about the SGA components and their dynamic resizing:

VIEW	DESCRIPTION
v$sga	Displays summary information about the system global area (SGA)
v$sgainfo	Displays size information about the SGA, including the sizes of different SGA components, the granule size, and free memory
v$sgastat	Displays detailed information about the SGA
v$sga_dynamic_components	Displays information about the dynamic SGA components. This view summarizes information based on all completed SGA resize operations since instance startup.
v$sga_dynamic_free_memory	Displays information about the amount of SGA memory available for future dynamic SGA resize operations
v$sga_resize_ops	Displays information about the last 100 completed SGA resize operations
v$sga_current_resize_ops	Displays information about SGA resize operations which are currently in progress.

Table 14.3: *Oracle V$ Performance Views*

Determining the optimal size for the data buffers is a critical task for very large databases. It is economically prohibitive to cache an entire database in RAM as databases grow ever larger, perhaps reaching sizes in the hundreds of billions of bytes.

The difficulty Oracle professionals face is finding the point of diminishing marginal returns as additional RAM resources are allocated to the database. Successfully determining the point of diminishing marginal return and effectively optimizing RAM can save a company hundreds of thousands, if not millions, of dollars in RAM expenses.

Among the features that Oracle has automated within AMM is the *v$db_cache_advice* view. This view can help predict the benefit of adding buffers to the data buffer cache. It estimates the miss rate for twenty potential buffer cache sizes, ranging from 10 percent of the current size to 200 percent of the current size. This tool allows the Oracle DBA to accurately predict the optimal size for each RAM data buffer. A few examples will help illustrate the process.

In order to use the new view, RAM memory must be pre-allocated to the data buffers, just as it was in the Oracle 7 *x$kcbcbh* utility. Setting the *init.ora* parameter, *db_cache_advice,* to the value of ON or READY enables the cache advice feature. These values can be set while the database is running by using the *alter system* command, taking advantage of the predictive feature dynamically. However, since the additional RAM buffers must be allocated before the *db_cache_size* can use *v$db_cache_advice,* the DBA may wish to use the utility only once to determine the optimal size.

The *v$db_cache_advice* view is similar to an Oracle 7 utility that also predicted the benefit of adding data buffers. The Oracle 7 utility used the *x$kcbrbh* view to track buffer hits and the *x$kcbcbh* view to track buffer misses. Also, there is no way to get cache advice on Oracle 8 since *db_block_lru_statistics* was made obsolete. The DBHR can provide data similar to *v$db_cache_advice,* and most Oracle tuning professionals use both tools to monitor the effectiveness of data buffers and monitor how AMM adjusts the sizes of the buffer pools.

The following query can be used to perform the cache advice function once the *db_cache_advice* has been enabled and the database has run long enough to give representative results.

🖫 **display_buffer_cache_advice.sql**

```
column c1    heading 'Cache Size (m)'       format 999,999,999,999
column c2    heading 'Buffers'              format 999,999,999
column c3    heading 'Estd Phys|Read Factor' format 999.90
column c4    heading 'Estd Phys| Reads'     format 999,999,999

select
   size_for_estimate        c1,
   buffers_for_estimate     c2,
   estd_physical_read_factor c3,
   estd_physical_reads      c4
from
   v$db_cache_advice
where
   name = 'DEFAULT'
and
   block_size  = (SELECT value FROM V$PARAMETER
                  WHERE name = 'db_block_size')
and
   advice_status = 'ON';
```

The output from the script is shown below. The values range from 10 percent of the current size to double the current size of the *db_cache_size*.

Cache Size (MB)	Buffers	Estd Phys Read Factor	Estd Phys Reads	
30	3,802	18.70	192,317,943	← 10% size
60	7,604	12.83	131,949,536	
91	11,406	7.38	75,865,861	
121	15,208	4.97	51,111,658	

```
152        19,010        3.64     37,460,786
182        22,812        2.50     25,668,196
212        26,614        1.74     17,850,847
243        30,416        1.33     13,720,149
273        34,218        1.13     11,583,180
304        38,020        1.00     10,282,475 Current Size
334        41,822         .93      9,515,878
364        45,624         .87      8,909,026
395        49,426         .83      8,495,039
424        53,228         .79      8,116,496
456        57,030         .76      7,824,764
486        60,832         .74      7,563,180
517        64,634         .71      7,311,729
547        68,436         .69      7,104,280
577        72,238         .67      6,895,122
608        76,040         .66      6,739,731 ← 2x size
```

The output shows neither a peak in total disk I/O nor a marginal trend with additional buffer RAM. This result is typical of a data warehouse database that reads large tables with full-table scans. In this case, there is no specific optimal setting for the *db_cache_size* parameter. Oracle will devour as much data buffer RAM as is fed to it, and disk I/O will continue to decline. However, there is no tangential line that indicates a point of diminishing returns for this application.

This predictive model is the basis for Oracle AMM. When the data from Oracle's buffer caching advisory is plotted, the tradeoff is clearly visible as shown in Figure 14.7.

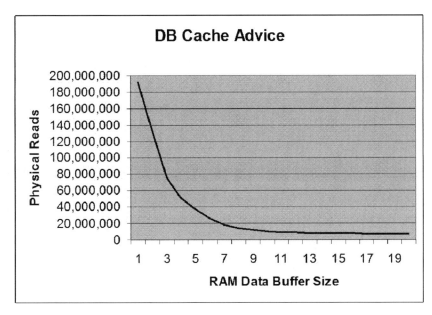

Figure 14.7: A plot from the output of ***v$db_cache_advice***

The *v$db_cache_advice* view is now run dynamically in the *sysaux_xxx* views. It is similar to an Oracle 7 utility that also predicted the benefit of adding data buffers. The Oracle 7 utility used the *x$kcbrbh* view to track buffer hits and the *x$kcbcbh* view to track buffer misses. The DBHR can provide data similar to *v$db_cache_advice*, and most Oracle tuning professionals use both tools to monitor the effectiveness of data buffers.

If the advisory output shows neither a peak in total disk I/O nor a marginal trend with additional buffer RAM, the advisory utility may not apply, and the DBA might consider disabling ASMM. Taking the above into account, Oracle will apply this simple rule: *db_cache_size* should be increased if spare memory is available and marginal gains can be achieved by adding buffers.

The main point of this relationship between RAM buffering and physical reads is that all Oracle databases have data that is accessed with differing popularity. In sum, the larger the working set of frequently referenced data blocks, the greater the benefit from speeding up block access.

The next section provides insight into the internal mechanism of Oracle AMM and how it reacts to changes in buffer demands.

AMM and Oracle Instance Tuning

To fully understand ASMM, look at what happens at a detailed level within the buffers. Figure 14.8 shows that a marginal increase in data buffer blocks is asymptotic to disk I/O. In databases with a very small *db_cache_size*, a large reduction in disk I/O is achieved with a small increase in the size of a small RAM buffer, as shown in the following diagram.

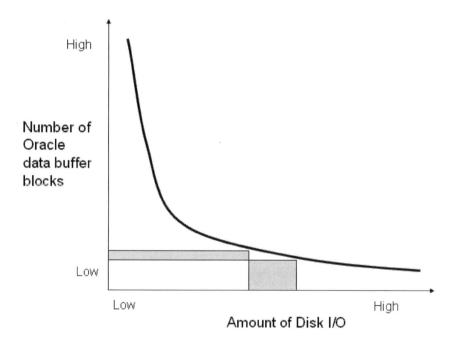

Figure 14.8: *Reduction in Disk I/O From an Increase to RAM Data Buffer*

This shows that a small increase in the size of *db_cache_size* results in a large reduction in actual disk I/O. This happens because the cache is now larger and frequently referenced data blocks can now stay resident in the RAM data buffer. However, the impressive reduction in disk I/O does not continue indefinitely. As the total RAM size begins to approach the database size, the marginal reduction in disk I/O begins to decline as shown in Figure 14.9.

This low marginal cost is due to the fact that all databases have data that is accessed infrequently. Infrequently accessed data does not normally have a bearing on the repeated reads performed by traditional OLTP applications, and this is why there is a marked decline in the marginal benefit as the database approaches full RAM caching.

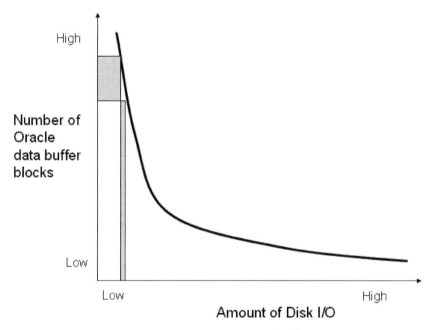

Figure 14.9: *Large Buffers' Changes Result in Small I/O Gains*

As a general guideline, all memory available on the host should be tuned, and the *db_cache_size* should be allocating RAM resources up to the point of diminishing returns, as shown in Figure 14.10.

This is the point where additional buffer blocks do not significantly improve the buffer hit ratio.

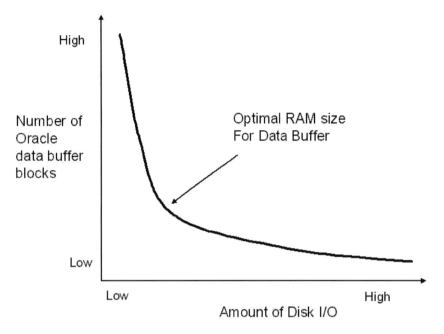

Figure 14.10: *The Optimal Size of the RAM Data Buffer*

Taking the above into account, the thrifty DBA will apply this simple rule: *db_cache_size* should be increased if spare memory is available and marginal gains can be achieved by adding buffers. Of course, increasing the buffer blocks increases the amount of RAM running on the database.

Hence, the database management system may place more demands on the processor than it can handle. The administrator must carefully juggle the amount of available memory with the limitations of the hardware in determining the optimal size of buffer blocks.

In Oracle 9i and earlier, the DBA needed to prepare a strategy for enabling cache advice. Setting the *dba_cache_advice* = on while the database is running will cause Oracle to grab RAM pages from the shared pool RAM area, with potentially disastrous consequences for the objects in the library cache.

For complex databases that can benefit from Oracle's full array of features, the DBA can control not only the size of each data buffer, but also the blocksize of each individual buffer. For example, suppose the database tends to cluster records on a single database block while the other data blocks remain small. Realizing that the I/O for a 32K block is virtually the same as the I/O for a 4K block, the database designer might choose to make some of the buffers larger to minimize I/O contention.

With the cache advice utility, Oracle provides another tool to streamline database performance by predicting the optimal size of the RAM buffer pools. The following sections will plot the average DBHR for an Oracle database over different intervals.

Plotting the Data Buffer Usage by Hour of the Day

The AWR can easily compute the average DBHR by the hour of the day. The *rpt_bhr_awr_hr.sql* script below performs this function. The script references the *stats$buffer_pool_statistics* table. This table contains the values used for computing the DBHR. These values are time specific and are only indicative of conditions at the time of the AWR snapshot. However, a technique that will yield that in an elapsed time measure of the hit ratio is needed.

To convert the values into elapsed time data, the *stats$buffer_pool_statistics* table can be joined against itself, and the original snapshot can be compared with each successive snapshot. Since the desired collection interval is hourly, the script presented below will compute each hourly buffer hit ratio. The hourly DBHR for each day can be derived by selecting the snap_time column with a mask of HH24.

🖫 rpt_bhr_awr_hr.sql

```
set pages 999;

column bhr format 9.99
column mydate heading 'yr.  mo dy Hr.'

select
   to_char(snap_time,'HH24')        mydate,
   avg(
   (((new.consistent_gets-old.consistent_gets)+
   (new.db_block_gets-old.db_block_gets))-
   (new.physical_reads-old.physical_reads))
   /
   ((new.consistent_gets-old.consistent_gets)+
   (new.db_block_gets-old.db_block_gets))
   ) bhr
from
   dba_hist_buffer_pool_stat old,
   dba_hist_buffer_pool_stat new,
   dba_hist_sga              sn
where
   new.name in ('DEFAULT','FAKE VIEW')
and
   new.name = old.name
and
   new.snap_id = sn.snap_id
and
   old.snap_id = sn.snap_id-1
and
   new.consistent_gets > 0
and
   old.consistent_gets > 0
having
   avg(
   (((new.consistent_gets-old.consistent_gets)+
   (new.db_block_gets-old.db_block_gets))-
   (new.physical_reads-old.physical_reads))
   /
   ((new.consistent_gets-old.consistent_gets)+
   (new.db_block_gets-old.db_block_gets))
```

```
    ) < 1
group by
    to_char(snap_time,'HH24');
```

The output from the DBHR hourly average script is shown in Figure 14.11. The report displays the average hit ratio for each day. The report provides insight, but the signature of the database becomes much more obvious if it is plotted. Oracle professionals use the AWR to extract the signatures for all of the important metrics and then plot the metrics to reveal the trend-based patterns. The signatures are typically gathered by hour of the day and day of the week.

Signatures become more evident over longer periods of time. Nevertheless, the plot of this database already presents some interesting trends.

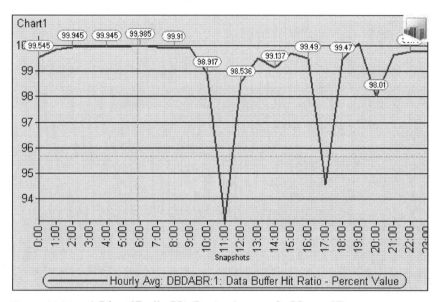

Figure 14.11: *A Plot of Buffer Hit Ratio Averages by Hour of Day*

Once the signature has been visualized, exactly when to take a closer look at the database performance will be known.

Plotting the Data Buffer Hit Ratio by Day of the Week

A similar analysis will yield the average DBHR by day of the week. This is achieved by changing the script *snap_time* format mask from HH24 to DAY.

```
set pages 999;

column bhr format 9.99
column mydate heading 'yr.  mo dy Hr.'

select
```

Oracle Tuning

```
   to_char(end_interval_time,'day')          mydate,
   avg(
   (((new.consistent_gets-old.consistent_gets)+
   (new.db_block_gets-old.db_block_gets))-
   (new.physical_reads-old.physical_reads))
   /
   ((new.consistent_gets-old.consistent_gets)+
   (new.db_block_gets-old.db_block_gets))
   ) bhr
from
   dba_hist_buffer_pool_stat old,
   dba_hist_buffer_pool_stat                  new,
   dba_hist_snapshot sn
where
   new.name in ('DEFAULT','FAKE VIEW')
and
   new.name = old.name
and
   new.snap_id = sn.snap_id
and
   old.snap_id = sn.snap_id-1
and
   new.consistent_gets > 0
and
   old.consistent_gets > 0
having
   avg(
   (((new.consistent_gets-old.consistent_gets)+
   (new.db_block_gets-old.db_block_gets))-
   (new.physical_reads-old.physical_reads))
   /
   ((new.consistent_gets-old.consistent_gets)+
   (new.db_block_gets-old.db_block_gets))
   ) < 1
group by
   to_char(end_interval_time,'day')
;
```

The output from the script is below. The days must be manually re-sequenced because they are given in alphabetical order. This can be done after pasting the output into a spreadsheet for graphing.

```
Day        BHR
---------  -----
friday      .89
monday      .98
saturday    .92
sunday      .91
thursday    .96
tuesday     .93
wednesday   .91
```

The following is another example of output from this script on a different database. The resulting graph is plotted as shown in Figure 14.12. The ION for Oracle tool can be used to run this report on any Oracle database.

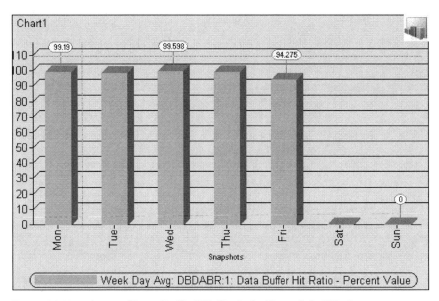

Figure 14.12: *Average Data Buffer Hit Ratio by Day of the Week*

This is all a DBA needs to know to plot and interpret data buffer hit ratios. It is also important to understand the value of trend analysis for indicating pattern signatures. The next step in the learning process is to look at some more AWR scripts for tuning the structure of the SGA, and the place to start is with an exploration of the library cache.

A script similar to the preceding DBHR scripts, applied to the library cache, can reveal deficiencies within the shared pool. The utility takes time-based Oracle tuning information, such as the library cache miss ratio, and stores it within Oracle tables.

Once the DBA is familiar with the structure of the tables and columns within these tables, simple Oracle queries like the following that will display trend-based information can be devised. The trend-based data can then be applied to predictive models that inform of the appropriate times to change the internal structure of the SGA.

```
set lines 80;
set pages 999;

column mydate heading 'Yr.  Mo Dy  Hr.'        format a16
column c1      heading "execs"                  format 9,999,999
column c2      heading "Cache Misses|While Executing" format 9,999,999
column c3      heading "Library Cache|Miss Ratio" format 999.99999

break on mydate skip 2;

select
   to_char(snap_time,'yyyy-mm-dd HH24')  mydate,
   sum(new.pins-old.pins)              c1,
   sum(new.reloads-old.reloads)        c2,
   sum(new.reloads-old.reloads)/
   sum(new.pins-old.pins)              library_cache_miss_ratio
from
   stats$librarycache old,
```

```
   stats$librarycache new,
   stats$snapshot     sn
where
   new.snap_id = sn.snap_id
and
   old.snap_id = new.snap_id-1
and
   old.namespace = new.namespace
group by
   to_char(snap_time,'yyyy-mm-dd HH24');
```

The output below indicates a RAM shortage in the shared pool between 9:00 and 10:00 AM.

```
                       Cache Misses      Library Cache
Yr. Mo Dy  Hr.  execs  While Executing   Miss Ratio
-------------- ------- ---------------   -------------
2001-12-11 10   10,338          6,443          .64
2001-12-12 10  182,477         88,136          .43
2001-12-14 10  190,707        101,832          .56
2001-12-16 10   72,803         45,932          .62
```

The DBA merely needs to schedule additional RAM for the *shared_pool_size* during the deficient period.

From the example above, it is apparent that a high number of library cache misses indicate that the shared pool is too small. To further summarize, a DBHR of less than 90 percent for any of the seven Oracle data buffer pools indicates that memory should be moved from other database regions and reallocated to the data buffer area.

Also, whenever the percentage of optimal executions within the PGA is less than 95, the value of the PGA aggregate target parameter should be increased. The next step is to evaluate those times at which a dynamic reconfiguration of Oracle should be triggered.

Once the basics of buffer block size allocation are understood, time can be spent taking a closer look at the internal mechanisms of the data buffers.

Internals of the Oracle Data Buffers

This section is a little more advanced and provides information about the internal mechanisms of the Oracle data buffers.

Oracle has always had RAM buffers with the goal of preventing expensive data block rereads from disk; however, the way the buffers internally handle the incoming data has evolved radically. Prior to Oracle 8i, an incoming data block was placed at the front of the list in the buffer, and subsequent to the release of Oracle 8i, the incoming block is placed in the middle of the buffer chain. New blocks are inserted into the middle of the buffer and their positions are adjusted according to access activity. This scheme effectively partitions each data buffer into two sections: a hot section that contains the data used most recently and a cold section containing the data used least recently.

This is a tremendous advance over the performance of earlier buffers. The midpoint insertion method essentially creates two subregions within the KEEP, RECYCLE, and DEFAULT pools. Each buffer pool has a hot and cold area, and only the data blocks that are requested repeatedly will migrate into the hot area of each pool. This method greatly improves the efficiency of the data buffers.

The size of the hot regions is internally configured by three hidden parameters:

- _db_percent_hot_default
- _db_percent_hot_keep
- _db_percent_hot_recycle

Oracle Corporation does not recommend changing these parameters. These parameters should only be altered by advanced DBAs who thoroughly understand the internal mechanisms of data buffers and wish to alter the performance of the buffers.

Finding Hot Blocks inside the Oracle Data Buffers

The relative performance of the data buffer pools is shown in Oracle 8i by the internal *x$bh* view. This view shows the following columns:

- **tim:** The tim column governs the amount of time between touches and is related to the new *db_aging_touch_time* parameter.

- **tch:** The tch column gives the number of times a buffer is touched by user accesses. This is the count that directly relates to the promotion of buffers from the cold region into the hot, based on having been touched the number of times specified by the *db_aging_hot_criteria* parameter.

Since the *tch* column gives the number of touches for a specific data block, the hot blocks within the buffer can be displayed with a simple dictionary query like the one shown below:

```
SELECT
    obj      object,
    dbarfil  file#,
    dbablk   block#,
    tch      touches
FROM
    x$bh
WHERE
    tch > 10
ORDER BY
    tch desc;
```

This advanced query is especially useful for tracking objects in the DEFAULT pool. It was pointed out earlier that there should be enough data blocks in the KEEP pool to fully cache the table or index. If hot blocks are found in the DEFAULT pool, they should be moved into the KEEP pool.

The next section presents a technique for viewing the actual objects inside the data buffers and the scripts that will show their contents.

Viewing the Data Buffer Contents

The Oracle *v$bh* view shows the contents of the data buffers as well as the number of blocks for each type of segment in the buffer. This view is primarily useful for indicating the amount of table and index caching in multiple data blocks. Combining the *v$bh* view with *dba_objects* and *dba_segments* provides a block-by-block listing of the data buffer contents and indicates how well the buffers are caching tables and indexes. This is very important in Oracle since the data buffer sizes can be altered dynamically.

There are several data dictionary tricks that can be used when writing a script for mapping data objects to RAM buffers:

- **Duplicate object names:** When joining *dba_objects* to *dba_segments*, the name, type, and owner are all required to distinguish the object sufficiently.

- **Multiple blocksizes:** To show objects in the separate instantiated buffers such as *db_2k_cache_size*, the blocksize for the object must be displayed. This is achieved by computing the blocksize from *dba_segments*, dividing bytes by blocks.

- **Partitions:** With a standard equi-join, every object partition joins to every segment partition for a particular object. Hence, the following qualification is required to handle partitions:

```
and nvl(t1.subobject_name,'*') = nvl(s.partition_name,'*')
```

- **Clusters:** Clusters present a challenge when joining the *v$bh* row with its corresponding database object. Instead of joining the *bh.objd* to *object_id*, it needs to be joined into *data_object_id*.

- **Multiple caches:** There are situations where a particular block may be cached more than once in the buffer cache. This is a mystifying concept, but it is easily overcome by creating the following in-line view:

```
(select distinct objd, file#, block# from v$bh where status != 'free')
```

Many thanks to Randy Cunningham for developing this great script that can be used to watch the data buffers. His *buf_blocks.sql* script, which is listed below, only works with Oracle 9i and beyond.

🖫 buf_blocks.sql

```
set pages 999
set lines 92

ttitle 'Contents of Data Buffers'

drop table t1;

create table t1 as
select
    o.owner          owner,
    o.object_name    object_name,
```

```
     o.subobject_name subobject_name,
     o.object_type      object_type,
     count(distinct file# || block#)          num_blocks
from
     dba_objects   o,
     v$bh          bh
where
     o.data_object_id   = bh.objd
and
     o.owner not in ('SYS','SYSTEM')
and
     bh.status != 'free'
group by
     o.owner,
     o.object_name,
     o.subobject_name,
     o.object_type
order by
     count(distinct file# || block#) desc
;

column c0 heading "Owner"                          format a12
column c1 heading "Object|Name"                    format a30
column c2 heading "Object|Type"                    format a8
column c3 heading "Number of|Blocks in|Buffer|Cache" format 99,999,999
column c4 heading "Percentage|of object|blocks in|Buffer" format 999
column c5 heading "Buffer|Pool"                    format a7
column c6 heading "Block|Size"                     format 99,999

select
     t1.owner                                      c0,
     object_name                                   c1,
     case when object_type = 'TABLE PARTITION' then 'TAB PART'
          when object_type = 'INDEX PARTITION' then 'IDX PART'
          else object_type end c2,
     sum(num_blocks)                               c3,
     (sum(num_blocks)/greatest(sum(blocks), .001))*100 c4,
     buffer_pool                                   c5,
     sum(bytes)/sum(blocks)                        c6
from
     t1,
     dba_segments s
where
     s.segment_name = t1.object_name
and
     s.owner = t1.owner
and
     s.segment_type = t1.object_type
and
     nvl(s.partition_name,'-') = nvl(t1.subobject_name,'-')
group by
     t1.owner,
     object_name,
     object_type,
     buffer_pool
having
     sum(num_blocks) > 10
order by
     sum(num_blocks) desc
;
```

A sample listing from this exciting report is shown next. The report lists the tables and indexes that reside inside the data buffer at the exact moment that the script was executed. This is important information for the Oracle professional who needs to know how many blocks for each object reside in the RAM buffer. To effectively manage the limited RAM resources, the Oracle DBA must be able to know the ramifications of decreasing the size of the data buffer caches.

The following is the report from *buf_blocks.sql* when run against a large Oracle data warehouse.

Contents of Data Buffers

Owner	Object Name	Object Type	Number of Blocks in Buffer Cache	Percentage of object in Buffer Blocks	Buffer Pool	Block Size
DW01	WORKORDER	TAB PART	94,856	6	DEFAULT	8,192
DW01	HOUSE	TAB PART	50,674	7	DEFAULT	16,384
ODSA	WORKORDER	TABLE	28,481	2	DEFAULT	16,384
DW01	SUBSCRIBER	TAB PART	23,237	3	DEFAULT	4,096
ODS	WORKORDER	TABLE	19,926	1	DEFAULT	8,192
DW01	WRKR_ACCT_IDX	INDEX	8,525	5	DEFAULT	16,384
DW01	SUSC_SVCC_IDX	INDEX	8,453	38	KEEP	32,768
DW02	WRKR_DTEN_IDX	IDX PART	6,035	6	KEEP	32,768
DW02	SUSC_SVCC_IDX	INDEX	5,485	25	DEFAULT	16,384
DW02	WRKR_LCDT_IDX	IDX PART	5,149	5	DEFAULT	16,384
DW01	WORKORDER_CODE	TABLE	5,000	0	RECYCLE	32,768
DW01	WRKR_LCDT_IDX	IDX PART	4,929	4	KEEP	32,768
DW02	WOSC_SCDE_IDX	INDEX	4,479	6	KEEP	32,768
DW01	SBSC_ACCT_IDX	INDEX	4,439	8	DEFAULT	32,768
DW02	WRKR_WKTP_IDX	IDX PART	3,825	7	KEEP	32,768
DB_AUDIT	CUSTOMER_AUDIT	TABLE	3,301	99	DEFAULT	4,096
DW01	WRKR_CLSS_IDX	IDX PART	2,984	5	KEEP	32,768
DW01	WRKR_AHWO_IDX	INDEX	2,838	2	DEFAULT	32,768
DW01	WRKR_DTEN_IDX	IDX PART	2,801	5	KEEP	32,768

This is an interesting report because there are three object types: tables, indexes, and partitions. The subsets of the DEFAULT pool for KEEP and RECYCLE are also evident. Also, all indexes are defined in the largest supported blocksize (*db_32k_cache_size*), and multiple buffer pools of 4K, 8K, 16K and 32K sizes are defined.

The output of this script can be somewhat confusing due to the repeated DEFAULT buffer pool name. In earlier releases of Oracle, the KEEP and RECYCLE buffer pools are subsets of *db_cache_size* and can only accommodate objects with the DEFAULT *db_block_size*. In later releases, the KEEP and RECYCLE pools become independent pools.

Conversely, any blocksizes that are not the default *db_block_size*, go into the buffer pool named DEFAULT. The output listing shows that there are really six mutually exclusive and independently sized buffer pools and four of them are called DEFAULT.

Internals of the Oracle Data Buffers

Gathering *v$bh* Status for Multiple Buffer Pools

When using multiple blocksizes, standard *v$bh* scripts would report large amounts of free buffers even when the default pool was full and needed more when the optional areas had free. So here is a first cut at finding the status of the blocks by blocksize in the buffer.

🖫 **all_vbh_status.sql**

```
set pages 50
@title80 'All Buffers Status'
spool rep_out\&&db\all_vbh_status
select
  '32k '||status as status,
  count(*) as num
from
 v$bh
where file# in(
   select file_id
     from dba_data_files
     where tablespace_name in (
       select tablespace_name
         from dba_tablespaces
         where block_size=32768))
group by '32k '||status
union
select
  '16k '||status as status,
   count(*) as num
from
 v$bh
where
  file# in(
   select file_id
     from dba_data_files
     where tablespace_name in (
       select tablespace_name
         from dba_tablespaces
         where block_size=16384))
group by '16k '||status
union
select
  '8k '||status as status,
  count(*) as num
from
 v$bh
where
  file# in(
   select file_id
     from dba_data_files
     where tablespace_name in (
       select tablespace_name
         from dba_tablespaces
         where block_size=8192))
group by '8k '||status
union
select
  '4k '||status as status,
  count(*) as num
from
 v$bh
where
 file# in(
  select file_id
```

```
    from dba_data_files
    where tablespace_name in (
      select tablespace_name
      from dba_tablespaces
      where block_size=4096))
group by '4k '||status
union
select
  '2k '||status as status,
  count(*) as num
from
  v$bh
where
  file# in(
    select file_id
    from dba_data_files
    where tablespace_name in (
      select tablespace_name
      from dba_tablespaces
      where block_size=2048))
group by '2k '||status
union
select
  status,
  count(*) as num
from
  v$bh
where status='free'
group by status
order by 1
/
spool off
ttitle off
```

Here is a sample of the *v$bh* output for a database with multiple blocksizes:

```
STATUS      NUM
---------   ----------
32k cr       1456
32k xcur    30569
8k  cr      32452
8k  free        6
8k  xcur   340742
free        15829
```

It is interesting to run this report repeatedly because the Oracle data buffers are so dynamic. Running the script frequently allows the DBA to view the blocks entering and leaving the data buffer. The midpoint insertion method can be seen in action and the hot and cold regions can be seen as they update.

The *v$segment_statistics* view is a goldmine for funding wait events that are associated with a specific Oracle table. The following script was written to show run-time details about a segment, usually a table or an index. This powerful script interrogates the *v$segment_statistics* view by use of a *case* statement. Examination of the script will yield how the *v$segment_statistics* view is grouped by *object_name*. For each object, counts of the major object wait events are displayed, as seen in the *case* expression. The most important of these object-level wait events will provide clues into the source of the contention.

Internals of the Oracle Data Buffers   **651**

For example, buffer busy waits and ITL waits all have a clear set of causes. Knowing this information is critical to understanding the root cause of the contention.

When reviewing objects for possible tuning issues, it is handy to have statistics such as the number of internal transaction list (ITL) waits, buffer busy waits, and row lock waits that the object has experienced. Combined with the number of logical and physical reads the object has experienced, the above statistics give a complete picture of the usage of the object in question.

The *v$segment_statistics* provides a *statistic_name* and value column for each table. Unfortunately, this format does not lend itself to easy use. By utilizing the crosstab technique, a report can easily be created to show these vital tuning statistics for the system. An example of this type of cross tab report is shown below.

obj_xtab.sql

```
-- Crosstab of object and statistic for an owner
-- by Mike Ault www.oracle-script.com

col "Object" format a20
set numwidth 12
set lines 132
set pages 50
@title132 'Object Wait Statistics'
spool rep_out\&&db\obj_stat_xtab

select * from
(
   select
      DECODE
      (GROUPING(a.object_name), 1, 'All Objects', a.object_name)
   AS "Object",
sum(case when
   a.statistic_name = 'ITL waits'
then
   a.value else null end) "ITL Waits",
sum(case when
   a.statistic_name = 'buffer busy waits'
then
   a.value else null end) "Buffer Busy Waits",
sum(case when
   a.statistic_name = 'row lock waits'
then
   a.value else null end) "Row Lock Waits",
sum(case when
   a.statistic_name = 'physical reads'
then
   a.value else null end) "Physical Reads",
sum(case when
   a.statistic_name = 'logical reads'
then
   a.value else null end) "Logical Reads"
from
   v$segment_statistics a
where
   a.owner like upper('&owner')
group by
   rollup(a.object_name)) b
where (b."ITL Waits">0 or b."Buffer Busy Waits">0)
/
```

```
spool off
clear columns
ttitle off
```

The cross tab report generates a listing showing the statistics of concern as headers across the page rather than listings going down the page and summarizes them by object. This allows the easy comparison of total buffer busy waits to the number of ITL or row lock waits. This ability to compare the ITL and row lock waits to buffer busy waits allows for determination of what objects may be experiencing contention for ITL lists.

It also determines what objects may be experiencing excessive locking activity and through comparisons, which objects are highly contended for without the row lock or ITL waits. An example of the output of the report, edited for length, is shown below.

Object Reads	ITL Waits	Buffer Busy Waits	Row Lock Waits	Physical Reads	Logical
BILLING 410219712	0	63636	38267	1316055	
BILLING_INDX1 21776800	1	16510	55	151085	
...					
DELIVER_INDX1 60809744	1963	36096	32962	1952600	
DELIVER_INDX2 342857488	88	16250	9029	18839481	
DELIVER_PK 416206384	2676	99748	29293	15256214	
...					
All Objects 20947864752	12613	20348859	1253057	1139977207	

In the above report, the *billing_indx1* index has a large amount of buffer busy waits but cannot be accounted for from the ITL or row lock waits. This indicates that the index is being constantly read and the blocks then aged out of memory forcing waits as they are reread for the next process. On the other hand, almost all of the buffer busy waits for the *deliver_indx1* index can be attributed to ITL and row lock waits. In situations where there are large numbers of ITL waits, consider the increase of the *initrans* setting for the table to remove this source of contention.

If the predominant wait is row lock waits, then the DBA needs to determine if the proper use of locking and cursors is being utilized in the application. For example, the *select_for* update type code may be overused. If, on the other hand, all the waits are unaccounted for buffer busy waits, then consideration needs to be given to increasing the amount of database block buffers in the SGA. This object wait cross tab report can be a powerful addition to the tuning arsenal.

The *buf_blocks.sql* script, shown previously in this chapter, is even more important when considering a decrease in a cache size. When an *alter system* command is issued to decrease the cache size, Oracle will grab pages from the least recently used (LRU) end of the buffer. Depending on the amount of RAM removed, an *alter system* command will uncache data blocks that may be needed by upcoming SQL statements.

Internals of the Oracle Data Buffers

Finding the Cause of Buffer Busy Waits

The resolution of buffer busy wait events is one of the most confounding problems with Oracle. In an I/O-bound Oracle system, buffer busy waits are common, as evidenced by any system with read (sequential/scattered) waits in the top 5 waits in the Oracle AWR report, like the following sample AWR report:

```
Top 5 Timed Events
                                                        % Total
  Event                        Waits        Time (s)    Ela Time
  -------------------------    -----------  ----------- -----------
  db file sequential read       2,598        7,146       48.54
  db file scattered read       25,519        3,246       22.04
  library cache load lock         673        1,363        3.26
  CPU time                      2,154          934        7.83
  log file parallel write      19,157          837        5.68
```

Reducing buffer busy waits reduces the total I/O on the system. This can be accomplished by tuning the SQL to access rows with fewer block reads by adding indexes, adjusting the database writer, or adding freelists to tables and indexes. Even if there is a huge *db_cache_size,* there may still be buffer busy waits and, in this case, increasing the buffer size will not help.

Can buffer busy waits be fixed?

The most common remedies for high buffer busy waits include database writer (DBWR) contention tuning, adding freelists, implementing Automatic Segment Storage Management (ASSM, a.k.a bitmap freelists), and, of course, adding a missing index to reduce buffer touches.

The *v$system_event* performance view can also be queried to look at system-wide wait events. Shown here, this view provides the name of the wait event, the total number of waits and timeouts, the total time waited, and the average wait time per event:

```
select *
from
   v$system_event
where
   event like '%wait%';
```

```
EVENT                TOTAL_WAITS TOTAL_TIMEO TIME_WAITED  AVERAGE_WAIT
-------------------- ----------- ----------- ------------ -----------
buffer busy waits       636,528       1,557      549,700   .863591232
write complete waits      1,193           0       14,799   12.4048617
```

```
free buffer waits        1,601          0          622   .388507183
```

The type of buffer causing the wait can be queried using the *v$waitstat* view. This view lists the waits for each buffer type for buffer busy waits, where *count* is the sum of all waits for the class of block, and *time* is the sum of all wait times for that class:

```
select * from v$waitstat;

CLASS                   COUNT       TIME
------------------  ----------  ----------
data block           1,961,113   1,870,278
segment header          34,535     159,082
undo header            233,632      86,239
undo block               1,886       1,706
```

When an Oracle session needs to access a block in the buffer cache, but is unable to because the buffer copy of the data block is locked, a buffer busy wait occurs. This buffer busy wait condition happens for two reasons:

3. Another session has the buffer block locked in a mode that is incompatible with the waiting session's request.

4. The block is being read into the buffer by another session, so the waiting session must wait for the block read to complete.

Unfortunately, there is nothing that can be done until the blocks that are in conflict are identified along with the reasons that the conflicts are occurring since buffer busy waits are due to contention between particular blocks. Therefore, this type of tuning involves identifying and eliminating the cause of the block contention.

The following *v$session_wait* performance view can offer some insight into what is being waited for and why the wait is occurring.

```
SQL> desc v$session_wait

 Name                                      Null?    Type
 ----------------------------------------- -------- -------------------
 SID                                                NUMBER
 SEQ#                                               NUMBER
 EVENT                                              VARCHAR2(64)
 P1TEXT                                             VARCHAR2(64)
 P1                                                 NUMBER
 P1RAW                                              RAW(4)
 P2TEXT                                             VARCHAR2(64)
 P2                                                 NUMBER
 P2RAW                                              RAW(4)
 P3TEXT                                             VARCHAR2(64)
 P3                                                 NUMBER
 P3RAW                                              RAW(4)
 WAIT_TIME                                          NUMBER
 SECONDS_IN_WAIT                                    NUMBER
 STATE                                              VARCHAR2(19)
```

There are three columns of the *v$session_wait* view that are of particular interest for a *buffer busy wait* event:

- **P1:** The absolute file number for the data file involved in the wait

- **P2:** The block number within the data file referenced in P1 that is being waited upon

- **P3:** The reason code describing why the wait is occurring

The following is an Oracle data dictionary query for these values:

```
select
   p1 "File #".
   p2 "Block #",
   p3 "Reason Code"
from
   v$session_wait
where
   event = 'buffer busy waits';
```

The next query should show the name and type of the segment, but only if the output from repeatedly running the above query shows a block or range of blocks is experiencing waits:

```
select
   owner,
   segment_name,
   segment_type
from
   dba_extents
where
   file_id = &P1
and
  &P2 between block_id and block_id + blocks -1;
```

Once the segment is established, the *v$segment_statistics* performance view facilitates real-time monitoring of segment-level statistics. This enables a DBA to recognize performance issues related to individual tables or indexes, as shown below.

```
select
   object_name,
   statistic_name,
   value
from
   V$SEGMENT_STATISTICS
where
   object_name = 'SOURCE$';
```

The sample script output below shows various I/O related statistics against the source$ table:

OBJECT_NAME	STATISTIC_NAME	VALUE
SOURCE$	logical reads	11,216
SOURCE$	buffer busy waits	210
SOURCE$	db block changes	32
SOURCE$	physical reads	10,365
SOURCE$	physical writes	0
SOURCE$	physical reads direct	0
SOURCE$	physical writes direct	0

```
SOURCE$        ITL waits                          0
SOURCE$        row lock waits
```

By using the P1 value from *v$session_wait* to find the file_id, the *dba_data_files* can also be queried to determine the file_name for the file involved in the wait.

```
SQL> desc dba_data_files
```

```
Name                                    Null?    Type
---------------------------------------- -------- ----------------
FILE_NAME                                         VARCHAR2(513)
FILE_ID                                           NUMBER
TABLESPACE_NAME                                   VARCHAR2(30)
BYTES                                             NUMBER
BLOCKS                                            NUMBER
STATUS                                            VARCHAR2(9)
RELATIVE_FNO                                      NUMBER
AUTOEXTENSIBLE                                    VARCHAR2(3)
MAXBYTES                                          NUMBER
MAXBLOCKS                                         NUMBER
INCREMENT_BY                                      NUMBER
USER_BYTES                                        NUMBER
USER_BLOCKS                                       NUMBER
```

In Oracle, the same information can be found through the use of a new ASH view called *v$active_session_history*. This view shows the real time history for various session wait events including buffer busy waits that occurred in the recent past. The following Oracle query can be used as a substitute for all of the above queries:

```
select
   h.p3 "Reason Code",
   h.time_waited "Time Waited",
   o.object_name "Object",
   f.file_name "Datafile",
   h.current_block# "Block Waited"
from
   v$active_session_history h,
   dba_objects o,
   dba_data_files f
where
   h.event = 'buffer busy waits' and
   h.current_obj# = o.object_id and
   h.current_file# = f.file_id and
   h.session_state = 'WAITING';
```

Retrieving the reason code, P3, from the *v$session_wait* or ASH query for a buffer busy wait event will give information as to why the session is waiting. The following table lists the P3 reason codes and their definitions.

CODE	REASON FOR WAIT
-	A modification is happening on a SCUR or XCUR buffer but has not yet completed.
0	The block is being read into the buffer cache.
100	The goal is to NEW the block, but the block is currently being read by another session, most likely for undo.

110	The goal is to have the CURRENT block either shared or exclusive, but the block is being read into cache by another session; therefore, the DBA has to wait until it's read() is completed.
120	The goal is to get the block in current mode, but someone else is currently reading it into the cache. The solution is to wait for the user to complete the read. This occurs during buffer lookup.
130	The block is being read by another session, no other suitable block image was found, so the DBA must wait until the read is completed. This may also occur after a buffer cache assumes deadlock. The kernel cannot get a buffer in a certain amount of time and assumes a deadlock; therefore, it will read the CR version of the block.
200	The goal is to NEW the block, but someone else is using the current copy; therefore, the DBA has to wait for that user to finish.
210	The session wants the block in SCUR or XCUR mode. If this is a buffer exchange or the session is in discrete TX mode, the session waits for the first time and the second time escalates the block as a deadlock, so it does not show up as waiting very long. In this case, the statistic exchange deadlock is incremented, and the CPU for the buffer deadlock wait event is revealed.
220	During buffer lookup for a CURRENT copy of a buffer, the buffer has been found, but someone holds it in an incompatible mode, so the DBA has to wait.
230	The system is trying to get a buffer in CR/CRX mode, but a modification has started on the buffer that has not yet been completed.
231	CR/CRX scan found the CURRENT block, but a modification has started on the buffer that has not yet been completed.

Table 14.2: Reason Codes

To reiterate, buffer busy waits are prevalent in I/O-bound systems with high DML updates. I/O contention is sometimes the result of waiting for access to data blocks and can be caused by multiple Oracle tasks repeatedly reading the same blocks, as when many Oracle sessions scan the same index.

For resolving each type of contention situations, the following rules of thumb may be useful:

- **Undo header contention:** Increase the number of rollback segments.
- **Segment header contention:** Increase the number of *freelists* and use multiple *freelist groups*, which can make a difference even within a single instance.

- **Freelist block contention:** Again, increase the *freelists* value. Also, when using Oracle Parallel Server or Real Application Clusters, the DBA must be certain that each instance has its own *freelist groups*.

- **Data block contention:** Identify and eliminate hot blocks from the application via changing *pctfree* and or *pctused* values to reduce the number of rows per data block. Check for repeatedly scanned indexes. Since each transaction updating a block requires a transaction entry, the DBA might increase the *initrans* value.

Oracle provides the *v$segment_statistics* view to help monitor buffer busy waits, and the *v$system_event* view is provided to identify the specific blocks for the buffer busy wait. The identification and resolution of buffer busy waits can be very complex and confusing. Determining and correcting the causes of buffer busy waits is not an intuitive process, but the results of these efforts can be quite rewarding.

For great scripts to interrogate *v$segment_statistics*, see the scripts in Chapter 15, *Tablespace & Object Tuning*.

The Downside of Mega Data Buffers

The 64-bit Oracle database now allows for far larger SGA regions. Unfortunately, a 32-bit word size can only address 2 to the 32nd power, or about 4 gigabytes of RAM. All 64-bit servers have a larger word size of 2 to the 64th power that allows for up to 18 billion gigabytes. That is 18 exabytes! Hence, many Oracle DBAs are running SGAs larger than 20 gigabytes with most of it dedicated to the data buffer caches.

There are downsides to having a large *db_cache_size*. While direct access to data is done with hashing, there are times when Oracle performance might slow down with a large cache. In these cases, objects may be segregated into a distinct, smaller buffer cache.

- **Objects with high invalidations:** Whenever a program issues a truncate table, uses non-Global temporary tables, or runs a large data purge, Oracle performance might suffer.

- **High update objects:** Tables and indexes that experience high Data Manipulation Lock (DML) activity may perform better if mapped into a separate buffer cache.

- **RAC systems:** Systems using Oracle RAC may experience high cross-instance calls when using a large *db_cache_size* in multiple RAC instances. This inter-instance pinging can cause excessive overhead, and that is why RAC DBAs try to segregate RAC instances to access specific areas of the database.

If a DBA has a system that has any of these characteristics, special operations to reduce the stress on the RAM will need to be performed. In these types of systems, the data buffer caches can be downsized prior to these operations, the buffer can be flushed if Oracle is in use, and then the data buffer region can be resized using a script like the following:

💾 **resize_sga.ksh**

```
#!/bin/ksh
```

```
# First, we must set the environment . . . .
ORACLE_SID=$1
export ORACLE_SID
ORACLE_HOME=`cat /etc/oratab|grep ^$ORACLE_SID:|cut -f2 -d':'`
#ORACLE_HOME=`cat /var/opt/oracle/oratab|grep ^$ORACLE_SID:|cut -f2 -d':'`
export ORACLE_HOME
PATH=$ORACLE_HOME/bin:$PATH
export PATH


# ************************************************************
#
# This will reduce the size of the data buffer
# immediately preceding a large truncate or data purge
#
# ************************************************************


$ORACLE_HOME/bin/sqlplus -s /nologin<<!
connect system/manager as sysdba;
alter system set db_cache_size=10m;
alter system flush buffer_cache;
exit
!


# ************************************************************
# Now we can invoke the specialty task.
# ************************************************************

nohup purge_job.ksh > /tmp/purge.lst 2>&1 &

$ORACLE_HOME/bin/sqlplus -s /nologin<<!
connect system/manager as sysdba;
alter system set db_cache_size=1500m;
exit
!
```

DBAs must remember that the ASMM does not yet analyze detailed workloads. Oracle has provided the KEEP and RECYCLE pools so that intelligence can be added to the database and appropriate objects can be assigned to the right buffer pool. The next section covers the allocation process.

Allocating Oracle Objects into Multiple RAM data Buffers

Since very few Oracle databases can afford the cost of full RAM caching, many rules have been developed for the segregation and isolation of cached objects. Some of these rules of thumb will yield clues about the best way to utilize solid-state disk (SSD) in a solid-state Oracle environment:

- **Segregate large-table full-table scans:** Tables that experience large-table full-table scans will benefit from the largest supported blocksize and should be placed in a tablespace with the largest blocksize.

- **Use the RECYCLE pool:** If the *db_cache_size* is not set to the largest supported blocksize for the server, the *db_recycle_cache_size* parameter should not be used. Instead, use a *db_32k_cache_size* or whatever the maximum size for the system is, and assign all tables that experience frequent large-table full-table scans to the largest buffer cache in the database.

- **Segregate indexes:** In many cases, Oracle SQL statements will retrieve index information via an index range scan, scanning the b-tree or bitmap index for ranges of values that match the SQL search criteria. Hence, it is beneficial to have as much of an index residing in RAM as possible. One of the first things the Oracle 9i DBA should do is to migrate all of their Oracle indexes into a large blocksize tablespace. Indexes will always favor the largest supported blocksize.

- **Segregate random access reads:** For those databases that fetch small rows randomly from the disk, the Oracle DBA can segregate these types of tables into 2K Tablespaces. While disk is becoming cheaper every day, no one wants to waste any available RAM by reading in more information to RAM than is actually going be used by the query. Hence, many Oracle DBAs will use small blocksizes in cases of tiny, random access record retrieval.

- **Segregate Locator Object (LOB) column tables:** For those Oracle tables that contain raw, long raw, or in-line LOBs, moving the table rows to large blocksize will have an extremely beneficial effect on disk I/O. Experienced DBAs will check *dba_tables.avg_row_len* to make sure that the blocksize is larger than the average size. Row chaining will be reduced while at the same time the entire LOB can be read within a single disk I/O, thereby avoiding the additional overhead of having Oracle to go out to read multiple blocks.

- **Segregate large-table full-table scan rows:** When the RECYCLE pool was first introduced in Oracle 8i, the idea was that the full-table scan data blocks, which are not likely to be reread by other transactions, could be quickly flushed through the Oracle SGA, thereby reserving critical RAM for those data blocks which are likely to be reread by another transaction. In Oracle 9i, the RECYCLE pool can be configured to use a smaller blocksize.

- **Check the average row length:** The blocksize for a tables' tablespace should always be greater than the average row length for the dba_tables.avg_row_len table. If the blocksize is smaller than the average row length, rows chaining occurs and excessive disk I/O is incurred.

- **Use large blocks for data sorting:** The TEMP tablespace will benefit from the largest supported blocksize. This allows disk sorting to happen in large blocks with a minimum of disk I/O.

Recent TPC-C benchmarks make it clear that very large RAM regions are a central component in high performance Oracle databases. The 2004 UNISYS Oracle Windows benchmark exceeded 300,000 transactions per minute using a Windows-based 16-CPU server with 115 gigabytes of Oracle data buffer cache. The following are the actual Oracle parameters that were used in the benchmark, and the benefit of large scale RAM caching becomes more evident:

- *db_16k_cache_size* = 15010M

- *db_8k_cache_size* = 1024M

- *db_cache_size* = 8096M

- *db_keep_cache_size* = 78000M

At this point, it should be clear that RAM resources are an important factor in maintaining the performance of I/O-intensive Oracle systems.

Automatically Generate KEEP Syntax

A DBA can easily write a script that automatically identifies candidates for the KEEP pool and generates the syntax to move the tables into the pool. The placement criteria for tables and indexes into the KEEP buffer are straightforward:

- **Frequently accessed tables:** The threshold for access can be adjusted in the script.

- **High buffer residency:** Any table that has more than 80% of its blocks in the data buffer should be cached in the KEEP pool.

The approach to identifying tables for the KEEP pool is simple. All objects that have more than 80% of their data blocks in the buffer should be assigned to the KEEP pool. The following section contains scripts for each of these methods.

Automating the Assignment of KEEP Pool Contents

Another method for identifying tables and indexes for the KEEP pool involves the examination of the current blocks in the data buffer. For the *buf_keep_pool.sql* query, the rules are simple.

5. Use the KEEP pool if the object consumes more than 10% of the total size of the data buffer.

6. Use the KEEP pool if more than 50% of the objects blocks already resides in the data buffer, according to an *x$bh* query.

It is highly unlikely that an undeserving table or index would meet this criterion. Of course, this script would need to be run at numerous times during the day because the buffer contents change very rapidly.

The following script can be run every hour via *dbms_job* and will automate the monitoring of KEEP pool candidates. Every time it finds a candidate, execute the syntax and adjust the total KEEP pool size to accommodate the new object.

💾 buf_keep_pool.sql

```
set pages 999
set lines 92


spool keep_syn.lst

drop table t1;

create table t1 as
select
   o.owner          owner,
   o.object_name    object_name,
   o.subobject_name subobject_name,
   o.object_type    object_type,
   count(distinct file# || block#)        num_blocks
from
   dba_objects   o,
   v$bh          bh
where
   o.data_object_id  = bh.objd
and
   o.owner not in ('SYS','SYSTEM')
and
   bh.status != 'free'
group by
   o.owner,
   o.object_name,
```

```
      o.subobject_name,
      o.object_type
order by
      count(distinct file# || block#) desc
;

select
      'alter '||s.segment_type||' '||t1.owner||'.'||s.segment_name||' storage (buffer_pool
keep);'
from
      t1,
      dba_segments s
where
      s.segment_name = t1.object_name
and
      s.owner = t1.owner
and
      s.segment_type = t1.object_type
and
      nvl(s.partition_name,'-') = nvl(t1.subobject_name,'-')
and
      buffer_pool <> 'KEEP'
and
      object_type in ('TABLE','INDEX')
group by
      s.segment_type,
      t1.owner,
      s.segment_name
having
      (sum(num_blocks)/greatest(sum(blocks), .001))*100 > 80
;


spool off;
```

The following is sample of the output from this script.

```
alter TABLE BOM.BOM_DELETE_SUB_ENTITIES storage (buffer_pool keep);
alter TABLE BOM.BOM_OPERATIONAL_ROUTINGS storage (buffer_pool keep);
alter INDEX BOM.CST_ITEM_COSTS_U1 storage (buffer_pool keep);
alter TABLE APPLSYS.FND_CONCURRENT_PROGRAMS storage (buffer_pool keep);
alter TABLE APPLSYS.FND_CONCURRENT_REQUESTS storage (buffer_pool keep);
alter TABLE GL.GL_JE_BATCHES storage (buffer_pool keep);
alter INDEX GL.GL_JE_BATCHES_U2 storage (buffer_pool keep);
alter TABLE GL.GL_JE_HEADERS storage (buffer_pool keep);
alter TABLE INV.MTL_DEMAND_INTERFACE storage (buffer_pool keep);
alter INDEX INV.MTL_DEMAND_INTERFACE_N10 storage (buffer_pool keep);
alter TABLE INV.MTL_ITEM_CATEGORIES storage (buffer_pool keep);
alter TABLE INV.MTL_ONHAND_QUANTITIES storage (buffer_pool keep);
alter TABLE INV.MTL_SUPPLY_DEMAND_TEMP storage (buffer_pool keep);
alter TABLE PO.PO_REQUISITION_LINES_ALL storage (buffer_pool keep);
alter TABLE AR.RA_CUSTOMER_TRX_ALL storage (buffer_pool keep);
alter TABLE AR.RA_CUSTOMER_TRX_LINES_ALL storage (buffer_pool keep);
alter INDEX WIP.WIP_REQUIREMENT_OPERATIONS_N3 storage (buffer_pool keep);
```

In sum, there are two ways to identify tables and indexes for full caching in the KEEP pool. The first step is to explain all of the SQL in the databases that are looking for small-table full-table scans. Next, the data buffer cache should be examined repeatedly in order to identify any objects that have more than

---

80% of their blocks in RAM. The next section covers how the job is finished and how the KEEP pool can be resized to accommodate the new objects.

Sizing the KEEP Pool

Once the tables and indexes have been loaded into the KEEP buffer pool, the *buffer_pool_keep* parameter must be increased by the total number of blocks in the migrated tables.

The following script will total the number of blocks that the KEEP pool requires, insuring 100 percent data caching. The script adds 20 percent to the total to allow for growth in the cached objects. Run this script frequently to make sure the KEEP pool always has a DBHR of 100 percent.

```
prompt The following will size your init.ora KEEP POOL,
prompt based on Oracle8 KEEP Pool assignment values
prompt

select
'BUFFER_POOL_KEEP = ('||trunc(sum(s.blocks)*1.2)||',2)'
from
   dba_segments s
where
   s.buffer_pool = 'KEEP';
;
```

This script outputs the Oracle parameter that resizes the KEEP pool for the next restart of the Oracle instance. The parameter is placed in the *init.ora* file. Oracle10g deprecates *buffer_pool_keep* and it cannot be modified with an alter system command.

```
buffer_pool_keep=(1456, 3)
```

Now the database can be bounced and the parameter change will take effect.

Advanced KEEP Pool Candidate Identification

The KEEP pool is an excellent storage location for small-table full-table scans. It can also be a good place to store data blocks from frequently used segments that consume a lot of block space in the data buffers. These blocks are usually found within small reference tables that are accessed through an index and do not appear in the full-table scan report.

The *x$bh* internal view is the only window into the internals of the Oracle database buffers. The view contains much detailed information about the internal operations of the data buffer pools. Both the number of objects in a specific type and the number of touches for that object type can be counted in the *x$bh* table. It can even be used to create a snapshot of all the data blocks in the buffer.

The query shown below utilizes the *x$bh* view to identify all the objects that reside in blocks averaging over five touches and occupying over twenty blocks in the cache. It finds tables and indexes that are referenced frequently and are good candidates for inclusion in the KEEP pool.

```
-- You MUST connect as SYS to run this script
connect sys/manager;

set lines 80;
set pages 999;

column avg_touches             format 999
column myname heading 'Name' format a30
column mytype heading 'Type' format a10
column buffers                 format 999,999

SELECT
   object_type  mytype,
   object_name     myname,
   blocks,
   COUNT(1) buffers,
   AVG(tch) avg_touches
FROM
   sys.x$bh     a,
   dba_objects b,
   dba_segments s
WHERE
   a.obj = b.object_id
and
   b.object_name = s.segment_name
and
   b.owner not in ('SYS','SYSTEM')
GROUP BY
   object_name,
   object_type,
   blocks,
   obj
HAVING
   AVG(tch) > 5
AND
   COUNT(1) > 20;
```

The script will only run on Oracle 8i and subsequent versions. This is because the *tch* column was not added until Oracle 8.1.6.

The output from the script is shown next. It identifies the active objects within the data buffers based on the number of data blocks and the number of touches.

Type	Name	BLOCKS	BUFFERS	AVG_TOUCHES
TABLE	PAGE	104	107	44
TABLE	SUBSCRIPTION	192	22	52
INDEX	SEQ_KEY_IDX	40	34	47
TABLE	SEC_SESSIONS	80	172	70
TABLE	SEC_BROWSER_PROPERTIES	80	81	58
TABLE	EC_USER_SESSIONS	96	97	77
INDEX	SYS_C008245	32	29	270

The big decision now is whether the hot objects are to be segregated into the KEEP pool. In general, there should be enough RAM available to store the entire table or index. Using the example, if consideration is given to adding the page table to the KEEP pool, 104 blocks would have to be added to the Oracle *buffer_pool_keep* parameter.

The Downside of Mega Data Buffers

The results from this script will differ every time it is executed because the data buffers are dynamic, and data storage is transient. Some DBAs schedule this script as often as every minute if they need to see exactly what is occurring inside the data buffers.

Automating KEEP Pool Assignment

The Oracle documentation states:

> "A good candidate for a segment to put into the KEEP pool is a segment that is smaller than 10% of the size of the DEFAULT buffer pool and has incurred at least 1% of the total I/Os in the system."

It is easy to locate segments that are less than 10% of the size of their data buffer, but Oracle does not have a mechanism to track I/O at the segment level. To get around this issue, some DBAs place each segment into an isolated tablespace so that the AWR can show the total I/O. However, this is not a practical solution for complex schemas with hundreds of segments.

Since the idea of the KEEP is to fully cache the object, the goal is to locate those objects that are small and experience a disproportional amount of I/O activity. Using this guideline, there are two approaches. Unlike the recommendation from the Oracle documentation, these approaches can be completely automated:

- Cache tables & indexes where the table is small (<50 blocks) and the table experiences frequent full-table scans.

- Cache any objects that consume more than 10% of the size of their data buffer.

The first method that uses *v$sql_plan* to examine all execution plans, searching for small-table full-table scans, is found in *get_keep_pool.sql*. This can automatically generate the KEEP syntax for any small table, with the DBA adjusting the table size threshold, for tables that have many full-table scans.

🖫 **get_keep_pool.sql**

```
select
   'alter table '||p.owner||'.'||p.name||' storage (buffer_pool keep);'
from
   dba_tables    t,
   dba_segments  s,
   dba_hist_sqlstat a,
   (select distinct
      pl.sql_id,
      pl.object_owner owner,
      pl.object_name name
   from
      dba_hist_sql_plan pl
   where
      pl.operation = 'TABLE ACCESS'
      and
      pl.options = 'FULL') p
```

```
where
   a.sql_id = p.sql_id
   and
   t.owner = s.owner
   and
   t.table_name = s.segment_name
   and
   t.table_name = p.name
   and
   t.owner = p.owner
   and
   t.owner not in ('SYS','SYSTEM')
   and
   t.buffer_pool <> 'KEEP'
having
   s.blocks < 50
group by
   p.owner, p.name, t.num_rows, s.blocks
UNION
-- *************************************************************
-- Next, get the index names
-- *************************************************************
select
   'alter index '||owner||'.'||index_name||' storage (buffer_pool keep);'
from
   dba_indexes
where
   owner||'.'||table_name in
(
select
   p.owner||'.'||p.name
from
   dba_tables          t,
   dba_segments        s,
   dba_hist_sqlstat    a,
   (select distinct
     p1.sql_id,
     p1.object_owner owner,
     p1.object_name name
   from
     dba_hist_sql_plan p1
   where
     p1.operation = 'TABLE ACCESS'
     and
     p1.options = 'FULL') p
where
   a.sql_id = p.sql_id
   and
   t.owner = s.owner
   and
   t.table_name = s.segment_name
   and
   t.table_name = p.name
   and
   t.owner = p.owner
   and
   t.owner not in ('SYS','SYSTEM')
   and
   t.buffer_pool <> 'KEEP'
having
   s.blocks < 50
group by
   p.owner, p.name, t.num_rows, s.blocks
)
```

By running this script, the Oracle *v$* views can be used to generate suggestions for the KEEP syntax, based on the number of blocks in the object.

```
alter index DING.PK_BOOK storage (buffer_pool keep);
alter table DING.BOOK storage (buffer_pool keep);
alter table DING.BOOK_AUTHOR storage (buffer_pool keep);
alter table DING.PUBLISHER storage (buffer_pool keep);
alter table DING.SALES storage (buffer_pool keep);
```

Another method for identifying tables and indexes for the KEEP pool examines the current blocks in the data buffer. For this query, the rules are simple. Any object that has more than 80% of its data blocks in the data buffer should probably be fully cached.

It is highly unlikely that an undeserving table or index would meet this criterion. Of course, this script would need to be run numerous times during the day because the buffer contents change very rapidly. The script in *keep_syn.sql* can be run every hour via *dbms_job*, and automates the monitoring of KEEP pool candidates. Every time it finds a candidate, execute the syntax and adjust the total KEEP pool size to accommodate the new object.

🖫 keep_syn.sql

```
set pages 999
set lines 92


spool keep_syn.lst

drop table t1;

create table t1 as
select
    o.owner          owner,
    o.object_name    object_name,
    o.subobject_name subobject_name,
    o.object_type    object_type,
    count(distinct file# || block#)          num_blocks
from
    dba_objects  o,
    v$bh         bh
where
    o.data_object_id  = bh.objd
and
    o.owner not in ('SYS','SYSTEM')
and
    bh.status != 'free'
group by
    o.owner,
    o.object_name,
    o.subobject_name,
    o.object_type
order by
    count(distinct file# || block#) desc
;

select
    'alter '||s.segment_type||' '||t1.owner||'.'||s.segment_name||' storage (buffer_pool
keep);'
from
```

```
   t1,
   dba_segments s
where
   s.segment_name = t1.object_name
and

   s.owner = t1.owner
and
   s.segment_type = t1.object_type
and
   nvl(s.partition_name,'-') = nvl(t1.subobject_name,'-')
and
   buffer_pool <> 'KEEP'
and
   object_type in ('TABLE','INDEX')
group by
   s.segment_type,
   t1.owner,
   s.segment_name
having
   (sum(num_blocks)/greatest(sum(blocks), .001))*100 > 80
;
```

The following is a sample of the output from this script:

```
alter TABLE IS.GL_JE_BATCHES storage (buffer_pool keep);
alter INDEX IS.GL_JE_BATCHES_U2 storage (buffer_pool keep);
alter TABLE IS.GL_JE_HEADERS storage (buffer_pool keep);
```

Once the segments for assignment to the KEEP pool have been identified, the DBA will need to adjust the *db_keep_cache_size* parameter to ensure that it has enough blocks to fully cache all of the segments that are assigned to the pool. Of course, there are many exceptions to this automated approach. For example, these scripts do not handle table partitions and other object types. Hence, these scripts should be used as a framework for a KEEP pool caching strategy and should not be run as-is.

The next section provides information on scripts that can be used to automate the identification of objects for the RECYCLE pool. The identification of candidates for the RECYCLE pool is very similar to the KEEP pool process.

Tuning the RECYCLE Pool

Oracle 8 introduced the RECYCLE pool as a reusable data buffer for transient data blocks. Transient data blocks are blocks that are read as parts of large-table full-table scans and are not likely to be needed again soon. The goal is to use the RECYCLE pool for segregating large tables involved in frequent full-table scans.

To locate these large-table full-table scans, the *plan9i.sql* script which can be obtained from the code depot can be used once again:

```
                 full table scans and counts

OWNER       NAME                    NUM_ROWS C K   BLOCKS  NBR_FTS
---------   --------------------    -------- - -   ------- -----APPLSYS

FND_CONC_RELEASE_DISJS             39 N K       2  98,864
```

APPLSYS	FND_CONC_RELEASE_PERIODS	39 N K	2	98,864
APPLSYS	FND_CONC_RELEASE_STATES	1 N K	2	98,864
SYS	DUAL	N K	2	63,466
APPLSYS	FND_CONC_PP_ACTIONS	7,021 N	1,262	52,036
APPLSYS	FND_CONC_REL_CONJ_MEMBER	0 N K	22	50,174

One table in the listing is a clear candidate for inclusion in the RECYCLE pool. The *fnd_conc_pp_actions* table contains 1,262 blocks and experienced 52,036 full-table scans.

After candidates for the RECYCLE pool have been identified, a script that reads the plan table generated from plan9i.sql can be run. This query will search for large tables of over 10,000 blocks that are subject to full-table scans and are not already in the RECYCLE pool.

Caution!

The prudent DBA should verify that the large-table full-table scan is legitimate before blindly assigning a table to the RECYCLE pool.

Many queries are structured to perform full-table scans on tables, even though far less than 40 percent of the table rows will be referenced. A better-designed query will only perform large-table full-table scans in systems such as data warehouses that require frequent SUM or AVG queries that touch most or all of the table rows.

9i_recycle_syntax.sql

```
set pages 999;
set heading off;
set feedback off;

ttitle off;

spool keep_syntax.sql

-- ************************************************************
-- First, get the table list
-- ************************************************************
select
   'alter table '||p.owner||'.'||p.name||' storage (buffer_pool recycle);'
from
   dba_tables   t,
   dba_segments s,
   v$sqlarea    a,
   (select distinct
     address,
     object_owner owner,
     object_name name
   from
     v$sql_plan
   where
     operation = 'TABLE ACCESS'
     and
     options = 'FULL') p
```

```
where
   a.address = p.address
   and
   t.owner = s.owner
   and
   t.table_name = s.segment_name
   and
   t.table_name = p.name
   and
   t.owner = p.owner
   and
   t.owner not in ('SYS','SYSTEM')
   and
   t.buffer_pool <> 'RECYCLE'
having
   s.blocks > 10000
group by
   p.owner, p.name, t.num_rows, s.blocks
UNION
-- ***********************************************************
-- Next, get the index names
-- ***********************************************************
select
   'alter index '||owner||'.'||index_name||' storage (buffer_pool recycle);'
from
   dba_indexes
where
   owner||'.'||table_name in
(
select
   p.owner||'.'||p.name
from
   dba_tables    t,
   dba_segments s,
   v$sqlarea     a,
   (select distinct
     address,
     object_owner owner,
     object_name name
   from
     v$sql_plan
   where
     operation = 'TABLE ACCESS'
     and
     options = 'FULL') p
where
   a.address = p.address
   and
   t.owner = s.owner
   and
   t.table_name = s.segment_name
   and
   t.table_name = p.name
   and
   t.owner = p.owner
   and
   t.owner not in ('SYS','SYSTEM')
   and
   t.buffer_pool <> 'RECYCLE'
having
   s.blocks > 10000
group by
   p.owner, p.name, t.num_rows, s.blocks
)
;
```

```
spool off;
```

The output from this script is shown below:

```
SQL> @9i_recycle_syntax
```

```
alter table APPLSYS.FND_CONC_PP_ACTIONS storage (buffer_pool recycle);
```

As a general rule, check the SQL source to verify that a full-table query is retrieving over 40 percent of the table rows before adding any table to the RECYCLE pool.

The *x$bh* view can be used as another approach for finding RECYCLE candidates, similar to what was done for the KEEP pool. This topic is addressed in the next section.

Advanced RECYCLE Pool Tuning

The query below uses *x$bh.tch* to identify objects in the buffer cache that are larger than five percent of the total cache and have single touch buffer counts.

A significant amount of cache space is filled with these blocks that have only been used once. They are good candidates for inclusion in the RECYCLE buffer pool. Upon careful examination, DBAs will find that the script below will identify the percentage of an object's block in the buffer.

```
set lines 80;
set pages 999;

column avg_touches format 999
column myname heading 'Name' format a30
column mytype heading 'Type' format a10
column buffers format 999,999

select
   object_type  mytype,
   object_name    myname,
   blocks,
   COUNT(1) buffers,
   100*(COUNT(1)/totsize) pct_cache
from
   sys.x$bh     a,
   dba_objects b,
   dba_segments s,
   (select value totsize from v$parameter
        where name = 'db_cache_size')
where
   a.obj = b.object_id
and
   tch=1  -- This line only works in 8.1.6 and above
and
   b.object_name = s.segment_name
and
   b.owner not in ('SYS','SYSTEM')
group by
   object_type,
   object_name,
   blocks,
   totsize
```

```
having
  100*(COUNT(1)/totsize) > 5
;
```

DBAs must remember that Oracle releases prior to 8.1.6 do not support the reference to the touch (*tch*) column. The report can still be useful with releases prior to 8.1.6, but there is no way of knowing how many times the objects have been touched since their entry into the data pool.

A sample report from this script is shown below. These tables and indexes occupy over five percent of the data buffer space and have only been touched once. This behavior is characteristic of large-table full-table scans.

```
Type      Name                                BLOCKS  BUFFERS PCT_CACHE
--------- ----------------------------------- ------- ------- ---------
INDEX     WIP_REQUIREMENT_OPERATIONS_U1          1042     334      5.57
TABLE     MTL_DEMAND_INTERFACE                    847     818     13.63
TABLE     MTL_SYSTEM_ITEMS                       4227     493      8.22
```

It is important to take into consideration both the number of blocks in the table and how often the table appears in the query output when determining whether or not to add objects to the RECYCLE pool.

Selecting candidates for the RECYCLE pool is an iterative process, just as it is for the KEEP pool. Data buffers are constantly changing, and the DBA may choose to run this script every minute over a period of several hours to get as complete a picture as possible of block activity within the data buffer.

This information covered how to monitor and tune the data buffer pools, so now it is time to return to a more general consideration of large blocksizes and their behavior inside the Oracle data buffers.

Large Blocks and Oracle Instance Caching

When an SQL query retrieves a result set from an Oracle table, it is probably gathering the table rows through an index. Many Oracle tuning experts have recommended that databases created prior to Oracle 10g be redefined with large blocksizes. The performance gains realized from switching a 2K blocksize database to an 8K block size have perplexed many DBAs. Resistance to increasing the blocksize was typically expressed as "Why will moving to a large blocksize improve a database that only randomly fetches small rows?" The answer to this question is not so simple, but it involves indexes.

Many DBAs fail to consider index trees and the index range scan process of sequential retrieval of the index when choosing a blocksize. Nested loop joins usually indicate an index range scan, and the vast majority of rows are accessed using indexes.

Locating indexes in larger size blocks reduces I/O and further improves throughput for the entire database because index range scans gather index nodes sequentially. If this is the case, why not just create the database with large blocksizes and forget about multiple blocksizes?

The answer to this question is also complex. RAM buffer memory cannot be utilized with maximum efficiency unless the tables are segregated according to the distribution of related data between them. In allocating blocksizes, the same general rules can be applied, with some modification in understanding.

Small Blocksize

Tables containing small rows that are accessed randomly should be placed into tablespaces with smaller blocksizes. This way, more of the buffer RAM remains available to store rows from other tables that are referenced frequently.

Larger Blocksize

Larger blocksizes are suitable for indexes, row ordered tables, single-table clusters, and tables with frequent full-table scans. In this way, a single I/O will retrieve many related rows, and future requests for related rows will already be available in the data buffer.

Some objects that may benefit from a larger blocksize, such as 16K or 32K, include:

- Some indexes, such as those that experience index range scans
- Large tables that are the target of full table scans
- Tables with large objects, such as BLOB, CLOB, data
- Tables with large row sizes that might blossom into chained/migrated rows
- Temporary tablespaces used for sorting

The simple goal is to maximize the amount of RAM available to the data buffers by setting the blocksize according to the amount of I/O the table or index sees. Smaller blocksizes are appropriate for randomly accessed small rows while larger blocks are more suitable for rows that are sequentially accessed.

To illustrate, suppose a query retrieves 100 random 80-byte rows from Oracle. Since the rows are randomly accessed, it is safe to assume that no two rows exist on the same block, implying that it is necessary to read 100 blocks to fulfill the task. If the blocks are sized at 16K, the *db_16k_cache_size* buffer will need 16 MB (16K * 100) of RAM. If the blocks are sized at 2K instead, only 2 MB of RAM is needed in the buffer for the 100 I/Os. Using the smaller blocksize would save 14 MB of RAM for this query alone. This is RAM that will be available elsewhere to hold other data.

Maximizing Oracle Block Space Usage

The RAM that is allocated to the data buffers will have to be carefully managed until memory becomes cheap enough to cache the entire database. Properly allocating tables and indexes according to block size is a balancing act. If the data blocks are set too large, valuable buffer space is wasted holding row data that will never be referenced. If the blocks are set too small, Oracle is forced to perform more disk I/O to satisfy a query.

The following are some further general guidelines that can be used for allocating data blocksizes:

- **Segregate large-table full-table scans:** Tables subject to large-table full-table scans will benefit from the largest supported blocksize. They should be placed in a tablespace with the largest blocksize.

- **Set *db_recycle_cache_size* carefully:** If *db_cache_size* is not set to the largest supported blocksize, the *db_recycle_cache_size* parameter should be used. Instead, a *db_32k_cache_size*, or whatever the max size is, should be created, and then assign all tables and indexes subject to large-table full-table scans to the largest data buffer in the database.

The data dictionary will use the default blocksize. Make sure that the dictionary, the SYSTEM tablespace for example, is always fully cached in a data buffer pool. The blocksize, per se, of the dictionary is less important than having enough RAM in the SYSTEM tablespace buffer to fully cache all of the dictionary blocks.

Finding Baselines

Oracle databases are always changing, and the databases that are examined at 10:00 AM may be completely different than the databases that exist at 3:00 PM. Does this mean that a broad brush application of SSD is not valid? When the performance of Oracle disk I/O is examined over different time periods, regular signatures appear when the I/O information is aggregated by hours of the day and day of the week as shown in Figure 14.13.

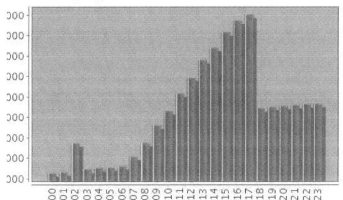

Figure 14.13: *Average Disk Reads by Hour of the Day*

Most Oracle professionals will use Oracle 9i STATSPACK or Oracle AWR information to gather these baselines. Once the repeating I/O trends have been identified, the DBA will be able to apply a broad brush to the use of SSD, placing the fast I/O devices where they will do the most good.

I/O information can be captured at the file level and this can give insight into the best data files to place on super fast SSD. The following script extracts the physical read information from the Oracle *dba_hist_filestatxs* view:

```
break on begin_interval_time skip 2

column phyrds   format 999,999,999
column begin_interval_time format a25

select
   begin_interval_time,
   filename,
   phyrds
from
   dba_hist_filestatxs
 natural join
   dba_hist_snapshot
;
```

The sample output below shows a running total of physical reads by datafile. The snapshots are collected every half-hour. Starting from this script, the DBA could easily add a *where* clause criteria and create a unique time-series exception report.

```
SQL> @reads

BEGIN_INTERVAL_TIME          FILENAME                                   PHYRDS
-------------------------     ------------------------------------     --------
24-FEB-04 11.00.32.000 PM    E:\ORACLE\ORA92\FSDEV\SYSTEM01.DBF       164,700
                             E:\ORACLE\ORA92\FSDEV\UNDOTBS01.DBF       26,082
                             E:\ORACLE\ORA92\FSDEV\SYSAUX01.DBF       472,008
                             E:\ORACLE\ORA92\FSDEV\USERS01.DBF          1,794
                             E:\ORACLE\ORA92\FSDEV\T_FS_LSQ.ORA         2,123


24-FEB-04 11.30.18.296 PM    E:\ORACLE\ORA92\FSDEV\SYSTEM01.DBF       167,809
                             E:\ORACLE\ORA92\FSDEV\UNDOTBS01.DBF       26,248
                             E:\ORACLE\ORA92\FSDEV\SYSAUX01.DBF       476,616
                             E:\ORACLE\ORA92\FSDEV\USERS01.DBF          1,795
                             E:\ORACLE\ORA92\FSDEV\T_FS_LSQ.ORA         2,244


25-FEB-04 12.01.06.562 AM    E:\ORACLE\ORA92\FSDEV\SYSTEM01.DBF       169,940
                             E:\ORACLE\ORA92\FSDEV\UNDOTBS01.DBF       26,946
                             E:\ORACLE\ORA92\FSDEV\SYSAUX01.DBF       483,550
                             E:\ORACLE\ORA92\FSDEV\USERS01.DBF          1,799
                             E:\ORACLE\ORA92\FSDEV\T_FS_LSQ.ORA         2,248
```

A little tweaking to the reads.sql script and it will report on physical writes, read time, write time, single block reads, and a host of other interesting metrics from the *dba_hist_filestatxs* view.

Learning Instance Tuning from Performance Benchmarks

A close look at the benchmark methodology leads to the conclusion that blistering transaction speed cannot be attributed solely to high-speed hardware platforms. In order to appreciate the nature of these benchmarks, a closer look at how the Oracle professionals designed the database to accommodate high-speed data retrieval is needed.

Oracle Windows Benchmark

The benchmark where UNISYS set the world record for price-performance, achieving over a quarter of a million transactions per minute using Oracle on Windows has already been mentioned in this text. The $1,400,000 server had 16 Intel Itanium 2 processors running at 1.5GHz, each with 6MB of Level 3 (iL3) cache and 128GB of memory. The techniques used by the Oracle DBA in this benchmark included:

- Oracle multiple blocksizes

- 115 gigabyte total SGA data buffer cache (*db_cache_size*, *db_32k_cache_size*)

- 78 gigabyte KEEP pool (*db_keep_cache_size*)

HP Linux Benchmark

This world record benchmark used a $6,000,000 HP server with 64-Intel Itanium2 processors and 768 gigabytes of RAM and achieved over one million transactions per minute.

This voluminous benchmark disclosure report numbered 206 pages and offered some interesting clues into the way that the Oracle DBA configured Oracle for this world record benchmark:

- **Real Application Clusters:** The benchmark used 16 Oracle instances, each mapping to four processors.

- **Multiple blocksizes:** This world record used four separate blocksizes (2k, 4k, 8k, 16k) to isolate RAM data buffers and place objects within the most appropriate blocksizes.

- **Oracle hidden parameters:** The benchmark DBA employed several Oracle hidden parameters to boost performance. Like most vendors, they take advantage of hardware specific performance features:

    - *_in_memory_undo* = false

    - *_cursor_cache_frame_bind_memory* = true

    - *_db_cache_pre_warm* = false

    - *_in_memory_undo* = false

    - *_check_block_after_checksum* = false

    - *_lm_file_affinity*

- Large RAM data buffers: For each of the 16 RAC nodes, this benchmark used about 44 gigabytes of RAM data buffers each, distributed into five separate RAM data block buffers. The total RAM data block buffer storage was over 700 billion bytes. The following are the data block buffer parameters for each RAC node:

    - *db_cache_size* = 4000M

    - *db_recycle_cache_size* = 500M

- *db_8k_cache_size* = 200M

- *db_16k_cache_size* = 4056M

- *db_2k_cache_size* = 35430M

- Single table hash cluster: The benchmark used single-table hash clusters to speed access to specific rows, bypassing index access with faster hash access to rows. Their hash cluster used the RECYCLE pool because single-table hash cluster access is random by nature and another task is unlikely to need the block in the buffer.

There are some important lessons in these benchmarks for the Oracle professional desiring to hypercharge their application:

- **Multiple blocksizes:** Using multiple blocksizes allows for segregating data blocks in the SGA data buffer cache. Multiple blocksizes are also beneficial for improving the speed of sequential access tablespaces, indexes and temp tablespace by using the *db_32k_cache_size* parameter.

- **Large data buffers:** Both of these benchmarks had over 100 gigabytes of data buffer cache (*db_cache_size*, *db_keep_cache_size*, *db_32k_cache_size*). Caching of data can improve the rate of logical I/O to physical disk I/Os and experts say that logical I/O is 20 to 200 times faster than disk access.

- **Hash clusters:** Oracle hash cluster tables can improve random row access speed by up to four times because the hash can get the row location far faster than index access. Also, multiple table hash clusters can store logically related rows on a single data block, allowing access to a whole unit of data in a single physical I/O.

Now look at some general rules for adjusting the shared pool.

Rules for adjusting *shared_pool_size*

There are several queries used for determining when the Oracle shared pool is too small. The library cache miss ratio tells whether to add space to the shared pool, and it represents the ratio of the sum of library cache reloads to the sum of pins. In general, if the library cache miss ratio is greater than one, consider adding to the *shared_pool_size*. Library cache misses occur during the parsing and preparation of the execution plans for SQL statements.

The compilation of an SQL statement consists of two phases: the parse phase and the execute phase. When the time comes to parse an SQL statement, Oracle checks to see if the parsed representation of the statement already exists in the library cache. If not, Oracle will allocate a shared SQL area within the library cache and then parse the SQL statement. At execution time, Oracle checks to see if a parsed representation of the SQL statement already exists in the library cache. If not, Oracle will reparse and execute the statement.

The following script will compute the library cache miss ratio. The script sums all of the values for the individual components within the library cache and provides an instance-wide view of the health of the library cache.

```
set lines 80;
set pages 999;
```

```
column mydate heading 'Yr.  Mo Dy  Hr.'         format a16
column c1 heading "execs"                       format 9,999,999
column c2 heading "Cache Misses|While Executing" format 9,999,999
column c3 heading "Library Cache|Miss Ratio"    format 999.99999

break on mydate skip 2;

select
   to_char(snap_time,'yyyy-mm-dd HH24')   mydate,
   sum(new.pins-old.pins)                 c1,
   sum(new.reloads-old.reloads)           c2,
   sum(new.reloads-old.reloads)/
   sum(new.pins-old.pins)                 library_cache_miss_ratio
from
   stats$librarycache old,
   stats$librarycache new,
   stats$snapshot      sn
where
   new.snap_id = sn.snap_id
and old.snap_id = new.snap_id-1
and old.namespace = new.namespace
group by
   to_char(snap_time,'yyyy-mm-dd HH24')
;
```

The following is the 10g and beyond version of the script:

```
set lines 80;
set pages 999;

column mydate heading 'Yr.  Mo Dy  Hr.'         format a16
column c1 heading "execs"                       format 9,999,999
column c2 heading "Cache Misses|While Executing" format 9,999,999
column c3 heading "Library Cache|Miss Ratio"    format 999.99999

break on mydate skip 2;

select
   to_char(sn.end_interval_time,'yyyy-mm-dd HH24')  mydate,
   sum(new.pins-old.pins)                 c1,
   sum(new.reloads-old.reloads)           c2,
   sum(new.reloads-old.reloads)/
   sum(new.pins-old.pins)                 library_cache_miss_ratio
from
   dba_hist_librarycache old,
   dba_hist_librarycache new,
   dba_hist_snapshot      sn
where
   new.snap_id = sn.snap_id
and old.snap_id = new.snap_id-1
and old.namespace = new.namespace
group by
   to_char(sn.end_interval_time,'yyyy-mm-dd HH24')
;
```

The output is shown next. This report can easily be customized to give an alert when there are excessive executions or library cache misses.

```
                      Cache Misses  Library Cache

Yr.  Mo Dy  Hr.        execs While Executing   Miss Ratio
----------------  ---------- --------------- ----------------------
```

```
2001-12-11 10        10,338        3              .00029
2001-12-12 10       182,477      134              .00073
2001-12-14 10       190,707      202              .00106
2001-12-16 10         2,803       11              .00392
```

Once this report identifies a time period where there may be a problem, STATSPACK provides the ability to run detailed reports to show the behavior of the objects within the library cache.

In the preceding example, there is clearly a RAM shortage in the shared pool between 10:00 AM and 11:00 AM each day. In this case, the shared pool could be reconfigured dynamically with additional RAM memory from the *db_cache_size* during this period.

Sizing the Shared Pool with the Oracle Advisory Utility

Starting in Oracle 9i release 2, there is an advisory called *v$shared_pool_advice*, and there is talk of expanding the advice facility to all SGA RAM areas in future releases of Oracle. It is also included in the standard AWR reports, *$oracle_home/rdbms/admin/awrrpt.sql*.

The *v$shared_pool_advice* view shows the marginal difference in SQL parses as the shared pool changes in size from 10% of the current value to 200% of the current value. The Oracle documentation contains a complete description for the setup and use of shared pool advice, and it is very simple to configure. Once it is installed, a simple script can be run to query the *v$shared_pool_advice* view and locate the marginal changes in SQL parses for different *shared_pool* sizes.

```
set lines   100
set pages   999

column      c1      heading 'Pool  |Size(M)'
column      c2      heading 'Size|Factor'
column      c3      heading 'Est |LC(M)   '
column      c4      heading 'Est LC|Mem. Obj.'
column      c5      heading 'Est |Time|Saved|(sec)'
column      c6      heading 'Est |Parse|Saved|Factor'
column      c7      heading 'Est|Object Hits'   format 999,999,999

SELECT
   shared_pool_size_for_estimate    c1,
   shared_pool_size_factor          c2,
   estd_lc_size                     c3,
   estd_lc_memory_objects           c4,
   estd_lc_time_saved               c5,
   estd_lc_time_saved_factor        c6,
   estd_lc_memory_object_hits       c7
FROM
   v$shared_pool_advice;
```

The following is a sample of the output:

Pool Size(M)	Size Factor	Est LC(M)	Est LC Mem. Obj.	Est Time Saved (sec)	Est Parse Saved Factor	Est Object Hits
48	.5	48	20839	1459645	1	135,756,032

64	.6667	63	28140	1459645	1	135,756,101
80	.8333	78	35447	1459645	1	135,756,149
96	1	93	43028	1459645	1	135,756,253
112	1.1667	100	46755	1459646	1	135,756,842
128	1.3333	100	46755	1459646	1	135,756,842
144	1.5	100	46755	1459646	1	135,756,842
160	1.6667	100	46755	1459646	1	135,756,842
176	1.8333	100	46755	1459646	1	135,756,842
192	2	100	46755	1459646	1	135,756,842

The statistics for the shared pool in this example fall in a wide range from 50% of the current size to 200% of the current size. These statistics can give a great idea about the proper size for the *shared_pool_size*. If the SGA region sizes are selected automatically with the alter system commands, creating this output and writing a program to interpret the results is a great way to ensure that the shared pool and library cache always have enough RAM.

The next section will provide information on the Program Global Area (PGA) RAM regions.

Rules for Adjusting the Data Buffer Sizes

The following report can be used to alert when the data buffer hit ratio falls below the preset threshold. It is very useful for pinpointing those times when decision support-type queries are being run, since a large number of large-table full-table scans may make the data buffer hit ratio drop. This script also reports on all three data buffers, including the KEEP and RECYCLE pools, and it can be customized to report on individual pools.

The KEEP pool should always have enough data blocks to cache all table rows, while the RECYCLE pool should get a very low buffer hit ratio since it seldom rereads data blocks. If a low data buffer hit ratio is combined with expressive disk I/O, the DBA may want to increase *db_cache_size* (*db_block_buffers* in Oracle 8i and earlier).

```
yr. mo dy Hr.   Name     bhr
------------- --------   -----
2001-01-27 09 DEFAULT     45
2001-01-28 09 RECYCLE     41
2001-01-29 10 DEFAULT     36
2001-01-30 09 DEFAULT     28
2001-02-02 10 DEFAULT     83
2001-02-02 09 RECYCLE     81
2001-02-03 10 DEFAULT     69
2001-02-03 09 DEFAULT     69
```

These results indicate those times when the DBA might want to dynamically increase the value of the *db_cache_size* parameter. In the case of the preceding output, the *db_cache_size* could be increased each day between 8:00 AM and 10:00 AM, stealing RAM memory from *pga_aggregate_target*.

Remember, we can dynamically modify almost all of the Oracle memory pools, and we have the ability to dynamically reconfigure the Oracle instance while it is running, whether in reaction to a current performance problem or in anticipation of an impending performance problem.

Monitoring RAM usage

Oracle provides us with many ways to monitor our SGA and PGA RAM. Here are some useful scripts that I use to view instance RAM usage.

With each new release, Oracle enhances the *v$* views to include information about RAM memory utilization. Oracle has implemented RAM memory monitoring by enhancing the *v$process* view. The new columns in the *v$process* view allow you to show details about the program global area (PGA) regions for all current Oracle processes. The PGA is a dedicated area of RAM memory used by individual processes to perform RAM intensive functions, such as sorting.

The three new columns in the *v$process* view include *pga_used_memory*, *pga_allocated_memory*, and *pga_max_memory*. From these metrics, you can see the actual RAM utilization for individual background processes within the Oracle environment and also look at the RAM demands of individual connections to the database. To illustrate, consider the following query:

🖫 pga_parogram_used_ram.sql

```
col c1 heading 'Program|Name'         format a30
col c2 heading 'PGA|Used|Memory'      format 999,999,999
col c3 heading 'PGA|Allocated|Memory' format 999,999,999
col c4 heading 'PGA|Maximum|Memory'   format 999,999,999

select
   program         c1,
   pga_used_mem    c2,
   pga_alloc_mem   c3,
   pga_max_mem     c4
from
   v$process
order by
   c4 desc;
```

Here we see the output, showing the RAM usage for each user on the database:

PROGRAM	PGA_USED_MEM	PGA_ALLOC_MEM	PGA_MAX_MEM
oracle@janet (PMON)	120,463	234,291	234,291
oracle@janet (DBW0)	1,307,179	1,817,295	1,817,295
oracle@janet (LGWR)	4,343,655	4,849,203	4,849,203
oracle@janet (CKPT)	194,999	332,583	332,583
oracle@janet (SMON)	179,923	775,311	775,323
oracle@janet (RECO)	129,719	242,803	242,803
oracle@janet (TNS V1-V3)	1,400,543	1,540,627	1,540,915
oracle@janet (P000)	299,599	373,791	635,959
oracle@janet (P001)	299,599	373,791	636,007
oracle@janet (TNS V1-V3)	1,400,543	1,540,627	1,540,915
oracle@janet (TNS V1-V3)	22,341	1,716,253	3,625,241

This example provides insight into the behavior of the Oracle database engine. For example, you can see that Oracle's log writer (LGWR) process is the highest consumer of PGA RAM memory, which makes

---

sense because the Oracle Log Writer process must transfer redo log images from Oracle's Log Buffer (in RAM memory) to the online redo log filesystem.

You can also see high RAM memory utilization for Oracle's Database Writer (DBW0) process. This also makes sense, because Oracle's asynchronous I/O process must make extensive use of RAM memory resources to ensure that all database changes are successfully written to the database.

RAM for individual processes

But the real value in viewing RAM usage in Oracle is to see RAM utilization for individual processes. Oracle uses a shared RAM region called *pga_aggregate_target*. When using the Oracle multithreaded server, the *pga_aggregate_target* parameter works similar to Oracle's large pool but with one important difference.

By having a shared RAM memory area, individual Oracle processes are free to use up to 5 percent of the total amount of memory within the pool when performing sorting and hash join activities. This is a huge improvement over the Oracle8*i* requirement that each PGA region be restricted according to the value of the *sort_area_size* initialization parameter.

Oracle also provides a useful *v$pgastat* view. The *v$pgastat* view shows the total amount of RAM memory utilization for every RAM memory region within the database. This information can tell you the high water mark of RAM utilization, and allow you to size RAM memory demands according to the relative stress on the system. Here is a simple query against *v$pgastat*:

```
column name format a40
column value format 999,999,999

select
   name,
   value
from
   v$pgastat
order by
   value desc;
```

Here is the output, showing total RAM usage:

```
NAME                                                VALUE
------------------------------------------------    ----------
aggregate PGA auto target                           736,052,224
global memory bound                                      21,200
total expected memory                                  141,144
total PGA inuse                                      22,234,736
total PGA allocated                                 55,327,872
```

```
maximum PGA allocated                              23,970,624
total PGA used for auto workareas                     262,144
maximum PGA used for auto workareas                 7,333,032
total PGA used for manual workareas                         0
maximum PGA used for manual workareas                       0
estimated PGA memory for optimal                      141,395
maximum PGA memory for optimal                    500,123,520
estimated PGA memory for one-pass                     534,144
maximum PGA memory for one-pass                    52,123,520
```

From this listing, you can see the value of *pga_aggregate_target* and the high water marks for all RAM memory areas used by this instance. But let's take a look at optimal, one pass, and multipass RAM memory executions.

When an Oracle process requires an operation, such as a sort or a hash join, it goes to the shared RAM memory area within *pga_aggregate_target* region and attempts to obtain enough contiguous RAM frames to perform the operation.

If the process is able to acquire these RAM frames immediately, it is marked as an optimal RAM access. If the RAM acquisition requires a single pass through *pga_aggregate_target*, the RAM memory allocation is marked as one pass. If all RAM is in use, Oracle may have to make multiple passes through *pga_aggregate_target* to acquire the RAM memory. This is called multipass.

Remember, RAM memory is extremely fast, and most sorts or hash joins are completed in microseconds. Oracle allows a single process to use up to 5 percent of the *pga_aggregate_target*, and parallel operations are allowed to consume up to 30 percent of the PGA RAM pool.

Multipass executions indicate a RAM shortage, and you should always allocate enough RAM to ensure that at least 95 percent of connected tasks can acquire their RAM memory optimally.

You can also obtain information about workarea executions by querying the *v$sysstat* view shown here:

🖫 pga_workareas.sql

```
col c1 heading 'Workarea|Profile' format a35
col c2 heading 'Count'           format 999,999,999
col c3 heading 'Percentage'      format 99

select
   name                                       c1,
   cnt                                        c2,
   decode(total, 0, 0, round(cnt*100/total)) c3
from
(
   select name,value cnt,(sum(value) over ()) total
   from
      v$sysstat
   where
   name like 'workarea exec%'
);
```

Below we see the output, showing the efficiency of our RAM operations.

```
PROFILE                            CNT      PERCENTAGE
---------------------------     ----------  ----------
workarea executions - optimal      5395         98
workarea executions - onepass       284          2
workarea executions - multipass       0          0
```

At least 95 percent of the tasks should have optimal workarea executions. In the output above, you can see all workarea executions that were able to execute *optimal, onepass*, and *multipass* modes.

This listing provides valuable information regarding the appropriate size for the *pga_aggregate_target* region. It can also indicate an over-allocation of the RAM memory region. If the percentage of optimal workarea executions consistently stays at 98 to 100 percent, you can safely steal RAM frames from *pga_aggregate_target* and reallocate them to other areas of the Oracle SGA (such as *db_cache_size*) that may have a greater need for the RAM memory resources.

Viewing individual RAM work areas

Oracle also provides data dictionary views that show the amount of RAM memory used by individual steps within the execution plan of SQL statements. This can be invaluable for the appropriate sizing of *hash_area_size, pga_aggregate_target* and other RAM-intensive parameters.

The *v$sql_workarea_active* view shows the amount of RAM usage by each individual workarea within the Oracle database.

Also, Oracle provides several methods for joining tables together, each with widely varying RAM memory usage. The Oracle SQL optimizer can choose sort merge joins, nested loop joins, hash joins, and star joins methods. In some cases, the hash join can run faster than a nested loop join, but hash joins require RAM memory resources and a high setting for the *hash_area_size* and *pga_aggregate_target* parameter.

For a more comprehensive view of all tasks using RAM resources, you can use this query using the *v$sql_workarea_active* view:

🖫 show_pga_ram_details.sql

```
select
    to_number(decode(SID, 65535, NULL, SID)) sid,
    operation_type                  OPERATION,
    trunc(WORK_AREA_SIZE/1024)      WSIZE,
```

```
   trunc(EXPECTED_SIZE/1024)              ESIZE,
   trunc(ACTUAL_MEM_USED/1024)            MEM,
   trunc(MAX_MEM_USED/1024)               "MAX MEM",
   number_passes                          PASS
from
   v$sql_workarea_active
order by 1,2;
```

Below we see the output, showing RAM usage for specific step of SQL execution plans:

```
SID OPERATION              WSIZE     ESIZE        MEM    MAX MEM PASS
--- -------------------    -----  --------   --------   -------- ----
 27 GROUP BY (SORT)           73        73         64         64    0
 44 HASH-JOIN               3148      3147       2437       6342    1
 71 HASH-JOIN              13241     19200      12884      34684    1
```

Above, we can see the amount of RAM used for each step of SQL execution. One SQL statement is performing a Group By sort using 73 KB of RAM memory. You can also see the system ID (SID) for two SQL statements that are performing hash joins. These hash joins are using the 3 and 13 MB respectively to build their in-memory hash tables.

Tracking hash joins

Because hash joins are so tightly controlled by available memory, the savvy DBA might track hash joins over time. You can use SQL scripts to track system-wide hash joins.

🖫 track_hash_joins.sql

```
select
  to_char(
    sn.begin_interval_time,
    'yy-mm-dd hh24'
  )                                       snap_time,
  count(*)                                ct,
  sum(st.rows_processed_delta)            row_ct,
  sum(st.disk_reads_delta)                disk,
  sum(st.cpu_time_delta)                  cpu
from
  dba_hist_snapshot    sn,
  dba_hist_sqlstat     st,
  dba_hist_sql_plan    sp
where
  st.snap_id = sn.snap_id
and
  st.dbid = sn.dbid
and
  st.instance_number = sn.instance_number
and
  sp.sql_id = st.sql_id
```

```
and
    sp.dbid = st.dbid
and
    sp.plan_hash_value = st.plan_hash_value
and
    sp.operation = 'HASH JOIN'
group by
    to_char(sn.begin_interval_time,'yy-mm-dd hh24')
having
        count(*) > &hash_thr;
```

The sample output might look the following, showing the number of hash joins during the snapshot period along with the relative I/O and CPU associated with the processing. The values for *rows_processed* are generally higher for hash joins which do full-table scans as opposed to nested loop joins with generally involved a very small set of returned rows.

```
Hash Join Thresholds by hour

                   Hash
                   Join        Rows        Disk         CPU
Date               Count    Processed      Reads        Time
-----------------  -----   ----------   ----------   ----------
04-10-12 17         22        4,646         887      39,990,515
04-10-13 16         25        2,128         827      54,746,653
04-10-14 11         21       17,368       3,049      77,297,578
04-10-21 15         60        2,805       3,299       5,041,064
04-10-22 10         25        6,864         941       4,077,524
04-10-22 13         31       11,261       2,950      46,207,733
04-10-25 16         35       46,269       1,504       6,364,414
```

Oracle hash joins are dependent upon your system and session parameter settings.

Viewing RAM usage for hash joins in SQL

Oracle has the ability to display RAM memory usage along with execution plan information.

To get this information you need to gather the address of the desired SQL statement from the *v$sql* view. For example, if you have a query that operates against the *customer* table, you can run the following query to get the address:

```
select
```

```
   address
from
   v$sql
where
   sql_text like '%CUSTOMER%';

88BB460C

1 row selected.
```

Now that we have the address of the SQL statement in RAM, we can plug it into the following script to get the execution plan details and the PGA memory usage for the SQL statement.

🖫 show_ram_plan.sql

```
select
   operation,
   options,
   object_name                          name,
   trunc(bytes/1024/1024)               "input(MB)",
   trunc(last_memory_used/1024)         last_mem,
   trunc(estimated_optimal_size/1024)   opt_mem,
   trunc(estimated_onepass_size/1024)   onepass_mem,
   decode(optimal_executions, null, null,
          optimal_executions||'/'||onepass_executions||'/'||
          multipasses_exections)                "O/1/M"
from
   v$sql_plan      p,
   v$sql_workarea  w
where
   p.address=w.address(+)
and
   p.hash_value=w.hash_value(+)
and
   p.id=w.operation_id(+)
and
   p.address='88BB460C';
```

Here is the listing from this script. This is important because it reveals the RAM used for each step in the SQL.

```
OPERATION     OPTIONS  NAME input(MB) LAST_MEM OPT_MEM ONEPASS_MEM O/1/M
------------  -------- ---- --------- -------- ----------- ----------- ----
SELECT STATE
```

```
SORT         GROUP BY    4582         8        16        16    26/0/0
HASH JOIN         SEMI    4582      5976      5194      2187    16/0/0
TABLE ACCESS FULL      ORDERS       51
TABLE ACCESS FULL      LINEITEM   1000
```

Here we see the details about the execution plan along with specific memory usage details. This is an exciting new advance in Oracle and gives the Oracle DBA the ability to have a very high level of detail about the internal execution of any SQL statement.

Conclusion

The proper settings for the Oracle instance parameters are the single most important aspect of Oracle tuning. Oracle parameters control the sizes of the SGA regions, the SQL optimization process, and the ability of Oracle to invoke automatic tuning activities such as cursor sharing, automatic query rewrite and automatic memory management.

The main points of this chapter include:

- Oracle instance tuning involves adjusting important *init.ora* parameters, configuring the SGA regions and adjusting the disk I/O blocksizes.

- Oracle server kernel parameter, especially I/O configuration, has a huge influence on Oracle instance performance.

- The most important Oracle parameters are those that govern the SQL optimizer and the sizes of the SGA regions.

- Oracle provides hidden instance parameters and these can be very helpful on specific hardware. The TPC Oracle benchmarks (www.tpc.org) should be consulted to see the hidden Oracle parameters used by hardware vendors to see how they are used.

- Oracle has created a special KEEP pool to ensure that frequently references data blocks stay inside the SGA. It is the job of the DBA to identify and cache all high impact tables and indexes in the KEEP pool.

- Benchmarks show that multiple blocksizes should be defined so that Oracle objects can be mapped to the most beneficial blocksize.

- Any tablespaces whose objects experience full-scans should be placed into a large blocksize. This includes certain indexes, the TEMP tablespace, and data warehouse tables.

- Objects that experience high invalidations, such as truncate table or high DML, should be segregated into a separate data buffer, sometimes with a small size.

This chapter has been extensive, but it lays the foundation for a look at proactive SQL Tuning which is a very complex and important component of Oracle tuning. Once we have an optimized instance, then it is time to tackle the SQL. Now that we have covered instance tuning, we can move on and discuss how we can tune our performance at the tablespace and table level.

Tablespace & Object Tuning

Poorly optimized objects cause poor response time

Oracle Tablespace Tuning

Oracle tuning has already been covered for the instance and disk I/O tuning, but there are many tuning options that apply directly to Oracle tablespaces and objects such as tables and indexes.

As a quick review, the Oracle data files on disk are considered physical structures and the tablespace definition maps the data files to the logical tablespace. In other words, the tablespace is the separation point between the logical machinations of Oracle and the physical machinations of the disks and operating system environment.

Historically, space management was one of the most time consuming tasks for DBAs. According to surveys conducted by Oracle Corporation, Oracle DBAs spent about twenty percent of their work time performing space management activities, doing activities like ensuring that tables can extend, load-balancing data files on disk and ensuring the tablespaces are sized properly for the objects inside them. Today, there are many options for tablespace management.

Inside Oracle Tablespace Tuning

Over the past few years, Oracle has been automating and improving the internal administration of tables and indexes. However, the DBA must always be wary of any "one size fits all" approach, because it may not be optimal for the database.

Oracle has introduced two new tablespace parameters that automate storage management functions:

- **Locally Managed Tablespace (LMT):** The LMT is implemented by adding the *extent management local* clause to the tablespace definition. LMTs automate extent management and remove the ability to specify the *next* storage parameter. The only exception is when *next* is used with *minextents* at table creation time. The LMT is the default in Oracle 10g and beyond.

- **Automatic Segment Space Management (ASSM):** ASSM replaces the old-fashioned one-way linked lists of free data blocks with bitmap structures. The ASSM tablespace is implemented by adding the *segment space management auto* clause to the tablespace definition. ASSM tablespaces automate freelist management and remove the ability to specify *pctused*, *freelists*, and *freelist groups'* storage parameters. The ASSM cannot be used unless LMTs are also used on a tablespace.

 **Watch out for ASSM bottlenecks!**

Beware that ASSM is not appropriate for high-update tablespaces. During high DML load rates, there may be buffer wait contention.

Remember, LMT and ASSM are optional and they can be used in the same instance with traditional tablespaces.

The combination of bitmap freelists (ASSM) and LMTs has greatly simplified and improved the internal management of data blocks within Oracle tablespaces, but it is not always the best choice for high performance. The use of bitmap freelists removes the need to define multiple freelists for tables and indexes that experience high volume concurrent DML and provides a simple solution to the problem of segment header contention, but ASSM has been known to cause bottlenecks under high DML activity.

Remember, there is always a tradeoff between any one-size-fits-all solution and the power of being able to set individual object parameters for tables and indexes. The choice of LMT and ASSM for tablespace management depends heavily on the application, and real-world Oracle tablespaces will implement LMT and ASSM tablespaces only after careful consideration.

There is some debate about whether any one-size-fits-all approach is best for Oracle. In large databases, individual object settings can make a huge difference in both performance and storage. The setting for *pctused* governs *freelist* relinking as space is freed by *update* and *delete* statements.

Despite the changes in automation, one parameter remains with a profound impact on table performance, the *pctfree* table parameter.

The Issue of *pctfree*

The *pctfree* parameter is used to specify the amount of free space on a data block to reserve for future row expansion. The *pctfree* and *pctused* parameters tell Oracle when to link and unlink a block from the freelist chain, and *pctfree* is the unlink threshold.

The DBA must reserve enough room on each data block for existing rows to expand without fragmenting onto other blocks. The purpose of *pctfree* is to tell Oracle when to remove a block from the object's freelist. Since the Oracle default is *pctfree=10*, blocks remain on the freelist while they are less than 90 percent full. Once an insert makes the block grow beyond 90 percent full, it is removed from the freelist, leaving 10 percent of the block for row expansion.

Furthermore, the data block will remain off the freelist even after the space drops below 90 percent. Only after subsequent deletes cause the space to fall below the *pctused* threshold of 40 percent will Oracle put the block back onto the freelist. Remember, *pctfree* is only used at insert or update time. Whenever new storage causes the block to cross the *pctfree* threshold, the data block will be unlinked from the freelist chain, thereby making the block unavailable for further updates.

If *pctfree* is set improperly, SQL update statements can cause a huge amount of row fragmentation and chaining. The setting for *pctfree* is especially important where a row is initially stored small and expanded at a later time. In such systems, it is not uncommon to set *pctfree* equal to 95, telling Oracle to reserve 95 percent of the data block space for subsequent row expansion.

The setting for *pctfree* sets the value for the percent of a block to reserve for updates. A block will remain on a freelist until it reaches blocksize * (1-(*ptcfree*/100)) full or greater. Here are the main issues with incorrect settings:

- **High migrated/chained rows:** If *pctfree* is too small, adequate space may not be reserved in the block for update of variable sized rows in the block or may not have enough space for a complete row insert. In this case, a block chaining will occur where the data is migrated to a new block and a pointer will be established from the old block to a new block.

- **High I/O:** This will result in doubling the I/O required to retrieve this data. For new data blocks, the space available for inserts is equal to the block size minus the sum of the block overhead (84-107 bytes) and free space (*pctfree/100 * blocksize*). When existing data is updated, Oracle uses any available space in the block. So updates will eventually reduce the available space in a block to less than *pctfree*, the space reserved for updates but not accessible to inserts. This removes the block from the freelist on which it resides.

All professional DBAs know that minimizing chained rows is a fundamental job role and they recognize that row migration (chaining) is a function of:

- blocksize
- pctfree
- load time average row length
- Expected row expansion (bytes per row)

The Freelist Unlink Process

Blocks with total filled volume less than $blocksize$ – overhead – (blocksize*(1-($pctfree$/100)) are available for inserts. When an *insert* statement is issued, Oracle checks a freelist of the table for the first available data block and uses it if possible.

If the free space in the selected block is not large enough to accommodate the data in the *insert* statement, and the block is at least filled to the value *pctused*, then Oracle will remove the block from the freelist. Multiple freelists for each segment can reduce contention for freelists when concurrent inserts take place.

The Issue of *pctused*

This storage parameter determines when a block can relink onto the table freelist after *delete* operations. Setting a low value for *pctused* will result in high performance. A higher value of *pctfree* will result in efficient space reuse but will slow performance.

As rows are deleted from a table, the database blocks become eligible to accept new rows. This happens when the amount of space in a database block falls below *pctused*, and a freelist relink operation is triggered. For example, with *pctused*=60, all database blocks that have less than 60 percent will be on the freelist, as well as other blocks that dropped below *pctused* and have not yet grown to *pctfree*. Once a block deletes a row and becomes less than 60 percent full, the block goes back on the freelist.

As rows are deleted, data blocks become available when a block's free space drops below the value of *pctused* for the table, and Oracle relinks the data block onto the freelist chain. As the table has rows inserted into it, it will grow until the space on the block exceeds the threshold *pctfree*, at which time the block is unlinked from the freelist.

Improper settings for *pctused* can cause huge degradation in the performance of SQL *insert*s. If a data block is not largely empty, excessive I/O will happen during SQL inserts because the reused Oracle data blocks already contain rows, and the block will fill up faster causing extra I/O. Taken to the extreme, improper settings for *pctused* can create a situation in which the free space on the data block is smaller than the average row length for thc table. In these cases, Oracle will try five times to fetch a new block from the freelist chain. After five attempts, Oracle will raise the high water mark for the table and grab five completely empty data blocks for the insert.

With ASSM, the *pctused* parameter no longer governs the relink threshold for a table data block, and the DBA must rely on the judgment of Oracle to determine when a block is empty enough to be placed back onto the freelist. Unlike *pctfree*, in which Oracle cannot tell in advance how much row expansion will occur, Oracle does have information about the right time to relink a data block after the row space shrinks. Since Oracle knows the average row length for the table rows, *dba_tables.avg_row_len*. With that information, Oracle should be able to adjust *pctused* to ensure that the relinked data block will have room for the insertion of new rows.

Setting Pctfree and Pctused

As any experienced DBA understands, the settings for *pctused* can have a dramatic impact on the performance of an Oracle database. Many new Oracle DBAs fail to realize that *pctused* is only used to relink a full data onto the table freelist. A relink only occurs when a *delete* or *update* statement has reduced the free space in the data block. The setting for *pctused* will determine the amount of row space in this newly relinked data block. The default settings for all Oracle tables are *pctused=40*. The *pctused=40* setting means that a block must become less than 40 percent full before being relinked on the table freelist.

Take a closer look at how the *pctused* operator works and how it affects the operation of relinks onto the table freelist. A data block becomes available for reuse when a block's free space drops below the value of *pctused* for the table. This happens when the amount of space in a database block falls below *pctused*, and a freelist relink operation is triggered. For example, with *pctused=60*, all database blocks that have less than 60 percent data will be on the freelist, as well as other blocks that dropped below *pctused* and have not yet grown to *pctfree*. Once a block deletes a row and becomes less than 60 percent full, the block goes back on the freelist.

There is a direct tradeoff between the setting for *pctused* and database performance on insert operations. In general, the higher the setting for *pctused*, the less free space will be on reused data blocks at *insert* time. Hence, *insert* tasks will need to do more frequent I/Os than they would if they were inserting into empty blocks. In short, the value for *pctused* should only be set above 40 when the database is short on disk space, and it must make efficient reuse of data block space.

It should now be very clear that the DBA needs to consider the average row length when customizing the values for *pctfree* and *pctused*. Set *pctfree* such that room is left on each block for row expansion, and then set *pctused* so that newly linked blocks have enough room to accept rows.

Herein lies the tradeoff between effective space usage and performance. If *pctused* is set to a high value, say 80, then a block will quickly become available to accept new rows, but it will not have room for a lot of rows before it becomes logically full again. In the most extreme case, a relinked free block may only have enough space for a single row before causing another I/O. The script in *pctused.sql* allows for adjusting the setting for *pctfree* and *pctused* as a function of the number of rows that the DBA wants to store between I/Os.

Know about *pctused* and performance!

The lower the value for *pctused,* the less I/O there will be at insert time, and the faster the system will run. The downside is that a block will be nearly empty before it becomes eligible to accept new rows.

Because row length is a major factor in intelligently setting *pctused*, a script can be written that allows the DBA to specifically control how many rows will fit onto a reused data block before it unlinks from the freelist. The script shown in the listing below generates the table alteration syntax. Please note that this script only provides general guidelines and the default *pctused=40* should be left out unless the system is low on disk space or unless the average row length is very large.

🖫 **pctused.sql**

```
set heading off;
set pages 9999;
set feedback off;

spool pctused.lst;

define spare_rows = 2;

define blksz = 8192;

select
' alter table '||owner||'.'||table_name||
' pctused '||least(round(100-((&spare_rows*avg_row_len)/(&blksz/10))),95)||
' '||
' pctfree '||greatest(round((&spare_rows*avg_row_len)/(&blksz/10)),5)||
';'
from
dba_tables
where
avg_row_len > 1
and
avg_row_len < 2000
and
table_name not in
(select table_name from dba_tab_columns b
where
data_type in ('RAW','LONG RAW', 'CLOB', 'BLOB', 'XMLTYPE')
)
order by owner, table_name
;

spool off;
```

Note that the script below allows the DBA to define the blocksize and the number of rows for which they want to leave room after the block relinks onto the freelist. The file in *pctused.lst* will now contain the *alter table* syntax to reset *pctused*. Again, this script is generally used when the database is very tight on space and the DBA wants to make the tradeoff between efficient space reuse and insert performance.

Excessive migrated rows are often the result of a DBA error, usually by failing to anticipate the future row expansion. An improper *pctfree*, precipitating a high *chain_cnt*, is a DBA error and quite rare. Usually migrated rows are the result of large objects in small blocks and the most common remedy to deploy a larger blocksize.

Freelists and Performance

Many people who experience segment header contention, i.e. buffer busy wait or read by other sessions, are confused about the proper use of multiple freelists versus multiple *freelist_groups* for a table or index. Oracle allows tables and indexes to be defined with multiple freelists. All tables and index freelists should be set to the high watermark of concurrent *insert* or *update* activity. Too low a value for freelists will cause poor Oracle performance.

As may be known, multiple freelists add additional process freelists within a single segment header, while multiple freelist groups add multiple segment headers. However, there is growing evidence that some segment header contention can be relieved in non-RAC systems by adding multiple freelist groups to tables and indexes. This is especially useful for partitioned tables and systems with extremely high DML activity.

A Case Study in Multiple Freelists

A client called from Michigan once with a complaint that the company order-processing center was unable to keep up with adding new orders into Oracle. The client had just expanded its telephone order-processing department and had doubled the order-processing staff to meet a surge in market interest. The VP was frantic, saying that 400 order-entry clerks were getting 30-second response time and they were forced to manually write down order information.

I checked *v$session* and found 450 connected users, and a quick review of *v$sql* revealed that at virtually all the DML were inserts into a *customer_order* table. The top timed event was buffer busy waits and it was clear that there were enqueues on the segment header blocks for the table and its indexes.

Now, the supposedly proper fix for this issue is to create a new tablespace for the table and index using ASSM, also known as bitmap freelists. I could then reorganize the table online with the *dbms_redefinition* utility and *alter index cust_pk* to rebuild the index into the new tablespace. However, it would take me several hours to build and execute the jobs and the VP said that he was losing over $500 per minute.

The system was on release 9.2.0.4, so I was able to immediately relieve the segment header contention with these commands:

```
alter table customer_order freelists 5;
alter index cust_pk freelists 5;
```

Note: I did not know the length of the enqueues on the segment header, so I added the additional freelists, one at a time, until the buffer busy waits disappeared.

The additional freelists did the trick and the segment header contention disappeared. However, I knew that this was only a stop-gap fix and as soon as they ran their weekly purge, a single process, that only one of the five freelists would get the released blocks, causing the table to extend unnecessarily.

ASSM and Tablespace Performance

Before exploring the differences between bitmap freelists and traditional freelists, the DBA must understand more about how bitmap freelists are implemented. The process starts with the creation of a tablespace with the *segment space management auto* parameter. ASSM is only valid for locally managed tablespaces with *extent management local* syntax.

```
create tablespace
   asm_test
```

```
datafile
   'c:\oracle\oradata\diogenes\asm_test.dbf'
size
   5m
EXTENT MANAGEMENT LOCAL
SEGMENT SPACE MANAGEMENT AUTO;
```

Once a table or index is allocated in this ASSM tablespace, the values for *pctused* for individual objects will be ignored, and Oracle will automatically manage the freelists for the tables and indexes inside the tablespace. For objects created in this tablespace, the *next* extent clause is now obsolete because of the locally managed tablespace, except when a table is created with the *minextents* and *next* clauses.

The Oracle 10g ASMM feature, the default on Oracle 10g, should anticipate high updates and allocate additional data buffers during high update periods. The *initial* parameter is still required because Oracle cannot know in advance the size of the initial table load. When using ASSM, the minimum value for initial is three blocks.

Prior to Oracle 9i, buffer busy waits were a major issue for systems with high concurrent inserts. As a review, a buffer busy wait often occurs when a data block is inside the data buffer cache, but it is unavailable because it is locked by another DML transaction. Without multiple freelists, every Oracle table and index has a single data block at the head of the table to manage the free block for the object. Whenever any SQL insert ran, it had to go to this segment header block and get a free data block on which to place its row.

Oracle's ASSM feature claims to improve the performance of concurrent DML operations significantly since different parts of the bitmap can be used, simultaneously eliminating serialization for free block lookups. According to Oracle benchmarks, using bitmap freelists removes all segment header contention and allows for fast concurrent insert operations as shown in Figure 15.1.

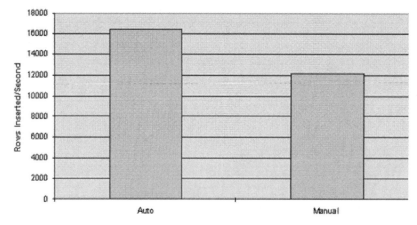

Figure 15.1: *Oracle Corp. Benchmark on SQL Insert Speed with Bitmap Freelists*

The following section will introduce how the Oracle DBA can use these object management parameters to control every aspect of row storage on the data blocks.

Internal Freelist Management

With ASSM, Oracle controls the number of bitmap freelists, providing up to 23 freelists per segment. Internally within Oracle, a shortage of freelists is manifested by a buffer busy wait. In traditional non-bitmap freelists, Oracle has a manual mechanism for the DBA to use to allocate a new segment header block with another freelist whenever buffer busy waits are detected for the segment. Oracle first introduced dynamic freelist addition in Oracle 8i.

The following section will provide information on how the bitmap freelists of ASSM control free blocks within a segment.

Characteristics of Bitmap Segment Management

Bitmap space management uses four bits inside each data block header to indicate the amount of available space in the data block. Unlike traditional space management with a fixed relink and unlink threshold, bitmap space management allow Oracle to compare the actual row space for an insert with the actual available space on the data block. This enables better reuse of the available free space, especially for objects with rows of highly varying size. Table 15.1 shows the values inside the four-bit space:

VALUE	MEANING
0000	Unformatted Block
0001	Block is logically full
0010	<25% free space
0011	>25% but <50% free space
0100	> 50% but <75% free space
0101	>75% free space

Table 15.1: *Bitmap Value Meanings*

The value column of this bitmap table indicates how much free space exists in a given data block. In traditional space management, each data block must be read from the *freelist* to see if it has enough space to accept a new row. In Oracle, the bitmap is constantly kept up to date with changes to the block and there is also a reduction of wasted space because blocks can be kept fuller because the overhead of *freelist* processing has been reduced.

Another benefit of ASSM is that concurrent DML operations improve significantly. This is because different parts of the bitmap can be used simultaneously, thereby eliminating the need to serialize free space lookups.

The bitmap segment control structures of ASSM are much larger than traditional one-way linked-list *freelist* management. Since each data block entry contains the four-byte data block address and the four-bit free space indicator, each data block entry in the space management bitmap will consume approximately six bytes of storage.

It is also important to note that the space management blocks are not required to be the first blocks in the segment. In Oracle 8, the segment headers were required to be the first blocks in the segment. In Oracle 8i this restriction was lifted, and the DBA could allocate additional *freelists* with the *alter table* command, causing additional non-contiguous segment headers.

In Oracle, Oracle automatically allocates new space management blocks when a new extent is created and maintains internal pointers to the bitmap blocks as shown in Figure 15.2:

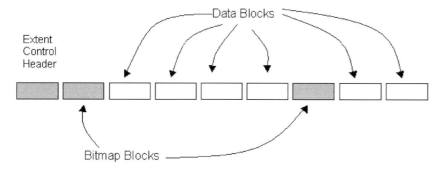

Figure 15.2: *Non-contiguous Bitmap Blocks Within a Segment*

Just like traditional freelists, the bitmap block (BMB) is stored in a separate data block within the table or index. Since Oracle does not publish the internals of space management, the structure must be inferred from block dumps. Therefore, this information may not be completely accurate, but it will give a general idea about the internal mechanisms of Oracle ASSM.

Unlike a linear-linked list in traditional freelists, bitmap blocks are stored in a b-tree structure, much the same as a bitmap. Since Oracle can use the freelists blocks much like a bitmap index, multiple transactions can simultaneously access free blocks without locking or concurrency problems.

The next section will provide a look inside the segment header and a closer look at bitmap space management techniques within ASSM.

New High Watermark Pointers

The high watermark in the segment header has also changed in Oracle 9i bitmap blocks. Instead of having a single pointer to the highest free block in an object, the b-tree index structure allows for a range of high watermark blocks. Therefore, two pointers for the high watermark can be seen.

- **The low high watermark (LHWM):** All blocks below this block have been formatted for the table.

- **The high high watermark (HHWM):** All blocks above this block have not been formatted. Internally, the HHWM is required to ensure that Oracle direct load operations can access contiguous unformatted blocks.

The following sections will explore each block in detail to understand how space is managed in bitmap segment control.

Extent Control Header Block

This block contains the high-high watermark, the low-high watermark, the extent map, and the data block addresses for each of the three levels of bitmap blocks.

The extent map lists all of the data block addresses for each block within each extent within the segment and shows the four-bit free space of each block within the extent. Since the extent size is controlled by Oracle locally managed tablespaces, each extent size within the tablespace is uniform, regardless of the *next* extent size for each object in the tablespace. The first three blocks of the first extend list, blocks zero through two, are used for metadata and are not available for segment block addresses.

For each extent in the segment, Oracle keeps an entry pointing to the bitmap for that segment as shown in Figure 15.3.

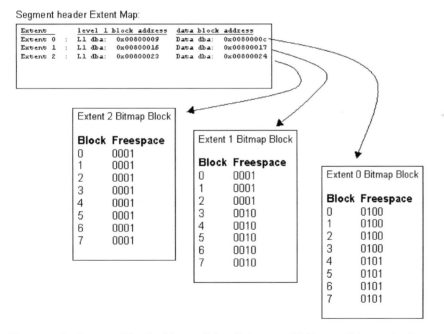

Figure 15.3: *Segment Header Extent Map Points to All Extent Bitmaps in Segments*

Oracle also has pointers to the last bitmap block within each logical bitmap level as shown in Figure 15.4.

ASSM and Tablespace Performance

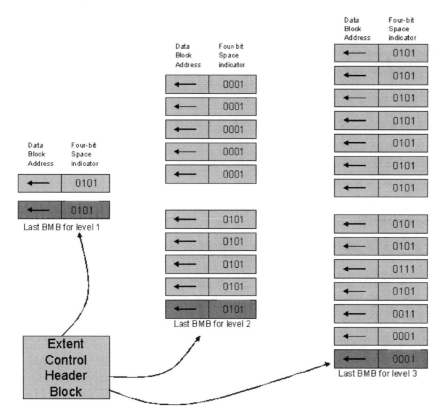

Figure 15.4: *Pointers to Last Bitmap Block on Each Bitmap Level*

This new pointer structure allows Oracle to quickly access multiple bitmaps to improve concurrency of high volume inserts.

Using ASSM with RAC

The performance and manageability gains provided by Oracle data management features are particularly noticeable in a Real Application Cluster (RAC) environment, especially the creation of multiple freelist groups for each node in the RAC cluster. The ASSM eliminates the need to alter the number of freelists and freelist groups when new instances are brought online, thereby saving the downtime associated with such table reorganizations. It also avoids the tuning effort previously required for multiple instance environments.

An Oracle internal benchmark comparing the performance of automatic and manual segment space management showed that the ASSM feature provided a 35% performance gain over an optimally tuned segment using the manual mode. This benchmark was conducted on a two-node RAC database by inserting about 3 million rows in a table. More details are available from Oracle Metalink Note 180608.1.

The new *dbms_space.space_usage* procedure can be used for reporting the space position in BMB segments. This procedure provides the space usage ratio within each block. The *block_count.sql* script below can be used to show how to get information about the blocks. It uses the *dbms_space.space_usage* procedure to examine the blocks within the specified table and count up the free space ranges for all data blocks in the table. The *block_count.sql* script below can be used to show how to get information about the blocks:

💾 block_count.sql

```
-- ***************************************************
-- Copyright © 2009 by Rampant TechPress
-- ***************************************************

Set serveroutput on

DECLARE
 v_unformatted_blocks number;
 v_unformatted_bytes number;
 v_fs1_blocks number;
 v_fs1_bytes number;
 v_fs2_blocks number;
 v_fs2_bytes number;
 v_fs3_blocks number;
 v_fs3_bytes number;
 v_fs4_blocks number;
 v_fs4_bytes number;
 v_full_blocks number;
 v_full_bytes number;

BEGIN
dbms_space.space_usage ('SYSTEM', 'TEST', 'TABLE', v_unformatted_blocks,
v_unformatted_bytes, v_fs1_blocks, v_fs1_bytes, v_fs2_blocks, v_fs2_bytes, v_fs3_blocks,
v_fs3_bytes, v_fs4_blocks, v_fs4_bytes, v_full_blocks, v_full_bytes);
dbms_output.put_line('Unformatted Blocks = '||v_unformatted_blocks);
dbms_output.put_line('FS1 Blocks       = '||v_fs1_blocks);
dbms_output.put_line('FS2 Blocks       = '||v_fs2_blocks);
dbms_output.put_line('FS3 Blocks       = '||v_fs3_blocks);
dbms_output.put_line('FS4 Blocks       = '||v_fs4_blocks);
dbms_output.put_line('Full Blocks      = '||v_full_blocks);
end;

The script yields the following output:

  Unformatted Blocks = 0
  FS1 Blocks        = 0
  FS2 Blocks        = 0
  FS3 Blocks        = 0
  FS4 Blocks        = 1
  Full Blocks       = 9

Where:

  FS1 means 0-25%    free space within a block
  FS2 means 25-50%   free space within a block
  FS3 means 50-75%   free space within a block
  FS4 means 75-100%  free space within a block
```

In summary, the ASSM and the new online space management packages can significantly help the space-related management chores, especially in RAC environments.

Potential Performance Issues with ASSM

The Oracle community has mixed feelings about using ASSM tablespaces. Among the top points about ASSM, there are both pros and cons. The next two sections address these pros and cons.

Pros of ASSM:

- Varying row sizes: ASSM is better than a static *pctused*. The bitmaps make ASSM tablespaces better at handling rows with wide variations in row length.

- Great for RAC: the bitmap freelists remove the need to define multiple freelists groups for RAC and provide overall improved freelist management over traditional freelists

Cons of ASSM:

- Slow for full-table scans: several studies have shown that large-table full-table scans (FTS) will run longer with ASSM than standard freelists. ASSM FTS tablespaces are consistently slower than freelist FTS operations. This implies that ASSM may not be appropriate for decision support systems and warehouse applications unless partitioning is used with Oracle Parallel Query (OPQ).

- Slower for high-volume concurrent inserts: numerous experts have conducted studies that show that tables with high volume bulk loads perform faster with traditional multiple freelists

- ASSM will influence index clustering: for row ordered tables, ASSM can adversely affect the *clustering_factor* for indexes. Bitmap freelists are less likely to place adjacent rows on physically adjacent data blocks, and this can lower the *clustering_factor* and the CBO's propensity to favor an index range scan.

The combination of bitmap freelists, ASSM, and LMT has greatly simplified and improved the internal management of data blocks within Oracle tablespaces. The use of bitmap freelists removes the need to define multiple freelists for tables and indexes that experience high volume concurrent DML and provides a simple solution to the problem of segment header contention.

However, the savvy DBA recognizes the tradeoff between one-size-fits-all convenience and the power of being able to set individual object parameters for tables and indexes. The choice of LMT and ASSM for tablespace management depends heavily on the application, and real-world Oracle tablespaces will implement LMT and ASSM tablespaces only after careful consideration.

Faster SQL with Database Reorganizations

Ever since the earliest days of data processing, database experts have known that the physical layout of the data on disk can affect the speed of queries. Clustering data together can reduce logical I/O and disk reads, making queries run far faster. Oracle also offers cluster tables to allow related row data to be clustered together in the same data blocks.

Oracle provides table and index maintenance tools that allow the DBA to re-optimize data while the database accepts updates with the Oracle *dbms_redefinition* package. To keep the databases running quickly, Oracle chooses not to incur the overhead of coalescing table rows and restructuring indexes during peak update times. This is why the DBA maintenance utilities exist. The trick is to understand when a table or index will benefit from reorganization.

Oracle has offered some huge improvements in indexing, especially related to the detection of missing indexes and materialized views. Another key improvement is the automation of index histogram detection for the SQL optimizer. Not to stop there, Oracle has also provided improvements to table maintenance. Oracle Database 10g included the following online data reorganization enhancements:

- Online table redefinition enhancements

- Easy cloning of indexes, grants, constraints, and more

- Conversion from LONG to LOB online

- Allowing unique index instead of primary key

- Changing tables without recompiling stored procedures

- Online segment shrink

Despite all of the wonderful automated tools at their disposal, the Oracle DBA must still perform routine table and index maintenance in order to keep highly active databases performing at peak levels.

Experience has shown that rebuilding tables and indexes improves the speed of queries, and there has been a great debate concerning the pros and cons of rebuilding Oracle indexes. There are two schools of thought on this important issue, and both sides make strong arguments for their case. The two viewpoints are as follows:

- Oracle Index Rebuilding is a waste of time: Some claim that indexes are always self-balancing and rarely need rebuilding. Even after an Oracle index rebuild, many say that SQL query performance is rarely faster.

- Oracle Index Rebuilding improves performance: Others note that indexes on tables with high DML, such as SQL inserts, updates and deletes, will be heavily fragmented with many empty blocks and a suboptimal access structure. These DBAs claim to see huge performance improvements after rebuilding a busy Oracle index.

On the surface, both stances sound like good arguments, but the DBA must dig deeper to fully understand index maintenance. The following is a logical approach to the issue of Oracle index rebuilding, and it starts with these assertions:

- **It is about I/O:** If SQL performance is faster after an index is rebuilt, it is because the query does fewer index block reads. This should be evident in the consistent gets and logical reads from the data buffer.

- **Only some index access methods will benefit from a rebuilt index:** Index fast full scans and some index range scans will run faster after a rebuild. Similar to how a full-table scan can take a long time when reading a table with many empty blocks, reading a range of a sparse index will result in excessive logical reads, as empty index nodes are accessed by the SQL query execution. Index unique scans will not improve after a rebuild, since they only read their participating nodes.

- **Oracle indexes can get clogged with empty and near empty index blocks:** As massive deletes take place, large chunks of an index are logically deleted, meaning that they are passed over by the pointers but still remain in the structure. These remaining empty blocks can have an effect on performance. Block-by-block scans, like those affected by *db_file_multiblock_read_count*, and some index range scans will perform fewer reads. This results in less I/O and better performance.

Managing Row Chaining in Oracle

Improper settings for *pctfree* and *pctused* can also cause database fragmentation. Whenever a row in an Oracle database expands because of an update, there must be sufficient room on the data block to hold the expanded row. If a row spans several data blocks, the database must perform additional disk I/O to fetch the block into the SGA. This excessive disk I/O can cripple the performance of the database.

The space reserved for row expansion is controlled by the *pctfree* parameter. Row chaining is especially problematic in cases where a row with many *varchar* datatypes is stored with *null* values, and subsequent update operations populate the varchar columns with large values. Fortunately, row chaining is relatively easy to detect. One important area of Oracle DBA work is tracking chained row fetches, i.e. *table fetch continued row name* in *v$sysstat* and *stats$sysstat*.

Watched for chained rows!
Remember, migrated/chained rows always cause double the I/O for a row fetch and the primary job of the Oracle tuning professional is to reduce disk I/O.

The presence of any of the following conditions may cause a *table fetch continued row* (chained row fetch):

- **Raw, long raw, BLOB or CLOB columns:** These may manifest as chained row fetches if the *avg_row_len > db_block_size*.

- **Tables with > 255 columns:** These are stored in 255 row-pieces, and show as migrated/chained rows.

- **Pctfree too small:** Did not allow enough room on the data block for the row to expand via SQL Update statements, causing rows to chain onto adjacent blocks.

The DBA can reduce migrated/chained rows by reorganizing the table with the *dbms_redefinition* utility or CTAS. Large-object related row chaining can be reduced by moving the object into a tablespace with a 32k blocksize. It is tempting to gather the *table fetch continued row* statistic from *v$sysstat* or *stats$sysstat*. For example, consider this report.

```
column table_fetch_continued_row  format 999,999,999

select
   to_char(snap_time,'yyyy-mm-dd hh24'),
   avg(newmem.value-oldmem.value)table_fetch_continued_row
from
   perfstat.stats$sysstat oldmem,
```

```
   perfstat.stats$sysstat newmem,
   perfstat.stats$snapshot    sn
where
   snap_time > sysdate-&1
and
   newmem.snap_id = sn.snap_id
and
   oldmem.snap_id = sn.snap_id-1
and
   oldmem.name = 'table fetch continued row'
and
   newmem.name = 'table fetch continued row'
and
   newmem.value-oldmem.value > 0
having
   avg(newmem.value-oldmem.value) > 10000
group by
   to_char(snap_time,'yyyy-mm-dd hh24');
```

Note that the following output only reports total chained row fetches per hour, regardless of the amount of total rows read. The existing report is silly because it only reports the total chained row fetches per hour, a meaningless number because it is not known if it is 1% or 80% of the total row fetches:

```
yr.  mo dy Hr.   TABLE_FETCH_CONTINUED_ROW
---------------  -------------------------
2003-10-23 08                    4,462,409
2003-10-23 09                    2,962,667
2003-10-23 10                    7,178,844
```

In the example above, the 4 million chained row fetches would be fine if 10 trillion rows were read, bad if 5 million rows are read.

In Oracle, the DBA can get the total row fetches by summing the *v$sysstat value* for *name = 'table scan rows gotten'* plus *'table fetch by rowid'*. A more meaningful report is shown below. This report only shows the alerts for those hours when total chained row fetches exceed 5% of total row fetches.

Row		Table Fetch	migrated/chained rows	Continued
yr. mo dy Hr.	Fetched	Row	Percent	
---------------	---------	-------------	-----	
2003-10-23 08	53,372,282	4,462,409	6%	
2003-10-24 09	46,282,383	2,962,667	14%	
2003-10-28 10	14,373,264	7,178,844	50%	

A script has been created that will run against the Oracle data dictionary and will produce a report showing the tables with excessive migrated/chained rows. Note that it is important to analyze all of the tables in the Oracle database with the *dbms_stats* before running this script.

💾 chained_row.sql

```
-- ********************************
-- This script relies on current CBO statistics
-- ********************************

spool chain.lst;
set pages 9999;
```

```
column c1 heading "Owner"    format a9;
column c2 heading "Table"    format a12;
column c3 heading "PCTFREE"  format 99;
column c4 heading "PCTUSED"  format 99;
column c5 heading "avg row"  format 99,999;
column c6 heading "Rows"     format 999,999,999;
column c7 heading "Chains"   format 999,999,999;
column c8 heading "Pct"      format .99;

set heading off;
select 'Tables with migrated/chained rows and no BLOB columns.' from dual;
set heading on;

select
    owner             c1,
    table_name        c2,
    pct_free          c3,
    pct_used          c4,
    avg_row_len       c5,
    num_rows          c6,
    chain_cnt         c7,
    chain_cnt/num_rows c8
from dba_tables
where
owner not in ('SYS','SYSTEM')
and
table_name not in
 (select table_name from dba_tab_columns
   where
 data_type in ('RAW','LONG RAW', 'BLOB', 'CLOB')
 )
and
chain_cnt > 0
order by chain_cnt desc
;
```

Here important information is seen including the table name and settings for *pctfree* and *pctused*, the average row length (*avg_row_len*) and a count of the chained rows at the time of the last analyze:

Owner	Table	PCTFREE	PCTUSED	avg row	Rows	Chains	Pct
SAPR3	ZG_TAB	10	40	80	5,003	1,487	.30
SAPR3	ZMM	10	40	422	18,309	509	.03
SAPR3	Z_Z_TBLS	10	40	43	458	53	.12
SAPR3	USR03	10	40	101	327	46	.14
SAPR3	Z_BURL	10	40	116	1,802	25	.01
SAPR3	ZGO_CITY	10	40	56	1,133	10	.01

Large objects will fragment!
It is common to experience lots of chaining in tables that contain raw, BLOB, CLOB and long raw columns, because the row length exceeds the *db_block_size*.

Once the tables have been identified with migrated/chained rows, the DBA must increase *pctfree* for the tables and then reorganize the tables using data pump, *alter table xxx move, create table as select* or *dbms_redefinition* to remove the chains. While there are several third-party products for reorganizing tables, table reorganization is most commonly done by running Oracle utilities such as *dbms_redefinition*.

Remember, for efficient space reuse, set a high value for *pctused*. A high value for *pctused* will effectively reuse space on data blocks, but at the expense of additional I/O. A high *pctused* means that relatively full blocks are placed on the freelist. Hence, these blocks will be able to accept only a few rows before becoming full again, leading to more I/O.

For better performance, set a low value for *pctused*. A low value for *pctused* means that Oracle will not place a data block onto the freelist until it is nearly empty. The block will be able to accept many rows until it becomes full, thereby reducing I/O at insert time. Remember that it is always faster for Oracle to extend into new blocks than to reuse existing blocks. For superfast space acquisition on SQL inserts, turn off freelist link/unlinks. It takes fewer resources for Oracle to extend a table than to manage freelists.

In effect, freelists can be turned off by setting *pctused* to 1. This will cause the freelists to be populated exclusively from new extents. Of course, this approach requires lots of extra disk space, and the table must be reorganized periodically to reclaim space within the table.

A Summary of Object Tuning Rules

The following rules govern the settings for the *init.ora* parameters *freelists, freelist groups, pctfree,* and *pctused*. Now review the general guidelines for setting object storage parameters.

Always set *pctused* to allow enough room to accept a new row. Free blocks that do not have enough room to accept a row are undesirable. If this happens, it will cause a slowdown since Oracle will attempt to read five dead free blocks before extending the table to get an empty block.

The presence of migrated/chained rows in a table means that *pctfree* is too low or that *db_block_size* is too small. In most cases within Oracle, raw and long raw columns make huge rows that exceed the maximum blocksize for Oracle, making migrated/chained rows unavoidable.

If a table has simultaneous *insert* SQL processes, it needs to have simultaneous *delete* processes. Running a single purge job will place all of the free blocks on only one freelist, and none of the other freelists will contain any free blocks from the purge.

The *freelists* parameter should be set to the high watermark of updates to a table. For example, if the customer table has up to 20 end users performing inserts at any time, then the customer table should have *freelists=20. Freelist groups* should be set to the number of RAC nodes and instances that access the table. For partitioned objects and cases of segment header contention, *freelist_groups* may be set for non-RAC systems.

The value of *pctused* and *pctfree* can easily be changed at any time with the *alter table* command, and the observant DBA should be able to develop a methodology for deciding the optimal settings for these parameters. There is a direct tradeoff between effective space utilization and high performance:

- **For efficient space reuse:** A high value for *pctused* will effectively reuse space on data blocks but at the expense of additional I/O. A high *pctused* means that relatively full blocks are placed on the freelist. Therefore, these blocks will be able to accept only a few rows before becoming full again, leading to more I/O.

- **For high performance:** A low value for *pctused* means that Oracle will not place a data block onto the freelist until it is nearly empty. The block will be able to accept many rows until it becomes full, thereby reducing I/O at insert time. It is always faster for Oracle to extend into new blocks than to reuse existing blocks. It takes fewer resources for Oracle to extend a table than to manage freelists, and freelist management can be turned off by setting *pctused* to a value of one. This will cause the freelists to be populated exclusively from empty blocks. Of course, this approach requires lots of extra disk space, and the table must be reorganized periodically to reclaim the wasted storage.

The *pctused* parameter should always be set large enough to allow plenty of room to accept a new row. The DBA never wants to have free blocks that do not have enough room to accept a row. If this happens, a slowdown will be the result since Oracle will attempt to read five dead free blocks before extending the table to get a completely empty block.

The presence of chained rows in a table means that *pctfree* is too low. In most cases within Oracle, raw and long raw columns make huge rows that exceed the maximum blocksize for Oracle, making row fragmentation unavoidable. If a table has simultaneous *insert* dialog processes, it needs to have multiple freelists to reduce segment header contention, and the application should parallelize the *delete* processes to evenly repopulate each freelist. Running a single purge job will place all of the free blocks on only one freelist, and none of the other freelists will contain any free blocks from the purge job.

Multiple freelists can also waste disk. Tables with dozens of freelists may exhibit the sparse table phenomenon as the table grows and each freelist contains free blocks that are not known to the other freelists. If these tables consume too much space, the Oracle DBA faces a tough decision. To maximize space reuse, the data block should be placed onto a freelist as soon as it is capable of receiving more than two new rows.

Therefore, a fairly high value for *pctused* is desired to maximize space reuse. On the other hand, this would result in slower runtime performance since Oracle will only be able to insert a few rows before having to perform an I/O to get another block. Now move on and take a look at proactive tablespace management techniques.

Reorganizing Tables for High Performance

Like other commercial databases, Oracle chose not to take the time to keep tables and indexes in a pristine state. Hence, periodic reorganization is required to keep tables and indexes performing at optimal levels.

Until Oracle 10g gave the *dbms_redefinition* package, there was no way to compact tables without affecting the end user activity. To understand table fragmentation, consider the illustration in Figure 15.5. The small squares indicate rows stored in the segment.

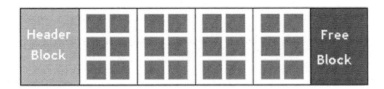

Figure 15.5: *A Table Segment Illustration*

When end users insert rows into this table, Oracle fills-up all empty blocks that were defined with the initial parameter (Figure 15.6).

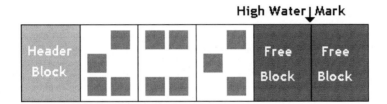

Figure 15.6: *Rows Deleted, Data Segment Wastes the Space, HWM Remains the Same*

The High WaterMark (HWM) represents the highest data block used by a table. For performance reasons, Oracle does not reclaim free space below the High WaterMark. This is because Oracle reserves that free space for future row inserts and possible row growth after updates. As a result, it is not uncommon to see excessive full-table scan times in tables where the High WaterMark has been raised, and lots of rows are then deleted. Even though the table is now small, full scans will go up to the HWM for the table.

Also, when Oracle inserts rows through the direct path method, i.e. the *append* hint, it always places new rows in data blocks above the HWM. Take a closer look at why, when and how to reorganize Oracle tables.

Online Reorganization

Starting with *dbms_redefinition* in 10g, a DBA can now go to an *online reorg* and restructure a table back into a pristine state while that table is still available for updates. Oracle also has the ability to reclaim space from a segment by shrinking a table with the *alter table xxx shrink space compact* syntax, a powerful tool for effective and easy Oracle table tuning.

Shrinking a table will coalesce unused space available to other segments in the tablespace and may improve the performance of queries and DML operations. However, the DBA needs to know what tables experience high space waste in order to know what tables to reorganize. The *awr_list_seg_block_space.sql* script below reports percentages of free space for data segments:

💾 awr_list_seg_block_space.sql

```
drop type BlckFreeSpaceSet;
drop type BlckFreeSpace;

create type BlckFreeSpace as object
(
 seg_owner varchar2(30),
 seg_type varchar2(30),
 seg_name varchar2(100),
 fs1 number,
 fs2 number,
 fs3 number,
 fs4 number,
 fb  number
 );

create type BlckFreeSpaceSet as table of  BlckFreeSpace;

create or replace function BlckFreeSpaceFunc (seg_owner IN varchar2, seg_type in varchar2
default null) return BlckFreeSpaceSet
pipelined
is
    outRec BlckFreeSpace := BlckFreeSpace(null,null,null,null,null,null,null,null);
    fs1_b number;
    fs2_b number;
    fs3_b number;
    fs4_b number;
    fs1_bl number;
    fs2_bl number;
    fs3_bl number;
    fs4_bl number;
    fulb number;
    fulbl number;
    u_b number;
    u_bl number;
begin
  for rec in (select s.owner,s.segment_name,s.segment_type from dba_segments s where owner =
seg_owner and segment_type = nvl(seg_type,segment_type) )
  loop
    dbms_space.space_usage (
        segment_owner       => rec.owner,
        segment_name        => rec.segment_name,
        segment_type        => rec.segment_type,
        fs1_bytes           => fs1_b,
        fs1_blocks          => fs1_bl,
        fs2_bytes           => fs2_b,
        fs2_blocks          => fs2_bl,
        fs3_bytes           => fs3_b,
        fs3_blocks          => fs3_bl,
        fs4_bytes           => fs4_b,
        fs4_blocks          => fs4_bl,
        full_bytes          => fulb,
        full_blocks         => fulbl,
        unformatted_blocks  => u_bl,
        unformatted_bytes   => u_b
    );

  outRec.seg_owner := rec.owner;
  outRec.seg_type := rec.segment_type;
```

```
    outRec.seg_name := rec.segment_name;

   outRec.fs1 := fs1_bl;
   outRec.fs2 := fs2_bl;
   outRec.fs3 := fs3_bl;
   outRec.fs4 := fs4_bl;
   outRec.fb  := fulbl;

   Pipe Row (outRec);

  end loop;
  return;
end;
/
```

The following script can be used to quickly generate a report showing which tables are good candidates for segment shrinking:

```
col seg_owner heading 'Segment|Owner'  format a10
col seg_type  heading 'Segment|Type'   format a10
col seg_name  heading 'Segment|Name'   format a30

col fs1 heading '0-25%|Free Space'    format 9,999
col fs2 heading '25-50%|Free Space'   format 9,999
col fs3 heading '50-75%|Free Space'   format 9,999
col fs4 heading '75-100%|Free Space'  format 9,999
col fb  heading 'Full|Blocks'         format 9,999

accept user_name prompt 'Enter Segment Owner: '

break on seg_owner

select
  *
from
  Table ( BlckFreeSpaceFunc ('&user_name', 'TABLE' ) )
order by
  fs4 desc
;
```

The following is the sample output of the above script for the *perstat* schema that owns STATSPACK utility:

Segment Owner	Segment Type	Segment Name	0-25% Free Space	25-50% Free Space	50-75% Free Space	75-100% Free Space	Full Blocks
PERFSTAT	TABLE	STATS$EVENT_HISTOGRAM	0	0	2	47	321
	TABLE	STATS$LATCH	0	0	1	35	522
	TABLE	STATS$SQL_SUMMARY	0	1	0	28	1,285
	TABLE	STATS$SYSSTAT	1	0	1	13	355

	TYPE			NAME		
0	TABLE	7	13	STATS$LIBRARYCACHE	0	0
1	TABLE	7	5	STATS$SQL_WORKAREA_HISTOGRAM	0	0
1	TABLE	6	43	STATS$ROWCACHE_SUMMARY	0	0
1	TABLE	6	66	STATS$ENQUEUE_STATISTICS	0	0
1	TABLE	6	5	STATS$RESOURCE_LIMIT	1	0
0	TABLE	5	0	STATS$TIME_MODEL_STATNAME	0	0
0	TABLE	5	0	STATS$DATABASE_INSTANCE	0	0
0	TABLE	5	0	STATS$LEVEL_DESCRIPTION	0	0
0	TABLE	5	0	STATS$IDLE_EVENT	0	0
1	TABLE	5	13	STATS$WAITSTAT	1	0
0	TABLE	5	0	STATS$STATSPACK_PARAMETER	0	0
0	TABLE	4	0	STATS$TEMP_HISTOGRAM	0	1
0	TABLE	4	0	STATS$INSTANCE_RECOVERY	0	1
1	TABLE	4	0	STATS$SQL_STATISTICS	0	0
2	TABLE	4	44	STATS$SGASTAT	0	0
1	TABLE	4	0	STATS$THREAD	0	0
1	TABLE	4	14	STATS$ROLLSTAT	0	1
0	TABLE	4	301	STATS$PARAMETER	1	0

As can be seen from the 75-100% free space column, *stats$event_histogram*, *stats$latch*, *stats$sql_summary*, and *stats$sysstat* are good candidates for segment shrinking. The following *alter table enable row movement* and *alter table shrink space compact* statements can be issued to shrink the segments mentioned:

```
SQL> alter table stats$event_histogram enable row movement;
```

Table altered.

```
SQL> alter table stats$event_histogram shrink space compact;
```

Table altered.

```
SQL> alter table stats$latch enable row movement;
```

Table altered.

```
SQL> alter table stats$latch shrink space compact;
```

```
Table altered.

SQL> alter table stats$sql_summary enable row movement;

Table altered.

SQL> alter table stats$sql_summary shrink space compact;

Table altered.

SQL> alter table stats$sysstat   enable row movement;

Table altered.

SQL> alter table stats$sysstat   shrink space compact;

Table altered.
```

In order to verify that Oracle has indeed reclaimed the space, the report can be run again. See how much space was reclaimed.

```
SQL> @ awr_report_seg_block_space.sql
```

Segment Owner	Segment Type	Segment Name	0-25% Free Space	25-50% Free Space	50-75% Free Space	75-100% Free	Full Blocks
PERFSTAT	TABLE	STATS$LIBRARYCACHE	0	0	0	7	13
	TABLE	STATS$SQL_WORKAREA_HISTOGRAM	0	0	1	7	5
	TABLE	STATS$ROWCACHE_SUMMARY	0	0	1	6	43
	TABLE	STATS$RESOURCE_LIMIT	1	0	1	6	5
	TABLE	STATS$ENQUEUE_STATISTICS	0	0	1	6	66
....							
	TABLE	STATS$SHARED_POOL_ADVICE	1	0	0	2	17
	TABLE	STATS$BUFFER_POOL_STATISTICS	0	0	2	2	1
	TABLE	STATS$EVENT_HISTOGRAM	0	1	0	1	320
	TABLE	STATS$SYSSTAT	0	0	1	1	356
	TABLE	STATS$SGA	0	1	1	1	2
	TABLE	STATS$BUFFERED_QUEUES	0	1	2	1	1
	TABLE	STATS$PGASTAT	1	1	1	1	9
	TABLE	STATS$SYS_TIME_MODEL	0	1	1	1	10
.....							
	TABLE	STATS$PGA_TARGET_ADVICE	1	0	1	0	11
	TABLE	STATS$LATCH_PARENT	0	0	0	0	0

		TABLE	STATS$LATCH_CHILDREN	0	0	0
0	0	TABLE	STATS$LATCH	0	1	1
0	521	TABLE	STATS$DB_CACHE_ADVICE	0	1	0
0	27	TABLE	STATS$SQL_SUMMARY	1	0	0
0	1,284	TABLE	STATS$SEG_STAT_OBJ	0	0	0
0	0	TABLE	STATS$SQL_PLAN	0	0	0
0	0	TABLE	STATS$SESS_TIME_MODEL	0	0	0
0	0	TABLE	STATS$DLM_MISC	0	0	0
0	0	TABLE	STATS$CR_BLOCK_SERVER	0	0	0
0	0	TABLE	STATS$CURRENT_BLOCK_SERVER	0	0	0
0	0	TABLE	STATS$CLASS_CACHE_TRANSFER	0	0	0
0	0					

In the listing above the shrunken tables consume much less space than they did before the reorganization. However, the HWM still has not been reset. The HWM for tables can be reset using a SQL statement like *alter table shrink space*. The shrink operation is performed completely online without affecting end users. If the *cascade* option is added to the *shrink* clause, Oracle will also compact indexes created on the target table.

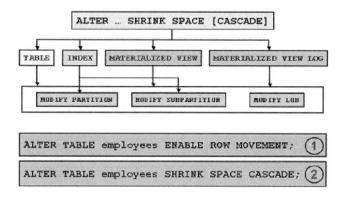

Figure 15.7: *Database Objects That Support the Shrink Space Operation*

Figure 15.7 shows database objects that support the *shrink space* operation. Oracle provides the ability to perform an in-place reorganization of data for optimal space utilization by shrinking it. This feature also provides the ability to both compact the space used in a segment and then de-allocate it from the segment.

The de-allocated space is returned to the tablespace and becomes available to other segments within the tablespace. By performing *shrink*, the data in the table is compacted and the high watermark of the segment is pushed down to the last populated data block. This makes full-table scans read less blocks and hence, run faster. Also, during compaction, row chaining is eliminated whenever possible.

Reorg in real-time!
Remember, an *alter table shrink space* can be done anytime, and the table will still accept updates. However, shrinking during low activity periods is recommended.

The DBA can also schedule segment shrinks using *dbms_scheduler* as a nightly job without requiring any additional space to be provided to the database. For more details, see Dr. Hall's book, *Oracle Job Scheduling*, by Rampant TechPress. Segment shrink works on heaps, IOTs, LOBs, materialized views and indexes with row movement enabled in tablespaces with ASSM.

Now explore how to predict the benefits of table reorganization.

Segment Space Growth Prediction

All databases will grow over the course of time, and planning for growth is a very important chore. One of the most important features of Oracle is its ability to predict the growth of the segments. The *object_growth_trend* prediction mechanism is based on data collected and stored by the AWR, and can be used to create growth trend reports for the key tables.

The query below allows the estimation of the segment growth trend for the *stats$sysstat* table:

```
SQL> select
*
from
table(dbms_space.OBJECT_GROWTH_TREND
('PERFSTAT','STATS$SYSSTAT','TABLE'));
```

The output of this query might look like this, showing the growth trend for the table. This is very useful for forecasting database growth and planning future disk storage needs:

TIMEPOINT	SPACE_USAGE	SPACE_ALLOC	QUALITY
02.10.04 15:58:04,218000	592359	1048576	INTERPOLATED
03.10.04 15:58:04,218000	592359	1048576	INTERPOLATED
04.10.04 15:58:04,218000	592359	1048576	INTERPOLATED
05.10.04 15:58:04,218000	592359	1048576	INTERPOLATED
06.10.04 15:58:04,218000	592359	1048576	INTERPOLATED
17.10.04 15:58:04,218000	592359	1048576	INTERPOLATED
18.10.04 15:58:04,218000	592359	1048576	INTERPOLATED
19.10.04 15:58:04,218000	592359	1048576	INTERPOLATED
20.10.04 15:58:04,218000	592359	1048576	INTERPOLATED
21.10.04 15:58:04,218000	592359	1048576	GOOD

```
22.10.04 15:58:04,218000          786887    1048576  INTERPOLATED
23.10.04 15:58:04,218000          826610    1048576  INTERPOLATED
24.10.04 15:58:04,218000          839843    1048576  INTERPOLATED
25.10.04 15:58:04,218000          846459    1048576  INTERPOLATED
26.10.04 15:58:04,218000         3072829    3145728  INTERPOLATED
27.10.04 15:58:04,218000         3072829    3145728  INTERPOLATED
28.10.04 15:58:04,218000         3072829    3145728  INTERPOLATED
29.10.04 15:58:04,218000         3072829    3145728  INTERPOLATED
30.10.04 15:58:04,218000         3072829    3145728  INTERPOLATED
31.10.04 15:58:04,218000         3072829    3145728  INTERPOLATED
01.11.04 15:58:04,218000         3072829    3145728  INTERPOLATED
02.11.04 15:58:04,218000         3678280    3678280  PROJECTED
03.11.04 15:58:04,218000         3764774    3764774  PROJECTED
04.11.04 15:58:04,218000         3851267    3851267  PROJECTED
05.11.04 15:58:04,218000         3937760    3937760  PROJECTED
06.11.04 15:58:04,218000         4024253    4024253  PROJECTED
```

The *space_usage* column shows how many bytes the *stats$sysstat* table actually consumes, and *space_alloc* reports the size, in bytes, of space used by the table.

The next section will provide an introduction to an important tool for tuning SQL, the *clustering_factor* column in the *dba_indexes* view.

Tuning SQL Access with *clustering_factor*

With each new release of Oracle, the CBO improves. The consideration of external influences such as CPU cost and I/O cost when formulating an execution plan came with the release of Oracle 9i. As Oracle evolved into release Oracle 11g, there have been improvements in the ability of the CBO to get the optimal execution plan for a query. Despite these advances, it is still important to understand the mechanism.

Before attempting to understand how Oracle decides on an execution plan for a query, it is important to first learn the rules Oracle uses when it determines whether to use an index.

The most important characteristics of column data are the clustering factor for the column and the selectivity of column values, even though other important characteristics within tables are available to the CBO.
The optimizer's decision to perform a full-table versus an index range scan is influenced by the *clustering_factor* column located inside the *dba_indexes* view, *db_block_size* and *avg_row_len*. It is important to understand how the CBO uses these statistics to determine the fastest way to deliver the desired rows.

Conversely, a high *clustering_factor*, where the value approaches the number of rows in the table (*num_rows*), indicates that the rows are not in the same sequence as the index, and additional I/O will be required for index range scans. As the *clustering_factor* approaches the number of rows in the table, the rows are out of sync with the index.

A column called *clustering_factor* in the *dba_indexes* view offers information on how the table rows are synchronized with the index. When the clustering factor is close to the number of data blocks and the column value is not row ordered when the *clustering_factor* approaches the number of rows in the table, the table rows are synchronized with the index.

To illustrate this, the following query will filter the result set using a column value:

```
select
   customer_name
from
   customer
where
   customer_state = 'North Carolina';
```

In this example, an index scan is faster for this query if the percentage of customers in New Mexico is small and the values are clustered on the data blocks. The decision to use an index versus a full-table scan is at least partially determined by the percentage of customers in New Mexico.

Four factors synchronize to help the CBO choose whether to use an index or a full-table scan:

7. The selectivity of a column value

8. The *db_block_size*

9. The *avg_row_len*

10. The cardinality

An index scan is usually faster if a data column has high selectivity and a low *clustering_factor* as shown in Figure 15.8.

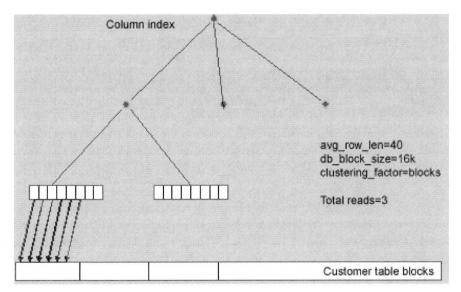

Figure 15.8: *Column with a Low Clustering Factor, Small Rows and Large Blocks*

If there is a frequent query that performs large index range scans, the table can be forced to have the same order as the index. By maintaining row order, suboptimal full-table scans are removed. Placing all adjacent rows in the same data block can often allow some queries to run much faster.

Table row order can be forced with a single-table table cluster or by reorganizing the table with the *create table as select* syntax, using the SQL ORDER BY clause to force the row order. This is especially important when a majority of the SQL references a column with a high *clustering_factor,* a large *db_block_size,* and a small *avg_row_len.*

Even when a column has high selectivity, a high *clustering_factor* and a small *avg_row_len,* there is still an indication that column values are randomly distributed in the table. In this case, an additional I/O will be required to obtain the rows.

On the other hand, as the *clustering_factor* nears the number of rows in the table, the rows fall out of sync with the index. A high *clustering_factor,* in which the value is close to the number of rows in the table *(num_rows),* indicates that the rows are out of sequence with the index and an additional I/O may be required for index range scans.

An index range scan can cause a huge amount of unnecessary I/O as shown in Figure 15.9. Full-table scans are much more efficient.

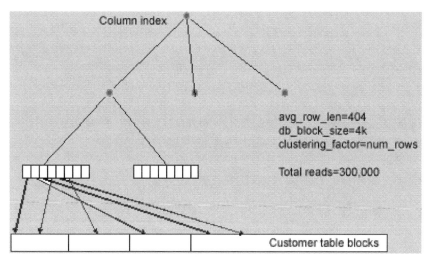

Figure 15.9: *Column with High Clustering Factor Small Blocks and Large Rows*

Oracle developers have recognized that certain types of queries will run thousands of times faster when related data is placed together on disk. Oracle provides several tools for keeping an optimal *clustering_factor* for important queries:

- **Multi-table table clusters:** If the system always accesses related data together, using a multi-table cluster can greatly improve query performance. For example, if the system always displays customer row data with data from the orders table, the customer row and all of the orders can be placed on a single data block, requiring only a single consistent get to acquire all of the required data.

- **Single-table table clusters:** This technique allows Oracle to guarantee that data blocks are stored in column value order, allowing index range scans to run very quickly.

Oracle cluster tables have overhead, namely wasted disk space that must be reserved using *pctfree*, in order for new rows to be placed on the proper block. There is also the overhead of maintaining overflow areas when it is impossible to store rows on their target block.

Many Oracle DBAs will choose to manually reorganize tables using the *dbms_redefinition* package, the *create table as select* or *alter table move* syntax using an *order by* and a *parallel* clause.

Since it is apparent that the placement of data on disk affects SQL performance, a closer look at changing the organization of the tables and indexes to speed up SQL execution speed is a good next step.

Not all Indexes are Used in Range Scans

When deciding to segregate indexes into larger blocksizes, it is important to understand that the indexes that are most subject to frequent index range scans and fast-full scans will benefit the most from a larger blocksize.

When Oracle joins two tables with a nested loop, only one of the indexes may be accessed as a range. The optimizer always performs an index range scan on one index, gathers the *rowid* values, and does fetch by *rowid* on the matching rows in the other table. For example:

```
select
   customer_name,
   order_date
from
   customer
   orders
where
   customer.cust_key = orders.cust_key;
```

The Oracle documentation notes that a nested loop involves two loops:

> *"In a nested loop join, for every row in the outer row set, the inner row set is accessed to find all the matching rows to join. Therefore, in a nested loop join, the inner row set is accessed as many times as the number of rows in the outer row set."*

Oracle will only scan one index, build a set of keys and then probe the rows from the other table as represented in Figure 15.10.

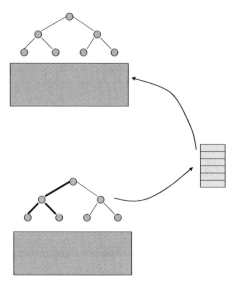

Figure 15.10: *Table Joins Include Index Range Scans and Index Unique Scans*

If this nested loop never uses the customer index, some may wonder why it is there at all. The answer is: For index unique scans. In an index unique scan, a single row is accessed within the index, as seen in this query:

```
select
   customer_last_name,
   customer_address
from
   customer
where
   cust_key = 123;
```

In sum, the DBA must find out how their indexes are being used by the SQL. An index that never experiences range scans will not benefit from a larger blocksize. The question becomes one of finding those indexes that experience a large number of range scans.

It is possible to identify those indexes with the most index range scans with the following simple AWR script.

💾 **index_range_scans.sql**

```
col c1  heading 'Object|Name'        format a30
col c2  heading 'Option'             format a15
col c3  heading 'Index|Usage|Count'  format 999,999

select
  p.object_name c1,
  p.options     c2,
  count(1)      c3
from
```

```
    dba_hist_sql_plan p,
    dba_hist_sqlstat  s
where
   p.object_owner <> 'SYS'
and
   p.options like '%RANGE SCAN%'
and

   p.operation like '%INDEX%'
and
   p.sql_id = s.sql_id
group by
   p.object_name,
   p.operation,
   p.options
order by
  1,2,3;
```

The following is the output showing overall total counts for each object and table access method.

| | | Index Usage |
Object Name	Option	Count
CUSTOMER_CHECK	RANGE SCAN	4,232
AVAILABILITY_PRIMARY_KEY	RANGE SCAN	1,783
CON_UK	RANGE SCAN	473
CURRENT_SEVERITY	RANGE SCAN	323
CWM$CUBEDIMENSIONUSE_IDX	RANGE SCAN	72
ORDERS_FK	RANGE SCAN	20

This script will quickly identify indexes that will benefit the most from a 32k blocksize.

This index list can be double verified by using the AWR to identify indexes with high disk reads during each AWR snapshot period. The sample script below shows the top five tables accessed by physical disk reads for every snapshot interval:

busy_table_io.sql

```
col c0 heading 'Begin|Interval|time'  format a8
col c1 heading 'Table|Name'           format a20
col c2 heading 'Disk|Reads'           format 99,999,999
col c3 heading 'Rows|Processed'       format 99,999,999

select
*
from (
select
    to_char(s.begin_interval_time,'mm-dd hh24') c0,
    p.object_name c1,
    sum(t.disk_reads_total) c2,
    sum(t.rows_processed_total) c3,
    DENSE_RANK() OVER (PARTITION BY to_char(s.begin_interval_time,'mm-dd hh24') ORDER BY
SUM(t.disk_reads_total) desc) AS rnk
from
  dba_hist_sql_plan p,
  dba_hist_sqlstat t,
```

```
  dba_hist_snapshot s
where
  p.sql_id = t.sql_id
and
  t.snap_id = s.snap_id
and
  p.object_type like '%TABLE%'
group by
  to_char(s.begin_interval_time,'mm-dd hh24'),
  p.object_name
order by
c0 desc, rnk
)
where rnk <= 5
;
```

The following is the sample output from the above script:

Begin Interval time	Table Name	Disk Reads	Rows Processed	RNK
10-29 15	CUSTOMER_CHECK	55,732	498,056	1
10-29 15	CON_UK	18,368	166,172	2
10-29 15	CURRENT_SEVERITY	11,727	102,545	3
10-29 15	ORDERS_FK	5,876	86,671	4
10-29 15	SYN$	2,624	23,674	5
10-29 14	CUSTOMER_CHECK	47,756	427,762	1
10-29 14	CON_UK	15,939	142,878	2
10-29 14	CURRENT_SEVERITY	6,976	113,649	3
10-29 14	X$KZSRO	4,772	119,417	4
10-29 14	ORDERS_FK	2,274	20,292	5
10-29 13	CUSTOMER_CHECK	25,704	213,786	1
10-29 13	CON_UK	8,568	71,382	2
10-29 13	OBJ$	3,672	30,474	3
10-29 13	X$KZSRO	2,448	20,328	4
10-29 13	SYN$	1,224	10,146	5

This report shows the tables with the highest disk reads. This information is very important for disk tuning.

The *dba_hist_sql_plan* table can also be used to gather counts about the frequency of participation of objects inside of queries. Below is a useful query to quickly see what is going on between the tables and the SQL that accesses them.

🖫 count_table_access.sql

```
col c1 heading 'Object|Name'        format a30
col c2 heading 'Operation'          format a15
col c3 heading 'Option'             format a15
```

```
col c4 heading 'Object|Count'          format 999,999

break on c1 skip 2
break on c2 skip 2

select
  p.object_name  c1,
  p.operation    c2,
  p.options      c3,
  count(1)       c4
from
   dba_hist_sql_plan p,
   dba_hist_sqlstat  s
where
   p.object_owner <> 'SYS'
and
   p.sql_id = s.sql_id
group by
   p.object_name,
   p.operation,
   p.options
order by
  1,2,3;
```

The following output shows overall total counts for each object and table access method.

Object Name	Operation	Option	Object Count
CUSTOMER	TABLE ACCESS	FULL	305
CUSTOMER _CHECK	INDEX	RANGE SCAN	2
CUSTOMER_ORDERS	TABLE ACCESS	BY INDEX ROWID	311
CUSTOMER_ORDERS		FULL	1
CUSTOMER_ORDERS_PRIMARY	INDEX	FULL SCAN	2
CUSTOMER_ORDERS_PRIMARY		UNIQUE SCAN	311
AVAILABILITY_PRIMARY_KEY		RANGE SCAN	4
CON_UK		RANGE SCAN	3
CURRENT_SEVERITY_PRIMARY_KEY		RANGE SCAN	1
CWM$CUBE	TABLE ACCESS	BY INDEX ROWID	2
CWM$CUBEDIMENSIONUSE		BY INDEX ROWID	2
CWM$CUBEDIMENSIONUSE_IDX	INDEX	RANGE SCAN	2
CWM$CUBE_PK		UNIQUE SCAN	2
CWM$DIMENSION_PK		FULL SCAN	2
MGMT_INV_VERSIONED_PATCH	TABLE ACCESS	BY INDEX ROWID	3
MGMT_JOB		BY INDEX ROWID	458
MGMT_JOB_EMD_STATUS_QUEUE		FULL	181
MGMT_JOB_EXECUTION		BY INDEX ROWID	456
MGMT_JOB_EXEC_IDX01	INDEX	RANGE SCAN	456

Tuning SQL Access with clustering_factor

MGMT_JOB_EXEC_SUMMARY	TABLE ACCESS	BY INDEX ROWID	180
MGMT_JOB_EXEC_SUMM_IDX04	INDEX	RANGE SCAN	180
MGMT_JOB_HISTORY	TABLE ACCESS	BY INDEX ROWID	1
MGMT_JOB_HIST_IDX01	INDEX	RANGE SCAN	1
MGMT_JOB_PK		UNIQUE SCAN	458
MGMT_METRICS	TABLE ACCESS	BY INDEX ROWID	180

Using the output above, it is easy to monitor object participation within the SQL queries. This output also shows the mode by which an object was accessed by Oracle.

Why is it important to know how tables and indexes are accessed? Objects that experience multi-block reads may perform faster in a larger blocksize and also reduce SGA overhead.

Next, let's examine index maintenance so that we understand when it is necessary to reorganize of rebuild indexes.

Rebuilding Indexes

Some people suggest that indexes require rebuilding when deleted leaf rows appear or when the index has a suboptimal number of block gets per access. While it is tempting to write a script that rebuilds every index in the schema, bear in mind that the schema may contain many thousands of indexes, and a complete rebuild can be very time consuming.

Hence, it is important to develop a method to identify those indexes that will get improved performance with a rebuild. Look at one method for accomplishing this task.

Oracle MetaLink note 122008.1 has the officially authorized script to detect indexes that benefit from rebuilding. This script detects indexes for rebuilding using these rules: Rebuild the index when these conditions are true:

11. Deleted entries represent 20% or more of the current entries

12. The index depth is more than 4 levels

Oracle's index rebuilding guidelines appearing in Metalink note 77574.1 (dated April 2007) recommend that indexes be periodically examined to see if they are candidates for an index rebuild.

However, when large numbers of adjacent rows are deleted, it is highly unlikely that Oracle will have an opportunity to reuse the deleted leaf rows, and these represent wasted space in the index. In addition to wasting space, large volumes of deleted leaf nodes will make index fast-full scans run for longer periods.

- **The number of deleted leaf rows:** The term "deleted leaf node" refers to the number of index inodes that have been logically deleted as a result of row deletes. Remember that Oracle leaves dead index nodes in the index when rows are deleted. This is done to speed up SQL deletes, since Oracle does not have to allocate resources to rebalance the index tree when rows are deleted.

- **Index height:** The height of the index refers to the number of levels that are spawned by the index as a result in row inserts. When a large amount of rows are added to a table, Oracle may spawn additional levels of an index to accommodate the new rows. Hence, an Oracle index may have four levels, but only in those areas of the index tree where the massive inserts have occurred. Oracle indexes can support many millions of entries in three levels, and any Oracle index that has four or more levels would benefit from rebuilding.

- **Gets per index access:** The number of gets per access refers to the amount of logical I/O that is required to fetch a row with the index. A logical get is not necessarily a physical I/O since much of the index may reside in the Oracle buffer cache. However, any SAP index with a number greater than 10 would probably benefit from an index rebuild.

Unfortunately, Oracle does not make it easy to capture this information. In Oracle, these commands must be issued:

```
analyze index index_name compute statistics
analyze index index_name validate structure
```

After analyzing the report above, the DBA may want to consider rebuilding any index where the height is more than three levels, since three levels will support millions of index entries. Note that Oracle indexes will spawn to a fourth level only in areas of the index where a massive insert has occurred, such that 99% of the index has three levels, but the index is reported as having four levels.

It might be appropriate to rebuild an index if the block gets per access is greater than five, since excessive block gets indicate a fragmented b-tree structure. Another rebuild condition would be cases where deleted leaf nodes comprise more than 20% of the index nodes.

Now that the candidates for an index rebuild have been identified, the DBA can run the following script during SAP system downtime to rebuild all of the indexes.

```
Set heading off;
Set pages 9999;
Spool run_rebuild.sql;

select 'alter index sapr3.'||
index_name||
' rebuild tablespace '||
tablespace_name||';'
from dba_indexes
where owner = 'SAPR3';

spool off;
@run_rebuild


The ALTER INDEX index_name REBUILD command is very safe way to rebuild indexes. Here is the
syntax of the command:

alter index index_name
rebuild
tablespace tablespace_name
storage (initial new_initial next new_next freelists new_freelist_number )
```

Rebuilding Indexes

Unlike the traditional method where the index is dropped and recreated, the *rebuild* command does not require a full-table scan of the table, and the subsequent sorting of the keys and ROWIDs. Rather, the *rebuild* command will perform the following steps:

13. Walk the existing index to get the index keys

14. Populate temporary segments with the new tree structure

15. Once the operation has completed successfully, drop the old tree, and rename the temporary segments to the new index

Carefully following the steps described above eliminates any worry about accidently losing an index while rebuilding indexes. If the index cannot be rebuilt for any reason, Oracle will abort the operation and leave the existing index intact. Only after the entire index has been rebuilt does Oracle transfer the index to the new b-tree. Most Oracle administrators run this script, and then select the index that they would like to rebuild. Note that the *tablespace* clause should always be used with the *alter index rebuild* command to ensure that the index is not rebuilt within the default tablespace, usually SYS.

Be aware that it is always a good idea to move an index into another tablespace and there must be enough room in that tablespace to hold all of the temporary segments required for the index rebuild, so most Oracle administrators will double-size index tablespaces with enough space for two full index trees.

When to Rebuild Indexes

Today, a battle is raging between the academics who do not believe that indexes should be rebuilt without expensive studies and the pragmatists who rebuild indexes on a schedule because their end-users report faster response times.

To date, none of the world's Oracle experts has determined a reliable rule for index rebuilding, and no expert has proven that index rebuilds rarely help. Getting statistically valid proof from a volatile production system would be a phenomenal challenge. In a large production system, it would be a massive effort to trace LIO from specific queries to specific indexes before and after the rebuild.

- **Academic approach:** Many Oracle experts claim that indexes rarely benefit from rebuilding, yet none has ever proffered empirical evidence that this is the case, or what logical I/O conditions arise in those rare cases where indexes benefit from rebuilding.

- **Pragmatic approach:** Many IT managers force their Oracle DBAs to periodically rebuild indexes because the end-user community reports faster response times following the rebuild. The pragmatists are not interested in proving anything, they are just happy that the end-users are happy. Even if index rebuilding were to be proven as a useless activity, the Placebo Effect on the end-users is enough to justify the task.

The only time indexes need to be rebuilt is when the cost to rebuild is less than the performance gained. The first one is obvious. Pack the tables and indexes, i.e. rebuild into the soon to be read-only tablespace, tightly and they will stay that way. The second is much more difficult.

First, it is a continuing process since the index will move toward fluff with use. Second, there is the cost of rebuilding the index and the cost of the additional redo as the index changes. There is only one method to determine if rebuilding an index benefits the database: testing.

Ceteris Paribas, SQL response time for full-scan and logically-sequential range scans is a function of the density of the index block. Index blocks that are made sparse as a result of delete activity will cause additional I/O. Index rebuilding is risk free when done properly, moving the indexes between two tablespaces.

Here are some generally accepted observations about Oracle indexes. Note: By their very nature, all observations cannot be validated without exposing proprietary details. Hence, make sure to check the credentials and qualifications of all claims.

- **Index rebuilds can improve SQL performance:** On indexes with heavy delete activity, rebuilding has been proven to improve SQL performance for range queries. One DBA noted "our observation was that on 20 million row tables and upward, as little as 5% deletes, regardless of other factors, would cause sufficient performance degradation to justify an index rebuild."

- **Index rebuilds can be safely automated:** For shops that are concerned about space reclamation, batch jobs can be implemented to reliably rebuild all indexes automatically. I've personally used crontab jobs for index rebuilding when my clients insisted on scheduled index rebuilding, and there is a very low risk of causing a production problem, provided that the rebuilds are performed during regularly scheduled maintenance windows using Oracle Best Practices.

- **Index rebuilds can release free space:** It is well documented that index rebuilding/coalesce will release lost space (see the Oracle Segment Advisor) and in rare cases, an index rebuild may cause a performance boost, but only under certain conditions.

Using Oracle's model, the DBA compares allocated space to used space to locate sparse indexes, and many DBAs have postulated equations and formulae for identifying suboptimal indexes. But when rebuilding for performance, the DBA must also inspect the workload to find reproducible evidence of unnecessary I/O, e.g. too many blocks read for an index range scan or an index fast-full-scan.

Oracle's segment advisor has built primitive predictive models to suggest reorganization opportunities, but like any DSS, the rules are not fully quantifiable. The DSS only supplies the well-structured quantitative component, but it is still a semi-structured problem, requiring a real human expert to make the right decision.

The question remains, can an automated tool inspect the workload and the indexes and make a rebuild recommendation? I say yes, but it can never be fully automated without human input. Take a closer look.

No two systems are alike, and the methods used by DBAs are as varied as the applications themselves. It is suggested that well-structured rules exist for index rebuilding, but they are somewhat complex and require empirical evidence about:

- Specific conditions within the real-world workload, i.e. too-long IRS and IFFS

- Indexes which are sparsely populated as a result of DML

- Knowledge of future index expansion

Some DBAs will use an empirical approach and rebuild suspect indexes during scheduled downtime, measuring later changes or replying upon first-hand end-users for feedback. Others are ordered to rebuild regularly, based on superstition and bad advice.

While it is easy to measure the space savings of an index rebuild, it is more challenging to correlate range-scan and full-scan SQL before-and-after an index rebuild. Some DBAs who have a high-DML system may use scripts such as the *plan9i.sql* script, available online, to identify range-scan and full-scan SQL statements. If significant scans are identified, a representative DML and query-only workload can be captured and used in a simple test.

- In test, rebuild the target index

- Run the query-only workload, measuring total logical I/O (buffer touches)

- Replay the DML load/update/purge/jobs

- Run the query-only workload, measuring total logical I/O (buffer touches)

Again, every situation is unique, and this is only one of dozens of ways that a DBA might approach this problem.

What Types of Applications Have Index Rebuilding Opportunities?

Some people claim that systems which see a performance benefit from index rebuilding are rare, and the term rarity is in the eyes of the beholder. In some super-dynamic applications, i.e. Pharmaceuticals or scientific research applications, it is not rare at all to get a benefit from index rebuilding. These types of systems were one reason that 10g introduced dynamic sampling. A table can be huge in the AM and tiny in the afternoon, and skewed values change with each batch load.

While I can only speak from my own experience, I have noted that systems that are characterized by large batch loads, updates and purges are the ones most likely to have indexes. These include many ERP products such as SAP, especially M&I systems (Oracle INV and MFG modules), but only where raw materials and shipped goods are updated via batch jobs, i.e. EDI feeds.

Also problematic are scientific applications, especially LIMS (Laboratory Information Management System), which constantly load, modify and purge large sets of experimental data. For example, consider the popular Clintrial software, a LIMS that uses Oracle. In Clintrial, experimental results are initially stored as small rows. Later, as more data is collected, the varchar columns expand, causing massive row chaining, and fragmenting the daylights out of secondary indexes as key values are changed. In the Clintrial databases I have worked with, most data updates are done via large batch loads from SAS, and as a typical DSS, the queries tend to do lots of large range scans, aggregations and index full-scans.

To plan for this expected growth, set *pctfree* to allow only a few rows per block, thereby avoiding the chained row issue. The problem, of course, is having a priori knowledge of how the application will process its rows. In my world, the scientists start complaining about slow response times, and while the row chaining issue has been alleviated, the indexes still needed to be rebuilt.

In practice, many of these shops drop the indexes before the batch jobs and rebuild them again afterwards, but some choose to perform periodic index maintenance.

Can Indexes Be Found That Will Benefit From a Rebuild?

Many Oracle professionals have attacked the practice of rebuilding Oracle indexes on a regularly scheduled basis, correctly noting that the space reclamation and index performance does not always significantly change when an index is rebuilt. This has lead to the incorrect assertion that Oracle indexes are always optimized and never require rebuilding. Others attempt to create a set of index characteristics that accurately determine when an index will benefit from rebuilding.

In reality, many Oracle databases experience a huge benefit from periodic index rebuilding. Oracle recognized this benefit of index rebuilding when the Oracle 9i online index rebuild feature made it possible to rebuild an Oracle index while the index is being updated using the *alter index xxx rebuild online tablespace yyy;* syntax.

Reliably predicting when to reorganize tables and indexes is an important decision, and one that can be automated. This has become the Holy Grail for many Oracle professionals with numerous articles and debates about predicting the benefit from a reorg. Some purists say that it is better to design the table/indexes never to fragment in the first place, but the reality of the Oracle DBA is that high attrition, vendor packages and the inability to control the developers makes this a very important real-world problem.

The goal is to create a reliable predictive model that will suggest tables and indexes which will measurably benefit from reorganization, predict the reduction in I/O, meaning logical I/O - *consistent gets* and physical I/O - *physical reads*, after the reorganization, and suggest changes that will prevent a reoccurrence of the fragmentation, i.e. new *pctfree*, new blocksize and such:

- Oracle tables/indexes can be reorganized, sometimes resulting in faster SQL execution speeds.

- AWR (STATSPACK) has a history of how the tables were accessed by historical SQL, *dba_hist_sql_plan* and *stats$sql_plan*, for example, including the I/O and CPU costs associated with each step of SQL execution.

- The current internal structure of every table/index, e.g. *chain_cnt, clustering_factor,* and more, can be seen.

Most databases have repeating patterns of behavior, and historical SQL is usually representative of future activity. The model should be able to see if the table/index history has simply by examining the historical access patterns.

The steps to solving this problem are simple, but the process logic is complex:

16. **Gather table/index structure information:** There are many examples of routines that can perform an *alter index xxx validate structure* command and store the results in a table for analysis.

17. **Analyze historical patterns of usage:** Alter the *plan9i.sql* script to access the *stats$sql_plan* table and see exactly how table/indexes are accessed by the SQL, and how often, too.

18. **Add the decision rules:** Design an expert-system algorithm that will interrogate the data from steps 1 and 2 and create the list of tables/indexes, predicted I/O reductions, and suggested structural changes.

19. **Test and refine the rules:** Iterate through step 3, successively refining the rules based on actual results.

Here is a list of possible conditions that may contribute to table/index fragmentation. Remember, there is no need to pre-justify the chosen rule set. The only thing that counts is that the rules make accurate predictions.

Index fast-full-scans will run faster after index reorganization whenever the density of the index entries becomes greater. In other words, it takes less time to read 100,000 entries from a 100 block index than reading the entries from a 500 block index.

Multi-block index scans (*index_ffs*) will run faster when the table data blocks are arranged in index-key order and when the data blocks have a high number of row entries, as evidenced by *clustering_factor* in *dba_indexes*.

Large-table full-table scans may run faster after table reorganization, especially when the table has excessive chained or relocated rows or low block density after massive DML activity, i.e. updates and deletes. Remember, rebuilding indexes can be a low-risk, low resource task, but that does not mean that indexes should be rebuilt will-nilly and without justification.

- **Index rebuilds are low risk:** Because the new index is created in temporary segments, Oracle will never destroy the old index until the new index has been created.

- **Index rebuilds are unobtrusive:** Oracle indexes can be rebuilt online without interruption to availability and DML activity.

- **Index rebuilds are cheap:** The cost of the duplicate disk to store a new index tree is negligible, as are the computing resources used during a rebuild. Many Oracle professionals forget that unused server resources can never be reclaimed, and servers depreciate so fast that the marginal cost of utilizing extra CPU and RAM are virtually zero.

Now that the issues with index performance management have been explained, this chapter will wrap up with an examination of how to manage objects with parallel DDL. Parallelism is an indispensible tool for performance management in a busy environment.

Oracle Parallel DDL

DDL operations, such as create table and create index, can be paralleled if a *parallel* clause or an *alter session force parallel ddl;* declaration is specified in the syntax. The parallel DDL statements for non-partitioned tables and indexes are:

```
CREATE INDEX
CREATE TABLE ... AS select
ALTER INDEX ... REBUILD
```

The parallel DDL statements for partitioned tables and indexes are:

```
CREATE INDEX
CREATE TABLE ... AS select
ALTER TABLE ... MOVE PARTITION
ALTER TABLE ... SPLIT PARTITION
ALTER TABLE ... COALESCE PARTITION
ALTER INDEX ... REBUILD PARTITION
ALTER INDEX ... SPLIT PARTITION
```

DDL operations can be paralleled if a *parallel* clause or declaration is specified in the syntax. The parallel DDL statements for non-partitioned tables and indexes are:

```
CREATE INDEX
CREATE TABLE ... AS select
ALTER INDEX ... REBUILD
```

The parallel DDL statements for partitioned tables and indexes are:

```
CREATE INDEX
CREATE TABLE ... AS select
ALTER TABLE ... MOVE PARTITION
ALTER TABLE ... SPLIT PARTITION
ALTER TABLE ... COALESCE PARTITION
ALTER INDEX ... REBUILD PARTITION
ALTER INDEX ... SPLIT PARTITION
```

The *alter session force parallel DDL* statement can be used to override the *parallel* clauses of subsequent DDL statements in a session. The DOP is determined by the specification in the *parallel* clause unless an *alter session force parallel DDL* statement overrides it. A rebuild of a partitioned index is never paralleled.

When indexes and tables are created in parallel, each parallel execution server allocates a new extent and fills the extent with the table or index data. Hence, if an index is created with a DOP of four, the index will have at least four extents initially. The parallel allocation of extents is the same for indexes that are built in parallel or partitions that are being moved, split, or rebuilt in parallel. While serial operations only require that the schema object has at least one extent, parallel creations initially require that tables or indexes have at least as many extents as there are parallel execution servers creating the schema object. After creation, the extents may be coalesced, but there must be a plan for the additional space that may be required for the initial multiple extents caused by parallel DDL operations.

Rules for Paralleling Create Table as Select (CTAS)

Create Table As Select (CTAS) is a very widely used and useful operation while dealing with the reorganization of large tables. The CTAS statement contains two parts: a *create* part (DDL) and a *select* part (query). Oracle can parallelize both parts of the statement. The *create* part of the CTAS must follow the same rules that apply to other DDL operations. The following conditions must be satisfied if the query part of a CTAS statement is to be parallelized:

- The query includes a *parallel* hint specification, the *create* part of the statement has a *parallel* clause, or objects referred to in the query have a parallel declaration.

- At least one of the tables specified in the query requires a full-table scan or an index-range scan spanning multiple partitions.

The DOP for the query part of CTAS is then determined as follows:

- The query part of the CTAS uses the settings specified in the *parallel* clause of the *create* part.

- When the *parallel* clause is not specified, the default DOP will be the number of CPUs.

- When the *create* is done as a serial operation, the DOP is determined by the query settings.

The *create* operation of CTAS can be paralleled only by a *parallel* clause or an *alter session force parallel ddl* statement. The DOP for the *create* operation, and for the *select* operation if it is paralleled, is specified by the parallel clause of the *create* statement, unless it is overridden by an *alter session force parallel ddl* statement.

Invoking Parallelism

There are several ways to invoke Oracle parallel query, and some of them are very dangerous because they influence the costs assigned to full-table scans.

- **Session-level parallelism:** Using the alter session force parallel query syntax.

- **SQL-level parallel query:** This *parallel* hint is the preferred method for invoking parallel query, selectively, based on the operation:

```
select /*+ parallel (c, 31) (e, 31) */ . . . .
```

Parallel DBA Operations

With 24/7 e-commerce databases on the Web, the Oracle DBA is challenged to perform maintenance duties as fast as possible. Oracle has several tools that can implement the parallelization approach to improve manageability and speed up the processing performance of Oracle database administration.

There are several areas where it is appropriate to use parallel operations to speed Oracle maintenance.

- **Parallelize the Oracle backup:** The time required for backups can be both multiplexed, through RMAN, and parallelized with such third-party tools as Legato, ADSM, or Veritas to speed the elapsed time for the backup. Creating a separate backup thread for each available tape drive will accomplish this. Hence, a backup that takes eight hours with one tape drive will only take 30 minutes with 16 tape drives.

- **Parallelize the index rebuilds:** Oracle indexes become out-of-balance and inefficient in highly active e-commerce databases. It is possible to submit many index rebuild tasks concurrently by performing parallel *alter index rebuild* commands. This can also be done within an OPS environment without excessive pinging, so long as the Web servers are disconnected from the database.

- **Parallelize the table reorganizations:** Oracle tables will fragment and become less efficient over time, and the DBA sometimes needs to reorganize the tables to improve performance. Before Oracle 9i, if the Oracle tables are being reorganized to re-sequence the rows, parallelism cannot be used with the *create table as select* (CTAS) statement because it is necessary to use an *index* hint to force the sequence of the rows. An *index* hint and a *parallel* hint cannot be used in the same statement. However, concurrent CTAS tasks can be submitted, one for each table, such that the elapsed time for the reorganization becomes the maximum time required for the largest table.

Oracle is the world's most flexible database and there are several ways to do everything, including creating an index in parallel.

Create an Index in Parallel

These techniques will start a parallel full scan of the target table to build the index in parallel:

```
SQL> alter session force parallel dml;
SQL> create index myidx . . .
```

Oracle provides a SQL hint to force a full-index scan. The DBA can also force a fast full-index scan by specifying the *index_ffs* hint, and this is commonly combined with the *parallel_index* hint to improve performance. For example, the following query forces the use of a fast full-index scan with parallelism:

```
select /*+ index_ffs(car pk_auto) parallel_index(car pk_auto)*/
distinct color,
count(*)
from
car
group by color;
```

Create an Index for Parallel Full Scans

The *parallel* clause can also be specified to make an index parallel, but parallelism is only invoked when the optimizer chooses an index fast-full scan. Setting parallelism on an index is only recommended for shops which process large batch jobs and use *all_rows* optimization because setting parallelism on an index changes the optimizer's propensity to perform index fast-full scans. For typical OLTP transaction-oriented systems, index parallelism should be specified at the session level or with a *parallel* hint.

Here are examples of *create index in parallel* and *alter index parallel*:

```
CREATE INDEX
   myidx
   ON
   customer(sex, hair_color, customer_id)
PARALLEL 35;
ALTER INDEX myidx parallel 35;
```

It can also be checked with this query:

```
select degree from dba_indexes where index_name='MYIDX';
```

Conclusion

This chapter is all about tables and tablespaces and showing that tablespaces and objects can be configured to match the SQL workload for optimal performance. The key points of this chapter include:

- The settings for *pctfree* and *pctused* have a profound impact on performance for some operations.

- The bitmap freelists of ASSM greatly improve simultaneous *insert* concurrency, but it may have a detrimental effect for very high DML periods.

- The DBA may need to manually control *freelist* unlinking and relinking to reduce row fragmentation and improve performance.

- ASSM removes the need to specify *freelist groups* in RAC.

- The new *dbms_space* procedures allow the DBA to see growth trends within specific objects.

It is now time to move on to the core of Oracle tuning, the tuning of specific SQL statements. Remember, all instance tuning must be done before starting SQL tuning because changes to the instance can change the execution plans of hundreds of SQL statements.

Inside Oracle SQL Tuning

"I think we need to tune your SQL"

Introduction to Oracle SQL

Many Oracle professionals do not know that databases existed for decades before the advent of Oracle. Ever since the 1970s, DBAs have managed large online systems and written queries to extract their data. While SQL is the de-facto standard for data access in relational databases, it is important to note that the acronym SQL is a bit of a misnomer.

This chapter is only a taste of a much larger topic, and I have an entire book on this subject. For a complete methodology and treatment of SQL tuning, see my book *Advanced SQL Tuning: The Definitive Reference*.

It can be argued that SQL is neither structured, query-only nor a language:

- **Structured:** Like any other procedural tool, SQL can be written in an unstructured fashion. As of 2010, many people are using Oracle SQL as a full-blown procedural language as noted in Oracle ACE Laurent Schneider's book *"Advanced Oracle SQL Programming"*.

- **Query:** SQL is not query-only and a subset of SQL called DML (Data Manipulation Language) performs updates, inserts and deletes.

- **Language:** SQL is not a true language per-se, yet it is embedded inside languages. SQL does not support all of the traditional language constructs (IF branching, looping_ and SQL are embedded into languages). In Oracle, SQL is embedded into C++ with the Pro*C pre-compiler, Java, PL/SQL and a host of other languages.

However, SQL is becoming more like a programming language, especially after the introduction of the SQL-99 enhancements. As implemented by Oracle, this includes the following new table join syntax:

- **The *with* clause:** Complex queries can now be pre-materialized in-line, just like with global temporary tables

- **natural join:** This is a useful Oracle syntax feature that improves the readability of SQL by removing join criteria from the *where* clause

- **The *using* clause:** This allows the specification of the join key by name

- **The *on* clause:** This syntax allows the specification of column names for join keys in both tables

Enhancements to SQL now allow the simulation of Boolean branching. Oracle SQL allows the addition of Boolean logic and branching using the *decode* and *case* clauses. The *case* statement is a more flexible extension of the *decode* statement. In its simplest form, the Oracle *case* function is used to return a value when a match is found:

```
select
  last_name, commission_pct,
  (case commission_pct
    when 0.1 then 'Low'
    when 0.15 then 'Average'
    when 0.2 then 'High'
    else 'N/A'
  end ) Commission
from
  employees
order by
  last_name;
```

A more complex version is the searched case expression where a comparison expression is used to find a match:

```
select
  last_name, job_id, salary,
  (case
    when job_id like 'SA_MAN' and salary < 12000 then '10%'
    when job_id like 'SA_MAN' and salary >= 12000 then '15%'
    when job_id like 'IT_PROG' and salary < 9000 then '8%'
    when job_id like 'IT_PROG' and salary >= 9000 then '12%'
    else 'NOT APPLICABLE'
  end ) Raise
from
  employees;
```

Oracle SQL continues to evolve from an extraction-only access method into a full-blown language in its own right. Before taking a closer look at the evolution of Oracle SQL and seeing how tuning SQL is critical to all Oracle databases, be aware that this chapter offers only a taste of the complex world of SQL tuning.

The Origin of SQL

Back in the 1970s, I was a junior programmer and DBA, and I remember the pre-relational data access methods used by the predecessors to Oracle, namely the IMS and IDMS database engines. Data access was not for beginners, and end users were required to attend three-day classes on pre-relational data extraction tools such as the Cullinet "Culprit" access language.

Clearly, something needed to be done if easy data access was to become available to the end user community. Early attempts focused on natural language interfaces to databases, such as Excalibur Corporations Savvy tool, which attempted to translate a free-form query into a structured form that a database could understand.

The following is an example of the cumbersome navigational queries in the CODASYL DBTG Network database:

```
    MOVE 'JONES' TO CUST-DESC.
    OBTAIN CALC CUSTOMER.
    MOVE CUSTOMER-ADDRESS TO OUT-REC.
    WRITE OUT-REC.
    FIND FIRST ORDER WITHIN CUSTOMER-ORDER.
       PERFORM ORDER-LOOP UNTIL END-OF-SET.
 *************
  ORDER-LOOP.
 *************
       OBTAIN FIRST ORDER-LINE-REC WITHIN ORDER-LINE.
     PERFORM ORDER-LINE-LOOP UNTIL END-OF-SET.
     FIND NEXT ORDER WITHIN CUSTOMER-ORDER.
 *************
  ORDER-LINE-LOOP.
 *************
       OBTAIN NEXT ORDER-LINE-REC WITHIN ORDER-LINE.
       MOVE QUANTITY-ORDERED TO OUT-REC.
       WRITE OUT-REC.
       OBTAIN OWNER WITHIN ORDER-LINE-PRODUCT
       MOVE PRODUCT-NAME TO OUT-REC.
       WRITE OUT-REC.
```

Dr. Ted Codd and Chris Date first introduced the concept of the Structured Query Language (SQL) in 1979 as a replacement for this type of data access.

As noted in the introduction to this chapter, SQL is technically not a query language. SQL performs much more than queries; it allows updates, deletes, and inserts. SQL is also not a language, yet it is embedded within procedural languages such as Java or C++. Consequently, the name of Structured Query Language seemed a logical name for Dr. Codd's new tool.

In theory, SQL offers three classes of operators: select, project, and join.

- **Select:** The select operator serves to shrink the table vertically by eliminating unwanted rows (tuples)

- **Project:** The project operator serves to shrink the table horizontally by removing unwanted columns

- **Join:** The join operator allows the dynamic linking of two tables that share a common column value

Most commercial implementations of SQL do not directly support the project operation, and projections are achieved by specifying the columns desired in the output. The join operation is achieved by stating the selection criteria for two tables and equating them with their common columns.

Understanding SQL Tuning

Before relational databases were introduced, building queries required knowledge of the internal structures of a database, forcing developers to build tuning directly into their queries. The SQL standard imposed a declarative solution to this problem. DBAs could now rely on the database optimizer to determine important data access methods, such as what indexes to use and the optimal sequence to join multiple tables together.

In today's world, it is not enough for a developer to simply write an SQL statement that provides the correct answer. Even a seemingly simple query can bring a database to its knees, and DBAs and developers must all understand SQL tuning concepts. SQL is declarative, so there can be many ways to formulate a query. Multiple queries formulated in different ways can each return identical results, but may do so with far different execution times.

Oracle SQL tuning is a phenomenally complex subject. Entire books have been devoted to the nuances of Oracle SQL tuning, one of the most notable being *Oracle SQL & CBO Internals* by Kimberly Floss.

This chapter provides a review of the following areas of SQL tuning:

- the goals of SQL tuning
- simplifying complex SQL
- SQL optimization instance parameters
- statistics and SQL optimization
- Oracle and CBO statistics
- Oracle tuning with hints
- Oracle SQL profiles
- AWR and SQL tuning
- ADDM and SQL tuning

The first three sections are an overview of general Oracle tuning concepts. These sections will provide a good foundation to build upon, covering the basic tools and techniques for tuning and optimizing SQL.

The focus will then shift to the new Oracle SQL profiles. After that, the internals of AWR will be covered, in addition to showing how the SQL Tuning and SQL Access Advisor use time-series metadata to provide advice on query changes or enhancements.

Holistic Oracle SQL Tuning

Oracle professionals should perform holistic tuning before delving into the tuning of specific SQL statements. This approach has been the bread and butter of successful corporate DBAs since the earliest days of Oracle 6.

In Oracle 11g, this holistic approach is codified in the SQL Performance Analyzer (SPA), a new tool designed to simplify the setting of optimizer statistics and initialization parameters. When using SPA, the DBA chooses a representative workload and runs it, comparing the overall SQL execution plans with different sets of CBO statistics and settings for the silver bullet initialization parameters.

Prior to Oracle 10g, adjusting the *optimizer_index_cost_adj* parameter was the only cost-effective way for large shops to compensate for sampling issues in *dbms_stats*. As of 10g, the use of *dbms_stats.gather_system_stats* and the improved sampling within *dbms_stats* has made adjustments to these parameters far less important. Today, the savvy DBA will optimize their CBO statistics before adjusting their silver bullet parameters.

Dealing with Time Constraints

In a busy Oracle shop, the DBA often does not have the luxury of undertaking the time consuming task of reorganizing fragmented tables with *dbms_redefinition* and manually gathering optimal CBO statistics. The task of identifying columns that require histograms is especially time consuming. Because of the strain these procedures cause, some database managers optimize their workload by lowering the value for *optimizer_index_cost_adj* or adjusting other broad-brush *optimizer* parameters.

Best Practices for SQL Optimization

As we will see, the Oracle SQL optimizer tries to be fully automated, but there are tasks that you will need to perform to ensure that your SQL always chooses the "best" execution plan. The following sections will cover some of the best practices for SQL optimization that I've used in large corporations.

Proper Development Environment

Many infrastructure issues must be addressed in order to avoid surprises with SQL optimization. Shops that do not create this infrastructure are plagued by constantly changing SQL execution plans and poor database performance. The key to success with the Cost Based Optimizer (CBO) is stability. Ensuring success with the CBO involves several important infrastructure issues.

- **Reanalyze statistics only when necessary:** One of the most common mistakes made by Oracle DBAs is frequently reanalyzing the schema. Remember, the sole purpose of reanalyzing is to change the execution plans for the SQL. Like the saying goes: If it ain't broke; don't fix it. If a DBA is satisfied with current SQL performance, reanalyzing a schema can cause significant performance problems and undo the tuning efforts of the development staff. In practice, very few shops are sufficiently dynamic to require periodic schema reanalysis.

- **Force developers to tune their SQL:** Many developers falsely assume that their sole goal is to write SQL statements that deliver the correct data from Oracle. In reality, formulating the SQL is only half their job. Successful Oracle shops always require that developers ensure that their SQL accesses the database in an optimal fashion and require migration forms that include the execution plan for all new SQL.

- **Carefully manage CBO statistics:** Successful Oracle shops carefully manage the CBO statistics to ensure that the CBO works the same in both test and production environments. A savvy DBA will collect high quality statistics and migrate their production statistics into their test environments. This approach ensures that all SQL migrating into production has the same execution plan as it did in the test database. Because the CBO relies on information about database objects, it is imperative that the CBO have the best possible statistics, and that the same excellent statistics are used in the production, test, quality assurance and development instances.

- **Rarely change CBO parameters:** Unnecessarily changing CBO parameters can be a very dangerous activity. A single parameter change can adversely affect the performance of an entire enterprise. Changes to critical CBO parameters such as *optimizer_mode*, *optimizer_index_cost_adj*, and *optimizer_index_caching* should only be made after careful system testing.

- **Ensure static execution plans:** Nobody likes surprises, and successful CBO shops lock down SQL execution plans. Oracle provides SQL profiles or the older stored outline options for freezing execution plans.

Maintaining A SQL Infrastructure

It is an important job of the Oracle DBA to properly gather and distribute statistics for the CBO. The goal of the DBA is to keep the most accurate production statistics for the current processing. In some cases, there may be more than one set of optimal statistics. For example, the best statistics for OLTP processing may not be the best statistics for the data warehouse processing that occurs each evening.

In this case, the DBA will keep two sets of statistics and import them into the schema when processing modes change. Exporting CBO statistics is done with the *export_system_stats* procedure in the *dbms_stats* package. In this example, CBO statistics are exported into a table called *stats_table_oltp*:

```
dbms_stats.export_system_Stats('stats_table_oltp');
```

Once captured, the *import_system_stats* procedure in *dbms_stats* can be used to move the table to other instances. This should be done in order to overlay the CBO statistics when processing modes change:

```
dbms_stats.import_system_stats('stats_table_oltp');
dbms_stats.import_system_stats('stats_table_dss');
```

It is important to remember that once CBO parameters are optimized, they should be left alone. Many Oracle shops mistakenly change the fundamental characteristics of their CBO by changing the global CBO parameters. Especially dangerous are changes to *optimizer_mode* and *optimizer_index_cost_adj*, and these changes should only be made when a sound reason exists. Other CBO parameters such as *pga_aggregate_target*, *hash_area_size,* and *sort_area_size* are less dangerous and and can be set at the system or session levels to change.

Some shops try to ensure consistency of SQL execution with static execution plans. Remember, reanalyzing a schema can cause thousands of SQL statements to change execution plans. Many Oracle shops have implemented standards that require that all SQL, when tested and approved in their test environment, function identically in production.

Some techniques for assisting developers in tuning their SQL include:

- Training them to use the Autotrace and TKPROF utilities and to interpret SQL execution results. Oracle University has several excellent classes on CBO optimization techniques.

- Forcing all SQL that is migrating into production to have verification that the SQL has been tuned

- Making performance an evaluation criterion. Instead of noting that the best developer is the developer who writes SQL the fastest, add the mandate that a good developer also writes SQL that performs efficiently.

Migrating statistics is also a way to help developers achieve their SQL tuning mandate. The DBA can migrate the statistics that were used in SQL testing into the production environment when the SQL is migrated. However, the DBA must ensure that a migration of statistics from test into production does not adversely affect the execution plans of other SQL that touch the target table. Hence, the DBA will carefully manage the CBO statistics, ensuring that no SQL changes execution plans after it is migrated into production. Next, see how holistic workload tuning has changed within each release of Oracle.

A Release-centric Approach to Holistic Optimization

Each release of Oracle brings enhancements and changes to the way that the Oracle DBA optimizes their system-wide workloads. In general, these approaches to global SQL optimization are highly dependent on the release of Oracle:

Oracle 6 – Oracle 7 enhancements

In Oracle 7, there were significant shortcomings to the Cost Based Optimizer and many Oracle professionals were forced to tweak the CBO throttles to achieve the largest amount of optimized SQL.

These techniques include setting optimizer_mode=rule and adjusting optimizer_index_cost_adj. This time also brought the introduction of the CBO histogram, an important feature for SQL optimization.

Oracle 8 – Oracle 8i enhancements

In the Oracle 8 series of releases, the CBO was ready for primetime. Oracle 8 introduced materialized views and enhanced CBO statistics collection. DBAs saw the introduction of function-based indexes to alleviate unnecessary full-table scans. This release also introduced the *dbms_stats* package that allowed for a better collection of schema metadata.

This metadata proved to be very helpful for the CBO, allowing it to make more intelligent decisions. The Rule Based Optimizer (RBO) remained a popular tuning tool for simple databases, and the adjustment of SQL workload optimization relied on changing *optimizer_mode*, *optimizer_index_cost_adj* and *optimizer_index_caching*.

We also saw the implementation of global temporary tables (a precursor to subquery factoring using the *with* clause) to materialize intermediate query steps. Best of all, the BSTAT-ESTAT utility was enhanced with the STATSPACK tool to allow for the historical storage of tuning information, indispensable for proactive workload tuning.

Oracle 9i enhancements

With Oracle 9i, DBAs were introduced to the new *v$sql_plan* view that helped them tune SQL proactively. In addition, version 9i had an enhanced *dbms_stats* package that was more intelligent than ever before. Despite these advances however, the DBA was still frequently forced to optimize their SQL by adjusting the optimizer parameters.

Oracle 9i brought the ability to collect a deep sample with *dbms_stats* and save them. This tool proved especially useful for large shops where production CBO statistics could be exported and imported into test and development instances.

This practice allowed developers to optimize their SQL before introducing it into production. Oracle 9i also premiered the *dbms_redefinition* package that allowed DBAs to reorganize fragmented tables online.

Oracle 10g enhancements

Oracle 10g greatly aided the optimization of large SQL workloads with the introduction of dynamic sampling and root-cause optimization with *dbms_stats*. Oracle acknowledged that the root cause of sub-optimal SQL execution plans related to the quality of CBO statistics, and they introduced enhancements to *dbms_stats* to allow for automatic histogram creation and the *gather_system_stats* procedure to collecting all-important external information, most notably the average disk access timings for index access (sequential reads) and full-scan access (scattered reads).

This changed the landscape for SQL Tuning, as it was then possible to address the root cause of suboptimal execution plans. However, many DBAs that were under time constraints were unable to undertake the time consuming analysis required to verify that they have optimal statistics, and they resorted to the quick fix of adjusting the optimizer parameters.

Oracle 10g Release 2 enhancements

Starting in Oracle 10g release 2, Oracle recommended not setting the *db_file_multiblock_read_count* parameter, allowing Oracle to empirically determine the optimal setting.

Oracle 11g enhancements

In Oracle 11g, DBAs see the promise of a greatly improved *dbms_stats* package, running 2x faster and automatically collecting a statistically significant sample size. They also see the promise of better detection of columns for histograms.

Oracle technical support claims that adjusting the CBO statistics addresses the root cause of sub-optimal execution and that changes to the *optimizer_index_cost_adj* are rarely required. However, DBAs still need to set the optimal *optimizer_mode* and *optimizer_index_caching*. We can run scripts to intelligently identify and set an appropriate value for *optimizer_index_caching*.

In sum, the techniques for holistic SQL optimization change radically by release level, and in Oracle 10g and Oracle 11g, it is now less time consuming to fix the root cause of CBO issues through the adjustment of the CBO statistics.

The general holistic SQL optimization steps for 9i, 10g and 11g include addressing the root cause, bad statistics, whenever feasible:

- Verify a correct sample size using *dbms_stats* and determine an intelligent threshold for reanalyzing statistics.

- Find the low hanging fruit, such as any high impact sub-optimal SQL, and add histograms to improve access for queries against skewed and out-of-bounds queries.

- Add histograms where necessary and if applicable to improve the CBO's ability to determine the optimal table join order.

- Run *dbms_stats.gather_system_stats* to get external I/O tuning for full-scan vs. index I/O

- Intelligently set *optimizer_mode* and *optimizer_index_caching*, testing with a representative workload in a real world environment

- Optimize the silver bullet parameters (*db_cache_size, db_file_multiblock_read_count*, and such)

- Set *optimizer_index_cost_adj,* if required, to fix any remaining suboptimal execution plans

- Finally, tune individual SQL statements using SQL profiles

What is the Best Optimizer Philosophy?

Some Oracle professionals subscribe to the theory that for any SQL query, there exists one and only one, optimal execution plan. Once this optimal execution plan is determined, it should be made persistent using optimizer plan stability. In contrast, other shops want their SQL to change execution plans whenever there has been a significant change to the CBO statistics.

Stable shops where the table statistics rarely change should employ optimizer plan stability in order to make execution plans persistent. Shops where the CBO statistics frequently change should tune their queries without optimizer plan stability. This way, the run-time optimizer is free to choose the most appropriate execution plan based on the CBO statistics.

The choice of SQL philosophy has a dramatic impact on the approach to SQL tuning and statistics maintenance. The following should be taken into careful consideration when making tuning decisions:

- Table and index statistics: The dynamic philosophy relies heavily on the table and index statistics, and these statistics must be recomputed each time a table has a significant change. In contrast, the static philosophy does not rely on statistics.

- SQL profiles: The choice of using SQL profiles and optimizer plan stability to freeze SQL execution plans depends heavily on the type of workload. The dynamic shop does not use optimizer plan stability because it wants the freedom for the execution plan to change whenever there is a major change to the data inside the tables. Conversely, the static shop relies on optimizer plan stability to make its tuning changes permanent and to improve SQL execution time by avoiding the reparsing of SQL statements.

- Adaptive cursor sharing: the dynamic shop often has SQL that is generated by ad-hoc query tools with hard-coded literal values embedded within the SQL. Hard-coded literal values make the SQL statements non-reusable unless cursor_sharing=force is set in the Oracle initialization file. Shops that are plagued with non-reusable SQL can adopt either the persistent or the dynamic philosophy. To use optimizer plan stability with non-reusable SQL, the DBA will set cursor_sharing=force and then extract the transformed SQL from the library cache and use optimizer plan stability to make the execution plan persistent.

Next is a closer look at the two competing SQL philosophies.

The Persistent SQL Philosophy

If a shop has relatively static tables and indexes, DBAs generally adopt the persistent SQL philosophy. This philosophy states that there exists only one optimal execution plan for any SQL statement. Shops that subscribe to this philosophy are characterized by stable applications that have been tuned to use host variables, instead of literal values, in all SQL queries.

Persistent shops also have tables and indexes whose recomputed statistics rarely change the execution plan for their SQL queries, regardless of how often the statistics are recomputed. Many persistent shops have all of their SQL embedded inside PL/SQL packages, and the applications will call their SQL using a standard PL/SQL function of a stored procedure call. This insulates the SQL from the application programs and ensures that all applications execute identical SQL. It also guarantees that all of the SQL has been properly tuned.

Choosing the persistent approach means that all tuned SQL will utilize optimizer plan stability and the CBO statistics will be used only for ad-hoc queries and new queries that have not yet been tuned. Of course, there is also a performance benefit to using optimizer plan stability because the SQL statements are pre-parsed and ready to run. This approach is generally used in shops where experience has shown that the execution plans for SQL rarely change after the CBO statistics have been reanalyzed.

The persistent SQL philosophy requires the DBA to write scripts to detect all SQL statements that do not possess stored outlines, and also to tune those queries on behalf of the developers. The persistent SQL philosophy also requires less reliance on CBO statistics, and tables are generally only analyzed when they are first migrated into the production environment. Since optimizer plan stability does not rely on statistics, the server overhead of periodically re-computing statistics for the CBO is avoided.

The Dynamic SQL Philosophy

The dynamic SQL philosophy is the belief that Oracle SQL should change execution plans in tandem with the changes to the CBO statistics. Shops that subscribe to the dynamic SQL philosophy are typically characterized by highly volatile environments where tables and indexes change radically and frequently. These shops frequently reanalyze their CBO statistics and allow the CBO to choose the execution plan based upon the current status of their CBO statistics.

A shop that employs the dynamic SQL philosophy would likely have tables that are grown for a length of time and then purged. In these types of environments, the *num_rows* and *avg_row_len* for the tables are frequently changing, as are the distributions of index values. This change in statistics, in turn, causes the CBO to choose a different execution plan for the SQL queries.

Decision-support environments and scientific databases often adopt this philosophy because entirely new subsets of data are loaded into tables, the data is analyzed, the tables truncated and a wholly different set of data is loaded into the table structures.

Another common characteristic of dynamic shops is the difficulty of SQL tuning. Oracle databases that are accessed by casual users via ODBC and third-party tools such as Crystal Reports or Microsoft Access are often forced into the dynamic philosophy because the incoming SQL is always different. However, it is very important to note that the use of third-party application suites, such as SAP and PeopleSoft, does not always require the adoption of the dynamic philosophy. The SQL from these types of application suites can be captured in the library cache, and optimizer plan stability can be used to make the execution plan persistent.

Dynamic shops require a very different approach to SQL tuning than persistent SQL shops do. Each time data is loaded or changed, the affected tables and indexes must be reanalyzed. As a result, dynamic shops often incorporate the *dbms_stats* package directly into their load routines.

In Oracle, the DBA for dynamic shops must be aware of changes to the distribution of index column values. When column values for any index become skewed, they must create column histograms for the index so the optimizer can choose between a full-table scan and an index range scan to service queries.

Many companies adopt a SQL philosophy without completely realizing the ramifications of their chosen approach. In practice, most shops tend to begin with a dynamic philosophy and then migrate towards the static approach over time. DBAs will often make this change when experience indicates that their execution plans rarely change following reanalysis of the tables and indexes.

The following section provides a quick, simple review of the goals of SQL tuning.

Goals of SQL Tuning

There are many approaches to SQL tuning. This section describes a fast, holistic method of SQL tuning. This method involves optimizing the SGA, setting the all-important optimizer parameters and adjusting CBO statistics based on current system load. Once the best overall optimization is achieved, effective tuning also includes drilling down into the specific cases of sub-optimal SQL and changing their execution plans with SQL profiles, specialized CBO stats or hints.

Despite the inherent complexity of tuning SQL, there are general guidelines that every effective Oracle DBA follows in order to improve the overall performance of their Oracle systems. The goals of SQL tuning are simple:

- Replace unnecessary large-table full-table scans with index scans

- Cache small-table full-table scans

- Ensure optimal table join order

- Verify optimal index usage

- Verify optimal join techniques

- Tune complex subqueries to remove redundant access

These goals may seem deceptively simple, yet comprise 90 percent of SQL tuning. They do not require a thorough understanding of the internals of Oracle SQL. Let's begin by examining the optimal table join order.

Determine Optimal Table Join Order

One of the most common problems with complex SQL occurs when the tables are not joined in the optimal order. Oracle tries to make the first table join (the driving table) produce the smallest number of rows to reduce the intermediate row baggage that must be input to later table joins. Oracle 11g extended optimizer statistics, histograms and the ordered or leading hints are great ways to verify optimal table join order.

Remove Unnecessary Large-table Full-table Scans

While not all large-table full-table scans are problematic, a large-table full-table scan is a common symptom of a SQL execution problem. Large-table full-table scans in an explain plan (TABLE

ACCESS FULL) should always be examined to verify that it is not due to a database problem, such as a missing index.

Unnecessary large-table full-table scans "full-table scans" are an important symptom of sub-optimal SQL and cause unnecessary I/O that can drag down an entire database.

The first step in validating a full-table scan is to evaluate the SQL based on the number of rows returned by the query and your own guess about the number of trips to the data blocks that would be needed to fetch the rows.

Oracle says that if the query returns less than 40 percent of the table rows in an ordered table or seven percent of the rows in an unordered table, the query can be tuned to use an index in lieu of the full-table scan, but in reality there is no fixed number because it depends on many factors like the *db_block_size* and *db_file_multiblock_read_count*.

This decision is partly based on the index key value described by *clustering_factor* in the *dba_indexes* view. However, it is not a simple process.

The choice of a full table scan vs. index access as the "best" access plan for a SQL statement depends on many factors. The most common cause of unnecessary full-table scans is a *optimizer_mode* that favors full-table scans (like *all_rows*) or a missing index, especially a function-based indexes.

These factors are listed in their order of importance:

- **Sub-optimal optimizer_mode:** The all_rows mode minimizes computing resources and favors full-table scans, while the first_rows_n mode favors index access.

- **Missing indexes:** Missing indexes, (especially missing function-based indexes) will cause in unnecessary large-table full-table scans.

- **Bad CBO statistics:** Missing or stale SQL optimizer statistics (gathered via *dbms_stats*) will cause Oracle to mis-judge the execution plan for a SQL query.

- **Missing CPU and disk statistics:** Missing system statistics (gathered with *dbms_stats.gather_system_stats*) will prevent the optimizer from making a smart decision about invoking multi-block I/O.

- **Histograms:** For skewed data columns, missing column histograms will influence the choice of index vs. full-table scan access.

- **Index clustering:** The physical row order on the data blocks is important to know when choosing an index, and the clustering of the table rows to the desired index (as displayed in *dba_indexes clustering factor*)

- **Sub-optimal setting for *db_file_multiblock_read_count:*** The optimization of *db_file_multiblock_read_count* has been automated in 10g release 2 and beyond to prevent errors.

- **Sub-optimal setting for *optimizer_index_cost_adj:*** This is a throttle that makes index access more attractive to the optimizer, and lowering the value of *optimizer_index_cost_adj* will cause the SQL optimizer to favor indexes.

- **Sub-optimal setting for *optimizer_index_caching:*** The *optimizer_index_caching* parameter is set by the DBA to help the optimizer know, on average, how much of an index resides inside the data buffer.

- **Parallel query:** Enabling Oracle parallel query (OPQ) will influence the optimizer that full-scans are less expensive, and it may change the execution plans for hundreds of SQL statements. If you are on an SMP server with dozens of CPU's a full-table scan can be parallelized for faster execution. However, you should never read a data block unless it is needed to get rows for your SQL result set. Remember, parallel query only effects full-table scans, and it has no effect when performing index access.

- **Disk blocksize:** The number of rows that resides on each disk data block influences the choice between a full-table scan of an index scan. This is especially true when you are using RAID with a smaller stripe size, and reading a table with a 2k block size would take significantly more I/O and reading a table with a 32k block size.

Fix the root cause, not the symptom!

Do not doink with *optimizer_index_cost_adj* until you have checked for the right *optimizer_mode* and ensured that you have fresh table and system statistics. Fix the problem, not the symptom.

Look Out!

In sum, your decision about removing a full-table scan should be based on a careful examination of the amount of logical I/O (consistent gets) of the index scan versus the costs of the full-table scan, based on the number of rows returned by the query.

Now that we get the general idea of examining large-table full-table scans, let's take a look at how to locate full-scan operations.

Locating full-scan operations

I have several free scripts on the web that you can invoke to find SQL that invokes full-scans, located on www.dba-oracle.com. The most common script ids called *plan9i.sql*, and you can use this script to display all operations that have full-table scans.

I also have a time-series version of this script called *plan10g.sql*, for those who have purchased a pack license to query the *dba_hist_sqlstat* table. Un.ike *plan91.sql*, the *plan10g.sql* shows the SQL over time, for each snapshot period.

Let's take a look at this very important full table scan report:

```
Full table scans and counts
```

OWNER	NAME	NUM_ROWS	C	K	BLOCKS	NBR_FTS
SYS	DUAL		N		2	97,237
SYSTEM	SQLPLUS_PRODUCT_PRO		N	K	2	16,178
DONALD	PAGE	3,450,209	N		932,120	9,999
DONALD	RWU_PAGE	434	N		8	7,355
DONALD	PAGE_IMAGE	18,067	N		1,104	5,368
DONALD	SUBSCRIPTION	476	N	K	192	2,087
DONALD	PRINT_PAGE_RANGE	10	N	K	32	874
ARSD	JANET_BOOKS	20	N		8	64
PERFSTAT	STATS$TAB_STATS		N		65	10

Moving from left to right we see the following columns:

- **Table owner and table name**

- **num_rows**: This is the current number of rows as per the last analyze with *dbms_stats*.

- **C**: This is the old Oracle7 "cache" utility, now obsolete.

- **K:** This flag indicates whether the table resides in the KEEP pool. This is important for small tables that experience frequent full-scan operations, to ensure that they are kept on the RAM data buffers for fast repeated access.

- **Blocks**: This is the number of blocks in the table. This is an important column because it's the number of blocks in the table, not necessarily the number of rows, which determines whether s full-scan is appropriate.

- **nbr_fts**: This is the number of full-table scans, as reported by *v$sql_plan* of *dba_hist_sql_plan* respectively.

In the report above we see several tables that have a large number of full-scan operations.

Tuning large-table full-table scans

We also use this report to identify large tables that experience full-table scans. While full-table scans may be legitimate, full-scans are an indicator of possible sub-optimal execution:

	Full table scans and counts					
OWNER	NAME	NUM_ROWS	C	K	BLOCKS	NBR_FTS
SYS	DUAL		N		2	97,237
SYSTEM	SQLPLUS_PRODUCT_PRO		N	K	2	16,178
DONALD	PAGE	3,450,209	N		932,120	9,999
DONALD	RWU_PAGE	434	N		8	7,355
DONALD	PAGE_IMAGE	18,067	N		1,104	5,368
DONALD	SUBSCRIPTION	476	N	K	192	2,087
DONALD	PRINT_PAGE_RANGE	10	N	K	32	874
ARSD	JANET_BOOKS	20	N		8	64
PERFSTAT	STATS$TAB_STATS		N		65	10

Of course, not all large-table full-table scans are evil, but they warrant inspection. Also, this report is useful for identifying large-table full-table scans that can be parallelized. While we cover parallel scans in a later chapter, note that we can parallelize legitimate large-table full-table scans with a degree of *cpu_count-1*. For non-warehouse databases, it's also a good idea to turn-on parallel query at the query level, using a *parallel* hint.

This report shows us the table name, and we can run a quick query to display all SQL that accesses this table. We can then gather an explain plan for these statement to inspect the access plans:

```
select
   sql_text
from
   v$sql
where
   upper(sql_text) like('%TABLENAME%)':
```

For SQL statements that invoke full-scan operations, we carefully inspect the where clause to see if there is an indexing opportunity.

Tuning small-table full-table scans

This report listing from *plan91.sql* (download from www.dba-oracle.com), shows both large and small table scans. We use the "*blocks*" column to identify small tables with small-table full-table scans:

```
                    Full table scans and counts

OWNER          NAME                   NUM_ROWS C K    BLOCKS   NBR_FTS
-------------- ---------------------- -------- - - --------- ---------
SYS            DUAL                             N            2    97,237
SYSTEM         SQLPLUS_PRODUCT_PRO             N K           2    16,178
DONALD         PAGE                  3,450,209 N       932,120     9,999
DONALD         RWU_PAGE                    434 N             8     7,355
DONALD         PAGE_IMAGE               18,067 N         1,104     5,368
DONALD         SUBSCRIPTION                476 N   K       192     2,087
DONALD         PRINT_PAGE_RANGE             10 N   K        32       874
ARSD           JANET_BOOKS                  20 N             8        64
PERFSTAT       STATS$TAB_STATS              N             65        10
```

Above, we see that the *rwu_page* table resides on only 8 data blocks and has experienced 7,355 full-scan operations. For any legitimate small-table full-table scans we can quickly cache the table into the KEEP pool with this syntax:

```
alter table
   rwu_page
storage (buffer_pool keep);
```

In most cases, small tables will "self cache" themselves because the table will ping itself to the most-recently-used (MRU) end of the data buffer each time that the table is referenced, but placing these tables into the KEEP area is a best practice because if have applied an intelligent criteria to this assignment.

Now that we get the general idea of examining large-table full-table scans, let's take a look at how our server RAM resources are used to tune SQL statements.

Optimizing SQL RAM Resources

Just like a program, a SQL statement requires Oracle RAM memory for efficient performance. The following areas are where RAM effects SQL execution speed:

- **Library cache RAM:** An optimal shared pool reduces SQL parsing and makes SQL run faster

- **Data buffer RAM:** Fetching a data block from the RAM data buffers can be hundreds of times faster than disk access

- *hash* **join RAM:** The more RAM available for *hash* joins via *pga_aggregate_target* or *hash_area_size*, the greater the propensity for the Oracle SQL optimizer to choose a fast *hash* join

- **Sorting RAM:** The more RAM available for row resequencing via *pga_aggregate_target* or *sort_area_size*, the faster the processing of SQL *order by* and *group by* directives

But there are times when a DBA must override the Oracle defaults for *hash* joins and sorting. To prevent runaway tasks from hogging resources, Oracle has a built-in governor that prevents any individual session from consuming too many RAM resources. In the hands of a savvy DBA, these governors can be adjusted, resulting in more efficient processing for large batch jobs. The next section will delve deeper into these types of adjustments.

Cache Small-table Full-table Scans

For cases in which a full-table scan is the fastest access method, the tuning professional should ensure that a dedicated data buffer is available for the rows. To accomplish this in Oracle 7, an *alter table xxx cache* command can be issued. In Oracle 8 and beyond, the small-table can be cached by forcing it into the KEEP cache.

Logical reads (consistent gets) are often 100x faster than disk reads. Small and frequently referenced objects such as tables, clusters and indexes should be fully cached in the KEEP cache. Most DBAs check *x$bh* periodically, moving any table that has 80% or more of its blocks in the buffer into the KEEP cache. In addition to this procedure, *dba_hist_sqlstat* should be checked for tables that experience frequent small-table full-table scans.

Verify Optimal Index Usage

Optimal Index Usage is especially important for improving the speed of queries. Oracle sometimes has a choice of indexes, and the tuning professional must examine each index to ensure that Oracle is using the proper index. DBAs should also be wary of bitmapped and function-based indexes.

Determining the index usage is especially important for improving the speed of queries with multiple *where* clause predicates. Oracle sometimes has a choice of indexes, and it is our responsibility as the DBA to examine each index and ensure that Oracle is using the best index, meaning the one that returns the result with the least consistent gets. The problem occurs when the optimizer cannot find an index, or when the most restrictive *where* clause in the SQL is not matched with an index. When the optimizer cannot find an appropriate index to access table rows, the optimizer will always invoke a full-table scan, reading every row in the table. Hence, a large-table full-table scan might indicate a sub-optimal SQL statement that can be tuned by adding an index that matches the *where* clause of the query.

Verify Optimal Join Techniques

Some queries will perform faster with nested loops joins, some with hash joins, while others work best with sort-merge joins. It is difficult to predict which join technique will be fastest. To test their efficacy, many Oracle tuning experts will test run the SQL with each different table join method.

The optimizer has many join methods available including a merge join, a nested loop join, a hash join and a star join. In order to choose the right join method, the optimizer must guess the size of the intermediate result sets from multi-way table joins.

To make this guess, the optimizer uses incomplete information. Even if histograms are present, the optimizer cannot know for certain the exact number of rows that will be returned from a join. The most common remedy is to use hints to change the join type (*use_nl, use_hash*), re-size *hash_area_size* or *pga_aggregate_target* or reanalyze the statistics and histograms on the target tables.

Tuning by Simplifying SQL Syntax

There are several methods for simplifying complex SQL statements. In fact, Oracle will sometimes automatically rewrite SQL to make it more efficient. Some options for simplification include:

- Rewrite the query into a more efficient form
- Use the *with* clause
- Use global temporary tables
- Use materialized views

The following example shows how SQL can be rewritten. For a simple example of SQL syntax and execution speed, the following queries can be used. All of these SQL statements produce the same results, but have widely varying execution plans and execution performance.

```
-- A non-correlated sub-query
```

```
select
  book_title
from
  book
where
  book_key not in (select book_key from sales);
```

Execution Plan
----
    0   SELECT STATEMENT Optimizer=CHOOSE (Cost=1 Card=1 Bytes=64)
    1   0   FILTER
    2   1   TABLE ACCESS (FULL) OF 'BOOK' (Cost=1 Card=1 Bytes=64)
    3   1   TABLE ACCESS (FULL) OF 'SALES' (Cost=1 Card=5 Bytes=25)

-- An outer join

```
select
  book_title
from
  book   b,
  sales  s
where
  b.book_key = s.book_key(+)
and
  quantity is null;
```

Execution Plan
----
0   SELECT STATEMENT Optimizer=CHOOSE (Cost=3 Card=100 Bytes=8200)

1   0 FILTER
2   1   FILTER
3   2   HASH JOIN (OUTER)
4   3   TABLE ACCESS (FULL) OF 'BOOK' (Cost=1 Card=20 Bytes=1280)
5   3   TABLE ACCESS (FULL) OF 'SALES' (Cost=1 Card=100 Bytes=1800)

-- A Correlated sub-query

```
select
  book_title
from
  book
where
  book_title not in (
                select
                distinct
                  book_title
                from
                  book,
                  sales
                where
                  book.book_key = sales.book_key
                and
                  quantity > 0);
```

Execution Plan
----
0   SELECT STATEMENT Optimizer=CHOOSE (Cost=1 Card=1 Bytes=59)
```

Locating full-scan operations                                                                    **755**
```

```
1   0   FILTER
2   1     TABLE ACCESS (FULL) OF 'BOOK' (Cost=1 Card=1 Bytes=59)
3   1     FILTER
4   3       NESTED LOOPS (Cost=6 Card=1 Bytes=82)
5   4         TABLE ACCESS (FULL) OF 'SALES' (Cost=1 Card=5 Bytes=90)
6   4         TABLE ACCESS (BY INDEX ROWID) OF 'BOOK' (Cost=1 Card=1)
7   6           INDEX (UNIQUE SCAN) OF 'PK_BOOK' (UNIQUE)
```

As shown above, the formulation of the SQL query has a dramatic impact on the execution plan for the SQL. The order of the *where* clause predicates can make a significant difference. Savvy Oracle developers know the most efficient way to code Oracle SQL for optimal execution plans, and the more successful Oracle shops train their developers to formulate efficient SQL.

Roadblocks to SQL Tuning

If a DBA decides to use a vendor package with Oracle, they may be faced with the common problem of trying to tune and optimize a system that is unfamiliar or that cannot be changed. Oracle shops are now choosing to use giant enterprise resource planning (ERP) solutions like Oracle Applications, SAP and PeopleSoft. There are also thousands of application vendors that are choosing to use Oracle as their database.

From small departmental applications to giant ERP packages, customers are now asserting their right to be provided with reliable documentation about the proper configuration for Oracle. This is especially true for vendors of departmental applications. These vendors are typically growing their client base and moving from small simple databases (MySQL, SQL Server) to a more robust database like Oracle.

SQL Profiles

One inherent problem in SQL has to do with the dynamic nature of SQL performance. SQL was designed to be very sensitive to external influences. Any number of routine changes, like adding an index or reanalyzing statistics, can influence SQL execution plans.

This instability of SQL is a godsend for some shops and a nightmare for others. Many shops seek to freeze SQL execution plans after tuning to ensure that they do not have any unplanned performance problems.

The Oracle SQL Tuning Advisor allows the implementation of tuning suggestions in the form of SQL profiles that will improve performance, SQL profiles can be used the same way as stored outlines, i.e. optimizer plan stability. The SQL profile is a collection of the historical information of prior runs of the SQL statement, comparison details of the actual and estimated cardinality and predicate selectivity and so on. A SQL profile is stored persistently in the data dictionary; therefore, it does not require any application code changes.

A SQL profile also helps generate a better execution plan than the normal optimization because it is tested against a real-world workload in the SQL Tuning Set (STS). Additional tasks like checking for advanced predicate selectivity, correlation between columns, join skews and complex predicates such as functions help in profiling the SQL statement. Once a SQL statement is profiled and stored, differing execution plans can be invoked at will.

As a review, stored outlines (optimizer plan stability) allow the DBA to freeze SQL execution plans, and more importantly, change execution plans without touching the SQL source. This is a critical tool for tuning third-party vendor systems where it is not possible to touch the source code. In earlier releases of Oracle, the storing of plan outlines for SQL statements was known as optimizer plan stability and ensures that changes in the Oracle environment do not affect the way a SQL statement is optimized by the CBO.

Tracing SQL Execution History

Shops that want static SQL execution plans can use a variety of methods to track when execution plans change over time as a result of *dynamic_sampling* or a reanalyzing of the optimizer statistics. SQL Plan history analysis is not an easy chore. As the world's most robust and complex RDBMS, Oracle offers something for everyone. It can be confusing to optimize Oracle because of its plethora of features.

One wonderful benefit of Oracle is the ability to have SQL execution plans change when the characteristics of the underlying table change. For shops where a table is huge one day and small the next, where column distribution varies wildly, dynamic SQL is a godsend.

However, dynamic SQL changes are not so great for stable shops where there exists only one optimal execution plan for any given SQL statement. Because SQL plans will change whenever changes are made to the instance, any SQL statement will have a history of execution plans. Here are some common acts that will change execution plans:

- Enabling dynamic sampling

- Reanalyze the schema statistics. This is done automatically starting in 10g

- Changing an optimizer parameter (*optimizer_mode, optimizer_index_cost_adj*)

- Enabling parallelism

This execution plan history can be seen by running scripts against the STATSPACK (*stats$sql_plan and stats$sql_plan_usage*) or the AWR (*dba_hist_sql_plan*) tables. Once the *sql_id* for a statement has been acquired, the built-in *dbms_xplan.display_awr* procedure can be used to see the different execution plans for the query.

The *dbms_xplan.display_awr* allows a DBA to input only a *sql_id*, and Oracle will show the explain plans for that *sql_id* as recorded in the AWR. This simple query will show changes to SQL explain plan history once the extra cost licenses for AWR are purchased:

```
select
  *
from
  table(dbms_xplan.display_awr('&sqlid'));
```

Oracle 11g has introduced a wealth of new tools to help DBAs freeze the optimal SQL execution plan. When frozen, the execution plan will not change when the data changes. Also, the Oracle CBO group coined the term "plan regression" for changes that result in a sub-optimal execution plan. While Oracle

11g has tools for tracking explain plans, it is still possible to choose manual methods, gather changes to execution plans from STATSPACK or the extra-cost AWR tables.

Oracle SQL as a Database Access Method

Today in Oracle11g, both the cost-based optimizer (CBO) and the rule-based optimizer (RBO) are commonly used to derive the execution plan for Oracle SQL statements. Back in the 1990's Oracle announced a plan to retire the RBO with Oracle8, but they forgot that their own applications used rule-based optimization, well into Oracle 9i! With each new release they continue to threaten to remove the rule-based SQL optimizer.

The rule-based optimizer is very elegant in its simplicity and often makes execution choices faster than the CBO. In fact, Oracle Applications products used the RBO up until 2001 when the Oracle Apps 11i product was introduced. It is only since the release of Oracle 8i (8.1.6) that the CBO has become faster than the RBO in all cases.

While it is very tempting to go into the relative advantages of the RBO and CBO within each successive release of Oracle, it would perhaps be more useful to simply include some general observations about the characteristics of the rule-based optimizer:

- **Always use the index:** If an index can be used to access a table, choose the index. Indexes are always preferable over a full-table scan of a sort merge join. A sort merge join does not require an index.

- **Always starts with the driving table:** The last table in the *from* clause will be the driving table. For the RBO, this should be the table that chooses the fewest number of rows. The RBO uses this driving table as the first table when performing nested loop join operations.

- **Full-table scans as a last resort:** The RBO is not aware of Oracle parallel query and multi-block reads, and does not consider the size of the table. Hence, the RBO dislikes full-table scans and will only use them when no index exists.

- **Any index will do:** The RBO will sometimes choose a less than ideal index to service a query. This is because the RBO does not have access to statistics that show the selectivity of indexed columns.

- **Simple is sometimes better:** Prior to Oracle 8i, the RBO often provided a better overall execution plan for some databases.

The biggest shortcoming of the RBO is that it will often choose the wrong index to access a table. This is because the RBO does not have access to the statistics about the relative selectivity and cardinality of the indexes column.

The *rule* Hint is still Popular in Oracle 11g

Since the release of Oracle 8, Oracle has threatened to phase out the rule-based optimizer. For Oracle applications, it was ironic that Oracle apps used the RBO, and Oracle made a big deal out of announcing that Oracle Applications 11i eBusiness suite was moving to the cost-based SQL optimizer (CBO).

Of course, a close examination of the actual SQL in *v$sql* reveals that hundreds of the SQL statements have the rule hint!

The *rule* hint is a trick used by many SQL tuning professionals, and it is the first thing that experts try when tuning a SQL statement since it points to problems with optimizer statistics (see *dbms_stats* and CBO histograms).

Also see MetaLink Note# 375386 where Oracle notes sub-optimal execution plans for RMAN in 10g release 2. The solution? Forget about fixing the CBO statistics. Oracle recommends this fix, added to the RMAN script:

```
"alter session set optimizer_mode=RULE";
```

Now that *rule* hints have been covered, it is time to take a look at a very important area of Oracle SQL tuning: the use of indexes to speed up SQL queries.
Next up is the section covering the use of regular expressions to tune SQL queries.

The next section will cover how the library cache impacts Oracle performance.

The Library Cache and Oracle SQL Performance

Just as the data buffers serve to cache data blocks for faster subsequent access, the library cache area of the shared pool is designed to hold SQL statements for faster subsequent re-use. Unlike data, SQL can have many states. The executable SQL may allow for different variables and the shared pool must accommodate versions of the same SQL statement.

When a SQL statement is executed with multiple child cursors, multiple versions are created within the library cache of the shared pool. A DBA can query the *v$sqlarea* view for details on child cursors, using the *sharable_mem* and *persistent_mem* columns.

The *v$sql* columns can also be queried:

- *sharable_mem*: Amount of shared memory used by the child cursor (in bytes)
- *persistent_mem*: Fixed amount of memory used for the lifetime of the child cursor (in bytes)
- **invalidations:** Number of times this child cursor has been invalidated
- *parse_calls*: Number of parse calls for this child cursor
- *disk_reads*: Number of disk reads for this child cursor
- *direct_writes*: Number of direct writes for this child cursor
- *buffer_gets*: Number of buffer gets for this child cursor
- *parsing_user_id*: User ID of the user who originally built this child cursor
- *parsing_schema_id*: Schema ID that was used to originally build this child cursor

- *parsing_schema_name*: Schema name that was used to originally build this child cursor

- *kept_versions*: Indicates whether this child cursor has been marked to be kept pinned in the cache using the *dbms_shared_pool* package

- **address:** Address of the handle to the parent for this cursor

- *type_chk_heap*: Descriptor of the type check heap for this child cursor

- *child_address*: Address of the child cursor

For working scripts against these views, see the Oracle script collection at www.oracle-script.com.

The STATSPACK report scripts *sprepsql.sql* and *sprsqins.sql* are used to generate the STATSPACK report for SQL statements, statistics and plan usage. This STATSPACK SQL report, in *$oracle_home/admin/rdbms/admin*, shows the shareable memory used by a SQL cursor. This figure is the sum of all memory used by the SQL, including child cursors.

Steve Adams notes the library cache structures for SQL with multiple children and the multiple cursor structure within the shared pool library cache (http://www.ixora.com.au/q+a/0104/19005414.htm):

> *"For each SQL statement, the library cache contains a parent cursor for the text of the SQL statement.*
> *The parent cursor is comprised of a handle that can be looked up by hash value via the library cache hash table, and an object that contains pointers to each of its child cursors.*
>
> *Each child cursor is also comprised of a handle and an object. The child object is comprised of two heaps numbered 0 and 6. Heap 0 contains all the identifying information for a particular version of the SQL statement and heap 6 contains the execution plan. This distinction between parent and child cursors is maintained even when there is only one version of each SQL statement.*
>
> *For parent cursors, the convention used in the x$ tables is that the parent address is the same as the handle address. V$open_cursors, v$sql and so on are only interested in child cursors and so they exclude parent cursors by requiring that the two addresses are different. The columns that you mentioned are of course the two addresses."*

In STATSPACK, the collection threshold *p_def_version_count_th* can be used to govern the threshold for the SQL child cursors.

Frank Pachot published the following SQL, intended to be run right after an SQL is executed. The previously run SQL statement can be identified by the *v$session.prev_sql_addr* column.

> *"When you have the same statement that has several versions (child), the view v$sql_shared_cursor shows the reason why the statement cannot be shared. More detail on reasons in Metalink note 120655.1"*

⊟ **sql_shared_cursor.sql**

```
select version_count,address,hash_value,parsing_schema_name,reason,sql_text from (
select
 address,''
 ||decode(max(                    UNBOUND_CURSOR),'Y',                    ' UNBOUND_CURSOR')
 ||decode(max(                SQL_TYPE_MISMATCH),'Y',                ' SQL_TYPE_MISMATCH')
 ||decode(max(               OPTIMIZER_MISMATCH),'Y',               ' OPTIMIZER_MISMATCH')
 ||decode(max(                 OUTLINE_MISMATCH),'Y',                 ' OUTLINE_MISMATCH')
 ||decode(max(               STATS_ROW_MISMATCH),'Y',               ' STATS_ROW_MISMATCH')
 ||decode(max(                 LITERAL_MISMATCH),'Y',                 ' LITERAL_MISMATCH')
 ||decode(max(               SEC_DEPTH_MISMATCH),'Y',               ' SEC_DEPTH_MISMATCH')
 ||decode(max(             EXPLAIN_PLAN_CURSOR),'Y',             ' EXPLAIN_PLAN_CURSOR')
 ||decode(max(            BUFFERED_DML_MISMATCH),'Y',            ' BUFFERED_DML_MISMATCH')
 ||decode(max(                PDML_ENV_MISMATCH),'Y',                ' PDML_ENV_MISMATCH')
 ||decode(max(               INST_DRTLD_MISMATCH),'Y',               ' INST_DRTLD_MISMATCH')
 ||decode(max(                SLAVE_QC_MISMATCH),'Y',                ' SLAVE_QC_MISMATCH')
 ||decode(max(               TYPECHECK_MISMATCH),'Y',               ' TYPECHECK_MISMATCH')
 ||decode(max(               AUTH_CHECK_MISMATCH),'Y',              ' AUTH_CHECK_MISMATCH')
 ||decode(max(                    BIND_MISMATCH),'Y',                    ' BIND_MISMATCH')
 ||decode(max(                DESCRIBE_MISMATCH),'Y',                ' DESCRIBE_MISMATCH')
 ||decode(max(                LANGUAGE_MISMATCH),'Y',                ' LANGUAGE_MISMATCH')
 ||decode(max(             TRANSLATION_MISMATCH),'Y',             ' TRANSLATION_MISMATCH')
 ||decode(max(           ROW_LEVEL_SEC_MISMATCH),'Y',           ' ROW_LEVEL_SEC_MISMATCH')
 ||decode(max(                     INSUFF_PRIVS),'Y',                     ' INSUFF_PRIVS')
 ||decode(max(                 INSUFF_PRIVS_REM),'Y',                 ' INSUFF_PRIVS_REM')
 ||decode(max(             REMOTE_TRANS_MISMATCH),'Y',            ' REMOTE_TRANS_MISMATCH')
 ||decode(max(          LOGMINER_SESSION_MISMATCH),'Y',        ' LOGMINER_SESSION_MISMATCH')
 ||decode(max(               INCOMP_LTRL_MISMATCH),'Y',             ' INCOMP_LTRL_MISMATCH')
 ||decode(max(             OVERLAP_TIME_MISMATCH),'Y',             ' OVERLAP_TIME_MISMATCH')
 ||decode(max(             SQL_REDIRECT_MISMATCH),'Y',             ' SQL_REDIRECT_MISMATCH')
 ||decode(max(             MV_QUERY_GEN_MISMATCH),'Y',             ' MV_QUERY_GEN_MISMATCH')
 ||decode(max(             USER_BIND_PEEK_MISMATCH),'Y',          ' USER_BIND_PEEK_MISMATCH')
 ||decode(max(                TYPCHK_DEP_MISMATCH),'Y',              ' TYPCHK_DEP_MISMATCH')
 ||decode(max(               NO_TRIGGER_MISMATCH),'Y',              ' NO_TRIGGER_MISMATCH')
 ||decode(max(                FLASHBACK_CURSOR),'Y',                ' FLASHBACK_CURSOR')
 ||decode(max(            ANYDATA_TRANSFORMATION),'Y',           ' ANYDATA_TRANSFORMATION')
 ||decode(max(               INCOMPLETE_CURSOR),'Y',               ' INCOMPLETE_CURSOR')
 ||decode(max(             TOP_LEVEL_RPI_CURSOR),'Y',             ' TOP_LEVEL_RPI_CURSOR')
 ||decode(max(             DIFFERENT_LONG_LENGTH),'Y',            ' DIFFERENT_LONG_LENGTH')
 ||decode(max(            LOGICAL_STANDBY_APPLY),'Y',            ' LOGICAL_STANDBY_APPLY')
 ||decode(max(                 DIFF_CALL_DURN),'Y',                  ' DIFF_CALL_DURN')
 ||decode(max(                 BIND_UACS_DIFF),'Y',                  ' BIND_UACS_DIFF')
 ||decode(max(           PLSQL_CMP_SWITCHS_DIFF),'Y',          ' PLSQL_CMP_SWITCHS_DIFF')
 ||decode(max(              CURSOR_PARTS_MISMATCH),'Y',           ' CURSOR_PARTS_MISMATCH')
 ||decode(max(               STB_OBJECT_MISMATCH),'Y',             ' STB_OBJECT_MISMATCH')
 ||decode(max(                ROW_SHIP_MISMATCH),'Y',                ' ROW_SHIP_MISMATCH')
 ||decode(max(                PQ_SLAVE_MISMATCH),'Y',                ' PQ_SLAVE_MISMATCH')
 ||decode(max(             TOP_LEVEL_DDL_MISMATCH),'Y',           ' TOP_LEVEL_DDL_MISMATCH')
 ||decode(max(                MULTI_PX_MISMATCH),'Y',                ' MULTI_PX_MISMATCH')
 ||decode(max(             BIND_PEEKED_PQ_MISMATCH),'Y',         ' BIND_PEEKED_PQ_MISMATCH')
 ||decode(max(              MV_REWRITE_MISMATCH),'Y',              ' MV_REWRITE_MISMATCH')
 ||decode(max(             ROLL_INVALID_MISMATCH),'Y',            ' ROLL_INVALID_MISMATCH')
 ||decode(max(            OPTIMIZER_MODE_MISMATCH),'Y',          ' OPTIMIZER_MODE_MISMATCH')
 ||decode(max(                       PX_MISMATCH),'Y',                    ' PX_MISMATCH')
 ||decode(max(              MV_STALEOBJ_MISMATCH),'Y',             ' MV_STALEOBJ_MISMATCH')
 ||decode(max(           FLASHBACK_TABLE_MISMATCH),'Y',         ' FLASHBACK_TABLE_MISMATCH')
 ||decode(max(               LITREP_COMP_MISMATCH),'Y',             ' LITREP_COMP_MISMATCH')
 reason
from
   v$sql_shared_cursor
group by
   address
) join v$sqlarea using(address) where version_count>&versions
order by version_count desc,address
;
```

The next section will cover how SQL can be made reentrant.

Using *cursor_sharing=force*

Some Oracle databases with high ad-hoc query activity, such as those utilizing Crystal Reports or Business Objects, cannot avoid in-line literals inside the SQL, and that is why Oracle introduced the *cursor_sharing* parameter. This use of *cursor_sharing=force* has been a huge benefit for databases plagued with literals, i.e. non-reentrant SQL, in their library cache.

The dynamic shop often has SQL that is generated by ad-hoc query tools with hard-coded literal values embedded within the SQL. Hard-coded literal values make the SQL statements non-reusable unless *cursor_sharing=force* is set in the Oracle initialization file.

As mentioned earlier, shops that are plagued with non-reusable SQL can adopt either the persistent or the dynamic execution plan philosophy. To use optimizer plan stability with non-reusable SQL, the *cursor_sharing=force* should be set and then the transformed SQL extracted from the library cache. Optimizer plan stability should be used to make the execution plan persistent.

Back in version 8i when the *cursor_sharing* initialization parameter was first introduced, many DBAs thought it was a great idea. However, after several false starts, multiple bugs and lackluster performance, most users shelved the idea of *cursor_sharing* until a more stable release.

Essentially, there are two options for the *cursor_sharing* parameter:

- *exact:* Meaning that the cursors have to be exactly in order to be shared
- *force:* Meaning every literal is replaced with a bind variable.

Many Oracle shops that use purchased packages are stuck with poorly implemented applications from third parties. Many of these packages do not allow for the alteration of source code, so the ability to force bind variable is a good feature.

However, it is not always a good idea to force bind variables for 100% of statements. When a bind variable is volatile, meaning the value of the bind variable affects the execution plan for the SQL, it is not a good idea to replace the literals in a statement with a bind variable. Fortunately, there is the *similar* option which only substitutes when the bind variable will not affect the execution plan.

The next section will cover some recent cursor sharing enhancements.

Oracle Cursor Sharing Enhancements

An exciting internal feature of Oracle 11g allows the cost-based SQL optimizer to change execution plans even when optimizer plan stability is used. This is called peeking and allows the cost-based SQL optimizer to change execution plans when the value of a bind variable could cause a significant change to the execution plan for the SQL.

Watch the Release!

While *cursor_sharing=similar* has been around since Oracle 9i, it originally had a few bugs. It has become more useable as of Oracle 11g.

Cursor sharing has a processing overhead at optimization time, and it should only be used if an application generates dynamic SQL or with applications that must embed literal values. PL/SQL applications should be written for the SQL to use bind variables, and these systems will not benefit from cursor sharing.

To illustrate with a simple example, the *cursor_sharing* parameter has been set to *force*. This will change all SQL literal values to host variables inside the library cache.

Now assume that there is an index on a region column of a customer table. The region column has four values: north; south; east; and west. The data values for the region column are highly skewed with 90% of the values in the south region.

Because of this, the cost-based SQL optimizer would be faster performing a full-table scan when south is specified and an index range scan when east, west, or north is specified. When using cursor sharing, the cost-based SQL optimizer changes any literal values in the SQL to bind variables. The statement would be changed as follows:

```
select
   customer_stuff
from
   customer
where
   region = 'west';
```

The transformation replaces the literal west with a host variable:

```
select
   customer_stuff
from
   customer
where
   region = ':var1';
```

In Oracle 11g with *cursor_sharing=similar*, the cost-based SQL optimizer peeks at the values of user-defined bind variables on the first invocation of a cursor. This lets the optimizer determine the selectivity of the *where* clause operator and change the execution plan whenever the south value appears in the SQL. This enhancement greatly improves the performance of cursor sharing when a bind variable is used against a highly skewed column.

With *cursor_sharing=similar*, Oracle will switch in the bind variables when doing so makes no difference to the outcome. Oracle will use literal values if using bind variables would make a significant difference to the outcome. Remember that Oracle's bind peeking is only useful when dealing with highly skewed column distributions. Peeking is beneficial when Oracle detects that the value of a column literal will affect the execution plan. For index columns without excessive skew, peeking is a wasted step.

To get an idea how cursor sharing can improve SQL execution, examine this simple case study:

A Case Study in Cursor Sharing

An Oracle 11g database had experienced poor performance immediately after a new manufacturing plant was added to the existing database. A standard STATSPACK report was used to isolate the top 5 wait events. The report looked similar to this:

```
Top 5 Wait Events
~~~~~~~~~~~~~~~~~~                        Wait      % Total
Event                          Waits   Time (cs)   Wt Time
------------------------------ ------------ ------------ -------
enqueue                          25,901    479,654   46.71
db file scattered read       10,579,442    197,205   29.20
db file sequential read         724,325    196,583    9.14
latch free                    1,150,979     51,084    4.97
log file parallel write         148,932     39,822    3.88
```

A review of the SQL section of the STATSPACK report revealed that almost all of the SQL used literals in the *where* clause of all queries.

```
Where
   customer_state = 'Alabama'
and
   customer_type = 'LAWYER';
```

In this case, the *cursor_sharing* parameter was the only fast solution because the application was a vendor package with dynamically generated SQL. This package could not easily be changed without using Optimizer Plan Stability (Stored Outlines), which is a very time-consuming task.

Setting *cursor_sharing=force* greatly reduced the contention on the library cache and reduced CPU consumption. The end users reported a 75 percent improvement in overall performance.

The next section will cover table syntax.

Oracle ISO 99 Table Syntax

In Oracle 9i, Oracle made some important enhancements to the SQL, including a host of exciting execution plans, support for scalar subqueries and support for the ISO 99 SQL standard. As implemented by Oracle, this included the following *table join* syntax:

- *cross* join: This creates a Cartesian product of the rows in both tables, just like in Oracle 8i when the *where* clause is forgotten

- *natural* join: This is a useful Oracle 9i syntax feature that improved the readability of SQL by removing join criteria from the *where* clause

- The USING clause: This allows a DBA to specify the join key by name.

- The ON clause: This syntax allows a DBA to specify the column names for join keys in both tables.

- *left outer* join: Tthis returns all the rows from the table on the left side of the join, along with the values from the right-hand side or nulls if a matching row does not exist.

- *right outer* join: This returns all the rows from the table on the right side of the join, along with the values from the left-hand side or nulls if a matching row does not exist.

- *full outer* join: This returns all rows from both tables, filling in any blanks with nulls. NOTE: There is no equivalent for this for those still using Oracle 8i.

Most of these enhancements were introduced to allow non-Oracle applications to quickly port onto an Oracle database, and it is important to remember that these are just syntax differences. Remember, the ISO 99 standard did not bring any new functionality to Oracle SQL, it just added new syntax.

The *cross* Join

In Oracle, the *cross join* syntax produces a Cartesian product, very much the same as forgetting to add a *where* clause when joining two tables:

```
Select
  last_name, dept_id
from
  emp, depts;
```

In Oracle 9i and beyond, the *cross join* syntax can be used to achieve the same result:

```
Select
  last_name, dept_id
from
  emp
cross join
  dept;
```

The *natural* Join

The *natural join* syntax is great because it automatically detects the join keys based on the name of the matching column in both tables. This simplified Oracle 9i SQL because the *where* clause only contained filtering predicates. Of course, the use of *natural* join requires that both columns have identical names in each table. It is interesting to note that this feature works even without primary or foreign key referential integrity.

Oracle 8i:

```
Select
  book_title, sum(quantity)
from
  book, sales
where
  book.book_id = sales.book_id
group by
  book_title;
```

Oracle 9i and beyond:

```
Select
  book_title, sum(quantity)
from
  book
natural join
  sales
group by
  book_title;
```

The USING Clause

The USING clause is used when several columns share the same name, but the DBA does not want to join using all of these common columns. The columns listed in the USING clause cannot have any qualifiers in the statement, including the *where* clause:

Oracle 8i:

```
Select
  dept_id, city
from
  departments, locations
where
  departments.location_id = location.location_id;
```

Oracle 9i and beyond:

```
select
  department_name, city
from
  departments
join
  locations
using
  (location_id);
```

The ON Clause

The ON clause is used to join tables where the column names do not match in both tables. The join conditions are removed from the filter conditions in the *where* clause:

Oracle 8i:

```
Select
  department_name, city
from
  department, location
where
  department.location_id = location.loc_id;
```

Oracle 9i and beyond:

```
Select
  department_name, city
from
  department d
join location
  l
on
  (d.location_id = l.loc_id);
```

Mutable Joins

Mutable joins are those where more than two tables are joined. The ISO SQL 99 standard always assumes the tables are joined from the left to the right, with the join conditions only being able to reference columns relating to the current join and any previous joins to the left.

Oracle 8i:

```
Select
  emp_id, city_name, dept_name
from
  location l, department d, emp e
where
  d.location_id = l.location_id
and
  d.department_id = e.department_id;
```

Oracle 9i and beyond:

```
Select
  emp_id, city_name, dept_name
from
  locations l
join
  departments d on (d.location_id = l.location_id)
join
  employees e    on (d.department_id = e.department_id);
```

Outer Join Syntax

The ISO 99 standard removed the onerous plus sign (+) from Oracle outer joins and makes outer join SQL easier to understand.

left outer Join

In a *left outer* join, all rows in the left-hand table are returned, even if there is no matching column in the joined tables. In this example, all employee last names are returned, even those employees who are not yet assigned to a department:

Oracle 8i:

```
Select
  last_name, d.department_id
from
  emp  e, dept d
where
  e.department_id = d.department_id(+);
```

Oracle 9i and beyond:

```
Select
  last_name, d.department_id
from
```

```
  emp e
left outer join
  Dept d
On
  e.department_id = d.department_id;
```

right outer Join

In a *right outer* join, all rows in the right-hand table are returned, even if there is no matching column in the joined tables. In this example, all department IDs are returned, even for those departments without any employees:

Oracle 8i:

```
Select
  last_name, d.department_id
from
  employees e, departments d
where
  e.department_id(+) = d.department_id;
```

Oracle 9i and beyond:

```
Select
  last_name, d.department_id
from
  employees e
right outer join
  departments d
on
  (e.department_id = d.department_id);
```

The ISO 99 standard has been another example of Oracle's commitment to enhancing its implementation of SQL. The most popular of these enhancements are the *natural* join, which simplifies SQL syntax, and the *left outer* join and *right outer* join, which eliminate the need for the clumsy (+) syntax.

Starting with Oracle 9i, the confusing *outer* join syntax using the (+) notation has been superseded by ISO 99 outer join syntax. There are three types of outer joins; *left*, *right*, and *full* outer join. The purpose of an outer join is to include non-matching rows. The outer join returns missing columns as *null* values. Review the syntax differences between these variations in join syntax:

left outer join, Oracle 8i:

```
select
   last_name,
   department_name
from
   employees e,
   departments d
where
   e.department_id = d.department_id(+);
```

left outer join, Oracle 9i:

```
select
   last_name,
   department_name
from
   employees e
left outer join
   departments d
on
   e.department_id = d.department_id;
```

The next section will cover a non-traditional table type, the external table, and show how SQL is optimized for querying data outside Oracle.

External Tables and SQL

One of the most exciting advances in Oracle 9i was the ability to access non-Oracle files with Oracle SQL. This functionality, called external tables, brought with it important ramifications for systems where external files need to be available for non-database applications and appear to be a table within Oracle.

External tables allow a DBA to define the structure of almost any flat file on a server and have it appear to Oracle as if it were a real table, as diagrammed in Figure 16.1.

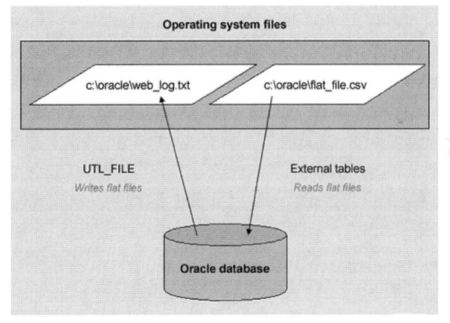

Figure 16.1: *The Oracle Read and Write Interfaces to OS Files*

Oracle lets a database program write to flat files using the *utl_file* utility. Combined with external table's read ability, this topology removed the requirement that all Oracle data reside inside Oracle tables, opening new applications for Oracle. The next section will take a closer look at how this feature works.

Defining an External Table

In this example, the goal is to get Oracle to refer to this comma-delimited flat file:

```
7369,SMITH,CLERK,7902,17-DEC-80,800,20
7499,ALLEN,SALESMAN,7698,20-FEB-81,1600,300,30
7521,WARD,SALESMAN,7698,22-FEB-81,1250,500,30
7566,JONES,MANAGER,7839,02-APR-81,2975,,20
7654,MARTIN,SALESMAN,7698,28-SEP-81,1250,1400,30
7698,BLAKE,MANAGER,7839,01-MAY-81,2850,,30
7782,CLARK,MANAGER,7839,09-JUN-81,2450,,10
7788,SCOTT,ANALYST,7566,19-APR-87,3000,,20
7839,KING,PRESIDENT,,17-NOV-81,5000,,10
7844,TURNER,SALESMAN,7698,08-SEP-81,1500,0,30
7876,ADAMS,CLERK,7788,23-MAY-87,1100,,20
```

The file contains the following employee information:

- Employee ID
- Last name
- Job description
- Manager's employee ID
- Hire date
- Salary
- Commission
- Department

So, how can this file be defined to Oracle? First, an Oracle directory entry must be created in the data dictionary that points to the Windows directory where the flat file resides. In this example, the directory will be named *test dir*. It will be pointed to c:\docs\pubsdb\queries:

```
SQL> create directory testdir as 'c:\docs\pubsdb\queries';
```

Now that the directory exists, the structure of the external file can be defined to Oracle:

```
create table
   emp_ext
(
   empno    number(4),
   ename    varchar2(10),
   job      varchar2(9),
   mgr      number(4),
   hiredate date,
   sal      number(7,2),
   comm     number(7,2),
   deptno   number(2)
)
organization external
(
   type oracle_loader
   default directory testdir
```

```
   access parameters
   (
      records delimited by newline
      fields terminated by ','
   )
location ('emp_ext.csv')
)
reject limit 1000;
```

In this syntax, the column of the external table has been defined in much the same way as an internal Oracle table. The external definitions occur in the ORGANIZATION EXTERNAL clause:

- default directory testdir is the directory where the file resides

- records delimited by newline is the new line character

- fields terminated by ',' indicate the column termination character

- location ('emp_ext.csv') identifies the name of the external file

External Definitions for the Comma-delimited File

Now that the external table has been defined, it is possible to run reports against the external table using SQL, just as if the table resided inside the database. In the query below, note the use of the sophisticated *rollup* parameter to summarize salaries by both department and job title.

```
ttitle 'Employee Salary|Cubic Rollup'

col  deptno    heading 'Department|Number'
col  job       heading 'Job|Title'
col  num_emps  heading 'Number of|Employees' format 9,999
col  sum_sal   heading 'Total|Salary'        format $99,999

select
   deptno,
   job,
   count(*)  num_emps,
   sum(sal)  sum_sal
from
   emp_ext
group by
   rollup
   (
      deptno,
      job
   );
```

Listing C

```
Wed Jun 12                                   page    1
                   Employee Salary
                   Cubic Rollup

Department Job       Number of    Total
   Number Title      Employees    Salary
---------- --------- ---------    --------
       10 MANAGER            1    $2,450
       10 PRESIDENT          1    $5,000
       10                    2    $7,450
```

```
20 ANALYST            1    $3,000
20 CLERK              1    $1,100
20 MANAGER            1    $2,975
20                    3    $7,075
30 MANAGER            1    $2,850
30 SALESMAN           4    $5,600
30                    5    $8,450
                     10   $22,975
```

Limitations on External Tables

Because external tables are still fairly new in relative terms, their use has not been perfected. This feature has several limitations, including:

- **No support for DML:** External tables are read-only, but the base data can be edited in any text editor.
- **Poor response for high-volume queries:** External tables have a processing overhead, perform full scans and are not suitable for large tables.

Accessing flat files via Oracle has a number of uses. It is also possible to define spreadsheets to Oracle. This technique has important ramifications for shops where users can control system-wide parameters inside desktop spreadsheets and Oracle knows immediately about changes:

- The external file must be comma-delimited and stored on the server as a file with a *.csv* extension
- External spreadsheets are not good for large files because the entire file must be reread into Oracle whenever a change is saved to the spreadsheet
- End users must never reformat the data columns inside the spreadsheet environment

Remember, when defining the flat file as an external table, the file remains on the operating system as a flat file, where it can be read and updated with a variety of tools, including spreadsheets. Using Microsoft's Excel spreadsheets, the external table data can be read just as if it were standard spreadsheet data as shown in Figure 16.2.

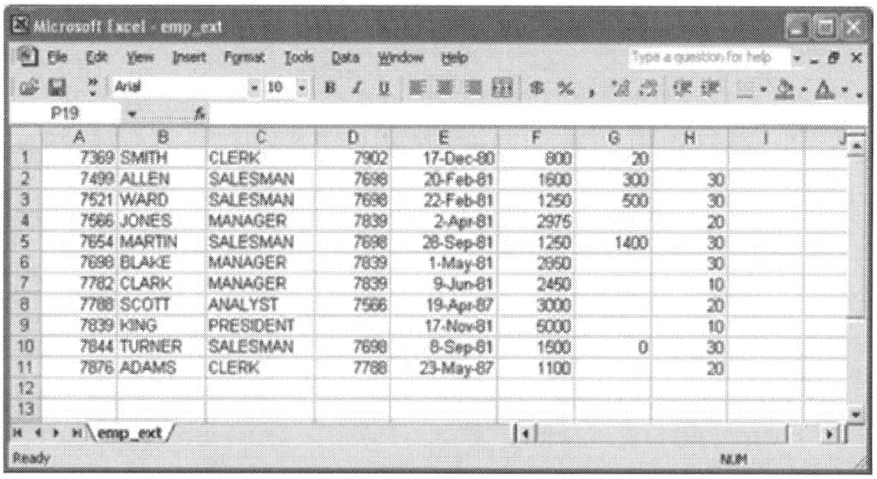

	A	B	C	D	E	F	G	H
1	7369	SMITH	CLERK	7902	17-Dec-80	800	20	
2	7499	ALLEN	SALESMAN	7698	20-Feb-81	1600	300	30
3	7521	WARD	SALESMAN	7698	22-Feb-81	1250	500	30
4	7566	JONES	MANAGER	7839	2-Apr-81	2975		20
5	7654	MARTIN	SALESMAN	7698	28-Sep-81	1250	1400	30
6	7698	BLAKE	MANAGER	7839	1-May-81	2850		30
7	7782	CLARK	MANAGER	7839	9-Jun-81	2450		10
8	7788	SCOTT	ANALYST	7566	19-Apr-87	3000		20
9	7839	KING	PRESIDENT		17-Nov-81	5000		10
10	7844	TURNER	SALESMAN	7698	8-Sep-81	1500	0	30
11	7876	ADAMS	CLERK	7788	23-May-87	1100		20

Figure 16.2: *An External Table Inside an Excel Spreadsheet*

End users can manage critical tables inside easy-to-use spreadsheets. Oracle immediately notices whenever a change is made to the spreadsheet. However, there are important limitations to using spreadsheets as Oracle tables, the foremost being excessive disk I/O whenever the spreadsheet has changed.

Internals of External Tables

It is important to recognize that Oracle data inside spreadsheets will not be accessible as quickly as internal row data. Oracle cannot maintain row-level locking because the operating system is in command rather than Oracle. When a spreadsheet is defined as an external table, Oracle has no way of knowing when individual row data changes. The operating system will only tell Oracle that the entire spreadsheet has changed.

In addition, data blocks that are read from an external table are not placed inside the Oracle data buffers. The dictionary query below demonstrates that Oracle does not read the external table rows into the RAM data cache.

```
select
        bp.name             pool_name,
        ob.name             object,
        ob.subname      sub_name,
        sum(buf_count)  buffer_blocks
from
        (select set_ds, obj, count(*) buf_count
        from x$bh group by set_ds, obj)      bh,
        obj$                                 ob,
        x$kcbwds                             ws,
        v$buffer_pool                        bp
where
   ob.dataobj# = bh.obj
and
   ob.owner# > 0
and
   bh.set_ds = ws.addr
and
   ws.set_id between bp.lo_setid and bp.hi_setid
group by
        bp.name,
        ob.name,
        ob.subname
order by
        bp.name,
        ob.name,
        ob.subname
;
```

As shown in the listing below, selections from the table do not reside in the data buffers following a SQL query.

```
SQL> select ename from pubs.emp_ext;

SQL> @buf_data

POOL_NAME OBJECT                     SUB_NAME                    BLOCKS
--------- -------------------------- ------------------------- --------
DEFAULT   PUBLISHER                                                   2
          REPCAT$_REPPROP                                             1
```

```
SNS$BINDINGS$                          2
SNS$INODE$                             2
SNS$NODE_INDEX                         1
SNS$REFADDR$                           3
SNS$REFADDR_INDEX                      3
SYS_C001042                            1
SYS_C001414                            1
```

Oracle does not make it clear whether a separate buffering mechanism is used for external tables. With this lack of buffering, Oracle must reread the entire spreadsheet for each SQL invocation that accesses the external table.

To maintain data integrity, Oracle must detect when the spreadsheet data has changed, but there is no way to discover when specific spreadsheet values have changed. When Oracle detects that the flat file has been updated, all data in the RAM data buffers becomes invalid, and the entire spreadsheet must be reread. This is the primary reason external tables are not efficient for large volumes of data.

Because Oracle reads operating system files in data blocks, a DBA can compute the amount of disk I/O by determining the number of spreadsheet blocks with a simple shell script. In this script, the Oracle database has 8 KB block sizes:

```
bytes=`ls -al|grep emp_ext.csv|awk '{ print $5 }'`
num_bytes=`expr $bytes`
blocks=`expr $num_bytes / 8192`
echo $blocks
```

The results of this script will show exactly how many disk reads are required to access the Oracle external table whenever a change is made.

Limitations of Comma-delimited Spreadsheet Files

In order for Oracle to successfully read comma-delimited (*csv*) files, it is important to avoid making spreadsheet-specific changes, This is because Excel will change the internal storage of the column to accommodate the formatting. For example, assume that the salary column is reformatted for comma display, as shown in Figure 16.3:

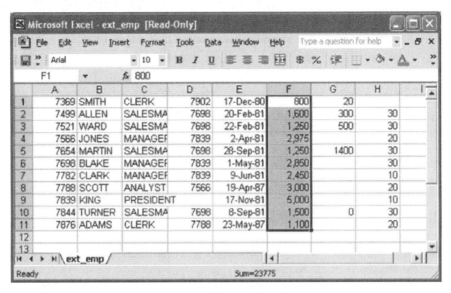

Figure 16.3: *Reformatting a Comma-delimited (csv) Spreadsheet*

Once the file has been saved, Oracle can no longer read the salary column because the column has been stored in quotes. To Oracle, this defines the column as a character:

```
7369,SMITH,CLERK,7902,17-Dec-80,800,20,
7499,ALLEN,SALESMAN,7698,20-Feb-81,"1,600",300,30
7521,WARD,SALESMAN,7698,22-Feb-81,"1,250",500,30
7566,JONES,MANAGER,7839,2-Apr-81,"2,975",,20
7654,MARTIN,SALESMAN,7698,28-Sep-81,"1,250",1400,30
7698,BLAKE,MANAGER,7839,1-May-81,"2,850",,30
7782,CLARK,MANAGER,7839,9-Jun-81,"2,450",,10
7788,SCOTT,ANALYST,7566,19-Apr-87,"3,000",,20
7839,KING,PRESIDENT,,17-Nov-81,"5,000",,10
7844,TURNER,SALESMAN,7698,8-Sep-81,"1,500",0,30
7876,ADAMS,CLERK,7788,23-May-87,"1,100",,20
```

The accidental reformatting of the file makes it unreadable by Oracle. Special consideration must be taken to instruct end users to never change the formatting of the associated spreadsheet.

Tuning Distributed SQL Queries

Generally, the limiting factor in SQL performance of a distributed query (over a db-link) is the speed of the network. DBAs should make sure that they have a high-speed network with proper SDU, but there are other issues besides speed to consider:

- **tnsnames.ora:** Some recommend a separate listener and a larger value for SDU to accommodate jumbo Ethernet frames. By using a separate listener for the gigabit network with a larger SDU, DBAs can better exploit jumbo Ethernet frames.

- **Pull vs. Push:** In general, performance can be faster if data is pulled rather than pushed. An example of pushing the data would be performing the join on a remote table. It would be better to pull the data by calling the remote table from the master instance. This is especially true if a large sort is required, because the rows may be transferred to the remote host for sorting, and then back again afterwards.

- *driving_site* **hint:** the *driving_site* hint forces query execution to be done at a different site than the initiating instance. This is done when the remote table is much larger than the local table. It is also good when the work (join, sorting) is to be done remotely to save the back-and-forth network traffic. In this example, the *driving_site* hint is used to force the work to be done on the site where the huge table resides:

```
select /*+DRIVING_SITE(h)*/
   ename
from
  tiny_table          t,
  huge_table@remote h
where
   t.deptno = h.deptno;
```

- **Views:** Some experts recommend creating a view on the remote site referencing the local tables and calling the remote table via the local view.

```
create view local_cust as select * from cust@remote;
```

It is possible to get the same effect by using an inline view:

```
select /*+ DRIVING_SITE(a) */
*
from (select stuff from emp@remote) a
```

- **Sorting:** If the SQL performs a sort, everyone should be aware that the sort will be performed on the local database. This is one reason why it is bad to use a push approach, because the rows will traverse back-and-forth.

- **Parallelism:** Parallel query across a database link can be quite complex. In a distributed environment, pieces of a table may reside on many remote servers. For example, assume a distributed architecture where local customer tables are kept on each instance. All of the remote rows can be accessed in a single query, using inter-instance parallel execution. In this example, the query is executed from the *north_carolina* instance, accessing two remote instances in parallel:

```
select customer_name, sum(purchase_amount) from sales
union
select customer_name, sum(purchase_amount) from sales@san_francisco
union
select customer_name, sum(purchase_amount) from sales@new_york
group by
   customer_name;
```

In this case, the *north_carolina* instance drives the distributed parallel query and it is the *north_carolina* instance that must gather and sort the result set.

Also, note that there are many hidden parameters that influence OPQ performance. Always consult Oracle technical support before changing an undocumented parameter:

```
NAME                                    VALUE
-----------------------------------    --------------------
_parallel_adaptive_max_users            1
_parallel_default_max_instances         1
_parallel_execution_message_align       FALSE
_parallel_fake_class_pct                0
_parallel_load_bal_unit                 0
_parallel_load_balancing                TRUE
_parallel_min_message_pool              64560
_parallel_recovery_stopat               32767
_parallel_server_idle_time              5
_parallel_server_sleep_time             10
_parallel_txn_global                    FALSE
_parallelism_cost_fudge_factor          350
```

Monitoring parallel query for remote distributed queries is also challenging. As noted, SQL can be nested inside SQL, and subqueries can be placed anywhere; in the *select* clause, in the *from* clause and in the *where* clause. The next section will take a closer look at subqueries.

Subqueries and SQL

A subquery is a condition where an SQL query is nested or placed inside another SQL query. The ISO 99 SQL standard allows for SQL queries to be embedded inside other SQL statements in several ways. SQL queries can be placed inside the *select* clause (scalar subqueries), inside the *from* clause (in-line views), and inside the *where* clause (basic subqueries).

The ability to nest SQL statements inside each other provides tremendous power to SQL and allows SQL statements to perform extremely complex processing without using a procedural language like PL/SQL.

In relational terminology, the main query is called the outer query, and the subquery is often referred to as the inner query.

Basic SQL Subqueries

When a DBA sees a SQL statement that specifies a subquery, they first need to carefully check the *where* clause and determine if the subquery is a non-correlated subquery or a correlated subquery.

A correlated subquery is a query where the key in the subquery is correlated with a column that is selected in the outer query using the = operator. A non-correlated subquery is a query where the subquery executes independently of the outer query, passing a result set to the outer query at the end of its execution. Non-correlated subqueries are commonly seen when using the *in, not in, exists*, and *not exists* SQL clauses.

In a basic subquery, an SQL statement is embedded inside the *where* clause of the query. The query below can be used to locate all authors who have not yet published a book.

```
select
   author_last_name
```

```
from
    author
where
    author_key not in
        (select author_key from book_author);
```

This type of query is called a non-correlated subquery because the subquery does not make any references to the outside query. The output should look like the following:

```
AUTHOR_LAST_NAME
------------------------------------------
clark
mee
```

In this example, the query selected all authors who have not yet published their first book. Internally, this query reads all *author_key* values from the book_author table and then compares this result set with the *author_key* value in the author table. The savvy Oracle SQL tuner is always on the lookout for both correlated and non-correlated subqueries for several reasons. The foremost is to search for opportunities for replacing the subquery with a standard join, and the other is to examine the uniqueness of the indexes in the subquery to see if changing the index structure can change the table access method.

```
-- Form one:  Using non-correlated subquery)
select
  book_title
from
  book
where
  book_key not in (select book_key from sales);
```

```
Execution Plan
----------------------------------------------------------
   0        SELECT STATEMENT Optimizer=CHOOSE (Cost=1 Card=1 Bytes=64)
   1     0    FILTER
   2     1      TABLE ACCESS (FULL) OF 'BOOK' (Cost=1 Card=1 Bytes=64)
   3     1      TABLE ACCESS (FULL) OF 'SALES' (Cost=1 Card=5 Bytes=25)
```

```
-- Form two:  Using outer join
select
  book_title
from
  book  b,
  sales  s
where
  b.book_key = s.book_key(+)
and
  quantity is null;
```

```
Execution Plan
----------------------------------------------------------
0    SELECT STATEMENT Optimizer=CHOOSE (Cost=3 Card=100 Bytes=8200)

1  0 FILTER
2  1    FILTER
3  2      HASH JOIN (OUTER)
4  3        TABLE ACCESS (FULL) OF 'BOOK' (Cost=1 Card=20 Bytes=1280)
5  3        TABLE ACCESS (FULL) OF 'SALES' (Cost=1 Card=100 Bytes=1800)
```

```
-- Form three: using correlated subquery
select
  book_title
from
  book
where
  book_title not in (
                  select
                  distinct
                    book_title
                  from
                    book,
                    sales
                  where
                    book.book_key = sales.book_key
                  and
                    quantity > 0);
```

Execution Plan
----
0   SELECT STATEMENT Optimizer=CHOOSE (Cost=1 Card=1 Bytes=59)
1 0   FILTER
2 1   TABLE ACCESS (FULL) OF 'BOOK' (Cost=1 Card=1 Bytes=59)
3 1   FILTER
4 3   NESTED LOOPS (Cost=6 Card=1 Bytes=82)
5 4   TABLE ACCESS (FULL) OF 'SALES' (Cost=1 Card=5 Bytes=90)
6 4   TABLE ACCESS (BY INDEX ROWID) OF 'BOOK' (Cost=1 Card=1)
7 6   INDEX (UNIQUE SCAN) OF 'PK_BOOK' (UNIQUE)

Scalar Subqueries

Scalar subqueries are a powerful enhancement, first introduced in Oracle 9i SQL. They allow for quick formulation of extremely complex SQL statements. Oracle's introduction of scalar subquery support is another example of the company's commitment to keeping pace with the evolution of the SQL language.

Oracle has long supported the notion of an in-line view, whereby a subquery can be placed in the *from* clause, just as if it were a table name. There is an Oracle query displaying tablespace sizes.

```
select
  df.tablespace_name                              "Tablespace",
  block_size                                      "Block Size",
  (df.totalspace - fs.freespace)                  "Used MB",
  fs.                                             "Free MB",
  df.totalspace                                   "Total MB",
  round(100 * (fs.freespace / df.totalspace))     "Pct. Free"
from
  dba_tablespaces                                 ts,
  (select tablespace_name,
      round(sum(bytes) / 1048576) TotalSpace
   from dba_data_files . . .
```

In the simple example below, the SQL subqueries are placed inside the *from* clause and assigned the aliases of *df* and *fs*. The *df* and *fs* subquery values are then referenced inside the *select* clause.

Tuning Distributed SQL Queries

This query sums and compares two ranges of values from two tables, all in a single query. For some readers, seeing SQL inside the *from* clause is probably quite strange, and the scalar subquery is even stranger! The scalar subquery is a take-off of the in-line view whereby SQL subqueries can be placed inside the *select* clause. The following sections will introduce a few examples.

Scalar Subquery Performance

Once a DBA becomes acquainted with the syntax, they often find scalar subqueries to be very powerful. Scalar subqueries are especially useful for combining multiple queries into a single query. The following uses scalar subqueries to compute several different types of aggregations (*max* and *avg*), all in the same SQL statement. Note that this query uses both scalar subqueries and in-line views.

```
select
   (select max(salary) from emp)          highest_salary,
   emp_name                               employee_name,
   (select avg(bonus) from commission)   avg_comission,
   dept_name
from
   emp,
   (select dept_name from dept where dept = 'finance')
;
```

Scalar subqueries are also handy for inserting into tables, based on values from other tables. Below, a scalar subquery is used to compute the maximum credit for Bill and insert this value into a *max_credit* table.

```
insert into
   max_credit
(
   name,
   max_credit
)
values
(
   'Bill',
   select max(credit) from credit_table where name = 'BILL'
);
```

The scalar subquery above is quite useful for Oracle data warehouse applications. In an Oracle data warehouse, it is common for the DBA to pre-aggregate values to speed up query execution, and scalar subqueries are a powerful helper in aggregation. The example below populates an *emp_salary_summary* table with many types of aggregate values from the base tables.

```
insert into
   emp_salary_summary
(
   sum_salaries
   max_salary,
   min_salary,
   avg_salary,
values
(
   (select sum(salary) from emp),
   (select max(salary) from emp),
   (select min(salary) from emp),
```

```
(select avg(salary) from emp);
```

Restrictions on Scalar Subqueries

Scalar subqueries are restricted to returning a single value because they select a finite value. Scalar subqueries could be used in earlier versions of Oracle in some parts of a SQL statement, but Oracle has extended their use to almost any place where an expression can be used, including:

- *case* expressions

- *select* statements

- *values* clauses of *insert* statements

- *where* clauses

- ORDER BY clauses

- parameters of a function

There are also important restrictions on scalar subqueries. Scalar subqueries cannot be used for:

- default values for columns

- RETURNING clauses

- hash expressions for clusters

- functional index expressions

- *check* constraints on columns

- WHEN condition of triggers

- GROUP BY and HAVING clauses

- *start with* and *connect by* clauses

Subqueries can often be rewritten to use a standard outer join, resulting in faster performance. It is important to consider that an outer join uses the plus sign (+) operator to tell the database to return all non-matching rows with NULL values. Hence, by combining the outer join with a null test in the *where* clause, the result set can be reproduced without using a subquery.

```
select
   b.book_key
from
   book   b,
   sales  s
where
   b.book_key = s.book_key(+)
and
   s.book_key is NULL
;
```

The execution plans for these types of queries will be covered in more detail later, but for now, be aware that subqueries can often be rewritten to improve the speed of the query and the resource demands on the database.

Tuning Distributed SQL Queries

781

The next section will take a look at another class of subqueries. These subqueries are placed inside the *from* clause of the outer query.

In-line Views (Subqueries in the *from* Clause)

The in-line view is a construct in Oracle SQL where a query can be placed in the SQL *from* clause, just as if the query were a table name. A common use for in-line views in Oracle SQL is to simplify complex queries by removing join operations and condensing several separate queries into a single query.

The best example of the in-line view is the common Oracle DBA script that is used to show the amount of free space and used space within all Oracle tablespaces. Carefully note that the *from* clause in this SQL query specifies two sub-queries that perform summations and grouping from two views, *dba_data_files* and *dba_free_space*.

In ANSI standard SQL, it is quite difficult to compare two result sets that are summed together in a single query. This is a common problem with Oracle SQL where specific values must be compared to a summary. Without the use of an in-line view, several separate SQL queries would need to be written, one to compute the sums from each view and another to compare the intermediate result sets.

The following code yields a great report for displaying the actual amount of free space within an Oracle tablespace.

```
column "Tablespace" format a13
column "Used MB"    format 99,999,999
column "Free MB"    format 99,999,999
colimn "Total MB"   format 99,999,999
select
   fs.tablespace_name                        "Tablespace",
   (df.totalspace - fs.freespace)            "Used MB",
   fs.freespace                              "Free MB",
   df.totalspace                             "Total MB",
   round(100 * (fs.freespace / df.totalspace)) "Pct. Free"
from
   (select
      tablespace_name,
      round(sum(bytes) / 1048576) TotalSpace
   from
      dba_data_files
   group by
      tablespace_name
   ) df,
   (select
      tablespace_name,
      round(sum(bytes) / 1048576) FreeSpace
   from
      dba_free_space
   group by
      tablespace_name
   ) fs
where
   df.tablespace_name = fs.tablespace_name;
```

This SQL quickly compares the sum of the total space within each tablespace to the sum of the free space within each tablespace. When run against a database, the above code should return output similar to this:

```
SQL> @tsfree

Tablespace Used    MB Free                MB Total    MB Pct. Free
---------- ----    -------                --------    ------------
CWMLITE    6       14            20             70
DRSYS      8       12            20             60
EXAMPLE    153     0             153            0
INDX               0       25             25             100
SYSTEM     240     85            325            26
TOOLS      7       3             10             30
UNDOTBS    1       199           200            100
USERS      1       24            25             96
```

Inside Oracle Views

A view is simply the representation of a SQL statement that is stored in memory so that it can easily be re-used. For example, the following is an example of a frequently used query:

```
Select
    Empid
from
    emp;
```

I might well want to make this a view, although in reality a working DBA would probably never create a view for a statement this simple. To create a view, use the *create view* command as seen in this example:

```
create view
    view_emp
as
select
    empid
from
    emp;
```

This command creates a new view called *view_emp*. Note that this command does not result in anything being actually stored in the database except for a data dictionary entry that defines this view. This means that every time this view is queried, Oracle has to go out and execute the view and query the database data. The query can be viewed like this:

```
Select
    *
From
    view_emp
where
    empid between 500 and 1000;
```

And Oracle will transform the query into this:

```
Select
    *
from
    (select empid from emp)
where
    empid between 500 and 1000;
```

Benefits of Oracle Views

Oracle views offer some compelling benefits. These include:

- **Commonality of code:** Since a view is based on one common set of SQL, this means that when it is called, it is less likely to require parsing. This is because the same underlying SQL is always called. However, since a DBA can add additional *where* clauses when calling a view, it is still necessary to use bind variables. Additional *where* clauses without a bind variable can still cause a hard parse!

- **Security:** Views have long been used to hide the tables that actually contain the data being queried. Views can be used to restrict the columns to which a user has been given access. Using views for security on less complex databases is usually not a bad thing. As databases become more complex, this solution becomes harder to scale and other solutions will be needed.

- **Predicate pushing:** Oracle supports pushing of predicates into a given view. Assume a DBA has a set of layered views, like this:

```
-- View One
create view
   vw_layer_one
as select
   *
from
   emp;

-- view two
create view
   vw_layer_two_dept_100
as select
   *
from
   vw_layer_one
where
   deptno=100;
```

Then assume the following query is issued:

```
select
   *
From
   vw_layer_two_dept_100
where
   empid=100;
```

The predicate in this statement is the where *empid*=100 statement. This may be one of tens or even hundreds of predicates. Oracle will, in many cases, push those predicates down into the views being called. Thus, Oracle will transform the *vw_layer_one* view into a SQL statement that looks like this:

```
create view
   vw_layer_one
as select
   *
from
   emp
where
   deptno=100
and
   empid=100;
```

Note that both the predicate from view two (where *deptno*=100) and the predicate from the SQL statement being executed (where *empid*=100) are pushed down into the final view that is executed. This can have significant performance benefits because now the bottom view can use an index if one exists on deptno and/or empid.

Predicate pushing has a number of restrictions that are beyond the scope of this book. These can be found in the Oracle documentation. Also, any predicate pushing may result in a hard parse of the underlying SQL that is executed. Hence, it is important to make sure to use bind variables instead of literals in SQL code calling views. For the best performance, the SQL in this example should look something like this:

```
select
   *
from
   vw_layer_two_dept_100
where
   empid=:b100;
```

An Oracle view is the encapsulation of a complex query into a single pseudo-table that behaves like a single table. In this example, a view is created:

```
create or replace view
   cust_view
as
select
   customer_name,
   order_nbr,
   item_desc
from
   customer     c,
   order        o,
   item         i,
where
   c.cust_nbr = o.cust_nbr
and
   o_item_nbr = i.item_nbr;
```

The pseudo table in the following query hides the complexity of the underlying query and has no effect on the performance of the underlying SQL:

```
Select
   *
From
   cust_view
where
   cust_nbr = 123;
```

In this example, every time the *cust_view* is queried, Oracle will join the three tables at runtime.

Since views do not improve performance, why use them? Most Oracle shops that employ views do so for end-user queries. Any query that can benefit from hidden complexity or uniform join methods is a candidate from using views.

The Downside to Using Views

Views are very handy, but they often get badly abused. I have seen views that return 50 columns and have 40 predicates used to return just two or three columns that could easily have been retrieved from a simple SQL query. This is clearly a case of view abuse and can lead to badly performing views.

Stacked views can also mask performance problems. Again, they can result in innumerable columns being returned when all that is needed are a few of those columns. Also, predicate pushing tends to break down as more views are stacked on top of more views. If there is a plan to stack views, it is important to carefully review the rules for predicate pushing in the Oracle documentation. They are rather long and involved.

Some shops create complex views to represent large subsets of their schema and allow developers and end users to access these views. This approach often leads to poor performance. Here are some situations to avoid when working with complex views:

- **Querying subsets:** Developers will often query a subset of the complex view, not realizing that all tables in the view will be joined.

- **Adding complex *where* clauses:** Queries against views with complex *where* clauses will often override any tuning hints that are placed within the view, causing suboptimal execution plans.

- **Hinting the view:** A view cannot be treated as a finite table, and adding SQL hints to view queries will often result in suboptimal execution plans. Remember, any time the optimizer gets confused, it will perform an unnecessary full-table scan. While hints can be used for specific SQL optimization, the use of views is strongly discouraged with hints because they can be invoked in many contexts.

To summarize, Oracle views are an encapsulation of a complex query and must be used with care. Here are the key facts to remember:

- Views are not intended to improve SQL performance. When it is necessary to encapsulate SQL, it should be placed inside a stored procedure rather than using a view.

- Views hide the complexity of the underlying query, making it easier for inexperienced programmers and end users to formulate queries.

- Views can be used to tune queries with hints, provided that the view is always used in the proper context.

Combining Hints and Views

Although DBAs must be careful when using hints against a view, the following are two ways they can be used without creating performance problems:

1. Hints can be embedded inside the view definition. This is useful for cases where a view will be called without a *where* clause, but it can be quite damaging to performance when the view result set is altered by calling the view with a complex *where* clause.

2. Hints can be added in the calling query. The danger with using hints in views is that the context of the query may change. When this happens, any existing hints within the view

definition may be ignored, which can confuse the SQL optimizer and result in an unnecessary full-table scan.

When views are invoked with certain *where* clauses, the context of the view may change, as will the functionality of any SQL hints that may be embedded inside the view.

This simple example shows how such a context change can occur:

```
select
   cust_name,
   cust_address
from
   cust_view
where
   cust_nbr = 123;
```

This illustrates how a view can be invoked to perform a three-way table join on execution, but the *where* clause in the SQL indicates that the user is interested only in data within a single table. Any SQL hints that might be embedded inside the view may be ignored.

Parsing SQL Syntax

Oracle SQL is parsed before execution, and a hard parse includes these steps:

- **Loading into shared pool:** The SQL source code is loaded into RAM for parsing (the hard parse step).

- **Syntax parse:** Oracle parses the syntax to check for misspelled SQL keywords.

- **Semantic parse:** Oracle verifies all table and column names from the dictionary and checks to see if the DBA is authorized to see the data.

- **Optimization:** Oracle then creates an execution plan based on the schema statistics or possibly dynamic sampling in 10g.

Create Executable

Next, Oracle builds an executable file with native file calls to service the SQL query.

Oracle provides the *shared_pool_size* parameter to cache SQL so that it is not necessary to parse over and over again. However, SQL can age-out if the *shared_pool_size* is too small or if it is cluttered with non-reusable SQL, i.e. SQL that has literals like *where name="fred* in the source.

What is the difference between a hard parse and a soft parse in Oracle? A soft parse does not require a shared pool reload or the associated RAM memory allocation. A general high parse call (> 10/sec.) indicates that the system has many incoming unique SQL statements, or that the SQL is not reentrant, i.e. not using bind variables.

A hard parse is when SQL must be reloaded into the shared pool. A hard parse is worse than a soft parse because of the overhead involved in shared pool RAM allocation and memory management. Once loaded, the SQL must then be completely rechecked for syntax and semantics and an executable generated.

Excessive hard parsing can occur when the *shared_pool_size* is too small and reentrant SQL is paged out, or when there are non-reusable SQL statements without host variables. See the *cursor_sharing* parameter for an easy way to make SQL reentrant. It is best to always use host variables in the SQL so that they can be reentrant.

SQL *where* Clause Order Can be Important to Performance

Many people believe that the Oracle cost-based SQL optimizer does not consider the order that the Boolean predicates appear in the *where* clause. However, there is some evidence that this is not completely true, as shown by the *ordered_predicates* SQL hint.

The *ordered_predicates* hint is specified in the *where* clause of a query and is used to specify the order in which Boolean predicates should be evaluated. In the absence of *ordered_predicates*, Oracle uses the following steps to evaluate the order of SQL predicates:

- Subqueries are evaluated before the outer Boolean conditions in the *where* clause.

- All Boolean conditions without built-in functions or subqueries are evaluated in reverse from the order they are found in the *where* clause, with the last predicate being evaluated first.

- Boolean predicates with built-in functions of each predicate are evaluated in increasing order of their estimated evaluation costs.

Some of the things that influence the order of application of the predicates are:

- their position in the *where* clause

- the kind of operators involved

- automatic datatype conversion

- the presence of bind variables

- joins

- the optimizer mode (Rule or Cost)

- the cost model (IO or CPU)

- the Query Rewrite feature

- distributed operations

- view merging

- query un-nesting

- other documented and undocumented Parameters

- hints

It is also important to note the bug in Oracle 9i where adjusting *optimizer_index_cost_adj* will cause CPU costs to be considered in execution plans. More importantly, setting the SQL optimizer cost model, whether CPU or I/O, will also affect the way that the optimizer evaluates predicate.

Interrogating SQL Execution Plans

The script below examines the execution plans of *plan9i.sql* and reports on the frequency of every type of table and index access including full-table scans, index range scans, index unique scans and index full scans. The script goes to the appropriate view, *v$sql_plan* in *plan9i.sql* and *dba_hist_sql_plan* in *plan10g.sql*, and parses the output, counting the frequency of execution for each type of access.

The following *plan9i.sql* script will show the SQL that is currently inside the library cache.

🖫 **plan9i.sql**

```
set echo off;
set feedback on

set pages 999;

column nbr_FTS   format 999,999
column num_rows  format 999,999,999
column blocks    format 999,999
column owner     format a14;
column name      format a24;
column ch        format a1;

column object_owner heading "Owner"          format a12;
column ct           heading "# of SQL selects" format 999,999;

select
   object_owner,
   count(*)    ct
from
   v$sql_plan
where
   object_owner is not null
group by
   object_owner
order by
   ct desc
;
--spool access.lst;

set heading off;
set feedback off;

set heading on;
set feedback on;
ttitle 'full table scans and counts|  |The "K" indicates that the table is in the KEEP Pool
(Oracle8).'
select
   p.owner,
   p.name,
   t.num_rows,
--   ltrim(t.cache) ch,
   decode(t.buffer_pool,'KEEP','Y','DEFAULT','N') K,
   s.blocks blocks,
```

```
   sum(a.executions) nbr_FTS
from
   dba_tables   t,
   dba_segments s,
   v$sqlarea a,
   (select distinct
      address,
      object_owner owner,
      object_name name
   from
      v$sql_plan
   where
      operation = 'TABLE ACCESS'
      and
      options = 'FULL') p
where
   a.address = p.address
   and
   t.owner = s.owner
   and
   t.table_name = s.segment_name
   and
   t.table_name = p.name
   and
   t.owner = p.owner
   and
   t.owner not in ('SYS','SYSTEM')
having
   sum(a.executions) > 9
group by
   p.owner, p.name, t.num_rows, t.cache, t.buffer_pool, s.blocks
order by
   sum(a.executions) desc;

column nbr_RID  format 999,999,999
column num_rows format 999,999,999
column owner    format a15;
column name     format a25;

ttitle 'Table access by ROWID and counts'
select
   p.owner,
   p.name,
   t.num_rows,
   sum(s.executions) nbr_RID
from
   dba_tables t,
   v$sqlarea s,
   (select distinct
      address,
      object_owner owner,
      object_name name
   from
      v$sql_plan
   where
      operation = 'TABLE ACCESS'
      and
      options = 'BY ROWID') p
where
   s.address = p.address
   and
   t.table_name = p.name
   and
   t.owner = p.owner
having
```

```
   sum(s.executions) > 9
group by
   p.owner, p.name, t.num_rows
order by
   sum(s.executions) desc;

--*************************************************
```

Next is the AWR version of the SQL execution plan script. Unlike the *plan9i.sql* script that only extracts current SQL from the library cache, the *plan10g.sql* script accesses the AWR *dba_hist_sqlplan* table and yields a time-series view of the ways that Oracle is accessing tables and indexes.

🖫 plan10g.sql

```
spool plan.lst

set echo off
set feedback on

set pages 999;
column nbr_FTS    format 99,999
column num_rows format 999,999
column blocks     format 9,999
column owner      format a10;
column name       format a30;
column ch         format a1;
column time       heading "Snapshot Time"         format a15

column object_owner heading "Owner"               format a12;
column ct           heading "# of SQL selects" format 999,999;

break on time

select
   object_owner,
   count(*)    ct
from
   dba_hist_sql_plan
where
   object_owner is not null
group by
   object_owner
order by
   ct desc
;


--spool access.lst;

set heading on;
set feedback on;

ttitle 'full table scans and counts|  |The "K" indicates that the table is in the KEEP Pool
(Oracle8).'
select
   to_char(sn.end_interval_time,'mm/dd/rr hh24') time,
   p.owner,
   p.name,
   t.num_rows,
--   ltrim(t.cache) ch,
   decode(t.buffer_pool,'KEEP','Y','DEFAULT','N') K,
   s.blocks blocks,
```

Inside Oracle Views

```
     sum(a.executions_delta) nbr_FTS
from
   dba_tables  t,
   dba_segments s,
   dba_hist_sqlstat a,
   dba_hist_snapshot sn,
   (select distinct
     pl.sql_id,
     object_owner owner,
     object_name name
   from
     dba_hist_sql_plan pl
   where
     operation = 'TABLE ACCESS'
     and
     options = 'FULL') p
where
   a.snap_id = sn.snap_id
   and
   a.sql_id = p.sql_id
   and
   t.owner = s.owner
   and
   t.table_name = s.segment_name
   and
   t.table_name = p.name
   and
   t.owner = p.owner
   and
   t.owner not in ('SYS','SYSTEM')
having
   sum(a.executions_delta) > 1
group by
   to_char(sn.end_interval_time,'mm/dd/rr hh24'),p.owner, p.name, t.num_rows, t.cache,
t.buffer_pool, s.blocks
order by
   1 asc;


column nbr_RID  format 999,999,999
column num_rows format 999,999,999
column owner     format a15;
column name      format a25;

ttitle 'Table access by ROWID and counts'
select
   to_char(sn.end_interval_time,'mm/dd/rr hh24') time,
   p.owner,
   p.name,
   t.num_rows,
   sum(a.executions_delta) nbr_RID
from
   dba_tables t,
   dba_hist_sqlstat  a,
   dba_hist_snapshot sn,
   (select distinct
     pl.sql_id,
     object_owner owner,
     object_name name
   from
     dba_hist_sql_plan pl
   where
     operation = 'TABLE ACCESS'
     and
     options = 'BY USER ROWID') p
```

```
where
   a.snap_id = sn.snap_id
   and
   a.sql_id = p.sql_id
   and
   t.table_name = p.name
   and
   t.owner = p.owner
having
   sum(a.executions_delta) > 9
group by
   to_char(sn.end_interval_time,'mm/dd/rr hh24'),p.owner, p.name, t.num_rows
order by
   1 asc;

--***************************************************
--   Index Report Section
--***************************************************

column nbr_scans   format 999,999,999
column num_rows    format 999,999,999
column tbl_blocks format 999,999,999
column owner       format a9;
column table_name format a20;
column index_name format a20;

ttitle 'Index full scans and counts'
select
   to_char(sn.end_interval_time,'mm/dd/rr hh24') time,
   p.owner,
   d.table_name,
   p.name index_name,
   seg.blocks tbl_blocks,
   sum(s.executions_delta) nbr_scans
from
   dba_segments seg,
   dba_indexes d,
   dba_hist_sqlstat    s,
   dba_hist_snapshot sn,
   (select distinct
     p1.sql_id,
     object_owner owner,
     object_name name
   from
     dba_hist_sql_plan p1
   where
     operation = 'INDEX'
     and
     options = 'FULL SCAN') p
where
   d.index_name = p.name
   and
   s.snap_id = sn.snap_id
   and
   s.sql_id = p.sql_id
   and
   d.table_name = seg.segment_name
   and
   seg.owner = p.owner
having
   sum(s.executions_delta) > 9
group by
   to_char(sn.end_interval_time,'mm/dd/rr hh24'),p.owner, d.table_name, p.name, seg.blocks
order by
   1 asc;
```

```
ttitle 'Index range scans and counts'
select
   to_char(sn.end_interval_time,'mm/dd/rr hh24') time,
   p.owner,
   d.table_name,
   p.name index_name,
   seg.blocks tbl_blocks,
   sum(s.executions_delta) nbr_scans
from
   dba_segments seg,
   dba_hist_sqlstat s,
   dba_hist_snapshot sn,
   dba_indexes d,
   (select distinct
      pl.sql_id,
      object_owner owner,
      object_name name
   from
      dba_hist_sql_plan pl
   where
      operation = 'INDEX'
      and
      options = 'RANGE SCAN') p
where
   d.index_name = p.name
   and
   s.snap_id = sn.snap_id
   and
   s.sql_id = p.sql_id
   and
   d.table_name = seg.segment_name
   and
   seg.owner = p.owner
having
   sum(s.executions_delta) > 9
group by
   to_char(sn.end_interval_time,'mm/dd/rr hh24'),p.owner, d.table_name, p.name, seg.blocks
order by
   1 asc;

ttitle 'Index unique scans and counts'
select
   to_char(sn.end_interval_time,'mm/dd/rr hh24') time,
   p.owner,
   d.table_name,
   p.name index_name,
   sum(s.executions_delta) nbr_scans
from
   dba_hist_sqlstat s,
   dba_hist_snapshot sn,
   dba_indexes d,
   (select distinct
      pl.sql_id,
      object_owner owner,
      object_name name
   from
      dba_hist_sql_plan pl
   where
      operation = 'INDEX'
      and
      options = 'UNIQUE SCAN') p
where
   d.index_name = p.name
```

```
   and
   s.snap_id = sn.snap_id
   and
   s.sql_id = p.sql_id
having
   sum(s.executions_delta) > 9
group by
   to_char(sn.end_interval_time,'mm/dd/rr hh24'),p.owner, d.table_name, p.name
order by
   1 asc;

spool off
```

The output is shown below, and it is the same in 9i and 10g. A good way to start the review of the results is by looking at the counts of full-table scans for each AWR snapshot period. This report gives all the information needed to select candidate tables for the KEEP pool. The database will benefit from placing small tables, which constitutes less than two percent of *db_cache_size* that are subject to frequent full-table scans in the KEEP pool. The report from an Oracle Applications database below shows full-table scans on both large and small tables.

The goal is to use the RECYCLE pool for segregating large tables involved in frequent full-table scans. To locate these large-table full-table scans, consult the *plan9i.sql* full-table scan report for a 9i and beyond database:

```
                         full table scans and counts
Snapshot Time    OWNER         NAME                         NUM_ROWS C K    BLOCKS   NBR_FTS
-------------    ----------    -----------------------      -------- - -    --------  ----
-    12/08/04 14    APPLSYS     FND_CONC_RELEASE_DISJS             39 N K         2
98,864
                 APPLSYS       FND_CONC_RELEASE_PERIODS           39 N K         2    98,864
                 APPLSYS       FND_CONC_RELEASE_STATES             1 N K         2    98,864
                 SYS           DUAL                                  N K         2    63,466
                 APPLSYS       FND_CONC_PP_ACTIONS             7,021 N     1,262    52,036
                 APPLSYS       FND_CONC_REL_CONJ_MEMBER            0 N K        22    50,174

12/08/04 15      APPLSYS       FND_CONC_RELEASE_DISJS             39 N K         2    33,811
                 APPLSYS       FND_CONC_RELEASE_PERIODS           39 N K         2     2,864
                 APPLSYS       FND_CONC_RELEASE_STATES             1 N K         2    32,864
                 SYS           DUAL                                  N K         2    63,466
                 APPLSYS       FND_CONC_PP_ACTIONS             7,021 N     1,262    12,033
                 APPLSYS       FND_CONC_REL_CONJ_MEMBER            0 N K        22    50,174
```

One table in the listing is a clear candidate for inclusion in the *recycle* pool. The *fnd_conc_pp_actions* table contains 1,262 blocks and has experienced many full-table scans. Examining this report, it should be easy to quickly identify three files that should be moved to the KEEP pool by selecting the tables with less than 50 blocks that have no "K" designation.

Oracle developed the KEEP pool to fully cache blocks from frequently accessed tables and indexes in a separate buffer. When determining the size of the KEEP pool, the number of bytes comprising all tables that will reside in the KEEP area must be summed. This will ensure that the *keep cache* buffer is large enough to fully cache all the tables that have been assigned to it.

Oracle requires that a table only reside in a tablespace of the same blocksize as the buffer assigned to the table. For example, if the default buffer is set at 32K, the following ALTER command would not work if the customer table resides in a 16K tablespace. The default *keep* and *recycle* designations only apply to the default blocksize. *Keep* and *recycle* buffers cannot be assigned different sizes than that of the default *db_block_size*.

```
alter table customer storage (buffer_pool KEEP);
```

The whole reason for the existence of the KEEP pool is to always have a data buffer hit ratio of 100 percent. The blocksize of the KEEP pool is not important because all blocks, once loaded, will remain in RAM memory. A KEEP pool might be defined as a 32K blocksize because a large *recycle* buffer was needed to improve the performance of full-table scans.

CAUTION!

Selecting tables for the KEEP pool requires inspecting the data cache over time. These reports include only SQL that happens to be in the library cache at the time the report is run.

Since the goal for the data buffer hit ratio of the KEEP pool is 100 percent, each time a table is added to KEEP, the number of blocks in that table must also be added to the KEEP pool parameter in the Oracle file.

These scripts show the counts for indexes that are accessed via ROWID, which is indicative of non-range scan access. The result of these scripts is shown below.

```
Table access by ROWID and counts
Wed Dec 22
```

Snapshot Time	OWNER	NAME	NUM_ROWS	NBR_RID
12/16/04 19	SYSMAN	MGMT_TARGET_ROLLUP_TIMES	110	10
12/17/04 06	SYSMAN	MGMT_TARGET_ROLLUP_TIMES	110	10
12/17/04 07	SYSMAN	MGMT_TARGET_ROLLUP_TIMES	110	10
12/17/04 08	SYSMAN	MGMT_TARGET_ROLLUP_TIMES	110	10
12/17/04 12	SYSMAN	MGMT_TARGET_ROLLUP_TIMES	110	10
12/17/04 13	SYSMAN	MGMT_TARGET_ROLLUP_TIMES	110	10
12/17/04 14	SYS	VIEW$	2,583	84
	SYSMAN	MGMT_TARGET_ROLLUP_TIMES	110	10
12/17/04 17	SYS	VIEW$	2,583	82
12/17/04 18	SYSMAN	MGMT_TARGET_ROLLUP_TIMES	110	10
12/17/04 20	SYSMAN	MGMT_TARGET_ROLLUP_TIMES	110	10
12/17/04 21	SYSMAN	MGMT_TARGET_ROLLUP_TIMES	110	10
12/17/04 22	SYSMAN	MGMT_TARGET_ROLLUP_TIMES	110	10
12/17/04 23	SYSMAN	MGMT_TARGET_ROLLUP_TIMES	110	10
12/18/04 00	SYSMAN	MGMT_TARGET_ROLLUP_TIMES	110	10
12/18/04 01	SYSMAN	MGMT_TARGET_ROLLUP_TIMES	110	20
12/18/04 02	SYSMAN	MGMT_TARGET_ROLLUP_TIMES	110	10
12/18/04 03	SYSMAN	MGMT_TARGET_ROLLUP_TIMES	110	10

Snapshot Time	OWNER	TABLE_NAME	INDEX_NAME	TBL_BLOCKS	NBR_SCANS

12/18/04 04	SYSMAN	MGMT_TARGET_ROLLUP_TIMES		110	10
12/18/04 05	SYSMAN	MGMT_TARGET_ROLLUP_TIMES		110	10
12/18/04 09	SYSMAN	MGMT_TARGET_ROLLUP_TIMES		110	20
12/18/04 11	SYSMAN	MGMT_TARGET_ROLLUP_TIMES		110	20

Counts of index full scans and index range scans can also be acquired, and this data is very useful for locating those indexes that might benefit from segregation onto a larger blocksize.

```
Index full scans and counts
```

Snapshot Time NBR_SCANS	OWNER	TABLE_NAME	INDEX_NAME	TBL_BLOCKS
12/08/04 14 59	SYSMAN	MGMT_FAILOVER_TABLE	PK_MGMT_FAILOVER	8
12/08/04 15 58	SYSMAN	MGMT_FAILOVER_TABLE	PK_MGMT_FAILOVER	8
12/08/04 16 16	SYS	WRH$_TEMPFILE	WRH$_TEMPFILE_PK	8
59	SYSMAN	MGMT_FAILOVER_TABLE	PK_MGMT_FAILOVER	8
12/08/04 17 483	SYS	WRH$_STAT_NAME	WRH$_STAT_NAME_P	8
58	SYSMAN	MGMT_FAILOVER_TABLE	PK_MGMT_FAILOVER	8
12/08/04 18 59	SYSMAN	MGMT_FAILOVER_TABLE	PK_MGMT_FAILOVER	8
12/08/04 19 58	SYSMAN	MGMT_FAILOVER_TABLE	PK_MGMT_FAILOVER	8
12/08/04 20 59	SYSMAN	MGMT_FAILOVER_TABLE	PK_MGMT_FAILOVER	8
12/08/04 21 58	SYSMAN	MGMT_FAILOVER_TABLE	PK_MGMT_FAILOVER	8
12/08/04 22 58	SYSMAN	MGMT_FAILOVER_TABLE	PK_MGMT_FAILOVER	8
12/08/04 23 59	SYSMAN	MGMT_FAILOVER_TABLE	PK_MGMT_FAILOVER	8
12/09/04 00 58	SYSMAN	MGMT_FAILOVER_TABLE	PK_MGMT_FAILOVER	8
12/09/04 01 59	SYSMAN	MGMT_FAILOVER_TABLE	PK_MGMT_FAILOVER	8
12/09/04 02 59	SYSMAN	MGMT_FAILOVER_TABLE	PK_MGMT_FAILOVER	8
12/09/04 03 59	SYSMAN	MGMT_FAILOVER_TABLE	PK_MGMT_FAILOVER	8
12/09/04 04 58	SYSMAN	MGMT_FAILOVER_TABLE	PK_MGMT_FAILOVER	8
12/09/04 05 59	SYSMAN	MGMT_FAILOVER_TABLE	PK_MGMT_FAILOVER	8
12/09/04 06 58	SYSMAN	MGMT_FAILOVER_TABLE	PK_MGMT_FAILOVER	8
12/09/04 07 59	SYSMAN	MGMT_FAILOVER_TABLE	PK_MGMT_FAILOVER	8
12/09/04 08 58	SYSMAN	MGMT_FAILOVER_TABLE	PK_MGMT_FAILOVER	8

```
12/09/04 09     SYSMAN    MGMT_FAILOVER_TABLE     PK_MGMT_FAILOVER          8
59

Index range scans and counts

Snapshot Time   OWNER    TABLE_NAME             INDEX_NAME               TBL_BLOCKS
NBR_SCANS
--------------- --------- --------------------- ----------------------- -------
---
12/08/04 14     SYS      SYSAUTH$               I_SYSAUTH1                        8
345
                SYSMAN   MGMT_JOB_EXECUTION     MGMT_JOB_EXEC_IDX01               8
1373
                SYSMAN   MGMT_JOB_EXEC_SUMMARY  MGMT_JOB_EXEC_SUMM_IDX04          8
59
                SYSMAN   MGMT_METRICS           MGMT_METRICS_IDX_01              80
59
                SYSMAN   MGMT_PARAMETERS        MGMT_PARAMETERS_IDX_01            8
179
                SYSMAN   MGMT_TARGETS           MGMT_TARGETS_IDX_02               8
61
12/08/04 15     SYS      SYSAUTH$               I_SYSAUTH1                        8
273
                SYSMAN   MGMT_JOB_EXECUTION     MGMT_JOB_EXEC_IDX01               8
1423
                SYSMAN   MGMT_JOB_EXEC_SUMMARY  MGMT_JOB_EXEC_SUMM_IDX04          8
58
```

Now that the use of the *v$sql_plan* view to see how tables and indexes are used by the SQL has been introduced, it is time to investigate techniques for finding the most resource intensive SQL for tuning.

Oracle SQL Optimizer Statistics

Some DBAs believe in the practice of running statistics by a schedule, such as once a week. Some believe in just calculating statistics when the data changes. Still others believe that statistics are only needed to fix a poor access path, and once things are good, they should not be touched. It is difficult to say who is correct.

Oracle automatically reanalyzes schema statistics based on the number of changes to rows in the table, but it may be sub-optimal, and many senior Oracle DBAs use more sophisticated methods for determining when to reanalyze CBO statistics. Although the Oracle CBO is one of the world's most sophisticated software achievements, it is still the job of the Oracle professional to provide valid statistics for the schema and understand how Oracle parameters affect the overall performance of the SQL optimizer.

Keep in mind, suboptimal SQL execution plans are a major reason for poorly performing Oracle databases, and because the CBO determines the execution plans, it is a critical component in Oracle optimization.

The *dbms_stats* utility is a great way to improve SQL execution speed. By using *dbms_stats* to collect top quality statistics, the CBO will usually make an intelligent decision about the fastest way to execute any

SQL query. The *dbms_stats* utility continues to improve, and the exciting new features of automatic sample size and automatic histogram generation greatly simplify the job of the Oracle professional.

The Oracle *dbms_stats* Package

One of the greatest problems with the Oracle CBO was the failure of the Oracle DBA to gather accurate schema statistics. Even with the *dbms_stats* package, the schema statistics were often stale. In addition, DBAs did not always create histograms for skewed data columns and data columns that are used to estimate the size of SQL intermediate result sets.

This resulted in a bum rap for Oracle's CBO, and beginner DBAs often falsely accused the CBO of failing to generate optimal execution plans. In reality, the cause of the suboptimal execution plan was the DBA's failure to collect complete schema statistics.

Oracle has automated the collection and refreshing of schema statistics in Oracle. This automates the DBA's task and ensures that Oracle will always gather good statistics and choose the best execution plan for any query. Using the enhanced *dbms_stats* package, Oracle will automatically estimate the sample size, detect skewed columns that would benefit from histograms, and refresh the schema statistics when they become stale. This automates a very important DBA task and ensures that Oracle always has the statistics that it needs to make good execution plan choices.

The following is an example of using the *dbms_stats* package:

```
begin
   dbms_stats.gather_schema_stats(
      ownname          => 'SCOTT',
      estimate_percent => dbms_stats.auto_sample_size,
      method_opt => 'for all columns size repeat',
      degree           => 7
   );
end;
/
```

However, there was always a nagging problem with the CBO. Even with good statistics, the CBO would sometimes determine a sub-optimal table join order, causing unnecessarily large intermediate result sets. For example, consider the complex *where* clause in the query below.

Even with the best schema statistics, it can be impossible to predict the optimal table join order, which is the table join order that has the smallest intermediate baggage. As one might expect, reducing the size of the intermediate row sets can greatly improve the speed of the query.

```
select
   stuff
from
   customer
natural join
   orders
natural join
   item
natural join
   product
```

```
where
   credit_rating * extended_credit > .07
and
   (qty_in_stock * velocity) /.075 < 30
or
   (sku_price / 47) * (qty_in_stock / velocity) > 47;
```

In this example, the SQL invokes a 4-way table join that only returns 18 rows, but the query carries 9,000 rows in intermediate result sets, which slows the overall SQL execution speed. This phenomenon is illustrated in Figure 16.4.

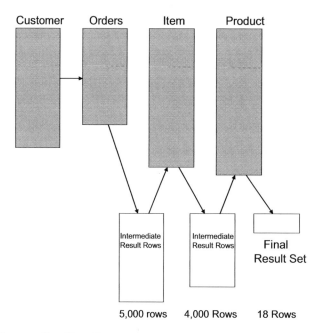

Figure16.4: *Suboptimal Intermediate Row Sets*

If there were a way to somehow predict the sizes of the intermediate results, the table join order can be re-sequenced to carry less intermediate baggage during the 4-way table join. The result for this particular example would yield only 3,000 intermediate rows between the table joins. This phenomenon is illustrated in Figure 16.5.

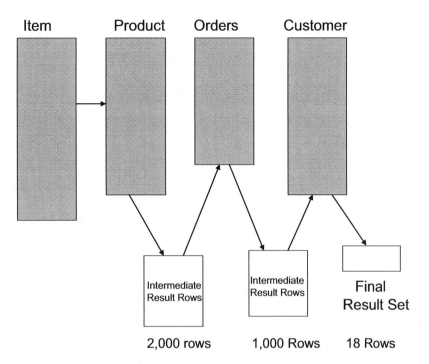

Item　　Product　　Orders　　Customer

Intermediate Result Rows　　Intermediate Result Rows　　Final Result Set

2,000 rows　　1,000 Rows　　18 Rows

Figure16.5: *Optimal Intermediate Row Sets*

For the following example, assume there is a three-way table join against tables that all contain over 10,000 rows each. This database has 50,000 student rows, 10,000 course rows and 5,000 professor rows. If the number of rows in the table determined the best table join order, I would expect that any 3-way table join would start by joining the professor and course tables, and then join the result set to the student table.

However, whenever there is a *where* clause, the total number of rows in each table does not matter if index access is being used. The following is a sample query:

```
select
   student_name
from
   professor
natural join
   course
natural join
   student
where
   professor = 'jones'
and
   course = 'anthropology 610';
```

```
Stan Nowakowski
Bob Crane
James Bakke
PattyO'Furniture
```

Despite the huge numbers of rows in each table, the final result set will only be four rows. If the CBO can guess the size of the final result, sampling techniques can be used to examine the *where* clause of the query and determine which two tables should be joined together first.

There are only two table join choices in the simplified example:

- Join *student* to *course* and *result* to *professor*

- Join *professor* to *course* and *result* to *student*

Which is better? The best solution will be the one where *result* is smallest. Because the query is filtered with a *where* clause, the number of rows in each table is incidental, and the real concern is the number of rows where *professor*='jones' and where *course*='Anthropology 610'.

If the specific output goal is known, the best table join order becomes obvious. Assume that Professor Jones is very popular and teaches 50 courses, and Anthropology 610 has a total of eight students. With this knowledge, it is clear that the size of the intermediate row baggage is very different. Figure 16.6 shows the following join of *professor* to *course* and *result* to *student*.

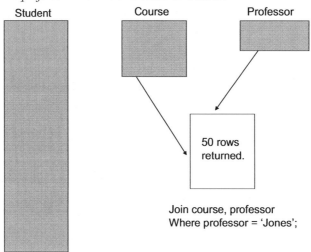

Figure16.6: *A Suboptimal Intermediate Row Size*

If the CBO were to join the *student* table to the *course* table first, the intermediate result set would only be eight rows, far less baggage to carry over to the final join as shown in Figure 16.7, which demonstrates the following join of *student* to *course* and *result* to *professor*.

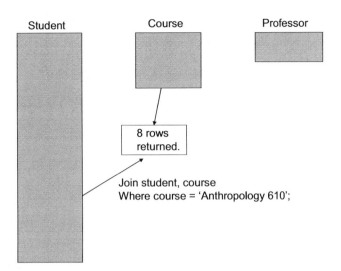

Figure16.7: *An Optimal Intermediate Row Size*

Now that there are only eight rows returned from the first query, it is easy to join the tiny eight-row result set into the *professor* table to get the final answer.

Managing Schema Statistics with *dbms_stats*

When a SQL statement is executed, the database must convert the query into an execution plan and choose the best way to retrieve the data. For Oracle, each SQL query has many choices for execution plans, including which index to use to retrieve table row, what order in which to join multiple tables together, and which internal join methods to use. Oracle has *nested loop* joins, *hash* joins, *star* joins, and sort merge join methods to decide between. These execution plans are computed by the Oracle CBO.

The choice of executions plans made by the Oracle SQL optimizer is only as good as the Oracle statistics. To always choose the best execution plan for a SQL query, Oracle relies on information about the tables and indexes in the query.

Starting with the introduction of the *dbms_stats* package, Oracle has provided a simple way for the Oracle professional to collect statistics for the CBO. The old-fashioned analyze table and *dbms_utility* methods for generating CBO statistics are obsolete. These methods are also somewhat dangerous to SQL performance because they do not always capture high-quality information about tables and indexes. The CBO uses object statistics to choose the best execution plan for all SQL statements.

The *dbms_stats* utility does a far better job in estimating statistics, especially for large partitioned tables, and the better stats result in faster SQL execution plans. Andrew Holdsworth of Oracle Corporation notes that *dbms_stats* is essential to good SQL performance, and it should always be used before adjusting any of the Oracle optimizer initialization parameters:

> *"The payback from good statistics management and execution plans will exceed any benefit of init.ora tuning by orders of magnitude."*

Most experts agree that the majority of common SQL problems can be avoided if statistics are carefully defined and managed. In order for the CBO to make an intelligent decision about the best execution plan for SQL, the CBO must have information about the table and indexes that participate in the query. This information includes:

- the size of the tables

- the indexes on the tables

- the distribution of column values

- the cardinality of intermediate result sets

Given this information, the CBO can make an informed decision and almost always generates the best execution plan. The following section will cover how to gather top quality statistics for the CBO, as well as how to create an appropriate CBO environment for the database.

Getting Top Quality Statistics with *dbms_stats*

The choice of execution plans is only as good as the optimizer statistics available to the query, and *dbms_stats* package is the best ways to get statistics, superseding the old-fashioned *analyze table* and *dbms_utility* methods. The *dbms_stats* utility does a far better job in estimating statistics, especially for large partitioned tables, and the better statistics result in faster SQL execution plans. The following is a sample execution of *dbms_stats* with the OPTIONS clause:

```
exec dbms_stats.gather_schema_stats( -
ownname          => 'SCOTT', -
options          => 'gather auto', -
estimate_percent => dbms_stats.auto_sample_size, -
method_opt       => 'for all columns size repeat', -
cascade          => true, -
degree           => 15 -
)
```

Here is a representative example of invoking *dbms_stats* in 10g:

```
dbms_stats.gather_schema_stats(
   ownname=>'<schema>',
   estimate_percent=>dbms_stats.auto_sample_size
   cascade=>TRUE,
   method_opt=>'FOR ALL COLUMNS SIZE AUTO');
```

There are several values for the *options* parameter:

- *gather:* This option re-analyzes the whole schema.

- *gather empty:* This option only analyzes objects that have no statistics.

- *gather stale:* This option is used with the monitoring feature and only reanalyzes tables with more than 10 percent modifications (inserts, updates, deletes).

- **_gather auto_.** This option will reanalyze objects that currently have no statistics and objects with stale statistics (objects with more than 10% row changes). Using the _gather auto_ option is like combining _gather stale_ and _gather empty_ options.

Both _gather stale_ and _gather auto dbms_stats_ options require monitoring. In Oracle 9i, table monitoring can be implemented with the _alter table xxx monitoring_ command, and in Oracle 10g and beyond, table monitoring is automatic. Oracle tracks changed tables with the _dba_tab_modifications_ view. Oracle compares the number of modifications with the _num_rows_ column in the _dba_tables_, based on the _sys.tab$_ fixed view, and the modifications are kept in _sys.mon_mos$_ table.

The _dba_tab_modifications_ contains the cumulative number of inserts, updates, and deletes that are tracked since the last analysis of statistics:

```
SQL>desc dba_tab_modifications;

Name                            Type
--------------------------------   ------------------
TABLE_OWNER                     VARCHAR2(30)
TABLE_NAME                              VARCHAR2(30)
PARTITION_NAME                  VARCHAR2(30)
SUBPARTITION_NAME               VARCHAR2(30)
INSERTS                         NUMBER
UPDATES                         NUMBER
DELETES                         NUMBER
TIMESTAMP                       DATE
TRUNCATED                       VARCHAR2(3)
```

The most interesting of the options is the _gather stale_ option. Since all statistics will become stale quickly in a robust OLTP database, it is important to remember that the rule for _gather stale_ is > 10% row change based on _num_rows_ at statistics collection time.

As a result, almost every table except read-only tables will be reanalyzed with the _gather stale_ option, making the _gather stale_ option best for systems that are largely read-only. For example, if only five percent of the database tables get significant updates, then only five percent of the tables will be reanalyzed with the _gather stale_ option.

To aid in intelligent histogram generation, Oracle uses the _method_opt_ parameter of _dbms_stats_. There are also important options within the _method_opt_ clause, namely _skewonly_, _repeat_ and _auto_:

- =>'for all columns size skewonly'
- =>'for all columns size repeat'
- =>'for all columns size auto'

The _skewonly_ option is very time intensive because it examines the distribution of values for every column within every index.

If _dbms_stats_ finds an index whose columns are unevenly distributed, it will create a histogram for that index to aid the cost-based SQL optimizer in making a decision about index versus full-table scan access.

For example, if an index has one column that is in 50 percent of the rows, a full-table scan is faster than an index scan to retrieve these rows.

```
-- ***********************************************************
-- SKEWONLY option—Detailed analysis
--
-- Use this method for a first-time analysis for skewed indexes
-- This runs a long time because all indexes are examined
-- ***********************************************************

begin
  dbms_stats.gather_schema_stats(
     ownname          => 'SCOTT',
     estimate_percent => dbms_stats.auto_sample_size,
     method_opt       => 'for all columns size skewonly',
      degree          => 7
  );
end;
```

If the statistics need to be reanalyzed, the reanalyze task will be less resource intensive with the *repeat* option. Using the *repeat* option, Oracle will only reanalyze indexes with existing histograms and will not search for other histogram opportunities. These statistics should be reanalyzed on a regular basis.

```
-- ***********************************************************
-- REPEAT OPTION - Only reanalyze histograms for indexes
-- that have histograms
--
-- Following the initial analysis, the weekly analysis
-- job will use the "repeat" option. The repeat option
-- tells dbms_stats that no indexes have changed, and
-- it will only reanalyze histograms for
-- indexes that have histograms.
-- ***********************************************************
begin
  dbms_stats.gather_schema_stats(
     ownname          => 'SCOTT',
     estimate_percent => dbms_stats.auto_sample_size,
     method_opt       => 'for all columns size repeat',
     degree           => 7
  );
end;
```

The dbms_stats procedure can be made to analyze schema statistics very quickly on SMP servers with multiple CPUs. Oracle allows for parallelism when collecting CBO statistics, which can greatly speed up the time required to collect statistics. A parallel statistics collection requires an SMP server with multiple CPUs.

The following section will introduce the importance of estimating the optimal sample size when gathering schema statistics.

Automating Statistics Sample Size with *dbms_stats*

The higher the quality of the schema statistics, the higher the probability that CBO will choose the optimal execution plan. Unfortunately, doing a complete analysis of every row of every table in a schema can often take days, and most shops must sample their database to get CBO statistics.

The goal of estimating the sample size is to take a large enough sample of the database to provide top quality data for the CBO while not adversely impacting server resources. Now that how the *dbms_stats* option works has been introduced, it will be useful see how to specify an adequate sample size for *dbms_stats*.

In earlier releases, the DBA had to guess what percentage of the database provided the best sample size. This led many to occasionally under analyze the schema. Starting with the Oracle 9i database, the *estimate_percent* argument was added to *dbms_stats* to allow Oracle to automatically estimate the best percentage of a segment to sample when gathering statistics. A sample invocation is below:

```
estimate_percent => dbms_stats.auto_sample_size
```

After collecting statistics with an automatic sample size, the accuracy of the automatic statistics sampling can be verified by looking at the *sample_size* column on any of these data dictionary views:

- *dba_object_tables*
- *dba_tab_col_statistics*
- *dba_tab_partitions*
- *dba_tab_subpartitions*
- *dba_part_col_statistics*
- *dba_subpart_col_statistics*
- *dba_tables*
- *dba_tab_cols*
- *dba_tab_columns*
- *dba_all_tables*
- *dba_indexes*
- *dba_ind_partitions*
- *dba_ind_subpartitions*

In practice, the *auto_sample_size* option of *dbms_stats* generally chooses a *sample_size* from five to 20 percent when using automatic sampling, depending on the size of the tables and the distribution of column values.

A sample size that is too small can impact the CBO, so it is important to always make sure to take a statistically significant sample size for every object in the schema. The next section will introduce some methods used to ensure that the SQL optimizer always has great schema statistics.

Column Skew and histograms

The distribution of values within an index will often affect the CBO's decision whether to perform a full-table scan or to use an index to satisfy a query. This can happen whenever the column referenced within a SQL query *where* clause has a non-uniform distribution of values, making a full-table scan faster than index access.

Since they affect performance, histograms should only be used when they are required for a faster CBO execution plan. Histograms incur additional overhead during the parsing phase of an SQL query. It can be used effectively only when:

- **A column's values cause the CBO to make an incorrect guess:** If the CBO makes a wrong assumption about the size of an intermediate result set, it may choose a sub-optimal execution plan. A histogram added to the column often provides the additional information required for the CBO to choose the best plan.

- **Significant skewing exists in the distribution of a column's data values:** The skew must be important enough to make the CBO choose another execution plan

- **A table column is referenced in one or more queries:** Never create histograms if queries do not reference the column. Novice DBAs may mistakenly create histograms on a skewed column, even if it is not referenced in a query.

The ability to seek columns that should have histograms, and then automatically create the histograms was introduced as a feature of the Oracle 9i *dbms_stats* package.

Before Oracle 9i, the DBA had to manually detect those data columns that needed histograms and manually create them using these guidelines:

- Create a histogram whenever a column is referenced by many SQL *where* clauses and when the data is heavily skewed, such that the optimal execution plan would change depending on the value in the *where* clause

- Create histograms when the optimizer cannot accurately predict the size of intermediate result sets in n-way table joins

Figure 16.8 below shows an example of skewed and non-skewed data columns.

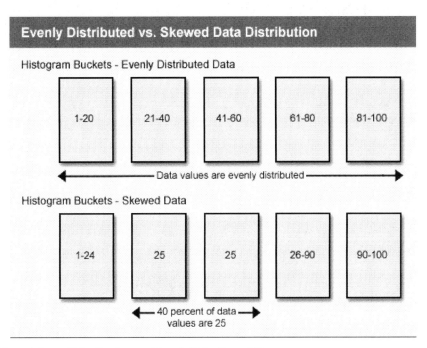

Figure 16.8: *Skewed Data Distribution vs. Evenly Distributed Data*

By using the *repeat* option, histograms are collected only on the columns that already have histograms. Like any other CBO statistic, histograms are static and need to be refreshed when column value distributions change. When refreshing statistics, the *repeat* option would be used as in the example below:

```
execute dbms_stats.gather_schema_stats(
 ownname         => 'SCOTT',
 estimate_percent => dbms_stats.auto_sample_size,
 method_opt => 'for all columns size repeat',
 degree          => dbms_stats.default_degree);
```

Since it examines the data distribution of values for every column within every index, the *skewonly* option introduces a very time-consuming build process. The *dbms_stats* package creates histograms to help the CBO make a table access decision, i.e. index versus a full-table scan when it finds an index whose column values are distributed unevenly. From the earlier *vehicle_type* example, if an index has one column value, e.g., CAR that exists in 65 percent of the rows, a full-table scan will be faster than an index scan to access those rows, as in this example:

```
execute dbms_stats.gather_schema_stats(
 ownname         => 'SCOTT',
 estimate_percent => dbms_stats.auto_sample_size,
 method_opt     => 'for all columns size skewonly',
 degree          => dbms_stats.default_degree);
```

Histograms are also effective with queries that have bind variables and queries with *cursor_sharing* enabled. In these cases, the CBO decides if the column value could affect the execution plan, and if it does, it substitutes a literal for the bind variable and proceeds to perform a hard parse.

Watch the Histograms!

Histograms should not be used arbitrarily. They should be used only when they allow the CBO to significantly improve query speed.

The following section will show the exciting SQL optimization feature, dynamic sampling, which was first introduced in Oracle 10g.

Automating Histogram Sampling with *dbms_stats*

One exciting feature of *dbms_stats* is the ability to automatically look for columns that should have histograms and create the histograms. Multi-bucket histograms add a huge parsing overhead to SQL statements, and histograms should only be used when the SQL will choose a different execution plan based upon the column value.

As mentioned earlier in this chapter, *skewonly*, *repeat* and *auto* are the important options of *dbms_stats*. In practice, there is a specific order for using these different options. Remember, analyzing for histograms is time-consuming, and histograms are used under two conditions:

- **Table join order:** The CBO must know the size of the intermediate result sets (cardinality) to properly determine the correct join order the multi-table joins.

- **Table access method:** The CBO needs to know about columns in SQL *where* clauses, where the column value is skewed such that a full-table scan might be faster than an index range scan. Oracle uses this skew information in conjunction with the *clustering_factor* columns of the *dba_indexes* view.

Hence, this is the proper order for using the *dbms_stats* package to locate proper columns for histograms:

- *skewonly* **option:** DBAs should use *skewonly* to do histograms for skewed columns. These are cases where the value will make a difference between a full-table scan and an index scan.

- **Monitor:** The next step is for the DBA to turn on monitoring. To do this, the DBA should issue the *alter table xx monitoring* and *alter index yyy monitoring* command for all segments in the schema.

- *auto* **option:** Once monitoring is in place, it will be necessary to reanalyze with the *auto* option to create histograms for join columns within tables. This is critical for the CBO to determine the proper join order for finding the driving table in multi-table joins.

- *repeat* **option:** Finally, use the *repeat* option to reanalyze only the existing histograms.

Periodically, the DBA will want to rerun the *skewonly* and *auto* options to identify any new columns that require histograms. Once located, the *repeat* option will ensure that they are refreshed with current values.

Starting with Oracle 10g, there are some new arguments available for *dbms_stats*.

granularity

This parameter is used in subprograms such as *gather_table_stats* and *gather_schema_stats*. This parameter indicates the granularity of the statistics, particularly for the partitioned tables. The DBA can gather the global statistics on a partitioned table, or they can gather global and partition-level statistics. It has two options. They are 1) *auto* and 2) *global and partition*.

When the *auto* option is specified, the procedure determines the granularity based on the partitioning type. Oracle collects global, partition-level, and sub-partition level statistics if sub-partition method is *list*. For other partitioned tables, only the global and partition level statistics are generated.

When the *global and partition* option is specified, Oracle gathers the global and partition level statistics. No sub-partition level statistics are gathered even if it is a composite partitioned object.

degree

With this parameter, it is possible to specify the degree of parallelism. In general, the *degree* parameter allows the DBA to parallelize the statistics gathering process. The degree parameter can take the value of *auto_degree*.

When *auto_degree* is specified, Oracle will determine the degree of parallelism automatically. It will be either 1 (serial execution) or *default_degree*, which is the system default value based on number of CPUs and initialization parameters, according to the size of the object. Take care if Hyper Threading is used, as the DBA will actually have less computational power than Oracle assumes.

DML Table Monitoring Changes

With Oracle Database 9i and beyond, the *statistcis_level* initialization parameter functions as a global option for the table monitoring mechanism. This mechanism overrides the table *level monitoring* clause. In other words, the *[no]monitoring* clauses are now obsolete.

If the *statistics_level* parameter is set to *basic*, the monitoring feature is disabled. When it is set to *typical*, which is the default setting or ALL, then the global table monitoring is enabled.

These changes are aimed at simplifying operations and also making them consistent with other related statistics. The modification monitoring mechanism is now enabled by default, and users of the *gather auto* or *stale* feature of *dbms_stats* no longer have to enable monitoring explicitly for every table under the default settings.

Watch out for "no operation" clauses and procedures!

It is still possible to use the monitoring clauses as well as *alter_schema_tab_monitoring* and *alter_database_tab_monitoring*, but these clauses and procedures are now considered as no operation. They execute without error but have no effect.

dbms_stats.gather_fixed_objects_stats Tips

Starting in version 10g, Oracle introduced a new procedure called *dbms_stats.gather_fixed_objects_stats*. It is used for analyzing the dictionary fixed structures, like the *x$* tables. The Oracle docs note that fixed objects should be analyzed only once unless the workload footprint changes. When this happens, the DBA must be connected to a *sys* (or a user with *sysdba*) to invoke *dbms_stats.gather_fixed_object_stats*.

Just like the workload statistics, Oracle recommends that the *x$* tables be analyzed only once, and during a typical database workload.

```
exec dbms_stats.gather_schema_stats('SYS',gather_fixed=>TRUE)

exec dbms_stats.gather_fixed_objects_stats('ALL');
```

Oracle also released the helpful new procedures:

- *dbms_stats.export_fixed_objects_stats*
- *dbms_stats.import_fixed_objects_stats*

These are used for migrating production workload statistics into test and development instances.

Oracle 11g New Features for *dbms_stats*

Oracle 11g has the challenge of making their wonderful cost-based optimizer (CBO) always generate the best execution plan for any SQL. This is a formidable challenge. Oracle understands that the quality of their metadata is critical to achieving this goal. Only by knowing the distribution of values with the tables can the CBO make the best decision regarding execution plans.

Prior to Oracle 10g, adjusting powerful optimizer parameters like *optimizer_index_cost_adj* was the only way to compensate for sample size issues with *dbms_stats*.

However, as of Oracle 10g, improvements in system statistics collection using *dbms_stats.gather_system_stats* to measure sequential versus scattered disk I/O speed, plus improved sampling within *dbms_stats* have made adjustments to the optimizer parameters a worst practice exercise in most cases. Ceteris Paribas, always adjust CBO statistics before adjusting optimizer parameters.

Improving CBO Statistics the Smart Way

Oracle performance guru Greg Rahn performed a representative test of the Oracle 11g enhancements to the *dbms_stats* package, correctly noting that skewed data distributions were problematic in 10g because the *dbms_stats* package did not manage skew and out of range values in an optimal fashion. Rahn also demonstrated several exciting improvements to *dbms_stats*:

- **Faster collection:** The *dbms_stats* package is approximately 2x faster when collecting statistics. Of course, the recommended procedure with *dbms_stats* is to collect a single, deep sample and save the statistics, but this performance feature is welcome, especially for very large shops.

- **Refined automatic sample size:** Rahn notes that the 11g *dbms_statsauto_sample_size* now collects a statistically significant sample, even for highly skewed data distributions.

Overall with version 11g, Oracle has taken great strides into improving the automated collection of CBO statistics, ensuring that SQL will be optimized with much less manual intervention. Traditionally, a skewed distribution within column values required manual intervention by adding column histograms.

Reanalyzing Optimizer Statistics

It is astonishing how many shops prohibit any unapproved production changes and yet reanalyze schema stats weekly. Evidently, they do not understand that the purpose of schema reanalysis is to change their production SQL execution plans, and they act surprised when performance changes!

Most Oracle experts only recommend scheduled reanalysis for highly dynamic databases, and most shops save one very deep sample with histograms, storing the statistic with the *dbms_stats.export_schema_stats* procedure. The only exceptions are highly volatile systems, i.e. lab research systems, where a table is huge one day and small the next.

For periodic reanalysis, many shops us the table monitoring option and also *method_opt=auto* after they are confident that all histograms are in place.

Saving and Re-using Optimizer Statistics

For data warehouses and databases using the *all_rows optimizer_mode*, Oracle 9i R2 and beyond have the ability to collect the external *cpu_cost* and *io_cost* metrics. The ability to save and re-use schema statistics is important for several types of Oracle shops:

- **Bi-modal shops:** Many shops get huge benefits from using two sets of stats; one for OLTP (daytime), and another for batch (evening jobs)

- **Test databases:** Many Oracle professionals will export their production statistics into the development instances so that the test execution plans more closely resemble the production database

Getting Top Quality Optimizer Statistics

Because Oracle schema statistics work best with external system load, it can be a good idea to schedule a valid sample during regular working hours. This can be done using *dbms_stats.auto_sample_size*. In the following code example, statistics are refreshed using the *auto* option, which works with the table monitoring facility to only reanalyze those Oracle tables that have experienced more than a 10% change in row content:

```
begin
   dbms_stats.gather_schema_stats(
      ownname          => 'SCOTT',
      estimate_percent => dbms_stats.auto_sample_size,
      method_opt       => 'for all columns size auto',
      degree           => 7
   );
end;
/
```

Tips for Optimizing the CBO with Statistics

There are several tips for optimizing the CBO with good statistics:

- Find skewed columns that are referenced in SQL. Many shops do not use *method_opt=skewonly* and suffer from poor execution plans on skewed column access.

- Find histograms for foreign key columns: Many DBAs forget that the CBO must have foreign-key histograms in order to determine the optimal table join order, i.e. the *ordered* hint.

- Fix the cause, not the symptom. For example, whenever there is a sub-optimal order for table joins, resist the temptation to add the *ordered* hint, and instead create histograms on the foreign keys of the join to force the CBO to make the best decision.

For new features, explore the Oracle 11g automatic histogram collection mechanism that interrogates *v$sql_plan* to see where the foreign keys are used. It claims to generate histograms when appropriate, all automatically.

Oracle Workload Statistics and SQL Performance

Experienced DBAs know that the external environment has a profound impact on SQL performance. The Oracle cost-based optimizer now has the ability to consider real-world timings for multiblock reads (*mreadtim*) and sequential read I/O times (*sreadtim*) within the *dbms_stats.gather_system_stats* procedure.

Oracle has two types of CBO statistics for estimating disk read times *workload* and *noworkload* statistics. The *noworkload* statistics gather data by submitting random reads against all data files, while the workload statistics increments internal counters to measure database I/O activity.

- **Noworkload statistics:** These include *cpuspeednw*, *ioseektim* and *iotfrspeed*.

- **Workload statistics:** These are gathered by *dbms_stats.gather_system_stats* and include *sreadtim*, *mreadtim*, *cpuspeed*, *mbrc*, *maxthr*, and *slavethr* representing workload statistics

If both *workload* and *noworkload* statistics are available, the optimizer uses the *workload* statistics in hopes of getting the best execution plan for the SQL. The output from *dbms_stats.gather_system_stats* is stored in the *aux_stats$* table. It can be queried as follows to see the current values for the database:

```
SQL> select sname, pname, pval1
  from sys.aux_stats$;

SNAME              PNAME       PVAL1
-------------      ---------   -------
SYSSTATS_INFO      STATUS
SYSSTATS_INFO      DSTART
SYSSTATS_INFO      DSTOP
SYSSTATS_INFO      FLAGS            1
SYSSTATS_MAIN      CPUSPEEDNW  502.005
SYSSTATS_MAIN      IOSEEKTIM       10
SYSSTATS_MAIN      IOTFRSPEED    4096
SYSSTATS_MAIN      SREADTIM     7.618
SYSSTATS_MAIN      MREADTIM    14.348
SYSSTATS_MAIN      CPUSPEED       507
SYSSTATS_MAIN      MBRC             6
SYSSTATS_MAIN      MAXTHR       32768
SYSSTATS_MAIN      SLAVETHR

13 rows selected.
```

Oracle workload statistics that are gathered with *dbms_stats.gather_system_stats* now gather real-workload I/O performance metrics:

- **sreadtim:** Single block read time in milliseconds
- **mreadtim:** Multiblock read time in ms
- **cpuspeed:** CPU speed
- **mbrc:** Average blocks read per multiblock read (see *db_file_multiblock_read_count*)
- **maxthr:** Maximum I/O throughput, for Oracle Parallel Query (OPQ) only
- **slavethr:** OPQ Factotum (slave) throughput (OPQ only)

The *dbms_stats.gather_system_stats* procedure measures important timings within the database and adjusts the optimizer's propensity to choose indexes vs. full-scans.

The Oracle 11g Performance Tuning Guide notes that the timing of the workload sample is important. Samples should be run during a time when the system is performing legitimate multiblock reads. Another option is to stage a workload that performs full-table scans. The documents also note that bad timing of a system statistics sample can cause less than optimal estimates for the timings of full-table scan I/O.

The *dbms_stats.gather_system_stats* procedure is especially useful for multi-mode Oracle shops that run OLTP during the day and DSS at night. The *dbms_stats.gather_system_stats* procedure is invoked as an elapsed time capture, making sure to collect the statistics during a representative heavy workload:

```
execute dbms_stats.gather_system_stats('Start');
```

```
-- one hour delay during high workload
execute dbms_stats.gather_system_stats('Stop');
```

The data collection mechanism of the *dbms_stats.gather_system_stats* procedure works in a similar fashion to the script that measures I/O times to optimize the *optimizer_index_cost_adj* parameter. The *dbms_stats.gather_system_stats* is also related to the undocumented *_optimizer_cost_model* parameter and the DBA's *db_file_multiblock_read_count* setting.

The *dbms_stats.gather_system_stats* procedure is very similar to the following script for setting *optimizer_index_cost_adj* where the relative costs of sequential and scattered read times are compared:

```
select
   sum(a.time_waited_micro)/sum(a.total_waits)/1000000 c1,
   sum(b.time_waited_micro)/sum(b.total_waits)/1000000 c2,
   (
      sum(a.total_waits) /
      sum(a.total_waits + b.total_waits)
   ) * 100 c3,
   (
      sum(b.total_waits) /
      sum(a.total_waits + b.total_waits)
   ) * 100 c4,
   (
      sum(b.time_waited_micro) /
      sum(b.total_waits)) /
      (sum(a.time_waited_micro)/sum(a.total_waits)
   ) * 100 c5
from
   dba_hist_system_event a,
   dba_hist_system_event b
where
   a.snap_id = b.snap_id
and
   a.event_name = 'db file scattered read'
and
   b.event_name = 'db file sequential read';
```

The sample that follows is the output from a real system showing an empirical test of disk I/O speed. DBAs can expect scattered reads (full-table scans) to be far faster than sequential reads (index probes) because of Oracle sequential prefetch, according to the setting for *db_file_multiblock_read_count*. It is important to note that this is obsolete as of Oracle 10g R2:

As seen below, the starting value for *optimizer_index_cost_adj* is based on the relative I/O costs, which is very similar to *dbms_stats.gather_system_stats*:

- scattered read (full table scans) are fast at 13ms (c3)

- sequential reads (index probes) take much longer 86ms (c4)

- starting setting for *optimizer_index_cost_adj* at 36:

C1	C2	C3	C4	C5
----------	----------	----------	----------	----------

```
13,824     5,072      13          86            36
```

Oracle 11g Extended Optimizer Statistics

Some of the most exciting new features of Oracle 11g are the improvements to the *dbms_stats* package, specifically the ability to aid complex queries by providing extended statistics to the CBO. The 11g extended optimizer statistics are intended to improve the optimizer's guesses for the cardinality of combined columns and columns that are modified by a built-in or user-defined function.

In Oracle 10g, dynamic sampling can be used to provide inter-table cardinality estimates, but dynamic sampling has important limitations. The 11g extended statistics in *dbms_stats* relieve much of the problem of sub-optimal table join orders.

In the absence of column histograms and extended statistics, the CBO must be able to guess the size of complex result sets information, and it sometimes gets it wrong. This is one reason why the *ordered* hint is one of the most popular SQL tuning hints. The *ordered* hint allows the specification that the tables be joined together in the same order that they appear in the *from* clause.

The new 11g *dbms_stats* package has several new procedures to aid in supplementing histogram data, and the state of these extended histograms can be seen in the *user_tab_col_statistics* view:

- *dbms_stats.create_extended_stats*

- *dbms_stats.show_extended_stats_name*

- *dbms_stats.drop_extended_stats*

In OLTP databases, it is very rare for the fundamental nature of a schema to change. Large tables remain large, and index columns rarely change distribution, cardinality, and skew. Periodic reanalysis of the total schema statistics should only be considered if the database matches the following criteria:

- **CPU-intensive databases:** Many scientific systems load a small set of experimental data, analyze the data, produce reports, and then truncate and reload a new set of experiments. There are also Oracle databases with super large data buffer caches, which reduce physical I/O at the expense of higher CPU consumption. For these types of systems, it may be necessary to reanalyze the schema each time the database is reloaded.

- **Highly volatile databases:** In these rare cases, the size of tables and the characteristics of index column data changes radically. For example, Laboratory Information Management Systems (LIMS) load, analyze and purge experimental data so frequently that it is very difficult to always have optimal CBO statistics. If a database has a table that has 100 rows one week and 10,000 rows the next week, it might be prudent to consider using Oracle dynamic sampling or a periodic reanalysis of statistics.

The following section will show how Oracle SQL optimization can be adjusted to evaluate I/O costs of CPU costs.

External Costing with the Optimizer

Over the past decade, Oracle has been enhanced to take external influences into consideration when determining the best execution plan. Because the Oracle database does not run in a vacuum, the optimizer must be able to factor in the costs of external disk I/O and the cost of CPU cycles for each SQL operation.

This process is especially critical for queries running *all_rows* optimization, where minimizing server resources is a primary goal. We now see these external costing values with Oracle SQL execution plans:

- *cpu_cost:* The Oracle SQL optimizer can now estimate the number of machine cycles required for an operation and factors this cost into the execution plan calculation. The CPU costs associated with servicing an Oracle query depends upon the current server configuration, which Oracle cannot see.

- *io_cost:* The CBO had been enhanced to estimate the number of physical block reads required for an operation. The I/O cost is proportional to the number of physical data blocks read by the operation.

Internally, Oracle uses both the CPU and I/O cost estimations in evaluating the execution plans, but these factors can be weighted according to the stress on the server. If the top five timed events include CPU, then the SQL may need to be optimized to minimize CPU resources. This equation becomes even more complex when parallel query is factored in, where many concurrent processes are servicing the query.

The best benefit for using CPU costing is for *all_rows* execution plans where cost is more important than with *first_rows* optimization.

The following section will provide a look at column histograms and how they help SQL execute faster.

Tuning SQL with Histograms

Histograms are an add-on feature to the *dbms_stats* procedure that store the distribution of column values in either height-balanced or weight-balanced buckets. Histograms may help the Oracle optimizer in two ways:

- **Skewed index:** Histograms are important when the column value requires the CBO to decide whether to use an index versus a full-table scan

- **Table join order:** Histograms can reveal the expected number of rows returned from a table query, i.e. *select * from customer where state = 'NC'*, thereby helping the optimizer determine the fastest table join order

Determining the Optimal Table Join Order

When large tables are joined and the result set is small, it is critical that Oracle knows the number of rows in each table after the query's *where* clause is considered, and histograms can help. If the cardinality of the table is too high, i.e. the intermediate row sizes are larger than they have to be, then histograms on the most selective column in the *where* clause will tip-off the optimizer and change the table join order.

Histograms are also used to predict cardinality and the number of rows returned, an important factor in determining the fastest table join order. In a situation where there is a *vehicle_type* index and 65 percent of the values are for the CAR type, when a query with *where vehicle_type* = 'CAR' is specified, a full-table scan would be the fastest execution plan. However, a query with *where vehicle_type* = 'TRUCK' would be faster when using access via an index.

For manually determining the best table join order to add an *ordered* or *leading* hint, the *where* clause of the query can be inspected along with the execution plan for the original query. The problem with forcing the sequence of table joins with the *ordered* hint is that it is not dynamic, and careful application of histograms can do the same job and apply to all queries.

How is Join Cardinality Estimated?

In the absence of column histograms, the Oracle CBO must be able to guess on information, and sometimes the guess is wrong. This is one reason why the *ordered* hint is one of the most popular SQL tuning hints, because it allows the DBA to specify that the tables be joined in the same order that they appear in the *from* clause, like this:

```
select /+ ordered */
   student_name
from
   student
natural join
   course
natural join
   professor
where
   professor = 'jones'
and
   course = 'anthropology 610';
```

If the values for the *professor* and *course* table columns are not skewed, it is unlikely that the 10g automatic statistics would have created histograms buckets in the *dba_histograms* view for these columns.

The Oracle CBO needs to be able to accurately estimate the final number of rows returned by each step of the query and then use schema metadata from running *dbms_stats* to choose the table join order that results in the least amount of baggage, in the form of intermediate rows, from each of the table join operations. This is a daunting task. When an SQL query has a complex *where* clause, it can be very difficult to estimate the size of the intermediate result sets, especially when the *where* clause transforms column values with mathematical functions. Oracle has made a commitment to making the CBO infallible, even when incomplete information exists.

Oracle 9i introduced the new dynamic sampling method for gathering run-time schema statistics, and it is now enabled by default in Oracle 10g and beyond. However, dynamic sampling is not for every database. The following section will reveal why this is the case.

Oracle join elimination

Oracle join elimination was introduced in 10gr2 and again in 11g to prevent unnecessary joins of tables that reside inside views. In essence, join elimination is a part of the 11g tuning transformations.

In essence, Oracle join elimination is transparent and simple. Prior to 10gr2, a view that had a 10-way join would always join all ten tables together, regardless of the number of tables that were required to service the query. Rather than calling this unnecessary table joining a bug, Oracle fixed the problem and called it "join elimination".

Prior to executing a view, Oracle interrogates the original query, working backwards to see of all of the tables inside the view are required to deliver the result set. If not, Oracle will not join superfluous tables, thereby cutting-down on the number of joins and improving response time.

The new join elimination transformation has the JE abbreviation that is used within an optimizer trace file to indicate a join elimination. For example, an optimizer trace file might refer to a join elimination thusly:

```
JE: eliminate table: DEPARTMENTS
```

Next, let's examine dynamic sampling.

Using Dynamic Sampling

The main objective of dynamic sampling is to create more accurate selectivity and cardinality estimates. This in turn helps the CBO generate faster execution plans. Dynamic sampling is normally used to estimate single-table predicate selectivity when collected statistics cannot be used, or when they are likely to lead to significant errors in estimation. Dynamic sampling is also used to estimate table cardinality for tables without statistics or for tables whose statistics are too out of date to trust.

The *optimizer_dynamic_sampling* initialization parameter controls the number of blocks read by the dynamic sampling query. The parameter can be set to a value from zero to ten. In 10g, the default for this parameter is set to two, automatically enabling dynamic sampling. The *optimizer_features_enable* parameter will turn off dynamic sampling if it is set to a version earlier than 9.2.0.

A value of zero means dynamic sampling will not be performed. Increasing the value of the parameter results in more aggressive dynamic sampling in terms of both the type of tables sampled, analyzed or unanalyzed, and the amount of I/O spent on sampling.

By default, Oracle will sample 32 random blocks. It is also important to know that dynamic sampling does not occur on tables that contain less than 32 blocks. There is also a new dynamic sampling hint, *dynamic_sampling (tablename level*, where *tablename* is the name of the table to be dynamically sampled and *level* is the same setting from zero to ten. The default value for the *level* is two, which will only sample tables that have not been analyzed with *dbms_stats*.

Oracle Tuning

```
select /*+ dynamic_sampling (customer 4) */
   customer_name, . . . .
```

The following are the level descriptions, and remember, the higher the level, the deeper the sampling. The sampling levels are cumulative and each level contains all of the sampling of the prior level:

- **Level 1:** Samples tables that appear in join or subquery conditions that have no indexes and have more blocks than 32, the default for dynamic sampling

- **Level 2 (default):** Samples all unanalyzed tables that have more than 32 blocks

- **Level 3:** Samples tables using a single column that applies selectivity to the table being sampled

- **Level 4:** Samples tables using two or more columns that apply selectivity to the table being sampled

- **Level 5:** Doubles the dynamic sample size and samples 64 blocks on tables

- **Level 6:** Quadruples the dynamic sample size and samples 128 blocks on tables

- **Level 7:** Samples 256 blocks on tables

- **Level 8:** Samples 1,024 blocks on tables

- **Level 9:** Samples 4,096 blocks on tables

- **Level 10:** Samples all of the block in the tables

 **Dynamic sampling is not for everyone!**

When *dynamic_sampling* was first introduced in Oracle 9i, it was used primarily for data warehouse systems with complex queries. Because it is enabled by default in Oracle10g and beyond, the DBA may want to turn off *dynamic_sampling* to remove unnecessary overhead if any of the following are true:

- The system utilizes an online transaction processing (OLTP) database with small, single-table queries

- Queries are not frequently re-executed as determined by the *executions* column in *v$sql* and *executions_delta* in *dba_hist_sqlstat*

- Multi-table joins have simple *where* clause predicates with single-column values and no built-in or mathematical functions

Dynamic sampling is ideal whenever a query is going to execute multiple times because the sample time is small compared to the overall query execution time.

By sampling data from the table at runtime, Oracle 10g can quickly evaluate complex *where* clause predicates and determine the selectivity of each predicate, using this information to determine the optimal table join order. The following section will introduce the Oracle SQL *sample* clause and show how it works.

Sampling Table Scans

A *sample* table scan retrieves a random sample of data of a selected size. The sample can be from a simple table or a complex *select* statement, such as a statement involving multiple joins and complex views.

Some simple SQL queries can be run to allow a peek inside dynamic sampling. The following SQL statement uses a sample block and a sample rows scan on the customer table. There are 50,000 rows in this table. The first statement shows a sample block scan and the last SQL statement shows a sample row scan.

```
select
   count(*)
from
   customer
   sample block(20);
```

```
  COUNT(*)
----------
     12268
```

```
select
   pol_no,
   sales_id,
   sum_assured,
   premium
from
   customer
   sample (0.02);
```

POL_NO	SALES_ID	SUM_ASSURED	PREMIUM
2895	10	2525	2
3176	10	2525	2
9228	10	2525	2
11294	11	2535	4
19846	11	2535	4
25547	12	2545	6
29583	12	2545	6
40042	13	2555	8
47331	14	2565	10
45283	14	2565	10

Just as the data can be sampled with SQL, the Oracle CBO can sample the data prior to formulating the execution plan. For example, the new *dynamic_sampling* SQL hint can be used to sample rows from the table:

```
select /*+ dynamic_sampling (customer 10) */
   pol_no,
   sales_id,
   sum_assured,
   premium
from
   customer;
```

```
    POL_NO   SALES_ID SUM_ASSURED     PREMIUM
---------- ---------- ----------- ---------- --
      2895         10        2525          2
      3176         10        2525          2
      9228         10        2525          2
     11294         11        2535          4
     19846         11        2535          4
     25547         12        2545          6
     29583         12        2545          6
     40042         13        2555          8
     47331         14        2565         10
     45283         14        2565         10
```

Dynamic sampling addresses an innate problem in SQL, and this issue is common to all relational databases. Estimating the optimal join order involves guessing the sequence that results in the smallest amount of intermediate row sets, and it is impossible to collect every possible combination of *where* clauses.

Dynamic sampling is almost a miracle for databases that have large n-way table joins that execute frequently. By sampling a tiny subset of the data, the Oracle CBO gleans clues as to the fastest table join order.

Fortunately, *dynamic_sampling* does not take a long time to execute, but it can cause unnecessary overhead for Oracle databases. Dynamic sampling is just another example of Oracle's commitment to making Oracle an intelligent, self-optimizing database.

Oracle Tuning with Hints

Oracle ensures that the cost-based SQL optimizer becomes more sophisticated with each release. With each new release, Oracle provides an increasing number of methods for changing the execution plans for SQL statements. While hints are used for tuning as well as documentation, the most common use for Oracle hints is as a debugging tool. The hints can be used to determine the optimal execution plan and then work backwards, adjusting the statistics to make the vanilla SQL simulate the hinted query.

Using Oracle hints can be very complicated, and Oracle developers only use hints as a last resort, preferring to alter the statistics to change the execution plan. Oracle contains more than 124 hints, and many of them are not found in the Oracle documentation. Table 16.1 contains a detailed list of these hints.

Hints		
all_rows	index_ss_asc	pq_nomap

and_equal	index_ss	push_pred
antijoin	index	push_subq
append	leading	remote_mapped
bitmap	like_expand	restore_as_intervals
buffer	local_indexesmaterialize	rewrite
bypass_recursive_check	merge	rule
bypass_ujvc	merge_aj	save_as_intervals
cache	merge_sj	scn_ascending
cache_cb	mv_merge	selectivity
cache_temp_table	nested_table_get_refs	semijoin
cardinality	nested_table_set_refs	semijoin_driver
choose	nested_table_set_setid	skip_ext_optimizer
civ_gb	nl_aj	sqlldr
collections_get_refs	nl_sj	star
cpu_costing	no_access	star_transformation
cube_gb	no_buffer	swap_join_inputs
cursor_sharing_exact	no_expand	sys_dl_cursor
defref_no_rewrite	no_expand_gset_to_union	sys_parallel_txn
dml_update	no_fact	sys_rid_order
domain_index_no_sort	no_filtering	tiv_gb
domain_index_sort	no_index	tiv_ssf
driving_site	no_merge	unnest
dynamic_sampling	no_monitoring	use_anti
dynamic_sampling_est_cdn	no_order_rollups	use_concat
expand_gset_to_union	no_prune_gsets	use_hash
fact	no_push_pred	use_merge
first_rows	no_push_subq	use_nl
force_sample_block	no_qkn_buff	use_semi
full	no_semijoin	use_ttt_for_gsets
gby_conc_rollup	no_stats_gsets	pq_nomap
global_table_hints	no_unnest	push_pred
hash	noappend	push_subq
hash_aj	nocache	remote_mapped
hash_sj	nocpu_costing	restore_as_intervals
hwm_brokered	noparallel	rewrite
ignore_on_clause	noparallel_index	rule
ignore_where_clause	norewrite	save_as_intervals
index_asc	or_expand	scn_ascending
index_combine	parallel	selectivity
index_desc	parallel_index	semijoin
index_ffs	piv_gb	semijoin_driver
index_join	piv_ssf	
index_rrs	pq_distribute	
index_ss	pq_map	

Hints are optimizer directives used for altering optimizer execution plans. Remember, an *optimizer* hint is placed inside comments within the SQL statement and is used in those rare cases when the optimizer makes an incorrect decision about the execution plan. Since hints are inside comments, it is important to ensure that the hint name is spelled correctly and that the hint is appropriate to the query.

For example, the following hint is invalid because *first_rows* access and parallel access are mutually exclusive. This is because parallel access always assumes a full-table scan, and *first_rows* favors index access.

```
-- An invalid hint
select /*+ first_rows parallel(emp,8)*/
   emp_name
from
   emp
order by
   ename;
```

Some Oracle professionals will place hints together to reinforce their wishes. For example, if there is a SMP server with eight or more CPUs, someone might have the idea to use Oracle Parallel Query to speed up legitimate full-table scans.

When using a parallel query, careful consideration must be given to whether or not to turn on parallelism at the table level. This influences the optimizer, causing it to see the full table scan as inexpensive. Most commonly, parallel query is specified on a query-by-query basis, combining the *full* hint with the *parallel* hint to ensure a fast parallel full-table scan:

```
-- A valid hint
select /*+ full parallel(emp,35)*/
   emp_name
from
   emp
order by
   ename;
```

Now that the general concept of hints has been introduced, it is an appropriate time to look at one of the most important hints for optimizer tuning, the *ordered* hint.

The *ordered* hint determines the driving table for the query execution and also specifies the order in which tables are joined. The *ordered* hint requests that the tables should be joined in the order that they are specified in the *from* clause, with the first table in the *from* clause specifying the driving table. Using the *ordered* hint can save the system a huge amount of parse time and speed SQL execution. This is because the optimizer is given the best order in which to join the tables.

For example, the following query uses the *ordered* hint to join the tables in their specified order in the *from* clause. In this example, the execution plan is further refined by specifying that the emp-to-dept join, use a hash join and the sal-to-bon join uses a nested loop join:

```
select
/*+ ordered use_hash (emp, dept) use_nl (sal, bon) */
from
   emp,
   dept,
   sal,
   bon
where . . .
```

The *ordered* hint is most commonly used in data warehouse queries or in SQL that joins more than five tables.

SQL execution is dynamic, and tuning a SQL statement for the current data may not be optimal in the future.

When hints appear to be ignored

Remember, hints are a last resort measure and you should only use the "good hints" like *ordered* and *ordered_predicates*, hints that give the SQL optimizer information that it cannot easily gather from the *dbms_stats* statistics.

A SQL hint is an "optimizer directive" and that, in theory, hints cannot be ignored, but in the real world, hints are ignored frequently. Oracle even has a hidden parameter called *_optimizer_ignore_hints* to make the optimizer ignore valid hints.

There are three main reasons why an invalid hint attempt is being ignored, syntax errors, semantic errors and invalid arguments:

⊟ **Syntax error hints are ignored:** Oracle does not report when a hint is mis-spelled and because hints are embedded into comments, syntax errors are common, and your hint attempt will be ignored. If the hint name spelled incorrectly, then the hint will not be ignored. Here we see a query with a misspelled hint name:

```
select /*+ indrex(erp, dept_idx) */ * from emp;
```

⊟ **Semantic error hints are ignored:** If a hint argument is spelled incorrectly, and not found in the data dictionary then a semantic hint error will cause the hint will not be ignored. Here we see a query with a misspelled table name, erp instead of emp:

```
select /*+ index(erp, dept_idx) */ * from emp;
```

A hint will also be ignored if it is specified improperly, with missing arguments. For example, the table name is mandatory for an index hint. For example, the following hint will be ignored because the table name is not specified in the index hint:

```
select /*+ index(dept_idx) */ * from emp;
```

- **Incompatible hints are ignored**: Incongruent hints are ignored, such as a hint that does not "make sense". In the context of the query, an incompatible is indeed ignored, such as a query that specifies incompatible access plans. For example, the following hints are inconsistent and one of the hints will be ignored:

  Ignored: Parallel hint with index hint

  Ignored: Full hint with index hint

- **Hints with bad parameters are ignored**: It's possible to have a valid hint (syntax and semantics) that is ignored because of a lack of server resources. For example, the use_hash hint is dependent upon there being enough RAM (as defined by pga_aggregate_target or hash_area_size). If these settings prohibit the optimizer from invoking a hash join, the use_hash hint will be ignored.

```
select /*+ use_hash(e,b) parallel(b, 15) */
   e.ename,
   hiredate,
   b.comm
from
   smalltab e,
   largetab b
where
   e.ename = b.ename;
```

Here are other cases where an invalid hint will be ignored:

Hint	When Ignored
cluster	When used with a noncluster table
hash	When used with a noncluster table
hash_aj	When no subquery exists
index	When the specified index does not exist
index_combine	When no bitmapped indexes exist
merge_aj	When no subquery exists
parallel	When a plan other than TABLE ACCESS FULL is invoked
push_subq	When no subquery exists

star	When improper indexes exists on the fact table
use_concat	When no multiple *or* conditions exist in the *where* clause
use_nl	When indexes do not exist on the tables

The next sections cover an age-old debate: Do Oracle indexes benefit from periodic rebuilding?

Oracle Indexes – Is Maintenance Required?

The question about whether Oracle indexes are self-balancing is largely a matter of semantics. As rows are added to an empty table, Oracle controls the addition of same level blocks until the higher level index node is unable to hold any more key pointer pairs. This process is called splitting. When the index can no longer split because the owner block is full, Oracle will spawn a whole new index level, keeping the index tree in perfect logical and physical balance.

Deletes are a different story. Physically, Oracle indexes are always balanced because empty blocks stay inside the tree structure after a massive delete. Logically, Oracle indexes are not self-balancing because Oracle does not remove the dead blocks as they become empty. Figure 16.9 shows an Oracle index before a massive delete.

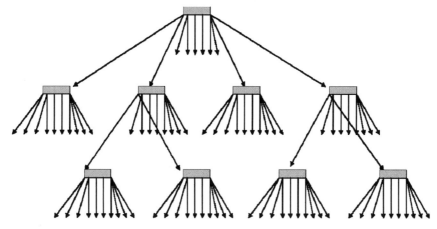

Figure16.9: *A Physical Index Before a Massive Row Delete*

After a massive delete, the physical representation of the index is precisely the same because the empty data blocks remain. This is illustrated in Figure 16.10. Unfortunately, this process leaves the logical internal pointer structure unbalanced. This is because Oracle goes around the deleted leaf nodes and places the empty index blocks back into the freelist, allowing these blocks to be reused anywhere in the index tree structure.

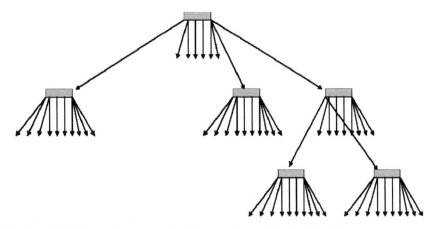

Figure 16.10: *The Logical Pointer Structure of an Index after a Massive Row Delete*

This type of sparse index is typical of an index on highly active tables with large-scale inserts, deletes and updates. There may be thousands of empty or almost empty index blocks, and the sparse data can cause excessive I/O. There are several types of Oracle execution steps that will run longer on this type of sparse index:

- Index Range Scans: Index range scans that must access many near empty blocks will have excessive I/O compared to a rebuilt index

- Index Fast Full Scans: It is important to remember that around 70% of an index can be deleted, yet the index can still have the same number of data blocks. Because of this, a full index scan may run many times slower before it is rebuilt.

The following section will provide a look at techniques for locating indexes for the Oracle KEEP pool.

Locating Tables and Indexes for the KEEP Pool

From the chapter on instance tuning it was noted that SQL performance can be enhanced by placing frequently referenced data in the RAM buffer caches:

> *"A good candidate for a segment to put into the KEEP pool is a segment that is smaller than 10% of the size of the default buffer pool and has incurred at least 1% of the total I/Os in the system."*

More concisely, a small table that is in high demand is a good candidate for *keep* caching.

Internally, it is critical to cache small-table full-table scans because the Oracle data buffer does not increase the touch count when blocks from full-table scans are referenced. Hence, small-table full-table scan blocks will age out of the data buffers very quickly, causing unnecessary disk I/O.

For details on caching in the KEEP pool, see the chapter on Oracle Instance Tuning.

Identifying Problem SQL

One short path to identifying performance problems in an Oracle database includes the following steps:

1. Find the sessions responsible for hogging the most resources like I/O or CPU

2. Identify the code these sessions are running.

3. Peel away the bad code these sessions have executed from the good and acceptable code.

4. Highlight the worst SQL and then tune it for better performance.

The following sections work through these four steps and illustrate how several performance views can assist in this process.

Find the Problem Sessions

Even if there is no database monitor that offers a top sessions view, it is easy to pinpoint the sessions that are giving the database grief. Database professionals have their own differing ideas about what constitutes a top session. Some feel that the sum total of physical I/O alone tells the story, while others look at CPU. Others still use a combination of physical and logical I/O.

Whatever the preference, the script in *top_20_sessions.sql* can be used to quickly show the top twenty sessions in an Oracle database. The initial sort is on physical I/O, but this can be changed to any other column desired.

🖫 top_20_sessions.sql

```
select * from
(select b.sid sid,
    decode (b.username,null,e.name,b.username) user_name,
    d.spid os_id,
    b.machine machine_name,
    to_char(logon_time,'dd-mon-yy hh:mi:ss pm') logon_time,
    (sum(decode(c.name,'physical reads',value,0)) +
    sum(decode(c.name,'physical writes',value,0)) +
    sum(decode(c.name,'physical writes direct',value,0)) +
    sum(decode(c.name,'physical writes direct (lob)',value,0))+
    sum(decode(c.name,'physical reads direct (lob)',value,0)) +
    sum(decode(c.name,'physical reads direct',value,0)))
    total_physical_io,
    (sum(decode(c.name,'db block gets',value,0)) +
    sum(decode(c.name,'db block changes',value,0)) +
    sum(decode(c.name,'consistent changes',value,0)) +
    sum(decode(c.name,'consistent gets',value,0)) )
    total_logical_io,
    (sum(decode(c.name,'session pga memory',value,0))+
    sum(decode(c.name,'session uga memory',value,0)) )
    total_memory_usage,
    sum(decode(c.name,'parse count (total)',value,0)) parses,
    sum(decode(c.name,'cpu used by this session',value,0))
    total_cpu,
    sum(decode(c.name,'parse time cpu',value,0)) parse_cpu,
    sum(decode(c.name,'recursive cpu usage',value,0))
    recursive_cpu,
```

```
       sum(decode(c.name,'cpu used by this session',value,0)) -
       sum(decode(c.name,'parse time cpu',value,0)) -
       sum(decode(c.name,'recursive cpu usage',value,0))
          other_cpu,
       sum(decode(c.name,'sorts (disk)',value,0)) disk_sorts,
       sum(decode(c.name,'sorts (memory)',value,0)) memory_sorts,
       sum(decode(c.name,'sorts (rows)',value,0)) rows_sorted,
       sum(decode(c.name,'user commits',value,0)) commits,
       sum(decode(c.name,'user rollbacks',value,0)) rollbacks,
       sum(decode(c.name,'execute count',value,0)) executions
from sys.v_$sesstat a,
     sys.v_$session b,
     sys.v_$statname c,
     sys.v_$process d,
     sys.v_$bgprocess e
where a.statistic#=c.statistic# and
      b.sid=a.sid and
      d.addr = b.paddr and
      e.paddr (+) = b.paddr and
      c.NAME in ('physical reads',
                 'physical writes',
                 'physical writes direct',
                 'physical reads direct',
                 'physical writes direct (lob)',
                 'physical reads direct (lob)',
                 'db block gets',
                 'db block changes',
                 'consistent changes',
                 'consistent gets',
                 'session pga memory',
                 'session uga memory',
                 'parse count (total)',
                 'CPU used by this session',
                 'parse time cpu',
                 'recursive cpu usage',
                 'sorts (disk)',
                 'sorts (memory)',
                 'sorts (rows)',
                 'user commits',
                 'user rollbacks',
                 'execute count'
)
group by b.sid,
         d.spid,
         decode (b.username,null,e.name,b.username),
         b.machine,
         to_char(logon_time,'dd-mon-yy hh:mi:ss pm')
order by 6 desc)
where rownum < 21
```

The above query can also be modified to exclude Oracle background processes, the *sys* and *system* user and more. The end result should be a current list of top offending sessions in the database as ranked by various performance metrics, which is the normal way to rank problem user accounts. Figure 16.11 shows a sample output of this query:

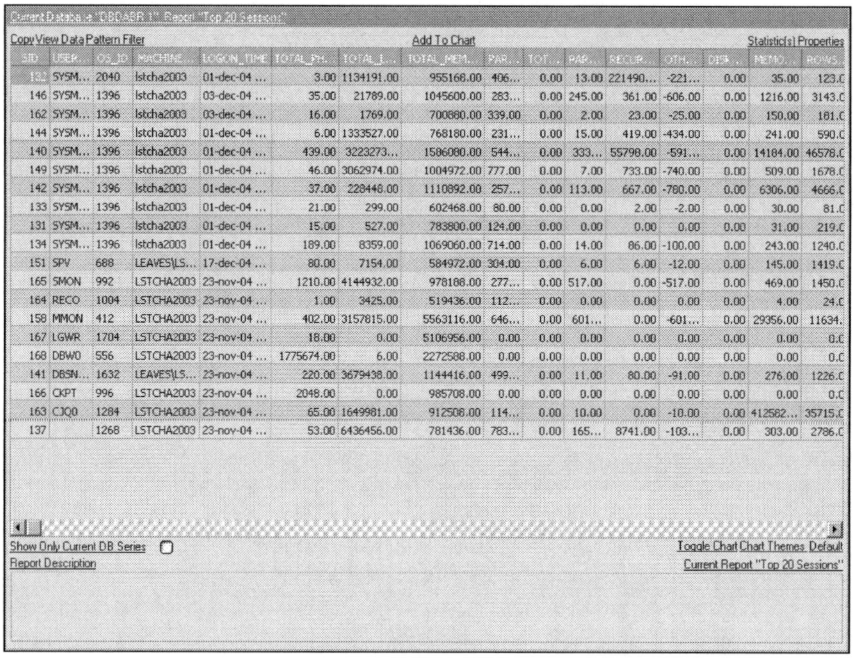

Figure 16.11: *The Sample top_20_sessions.sql Query Output*

Some DBAs feel that this method, while useful, lacks depth. Specifically, since DBAs know that a user's resource consumption is almost always tied to inefficient SQL, they would like to cut to the chase and find the problem sessions in a database that have, for example, caused most of the large table scans on the system or have submitted queries containing Cartesian joins.

Such a thing was difficult to determine in earlier versions of Oracle, but fortunately, 9i provided a new performance view that can be used to derive such data. The *v$sql_plan* view contains execution plan data for all submitted SQL statements. Such a view provides a wealth of information regarding the performance and efficiency of SQL statements and the sessions that submitted them.

For example, if a DBA wants to know what sessions have parsed SQL statements that caused large table scans, with large defined as being anything over one MB, on a system along with the total number of large scans by session, the following query could be submitted:

🖫 **high_scan_sql.sql**

```
select
    c.username username,
    count(a.hash_value) scan_count
from
    sys.v_$sql_plan a,
    sys.dba_segments b,
    sys.dba_users c,
    sys.v_$sql d
where
    a.object_owner (+) = b.owner
and
    a.object_name (+) = b.segment_name
```

```
and
    b.segment_type IN ('TABLE', 'TABLE PARTITION')
and
    a.operation like '%TABLE%'
and
    a.options = 'FULL'
and
    c.user_id = d.parsing_user_id
and
    d.hash_value = a.hash_value
and
    b.bytes / 1024 > 1024
group by
    c.username
order by
    2 desc
;
```

The output from the above query might look something like the following:

```
USERNAME     SCAN_COUNT
----------   ----------
SYSTEM              14
SYS                 11
ERADMIN              6
ORA_MONITOR          3
```

In like fashion, to uncover what sessions have parsed SQL statements containing Cartesian joins along with the number of SQL statements that contain such joins, the following query could be used:

💾 find_cartesian_joins.sql

```
select
    username,
    count(distinct c.hash_value) nbr_stmts
from
    sys.v_$sql a,
    sys.dba_users b,
    sys.v_$sql_plan c
where
    a.parsing_user_id = b.user_id
and
    options = 'CARTESIAN'
and
    operation like '%JOIN%'
and
    a.hash_value = c.hash_value
group by
    username
order by
    2 desc
;
```

A result set from this query could look similar to the following:

```
USERNAME   NBR_STMTS
---------  ---------
SYS                2
```

```
SYSMAN            2
ORA_MONITOR       1
```

The *v$sql_plan* view adds more meat to the process of identifying problem sessions in a database. When combined with the standard performance metrics query, DBAs can really begin to pinpoint the sessions that are wreaking havoc inside their critical systems.

Identify Resource-Intensive SQL

After identifying the top resource hogging sessions in a database, attention can then be turned to the code the DBA and others are executing that is likely causing system bottlenecks. As with top session monitors, many decent database monitors have a top SQL feature that can help ferret out bad SQL code. Without access to such tools, a script like the one shown in *high_resource_sql.sql* can be used.

🖫 high_resource_sql.sql

```
select sql_text,
       username,
       disk_reads_per_exec,
       buffer_gets,
       disk_reads,
       parse_calls,
       sorts,
       executions,
       rows_processed,
       hit_ratio,
       first_load_time,
       sharable_mem,
       persistent_mem,
       runtime_mem,
       cpu_time,
       elapsed_time,
       address,
       hash_value
from
(select sql_text ,
        b.username ,
 round((a.disk_reads/decode(a.executions,0,1,
 a.executions)),2)
       disk_reads_per_exec,
       a.disk_reads ,
       a.buffer_gets ,
       a.parse_calls ,
       a.sorts ,
       a.executions ,
       a.rows_processed ,
       100 - round(100 *
       a.disk_reads/greatest(a.buffer_gets,1),2) hit_ratio,
       a.first_load_time ,
       sharable_mem ,
       persistent_mem ,
       runtime_mem,
       cpu_time,
       elapsed_time,
       address,
       hash_value
from
   sys.v_$sqlarea a,
```

```
   sys.all_users b
where
   a.parsing_user_id=b.user_id and
   b.username not in ('sys','system')
order by 3 desc)
where rownum < 21
```

The code above will pull the top twenty SQL statements as ranked by disk reads per execution. The *rownum* filter at the end can be changed to show more or all SQL that has executed in a database. *where* predicates can be added that only show the SQL for one or more of the previously identified top sessions.

In Oracle 9i, the *cpu_time* and *elapsed_time* columns were added. This provided more data that could be used to determine the overall efficiency of an SQL statement. Figure 16.12 shows a sample output of this query:

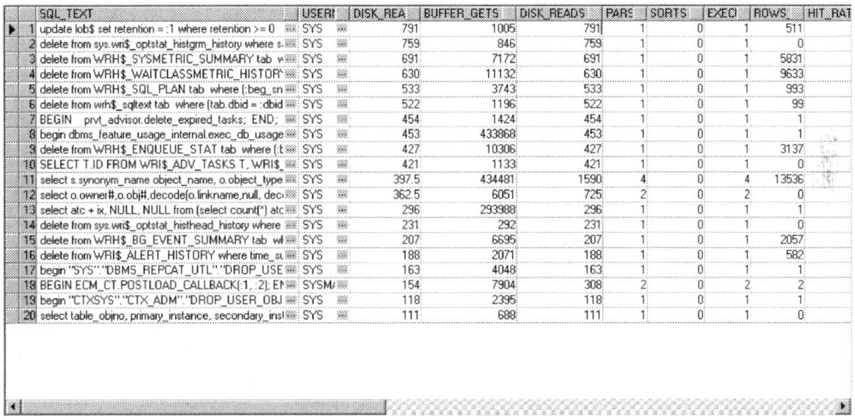

	SQL_TEXT	USER	DISK_REA	BUFFER_GETS	DISK_READS	PARS	SORTS	EXEC	ROWS	HIT_RAT
1	update lob$ set retention = :1 where retention >= 0	SYS	791	1005	791	1	0	1	511	
2	delete from sys.wri$_optstat_histgrm_history where s.	SYS	759	846	759	1	0	1	0	
3	delete from WRH$_SYSMETRIC_SUMMARY tab w	SYS	691	7172	691	1	0	1	5831	
4	delete from WRH$_WAITCLASSMETRIC_HISTOR	SYS	630	11132	630	1	0	1	9633	
5	delete from WRH$_SQL_PLAN tab where (:beg_sn	SYS	533	3743	533	1	0	1	993	
6	delete from wrh$_sqltext tab where (tab.dbid = :dbid	SYS	522	1196	522	1	0	1	99	
7	BEGIN prvt_advisor.delete_expired_tasks; END;	SYS	454	1424	454	1	0	1	1	
8	begin dbms_feature_usage_internal.exec_db_usage	SYS	453	433868	453	1	0	1	1	
9	delete from WRH$_ENQUEUE_STAT tab where (:t	SYS	427	10306	427	1	0	1	3137	
10	SELECT T.ID FROM WRI$_ADV_TASKS T, WRI$_	SYS	421	1133	421	1	0	1	0	
11	select s.synonym_name object_name, o.object_type	SYS	397.5	434481	1590	4	0	4	13536	
12	select o.owner#,o.obj#,decode(o.linkname,null, dec	SYS	362.5	6051	725	2	0	2	0	
13	select atc + ix, NULL, NULL from (select count(*) atc	SYS	296	293988	296	1	0	1	1	
14	delete from sys.wri$_optstat_histhead_history where	SYS	231	292	231	1	0	1	0	
15	delete from WRH$_BG_EVENT_SUMMARY tab wh	SYS	207	6695	207	1	0	1	2057	
16	delete from WRI$_ALERT_HISTORY where time_su	SYS	188	2071	188	1	0	1	582	
17	begin "SYS"."DBMS_REPCAT_UTL"."DROP_USE	SYS	163	4048	163	1	0	1	1	
18	BEGIN ECM_CT.POSTLOAD_CALLBACK(:1, :2); EN	SYSM	154	7904	308	2	0	2	2	
19	begin "CTXSYS"."CTX_ADM"."DROP_USER_OBJ	SYS	118	2395	118	1	0	1	1	
20	select table_objno, primary_instance, secondary_ins	SYS	111	688	111	1	0	1	0	

Figure 16.12: *The Sample high_resource_sql.sql Query Output*

The *v$sql_plan* view can also help identify problem SQL. For example, someone may want to know how many total SQL statements are causing Cartesian joins on a system. The following query can answer that question:

cartesian_sum.sql

```
select
   count(distinct hash_value) carteisan_statements,
   count(*)                   total_cartesian_joins
from
   sys.v_$sql_plan
where
```

```
    options = 'CARTESIAN'
and
    operation like '%JOIN%'
```

Output from this query will resemble the following, noting that it is possible for a single SQL statement to contain more than one Cartesian join:

```
CARTESIAN_STATEMENTS    TOTAL_CARTESIAN_JOINS
--------------------    ---------------------
                   3                        3
```

It is then possible to view the actual SQL statements containing the Cartesian joins, along with their performance metrics, by using a query like the following:

🖫 sql_cartesian.sql

```
select *
from
    sys.v_$sql
where
    hash_value in
        (select hash_value
         from
             sys.v_$sql_plan
         where
             options = 'CARTESIAN'
             and
             operation LIKE '%JOIN%' )
order by hash_value;
```

Another area of interest for DBAs is table scan activity. Most do not worry about small-table scans because Oracle can many times access small tables more efficiency through a full scan than through index access. Large table scans are another matter. Most DBAs prefer to avoid those where possible through smart index placement or intelligent partitioning.

Using the *v$sql_plan* view, it is possible to quickly identify any SQL statement that contains one or more large table scans. The following query indicates any SQL statement containing a large table scan, which is defined as a table over one MB. This query also provides a count of large scans, the total number of times the statement has been executed, and the sum total of all scans it has caused on the system:

🖫 large_scan_count.sql

```
select
    sql_text,
    total_large_scans,
        executions,
        executions * total_large_scans sum_large_scans
from
(select
        sql_text,
        count(*) total_large_scans,
        executions
```

```
from
      sys.v_$sql_plan a,
      sys.dba_segments b,
      sys.v_$sql c
where
      a.object_owner (+) = b.owner
   and
      a.object_name (+) = b.segment_name
   and
      b.segment_type IN ('TABLE', 'TABLE PARTITION')
   and
      a.operation LIKE '%TABLE%'
   and
      a.options = 'FULL'
   and
      c.hash_value = a.hash_value
   and
      b.bytes / 1024 > 1024
   group by
      sql_text, executions)
order by
  4 desc;
```

This query produces output like that shown in Figure 16.13. Should we worry more about a SQL statement that causes only one large table scan but has been executed 1000 times? Or should we be more concerned with a SQL statement that has ten large scans but has only been executed a handful of times?

	SQL_TEXT	TOTAL_L	EXECUTIONS	SUM_LARGE_SCANS
1	select name,type#,obj#,remoteowner,linkname,namespace, subname from obj$ v	1	71	71
2	select o.name,o.type#,o.obj#,o.remoteowner,o.linkname,o.namespace, o.subnan	1	16	16
3	select object_name, object_type from sys.user_objects o where o.object_type in	2	3	6
4	select s.synonym_name object_name, o.object_type from sys.all_synonyms s,	1	4	4
5	select name, type#, obj#, remoteowner, linkname, namespace, subname from ob	1	3	3
6	select object_name, object_type from sys.user_objects o where o.object_type in	2	1	2
7	SELECT NUM#,BOX_OR_TAB#,#PTYPE#,#SUBPTYPE#,#PCNT#,#SUBPCNT	2	1	2
8	SELECT /*+ full(o) */ U.NAME, COUNT(DECODE(O.TYPE#, 7,1, 8,1, 9,1, 11,1,	1	1	1
9	delete from WRH$_SQL_PLAN tab where (:beg_snap <= tab.snap_id and	1	1	1
10	delete from WRH$_BG_EVENT_SUMMARY tab where (:beg_snap <= tab.snap	1	1	1
11	select name,type#,obj#,remoteowner,linkname,namespace, subname from obj$ v	1	1	1
12	select name, type#, obj#, remoteowner, linkname, namespace, subname from ob	1	1	1
13	select name, type#, obj#, remoteowner, linkname, namespace, subname from ob	1	1	1
14	delete from wrh$_sqltext tab where (tab.dbid = :dbid and :beg_snap <= tab.	1	1	1
15	select grantor#,ta.obj#,o.type# from objauth$ ta, obj$ o where grantee#=:1 and t	1	1	1
16	select name, type#, obj#, remoteowner, linkname, namespace, subname from ob	1	1	1
17	select name, type#, obj#, remoteowner, linkname, namespace, subname from ob	1	1	1
18	delete from WRH$_WAITCLASSMETRIC_HISTORY tab where (:beg_snap <= t	1	1	1
19	delete from WRH$_SYSMETRIC_SUMMARY tab where (:beg_snap <= tab.snap	1	1	1
20	delete from WRH$_ENQUEUE_STAT tab where (:beg_snap <= tab.snap_id and	1	1	1
21	delete from WRH$_ALERT_HISTORY where time_suggested < :1	1	1	1
22	select max(bytes) from dba_segments	1	1	1

Figure 16.13: *The Sample large_scan_count.sql Query Output*

Each DBA will likely have an opinion on this, but regardless, it is apparent how such a query can assist in identifying SQL statements that have the potential to cause system slowdowns.

Now that a way to find suboptimal SQL execution has been introduced, it would be useful to have a way to change the SQL execution plans with special optimizer directives called hints. After the tuning hints have been introduced, it is easy to appreciate how SQL Profiles improve the SQL tuning process.

AWR and SQL Tuning

Just as the *v$sql_plan* view revolutionized Oracle 9i tuning, the Oracle AWR tables revolutionized SQL tuning. Most Oracle experts note that SQL optimization is one of the most important factors in database tuning, yet the transient nature of SQL execution has made it difficult to see the impact of SQL execution over time.

The AWR tables contain useful information about the time-series execution plans for SQL statements, and this repository can be used to display details about the frequency of usage for tables and indexes.

The following basic relationships between database objects and SQL statements are important, as shown in Figure 16.14:

Each SQL statement may generate many access plans: from the information on dynamic sampling and *dbms_stats*, the execution plans for SQL statements will change over time to accommodate changes in the data they access. It is important to understand how and when a frequently executed SQL statement changes its access plan.

Each object is accessed by many access plans: in most OLTP systems, tables and indexes show repeating patterns of usage. Clear patterns can be detected when averaging object access of day-of-the-week and hour-of-the-day.

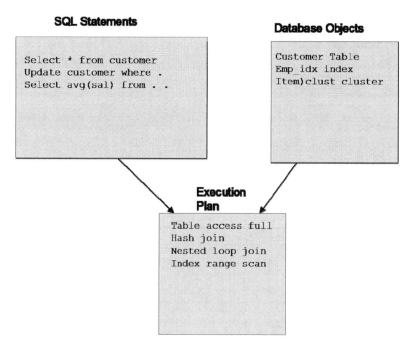

Figure 16.14: *Time-series Relationships Between SQL and Database Objects*

Figure 16.15 shows that there is a many-to-many relationship between any given SQL statement and the tables they access. Once this fundamental relationship is clear, the AWR tables can be used to perform time-based SQL tuning. The following AWR tables are for SQL tuning as shown in Figure 16.15:

- *dba_hist_sqlstat*

- *dba_hist_sql_summary*

- *dba_hist_sql_workarea*

- *dba_hist_sql_plan*

- *dba_hist_sql_workarea_histogram*

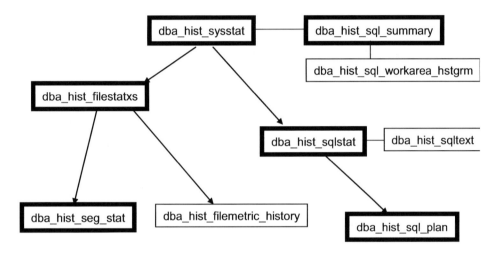

Figure 16.15: *The dba_hist views for SQL Tuning*

These simple tables represent a revolution in Oracle SQL tuning, and time-series techniques can be employed to optimize SQL with better results than ever before. The following section provides a closer look at these AWR tables and the amazing details that they can provide about SQL execution over time.

The *dba_hist_sqlstat* Table

This view is very similar to the *v$sql* view, but it contains important SQL metrics for each snapshot. These include important change information on disk reads and buffer gets, as well as time-series delta information on application, I/O and concurrency wait times.

💾 **awr_sqlstat_deltas.sql**

```
col c1 heading 'Begin|Interval|time'    format a8
col c2 heading 'SQL|ID'                 format a13
col c3 heading 'Exec|Delta'             format 9,999
```

```
col c4  heading 'Buffer|Gets|Delta'         format 9,999
col c5  heading 'Disk|Reads|Delta'          format 9,999
col c6  heading 'IO Wait|Delta'             format 9,999
col c7  heading 'Application|Wait|Delta'    format 9,999
col c8  heading 'Concurrency|Wait|Delta'    format 9,999


break on c1

select
  to_char(s.begin_interval_time,'mm-dd hh24')  c1,
  sql.sql_id                c2,
  sql.executions_delta      c3,
  sql.buffer_gets_delta     c4,
  sql.disk_reads_delta      c5,
  sql.iowait_delta          c6,
  sql.apwait_delta          c7,
  sql.ccwait_delta          c8
from
  dba_hist_sqlstat          sql,
  dba_hist_snapshot         s
where
  s.snap_id = sql.snap_id
order by
  c1,
  c2;
```

The following is a sample of the output. This allows visualization of the changes in SQL execution over time. For each snapshot period, it is possible to see the change in the number of times that the SQL was executed as well as important performance information about the performance of the statement.

Begin Interval time	SQL ID	Exec Delta	Buffer Gets Delta	Disk Reads Delta	IO Wait Delta	Application Wait Delta	Concurrency Wait Delta
10-10 16	0sfgqjz5cs52w	24	72	12	0	3	0
	1784a4705pt01	1	685	6	0	17	0
	19rkm1wsf9axx	10	61	4	0	0	0
	1d5d88cnwxcw4	52	193	4	6	0	0
	1fvsn5j51ugz3	4	0	0	0	0	0
	1uym1vta995yb	1	102	0	0	0	0
	23yu0nncnp8m9	24	72	0	0	6	0
	298ppdduqr7wm	1	3	0	0	0	0
	2cpffmjm98pcm	4	12	0	0	0	0
	2prbzh4qfms7u	1	4,956	19	1	34	5
10-10 17	0sfgqjz5cs52w	30	90	1	0	0	0
	19rkm1wsf9axx	14	88	0	0	0	0
	1fvsn5j51ugz3	4	0	0	0	0	0
	1zcdwkknwdpgh	4	4	0	0	0	0
	23yu0nncnp8m9	30	91	0	0	0	5
	298ppdduqr7wm	1	3	0	0	0	0
	2cpffmjm98pcm	4	12	0	0	0	0
	2prbzh4qfms7u	1	4,940	20	0	0	0
	2ysccdanw72pv	30	60	0	0	0	0
	3505vtqmvvf40	2	321	5	1	0	0

This report is especially useful because it is possible to track the logical I/O (buffer gets) versus physical I/O for each statement overtime, thereby yielding important information about the behavior of the SQL statement. This output gives a quick overview of the top SQL during any AWR snapshot period, and shows how their behavior has changed since the last snapshot period. Detecting changes in the behavior of commonly executed SQL statements is the key to time-series SQL tuning.

A *where* clause can easily be added to the above script and the I/O changes plotted overtime:

💾 **awr_sqlstat_deltas_detail.sql**

```
col c1  heading 'Begin|Interval|time'    format a8
col c2  heading 'Exec|Delta'             format 999,999
col c3  heading 'Buffer|Gets|Delta'      format 999,999
col c4  heading 'Disk|Reads|Delta'       format 9,999
col c5  heading 'IO Wait|Delta'          format 9,999
col c6  heading 'App|Wait|Delta'         format 9,999
col c7  heading 'Cncr|Wait|Delta'        format 9,999
col c8  heading 'CPU|Time|Delta'         format 999,999
col c9  heading 'Elpsd|Time|Delta'       format 999,999

accept sqlid prompt 'Enter SQL ID: '

ttitle 'time series execution for|&sqlid'

break on c1

select
  to_char(s.begin_interval_time,'mm-dd hh24')  c1,
  sql.executions_delta      c2,
  sql.buffer_gets_delta     c3,
  sql.disk_reads_delta      c4,
  sql.iowait_delta          c5,
  sql.apwait_delta          c6,
  sql.ccwait_delta          c7,
  sql.cpu_time_delta        c8,
  sql.elapsed_time_delta    c9
from
  dba_hist_sqlstat          sql,
  dba_hist_snapshot           s
where
  s.snap_id = sql.snap_id
and
  sql_id = '&sqlid'
order by
  c1;
```

The following output shows changes to the execution of a frequently used SQL statement and how its behavior changes overtime:

Begin Interval time	Exec Delta	Buffer Gets Delta	Disk Reads Delta	IO Wait Delta	App Wait Delta	Cncr Wait Delta	CPU Time Delta	Elpsd Time Delta
--------	--------	--------	------	-------	------	------	--------	--------

10-14 10	709	2,127	0	0	0	0	398,899	423,014
10-14 11	696	2,088	0	0	0	0	374,502	437,614
10-14 12	710	2,130	0	0	0	0	384,579	385,388
10-14 13	693	2,079	0	0	0	0	363,648	378,252
10-14 14	708	2,124	0	0	0	0	373,902	373,902
10-14 15	697	2,091	0	0	0	0	388,047	410,605
10-14 16	707	2,121	0	0	0	0	386,542	491,830
10-14 17	698	2,094	0	0	0	0	378,087	587,544
10-14 18	708	2,124	0	0	0	0	376,491	385,816
10-14 19	695	2,085	0	0	0	0	361,850	361,850
10-14 20	708	2,124	0	0	0	0	368,889	368,889
10-14 21	696	2,088	0	0	0	0	363,111	412,521
10-14 22	709	2,127	0	0	0	0	369,015	369,015
10-14 23	695	2,085	0	0	0	0	362,480	362,480
10-15 00	709	2,127	0	0	0	0	368,554	368,554
10-15 01	697	2,091	0	0	0	0	362,987	362,987
10-15 02	696	2,088	0	0	0	2	361,445	380,944
10-15 03	708	2,124	0	0	0	0	367,292	367,292
10-15 04	697	2,091	0	0	0	0	362,279	362,279
10-15 05	708	2,124	0	0	0	0	367,697	367,697
10-15 06	696	2,088	0	0	0	0	361,423	361,423
10-15 07	709	2,127	0	0	0	0	374,766	577,559
10-15 08	697	2,091	0	0	0	0	364,879	410,328

In the listing above, it is possible to see how the number of executions varies overtime.

The above example shows the average elapsed time for the SQL statement over time. Of course, the execution speed may change due to a number of factors:

- Different bind variables
- Database resource shortage
- High physical reads from data buffer shortage

With this information, it is possible to drill down into those specific times when SQL statements performed badly and see exactly why its execution time was slow.

The above script can be changed slightly in order to examine logical I/O (consistent gets) versus physical I/O (disk reads) averages for any given SQL statement.

The ratio of logical to physical reads changes depending on the day of the week. If execution speed for this SQL query is critical, the DBA would want to examine those times when it has high physical disk reads and consider segregating the tables that participate in this query into the KEEP pool.

💾 **sqlstathist.sql**

```
set echo off feed off lines 100 pages 9999
clear col
clear break

col beginttm      head 'Begin|Interval' format a14
col sqlid         head 'SQL|ID' format a13
col execsdlt      head 'Delta|Execs' format 99990
col bufgetwaitdlt head 'Delta|Buffer|Gets' format 9999990
col dskrdwaitdlt  head 'Delta|Disk|Reads' format 999990
```

```
col iowaitdlt        head 'Delta|IO Wait' format 9999990
col appwaitdlt       head 'Delta|Wait|App' format 9999990
col concurwaitdlt    head 'Delta|Wait|Concur' format 99990
break on beginttm skip 1


spool sqlstathist.lis


set echo off feed off lines 100 pages 9999
clear col
clear break

col beginttm         head 'Begin|Interval' format a14
col sqlid            head 'SQL|ID' format a13
col execsdlt         head 'Delta|Execs' format 99990
col bufgetwaitdlt    head 'Delta|Buffer|Gets' format 9999990
col dskrdwaitdlt     head 'Delta|Disk|Reads' format 999990
col iowaitdlt        head 'Delta|IO Wait' format 9999990
col appwaitdlt       head 'Delta|Wait|App' format 9999990
col concurwaitdlt    head 'Delta|Wait|Concur' format 99990
break on beginttm skip 1

spool sqlstathist.lis


select
   to_char(begin_interval_time,'mm-dd hh24:mi:ss') beginttm,
   sql_id sqlid,
   executions_delta execsdlt,
   buffer_gets_delta bufgetwaitdlt,
   disk_reads_delta dskrdwaitdlt,
   iowait_delta iowaitdlt,
   apwait_delta appwaitdlt,
   ccwait_delta concurwaitdlt
from
   dba_hist_snapshot sn,
   dba_hist_sqlstat ss
where
   ss.snap_id = sn.snap_id and
   begin_interval_time > (sysdate - 4/24)
order by
   beginttm,
   ( executions_delta + buffer_gets_delta +
     disk_reads_delta + iowait_delta +
     apwait_delta + ccwait_delta ) desc
/


spool off
clear break
clear col
```

The following section provides a look at another exciting new table, the *dba_hist_sql_plan* table, which stores time-series execution details.

The *dba_hist_sql_plan* Table

The *dba_hist_sql_plan* table contains time-series data about each object, table, index, or view involved in the query. The important columns include the cost, cardinality, *cpu_cost*, *io_cost* and *temp_space* required for the object.

The sample query below retrieves SQL statements that have high query execution cost identified by the Oracle optimizer.

🖫 awr_high_cost_sql.sql

```
col c1 heading 'SQL|ID'            format a13
col c2 heading 'Cost'              format 9,999,999
col c3 heading 'SQL Text'          format a200


select
  p.sql_id            c1,
  p.cost              c2,
  to_char(s.sql_text) c3
from
  dba_hist_sql_plan    p,
  dba_hist_sqltext     s
where
    p.id = 0
  and
    p.sql_id = s.sql_id
  and
    p.cost is not null
order by
  p.cost desc
;
```

The output of the above query might look like this, showing the high cost SQL statements over time:

```
SQL
ID                  Cost SQL Text
------------- ---------- --------------------------------------------------
847ahztscj4xw    358,456 select
                           s.begin_interval_time    c1,
                           pl.sql_id                c2,
                           pl.object_name           c3,
                           pl.search_columns        c4,
                           pl.cardinality        c5,
                           pl.access_predicates     c6,
                           pl.filter_predicates     c7
                         from
                           dba_hist_sql_plan pl,
                           dba_hist_snapshot s
                         order by
                           c1, c2
```

```
58du2p8phcznu          5,110 select
                             begin_interval_time   c1,
                             search_columns        c2,
                             count(*)              c3
                       from
                          dba_hist_sqltext
                       natural join
                          dba_hist_snapshot
                       natural join
                          dba_hist_sql_plan
                       where
                          lower(sql_text) like lower('%idx%')
                       group by
                          begin_interval_time,search_columns
```

There is much more information in *dba_hist_sql_plan* that is useful. The query below will extract important costing information for all objects involved in each query. SYS objects are not counted.

🖫 awr_sql_object_char.sql

```
col c1 heading 'Owner'              format a13
col c2 heading 'Object|Type'        format a15

col c3 heading 'Object|Name'        format a25
col c4 heading 'Average|CPU|Cost'   format 9,999,999
col c5 heading 'Average|IO|Cost'    format 9,999,999


break on c1 skip 2
break on c2 skip 2


select
  p.object_owner    c1,
  p.object_type     c2,
  p.object_name     c3,
  avg(p.cpu_cost)   c4,
  avg(p.io_cost)    c5
from
  dba_hist_sql_plan p
where
        p.object_name is not null
    and
        p.object_owner <> 'SYS'
group by
  p.object_owner,
  p.object_type,
  p.object_name
order by
  1,2,4 desc;
```

The following is a sample of the output. The results show the average CPU and I/O costs for all objects that participate in queries over time periods.

	Object	Object	Average CPU	Average IO
Owner	Type	Name	Cost	Cost

OLAPSYS	INDEX	CWM$CUBEDIMENSIONUSE_IDX	200	0
OLAPSYS	INDEX (UNIQUE)	CWM$DIMENSION_PK		
OLAPSYS		CWM$CUBE_PK	7,321	0
OLAPSYS		CWM$MODEL_PK	7,321	0
OLAPSYS	TABLE	CWM$CUBE	7,911	0
OLAPSYS		CWM$MODEL	7,321	0
OLAPSYS		CWM2$CUBE	7,121	2
OLAPSYS		CWM$CUBEDIMENSIONUSE	730	0
MYSCHEMA		CUSTOMER_DETS_PK	21,564	2
MYSCHEMA		STATS$SGASTAT_U	21,442	2
MYSCHEMA		STATS$SQL_SUMMARY_PK	16,842	2
MYSCHEMA		STATS$SQLTEXT_PK	14,442	1
MYSCHEMA		STATS$IDLE_EVENT_PK	8,171	0
SPV	INDEX (UNIQUE)	WSPV_REP_PK	7,321	0
SPV		SPV_ALERT_DEF_PK	7,321	0
SPV	TABLE	WSPV_REPORTS	789,052	28
SPV		SPV_MONITOR	54,092	3
SPV		SPV_SAVED_CHARTS	38,337	3
SPV		SPV_DB_LIST	37,487	3
SPV		SPV_SCHED	35,607	3
SPV		SPV_FV_STAT	35,607	3

This script can now be changed to allow the user to enter a table name and see changes in access details over time:

💾 awr_sql_object_char_detail.sql

```
accept tabname prompt 'Enter Table Name:'

col c0 heading 'Begin|Interval|time'  format a8
col c1 heading 'Owner'                format a10
col c2 heading 'Object|Type'          format a10
col c3 heading 'Object|Name'          format a15
col c4 heading 'Average|CPU|Cost'     format 9,999,999
col c5 heading 'Average|IO|Cost'      format 9,999,999


break on c1 skip 2
break on c2 skip 2

select
   to_char(sn.begin_interval_time,'mm-dd hh24')  c0,
   p.object_owner                                c1,
   p.object_type                                 c2,
   p.object_name                                 c3,
   avg(p.cpu_cost)                               c4,
```

```
  avg(p.io_cost)                              c5
from
  dba_hist_sql_plan p,
  dba_hist_sqlstat  st,
  dba_hist_snapshot sn
where
  p.object_name is not null
and
   p.object_owner <> 'SYS'
and
   p.object_name = 'CUSTOMER_DETS'
and
  p.sql_id = st.sql_id
and
  st.snap_id = sn.snap_id
group by
  to_char(sn.begin_interval_time,'mm-dd hh24'),
  p.object_owner,
  p.object_type,
  p.object_name
order by
  1,2,3 desc;
```

This script is great because it is possible to see changes to the table's access patterns over time, which is a very useful feature:

Begin Interval time	Owner	Object Type	Object Name	Average CPU Cost	Average IO Cost
10-25 17	MYSCHEMA	TABLE	CUSTOMER_DETS	28,935	3
10-26 15	MYSCHEMA		CUSTOMER_DETS	28,935	3
10-27 18	MYSCHEMA		CUSTOMER_DETS	5,571,375	24
10-28 12	MYSCHEMA		CUSTOMER_DETS	28,935	3

Now that the DBA has access to the important table structures, it is appropriate to examine how spectacular reports can be retrieved from the AWR data to reveal hidden bottlenecks. This data can show exactly how the database is performing.

Viewing Table and Index Access with AWR

One of the problems in Oracle 9i was the single bit-flag that was used to monitor index usage. The flag was set with the *alter index xxx monitoring usage* command, and DBAs could see if the index was accessed by querying the *v$object_usage* view.

The goal of any index access is to use the most selective index for a query. This would be the one that produces the smallest number of rows. The Oracle data dictionary is usually quite good at this, but it is up to the DBA to define the index. Missing function-based indexes are a common source of suboptimal SQL execution because Oracle will not use an indexed column unless the *where* clause matches the index column exactly.

Tracking SQL Nested Loop Joins

As a review, nested loop joins are the most common method for Oracle to match rows in multiple tables. Nested loop joins always invoke an index and they are never parallelized. The following *awr_nested_join_alert.sql* script is used to count nested loop joins per hour:

Transient SQL will not be collected!

These scripts will only track SQL that Oracle has been directed to capture via the SQL collection settings in AWR or STATSPACK. It will not collect transient SQL that did not appear in *v$sql* at snapshot time and not all SQL will appear in these reports.

🖫 awr_nested_join_alert.sql

```
col c1 heading 'Date'               format a20
col c2 heading 'Nested|Loops|Count' format 99,999,999
col c3 heading 'Rows|Processed'     format 99,999,999
col c4 heading 'Disk|Reads'         format 99,999,999
col c5 heading 'CPU|Time'           format 99,999,999


accept nested_thr char prompt 'Enter Nested Join Threshold: '

ttitle 'Nested Join Threshold|&nested_thr'

select
   to_char(sn.begin_interval_time,'yy-mm-dd hh24')  c1,
   count(*)                                          c2,
   sum(st.rows_processed_delta)                      c3,
   sum(st.disk_reads_delta)                          c4,
   sum(st.cpu_time_delta)                            c5
from
   dba_hist_snapshot sn,
   dba_hist_sql_plan  p,
   dba_hist_sqlstat   st
where
   st.sql_id = p.sql_id
and
   sn.snap_id = st.snap_id
and
   p.operation = 'NESTED LOOPS'
having
   count(*) > &hash_thr
group by
   begin_interval_time;
```

The output below shows the number of total nested loop joins during the snapshot period along with a count of the rows processed and the associated disk I/O. This report is useful where the DBA wants to know if increasing *pga_aggregate_target* will improve performance.

Nested Loop Join Thresholds

| | Nested | | | |
| | Loops | Rows | Disk | CPU |
Date	Count	Processed	Reads	Time
04-10-10 16	22	750	796	4,017,301
04-10-10 17	25	846	6	3,903,560
04-10-10 19	26	751	1,430	4,165,270
04-10-10 20	24	920	3	3,940,002
04-10-10 21	25	782	5	3,816,152
04-10-11 02	26	905	0	3,935,547
04-10-11 03	22	1,001	0	3,918,891
04-10-11 04	29	757	8	3,939,071
04-10-11 05	28	757	745	4,395,197
04-10-11 06	24	839	4	4,010,775

In the report above, nested loops are favored by SQL that returns a small number of *rows_processed* than hash joins, which tend to return largest result sets.

The following *awr_sql_index.sql* script exposes the cumulative usage of database indexes:

🖫 awr_sql_index.sql

```
col c0 heading 'Begin|Interval|time'  format a8
col c1 heading 'Index|Name'           format a20
col c2 heading 'Disk|Reads'           format 99,999,999
col c3 heading 'Rows|Processed'       format 99,999,999
select
  to_char(s.begin_interval_time,'mm-dd hh24')  c0,
  p.object_name                 c1,
  sum(t.disk_reads_total)       c2,
  sum(t.rows_processed_total) c3
from
      dba_hist_sql_plan p,
      dba_hist_sqlstat  t,
      dba_hist_snapshot s
where
      p.sql_id = t.sql_id
   and
      t.snap_id = s.snap_id
   and
      p.object_type like '%INDEX%'
group by
      to_char(s.begin_interval_time,'mm-dd hh24'),
      p.object_name
order by
      c0,c1,c2 desc;
```

The following is a sample of the output where the stress on every important index is shown over time. This information is important for placing index blocks into the KEEP pool to reduce disk reads and for determining the optimal setting for the important *optimizer_index_caching* parameter.

Begin

AWR and SQL Tuning   **849**

```
Interval  Index                        Disk          Rows
time      Name                        Reads     Processed
--------  --------------------   -----------   -----------
10-14 12  I_CACHE_STATS_1                              114
10-14 12  I_COL_USAGE$                 201          8,984
10-14 12  I_FILE1                        2              0
10-14 12  I_IND1                        93            604
10-14 12  I_JOB_NEXT                     1        247,816
10-14 11  I_KOPM1                        4          2,935
10-14 11  I_MON_MODS$_OBJ               12         28,498
10-14 11  I_OBJ1                    72,852            604
10-14 11  I_PARTOBJ$                    93            604
10-14 11  I_SCHEDULER_JOB2               4              0
10-14 11  SYS_C002433                  302          4,629
10-14 11  SYS_IOT_TOP_8540               0         75,544
10-14 11  SYS_IOT_TOP_8542               1          4,629
10-14 11  WRH$_DATAFILE_PK               2              0
10-14 10  WRH$_SEG_STAT_OBJ_PK          93            604
10-14 10  WRH$_TEMPFILE_PK                              0
10-14 10  WRI$_ADV_ACTIONS_PK           38          1,760
```

The above report shows the highest impact tables.

The following *awr_sql_index_access.sql* script will summarize index access by snapshot period.

💾 awr_sql_index_access.sql

```
col c1 heading 'Begin|Interval|Time'   format a20
col c2 heading 'Index|Range|Scans' format 999,999
col c3 heading 'Index|Unique|Scans' format 999,999
col c4 heading 'Index|Full|Scans' format 999,999

select
  r.c1   c1,
  r.c2   c2,
  u.c2   c3,
  f.c2   c4
from
(
select
  to_char(sn.begin_interval_time,'yy-mm-dd hh24')   c1,
  count(1)                                c2
from
   dba_hist_sql_plan p,
   dba_hist_sqlstat  s,
   dba_hist_snapshot sn
where
  p.object_owner <> 'SYS'
and
  p.operation like '%INDEX%'
and
  p.options like '%RANGE%'
and
  p.sql_id = s.sql_id
and
  s.snap_id = sn.snap_id
group by
  to_char(sn.begin_interval_time,'yy-mm-dd hh24')
```

```
order by
1 ) r,
(
select
   to_char(sn.begin_interval_time,'yy-mm-dd hh24')   c1,
   count(1)                               c2
from
   dba_hist_sql_plan p,
   dba_hist_sqlstat   s,
   dba_hist_snapshot sn
where
   p.object_owner <> 'SYS'
and
   p.operation like '%INDEX%'
and
   p.options like '%UNIQUE%'
and
   p.sql_id = s.sql_id
and
   s.snap_id = sn.snap_id
group by
   to_char(sn.begin_interval_time,'yy-mm-dd hh24')
order by
1 ) u,
(
select
   to_char(sn.begin_interval_time,'yy-mm-dd hh24')   c1,
   count(1)                               c2
from
   dba_hist_sql_plan p,
   dba_hist_sqlstat   s,
   dba_hist_snapshot sn
where
   p.object_owner <> 'SYS'
and
   p.operation like '%INDEX%'
and
   p.options like '%FULL%'
and
   p.sql_id = s.sql_id
and
   s.snap_id = sn.snap_id
group by
   to_char(sn.begin_interval_time,'yy-mm-dd hh24')
order by
1 ) f
where
      r.c1 = u.c1
   and
      r.c1 = f.c1;
```

The sample output below shows those specific times when the database performs unique scans, index range scans and index fast full scans:

Begin Interval Time	Index Range Scans	Index Unique Scans	Index Full Scans
04-10-21 15	36	35	2
04-10-21 19	10	8	2
04-10-21 20		8	2

04-10-21 21		8	2
04-10-21 22	11	8	3
04-10-21 23	16	11	3
04-10-22 00	10	9	1
04-10-22 01	11	8	3
04-10-22 02	12	8	1
04-10-22 03	10	8	3
04-10-22 04	11	8	2
04-10-22 05		8	3
04-10-22 06		8	2
04-10-22 07	10	8	3
04-10-22 08		8	2
04-10-22 09		8	2

SQL object usage can also be summarized by day-of-the-week:

🖫 awr_sql_object_avg_dy.sql

```
col c1 heading 'Object|Name'        format a30
col c2 heading 'Week Day'           format a15
col c3 heading 'Invocation|Count'   format 99,999,999

break on c1 skip 2
break on c2 skip 2

select

decode(c2,1,'Monday',2,'Tuesday',3,'Wednesday',4,'Thursday',5,'Friday',6,'Saturday',7,'Sunda
y') c2,
   c1,
   c3
from
(
select
   p.object_name                    c1,
   to_char(sn.end_interval_time,'d') c2,
   count(1)                         c3
from
   dba_hist_sql_plan    p,
   dba_hist_sqlstat     s,
   dba_hist_snapshot    sn
where
   p.object_owner <> 'SYS'
and
   p.sql_id = s.sql_id
and
   s.snap_id = sn.snap_id
group by
   p.object_name,
   to_char(sn.end_interval_time,'d')
order by
   c2,c1
)
;
```

The output below shows the top objects within the database during each snapshot period.

Week Day	Object Name	Invocation Count

```
 --------------       ------------------------------------   -----------
Monday            CUSTOMER                                44
                  CUSTOMER_ORDERS                         44
                  CUSTOMER_ORDERS_PRIMARY                 44
                  MGMT_CURRENT_METRICS_PK                 43
                  MGMT_FAILOVER_TABLE                     47
                  MGMT_JOB                               235
                  MGMT_JOB_EMD_STATUS_QUEUE               91
                  MGMT_JOB_EXECUTION                     235
                  MGMT_JOB_EXEC_IDX01                    235
                  MGMT_JOB_EXEC_SUMMARY                   94
                  MGMT_JOB_EXEC_SUMM_IDX04                94
                  MGMT_JOB_PK                            235
                  MGMT_METRICS                            65
                  MGMT_METRICS_1HOUR_PK                   43

Tuesday           CUSTOMER                                40
                  CUSTOMER    _CHECK                        2
                  CUSTOMER _PRIMARY                         1
                  CUSTOMER_ORDERS                         46
                  CUSTOMER_ORDERS_PRIMARY                 46
                  LOGMNR_LOG$                               3
                  LOGMNR_LOG$_PK                            3
                  LOGSTDBY$PARAMETERS                       2
                  MGMT_CURRENT_METRICS_PK                 31
                  MGMT_FAILOVER_TABLE                     42
                  MGMT_JOB                               200
                  MGMT_JOB_EMD_STATUS_QUEUE               78
                  MGMT_JOB_EXECUTION                     200
                  MGMT_JOB_EXEC_IDX01                    200
                  MGMT_JOB_EXEC_SUMMARY                   80
                  MGMT_JOB_EXEC_SUMM_IDX04                80
                  MGMT_JOB_PK                            200
                  MGMT_METRICS                            48

Wednesday         CURRENT_SEVERITY_PRIMARY_KEY             1
                  MGMT_CURRENT_METRICS_PK                 17
                  MGMT_CURRENT_SEVERITY                    1
                  MGMT_FAILOVER_TABLE                     24
                  MGMT_JOB                               120
                  MGMT_JOB_EMD_STATUS_QUEUE               46
                  MGMT_JOB_EXECUTION                     120
                  MGMT_JOB_EXEC_IDX01                    120
                  MGMT_JOB_EXEC_SUMMARY                   48
                  MGMT_JOB_EXEC_SUMM_IDX04                48
                  MGMT_JOB_PK                            120
                  MGMT_METRICS                            36
                  MGMT_METRICS_1HOUR_PK                   14
                  MGMT_METRICS_IDX_01                     24
                  MGMT_METRICS_IDX_03                      1
                  MGMT_METRICS_PK                         11
```

When these results are posted, the result is a well-defined signature that emerges for particular tables, access plans and SQL statements. Most Oracle databases are remarkably predictable, with the exception of DSS and ad-hoc query systems, and the DBA can quickly track the usage of all SQL components.

Understanding the SQL signature can be extremely useful for determining what objects to place in the KEEP pool, and determining the most active tables and indexes in the database. Once a particular SQL statement for which details are desired has been identified, it is possible to view its execution plan used by the optimizer to actually execute the statement. The query below retrieves an execution plan for a particular SQL statement of interest:

📁 **awr_sql_details.sql**

```
accept sqlid prompt 'Please enter SQL ID: '

col c1 heading 'Operation'          format a20
col c2 heading 'Options'            format a20
col c3 heading 'Object|Name'        format a25
col c4 heading 'Search Columns'     format 999,999
col c5 heading 'Cardinality'        format 999,999

select
   operation          c1,
   options            c2,
   object_name        c3,
   search_columns     c4,
   cardinality        c5
from
   dba_hist_sql_plan p
where
        p.sql_id = '&sqlid'
order by
   p.id;
```

This is one of the most important of all of the SQL tuning tools. The following is a sample of the output from this script:

Operation	Options	Name	Search Cols	Cardinality
SELECT STATEMENT			0	
VIEW			3	4
SORT	ORDER BY		4	4
VIEW			2	4
UNION-ALL			0	
FILTER			6	
NESTED LOOPS	OUTER		0	3
NESTED LOOPS	ANTI		0	3
TABLE ACCESS	BY INDEX ROWID	STATS$SYSTEM_EVENT	0	70
INDEX	RANGE SCAN	STATS$SYSTEM_EVENT_PK	3	70
INDEX	UNIQUE SCAN	STATS$IDLE_EVENT_PK	1	46
TABLE ACCESS	BY INDEX ROWID	STATS$SYSTEM_EVENT	0	1
INDEX	UNIQUE SCAN	STATS$SYSTEM_EVENT_PK	4	1
FILTER			0	
FAST DUAL			1	1

The following section will show how to count the frequency at which indexes are used within Oracle.

Tracking Full Scan Access with AWR

All of the specific SQL access methods can be counted and their behavior tracked over time. This is especially important for large-table full-table scans (LTFTS) because they are a common symptom of suboptimal execution plans, like missing indexes.

Once it has been determined that the LTFTS are legitimate, the DBA must know when they are executed so that a selective parallel query can be implemented, depending on the existing CPU consumption on the server. Oracle Parallel Query (OPQ) drives up CPU consumption and should be invoked specifically when the server can handle the additional load.

🖫 awr_full_table_scans.sql

```
ttitle 'Large Full-table scans|Per Snapshot Period'

col c1 heading 'Begin|Interval|time' format a20
col c4 heading 'FTS|Count'            format 999,999

break on c1 skip 2
break on c2 skip 2

select                  -
  to_char(sn.begin_interval_time,'yy-mm-dd hh24')  c1,
  count(1)                                          c4
from
  dba_hist_sql_plan    p,
  dba_hist_sqlstat     s,
  dba_hist_snapshot    sn,
  dba_segments         o
where
  p.object_owner <> 'SYS'
and
  p.object_owner = o.owner
and
  p.object_name = o.segment_name
and
  o.blocks > 1000
and
  p.operation like '%TABLE ACCESS%'
and
  p.options like '%FULL%'
and
  p.sql_id = s.sql_id
and
  s.snap_id = sn.snap_id
group by
  to_char(sn.begin_interval_time,'yy-mm-dd hh24')
order by
  1;
```

The output below shows the overall total counts for tables that experience large-table full-table scans.

```
Large Full-table scans
Per Snapshot Period

Begin
```

```
Interval                    FTS
time                        Count
-------------------------   --------
04-10-18 11                        4
04-10-21 17                        1
04-10-21 23                        2
04-10-22 15                        2
04-10-22 16                        2
04-10-22 23                        2
04-10-24 00                        2
04-10-25 00                        2
04-10-25 10                        2
04-10-25 17                        9
04-10-25 18                        1
04-10-25 21                        1
04-10-26 12                        1
04-10-26 13                        3
04-10-26 14                        3
04-10-26 15                       11
04-10-26 16                        4
04-10-26 17                        4
04-10-26 18                        3
04-10-26 23                        2
04-10-27 13                        2
04-10-27 14                        3
04-10-27 15                        4
04-10-27 16                        4
04-10-27 17                        3
04-10-27 18                       17
04-10-27 19                        1
04-10-28 12                       22
04-10-28 13                        2
04-10-29 13                        9
```

This data can be easily plotted to see the trend for a database as shown in Figure 16.16:

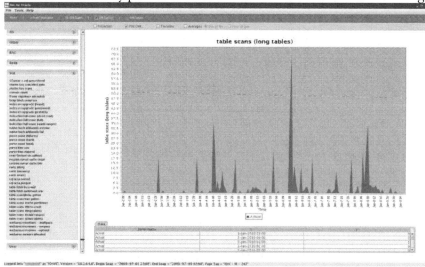

Figure 16.16: *Trends of Large-table Full-table Scans*

Search for Symptoms!

One of the most common manifestations of suboptimal SQL is a large-table full-table scan. Oracle may be forced to read every row in the table.

If the large-table full-table scans are legitimate, the DBA will want to know the periods in which they are invoked, so OPQ can be invoked to speed up the scans as shown in the *awr_sql_access_hr.sql* script that follows:

🖫 awr_sql_access_hr.sql

```
ttitle 'Large Table Full-table scans|Averages per Hour'

col c1 heading 'Day|Hour'               format a20
col c2 heading 'FTS|Count'              format 999,999

break on c1 skip 2
break on c2 skip 2

select
  to_char(sn.begin_interval_time,'hh24')  c1,
  count(1)                               c2
from
  dba_hist_sql_plan p,
  dba_hist_sqlstat  s,
  dba_hist_snapshot sn,
  dba_segments      o
where
  p.object_owner <> 'SYS'
and
  p.object_owner = o.owner
and
  p.object_name = o.segment_name
and
  o.blocks > 1000
and
  p.operation like '%TABLE ACCESS%'
and
  p.options like '%FULL%'
and
  p.sql_id = s.sql_id
and
  s.snap_id = sn.snap_id
group by
  to_char(sn.begin_interval_time,'hh24')
order by
  1;
```

The following output shows the average number of large-table full-table scans per hour.

```
Large Table Full-table scans
Averages per Hour

Day                          FTS
Hour                       Count
-------------------     --------
00                             4
10                             2
11                             4
12                            23
13                            16
14                             6
15                            17
16                            10
17                            17
18                            21
19                             1
23                             6
```

The script below shows the same data for day of the week:

💾 **awr_sql_access_day.sql**

```
ttitle 'Large Table Full-table scans|Averages per Week Day'

col c1 heading 'Week|Day'              format a20
col c2 heading 'FTS|Count'             format 999,999

break on c1 skip 2
break on c2 skip 2

select
  to_char(sn.begin_interval_time,'day')  c1,
  count(1)                          c2
from
   dba_hist_sql_plan p,
   dba_hist_sqlstat  s,
   dba_hist_snapshot sn,
   dba_segments      o
where
   p.object_owner <> 'SYS'
and
   p.object_owner = o.owner
and
   p.object_name = o.segment_name
and
   o.blocks > 1000
and
   p.operation like '%TABLE ACCESS%'
and
   p.options like '%FULL%'
and
   p.sql_id = s.sql_id
and
   s.snap_id = sn.snap_id
group by
  to_char(sn.begin_interval_time,'day')
order by
1;
```

The following sample query output shows specific times the database experienced large table scans.

```
Large Table Full-table scans
Averages per Week Day

Week                      FTS
Day                     Count
-------------------  --------
sunday                      2
monday                     19
tuesday                    31
wednesday                  34
thursday                   27
friday                     15
saturday                    2
```

The *awr_sql_scan_sums.sql* script below will show the access patterns of usage over time. If a DBA is really driven to know their system, all they need to understand is how SQL accesses the tables and indexes in the database to provide insight. The optimal instance configuration for large-table full-table scans is quite different than the configuration for an OLTP databases, and the report generated by the *awr_sql_scan_sums.sql* script will quickly identify changes in table access patterns.

🖫 awr_sql_scan_sums.sql

```
col c1   heading 'Begin|Interval|Time'            format a20
col c2   heading 'Large|Table|Full Table|Scans'   format 999,999
col c3   heading 'Small|Table|Full Table|Scans'   format 999,999
col c4   heading 'Total|Index|Scans'              format 999,999


select
  f.c1   c1,
  f.c2   c2,
  s.c2   c3,
  i.c2   c4
from
(
select
  to_char(sn.begin_interval_time,'yy-mm-dd hh24')  c1,
  count(1)                           c2
from
  dba_hist_sql_plan p,
  dba_hist_sqlstat  s,
  dba_hist_snapshot sn,
  dba_segments      o
where
  p.object_owner <> 'SYS'
and
  p.object_owner = o.owner
and
  p.object_name = o.segment_name
and
  o.blocks > 1000
and
  p.operation like '%TABLE ACCESS%'
and
  p.options like '%FULL%'
and
  p.sql_id = s.sql_id
```

```
and
   s.snap_id = sn.snap_id
group by
  to_char(sn.begin_interval_time,'yy-mm-dd hh24')
order by
1 ) f,
(
select
  to_char(sn.begin_interval_time,'yy-mm-dd hh24')   c1,
  count(1)                           c2
from
   dba_hist_sql_plan p,
   dba_hist_sqlstat  s,
   dba_hist_snapshot sn,
   dba_segments        o
where
   p.object_owner <> 'SYS'
and
   p.object_owner = o.owner
and
   p.object_name = o.segment_name
and
   o.blocks < 1000
and
   p.operation like '%INDEX%'
and
   p.sql_id = s.sql_id
and
   s.snap_id = sn.snap_id
group by
  to_char(sn.begin_interval_time,'yy-mm-dd hh24')
order by
1 ) s,
(
select
  to_char(sn.begin_interval_time,'yy-mm-dd hh24')   c1,
  count(1)                           c2
from
   dba_hist_sql_plan p,
   dba_hist_sqlstat  s,
   dba_hist_snapshot sn
where
   p.object_owner <> 'SYS'
and
   p.operation like '%INDEX%'
and
   p.sql_id = s.sql_id
and
   s.snap_id = sn.snap_id
group by
  to_char(sn.begin_interval_time,'yy-mm-dd hh24')
order by
1 ) i
where
     f.c1 = s.c1
  and
     f.c1 = i.c1
;
```

The sample output looks like the following where there is a comparison of index versus table scan access. This is a very important signature for any database because it shows, at a glance, the balance between index (OLTP) and data warehouse type access.

Begin Interval Time	Full	Large Table Table Scans	Full	Small Table Table Scans	Total Index Scans
04-10-22 15		2		19	21
04-10-22 16				1	1
04-10-25 10				18	20
04-10-25 17		9		15	17
04-10-25 18		1		19	22
04-10-25 21				19	24
04-10-26 12				23	28
04-10-26 13		3		17	19
04-10-26 14				18	19
04-10-26 15		11		4	7
04-10-26 16		4		18	18
04-10-26 17				17	19
04-10-26 18		3		17	17
04-10-27 13		2		17	19
04-10-27 14		3		17	19
04-10-27 15		4		17	18
04-10-27 16				17	17
04-10-27 17		3		17	20
04-10-27 18		17		20	22
04-10-27 19		1		20	26
04-10-28 12		22		17	20
04-10-28 13		2		17	17
04-10-29 13		9		18	19

This is a very important report because it shows the method with which Oracle is accessing data over time periods. This is especially important because it shows when the database processing modality shifts between OLTP (*first_rows* index access) to a batch reporting mode (*all_rows* full scans) as shown in Figure 16.17.

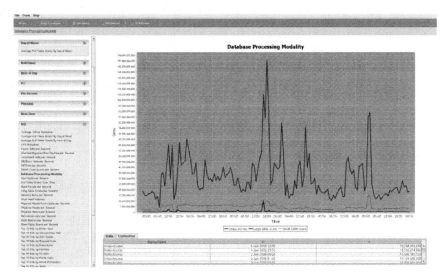

Figure 16.17: *Plot of Full Scans vs. Index Access*

The example in Figure 16.17 is typical of an OLTP database with the majority of access done via small-table full-table scans and index access. In this case, the large-table full-table scans must be carefully checked and their legitimacy verified for such things as missing indexes, and then they should be adjusted to maximize their throughput.

Of course, in an exceptionally busy database, there may be concurrent OLTP index access and full-table scans for reports, and it is the DBA's job to know the specific times when the system shifts table access modes as well as the identity of those tables that experience the changes.

The following *awr_sql_full_scans_avg_dy.sql* script can be used to roll-up average scans into daily averages.

🖫 awr_sql_full_scans_avg_dy.sql

```
col c1 heading 'Begin|Interval|Time'   format a20
col c2 heading 'Index|Table|Scans' format 999,999
col c3 heading 'Full|Table|Scans' format 999,999

select
  i.c1  c1,
  i.c2  c2,
  f.c2  c3
from
(
select
  to_char(sn.begin_interval_time,'day')  c1,
  count(1)                                c2
from
  dba_hist_sql_plan p,
  dba_hist_sqlstat  s,
  dba_hist_snapshot sn
where
  p.object_owner <> 'SYS'
and
  p.operation like '%TABLE ACCESS%'
and
  p.options like '%INDEX%'
and
  p.sql_id = s.sql_id
and
  s.snap_id = sn.snap_id
group by
  to_char(sn.begin_interval_time,'day')
order by
1 ) i,
(
select
  to_char(sn.begin_interval_time,'day')  c1,
  count(1)                                c2
from
  dba_hist_sql_plan p,
  dba_hist_sqlstat  s,
  dba_hist_snapshot sn
where
  p.object_owner <> 'SYS'
and
  p.operation like '%TABLE ACCESS%'
and
  p.options = 'FULL'
```

```
and
   p.sql_id = s.sql_id
and
   s.snap_id = sn.snap_id
group by
  to_char(sn.begin_interval_time,'day')
order by
1 ) f
where
     i.c1 = f.c1
;
```

The sample output is shown below:

```
Begin                    Index      Full
Interval                 Table      Table
Time                     Scans      Scans
--------------------     --------   --------
sunday                        393        189
monday                        383        216
tuesday                       353        206
wednesday                     357        178
thursday                      488        219
friday                        618        285
saturday                      400        189
```

For example, the signature shown in Figure 16.18 below indicates that Fridays have a large amount of full-table scans, probably as the result of weekly reporting.

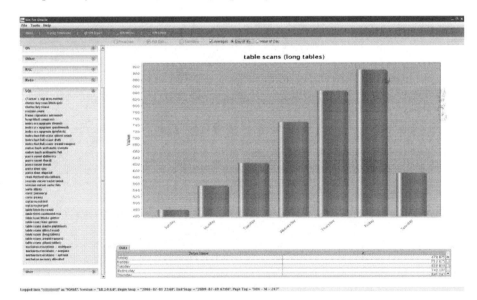

Figure 16.18: *Plot of Full Scans*

With this knowledge, the DBA can anticipate the changes in processing from index access to LTFTS access by adjusting instance configurations.

Whenever the database changes into a mode dominated by LTFTS, the data buffer sizes, such as *db_cache_size* and *db_nk_cache_size*, can be decreased. Since parallel LTFTS bypass the data buffers, the intermediate rows are kept in the *pga_aggregate_target* region. Hence, it may be desirable to use *dbms_scheduler* to anticipate this change and resize the SGA just in time to accommodate the regularly repeating change in access patterns.

One important use for the AWR tables is tracking table join methods over time.

Interrogating Table Join Methods

The decision between a *hash* join and a *nested loop* join depends on several factors:

- The relative number of rows in each table

- The presence of indexes on the key values

- The settings for static parameters like *index_caching* and *cpu_costing*

- The current setting and available memory in *pga_aggregate_target*

The use of *hash* joins with parallel full-table scans tends to drive up CPU consumption because *hash* joins do not use indexes and perform full-table scans often using parallel query. .

PGA memory consumption also increases when *hash* joins are used, but if AMM is enabled, it is not usually a problem.

The following query produces a report that alerts the Oracle DBA when the *hash* join operations count exceeds a specific threshold:

💾 **awr_hash_join_alert.sql**

```
col c1 heading 'Date'             format a20
col c2 heading 'Hash|Join|Count'  format 99,999,999
col c3 heading 'Rows|Processed'   format 99,999,999
col c4 heading 'Disk|Reads'       format 99,999,999
col c5 heading 'CPU|Time'         format 99,999,999


accept hash_thr char prompt 'Enter Hash Join Threshold: '

ttitle 'Hash Join Threshold|&hash_thr'

select
   to_char(sn.begin_interval_time,'yy-mm-dd hh24')  c1,
   count(*)                                          c2,
   sum(st.rows_processed_delta)                      c3,
   sum(st.disk_reads_delta)                          c4,
   sum(st.cpu_time_delta)                            c5
from
   dba_hist_snapshot  sn,
   dba_hist_sql_plan  p,
   dba_hist_sqlstat   st
where
   st.sql_id = p.sql_id
and
```

```
    sn.snap_id = st.snap_id
and
    p.operation = 'HASH JOIN'
having
    count(*) > &hash_thr
group by
    begin_interval_time;
```

The sample output might look the result set below. It shows the number of *hash* joins during the snapshot period along with the relative I/O and CPU associated with the processing. The values for *rows_processed* are generally higher for *hash* joins that do full-table scans rather than *nested loop* joins, which generally involved a very small set of returned rows.

```
Hash Join Thresholds

                   Hash
                   Join        Rows          Disk          CPU
Date               Count   Processed         Reads         Time
----------------   -----   ---------   -----------   ----------
04-10-12 17           22       4,646           887   39,990,515
04-10-13 16           25       2,128           827   54,746,653
04-10-14 11           21      17,368         3,049   77,297,578
04-10-21 15           60       2,805         3,299    5,041,064
04-10-22 10           25       6,864           941    4,077,524
04-10-22 13           31      11,261         2,950   46,207,733
04-10-25 16           35      46,269         1,504    6,364,414
```

hash join Tuning is Tricky!

The sorting default is that no single task may consume more than 5% of the *pga_aggregate_target* region before the sort pages out to the temp tablespace for a disk sort.

Now it's time to consider automating the tuning process.

Towards Automated SQL Tuning

Until the advent of the Oracle 10g intelligent SQL tuning advisors, the SQL Access advisor and SQL Tuning Advisor, SQL tuning was a time-consuming and tedious task. That all started to change in Oracle 10g, and it is even more exciting in Oracle 11g where Oracle has promised fully automated SQL tuning, via the new SQL Performance Analyzer (SPA), and improvements in the SQL advisories.

The Oracle 10g automatic tuning advisor allowed the implementation of tuning suggestions in the form of SQL profiles that will improve performance. Now with Oracle 11g, the DBA can tell Oracle to automatically apply SQL profiles for statements whenever the suggested profile gives three-times better performance than that of the existing statement. These performance comparisons are done by a new 11g administrative task that is executed during a user-specified maintenance window. In a nutshell, the 11g fully automated SQL tuning works like this:

1. **Define the SQL workload:** This is where a set of problematic SQL statements can be defined using exception thresholds. e.g. all SQL with > 100,000 disk reads, selected from the cursor cache or the AWR. This is called the SQL Tuning set (STS).

2. **Set-up a changed environment:** This is where the choice can be made to choose to change initialization parameters, test their performance against a previous release of the CBO, a very useful feature when testing upgrades, or conduct custom experiments on the effect of environmental changes on the SQL tuning set.

3. **Schedule & run the tests:** In this step, the workload is scheduled for execution during low usage periods so that an empirical sample of real-world execution times can be collected and compared using different execution plans

4. **Implement the changes:** During implementation, SQL statements can be flagged for changes, and they can be tuned with the SQL Tuning Advisor

Before drilling down into the nuances of the 11g fully automated SQL tuning features, it is important to review the goals of SQL tuning.

The Goals of Holistic SQL Tuning

Holistic tuning in Oracle 11g is a broad-brush approach that can save thousands of hours of tedious manual SQL tuning. By applying global changes, it is possible to tune hundreds of queries at once and implement them via SQL profiles.

DBAs who fail to do holistic SQL tuning first, especially those who tune SQL with optimizer directives, may find that subsequent global changes, e.g. optimizer parameter change, may un-tune their SQL. By starting with system-level tuning, an optimal baseline can be established before diving into the tuning of individual SQL statements:

- **Optimize the server kernel:** The disk and network I/O subsystem (RAID, DASD bandwidth, network) must always be tuned to optimize the I/O time, network packet size and dispatching frequency. Kernel settings have an indirect effect on SQL performance. For example, a kernel setting may speed up I/O, a change which is noted by the CBO workload statistics using *dbms_stats.gather_workload_stats*. This, in turn, directly influences the optimizer's access decisions.

- **Adjusting theoptimizer statistics:** Optimizer statistics must always be collected and stored to allow the optimizer to learn more about the distribution of the data to take more intelligent execution plans. Also, histograms can hypercharge SQL in cases of determining optimal table join order and when making access decisions on skewed *where* clause predicates. Also new in 11g, multi-column statistics can be gathered for use by the optimizer to determine optimal ways to run queries based upon multiple column criteria.

- **Adjust optimizer parameters:** *optimizer optimizer_mode, optimizer_index_caching* and *optimizer_index_cost_adj*

- **Optimize the instance:** The choice between *db_block_size, db_cache_size,* and OS parameters *db_file_multiblock_read_count, cpu_count,* and more can influence SQL performance

- **Tune the SQL Access workload with physical indexes and materialized views:** Just as the 10g SQL Access Advisor recommends missing indexes and missing materialized views, DBAs should always optimize their SQL workload with indexes. Function-based indexes are especially helpful for SQL tuning.

Now, Oracle 11g does not have all of the intelligence of a human SQL tuning expert, but the 11g SQL Performance Analyzer (SPA) is a great way to test for the effect of environmental changes to the Oracle environment.

The SQL Tuning Advisor

The SQL Tuning Advisor (STA) works with the Automatic Tuning Optimizer (ATO) to analyze historical SQL workload using data from the AWR, and it generates recommendations for new indexes and materialized views that will reduce the disk I/O associated with troublesome SQL statements.

The STA is primarily designed to replace the manual tuning of SQL statements and speed up the overall SQL tuning process. The SQL Tuning Advisor studies poorly executing SQL statements and evaluates resource consumption in terms of CPU, I/O and temporary space. The advisor receives one or more SQL statements as input and provides advice on how to optimize their execution plans, gives the rationale for the advice, the estimated performance benefit and the actual command to implement the advice.

The STA can be thought of as a container for conducting and analyzing many tuning tasks. It calls the optimizer internally and performs the analysis as follows:

- **Executes the stale or missing statistics analysis:** Makes a recommendation to collect, if necessary.

- **Plans the tuning analysis and creates a SQL Profile:** The SQL Profile is a collection of the historical information of prior runs of the SQL statement, comparison details of the actual and estimated cardinality, and predicate selectivity. SQL Profile is stored persistently in the data dictionary, so it does not require any application code changes.

- **Performs the access path analysis:** The optimizer recommends new indexes that produce a significantly faster execution path.

- **Restructure the SQL statement:** The optimizer identifies SQL statements that have bad plans and makes relevant suggestions to restructure them.

The plan analysis mode, which creates the SQL Profiles, is a significant stage where additional information for the query is collected by the optimizer. This analysis is not possible in the normal mode.

Such a SQL Profile helps generate a better execution plan than the normal optimization. Additional tasks like checking for advanced predicate selectivity, correlation between columns, join skews, and complex predicates such as functions help in profiling the SQL statement. Once a statement is profiled and stored, it can be used at will.

Using SQL Tuning Advisor Session

This tuning method has many stages. In the first stage, the SQL Advisor task can be created by taking SQL statement input from a variety of sources. They are as follows:

- High load SQL statements, identified by ADDM

- SQL statements that are currently in cursor cache from the *v$sql_plan* view

- SQL statements based on the range of snapshot IDs from the Automatic Workload Repository (AWR). By default, the AWR maintains data for up to seven days.

- Simple SQL Statement Text: A user can define a custom workload consisting of statements of interest to the user. These may be statements that are either in cursor cache or high-load to be captured by ADDM or AWR.

- SQL Tuning Set (STS): A SQL Tuning Set is a named set of SQL statements with their associated execution context and basic execution statistics.

The following is an example of a SQL tuning session, using this new functionality:

Step 1: Create a tuning task

There is a SQL statement, perhaps from a packaged application and it may not be possible to change the code.

```
create_tuning_task (
sql_text => 'select * from emp_history
where empid_id = :bnd_var',f
bind_list =>
sql_binds(anydata.ConvertNumber(100)),
usern_name => 'scott',
scope => 'comprehensive',
time_limit => 60,
task_name => 'bad_sql',
description => 'sql that performs poorly');
```

The time limit is set to 60, so the optimizer will spend up to 60 seconds analyzing this SQL statement. The comprehensive setting indicated that the optimizer should perform its additional analysis. Instead of using the above SQL, the *sql id* out of OEM or other catalog tables such as *sql_advisor_%* can be used.

```
create_tuning_task (sql_id =>
'abc123456xyz');
```

Step 2: Execute the tuning task

```
Execute_tuning_task (
Task_name => 'bad_sql');
```

The results of this execution have been put into the new catalog tables and can be seen by querying *dba_advisor_%* views such as *dba_advisor_findings* and *dba_advisor_recommendations*.

Step 3: See the results

```
set long 10000;
select report_tuning_task (task_name => 'bad_sql') from dual;
```

This will return a complete report of the results, including findings and recommendations. This report can also be run via OEM.

Step 4: Determine what is to be implemented and execute accordingly

```
accept_sql_profile (tastk_name => 'bad_sql',
name => 'use_this_profile');
```

This will store the profile in the catalog, which is similar to a stored outline in previous releases of Oracle. So, when using the optimizer in normal mode, instead of using the original access path when the bad SQL comes along, , this new profile will be used instead.

Following that introduction to the SQL Tuning Advisor, it will be helpful to investigate automated analyzers in more detail.

Inside the 11g SQL Performance Analyzer

The declarative nature of the SQL syntax has always made it difficult to perform SQL tuning. The basic tenet of cost-based SQL optimization is that the person who writes a SQL query simply declares what columns they want to see (the *select* clause), the tables where the columns reside (the *from* clause) and the filtering conditions (the *where* clause). It is up to the SQL optimizer to always determine the optimal execution plan. This is a formidable challenge, especially in a dynamic environment, which is why Oracle introduced the 10g new feature of CBO dynamic sampling.

Oracle tuning consultants have known for many years that the best way to tune an Oracle system is to take a top-down approach, finding the optimal configuration for external factors, i.e. OS kernel settings or disk I/O subsystem, and determining the best overall setting for the Oracle instance, i.e. *init.ora* parameters.

Holistic tuning involves tuning a representative workload, adjusting global parameters in order to optimize as much SQL as possible. Only then is it prudent to start tuning individual SQL statements. Many Oracle professionals who adopt a bottom-up approach by tuning the SQL first find all of their hard work undone when a change is made to a global setting, such as one of the SQL optimizer parameters or re-computing optimizer statistics.

Oracle's holistic SQL tuning approach is new and given the misleading marketing name "fully automated SQL tuning". Holistic tuning is well-known to working DBAs who have been doing manual workload-based optimization since Oracle 6. Now in 11g, Oracle gives an automated method.

The Oracle 11g SPA is primarily designed to speed up the holistic SQL tuning process, automating much of the tedium. Once a workload called a SQL Tuning Set (STS) is created, Oracle will repeatedly execute the workload using sophisticated predictive models using a regression testing approach to accurately identify the salient changes to execution plans based on the system's environmental changes.

Using SPA, impact of system changes on a workload can be reliably predicted. The SPA helps DBAs forecast changes in response times for SQL after making any change like parameter changes, schema changes, hardware changes, OS changes or Oracle upgrades. Any change that influence SQL plans is a good candidate for SPA.

Decision Support and Expert Systems Technology

Oracle had made a commitment to Decision Support Systems (DSS) Technology starting in Oracle 9i when they started to publish advisory utilities, the result of monitoring the Oracle instance and coming up with estimated benefits for making a change to the database configuration. In the world of applied artificial intelligence, an expert system, e.g. automated memory advisor (AMM) and automated storage management (ASM), solves a well-structured problem for the DBA, while a decision support system solves a semi-structured problem with the DBA who supplies the human intuition required to solve a complex problem.

Oracle has made a commitment to distinguishing themselves in the database marketplace, and this is one of the major reasons that they command a major market share. One of the most exciting areas of Oracle technology is automation, especially the self-management features. Oracle has now automated many critical components, including AMM and ASM. In addition, Oracle is now working to enhance more intelligent utilities including the Automated Database Diagnostic Monitor (ADDM), and the brand new 11g SQL Performance Analyzer (SPA).

The Oracle 11g SPA functions as a DSS, helping the DBA by automating the well-structured components of a complex tuning task, such as hypothesis testing. In SPA, the DBA defines a representative workload and then tests this workload empirically, running the actual queries against the database and collecting performance metrics. SPA allows the DBA to obtain real-world performance results for several types of environmental changes:

- **Initialization parameters:** Pre-test changes to global parameters, most often the Oracle optimizer parameters (*optimizer_mode, optimizer_index_cost_adj, optimizer_index_caching*). Prior to Oracle 10g, adjusting these optimizer parameters was the only way to compensate for sample size issues with *dbms_stats*.

- **Optimizer software levels:** Compare SQL execution between different releases of the CBO

- **Guided Workflow:** This is a hypothesis testing option that allows the creation of customized experiments and provides validation of hypotheses using empirical methods.

As of Oracle 10g and beyond, the use of *dbms_stats.gather_system_stats* and improved sampling within *dbms_stats* has made adjustments to these parameters far less important. Ceteris Parabus, always adjust CBO statistics before adjusting optimizer parms.

Instead of using theory and mathematical calculations, Oracle SPA tests the STS workload in a real-world environment, running the workload repeatedly while using heuristic methods to tally the optimal execution plan for the SQL. The DBA can then review the changes to execution plans and tune the SQL using the SQL Tuning Advisor to lock in the execution plans using SQL profiles. Holistic SQL tuning can save DBAs from the tedium of tuning SQL statements.

Inside the Oracle 11g SQL Performance Analyzer

The Oracle 11g SQL Performance Analyzer (SPA) is a step in the direction of fully automated SQL tuning, allowing the database administrator to create a STS workload, a unified set of SQL which comes from either the cursor cache (shared pool) or from the AWR. Exception thresholds can be used to select the SQL for each STS based on execution criteria such as disk reads, consistent gets, executions and such. Once the DBA has chosen their STS, SPA allows them to run the workload while changing Oracle environmental factors, namely the CBO release level, *init.ora* parameters and customized hypothesis testing using the guided workflow option.

The central question becomes which Oracle initialization parameters would be the most appropriate within the SPA? Because the SPA is used to measure changes in SQL execution plans, it only makes sense to choose those Oracle parameters that will influence the behavior of the Oracle optimizer.

These would include the basic Oracle optimizer parameters including *optimizer_index_cost_adj*, *optimizer_mode* and *optimizer_index_caching*, as well as other important initialization parameters. There are also non-optimizer parameters which effect SQL execution plan decisions:

- **db_file_multiblock_read_count.** When this parameter is set to a high value, the Oracle CBO recognizes that scattered multiblock reads may be less expensive than sequential reads, i.e. full-table scans and full index scans. **10gr2 Note:** Starting in Oracle 10g release 2, Oracle recommends not setting the *db_file_multiblock_read_count* parameter, allowing Oracle to empirically determine the optimal setting.

- **parallel_automatic_tuning.** When *parallel_automatic_tuning* is set to ON, the Oracle optimizer will parallelize legitimate full-table scans. Because parallel full-table scans can be done very quickly using parallel query, Oracle's CBO will assign a higher cost index access, making the optimizer friendlier to full-table scans.

- **hash_area_size** (if not overridden by *pga_aggregate_target*): The setting for *hash_area_size* governs the propensity of Oracle's optimizer to favor *hash* joins over *nested loop* and for *merge* joins. This makes it an ideal testing parameter for changes to Oracle memory regions so that one can see how they would be affected within a production environment.

- **pga_aggregate_target.** The settings for *pga_aggregate_target* have a profound impact on the behavior of Oracle SQL statements, making this an interesting test case for the SPA, especially with regard of the propensity of the Oracle optimizer to do in memory sorts and *hash* joins.

- **sort_area_size** (if not overridden by *pga_aggregate_target*): The *sort_area_size* parameter influences the CBO when deciding whether or not to perform index access or to perform a sort of the ultimate results set from the SQL query. The higher the value for *sort_area_size*, the more likely it will be that the Oracle 11g optimizer will invoke a backend sort because it knows that the sort can be performed in memory. Of course, this depends upon the Oracle optimizer's estimated cardinality for the results set of the SQL query.

The SPA allows the DBA to define the STS, as a source for the test, usually using historical SQL from the AWR tables.

The SPA receives one or more SQL statements as input via the SPA and provides advice on which tuning conditions have the best execution plans, gives the proof for the advice, shows an estimated performance benefit and allegedly has a facility to automatically implement changes that are more than 3x faster than the before condition.

Gathering the SQL Tuning Set

The STS can be thought of as a container for conducting and analyzing many SQL statements. The STS is fed to the SPA for real-world execution with before-and-after comparisons of changes to holistic environmental conditions, specifically CBO levels or changed *init.ora* parameters.

Internally, the SPA is stored as a database object that contains one or more SQL statements combined with their execution statistics and context such as particular schema, application module name, list of bind variables and more. The STS also includes a set of basic execution statistics such as CPU and elapsed times, disk reads and buffer gets, and number of executions.

When creating an STS, the SQL statements can be filtered by different patterns such as application module name or execution statistics, such as high disk reads. Once created, STS can be an input source for the SQL Tuning Advisor. Typically, the following steps are used to define how STS uses the *dbms_sqltune* package. The steps within the new 11g OEM screen for guided workflow are simple and straightforward, and serve as an online interface to the *dbms_sqltune.create_sqlset* procedure:

1. **Options:** Choose a name for an STS. This encapsulated SQL workload is created using the *dbms_sqltune.create_sqlset* procedure. For example, the following script can be used to create an STS called SQLSET1:

```
exec dbms_sqltune.create_sqlset ('MYSET1');
```

2. **Load methods:** This is where a DBA can choose the source for their SQL workload and to take historical SQL statements from AWR

3. **Filter options:** This is where filtering conditions can be chosen, based on specific tuning needs. For example, if the database is disk I/O bound, only SQL statements that have more than 100k disk reads might be chosen.

4. **Schedule:** This is an interface to the *dbms_scheduler* package. This allows a job to be defined and scheduled.

5. **Review:** In this important step, it is possible to see the actual source calls to *dbms_sqltune.create_sqlset* and the *dbms_scheduler.create_job* procedure call syntax.

There is an interface to the SPA in the Enterprise Manager in the OEM Advisor Central area, and a number of new to *dba_advisor* views have been added in 11g which will display information from the SQL Performance Advisor. The technology behind SPA is encapsulated inside a new package called *dbms_sqlpa*. The following list includes an overview for the procedures of the *dbms_sqlpa* package:

- *cancel_analysis_task:* This procedure cancels the currently executing task analysis of one or more SQL statements.

- *create_analysis_task:* This function creates an advisor task to process and analyze one or more SQL statements.

- *drop_analysis_task:* This procedure drops a SQL analysis task.

- *execute_analysis_task:* This function and procedure executes a previously created analysis task.

- *interrupt_analysis_task:* This procedure interrupts the currently executing analysis task.

- *report_analysis_task:* This function displays the results of an analysis task.

- *reset_analysis_task:* This procedure resets the currently executing analysis task to its initial state.

- *resume_analysis_task:* This procedure resumes a previously interrupted analysis task that was created to process a SQL tuning set.

- *set_analysis_task_parameter:* This procedure sets the SQL analysis task parameter value.

- *set_analysis_default_parameter:* This procedure Sets the SQL analysis task parameter default value

In sum, the new 11g SPA is a great way to test for holistic tuning changes. Remember, the savvy Oracle DBA will always adjust their Oracle initialization parameters to optimize as much of the workload as possible before diving into the tuning of specific SQL statements.

Oracle 11g Guided Workflow Screen

The OEM screen for the SPA guided workflow contains a pre-defined set of steps for holistic SQL workload tuning:

1. Create SPA Task, based on STS

2. Replay SQL tuning set in initial environment

3. Create replay trial using changed environment

4. Create replay trial comparison (using trials from step 2 and step 3)

5. View trial comparison report

Using the guided workflow functionality, SQL tuning set can be executed twice, once before and again after, saving the SQL execution results (disk reads, buffer gets) using some of the common SQL execution metrics found in the *dba_hist_sqlstat* table:

dba_hist_sqlstat Columns:

- fetches_total

- end_of_fetch_count_total

- sorts_total

- executions_total

- loads_total

- invalidations_total

- parse_calls_total

- disk_reads_total

- buffer_gets_total

- rows_processed_total

- cpu_time_total

- elapsed_time_total

Guided Workflow Items:

- *execute_elapsed_time*

- *elapsed_time*

- *parse_time*

- *execute_elapsed_time*

- *execute_cpu_time*

- *buffer_gets*

- *disk_reads*

- *direct_writes*

- *optimizer_cost*

It is important to note at this point, that the guided workflow does not measure these important SQL execution metrics such as sorts and fetches.

Comparing the SPA Results

The final step in SPA allows the quick isolate suboptimal SQL statements which can then be tuned with the 11g SQL Tuning Advisor, as shown in the previous section. When viewing the results, OEM can be used for a visual display of all delta values between the execution run. Most importantly, it is possible to do a side-by-side comparison of the before-and-after execution plans.

Oracle has always been ahead of the curve in automating well-structured DBA tasks, and the SPA is just the latest incarnation in real-world SQL tuning tools. Tools such as SPA free up the DBA to pursue other important DBA tasks, relieving them of the tedium of individually tuning SQL statements.

Oracle Automatic Database Diagnostics Monitor

With the extra-cost Oracle Performance pack and Diagnostic pack are purchased, access is granted to an automated tool called the Automatic Database Diagnostic Monitor (ADDM). Prior to Oracle10g, SQL tuning could not be automated and the DBA spent much of their time adding indexes, managing materialized views, changing *init.ora* parameters, testing hints, reading TKPROF output, examining explain plans and so on.

Oracle offers more automatic mechanisms for rudimentary SQL tuning. The AWR tables allow Oracle to collect and maintain detailed SQL execution statistics, and this stored data is then used by the ADDM.

The ADDM attempts to supply a root cause analysis along with recommendations on what to do to fix the problem. An ADDM output might contain information that there is read/write contention, a freelist problem or the need to use locally managed tablespaces. The ADDM tool can be accessed either via the command line interface or through the Oracle Enterprise Manager (OEM), but most people prefer the command line interface.

As noted earlier in the chapter, Oracle also has the SQL Tuning Advisor to assist with tuning SQL. This use of this tool is based on changes to the optimizer. The optimizer now has a tuning mode that is used when tuning SQL. The tuning mode causes the optimizer to go through four checks:

- **Analyze SQL Statistics:** Check for missing or stale CBO statistics

- **SQL Profiling:** Determine additional information that will make a statement run better and save it off for use later, similar to a stored outline

- **SQL Access Analysis:** Verify that the access path is the most optimal or make recommendations for a better one

- **SQL Structure Analysis:** Determine if tweaking the SQL will make it run better such as changing a *not in* to a *not exists*, for example.

The ADDM can identify high load SQL statements, which can, in turn, be fed into the SQL Tuning Advisor. The ADDM automatically detects common performance problems, including:

- Excessive I/O

- CPU bottlenecks

- Contention issues

- High parsing

- Lock contention

- Buffer sizing issues

- RAC tuning issues

The ADDM is invoked every 30 minutes or whenever specified. The DBA can begin with ADDM by creating a new snapshot with information populated in *dba_hist_snapshot*:

```
exec dbms_workload_repository.create_snapshot();
```

The *addm_rpt.sql* script can be used to view the output of the snapshot, including recommendations:

🖫 addm_rpt.sql

```
set long 1000000
set pagesize 50000

column get_clob format a80

select
    dbms_advisor.get_task_report(task_name, 'TEXT', 'ALL') as first_ADDM_report
from
    dba_advisor_tasks
where
```

```
     task_id=(
select
    max(t.task_id)
from
    dba_advisor_tasks t, dba_advisor_log l
where
    t.task_id = l.task_id
and
    t.advisor_name='ADDM'
and
    l.status= 'COMPLETED');
```

The following is an example of output that the ADDM generates. This result shows that the ADDM detected excessive physical reads and used the *v$db_cache_advice* method to determine that this instance would benefit from a larger data buffer cache:

```
FINDING 3: 5.2% impact (147 seconds)
------------------------------------
The buffer cache was undersized causing significant additional read I/O.

RECOMMENDATION 1: DB Configuration, 5.2% benefit (147 seconds)
ACTION: Increase SGA target size by increasing the value of parameter "sga_target"
by 24 M.

SYMPTOMS THAT LED TO THE FINDING:
Wait class "User I/O" was consuming significant database time. (5.3%  impact [150
seconds])
```

Using the *with* Clause to Simplify Complex SQL

Oracle SQL can run faster when complex subqueries are replaced with global temporary tables. Starting in Oracle 9i release 2, there was an incorporation of a subquery factoring utility implementing the SQL-99 *with* clause. The *with* clause is a tool for materializing subqueries to save Oracle from having to recompute them multiple times.

Use of the SQL *with* clause is very similar to the use of Global Temporary Tables (GTT), a technique that is often employed to improve query speed for complex subqueries. The following are some important notes about the Oracle *with* clause:

- The SQL *with* clause only works on Oracle 9i release 2 and beyond.

- The SQL *with* clause is used when a subquery is executed multiple times.

- The ANSI *with* clause is also useful for recursive queries, but this feature has not yet been implemented in Oracle SQL.

The following example shows how the Oracle SQL *with* clause works and see how the *with* clause and global temporary tables can be used to speed up Oracle queries.

All Stores With Above Average Sales

To keep it simple, the following example only references the aggregations once, where the SQL *with* clause is normally used when an aggregation is referenced multiple times in a query.

The following is an example of a request to see the names of all stores with above average sales. For each store, the average sales must be compared to the average sales for all stores as shown in Figure 16.19.

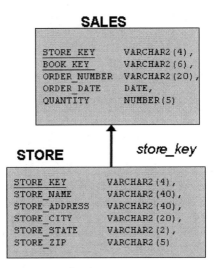

Figure 16.19: *The Relationship between store and sales*

Essentially, the query below accesses the *store* and *sales* tables, comparing the sales for each store with the average sales for all stores. To answer this query, the following information must be available:

- The total sales for all stores

- The number of stores

- The sum of sales for each store

To answer this in a single SQL statement, inline views will be employed along with a subquery inside a HAVING clause:

```
select
   store_name,
   sum(quantity)                                               store_sales,
   (select sum(quantity) from sales)/(select count(*) from store) avg_sales
from
   store  s,
   sales  sl
where
   s.store_key = sl.store_key
having
   sum(quantity) > (select sum(quantity) from sales)/(select count(*) from store)
group by
   store_name
```

While this query provides the correct answer, it is difficult to read and complex to execute as it is re-computing the sum of sales multiple times.

To prevent the unnecessary re-execution of the aggregation (sum(sales)), temporary tables could be created and used to simplify the query. The following steps should be followed:

1. Create a table named T1 to hold the total sales for all stores.

2. Create a table named T2 to hold the number of stores.

3. Create a table named T3 to hold the store name and the sum of sales for each store.

A fourth SQL statement that uses tables T1, T2, and T3 to replicate the output from the original query should then be written. The final result will look like this:

```
create table
   t1
as
select
   sum(quantity) all_sales
from
   stores;

create table
   t2
as
select
   count(*) nbr_stores
from
   stores;

create table
   t3
as
select
   store_name, sum(quantity) store_sales
from
   store
natural join
   sales;


select
   store_name
from
   t1,
   t2,
   t3
where
   store_sales > (all_sales / nbr_stores)
;
```

While this is a very elegant solution and easy to understand and has a faster execution time, the SQL-99 *with* clause can be used instead of temporary tables. The Oracle SQL *with* clause will compute the aggregation once, give it a name and allow it to be referenced, perhaps multiple times, later in the query.

The SQL-99 *with* clause is very confusing at first because the SQL statement does not begin with the word *select*. Instead, the *with* clause is used to start the SQL query, defining the aggregations, which can then be named in the main query as if they were real tables:

```
with
   subquery_name
as
```

```
  (the aggregation SQL statement)
select
  (query naming subquery_name);
```

Returning to the oversimplified example, the temporary tables should be replaced with the SQL *with* clause:

```
with
  sum_sales    AS
      select /*+ materialize */
      sum(quantity) all_sales from stores
  number_stores AS
      select /*+ materialize */
      count(*) nbr_stores from stores;
  sales_by_store AS
      select /*+ materialize */
      store_name, sum(quantity) store_sales from
      store natural join sales
select
  store_name
from
  store,
  sum_sales,
  number_stores,
  sales_by_store
where
  store_sales > (all_sales / nbr_stores)
;
```

Consider a GTT!

Depending on the release of Oracle in use, the global temporary tables (GTT) might be a better solution than the *with* clause because indexes can be created on the GTTs for faster performance.

Note the use of the Oracle undocumented *materialize* hint in the *with* clause. The Oracle *materialize* hint is used to ensure that the Oracle CBO materializes the temporary tables that are created inside the *with* clause, and its opposite is the undocumented *inline* hint. This is not necessary in Oracle 11g, but it helps ensure that the tables are only created one time.

Future Enhancement to the *with* Clause

Even though it is part of the ANSI SQL standard, as of Oracle 10g, it should be noted that the *with* clause is not yet fully functional within Oracle SQL, and it does not yet support the use of *with* clause replacement for *connect by* when performing recursive queries.

To show how the *with* clause is used in ANSI SQL-99 syntax, the following is an excerpt from Jonathan Gennick's work, *Understanding the With Clause*, showing the use of the SQL-99 *with* clause to traverse a recursive bill of materials hierarchy.

NOTE: This ANSI SQL syntax does NOT work (yet) with Oracle SQL.

```
with recursiveBOM
    (assembly_id, assembly_name, parent_assembly) as
(select
        parent.assembly_id,
        parent.assembly_name,
        parent.parent_assembly
from
        bill_of_materials parent
where
        parent.assembly_id=100
union all
select
        child.assembly_id,
        child.assembly_name,
        child.parent_assembly
from
        recursiveBOM parent, bill_of_materials child
where
        child.parent_assembly = parent.assembly_id)
select
        assembly_id, parent_assembly, assembly_name
from
        recursiveBOM;
```

The *with* clause allows components of a complex query to be pre-materialized, making the entire query run faster. This same technique can also be used with global temporary tables.

Before delving into the tuning of individual SQL statements, it will be useful to further examine how global Oracle parameters and statistics influence SQL execution. When tuning SQL, it is critical to optimize the instance as a whole before tuning individual SQL statements. This is especially important for proactive SQL tuning where the SQL may change execution plans based on changes in object statistics.

Fixing CBO Statistics

A client had just moved their system into production and was experiencing a serious performance problem. The emergency support DBA found that the *optimizer_mode=first_rows*, and there was only one table with statistics. The DBA was running cost based but seemed completely unaware of the necessity to analyze the schema for CBO statistics.

The trouble began when the DBA wanted to know the average row length for a table. After using a Google search to determine that the location of that information was the *dba_tables.avg_row_len* column, it was determined that the values were NULL. The DBA then went to MetaLink and learned gathering statistics with *dbms_stats* would fill in the *avg_row_len* column.

The CBO will dynamically estimate statistics for all tables with missing statistics, and when using *optimizer_mode=first_rows* with only one table analyzed, any SQL that touches the table will be optimized as a cost-based query. In this case, a multi-step silver bullet did the trick:

```
exec dbms_stats.delete_table_stats('username', 'tablename');

exec dbms_stats.gather_table_stats('username', 'tablename');
```

When the system immediately returned to an acceptable performance level, the DBA realized the importance of providing complete and timely statistics for the CBO using the *dbms_stats* utility.

Next, let's examine some special SQL tuning tricks.

Now that we see how rownum can help with tuning, lets xxx

Holistic SQL Tuning with Parameters

Making the CBO one of the most sophisticated tools ever created has cost Oracle Corporation millions of dollars. While the job of the CBO is to always choose the most optimal execution plan for any SQL statement, there are some things that the CBO cannot detect. This is when the DBA's expertise is needed.

The best execution plan for an SQL statement is affected by the types of SQL statements, the speed of the disks and the load on the CPUs. For instance, the best execution plan resulting from a query run at 4:00 a.m. when 16 CPUs are idle may be quite different from the same query at 3:00 p.m. when the system is 90 percent utilized. The CBO is not psychic, despite the literal definition of Oracle. Oracle can never know the exact load on the Oracle system; therefore, the Oracle professional must adjust the CBO behavior periodically.

Most Oracle professionals make these behavior adjustments using the instance-wide CBO behavior parameters such as *optimizer_index_cost_adj* and *optimizer_index_caching*. However, Oracle does not advise altering the default values for many of these CBO settings because the change scan affects the execution plans for thousands of SQL statements.

Some major adjustable parameters that influence the behavior of the CBO are shown below:

- ■ *parallel_automatic_tuning*: Full-table scans are parallelized when set to ON. Since parallel full-table scans are extremely quick, the CBO will give a higher cost to index access and will be friendlier to full-table scans.

- ■ *hash_area_size* (if not using *pga_aggregate_target*): The setting for the *hash_area_size* parameter governs the propensity of the CBO to favor hash joins over nested loops and sort merge table joins.

- ■ *db_file_multiblock_read_count*: The CBO, when set to a high value, recognizes that scattered (multi-block) reads maybe less expensive than sequential reads. This makes the CBO friendlier to full-table scans.

- ■ *optimizer_index_cost_adj*: This parameter changes the costing algorithm for access paths involving indexes. The smaller the value, the cheaper the cost of index access.

- ■ *optimizer_index_caching*: This parameter tells Oracle the amount the index is likely to be in the RAM data buffer cache. The setting for *optimizer_index_caching* affects the CBO's decision to use an index for a table join (nested loops) or to favor a full-table scan.

- ■ *optimizer_max_permutations*: This controls the maximum number of table join permutations allowed before the CBO is forced to pick a table join order. For a six-way table join, Oracle must evaluate six factorial (6!) or 720 possible join orders for the tables. This parameter has been deprecated in Oracle 10g.

- *sort_area_size* **(if not using** *pga_aggregate_target***):** The *sort_area_size* influences the CBO when deciding whether to perform an index access or a sort of the result set. The higher the value for *sort_area_size*, the more likely a sort will be performed in RAM, and the more likely that the CBO will favor a sort over pre-sorted index retrieval.

Note that *sort_area_size* is ignored when *pga_aggregate_target* is set and when *workarea_size_policy* =*auto*, unless one is using a specialized feature such as the MTS (shared servers). If dedicated server connections are used, the *sort_area_size* parameter is ignored.

New sorting algorithm makes resource claims!

Oracle 10g release 2 has a new sorting algorithm which claims to use less server resources (specifically CPU and RAM resources). A hidden parameter called *_newsort_enabled* (set to true or false) is used to turn on the new sorting method..

Remember, the *optimizer_index_cost_adj* parameter controls the CBO's propensity to favor index scans over full-table scans. In a dynamic system, as the type of SQL and load on the database changes, the idea *lvalue* for *optimizer_index_cost_adj* may change radically in just a few minutes.

Next, let's examine a very important Oracle tuning knob, the *optimizer_index_cost_adj* parameter.

Using *optimizer_index_cost_adj*

Prior to the getting ability to sample external I/O timings with *dbms_stats.gather_system_stats* in Oracle 9i, we frequently had to adjust our *optimizer_index_cost_adj* to make index access more attractive, but it's important to note that you should only change this parameter after investing other possible reasons for too frequent full scans.

These root cause reasons for unnecessary large-table full table scans might include:

- **Stale system statistics:** The *dbms_stats.gather_system_stats* procedure measures important timings within the database and adjusts the optimizer's propensity to choose indexes vs. full-scans. In Oracle we now see 11g extended optimizer statistics, an alternative to *dynamic_sampling* for estimating result set sizes.

- **Sub-optimal** *optimizer_mode* **choice:** The default *optimizer_mode* of *all_rows* is designed to choose execution plans that minimize computing resources and it favors full-scan access. If you want to minimize response time instead, you will want to change your optimizer_mode to *first_rows_n*.

- **Improper setting for** *db_file_multiblock_read_count*: Prior to 10g release 2 where this parameter setting was automated, a sub-optimal db_file_multiblock_read_count could cause the optimizer to choose unnecessary large-table full-table scans. See Chapter 13, Oracle I/O tuning for more details on this important parameter.

Even in a well-optimized Oracle 11g database, the default value of 100 for *optimizer_index_cost_adj* may not be right for your SQL workloads.

For OLTP systems, resetting this parameter to a smaller value between 10 and 30 may result in huge performance gains as SQL statements change from large-table full-table scans to index range scans. The Oracle environment can be queried so that the optimal setting for *optimizer_index_cost_adj* can be intelligently estimated.

The *optimizer_index_cost_adj* parameter defaults to a value of 100, but it can range in value from one to 10,000. A value of 100 means that equal weight is given to index versus multiblock reads. In other words, *optimizer_index_cost_adj* can be thought of as a "*how much do I like full-table scans?*" parameter.

With a value of 100, the CBO likes full-table scans and index scans equally, and a number lower than 100 tells the CBO index scans are faster than full-table scans. Although, with a super low setting such as *optimizer_index_cost_adj=1*, the CBO will still choose full-table scans for no-brainers such as tiny tables that reside on two blocks.

The following *optimizer_index_cost_adj.sql* script illustrates the suggested initial setting for *the optimizer_index_cost_adj*.

💾 optimizer_index_cost_adj.sql

```
col c1 heading 'Average Waits for|Full Scan Read I/O' format 9999.999
col c2 heading 'Average Waits for|Index Read I/O'     format 9999.999
col c3 heading 'Percent of| I/O Waits|for Full Scans' format 9.99
col c4 heading 'Percent of| I/O Waits|for Index Scans' format 9.99
col c5 heading 'Starting|Value|for|optimizer|index|cost|adj' format 999


select
   a.average_wait                                 c1,
   b.average_wait                                 c2,
   a.total_waits /(a.total_waits + b.total_waits) c3,
   b.total_waits /(a.total_waits + b.total_waits) c4,
   (b.average_wait / a.average_wait)*100          c5
from
   v$system_event  a,
   v$system_event  b
where
   a.event = 'db file scattered read'
and
   b.event = 'db file sequential read'
;
```

The following is the output from the script.

		Starting Value for optimizer
Percent of	Percent of	index

Average waits for full scan read I/O	Average waits for index read I/O	I/O waits for full scans	I/O waits for index scans	cost adj
1.473	.289	.02	.98	20

In this example, the suggested starting value of 20 for *optimizer_index_cost_adj* may be too high because 98 percent of the data waits are on index (sequential) block access. Weighting this starting value for *optimizer_index_cost_adj* to reflect the reality that this system has only two percent waits on full-table scan reads, a typical OLTP system with few full-table scans is a practical matter. It is not desirable to have an automated value for *optimizer_index_cost_adj* to be less than one or more than 100.

This same script may give a very different result at a different time of the day because these values change constantly as the I/O waits accumulate and access patterns change. Oracle 10g has the *dba_hist_sysmetric_summary* table for time-series analysis of this behavior.

Next, let's examine another important SQL tuning knob, the optimizer cost model, a single parameter that can have a profound impact on your entire database.

Setting the SQL Optimizer Cost Model

Starting with Oracle 9i, DBAs were given the ability to view the estimated CPU, temp and I/O costs for every SQL execution plan step. Oracle Corporation has noted that typical OLTP databases are becoming increasingly CPU-bound and has provided the ability for the DBA to make the optimizer consider the CPU costs associated with each SQL execution step.

In Oracle 10g and beyond, external I/O and CPU timing samples are gathered by default by a hidden job using *dbms_stats.gather_system_stats*, but in earlier releases we must manually execute the *dbms_stat.gather_system_stats* package to get CBO statistics.

As RAM prices fell and more shops cached their frequently-used data in large *db_cache_size* buffers, Oracle recognized this trend toward CPU-based optimization by providing the ability to choose CPU-based or I/O-based costing during SQL optimization with the 10g and beyond default being CPU-costing.

```
alter session set "_optimizer_cost_model"=choose;
alter session set "_optimizer_cost_model"=io;
alter session set "_optimizer_cost_model"=cpu;
```

This parameter can be used to choose the best optimizer costing model for a particular database, based on the I/O and CPU load.

The choice of relative weighting for these factors depends upon the existing state of the database. Databases using 32-bit technology and the corresponding 1.7 gigabyte limit on SGA RAM size tend to be I/O-bound with the top timed events being those performing disk reads:

```
Top 5 Timed Events
~~~~~~~~~~~~~~~~~~
                                                      % Total
Event                           Waits      Time (s) Ela Time
------------------------------- ----------- ---------- --------
```

```
db file sequential read                       xxxx    xxxx    30
db file scattered read                        xxxx    xxxx    40
```

Once 64-bit became popular, Oracle SGA sizes increased, more frequently referenced data was cached, and databases became increasingly CPU-bound. Also, solid-state disk (RAM SAN) has removed disk I/O as a source of waits:

```
Top 5 Timed Events
~~~~~~~~~~~~~~~~~~                                         % Total
Event                                Waits   Time (s) Ela Time
---------------------------------- ----------- ---------- --------
CPU time                             xxxx     xxxx      55.76
db file sequential read              xxxx     xxxx      27.55
```

The gathered statistics are captured via the *dbms_stats* package in 9.2 and above, and the following CPU statistics are captured automatically in 10g and stored in the *sys.aux_stat$* view.

- Single block disk read time, expressed in microseconds

- multiblock disk read-time, expressed in microseconds

- CPU speed, expressed in megahertz (mhz)

- The average *multiblock_read_count,* expressed in the number of blocks

A database where CPU is the top timed event may benefit from a change in the SQL optimizer to consider the CPU costs associated with each execution plan.

Using CPU costing may not be good for databases that are I/O-bound. Also, changing to CPU-based optimizer costing will change the predicate evaluation order of the query. MetaLink bulletin 276877.1 provides additional information on this.

Turning on CPU Costing

The default setting for the optimizer cost model is CHOOSE, meaning that the presence of CBO statistics will influence whether or not CPU costs are considered. According to the documentation, CPU costs are considered when SQL optimizer schema statistics are gathered with the *dbms_stat.gather_system_stats* package, which is the default behavior in Oracle 10g and beyond, and CPU costs will be considered in all SQL optimization.

It gets tricky because of Bug 2820066 where CPU cost is computed whenever *optimizer_index_cost_adj* is set to a non-default value. Unless the 9.2.0.6 server patch set has been applied, the Oracle database may be generating CPU statistics, regardless of the CBO stats collection method.

To ensure that CPU costing is in use, just set the undocumented *parameter _optimizer_cost_model=cpu.*

Turning on I/O Costing

I/O-bound databases, especially 32-bit databases, may want to utilize I/O-based SQL costing. The default optimizer costing in Oracle 11g is CPU, and it can be changed to I/O costing by using these techniques:

- Ensure that *optimizer_index_cost_adj* is set to the default value (Oracle 9i bug 2820066)

- Add a *no_cpu_costing* hint in the SQL

- Alter session set *_optimizer_cost_model=io*;

- Set *init.ora* hidden *parameter _optimizer_cost_model=io*

In sum, CPU cost is always computed regardless of optimizer mode when *optimizer_index_cost_adj* is set in unpatched Oracle versions less than 10.1.0.2.

The following section shows how to change from CPU-based to I/O-based SQL optimization when the processing characteristics of the database change on a regular basis.

Bi-modal Configuration for different SQL Workloads

It is not uncommon for databases to be bi-modal, operating OLTP during the day (CPU-intensive) and doing aggregations and rollups (I/O-intensive) at night.

The CPU and I/O statistics can now be captured using *dbms_stats* and then swapped them in as the processing mode changes. Most shops do this with the *dbms_scheduler* (*dbms_job*) package so that the statistics are swapped at the proper time.

With that introduction to the influence of parameters, it is time to examine other Oracle features that influence SQL execution. The most important system level factor is the schema statistics which have a huge influence on SQL execution.

Changing CBO SQL Optimizer Parameters

An emergency involving an Oracle 11g client from Phoenix, who was experiencing steadily degrading performance, involved a large number of large-table full-table scans which were suspected to being unnecessary. This suspicious information was found by a quick look in to *v$sql_plan* view using the plan *10g.sql* script that is found earlier in this chapter.

The top SQL was extracted from *v$sql* and timed as-is with an *index* hint. While it was unclear why the CBO was not choosing the index, the query with the *index* hint ran almost 20x faster. After and running a script against *v$bh and user_indexes*, we discovered that approximately 65 percent of the indexes were already inside the data buffer cache.

Based on similar systems, the next step was to lower *optimizer_index_cost_adj* to a value of 20 in hopes of forcing the CBO to lower the relative costs of index access.

```
optimizer_index_cost_adj=20
optimizer_index_caching=65
```

Changing Optimizer Parameters at the User Level

In the previous examples, global changes were made which will affect the entire system. The optimizer parameters can also be reset at the session level, changing the optimizer settings for a particular user. This is especially useful for changing the optimizer characteristics for batch jobs when it might be desirable to change the default *first_rows* optimization to *all_rows*, and change the optimizer weights for full-scan access and index caching:

```
create or replace trigger logon_batch
after logon on database
declare pragma autonomous_transaction;
begin
if user = 'SCOTT' then
execute immediate 'ALTER SESSION SET optimizer_mode=all_rows';
execute immediate 'ALTER SESSION SET optimizer_index_cost_adj=90';
execute immediate 'ALTER SESSION SET optimizer_index_caching=25';
end if;
end;
/
```

As a result of these actions, the execution plans for over 350 SQL statements were changed, and the overall system response time was cut in half.

Next's let's explore how to use special rownum tricks to optimizer special cases of Oracle SQL.

Tuning SQL with *"rownum"* Filters

Many people forget that the Oracle SQL optimizer is an in-house computer program, written by software engineers, and it's not something where the rules of scientific endeavor apply.

Hence, Oracle SQL has lots of special nuances and there are many counterintuitive tips and tricks for tuning Oracle SQL. The rownum pseudo column is interesting because there are a few legitimate uses for it:

- **Top-n queries:** The *rownum* can be used to materialize an in-line view. Beware, there are reports that using where rownum<n for top-n queries has the same net effect as using a first_rows_n hint in the query, changing the optimizer mode. This is not always a good thing, as adding the *where rownum<n* will invalidate the all_rows optimization, which may make a query run far slower. It's far better to materialize a subquery using the *with* clause.

- **Range-bounded queries:** In the discussion below, there are special cases where it may be safe to use rownum to speed-up special cases of range-bounded queries.

- **DML:** In some cases you can use rownum with DML, but only if you force the update to use an index with an index hint. See example here.

However, before we go into more details, note that complex subqueries can be tuned more efficiently by decomposing the subquery into separate queries by using the *with* clause.

Using *rownum* for top-n queries

As we have noted, *rownum* can be used to filter query results, but it may be done at the expense of poor performance.

For example, Oracle professional Yoni Sade notes that using the *where rownum<n* caused his query to run 20 times longer! This is an issue that he claims happens because his predicate (*where alert_level=3*) isn't being pushed into his inline view when the *rownum* is used:

```
select *
from (
    select * from all_alerts
    where alert_level=3
    order by alert_time desc);
```

It takes 5 seconds to get 1000 rows.

When I query to get the last 10 alerts:

```
select *
from (
    select * from my_view
    where alert_level=3
    order by alert_time desc)
where
    rownum<=10;
```

It takes 2 minutes (!)

In this case, in the second query with a *rownum* filter, Oracle must fully execute the subquery and sort the entire set before returning the top rows, in some cases, processing thousands of rows.

Using *rownum* can change optimizer mode!

This use of *rownum*< can cause performance problems. Using rownum may change the *all_rows* optimizer mode for a query to *first_rows*, causing unexpected sub-optimal execution plans.

Hot Tip!

One solution to this problem is to always include an *all_rows* hint when using *rownum* to perform a top-n query.

For top-n SQL queries, it's more efficient form of the query using the rank and over functions may perform faster, with the *window sort pushed rank* execution plan:

```
select
   *
from
   (select empno, sal, rank()
   over (order by sal desc ) rnk
   from emp)
where rnk <= 5;
```

Also, note that for tuning top-n queries we need to ensure that the subquery is using an index to minimize I/O.

Next, let's examine how using rownum might be used to speed-up range bounded SQL queries.

Using rownum with range bound queries

The "hack" for SQL tuning is used to force a subquery to use an index and invoke the *count stopkey* execution plan. For a simple example, consider a query to display all rows with a *max* date:

```
select
   emp_name,
   hire_date
from
   emp
where
   hire_date = (select max(hire_date) from emp);
```

In this case, it has been suggested that Oracle will perform an expensive full-scan operation to get the max hire date in the subquery.

Here is an example of tuning with *rownum=1*.

```
select
    emp_name,
    hire_date
from
    emp
where
    hire_date = (select max(hire_date) from emp)
and
    rownum=1;
```

Another approach might be to retrieve the subquery rows in pre-sorted order with an *index* hint:

```
select
    emp_name,
    hire_date
from
    emp
where
    hire_date = (select /+* hire_idx */ max(hire_date) from emp);
```

One great tips is where you can get make date range-bound queries to run faster by including the clause "*where rownum=1*" to the query.

In sum, the *rownum=1* is used to "short circuit" an index range scan, which is useful to speed up range-bounded queries that have overlapping end points. Internally, it is not complete clear how this *rownum=1* trick work, especially since it has been noted that the Oracle optimizer changes the overall optimizer mode behind the curtains.

It's important to note that rownum in SQL behavior has changed between releases and it behaved quite differently before Oracle10g.

Alternatives to rownum

Using *rownum* is very dangerous, especially in the hands of beginners, and there are always alternatives to using rownum:

- **The *with* clause:** Another approach to tuning rownum queries is to separate-out the subquery using the powerful *with* clause. Another benefit of separating-out the sorted subquery is that you can easily apply either a parallel hint or an index hint, if it's faster to retrieve the rows in pre-sorted order.

- **The rank or row_number analytics:** You can replace rownum in top-n queries with analytics functions, using rank() or row_number() instead, getting the same top-in result, but with much faster response time.

- **Optimizer goal hint:** In cases where rownum is used to change the optimizer mode to *first_rows_n*, it may be possible to negate this effect by using an *all_rows* hint.

- **Index hint:** In cases where rownum is used to force an index in a subquery, again, deploy an index hint to duplicate the faster execution plan.

Next, let's look at the importance of optimizer statistics and see how stake metadata can ruin the performance of our entire SQL workload.

Repairing Obsolete CBO Statistics Gathering

A client called and expressed confusion as to why their system was grinding to a halt. There was a serious degradation in SQL performance after the implementation of partitioned tablespaces in a 16-CPU Solaris 64-bit Oracle 11.1.0.7 system. The changes in the development and QA instances had been thoroughly tested.

As it turned out, *analyze table* and *analyze index* commands had been used to gather the CBO statistics. The *dbms_stats* utility gathers partition-wise statistics. There was not time to pull a deep sample collection, so a *dbms_stats* was issued with a ten percent sample size. It is parallelized with 15 parallel processes to speed-up the statistics collection:

```
exec dbms_stats.gather_schema_stats( -
   ownname          => 'SAPR4', -
   options          => 'GATHER AUTO', -
   estimate_percent => 10, -
   method_opt       => 'for all columns size repeat', -
   degree           => 15 -
)
```

In less than 30 minutes, the improved CBO statistics tripled the performance of the entire database.

Parallelizing Oracle SQL

One of the latest trends is for systems to have more and more CPUs inside a single server. Using symmetric multiprocessing (SMP) servers, it is not uncommon for an Oracle server to have 8, 16 or 32 CPUs, along with many gigabytes of RAM for the Oracle SGA regions.

Oracle has kept pace with these changes and offers a wealth of facilities to take advantage of multiple CPUs. Starting with Oracle 8i, Oracle implemented parallelism in virtually every database function, including SQL access (full-table scans), parallel data manipulation, and parallel recovery. The challenge for Oracle professionals is to configure their databases to use as many of the CPUs as possible.

One of the best ways to implement parallelism in an Oracle environment is to use Oracle Parallel Query (OPQ). How OPQ works and how it can be used to improve response time in large full-table scans, to invoke parallel rollbacks and more will be shown next.

Using OPQ in SQL

When Oracle has to perform a legitimate, large full-table scan, OPQ can make a dramatic difference in the response time. Using OPQ, Oracle partitions the table into logical chunks.

Once the table has been partitioned into pieces, Oracle fires off parallel query slaves, sometimes called factotum processes, and each slave simultaneously reads a piece of the large table. Upon completion of all slave processes, Oracle passes the results back to a parallel query coordinator, which will reassemble the data, perform a sort if required, and return the results back to the end user. OPQ can give almost infinite scalability, so very large full-table scans that used to take many minutes can now be completed with sub-second response times. This approach is illustrated in Figure 16.20:

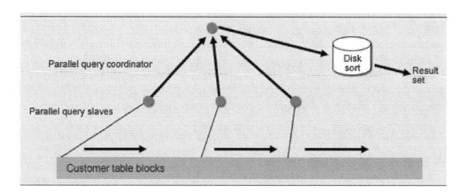

Figure 16.20: *Oracle Parallel Queries Divide and Conquer Approach*

OPQ is heavily influenced by the number of processors involved, and full-table scans can be hugely improved by running them in parallel, with the optimum normally achieved by using N-1 parallel processes where N=the number of CPUs on the dedicated Oracle server.

It is also very important to note that Oracle can detect the server environment, including the specific number of CPUs residing there. At startup time, Oracle examines the number of CPUs on the server and sets a parameter called *cpu_count*, which is used in the computation of the default values of several other important parameters.

Oracle Parallel Query Parameters

There are several initialization parameters that pertain to parallel query. The following are some of the parameters that Oracle sets at install time based upon the *cpu_count*:

- *fast_start_parallel_rollback*
- *parallel_max_servers*
- *log_buffer*
- *db_block_lru_latches*

It can also be seen that these parameters control parallel query function:

- *parallel_adaptive_multi_user*

- *optimizer_percent_parallel*

- *fast_start_parallel_rollback*

For a detailed description of these parameters, see Chapter 14, *Oracle Instance Tuning*. It is important to take into consideration that the number of CPUs can influence these parameters.

Parallel DML: Update, Merge, Delete

Updates, merges and deletes can only be paralleled on partitioned tables.

To specify parallel directives, follow one of the following methods:

- *alter session force parallel dml*

- Use an update, merge or delete *parallel* hint in the statement

- Use a PARALLEL clause in the definition of the table or reference object being updated or deleted

The precedence rule in this category of operations is:

 Hint --> Session --> Parallel declaration specification of the target table.

If the statement contains subqueries or updatable views, they may have their own separate parallel hints or clauses. Remember, these parallel directives do not affect decisions to parallelize the update, merge or delete activities.

Once it is decided to use parallel processing, the maximum DOP that can be achieved in *delete, merge* and *update* is equal to the number of partitions or subpartitions, in the case of composite subpartitions, in the table. Multiple partitions can be updated, merged into or deleted from by a single parallel execution, but each partition can only be updated or deleted by one parallel execution server at a time. Each parallel process transaction is a result of a different parallel execution server. Therefore, parallel DML requires multiple undo segments for performance.

However, there are some restrictions, quoting the Oracle documentation for accuracy, as shown below:

- A transaction can contain multiple parallel DML statements that modify different tables, but after a parallel DML statement modifies a table, no subsequent serial or parallel statement (DML or query) can access the same table again in that transaction.

- Parallel DML operations cannot be done on tables with triggers. Relevant triggers must be disabled in order to parallel DML on the table.

- A transaction involved in a parallel DML operation cannot be or become a distributed transaction.

- Clustered tables are not supported.

- Parallel DML: *insert .... select*

    - An *insert ... select* statement parallels its insert and select operations independently, except for the DOP. The insert operation will be paralleled if at least one of the following is true:

- The parallel hint is used in the *insert* in the DML statement.

- The table being inserted into was specified with a parallel declaration specification.

- The session is under the affect of an *alter session force parallel dml* statement.

The *select* statement follows its own set of rules as specified in the query section. Only one parallel directive is picked for deciding the DOP of the whole statement. Then the chosen DOP is applied to both the *select* and *insert* operations using the precedence rule:

Insert Hint directive --> Session --> Parallel declaration specification of the inserting table --> Maximum query directive.

Optimizing Oracle SQL Insert Performance

Before we begin our discussion of tuning SQL insert performance, we must remember that Oracle gives us several different options for putting rows into tables and some of them are faster than SQL.

A standard SQL insert may not be the fastest way to load table data as illustrated in Figure 16.21 below:

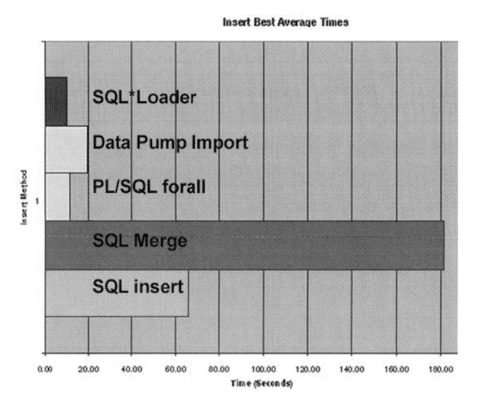

Figure 16.21: *Best Times of SQL Inserts*

As we see, the Oracle Data Pump import (*impdp*) utility and the *SQL*Loader* utility have faster performance than SQL for large volumes of data. For complete details on using these powerful utilities, see the book *Advanced Oracle Utilities: The Definitive Reference* by Bert Scalzo and Steven Callan.

As we will see in the section below on bulk DML operations, when data is pre-loaded into PL/SQL arrays (collections), using the powerful *forall* operator loads rows far faster than native SQL *insert* statements, in some cases more than 30 times faster.

Every system is different, and the type of insert must be customized for the application. Some applications require PL/SQL to issues the *insert* statements, while other systems use massive batch loads, while other shops process selective inserts. Every shop is different, but there are some *insert* tuning techniques that can work in a multitude of workloads.

High Impact *insert* tuning (gains to over 50% faster)

The following are some techniques that can increase insert speed significantly:

- **Manage segment header contention for parallel inserts:** Make sure to define multiple freelist or freelist groups to remove contention for the table header. Multiple freelists add additional segment header blocks, removing the bottleneck. ASSM (bitmap freelists) can be used to support parallel DML, but ASSM has some limitations.

- **Using SSD for insert tablespaces:** For databases that require high-speed loads, some shops define the insert table partition on solid-state RAM disk. These shops do their real-time inserts to SSD in order to maintain fast consistent response time, and transfer the data to traditional disk at a later time. The book *Oracle Solid-State Disk Tuning*, notes a respectable 30% improvement in insert speed when using SSD:

  > *"In the SSD verses ATA benchmark, the gains for insert and update processing as shown in the database loading and index build scenarios was a respectable 30%. This 30% was due to the CPU overhead involved in the insert and update activities."*

- **Parallelize the load:** Parallel DML can be invoked, i.e. using the *parallel* and *append* hint, to have multiple inserts into the same table. For this insert optimization, make sure to define multiple freelists and use the SQL *append* option. Mark Bobak notes that if parallel jobs are submitted to insert against the table at the same time, using the *append* hint may cause serialization, removing the benefit of parallel jobstreams.

- ***append* into tables:** By using the *append* hint, ensure that Oracle always grabs fresh data blocks by raising the high watermark for the table. If a parallel insert DML is being performed, the *append* mode is the default and there is no need to specify an *append* hint.

- **Use nologging:** If you are using the *insert* with the *append* clause, and you understand the how to fill-in gaps in your redo logs, you can use the *alter table* command to temporarily out the table into *nologging* mode, significantly improving the performance of the *insert* DML.

```
alter table customer nologging;
```

```
insert /*+ append */ into
    customer
values ('hello',';there');

alter table customer logging;
```

Know your redo logs!

You must remember that using nologging leaves a gap in your redo logs and you cannot use the recover database command to roll-forward though the time that the inserts occurred.

Look Out!

There are also some fine-tuning techniques for Oracle insert tuning.

Low-impact *insert* Tuning (gains 5% to 20% faster)

These following indicate specialized cases where marginal performance improvements can be seen under special circumstances:

- **Use a large blocksize:** Heavy insert/update tables can see faster performance when segregated into another blocksize which is mapped to a small data buffer cache. Smaller data buffer caches often see faster throughput performance. By defining large blocksizes for the target table, I/O is less because more rows fit onto a block before it becomes full.

- **Disable/drop indexes:** It can be faster to drop and rebuild indexes when doing large data loads. Also, remember that indexes will rebuild with less height if they are rebuilt in a tablespace with a 32k block size.

If the Oracle level processing for insert and update activities could be optimized for SSD, significant performance gains might be realized during these activities. When loading large volumes of data, there are several choices of tools, each with their own costs and performance benefits.

Here are some general guidelines for tuning Oracle insert SQL:

- **Add freelists:** Parallelized insert programs, each doing concurrent *insert* statements with enough freelists, can speed up insert performance

- **Use PL/SQL bulking:** PL/SQL often out-performs standard SQL inserts because of the array processing and bulking in the FORALL statement. Kent Crotty has shown examples where FORALL provides a 30x performance improvement on inserts, making PL/SQL as fast as SQL*Loader, one of the fastest ways to load Oracle data.

- **Use solid-state media:** Oracle with SSD can support over 500,000 rows per second for inserts, making it a great solution for shops that must "drink from the garden hose" during ETL insert feeds

- **Manage segment header contention for parallel inserts:** Make sure to define multiple freelist (or freelist groups) to remove contention for the table header. Multiple freelists add additional segment header blocks, removing the bottleneck. As noted in the techniques list for the high impact tuning approaches, ASSM (bitmap freelists) can be used to support parallel DML, but it has some limitations.

The following techniques were detailed in the section on High Impact Techniques. In some circumstances, their application would yield amazing performance improvements; however, depending on the system and its specific performance issues, these same techniques might have a lower yield:

- Parallelize the inserts
- append into tables

Let's look at the impact of our OS blocksize on SQL insert performance.

Blocksize and Insert Performance

Here is a small single-CPU, single-user benchmark showing the performance of loads into a larger blocksize:

```
alter system set db_2k_cache_size=64m scope=spfile;
alter system set db_16k_cache_size=64m scope=spfile;
startup force
create tablespace
   twok blocksize 2k; <-- using ASM defaults to 100m
create tablespace
   sixteenk blocksize 16k;
create table
   load2k tablespace twok
as
select
   *
from
   dba_objects; < creates 8k rows
drop table
   load2k; <- first create was to preload buffers


set timing on;
create
   table load2k tablespace twok
as
select
   *
from
   dba_objects;
create table
   load16k tablespace sixteen
as
select
   *
from
   dba_objects;
```

For a larger sample, the create processes are reissued with:

```
Select
   *
From
   dba_source;
-- (80k rows)
```

Even with this super-tiny sample on Linux using Oracle10g (with ASM), the results were impressive with a significant performance improvement using large blocksizes.

```
                                        16k
                     blksze             blksze
--------------------------------------------------------
8k table size        4.33 secs          4.16 secs
80k table size       8.74 secs          8.31 secs
```

Oracle Delete Tuning

A *delete* is like any other DML (Data Manipulation Language) statement, and Oracle provides several techniques for doing large batch deletes at a faster speed:

- **Implement partitioning:** Removing large volumes of adjunct data in a related partition is faster. By segregating the data to be deleted into a separate partition, super fast deletes become easy with the *alter tablespace xxx drop partition* syntax. If the user is not licensed for Oracle partitioning and the rows are loaded in-order, it is possible to roll-your-own partitioning using different tables names for each partition.

High Impact Techniques (over 20% faster):

- **Parallelize deletes:** Oracle parallel DML includes delete statements and large deletes can be parallelized for faster performance. Multiple, simultaneous delete statements can be submitted against the same table; however, just make sure that there are enough freelists (or ASSM) to handle the concurrency.

- **Drop indexes:** Dropping indexes before a mass delete and rebuilding them afterwards can improve delete performance because each individual delete would have to remove itself from the index, causing slowdowns. Oracle removes index entries without rebalancing the index tree (a logical delete), but this is still time-consuming, especially if there are lots of indexes on the target table.

Low Impact Techniques (between 5% and 20% faster)

These specialized cases where marginal performance improvements can be seen under special circumstances:

- **Have a larger blocksize:** Heavy insert/update tables can see faster performance when segregated into another blocksize which is mapped to a small data buffer cache. Smaller data buffer caches often see faster throughput performance. The time delay in an Oracle delete is largely the time spent writing the new blocks to disk and placing the table into a 32k blocksize will marginally speed-up delete DML because there will be more rows deleted before a physical write. This speed difference can range from zero up to ten percent depending on the type of delete and the sequencing of the rows.

- **Use bulk binds:** In certain cases, using bulk collect/forall can improve delete performance. Bulk binds are a PL/SQL technique where, instead of multiple individual *delete* statements, all of the operations are carried out at once in bulk. This avoids the context-switching that happens when the PL/SQL engine has to pass over to the SQL engine.

Using Bulking for Delete Performance

The bulk delete operation is the same regardless of server version. Using the *forall_test* table, a single predicate is needed in the *where* clause, but for this example both the *id* and *code* columns are included as if they represented a concatenated key.

The *delete_forall.sql* script listed below is used for this test. The script contains rollback statements, which are necessary to make sure the bulk operation has something to delete. Since the script uses separate collections for each bind, it is suitable for all versions of Oracle that support bulk operations.

🖫 **delete_forall.sql**

```
set serveroutput on
declare
  type t_id_tab is table of forall_test.id%TYPE;
  type t_code_tab is table of forall_test.code%TYPE;
  l_id_tab      t_id_tab    := t_id_tab();
  l_code_tab    t_code_tab := t_code_tab();
  l_start       number;
  l_size        number      := 10000;
begin
  -- Populate collections.
  for i in 1 .. l_size loop
    l_id_tab.extend;
    l_code_tab.extend;
    l_id_tab(l_id_tab.last)      := i;
    l_code_tab(l_code_tab.last) := to_char(i);
  end loop;
  -- Time regular updates.
  l_start := dbms_utility.get_time;
  for i in l_id_tab.first .. l_id_tab.last loop
delete from
  forall_test
where
  id   = l_id_tab(i)
and
  code = l_code_tab(i);
end loop;

  rollback;
  dbms_output.put_line('Normal Deletes : ' ||
                       (dbms_utility.get_time - l_start));
  l_start := dbms_utility.get_time;
  -- Time bulk updates.
  forall i in l_id_tab.first .. l_id_tab.last
delete
  from forall_test
where
  id   = l_id_tab(i)
and
  code = l_code_tab(i);
  dbms_output.put_line('Bulk Deletes   : ' ||
                       (dbms_utility.get_time - l_start));
  rollback;
end;
```

Before running the *delete_forall.sql* script, make sure the *forall_test* table is populated using the *insert_forall.sql* script or there will be no records to delete.

```
SQL> @delete_forall.sql
```

```
Normal Deletes : 416
Bulk Deletes   : 204

PL/SQL procedure successfully completed.
```

The performance of the bulk delete is similar to the performance of the bulk update; the bulk operation is approximately twice the speed of the conventional operation.

Oracle Update Tuning

The SQL standard for DML *update* statements can be complex and convoluted. There are best practices that can help with writing efficient *update* statements.

High impact techniques (over 20% faster):

- **Use CTAS in lieu of large updates:** Copying a table with a *where* clause is often faster than doing a massive *update*. Simply include the set condition in the *where* clause.

- **Simplify the *where* predicates:** This can result in faster update execution plans.

- **Have a small, separate data cache for high DML tables:** Research suggests that heavy insert/update tables can see faster performance when the table is mapped to a small RAM data buffer. This is because the database writer, the DBWR background process, performs a full-scan operation on the RAM heap, searching for dirty blocks. The tinier the buffer, the more efficiently the DBWR may flush the dirty (updated) blocks, writing them back to the disk.

Low-impact techniques (between 5% and 20% faster):

- **Use a larger blocksize:** Heavy insert/update tables can see faster performance when segregated into another blocksize which is mapped to a small data buffer cache

- **Use bulk PL/SQL operators:** In some cases, using PL/SQL for bulk deletes is faster than native SQL

The following section takes a closer look at these techniques and how they apply to common tuning situations.

CTAS vs. SQL Update statements

When the majority of rows in a table are being updated, using Create Table As Select (CTAS) is often more efficient performance than a standard *update*. For example, assume that the following *update* changed 75% of the table rows:

```
update
   mytab
set
   status = 'new'
where
   status = 'old';
```

In this case, a parallelized CTAS may perform far faster

Note: Make sure that there is an SMP server before using the parallel degree option.

```
create table
   new_mytab
nologging as
select
   /*+ full parallel(mytab,35)*/
   decode (status,'new','old',status,
   col2, col3, col4
from
   mytab;

-- rebuild indexes, triggers and constraints to new_mytab

rename
   mytab
      to bkup_mytab;
rename
   new_mytab
      to mytab;
```

Include the *set* Condition in the *where* Clause

This note shows a case where the developer forgot to include the set condition in the *update where* clause, causing high redo waits such as log file parallel write waits and log file sync waits. Simply including the existing state of the *set* clause can result in a huger performance improvement for *update* statements:

```
-- zillion row update
update
   history
set
   flag=0
where
   class='X'
```

```
-- hundred row update
Update
   History
set
   flag=0
where
   class='X'
and
   flag!=0
```

Consider a Small, Separate Data Cache for High DML Tables

As more people adopt the new mainframe computers, 64-bit servers with giant data buffers, there is a delay caused by the database writer process having to scan through giant data buffers seeking dirty blocks. As hardware prices decline and capacity increases, many shops are replacing their platter-style disks with solid-state disks, using solid state disk (SSD) to create a small data buffer. This provides faster throughput for update-bound databases, and the specialty fast update area looks just like a disk.

Because it appears to the OS as a standard storage device, the SSD can be mapped to those tables that experience a high DML rate. The high cost of SSD, currently about $1k/gig, may prohibit SSD adoption by large warehouse systems, e.g. multi-terabyte. If traditional platter disks are still in use, small amounts of SSD can be bought and applied directly to problematic I/O areas.

The high-updates objects, i.e. tables and indexes, can be segregated into a separate blocksize so that they can have a separate, small data buffer. By segregating high activity tables into a separate, smaller data buffer, Oracle has far less RAM frames to scan for dirty block, improving the throughput and also reducing CPU consumption. This is especially important for high update tables with more than 100 row changes per second.

MetaLink Note: 223299.1 also embraces the importance of multiple blocksizes, listing the multiple buffer regions as among the most powerful tuning techniques.

Simplifying the *where* Clause Predicates

The most common issue with updates is the requirement to have a complex *select* statement in the *where* clause to identify the rows to be updated. The best techniques for simplifying *update where* clauses include:

- Predicate pushing
- Rewriting subqueries as outer joins (if possible)
- Oracle SQL subquery un-nesting
- Partitioning pruning
- Avoid *in* and *not in*: it is a good idea to discourage the use of the *not in* clause, which invokes a sub-query, and to prefer *not exists*, which invokes a correlated subquery.

Using Bulk *operations to replace SQL* Updates

In some cases, using PL/SQL with bulking operations is a faster alternative to a SQL *update* statement. Whenever there is a PL/SQL based application, the speed of updates can be greatly improved with bulk binding, which is the use of the *bulk collect* and *forall* operators.

In this simple test, a *forall_test* table is used to compare the performance of individual updates against bulk updates. The script using forall is called *update_forall.sql*.

Check out the *row* keyword!

Note the use of the *row* keyword in the following bulk operation (*set row = l_tab(i)*). This *row* keyword allows updates using the whole record definition. There will be no need to reference each-and-every individual elements of the record!

Here is the test script that does SQL updates with the *forall* operator:

🖫 update_forall.sql

```
set serveroutput on
declare
  type t_id_tab is table of forall_test.id%TYPE;
  type t_forall_test_tab is table of forall_test%ROWTYPE;
  l_id_tab   t_id_tab            := t_id_tab();
  l_tab      t_forall_test_tab := t_forall_test_tab ();
  l_start    number;
  l_size     number              := 10000;
begin
  -- Populate collections.
  for i in 1 .. l_size loop
    l_id_tab.extend;
    l_tab.extend;
    l_id_tab(l_id_tab.last)       := i;
    l_tab(l_tab.last).id          := i;
    l_tab(l_tab.last).code        := to_char(i);
    l_tab(l_tab.last).description := 'Description: ' || to_char(i);
  end loop;

  -- Time regular updates.
  l_start := dbms_utility.get_time;
  for i in l_tab.first .. l_tab.last loop
    update
       forall_test
    set
       row = l_tab(i)
    where
       id  = l_tab(i).id;
  end loop;

  dbms_output.put_line('Normal Updates : ' ||
                      (dbms_utility.get_time - l_start));
  l_start := dbms_utility.get_time;
  -- Time bulk updates.

  -- *****************************************************
  -- ***  Here is the forall
  -- *****************************************************
  forall i in l_tab.first .. l_tab.last
    update
       forall_test
    set
       row = l_tab(i)
    where
       id  = l_id_tab(i);

  dbms_output.put_line('Bulk Updates   : ' ||
```

```
                              (dbms_utility.get_time - l_start));
  commit;
end;
/
```

Bulking SQL Updates

The *update_forall.sql* script has a similar internal structure to the *insert_forall.sql* script described earlier. The main difference is the *update* statement requires a *where* clause that references the table's *id* column allowing individual rows to be targeted. If the bulk operation were altered to reference the *id* column within the collection, the following compilation error would be produced.

```
  -- Incorrect bulk operation.
  forall i in l_tab.first .. l_tab.last
    update
      forall_test
    set
      row = l_tab(i)
    where
      id  = l_tab(i).id;
```

```
Errors for PROCEDURE UPDATE_FORALL:

LINE/COL ERROR
-------- ----------------------------------------------------------
36/5     PL/SQL: SQL Statement ignored
38/18    PL/SQL: ORA-22806: not an object or REF
38/18    PLS-00382: expression is of wrong type
38/18    PLS-00436: implementation restriction: cannot reference
         fields of BULK In-BIND table of records
```

Before running the script, make sure the *forall_test* table is populated using the *insert_forall.sql* script or there will be no records to update. The results from the *update_forall.sql* script are listed below.

```
SQL> @update_forall.sql


Normal Updates : 202
Bulk Updates   : 104

PL/SQL procedure successfully completed.
```

In this example, the use of *forall* creates approximately twice the speed of the conventional PL/SQL update method.

Bulking SQL Inserts

In some cases, using the PL/SQL *forall* bulking operator can make inserts an order of magnitude faster than SQL. Loading data from an Oracle table from a PL/SQL array involves expensive *"context switches"*, and the PL/SQL *forall* operator speed is an amazing alternative to SQL *insert* DML..

Kent Crotty, author of the bestselling book *"**Easy Oracle Application Express**"* conducted a benchmark and found that using *forall* bulking in PL/SQL was an astonishing 30 times faster than using vanilla SQL inserts:

```
DECLARE
TYPE prod_tab IS TABLE OF products%ROWTYPE;
products_tab    prod_tab := prod_tab();
start_time  number;  end_time    number;
BEGIN
-- Populate a collection - 100000 rows
SELECT * BULK COLLECT INTO products_tab FROM products;

EXECUTE IMMEDIATE 'TRUNCATE TABLE products';
Start_time := DBMS_UTILITY.get_time;
FOR i in products_tab.first .. products_tab.last LOOP
 INSERT INTO products (product_id, product_name, effective_date)
   VALUES (products_tab(i).product_id, products_tab(i).product_name,
        products_tab(i).effective_date);
END LOOP;
end_time := DBMS_UTILITY.get_time;
DBMS_OUTPUT.PUT_LINE('Conventional Insert: '||to_char(end_time-start_time));

EXECUTE IMMEDIATE 'TRUNCATE TABLE products';
Start_time := DBMS_UTILITY.get_time;
FORALL i in products_tab.first .. products_tab.last
 INSERT INTO products VALUES products_tab(i);
end_time := DBMS_UTILITY.get_time;
DBMS_OUTPUT.PUT_LINE('Bulk Insert: '||to_char(end_time-start_time));
COMMIT;
END;
```

Crotty notes a great speed improvement with very few code changes, from 622 seconds to only 22 seconds:

```
SQL> /
Conventional Insert: 686
Bulk Insert: 22
```

Next, let's move on and look at one of the most important areas of SQL tuning, the use of indexes. Indexes, more than any other tool, offer us the ability to minimize data block touches and get the rows that we need quickly and efficiently.

Oracle tuning with indexes

When discussing Oracle indexes it's important to understand that indexes are used to maintain referential integrity, to remove full-table scans and to speed up SQL by providing a direct path to matching table rows. An Oracle database can run without any indexes at all, but it's your job to create and maintain the optimal set of indexes for the SQL workload.

SQL Tuning with Indexes

Oracle is the world's most powerful and flexible database and it has numerous index types to improve the speed of Oracle SQL queries. Disk storage has become unbelievably inexpensive and Oracle leverages upon cheap storage with new indexing types, based upon algorithms that dramatically increase the speed with which Oracle queries are serviced.

This chapter explores the internals of Oracle indexing; reviewing the standard b-tree index, bitmap indexes, function-based indexes, and index-only tables (IOTs); and demonstrates how these indexes may dramatically increase the speed of Oracle SQL queries.

Because indexes are such an important component to SQL tuning, this chapter is quite large and covers these important topics:

- Types of Oracle Indexes

    o Single-column b-tree indexes
    o Multi-column b-tree indexes
    o Bitmap indexes
    o Bitmap join indexes

- Tuning SQL with function-based indexes
- Tuning SQL with the CASE statement
- Tuning SQL with regular expressions
- Using Index-only tables

- Finding missing indexes
- Removing superfluous indexes
- Removing un-used indexes

- Index usage and clustering
- Forcing index usage
- Index maintenance
- Index monitoring
- Rebuilding indexes for SQL performance

With respect to SQL optimization, Oracle uses indexes to alleviate the need for large-table, full-table scans and disk sorts. In the absence of an index, the SQL optimizer may not be able to find an efficient way to service the SQL query and invoke an expensive full table scan.

Not all full-scans are bad!

If your SQL *optimizer_mode is* set to minimize computing resources (*all_rows*), a full-scan on a small table may be more efficient than index access.

In addition to speeding up SQL, Oracle indexes are also used to enforce the uniqueness of columns and to maintain one-to-many and many-to many data relationships (as defined by primary and foreign keys constraints).

When you create a primary or unique foreign key, Oracle builds indexes on your behalf and then uses these indexes to enforce the data relationships between all parent and child rows.

For example, in a one-to-many relationship, Oracle will not allow a child row to exist without a matching parent row, and every insert of a row to the child table will cause Oracle to lookup the parent key to ensure that the logical data relationship is maintained.

Be careful when disabling referential integrity!

While Oracle does not recommend it, some applications such as SAP will turn-off primary and foreign key constraints in order to improve DML performance and reduce overhead.

While some "trustworthy" applications will deliberately disable indexes for primary and foreign keys, this techniques only works in systems where the end-user cannot access the database with any ad-hoc interfaces such as SQL*Plus or ODBC.

Turning-off referential integrity is risky, but it has been done successfully for applications that require high performance data loading. In some applications, referential integrity is temporarily disabled and re-enabled after batch data loads.

The types of Oracle indexes

As we may know, Oracle offers a wealth of index structures, each with their own benefits and drawbacks. Here are some of the most common:

- **Single-column B-tree indexes**: This is the standard tree index that Oracle has been using since the earliest releases.

- **Multi-column b-tree indexes:** You can define multiple columns to match any SQL *where* clause, providing super-fast access to your desired rows. These *concatenated* indexes allow you to combine many table columns together into a single index.

- **Bitmap indexes:** Bitmap indexes are used where an index column has a relatively small number of distinct values (low cardinality). Bitmap indexes are designed for super-fast access for read-only databases, but are not suitable for systems with frequent updates.

- **Bitmap join indexes**: This is an index structure whereby data columns from other tables appear in a multi-column index of a junction table. This is the only create index syntax to employ a SQL-like from clause and where clause.

- **Index-only tables** – In cases where every column in the table is needed by a multi-column index, the table itself becomes redundant, and the table rows can be maintained within the index tree.

- **Reverse key indexes** – To improve SQL *insert* performance, you can build an index with the *reverse* keyword, internally reversing the keys. The reverse key index behaves like an ordinary b-tree index, but it performs faster in RAC systems. See chapter 19, ***Oracle DML Tuning*** for details on using reverse key indexes.

While Oracle will only use one index to access any given table (with rare exceptions), in complex n-way table joins we may see many index types in our plan including bitmap indexes, a single-column b-tree index, or multi-column b-tree indexes.

Now let's get started and look deeper into each types of Oracle index and see how they are used to speed-up SQL queries by reviewing standard Oracle b-tree indexes.

The Oracle b-tree index

The oldest and most popular type of Oracle index is the tried and true b-tree index, a basic index type that has not changed since the earliest releases of Oracle and remains the most widely used index type within a typical Oracle database.

Conceptually, Oracle uses a rows location as a pointer to a row. Just as your home address uniquely identifies where you live, an Oracle ROWID uniquely identified where an index rows resides.

You can conceptualize a b-tree index as a long list of key-and ROWID pairs, organized in a tree form for fast lookup of a symbolic key. However, in reality, the higher level index nodes with have start and end key values, while the lowest level tree nodes contain the actual ROWID and key pairs. The amount of key pairs in the lowest level nodes depends upon the key length and the index blocksize.

Oracle can read an index "sideways" (via the index fast full scan), but the most common access method is traversing an index via dropping-down into the index using the key value: (Figure 16.22).

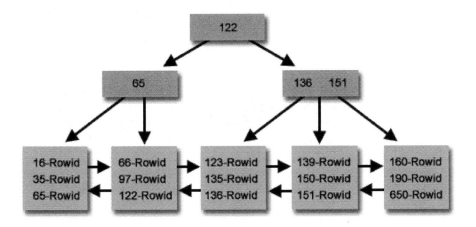

Figure 16.22: *An Oracle b-tree index*

In addition to speeding access to table rows, b-tree indexes are also used to avoid large sorting operations. In most queries with an *order by* clause, Oracle will retrieve the rows and then sort them in RAM.

However, the optimizer can also choose to use the index to fetch the rows in pre-sorted order. For example, a SQL query requiring 10,000 rows to be presented in sorted order will often use a b-tree index to avoid the very large sort required to deliver the data to the end user.

We can quickly drop through the tree to find the symbolic key, and once we have the corresponding ROWID we can fetch the rows directly (Figure 16.23):

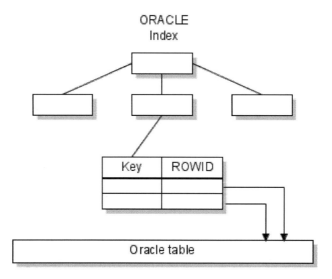

Figure 16.23: *Index traversal for a b-tree index*

Oracle offers several options when creating an index using the default b-tree structure. You can create an index on multiple columns (a *concatenated* index) to improve access speeds for queries with multiple where clause predicates. You can also specify that different columns be sorted in different orders with one column sorted *ascending* and the next column in *descending* order. This is very handy because you can make an index match the sort order of a report and fetch the report rows quickly, in pre-sorted order.

For example, we could create a b-tree index on a column called *last_name* in ascending order and have a second column within the index that displays the salary column in descending order.

```
create index
    name_salary_idx
on
    person
(
    last_name    asc,
    salary       desc
);
```

While b-tree indexes are great for simple queries, they are not very good for low-cardinality columns. These are columns with a relatively low number of distinct values do not have the selectivity required in order to benefit from standard b-tree index structures.

In order to properly manage the blocks, Oracle controls the allocation of pointers within each data block. As an Oracle tree grows (via inserting rows into the table), Oracle fills the block, and when full it splits, creating new index nodes (data blocks) to manage the symbolic keys within the index. Hence, an Oracle index block may contain two types of pointers:

1. Pointers to other index nodes (data blocks)

2. ROWID pointers to specific table rows

Oracle manages the allocation of pointers within index blocks, and this is the reason why we are unable to specify a *pctused* value (the freelist re-link threshold) for indexes. When we examine an index block structure, we see that the number of entries within each index node is a function of two values:

1. The length of the symbolic key
2. The blocksize for the index tablespace

Each data block within the index contains "nodes" in the index tree, with the bottom nodes (leaf blocks), containing pairs of symbolic keys and ROWID values.

As a single task inserts rows into an empty Oracle b-tree, the index until the block is full (based on your specification of the *pctfree* parameter for the index). At that point, inserts of more rows will cause the index tree to split, creating a new index node (on a new data blocks) to manage the symbolic keys within the index. Hence, an Oracle index block may contain pointers to other index nodes or ROWID/Symbolic-key pairs.

Creating a b-tree index

Conceptually a b-tree index can be thought of as a set of symbolic keys and ROWID pairs that allow the SQL to lookup the symbolic key and quickly find the matching ROWID. Once your SQL has the ROWID, it can proceed directly to the desired data block and fetch the row.

When you create an index, it's important to note that Oracle b-tree indexes have two layers, a logical layer (the key and ROWID pairs) and physical layer, consisting of the disk data blocks. Because Oracle's software engineers chose to map the boundary of a logical index node to a disk data block, the blocksize impacts the structure of the index tree. The Oracle block size serves as the boundaries for each index node (called the "the index node, or *inode* for short), and the index blocksize determines how many pairs of symbolic keys and ROWID's may fit on each index node.

As an index grows, we see two types of expansion operations:

- **Splitting** – As data block become logically full (according to your setting for the *pctfree* index parameter), each index block are marked as full, and the disk data block removed from the index freelist. Subsequent index growth will require Oracle to fetch a new data block from the freelist, thereby adding a new node to the index tree.

- **Spawning** – At predetermined size threshold, Oracle will decide to "spawn" the b-tree to create a new level. The number of levels for any given index can be viewed in the *blevel* column of the *dba_indexes* view. The most common height of an index is three levels, but large data warehouses will see indexes spawn into four tree levels.

Now that we understand how the logical tree nodes are tied to the physical disk blocks, let's examine how the size of the disk data block impacts the b-tree structure.

Does block size matter?

Because the index block size is directly tied to the index node structure, an index in a 2k blocksize with have less index keys per node than an index that uses a 32k blocksize, and an index in a 2k blocksize will also spawn into more levels than a index in a 32k blocksize.

According to Christopher Foot, author of the *OCP Instructors Guide for Oracle DBA Certification*, larger index block sizes might improve the key density and improve the run-time index performance, with less tree levels to traverse in order to fetch the required ROWID:

> "A bigger block size means more space for key storage in the branch nodes of B-tree indexes, which reduces index height and improves the performance of indexed queries."

While in most cases the index blocksize does not have an appreciable effect on SQL performance, very large mission critical databases with frequently deploy multiple blocksizes for indexes under these conditions:

- **Preventing index key fragmentation** – Indexes on large column datatypes (e.g. VARCHAR(2000), CLOB, LONG) should have a large enough blocksize to hold multiple rows on a single data block. For example, a 8k blocksize would not be appropriate for an index on a 10k symbolic key.

- **Small blocksizes and RAC** – Oracle Real Application Clusters (RAC) system can reduce pinging if we place indexes in a smaller blocksize. This minimizes the overhead of block transfers across the cache fusion layer.

- **Small blocksizes to reduce contention** – In cases of super-high concurrent DML, placing an index into a smaller blocksize can increase throughout. In some high-performance systems, high-DML indexes will be segregated into non-standard blocksizes with smaller data buffers, thereby improving DML performance by reducing the amount of data buffer block to scan when seeking dirty blocks.

- **Large blocksize for large reads** – In certain cases, a DBA will place an index that experiences lots of multi-block range scans, index fast full scans into a larger blocksize, thereby increasing the amount of data retrieved in a single read operation.

Today, most large corporate Oracle systems will deploy the multiple blocksize feature of Oracle because it provides buffer segregation and the ability to place objects with the most appropriate blocksize to reduce buffer waste. Some of the world record TPC Oracle benchmarks use very large data buffers and multiple blocksizes, see www.tpc.org for details.

Now that we understand what happens when a b-tree index grows, let's examine what happens when an index contracts. Whenever possible, Oracle attempts to keep the index data blocks evenly balanced, but when rows are deleted en-masse, Oracle deliberately chooses not to incur the runtime overhead of re-balancing the index disk data block.

As you might imagine, it would take considerable overhead to move rows around to evenly balance the tree entries across the data blocks, and the Oracle engineers wisely chose a "logical delete" feature. As rows are deleted, Oracle maintains an internal threshold (similar to the *pctused* threshold for tables), where Oracle marks a data block as empty, without physically taking the overhead to wipe the disk block clean.

In cases where large batch jobs delete millions of rows from tables, massive empty spaces appears on the data block, leading to an index fragmentation condition called *index browning*. Just as a lightening strike can cause a section of a tree to become dead, Oracle indexes will have large numbers of near-empty data blocks that cause index scan operations to take longer than required.

If you have purchased the extra-cost Oracle Segment Advisor software, Oracle can be configured to notify you about this condition and you can also see the section on index monitoring later in this chapter for scripts that you can run to detect index browning.

Also, note the important content later in this chapter on using multi-column indexes, a technique where a single index may be used to replace several smaller indexes and improve overall indexing strategies.

Next, let's look at how bitmap indexes are used in read-only database for super-fast access to low cardinality columns.

Tuning SQL with bitmapped indexes

Oracle bitmap indexes are very different from standard b-tree indexes. In bitmap structures, a two-dimensional array is created with one column for every row in the table being indexed. Each column represents a distinct value within the bitmapped index. This two-dimensional array represents each value within the index multiplied by the number of rows in the table.

At row retrieval time, Oracle decompresses the bitmap into the RAM data buffers so it can be rapidly scanned for matching values. These matching values are delivered to Oracle in the form of a Row-ID list, and these Row-ID values may directly access the required information.

It's very easy for a beginner to forget that bitmap indexes are only for low-cardinality columns (columns with only a few unique values like *gender, color, year of birth*, or *ethnicity*), and you can only be effective with bitmap indexes in read-only tables, where new rows are loaded at night and the bitmaps rebuilt.

Distinct key values and bitmap indexes!

The maximum cardinality for bitmap indexes is a function of the number of distinct values and the size of the key, but far and away it is the number of distinct values that is the largest contributing factor to the maximum number of distinct values you can have in a bitmap index.

As the number of distinct values increases, the size of the bitmap increases exponentially, such that an index with 100 values may perform thousands of times faster than a bitmap index on 1,000 distinct column values. The answer, as with all Oracle tuning questions is "It depends". To understand this, remember that when you create a bitmap, it is a two dimensional matrix with two axis:

- **The number of rows in the table**: A million rows table will have a million row bitmap index
- **The number of distinct keys**: The cardinality of the bitmap column is important because there will be one entry in the axis of the bitmap index for each distinct value. The size of these keys also reflects here, since the size of the bitmap index is directly influenced by the size of the key values.

Also, remember that bitmap indexes are only suitable for static tables and materialized views which are updated at night and rebuilt after batch row loading.

Bitmaps are for read-only tables!

Bitmap indexes should be for tables that are read-only during query time. The DML overhead of maintaining bitmap indexes is huge.

So, which are the right maximum values for your bitmap index? Who knows? You will need to run performance benchmarks on your unique database to see!

Benchmarks have shown these trends in SQL performance and the number of distinct bitmap index values (as a percentage of total table rows), and the clustering factor for the index column. All else being equal, cardinality is one of the most important factors in deciding to use a bitmap index, but there are rare cases where a bitmap on a column with 10,000 key values might be appropriate.

Remember how bitmap indexes are generally used. Because they are low cardinality, they have very little value by themselves, and the power comes when Oracle combines multiple bitmaps in a bitmap merge operation.

The real benefit of bitmapped indexing occurs when one table includes multiple bitmapped indexes.

Alone, each individual column has low cardinality is not very selective, but the creation of multiple bitmapped indexes provides a very powerful method for rapidly answering difficult SQL queries.

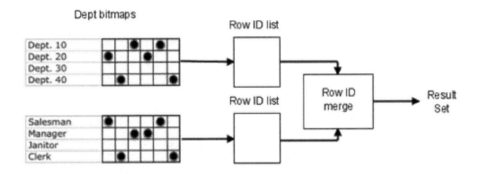

Figure 16.24: *A bitmap merge operation*

Consider a case where we have multiple columns with low cardinality values, such as *car_color, car_make, car_model,* and *car_year.* Each column contains less than 100 distinct values by themselves, and a b-tree index would be fairly useless in a database of 20 million vehicles.

However, combining these indexes together in a query can provide blistering response times a lot faster than the traditional method of reading each one of the 20 million rows in the base table. For example, assume we wanted to find old blue Toyota Corollas manufactured in 1981:

```
-- ***************************************************
-- SQL will multiple low-cardinality specifications
-- ***************************************************

select
   license_plat_nbr
from
   vehicle
where
   color = 'maroon'
and
   make = 'ford'
and
   year = 2011;
```

Tuning SQL with bitmapped indexes   **915**

Oracle uses a specialized optimizer method called a bitmapped index merge to service this query. In a bitmapped index merge, each Row-ID, or RID, list is built independently by using the bitmaps, and a special merge routine is used in order to compare the RID lists and find the intersecting values. Using this methodology, Oracle can provide sub-second response time when working against multiple low-cardinality columns (Figure 16.25):

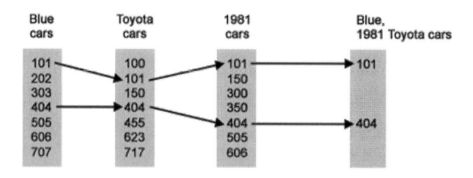

Figure 16.25: *Oracle bitmap merge join*

When using bitmapped indexes, we must remember several very important points:

- **Tables must be read-only:** The run-time overhead for updating a bitmap is huge, and bitmapped indexes are designed for databases where data is loaded in batch mode and the bitmaps re-created after each data load.

- **Columns must be low cardinality:** Each unique value of a bitmap index increases the size of an index, and as a general rule, and column with more than a few hundred distinct values will not perform well with a bitmap index.

- **Combinatorial SQL is best for bitmaps:** Any single bitmap index is of very limited value, and the real power of a bitmap index happens when a SQL query has predicates from multiple low-cardinality columns.

Now, that we understand the power of bitmap indexes, let's move on and look at a cousin of the bitmapped index, the bitmap join index, a novel way of pre-joining related table columns for fast row retrieval.

SQL Tuning with bitmap join indexes

Oracle9*i* first added the bitmap join index to its mind-boggling array of table join methods. This new table access method requires that you create an index that performs the join at index creation time and that creates a bitmap index of the keys used in the join. But unlike most relational database indexes, the indexed columns don't reside in the table.

Oracle has revolutionized index creation by allowing a *where* clause to be included in the index creation syntax. This feature revolutionizes the way relational tables are accessed via SQL.

The bitmap join index is extremely useful for table joins that involve low-cardinality columns (e.g. a column with less than 300 distinct values). However, bitmap join indexes aren't useful in all cases. You shouldn't use them for OLTP databases because of the high overhead associated with updating bitmap indexes. Let's take a closer look at how this type of index works.

How bitmap join indexes work

To illustrate bitmap join indexes, I'll use a simple example, a many-to-many relationship where we have parts and suppliers with an inventory table serving as the junction for the many-to-many relationship. Each part has many suppliers and each supplier provides many parts (Figure 6.26).

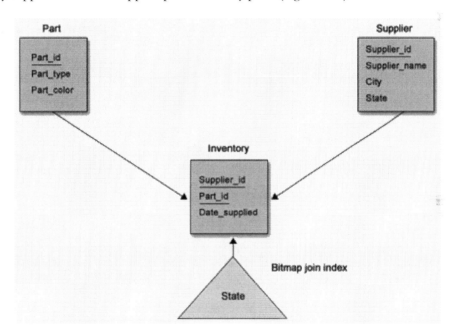

Figure 16.26: *A bitmap join index on a many-to-many relationship*

Note that this bitmap join index specified the join criteria for the three tables and created a bitmap index on the junction table (Inventory) with the *part_type* and *state* keys.

For this example, I'll assume the database has 300 types of parts and the suppliers provide parts in all 50 states. So there are 50 distinct values in the *state* column and only 300 distinct values in the *part_type* column.

Note that we create an index on the Inventory using columns contained in the *Supplier* and *Part* tables. The idea behind a bitmap join index is to pre-join the low cardinality columns, making the overall join faster.

It is well known that bitmap indexes can improve the performance of Oracle queries where the predicates involve the low cardinality columns, but this technique has never been employed in cases where the low cardinality columns reside in a foreign table.

To create a bitmap join index, issue the following Oracle DDL: (Note the inclusion of the *from* and *where* clauses inside the *create index* syntax.).

```
create bitmap index
   part_suppliers_state
on
   inventory(
      parts.part_type,
      supplier.state)
from
   inventory i,
   parts p,
   supplier s
where
   i.part_id=p.part_id
and
   i.supplier_id=p.supplier_id;
```

This is a fascinating idea, the concept of placing a SQL *where* clause in a *create index* statement! As we see, the bitmap join index syntax borrows the ANSI *from* clause and *where* clause from SQL.

Bitmap join index example

To see how bitmap join indexes work, look at this example of a SQL query. Let's suppose you want a list of all suppliers of pistons in North Carolina. To get that list, you would use this query:

```
select
   supplier_name
from
   parts
natural join
   inventory
natural join
   suppliers
where
   part_type = 'piston' and state='nc';
```

Prior to Oracle9i, this form of SQL query would be serviced by a *nested loops* join or *hash* join of all three tables. With a bitmap join index, the index has pre-joined the tables, and the query can quickly retrieve a row ID list of matching table rows in all three tables.

Oracle benchmarks claim that bitmap join indexes can run a query more than eight times faster than traditional indexing methods. However, this speed improvement is dependent upon many factors, and the bitmap join is not a panacea. Some restrictions on using the bitmap join index include:

- The indexed columns must be of low cardinality—usually with less than 100 distinct values.

- The query must not have any references in the *where* clause to data columns that are not contained in the index.

- The overhead when updating bitmap join indexes is substantial. For practical use, bitmap join indexes are dropped and rebuilt each evening about the daily batch load jobs. This means that bitmap join indexes are useful only for Oracle data warehouses that remain read-only during the processing day.

Remember: Bitmap join indexes can tremendously speed up specific data warehouse queries but at the expense of pre-joining the tables at bitmap index creation time. You must also be concerned about high-volume updates. Bitmap indexes are notoriously slow to change when the table data changes, and this can severely slow down *insert* and *update* DML against the target tables.

Exclusions for bitmap join indexes

Oracle imposes restrictions on when the SQL optimizer is allowed to invoke a bitmap join index. For queries that have additional criteria in the *where* clause that doesn't appear in the bitmap join index, Oracle will be unable to use this index to service the query. For example, the following query will not use the bitmap join index:

```
select
    supplier_name
from
    parts
natural join
    inventory
natural join
    suppliers
where
    part_type = 'piston'
and
    state = 'nc' and part_color = 'yellow';
```

Oracle has introduced extremely sophisticated execution plan features that can dramatically improve query performance, but these features cannot be used automatically. The Oracle professional's challenge is to understand these new indexing features, analyze the trade-offs of additional indexing, and judge when the new features can be used to speed queries.

When Oracle SQL chooses the wrong index

Back in the day when Oracle used the rule-based optimizer (up until 2007 in Oracle apps), the rule-based optimizer would commonly choose an index with poor selectivity.

If your goal for SQL tuning for fast response time, we seek to get the rows that we want with a minimum of data block touches. With respect to indexes, one sure sign of Oracle choosing a "wrong" index (one with less that optimal selectivity) is excessive *db file sequential read*, the type of disk read that indicates index access. You can easily run the Oracle *tkprof* utility to see the I/O details for any SQL statement.

Oracle SQL has metadata that shows the selectivity of the index, and it's rare to see Oracle choose a less-than stellar index, unless, of course, you have a "missing" index. However, there are cases where Oracle SQL chooses the wrong index, even in Oracle 11g.

Beware of high sequential reads!

Oracle can tell you if you are using a "wrong" index. One sure sign of a sub-optimal index are cases where you see too many *db file sequential read* events to justify fetching the row set.

Beware of the fast fix

If you report a sub-optimal index bugs to Oracle technical support, resist the temptation to set your *optimizer_features_enable* parameter. This is a fast fix "workaround" approach that fixes the issue, but does not address the root cause issue that caused the optimizer to choose the wrong index. Instead of downgrading the optimizer functionality to an earlier release, insist that Oracle resolve the root cause issue and issue a patch for the problem.

Next, let's look at techniques for forcing the optimizer to use an index. While this technique is rarely used in production environments, it is a great SQL tuning tool, allowing you to test your query execution time with different indexes.

Forcing index usage

One of the most common problems that I hear is "*Why is Oracle not using my index?*" Usually, this is because the table is so small that full-scan access is always faster and cheaper, but there are cases when you deliberately want to alter the execution of a SQL statement to change index access. Here are some common techniques:

- Changing optimizer parameters (optimizer_mode, optimizer_index_cost_adj)

- Adding column histograms (with dbms_stats)

- Changing index attributes (unique vs nonunique)

- Using an index hint

In general, index access usually starts returning rows faster than full-scan activity, but there are exceptions. Remember, it's the cost of the read-write head movement time on an I/O that takes-up most of the latency, and a multi-block read from a full scan that scan a dozen data blocks will always take less time than a dozen individual disk reads on discontiguous block.

Obviously, if I only want a dozen rows from a million row table, using an index would be the best access method, but what about a query that reads 30% of the table rows? What about a query that reads 60% of the table rows?

What is the threshold for using an index? The answer depends primarily upon the number of rows requested and the density of the rows per block, which, in turn, are a function of *avg_row_len* and *db_xxk_block_size*. But in the real world it's not that simple, since there are many other intervening factors such as how much if an index is cached in RAM (see the *optimizer_index_caching* parameter), and the selectivity of the target index.

Are you under-indexed?

When I evaluate an OLTP database, I check is how much space is used for indexes vs. data. A properly indexed OLTP database will have at least 30% of space dedicated to indexes, often as much as 60%.

Let's start our investigation of Oracle indexing by examining how Oracle has incorporate data functions into indexes, allowing us total freedom to create an index on anything that we see in the *where* clause of a SQL statement.

Why doesn't Oracle use my index?

A very common question with SQL tuners is *"Why isn't Oracle using my index?"* Oracle SQL not using an index is a common complaint, and it's often because the optimizer thinks that a full-scan is cheaper than index access. Oracle not using an index can be due to:

- **Bad/incomplete statistics** – Make sure to re-analyze the table and index with *dbms_stats* to ensure that the optimizer has good metadata.

- **Wrong optimizer_mode** – The *first_rows_n* optimizer mode is to minimize response time, and it is more likely to use an index than the default *all_rows* mode.

- **Bugs** – See these important notes on optimizer changes in 10g that cause Oracle not to use an index.

- **Cost adjustment** – In some cases, the optimizer will still not use an index, and you must decrease *optimizer_index_cost_adj*.

Try a rule hint!

For testing unnecessary large table full table scans, try a *rule* hint (*select /*+ RULE */ col1*). If the query uses the index with a *rule* hint, you have an issue with the CBO.

The Oracle cost-based optimizer carefully evaluates every query when making the decision whether to invoke a full-table scan or index access, and you can force index usage with in index hint. The goal of the SQL optimizer is to only force an index when it's the "best" access plan, given your optimization goals (Figure 16.27)

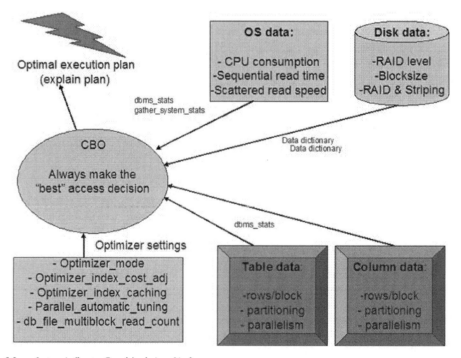

Figure 16.27: *Many factors influence Oracle's choice of index*

Some of the variables that influence the decision to force or ignore an index include:

- **The numbers of blocks in the table:** Small tables are accessed faster with a full scan and forcing index usage may hurt performance.

- **System statistics:** the *dbms_stats.gather_system_stats* procedure measures external timing for index access (sequential reads) and full-scan access (scattered reads). If Oracle sees expensive index disk reads, it may ignore an index.

- **System parameters:** There are several initialization parameters that can impact the propensity of the optimizer to choose an index:

  o **db_file_multiblock_read_count:** Prior to Oracle 10.2 (when this setting became automatic), this parameter helped govern the relative costs of full-scan vs. index costs.

  o **sort_area_size** (if not using *pga_aggregate_target*): The sort_area_size influences the CBO when deciding whether to perform an index access or a sort of the result set. The higher the value for sort_area_size, the more likely that a sort will be performed in RAM, and the more likely that the CBO will favor a sort over presorted index retrieval.

- **Optimizer parameter values:** You can adjust several optimizer parameters to force Oracle to use an index:

  o **optimizer_mode:** The *all_rows* access method often favors a parallel full-table scan over an index scan. The *first_rows_n optimizer_mode* will often stop Oracle from ignoring an index because it favors index access over computing resources.

  o **optimizer_index_cost_adj:** This parameter alters the costing algorithm for access paths involving indexes. The smaller the value, the lower the cost of index access.

  o **Optimizer_index_caching** – The *optimizer_index_caching* parameter is set by the DBA to help the optimizer know, on average, how much of an index resides inside the data buffer. The setting for *optimizer_index_caching* affects the CBO's decision to use an index for a table join (nested loops) or to favor a full-table scan.

For an example of how parameters can effect index usage, a developer may be tempted to switch to the *all_rows optimizer_mode* (or add an *all_rows* hint to their SQL), believing that it will improve throughput, while not realizing that *all_rows* favors full-scans over index usage.

In a similar example, some developers will mistakenly add a *parallel* hint to a SQL statement to improve performance, not realizing that Oracle parallel query only works with full-scans.

As we see, the Oracle SQL optimizer is very intelligent, and he will often bypass an index whenever a full-scan or a more selective index can be used.

Now, let's explore the most powerful indexing tool of all, the function-based index. The FBI is the single most frequently overlooked of all of the SQL tuning tools.

Using *nls_date_format* with *date* indexes

One of the single most common SQL coding errors is a developer specifying a date check in their where clause that invalidates the data index causing a sub-optimal SQL execution plan. In more serious cases, improperly specific date references in a SQL where clause can cause production crashes, especially when the SQL only fails with specific date values.

Hence, properly specifying date values is critical to proper SQL coding, and many SQL experts always advise explicitly specifying the date conversion to that the predicate compares values, date to date:

```
select
   stuff
from
   mytab
where
   order_date > to_date('14-MAY-2009','DD-MON-YYYY');
```

As a best practice, the left-hand side column should be free of any built-in functions that will make the index unusable.

We can use function-based indexes to make an index match the where clause exactly, but in many cases the index can be used with a few adjustments to the syntax of the data statement and adjusting the *nls_date_format* parameter.

One maddening feature of relational databases is the implicit *date* datatypes and the problems making the SQL use a generic index upon a *date* column.

In SQL we always see an implicit type conversion when a SQL statement does a date check. To understand this issue, consider these queries:

```
--**********************************************************
-- This will use the index because nls_date_format matches
--**********************************************************
alter session set nls_date_format= 'DD-MON-YYYY';
select stuff from mytab where order_date > '14-MAY-2009';

alter session set nls_date_format = 'MON';
select stuff from mytab where order_date = 'MAR';

alter session set nls_date_format = 'DAY';
select stuff from mytab where order_date = 'TUESDAY';
```

```
--*********************************************************
-- These may not use the order_date index because of
-- the nls_date_format mismatch
--*********************************************************
alter session set nls_date_format= 'DD-MON-RR';
select stuff from mytab where order_date > '14-MAY-2009';

alter session set nls_date_format = 'DAY';
select stuff from mytab where order_date = 'APRIL';

alter session set nls_date_format = 'MON';
select stuff from mytab where order_date = 'TUESDAY';
```

Why does the second set of queries fail to use an index? This is because Oracle always does an implicit conversion of the right-hand side of the query to change your predicate into a date datatype.

Problems occur when the system's default *nls_date_format* do not match the database where the original query was written and tested. This can lead to super-serious production problems, especially when the implicit conversion makes the SQL work with some dates and not others.

Your setting for *nls_territory* and *nls_date* can affect your *nls_date_format*, such that SQL may not use an index when moved onto another platform. Always test your SQL to ensure that the date index is being used.

These cases are rare, but it's when problems occur, the results can be devastating. As a developer best practice, many shops require the SQL coder to explicitly perform the conversion using the *to_date* built-in function. This also has the side benefit of not requiring you to carefully monitor your current value for *nls_date_format*:

```
--*************************************************************
-- To be safe, match the data datatypes and specify the date format:
--*************************************************************
select stuff from mytab
where
    order_date > to_date('14-MAY-2009','DD-MON-YYYY');

select stuff from mytab
where
    order_date = to_date('APRIL','MON');

select stuff from mytab
where
    order_date = to_date('TUESDAY','DAY');
```

Now that we see how the *nls_date_format* can help Oracle use indexes, let's examine how to write the correct syntax for complex date manipulation in SQL.

Forcing index usage

Managing complex date comparisons in SQL

As we see, it's easy to put a date check in SQL, but not so easy to ensure that the SQL uses the matching date index. To aid in specifying complex date predicates, Oracle offers a host of powerful functions for comparing date column values.

For example, assume that we needed a query to display data from the first Monday of each quarter year. In this case, we can elegantly use the *add_months* function to return the answer, while ensuring that the query is able to use the data index:

```
select
   stuff
from
   mytab
where
   'next_day(add_months(trunc(sysdate, ''q''), 3), ''monday'')'
```

Let's look at some more examples of using date BIF's for complex SQL where clause specifications.

Using the *months_between* date function

This Oracle date function returns the months between two dates. For example, if we wanted to know how many months an employee has worked for the company, we can use this Oracle date function.

```
select
  months_between(sysdate,emp_date_of_hire)
from
  emp;

MONTHS_BETWEEN(SYSDATE,EMP_DATE_OF_HIRE)
----------------------------------------              58.7710805
                              70.7710805
                              34.7710805
```

Notice that this Oracle date function returns the fraction of a month. You could use trunc or round to make the results more readable.

Using the *add_months* date function

The *add_months* Oracle date function gives you the same day, n number of months away. Note that the "n" can be positive or negative, so you can go backwards in time.

```
select
  sysdate,
  add_months(sysdate,1),
```

```
  add_months(sysdate,2),
  add_months(sysdate,3),
  add_months(sysdate,4),
  add_months(sysdate,5),
  add_months(sysdate,6)
from
  dual;

SYSDATE    ADD_MONTH ADD_MONTH ADD_MONTH ADD_MONTH ADD_MONTH ADD_MONTH
--------- --------- --------- --------- --------- --------- ---------
24-JAN-05 24-FEB-05 24-MAR-05 24-APR-05 24-MAY-05 24-JUN-05 24-JUL-05


select
  sysdate,
  add_months(sysdate,-1),
  add_months(sysdate,-2),
  add_months(sysdate,-3),
  add_months(sysdate,-4),
  add_months(sysdate,-5),
  add_months(sysdate,-6)
from
  dual;

SYSDATE    ADD_MONTH ADD_MONTH ADD_MONTH ADD_MONTH ADD_MONTH ADD_MONTH
--------- --------- --------- --------- --------- --------- ---------
24-JAN-05 24-DEC-04 24-NOV-04 24-OCT-04 24-SEP-04 24-AUG-04 24-JUL-04
```

Using the *last_day* date function

The *last_day* Oracle date function returns the last day of the month of the input date. If you want to find the first day of the next month, you can add one to the *last_day* results.

```
select
  sysdate,
  last_day(sysdate)    eom,
  last_day(sysdate)+1 fom
from dual;

SYSDATE    EOM        FOM
--------- --------- ---------
24-JAN-05 31-JAN-05 01-FEB-05
```

Using the *next_day* date function

The *next_day* Oracle date function returns the date of the *day_of_week* after date d. *day_of_week* can be the full name or abbreviation.

Below, we use *next_day()* to get the date for the next Monday, next Friday, and the first Tuesday of next month.

```
select
  sysdate,
  next_day(sysdate,'monday') "next mon",
  next_day(sysdate,'friday') "next fri",
  next_day(last_day(sysdate)+1,'tuesday') "first tue"
from dual;


SYSDATE    Next Mon  Next Fri  First Tue
---------  --------- --------- ---------
24-JAN-05 31-JAN-05 28-JAN-05 08-FEB-05
```

Using the *round* date function

The *round* function is commonly used to round-off numbers, but you can also use *round()* with dates. The *round()* function returns the date rounded to the format.

In this example, the current date (24 January 2005) is rounded to the closest month and year:

```
select
  sysdate,
  round(sysdate,'month') month,
  round(sysdate,'year')  year
from
  dual;


SYSDATE    MONTH      YEAR
---------  --------- ---------
24-JAN-05 01-FEB-05 01-JAN-05
```

Notice that SYSDATE is past midmonth so the month was rounded to the next month. We are not past midyear, however, so the year was rounded to the beginning of the current year.

Using the *trunc* date function

As with the numeric *trunc* function, the date version simply truncates the date to the level specified in the format. The trunc function is often used to "chop-off" unwanted parts of a date. IN the example, below we use trunc to convert the data to the first day of the current month, and the first day of the current year:

```
select
  sysdate,
```

```
  trunc(sysdate,'month')  month,
  trunc(sysdate,'year')   year
from
  dual;


SYSDATE   MONTH     YEAR
--------- --------- ---------
24-JAN-05 01-JAN-05 01-JAN-05
```

Now that we understand how to specify dates in SQL to ensure index usage, let's look at cases where it's necessary to create a function-based index to match a complex where clause specification.

Index usage and built-in functions

Oracle provides many built-in functions (or BIFs) that can be used to transform table column data. This feature can save developers and programmers a great deal of time, automating the cumbersome task of translating incoming column values into Oracle (e.g. *update customer set date_of_birth = to_date('03-25-1956','MM-DD-YYYY');*). BIFs can also be used to format non-displayable native datatypes. For example, one BIF formats the *date* datatype into a readable format.

Here are some common BIFs that can be used to simplify SQL queries:

- **decode:** This function is used to translate values in a SQL statement from an abbreviation into a readable value. One example is using this function to translate a state abbreviation into the full state name.

- **to_char:** This function is used to convert numeric columns into character representations. This is often used with the *date* datatype.

- **upper:** This function is used to ensure that the retrieval of case-sensitive data is properly serviced.

- **lower:** This function is used to convert text to lower case. This is particularly useful when searching for lines of text.

- **substr:** This function is used to extract sub-strings from larger datatype columns, for instance the area code of a phone number.

Concerning Oracle tuning, it is important to note that using BIFs will often cause the SQL optimizer to perform a full-table scan because the BIF in the where clause has not been matched with a function-based index. This can be avoided by creating a function-based index to match the BIF used.

A common use of an Oracle BIF is the use of the *to_char* function to translate a column containing the *date* datatype. The following query displays the number of STATSPACK snapshots occurring in the month of January.

```
select
  count(*)
from
  perfstat.stats$snapshot
```

```
where
   to_char(snap_time,'Mon') = 'Jan;
```

Remember that when using a generic index in the *snap_time* column, the *to_char* function is not able to use the *date* index. With the use of BIFs however, an index can be created on *to_char(snap_time,'Mon')*, thereby avoiding a full-table scan for the SQL query.

Finding BIF's

When performing system-wide tuning, we must remember that an invalidated index column might not always invoke a full-table scan, and instead, the SQL might just choose a less selective index instead.

You should always be on the lookout for BIFs in the *where* clause of SQL statements. The following SQL can be run against the v$sqlarea view to quickly identify SQL statements that might have a BIF in their where clause.

🖫   find_bif.sql

```
set lines 2000;

select
   sql_text,
   disk_reads,
   executions,
   parse_calls
from
   v$sqlarea
where
   lower(sql_text) like '% substr%'
or
   lower(sql_text) like '% to_char%'
or
   lower(sql_text) like '% decode%'
order by
   disk_reads desc
;
```

With each release of Oracle we see dozens of new features, and it's hard to understand that tuning features are right for you. For SQL tuning, the function-based indexes ranks among one of the most powerful Oracle features.

Tuning SQL with Function-based Indexes (FBI)

When function-based indexes (FBI's) were quietly introduced in Oracle 8i, many Oracle professional still fail to fully utilize function-based indexes as one of the single most powerful Oracle tuning tools.

One of the most important advances in Oracle indexing is the introduction of function-based indexing. Function-based indexes allow creation of indexes on expressions, internal functions, and user-written functions in PL/SQL and Java. Function-based indexes ensure that the Oracle designer is able to use an index for its query.

Prior to function-based indexes, using a built-in function would often "invalidate" the index and cause an expensive full table scan. Examples of SQL with function-based queries might include the following:

```
select * from customer where substr(cust_name,1,4) = 'BURL';

select * from customer where to_char(order_date,'MM') = '01';

select * from customer where upper(cust_name) = 'JONES';

select * from customer where initcap(first_name) = 'Mike';
```

In Oracle, Oracle always interrogates the *where* clause of the SQL statement to see if a matching index exists. By using function-based indexes, the Oracle designer can create a matching index that exactly matches the predicates within the SQL *where* clause. This ensures that the query is retrieved with a minimal amount of disk I/O and the fastest possible speed.

Oracle DBAs know that there are many "silver bullet" techniques, single changes that have a profound impact on the entire SQL workload. These include any global setting that affects the execution plans of SQL statements:

- Parameter settings (optimizer_mode, optimizer_index_cost_adj)
- New CBO statistics
- New patchsets/ new releases
- Indexes (especially function-based indexes)
- Materialized views

Out of these powerful tools, the most readily available is the adding of a "missing" index, especially a function-based index.

If the goal of an index is to fetch the desired row-set with a minimum of databases "touches" (e.g. *consistent_gets*), then a function-based index is a Godsend because anything that you see in the *where* clause of a SQL statement may have a matching function-based index.

In almost all cases, the use of a built-in function like *to_char, decode, substr,* etc. in an SQL query may cause a full-table scan of the target table. For example, consider this query:

```
-- select March sales

select
```

Managing complex date comparisons in SQL **931**

```
   sum(sales)
from
   mysales
where
   to_char(order_date, 'MON') = 'MARCH';
```

In this case, without a specific index on (*to_char(order_date,'MON'*), the above query will be forced to read every row in the *sales* table, even though an index already exists on the *order_date* column.

To avoid this problem, many Oracle DBAs will create corresponding indexes that make use of function-based indexes. If a corresponding function-based index matches the built-in function of the query, Oracle will be able to service the query with an index range scan thereby avoiding a potentially expensive full-table scan.

The following is a simple example. Suppose that you have identified a SQL statement with hundreds of full-table scans against a large table with a built-in function (BIF) in the *where* clause of the query. After examining the SQL, it is simple to see that it is accessing a customer by converting the customer name to uppercase using the upper BIF.

```
select
   c.customer_name,
   o.order_date
from
   customer c,
   order    o
where
  upper(c.customer_name) = upper(:v1)
and
   c.cust_nbr = o.cust_nbr
;
```

Running the explain plan utility confirms your suspicion that the upper BIF is responsible for an unnecessary large-table full-table scan.

OPTIONS	OBJECT_NAME	POSITION
SELECT STATEMENT		4
NESTED LOOPS		1
TABLE ACCESS		
FULL	CUSTOMER	1
TABLE ACCESS		
BY INDEX ROWID	ORDER	2
INDEX		
RANGE SCAN	CUST_NBR_IDX	1

The table access full customer option confirms that this BIF not using the existing index on the *customer_name* column. Since a matching function-based index may change the execution plan, a function-based index can be added on *upper(customer_name)*.

It can be risky to add indexes to a table because the execution plans of many queries may change as a result. This is not a problem with a function-based index because Oracle will only use this type of index when the query uses a matching BIF.

```
create index
   upper_cust_name_idx
on
   customer
      (upper(customer_name))
  tablespace
     customer_idx
;

exec dbms_stats.gather_index_stats('scott', ' upper_cust_name_idx');
```

Now, the SQL can be re-explained to show that the full-table scan has been replaced by an index range scan on the new function-based index.

For this query, the execution time has been decreased from 45 seconds to less than two seconds.

```
OPERATION
----------------------------------------------------------------------
OPTIONS                    OBJECT_NAME                    POSITION
----------------------------  ------------------------------  ----------
SELECT STATEMENT
                                                               5
  NESTED LOOPS
                                                               1
    TABLE ACCESS
BY INDEX ROWID             CUSTOMER                          1
      INDEX
RANGE SCAN                 CUST_NBR_IDX                      1
    TABLE ACCESS
BY INDEX ROWID             ORDER                             2
      INDEX
RANGE SCAN                 UPPER_CUST_NAME_IDX               1
```

This simple example serves to illustrate the foremost SQL tuning rule for BIFs. Whenever a BIF is used in a SQL statement, a function-based index must be created.

However, you always need to carefully examine the where clause of a query to see if there are alternatives to using a function-based index.

For example, at first glance these *where* clause predicates might be candidates for a function-based index:

```
-- Will not use ship_date index
where trunc(ship_date) > trunc(sysdate-7);

-- Will not use ship_date index
where to_char(ship_date,'YYYY-MM-DD') = '2004-01-04';
```

As we now know, even though the *ship_date* column has an index, the *trunc* and *to_char* built-in functions will invalidate the index, causing sub-optimal execution with unnecessary I/O. However, in these cases you can re-formulate the where clause to make the *ship_date* index work, without having to create a function-based index:

```
-- Uses ship_date index
where ship_date >= trunc(sysdate-7) + 1;

-- Uses ship_date index
where ship_date = to_date('2004-01-04','YYYY-MM-DD');
```

Remember, whenever possible you always want to use an existing index before creating a function-based index.

Now let's look at how you can use a function-based index with a *case* statement, a powerful tuning tool for complex queries.

Using *case* statements with a function-based index

Using function-based indexes (FBI) you can create an index on any built-in function, including a *case* expression. Here we use *case* within the create index syntax:

```
create index
   case_index
as
   (case SOURCE_TRAN
    when 'PO' then PO_ID
    when 'VOUCHER' then voucher_id
    ELSE journal_id
    end = '0000000001'
end);
```

Once created, you need to create CBO statistics, but beware that there are numerous bugs and issues when analyzing a function-based index.

```
exec dbms_stats.gather_index_stats('OWNER', 'CASE_INDEX');

exec dbms_stats.gather_table_stats(
   ownname=>null,
   tabname=> 'CASE_TAB,
   estimate_percent=>null,
   cascade=>true,
   method_opt=> 'FOR ALL HIDDEN COLUMNS SIZE 1'
);

exec dbms_stats.gather_table_stats(
ownname => 'OWNER',
tabname => 'CASE_TAB',
cascade => TRUE);
```

As a final step, run the execution plan for the query and ensure that your SQL with *case* is using the appropriate index.

Tip! Index on *decode* statements!

You can use a function-based index with a *decode* statement! This is an important feature, being able to transform column data and index upon the transformation.

Now, let's move on and look at how to manage indexes on complex functions.

Indexing on complex functions

After considering the power of the function-based index we might ask if there is any limit to the ability to index into complex expressions. Jonathan Gennick shows a great example where we use Oracle regular expressions to extract "acreage" references from inside a text string, ignoring important factors such as case sensitivity and words stems (acre, acres, acreage):

```
COLUMN park_name format a30
COLUMN acres      format a13

select
  park_name,
  REGEXP_SUBSTR(description,'[^ ]+[- ]acres?',1,1,'i') acres
from
   michigan_park
where
   REGEXP_LIKE(description, '[^ ]+[- ]acres?','i');
```

Here is the output, where we see that the regular expression has parsed-out the acreage figures, just as-if they were a discrete data column with the table:

```
PARK_NAME                       ACRES

Mackinac Island State Park      1800 acres
Muskallonge Lake State Park     217-acre
Porcupine Mountains State Park  60,000 acres
Tahquamenon Falls State Park    40,000+ acres
```

The only problem with this query is that it will always perform a large-table full-table scan on the *michigan_park* table, causing unnecessary overhead for Oracle.

However, using the powerful function-based indexes we could eliminate the unnecessary overhead by using the regular expression directly in the index.

```
create index
  parks_acreage
on
  michigan_parks
  (REGEXP_LIKE(description, '[^ ]+[- ]acres?','i'));
```

The rules for choosing a function-based index on a complex expression (regular expression, decode) is a trade-off between several factors:

- **The number of blocks in the table**: A full-table scan of a super-large table can cause I/O contention.

- **The percentage of rows returned**: If the regular expression returns only a small percentage of the total table rows, a regular expression index will greatly reduce I/O.

- **The frequency of the query**: If the query is executed frequently, Oracle may do millions of unnecessary full-table scans.

- **The tolerance for slower row inserts**: Parsing the text column at insert time (to add the row to the regular expression index) will slow-down inserts.

This trade-off represents an age-old quandary. If we build the regular expression once (at insert time) it can be used over-and-over again with little overhead. Conversely, using regular expressions in SQL without a supporting index will cause repeated full-table scans.

Statistics and function-based indexes

A common issue with Oracle DBA's and developers is "*Why does Oracle not using my function-based index*"?

Because a function-based index applies a function to a data column, special steps must be taken for the optimizer to be able to utilize a function-based index. The Oracle documentation notes that collecting statistics (and histograms) is an important prerequisite:

"You should analyze the table after creating a function-based index, to allow Oracle to collect column statistics equivalent information for the expression.

Optionally, you can collect histograms for the index expressions by specifying for all hidden columns size *number_of_buckets* in the *method_opt* argument to the *dbms_stats* procedures."

Tip! Be careful with automatic analysis!

The Oracle documentations says that in 10g and beyond it's not necessary to analyze an index after the index is created. However. Most DBA's will analyze manually.

Here are some methods for analyzing a function-based index, but beware that they may not work on all releases of Oracle for reasoned noted below:

```
--  Gather index stats for function-based index

exec dbms_stats.gather_index_stats('OWNER', 'CASE_INDEX');

--  Gather table stats for function-based index exec

dbms_stats.gather_table_stats(
   ownname=>null,
   tabname=> 'CASE_TAB,
   estimate_percent=>null,
   cascade=>true,
   method_opt=> 'FOR ALL HIDDEN COLUMNS SIZE 1'
);

exec dbms_stats.gather_table_stats(
ownname => 'OWNER',
tabname => 'CASE_TAB',
cascade => TRUE);
```

As we have noted, function-based indexes are "tricky" to get working, and you must carefully verify your SQL execution plans to ensure that they are working before migrating them into production.

There are reports of function-based indexes not being used by the CBO, some due to bugs and others due to issues with the *dbms_stats* analysis routine. See bug 2782919, titled "GATHER_TABLE_STATS FAILS ON TABLE WITH FUNCTION-BASED INDEX".

Conclusions on function-based indexes

In sum, function-based indexes are one of the true "Silver Bullet" techniques, a single action that can have a profound impact on your entire SQL workload. There are several points to remember about function-based indexes:

- A single FBI might optimizer hundreds of SQL statements, reducing system-wide I/O.

- Function-based indexes can match anything in a *where* clause, even derived data like that from a decode   statement.

- It's important to collect CBO stats (and possible histograms to ensure that the FBI is used properly by the optimizer.

Even though using a function-based index is tricky, it is well worth the effort since the function-based indexes allow you to go directly to the target data blocks that contain the rows that you desire.

Next, let's look at tuning with Oracle regular expressions.

SQL tuning with regular expression indexes

Oracle Regular Expression syntax has profound implications for Oracle tuning, especially in the area of indexing where indexes can be created on regular expressions, eliminating expensive full-table scans in-favor of fast index access. Regular expressions are extremely powerful for extracting facts from large text columns, especially the *regexp_like* syntax.

Oracle expert Jonathan Gennick notes that regular expression can be used in an Oracle index, a powerful tool for improving the speed of complex SQL queries, and notes that regular expression indexes (a type of function-based index) can dramatically reduce database overhead for pattern-matching queries.

Here are some little know facts about regular expressions:

- They can be used with bind variables
- They can be included in function-based indexes

Indexing on regular expressions

In Parsing with regular expressions *regexp_like* Jonathan Gennick shows a great example where we use Oracle regular expressions to extract "acreage" references from inside a test string, ignoring important factors such as case sensitivity and words stems (acre, acres, acreage):

```
column park_name format a30
column acres      format a13

select
  park_name,
  regexp_substr(description,'[^ ]+[- ]acres?',1,1,'i') acres
from
   michigan_park
  where
   regexp_like(description, '[^ ]+[- ]acres?','i');
```

Here is the output, where we see that the regular expression has parsed-out the acreage figures, just as-if they were a discrete data column with the table:

```
PARK_NAME                        ACRES
_____     _____
Mackinac Island State Park       1800 acres
```

```
Muskallonge Lake State Park        217-acre
Porcupine Mountains State Park     60,000 acres
Tahquamenon Falls State Park       40,000+ acres
```

The only problem with this query is that it will always perform a large-table full-table scan on the *michigan_park* table, causing unnecessary overhead for Oracle.

However, using the powerful function-based indexes we could eliminate the unnecessary overhead by using the regular expression directly in the index.

```
create index
   parks_acreage
ON
   michigan_parks
 (REGEXP_LIKE(description, '[^ ]+[- ]acres?','i'));
```

However, Laurent Schneider notes that it is illegal to have an index on a Boolean function, but you could have an index on a case expression returning 1. Note the *where* clause in this *create index* syntax:

```
create index
    i
on
   michigan_parks
   (case when
      description like '_% acre%'
    or
      description like '_%-acre%'
    then 1 end);

select
   *
from
   michigan_parks
where
   (case when
      description like '_% acre%'
    or
      description like '_%-acre%' then 1 end)
is not null;
```

This simple index definition would create a yes/no index on all park records that contain a reference to "acre", "acres", "acreage". The database overhead would be once, when each rows is added to the table, and not over-and-over again when queries are executed.

The rules for choosing a function-based index on a complex expression (regular expression, decode) is a trade-off between several factors:

■ **The number of blocks in the table:** A full-table scan of a super-large table can cause I/O contention.

- **The percentage of rows returned**: If the regular expression returns only a small percentage of the total table rows, a regular expression index will greatly reduce I/O.

- **The frequency of the query**: If the query is executed frequently, Oracle may do millions of unnecessary full-table scans.

- **The tolerance for slower row inserts**: Parsing the text column at insert time (to add the row to the regular expression index) will slow-down inserts.

It's the age-old quandary. If we build the regular expression once (at insert time) it can be used over-and-over again with little overhead. Conversely, using regular expressions in SQL without a supporting index will cause repeated full-table scans.

Doing case sensitive searches with indexes

Oracle 10g release 2 introduced a case insensitive search method for SQL that avoids index invalidation and unnecessary full-table scans. You can also employ Oracle text indexes to remove full-table scans when using the LIKE operator. Prior to Oracle10g release 2 case insensitive queries required special planning:

Step 1: Transform data in the query to make it case insensitive (note that this can invalidate indexes without a function-based index):

```
create index
   upper_full_name
on
   customer (upper(full_name));

select
   full_name
from
   customer
where
   upper(full_name) - 'DON BURLESON';
```

Step 2: Use a trigger to transform the data to make it case insensitive (or store the data with the *to_lower* or *to_upper* BIF.

Step 3: Use Alter session commands:

```
alter session set NLS_COMP=ANSI;
alter session set NLS_SORT=GENERIC_BASELETTER;
select * from customer where full_name = 'Don Burleson'
```

In Oracle10g release 2 and beyond we see this new approach to case insensitive searches. We start with setting these initialization parameters:

```
nls_sort=binary_ci

nls_comp=ansi
```

Next we create a sample index:

```
create index
   caseless_name_index
on
   customer
(
   nlssort( full_name, 'NLS_SORT=BINARY_CI')
);

alter session set nls_sort=binary_ci;

select * from customer where full_name = 'Don Burleson';
```

Now let's move on and look at Oracle*text indexes, a specialized index for read-only data.

SQL Tuning with Oracle*Text Indexes

One serious SQL performance problem occurs when you use the SQL "*like* clause" operator to find a string within a large Oracle table column (e.g. *varchar(2000)*, *clob*, *blob*):

```
select stuff from bigtab where text_column like '%ipod%';

select
   stuff
from
   bigtab
where
   full_name like '%JONES';
```

Because standard Oracle cannot index into a large column, there "like" queries cause full-table scans, and Oracle must examine every row in the table, even when the result set is very small. These unnecessary full-table scans are a problem:

- Large-table full-table scans increase the load on the disk I/O sub-system.

- Small table full table scans (in the data buffer) cause high consistent gets and drive-up CPU consumption.

The Oracle*Text utility (formally called Oracle ConText and Oracle Intermedia) allows us to parse through a large text column and index on the words within the column.

Unlike ordinary b-tree or bitmap indexes, Oracle *context*, *ctxcat* and *ctxrule* indexes are NOT updated as content is changed. Since most standard Oracle databases will use the *ctxcat* index with standard relational tables, you must decide on a refresh interval.

Hence, Oracle Text indexes are only useful for removing full-table scans when the tables are largely read-only and/or the end-users don't mind not having 100% search recall:

- The target table is relatively static (e.g. nightly batch updates)

- Your end-users would not mind "missing" the latest row data

Oracle Text works with traditional data columns and also with XML, MS-Word docs and Adobe PDF files that are stored within Oracle. Oracle Text has several index types:

- ***ctxcat* Indexes**: A *ctxcat* index is best for smaller text fragments that must be indexed along with other standard relational data (VARCHAR2).

```
where catsearch(text_column, 'ipod')> 0;
```

- ***context* Indexes**: The *context* index type is used to index large amounts of text such as Word, PDF, XML, HTML or plain text documents.

```
where contains(test_column, 'ipod', 1) > 0
```

- ***ctxrule* Indexes**: A *ctxrule* index can be used to build document classification applications.

These types of indexes allow you to replace the old-fashioned SQL "*like*" syntax with "*contains*" or "*catsearch*" SQL syntax:

When we execute the query with the new index we see that the full-table scan is replaced with an index scan, greatly reducing execution speed and improving hardware stress:

```
Execution Plan
----------------------------------------------------------
   0      SELECT STATEMENT Optimizer=FIRST_ROWS
   1    0   SORT (ORDER BY)
   2    1     TABLE ACCESS (BY INDEX ROWID) OF 'BIGTAB'
   3    2       DOMAIN INDEX OF 'TEXT-COLUMN_IDX'
```

Next let's look at how to resynchronize Oracle text indexes after an update.

Oracle Text Index re-synchronization

Because rebuilding an Oracle Text index (*context, ctxcat, ctxrule*) requires a full-table scan and lots of internal parsing, it is not practical to use triggers for instantaneous index updates.

Updating Oracle Text indexes is easy and they can be schedules using *dbms_job* or the Oracle 10g *dbms_scheduler* utility package: Oracle text provides a *ctx_ddl* package with the *sync_index* and *optimize_index* procedures:

```
exec ctx_ddl.sync_index('text_column_idx');

exec ctx_ddl.optimize_index('text_column_idx','full');
```

For example, if you create a nightly dbms_scheduler job to call *sync_index,* your index will be refreshed, but the structure will become sub-optimal over time. Oracle recommends that you periodically use the *optimize_index* package to periodically re-build the whole index from scratch. Index optimization can be performed in three modes (*fast, full* or *token*).

In sum, the Oracle Text indexes are great for removing unnecessary full-table scans from static Oracle tables and they can reduce I/O by several orders of magnitude, greatly improving overall SQL performance.

Tuning SQL with Index Organized Tables

Beginning with Oracle8, Oracle recognized that a table with an index on every column did not require table rows. In other words, Oracle recognized that by using a special table-access method called an index fast full scan, the index could be queried without actually touching the data itself.

Oracle codified this idea with its use of Index Organized Table (IOT) structure. When using an IOT, Oracle does not create the actual table but instead keeps all of the required information inside the Oracle index.

At query time, the Oracle SQL optimizer recognizes that all of the values necessary to service the query exist within the index tree, at which time the Oracle cost-based optimizer has a choice of either reading through the index tree nodes to pull the information in sorted order or invoke an index fast full scan, which will read the table in the same fashion as a full table scan, using sequential prefetch (as defined by the *db_file_multiblock_read_count* parameter).

The multiblock read facility allows Oracle to very quickly scan index blocks in linear order, quickly reading every block within the index tablespace. Here is an example of the syntax to create an IOT.

```
create table
   emp_iot
(
```

```
   emp_id     number,
   ename      varchar2(20),
   sal        number(9,2),
   deptno     number,
   constraint
      pk_emp_iot_index
   primary key
      (emp_id)
)
organization
   index
tablespace
   demo_ts_01
pcthreshold
   20
including
   ename
;
```

In sum, the index-only tablespace is perfect for queries where all of the column data can be contained within the index tree, alleviating the need for a traditional table.

Testing new Oracle indexes

Adding a missing index is a powerful silver bullet for Oracle tuning because a single new index can affect the performance of thousands of SQL queries. But remember, the changes are not guaranteed to always be good. Remember, Silver bullets work both ways. While a silver bullet causes a profound change to a workload, the change might also be a bad one, and careful testing is always required.

While the Oracle optimizer is not likely to choose a sub-optimal plan when a new index is added, it's possible, and when testing a new index for migration to production, complete workload testing is de-rigueur.

In Oracle 11g we see a new *init.ora* parameter to assist with index testing, the *optimizer_use_invisible_indexes* parameter. While the default for *optimizer_use_invisible_indexes* is false, we can change the setting for our session to test new indexes:

```
alter session set optimizer_use_invisible_indexes=true;
```

When setting optimizer_use_invisible_indexes=true, Oracle will allow us to test the effect of a new indexes solely within our session without effecting any other SQL. If the DBA sees that the new index has the desired effect they can alter the index to make it "visible" to the optimizer.

```
alter index myindex visible;
```

Don't do this in production!

The *optimizer_use_invisible_indexes* parameter should never be used on a production database. A test or QA database is the place to test new indexes, never production!

In the real-world, we would always test any new indexes in a QA database, by capturing a representative SQL workload and testing the workload using the Oracle 11g SQL Performance Manager (SPM) with the new index. Only then, can we confidently migrate the new index into our production environment.

Testing SQL workloads with invisible indexes

During an observation period, you create the new index in a QA environment and play some SQL tuning Sets (STS) to monitor the database performance to determine whether or not to keep the new index.

If our performance is negatively affected, the index would need to be rebuilt before it could be used again.

Another potential use for invisible indexes is in situations where specific applications require an index temporarily. For example, an index can be created as invisible to allow specific SQL statements to use the index while leaving the rest of the database unaffected. Creating a visible index for this same purpose would cause the optimizer to consider the new index for all execution plans on that object.

Consider the introduction of a reporting application into a large production database. Shortly after the go-live, a query in the application is found to be running slow. The query is consuming excessive amounts of resources due to a full table scan on a large, highly referenced table, *order_lines*.

After identifying this query, there is a realization that creating an index on column *order_lines.attribute7* would immediately resolve this particular issue. This issue needs to be resolved as soon as possible without impacting any other processes that use this object.

In this situation, creating an invisible index as a temporary solution until the application code can be reviewed would be an ideal solution. This method would alleviate the immediate problem without potentially affecting other users and processes that use the *order_lines* table.

Below, we create an invisible index on *order_lines.attribute7*:

```
create index
    order_lines_inv
on
    order_lines(attribute7) invisible;
```

This one query can be modified to explicitly use the invisible index with an *index* hint:

```
select /*+ index (order_lines order_lines_inv) */
    id
from
    order_lines
where
    attribute7 = 11001;
```

If the application code cannot be modified, it is possible to instruct the optimizer to include invisible indexes at the session level:

```
alter session set optimizer_use_invisible_indexes = true;
```

Keep in mind that rebuilding an invisible index will make it visible.

Invisible indexes are an attractive feature for the process of dropping an index. They are also useful when a specific application needs the benefit of a temporary index without impacting the database on a wider scale.

Be prudent with invisible indexes

Since the database must still maintain an invisible index for all DML operations, invisible indexes should not be used unless absolutely necessary.

Next, let's see how we can perform index monitoring.

Monitoring index usage

STATSPACK and AWR are perfect for holistic tuning because you can not only monitor the usage of specific indexes, you can see how your indexes are being used for your entire SQL workload, super-valuable information for SQL tuning.

For specific time periods, you can also summarize index access by snapshot period.

🖫 awr_sql_index_access.sql

```
col c1 heading 'Begin|Interval|Time'   format a20
col c2 heading 'Index|Range|Scans' format 999,999
col c3 heading 'Index|Unique|Scans' format 999,999
col c4 heading 'Index|Full|Scans' format 999,999

select
  r.c1  c1,
  r.c2  c2,
  u.c2  c3,
```

```
      f.c2   c4
from
(
select
  to_char(sn.begin_interval_time,'yy-mm-dd hh24')   c1,
  count(1)                                          c2
from
   dba_hist_sql_plan p,
   dba_hist_sqlstat  s,
   dba_hist_snapshot sn
where
   p.object_owner <> 'SYS'
and
   p.operation like '%INDEX%'
and
   p.options like '%RANGE%'
and
   p.sql_id = s.sql_id
and
   s.snap_id = sn.snap_id
group by
  to_char(sn.begin_interval_time,'yy-mm-dd hh24')
order by
1 ) r,
(
select
  to_char(sn.begin_interval_time,'yy-mm-dd hh24')   c1,
  count(1)                                          c2
from
   dba_hist_sql_plan p,
   dba_hist_sqlstat  s,
   dba_hist_snapshot sn
where
   p.object_owner <> 'SYS'
and
   p.operation like '%INDEX%'
and
   p.options like '%UNIQUE%'
and
   p.sql_id = s.sql_id
and
   s.snap_id = sn.snap_id
group by
  to_char(sn.begin_interval_time,'yy-mm-dd hh24')
order by
1 ) u,
(
select
  to_char(sn.begin_interval_time,'yy-mm-dd hh24')   c1,
  count(1)                                          c2
from
   dba_hist_sql_plan p,
   dba_hist_sqlstat  s,
   dba_hist_snapshot sn
where
   p.object_owner <> 'SYS'
and
   p.operation like '%INDEX%'
and
   p.options like '%FULL%'
and
   p.sql_id = s.sql_id
and
   s.snap_id = sn.snap_id
group by
```

Monitoring index usage

```
     to_char(sn.begin_interval_time,'yy-mm-dd hh24')
order by
1 ) f
where
     r.c1 = u.c1
  and
     r.c1 = f.c1
;
```

The sample output below shows those specific times when the database performs unique scans, index range scans and index fast full scans:

Begin Interval Time	Index Range Scans	Index Unique Scans	Index Full Scans
04-10-21 15	36	35	2
04-10-21 19	10	8	2
04-10-21 20		8	2
04-10-21 21		8	2
04-10-21 22	11	8	3
04-10-21 23	16	11	3
04-10-22 00	10	9	1
04-10-22 01	11	8	3
04-10-22 02	12	8	1
04-10-22 03	10	8	3
04-10-22 04	11	8	2
04-10-22 05		8	3
04-10-22 06		8	2
04-10-22 07	10	8	3
04-10-22 08		8	2
04-10-22 09		8	2

In Oracle10g and beyond, it is easy to see what indexes are used, when they are used and the context in which they are used. The following is a simple AWR query that can be used see index usage for a specific index over time. Note how it shows the number of times that an index is used each hour:

🖫 awr_count_index_details.sql

```
col c1 heading 'Begin|Interval|time'  format a20
col c2 heading 'Search Columns'       format 999
col c3 heading 'Invocation|Count'      format 99,999,999


break on c1 skip 2

accept idxname char prompt 'Enter Index Name: '

ttitle 'Invocation Counts for index|&idxname'
```

```
select
   to_char(sn.begin_interval_time,'yy-mm-dd hh24')   c1,
   p.search_columns                                  c2,
   count(*)                                          c3
from
   dba_hist_snapshot   sn,
   dba_hist_sql_plan   p,
   dba_hist_sqlstat    st
where
   st.sql_id = p.sql_id
and
   sn.snap_id = st.snap_id
and
   p.object_name = '&idxname'
group by
   begin_interval_time,search_columns;
```

The query will accept an index name and produce an output showing a summary count of the index specified during the snapshot interval. This can be compared to the number of times that a table was invoked from SQL. Here is a sample of the output from this index usage script:

```
Invocation Counts for cust_index

Begin
Interval                          Invocation
time           Search Columns        Count
------------   --------------    -----------
04-10-21 15                 1             3
04-10-10 16                 0             1
04-10-10 19                 1             1
04-10-11 02                 0             2
04-10-11 04                 2             1
04-10-11 06                 3             1
04-10-11 11                 0             1
04-10-11 12                 0             2
04-10-11 13                 2             1
04-10-11 15                 0             3
04-10-11 17                 0            14
04-10-11 18                 4             1
04-10-11 19                 0             1
04-10-11 20                 3             7
04-10-11 21                 0             1
```

Watch for seldom-used indexes

Using the query above, seek out seldom-used indexes that may be associated with weekly or monthly jobs. For these, consider building the index specifically for the infrequent job and then dropping the index until the next invocation.

Monitoring for Index Range Scans

When deciding to segregate indexes into larger blocksizes it is important to understand that those indexes that are subject to frequent index range scans and fast-full scans will benefit the most from a larger blocksize.

When Oracle joins two tables together with a nested loop, only one of the indexes may be accessed as a range. The optimizer always performs an index range scan on one index, gathers the *rowid* values, and does fetch by *rowid* on the matching rows in the other table. For example:

```
select
    customer_name,
    order_date
from
    customer
    orders
where
    customer.cust_key = orders.cust_key;
```

The Oracle documentation notes that a nested loop involves two loops:

> "In a nested loop join, for every row in the outer row set, the inner row set is accessed to find all the matching rows to join.
>
> Therefore, in a nested loop join, the inner row set is accessed as many times as the number of rows in the outer row set."

Oracle will only scan one index, build a set of keys, and then probe the rows from the other table (Figure 16.28).

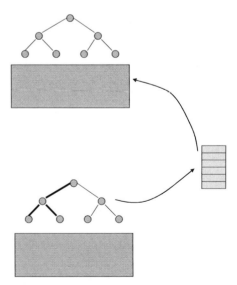

Figure 16.28: *Table joins include index range scans and index unique scans*

So, if this nested loop never uses the customer index, why is it there? The answer is, for index unique scans. In an index unique scan, a single row is accessed within the index, as seen in this query:

```
select
   customer_last_name,
   customer_address
from
   customer
where
   cust_key = 123;
```

In sum, the DBA must find out how their indexes are being used by the SQL. An index that never experiences range scans would not benefit from a larger blocksize. The question becomes one of finding those indexes that experience lots of range scans, and AWR can help.

It is possible to identify those indexes with the most index range scans with the following simple AWR script.

index_range_scans.sql

```
col c1 heading 'Object|Name'         format a30
col c2 heading 'Option'              format a15
col c3 heading 'Index|Usage|Count'   format 999,999

select
  p.object_name c1,
  p.options     c2,
  count(1)      c3
from
   dba_hist_sql_plan p,
   dba_hist_sqlstat  s
where
   p.object_owner <> 'SYS'
and
   p.options like '%RANGE SCAN%'
and

   p.operation like '%INDEX%'
and
   p.sql_id = s.sql_id
group by
   p.object_name,
   p.operation,
   p.options
order by
  1,2,3;
```

The following is the output showing overall total counts for each object and table access method.

Object Name	Option	Index Usage Count
----------------------------	---------------	--------

```
CUSTOMER_CHECK                  RANGE SCAN           4,232
AVAILABILITY_PRIMARY_KEY        RANGE SCAN           1,783
CON_UK                          RANGE SCAN             473
CURRENT_SEVERITY                RANGE SCAN             323
CWM$CUBEDIMENSIONUSE_IDX        RANGE SCAN              72
ORDERS_FK                       RANGE SCAN              20
```

This will quickly identify indexes that will benefit the most from a 32k blocksize.

This index list can be double verified by using the AWR to identify indexes with high disk reads during each AWR snapshot period. The sample script below exposes the top five tables accessed mostly heavily by physical disk reads for every snapshot interval:

busy_table_io.sql

```
col c0 heading 'Begin|Interval|time' format a8
col c1 heading 'Table|Name'          format a20
col c2 heading 'Disk|Reads'          format 99,999,999
col c3 heading 'Rows|Processed'      format 99,999,999

select
*
from (
select
    to_char(s.begin_interval_time,'mm-dd hh24') c0,
    p.object_name c1,
    sum(t.disk_reads_total) c2,
    sum(t.rows_processed_total) c3,
    DENSE_RANK() OVER (PARTITION BY to_char(s.begin_interval_time,'mm-dd hh24') ORDER BY
SUM(t.disk_reads_total) desc) AS rnk
from
  dba_hist_sql_plan p,
  dba_hist_sqlstat t,
  dba_hist_snapshot s
where
  p.sql_id = t.sql_id
and
  t.snap_id = s.snap_id
and
  p.object_type like '%TABLE%'
group by
  to_char(s.begin_interval_time,'mm-dd hh24'),
  p.object_name
order by
c0 desc, rnk
)
where rnk <= 5
;
```

The following is the sample output from the above script:

```
Begin
Interval  Table                 Disk        Rows
time      Name                  Reads       Processed     RNK
--------  ------------------    --------    ----------    ---------
10-29 15  CUSTOMER_CHECK          55,732       498,056        1
10-29 15  CON_UK                  18,368       166,172        2
```

10-29 15	CURRENT_SEVERITY	11,727	102,545	3
10-29 15	ORDERS_FK	5,876	86,671	4
10-29 15	SYN$	2,624	23,674	5
10-29 14	CUSTOMER_CHECK	47,756	427,762	1
10-29 14	CON_UK	15,939	142,878	2
10-29 14	CURRENT_SEVERITY	6,976	113,649	3
10-29 14	X$KZSRO	4,772	119,417	4
10-29 14	ORDERS_FK	2,274	20,292	5
10-29 13	CUSTOMER_CHECK	25,704	213,786	1
10-29 13	CON_UK	8,568	71,382	2
10-29 13	OBJ$	3,672	30,474	3
10-29 13	X$KZSRO	2,448	20,328	4
10-29 13	SYN$	1,224	10,146	5

This report shows the tables with the highest disk reads which is very important information for disk tuning.

The *dba_hist_sql_plan* table can also be used to gather counts about the frequency of participation of objects inside queries. This is a great query to quickly see what's going on between the tables and the SQL that accesses them.

💾 count_table_access.sql

```
col c1 heading 'Object|Name'      format a30
col c2 heading 'Operation'        format a15
col c3 heading 'Option'           format a15
col c4 heading 'Object|Count'     format 999,999

break on c1 skip 2
break on c2 skip 2

select
  p.object_name c1,
  p.operation   c2,
  p.options     c3,
  count(1)      c4
from
  dba_hist_sql_plan p,
  dba_hist_sqlstat  s
where
  p.object_owner <> 'SYS'
and
  p.sql_id = s.sql_id
group by
  p.object_name,
  p.operation,
  p.options
order by
  1,2,3;
```

The following output shows overall total counts for each object and table access method.

Object Name	Operation	Option	Object Count
CUSTOMER	TABLE ACCESS	FULL	305

CUSTOMER _CHECK	INDEX	RANGE SCAN	2
CUSTOMER_ORDERS	TABLE ACCESS	BY INDEX ROWID	311
CUSTOMER_ORDERS		FULL	1
CUSTOMER_ORDERS_PRIMARY	INDEX	FULL SCAN	2
CUSTOMER_ORDERS_PRIMARY		UNIQUE SCAN	311
AVAILABILITY_PRIMARY_KEY		RANGE SCAN	4
CON_UK		RANGE SCAN	3
CURRENT_SEVERITY_PRIMARY_KEY		RANGE SCAN	1
CWM$CUBE	TABLE ACCESS	BY INDEX ROWID	2
CWM$CUBEDIMENSIONUSE		BY INDEX ROWID	2
CWM$CUBEDIMENSIONUSE_IDX	INDEX	RANGE SCAN	2
CWM$CUBE_PK		UNIQUE SCAN	2
CWM$DIMENSION_PK		FULL SCAN	2
MGMT_INV_VERSIONED_PATCH	TABLE ACCESS	BY INDEX ROWID	3
MGMT_JOB		BY INDEX ROWID	458
MGMT_JOB_EMD_STATUS_QUEUE		FULL	181
MGMT_JOB_EXECUTION		BY INDEX ROWID	456
MGMT_JOB_EXEC_IDX01	INDEX	RANGE SCAN	456
MGMT_JOB_EXEC_SUMMARY	TABLE ACCESS	BY INDEX ROWID	180
MGMT_JOB_EXEC_SUMM_IDX04	INDEX	RANGE SCAN	180
MGMT_JOB_HISTORY	TABLE ACCESS	BY INDEX ROWID	1
MGMT_JOB_HIST_IDX01	INDEX	RANGE SCAN	1
MGMT_JOB_PK		UNIQUE SCAN	458
MGMT_METRICS	TABLE ACCESS	BY INDEX ROWID	180

Using the output above, it is easy to monitor object participation, especially indexes, in the SQL queries and the mode with which an object was accessed by Oracle.

Why is it important to know how tables and indexes are accessed? Objects that experience multi-block reads may perform faster in a larger blocksize and also reduce SGA overhead.

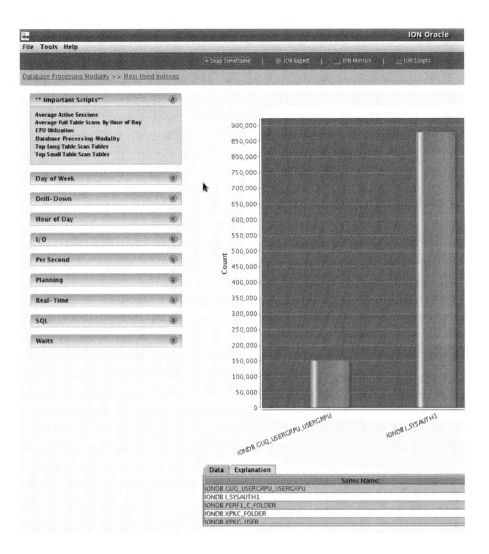

Figure 16.29: *Using Ion to find the most popular indexes*

The problem has always been that it is very difficult to know what indexes are the most popular. In Oracle10g we can easily see what indexes are used, when they are used and the context where they are used. Here is a simple AWR query to plot index usage:

💾 **index_usage_hr.sql**

```
col c1 heading 'Begin|Interval|time' format a20
col c2 heading 'Search Columns'     format 999
col c3 heading 'Invocation|Count'   format 99,999,999
```

```
break on c1 skip 2

accept idxname char prompt 'Enter Index Name: '

ttitle 'Invocation Counts for index|&idxname'

select
   to_char(sn.begin_interval_time,'yy-mm-dd hh24')   c1,
   p.search_columns                                  c2,
   count(*)                                          c3
from
   dba_hist_snapshot   sn,
   dba_hist_sql_plan   p,
   dba_hist_sqlstat    st
where
   st.sql_id = p.sql_id
and
   sn.snap_id = st.snap_id
and
   p.object_name = '&idxname'
group by
   begin_interval_time,search_columns;
```

This will produce an output like this, showing a summary count of the index specified during the snapshot interval. This can be compared to the number of times that a table was invoked from SQL. Here is a sample of the output from this script:

```
Invocation Counts for cust_index


Begin
Interval                         Invocation
time            Search Columns      Count
--------------- --------------- -----------
04-10-21 15                   1           3
04-10-10 16                   0           1
04-10-10 19                   1           1
04-10-11 02                   0           2
04-10-11 04                   2           1
04-10-11 06                   3           1
04-10-11 11                   0           1
04-10-11 12                   0           2
04-10-11 13                   2           1
04-10-11 15                   0           3
04-10-11 17                   0          14
04-10-11 18                   4           1
04-10-11 19                   0           1
04-10-11 20                   3           7
04-10-11 21                   0           1
```

Figure 16.30 shows a sample screenshot of output produced by the Ion tool for index access.

Most Used Indexes

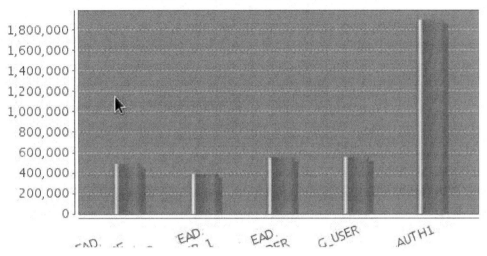

Figure 16.30 *Index Invocation Count in Ion Tool*

As we see, the AWR SQL tuning tables offer a wealth of important time metrics.

💾 awr_sql_index_freq.sql

```
col c1  heading  'Object|Name'          format a30
col c2  heading  'Operation'            format a15
col c3  heading  'Option'               format a15
col c4  heading  'Index|Usage|Count'    format 999,999

break on c1 skip 2
break on c2 skip 2

select
  p.object_name  c1,
  p.operation    c2,
  p.options      c3,
  count(1)       c4
from
   dba_hist_sql_plan  p,
   dba_hist_sqlstat   s
where
   p.object_owner <> 'SYS'
and
```

```
    p.operation like '%INDEX%'
and
    p.sql_id = s.sql_id
group by
    p.object_name,
    p.operation,
    p.options
order by
    1,2,3;
```

Here is the output where we see overall total counts for each object and table access method.

```
                                                                  Index
Object                                                            Usage
Name                        Operation      Option                 Count
--------------------------- -------------- -------------------- --------
CUSTOMER  _CHECK            INDEX          RANGE SCAN                  4
CUSTOMER  _PRIMARY                         UNIQUE SCAN                 1
CUSTOMER_ORDERS_PRIMARY                    FULL SCAN                   1
CUSTOMER_ORDERS_PRIMARY                    UNIQUE SCAN               247
AVAILABILITY_PRIMARY_KEY                   RANGE SCAN                  4
CON_UK                                     RANGE SCAN                  3
CURRENT_SEVERITY_PRIMARY_KEY               RANGE SCAN                  2
CWM$CUBEDIMENSIONUSE_IDX                   RANGE SCAN                  2
CWM$CUBE_PK                                UNIQUE SCAN                 2
CWM$DIMENSION_PK                           FULL SCAN                   2
CWM$MODEL_PK                               UNIQUE SCAN                 2
LOGMNR_LOG$_PK                             FULL SCAN                   3
LOGMNR_SESSION_PK                          UNIQUE SCAN                 1
MBAB_PK                                    UNIQUE SCAN                 1
MBAP_PK                                    UNIQUE SCAN                 1
MBA_PK                                     UNIQUE SCAN                 1
MBFAC_PK                                   RANGE SCAN                  1
MBPFB_PK                                   RANGE SCAN                  1
MGMT_ARU_OP_PK                             UNIQUE SCAN                 1
MGMT_ARU_PRD_PK                            UNIQUE SCAN                 1
MGMT_ARU_RLS_PK                            UNIQUE SCAN                 1
MGMT_BUG_FIX_APPLIC_CL_IDX                 RANGE SCAN                  1
MGMT_CURRENT_METRICS_PK                    RANGE SCAN                 20
MGMT_CURRENT_METRICS_PK                    UNIQUE SCAN               156
MGMT_ECM_SNAP_IDX                          RANGE SCAN                  3
MGMT_EMD_PING_PK                           UNIQUE SCAN                 1
MGMT_INV_COMPONENT_IDX                     FAST FULL SCAN              2
MGMT_INV_COM_CONT_IDX                      RANGE SCAN                  1
MGMT_INV_PATCH_CONT_IDX                    RANGE SCAN                  1
MGMT_JOB_EXEC_IDX01                        RANGE SCAN                921
MGMT_JOB_EXEC_SUMM_IDX04                   RANGE SCAN                364
MGMT_JOB_HIST_IDX01                        RANGE SCAN                  3
MGMT_JOB_PK                                UNIQUE SCAN               923
```

We can also sum-up this data by snapshot period giving us a overall view of how Oracle is accessing our table data.

🖫 awr_access_counts.sql

```
ttile 'Table Access|Operation Counts|Per Snapshot Period'

col c1 heading 'Begin|Interval|time'     format a20
col c2 heading 'Operation'               format a15
col c3 heading 'Option'                  format a15
col c4 heading 'Object|Count'            format 999,999
```

```
break on c1 skip 2
break on c2 skip 2

select
  to_char(sn.begin_interval_time,'yy-mm-dd hh24')   c1,
  p.operation     c2,
  p.options       c3,
  count(1)        c4
from
  dba_hist_sql_plan p,
  dba_hist_sqlstat  s,
  dba_hist_snapshot sn
where
  p.object_owner <> 'SYS'
and
  p.sql_id = s.sql_id
and
  s.snap_id = sn.snap_id
group by
  to_char(sn.begin_interval_time,'yy-mm-dd hh24'),
  p.operation,
  p.options
order by
  1,2,3;
```

Here is the output where we see overall total counts for each object and table access method.

Begin Interval time	Operation	Option	Object Count
04-10-15 16	INDEX	UNIQUE SCAN	1
04-10-15 16	TABLE ACCESS	BY INDEX ROWID	1
04-10-15 16		FULL	2
04-10-15 17	INDEX	UNIQUE SCAN	1
04-10-15 17	TABLE ACCESS	BY INDEX ROWID	1
04-10-15 17		FULL	2
04-10-15 18	INDEX	UNIQUE SCAN	1
04-10-15 18	TABLE ACCESS	BY INDEX ROWID	1
04-10-15 18		FULL	2
04-10-15 19	INDEX	UNIQUE SCAN	1
04-10-15 19	TABLE ACCESS	BY INDEX ROWID	1
04-10-15 19		FULL	2
04-10-15 20	INDEX	UNIQUE SCAN	1
04-10-15 20	TABLE ACCESS	BY INDEX ROWID	1
04-10-15 20		FULL	2
04-10-15 21	INDEX	UNIQUE SCAN	1
04-10-15 21	TABLE ACCESS	BY INDEX ROWID	1
04-10-15 21		FULL	2

Here is a script that will summarize index access by snapshot period.

 █ **awr_sql_index_access.sql**

```
col c1 heading 'Begin|Interval|Time'   format a20
col c2 heading 'Index|Range|Scans' format 999,999
col c3 heading 'Index|Unique|Scans' format 999,999
col c4 heading 'Index|Full|Scans' format 999,999

select
  r.c1   c1,
  r.c2   c2,
  u.c2   c3,
  f.c2   c4
from
(
select
  to_char(sn.begin_interval_time,'yy-mm-dd hh24')   c1,
  count(1)                              c2
from
   dba_hist_sql_plan p,
   dba_hist_sqlstat  s,
   dba_hist_snapshot sn
where
   p.object_owner <> 'SYS'
and
   p.operation like '%INDEX%'
and
   p.options like '%RANGE%'
and
   p.sql_id = s.sql_id
and
   s.snap_id = sn.snap_id
group by
  to_char(sn.begin_interval_time,'yy-mm-dd hh24')
order by
1 ) r,
(
select
  to_char(sn.begin_interval_time,'yy-mm-dd hh24')   c1,
  count(1)                              c2
from
   dba_hist_sql_plan p,
   dba_hist_sqlstat  s,
   dba_hist_snapshot sn
where
   p.object_owner <> 'SYS'
and
   p.operation like '%INDEX%'
and
   p.options like '%UNIQUE%'
and
   p.sql_id = s.sql_id
and
   s.snap_id = sn.snap_id
group by
  to_char(sn.begin_interval_time,'yy-mm-dd hh24')
order by
1 ) u,
(
```

```
select
  to_char(sn.begin_interval_time,'yy-mm-dd hh24')  c1,
  count(1)                           c2
from
  dba_hist_sql_plan p,
  dba_hist_sqlstat  s,
  dba_hist_snapshot sn
where
  p.object_owner <> 'SYS'
and
  p.operation like '%INDEX%'
and
  p.options like '%FULL%'
and
  p.sql_id = s.sql_id
and
  s.snap_id = sn.snap_id
group by
  to_char(sn.begin_interval_time,'yy-mm-dd hh24')
order by
1 ) f
where
    r.c1 = u.c1
  and
    r.c1 = f.c1
;
```

Here is the sample output showing those specific times when your database performs unique scans, index range scans and index fast full scans:

Begin Interval Time	Index Range Scans	Index Unique Scans	Index Full Scans
04-10-21 15	36	35	2
04-10-21 19	10	8	2
04-10-21 20		8	2
04-10-21 21		8	2
04-10-21 22	11	8	3
04-10-21 23	16	11	3
04-10-22 00	10	9	1
04-10-22 01	11	8	3
04-10-22 02	12	8	1
04-10-22 03	10	8	3
04-10-22 04	11	8	2
04-10-22 05		8	3
04-10-22 06		8	2
04-10-22 07	10	8	3
04-10-22 08		8	2
04-10-22 09		8	2
04-10-22 10		10	4
04-10-22 11	11	8	1
04-10-22 12	9	7	3
04-10-22 13		7	2
04-10-22 14		8	2
04-10-22 15	10	8	3
04-10-22 17		9	3

04-10-22 18	11	9	3
04-10-22 19	10	9	3
04-10-22 20	11	9	2
04-10-22 21	10	8	3
04-10-22 22	11	8	1
04-10-22 23		9	3

If you have a non-OLTP database that regularly performs large full-table and full-index scans, it is helpful to know those times when the full scan activity is high.

💾 awr_sql_full_scans.sql

```
col c1 heading 'Begin|Interval|Time'   format a20
col c2 heading 'Index|Table|Scans' format 999,999
col c3 heading 'Full|Table|Scans' format 999,999

select
  i.c1   c1,
  i.c2   c2,
  f.c2   c3
from
(
select
  to_char(sn.begin_interval_time,'yy-mm-dd hh24')  c1,
  count(1)                         c2
from
  dba_hist_sql_plan p,
  dba_hist_sqlstat  s,
  dba_hist_snapshot sn
where
  p.object_owner <> 'SYS'
and
  p.operation like '%TABLE ACCESS%'
and
  p.options like '%INDEX%'
and
  p.sql_id = s.sql_id
and
  s.snap_id = sn.snap_id
group by
  to_char(sn.begin_interval_time,'yy-mm-dd hh24')
order by
1 ) i,
(
select
  to_char(sn.begin_interval_time,'yy-mm-dd hh24')  c1,
  count(1)                         c2
from
  dba_hist_sql_plan p,
  dba_hist_sqlstat  s,
  dba_hist_snapshot sn
where
  p.object_owner <> 'SYS'
and
  p.operation like '%TABLE ACCESS%'
and
  p.options = 'FULL'
and
  p.sql_id = s.sql_id
```

```
and
    s.snap_id = sn.snap_id
group by
  to_char(sn.begin_interval_time,'yy-mm-dd hh24')
order by
1 ) f
where
    i.c1 = f.c1
;
```

Here is the output where we see a comparison of index-full scans vs. full-table scans.

Begin Interval Time	Index Table Scans	Full Table Scans
04-10-21 15	53	18
04-10-21 17	3	3
04-10-21 18	1	2
04-10-21 19	15	6
04-10-21 20		6
04-10-21 21		6
04-10-21 22	16	6
04-10-21 23	21	9
04-10-22 00	16	6
04-10-22 01		6
04-10-22 02	17	6
04-10-22 03	15	6
04-10-22 04	16	6
04-10-22 05		6
04-10-22 06		6
04-10-22 07	15	6
04-10-22 08		6
04-10-22 09		6
04-10-22 10	18	8
04-10-22 11	16	6
04-10-22 12	14	6
04-10-22 13		6
04-10-22 14		6
04-10-22 15	15	11
04-10-22 16	1	7
04-10-22 17	15	6
04-10-22 18	16	6
04-10-22 19	15	6

As we can see, knowing the signature for large-table full-table scans can help us in both SQL tuning and instance tuning. For SQL tuning, this report will tell us when to drill-down to verify that all of the large-table full-table scans are legitimate, and one verified, this same data can be used to dynamically reconfigure the Oracle instance to accommodate the large scans.

Monitoring SQL workload activity

The Ion for Oracle tool will instantly display SQL processing modality over time, quickly displaying any databases processing signature (Figure 16.31):

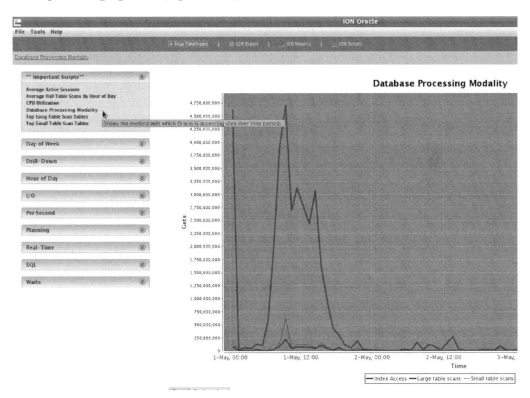

Figure 16.31: *Using Ion to display SQL workload processing modality*

Verifying optimal index usage

This is especially important for improving the speed of queries. Oracle sometimes has a choice of indexes, and the tuning professional must examine each index and ensure that Oracle is using the proper index. This also includes the use of bitmapped and function-based indexes.

Determining the index usage is especially important for improving the speed of queries with multiple *where* clause predicates. Oracle sometimes has a choice of indexes, and the tuning professional must examine each index and ensure that Oracle is using the best index, meaning the one that returns the result with the least consistent gets.

This problem occurs when the optimizer cannot find an index or the most restrictive where clause in the SQL is not matched with an index.

When the optimizer cannot find an appropriate index to access table rows, the optimizer will always invoke a full-table scan, reading every row in the table. Hence, a large-table full-table scan might indicate a sub-optimal SQL statement that can be tuned by adding an index that matches the where clause of the query.

Ion for Oracle instantly displays all tables and there predicate usage over time, very handy.

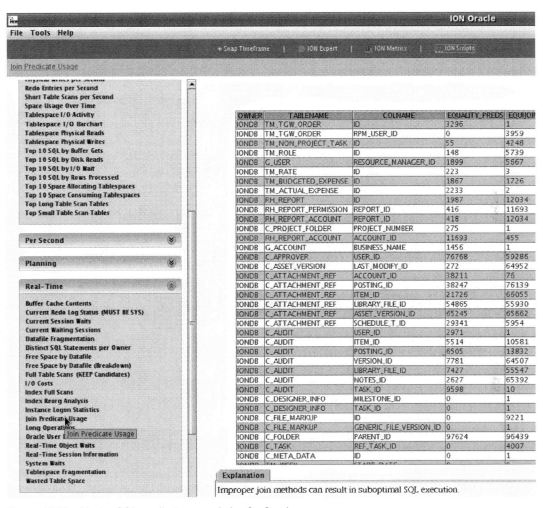

Figure 16.32: *Display SQL predicate usage in Ion for Oracle*

Next, let's explore techniques for locating new indexing opportunities, removing superfluous indexes and deleting un-unused indexes.

Finding indexing opportunities

As we know, one common symptom of a missing or invalidated index is that the SQL will perform an unnecessary large-table full-table scan. Sub-optimal index access to a table occurs when the optimizer cannot find an index or the most restrictive where clause in the SQL is not matched with an index.

This is especially true when SQL uses built-in functions and you have forgotten to create a matching function-based index. Make to read the section in this chapter on function-based indexes, one of the most powerful SQL tuning tools within Oracle.

When the optimizer cannot find an appropriate index to access table rows, the optimizer will always invoke a full-table scan, reading every row in the table. Hence, a large-table full-table scan might indicate a sub-optimal SQL statement that can be tuned by adding an index that matches the *where* clause of the query.

It's your job to find all missing indexes

While the extra-cost SQLAccess advisor will examine a SQL workload and identify missing indexes, you don't need an expensive tool to locate index opportunities.

We have the *plan9i.sql* script can be run to show all full-table scans and indicates the table size in both number of rows and data blocks, a great starting point for finding missing indexes.

find_full_scans.sql

To download this script, please do a web search for "plan9i.sql"

Here is the resulting report:

```
                    Full table scans and counts
          Note that "K" indicates in the table is in the KEEP pool.
```

```
OWNER           NAME                      NUM_ROWS  C K    BLOCKS   NBR_FTS
-------------   -----------------------   --------- - -  --------  --------
SYS             DUAL                                N            2   97,237
SYSTEM          SQLPLUS_PRODUCT_PROFILE             N K          2   16,178
DONALD          PAGE                      3,450,209 N      932,120    9,091
DONALD          RWU_PAGE                        434 N            8    7,355
DONALD          PAGE_IMAGE                   18,067 N        1,104    5,368
```

If you are licensed for the extra-cost AWR, (by purchasing the Oracle tuning pack and the Oracle diagnostic pack) you can also see this report by time-slice using the *plan10g.sql* script.

This script queries the *dba_hist_sql_plan* table to quickly find all tables that experience full-table scans. If you want to interrogate your current library cache, you can use the *plan9i.sql* script to see full-table scans from *v$sql_plan*.

Here is a sample of the output, showing full-table scans between AWR snapshot intervals:

```
                       full table scans and counts
Snapshot Time   OWNER      NAME                     NUM_ROWS C K    BLOCKS   NBR_FTS
-------------   -------    ----------------------   -------- - -   -------   -------
12/08/04 14     APPLSYS    FND_CONC_RELEASE_DISJS         39 N K        2    98,864
                APPLSYS    FND_CONC_RELEASE_PERIODS       39 N K        2    98,864
                APPLSYS    FND_CONC_RELEASE_STATES         1 N K        2    98,864
                SYS        DUAL                              N K        2    63,466
                APPLSYS    FND_CONC_PP_ACTIONS         7,021 N      1,262    52,036
                APPLSYS    FND_CONC_REL_CONJ_MEMBER        0 N K       22    50,174

12/08/04 15     APPLSYS    FND_CONC_RELEASE_DISJS         39 N K        2    33,811
                APPLSYS    FND_CONC_RELEASE_PERIODS       39 N K        2     2,864
                APPLSYS    FND_CONC_RELEASE_STATES         1 N K        2    32,864
                SYS        DUAL                              N K        2    63,466
                APPLSYS    FND_CONC_PP_ACTIONS         7,021 N      1,262    12,033
                APPLSYS    FND_CONC_REL_CONJ_MEMBER        0 N K       22    50,174
```

This report shows that the *page* table is rather large at 932,000 data blocks and the *page* table has experienced 9,000 full-table scans.

Remember, while full-table scans are not "bad", per se, they are an indicator that you may have a missing index, and excessive full-table scans on large tables should be investigated. High full-table scans on small tables could also be checked to ensure that they reside in your KEEP pool.

When performing SQL tuning, you should find this "suspicious", and examine the specific SQL to see if any of these scans are unnecessary, possible because of missing function-based indexes.

Once you have located a suspicious table that is experiencing large-table full-table scans, you can use this *get_sql.sql* script can be run to see the actual SQL that references the suspicious table.

💾 get_sql.sql

```
set lines 2000;

select
  sql_text,
  disk_reads,
  executions,
  parse_calls
```

```
from
   v$sqlarea
where
   lower(sql_text) like '% page %'
order by
   disk_reads desc
;
```

The following SQL statement is extracted from the output of the *get_sql.sql* script. After examination, it is obvious that the script is accessing customers by converting the customer name to uppercase using the *upper* BIF.

```
select
   p.page_name,
   o.order_date
from
   page      p,
   order     o
where
   upper(p.page_name) = upper(:v1)
and
   p.cust_nbr = o.cust_nbr
;
```

The *explain plan* utility can be now be ran against this SQL, confirming that this query is performs a full-table scan:

```
OPTIONS                         OBJECT_NAME                     POSITION
------------------------------- ------------------------------- ----------
SELECT STATEMENT
                                                                4
   NESTED LOOPS
                                                                1
      TABLE ACCESS
FULL                            PAGE                            1
      TABLE ACCESS
BY INDEX ROWID                  ORDER                           2
         INDEX
RANGE SCAN                      CUST_NBR_IDX                    1
```

A look at the *table access full page* option shows that the BIF is indeed responsible for the full-table scan. A matching function-based index can be added on *upper(page_name)* can now be used to remedy this issue.

It is important to remember that is not 100% safe to add indexes to tables, as this can often change the execution plan for the query and slow-down insert and update times.

```
create index
   upper_page_name_idx
on
   page
        (upper(page_name))
  tablespace ts_page
  pctfree 10;
```

Next, we re-run the SQL and see that the full-table scan has been replaced with an index range scan on our new function-based index. The resulting execution time has been reduced from 45 seconds to less than 2 seconds.

```
OPERATION
------------------------------------------------------------------------
OPTIONS                     OBJECT_NAME                   POSITION
--------------------------  ----------------------------  ----------
SELECT STATEMENT
                                                          5
  NESTED LOOPS
                                                          1
    TABLE ACCESS
BY INDEX ROWID              PAGE                          1
      INDEX
RANGE SCAN                  PAGE_NBR_IDX                  1
    TABLE ACCESS
BY INDEX ROWID              ORDER                         2
      INDEX
RANGE SCAN                  UPPER_PAGE_NAME_IDX           1
```

In sum, we see that it's relatively easy to detect "missing" function-based Oracle indexes and add them to tune our SQL.

Find SQL that uses sub-optimal indexes

Every Oracle tuning expert will let you to never assume that all optimal indexes, exist, especially function-based indexes. Remember, with rare exceptions, Oracle can only choose one index to access any given table in a SQL statement, and it's your job to ensure that the most restrictive index exists!

For beginners, Oracle has created several frameworks that will examine the access plans for SQL tuning sets and identify index and materialized view opportunities. These extra-cost tools include:

- **SQLAccess Advisor:** The Oracle SQLAccess advisor will examine workloads in an attempt to locate missing indexes and missing materialized views.

- **Real Application Testing:** The RAT framework allows you to replay a SQL tuning set, seeking tuning opportunities. The RAT framework, in turn, works with the 11g SQL tuning advisor to locater missing indexes.

For complete details on using the extra-cost Oracle Real Application Testing (RAT) and the SQL Performance Analyzer (SPA), see chapter 20, Oracle SQL Tuning Advisors.

While these tools are getting getter with each release of Oracle, a human SQL tuning expert can do a better job than any automated tool at finding missing indexes. While every expert has their own approach, locating missing indexes involves the following steps:

- **Locate high impact SQL** – You can search for high impact SQL using several criteria (*disk reads, executions*) and you can find historical SQL in any of these three locations:

- o   Search *v$sql* for frequently executed SQL (using the *executions* column)

- o   Search the *stats$sql_plan* table in STATSPACK

- o   Search the *dba_hist_sql_plan* in AWR (extra cost option)

- **Examine execution statistics** – For each high-impact SQL statement, compare the number of rows returned to the number of consistent gets required to fetch the rows. SQL with a missing index will use a sub-optimal index (or do a full table scan), showing too many buffer touches than are necessary to fetch the result row set.

- **Create a new index** – In your test or development environment, create the new index and re-run the SQL to see if the number of consistent gets is reduced. Remember, a new index may help more than just the SQL statement that you are tuning.

- **Implement the index** – Migrate the index into production and re-sample the workload to find the next "high-impact" SQL statement to tune.

- **Repeat as needed**: Finally, repeat the first step iteratively to tune the next SQL statement.

Finding SQL with excessive I/O

The best way to search for SQL that might be used a less than optimal indexes is to compare the rows returned with the number of block fetches, all the while being conscious of aggregate queries that require full-scans (min, max, sum, avg, &c).

For example, consider three queries that return ten rows, but each with very different numbers of data block reads:

- **Clustered data** – A SQL where the related rows are physically clustered together on the same data block (using sorted hash cluster tables) will fetch the ten rows with three data block reads.

- **Well tuned SQL** – With un-clustered data and a selective index, the ten rows can be fetched in less than 20 data block reads.

- **Sub-optimal index** – With a SQL with a missing index, fetching the ten rows might take hundreds of data block reads.

- **No indexes** – In a SQL with not appropriate indexes, a full-table scan is required and fetching the ten rows might require thousands of data block reads.

So as we see, one hallmark of sub-optimal SQL execution is an unusually high number of data block reads for the number of rows being returned.

Toss out aggregations!

When fishing for sub-optimal SQL, you need to filter out aggregations (min, max, avg, sum) because they types of queries will need to perform full table scans of use query-rewrite for materialized views.

Now that we understand the characteristics of sub-optimal index access, let's take a closer look at how to write scripts against the data dictionary, STATSPACK and AWR to identify queries with excessive I/O.

Finding sub-optimal SQL in the library cache

Here is a rough sample query that you can run against *v$sqlarea* to locate queries with possible sub-optimal indexes. Of course, you will need to customize this SQL to match your exact SQL workloads. In this example, we must remember that this will only extract SQL that is currently in your library cache, yet SQL is re-pinged to the front of the most-recently-used list each time that the SQL is executed.

🖫 **get_sub_optimal_cached_sql.sql**

```
set linesize 80 pagesize 80 trimspool on

ttitle "Top 10 Expensive SQL | Consistent Gets per Rows Fetched"

column sql_id heading "SQL ID"
column c2     heading "Avg Gets per Row"
column c3     heading "Total Gets"
column c4     heading "Total Rows"

select
   *
from
   (select
      sq.sql_id,
      round(sum(buffer_gets_delta) /
      decode(sum(rows_processed_delta), 0, 1,
      sum(rows_processed_delta))) c2,
      sum(buffer_gets_delta) c3,
      sum(rows_processed_delta) c4
   from
      dba_hist_snapshot sn,
      dba_hist_sqlstat sq,
      dba_hist_sqltext st
   where
      sn.snap_id = sq.snap_id
   and
      sn.dbid = sq.dbid
   and
      sn.instance_number = sq.instance_number
   and
      sn.dbid = st.dbid
   and
```

```
        sq.sql_id = st.sql_id
   and
        lower(sql_text) not like '%sum(%'
   and
        lower(sql_text) not like '%min(%'
   and
        lower(sql_text) not like '%max(%'
   and
        lower(sql_text) not like '%avg(%'
   and
        lower(sql_text) not like '%count(%'
   and
        sn.snap_id between &beginsnap and &endsnap
   and
        sq.parsing_schema_name not in ('SYS', 'SYSMAN', 'SYSTEM', 'MDSYS', 'WMSYS', 'TSMSYS',
'DBSNMP', 'OUTLN')
group by
   sq.sql_id
order by
   2 desc)
where
   rownum < 11
/
```

Here is a listing from this query:

```
@get_sub_optimal_cached_sql.sql

Enter value for beginsnap: 48810
Enter value for endsnap: 48913

old   11: and sn.snap_id between &beginsnap and &endsnap
new   11: and sn.snap_id between 48810 and 48913
```

```
Sun Jan 10                                                   page      1
                      Top 10 Expensive SQL
              Consistent Gets per Rows Fetched

SQL ID          Avg Gets per Row       Total Gets Total Rows
-------------   ----------------       ---------- ----------
9m73y3n44dmgy        606,665,271      606,665,271          0
a5zs0psr0m2p9         24,997,386       49,994,772          2
a7m9jw016q6hf         17,280,238       17,280,238          0
5zzvgcvxcxtth          8,278,019        8,278,019          0
bc5kw9qc0v0dm          8,049,460        8,049,460          0
8nus8twjpc3r9          8,018,029      192,432,698         24
cg5rg1vzw5uaz          5,168,572        5,168,572          0
9ncywvmgtakg3          4,004,378        4,004,378          0
dj6bagqucttx9          2,199,463      892,982,149        406
7uv8ra7n7vdps          1,899,353        1,899,353          0
```

As we see, this query shows the most expensive SQL statements by average gets per row.

Finding index opportunities in AWR

If you have purchased the extra-cost options required to use the Automatic Workload Repository (AWR), you can query the AWR tables to locate SQL with indexing opportunities. Please note that the free STATSPACK utility will do exactly the same job of capturing historical SQL.

See my book "***Oracle Tuning: The Definitive Reference***" for details on setting AWR SQL collection thresholds.

Here is a script that shows expensive SQL statements by time period. Note that you can constrain the list to display the top-n most expensive queries and adjust the I/O threshold for the display.

🖫 **awr_expensive_sql.sql**

```
set linesize 80 pagesize 80 trimspool on

ttitle "Top 10 Expensive SQL | Disk Reads per Rows Fetched"

column sql_id heading "SQL ID"
column c2 heading "Avg Reads per Row"
column c3 heading "Total Reads"
column c4 heading "Total Rows"

select
   *
from
   (select
      sq.sql_id,
      round(sum(disk_reads_delta) /
      decode(sum(rows_processed_delta),
      0,
      1,
      sum(rows_processed_delta))) c2,
   sum(disk_reads_delta) c3,
   sum(rows_processed_delta) c4
from
   dba_hist_snapshot sn,
   dba_hist_sqlstat  sq,
   dba_hist_sqltext  st
where
   sn.snap_id = sq.snap_id
and
   sn.dbid = sq.dbid
and
   sn.instance_number = sq.instance_number
and
   sn.dbid = st.dbid and sq.sql_id = st.sql_id
and
   lower(sql_text) not like '%sum(%'
and
   lower(sql_text) not like '%min(%'
and
   lower(sql_text) not like '%max(%'
and
   lower(sql_text) not like '%avg(%'
and
   lower(sql_text) not like '%count(%'
```

```
and
    sn.snap_id between &beginsnap and &endsnap
and
    sq.parsing_schema_name not in ('SYS', 'SYSMAN', 'SYSTEM', 'MDSYS', 'WMSYS', 'TSMSYS',
'DBSNMP', 'OUTLN')
group by
    sq.sql_id
order by
    2 desc)
where
    rownum < 11
/
```

Here is the output from this script, showing the most expensive SQL based on disk I/O

```
@awr_expensive_sql.sql

Enter value for beginsnap: 48810
Enter value for endsnap: 48913

old  11: and sn.snap_id between &beginsnap and &endsnap
new  11: and sn.snap_id between 48810 and 48913
```

```
Sun Jan 10                                                   page     1
                    Top 10 Expensive SQL
                  Disk Reads per Rows Fetched

SQL ID          Avg Reads per Row    Total Reads  Total Rows
-------------   ----------------     -----------  ----------
a5zs0psr0m2p9            346,838         693,675           2
7uv8ra7n7vdps            217,933         217,933           0
cg5rg1vzw5uaz            139,402         139,402           0
5zzvgcvxcxtth            128,271         128,271           0
a7m9jw016q6hf            117,039         117,039           0
8nus8twjpc3r9            101,795       2,443,082          24
9m73y3n44dmgy             56,664          56,664           0
bc5kw9qc0v0dm             45,732          45,732           0
9ncywvmgtakg3             44,728          44,728           0
7181d5ckdz09m             22,864       1,188,947          52
```

Next, let's look at the issue of superfluous and un-used indexes and understand why it's important to remove them from your production environment.

Locating un-used indexes

It a critical task to constantly monitor for un-used indexes by examining the characteristics of the SQL workload to see how often the SQL is used. Un-used indexes have several shortcomings:

- **Disk space waste** – Un-used disks waste significant amounts of disk space. Disk is cheap, but lots of indexes can still waste a significant amount of disk.

- **Slow inserts and updates** – With many indexes on a table, inserts can take large amounts of time, since all indexes must be updated at DML time.

As we have noted, it's impossible to know whether an index is used unless we have a way to track what SQL statements use the index.

The methods for identifying un-used indexes are release specific, so let's examine techniques for locating unused indexes by release.

Finding un-used indexes in Oracle 8i and earlier

In Oracle8i and earlier releases this was major undertaking since you had to capture SQL directly from the library cache, generate an execution plan, and save the indexes.

Over time, you collect a list of used indexes, and this list can be compared to the master index list in *dba_indexes* to find the un-used indexes. For the script to locate un-used indexes is unsupported releases, please Google for the query *access_index.sql* (available on www.dba-oracle .com).

Finding un-used indexes in Oracle 9i

Starting in Oracle9i, we get the *v$object_usage* view to tell us when an index is used. This is a primitive marker because it is only a bit flag, only indicating if an index is used and not noting whether the index was used once or a million times. You can use this simple command to set the bit flag to monitor usage for an index:

```
alter index
    myindex
monitoring usage;
```

Once implemented you simple query the *used* column of *v$object_usage* to see if the index was used:

```
select
    used
from
    v$object_usage
```

```
where
   index_name = 'MYINDEX';
```

Beware of index monitoring!

There is overhead to turning-on index monitoring
because all SQL statements in the library cache will
be invalidated. Hence, it is best to turn-on index
monitoring immediately after starting the instance.

In order to use index monitoring to find un-used indexes, it's important to leave index monitoring on long
enough to ensure that all possible SQL statement have executed. For example, a monthly job might use an
index, and the monitoring must be turned-on for a whole month. Of course, in a case like this, it may be a
better practice to create the index for the monthly job right before execution, and then dropping the index.

While the index usage in a bit flag, it might be helpful to know the number of times that the index was
invoked. In Oracle9i you can use STATSPACK for this, querying the *stats$sql_plan* table.

Finding un-used indexes in Oracle 10g and beyond

In Oracle 10g and beyond, you can more accurately count the number of times that an index was invoked
by using the STATSPACK or AWR tables. If you have not purchased the packs required to query the
AWR tables, you can use this query against the *stats$sql_plan* and stats$sql_plan_usage tables:

🖫 **statspack_unused_indexes.sql**

```
ttitle "Unused Indexes by Time Period"

col owner heading "Index Owner" format a30
col index_name heading "Index Name" format a30

set linesize 95 trimspool on pagesize 80

select *
from
   (select
      owner,
      index_name
   from
      dba_indexes di
   where
      di.index_type != 'LOB'
   and
      owner not in ('SYS', 'SYSMAN', 'SYSTEM', 'MDSYS', 'WMSYS', 'TSMSYS', 'DBSNMP',
'OUTLN')
minus
```

```
select
   index_owner owner,
   index_name
from
   dba_constraints dc
where
   index_owner not in ('SYS', 'SYSMAN', 'SYSTEM', 'MDSYS', 'WMSYS', 'TSMSYS', 'DBSNMP',
'OUTLN')
minus
select
   p.object_owner owner,
   p.object_name  index_name
from
   stats$snapshot       sn,
   stats$sql_plan       p,
   stats$sql_summary    st,
   stats$sql_plan_usage spu
where
   st.sql_id = spu.sql_id
and
   spu.plan_hash_value = p.plan_hash_value
and
   st.hash_value = p.plan_hash_value
and
   sn.snap_id = st.snap_id
and
   sn.dbid = st.dbid
and
   sn.instance_number = st.instance_number
and
   sn.snap_id = spu.snap_id
and
   sn.dbid = spu.snap_id
and
   sn.instance_number = spu.instance_number
and
   sn.snap_id between &begin_snap and &end_snap
and
   p.object_type = 'INDEX'
)
where owner not in ('SYS', 'SYSMAN', 'SYSTEM', 'MDSYS', 'WMSYS', 'TSMSYS', 'DBSNMP',
'OUTLN')
order by 1, 2
/
```

Note in the script above the clause to ensure that the index is not used to enforce a primary key or foreign key relationship. Even though an index may appear to be used by SQL, it may be heavily used to enforce primary key and foreign key constraints.

```
Enter value for begin_snap: 48795

Enter value for end_snap: 48923

old  22:     sn.snap_id between &begin_snap and &end_snap
new  22:     sn.snap_id between 48795 and 48923
```

Monitoring SQL workload activity   **977**

```
                  Unused Indexes by Time Period

Index Owner                          Index Name
-----------------------------        -----------------------------
ROBOHEAD                             CIX_ACCTERM_TID
ROBOHEAD                             CIX_ACTEXP_BETID
ROBOHEAD                             CIX_ACTEXP_CID
ROBOHEAD                             CIX_ACTEXP_ETID
ROBOHEAD                             CIX_ACTEXP_PID
ROBOHEAD                             CIX_ACTLOG_DID_DTYP_LFID
ROBOHEAD                             CIX_APPROVAL_STATUS
ROBOHEAD                             CIX_APPROVER_USERID
ROBOHEAD                             CIX_ATTREF_SCHT
ROBOHEAD                             CIX_AUDIT_NOTESID
```

When dropping un-used indexes, also watch out for any indexes that may be used internally to enforce primary key foreign key relationships.

Depending upon how you define the primary key or foreign key index, the index may have a name or it may appear as a system owned index, beginning with SYS. Below we see a sample of the output from this script, showing un-used, non-constraint indexes by time period.

If you have a license for the Oracle performance pack and the Oracle Diagnostic pack, then you can run this query to see un-used indexes:

🖫 awr_unused_indexes.sql

```
ttitle "Unused Indexes by Time Period"

col owner heading "Index Owner" format a30
col index_name heading "Index Name" format a30

set linesize 95 trimspool on pagesize 80

select * from
(select owner, index_name
from dba_indexes di
where
   di.index_type != 'LOB'
minus
select index_owner owner, index_name
from dba_constraints dc
minus
select
   p.object_owner owner,
   p.object_name index_name
from
   dba_hist_snapshot   sn,
   dba_hist_sql_plan    p,
   dba_hist_sqlstat    st
where
   st.sql_id = p.sql_id
and
   sn.snap_id = st.snap_id and sn.dbid = st.dbid and sn.instance_number = st.instance_number
and
```

```
      sn.snap_id between &begin_snap and &end_snap
and
      p.object_type = 'INDEX'
)
where owner not in ('SYS', 'SYSMAN', 'SYSTEM', 'MDSYS', 'WMSYS', 'TSMSYS', 'DBSNMP',
'OUTLN')
order by 1, 2
/
```

Dropping un-used indexes

Now that we have identified the un-used indexes, (being very careful to sample over a long enough time period to ensure that you have not missed any queries), the final steps are SIMPLE:

1. Take a backup of the index DDL using *dbms_metadata*.

2. Drop the index

For taking a backup of an un-used index, I recommend using the *dbms_metadata* package to punch-off a copy of the index DLL from the data dictionary:

```
set heading off;
set echo off;
Set pages 999;
set long 90000;

spool ddl_list.sql
select dbms_metadata.get_ddl('TABLE','DEPT','SCOTT') from dual;
select dbms_metadata.get_ddl('INDEX','DEPT_IDX','SCOTT') from dual;
spool off;
```

Next, let's see how to locate infrequently-used indexes.

Locating infrequently used indexes

It's not uncommon for infrequently-used indexes to consume more resources than they save when they are used. For highly active tables, each and every DML statement requires Oracle to keep the index current, and you must carefully weigh the relative saving of the index on the infrequent SQL against the continuous overhead of maintaining the index.

Disk space is cheap so the cost of the disk required to store the index is usually negligible. Infrequently-used indexes do not impose a heavy overhead for static tables that are rarely updated, but they can wreak havoc on volatile table, causing a measurable amount of operational overhead for very little benefit.

Remember, indexes always add overhead to DML operations, and it may often be a good practice for weekly and monthly jobs to drop the index and consider one of these alternative methods:

1. Create   the   index,   run   the   job   and   then   drop   the   index.

2. Allow the infrequent job to choose another plan that does not involve the index.

The below query can be used to find infrequently-used indexes.

When using the query below, adjust the count to match your specific workload (my default is 50 invocations). You can also change the date format mask to change the aggregation period (currently set to monthly (*mon*).

awr_infrequent_indexes.sql

```
ttitle "Infrequently-used indexes by month"

col c1 heading "Month"              format a20
col c2 heading "Index Owner"        format a30
col c3 heading "Index Name"         format a30
col c4 heading "Invocation|Count" format 99

set linesize 95 trimspool on pagesize 80

select
   to_char(sn.begin_interval_time,'Month') c1,
   p.object_owner c2,
   p.object_name c3,
   sum(executions_delta) c4
from
   dba_hist_snapshot    sn,
   dba_hist_sql_plan    p,
   dba_hist_sqlstat     st
where
   st.sql_id = p.sql_id
and
   sn.snap_id = st.snap_id
and
   sn.dbid = st.dbid
and
   sn.instance_number = st.instance_number
and
   p.object_type = 'INDEX'
and
   p.object_owner not in ('SYS', 'SYSMAN', 'SYSTEM', 'MDSYS', 'WMSYS', 'TSMSYS', 'DBSNMP')
group by
   to_char(sn.begin_interval_time, 'Month'),
   p.object_owner,
   p.object_name
```

```
having
    sum(executions_delta) < 50
order by
    1, 4 desc, 2, 3
/
```

Here is the output of the infrequent index report usage report:

```
Sun Jan 10                                              page 1
                Infrequently-used indexes by month

                                                    Invocation
Month              Index Owner    Index Name            Count
-----------------  -------------- -------------------- ----------
January            ROBOHEAD       CIX_ATTREF_LIBFID        44
January            ROBOHEAD       CIX_THUBNL_FAID          44
January            ROBOHEAD       CIX_AUDIT_TASKID         42
January            ROBOHEAD       CIX_FOLDER_GID           28
January            ROBOHEAD       PERF2_C_FOLDER_SEC       13
January            ROBOHEAD       CIX_AUDIT_TASK_ID        11
January            ROBOHEAD       CIX_PF_SI                11
January            ROBOHEAD       IX_ACCOUNT_1              8
January            ROBOHEAD       CIX_AUDIT_NOTESID         3
January            ROBOHEAD       CIX_SAVERPT_UID_TYPE      3
January            ROBOHEAD       CIX_FLDRTRCK_FLDR         2
January            PERFSTAT       DBA_HIST_IDX_STAT_DATE_IDX 1
January            ROBOHEAD       CIX_AL_UI                 1
```

Again, you need to carefully perform a cost-benefit analysis against any infrequently-used indexes:

- **Benefit** – It's easy to see the benefit because the SQL is infrequently used. Simply run the query in your QA database once with the index and again without the index.

- **Cost** – As noted the cost of an infrequently used index is directly proportional to the amount of updates to the target table. For each DML, the overhead to maintain the index may not be measurable, but it can add-up fast for highly active tables that perform thousands of updates per day.

Now that we understand the issue of infrequent indexes, let's move on and explore the issue of redundant indexes.

The problem of too many indexes

Over the years, it's not uncommon to create indexes and not notice when the jobs that use them are removed from the SQL workload.

For example, I once went on site to a shop that was complaining that each tale insert was taking 45 seconds per row! Upon inspection, the table had 80 columns bit it had over 120 indexes! The DBA did not understand how to add indexes, and after he was fired for inept work, we were faced with cleaning up this horrendous mess.

We could not simply delete all of the indexes because the system was live in production, and we had to carefully inspect each index and compare it to historical SQL execution plans to locate those indexes that could be safely removed without impacting run-time performance.

One common misconception by developers is that every predicate in a SQL *where* clause should be indexed, but this is not true. Because Oracle supports multi-column indexes, it's easy to accidently create "duplicate" indexes, indexes that add overhead to DML and do not aid in speeding-up SQL execution.

Aggressively remove duplicitous indexes!

Management commonly hires clandestine experts to review the technical ability of a DBA. One sure-fire way to get fired is to waste computing resources by allowing your database to have duplicate indexes.

Now that we understand how important it is to remove duplicate indexes, let's look at some common methods for finding indexes that can be safely dropped without effecting SQL execution.

You can query the *dba_ind_columns* view to quickly locate indexes with duplicate columns, but the real challenge comes when you need to decide which index to drop:

This script looks for indexes on tables with the same leading column, then for indexes with the same two leading columns. This duplicate index column report provides a good starting point for trying to reduce redundancy in indexes.

💾 **Find_duplicate_index_columns.sql**

```
set linesize 150 trimspool on pagesize 80

column index_owner format a20
column column_name format a30
column position format 9
column nextcol format a18 heading "Next Column Match?"

select
   a.index_owner,
   a.column_name,
   a.index_name index_name1,
   b.index_name index_name2,
   a.column_position position,
(select
    'YES'
from
    dba_ind_columns x,
    dba_ind_columns y
where
    x.index_owner = a.index_owner
and
    y.index_owner = b.index_owner
and
    x.index_name = a.index_name
and
    y.index_name = b.index_name
```

```
   and
      x.column_position = 2
   and
      y.column_position = 2
   and
      x.column_name = y.column_name) nextcol
from
   dba_ind_columns a,
   dba_ind_columns b
where
   a.index_owner not in ('SYS', 'SYSMAN', 'SYSTEM', 'MDSYS', 'WMSYS', 'TSMSYS', 'DBSNMP')
and
   a.index_owner = b.index_owner
and
   a.column_name = b.column_name
and
   a.table_name = b.table_name
and
   a.index_name != b.index_name
and
   a.column_position = 1
and
   b.column_position = 1
/
```

Here is a sample of the output from this script:

```
INDEX_OWNER     COLUMN_NAME     INDEX_NAME1                      INDEX_NAME2
POS MT
------------ --------------- -------------------------- --------------------------
--
ROBOHEAD        MARKUP_STATUS   IX_ASSET_VERSION_MRKUP_TYPE
IX_ASSET_VERSION_MRKSCLTYPE    1
ROBOHEAD        MARKUP_STATUS   IX_ASSET_VERSION_MRKSCLTYPE
IX_ASSET_VERSION_MRKUP_TYPE    1
ROBOHEAD        ID              PERF1_C_ASSET_VERSION            XPKC_ASSET_VERSION
1
ROBOHEAD        ID              XPKC_ASSET_VERSION               PERF1_C_ASSET_VERSION
1
ROBOHEAD        TASK_ID         CIX_AUDIT_TASKID                 CIX_AUDIT_TASK_ID
1
ROBOHEAD        TASK_ID         CIX_AUDIT_TASK_ID                CIX_AUDIT_TASKID
1
ROBOHEAD        ID              CIX_FOLDER_FID_PRNT              PERF1_C_FOLDER
1 YES
ROBOHEAD        ID              CIX_FOLDER_FID_PRNT              XPKC_FOLDER
1
ROBOHEAD        ID              PERF1_C_FOLDER                   CIX_FOLDER_FID_PRNT
1 YES
```

As we see, this query locates indexes with the same leading column and for indexes with the same two leading columns. While this query does not provide every possible duplicate column, it does give you the general idea on how to locate redundant index columns and it serves as a good starting point for identifying index redundancy.

Next, let's examine some techniques for determining which redundant indexes to drop.

Determining which index to delete

If your optimizer mode is set to minimize SQL response time (*optimizer_mode=first_rows_n*), the cost-based optimizer chooses which index to satisfy a query, he examines the metadata statistics (from *dbms_stats*) to locate the index that it thinks will be the most selective, the index that will result in the least amount of data block reads.

1. First, the optimizer evaluates all of the predicates in the *where* clause and locates the predicate that is the most unique (the one that will return the smallest result set).

2. For that index column, Oracle then searches for a matching index, either a single column index, or a multi-column index where the column is the leading column. Failing that, Oracle next tries to find an index on the next most restrictive column (based on the optimizer's cardinality estimates). This might be an index on another column in the where clause or on a multi-column index that contains the restrictive item as a secondary key (using the index skip scan method).

Remember, for any given table, Oracle will only choose one index to access the table (unless there bitmap indexes (the bitmap merge plan), or in 9i and earlier, when the *and_equal* hint is used).

Let's look at some example of redundant index columns. Consider this example below for a multi-column customer table. As we see, the *cust_id* column appears in three indexes and *cust_name* appears in several indexes. Which index is it safe to remove?

Index name	Index column
cust_id_idx	cust_id (primary_key)
cust_id_name_idx	cust_id, cust_name
cust_name_id_idx	cust_name, cust_id
cust_details_idx	cust_id, cust_name, cust_type

In this example, we can safely remove the *cust_name_id_idx* because all of its columns are completely contained in the *cust_details_idx*:

Index name	Index column
cust_id_idx	cust_id (primary key)
cust_id_name_idx	cust_id, cust_name
cust_name_id_idx	cust_name, cust_id
cust_details_idx	cust_id, cust_name, cust_type

Now, we have pared-down the index, but we still see two redundant *cust_id* columns:

Index name	Index column
cust_id_idx	cust_id (primary key)
cust_id_name_idx	cust_id, cust_name
cust_name_id_idx	cust_name, cust_id

In this example, the redundancy is necessary because the *cust_id_idx* is a primary key constraint. Also, the redundancy is acceptable in the *cust_name_id_idx* if there is a frequently-executed SQL statement that required both of these columns in the *where* clause.

At this point, you may be tempted to examine your SQL workload and attempt to create a large multi-column index in an attempt to create a single index to serve all of your queries.

Let's take a look at the dynamics of multi-column indexes and see how they are used for optimal SQL execution.

Large Multi-column Indexes

Multi-column indexes with more than 3 columns may not provide more efficient access than a two-column index. The objective of the index is to reduce the amount of rows returned from a table access. Therefore each added column must substantially reduce the number of returned rows to be effective.

For example, assuming a large table, on a query with 5 or more *where (and)* clauses using a 5-column index may return only 1 row. However using a 3-column index may return only 50 rows. A two-column index returns 200 rows. The time it takes to extract the one row from the 200 rows using nested-loops is negligible.

Thus the two-column index may be almost as efficient (fast) as the 5-column index. The key is to index the most restrictive columns. Another tradeoff is a table with multiple column indexes where the leading column(s) are the same.

For instance, a table with four 3-column indexes where the leading two columns are the same may work very efficiently on select statements but cause a heavy penalty on inserts and updates. Just one 2-column index on the leading two columns may provide acceptable query performance while greatly improving DML.

Small tables with two or three columns may benefit by being rebuilt as an Index Organized Table (IOT). A 2-column table with a primary key and a two-column index has 1.5 times the data in indexes that are in the table. Making the table an Index Organized Table reduced the need for indexes because the table is the index. Also IOTs can have indexes on non-leading columns if required. Again this has to be balanced with the overhead of maintaining the IOT.

Lastly, do not be afraid to use temporary indexes, creating and destroying the index when needed by a daily, weekly or monthly job.

For example, assume a nightly batch job that requires 6 hours to run, but it will run in 30 minutes with an index, but this index in not needed for any other SQL. In this case, you might want to create the index before running the report and drop it upon completion.

I work with clients that drop certain indexes to expedite the bill run, then recreate then for the normal application. They create indexes each night and drop them in the morning. There is nothing wrong with dynamically changing you database to respond to varying tasks if it results in efficiency.

Next, let's move on an examine how to tune SQL queries by creating selective indexes to speed up our queries.

Row clustering and SQL Performance

The CBO's decision to perform a full-table vs. an index range scan is influenced by the *clustering_factor* column (located inside the *dba_indexes* view), *db_block_size*, and *avg_row_len*. It is important to understand how the CBO uses these statistics to determine the fastest way to deliver the desired rows.

Conversely, a high *clustering_factor*, where the value approaches the number of rows in the table (*num_rows*), indicates that the rows are not in the same sequence as the index, and additional I/O will be required for index range scans. As the *clustering_factor* approaches the number of rows in the table, the rows are out of sync with the index.

Let's look at some important tool for tuning SQL, the *clustering_factor* column in the *dba_indexes* view.

By design, Oracle is a high-performance engine, and Oracle deliberately uses tricks to make Oracle run super-fast, things like delaying index maintenance when rows are deleted. Similarly, Oracle tables can fragment, causing full-scan SQL operations to run far longer than necessary. For table reorganization we have several utilities to returning a table to it's "pristine" state:

- **Online reorganization** – Oracle uses the *dbms_redefinition* package to embed Create Table As Select statement (CTAS), such that a table can be reorganized while it is still accepting updates.

- **Deallocate unused space**: Oracle notes that the "deallocate unused space" clause is used to explicitly deallocate unused space at "the end" of a segment and makes that space available for other segments within the tablespace.

```
alter table xxx deallocate unused space;
alter index xxx deallocate unused space;
```

  Internally, Oracle deallocates unused space beginning from the end of the objects (allocated space) and moving downwards toward the beginning of the object, continuing down until it reaches the high water mark (HWM). For indexes, "deallocate unused space" coalesces all leaf blocks within same branch of b-tree, and quickly frees up index leaf blocks for use.

- **The coalesce statement**: Unlike the "deallocate unused space" syntax which removes space above the high-water mark, "coalesce" puts together discontiguous fragmented extents.

There are two type of space fragmentation in Oracle. First is the honeycomb fragmentation, when the free extents are side by side, and the "Swiss Cheese" fragmentation, when the extents are separated by live segments.

```
alter table xxx coalesce;

alter index xxx coalesce;
```

- **Shrink space**: Using the "*alter table xxx shrink space compact*" command also has the benefit of making full-table scans run faster, as less block accesses are required. With standard Oracle tables, you can reclaim space with the "alter table shrink space" command:

```
SQL> alter table mytable enable row movement;
Table altered

SQL> alter table mytable shrink space;
Table altered
```

Row ordering matters!

In some systems where a table is always accessed by the same key sequence, re-ordering the table into the same order as the queries can dramatically reduce I/O and improve SQL performance.

With the introduction of these table reorg tools, the DBA gets a powerful tool for effective and easy database space management.

When reorganizing tables to improve SQL performance, keep this in-mind:

- Only tables that experience multi-block reads (full-table scans) may see an appreciable SQL performance benefit.

- Some shops will use sorted hash cluster tables to maintain row sequence order (in the same order as the most common indexed retrieval), and you can reorganize a table with an "order by" clause to make the rows in the same sequence as the index.

But it's not just tables that require periodic maintenance, it's also indexes.

Index reorganization and SQL Performance

When you rebuild an index, Oracle uses the current index to create the new index and read the existing index, front to back, building the new index in the target tablespace as temporary segments. Upon completion of reading the old index, the old index is dropped and the temporary segments become the fresh new index tree.

In general, index rebuilding greatly reduces index size in cases of indexes with lots of logically deleted entries, and this index size reduction, in turn, will improve the performance of SQL that does full-scan or index range scan operations.

Oracle has provided utilities to reorganize indexes for over a decade, and there is no dispute that SQL scan operations (index full scans, index fast-full scans, index range scans) will run longer against fragmented tables and indexes.

Production DBA's spend weekends reorganizing their data structures, returning them back into their original, pristine state, in preparation for the return of the end-users on Monday morning.

Rebuilding high-DML indexes in a schedule can be a DBA best practice under certain conditions:

- You can schedule a job to rebuild and index (and address errors) in just a few minutes. Because most DBA's are salaried professionals, the DBA cost is negligible.

- During a weekly maintenance window the server sits idle. Because hardware depreciates rapidly, regardless of use, the cost of rebuilding indexes is essentially zero.

When rebuilding indexes may help SQL performance

It's quite true that rebuilding indexes does not always help performance, but there are many times when rebuilding an index does help performance, especially for indexes that experience high DML activity and have multiple freelists and experience index range scans or index fast-full scans.

Watch the SQL workload!

Index access patterns matter! Only indexes that experience range scans will benefit from index rebuilding or coalescing.

The reason that SQL performance is improved after index maintenance is that the index is returned to its original pristine optimal state. Index performance suffers because many tasks compete from many freelists to get blocks as the index grows; the physical structure of the index data blocks becomes scrambled.

In general, rebuilding indexes may not improve SQL performance, especially when the SQL is performing index unique scans", dropping through the index tree to find a single ROWID. However, in rare cases index rebuilding has been shown to improve SQL performance:

- **Full table scans** – By reorganizing a fragmented index, the index becomes physically smaller, and less block reads are required to complete a full-table scan.

- **Index range scans** – For multi-block range scan operations, index rebuilding can reduce overall I/O.

In sum, you must do more than examine the index; you must also examine the SQL workload against the indexes to find the indexes that experience frequent multi-block read operations.

In an index with a single freelist, index range scans need only perform a single movement of the read-write head on disk, and the contiguous data locks can be read as fast as the disk can spin. In a large multi-user environment, index blocks become discontiguous and the benefits of multiblock reads for index range scans are lost.

When rebuilding indexes will hurt performance

While the "pristine" state of an index is generally optimal, there are rare cases where rebuilding indexes will cause *insert* DML to run more slowly.

For example, many systems achieve a "steady state", whereby index blocks will move change sizes on a regularly basis. In such systems, batch delete operations may cause lots of "dead" index data blocks, but subsequent insert jobs will re-use these blocks.

Again, every application is different, and the DBA can carefully test index rebuilding performance by testing them against SQL workloads. For details on testing index performance, see the book ***Database Benchmarking*** by Bert Scalzo.

Index behavior and Oracle blocksize

Because the blocksize affects the number of keys within each index node, it follows that the blocksize will have an effect on the structure of the index tree. All else being equal, large 32k blocksizes will have more keys per data block, resulting in a flatter index than the same index created in a 2k tablespace. A large blocksize will also reduce the number of consistent gets during index access, improving performance for scattered reads and range scan access.

While most Oracle databases will not see any appreciable benefit from multiple blocksizes, mission-critical applications can see a real benefit. In very large, high-activity databases, some Oracle tuning experts utilize the multiple blocksize feature of Oracle because it provides buffer segregation and the ability to place objects with the most appropriate blocksize to reduce buffer waste.

Choosing candidates for index maintenance

If you are a shop without a scheduled downtime window to rebuild/coalesce your indexes, it may be helpful to use an empirical approach to identify indexes that might benefit from a rebuild. As months pass, you gather feedback on your SQL performance for the specific indexes using STATSPACK or AWR, and successively refine your program to detect indexes that required maintenance.

Every SQL workload is different and no single rule set applies to every database. However, the propensity of an index becoming unbalanced is largely a function of these factors:

- **DML workload**: Databases with high batch delete jobs and frequent index key updates can fragment heavily.

- **Key length and blocksize** – Because Oracle indexes use block boundaries and index node boundaries, the index blocksize and key length factors into index fragmentation.

Oracle ACE Andrew Kerber notes this generic script to identify indexes that might benefit from index reorganization:

"I eventually wrote a simple query that generates a list of candidates for index rebuilds, and the commands necessary to rebuild the indexes once the tables reached a point where it was necessary.

The query reads a table we built called *table_modifications* that we loaded each night from *dba_tab_modifications* before we ran statistics. Monitoring must be turned on to use the *dba_tab_modifications* table."

🖫 find_sparse_indexes.sql

```
select
'exec analyzedb.reorg_a_table4('||''''||rtrim(t.table_owner)||''''||','||''''||
rtrim(t.table_name)||''''||');',
   t.table_owner||'.'||t.table_name name,
   a.num_rows,
   sum(t.inserts) ins,
   sum(t.updates) upd,
   sum(t.deletes) del,
   sum(t.updates)+sum(t.inserts)+sum(t.deletes) tot_chgs,
to_char((sum(t.deletes)/(decode(a.num_rows,0,1,a.num_rows)))*100.0,'999999.99') per_del,
```

```
round(((sum(t.updates)+sum(t.inserts)+sum(t.deletes))/(decode(a.num_rows,0,1,a.num_rows))
*100.0),2) per_chg
from
   analyzedb.table_modifications t,
   all_tables a
where
   t.timestamp >= to_date('&from_date','dd-mon-yyyy')
and
   t.table_owner = a.owner and t.table_owner not in ('SYS','SYSTEM') and
t.table_name=a.table_name
having
   (sum(t.deletes)/(decode(a.num_rows,0,1,a.num_rows)))*100.0 >=5
group by
   t.table_owner, t.table_name, a.num_rows
order by
   num_rows desc, t.table_owner, t.table_name;
```

Again, not all indexes will benefit from periodic index rebuilding, and it's a good practice to test and re-test scripts to examine your index tree structure to find sparse indexes.

In sum, here are some DBA best practices for rebuilding indexes:

- Properly executed during scheduled downtime, index rebuilding/coalescing is a zero-cost, zero-risk activity.

- For databases without scheduled maintenance windows, it is necessary to write scripts to detect indexes that may benefit from a rebuild. This involves examining the index trees as well as historical SQL activity.

- An index will benefit from a rebuild/coalesce if it experiences a significant number of full scan operations (index fast-full scans, index range scans). You can write queries against AWR (*dba_hist_sql_plan*) of STATSPACK (*stats$sql_plan*) to see how often an index experiences multi-block scan activity.

- By definition, a freshly rebuilt index is in its pristine state. When a DBA rebuilds an index, they will examine historical workloads and adjust PCTFREE to accommodate future DML activity.

Now let's move on and look at some new tools and techniques for testing the efficiency of Oracle indexes.

Oracle indexes are a software tool that Oracle SQL can use to avoid expensive full-scan operations against tables and ensure that we get our rows back with a minimum of data file touches. The main points of this chapter include:

- Oracle has specialized indexes for specialized types of applications (bitmap index, Context indexes) but the b-tree index is far and away the most common type of index.

- Indexes consume system resources. Using an index can consume disk space and slow-down DML, but that's the price we pay for getting rows back fast.

Index reorganization and SQL Performance

- Oracle indexes can retrieve rows in pre-sorted order, avoiding expensive back-end sort operations.

- Oracle optimizer parameters such as *optimizer_index_cost_adj* have a profound effect of the optimizer's propensity to invoke an index.

- Applying histogram statistics on indexes columns can improve the performance of SQL against columns that have heavily skewed values.

- Locating missing indexes is a powerful Oracle silver bullet. Adding a new index can change the entire landscape of SQL performance.

- The *first_rows_n* optimizer modes favor index access while the default *all_rows* optimizer mode favors full-scan operations because it tries to minimize computing resources.

- Function-based indexes are among the most powerful of all SQL tuning tools because you can match anything in your SQL where clause with an index. Function-based indexes are a commonly over-looked feature.

- Oracle DBA examine the SQL workload with scripts to see exactly how tables are accessed via indexes.

- Heavily updated indexes can become sub-optimal for SQL that performs scan operations, and periodic rebuilding or coalescing can keep SQL performance at optimal levels,

Conclusion

This chapter has provided a basic overview of SQL tuning in Oracle, with a focus on the newest and most useful historical SQL tuning features. For an advanced treatment of Oracle SQL tuning, see the book *Advanced Oracle SQL Tuning: The Definitive Reference*. The main points of this chapter include:

- The goals of SQL tuning involve verifying the best execution plan for any statements.

- The "best" execution plan is either the plan that starts returning rows the fastest or the plan that executes the query with the smallest resource consumption.

- System-wide SQL performance is governed by your metadata (as gathered by *dbms_stats*) and by the optimal settings for the important optimizer parameters and SGA pool parameters, and you must determine the optimal settings for these for your workload as a whole, before undertaking detailed tuning.

- You may have multiple types of SQL workloads, requiring that you create different sets of CBO statstucs and optimizer settings for each workload.

- Oracle has embraced a holistic SQL tuning approach with the SQL Performance Advisor (SPA) and Real Application Testing (RAT).

- Holistic tuning must always be done first, before tuning any individual statement because if you do holistic tuning after, you tuning changes might be un-done.

- Indexes are critical to fast SQL tuning response time, and locating missing indexes is a big part of SQL tuning.

- Oracle 10g and beyond now automatically collect and refresh schema statistics using the *dbms_stats* package

- Histogram collection can now be easily automated, and some of these databases choose to put histograms on all key columns to improve the accuracy of table join order. One common cause of suboptimal SQL is missing materialized view and indexes, especially function-based indexes.

- The SQLTuning Advisor and SQLAccess Advisor provide an easy method for identifying and tuning SQL with suboptimal execution plans. Oracle provides a wealth of hints to change the optimizer execution plans. SQL Profiles are a great improvement over the stored outlines of the optimizer plan stability.

- The STATSPACK and *dba_hist* tables contain a wealth of historical information about historical SQL execution statistics. Time-series analysis of execution plans within SQL can yield important insights into holistic tuning for SQL statements.

In the hands of a level-headed seasoned Oracle professional, Oracle's SQL tuning tools allow us to transform a slow and sluggish system and into a high performance screamer.

Next, let's move on and take a look at tuning very large databases (VLDB) and examine the Oracle arsenal of tuning tools for data warehouses.

Oracle Data Warehouse Tuning

CHAPTER

17

"We may need a hardware upgrade."

Oracle Data Warehouse Tuning

The intent of this chapter is to show how very large databases are used in data warehouse and decision support systems, and to review tools and techniques that can be used by Oracle data warehouse administrators for time-series warehouse tuning.

As corporate data warehouse systems grow from small-scale applications into industry-wide systems, the IT manager must be postured to help the system grow without service interruption.

Every data warehouse project needs programmers with specialized skills in coding the all-important components of the warehouse. Skills for a data warehouse might include online systems programming (e.g. Application Express) as well as knowledge of Oracle PL/SQL programming, Oracle SQL, Java and regular expression syntax. The data warehouse DBA is responsible for tuning the following data warehouse components:

- **Data cleansing sub-system:** The programmer would need to create an interactive online system for the Informaticist to be able to locate and scrub incoming data anomalies.

- **Decision support systems:** A programmer is required to create online systems for the end-users where aggregations can be displayed.

- **Expert systems:** For applications with well-defined decision rules, the programmer may be called upon to create expert systems to scan Oracle data and apply sophisticated rules to the data warehouse.

Of course, every shop is different, but these are the minimum job roles and skills required to be successful in getting a fast payback from an investment in Oracle data warehouse technology.

Oracle does their part to fill this niche since Oracle allows us infinite scalability; however, we must always remember that Oracle does not run in a vacuum and that scalable server hardware is required for seamless growth.

What Does a Data Warehouse Need?

Since the earliest days of Decision Support Systems (DSS) in the 1960s, database professionals have recognized that internal processing for data warehouse applications is very different than that of Online Transaction Processing Systems (OLTP).

Data warehouse applications can read trillions of bytes of information or more, thus making them very I/O intensive. These systems require specialized servers that can support the typical processing load associated with them.

Most data warehouses are bi-modal. During the data they run in read-only mode, and we optimize the instance for fast SQL throughout. A data warehouse also has an evening batch window when new data is loaded, indexed and summarized, and instance is normally re-configured to be optimized for high-speed data loading and aggregation.

The server must have on-demand CPU and RAM resources as well as a database management system capable of dynamically reconfiguring its resources to accommodate these shifts in processing.

In the 1970s, Moore's law was introduced, stating that processor costs were always falling while speed continued to improve. However, as Oracle professionals, we must understand that Moore's law does not apply to RAM. While RAM costs continue to fall every year, the speed of RAM access is constrained by silicon technology and did not improve over at least three decades as shown in Figure 17.1.

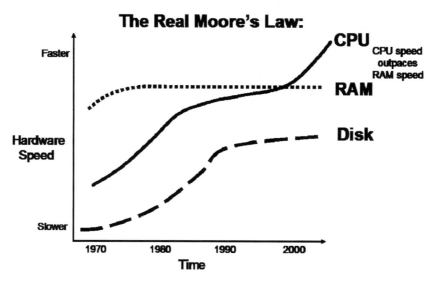

Figure 17.1: *Speed Improvements of CPU versus RAM*

Because RAM speed has not improved like CPU speed, RAM must be localized near the CPUs to keep them running at full capacity, and this is a main feature of many of the new Intel-based servers. Non Uniform Memory Access (NUMA) has been on hand for years in high-end UNIX servers that are running Symmetric Multi-processor (SMP) configurations.

In order to process large volumes of data quickly, the server must be able to support parallel large-table full-table scans for data warehouse aggregation. One of the biggest improvements in multi-CPU servers is their ability to utilize Oracle parallel features for table summarization, aggregation, DBA maintenance and parallel data manipulation.

For example, this divide and conquer approach makes large-table full-table scans run seven times faster on an 8-CPU server and 15x faster on a 16-way SMP server. These relationships are illustrated in Figure 17.2.

- Full-table scans can run 15x faster
- Parallel DML
- Parallel table reorganizations

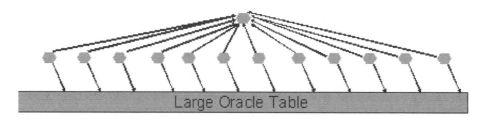

Figure 17.2: *Data Warehouse Large-table Full-table Scans Can Be Parallelized for Super-fast Response*

Historically, data warehouse applications have been constrained by I/O, but all of this is changing with the introduction of specialized data warehouse techniques, all with the goal of keeping the server CPUs running at full capacity. These techniques include:

- **Partitioning:** By having the database place data physically near other related data, excessive I/O is reduced.

- **Materialized views:** By pre-summarizing data and pre-joining tables, server resources become less I/O intensive at runtime.

- **Advanced indexing:** Databases now offer specialized techniques such as *bitmap join* indexes and specialized internal table join techniques such as STAR transformation schemes that help shift the processing burden away from I/O.

All of these techniques have helped remove the I/O bottleneck and make data warehouse applications more CPU-intensive. There are many server resources required for large data warehouse applications. These features include:

- **Large RAM:** All 64-bit servers have a larger word size, two to the 64th power, which allows for up to 16 exabytes! This allows for huge scalability as the processing demand grows and allows the database to have many gigabytes of data buffer storage.

- **Fast CPU:** Intel's 64-bit Itanium 2 architecture is far faster than the older 32-bit chipsets. The advanced features built into the Itanium 2 chipset allow much more real work to be done for each processor cycle. Combined with the Oracle NUMA RAM support, computationally intensive DSS queries will run at lightning speeds.

- **High parallelism:** Each CPUs is interconnected to local memory modules and an inter-node crossbar interconnect controller via a high-speed bus. This design allows large-scale parallel processing for Oracle full-table scans, which are the scattered reads that are the hallmark of Oracle warehouse systems.

- **High Performance I/O architecture:** The I/O subsystem also influences scalability and performance. Enterprise systems must provide the channel capacity required to support large databases and networks. For example, the Itanium 2 system architecture can support up to 64 peripheral component interconnect (PCI or PCI-X) 64-bit channels operating at speeds from 33 MHz to 100 MHz.

The advent of large RAM regions is also beneficial to the data warehouse. In most data warehouses, a giant central fact table exists, surrounded by smaller dimension tables. This schema is illustrated in Figure 17.3.

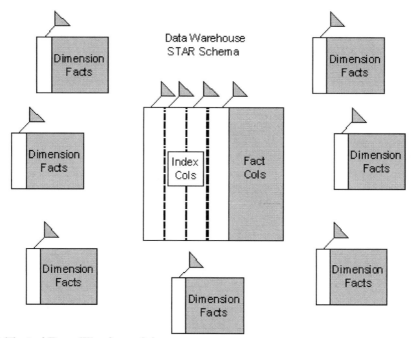

Figure 17.3: *A Typical Data Warehouse Schema*

In a typical *star schema,* the larger full-table scans can never be cached, but it is important to be able to control the caching of the dimension tables and indexes. When using a 64-bit server with fast RAM access, the Oracle KEEP pool and multiple buffer caches can be configured to guarantee that the smaller, frequently referenced objects always remain in the data buffers. This will shift the database bottleneck away from I/O. Once the bottleneck has been shifted from I/O to CPU, performance can be scaled by adding more processors.

These *star_transformation* joins can be successfully used to enable a data warehouse as explained next.

Oracle *star transformations* and SQL

To enable a data warehouse, the following suggested initialization parameter settings might be used:

- *cursor_space_for_time* = TRUE
- *db_cache_size* = XXX
- *db_block_size* = 32k
- *db_file_multiblock_read_count* = 128 or unset
- *filesystemio_options* = SETALL
- *pga_aggregate_target* = XXX
- *optimizer_index_cost_adj* = XXX

- *optimizer_index_caching* = XXX

- *query_rewrite_enabled* = TRUE

- *shared_pool_size* = 150M

- *star_transformation_enabled* = TRUE

- *workarea_size_policy* = AUTO

- *session_cached_cursors* = 100

- *log_buffer* = XXX or unset

- *bitmap_merge_area_size* = XXX

- *create_bitmap_area_size* = XXX

For *star_transformation* join plans, the following requirements must be considered:

- *star_transformation_enabled* = TRUE

- No hint *star*. So forcing a *star_query* excludes *star_transformation*

- No bind variable in *select* statement

- No *connect by* and *start with*

- For fact table columns involved in *equijoin* predicate, there must be bitmap index defined on them.

- More than two bitmap indexes on fact table

- Fact table must have more than 15,000 rows

- Fact table cannot be a view

- Fact table cannot be a remote table

- No hint *full* on fact table

Failure to set proper parameters can result in a botched attempt to initiate a *star_transformation* join as shown by the following example.

Bad *star transformation* Plan

The following is an example of a failed attempt at a *star_transformation* join. In this case, the *star_transformation* hint is ignored because other prerequisite settings have not been made:

```
alter session set "_always_star_transformation"= true;

select /*+ star_transformation */
   wdate,
   hour,
   minute,
   sum(bytes)
from
   network_fact      nf,
   date_dimension    ddi,
```

```
   hour_dimension    hdi,
   minute_dimension mdi
where
   nf.date_key=ddi.date_key
and
   nf.hour_key=hdi.hour_key
and
   nf.minute_key=mdi.minute_key
and
   wdate>=to_date('2004/10/14 21', 'yyyy/mm/dd hh24')
and
   wdate<=to_date('2004/10/15 21', 'yyyy/mm/dd hh24')
group by
   wdate, hour, minute;
```

The SQL looks fine, but we can only tell if the star query is invoked by inspecting the execution plan for the SQL.

```
Execution Plan
----------------------------------------------------------
    0        SELECT STATEMENT Optimizer=CHOOSE
    1     0   SORT (GROUP BY)
    2     1    HASH JOIN
    3     2     TABLE ACCESS (FULL) OF 'MINUTE_DIMENSION'
    4     2     HASH JOIN
    5     4      MERGE JOIN (CARTESIAN)
    6     5       TABLE ACCESS (FULL) OF 'DATE_DIMENSION'
    7     5       BUFFER (SORT)
    8     7        TABLE ACCESS (FULL) OF 'HOUR_DIMENSION'
    9     4      TABLE ACCESS (FULL) OF 'NETWORK_FACT'
```

Once we go through all of the prerequisites and adjust our initialization parameters, the same SQL performs far faster because it can invoke the star query transformation. The following is what a successful *star_transformation* join looks like:

```
Execution Plan
----------------------------------------------------------
    0        SELECT STATEMENT Optimizer=CHOOSE
    1     0   NESTED LOOPS
    2     1    HASH JOIN
    3     2     HASH JOIN
    4     2      TABLE ACCESS (FULL) OF 'MINUTE_DIMENSION'
    5     2     PARTITION CONCATENATED
    6     2      TABLE ACCESS BY ROWID
    7     2       BITMAP CONVERSION TO ROWIDS
    8     2      BITMAP AND
    9     2      BITMAP MERGE
   10     2      BITMAP KEY ITERATION
   11     2       SORT BUFFER
   12     2      TABLE ACCESS (FULL) OF 'MINUTE_DIMENSION'
                BITMAP INDEX RANGE SCAN I_C1
                BITMAP MERGE
                BITMAP KEY ITERATION
                SORT BUFFER
              TABLE ACCESS ... D2
                BITMAP INDEX RANGE SCAN I_C2
 BITMAP MERGE
```

```
BITMAP KEY ITERATION
SORT BUFFER
  TABLE ACCESS ... D3
  BITMAP INDEX RANGE SCAN I_C3
    TABLE ACCESS ... D2
    TABLE ACCESS BY ... D3
```

Why Oracle for the Data Warehouse?

The large data buffer caches in most OLTP Oracle systems can cause them to be CPU-bound, but Oracle data warehouses are another story because they tend to perform lots of large-table full-table scans, often in parallel. Parallel large table scans bypass the SGA data buffers changing the entire tuning landscape for the database.

With terabytes of information to aggregate and summarize, most Oracle data warehouses are I/O-bound and it is critical that a server that optimizes disk I/O throughput is chosen for the system.

Oracle has always made very large database (VLDB) technology a priority as evidenced by their introduction of partitioned structures, advanced bitmap indexing and materialized views. Oracle provides some features ideal for the data warehouse application:

- **Read-only tablespaces:** In a time-series warehouse where information eventually becomes static, using tablespace partitions and marking the older tablespaces as read-only can greatly improve performance. When a tablespace is marked as read-only, Oracle can bypass this read consistency mechanism, reducing overhead and resulting in faster throughput.

- **Automatic Storage Management (ASM):** This revolutionary method for managing the disk I/O subsystem removes the tedious and time-consuming chore of I/O load balancing and disk management. Oracle ASM allows all disks to be logically clustered into disk groups and data files spread across all devices using the Oracle Stripe and Mirror Everywhere (SAME) standard. By making the disk backend Just a Bunch of Disks (JBOD), Oracle manages this critical aspect of the data warehouse.

- **Multi-level partitioning of tables and indexes:** Oracle now has multi-level intelligent partitioning methods that allow Oracle to store data in a precise scheme. By controlling where data is stored on disk, Oracle SQL can reduce the disk I/O required to service any query.

- **Advanced data buffer management:** Using the Oracle multiple blocksizes and KEEP pool, it is possible to pre-assign warehouse objects to separate data buffers and ensure that the working set of frequently referenced data is always cached. Oracle also offers Automatic Memory Management (AMM) whereby Oracle will automatically re-assign RAM frames between the *db_cache_size* and the *pga_aggregate_target* region to maximize throughput of the data warehouse.

- **Materialized views:** Oracle's materialized views (MV) use Oracle replication locally or remotely to allow the DBA to pre-summarize and pre-join tables. Best of all, Oracle MVs are integrated with the Oracle query rewrite facility, so that any queries that might benefit from the pre-summarization will be automatically rewritten to reference the aggregate view. This will avoid a very expensive and unnecessary large-table full-table scan.

- **Automated Workload Repository (AWR) analysis:** The AWR provides a time-series component to warehouse tuning that is critical for the identification of materialized views and holistic warehouse tuning. The most important data warehouse tracking with AWR includes tracking large-table full-table scans, *hash* joins which might be replaced with *star* joins and tracking of RAM usage within the *pga_aggregate_target* region.

It is easy to identify when an Oracle warehouse is disk I/O bound. In the top 5 timed event report below it is clear that this typical data warehouse system is constrained by disk I/O resulting from the high percentage of full-table and full-index scans.

```
Top 5 Timed Events
~~~~~~~~~~~~~~~~~~~                                         % Total
Event                        Waits      Time (s)    Ela Time
-------------------------    -------    ----------  --------
db file scattered read        2,598       7,146      58.54
db file sequential read      25,519       3,246      12.04
library cache load lock         673       1,363       9.26
CPU time                                  1,154       7.83
log file parallel write      19,157         837       5.68
```

This listing shows that scattered reads, or full scans, constitute the majority of the total database time. This is very typical of a data warehouse that performs aggregations via SQL. It is also common during the refresh period for Oracle materialized views. The problem is the I/O bottleneck that is introduced during these periods.

Due to the fact that the typical data warehouse is so data intensive, there is always a problem fully utilizing the CPU power. Several platforms have addressed this issue by leveraging on Non-Uniform Memory Access (NUMA), whereby Windows and Oracle are automatically configured to exploit NUMA to keep the CPUs busy. The *data buffer hit ratio* is not relevant for data warehouses, systems that commonly perform full-table scans or those that use *all_rows* SQL optimization.

While a 30 GB *db_cache_size* might be appropriate for an OLTP shop or a shop that uses a large working set, a large SGA does not benefit data warehouse and decision support systems (DSS) where most data access is performed by a parallelized full-table scan. When Oracle performs a parallel full-table scan, the database blocks are read directly into the Program Global Area (PGA), bypassing the data buffer RAM as illustrated in Figure 17.4.

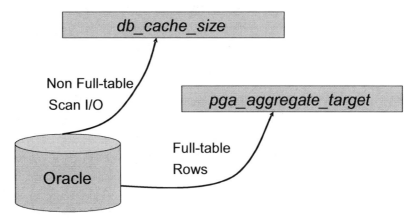

Figure 17.4: *Parallel Full Scans Bypass SGA* Data Buffers

The figure above shows that having a large *db_cache_size* does not benefit parallel large-table full-table scans, as this requires memory in the *pga_aggregate_target* region instead. Oracle's multiple data buffer features can be used to segregate and cache dimension tables and indexes, all while providing sufficient RAM for the full scans. When the processing mode changes during evening Extract, Transform and Load (ETL) and rollups, Oracle AMM will automatically detect the change in data access and re-allocate the RAM regions to accommodate the current processing.

All 64-bit servers have a larger word size (2 to the 64th power) that allows for up to 16 exabytes of addressable RAM. It may be tempting to create a super large RAM data buffer. Data warehouse systems tend to bypass the data buffers because of parallel full-table scans, and maximizing disk I/O throughput is the single most critical bottleneck.

Most SMP servers have a specialized high speed RAM called a L2 cache that is localized near the CPUs as shown in Figure 17.5.

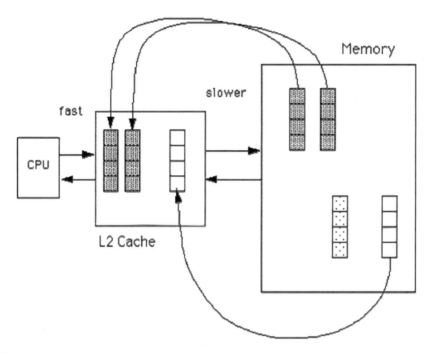

Figure 17.5: *The Non-uniform Memory Access Architecture*

Best of all, Oracle has been enhanced to recognize NUMA systems and adjust memory and scheduling operations accordingly. NUMA technology allows for faster communication between distributed memory in a multi-processor server. Better than the archaic UNIX implementations of the past decade, NUMA is fully supported by Linux and Windows and Oracle automatically use NUMA hardware in SMP servers.

Now that the use of Oracle for the warehouse has been clearly justified, it is important to examine why many shops are moving from Linux to Windows for their mission critical warehouse applications. While the automated features of Oracle AMM, ASM and automatic query rewrite simplify the role of the Oracle DBA, other advanced Oracle features can be leveraged to get fast data warehouse performance:

- **Extensive materialized views:** Mentioned previously, the Oracle *dbms_advisor* utility will automatically detect and recommend, then a materialized view will reduce disk I/O.

- **Automated Workload Repository:** The AWR is a critical component for data warehouse predictive tools such as the *dbms_advisor* package. The AWR allows the generation of time-series reports of SQL access paths and the intelligent creation of the most efficient materialized views for the warehouse.

- **Data caching:** Small, frequently referenced dimension tables should be cached using the Oracle KEEP pool.

- ***star query* optimization:** The Oracle *star query* features make it easy to make complex DSS queries run at fast speeds.

- **Asynchronous change data capture:** Change data capture allows incremental extraction, which allows only changed data to be extracted easily. For example, if a data warehouse extracts data from an operational system on a weekly basis, the data warehouse requires only the data that has changed since the last extraction, which would be only the data that has been modified in the past seven days.

- **Oracle Streams:** Streams-based feed mechanisms can capture the necessary data changes from the operational database and send it to the destination data warehouse. The use of redo information by the Streams capture process avoids unnecessary overhead on the production database.

Next, let's take a look at scaling an Oracle data warehouse.

Scaling the Oracle Data Warehouse

New generation Intel-based servers are pushing hard on the Oracle industry. Hardware vendors are calling out to Oracle professionals, each promising lower Total Cost of Ownership (TCO), faster performance and easy scalability. With so many choices, migrating onto a 64-bit platform can be a confusing proposition. In general, the following are competing approaches to scaling the Oracle data warehouse:

- **Step 1: Scale up:** Vendors promise on-demand computing resources, lower TCO and easy scalability. Their huge servers offer savings from CPU and RAM consolidation, reduced human management costs and seamless allocation of resources.

- **Step 2: Scale out:** Grid vendors offer solutions where server blades can be added to Oracle as processing demand increases. While grid computing offers infinite scalability, no central point of failure and the use of fast cheap server blades, it does have the same in-the-box parallelism that is found within a monolithic server. Unlike the scale up approach, Oracle grid computing is not automatic and requires additional costs and additional training as well as sophisticated monitoring and management software.

Most Oracle data warehouse shops practice the scale up approach first. Remember, you only need to scale out when you reach the processing limits of the server, which is a very rare occurrence for today's data warehouses. Many Oracle warehouse professionals have learned that scaling out with Real Application Clusters (RAC) and Grid is not an optimal solution. Instead, they choose the scale up approach within a single server for many compelling reasons:

- **High parallelism:** Complex data warehouse queries need easy parallel query capability and many on-board CPUs to maximize throughput.

- **Simplicity:** Oracle clustering solutions are complex to configure and manage. For the Oracle data warehouse, a large monolithic server provides complete on-demand resource allocation and scalability.

- **Low cost:** Oracle RAC licenses are expensive, and the DBA staff needs expensive specialized training to master the complex inter-node communications.

- **Seamless scalability:** Unlike the scale out approach, a scale up Oracle data warehouse will be instantly able to leverage new server resources without any changes to the environment.

There is also a common misconception that using a single server with scale up capabilities introduces a single point of failure problem. In reality, hardware redundancy on servers offers further protection against failure including redundant cooling, power and dual air conditioning with on-board power management, hot-pluggable components, automated failure diagnosis and recovery and proactive failover mechanisms.

The scale up approach is the natural reaction to the rampant distribution of Oracle systems onto small, independent servers. This architecture saves money on hardware costs at the expense of having to hire a huge system administration and DBA staff. The appeal of consolidation is the avoidance if the high overhead and expense of such server farms.

Due to the advances in 64-bit server technology, the concept of using a large SMP server for Oracle data warehousing has become very popular. The scale up approach provides on-demand resource allocation by sharing CPU and RAM between many resources, requiring less maintenance and human resources to manage fewer servers. More importantly, the scale up approach provides optimal utilization of RAM and CPU resources and gives the warehouse high availability through fault tolerant components. This approach provides a high degree of scalability and flexibility for high performance and also provides high availability and low total cost of ownership (TCO).

The scale out approach is designed for super large Oracle databases that support many thousands of concurrent users. Unless the system is facing a CPU bottleneck as a result of high transaction concurrency, it is likely that the system will benefit more from a scale up approach.

Parallel Query for Data Warehouses

It is a common misconception that parallel processors (SMP or MPP) are necessary in order to use and benefit from parallel processing. Even on the same processor, multiple processes can be used to speed up queries. Data warehouses generally employ parallel technology to perform warehouse loading and query functions. These include:

- **Parallel backup/recovery:** Some parallel tools are capable of backup rates in excess of 40 gigabytes per hour.
- **Parallel query (SMP & MPP):** Multiple processes are used to retrieve table data.
- **Parallel loading:** Multiple processes are used to simultaneously load many tables.
- **Parallel indexing:** Multiple processes are used to create indexes.

Oracle Data Warehouse Tuning TPC-H Benchmarks

Vendors spend millions of dollars tuning their benchmarks, and the TPC disclosure reports are a goldmine of Oracle tuning tips. Much can be learned about Oracle tuning by reading the TPC benchmark full disclosure reports.

The previous world record for Oracle TPC-H (data warehouse) benchmark was 1,500 QphH (query per hour), and this record has now been broken with an HP Superdome at 1,700 QphH. This benchmark used:

- **Large data blocks:** 32k blocksize

- **Huge PGA:** 50g PGA region size (*pga_aggregate_target*)

- **Huge SGA:** 90g SGA target (*sga_target*)

However, the most recent world records are even more impressive, with this world record TPC-H Oracle data warehouse benchmark report.

- **Tiny disks:** Smaller disks give higher bandwidth and this benchmark used tiny 32GB disks

- **Huge RAM buffers:** This benchmark used a 30GB data buffer and a 150GB *pga_aggregate_target*.

The next section will delve more into the Oracle tuning tips hidden inside this benchmark.

The Oracle TPC-H Benchmark Server

This benchmark noted 170k data warehouse transactions per hour, using an HP superdome, with a 3-year server cost of $6.6m, using an astounding 512 gigabytes of RAM:

- Processors = 64 CPUs, each 64-bit (Intel Itanium2)

- Database size = 10,000 gig - made-up of tiny 32 gig platters

- Server RAM = 512 gig - Yes, that is half a trillion bytes of RAM

Tuning Tricks for Oracle Data Warehouse Configuration

The following list includes the tricks that Oracle used to get super-fast performance in this data warehouse test, and should stand as a lesson for anyone who tunes a data warehouse environment:

- **Tiny disks:** Each disk is only 32 gigabytes, and each disk is not full. This provides higher bandwidth.

- **RAID 10:** This benchmark used Oracle ASM with SAME (Stripe And Mirror Everywhere, a.k.a. RAID1+0)

- **Giant RAM regions:** Remember that disks are now 50 years old, and there is a limit to this 1950s technology of magnetic-coated platters. This benchmark used a 30-gigabyte data buffer (*db_cache_size*) and *pga_aggregate_target* = 150g. This benchmark also chose a giant shared pool with *shared_pool_size* = 50g.

- **Large data blocks:** Numerous tests have shown that Oracle indexes build cleaner tree structures in 32k blocks, plus a single I/O results in more data being delivered into the SGA/PGA.

- **Server-specific parameters:** There are special parameters for most server types that can dramatically help performance. In this case, the test used the Oracle parameter *hpux_sched_noage* and the HP-UX parameter *async_buf_conf*.

- **Huge log buffer:** Oracle used to recommend keeping the *log_buffer* small (under 20MB), but this experience is that a larger *log_buffer* can increase throughput for high DML transactions. This benchmark used *log_buffer*=268,435,456, about 250 megabytes!

- **Adjust Oracle optimizer parameters:** Adjusting *optimizer_index_cost_adj* has a profound system-wide influence on the cost-based SQL optimizer. Most OLTP systems use a smaller value (10-50) for influence higher index usage, and data warehouses use a larger value (100-300) to prefer full-table-scans. This benchmark used *optimizer_index_cost_adj* = 200.

- **High query parallelism:** Servers with multiple CPUs can greatly increase the speed of full-table scans with Oracle parallel query.

This benchmark used these parallel parameters:

- *parallel_adaptive_multi_user* = TRUE

- *parallel_execution_message_size* = 65535

- *parallel_max_servers* = 1600

- *parallel_min_servers* = 1600

- *parallel_threads_per_cpu* = 3

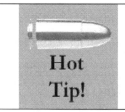

	Prior to 11g, adjusting the optimizer parameter was the only way to compensate for sample size issues with *dbms_stats*. Remember, always try adjusting CBO statistics before adjusting optimizer parameters.
Hot Tip!	

Clearly, reviewing the TPC results from www.tpc.org can give one a wealth of details and tips for tuning an Oracle data warehouse. The next section will cover some of the skills required to be successful in tuning an Oracle data warehouse.

Data Warehouse Design for High Performance

The design approach for any new Oracle data warehouse will leverage on the Oracle-supplied productivity packages such as Oracle 10g Discoverer and Oracle Warehouse Builder (OWB). Rapid development and implementation of basic decision support functionality is a major priority so that the end-users may begin to enjoy the benefits of a new Oracle data warehouse system.

The overall success of large Oracle warehouse projects requires small, incremental successes and a phased roll-out with basic functionality delivered first. The main pre-implementation phases an Oracle data warehouse project will include:

- Initial design or re-design of an existing data warehouse using Oracle with partitioning.

- Migration of existing data into the new Oracle data warehouse structure.

- Modeling the ETL processes from the data sources and developing the appropriate schema transformation rules (*star*, *hybrid* or *snowflake*).

- Implementing a complete ETL using the Oracle Warehouse Builder (OWB).

- Creation of primary materialized views and data refresh mechanisms.

Oracle data warehouse projects often suffer from chronic problems and operational issues:

- **Low staffing:** The existing DBA staff is caught up in operational details and is unable to find the time to perform the advanced Business Intelligence (BI) and data mining activities.

- **Cumbersome data loading:** The existing ETL process is non-uniform and requires significant manual intervention.

- **Non-usage of warehouse features:** The back-end Oracle data warehouse database does not utilize Oracle warehouse features such as bitmap indexes, partitioning or materialized views.

- **Non–scalable:** Adding additional users and/or data with a loss in performance. The existing database schema does not scale due to improper design, bad indexing or a combination of factors. By using the latest techniques and features, the new data warehouse will be scalable as well as performing at its peak efficiency.

- **Data consolidation issues:** Sites often need to incorporate data feeds from multiple external data centers. The data must be transformed into a unified, consistent format and a method for seamless growth must be assured.

- **Data transparency issues:** For example, as patients in a hospital system travel between treatment centers with separate databases, it can be difficult to track their treatments and progress. In a centralized, consolidated data warehouse environment, this becomes a non-issue.

- **Limited reporting:** The existing warehouse does not easily support ad-hoc or customized queries.

Next, let's explore a staged approach to success in data warehouse implementation.

Oracle Data Warehouse Evolution

An evolutionary approach is critical to the success of an Oracle data warehouse project. Once the database is back-filled, the end-users will be granted access to basic user functions. As they become comfortable with the base functionality, more advanced query support can be provided as follows:

- Ad-hoc query

- Aggregation and multidimensional display

- Correlation analysis

- Hypothesis testing

- Data Mining

End-user Query Approach

Once the new data warehouse and ETL have been created, Oracle Discoverer can be used for basic OLAP and DSS functionality. Some of the types of queries required by the new system might include:

- **Ad-hoc query:** The Discoverer 10g end-user layer will be configured to allow for the ad-hoc display of summary and detailed level data.

- **Aggregation and multidimensional display:** Oracle warehouse builder structures can be developed to summarize, aggregate and rollup salient information for display using the Oracle 10g Discoverer interface.

- **Basic correlations:** The front end should allow the end-user to specify dimensions and request a correlation matrix between the variables with each dimension. The system will start with one-to-one correlations and evolve to support multivariate chi-square methods.

- **Identify hidden correlations:** The end-users need the ability to identify populations, e.g. Eskimos with alcoholism, and then track this population across various external factors, e.g. treatments and drugs. These Oracle Decision Support System (DSS) interfaces require the ability for the end-user to refine their decision rules and change the salient parameters of their domain, i.e. the confidence interval for the predictions.

The main tasks in any Oracle data warehouse engagement include mentoring and technical assistance for these major activities:

- **Cost justification:** Data warehouses often have a very fast payback period as they can pay for themselves very quickly by helping management control costs.

- **Re-Design architecture:** The existing system requires a new structure, and an analysis of existing and new data requirements will allow for the design of a *star* or *snowflake* design.

- **Implement physical features:** The redesigned database utilizes important Oracle warehouse features designed to provide high performance and maintenance. These include data partitioning, read-only tablespaces, bitmap indexes and materialized views. Data warehouse queries are also designed to support Oracle *star transformation* queries.

- **Automate Extract, Transformation and Loading (ETL):** A new ETL system is implemented to allow for a minimum of human intervention. A data feed architecture is designed and intelligent rules are applied to unify the data and allow for a central repository. There is also an exception reporting mechanism to allow for minimal human intervention.

While no two Oracle data warehouse projects are identical, they share common interfaces and activities. These compose "best practices" and form a foundation for the successful evolution of the Oracle data warehouse.

Data Warehouse Tuning Skills

Implementing a useful Oracle data warehouse requires far more than just technical skill. More than any other type of Oracle database, Oracle data warehouses have a super-fast payback period and many companies realize tangible benefits, such as increased sales, in just a few months. For medical data warehouses, the benefits are even greater as lives are saved from analyzing the efficacy of different treatments.

Of course, it takes a skilled DBA to properly manage the large volumes of data, but the real value from any data warehouse requires knowledgeable professionals from other areas. Without Informaticists (data content experts) and statisticians, the value remains buried deep inside trillions of bytes of data. Any successful data warehouse project requires these team members:

- Project Manager
- Warehouse Informaticist
- Statistician
- Oracle warehouse DBA
- Warehouse programmers

The following sections cover these critical best practice data warehouse team roles and show how their job duties overlap.

Data Warehouse Project Manager

To get the job done properly, the data warehouse project manager must have enough technical savvy to understand the technical challenges and assign the appropriate professional to each task. Almost all successful data warehouse project managers have Oracle DBA skills, an absolute requirement for understanding all-important architectural issues such as partitioning schemes.

They must also have knowledge about the subject matter internals of the data warehouse, and most of all, they must have the quantitative skills to manage the complex data mining and longitudinal studies that are required from the warehouse. The ideal data warehouse project manager will have proficiency as an Oracle DBA, plus they must possess at least two years of Calculus and a working knowledge of multivariate statistics, especially chi-square techniques.

The Data Warehouse Informaticist

An Informaticist is an absolute necessity for the data warehouse. Only someone with intimate knowledge of the data will be able to provide direction to the Oracle DBA staff on decision rules for identifying data anomalies and ensuring that the decision rules inside advanced analysis, e.g. studying user-defined cohorts, are valid. In medical systems, a Medical Informaticist is used, someone with the rare combination of the following:

- M.D. degree
- Technical knowledge of statistics, advanced analytics and computer programming
- Oracle skills including Oracle SQL, Discoverer and PL/SQL programming

Medical Informaticists in Oracle with an M.D. degree are among the most highly paid of all Oracle professionals with many earning over $200,000.00 per year, sometimes more than the CIO!

The Warehouse Statistician

Performing advanced analytics in an Oracle data warehouse requires skills that are far beyond those of an ordinary Oracle system. Many shops employ professionals with advanced degrees in areas that are statistics-centered, drawing from people with doctorates in Economics, Experimental Psychology and Sociology. To perform complex and valid studies, the warehouse team must have a statistician with these skills:

- Multivariate statistics: Even a simple longitudinal study requires knowledge of the application of applied multivariate statistics.

- Artificial Intelligence (AI): Oracle Data Mining (ODM) product is heavily centered on the application of AI for the mining algorithms and the statistician should have a firm grounding in fuzzy logic, pattern matching and the use of advanced Boolean logic.

The Data Warehouse Oracle Tuning Professional

The data warehouse DBA has specialized skills beyond an ordinary database administrator and must understand all of the ancillary areas of Oracle data warehousing. Most are senior Oracle DBAs with more than a decade of progressive full-time experience, and the best practice is to use a DBA with these skills:

- **Oracle Business Intelligence Enterprise Edition:** The OBIEE product melds advanced reporting technologies acquired from Hyperion, and provides a complete data warehouse toolkit stack, including all ETL and reporting tools.

- **Oracle Discoverer:** The DBA is responsible for the installation and configuration of Oracle Discoverer, especially the web-based Discoverer OLAP tool which requires installation of Oracle 10g Application Server. The Oracle data warehouse DBA must also understand how to build supporting structures for OLAP and drill-down, including materialized views, and STAR schema transformations.

- **Oracle Warehouse Builder:** The Oracle data warehouse DBA must have an intimate knowledge of Oracle Warehouse Builder because the ETL (Extract Transform and Load) processes are a critical component of any warehouse. The warehouse DBA must understand OWB mappings, the mechanisms for creating aggregation and rollups and the methods for creating complex job streams in OWB to make the ETL processes have complete error checking and notification.

- **Oracle VLDB tools:** The Oracle data warehouse DBA needs to be proficient in all areas relating to very large databases, including Oracle multi-level partitioning, the creation and maintenance of materialized views and warehouse-specific skills such as *bitmap* indexes, *star* schemas and OLAP.

- Intimate knowledge of Oracle tuning is an absolute requirement for the Oracle data warehouse DBA because of the huge amounts of data and the requirements for fast response time for the decision support components of the data warehouse. It is also necessary to understand shared pool internals, Oracle SQL tuning, warehouse-related hints such an *ordered* and *star*, Oracle wait event tuning and knowledge of the Automated Workload Repository.

Conclusion

Data warehouse tuning is all about minimizing disk I/O. Oracle data warehouses are disk intensive and require an architecture that helps to keep the CPUs running at full capacity. As server resources become like commodities, IT managers will have to choose the platform that offers reliability, scalability and, above all, the lowest total cost of ownership. It is also vital to assemble an appropriately skilled team in order to successfully implement and Oracle data warehouse in a way to maximize the return on investment. Overall, the best advice is to go with the low TCO.

This chapter has shown the main tools and techniques that can be used by the Oracle data warehouse administrator for time-series warehouse tuning. It also covered the essential skills necessary for making sound tuning decisions and ensuring that the complex Oracle data warehouse performs its intended function properly.

Now that we understand Data Warehouse tuning issues, let's move on and explore Oracle Tuning with the Oracle Enterprise Manager (OEM).

OEM Tuning

OEM can advise you about pending performance problems.

Introduction to OEM

One of the reasons that Oracle achieved dominance in the early 1990s was their commitment to provide Oracle on over 60 hardware platforms running on everything from a mainframe to a Macintosh. In order to achieve this transparency between diverse hardware platforms, Oracle invested heavily in leveraging upon the strengths of each operating system while still providing a hardware independent look-and-feel.

Oracle's quest for platform-independent DBA management layers has gone though several incarnations over the past decade, from the archaic SQL*DBA command-line utility to the original Oracle Enterprise Manager (OEM).

The original OEM (circa 1996) was rejected by some experienced Oracle professionals as a simple SQL command generator, and seasoned DBAs preferred to enter the commands manually from SQL*Plus. Any DBA caught using OEM was immediately suspected of not knowing the Oracle command syntax.

The New OEM

Oracle recognized the need to improve the functionality of OEM for tuning activities and employed some of the world's leading Oracle experts including Kyle Hailey, John Beresniewicz, Gaja Krishna Vaidyanatha and Graham Wood to help rebuild the OEM performance interface.

Bearing little resemblance to its OEM predecessor, the new OEM performance interfaces were designed by practicing Oracle tuning experts, and the new OEM offers an unparalleled performance management interface, worthy of the most seasoned Oracle DBA.

OEM is great for learning!

Because OEM encapsulates all of the complex Oracle command syntax into a point-and-click GUI, it is perfect for beginners and semi-skilled technicians.

The OEM performance screens are straightforward and intuitive, making it easy to identify and correct performance issues. These new OEM tuning features include many powerful new elements:

- **Automatic display of performance information:** The OEM performance screens enable a stunning visual display of important Oracle performance metrics. The monitoring and diagnostic abilities of Oracle are enabled by the AWR, which collects and stores historical run-time performance data as an integral part of the Oracle database kernel.

- **Incorporation of external information:** OEM samples server-side metrics and incorporates CPU consumption, run-queue length, physical I/O and RAM paging information. This enables a comprehensive picture of overall Oracle performance.

- **Easy exception reporting mechanism:** OEM allows the customizing of alert thresholds to notify DBAs before their database experiences a performance problem. Since OEM is always watching, they are free to perform other important tasks, and customized thresholds can be set for hundreds of AWR metrics to guarantee that they will have the chance to address a pending problem before it affects their end-users.

- **Automated performance diagnostics:** Using the optional Database Diagnostic Pack and Database Tuning Pack components, OEM has a native interface to ADDM, allowing OEM to make intelligent performance recommendations.

- **Improved interface:** OEM has a secure web-based HTML interface for remote access and the OEM2GO PDA interface, making it easy for the Oracle professional to manage their Oracle database anywhere in the world.

This chapter focuses on using the OEM performance screens to quickly locate performance bottlenecks. The core point of this chapter is OEM's use of intelligent time-series metric display to provide a framework for easy top-down time-series performance monitoring. This chapter covers the following topics:

- **Navigating the OEM tuning architecture:** This section explores the hierarchy of the OEM tuning screens and how they are organized. It also reviews the performance screen and the session details screens to show how the DBA can drill down to find even the most subtle tuning issue.

- **Customizing OEM alerts:** The Oracle OEM allows for the easy creation of sophisticated notifications using hundreds of Oracle metrics. These custom alerts are deployed via e-mail, telephone, pager, or OEM2GO on a PDA.

- **Using OEM to troubleshoot a performance issue:** This section shows how to drill down into the OEM performance display to reveal how easy it is to locate transient performance issues.

- A quick review of the OEM screen hierarchy showing how OEM interfaces with the Oracle data dictionary and kernel tables to provide a complete logical interface is merited.

At the most simplistic level, the OEM performance screens are a Graphical User Interface (GUI) for the display and manipulation of Oracle performance information. Oracle has revolutionized the database industry by incorporating database performance information inside special built-in performance history tables.

Prior to Oracle 10g Enterprise Manager, tuning a complex performance issue was extremely time-consuming. The Oracle professional had to manually collect time-series performance information, trace dumps, STATSPACK reports and wade through reams of complex data to find the root cause of the sub-optimal performance.

Everything changes with OEM, which now filters through the AWR and ASH repository, quickly focusing on the important metrics. A brief tour of the OEM performance screens reveals how easy it is to spot and correct performance issues.

As previously noted, OEM was designed by practicing Oracle tuning professionals to provide a top-down, intuitive approach to Oracle monitoring. Using any web browser, secure access to the OEM performance screen can be acquired anywhere on the planet as shown in Figure 18.1.

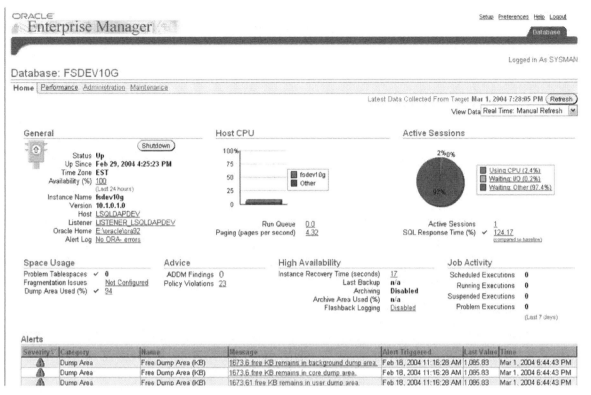

Figure 18.1: *The OEM Performance Home Screen for Enterprise Manager*

This summary screen provides a complete overview of the current status of the database. All aspects of the database instance including tablespace and session summary information is shown. Exciting external metrics with hyperlinks to the *listener, oracle_home, dump files* and *alert log* directories are also shown.

Tuning with Metrics and Exceptions

From this main OEM performance screen, the DBA can quickly drill down and view all AWR metrics and scroll through the complete list of automatically captured statistics as shown in Figure 18.2.

ORACLE
Enterprise Manager

All Metrics

Expand All | Collapse All

Metrics	Thresholds
▼ FSDEV10G	
▷ Alert Log	Some
▷ Alert Log Content	None
▷ Alert Log Error Status	All
▷ Archive Area	Some
▷ Data Guard	Some
▷ Database Files	None
▷ Database Job Status	All
▷ Database Limits	Some
▷ Database Services	None
▷ Deferred Transactions	All
▷ Dump Area	Some
▷ Efficiency	None
▷ Invalid Objects	None
▷ Invalid Objects by Schema	All
▷ Num of Sessions Waiting (EvtCLs)	None
▷ Recovery Area	None
▷ Response	Some
▷ SGA Pool Wastage	None
▷ SQL Response Time	All
▷ Session Suspended	None
▷ Snap Shot Too Old	None
▷ System Response Time Per Call	None
▷ Tablespaces Full	All
▷ Tablespaces With Problem Segments	Some
▷ Throughput	None
▷ User Audit	Some
▷ User Block	Some
▷ Wait Bottlenecks	None

Figure 18.2: *Partial Listing of the AWR Metrics from Inside OEM*

This feature allows the DBA to drill down into important Oracle performance areas including instance efficiency, SQL response time, SGA pool wastage, and wait bottlenecks.

There is more to the data collection than instance-wide metrics. OEM can be customized to send alerts for whatever combination of metric values desired. For example, the OEM Grid controller is used to add an additional RAC node to the system during this period, just in time to meet the increased processing demands as shown in Figure 18.3.

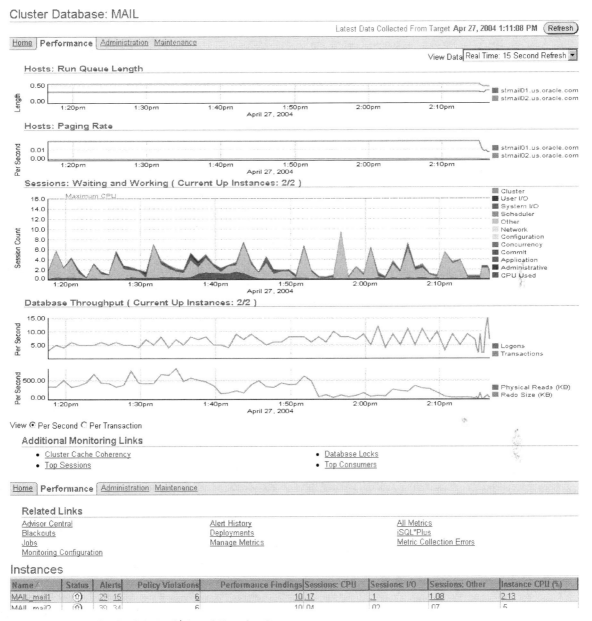

Figure 18.3: *The OEM Grid/RAC Display Screen*

Now that it has been shown how OEM incorporates external metrics, the ways OEM makes it easy to view Active Session History (ASH) information will be revealed. The ASH component, which was introduced in Oracle 10g, allows the DBA to quickly spotlight the important wait events associated with any Oracle task.

Active Session History in Enterprise Manager

Oracle now has an Active Session History (ASH) component that automatically collects detailed metrics on individual Oracle sessions. OEM also has an interface to the ASH component of AWR. The ASH uses special *dba_hist* views to collect and store highly detailed system event information, thereby allowing immediate access to every detail about Oracle execution.

Together, the AWR and ASH metrics form the foundation for a complete Oracle tuning framework, and Enterprise Manager provides the vehicle. Now that the underlying mechanism is shown, the DBA can explore how OEM gives an intelligent window into this critical Oracle tuning information.

While this functionality of OEM is amazing in its own right, Oracle has taken the AWR model beyond the intelligent display of performance metrics. Using true Artificial Intelligence (AI), OEM now has a built-in interface to the Automatic Database Diagnostic Monitor, pronounced "Adam", and the intelligent SQL Tuning and SQL Access Advisors.

The next section explores the Automated Alert mechanism within Enterprise Manager. This is a very important feature for Oracle tuning because it allows alert thresholds to be predefined and notifications about pending database problems to be sent. This gives the DBA the critical time necessary to fix the issue before the end-users suffer.

The use of the Enterprise Manager with ADDM and the SQL Tuning Advisor can save the DBA from the tedium of manually tuning hundreds of SQL statements. SQL profiles allow DBAs to rapidly and reliably complete a complex tuning effort in just a few hours.

Easy Customization of OEM Alerts

The Oracle Enterprise Manager recognizes that no DBA has the time to constantly monitor all of the metrics in real-time and provides an easy-to-use exception reporting mechanism. Figure 18.4 shows the Manage Metrics screen in which the DBA can easily define a customized alert mechanism for a database.

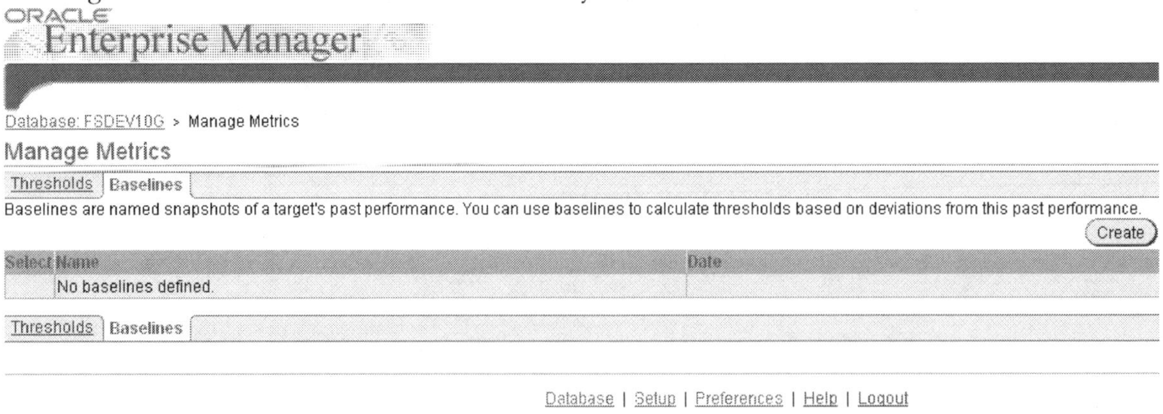

ORACLE
Enterprise Manager

Database: FSDEV10G > Manage Metrics

Manage Metrics

| Thresholds | Baselines |

Baselines are named snapshots of a target's past performance. You can use baselines to calculate thresholds based on deviations from this past performance.

(Create)

Select Name	Date
No baselines defined.	

| Thresholds | Baselines |

Database | Setup | Preferences | Help | Logout

Figure 18.4: *The OEM Manage Metrics Screen*

When a drill down into the metric list occurs, OEM displays hundreds of individual tuning metrics and provides the ability to set personalized alert thresholds as shown in Figure 18.5. OEM allows the DBA to specify any scalar thresholds, such as greater than or less than, and has full pattern matching capabilities for text-based alerts such as alert log messages.

SQL Response Time (%)	>	500	
Scans on Long Tables (per second)	>		
Scans on Long Tables (per transaction)	>		
Segments Approaching Maximum Extents Count	>	0	
Segments Not Able to Extend Count	>	0	
Service CPU Time (per user call)	>		
Service Response Time (per user call)	>		
Session Limit Usage (%)	>	80	
Session Logical Reads (per second)	>		
Session Logical Reads (per transaction)	>		
Session Terminated Alert Log Error	Contains	ORA-	
Session Terminated Alert Log Error Status	>	0	
Shared Pool Free (%)	<		
Soft Parse (%)	<		
Sorts in Memory (%)	<		
Sorts to Disk (per second)	>		
Sorts to Disk (per transaction)	>		
System Response Time (centi-seconds)	>		
Tablespace Space Used (%)	>	85	97

Figure 18.5: *Setting Alert Thresholds within OEM*

For example, DBAs can set an OEM threshold to send them a pager alert or use OEM2GO whenever their critical metrics change. There are several critical instance-wide performance metrics displayed in Figure 18.5:

- *SQL Response Time (%)*

- *System Response Time (centi-seconds)*

- *Shared Pool Free (%)*

Because of the time-series nature of AWR, it is easy to trigger an exception alert when the marginal values of any metrics change. All metrics denoted with the (%) are delta-based, meaning that OEM triggers an alert whenever any metric moves by more than a specified percentage, regardless of its current value. This delta-based mechanism is used to allow time to repair a pending performance issue before it cripples the end-users.

For automated notification, a SNMP interface can be easily configured to have OEM send the DBA a notification e-mail whenever the threshold value has been exceeded. This alert can be an e-mail, a telephone message or an alert on the OEM2GO PDA device.

Instance Efficiency Metrics

OEM also allows the customization of important instance efficiency metrics as shown in Figure 18.6. These track overall SGA efficacy each time an AWR snapshot is collected. The AWR snapshot frequency is customizable and OEM displays the last snapshot collection date in the third column of the display.

▼ Efficiency	None	Last Collected Mar 1, 2004 7:07:15 PM
Buffer Cache Hit (%)	Not Set	Last Collected Mar 1, 2004 7:07:15 PM
CPU Usage (per second)	Not Set	Last Collected Mar 1, 2004 7:07:15 PM
CPU Usage (per transaction)	Not Set	Last Collected Mar 1, 2004 7:07:15 PM
Cursor Cache Hit (%)	Not Set	Last Collected Mar 1, 2004 7:07:15 PM
Data Dictionary Hit (%)	Not Set	Last Collected Mar 1, 2004 7:07:15 PM
Database CPU Time (%)	Not Set	Last Collected Mar 1, 2004 7:07:15 PM
Library Cache Hit (%)	Not Set	Last Collected Mar 1, 2004 7:07:15 PM
Library Cache Miss (%)	Not Set	Last Collected Mar 1, 2004 7:07:15 PM
PGA Cache Hit (%)	Not Set	Last Collected Mar 1, 2004 7:07:15 PM
Parallel Execution Downgraded 1 to 25% (per second)	Not Set	Last Collected Mar 1, 2004 7:07:15 PM

Figure 18.6: *Setting Instance Efficiency Alert Thresholds*

Instance efficiency metrics are especially valuable when tracked over time. For example, the DBA can request a customized alert when the following changes occur:

- *PGA cache hit (%)* drops by more than 10%.

- *PGA multi-pass executions* increase above 5%.

This custom alert might indicate a change in SQL processing on the server that may be experiencing excessive disk sorting. By alerting the DBA before the problem is fully manifested, OEM can be used to give the DBA an opportunity to adjust the resources just in time to address the issue before the end-users experience a response time delay.

Alerts Notification and Setup

OEM can be used to send alert notifications to the DBA by pager or email. The following is an example of setting up an email notification for critical alerts using OEM. From the Database Control page, click the Setup link visible in the header as well as footer areas.

Figure 18.7: *Setting Up Alerts*

Click Notification Methods on the Setup page as shown in Figure 18.8.

Complete the information needed for the Mail Server portion on this screen. Users should get help from the network administrator or refer to online help to know more about the mail server names, as an examination on it is beyond the scope of this book.

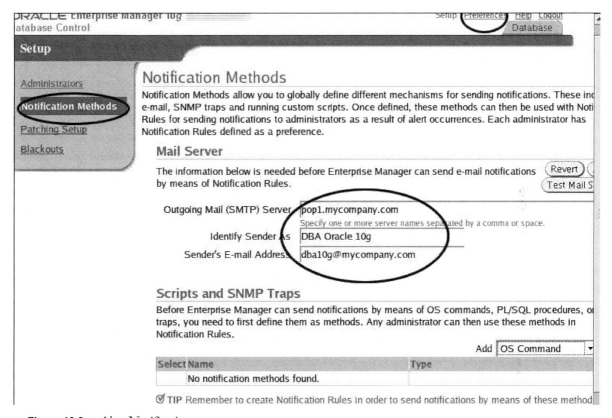

Figure 18.8: *Alert Notification*

From any Database Control page, click on the Preferences link visible in header or footer areas. See Figure 18.8 above.

Select General and enter an email address in the E-mail Address section. Select Notification Rules to modify any default notification rules. This page will show how to change the severity settings for receiving notification.

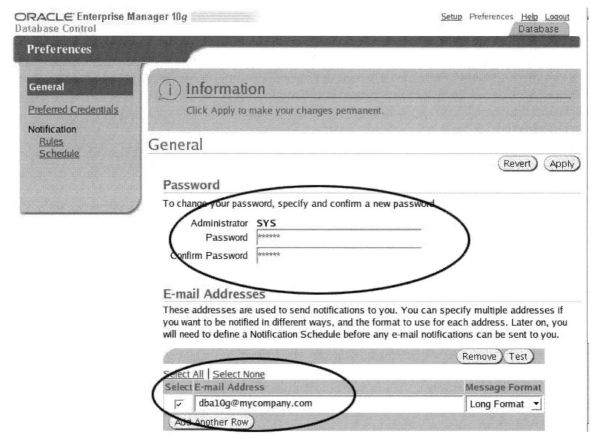

Figure 18.9: *OEM Alert Notification Setup Screen*

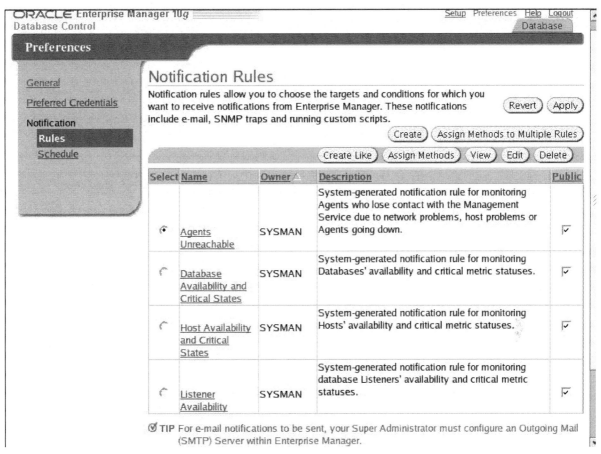

Figure 18.10: *Notification Rules*

Responding to OEM Alerts

Whenever an alert is received, many DBAs run ADDM or another advisor to get more detailed diagnostics of system or object behavior. The DBA can also opt to enable a corrective script to run on receiving an alert as mentioned in the Managing Metric Thresholds section.

If a Tablespace Space Usage alert is received, remedial actions can be taken by running the Oracle Segment Advisor on the tablespace to identify objects for shrinking. Those objects can then be coalesced or extended. All of the job details, including the schedule, job definition and the broken flag, can be edited within Enterprise Manager by double clicking on the job of interest. Figure 18.11 shows the Edit Job dialog.

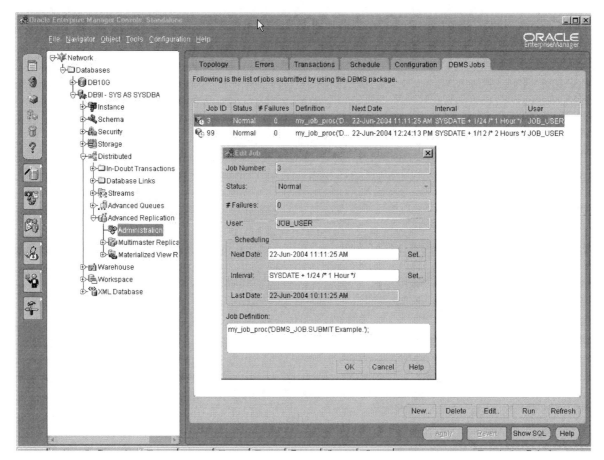

Figure 18.11: *OEM - Edit Job*

The run procedure on this screen allows the DBA to run a specified job immediately, with the *next_date* recalculated from that point. The *force* parameter indicates that the job queue affinity can be ignored, allowing any instance to run the job.

Job information is also available from Oracle Enterprise Manager (OEM) (Network > Databases > Your-Instance > Distributed > Advanced Replication > Administration > DBMS Job Tab).

Overview of *dbms_scheduler* Functions

The *dbms_scheduler* package is the recommended way to schedule jobs in Oracle. The *dbms_job* package is still present, but only for backward compatibility. The jobs created using the *dbms_job* package are very much standalone in their nature in that they are defined with their own schedules and actions. In addition to this, the *dbms_scheduler* package allows the DBA to define standard programs and schedules which can be used by many jobs. Before creating jobs, the DBA should learn how to define these standard elements. To access the *dbms_scheduler* package, a user must be granted the Create Job privilege. This has already been granted to the test user during the setup.

Job classes, windows, and window groups provide a link between the scheduler and the resource manager, allowing jobs to run with a variety of resource profiles. They are considered part of the scheduler administration and as such require the Manage Scheduler privilege. Coverage of the resource manager is beyond the scope of this chapter, so the sections that deal with administration objects will focus on how to create each type of object, rather than how they should be used.

Support for the scheduler is built into the OEM 10g Database Control. The majority of the scheduler objects can be managed via links from the administration page. Figure 18.12 shows the administration page with the scheduler links on the right hand side towards the bottom of the screen.

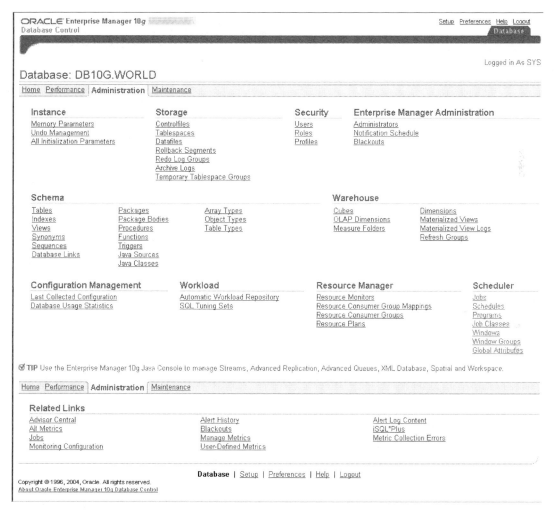

Figure 18.12: *OEM 10g DB Control - Administration*

Program information is also available from the OEM 10g DB Control via the Scheduler Programs screen shown in Figure 18.13.

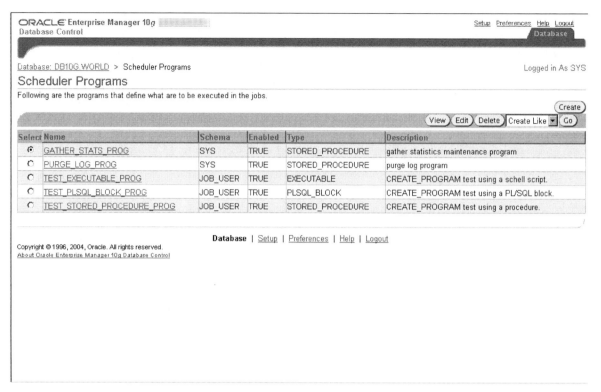

Figure 18.13: *OEM 10g DB Control - Scheduler Programs*

Schedules are created in the OEM 10g DB Control via the Create Schedule screen shown in Figure 18.14.

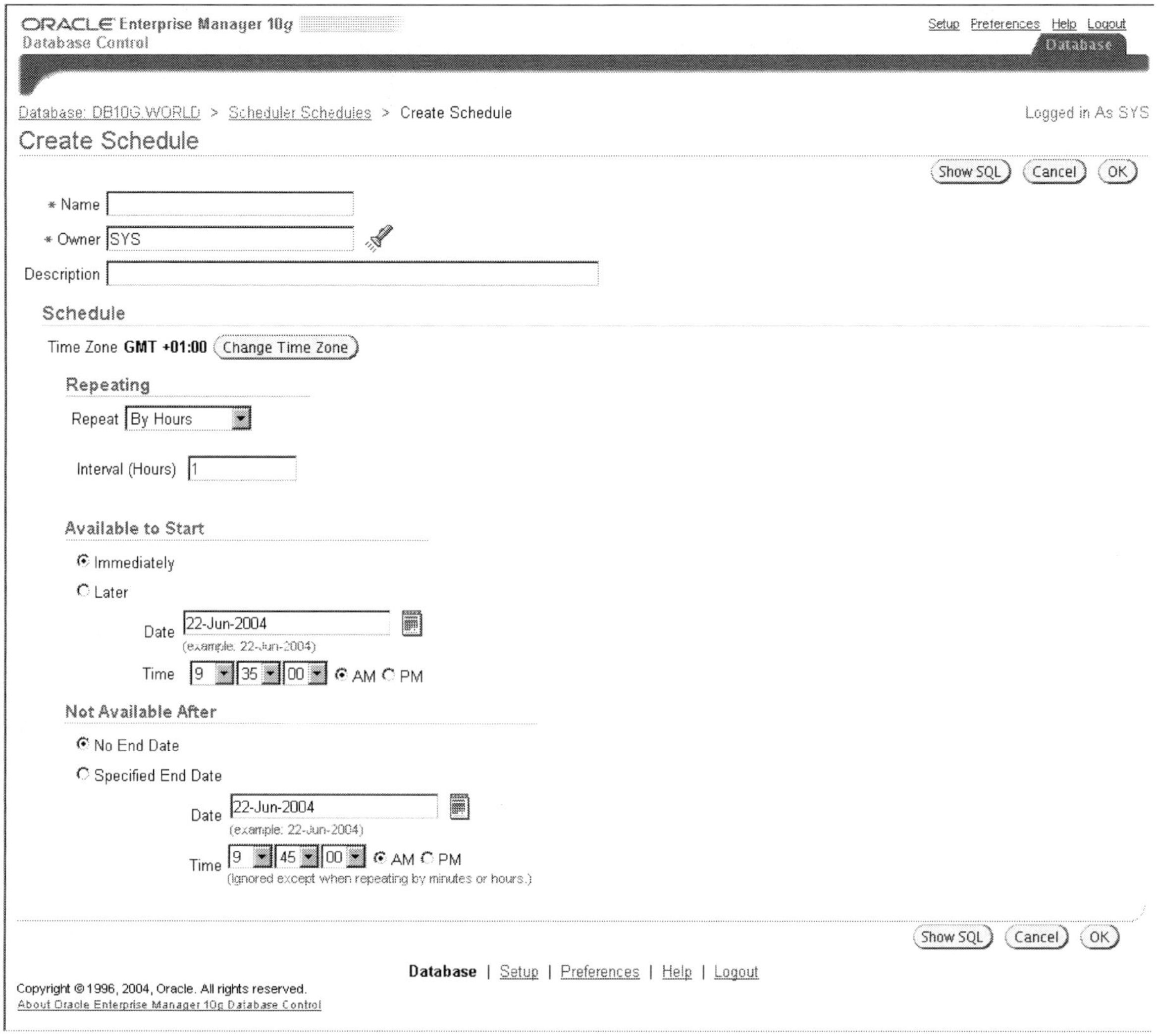

Figure 18.14: *OEM 10g DB Control - Create Schedule*

Information about schedules can be displayed using the *dba_scheduler_schedules* view. The following script uses this view to display information about schedules for a specified user or all users.

```
-- Parameters:
--    1) Specific USERNAME or ALL which doesn't limit output.
-- *****************************************************************

set verify off

SELECT
   owner,
   schedule_name,
   repeat_interval
FROM
   dba_scheduler_schedules
WHERE]
```

Overview of dbms_scheduler Functions

```
   owner = decode(upper('&1'), 'ALL', owner, upper('&1'))
;
```

The following is an example of the output.

```
SQL> @schedules job_user

OWNER                               SCHEDULE_NAME
----------------------------        ----------------------------
REPEAT_INTERVAL
--------------------------------------------------------------
JOB_USER                            TEST_HOURLY_SCHEDULE
freq=hourly; byminute=0


1 row selected.
```

Alternatively, the Scheduler Schedules screen of the OEM 10g DB Control shown in Figure 18.15 can be used to display schedule information.

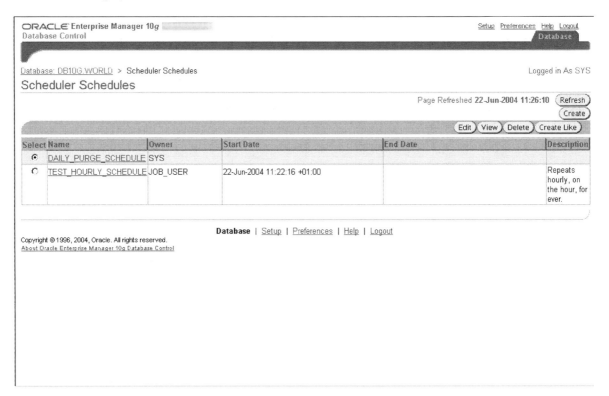

Figure 18.15: *OEM 10g DB Control - Scheduler Schedules*

The *dbms_job* screen can also be used for scheduling as shown in Figure 18.16.

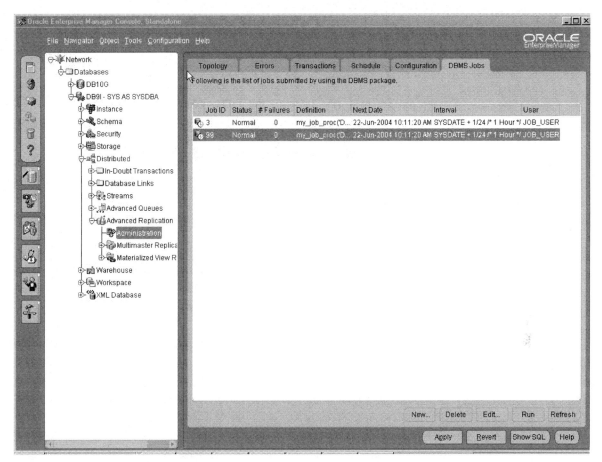

Figure 18.16: *OEM - DBMS Jobs*

Once a job is scheduled, changes to some of its attributes can be achieved using the *what, next_date, instance, interval* and *change* procedures whose call specifications are displayed below.

```
PROCEDURE what (
  job       IN  BINARY_INTEGER,
  what      IN  VARCHAR2)

PROCEDURE next_date (
  job       IN  BINARY_INTEGER,
  next_date IN  DATE)

PROCEDURE instance (
  job       IN  BINARY_INTEGER,
  instance  IN  BINARY_INTEGER,
  force     IN  BOOLEAN DEFAULT FALSE)

PROCEDURE interval (
  job       IN  BINARY_INTEGER,
  interval  IN  VARCHAR2)

PROCEDURE change (
  job       IN  BINARY_INTEGER,
```

```
what        IN  VARCHAR2,
next_date   IN  DATE,
interval    IN  VARCHAR2,
instance    IN  BINARY_INTEGER DEFAULT NULL,
force       IN  BOOLEAN DEFAULT FALSE)
```

The *what*, *next_date*, *instance* and *interval* procedures allow the individual attributes of the same name to be altered, while the *change* procedure allows all of them to be altered in one go, effectively replacing the existing job. The examples below show how the procedures can be used.

```
BEGIN
  DBMS_JOB.what (
    job  => 99,
    what => 'my_job_proc(''DBMS_JOB.ISUBMIT Example (WHAT).'');');

  DBMS_JOB.next_date (
    job       => 99,
    next_date => SYSDATE + 1/12);

  DBMS_JOB.interval (
    job      => 99,
    interval => 'SYSDATE + 1/12 /* 2 Hours */');

  COMMIT;
END;
/
```

The DBA can change the entire job definition back using the *change* procedure. If the *what*, *next_date* or *interval* parameters are NULL, the existing value is unchanged.

```
BEGIN
  DBMS_JOB.change (
    job       => 99,
    what      => 'my_job_proc(''DBMS_JOB.ISUBMIT Example.'');',
    next_date => TO_DATE('22-JUN-2004 10:11:20', 'DD-MON-YYYY HH24:MI:SS'),
    interval  => 'SYSDATE + 1/24 /* 1 Hour */');

  COMMIT;
END;
/
```

Figures 18.17 and 18.18 show the Create Job (General) and Create Job (Schedule) screens respectively. These provide a web-based alternative to the *create_job* procedure.

Figure 18.17: *OEM 10g DB Control - Create Job (General)*

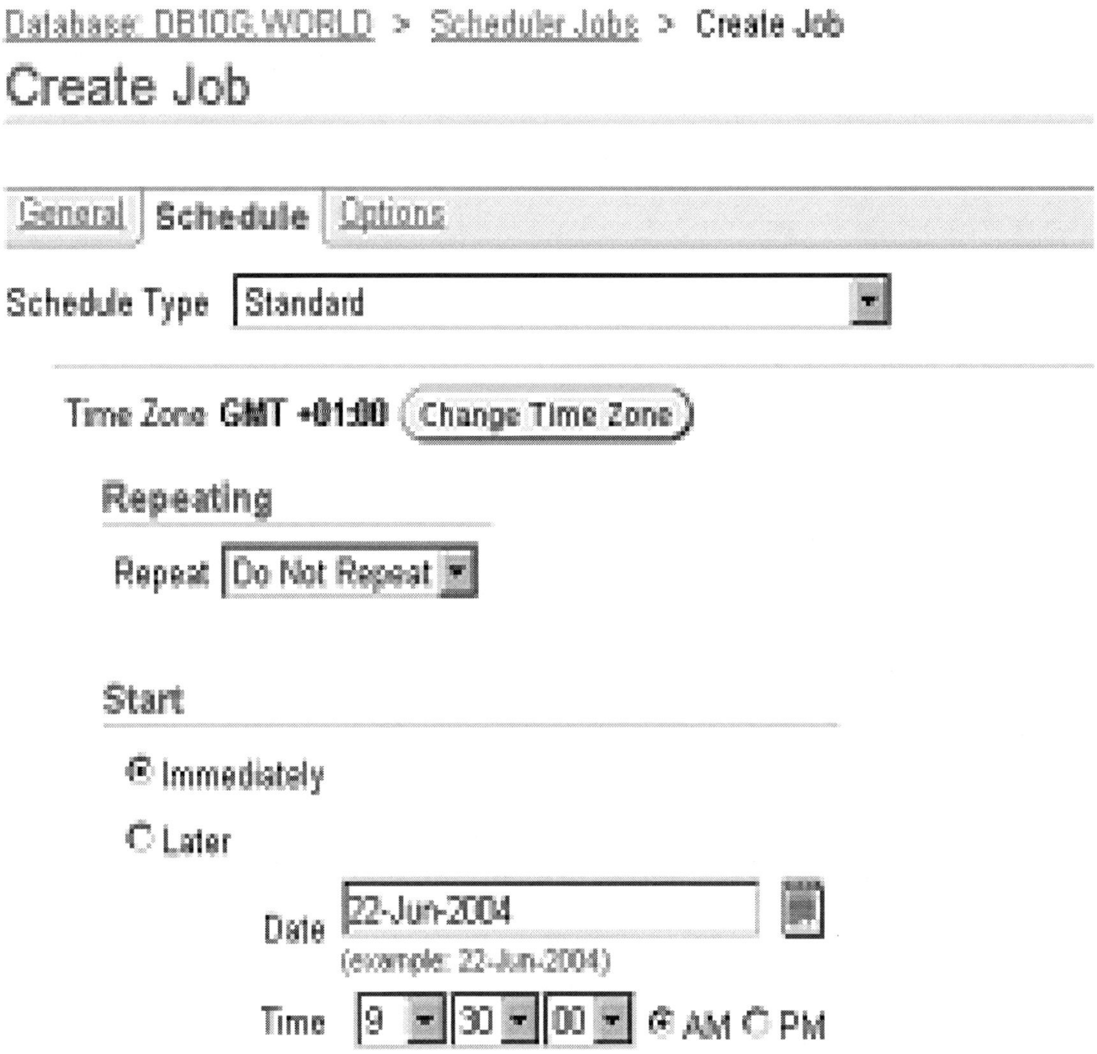

Create Job

| General | **Schedule** | Options |

Schedule Type | Standard ▾ |

Time Zone **GMT +01:00** (Change Time Zone)

Repeating

Repeat | Do Not Repeat ▾ |

Start

⦿ Immediately

○ Later

Date | 22-Jun-2004 | 📅
(example: 22-Jun-2004)

Time | 9 ▾ | 30 ▾ | 00 ▾ | ⦿ AM ○ PM

Figure 18.18: *OEM 10g DB Control - Create Job (Schedule)*

Information about jobs is displayed using the *dba_scheduler_jobs* view. The following script uses this view to display information about currently defined jobs.

```
- Parameters:
--     1) Specific USERNAME or ALL which doesn't limit output.
-- *****************************************************************

SET VERIFY OFF

SELECT
  owner,
  job_name,
  job_class,
  enabled,
  next_run_date,
  repeat_interval
FROM
  dba_scheduler_jobs
WHERE
  owner = decode(upper('&1'), 'ALL', owner, upper('&1'))
;
```

The output of the script for the current user is displayed below.

```
SQL> @jobs_10g job_user

OWNER                          JOB_NAME                       JOB_CLASS
ENABL
--------------------------- ----------------------------- ------
                                                                             -
next_RUN_DATE
----------------------------------------------------------------------
REPEAT_INTERVAL
----------------------------------------------------------------------
JOB_USER                       TEST_FULL_JOB_DEFINITION       DEFAULT_JOB_CLASS
TRUE
22-JUN-04 15.00.08.900000 +01:00
freq=hourly; byminute=0

JOB_USER                       TEST_PROG_SCHED_JOB_DEFINITION DEFAULT_JOB_CLASS
TRUE
22-JUN-04 15.00.16.200000 +01:00

JOB_USER                       TEST_PROG_JOB_DEFINITION       DEFAULT_JOB_CLASS
TRUE
22-JUN-04 15.00.09.600000 +01:00
freq=hourly; byminute=0

JOB_USER                       TEST_SCHED_JOB_DEFINITION      DEFAULT_JOB_CLASS
TRUE
22-JUN-04 15.00.16.200000 +01:00

4 rows selected.
```

Figure 18.19 shows the information displayed on the Scheduler Jobs screen in the OEM 10g DB Control.

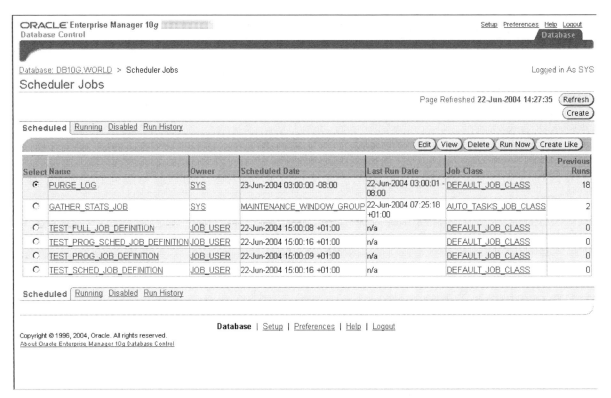

Figure 18.19: *OEM 10g DB Control - Scheduler Jobs*

Jobs are normally run asynchronously under the control of the job coordinator, but they can be controlled manually using the *run_job* and *stop_job* procedures.

```
PROCEDURE run_job (
  job_name            IN VARCHAR2,
  use_current_session IN BOOLEAN DEFAULT TRUE)

PROCEDURE stop_job (
  job_name            IN VARCHAR2,
  force               IN BOOLEAN DEFAULT FALSE)
```

The parameters of these procedures and their usage are as follows.

- *job_name*: A name which identifies a single job, a job class, or a comma separated list of job names

- *use_current_session*: When TRUE, the job is run in the user's current session; otherwise, a job slave runs it in the background.

- *force*: When FALSE, a job is stopped using the equivalent of sending a ctrl-c to the job. When TRUE, a graceful shutdown is attempted but if this fails, the slave process is killed. Using the *force* parameter requires the user to have the Manage Scheduler system privilege.

Figure 18.20 shows the Create Job Class screen in the OEM 10g DB Control.

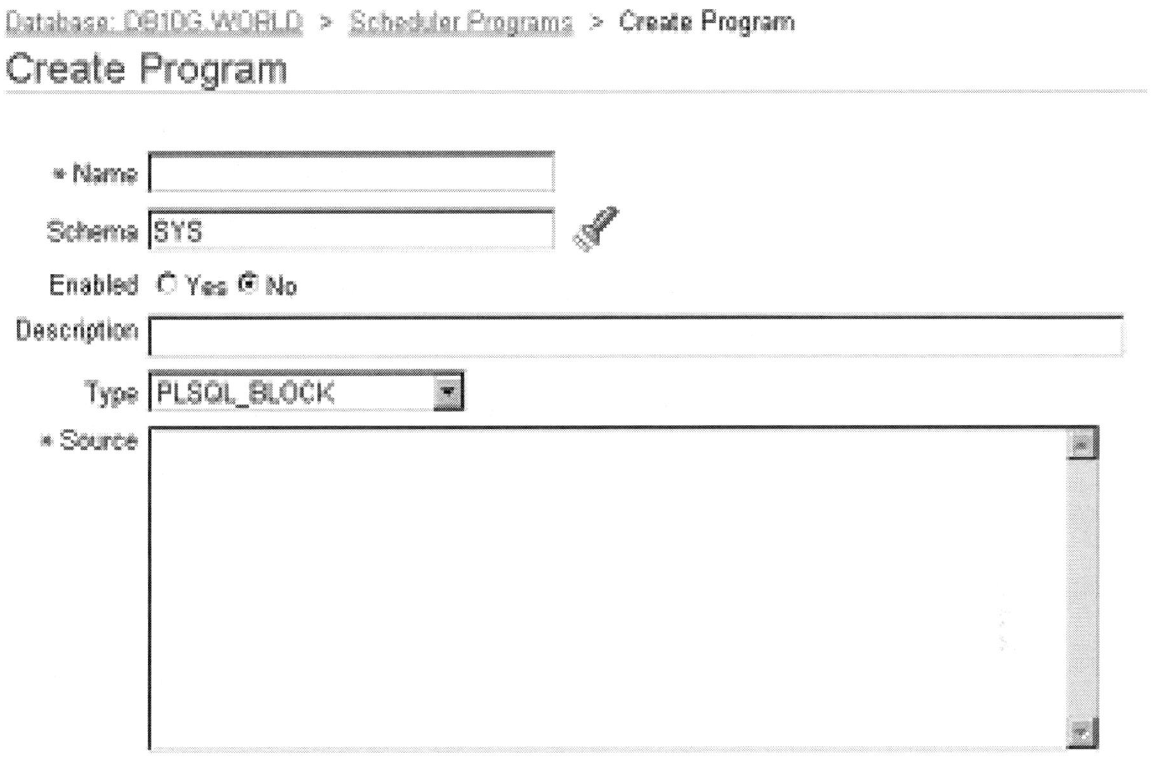

Create Program

Figure 18.20: *OEM 10g DB Control - Create Job Class*

Information about job classes can be displayed using the *dba_scheduler_job_classes* view. The following
script uses this view.

```
SELECT
   job_class_name,
   resource_consumer_group
FROM
   dba_scheduler_job_classes
;
```

The output from the script is displayed below.

```
SQL> @job_classes


JOB_CLASS_NAME                   RESOURCE_CONSUMER_GROUP
-------------------------------  -------------------------------
DEFAULT_JOB_CLASS
AUTO_TASKS_JOB_CLASS             AUTO_TASK_CONSUMER_GROUP
TEST_JOB_CLASS                   DEFAULT_CONSUMER_GROUP

3 rows selected.
```

Overview of dbms_scheduler Functions **1037**

Figure 18.21 shows the Scheduler Job Classes screen in the OEM 10g DB Control.

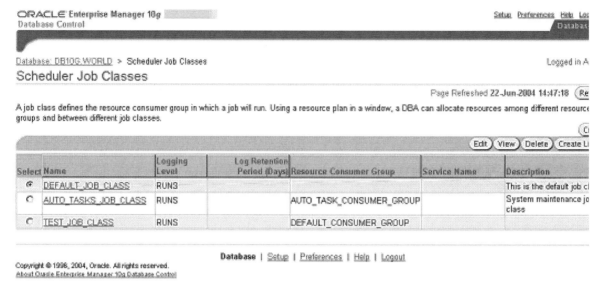

Figure 18.21: *OEM 10g DB Control - Scheduler Job Classes*

Jobs can be assigned to a job class during creation. It is also possible to assign a job to an alternative job class after creation using one of the *set_attribute* procedure overloads.

```
BEGIN
  -- Job defined and assigned to a job class.
  DBMS_SCHEDULER.create_job (
    job_name      => 'test_prog_sched_class_job_def',
    program_name  => 'test_plsql_block_prog',
    schedule_name => 'test_hourly_schedule',
    job_class     => 'test_job_class',
    enabled       => TRUE,
    comments      => 'Job defined and assigned to a job class ');
END;
/


BEGIN
  -- Assign an existing job to a job class.
  DBMS_SCHEDULER.set_attribute (
    name      => 'test_prog_sched_job_definition',
    attribute => 'job_class',
    value     => 'test_job_class');
END;
/
```

The output from the script shows that the job classes associated with these jobs have been set correctly.

```
job_user@db10g> @jobs_10g job_user

OWNER                         JOB_NAME                       JOB_CLASS
ENABL
----------------------------- ------------------------------ ------
```

```
next_RUN_DATE
-----------------------------------------------------------------
REPEAT_INTERVAL
-----------------------------------------------------------------
JOB_USER                        TEST_FULL_JOB_DEFINITION      DEFAULT_JOB_CLASS
TRUE
22-JUN-04 15.00.08.900000 +01:00
freq=hourly; byminute=0

JOB_USER                        TEST_PROG_SCHED_JOB_DEFINITION TEST_JOB_CLASS
TRUE
22-JUN-04 15.00.16.200000 +01:00

JOB_USER                        TEST_PROG_JOB_DEFINITION      DEFAULT_JOB_CLASS
TRUE
22-JUN-04 15.00.09.600000 +01:00
freq=hourly; byminute=0

JOB_USER                        TEST_SCHED_JOB_DEFINITION     DEFAULT_JOB_CLASS
TRUE
22-JUN-04 15.00.16.200000 +01:00

JOB_USER                        ARGUMENT_JOB_DEFINITION       DEFAULT_JOB_CLASS
TRUE
22-JUN-04 15.00.16.200000 +01:00

JOB_USER                        TEST_PROG_SCHED_CLASS_JOB_DEF TEST_JOB_CLASS
TRUE
22-JUN-04 15.00.16.200000 +01:00

6 rows selected.
```

Figure 18.22 shows the Create Window screen in the OEM 10g DB Control.

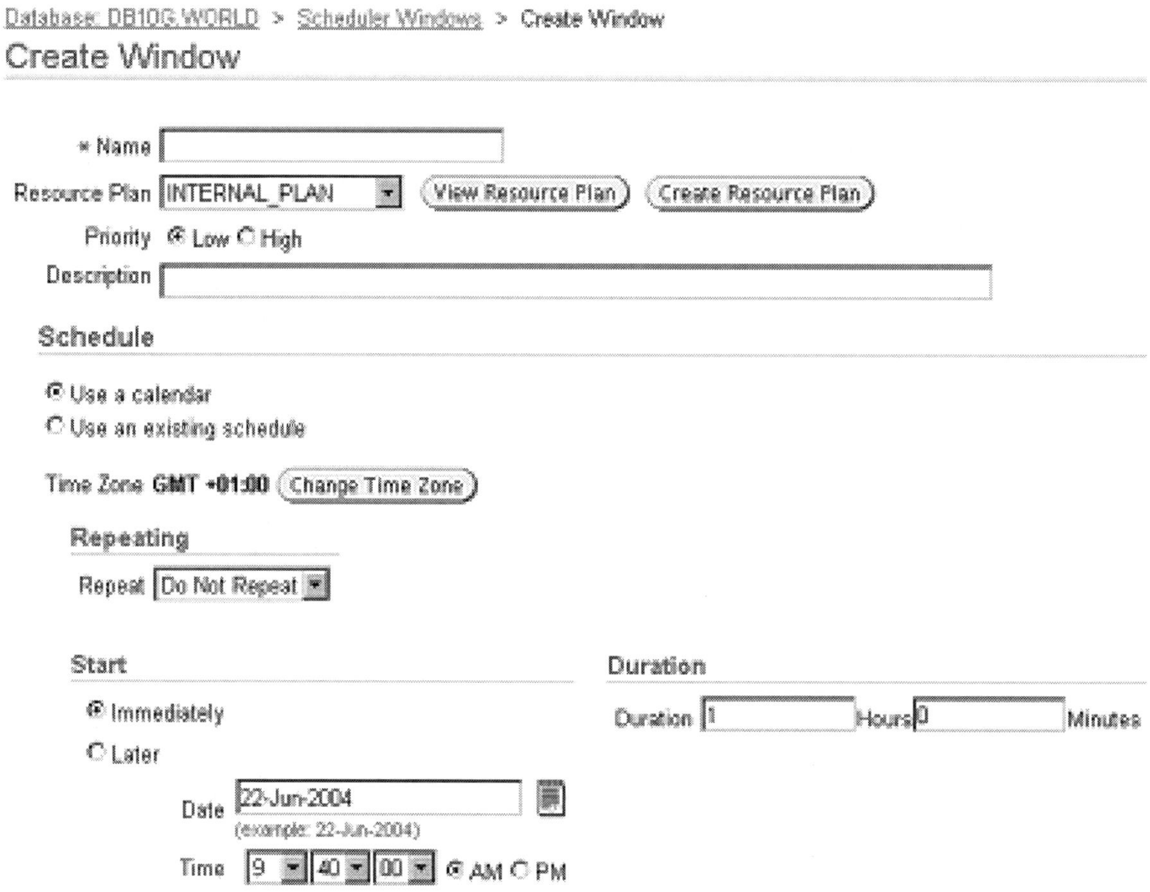

Create Window

```
*  Name  [                    ]
Resource Plan  [INTERNAL_PLAN  ▼]  ( View Resource Plan )  ( Create Resource Plan )
Priority  ⊙ Low  ○ High
Description  [                                        ]
```

Schedule

```
⊙ Use a calendar
○ Use an existing schedule

Time Zone  GMT +01:00  ( Change Time Zone )
```

Repeating

```
Repeat [Do Not Repeat ▼]
```

```
Start                                    Duration
  ⊙ Immediately                          Duration [1      ]Hours[0        ]Minutes
  ○ Later
        Date  [22-Jun-2004           ] 📅
              (example: 22-Jun-2004)
        Time  [9 ▼][40 ▼][00 ▼]  ⊙ AM ○ PM
```

Figure 18.22: *OEM 10g DB Control - Create Window*

Information about windows can be displayed using the *dba_scheduler_windows* view. The following script uses this view.

```
SELECT
   window_name,
   resource_plan,
   enabled,
   active
FROM
   dba_scheduler_windows
;
```

The output from the script is displayed below.

```
job_user@db10g> @windows.

WINDOW_NAME              RESOURCE_PLAN                ENABL ACTIV
------------------------ ---------------------------- ----- -----
TEST_WINDOW_1                                         TRUE  FALSE
TEST_WINDOW_2                                         TRUE  FALSE
```

```
WEEKEND_WINDOW                                                    TRUE    TRUE
WEEKNIGHT_WINDOW                                                  TRUE    FALSE

4 rows selected.
```

Figure 18.23 shows the Scheduler Windows screen in the OEM 10g DB Control.

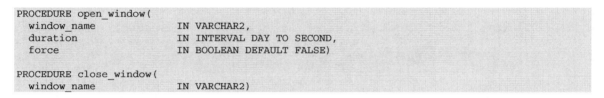

Figure 18.23: *OEM 10g DB Control - Scheduler Windows*

The server normally controls the opening and closing of windows, but they can be opened and closed manually using the *open_window* and *close_window* procedures.

```
PROCEDURE open_window(
  window_name               IN VARCHAR2,
  duration                  IN INTERVAL DAY TO SECOND,
  force                     IN BOOLEAN DEFAULT FALSE)

PROCEDURE close_window(
  window_name               IN VARCHAR2)
```

The parameters of these procedures and their usage are as follows:

- *window_name*: A name which uniquely identifies the window

- *duration*: The length of time in minutes the window should remain open.

- *force*: When FALSE, attempting to open a window when one is already open results in an error unless the currently open window is the one the DBA is attempting to open; in which case, the close time is set to the current system time plus the specified duration.

Closing a window causes all jobs associated with that window to be stopped.

Figure 18.24 shows the Create Window Group screen in the OEM 10g DB Control.

Create Window

* Name [   ]
Resource Plan [INTERNAL_PLAN ▼] (View Resource Plan) (Create Resource Plan)
  Priority ⦿ Low ○ High
Description [   ]

Schedule

⦿ Use a calendar
○ Use an existing schedule

Time Zone **GMT +01:00** (Change Time Zone)

Repeating

Repeat [Do Not Repeat ▼]

Start	Duration
⦿ Immediately	Duration [1] Hours [0] Minutes
○ Later	

Date [22-Jun-2004] ▦
(example: 22-Jun-2004)
Time [9 ▼] [40 ▼] [00 ▼] ⦿ AM ○ PM

Information about window groups can be displayed using the *dba_scheduler_window_groups* and *dba_scheduler_wingroup_members* views. The following script uses both views to display a summary of window group information.

```
PROMPT
PROMPT WINDOW GROUPS
PROMPT --------------

SELECT
   window_group_name,
   enabled,
   number_of_windowS
FROM
   dba_scheduler_window_groups
;

PROMPT
PROMPT WINDOW GROUP MEMBERS
PROMPT --------------------

SELECT
   window_group_name,
   window_name
FROM
   dba_scheduler_wingroup_members
;
```

The output from the script shows that the window group was created successfully.

```
SQL> @window_groups

WINDOW GROUPS
------------

WINDOW_GROUP_NAME                ENABL NUMBER_OF_WINDOWS
-------------------------------- ----- -----------------
MAINTENANCE_WINDOW_GROUP         TRUE                  2
TEST_WINDOW_GROUP                TRUE                  2

2 rows selected.


WINDOW GROUP MEMBERS
-------------------

WINDOW_GROUP_NAME                WINDOW_NAME
-------------------------------- --------------------------------
MAINTENANCE_WINDOW_GROUP         WEEKEND_WINDOW
MAINTENANCE_WINDOW_GROUP         WEEKNIGHT_WINDOW
TEST_WINDOW_GROUP                TEST_WINDOW_1
TEST_WINDOW_GROUP                TEST_WINDOW_2

4 rows selected.
```

Figure 18.25 shows the Scheduler Window Groups screen in the OEM 10g DB Control.

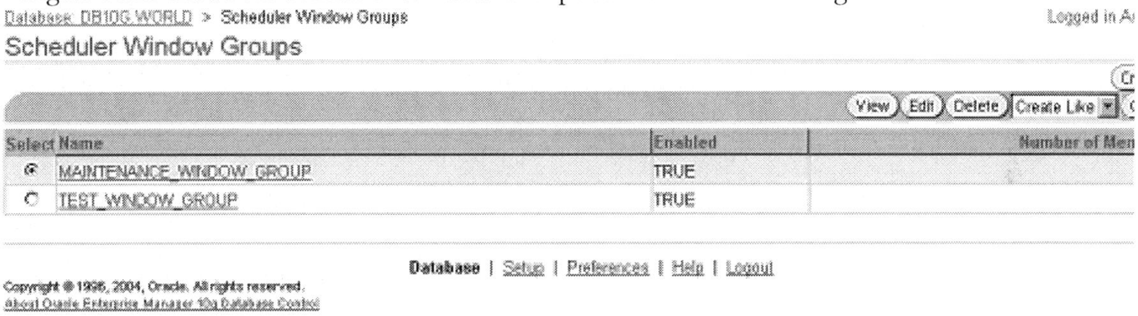

Figure 18.25: *OEM 10g DB Control - Scheduler Window Groups*

Windows can be added and removed from a group using the *add_window_group_member* and *remove_window_group_member* procedures respectively.

```
PROCEDURE add_window_group_member (
  group_name              IN VARCHAR2,
  window_list             IN VARCHAR2)

PROCEDURE remove_window_group_member (
  group_name              IN VARCHAR2,
  window_list             IN VARCHAR2)
```

The parameters of these procedures and their usage are listed as follows:

Overview of dbms_scheduler Functions

- *group_name*: A name that uniquely identifies the window group

- *window_list*: A comma separated list of windows to be added or removed from the window group

Figure 18.26 shows the Edit Window Group screen in the OEM 10g DB Control. Windows can be added and removed from a window group using this screen.

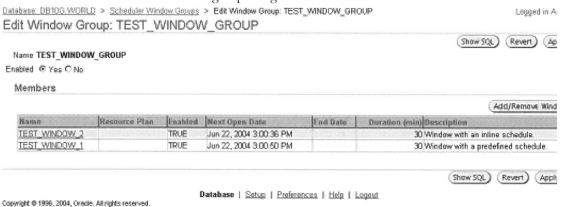

Figure 18.26: *OEM 10g DB Control - Edit Window Group*

Window groups are removed using the *drop_window_group* procedure.

```
PROCEDURE drop_window_group (
  group_name           IN VARCHAR2,
  force                IN BOOLEAN DEFAULT FALSE)
```

The parameters of this procedure and their usage are listed as follows:

- *group_name*: A name that uniquely identifies the window group

- *force*: When FALSE, an error is produced if any jobs reference the specified window group. When TRUE, any dependent jobs are disabled.

The following example shows how to drop a window group.

```
BEGIN
  DBMS_SCHEDULER.drop_window_group (
    group_name => 'test_window_group',
    force       => TRUE);
END;
/
```

The output from the script shows that the window group has been removed.

```
SQL> @window_groups

WINDOW GROUPS
-------------
```

```
WINDOW_GROUP_NAME                 ENABL NUMBER_OF_WINDOWS
------------------------------    ----- -----------------
MAINTENANCE_WINDOW_GROUP          TRUE                  2

1 row selected.


WINDOW GROUP MEMBERS
--------------------

WINDOW_GROUP_NAME                 WINDOW_NAME
------------------------------    ---------------------------------
MAINTENANCE_WINDOW_GROUP          WEEKEND_WINDOW
MAINTENANCE_WINDOW_GROUP          WEEKNIGHT_WINDOW

2 rows selected.
```

Now that information on scheduling with OEM has been presented, the next step is to investigate how to create custom OEM alerts with throughput metrics.

Throughput Metrics in OEM

Customized thresholds can be set for dozens of important Oracle throughput metrics as shown in Figure 18.27. These throughput metrics are critical for the senior Oracle professional because they can automate warning messages to allow time to fix an impending problem before end-users experience a performance slowdown. This is especially valuable when tuning a large OLTP database with high-volume I/O against many disk devices.

▼ Throughput	None	Last Collected Mar 1, 2004 7:07:15 PM
BG Checkpoints (per second)	Not Set	Last Collected Mar 1, 2004 7:07:15 PM
Branch Node Splits (per second)	Not Set	Last Collected Mar 1, 2004 7:07:15 PM
Branch Node Splits (per transaction)	Not Set	Last Collected Mar 1, 2004 7:07:15 PM
Consistent Read Changes (per second)	Not Set	Last Collected Mar 1, 2004 7:07:15 PM
Consistent Read Changes (per transaction)	Not Set	Last Collected Mar 1, 2004 7:07:15 PM
Consistent Read Gets (per second)	Not Set	Last Collected Mar 1, 2004 7:07:15 PM
Consistent Read Gets (per transaction)	Not Set	Last Collected Mar 1, 2004 7:07:15 PM
Cumulative Logons (per second)	Not Set	Last Collected Mar 1, 2004 7:07:15 PM
Cumulative Logons (per transaction)	Not Set	Last Collected Mar 1, 2004 7:07:15 PM
Cursor Blocks Created (per second)	Not Set	Last Collected Mar 1, 2004 7:07:15 PM
Cursor Blocks Created (per transaction)	Not Set	Last Collected Mar 1, 2004 7:07:15 PM
Cursor Undo Records Applied (per second)	Not Set	Last Collected Mar 1, 2004 7:07:15 PM
Cursor Undo Records Applied (per transaction)	Not Set	Last Collected Mar 1, 2004 7:07:15 PM
DBWR Checkpoints (per second)	Not Set	Last Collected Mar 1, 2004 7:07:15 PM
Database Block Changes (per second)	Not Set	Last Collected Mar 1, 2004 7:07:15 PM
Database Block Changes (per transaction)	Not Set	Last Collected Mar 1, 2004 7:07:15 PM
Database Block Gets (per second)	Not Set	Last Collected Mar 1, 2004 7:07:15 PM
Database Block Gets (per transaction)	Not Set	Last Collected Mar 1, 2004 7:07:15 PM
Enqueue Deadlocks (per second)	Not Set	Last Collected Mar 1, 2004 7:07:15 PM
Enqueue Deadlocks (per transaction)	Not Set	Last Collected Mar 1, 2004 7:07:15 PM
Enqueue Requests (per second)	Not Set	Last Collected Mar 1, 2004 7:07:15 PM
Enqueue Requests (per transaction)	Not Set	Last Collected Mar 1, 2004 7:07:15 PM
Enqueue Timeout (per second)	Not Set	Last Collected Mar 1, 2004 7:07:15 PM
Enqueue Timeout (per transaction)	Not Set	Last Collected Mar 1, 2004 7:07:15 PM
Enqueue Waits (per second)	Not Set	Last Collected Mar 1, 2004 7:07:15 PM

Figure 18.27: *OEM Throughput Metric Thresholds*

For a typical OLTP system where the main bottleneck is I/O throughput, setting these OEM thresholds allows the detection of a pending problem and time to fix it before the database encounters a problem. For example, a threshold alert might be set whenever the following conditions are true:

- *Buffer cache hit (%)* falls by more than 20%.

- *Database block gets* (per second) exceeds 5000 block gets per second.

In this simple example, the condition might signal an increase in physical disk I/O, perhaps due to uncached small-table full-table scans. By detecting the condition early, OEM is used to reallocate RAM to the *db_cache_size* or perhaps dynamically cache high-impact tables by placing them into the KEEP pool. Again, if OEM thresholds are used to alert the DBA at the first sign of the trend, time is available for the DBA to use OEM2GO to correct the issue before it becomes a performance problem.

Even though OEM displays almost every conceivable internal metric, it does not stop there. The AWR architecture goes beyond the bounds of the Oracle instance and collects external environment information, providing OEM with invaluable information about the external server-side environment.

OEM Outside the Instance

Using OEM, the Oracle professional can now get access to external information that has never been available before in a single interface. This is very important because it removes the need for the DBA to have any experience with the cumbersome OS command syntax required to display server-side information.

For example, in UNIX the DBA needs to know the command-line syntax of various UNIX utilities, such as *SAR*, *glance*, *top*, *lsattr* and *prtconf*, to display server metrics. The OEM screens now allow seamless access server-side performance metrics including:

- Oracle server-side file contents in the form of the alert log and trace dumps

- Oracle archive redo log file performance

- Server OS kernel performance parameter values

- Server OS characteristics such as the number of CPUs, amount of RAM, and network

- Historical capture of CPU and RAM activity

A quick look at the OEM display screens for external information shows how this relieves the DBA of knowing hundreds of server-side commands.
OEM quickly reveals the status of Oracle server-side file performance and error messages, including the alert log file, archived redo log status and file system status as shown in Figure 18.28.

Database: FSDEV10G > All Metrics

All Metrics

Expand All | Collapse All

Metrics	Thresholds	Collection Sta
▼ FSDEV10G		
▼ Alert Log	Some	Not Collected
Alert Log Error Trace File	Not Set	Not Collected
Alert Log Name	Not Set	Not Collected
Archiver Hung Alert Log Error	Set	Not Collected
Data Block Corruption Alert Log Error	Set	Not Collected
Generic Alert Log Error	Set	Not Collected
Session Terminated Alert Log Error	Set	Not Collected
▼ Alert Log Content	None	Not Collected
Content	Not Set	Not Collected
▼ Alert Log Error Status	All	Last Collected
Archiver Hung Alert Log Error Status	Set	Last Collected
Data Block Corruption Alert Log Error Status	Set	Last Collected
Generic Alert Log Error Status	Set	Last Collected
Session Terminated Alert Log Error Status	Set	Last Collected
▼ Archive Area	Some	Last Collected
Archive Area Used (%)	Set	Last Collected
Archive Area Used (KB)	Not Set	Last Collected
Free Archive Area (KB)	Not Set	Last Collected

Figure 18.28: *A Partial Listing of the AWR Metrics from Inside OEM*

The ability of OEM to monitor server-side metrics makes it a one-stop tool for monitoring both Oracle and the server. A Systems Administrator may no longer be required to buy expensive tools to monitor the server and the data files. Best of all, the Oracle professional now does not have to worry about a server-side problem, i.e. file-system full, causing an Oracle interruption.

From these OEM interfaces, the DBA can display and manage all server-side Oracle components without having to sign on to the server. This is a blessing for those Oracle professionals running UNIX servers who may not be fluent in cryptic UNIX commands and the complex vi editor. In Figure 18.29, the display of server ODS details including all OS kernel parameters is shown.

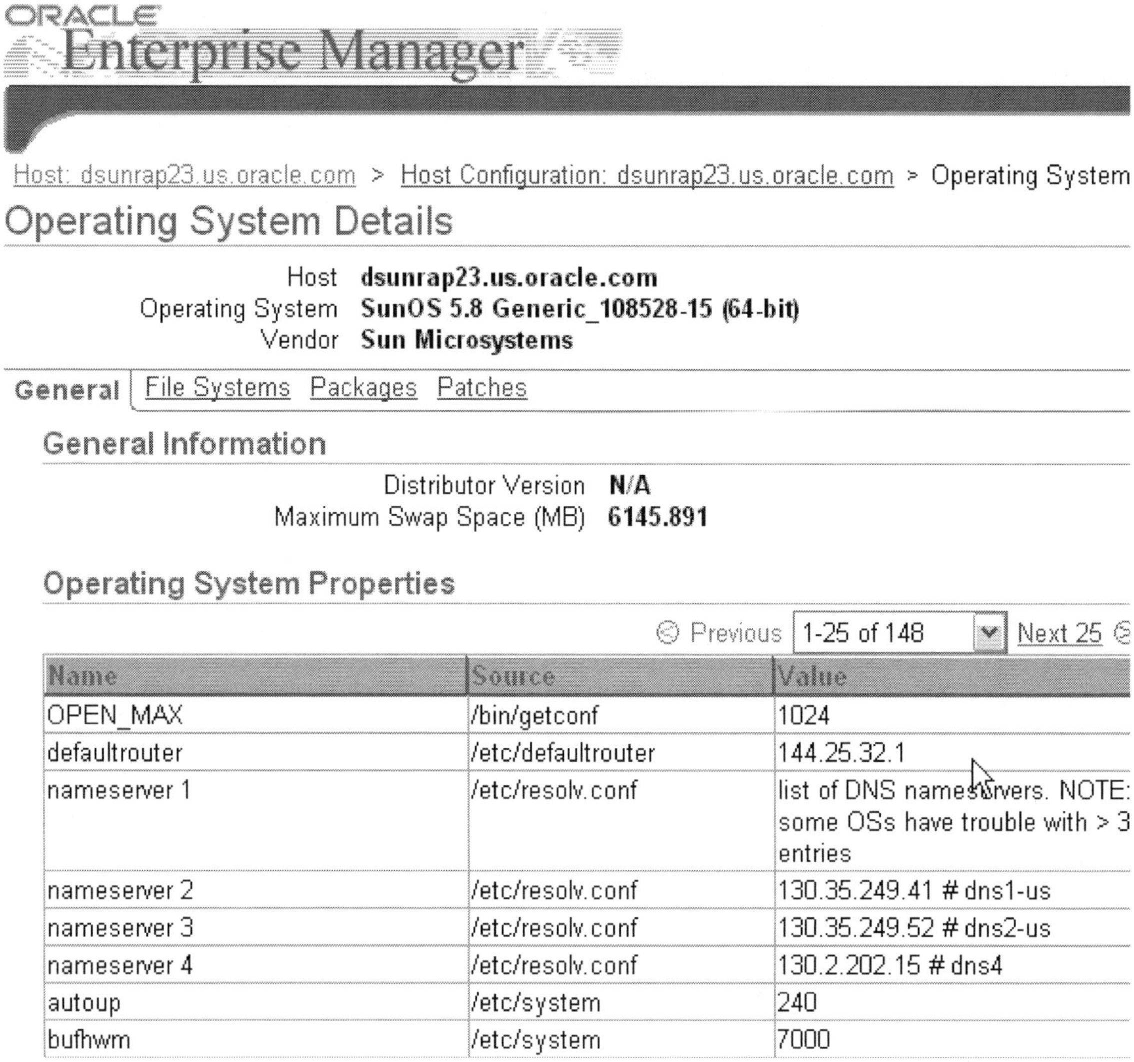

Host: dsunrap23.us.oracle.com > Host Configuration: dsunrap23.us.oracle.com > Operating System

Operating System Details

Host **dsunrap23.us.oracle.com**
Operating System **SunOS 5.8 Generic_108528-15 (64-bit)**
Vendor **Sun Microsystems**

General | File Systems Packages Patches

General Information

Distributor Version **N/A**
Maximum Swap Space (MB) **6145.891**

Operating System Properties

⊙ Previous | 1-25 of 148 ▾ | Next 25 ⊙

Name	Source	Value
OPEN_MAX	/bin/getconf	1024
defaultrouter	/etc/defaultrouter	144.25.32.1
nameserver 1	/etc/resolv.conf	list of DNS nameservers. NOTE: some OSs have trouble with > 3 entries
nameserver 2	/etc/resolv.conf	130.35.249.41 # dns1-us
nameserver 3	/etc/resolv.conf	130.35.249.52 # dns2-us
nameserver 4	/etc/resolv.conf	130.2.202.15 # dns4
autoup	/etc/system	240
bufhwm	/etc/system	7000

Figure 18.29: *The OEM Display of Server-side Performance Parameters*

The DBA can now throw away the checklist of cumbersome OS commands to display server hardware characteristics. For example, the following is a list of the cryptic commands the Oracle UNIX professional would have to know in order to display the number of CPUs on their Oracle server:

- Linux Command:

```
cat /proc/cpuinfo|grep processor|wc –l
```

- Solaris Command:

```
psrinfo -v|grep "Status of processor"|wc –l
```

- AIX Command:

```
lsdev -C|grep Process|wc -l
```

- HP/UX Command:

```
ioscan -C processor | grep processor | wc -l
```

The Oracle OEM issues these commands on the DBA's behalf and displays all hardware characteristics in an easy-to-read display as shown in Figure 18.30.

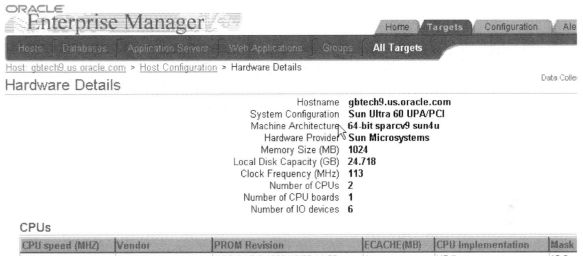

Figure 18.30: *The OEM Display of Server-side Hardware Configuration*

OEM does much more than display the server parameters and configuration information. Oracle tuning professionals know that a shortage of server resources may cause slow performance, and OEM now quickly displays the relevant CPU and RAM metrics. The main performance display screen in OEM shows a current summary of the CPU Run Queue and RAM paging as seen in Figure 18.31.

Host CPU

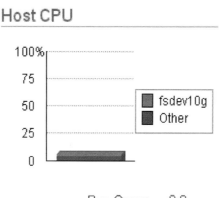

Run Queue   0.0
Paging (pages per second)   4.32

Figure 18.31: *The HOST CPU Section of the Main OEM Performance Screen*

Here the DBA can quickly see if a shortage of Oracle server resources is causing a performance bottleneck. Assuming that the instance and SQL have already been optimized, this server-side information can give immediate insights to server resource shortages:

- CPU dispatcher run queue: Whenever the server processors are overstressed, the run queue exceeds the number of CPUs. For example, a run queue value of nine on an 8-CPU server indicates the need to add more or faster CPUs.

- Server RAM paging: Whenever the RAM demands of a server exceed the real RAM capacity, the server's Virtual Memory (VM) utility will page, transferring RAM frames to a special swap disk on the server. Assuming the SGA and PGA regions are optimized, paging indicates the need to add RAM resources to the server.

The OEM also tracks server usage over time, allowing the DBA to quickly see those times when a hardware-related constraint is happening as shown in Figure 18.32. This display reveals the historical CPU usage, and a display of a self-defined threshold alert status, as defined by setting a threshold alert for the *Average CPU (%)* OEM metric, is noted.

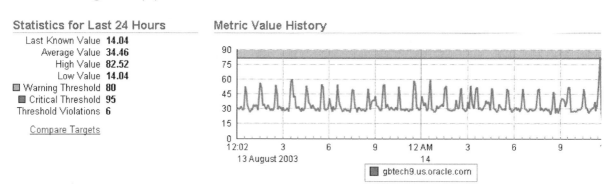

Figure 18.32: *The OEM Historical Tracking of CPU Consumption*

OEM also tracks server run queue waits over time and combines the CPU and Paging display into a single OEM screen so the DBA can tell when server-side waits on hardware resources are being experienced as shown in Figure 18.33. This is important because Oracle performance issues are often transient in nature, with short spikes in excessive CPU demands.

Because of the super-fast nature of CPU dispatching, a database might be CPU constrained for only a few minutes at a time during different times of the day. The time series OEM display can reveal a quick visual clue about those times when a CPU or RAM bottleneck is being experienced.

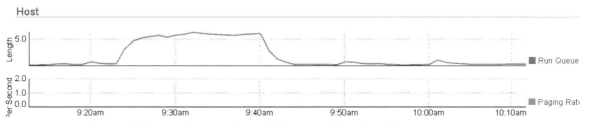

Figure 18.33: *Server CPU Run Queue and RAM Paging Values Over Time*

OEM has a drill down function which allows the DBA to easily click on any area of the graph to obtain detailed information.

Even though it is true that a CPU bottleneck exists when the run queue exceeds the number of processors, this condition does not always mean that the solution is to add processors.

Excessive CPU can be caused by many internal conditions including inefficient SQL statements that perform excessive logical I/O, non-reentrant SQL inside the library cache, and many other conditions. Fortunately, OEM allows the DBA to go back in time and find these conditions, even though the immediate run queue issue has passed.

Because of Oracle's commitment to extending OEM beyond the boundaries of the Oracle instance, all areas of server utilization can be tracked over time as shown in Figure 18.34. This figure illustrates the specific times when the server exceeds the maximum CPU capacity and the total time spent by active Oracle sessions, waiting and working.

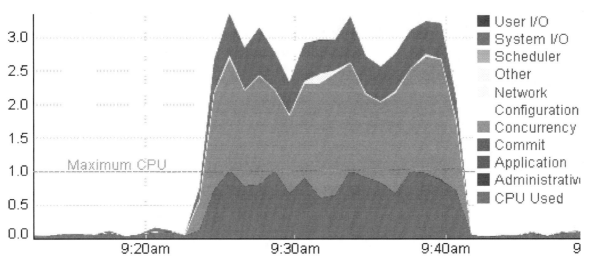

Figure 18.34: *Oracle Server Time series Resource Component Utilization*

Because of the clarity of the color OEM display, the total components of Oracle wait times including CPU time, concurrency management overhead (locks, latches), and I/O can be clearly seen. This display also shows the times when CPU usage exceeds the server capacity.

To fully understand how to customize OEM for maximum benefit, a brief tour of the OEM exception reporting mechanism and how it displays the predefined alerts will be provided.

Exception Tuning Inside Enterprise Manager

The Automatic Diagnostic component of the Oracle Performance OEM screen contains an alert area in which ADDM warns the DBA about historical performance exceptions. This exception-based reporting is very important to Oracle tuning because Oracle databases change rapidly, and transient performance issues are very difficult to detect without an exception-based mechanism.

Exception reports allow the Oracle professional to view specific times and conditions when Oracle processing demands have exceeded the server capacity. More important, these transient server exceptions give insight regarding repeating server trends.

Figure 18.35 is a representation of the OEM alert screen.

Alerts

Severity	Category	Name	Message	Alert Triggered	Last Value	Time
⚠	Response	User Logon Time (msec)	User logon time is 2797 msecs.	May 17, 2004 8:16:29 AM	907	May 17, 2004 9:21:29 AM
⚠	Invalid Objects by Schema	Owner's Invalid Object Count	84 object(s) are invalid in the FS_LSD schema.	Apr 27, 2004 8:35:58 PM	84	Apr 27, 2004 8:35:58 PM
⚠	Invalid Objects by Schema	Owner's Invalid Object Count	20 object(s) are invalid in the PUBLIC schema.	Apr 27, 2004 8:35:58 PM	20	Apr 27, 2004 8:35:58 PM
⚠	Invalid Objects by Schema	Owner's Invalid Object Count	21 object(s) are invalid in the SYS schema.	Apr 27, 2004 8:35:58 PM	21	Apr 27, 2004 8:35:58 PM

Related Alerts

Severity	Target Name	Target Type	Category	Name	Message	Alert Triggered	Last Value	Time
✕	localhost	Host	Load	CPU Utilization (%)	CPU Utilization is 100%	May 17, 2004 9:23:02 AM	100	May 17, 2004 9:23:02 AM
⚠	localhost	Host	Filesystems	Filesystem Space Available (%)	Filesystem C:\ has only 8.79% available space	Apr 5, 2004 6:37:44 PM	8.92	May 17, 2004 7:18:37 AM
⚠	localhost	Host	Load	Swap Utilization (%)	Swap Utilization is 84.64%	May 17, 2004 9:08:02 AM	83.39	May 17, 2004 9:23:02 AM

Figure 18.35: *The OEM Exception Reporting Screen*

In Figure 18.35, the Oracle alerts are located on the top half of the screen and the external server alerts are located on the bottom half. The server-related alerts are critical to Oracle performance because Oracle allows the DBA to relieve server stress by adding additional servers. Common server-related alerts might include:

- **CPU utilization:** Whenever the CPU run queue exceeds the number of processors on the server, the database is CPU-bound. Actions might include tuning SQL to reduce logical I/O or adding more CPU resources.

- **Filesystem shortage:** When using Oracle with autoextend datafiles, the only constraint to file growth is the limitation of the OS filesystem. Should a filesystem become unable to accommodate an automatic datafile expansion, Oracle halts the process until additional space is allocated. This monitoring task is critical to ensuring the continuous availability of the database.

- **Swap shortage:** The swap disk is used on a virtual processor to store infrequently used RAM frames. When the swap disk becomes full, more disks should be added.

This ability to perform server-side alerts is extremely valuable to the Oracle professional who must monitor both internal and external Oracle environments.

The next section shows techniques for extending the OEM functionality for trend-based reporting, and explores the Automated Database Diagnostic Monitor (ADDM) as well as the SQL Tuning Advisor within OEM. A real world Oracle 10g migration for an Oracle 8i application using the obsolete Rule-based SQL Optimizer (RBO) is also shown.

A good understanding of the basic functionality of OEM performance monitoring and how OEM accesses the new AWR database is needed before exploring how Enterprise Manager interprets AWR and ASH information. This information is used to diagnose performance issues with the Automatic Database Diagnostic Monitor.

The bottom of the following screen shows the Related Links, including the OEM Advisor Central link as shown in Figure 18.36:

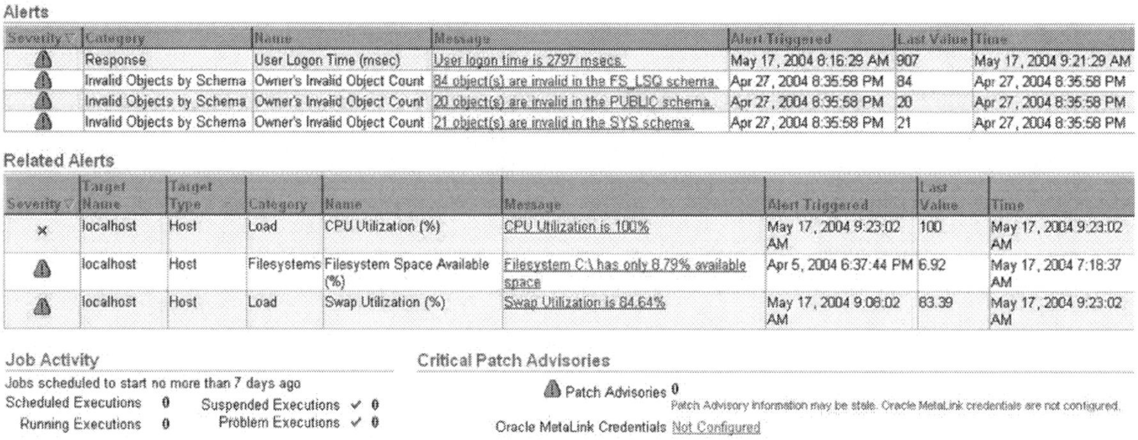

Figure 18.36: *The OEM Alerts Screen with Link to Advisor Central*

This link between the database and server exceptions provides a preview of the exceptional conditions and validates the recommendations from the Advisor Central area of OEM.

Next, attention can be focused on the examination of the OEM advisor area.

Advisor Central in OEM

The Advisor Central screen displays the three advisory areas of Enterprise Manager: the SQL Tuning Advisor, the ADDM, and the Segment Advisor as shown in Figure 18.37. This OEM information is externalized via the *dbms_advisor* package and the *dba_advisor_tasks* view.

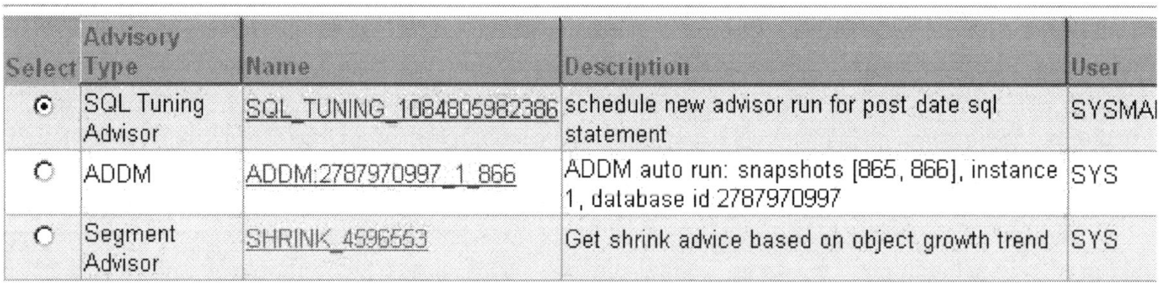

Select	Advisory Type	Name	Description	User
⊙	SQL Tuning Advisor	SQL_TUNING_1084805982386	schedule new advisor run for post date sql statement	SYSMAI
○	ADDM	ADDM:2787970997_1_866	ADDM auto run: snapshots [865, 866], instance 1, database id 2787970997	SYS
○	Segment Advisor	SHRINK_4596553	Get shrink advice based on object growth trend	SYS

Figure 18.37: *The OEM Advisor Central Screen*

Under the Advisors section of this screen, hyperlinks to the main Advisory areas are shown in Figure 18.38:

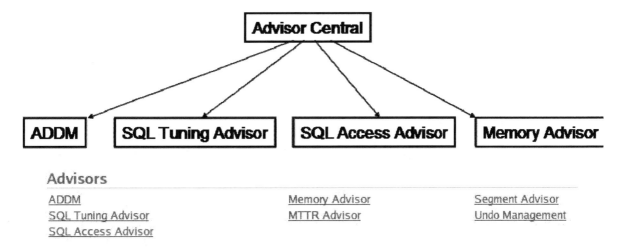

Figure 18.38: *The OEM Advisor Central Screen's Hyperlinks*

Each of the hyperlinks provides important advisory functions, yet each one addresses very different areas of Oracle tuning as follows:

- **ADDM:** The Automatic Database Diagnostic Monitor provides intelligent recommendations regarding Oracle changes that improve performance and throughput.

- **SQL Tuning Advisor:** This component prepares SQL tuning sets and SQL profiles for tuning sub-optimal SQL statements.

- **SQL Access Advisor:** This component displays execution plans for SQL statements and recommends changes to the SQL data access paths.

- **Automatic Memory Manager:** This component implements the dynamic SGA features in Oracle in which any of the following SGA areas can be resized, depending on the database load. If the DBA is not using the Automatic Memory Management (AMM) features to automatically adjust the SGA pools, the Memory Advisor should be used to provide the necessary recommendations for resizing the following SGA pools:

  - **Data Buffer Pool Advisory:** This component implements the *v$db_cache_advice* view and the *dba_hist_db_cache_advice* view. Whenever Oracle detects a shortage of RAM data buffers, Oracle may borrow RAM frames from other regions to allocate to the data buffers.

  - **Program Global Area (PGA) Advisory:** This component implements the *v$pga_target_advice* utility and is externalized in the *dba_hist_pgastat* view. The PGA monitors disk sorts and hash joins and determines the optimal setting for the PGA RAM region.

  - **Shared Pool Advisory:** This component adjusts the shared pool using the *v$shared_pool_advice* and the new *dba_hist_shared_pool_advice* view.

- Automatic Segment Advisor: This component advises on segment conditions including changes to data file and tablespace characteristics.

Automate index rebuilding!

The Oracle 11g Segment Advisor now identifies sparse indexes for rebuild to improve space utilization and performance.

These advisory functions are shown in detail later in this chapter, but it is important to note that OEM is an open-source tool, and all of the advisory information is externalized in a series of *dba_advisor* views, such as the following:

- *dba_advisor_actions*
- *dba_advisor_commands*
- *dba_advisor_definitions*
- *dba_advisor_def_parameters*
- *dba_advisor_directives*
- *dba_advisor_findings*
- *dba_advisor_journal*
- *dba_advisor_log*
- *dba_advisor_objects*
- *dba_advisor_object_types*
- *dba_advisor_parameters*
- *dba_advisor_rationale*
- *dba_advisor_recommendations*
- *dba_advisor_tasks*
- *dba_advisor_templates*
- *dba_advisor_usage*

To see the internals of the Automatic Segment Advisor, additional dictionary views are available. In the list below, SQLA represents the Access Advisor views, while SQLW represents the Workload tasks:

- *dba_advisor_sqla_rec_sum*
- *dba_advisor_sqla_wk_map*
- *dba_advisor_sqla_wk_stmts*
- *dba_advisor_sqlw_colvol*
- *dba_advisor_sqlw_journal*
- *dba_advisor_sqlw_parameters*
- *dba_advisor_sqlw_stmts*

- *dba_advisor_sqlw_sum*

- *dba_advisor_sqlw_tables*

- *dba_advisor_sqlw_tabvol*

- *dba_advisor_sqlw_templates*

Now, it is time to move on to an exploration of the ADDM. A review of the ADDM screens is started by clicking on the ADDM hyperlink. This reveals the ADDM Database Activity and ADDM Performance Analysis screens.

ADDM Main Screen

The ADDM hyperlink forwards the DBA to the main screen for ADDM. This screen is the heart of ADDM and shows the overview task bar for the main contributors to the response time.

The Database Activity chart on the top half of this screen provides vital Oracle tuning information because it reveals a time-based display of the main components of Oracle response time:

- Wait: This event is defined in the *dba_hist_waitclassmet_history* view and consists of all sources of waits on database processing including segment header waits, latch serialization, network and user I/O waits.

- I/O: This event is the physical disk I/O as captured in the *dba_hist_filestatxs* and *dba_hist_filemetric_history* views.

- CPU: High CPU consumption is typical for databases with large data buffer caches, sub-optimal logical I/O in the form of unnecessary consistent gets, or library cache contention. It can also be a legitimate condition requiring additional processor resources.

The database is constrained by physical disk I/O during the specified time period as shown in Figure 18.39.

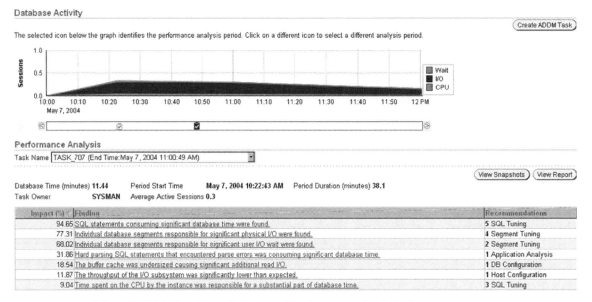

Figure 18.39: *The ADDM Database Activity and Performance Analysis Screen*

Under the performance analysis section, the DBA starts by choosing a specific task from the drop-down menu; TASK_707 on this screen. Figure 18.40 shows that for TASK_707, a host of diagnostic information is displayed.

Impact (%)	Finding	Recommendations
94.65	SQL statements consuming significant database time were found.	5 SQL Tuning
77.31	Individual database segments responsible for significant physical I/O were found.	4 Segment Tuning
68.02	Individual database segments responsible for significant user I/O wait were found.	2 Segment Tuning
31.86	Hard parsing SQL statements that encountered parse errors was consuming significant database time.	1 Application Analysis
18.54	The buffer cache was undersized causing significant additional read I/O.	1 DB Configuration
11.87	The throughput of the I/O subsystem was significantly lower than expected.	1 Host Configuration
9.04	Time spent on the CPU by the instance was responsible for a substantial part of database time.	3 SQL Tuning

Figure 18.40: *The Drop Down Menu*

The top finding on this screen is, "SQL Statements consuming significant database resources". When clicking on this hyperlink, the DBA drills down into the ADDM Performance Details screen shown in Figure 18.41.

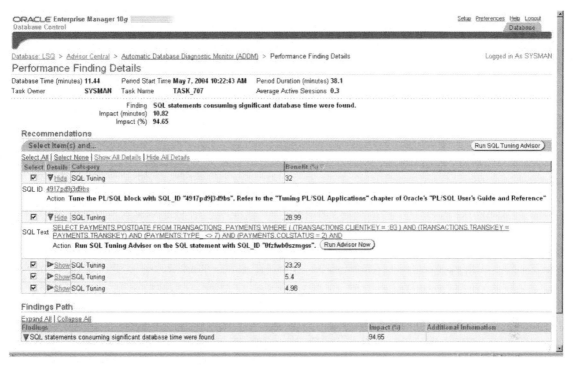

Figure 18.41: *The ADDM Performance Findings Details Screen*

The Performance Findings Details screen reveals a list of hyperlinks for SQL tuning recommendations. If the DBA clicks the Show Hyperlink on any of the SQL in this list, the source for each suspect SQL statement is displayed as a hyperlink, and clicking on this hyperlink takes the DBA into the next area of the OEM, the SQL Tuning Advisor. However, first an exploration of the ADDM recommendations is merited.

ADDM Recommendations

The ADDM recommendations screen is the result of the AWR data analysis, and it shows recommendations for current changes based upon historical information. The following figure (Figure 18.42) shows an ADDM recommendation to increase the size of the *sga_target* and the *db_cache_size*.

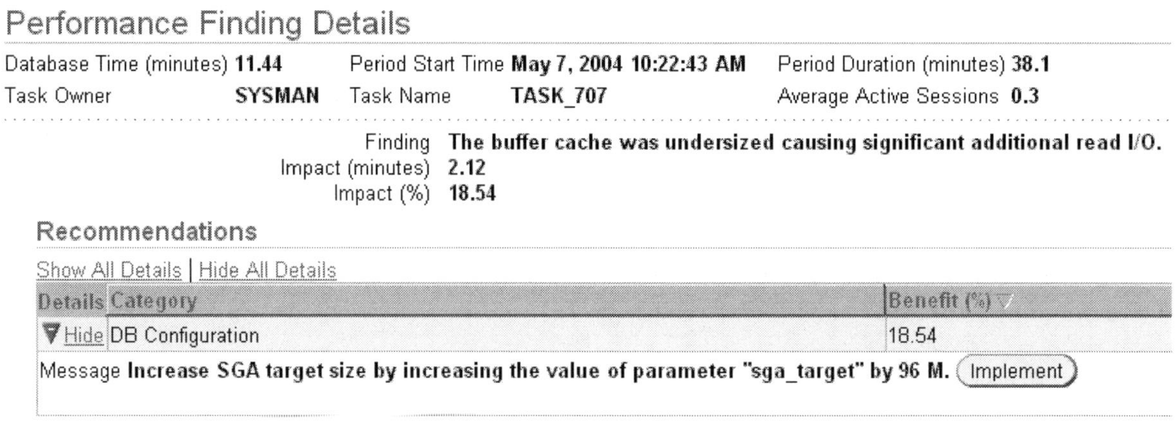

Performance Finding Details

Database Time (minutes) **11.44**	Period Start Time **May 7, 2004 10:22:43 AM**	Period Duration (minutes) **38.1**	
Task Owner **SYSMAN**	Task Name **TASK_707**	Average Active Sessions **0.3**	

Finding **The buffer cache was undersized causing significant additional read I/O.**
Impact (minutes) **2.12**
Impact (%) **18.54**

Recommendations

Show All Details | Hide All Details

Details	Category	Benefit (%) ▽
▼ Hide	DB Configuration	18.54

Message **Increase SGA target size by increasing the value of parameter "sga_target" by 96 M.** (Implement)

Figure 18.42: *A Ratio-based Recommendation for Increasing the Data Buffer Cache*

This advice is based on a predictive model similar to the *v$db_cache_advice* view from Oracle 9i in which the marginal benefit of adding additional RAM blocks to the data buffers is seen. If the reduction in physical I/O is substantially more than the cost of the RAM blocks, a recommendation for increasing the size of the buffer is appropriate.

This ADDM function uses data from the AWR *dba_hist_db_cache_advice*, *dba_hist_pga_target_advice* and the *dba_hist_shared_pool_advice* views. This function continuously monitors the marginal benefits of changes to the shared pool, data cache size and PGA region, dynamically morphing the region sizes with the goal of achieving the optimal size for the pool.

Another ADDM recommendation for investigating an issue within the shared pool is shown in Figure 18.43. ADDM has detected excessive hard parses within the library cache. Rather than blindly adding resources, ADDM correctly recommends an investigation of the application logic to eliminate parse errors.

Performance Finding Details

Database Time (minutes) **11.44**	Period Start Time **May 7, 2004 10:22:43 AM**	Period Duration (minutes) **38.1**	
Task Owner **SYSMAN**	Task Name **TASK_707**	Average Active Sessions **0.3**	

Finding **Hard parsing SQL statements that encountered parse errors was consuming significant database time.**
Impact (minutes) **3.64**
Impact (%) **31.86**

Recommendations

Show All Details | Hide All Details

Details	Category	Benefit (%) ▽
▼ Hide	Application Analysis	31.86

Action **Investigate application logic to eliminate parse errors.**

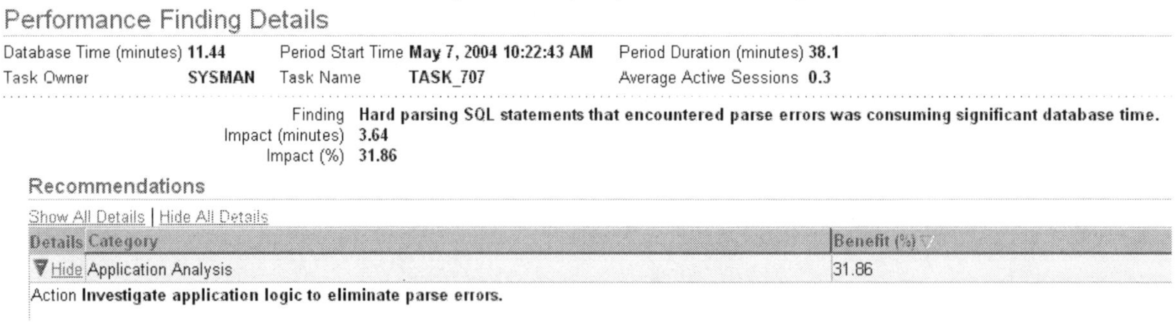

Figure 18.43: *The ADDM Recommendations for Excessive Hard Parses in the Library Cache*

Excessive hard parses occur when SQL is not reentrant. Non-reentrant code is sometimes associated with SQL that is never re-used because of the embedded literals values in the WHERE clause. If the library cache is clogged with SQL that is identical except for the literal values in the WHERE clause, using *cursor_sharing=force* replaces the literals with bind variables, making the SQL reusable and relieving the hard parsing problem.

The DBA must remember ADDM is not the only component that recommends changes. The SQL Tuning Advisor and the SQL Access Advisor also recommend changes to specific SQL statements. The following section presents a quick look at how OEM makes SQL tuning recommendations.

All these recommendations are stored in the SQL Access Advisor repository, a part of the Oracle database dictionary. The SQLA repository has many benefits such as being managed by the server and support of historical data.

Using the SQL Access Advisor through OEM

The following steps can be used to access the SQL Access Advisor through the Enterprise Manager. There are more details on the SQL Access Advisor later in this chapter.

The first step is to go to Advisor Central and click the SQL Access Advisor link as shown in Figure 18.44.

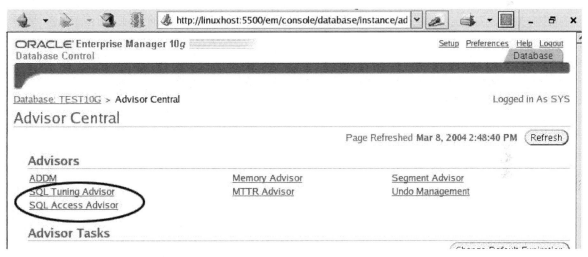

Figure 18.44: *SQL Access Advisor*

This starts the wizard. It then asks for workload source as shown in Figures 18.45 and 18.46.

Figure 18.45: *SQL Access Advisor – Workload Source (Top of Screen)*

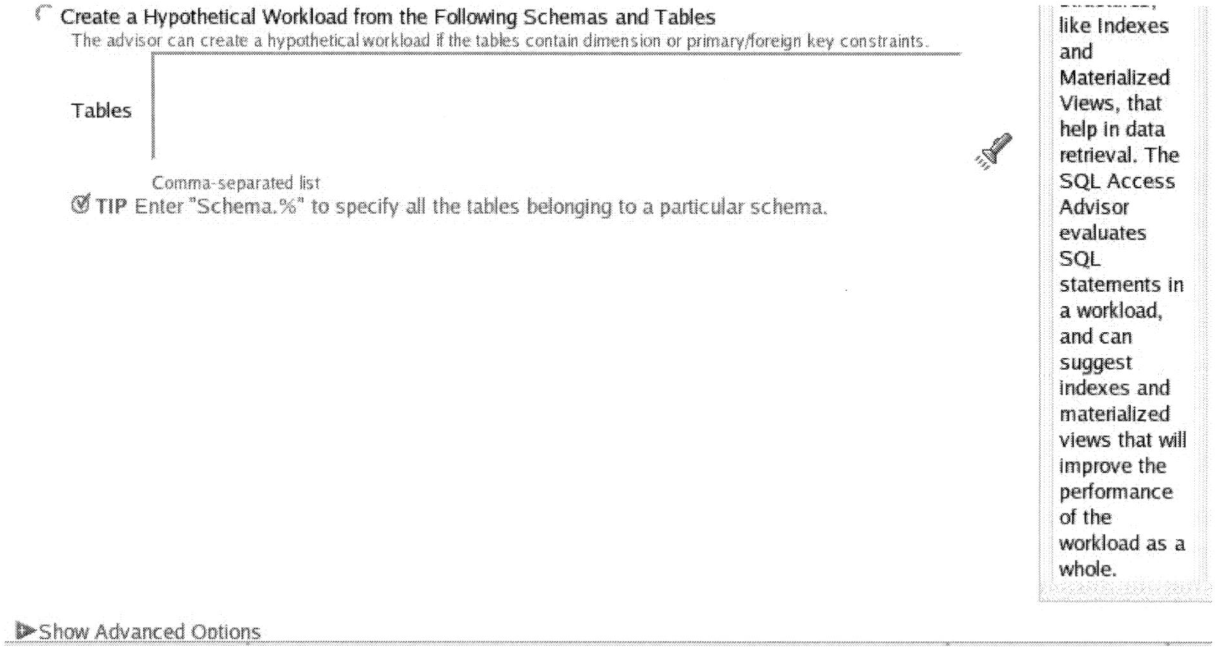

Figure 18.46: *SQL Access Advisor – Workload Source (Bottom of Screen)*

The Advisor should be selected to run in Comprehensive or Limited mode as shown in Figure 18.47.

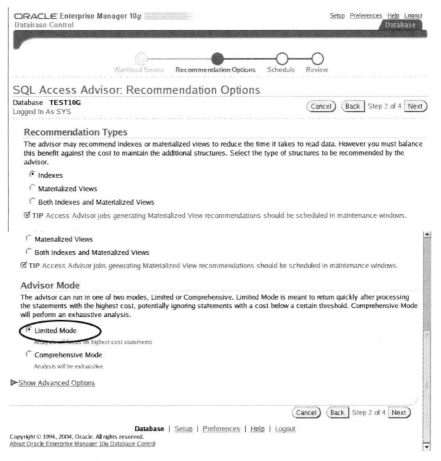

Figure 18.47: *SQL Access Advisor – Recommendation Options*

Clicking on Show Advanced Options shows the following screen represented in Figure 18.48.

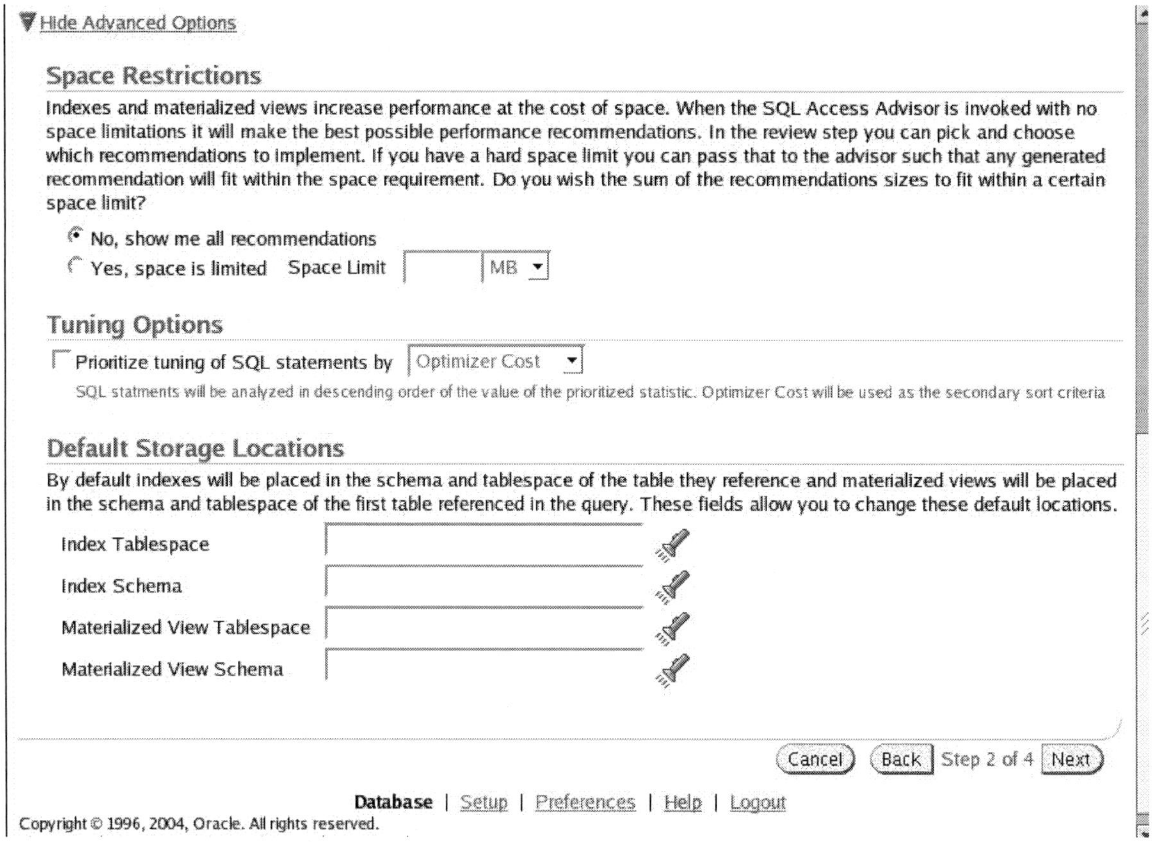

Figure 18.48: *SQL Access Advisor – Advanced Options*

The job should be scheduled and submitted as shown in Figures 18.49 and 18.50.

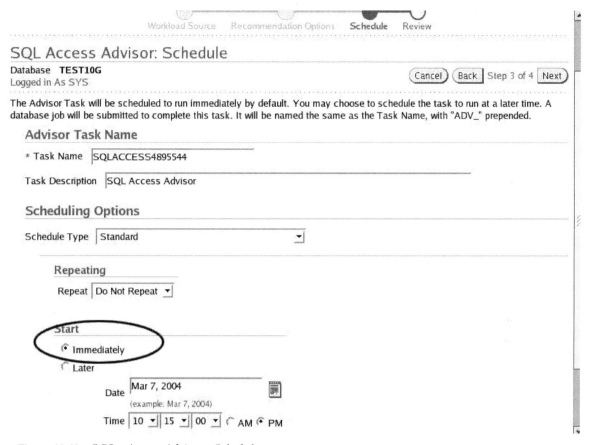

Figure 18.49: *SQL Access Advisor - Schedule*

Figure 18.50: *SQL Access Advisor - Review*

Results are available through the Advisor Central Page. Implement recommendations by clicking Schedule Implementation as shown in Figure 18.51.

Advisor Central

(i) Confirmation

Advisor Task created successfully: SQLACCESS4895544

Page Refreshed **Mar 7, 2004 10:22:51 PM** (Refresh)

Advisors

ADDM   Memory Advisor   Segment Advisor
SQL Tuning Advisor   MTTR Advisor   Undo Management
SQL Access Advisor

Advisor Tasks

(Change Default Expiration)

Search

Select an advisory type and optionally enter a task name to filter the data that is displayed in your results set.

Advisory Type   Task Name   Advisor Runs
[SQL Access Advisor ▼] [   ]   [All   ▼] (Go)

Results

(View Result) (Delete) Actions [Re-schedule ▼] (Go)

Select	Advisory Type	Name	Description	User	Status	Start Time ▽	End Time	Expires In (days)
⦿	SQL Access Advisor	SQLACCESS4895544	SQL Access Advisor	SYS	CREATED	Mar 7, 2004 10:22:50 PM		30

Figure 18.51: *Advisor Central - Results*

Understanding SQL Advisor Recommendations

The SQL Tuning Advisor and the SQL Access Advisor give specific recommendations regarding the best ways to tune the SQL execution. Figure 18.52 shows a sample screen from the SQL Access Advisor allowing the DBA to specify the types of SQL Access recommendations using indexes and materialized views.

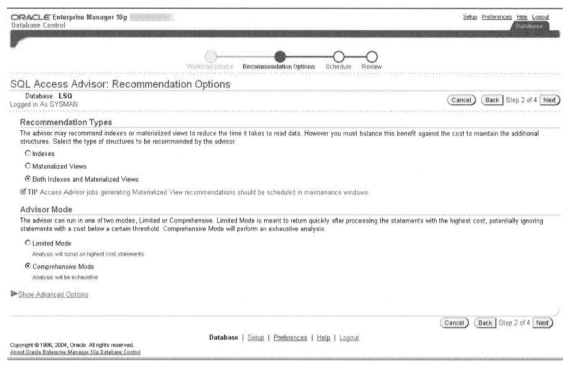

Figure 18.52: *Using the SQL Access Advisor*

The SQL Access Advisor allows the DBA to perform limited recommendations based on the top SQL or a comprehensive mode in which all-important SQL is analyzed.

This was a quick tour through the powerful new ADDM features of Oracle Enterprise Manager, and the main points of this section include:

- The Advisor Central screen displays time-series performance summaries, showing the top areas for performance recommendations from ADDM, the SQL Tuning Advisor, the SQL Access Advisor and the Memory Advisor.

- Using the time-series information stored in the AWR and ASH tables, the OEM advisory functions provide excellent insights into the root causes of transient Oracle tuning problems.

- The OEM Advisor utilities now collect performance information from the server, including the all-important CPU and I/O costs associated with each Oracle task.

- ADDM analyzes system-wide performance metrics. It also captures high-resource SQL and identifies those times when the database has exceeded pre-defined thresholds.

- ADDM will make intelligent recommendations regarding system-wide Oracle changes such as tablespace characteristics, sizes of the SGA pools, and changes to initialization parameters.

- ADDM is supplemented by the SQL Advisor utilities. The SQL Access Advisor makes specific recommendations about tuning opportunities, recommending new index and materialized views.

The SQL Tuning Advisor makes recommendations for specific SQL statements, using SQL profiles to alter the execution plans for specific SQL statements.

Now, it is time to explore the SQL advisory utilities and take a closer look at the operation of the SQL Access and SQL Tuning Advisors.

The SQL Tuning Advisor Links

At a high-level, the SQL Tuning Advisor samples historical SQL as captured in SQL Tuning Sets (STS) from the *dba_hist_sqlstat* and *dba_hist_sql_plan* views. The SQL Tuning Advisor can be launched from many places within Enterprise Manager:

- For high-load SQL statements identified by ADDM, SQL Tuning Advisor can be launched from the ADDM Finding Details screen.

- When selecting from the Top SQL statements, Advisor can be launched from the Top SQL Page.

- When the STS is the input for tuning, Advisor can be launched from the SQL Tuning Sets page.

The last input set for the SQL Tuning Advisor is user-input statements or the SQL Tuning Set. This could include untested SQL statements or a set of SQL statements currently under development. For tuning a set of SQL statements, a STS has to be constructed and stored, and fed to the SQL Tuning Advisor.

The OEM display screen for the SQL Tuning Advisor has the menu options shown in Figure 18.53.

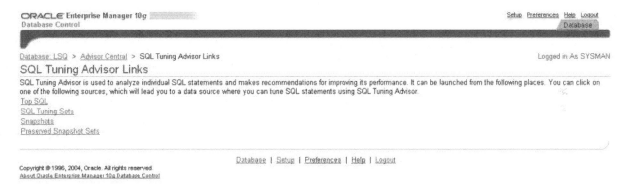

Figure 18.53: *The OEM SQL Tuning Advisor Links Screen*

While each of these is explained in detail later in this chapter, it is important to understand that this is the main anchor screen for the SQL Tuning advisory functions. For more sophisticated DBAs, Oracle provides the *dbms_sqltune* DBMS package as an interface to this powerful analytical tool.

This series of screens are arranged in a hierarchy of screens, showing each of the subscreens from the links screen shown in Figure 18.54.

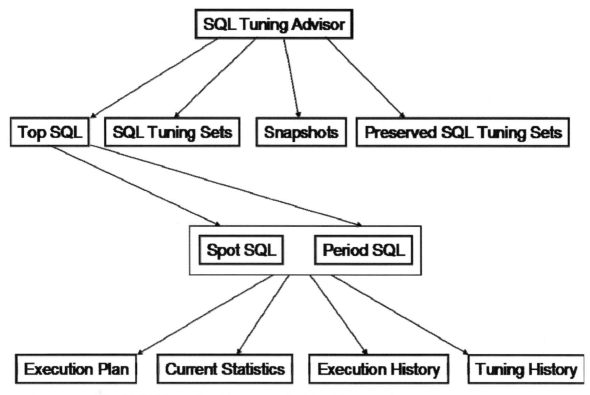

Figure 18.54: *The OEM Hierarchy of Screens for the SQL Tuning Advisor*

In addition to using Enterprise Manager, the SQL Tuning Advisor is obtained by using the PL/SQL package *dbms_sqltune*. This is a new package introduced in 10g, and it has comprehensive procedures that help to conduct the full SQL Advisor session. Some of the useful procedures include:

- *create_tuning_task*: This procedure creates a tuning task for a given SQL statement or for a cached cursor.

- *execute_tuning_task*: This procedure executes the tuning task and generates the tuning data.

- *report_tuning_task*: This procedure generates a complete report of the results of a task.

- *report_plans*: This procedure shows the SQL plans.

Most Oracle professionals find the Enterprise Manager interface far easier to use than the *dbms_sqltune* package. Therefore, a closer look at these SQL tuning functions is in order. The OEM SQL Tuning Advisor execution plan display is shown in Figure 18.55. From the top-level of the SQL Tuning Advisor screen, hyperlinks to the following OEM areas are shown:

- Top SQL: This OEM screen displays the most resource intensive SQL for any time period that is specified. As the time period changes, the top SQL is displayed along with the percentage of total elapsed time used by the statement, the CPU time consumed, the total wait time for the SQL and the average elapsed time per execution.

- SQL Tuning Sets (STS): SQL Tuning Sets are encapsulations of SQL statements. They contain the source for the SQL statement, the host variables used during historical execution, and performance metrics, and they allow a complete environment for testing the efficiency of a single SQL statement over time.

- Snapshots: SQL Snapshots are taken every hour and can be manipulated manually with the new *dbms_workload_repository* package.

- Preserved Snapshot Sets: A snapshot set, also known as a baseline, is a collection of multiple AWR snapshots. The preserved snapshot sets are then used to compare workload performance over specific periods.

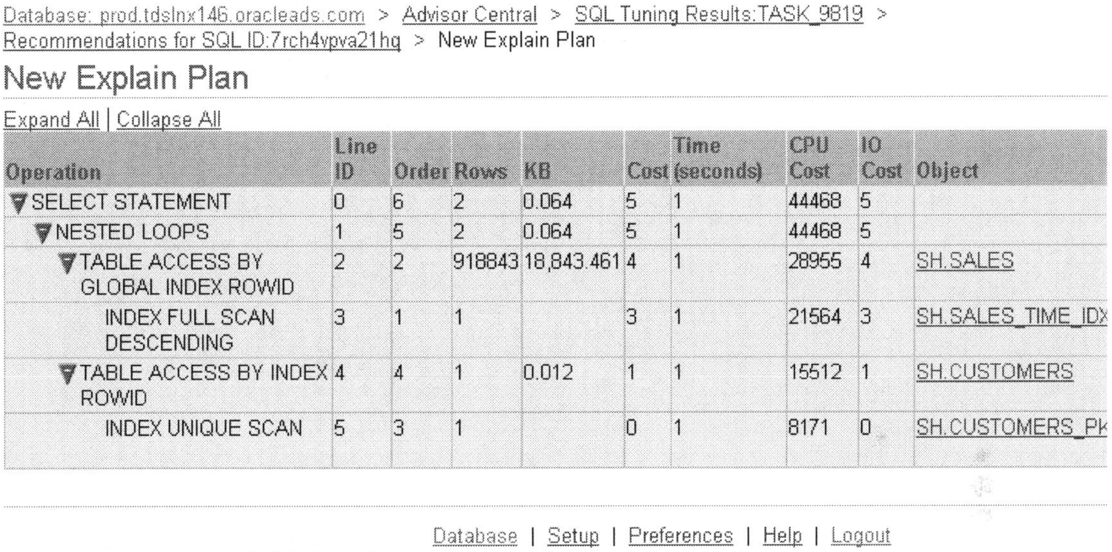

Database: prod.tdslnx146.oracleads.com > Advisor Central > SQL Tuning Results:TASK_9819 >
Recommendations for SQL ID:7rch4vpva21hq > New Explain Plan

New Explain Plan

Expand All | Collapse All

Operation	Line ID	Order	Rows	KB	Cost	Time (seconds)	CPU Cost	IO Cost	Object
▼SELECT STATEMENT	0	6	2	0.064	5	1	44468	5	
▼NESTED LOOPS	1	5	2	0.064	5	1	44468	5	
▼TABLE ACCESS BY GLOBAL INDEX ROWID	2	2	918843	18,843.461	4	1	28955	4	SH.SALES
INDEX FULL SCAN DESCENDING	3	1	1		3	1	21564	3	SH.SALES_TIME_IDX
▼TABLE ACCESS BY INDEX ROWID	4	4	1	0.012	1	1	15512	1	SH.CUSTOMERS
INDEX UNIQUE SCAN	5	3	1		0	1	8171	0	SH.CUSTOMERS_PK

Database | Setup | Preferences | Help | Logout

Figure 18.55: *New OEM SQL Tuning Advisor Explain Plan Display*

Drilling down into the top SQL areas shows how it captures the most resource-intensive SQL, allowing the DBA to explore the exact conditions leading to any Oracle performance bottleneck.

The Top SQL Screen

The Top SQL screen has two tabs, one for Period SQL and another for Spot SQL as shown in Figure 18.56. If the period tab is clicked, OEM presents a sliding time-series window so that the DBA can examine the top SQL over time right next to a time-based summary of active session information.

Do not rely on automation!

While the SQL Tuning Advisors are great for beginners, remember that they can never replace the intuition of a human SQL tuning expert.

The active session histogram allows the DBA to quickly zero in on the time period of interest, based on total waits, CPU or I/O during that period. This active session history data is stored inside the *dba_hist_active_session_history*, *dba_hist_waitclassmet_history* and *dba_hist_waitstat* views, so it is easy for Enterprise Manager to display the totals for these values in a colorful, easy-to-read fashion.

As the DBA moves the sliding right-hand bar, different sets of top SQL appear. The SQL for these statements are stored in the *dba_hist_sqltext*, *dba_hist_sql_plan* and *dba_hist_sqlstat* views, so it is easy for Enterprise Manager to access and display the top SQL as adjustments are made to the slide bar on the top SQL screen.

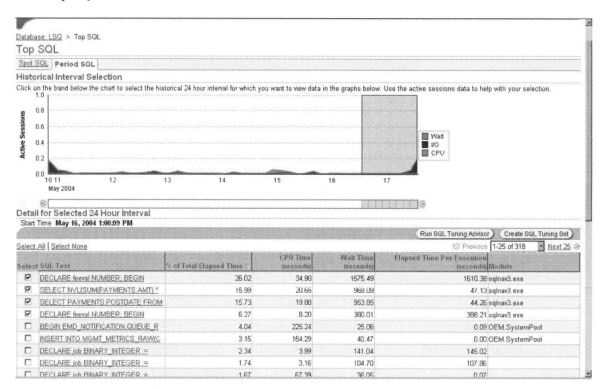

Figure 18.56: *The Period SQL Screen Showing Top SQL and Active Session Information*

The following section presents the details for the Top SQL statements.

Viewing SQL Details in OEM

When the DBA clicks on any of the SQL statements, the SQL details screen, represented in Figure 18.57, is shown. The SQL detail screen reveals the source for the SQL statement plus the following informational tabs:

- **Execution plan:** This displays the execution plan details including server CPU and I/O costs for each execution phase. It also includes hyperlinks to table details.

- **Current statistics:** This shows important details for the execution statistics for the SQL statement during a specified time, including the number of executions, average response time and CPU resources consumed.

- **Execution history:** This screen shows a graphical depiction of the SQL statement over time, plotting the average CPU and response time for the SQL statement.

- **Tuning history:** This shows the historical SQL advisor tuning set tasks for the SQL statement.

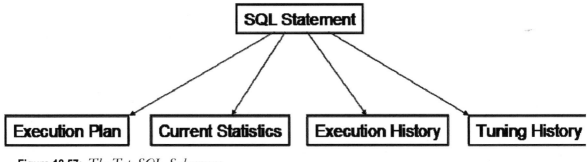

Figure 18.57: *The Top SQL Subscreens*

The tour begins with a look at the Execution Plan details tab.

The Execution Plan Tab

The details in the execution plan have been greatly enhanced from previous releases of Oracle. This fantastic execution plan display shows the RAM used by each step, the computed cost for each step and best of all, the external server details including the CPU and I/O costs for each phase of the SQL statement as shown in Figure 18.58.

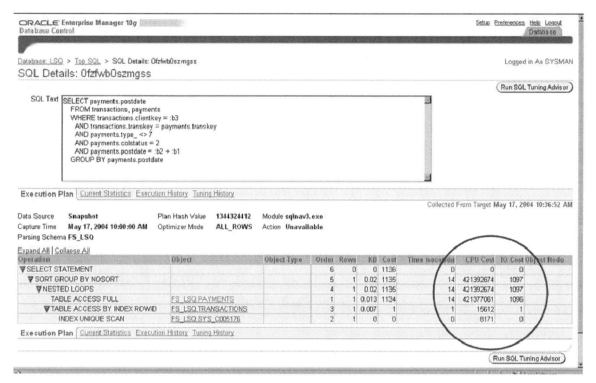

Figure 18.58: *SQL Details with Execution Plans and External Server CPU and I/O Costs*

Due to falling RAM prices, Solid State Disk (SSD) and the ability of 64-bit architectures to support huge data caches, many Oracle databases have shifted from being I/O-bound to being CPU-bound. Rather than focusing on the minimization of physical disk I/O, Oracle tuning often focuses on the reduction of logical I/Os (consistent gets), often by tuning the SQL to reduce buffer touches and by addressing specific task wait events using the use ASH views.

Of course, Oracle has recognized this shifting bottleneck as evidenced by the new CPU and I/O costing for SQL statements execution steps in Oracle. The table names for each table in the execution plan can be accessed to view details regarding the table column structure. The execution plan is only one of the areas in the detail display. To view more details, click on the Current Statistics.

Current Statistics Tab

The Current Statistics, shown in Figure 18.59, for the SQL statement are amazing. Unlike any earlier releases of Oracle, all resource components of the SQL can be seen, including important performance information from the *dba_hist_sys_time_model* view:

- Elapsed time to execute: This includes all response time components including network time.

- CPU per execution: This is the average CPU consumption per execution of the statement.

- Wait ratio: This is a ration measuring the amount of wait events for the SQL statement.

- Sharable memory: This shows the real RAM usage of the SQL for hash joins or sorting.

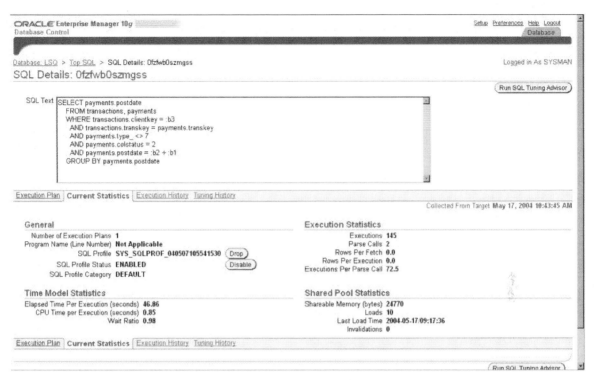

Figure 18.59: *Current Statistics for Historical SQL Execution*

Viewing this screen reveals important tuning information including the SQL profile name, the number of executions, the average elapsed time per execution, average CPU time per execution, and the average number of rows returned by the SQL. This data gives important insights into the areas for tuning improvement for the SQL.

For even more details, the DBA can use the Execution History tab.

Execution History Tab

The Execution History tab presents an easy-to-read display of the historical behavior of the SQL statement as shown in Figure 18.60. This is especially important to visualize changes to SQL performance after a database change, such as a new index or adding a materialized view.

The display shows the average CPU and elapsed time per hour, and a radio button allows the DBA to choose between displaying the total CPU and elapsed execution time, in seconds, or the average CPU and execution time per execution.

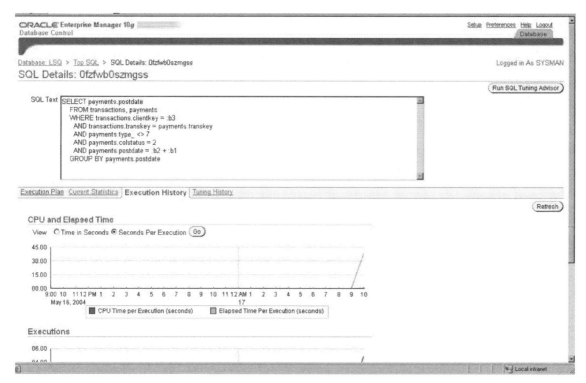

Figure 18.60: *Viewing Historical SQL Execution Details*

This screen also plots the number of executions over time so that those times when the SQL statement has the most impact on overall database performance can be viewed. Next, a look at the Tuning History tab is merited.

Tuning History Tab

The Tuning History screen shows a list of all previous advisor tasks and shows hyperlinks to the recommendations from both the SQL Tuning Advisor and the SQL Access Advisor as shown in Figure 18.61.

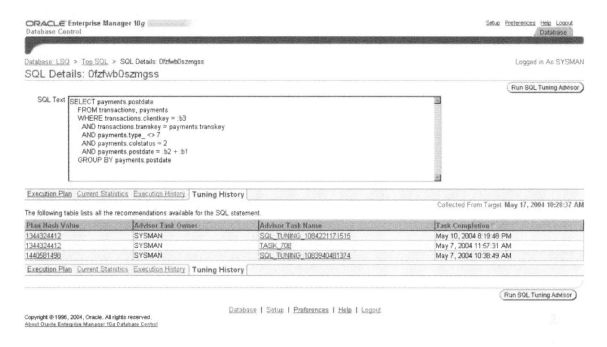

Figure 18.61: *Viewing Historical SQL Tuning Recommendations*

SQL workload tasks can be created to receive recommendations. However, as shown in the SQL Tuning History screen, SQL Tuning Advisor tasks are present and these are quite different from the SQL Tuning Advisor.

The SQL Tuning Advisor specifies the groupings of related SQL into SQL Tuning Sets, allowing Oracle to analyze them and to create SQL profiles that contain specific tuning recommendations for each statement. The following section presents a closer look at SQL Tuning Sets.

Oracle SQL Tuning Sets

STSs are different from SQL Advisor tasks in several areas. While a SQL Access Advisor task analyzes for missing index and materialized views, the SQL Tuning Advisor focuses on tuning the individual SQL by recommending changes to the execution plan via SQL Profiles.

The Oracle documentation describes the components of a STS as the following:

- A set of SQL statements

- Associated execution context such as user schema, application module name and action, list of bind values, and the cursor compilation environment

- Associated basic execution statistics such as elapsed time, CPU time, buffer gets, disk reads, rows processed, cursor fetches, the number of executions, the number of complete executions, optimizer cost, and the command type

All together, a STS encapsulates a set of SQL statements and generates SQL profiles that allow implementation of any recommended changes to the SQL execution plan. The following section shows how to create a STS.

Creating a SQL Tuning Set

A STS is usually created from the Top SQL screen by clicking the Create SQL Tuning Set hyperlink. This procedure presents a subscreen that provides a name and description for the set and includes all of the SQL from the Top SQL screen as shown in Figure 18.62.

Essentially, a STS is a named set of SQL statements with their associated execution context and basic execution statistics.

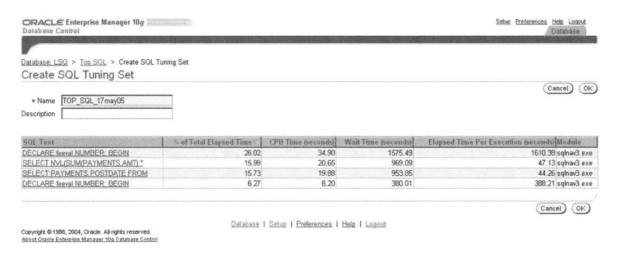

Figure 18.62: *Creating a SQL Tuning Set*

Once created, the SQL Tuning Advisor allows the DBA to schedule executions of the STS and view the specific recommendations from each execution. The following section explains how to view STS details.

Viewing SQL Tuning Set Details

Individual STSs are viewed by clicking on the Advisor Task name in the previous screen. Doing this presents a screen that displays a list of all SQL inside the STS as shown in Figure 18.63.

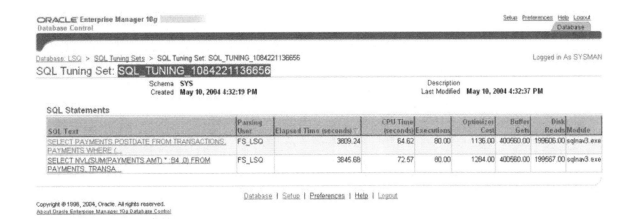

Database: LSQ > SQL Tuning Sets > SQL Tuning Set: SQL_TUNING_1084221136656

Logged in As SYSMAN

SQL Tuning Set: SQL_TUNING_1084221136656

Schema SYS
Created May 10, 2004 4:32:19 PM

Description
Last Modified May 10, 2004 4:32:37 PM

SQL Statements

SQL Text	Parsing User	Elapsed Time (seconds)	CPU Time (seconds)	Executions	Optimizer Cost	Buffer Gets	Disk Reads	Module
SELECT PAYMENTS.POSTDATE FROM TRANSACTIONS, PAYMENTS WHERE (...	FS_LSQ	3809.24	64.62	80.00	1136.00	400560.00	199606.00	sqlnav3.exe
SELECT NVL(SUM(PAYMENTS.AMT) * .84 ,0) FROM PAYMENTS, TRANSA...	FS_LSQ	3845.68	72.57	80.00	1264.00	400560.00	199567.00	sqlnav3.exe

Database | Setup | Preferences | Help | Logout

Figure 18.63: *Viewing SQL Inside a SQL Tuning Set*

This figure shows the details for the execution of a STS and the important execution metrics including the total elapsed time, total CPU time, and total optimizer costs as well as the number of logical I/Os (consistent gets) and total disk reads. This information is used as input to the SQL Profiles. A quick review of the SQL Tuning Advisor functionality is explained in the following section.

Using the SQL Access Advisor

The previous section explained how ADDM makes specific system-wide recommendations. An exploration of the SQL Access Advisor will reveal how it makes systemwide SQL recommendations relating to SQL execution.

Figure 18.64 below shows the distinctions between the tools from the Advisor Central.

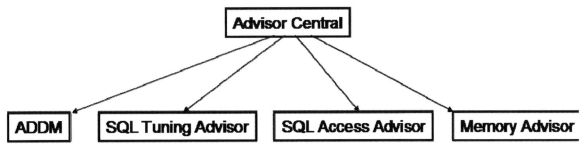

Figure 18.64: *The Advisor Central Performance Functional Areas*

It is important to understand the differences between these OEM advisor tools. The SQL Access Advisor makes global SQL tuning recommendations based on the workload that is specified. These global recommendations may include the creation of new indexes to remove unnecessary large-table full-table scans and the creation of materialized views to pre-aggregate summaries and pre-join highly normalized tables.

The SQL Access Advisor makes global recommendations on a workload while the SQL Tuning Advisor makes specific recommendations. The next section explores the important new features of the SQL advisors, and shows a real-world session with the SQL Access Advisor.

New Features of the SQL Advisors

While there are many important enhancements in Oracle 10g, the most important one is the integration and the at-your-fingertips access to all components of the task response time. The most important new features of the Oracle Enterprise Manager include:

- Server metrics: This exciting feature is the ability of Oracle to step out of the database areas and sample the server resources associated with every database operations.

- Integration: The OEM allows the DBA to easily see all aspects of performance to relieve the tedium of running scripts and executing specialized routines.

The server metrics are especially important for SQL tuning because of the server resources associated with every step within the execution plan for every SQL statement as shown in Figure 18.65.

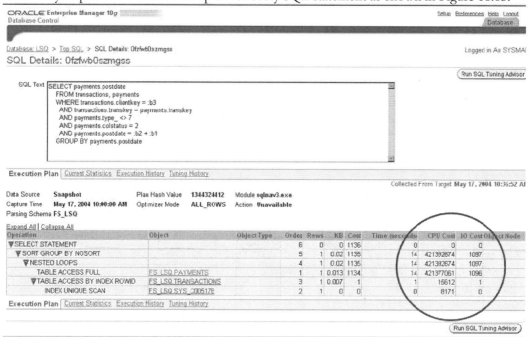

Figure 18.65: *SQL Details with External Server CPU and I/O Costs*

For any SQL statements, the components are displayed with hyperlinks for easy access.

By clicking on a table name in the execution plan in Figure 18.65, a detailed column representation of any table in the SQL query is easily viewed as shown in Figure 18.66.

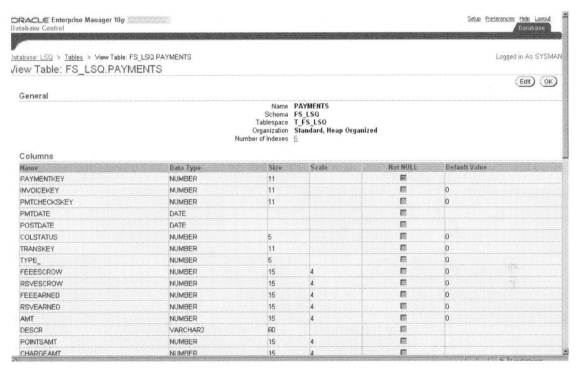

Figure 18.66: *Viewing Table Details in OEM*

This information includes the table description, the schema, and the tablespace and table organization method.

Now that the more important new features of the SQL advisors have been revealed, the following section shows how the SQL Access Advisor allows the DBA to make global changes that affect SQL execution.

Inside the SQL Access Advisor

The SQL Access Advisor allows the scheduling of system-wide SQL performance analysis and makes global recommendations to improve performance. Unlike the SQL Tuning Advisor, which only tunes a single SQL statement, the SQL Access Advisor recommends changes that might improve the performance of hundreds of SQL statements.

Using the SQL Access Advisor requires the following steps:

- Workload definition: This step allows the DBA to define the set of SQL statements to be used for the session.

- Definition options: This step allows the DBA to choose the scope of the analysis (indexes, materialized views, or both) and the type of analysis (limited or comprehensive).

- Schedule Advisor: This step allows the DBA to schedule an analysis of the high-resource SQL defined in the workload.

- Review recommendations: This step allows the DBA to see the recommendations and the justification for the recommendations.

The following section presents a closer look at each step of the process.

The SQL Access Advisor Workload Definition

The OEM workload screen allows the DBA to create a new workload or use a previously captured workload as shown in Figure 18.67. The source for the workload can be selected from the following four options:

- Use current and recent SQL activity: This option uses the *dba_hist_sqlstat*, *dba_hist_sqltext* and *dba_hist_sql_plan* views to collect and analyze SQL statements.

- Import a workload: This option is a pre-defined workload that has been stored in the new Oracle SQL repository.

- User-defined workload: This advanced feature allows the manual capture of SQL using a CTAS command and the result table as a workload. For example, here a *my_workload* table is created using personal criteria:

```
CREATE TABLE MY_WORKLOAD AS
SELECT
   sql_text,
   username
FROM
   dba_advisor_sqla_wk_stmts
WHERE
   executions > 400
and
   buffer_gets > 10000;
```

- Hypothetical workload: This advanced feature allows a comma-delimited list of tables to be entered and all SQL using these tables are included in the workload.

Figure 18.67: *The SQL Access Advisor Workload Source Definition Screen*

Once the workload is defined, the recommendation options can then be chosen.

The SQL Access Advisor Recommendation Options

The Recommendations Options screen in Figure 18.68 has two sections: the scope of the analysis and the type of analysis. This screen allows the workload to be analyzed for missing indexes and materialized view opportunities:

- Missing indexes: Indexes, especially function-based indexes, can greatly reduce the amount of logical I/O required for an SQL statement to retrieve its result set.

- Materialized views: If the target tables are not constantly changing, materialized views can be used to pre-join tables together or pre-summarize aggregate information. Materialized views can result in huge SQL performance improvements.

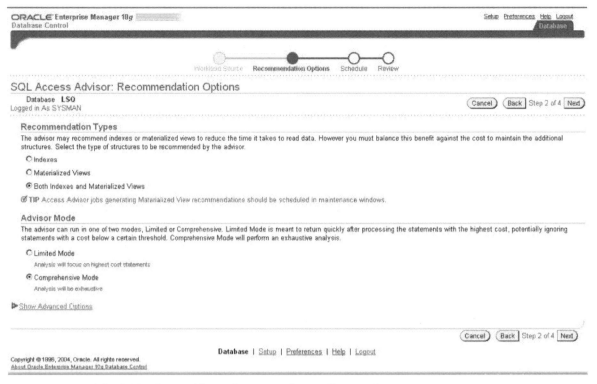

Figure 18.68: *The SQL Access Advisor Recommendations Options Screen*

The scope of the analysis can be limited, meaning that the SQL Access Advisor takes a quick look at the SQL and does not create SQL profiles; or comprehensive, meaning that detailed analysis is conducted and SQL profiles are created for the top SQL statements. Both the limited and comprehensive modes conduct the following activities against all SQL statements in the workload:

- **SQL access:** The SQL WHERE clause is interrogated and compared to the execution plan for each SQL statement to verify that the most efficient indexes are being used. If this step detects a missing index, it will be presented in the recommendations.

- **Statistics:** The statistics for all objects involved in each query are verified for quality and completeness.

- **Query structure:** The structure of the SQL statement is checked to ensure the optimal syntax format of the query. Because SQL is a declarative language, a query can be formulated in many ways to achieve the same result, some more efficient than others.

The SQL Profiles can then be used by the SQL Tuning Advisor.

The SQL Access Advisor Schedule Advisor

The Schedule Advisor screen allows the DBA to schedule an analytical session as shown in Figure 18.69. This screen allows the DBA to control every aspect of the analysis and provides intelligent recommendations for system-wide SQL tuning, including a justification for each recommendation.

Figure 18.69: *The SQL Access Advisor Scheduling Options*

When an analytical schedule is created, the following metrics are specified:

- **The name for the advisor session:** By specifying the name for the advisor session, multiple sessions are created and scheduled, each customized according to the type of database processing occurring at the specified time.

- **Scope:** The scope radio button allows the DBA to choose a limited analysis that only spends one wall-clock second on each SQL statement of the comprehensive option that analyzes each SQL statement and creates SQL profiles for all high-resource statements.

- **Schedule:** The scheduler option interfaces with the scheduler, using the *dbms_scheduler* package, to allow for a scheduled execution, or an immediate execution of a tuning session can be chosen.

The final pre-processing step in this process is a review of the previous definitions.

The SQL Access Advisor Review

The final consolidation of the workload, options and scheduling screen is now displayed in Figure 18.70. This figure shows a summary of all the previous screens and presents the opportunity to make changes before running the tuning task.

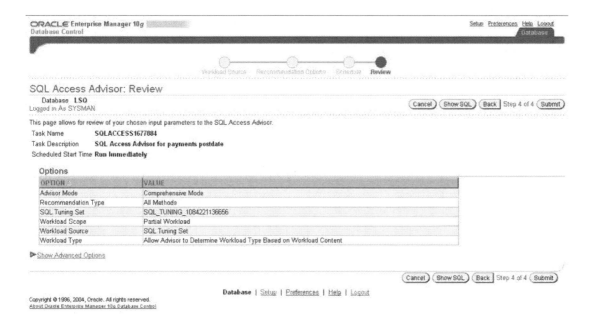

Figure 18.70: *The SQL Access Advisor Session Review Screen*

Now that the workload is specified, the type and scope of the analysis that scheduled the execution is chosen and the plan reviewed, the output from the SQL Access Advisor session is now ready for examination.

SQL Access Advisor Recommendations

The output of a SQL Access Advisor session is detailed in the Recommendations screen as shown in Figure 18.71.

Figure 18.71: *The SQL Access Advisor Recommendations Screen*

This screen makes specific recommendations for the creation of indexes and materialized views. It includes the definitions for these new database entities.

The creation of a new index or materialized view may immediately cause thousands of SQL statements to change their execution plans, so special care is required before implementing the recommendations in a production environment.

This section has been a quick review of the SQL Access Advisor to show how it relates to the Enterprise Manager Advisor Central screen and how the SQL Access Advisor makes recommendations about an entire pre-defined workload. The main points in this section were:

- The SQL Access Advisor allows the DBA to gather global recommendations for a workload. The SQL Tuning Advisor is more granular, tuning a single statement.

- The DBA defines the SQL used in the SQL Access Advisor task, and can choose current SQL, a user-defined set of SQL, a historical workload, or a hypothetical workload.

- A hypothetical workload is very useful because the DBA need only specify the tables that participate in the queries, and the SQL Access Advisor gathers the appropriate SQL statements to create the workload.

- The main functions of the SQL Access Advisor is to recommend missing indexes and materialized views, but a comprehensive task analysis will also create SQL Profiles that can be used within the SQL Tuning advisor.

The following section presents the most powerful and intelligent of all of the OEM advisory utilities, the Memory Advisors.

Inside the SQL Access Advisor **1087**

Using the Memory Advisor through OEM

The Memory Advisor can be used only when the Automatic Memory Management (AMM) feature is disabled. The Memory Advisor has three advisors that give recommendations on: the Shared Pool in the SGA, the Buffer Cache in the SGA, and the PGA.

The following steps can be used to access the Memory Advisor and tune its underlying structures.

The first step is to click on the Memory Advisor in the Advisor Central Page.

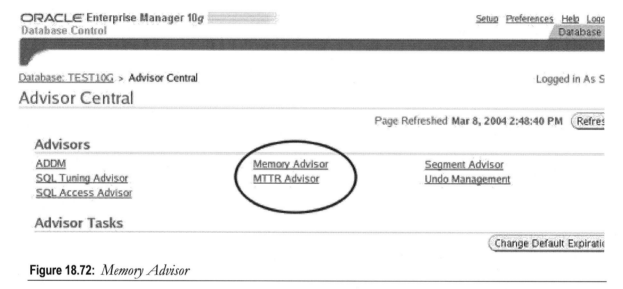

Figure 18.72: *Memory Advisor*

The Memory Parameters: SGA page will appear as shown in Figure 18.73. This page has all the details on memory usage for the SGA. The Shared Pool and the Buffer Cache are part of the SGA. Help can be clicked for more information on the structure shown here.

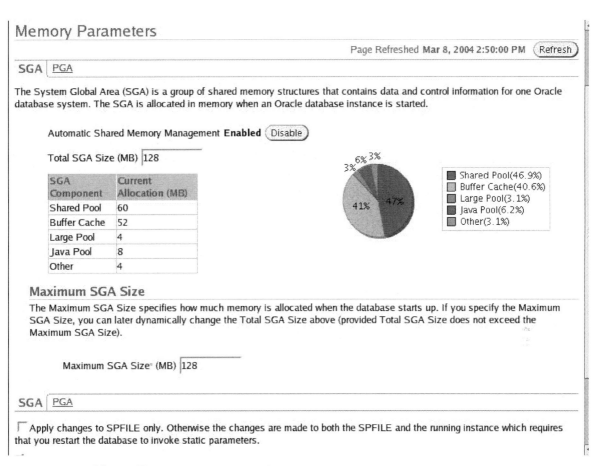

Figure 18.73: *Memory Parameters*

The Automatic Shared Memory Management has to be disabled to run the advisor. To accomplish this, the Shared Pool or the Buffer Cache should be chosen and the Advice link next to it should be clicked.

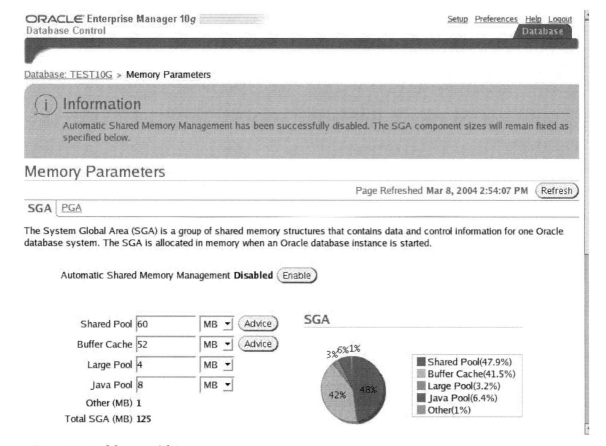

Figure 18.74: *Memory Advice*

The corresponding graphs appear as shown in Figures 18.75 and 18.76.

For Shared Pool size, the graph reveals that a shared pool size larger than 60 MB will not improve the performance much. So the recommended optimal shared pool size is 60 MB.

Shared Pool Size Advice

Shared Pool Size (MB) [60]

☑ TIP You can click on the curve in the graph to set new value.

Figure 18.75: *Memory Advice – Shared Pool Size*

Buffer Cache Size Advice

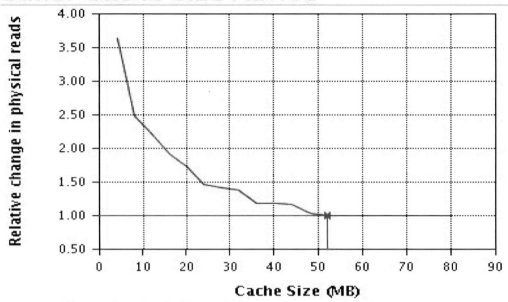

■ Change in physical reads for various cache sizes
✖ Current cache size

Cache Size (MB) | 52

☑ TIP You can click on the curve in the graph to set new value.

(Cancel) (OK)

Figure 18.76: *Memory Advice – Buffer Cache Size*

For Buffer Cache, the graph reveals that a buffer cache size larger than 52MB does not improve the performance as much as in Shared Pool. A bigger cache prompts less disk reads and improves the performance.

The PGA Advisor is run by clicking on the PGA property page. This is similar to running the SGA advisors. The cache hit percentage is plotted against memory size. Higher hit ratios in the range of 75% to 100% indicate better cache performance.

Memory Parameters

SGA | PGA

The Program Global Area (PGA) is a memory buffer that contains data and control information for a server process. A PGA is created by Oracle when a server process is started.

Aggregate PGA Target `38` `MB ▾` (Advice)

Current PGA Allocated (KB) **68178**

Maximum PGA Allocated (KB) **68946**

(since startup)

Cache Hit Percentage (%) **100**

(PGA Memory Usage Details)

☑ TIP The sum of PGA and SGA should be less than the total system memory minus memory required by the operating system and other applications.

SGA | PGA

☐ Apply changes to SPFILE only. Otherwise the changes are made to both the SPFILE and the running instance which requires that you restart the database to invoke static parameters.

☑ TIP * indicates controls, if changed, must restart database to invoke.

(Show SQL) (Revert) (Apply)

Database | Setup | Preferences | Help | Logout

Figure 18.77: *PGA Memory Parameters*

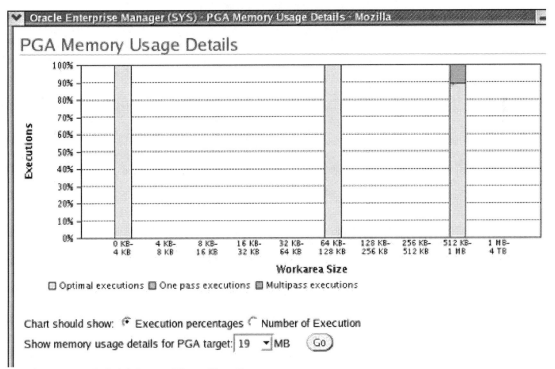

Figure 18.78: *PGA Memory Usage Details*

Using the Memory Advisor through OEM

1093

Persistence of Automatically Tuned Values

If the server parameter file (*spfile*) for the Oracle database is used, it will remember the sizes of the automatically tuned components across instance shutdowns. This allows Oracle to learn the characteristics of the workload each time an instance is started. It can start with the information from the last instance shutdown and continue evaluating the new workload.

Automated Maintenance Tasks

Oracle Database 10g is designed to handle routine maintenance tasks and schedule them at certain times of the day or week when the system load is low. For the designated time period, the use of a resource plan to control resource consumption of these tasks can be utilized. When the time elapses, the database can switch to a different resource plan with lower resource allocation.

Resource Management

Oracle Database 10g makes use of resource plans for different tasks. At the time of database installation, a Resource Manager consumer group called *auto_task_consumer_group* is pre-defined. Similarly, a Scheduler job class, *auto_tasks_job_class*, is also defined based on this consumer group. *gather_stats_job* is defined to run in the *auto_task_job_class* job class.

OEM has made quantum leaps in assisting the Oracle professional with creating an automated monitoring and performance display facility. The main points of this section include:

- OEM interfaces with the AWR to allow for the intelligent display of important performance metrics.

- The OEM performance screens are design in an intuitive top-down fashion and require little training to use.

- The DBA can create customized exception reporting mechanisms allowing OEM to send a notification in time to correct an issue before it causes a performance problem.

- The ASH component of AWR allows the DBA to view detailed Oracle session information within OEM.

The next section will present information on Oracle tuning tools.

Introduction to Online Oracle Tuning Tools

Historically, Oracle tuning professionals used SQL*Plus scripts, and many Oracle gurus wonder if any vendor will design a GUI that makes sense to the Oracle tuning DBA. Tuning Oracle is all about locating and fixing bottlenecks, and most DBAs pull out their native scripts rather than try to navigate their way through a convoluted interface.

Many DBAs will purchase a script collection such as the one at www.oracle-script.com. Oracle tuning experts are always skeptical of GUI tools that claim to assist with Oracle tuning, usually because the tool does not give them what they want to see.

For example, most Oracle tuning experts love the Automated Session History (ASH) cluster and the new ability to perform time-series tuning. The proliferation of third party tools, such as TOAD and Ion that were developed to compete with the OEM, speaks for itself; however, many Oracle professionals desire a time series tool that would allow them to do advanced trending and predictive analysis. It appears that these new self-collecting ASH GUI tools may be the wave of the future.

This chapter provides an overview of how popular third-party Oracle tuning tools might assist in Oracle tuning efforts.

- **Oracle dictionary scripts and tools:** The review will include a look at the Burleson Consulting Script collection from www.oracle-script.com.

- **Trend-based tools:** The review of trend-based tools will provide a quick look at Ion for Oracle because it is the only tool outside OEM that will plot time series data from the AWR and ASH. It has capabilities that are more advanced than OEM because it allows users to view Oracle trends by day of the week and hour of the day. The Ion Enterprise Edition also allows the same interface to Oracle 8i and Oracle 9i databases.

- **Wait event tuning tools:** There are several online tools that focus on a wait event tuning methodology. The DBFlash product by Confio software was chosen for this review because it is built around a wait event tuning framework.

The following section provides a review of custom Oracle dictionary scripts.

Using Custom Scripts for Oracle Tuning

In the real world, most Oracle experts use custom data dictionary scripts to investigate Oracle performance problems. One of the reasons that third-party tools cannot replace native scripts is that the Oracle data dictionary is very sophisticated, and there are hundreds of thousands of ways that Oracle metrics can be combined and displayed.

Oracle tuning scripts can also be very sophisticated in structure, especially when performing advanced tuning activities such as hypothesis testing and multivariate analysis. Even simple tasks can be far too complex for a GUI tool. For example, this simple script to display full-table scans would be nearly impossible to build from a GUI menu:

```
SELECT
   to_char(sn.end_interval_time,'mm/dd/rr hh24') time,
   p.owner,
   p.name,
   t.num_rows,
   decode(t.buffer_pool,'KEEP','Y','DEFAULT','N') K,
   s.blocks blocks,
   sum(a.executions_delta) nbr_FTS
FROM
   dba_tables    t,
   dba_segments s,
   dba_hist_sqlstat    a,
   dba_hist_snapshot sn,
   (select distinct
     pl.sql_id,
     object_owner owner,
     object_name name
   FROM
```

```
      dba_hist_sql_plan pl
   WHERE
      operation = 'TABLE ACCESS'
      and
      options = 'FULL') p
WHERE
   a.snap_id = sn.snap_id
   and
   a.sql_id = p.sql_id
   and
   t.owner = s.owner
   and
   t.table_name = s.segment_name
   and
   t.table_name = p.name
   and
   t.owner = p.owner
   and
   t.owner not in ('SYS','SYSTEM')
HAVING
   sum(a.executions_delta) > 1
GROUP BY
   to_char(sn.end_interval_time,'mm/dd/rr hh24'),p.owner, p.name, t.num_rows, t.cache,
t.buffer_pool, s.blocks
ORDER BY
   1 asc;
```

Native Oracle dictionary scripts also allow information to be displayed in novel ways and the creation of easy exception reports. To confound matters, every release of Oracle has changes to the underlying *x$* tables and *v$* views, and new scripts may need to be created for Oracle 9i and beyond.

With hundreds of thousands of possible tuning queries, how does the DBA manage to find the best possible solution? Most professional Oracle tuning professionals build collections of their top 500 scripts and organize them so that they can find the right script for desired outcome.

One extremely popular script collection is the BC collection available at www.oracle-script.com. This collection is organized with precise naming conventions to clue the DBA in the functions of each script. Within each script, all possible column values are displayed and the DBA can comment out those that they are not interested in observing.

To a knowledgeable DBA, finding the right script is simple. For example, to find all scripts referencing physical disk reads, the following *grep* command can be issued:

```
grep -i "physical reads" *.sql
```

Most hardcore Oracle tuning professionals do not like being forced to tune within the confines of the tool, and they enjoy the flexibility of being able to get any metric that they want. The exception to this rule is graphing time series data. For visual plotting, many Oracle DBAs cut and paste output data into MS Excel spreadsheets. The visualization of this data is one area where a third-party tool can assist the DBA.

Shortcomings of OEM

The OEM product is designed to be a comprehensive web-based interface for the DBA. In an attempt to do everything, it loses the direct focus and exception identification. For example, the top-level OEM screen is shown in Figure 18.79.

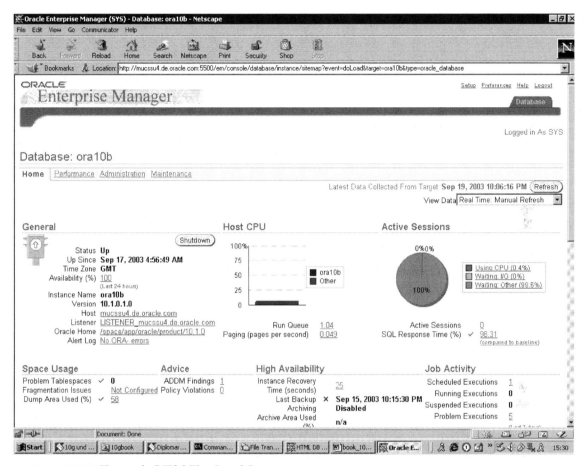

Figure 18.79: *Example OEM Top Level Screen*

This OEM screen is not focused directly on performance management. Rather, it is focused on the entire database, or databases, being monitored and their overall status. The user of OEM is presented with a sometimes bewildering array of options.

Another issue with OEM is that while the screen shows the ADDM findings and allows the user to view them as shown in Figure 18.80, the user must buy the additional license, or they could be found in default of their Oracle license agreement!

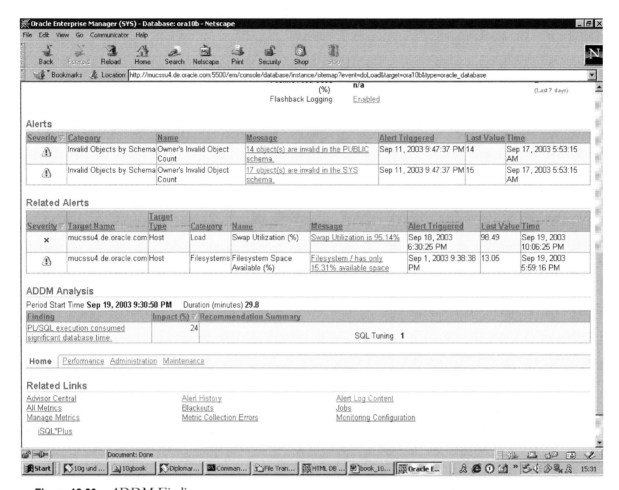

Figure 18.80: *ADDM Findings*

The OEM user must then drill down into the SQL analysis package, schedule an analysis job, wait for the analysis job to complete, then look at the analysis results and decide what, if any, recommendations to pursue. Oracle also cautions users that doing too detailed an analysis using the SQL Analyzer can impact the performance of their database and that it should be scheduled for off hours!

The ADDM addition to the OEM interface brings much needed depth to the Oracle product line and provides valuable input for the inexperienced DBA. With its distillation of Oracle experts' and consultants' tuning experience, it can provide the expertise lacking in many shops. However, this very strength can cause it to become a crutch, stifling the growth of key personnel and making them dependent on OEM. In addition, a more experienced DBA may recognize recommendations that would not be beneficial for their specific database, while an inexperienced DBA might take them as gospel and make decisions that could harm their database in the long run.

As shown in Figure 18.81, the SQL Detail screen is not forthcoming with wait event details specific to the problem SQL.

SQL Details: 7rch4vpva21hq

Run SQ

SQL Text
```
SELECT time_id, quantity_sold, amount_sold
  FROM sales s, customers c
  WHERE c.cust_id = s.cust_id
   AND cust_first_name = 'Dina'
  ORDER BY time_id DESC
```

Execution Plan Current Statistics **Execution History** Tuning History

CPU and Elapsed Time

View ⦿ Time in Seconds ○ Seconds Per Execution (Go)

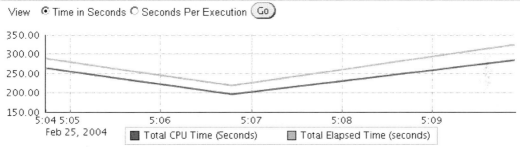

Figure 18.81: *SQL Detail Screen*

The SQL analysis tool provides the user with a set of recommendations, weighted by expected percentage of improvement as shown in Figure 18.82.

Shortcomings of OEM

1099

imendations for SQL ID:7rch4vpva21hq

ecommendation should be implemented.

Text

:ime_id, QUANTITY_SOLD, AMOUNT_SOLD from sales s, customers c where c.cust_id = s.cust_id and CUST_FIRST_NAMI
: id...

t Recommendation

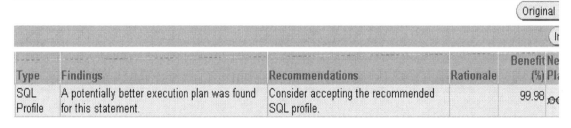

Type	Findings	Recommendations	Rationale	Benefit Ne (%) Pl;
SQL Profile	A potentially better execution plan was found for this statement.	Consider accepting the recommended SQL profile.		99.98

Figure 18.82: *Recommendations Screen*

The OEM allows for multiple statements to be placed together into a single SQL tuning job. Doing so requires the job to usually be run after peak hours.

The closest OEM comes to showing the detail of wait event information is in the Performance section of the interface, as shown in Figure 18.83.

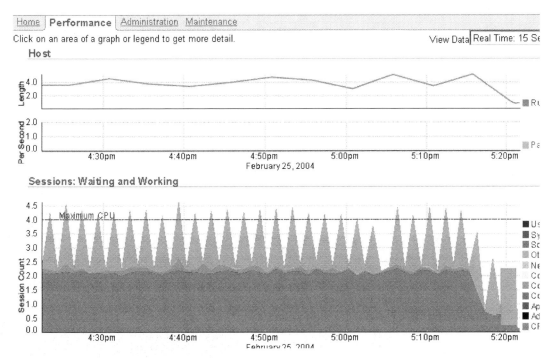

Figure 18.83: *OEM Performance Screen*

This screen only provides the overview of total system waits and requires a time specific drill down to get to more detailed data.

One nice feature of the OEM interface is before and after views of problem statement explain plans based on the implementation of tuning suggestions. A new explain plan is shown in Figure 18.84.

Any experienced DBA will likely confer that sometimes explain plans and cost figures do not actually represent the best performing SQL statements in the real world. For example, the explain plan in Figure 18.84, based on taking Oracle advice, shifts from a hash join to a nest loop, which may or may not provide better performance. The reality is that OEM does not always make the best recommendations about improving SQL performance. This is why the skilled DBA will always be in high demand.

Shortcomings of OEM   **1101**

New Explain Plan

Expand All | Collapse All

Operation	Line ID	Order	Rows	KB	Cost	Time (seconds)	CPU Cost	IO Cost	Object
▼SELECT STATEMENT	0	6	2	0.064	5	1	44468	5	
▼NESTED LOOPS	1	5	2	0.064	5	1	44468	5	
▼TABLE ACCESS BY GLOBAL INDEX ROWID	2	2	918843	18,843.461	4	1	28955	4	SH.SALES
INDEX FULL SCAN DESCENDING	3	1	1		3	1	21564	3	SH.SALES_TIME_ID:
▼TABLE ACCESS BY INDEX ROWID	4	4	1	0.012	1	1	15512	1	SH.CUSTOMERS
INDEX UNIQUE SCAN	5	3	1		0	1	8171	0	SH.CUSTOMERS_PI

Figure 18.84: *New Explain Plan Feature of OEM*

Conclusion

Oracle has made a major investment in the development of OEM with the goal of creating a one-stop interface for the myriad of Oracle administration duties. The tuning tools are littered throughout the dozens of complex and confusing screens.

On the other hand, third-party tools such as Ion and DBFlash provide a task-specific tool that provides the experienced DBA with a scalpel for use in surgically finding and correcting poorly performing SQL.

- **Intelligent approach:** By utilizing the Oracle wait interface and specific Oracle statistics and tying this information back to their source SQL statements, tools such as DBFlash allow for correction of the specific problems in an Oracle database SQL portfolio, eliminating the tuning of apparently bad SQL which, in fact, is not a problem at all. In contrast, Oracle's SQL Access Advisor makes global recommendations only on indexes and materialized views while the SQL Tuning Advisor makes specific recommendations; however, these recommendations may be made with limited intelligence. The SQL Access Advisor is a limited tool, and it can only recommend simple solutions such as new indexes and materialized views, ignoring the dozens of other SQL tuning options.

- **Less overhead:** While AWR, through use of the MMON background process, is more efficient at gathering statistics than the use of the Oracle job interface was for STATSPACK, it still has more performance impact than some third-party tools.

- **Less expensive:** Oracle ASH is a component of Oracle Enterprise Manager Diagnostic Pack and the Oracle Tuning Pack. These are extra cost features, and they must be licensed separately. The costs of these tuning packs can be prohibitively expensive for some shops.

- **Tightly focused:** The OEM screens are not focused on performance management, but rather the entire database, or databases, being monitored and their overall status. The OEM user can be presented with a bewildering array of options.

- **Fast problem identification:** In comparison to OEM, problem SQL can be quickly found by tools like Ion and DBFlash within a few mouse clicks. With the OEM interface and SQL Analyzer, the DBA may face an ordeal of scheduled analysis and correction jobs. The OEM interface practices an extreme amount of hand holding, and while reassuring to the inexperienced DBA, can be annoying to the more experienced DBA. The DBFlash interface assumes an experienced DBA is at the helm.

- **Fast tuning solutions:** Savvy DBAs know that long-term workload tests do not help tune most SQL. Oracle claims that many Oracle SQL statements will change execution plans as the workload changes. While this is true for a small number of shops, the vast majority of Oracle shops will find that there is one, and only one, optimal execution plan for any SQL statement.

This chapter has focused on the Oracle Enterprise Manager tuning components and how OEM displays AWR and ASH data in a visual form.

While the OEM performance screens are built in to the OEM console, many Oracle professionals are not aware that using these screens may require additional Oracle licenses. Third-party tools that bypass the AWR and ASH views can sometimes provide a more cost-effective solution.

Finally, it is noteworthy that many senior DBAs eschew GUI tools and use customized scripts to expose Oracle performance issues. The next chapter will explore techniques for tuning Oracle cluster systems and investigate Real Application Clusters (RAC) and tuning for Oracle Grid systems.

Oracle RAC and Grid Tuning

I know Grid, RAC, Streams and three other Oracle words.

Introduction to Tuning with RAC

The use of Oracle Real Application Clusters (RAC) is a complex and robust Oracle solution that provides infinite scalability and instant failover. Originally, this approach was named Oracle Parallel Server (OPS).

Oracle RAC is the flagship Oracle product, designed to provide high availability and scalability for large, mission-critical applications. Oracle RAC technology is the foundation of Oracle Grid computing. Grid computing contributes the "g" in Oracle 10g. When combined with the Transparent Application Failover (TAF) and Fast Application Notification (FAN) options, Oracle RAC can reconnect failed connections to a failover node without the client even being aware of a server failure.

Highly available and scalable server-based computer systems and applications are an essential part of today's 24x7 internet-based business environment. This availability and scalability are achieved by clustering technology and fault tolerant systems that allow seamless addition of computing resources to Oracle. This chapter will provide a closer look at high performance computing trends for Oracle RAC database systems.

Oracle RAC and Oracle Grid are unique and complex technologies and have very different tuning procedures. This chapter will cover the following RAC tuning topics:

- RAC and Grid in a nutshell

- Inside Oracle 10g Grid computing

- Configuring RAC and Grid for top performance

- RAC node load balancing for optimal performance

- RAC parallelism for high performance

- Monitoring RAC performance

A quick look into the Oracle RAC and Grid architecture is presented in the next section. Remember, these few pages only present a high-level overview of RAC tuning, and the whole story takes hundreds of pages. For the whole story of Oracle RAC tuning, I highly recommend the book, *Oracle RAC and Grid* by Oracle ACE Steve Karam (Rampant TechPress, 2010).

Oracle RAC in a Nutshell

In a nutshell, Oracle RAC is a complex database architecture where multiple RAM memory regions and processes and Oracle instances share a common set of database files. Figure 19.1 is an illustration of the complex RAC structure in Oracle.

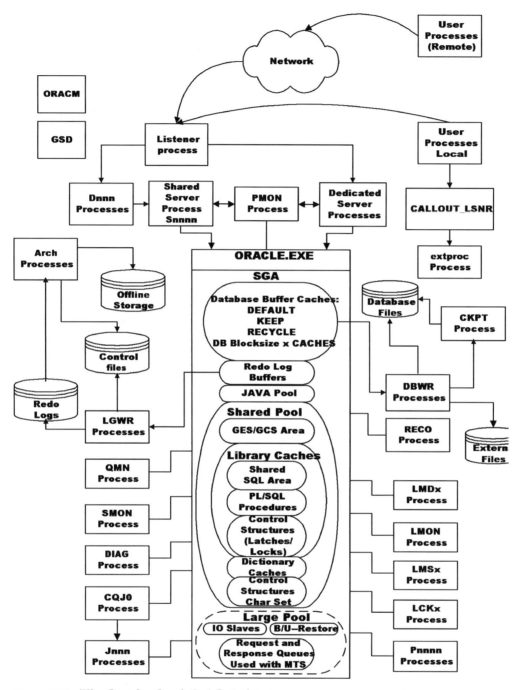

Figure 19.1: *The Complex Oracle RAC Architecture*

Because there are many Oracle instances sharing the same data files, a large component of Oracle RAC is managing concurrency between the database instances. These concurrencies are called nodes in RAC terminology. In order for the multiple Oracle instances to share data from the caches, a special set of processes called cache fusion manage the pinging of data blocks back and forth between the instances.

The essential differences between a RAC cluster and a non-RAC Oracle database are very simple. These differences pose unique challenges for the Oracle tuning professional, and this chapter will be dedicated to explaining these differences and showing how to tune a massively parallel database:

- **Multiple servers:** Because RAC has many database servers, each server is totally independent. When an Oracle system becomes CPU-bound and all tuning has been completed, a new RAC node can be added to the cluster.

- **Sharing data blocks between instances:** Because many Oracle databases have a working set of commonly referenced rows, such as lookup tables and shipping codes, Oracle RAC uses cache fusion processes to transfer these data blocks between multiple instances. Cache fusion is used to provide read consistency to the application across multiple instances. In many non-Oracle databases, read consistency is ensured by using locks. In contrast to that, the main mantra of the Oracle RDBMS is that readers do not block writers. On a single instance, this is achieved by reading blocks from the undo segments. It is less obvious how to do that when multiple instances are accessing the database. The process that creates the image of the block up to the requested point in time and ships it to the requesting instance over the private network interconnect is called the cache fusion. An alternative is the process by which the requesting database would force the database which owned the locks on the requested blocks to release them and flush the requested blocks to the disk. The requesting database would then read the blocks from the disk. That was the case in the predecessor of RAC, the OPS.

- **Dynamic resource allocation:** This ability to have many instances allows the RAC DBA to add additional servers, with a new instance on each server, whenever Oracle requires more processing power. Oracle Grid technology is all about the intelligent allocation of RAC server resources via the Oracle Enterprise Manager Grid control screens.

These differences appear simple on the surface, but there are some extremely complex techniques that are used to ensure the top performance of a RAC or Grid database.

It is critical to understand that Oracle RAC is not for every Oracle database, and it is almost always used in super-large, mission-critical systems and web databases that must support thousands of transactions per second. Oracle RAC is primarily used in these types of shops:

- **Low tolerance for downtime:** By having many servers, a failure on one node will not cause an outage because Oracle Transparent Application Failover (TAF) will resume all transactions on surviving nodes. This continuous availability feature is used by shops where downtime cost is greater than $100k per minute, and shops with more tolerance for downtime may use other Oracle failover technologies such as Oracle Streams and Oracle Data Guard.

- **High scalability:** For smaller databases, scale up scalability is best using a large monolithic server with 32 or 64 processors and hundreds of gigabytes of RAM. However, super-large Oracle shops need more horsepower, and RAC provides them with the ability to scale out, adding additional servers to RAC whenever they need more hardware resources.

For many systems, Oracle RAC and Grid allows the DBA true transparent scalability. In the past, in order to increase the number of servers in OPS, data and application changes were required and the scaling was far from transparent.

The following advantages come with Oracle RAC and Grid:

- No physical data partitioning is required.

- Vendor applications (SAP, Peoplesoft) will scale without modification.

This automatic, transparent scaling is due almost entirely to the cache fusion layer and the unique parallel architecture of RAC and Grid. Table 19.1 summarizes the main features of the single instance standalone database and the multi-instance RAC database.

SINGLE INSTANCE DATABASE	MULTI-INSTANCE RAC DATABASE
Only one instance to access and process database requests	Multiple instances accessing same database
One set of datafiles, redo files, undo and control files, and such	One set of datafiles and control files, but separate redo log files and undo for each instance
Locking and concurrency maintenance is confined to one instance	Locking and concurrency maintenance is extended to multiple instances
Dedicated storage structures for the instance	Multiple instances access the same shared storage structures
Weak on high availability and scalability	Provides high availability and scalability solution

Table 19.1: *Standalone versus Multi-Instance RAC Database*

By providing multiple instances such as a host and its associated resources to access the same database, a RAC system creates multiple database computing centers and improves scalability, but it is done at the cost of additional complexity and license costs.

Oracle Scalability and Grid Technology

Most savvy Oracle shops practice the scale up approach first, and then scale out after they reach the maximum capacity of their single server. Due to the advances in server technology, the concept of using a large server has become very popular. The following sections outline an approach used by many forward-thinking Oracle shops.

First Scale Up with SMP Servers

This scale up yields the following benefits:

- On-demand resource allocation by sharing CPU and RAM between many resources

- Less maintenance and human resources required to manage fewer servers

- Optimal utilization of RAM and CPU resources

- High availability through fault tolerant components

Next Scale Out with Multiple SMP Servers

This subsequent scale out will yield the following additional benefits:

- High availability through clustering servers with RAC

- Optimal utilization of servers

- Quicker implementation and easier maintenance with fewer servers

The scale out approach using RAC and Grid is designed for super- large Oracle databases that support many thousands of concurrent users. Unless a system has a need to support more than 10,000 transactions per second, it is likely that the scale up approach will be more than adequate.

Amazon is an excellent example of a scale out Oracle shop. Amazon announced plans to move their 14 trillion-byte Oracle database to Oracle RAC on Linux. Now Amazon uses load-balanced Linux Web servers to horizontally scale its Web presence.

Large-scale RAC databases use large servers, each with 32 or 64 processors and over a hundred gigabytes of RAM. As the capacities of the large servers are exceeded, a new server is genned into the RAC cluster. Figure 19.2 is an illustration of large-scale RAC databases with these large servers.

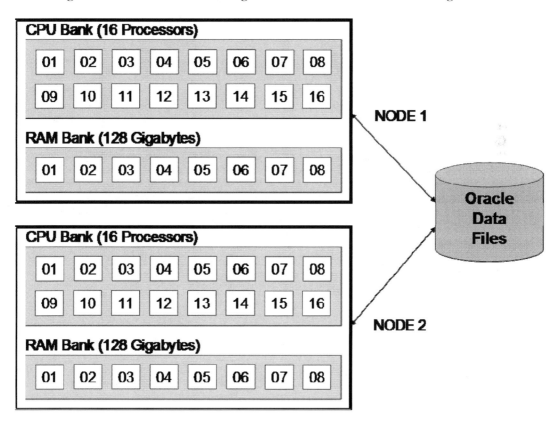

Large RAC clusters use large SMP servers and do not have the need for dynamic Grid facilities that are used in smaller clustered systems with server blades.

The next section will introduce how RAC is used within Oracle Grid for high performance database computing.

Oracle Grid in a Nutshell

At a high level, Oracle Grid computing is the on-demand sharing of computing resources within a tightly coupled network. For those old enough to remember data processing in the 1980s, the IBM mainframes were a primitive example of Grid computing. These mainframes had several CPUs, each independent, and the MVS/ESA operating system allocated work to the processors based on least recently used algorithms and customized task dispatching priorities. Of course, RAM and disk resources were available to all programs executing on the huge server.

However, Grid computing is fundamentally different from mainframes. In the 21st century, Grid computing performs a virtualization of distributed computing resources and allows for the automated allocation of resources as system demand changes. Each server is independent, yet ready to participate in a variety of processing requests from many types of applications.

Unlike large RAC deployments, Oracle Grid systems often employ small server blades, which are tiny servers with two to four processors and four to eight gigabytes of RAM as illustrated in Figure 19.3.

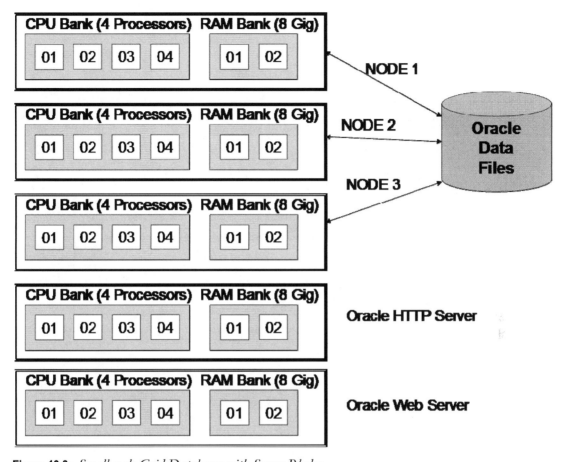

Figure 19.3: *Small-scale Grid Databases with Server Blades*

Oracle Grid computing also employs special software infrastructure using Oracle Streams to monitor resource usage and allocate requests to the most appropriate resource. This enables a distributed enterprise to function as if it were a single supercomputer as shown in Figure 19.4.

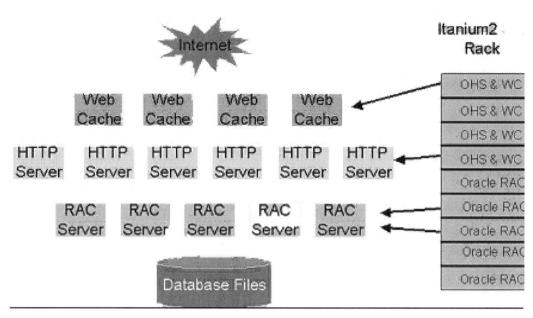

Figure 19.4: *Hardware Load Balancing for Oracle Application Server*

As components become stressed, the DBA can de-allocate a blade server from one Oracle component and reallocate that server to another part of the Oracle application. The software, such as RAC, Oracle HTTP Server, or Oracle web cache, must be pre-installed on each server blade.

The next section will provide a look at the new server blades and how they are used within Oracle Grid computing.

Blade Servers and Oracle RAC Tuning

Blade servers are often advertised hand-in-hand with Oracle Grid computing. It is critical to understand that blade servers are good for programs that do not require the symmetric multiprocessing (SMP) capabilities of large mid-range servers. For example, a blade server would not be appropriate for a RAC node that performs parallel query operations. That is because blade servers are normally small, one to four CPU servers, and Oracle parallel query works best when there are 32 or 64 CPUs for fast full-table scans on very large tables.

On the other hand, blade servers and RAC may be appropriate for small-scale OLTP applications because the nature of individual queries does not require multiple CPU resources.

Blade Servers and Oracle App Servers

Blade servers are also an option for Oracle Application Server 10g web cache servers or Oracle HTTP servers, because a new server can easily be added into the Oracle Application Server 10g server farm. In Oracle Application Server 10g, a rack of blade servers can be used and Oracle Web Server and Oracle HTTP server (OHS) software can be pre-installed. At runtime, the Oracle Application Server 10g administrator can add these server blades to their Oracle Application Server 10g farm, using each blade as either a Web cache server or an HTTP server, depending upon the stress on the system.

At this point, it should be very clear that there are a myriad of options for Oracle configurations. Given the complexity of cluster and Grid management, the best migration path may be to first scale up onto a large 64-bit server and add resources to the SMP on the server. Then, for additional high availability and increased flexibility, the scale out option can be explored.

Oracle RAC and Grid are complex technologies for complex applications. Even standard performance monitoring is challenging because multiple servers and instances must be monitored within the common database.

Now that the concepts of RAC and Grid have been presented, the following section will present information on Oracle Cache Fusion and how it manages inter-instance data block transfer.

The Revolution of Cache Fusion

Until later versions of Oracle 8i, an Oracle Parallel Server (OPS) database had to use a laborious process of copying blocks into and out of memory and to and from disks in order to share information in a single block between the multiple instances. This complex and slow disk-to-disk OPS data sharing mechanism resulted in serious performance issues if the database did not practice some kind of application partitioning, data partitioning and localized use.

Oracle 9i Real Application Clusters (RAC) relieved the limitations of the OPS disk-based block transfer method, but there were still performance issues related to the cache fusion layer. Cache fusion has several important jobs with the foremost job being able to maintain cache coherency and read consistency between database instances.

This cache coherency is maintained through the Global Services Directory and the various Global Enqueue processes. These processes monitor each data cache and transfer data block RAM to RAM across the high-speed cluster interconnect. The architecture of Cache Fusion is illustrated in Figure 19.5.

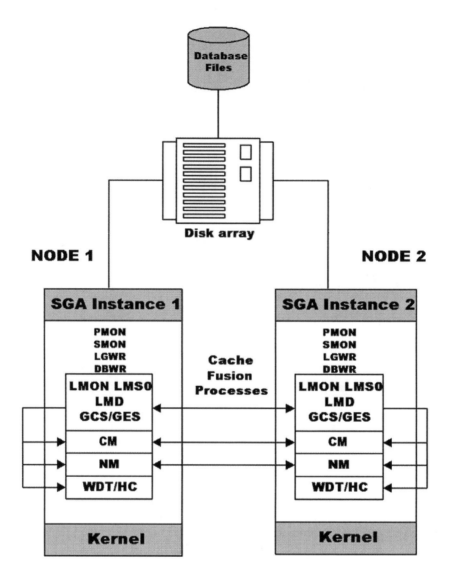

Cache Fusion Architecture

Figure 19.5: *The Cache Fusion Background Processes*

The cluster interconnect is the heart of cache fusion. Oracle has global directory services to manage data blocks inside the multiple instances and the use of intra-instance transportable locks to speed up data block transfers. The Cluster Interconnect architecture is illustrated in Figure 19.6.

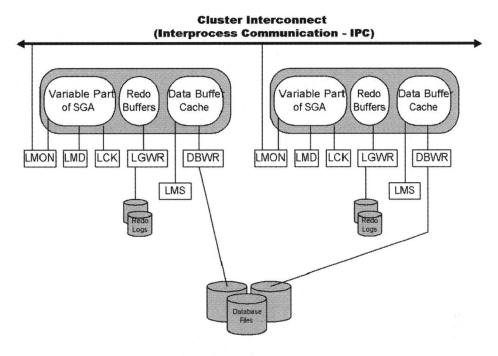

Figure 19.6: *The Cluster Interconnect IPC Architecture*

Even though data block transfers are now super fast, there is still a high amount of overhead in the cache fusion processes. It is the job of the Oracle DBA to devise methods to minimize this inter-instance block transfer. The disk subsystems within RAC must also be managed. Most RAC databases use Storage Area Networks (SAN) and use tools like the IBM FastT storage manager for the RAC nodes as shown in Figure 19.7:

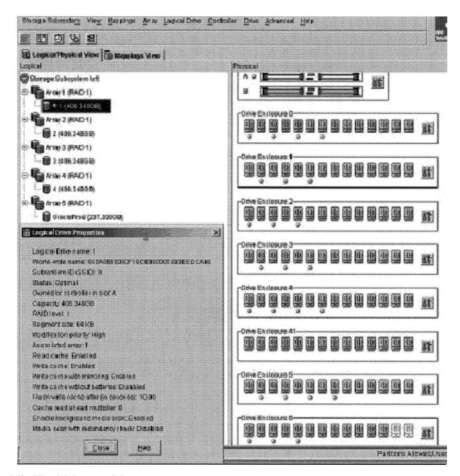

Figure 19.7: *The FastT Storage Manager*

Now that the basics of Oracle Cache Fusion have been presented, the following sections include information on how to tune Oracle RAC by load balancing traffic between the nodes.

Overview of RAC and Grid Tuning

There are only a few differences between an ordinary Oracle database and a Grid/RAC database. RAC and Grid yield some of the following superb abilities:

- Ability to load balance the transaction load between instances
- Ability to adjust inter-instance cache communication
- Ability to leverage parallel nodes
- Ability to provide on-demand server resources

These points form the core of all Oracle RAC tuning. The next section will start with a presentation of information on RAC load balancing as well as resource re-allocation and cache fusion tuning. The section will wrap up with information on RAC parallel tuning.

RAC Load Balancing

Load balancing has changed radically between OPS and RAC databases, but there are still two accepted approaches to RAC load balancing:

- **Data localization:** Business processes and the associated data are segregated by RAC node.

- **Automatic load balancing:** Using the TAF load balancing software, new connections are routed to the least loaded RAC node.

- **Hybrid:** A combination of data localization and automatic techniques are used, dedicating a set of nodes to the processing area and load-balancing connections within that group.

In OPS days, the expensive disk-to-disk data transfers meant that the DBA would carefully partition the application such that different types of applications would connect to different nodes. For example, in a database with order entry, inventory maintenance and customer management functions, clients from each of these areas would be directed to a separate node. The data localization load balancing method is illustrated in Figure 19.8.

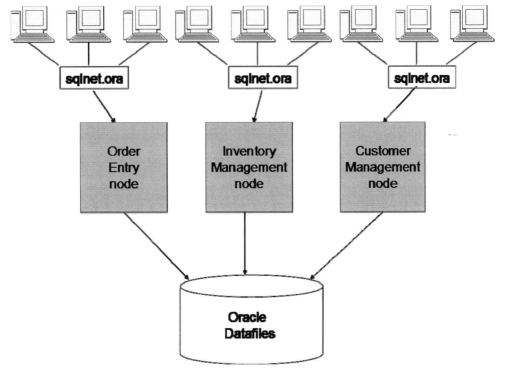

Figure 19.8: *The Data Localization Load Balancing Method*

This application-level partitioning ensured that all related data blocks were cached on the appropriate instance, and that the expensive disk-to-disk pinging of shared blocks between instances was minimized.

With the introduction of Oracle 9i RAC and TAF, another load balancing scheme called automatic load balancing became available. With this scheme, multiple Oracle RAC listeners with virtual IP addresses could be created, and the RAC listener could automatically direct transactions to the least loaded Oracle instance. This scheme is conceptually illustrated in Figure 19.9.

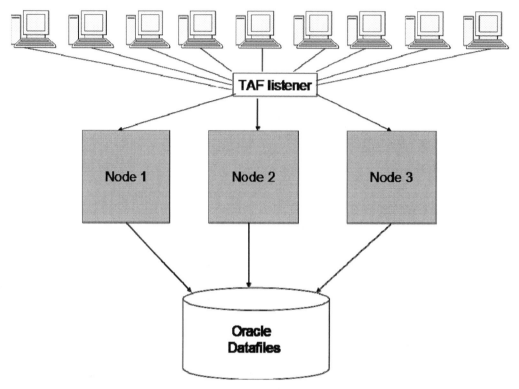

Figure 19.9: *The Automatic Load Balancing Method*

The automatic load balancing approach has several advantages for scalability and resources consumption because the Oracle RAC software manages instance load. On the other hand, databases with a large shared working set of frequently referenced data will find high data block transfers within the cache fusion processes. Oracle Grid databases almost exclusively use the automatic load balancing techniques.

There is a third approach that uses a hybrid of the automatic and localization approaches. This load balancing approach is used by large RAC shops where they want to load balance between a group of related nodes, thereby getting the automatic load balancing as well as the reduced cache fusion stress resulting from data localization. This hybrid scheme is illustrated in Figure 19.10.

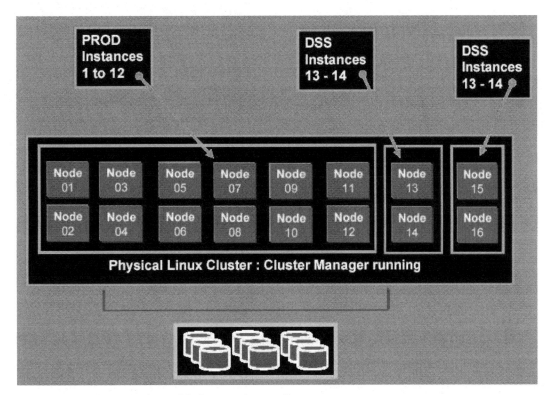

Figure 19.10: *The Hybrid Load-balancing Approach*

The DBA's choice of load balancing techniques depends on their database application. If the application does not share many common data blocks, automatic load balancing is the best choice. However, if the application has transactions that all share the same table rows, the server-side load balancing with RAC services might be the better choice.

Managing Inter-instance Data Block Transfers

The same data block may reside inside many SGA regions, so it is easy to run queries against the *v$bh* views on each node and the global *gv$bh* view on either node to find the data blocks that have been pinged via cache fusion.

The size of this working set of frequently referenced data blocks is important, and minimizing the amount of inter-instance block transfers can greatly improve RAC performance, especially if the working set is frequently updated.

The following script can be run on each instance to identify the data blocks that currently reside within each SGA. This is from Steve Karam's book, *Oracle Grid & Real Application Clusters.* A full set of Oracle RAC tuning scripts are also available from www.oracle-script.com.

```
break on report

compute sum of distinct_blocks on report
```

```
compute sum of blocks on report
set lines 132 pages 57
@title132 'Block Usage Inside SGA Block Buffers'

spool rep_out\&db\block_usage

SELECT a.INST_ID, decode(b.tablespace_name,null,'UNUSED',b.tablespace_name) ts_name,
       a.file# file_number,
       COUNT(a.block#) Blocks,
       COUNT (DISTINCT a.file# || a.block#) Distinct_blocks
  FROM GV$BH a, dba_data_files b
  WHERE a.file#=b.file_id(+)
  GROUP BY a.INST_ID, a.file#,decode(b.tablespace_name,null,'UNUSED',b.tablespace_name)
  order by a.inst_id
/
spool off
ttile off
```

Some inter-instance pinging is unavoidable due to the shared nature of almost all Oracle applications. However, there are many tricks that can be used by the Oracle DBA to minimize the work of the cache fusion layer. The following list shares some of these tricks:

- **Block spreading:** Small lookup tables can be spread across many data blocks to reduce the likelihood that another instance will need them.

- **Blocksize adjustment:** Many RAC databases that share large amounts of data blocks will perform better with a 2k blocksize because less data will be transferred between nodes.

- **Read only tablespaces:** The intelligent use of read-only tablespaces allows the DBA to minimize inter-instance communication, because Oracle does not have to maintain read consistency mechanisms.

The following sections provide a more in-depth look at each of these methods.

Block Spreading

Oracle RAC databases that have small, frequently referenced lookup tables can spread the rows across more data blocks. This can be illustrated with a simple example. Suppose that there is a State code lookup table with entries for all 50 states. Even on a 2k blocksize, all 50 rows fit into a single data block.

As competing instances access the lookup table, the same data block must be transferred between all of the nodes, and this can cause a huge overhead for the cache fusion background processes and slow down the entire database.

The solution is to adjust the *pctfree* threshold for the lookup table so that only a single row resides on each data block. Now, instead of consuming one data block, the lookup table resides on 50 separate blocks, and inter-instance communication is greatly minimized. This solution is illustrated in Figure 19.11.

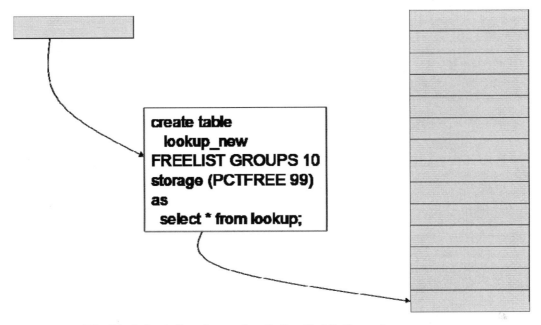

Figure 19.11: *The Block Spreading Approach to Relieve RAC Contention*

Of course, space is being wasted on each data block, but spreading out the table blocks makes a huge difference in overall performance. The *freelist groups* parameter allows multiple segment header blocks. Multiple *freelist groups* speed up *insert* operations because each node can acquire a separate header block, each with its own *freelist*.

The *freelist groups object* parameter should be set to the number of Oracle RAC nodes that update any table and index simultaneously. For partitioned objects and cases of segment header contention, *freelist groups* may be set for non-RAC systems. This will relieve the database from *buffer busy waits* caused by segment header contention.

Blocksize Adjustment

As a general rule, the RAC DBA should define all inter-instance shared blocks such that only the minimum amount of space is transferred across the cache fusion layer.

For example, if a shared shipping table with 80-byte rows will be frequently referenced by all nodes, a transaction will only want a single row in the table.

If the table is placed in a 32k blocksize, the entire table might fit onto only a few data blocks. However, if it is placed in a 2k blocksize, a smaller number of adjacent rows are transferred by cache fusion, thereby reducing the probability that another node will have to wait for the data block. This solution is illustrated in Figure 19.12.

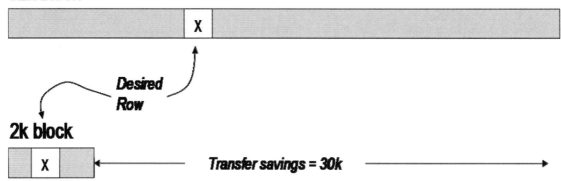

Figure 19.12: *Blocksize Adjustment to Reduce Cache Fusion Contention*

Oracle RAC supports multiple blocksizes, and the savvy Oracle DBA will adjust the data buffers according to the demands of their application.

All Oracle default caches and blocksizes in a RAC environment, as defined by *db_block_size*, must be identical, but there are other important differences between the configuration of a RAC database and a single-instance Oracle database, especially when using grid server blades.

Beginning with Oracle 9i RAC, Oracle allowed sub-caches to be configured that had different blocksizes than the default *db_block_size*, allowing *db_2k_block_size*, *db_4k_block_size*, *db_8k_block_size*, *db_16k_block_size* and *db_32k_block_size* (not available on all platforms) as sub-caches. For example, if the default *db_block_size* is 8K, then define a *db_2k_cache_size* to hold additional objects. However, all RAC nodes must have the sub-cache defined.

We must remember that the rules for caching in a RAC instance are very different than for a standard Oracle system. For example, numerous studies have shown that Oracle indexes often benefit from using the largest supported blocksize. This is not always true in RAC systems.

With Oracle systems now employing SSD instead of disk, and systems having giant *db_cache_size* regions, it is tempting to configure RAC with large data buffers. However, keep in mind that multi-instance Oracle is very different from a single-instance system:

- **Blade clusters have small buffer caches:** Most blade servers have only 2-gig or 4-gig of RAM. Hence, each RAC node is limited in the available *db_cache_size*.

- **RAC likes small blocksizes:** Because of the inter-instance block transfer via cache fusion, smaller blocksizes minimize pinging of blocks between instances. Most RAC DBAs will define the default *db_block_buffers* to 2k and then add a 4k buffer to isolate data objects.

- **RAC scales by the sum of RAM caches:** Unlike a single Oracle database with a 32-gigabyte RAM data cache, RAC systems achieve high caching by the sum of the individual RAM caches. Hence, a four-node RAC cluster with a 32-gigabyte RAM cache on each node would effectively have a total cache of 128 gigabytes.

Read-only Tablespaces

The Oracle RAC DBA can also minimize the cache fusion overhead by using Oracle read-only tablespaces. If Oracle is aware that a data block is read-only, a great amount of overhead is saved because Oracle does not have to monitor for competing DML and read consistency.

In larger RAC databases, the DBA may take the trouble to locate and segregate those blocks that are always read-only. This can be achieved with partitioned tables with only the most current partition being updatable.

Parallel Processing and RAC Performance

Parallel execution involves dividing a task into several smaller tasks and working on each of those smaller tasks in parallel. Oracle Parallel Query (OPQ), where multiple CPUs on a single instance can speed up large-table full-table scans, is already a familiar concept; however, RAC opens up a new area of inter-instance parallelism.

There are two ways to speed up tasks:

- Increasing the number of CPUs and use Oracle Parallel Query (OPQ), parallel DML, and such.

- Manually break down a complex task into multiple subtasks and assign each component to multiple processors to execute them concurrently.

In the first scenario of OPQ, a single-user task, such as a SQL query, can be parallelized to achieve higher speed and throughput by using multiple processors. Generally, Oracle's intra-query parallel execution improves performance for:

- Queries with large object full-scans

- Creation of large indexes

- Bulk inserts, updates, and deletes

- Data aggregations such as computing sums and averages

- DBA maintenance such as table and index reorganizations

Parallel processing involves the use of multiple processors to reduce the time needed to complete a given task. Instead of one processor executing an entire task, several processors work on separate tasks that are subordinate to the main task.

There are two types of parallelism that database users can utilize. They are: inter-query parallelism and intra-query parallelism. The differences between these two types of parallelism are outlined below:

- **Inter-query parallelism:** This can be done when individual transactions are independent and no transaction requires the output of other transactions to complete. Many CPUs can be kept busy by assigning each task or each query to a separate CPU. This is accomplished automatically by the server when the application submits the tasks and waits for each subsection to report back its results.

- **Intra-query parallelism:** To speed up execution of a large, complex query, it must first be decomposed into smaller problems. These smaller problems must be executed concurrently, in parallel, by assigning each sub problem concurrently to its CPUs. This intra-query parallelism is implemented with the Oracle parallel features such as OPQ.

Inter-query parallelism is an application design issue and is rare in Oracle RAC and Grid databases because most problems cannot be serialized into independent sub problems.

Conclusion

This chapter focused on detailed information on the Oracle RAC and Grid architectures and showed ways to improve the performance of these massively parallel database systems.

The information showed that Oracle Grid provides infinite scalability via on-demand generation of new servers into the RAC cluster, but limitations from the cache fusion layer were examined as were the requirement to transfer data blocks between instances. The main points of this chapter include:

- **RAC is not for every system:** Most small shops do not need RAC for scalability, although they may use RAC for continuous availability. RAC for scalability is only for large Oracle systems with more demands than can be met by a single server.

- **Oracle Grid uses smaller servers:** Unlike traditional RAC implementations with large servers, Oracle Grid computing uses small server blades.

- **Cache fusion is the key:** The Oracle RAC tuning expert is always concerned with minimizing the work of the cache fusion processes. The most common techniques involve block spreading, application partitioning, using small blocksizes and read-only tablespaces.

- **Load balancing is important:** The choice of data localization or automatic load balancing is an important RAC design consideration.

Index

$oracle_sid 49
_always_star_transformation 620
_db_aging_cool_count 620
_db_aging_freeze_cr 620
_db_aging_hot_criteria 620
_db_aging_stay_count 620
_db_aging_touch_time 620
_db_block_cache_clone 620
_db_block_cache_map 620
_db_block_cache_protect 620
_db_block_hash_buckets 616, 620
_db_block_hash_latches 616
_db_block_hi_priority_batch_size 620
_db_block_max_cr_dba 620
_db_block_max_scan_cnt 620
_db_block_med_priority_batch_size 620
_db_block_write_batch 616
_db_percent_hot_default 647
_db_percent_hot_keep 647
_db_percent_hot_recycle 647
_fast_full_scan_enabled 619
_kgl_latch_count 616
_latch_spin_count 616
_optimizer_cost_model 472, 484, 885, 886, 887
_parallelism_cost_fudge_factor 619
_pga_max_size 602, 611
_small_table_threshold 620
_smm_px_max_size 602, 608
10046 .... 393, 400
10046 trace event 431, 438
10046 trace file 445, 449
10046 wait event 557
32-bit shops 47
Active Session History 9, 294
Active Session History (ASH) 621, 1021
adaptive alert thresholds 42
Adaptive cursor sharing 747
adaptive threshold 41
add_window_group_member 1044
ADDM 33, 257, 876, 1058
addm_rpt.sql 876
ad-hoc display 81
ad-hoc query 1010
Advisor Central 1055, 1062, 1069, 1089
advisor_name 32
advisories 365
alert mechanism 1021
alert.log 434
all_rows 498, 819, 862
all_rows optimizer_mode 530
alter index rebuild 729, 735
alter session 30, 161, 433, 436, 440
alter system 11, 439
alter system command 634, 654
alter system flush shared_pool 154
alter table 697, 701, 711
alter table shrink space 717
AMM 99, 257, 267, 637
analysis job 1099
analyze table 805, 892
append option 896
Application Server 10g 1113

Apps 11i 759
ARCH 175, 177
Artificial Intelligence (AI) 1013
ASH 91
ASH tables 399, 563
ASH views 1075
ASSM 34, 693, 705, 896
asynch 514
auto option 811
auto_degree 812
auto_task_consumer_group 1095
auto_task_job_class 1095
auto_tasks_job_class 1095
autoextend 126, 127, 128, 130
Automated Database Diagnostic Monitor (ADDM) 1054
Automated Memory Management 40
Automated Session History 400, 422
Automated Session History (ASH) .. 558, 1096
automated SQL tuning 425
Automated Storage Management 55
Automated Workload Repository10, 424, 461, 1005
Automated Workload Repository (AWR) .1003
Automatic Database Diagnostic Monitor32, 51, 210, 1021
Automatic Diagnostic Database Advisor 40
automatic load balancing 1119
Automatic Maintenance Tasks 82
Automatic Memory Management .. 30, 99, 257
Automatic Memory Management (AMM)508, 589, 1002, 1056
Automatic Memory Manager 210, 1056
Automatic Memory Manager (AMM) 634
Automatic Segment Advisor 1056, 1057
Automatic segment management 162
Automatic Segment Management............. 695
Automatic Segment Space 34
Automatic Segment Space Management693, 699, 718
Automatic Shared Memory Management316, 1090
Automatic Shared Memory Management (ASMM) 510, 615
Automatic Storage Management 34
Automatic Storage Management (ASM) ..1002
Automatic Workload Repository 869
automatic_ipc 500, 501
average_waiter_count 380
avg_row_len 535, 709, 720, 721
AWR 33, 41, 83, 241, 255, 289
AWR baselines 425
AWR metrics 1018
AWR Report 305
AWR/STATSPACK report 74
awr_high_resource_sql.sql 835
awr_report_html 304, 312
awr_report_text 304, 312
awr_sql_scan_sums.sql 860
awrrpt.sql 26, 32, 300, 313
b*tree 35
baseline_name 302
begin_interval_time 243, 282, 286
begin_time 258, 379
BgnSnap 262
Bi-modal systems 47
bitmap 35
bitmap block 701, 702
bitmap freelists 693

bitmap indexes 527
bitmap join 35
bitmap space management 700
bitmap_merge_area_size.........................1000
blade servers 1113, 1123
block spreading 1121
block_count.sql 703
Blocking lock ratio 116
blocksize 457, 491, 674, 710, 723, 797
Bottleneck analysis..110, 117, 123, 124, 142, 180
break_poll_skip 500
bstat-estat 31
bstat-estat reports 309
Bubble fragmentation........................... 128
buf_blocks.sql 648
buf_keep_pool.sql 663
buffer busy wait 559, 655, 656, 657
buffer busy waits54, 225, 226, 227, 232, 329, 403, 410, 659, 697,
   699, 700, 1122
Buffer busy waits 162
buffer cache 364, 999
Buffer cache hit (%) 1047
Buffer cache hit ratio 115, 116, 144, 145, 151
Buffer Cache Hit Ratio (BCHR) 322
buffer cache size 1093
buffer hit ratio.................................... 321
buffer wait statistics.................................. 368
buffer_busy_wait 631
buffer_gets_th.. 298
buffer_pool_keep...................142, 628, 665, 666
buffer_pool_recycle 142, 628
bulk binds 899
C++ 739
cache buffers chain.............................. 327
cache buffers LRU chain......................... 327
cache fusion.................... 1108, 1114, 1122
cache hit 335
cache size 316
cardinality.......720, 805, 818, 820, 845, 855, 868
Cardinality 138
Cartesian joins 193, 194, 195, 199
cascade 302
catawr.sql 303
catdbsyn.sql 290
CBO30, 34, 281, 422, 497, 498, 499, 529, 571, 610, 759, 799, 803,
   818
CBO statistics....................................... 748
chained row fetches 707
chained/migrated rows 134, 136
change data capture 1005
close_window 1042
cluster interconnect 1115
clustering_factor571, 705, 719, 720, 721, 733, 987
clusters... 648
CODASYL DBTG 740
Confio Ignite 80
consistent gets28, 36, 256, 319, 706, 755, 843, 965
consistent_gets 631
convosync 515
correlation matrix 81
Cost Based Optimizer 742
Cost Based Optimizer (CBO) 619
cost-based optimizer 497
covariate analysis.................................... 497
CPU bottleneck 25

CPU costs...886
CPU dispatcher run queue..................... 1051
CPU dispatching..................................1052
CPU overhead......................................462
CPU run queue....................................1054
CPU run queue waits 25
cpu_cost 484, 498, 529, 819, 845, 846, 847
cpu_count..616, 618
CPU-bound 25, 29, 1075
CPU-bound database 405
Create Job 1027
create part (DDL)...................................734
Create Table As Select (CTAS) 734, 901
create_bitmap_area_size..........................1000
create_job...1033
create_snapshot.....................................299
create_tuning_task............................ 1071
crontab 544
cross join 766
CTAS 735
current statistics 1075
*cursor_sharing*155, 406, 615, 762, 764, 765, 811, 1062
cursor_space_for_time 999
data blocks 629
data buffer 627, 636
data buffer hit ratio................................ 631, 797
data buffer hit ratio (DBHR) 630
data buffer pools.................................. 49
data buffers...591
data dictionary views................................808
data localization 1118
Data Manipulation Language 738, 899
Data Manipulation Lock (DML) 660
data quality..41
data transmission delay............................506
data warehouse.................. 995, 998, 1010, 1011
data_object_id..648
Database block gets 1047
database blocksize 540
Database Control 1023
Database Diagnostic Pack.................32, 1016
Database Tuning Pack....................32, 1016
day\ mode 45
DB block gets......................................319
DB CPU 67
db file parallel write....................................551
db file scatter read 406
db file scatter reads 498
db file scattered read27, 167, 189, 462, 512, 551, 570
db file scattered read waits........................557
db file scattered reads 404
*db file sequential read*27, 232, 329, 406, 462, 512, 551, 572, 573,
   624, 765
db file sequential read waits.......................557
db file sequential reads 318, 403, 404, 498
db time 267, 271
DB time 67, 71
db_16k_cache_size....................................675
db_2k_cache_size 30, 648
db_32k cache_size................................ 30
db_32k_cache_size86, 529, 650, 661, 676, 678, 679
db_aging_hot_criteria 647
db_aging_touch_time 647
db_block_buffers........... 140, 141, 616, 628, 682
db_block_gets 631

db_block_lru_latches 616
db_block_lru_statistics 636
db_block_size372, 525, 532, 539, 571, 650, 710, 720, 721, 797, 999, 1123
db_cache_advice 636
db_cache_size11, 30, 39, 47, 48, 49, 79, 83, 84, 141, 148, 324, 372, 462, 463, 508, 509, 522, 542, 571, 577, 599, 615, 616, 620, 628, 630, 635, 636, 637, 638, 639, 641, 650, 655, 660, 661, 676, 678, 679, 681, 682, 683, 796, 865, 999, 1002, 1003, 1004, 1047, 1060
*db_file_multiblock_read_count*30, 372, 532, 533, 615, 707, 872, 882, 999
db_file_simultaneous_writes 616
db_files 616
*db_keep_cache_size*142, 462, 542, 615, 635, 670, 678, 679
db_nk_cache_size 142, 148
db_recycle_cache_size .. 142, 534, 635, 661, 676
db_time_in_wait 380
DB2 102
DBA 1013
dba_advisor 1057
dba_advisor_actions 1057
dba_advisor_commands 1057
dba_advisor_def_parameters 1057
dba_advisor_definitions 1057
dba_advisor_directives 1057
dba_advisor_findings 1057
dba_advisor_journal 1057
dba_advisor_log 1057
dba_advisor_object_types 1057
dba_advisor_objects 1057
dba_advisor_parameters 1057
dba_advisor_rationale 1057
dba_advisor_recommendations 1057
dba_advisor_sqla_rec_sum 1057
dba_advisor_sqla_wk_map 1057
dba_advisor_sqla_wk_stmts 1057
dba_advisor_sqlw_colvol 1057
dba_advisor_sqlw_journal 1057
dba_advisor_sqlw_parameters 1057
dba_advisor_sqlw_stmts 1057
dba_advisor_sqlw_sum 1058
dba_advisor_sqlw_tables 1058
dba_advisor_sqlw_tabvol 1058
dba_advisor_sqlw_templates 1058
dba_advisor_tasks 1055, 1057
dba_advisor_templates 1057
dba_advisor_usage 1057
dba_cache_advice 641
dba_data_files 93, 229, 394, 419, 658
dba_extents 564
dba_feature_usage_statistics 33
dba_hist25, 31, 52, 54, 88, 255, 258, 267, 300, 400, 406, 1021
dba_hist tables 64
dba_hist$buffer_pool_statistics table 631
*dba_hist_active_sess_history*91, 208, 210, 220, 229, 232, 233, 264, 294, 393, 402, 417, 418
dba_hist_active_session_history 1073
dba_hist_baselines 301, 304
dba_hist_bg_event_summary 245, 263
dba_hist_buffer_pool_stat 278
dba_hist_buffer_pool_stat table 631
dba_hist_buffer_pool_statistics 243, 245
dba_hist_db_cache_advice 1056, 1061
dba_hist_enqueue_stat 265
dba_hist_event_name 263

dba_hist_event_summary 243
dba_hist_filemetric_history 268, 389, 1058
dba_hist_filestatxs55, 94, 243, 244, 246, 286, 462, 482, 513, 575, 677, 1058
dba_hist_latch 243, 246, 274
dba_hist_latch_children 243, 246
dba_hist_latch_misses_summary 275
dba_hist_librarycache 243, 246, 276
dba_hist_metric_name 267
dba_hist_osstat 280
dba_hist_pga_target_advice 1061
dba_hist_pgastat 1056
dba_hist_rowcache_summary 243, 246, 277
dba_hist_seg_stat 284
dba_hist_service_name 294
dba_hist_service_stat 294
dba_hist_service_wait_class 294
dba_hist_sessmetric_history 268, 269
dba_hist_sgastat 243, 246
dba_hist_shared_pool_advice 1056, 1061
dba_hist_snapshot 243, 255, 282
dba_hist_sql_plan282, 725, 954, 1070, 1073, 1083
dba_hist_sql_summary 243, 246
dba_hist_sqlplan 790, 792
dba_hist_sqlstat282, 283, 603, 611, 754, 840, 841, 842, 848, 849, 850, 851, 852, 853, 856, 858, 859, 860, 861, 863, 865, 1070, 1073, 1083
dba_hist_sqltext 282, 283, 522, 1073, 1083
dba_hist_stat_name 244, 271
dba_hist_statname 273
*dba_hist_sys_time_model*69, 71, 271, 415, 621, 1075
dba_hist_sysmetric_history 269, 294, 384
dba_hist_sysmetric_summary268, 270, 294, 385
dba_hist_sysstat52, 54, 60, 86, 90, 95, 243, 244, 246, 271, 273, 463, 575
dba_hist_systat 257
dba_hist_system_event 243, 246, 261, 263
dba_hist_tempstatxs 286
dba_hist_waitclassmet_history271, 412, 1058, 1073
*dba_hist_waitstat*91, 92, 229, 243, 246, 264, 417, 419, 572, 1073
dba_hist_wr_control 208, 295
dba_histograms 820
dba_indexes 719, 733, 987
dba_jobs 73, 292
dba_objects 394, 623, 648
dba_scheduler_job_classes 1038
dba_scheduler_jobs 1035
dba_scheduler_schedules 1030
dba_scheduler_window_groups 1043
dba_scheduler_windows 1041
dba_scheduler_wingroup_members 1043
*dba_segments*648, 833, 838, 856, 858, 859, 860, 861
dba_tab_modifications 806
dba_tables 535, 662
dba_tables.avg_row_len 662, 695, 881
dba_users 622, 833, 834
DBHR 633, 645
dbid 301, 304
DbId 262
dbms_advisor 32, 1005, 1055
dbms_job 47, 48, 50, 663, 669, 887, 1027
dbms_mview 52
dbms_redefinition . 705, 707, 710, 712, 722, 742
dbms_scheduler30, 42, 47, 48, 50, 57, 85, 229, 589, 635, 718, 865, 887, 1027, 1086

dbms_session.set_ev().................................. 433
dbms_shared_pool 154
dbms_space.space_usage........................... 703
dbms_sqlpa 427, 873
dbms_sqltune 32, 51, 873, 1070, 1071
dbms_sqltune.create_sqlset 426
dbms_stat.gather_system_stats.......... 885, 886
dbms_stats34, 521, 708, 742, 745, 746, 748, 799, 800, 804, 806, 808, 810, 818, 882, 886, 887
dbms_stats.gather_workload_stats 427
dbms_utility................................. 34, 804, 805
dbms_workload_capture 453
dbms_workload_repository32, 208, 209, 295, 299, 303, 304, 312, 1072
dbms_xplan.display_awr 758
dbmsawr.sql 303
dbmspool.sql 290
DBWR 175, 177, 178
Decision Support System 53, 80, 320
Decision Support System (DSS) 1011
Decision Support Systems 871, 996
decision support systems (DSS) 1003
Decision Support Systems (DSS) 530
Default buffer cache 141
DEFAULT pool86, 624, 628, 629, 635, 647, 650
default_degree 812
deleted leaf node....................................... 727
deletes... 894
dictionary cache 348
dictionary cache 350
dictionary cache 370
dictionary-managed tablespace.......... 132, 133
dictionary-managed tablespaces 34
direct I/O 365, 513
directio... 514
Disk bottleneck 25
Disk enqueues 25
disk I/O.......................................482, 505, 570
disk I/O waits 558
disk_read_th 298
dispatcher timer....... 118, 119, 121, 122, 166, 167
dispatching priority 20
DISTINCT.. 160, 162
DML...................................... 693, 700, 731
driving \table..35
drop indexes 899
drop_window_group 1045
DSS 47, 48, 49, 53
duration 1042
dynamic sampling 821, 822, 824
dynamic_sampling 758
efficiency metrics....................................1023
elapsed time.. 69
end_interval_time..................................... 282
end_time.......................................258, 379
EndSnap 262
enqueue 122, 123, 167
enqueue statistics 338
enqueue waits... 284
enqueues................................28, 265, 267, 368
Enterprise Manager10, 29, 51, 209, 242, 257, 258, 463, 492, 873
enterprise resource planning..................... 757
equijoin predicate 1000
estimate_percent 892
ETL process 1009

event tables..248
exception reports...............................464, 1053
excessive logical I/O 28
execute_tuning_task 1071
execution history 1076
execution plan370, 497, 498, 499, 522, 529, 1074
executions_delta............................. 841, 842
executions_th..298
EXPLAIN 536
explain_rewrite... 52
extent management local 698
extent size...702
external tables 441, 770, 772
Extract, Transform, and Load (ETL) 1004
Extract, Transformation and Loading (ETL)1011
Fast Application Notification (FAN).......1105
fast_start_parallel_rollback 616, 618
fetch phase 451
fileio.sql script...548
filesystem..1054
filesystemio_options..................... 513, 514, 999
first_rows..498
first_rows optimizer_mode 529
flush_level...300
force............................... 1037, 1042, 1045
forcedirectio 514
forecasting 39
fragmentation...............................129, 130, 131
free_buffer_wait 631
freelist..694
freelist groups..................................... 1122
freelist_groups 406, 697, 710
freelists 35, 162, 229, 404, 406, 659, 711
from clause 759, 778, 780, 783, 826
full outer join 605, 606
full table scans 35
full-table scan 754
full-table scans 705
function-based indexes 35
Gallium Arsenide 486
gather auto 806
gather stale 806
gather_schema_stats 812
gather_stats_job 1095
gather_table_stats 812
get_io.sql script..550
get_iostat.ksh 517
get_vmstat.ksh 475, 477
glance 28, 1047
Graphical User Interface (GUI) 1017
grep 291, 1097
grid computing..17
Grid computing................................. 1105, 1111
GROUP BY 174
group_name 1045
GUI 1095
hard parse...788
hard parse elapsed time 416
hard parses 319
hash cluster 679
hash cluster tables 34
HASH JOIN FULL OUTER.....................606
hash joins 600
hash_area_size 161, 373, 521, 598, 601, 872, 882
hash_multiblock_io_count.........................615

HASH_VALUE 198
having clause 878
hidden parameters 615
high high watermark (HHWM) 702
high water mark (HWM) 595
high watermark 701
High WaterMark (HWM) 712
histogram 310
holistic tuning 870
hypothesis testing 81
Hypothesis testing 54
hypothetical workload 1083, 1088
I/O activity 363
I/O bound database 405
I/O overload 462
I/O session 569
I/O statistics 545
I/O-bound 1075
IN 172
index 728
Index Organized Tables 34
index range scan 661, 674, 721, 933, 934
index range scans ..527, 535, 722, 723, 951, 952
index rebuilding 730, 732
index rebuilds 733
index usage 36
index_ffs 736
indexes 829
Informaticists (data content experts) 1011
init.ora11, 85, 183, 313, 315, 367, 370, 372, 406, 500, 636, 665, 710, 875, 887
init.ora parameter 439
init.ora parameters 423, 872
initialization parameters 589, 614, 634
initrans 162
inline hint 880
insert ... select statement 894
insert statement 695
instance activity 331
instance configuration parameters 587
instance recovery 333
instance tuning 587
instance_number 301, 304
InstNum 262
inter-instance block transfers 1120
inter-instance parallelism 1124
internal transaction list (ITL) waits 653
inter-query parallelism 1124
INTERSECT 161
interval 209, 295
intra-instance transportable locks 1115
intra-query parallelism 1125
io_cost 819, 845, 846, 848
Ion 26
Ion Enterprise Edition 1096
Ion tool 72, 263
iostat 544, 550, 582
iostat utility 516
Itanium 2 .... 486, 489
Itanium 2 architecture 998
Java 739
Java API 82
java pool 367
Java pool 142
java_pool_size 141, 142

job_name 1037
Journal File System (JFS) 625
junk data 456
Keep buffer cache 141
keep cache 754
keep pool 796
KEEP pool86, 95, 233, 522, 523, 574, 633, 647, 662, 663, 665, 669, 682, 999, 1002, 1005, 1047
Laboratory Information Management Systems 818
Large pool 142
large_pool_size 141, 142, 599
large-scale RAC databases 1110
large-table full-table scans 534, 856, 997
latch contention 414
latch free 153, 167
latch hit percentage 321
latch sleeps 346
latch statistics 369
latch waits 403
latches 342
least-frequently-used (LRU) 596
left outer join 768
LGWR 175, 177
library cache 276, 349, 371
library cache hit 321
library cache latch 327, 369
library cache miss ratio 679, 680
Lightweight Onboard Monitor (LTOM) .. 429
listener.ora 500, 501
load profile 317
LOB 534
LOBs 662
Locally Managed Tablespace 693
Locally Managed Tablespaces 34
locally-managed tablespaces 34
lock element cleanup117, 118, 119, 120, 122, 166
log buffer space 234
Log Writer 327
*log_buffer*141, 142, 157, 234, 329, 345, 599, 615, 616, 1000, 1008
logical I/O (LIO) 626
logical reads 631, 706
long duration metrics 376
low high watermark (LHWM) 701
lsattr 1047
lsattr -El 592
lsdev 592
LTOM 429
Manage Scheduler 1028
Manageability Monitor 256, 294, 378
materialize hint 880
materialized views12, 998, 1002, 1003, 1005, 1068, 1069, 1078, 1081, 1084, 1088
max_interval 295, 304
max_retention 295
maximum transmission unit 501
Memory Advisor 352, 1056, 1089
memory_max_target 601
merges 894
method_opt 806, 892
metric baselines 41
metric group 377
metric_unit 269
min_interval 295, 304
min_retention 295
minextents 522, 699

MMON 300, 304
modify_snapshot_settings 208, 209
monitoring clause 812
Monolithic servers 17
Moore's law 996
Moore's Law 483
MS Windows 595, 612
mts_dispatchers 501
MTU 501
multiblock reads 455, 815
multiblock_read_count 886
multi-instance RAC database 1109
multiple blocksizes 523, 541, 679
multiple freelists 698, 705
multivariate statistics 82, 1013
mutable joins 768
MySQL 102
name 631
natural join 739, 766
nested loop join 722
nested loops join 588
nested loops joins 755
Network bottleneck 25
network bottlenecks 404
Network bottlenecks 28
Network latency 26
network overload 463
network-bound 29
new explain plan 1102
next 522
nice values 473
night\ mode 45
no_cpu_costing 887
Non Uniform Memory Access (NUMA) ... 997
Non-Uniform Memory Access (NUMA) .1003
NOT IN 120, 122
noworkload statistics 454, 815
Null event 118, 119, 121, 122, 166, 167
null values 707
num_rows 806
num_sql 297
Object fragmentation 132, 134
object partition joins 648
object_growth_trend 718
ODM 94
OEM 46, 493, 1017, 1095
OEM 10g DB Control 1028, 1036, 1040
OEM workload 1083
OEM2GO 1016, 1022, 1047
OLTP 44, 47, 49, 743, 839
on clause 767
on-demand CPU 996
online reorg 712
Online Transaction Processing (OLTP) ... 634
Online Transaction Processing Systems (OLTP) 996
open_window 1042
optimal join techniques 36
optimal parameter 340
optimizer 742
optimizer directives 826, 867
optimizer plan stability 102
Optimizer Plan Stability 765
optimizer statistics 427
optimizer_dynamic_sampling 821
optimizer_features_enable 821

*optimizer_index_caching*30, 529, 587, 588, 614, 619, 850, 882, 888, 1000
*optimizer_index_cost_adj*30, 406, 572, 614, 619, 882, 883, 885, 886, 887, 888, 999, 1008
optimizer_max_permutations 882
optimizer_mode30, 406, 498, 587, 614, 744, 746, 881
optimizer_percent_parallel 614, 616, 617
options 805
Oracle 10g Discoverer 1009
Oracle Data Guard 16
Oracle Data Miner 80
Oracle Discoverer 1013
Oracle Enterprise Manager 41, 382
Oracle Enterprise Manager (OEM) 1015
Oracle hints 824
Oracle HTTP server (OHS) 1113
Oracle instance tuning 30
Oracle Parallel Query571, 572, 705, 826, 856, 892
Oracle Parallel Query (OPQ) 616, 1124
Oracle Parallel Server 1105
Oracle Parallel Server (OPS) 1114
Oracle Streams 294, 1006, 1112
Oracle TPC-H 1007
Oracle Trace Analyzer 429
Oracle Wait Interface 91, 399, 417
Oracle Warehouse Builder (OWB) 1009
Oracle Web Server 1113
Oracle workload 43
oradebug 440
ORDER BY 174
order by clause 527
ordered hint 818, 820
ordered_predicates 789
OS buffer 513
OS parameters 613
outer join 769
page-in 596
page-out 596
parallel backup/recovery 1007
parallel clause 733, 736
parallel DDL statements 733
parallel indexing 1007
parallel loading 1007
parallel query 777, 1007
parallel query dequeue wait118, 119, 121, 122, 166, 167
parallel query idle wait - Slaves118, 119, 121, 122, 166, 167
parallel server tables 248
parallel_adaptive_multi_user 616, 617
*parallel_automatic_tuning*30, 617, 619, 872, 882
parallel_automatic_tuning (PAT) 616
parallel_index 736
parallel_max_servers 616, 618
parallel_threads_per_cpu 404
parallelism 404, 1006
Parallelize deletes 899
parse count (hard) 361
parse_calls_th 298
partitioning 998
pctfree 694, 695, 710, 1121
PCTFREE 404
pctfree / pctused 368
pctused 693, 695, 697, 699, 705, 710, 711
PCTUSED 227
Percentage of Maximum 41
perfstat 290, 293

persistent SQL philosophy 747
PGA......................................47, 333, 385, 602
PGA Advisor 1093
PGA cache hit (%) 1023
PGA management
    workarea_size_policy...161
PGA memory management 161
PGA multi-pass executions 1023
*pga_aggregate_target*30, 39, 47, 48, 49, 83, 161, 373, 463, 510,
    521, 548, 592, 598, 601, 602, 607, 608, 615, 683, 849, 865, 872,
    882, 883, 999, 1002, 1003, 1004, 1008
pga_size.sql 599
phys_reads.sql 53
physical disk I/O..542
physical disk I/O (PIO) 626
physical I/O waits 557
physical read waits....................................558
physical reads44, 79, 361, 366, 638, 677, 843, 877
physical_reads 631
physical_writes 631
physpctio.sql query....................................565
phywrts 575
pipe get 118, 119, 121, 122, 166, 167
PL/SQL lock timer..118, 119, 121, 122, 166, 167
PL/SQL packages 747
plan regression 758
plan9i.sql... 362, 731
pmon timer 118, 119, 120, 122, 166
predicate pushing 786
predictive modeling 43, 82
Predictive modeling....................................39
Proactive models..42
proactive tuning...................10, 11, 25, 58, 258
process events 433
processor affinity 20
Processor Queue Length 482
ProfitLogic..80
Program Global Area 29
Program Global Area (PGA) 597, 1003
project 741
project manager 1012
protocol.ora..500
prtconf.. 1047
QIO.. 515
QIOSTAT 515
query_rewrite_enabled 615, 1000
Quest Central..80
RAC 1106, 1123
RAC load balancing....................................1118
RAID 0+1....................................... 404
RAID 1+0 510
RAID 10 .... 510, 511, 551
RAID 5 .... 510, 511
RAID striping 505
RAID5 551
RAID-5..404
RAM.. 596, 599, 997
RAM bottleneck...25
RAM overload 463
RAM page-ins 25
RBO 759
RDBMS..758
rdbms ipc message 118, 119, 120, 122, 166
reactive tuning 10
read waits 572
read-only tablespaces..............................1124

read-write head delay 506
Real Application Cluster (RAC) 703
Real Application Clusters 424, 490
Real Application Clusters (RAC)..... 1006, 1105
Real Applications Clusters 16
rebuild command 729
recodify_snapshot_settings 256
Recommendations Options........................1084
Recycle buffer cache................................. 142
recycle pool.. 796
RECYCLE pool86, 205, 523, 624, 628, 662, 670, 673, 674, 679,
    682
redo allocation latch 327, 345
Redo log buffer.. 142
remove_window_group_member............1044
repeat 807, 810
report_plans..1071
report_tuning_task 1071
retention 295, 300, 304
right outer join 769
rollback segments 340
Rotational delay...................................... 507
row lock waits 654
ROWID values 535
rpt_bhr_all.sql 631
rpt_bhr_awr_hr.sql 641
RRDtool 60
RRDTool 88
run_job 1037
run_vmstat.ksh 478
runqueue value 473, 495
runqueue values....................................... 471
SAME 55, 94, 505, 510
SAME (Stripe and Mirror Everywhere) 1002
sample_size 808
sample_time 393
sar 28, 544
SAR...1047
SAS.. 80
scalar subqueries 780, 781
scale out 1110, 1114
scale out approach...................................1006
scale up 1109, 1114
scale up approach...................................1006
scattered disk reads 571
Schedule Advisor 1083, 1085
schema..101, 102
SDU 500, 501
Segment Advisor....................................1026, 1055
segment space management auto 698
segment statistics 369
select... 741
select clause 778
select part (query)................................ 734
select statement 618
sequential disk reads 571
server alerts...1054
server consolidation................................. 491
server metrics..1081
Server RAM paging 1051
server run queue waits 29
service statistics 356
sess_waits_ash.sql.................................. 66
session data unit 501
session events 433

Session ID (SID) 563
session_cached_cursors 1000
session_id 297
session_state.. 223
set events 433
set_attribute...1039
setall.. 514
SGA11, 30, 47, 48, 49, 99, 204, 257, 263, 296, 393, 596, 681, 682,
    1089
SGA sizing 594
SGA summary tables 248
sga_max_size 591, 594, 595, 601, 635
sga_target 367, 371, 594, 601, 1008, 1060
sharable_mem_th 298
shared pool116, 142, 143, 151, 152, 153, 154, 155, 156, 367
shared pool advice 681
Shared Pool Free (%)...............................1022
shared pool size 1091
shared_pool 48, 681
*shared_pool_size*11, 30, 39, 47, 83, 141, 142, 143, 156, 350, 370,
    463, 510, 599, 615, 646, 679, 788, 1000
short duration metrics 376
show parameters buffer............................ 628
show sga 141, 594, 597
shrink space.. 717
signature 42
signature analysis 41
Signature analysis 54
signatures 86
Significance Level 41
skewonly 806, 810, 811
slave wait 118, 119, 121, 122, 166, 167
smon timer...................... 118, 119, 120, 122, 166
SMP servers 403, 1004
snap_level 296
snap_time 641, 643
snapdeltafileio_awr.sql 580
snapfileio_10g.sql 578
snapshot set 1072
snapshots 41
soft parse 788
soft parses 319
Solid-state Disk (SSD) 506
Solid-State Disk (SSD) 1075
sort_area_retained_size 161
sort_area_size ..161, 162, 373, 597, 601, 872, 883
sp*.sql.. 294
SPA 873
space management blocks 701
space_alloc 719
space_usage... 719
spauto.sql 292, 294
spcpkg.sql.. 293
spcreate.sql......................................291, 293
spctab.sql... 293
spcusr.sql... 293
spdoc.txt.. 303
spdrop.sql.. 293
spdtab.sql... 293
spdusr.sql... 293
spfile 183, 1095
sppurge.sql 294, 300
sprepcon.sql... 294
sprepins.sql......................................294, 297
spreport.sql...............................294, 300, 312

sprepsql.sql 294
sprsqins.sql...294
SPSS 80
sptrunc.sql..294
spuexp.par...................................... 294, 301
SQL 738, 741, 743, 755, 758, 788
SQL Access Advisor33, 35, 281, 1056, 1062, 1068, 1078, 1080,
    1082, 1087
SQL Advisor 267
SQL details 1074
SQL Performance Advisor 9, 422
SQL Performance Analyzer11, 43, 422, 425, 452, 742
SQL Performance Analyzer (SPA) 542
SQL Plan Manager (SPM) 427
SQL profile 757
SQL profiles 747
SQL Profiles102, 427, 742, 838, 868, 1078, 1080, 1088
SQL query 1124
SQL Response Time (%) 1022
SQL Scripts
    9icartcount.sql 199
    9icartsql.sql 199
    9ilarge_scanusers.sql 190
    9iltabscan.sql 202
    9iplanstats.sql 201
    9itabscan.sql 200
    9iunused_indx.sql 203
    archhist.sql 178
    bgact.sql 177
    buffutl.sql 150
    bufobjwaits.sql 162
    cacheobjcnt.sql 149
    cartsession.sql 193
    cartsql.sql 193
    csesswaits.sql 121
    curriosql.sql 192
    currlwaits.sql 164
    datafileae.sql 128
    dictdet.sql 155
    fullsql.sql 198
    globaccpatt.sql 167
    globiostats.sql 165
    largescan9i.sql 172
    latchdet.sql 163
    libdet.sql 152
    libobj.sql 153
    libwait.sql 152
    lockcnt.sql 191
    maxext7.sql 132
    memhog.sql 159
    memsnap.sql 143, 151, 157, 160, 161, 162
    objdef.sql 133
    objwait.sql 122
    physpctio.sql 173
    poolhit.sql 145
    scatwait.sql 189
    sesshitrate.sql 145
    sesswaits.sql 120
    sgasize.sql 140
    sortdet.sql 182
    sortusage.sql 182
    sqlhitrate.sql 147
    syswaits.sql 118, 166
    top9isql.sql 196, 198
    topiousers.sql 175
    topsess.sql 183
    topsessdet.sql 186
    toptables.sql 170
    totpctio.sql 174
    totuserspace.sql 181
    tsfrag.sql 129
    userscans.sql 188
SQL Server 102
SQL Snapshots 1072
SQL statement 761
SQL tuning................................. 741, 749, 866
SQL Tuning 10, 25, 32, 51, 242

SQL Tuning Advisor25, 33, 210, 257, 281, 288, 757, 868, 875, 1054, 1055, 1056, 1060, 1062, 1068, 1070, 1071, 1078
SQL Tuning Set 757, 870
SQL Tuning Set (STS) 425
SQL Tuning Sets 1070, 1078
SQL Tuning Sets (STS) 541, 1070, 1072
SQL*DBA 1015
SQL*Loader 542
SQL*Net 403, 412, 463, 500, 501
SQL*Net break/reset to client118, 119, 120, 122, 166
SQL*Net message from client118, 119, 120, 122, 166
SQL*Net message to client118, 119, 120, 122, 166
SQL*Net more data to client.118, 119, 120, 122
SQL*Net wait events 28
SQL*Net waits 404
SQL*Plus53, 117, 141, 209, 257, 305, 313, 628, 1016, 1095
SQL*Trace 430
sql_id 283
sql_trace 432
SQLAccess 742
sqlnet.ora 500
SQLTuning 742
sqltxplain 428
SSD 629
stacked views 787
standalone database....................................1109
STAR query 1005
STAR schema 999
star_query 1000
star_transformation.................999, 1000, 1001
star_transformation_enabled 1000
start_capture 454
statistcis_level 812
statistician 1012
statistics_level........201, 299, 300, 382, 438, 574
stats$bg_event_summary 243, 245
stats$buffer_pool_statistics 243, 245
stats$buffer_pool_statistics table........ 631, 641
stats$buffered_queues 294
stats$buffered_subscribers 294
stats$event_histogram 715
stats$filestatxs...............243, 246, 389, 482, 513
stats$latch 243, 246, 715
stats$latch_children 243, 246
stats$librarycache 243, 246
stats$propagation_receiver 294
stats$propagation_sender 294
stats$rowcache_summary.................243, 246
stats$rule_set 294
stats$sesstat table 631
stats$sgastat...............................243, 246
stats$snapshot...248
stats$sql_summary 243, 246, 290, 302, 482, 715
stats$statspack_parameter..........................296
stats$streams_apply_sum 294
stats$streams_capture...............................294
stats$sysstat 243, 246, 715, 718, 719
stats$system_event 243, 246
stats$waitstat 243, 246
statscre.sql 290
statsctab.sql 291
STATSPACK41, 43, 83, 222, 241, 246, 250, 289, 424, 430, 511, 512, 521, 554, 570, 572, 574, 578, 595, 676, 745, 758, 761, 764
STATSPACK report 310
STATSPACK reports 252, 309

STATSPACK utility 714
statspack.snap 294, 299
STATSPACK/AWR report 309, 336
stop_job 1037
Storage Area Networks (SAN) 1116
Stripe and Mirror Everywhere . 55, 94, 505, 510
STS 871, 1079
suboptimal SQL 463
subquery 778, 779
Support Vector Machines 94
swap disk 1054
symmetric multiprocessing (SMP)...........1113
sys.aux_stat$..886
sys.v_$sysstat...................................547, 548
sys.v_$system_event 570
System Global Area 11, 29, 352
System Global Area (SGA)........................586
system latches...342
System Response Time 1022
system tables 248
syswaits.sql script 569
table fetch continued row......................... 168
table join 739, 746, 765
table join order 800, 820
table scan 823
table scans (long tables) 361
Tablespace fragmentation..........................131
tablespace partitions...............................1002
TAF 1118
tch column 647, 666
tcp.nodelay 500, 501
TDU 500, 501
throughput metrics...............................1046
tim column 647
time model approach...............................66
time model statistics................ 271, 355
Time Model Statistics report 74
time series trend charts 69
time series tuning....................................... 51
time_waited 220, 223, 380
time-based wait tuning.............................. 403
timed_statistics.....................................117
time-series tuning.................... 36, 236, 268, 269
TKPROF 449, 875
tnsnames.ora 500, 501
top 28, 1047
top 5 timed events 323
top five timed event 404
top five wait events 26
top SQL 357
Top SQL screen.......................................1072
top-down approach.................................. 9, 24
topiousers.sql query...................................567
toptables.sql query 554
Total Cost of Ownership (TCO) 1006
totpctio.sql query......................................565
touch count..............................620, 627, 830
trace events 431
trace file 446
trace report 448
transaction tables....................................248
Transparent Application Failover (TAF)1105, 1108
Transparent Network Substrate .. 101, 463, 499
trend-based reconfiguration 48
trend-based tools 1096

Index   **1133**

Tuning Advisors 40
tuning history 1077
undo segment statistics 341
undo segments 368
UNDO tablespace 162, 180
UNION 161
UNIX commands 1048
update statement 903
updates 894
use_current_session 1037
user_dump_dest 432, 438
using clause 767
utlbstat 241
utlestat 241
v$ views 401
v$active_sess_hist.............................. 209, 409
v$active_session_history32, 91, 208, 209, 219, 223, 224, 227, 228, 232, 393, 402, 621, 622, 623, 658
v$bh 648, 651
v$buffer_pool_statistics............................ 630
*v$db_cache_advice*83, 508, 511, 591, 636, 638, 877, 1056, 1061
v$enqueue_statistics................................... 265
v$event_histogram................................... 391
v$event_name 227, 263
v$eventmetric 258, 387
v$file_histogram 392
v$filemetric 388
v$filemetric_history 381, 388, 389
v$latch.. 274
v$librarycache 276
v$metric_name 267
v$metricgroup 267, 376
v$metricname 377
v$osstat 280
v$pga_target_advice 83, 1056
v$rowcache 277
v$segment_statistics284, 557, 560, 574, 652, 657, 660
v$segstat 284
v$segstat_name 284
v$servicemetric 389
v$servicemetric_history 389
v$services.. 389
v$sess_time_model.................................... 65
v$session........................223, 393, 401, 412, 441
v$session_event 411
*v$session_wait*220, 264, 400, 401, 409, 412, 557, 558, 559, 656, 657, 658
v$session_wait_class 391
*v$session_wait_history*208, 209, 226, 227, 392, 401, 412
v$sessmetric.. 385
v$shared_pool_advice 83, 350, 681, 1056
*v$sql*225, 282, 760, 822, 833, 835, 836, 837, 839, 840
v$sql_plan667, 790, 799, 833, 835, 836, 837, 869, 887
v$sql_shared_cursor 761
v$sqlarea 622
v$statname.. 271
v$sys_time_model 64, 271, 401, 412
v$sysmetric 383, 386
v$sysmetric_history 256, 269, 379, 383, 384
v$sysmetric_summary 256, 270, 383, 385
v$sysstat.................................273, 577, 602
v$sysstat value 708
v$system_event......261, 400, 557, 572, 655, 660
v$system_wait_class 391, 392
v$temp_histogram.................................. 392

v$waitclassmetric 258, 387
v$waitclassmetric_history 258, 380, 386, 387
v$waitstat........................264, 558, 656
v_$sql_plan 555
varchar 707
varyio 514
version_count_th......................................298
very large database (VLDB) 1002, 1013
very large databases (VLDB) 538
view 784
Views
    v$sessstat view... 190
    v$sql_plan 200
    v$sql_plan_statistics 201
    v$sqlarea 147
    v$sysstat 116
    v_$sql_plan 172, 190, 193, 194, 199, 200, 201, 202, 203
virtual circuit status. 118, 119, 121, 122, 166, 167
Virtual Memory 495
Virtual Memory (VM) 596
vmstat 28, 464, 473, 478, 512, 544, 582
vmstat capture 475
vmstat utility...325
wait event 260, 400
wait event histogram 330
Wait Event Interface 221
wait event tuning....................................402
wait events 261, 325, 451
wait_class 227
wait_count 56, 380
wait_time..223
wait_time_detail 419
wait_time_detail.sql 92
where clause244, 755, 766, 785, 787, 789, 802, 809, 819, 822, 842, 1061, 1085
WHERE clause 86
window_list 1045
window_name 1042
Windows Performance Manager 28
WISE tool 642
with clause 877, 879
workarea_size_policy 161, 883, 1000
Workload analysis 124, 180, 194
workload statistics.............................. 454, 816
wrh$ tables 258, 418
wrh$ views 401
wrh$_active_session_history 209, 223, 232
wrh$_active_session_history_bl 209
wrh$_bg_event_summary 209, 243
wrh$_buffer_pool_statistics 243
wrh$_event_name 209
wrh$_filemetric_history.............................389
wrh$_filestatxs..243
wrh$_latch 243
wrh$_latch_children 243
wrh$_librarycache 243
wrh$_metric_name 209
wrh$_rowcache_summary.........................243
wrh$_sessmetric_history 209
wrh$_sgastat...243
wrh$_sql_summary 243
wrh$_sys_time_model 209
wrh$_sys_time_model_bl 209
wrh$_sysmetric_history.............................209
wrh$_sysmetric_summary.........................209
wrh$_sysstat 209, 243, 244
wrh$_sysstat_bl 209

wrh$_system_event.............................209, 243
wrh$_system_event_bl..............................209
wrh$_waitclassmetric_history....................209
wrh$_waitstat....................................209, 243
wrh$_waitstat_bl..................................209
wri$ tables..258
wri$_alert_history 624
wri$_dbu_feature_metadata 33

wri$_dbu_feature_usage..............................33
wri$_dbu_usage_sample 33
wrm$ tables 258
wrm$_snapshot......................................244
x$bh 647, 663, 665, 673, 754
x$bh.tch 673
x$kcbcbh 636, 638
x$kcbrbh...636
